Sociological Theory

Ninth Edition

Sociological Theory

George Ritzer

University of Maryland

Jeffrey Stepnisky

Grant MacEwan University

Connect
Learn
Succeed™

SOCIOLOGICAL THEORY, NINTH EDITION

Published by McGraw-Hill, a business unit of The McGraw-Hill Companies, Inc., 1221 Avenue of the Americas, New York, NY, 10020. Copyright © 2014 by The McGraw-Hill Companies, Inc. All rights reserved. Printed in the United States of America. Previous editions © 2011, 2008, and 2004. No part of this publication may be reproduced or distributed in any form or by any means, or stored in a database or retrieval system, without the prior written consent of The McGraw-Hill Companies, Inc., including, but not limited to, in any network or other electronic storage or transmission, or broadcast for distance learning.

Some ancillaries, including electronic and print components, may not be available to customers outside the United States.

This book is printed on acid-free paper.

2 3 4 5 6 7 8 9 0 DOC/DOC 1 0 9 8 7 6 5

ISBN 978-0-07-802701-7
MHID 0-07-802701-2

Vice President, General Manager, Products & Markets: *Michael Ryan*
Executive Director of Development: *Lisa Pinto*
Managing Director: *Gina Boedeker*
Brand Manager: *Courtney Austermehle*
Marketing Specialist: *Alexandra Schultz*
Managing Development Editor: *Sara Jaeger*
Editorial Coordinator: *Adina Lonn*
Project Manager: *Jessica Portz*
Buyer: *Nicole Baumgartner*
Cover Designer: *Studio Montage, St. Louis, MO*
Cover Image: *Corey Holms/Getty Images RF*
Typeface: *10/12 Times Roman*
Compositor: *Cenveo® Publisher Services*
Printer: *R. R. Donnelley*

All credits appearing on page or at the end of the book are considered to be an extension of the copyright page.

Library of Congress Cataloging-in-Publication Data

Ritzer, George.
  Sociological theory / George Ritzer. — 9th ed.
    p. cm.
  ISBN 978-0-07-802701-7 (alk. paper)
  1. Sociology. 2. Sociologists—Biography I. Title.
HM585.R57   2013
301.01—dc23   2012044197

The Internet addresses listed in the text were accurate at the time of publication. The inclusion of a website does not indicate an endorsement by the authors or McGraw-Hill, and McGraw-Hill does not guarantee the accuracy of the information presented at these sites.

www.mhhe.com

About the Authors

George Ritzer is Distinguished University Professor at the University of Maryland. Among his awards: Honorary Doctorate from La Trobe University, Melbourne, Australia; Honorary Patron, University Philosophical Society, Trinity College, Dublin; American Sociological Association's Distinguished Contribution to Teaching Award. He has chaired four Sections of the American Sociological Association—Theoretical Sociology, Organizations and Occupations, History of Sociology, and was the first Chair of Global and Transnational Sociology. Among his books in theory are *Sociology: A Multiple Paradigm Science* (1975/1980) and *Metatheorizing in Sociology* (1991). In the application of social theory to the social world, his books include *The McDonaldization of Society* (7th ed., 2013), *Enchanting a Disenchanted World* (3rd ed., 2010), and *The Globalization of Nothing* (2nd ed., 2007). He is also the author of *Globalization: A Basic Text* (Blackwell, 2010). He edited the *Wiley-Blackwell Companion to Sociology* (2012), *The Blackwell Companion to Globalization* (2008), and co-edited the *Wiley-Blackwell Companions to Classical and Contemporary Major Social Theorists* (2011) and *Handbook of Social Theory* (2001). He was founding editor of the *Journal of Consumer Culture.* He also edited the eleven-volume *Encyclopedia of Sociology* (2007), the two-volume *Encyclopedia of Social Theory* (2005), and the five-volume *Encyclopedia of Globalization* (2012). He co-edited a special double issue (2012) of *American Behavioral Scientist* on prosumption. His books have been translated into over twenty languages, with over a dozen translations of *The McDonaldization of Society* alone.

Jeffrey Stepnisky is an Assistant Professor of Sociology at Grant MacEwan University in Edmonton, Alberta, Canada, where he teaches classical and contemporary social theory. He has published in the area of social theory, especially as it relates to questions of subjectivity. This includes a series of papers on the topic of antidepressant medications and contemporary selfhood. He is co-editor of the *Wiley-Blackwell Companion to Major Social Theorists* (2011) and has served as the managing editor for *The Encyclopedia of Social Theory* (2005) and *Journal of Consumer Culture.* In addition to this text he is co-author, with George Ritzer, of *Contemporary Sociological Theory and Its Classical Roots* (2013).

To David, With Love – GR
For Michelle and Nora – JS

Brief Contents

Contents

Biographical and Autobiographical Sketches

Preface

This new edition of *Sociological Theory*, like its eight predecessors, offers a comprehensive overview of the history of sociological theory from its inception to the latest theoretical developments. As with previous editions, our goal is to combine a discussion of the major classical theorists (Marx, Weber, Durkheim, and Simmel) with the most important contemporary theories and theorists. In one convenient volume, this book offers students a handy overview of much of what they need to know about sociological theory, both past and present.

In-depth discussions of theories (often enlivened with examples) are accompanied by informative and—we believe—engaging biographical sketches of many of the most important thinkers in the history of sociology. Once again, *Sociological Theory* offers two historical chapters surveying the early history of the field (Chapter 1) and recent developments (Chapter 6). These chapters provide an overview that allows students to put the work of each theorist in its historical, social, and political context.

A New Coauthor

A major change to this edition is the addition of Jeffrey Stepnisky as coauthor. Jeff is a former student of George Ritzer's and an Assistant Professor of Sociology at Grant MacEwan University in Edmonton, Canada. Jeff brings a fresh voice, and his involvement ensures that the text will continue into the future. As a teacher of undergraduate social theory classes, Jeff is enthusiastic about making theory relevant and accessible for students.

Changes in the Ninth Edition

As is always the case, we faced difficult decisions about what to add and what to cut. There are some important additions to this edition. In order to ensure that the text did not become too lengthy and cumbersome, we also removed or rewrote some sections. These decisions reflect the changing face of sociological theory. Among the major changes/additions are the following:

- The final section of Chapter 6, "Social Theory in the Twenty-First Century," has been rewritten to focus on four themes of recent theoretical interest: identity, consumption, globalization, and science and technology.

- In Chapter 8, the section on Henri Lefebvre has been rewritten to provide a more accessible version of the theory.
- In Chapter 8, the section on Immanuel Wallerstein has been updated to include his most recent work, including analysis of the global financial crisis that began in 2008.
- Chapter 9 on systems theory has been removed, but the important work of Niklas Luhmann has been incorporated into Chapter 7.
- The section on neofunctionalism has been removed from Chapter 7.
- A substantial new section on the sociology of emotion has been added to the chapter on symbolic interactionism (Chapter 9). Chapter 9 has been reorganized to accommodate this addition.
- A substantial new section on Charles Taylor that includes discussion of the self, the modern social imaginary, and religion has been added to the chapter on modernity (Chapter 14).
- Chapter 17 has been reorganized and rewritten to include substantial new material. This includes greater detail on the key concepts of queer theory and a discussion of the relationship between actor-network theory and science and technology studies.
- Chapter 17 also includes a substantial new section on affect theory.
- The text has been refreshed throughout, especially with the addition of new citations to the most recent work on various theories.

Thus, the text is much as it always has been but is renewed once again. The wonderful things about theory are both its continuity and its ever-changing character. We have tried to communicate those and other joys of sociological theory to readers in the early stages of their exposure to it.

Acknowledgments

We want to thank Patricia Lengermann and Gillian Niebrugge for revising Chapter 12, their pathbreaking chapter on contemporary feminist theory. Their chapter not only has made this book much stronger but also has had a strong influence on theorizing independent of the book. We also thank Matthias Junge for his contribution to the section on Niklas Luhmann (in Chapter 7) and Mike Ryan for his contribution to the section on queer theory (in Chapter 17). We also thank Doug Goodman (coauthor of the sixth edition) for his contributions, many of which continue to be found in this text. Thanks, as well, to those at McGraw-Hill who have provided continuing support throughout these revisions

Thanks also go to a panel of reviewers whose comments and suggestions helped to make this a better book:

James J. Chriss, *Cleveland State University*
Rebecca Jean Emigh, *University of California, Los Angeles*
David Allan Ford, *University of Central Oklahoma*
William J. Haller, *Clemson University*

Diane Kayongo-Male, *South Dakota State University*
Eleanor A. LaPointe, *Rutgers University*
Darek Niklas, *Rhode Island College*
Fabio Rojas, *Indiana University*

George Ritzer and Jeffrey Stepnisky

Classical Sociological Theory

C   H   A   P   T   E   R   **1**

A Historical Sketch of Sociological Theory: The Early Years

Chapter Outline

Introduction

Social Forces in the Development of Sociological Theory

Intellectual Forces and the Rise of Sociological Theory

The Development of French Sociology

The Development of German Sociology

The Origins of British Sociology

The Key Figure in Early Italian Sociology

Turn-of-the-Century Developments in European Marxism

A useful way to begin a book designed to introduce the range of sociological theory is with several one-line summaries of various theories:

- The modern world is an iron cage of rational systems from which there is no escape.
- Capitalism tends to sow the seeds of its own destruction.
- The modern world has less moral cohesion than earlier societies had.
- The city spawns a particular type of personality.
- In their social lives, people tend to put on a variety of theatrical performances.
- The social world is defined by principles of reciprocity in give-and-take relationships.
- People create the social worlds that ultimately come to enslave them.
- People always retain the capacity to change the social worlds that constrain them.

1

- Society is an integrated system of social structures and functions.
- Society is a "juggernaut" with the ever-present possibility of running amok.
- Although it appears that the Western world has undergone a process of liberalization, in fact it has grown increasingly oppressive.
- The world has entered a new postmodern era increasingly defined by the inauthentic, the fake, by simulations of reality.
- Paradoxically, globalization is associated with the worldwide spread of "nothing."
- Nonhuman objects are increasingly seen as key actors in networks.

This book is devoted to helping the reader better understand these and many other theoretical ideas, as well as the larger theories from which they are drawn.

Introduction

Presenting a history of sociological theory is an important task (S. Turner, 1998), but because we devote only two chapters (1 and 6) to it, what we offer is a highly selective historical sketch (Giddens, 1995). The idea is to provide the reader with a scaffolding that should help in putting the later detailed discussions of theorists and theories in a larger context. As the reader proceeds through the later chapters, it will prove useful to return to these two overview chapters and place the discussions in their context. (It will be especially useful to glance back occasionally to Figures 1.1 and 6.1, which are schematic representations of the histories covered in those chapters.)

The theories treated in the body of this book have a *wide range* of application, deal with *centrally important social issues,* and have *stood the test of time.* These criteria constitute the definition of *sociological theory* used in this book.[1]

A number of the theorists who are briefly discussed in Chapter 1 (for example, Herbert Spencer and Auguste Comte) will not receive detailed treatment later because they are of little more than historical interest. Other theorists (for example, Karl Marx, Max Weber, and Emile Durkheim) will be discussed in Chapter 1 in their historical context, and they will receive detailed treatment later because of their continuing importance. The focus is on the important theoretical work of sociologists or the work done by individuals in other fields that has come to be defined as important in sociology. To put it succinctly, this is a book about the "big ideas" in sociology that have stood the test of time (or promise to)—idea systems that deal with major social issues and that are far-reaching in scope.

We cannot establish the precise date when sociological theory began. People have been thinking about, and developing theories of, social life since early in history.

---

[1] Such a definition stands in contrast to the formal, "scientific" definitions (Jasso, 2001) that often are used in theory texts of this type. A scientific definition might be that a theory is a set of interrelated propositions that allows for the systematization of knowledge, explanation, and prediction of social life and the generation of new research hypotheses (Faia, 1986). Although such a definition has a number of attractions, it simply does not fit many of the idea systems that are discussed in this book. In other words, most classical (and contemporary) theories fall short on one or more of the formal components of theory, but they are nonetheless considered theories by most sociologists.

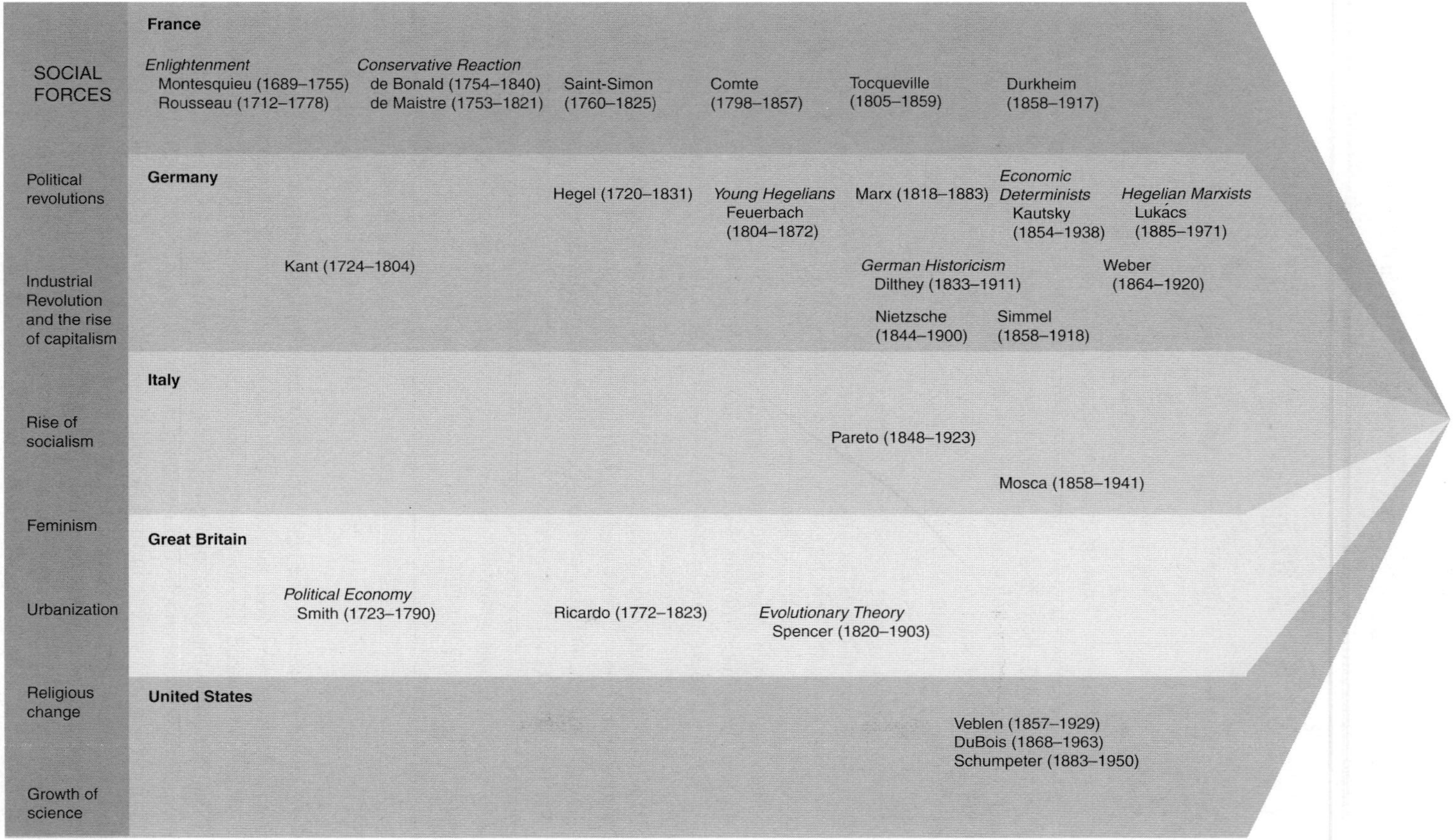

FIGURE 1.1 *Sociological Theory: The Early Years*

SOCIAL FORCES:
- Political revolutions
- Industrial Revolution and the rise of capitalism
- Rise of socialism
- Feminism
- Urbanization
- Religious change
- Growth of science

France

Enlightenment
Montesquieu (1689–1755)
Rousseau (1712–1778)

Conservative Reaction
de Bonald (1754–1840)
de Maistre (1753–1821)

Saint-Simon (1760–1825)
Comte (1798–1857)
Tocqueville (1805–1859)
Durkheim (1858–1917)

Germany

Kant (1724–1804)
Hegel (1720–1831)

Young Hegelians
Feuerbach (1804–1872)

Marx (1818–1883)

German Historicism
Dilthey (1833–1911)

Nietzsche (1844–1900)

Economic Determinists
Kautsky (1854–1938)

Simmel (1858–1918)
Weber (1864–1920)

Hegelian Marxists
Lukács (1885–1971)

Italy

Pareto (1848–1923)
Mosca (1858–1941)

Great Britain

Political Economy
Smith (1723–1790)
Ricardo (1772–1823)

Evolutionary Theory
Spencer (1820–1903)

United States

Veblen (1857–1929)
DuBois (1868–1963)
Schumpeter (1883–1950)

ABDEL RAHMAN IBN-KHALDUN

A Biographical Sketch

There is a tendency to think of sociology as exclusively a comparatively modern, Western phenomenon. In fact, however, scholars were developing sociological ideas and theories long ago and in other parts of the world. One example is Abdel Rahman Ibn-Khaldun.

Ibn-Khaldun was born in Tunis, North Africa, on May 27, 1332 (Alatas, 2011; Faghirzadeh, 1982). Born to an educated family, Ibn-Khaldun was schooled in the Koran (the Muslim holy book), mathematics, and history. In his lifetime, he served a variety of sultans in Tunis, Morocco, Spain, and Algeria as ambassador, chamberlain, and member of the scholars' council. He also spent two years in prison in Morocco for his belief that state rulers were not divine leaders. After approximately two decades of political activity, Ibn-Khaldun returned to North Africa, where he undertook an intensive five-year period of study and writing. Works produced during this period increased his fame and led to a lectureship at the center of Islamic study, Al-Azhar Mosque University in Cairo. In his well-attended lectures on society and sociology, Ibn-Khaldun stressed the importance of linking sociological thought and historical observation.

By the time he died in 1406, Ibn-Khaldun had produced a corpus of work that had many ideas in common with contemporary sociology. He was committed to the scientific study of society, empirical research, and the search for causes of social phenomena. He devoted considerable attention to various social institutions (for example, politics, economy) and their interrelationships. He was interested in comparing primitive and modern societies. Ibn-Khaldun did not have a dramatic impact on classical sociology, but as scholars in general, and Islamic scholars in particular, rediscover his work, he may come to be seen as being of greater historical significance.

But we will not go back to the early historic times of the Greeks or Romans or even to the Middle Ages. We will not even go back to the seventeenth century, although Olson (1993) has traced the sociological tradition to the mid-1600s and the work of James Harrington on the relationship between the economy and the polity. This is not because people in those epochs did not have sociologically relevant ideas, but because the return on our investment in time would be small; we would spend a lot of time getting very few ideas that are relevant to modern sociology. In any case, none of the thinkers associated with those eras thought of themselves, and few are now thought of, as sociologists. (For a discussion of one exception, see the biographical sketch of Ibn-Khaldun.) It is only in the 1800s that we begin to find thinkers who can be clearly identified as sociologists. These are the classical sociological thinkers we shall be interested in (Camic, 1997; for a debate about what makes theory classical, see R. Collins, 1997b; Connell, 1997), and we begin by examining the main social and intellectual forces that shaped their ideas.

Social Forces in the Development of Sociological Theory

All intellectual fields are profoundly shaped by their social settings. This is particularly true of sociology, which not only is derived from that setting but takes the social setting as its basic subject matter. We will focus briefly on a few of the most important social conditions of the nineteenth and early twentieth centuries, conditions that were of the utmost significance in the development of sociology. We also will take the occasion to begin introducing the major figures in the history of sociological theory.

Political Revolutions

The long series of political revolutions that were ushered in by the French Revolution in 1789 and carried over through the nineteenth century was the most immediate factor in the rise of sociological theorizing. The impact of these revolutions on many societies was enormous, and many positive changes resulted. However, what attracted the attention of many early theorists was not the positive consequences but the negative effects of such changes. These writers were particularly disturbed by the resulting chaos and disorder, especially in France. They were united in a desire to restore order to society. Some of the more extreme thinkers of this period literally wanted a return to the peaceful and relatively orderly days of the Middle Ages. The more sophisticated thinkers recognized that social change had made such a return impossible. Thus they sought instead to find new bases of order in societies that had been overturned by the political revolutions of the eighteenth and nineteenth centuries. This interest in the issue of social order was one of the major concerns of classical sociological theorists, especially Comte, Durkheim, and Parsons.

The Industrial Revolution and the Rise of Capitalism

At least as important as political revolution in shaping sociological theory was the Industrial Revolution, which swept through many Western societies, mainly in the nineteenth and early twentieth centuries. The Industrial Revolution was not a single event but many interrelated developments that culminated in the transformation of the Western world from a largely agricultural to an overwhelmingly industrial system. Large numbers of people left farms and agricultural work for the industrial occupations offered in the burgeoning factories. The factories themselves were transformed by a long series of technological improvements. Large economic bureaucracies arose to provide the many services needed by industry and the emerging capitalist economic system. In this economy, the ideal was a free marketplace where the many products of an industrial system could be exchanged. Within this system, a few profited greatly while the majority worked long hours for low wages. A reaction against the industrial system and against capitalism in general followed and led to the labor movement as well as to various radical movements aimed at overthrowing the capitalist system.

The Industrial Revolution, capitalism, and the reaction against them all involved an enormous upheaval in Western society, an upheaval that affected sociologists greatly. Four major figures in the early history of sociological theory—Karl Marx, Max Weber, Emile Durkheim, and Georg Simmel—were preoccupied, as were many lesser thinkers, with these changes and the problems they created for society as a whole. They spent their lives studying these problems, and in many cases they endeavored to develop programs that would help solve them.

The Rise of Socialism

One set of changes aimed at coping with the excesses of the industrial system and capitalism can be combined under the heading "socialism" (Beilharz, 2005g). Although some sociologists favored socialism as a solution to industrial problems, most were personally and intellectually opposed to it. On one side, Karl Marx was an active supporter of the overthrow of the capitalist system and its replacement by a socialist system. Although Marx did not develop a theory of socialism per se, he spent a great deal of time criticizing various aspects of capitalist society. In addition, he engaged in a variety of political activities that he hoped would help bring about the rise of socialist societies.

However, Marx was atypical in the early years of sociological theory. Most of the early theorists, such as Weber and Durkheim, were opposed to socialism (at least as it was envisioned by Marx). Although they recognized the problems within capitalist society, they sought social reform within capitalism rather than the social revolution argued for by Marx. They feared socialism more than they did capitalism. This fear played a far greater role in shaping sociological theory than did Marx's support of the socialist alternative to capitalism. In fact, as we will see, in many cases sociological theory developed in reaction against Marxian and, more generally, against socialist theory.

Feminism

In one sense there has always been a feminist perspective. Wherever women are subordinated—and they have been subordinated almost always and everywhere—they seem to have recognized and protested that situation in some form (Lerner, 1993). While precursors can be traced to the 1630s, high points of feminist activity and writing occurred in the liberationist moments of modern Western history: a first flurry of productivity in the 1780s and 1790s with the debates surrounding the American and French revolutions; a far more organized, focused effort in the 1850s as part of the mobilization against slavery and for political rights for the middle class; and the massive mobilization for women's suffrage and for industrial and civic reform legislation in the early twentieth century, especially the Progressive Era in the United States.

All of this had an impact on the development of sociology, in particular on the work of a number of women in or associated with the field—Harriet Martineau (Vetter, 2008), Charlotte Perkins Gilman (J. Allen, 2011), Jane Addams, Florence Kelley, Anna Julia Cooper, Ida Wells-Barnett, Marianne Weber, and Beatrice Potter Webb, to name a few. But their creations were, over time, pushed to the periphery of the profession, annexed, discounted, or written out of sociology's public record by the men who were organizing sociology as a professional power base. Feminist concerns filtered into sociology only on the margins, in the work of marginal male theorists or of the increasingly marginalized female theorists. The men who assumed centrality in the profession—from Spencer, through Weber and Durkheim—made basically conservative responses to the feminist arguments going on around them, making issues of gender an inconsequential topic to which they responded conventionally rather than critically in what they identified and publicly promoted as sociology. They responded in this way even as women were writing a significant body of sociological theory. The history of this gender politics in the profession, which is also part of the history of male response to feminist claims, is only now being written (for example, see Deegan, 1988; Fitzpatrick, 1990; Gordon, 1994; Lengermann and Niebrugge-Brantley, 1998; R. Rosenberg, 1982).

Urbanization

Partly as a result of the Industrial Revolution, large numbers of people in the nineteenth and twentieth centuries were uprooted from their rural homes and moved to urban settings. This massive migration was caused, in large part, by the jobs created by the industrial system in the urban areas. But it presented many difficulties for those people who had to adjust to urban life. In addition, the expansion of the cities produced a seemingly endless list of urban problems—overcrowding, pollution, noise, traffic, and so forth. The nature of urban life and its problems attracted the attention of many early sociologists, especially Max Weber and Georg Simmel. In fact, the first major school of American sociology, the Chicago school, was in large part defined by its concern for the city and its interest in using Chicago as a laboratory in which to study urbanization and its problems.

Religious Change

Social changes brought on by political revolutions, the Industrial Revolution, and urbanization had a profound effect on religiosity. Many early sociologists came from religious backgrounds and were actively, and in some cases professionally, involved in religion (Hinkle and Hinkle, 1954). They brought to sociology the same objectives they espoused in their religious lives. They wished to improve people's lives (Vidich and Lyman, 1985). For some (such as Comte), sociology was transformed into a religion (Wernick, 2000, 2005a, 2005b). For others, their sociological theories bore an unmistakable religious imprint. Durkheim wrote one of his major works on religion. Morality played a key role not only in Durkheim's sociology but also in the work of Talcott Parsons. A large portion of Weber's work also was devoted to the religions of the world. Marx, too, had an interest in religiosity, but his orientation was far more critical.

The Growth of Science

As sociological theory was being developed, there was an increasing emphasis on science, not only in colleges and universities but in society as a whole. The technological products of science were permeating every sector of life, and science was acquiring enormous prestige. Those associated with the most successful sciences (physics, biology, and chemistry) were accorded honored places in society. Sociologists (especially Comte, Durkheim, Spencer, Mead, and Schutz) from the beginning were preoccupied with science, and many wanted to model sociology after the successful physical and biological sciences. However, a debate soon developed between those who wholeheartedly accepted the scientific model and those (such as Weber) who thought that distinctive characteristics of social life made a wholesale adoption of a scientific model difficult and unwise (Lepenies, 1988). The issue of the relationship between sociology and science is debated to this day, although even a glance at the major journals in the field, at least in the United States, indicates the predominance of those who favor sociology as a science.

Intellectual Forces and the Rise of Sociological Theory

Although social factors are important, the primary focus of this chapter is the intellectual forces that played a central role in shaping sociological theory. In the real world, of course, intellectual factors cannot be separated from social forces. For example, in the discussion of the Enlightenment that follows, we will find that that movement was intimately related to, and in many cases provided the intellectual basis for, the social changes discussed above.

The many intellectual forces that shaped the development of social theories are discussed within the national context where their influence was primarily felt (Levine, 1995; Rundell, 2001). We begin with the Enlightenment and its influences on the development of sociological theory in France.

The Enlightenment

It is the view of many observers that the Enlightenment constitutes a critical development in terms of the later evolution of sociology (Hawthorn, 1976; Hughes, Martin, and Sharrock, 1995; Nisbet, 1967; Zeitlin, 1996). The Enlightenment was a period of remarkable intellectual development and change in philosophical thought.[2] A number of long-standing ideas and beliefs—many of which related to social life—were overthrown and replaced during the Enlightenment. The most prominent thinkers associated with the Enlightenment were the French philosophers Charles Montesquieu

---

[2] This section is based on the work of Irving Zeitlin (1996). Although Zeitlin's analysis is presented here for its coherence, it has a number of limitations: there are better analyses of the Enlightenment, there are many other factors involved in shaping the development of sociology, and Zeitlin tends to overstate his case in places (for example, on the impact of Marx). But on the whole, Zeitlin provides us with a useful starting point, given our objectives in this chapter.

(1689–1755) and Jean-Jacques Rousseau (1712–1778) (B. Singer, 2005a, 2005b). The influence of the Enlightenment on sociological theory, however, was more indirect and negative than it was direct and positive. As Irving Zeitlin puts it, "Early sociology developed as a reaction to the Enlightenment" (1996:10).

The thinkers associated with the Enlightenment were influenced, above all, by two intellectual currents—seventeenth-century philosophy and science.

Seventeenth-century philosophy was associated with the work of thinkers such as René Descartes, Thomas Hobbes, and John Locke. The emphasis was on producing grand, general, and very abstract systems of ideas that made rational sense. The later thinkers associated with the Enlightenment did not reject the idea that systems of ideas should be general and should make rational sense, but they did make greater efforts to derive their ideas from the real world and to test them there. In other words, they wanted to combine empirical research with reason (Seidman, 1983:36–37). The model for this was science, especially Newtonian physics. At this point, we see the emergence of the application of the scientific method to social issues. Not only did Enlightenment thinkers want their ideas to be, at least in part, derived from the real world, they also wanted them to be useful to the social world, especially in the critical analysis of that world.

Overall, the Enlightenment was characterized by the belief that people could comprehend and control the universe by means of reason and empirical research. The view was that because the physical world was dominated by natural laws, it was likely that the social world was too. Thus it was up to the philosopher, using reason and research, to discover these social laws. Once they understood how the social world worked, the Enlightenment thinkers had a practical goal—the creation of a "better," more rational world.

With an emphasis on reason, the Enlightenment philosophers were inclined to reject beliefs in traditional authority. When these thinkers examined traditional values and institutions, they often found them to be irrational—that is, contrary to human nature and inhibitive of human growth and development. The mission of the practical and change-oriented philosophers of the Enlightenment was to overcome these irrational systems. The theorists who were most directly and positively influenced by Enlightenment thinking were Alexis de Tocqueville and Karl Marx, although the latter formed his early theoretical ideas in Germany.

The Conservative Reaction to the Enlightenment

On the surface, we might think that French classical sociological theory, like Marx's theory, was directly and positively influenced by the Enlightenment. French sociology became rational, empirical, scientific, and change-oriented, but not before it was also shaped by a set of ideas that developed in reaction to the Enlightenment. In Seidman's view, "The ideology of the counter-Enlightenment represented a virtual inversion of Enlightenment liberalism. In place of modernist premises, we can detect in the Enlightenment critics a strong anti-modernist sentiment" (1983:51). As we will see, sociology in general, and French sociology in particular, have from the beginning been an uncomfortable mix of Enlightenment and counter-Enlightenment ideas.

The most extreme form of opposition to Enlightenment ideas was French Catholic counterrevolutionary philosophy, as represented by the ideas of Louis de Bonald (1754–1840) and Joseph de Maistre (1753–1821) (Reedy, 1994; Bradley, 2005a, 2005b). These men were reacting against not only the Enlightenment but also the French Revolution, which they saw partly as a product of the kind of thinking characteristic of the Enlightenment. Bonald, for example, was disturbed by the revolutionary changes and yearned for a return to the peace and harmony of the Middle Ages. In this view, God was the source of society; therefore, reason, which was so important to the Enlightenment philosophers, was seen as inferior to traditional religious beliefs. Furthermore, it was believed that because God had created society, people should not tamper with it and should not try to change a holy creation. By extension, Bonald opposed anything that undermined such traditional institutions as patriarchy, the monogamous family, the monarchy, and the Catholic Church.

Although Bonald represented a rather extreme form of the conservative reaction, his work constitutes a useful introduction to its general premises. The conservatives turned away from what they considered the "naive" rationalism of the Enlightenment. They not only recognized the irrational aspects of social life but also assigned them positive value. Thus they regarded such phenomena as tradition, imagination, emotionalism, and religion as useful and necessary components of social life. In that they disliked upheaval and sought to retain the existing order, they deplored developments such as the French Revolution and the Industrial Revolution, which they saw as disruptive forces. The conservatives tended to emphasize social order, an emphasis that became one of the central themes of the work of several sociological theorists.

Zeitlin (1996) outlined ten major propositions that he sees as emerging from the conservative reaction and providing the basis for the development of classical French sociological theory.

1. Whereas Enlightenment thinkers tended to emphasize the individual, the conservative reaction led to a major sociological interest in, and emphasis on, society and other large-scale phenomena. Society was viewed as something more than simply an aggregate of individuals. Society was seen as having an existence of its own with its own laws of development and deep roots in the past.

2. Society was the most important unit of analysis; it was seen as more important than the individual. It was society that produced the individual, primarily through the process of socialization.

3. The individual was not even seen as the most basic element within society. A society consisted of such component parts as roles, positions, relationships, structures, and institutions. Individuals were seen as doing little more than filling these units within society.

4. The parts of society were seen as interrelated and interdependent. Indeed, these interrelationships were a major basis of society. This view led to a conservative political orientation. That is, because the parts were held to be interrelated, it followed that tampering with one part could well lead to the undermining of other parts and, ultimately, of the system as a whole. This meant that changes in the social system should be made with extreme care.

5. Change was seen as a threat not only to society and its components but also to the individuals in society. The various components of society were seen as satisfying people's needs. When institutions were disrupted, people were likely to suffer, and their suffering was likely to lead to social disorder.

6. The general tendency was to see the various large-scale components of society as useful for both society and the individuals in it. As a result, there was little desire to look for the negative effects of existing social structures and social institutions.

7. Small units, such as the family, the neighborhood, and religious and occupational groups, also were seen as essential to individuals and society. They provided the intimate, face-to-face environments that people needed in order to survive in modern societies.

8. There was a tendency to see various modern social changes, such as industrialization, urbanization, and bureaucratization, as having disorganizing effects. These changes were viewed with fear and anxiety, and there was an emphasis on developing ways of dealing with their disruptive effects.

9. While most of these feared changes were leading to a more rational society, the conservative reaction led to an emphasis on the importance of nonrational factors (ritual, ceremony, and worship, for example) in social life.

10. Finally, the conservatives supported the existence of a hierarchical system in society. It was seen as important to society that there be a differential system of status and reward.

These ten propositions, derived from the conservative reaction to the Enlightenment, should be seen as the immediate intellectual basis of the development of sociological theory in France. Many of these ideas made their way into early sociological thought, although some of the Enlightenment ideas (empiricism, for example) were also influential.[3]

The Development of French Sociology

We turn now to the actual founding of sociology as a distinctive discipline—specifically, to the work of four French thinkers: Alexis de Tocqueville, Claude Saint-Simon, Auguste Comte, and especially Emile Durkheim.

Alexis de Tocqueville (1805–1859)

We begin with Alexis de Tocqueville even though he was born after both Saint-Simon and Comte. We do so because he and his work were such pure products of the Enlightenment (he was strongly and directly influenced by Montesquieu [B. Singer, 2005b], especially his *The Spirit of the Laws* [1748]) and because his work was not part of

---

[3] Although we have emphasized the discontinuities between the Enlightenment and the counter-Enlightenment, Seidman makes the point that there also are continuities and linkages. First, the counter-Enlightenment carried on the scientific tradition developed in the Enlightenment. Second, it picked up the Enlightenment emphasis on collectivities (as opposed to individuals) and greatly extended it. Third, both had an interest in the problems of the modern world, especially its negative effects on individuals.

ALEXIS DE TOCQUEVILLE

A Biographical Sketch

Alexis de Tocqueville was born on July 29, 1805, in Paris. He came from a prominent though not wealthy aristocratic family. The family had suffered during the French Revolution. Tocqueville's parents had been arrested but managed to avoid the guillotine. Tocqueville was well educated, became a lawyer and judge (although he was not very successful at either), and became well and widely read especially in the Enlightenment philosophy (Rousseau and Montesquieu) that played such a central role in much classical social theory.

The turning point in Tocqueville's life began on April 2, 1831, when he and a friend (Gustave de Beaumont) journeyed to the United States ostensibly to study the American penitentiary system. He saw America as a laboratory in which he could study, in their nascent state, such key phenomena to him as democracy, equality, and freedom. He traveled widely throughout much of the then-developed (and some undeveloped) parts of the United States (and a bit of Canada), getting as far west as Green Bay (Wisconsin) and Memphis (Tennessee) and New Orleans (Louisiana), traveling through large parts of the northeastern, middle Atlantic, and southern states, as well as some midwestern states east of the Mississippi River. He talked to all sorts of people along the way, asked systematic questions, took copious notes, and allowed his interests to evolve on the basis of what he found along the way. Tocqueville (and Beaumont) returned to France on February 20, 1832, having spent less than a year studying the vast physical and social landscape of the United States as it existed then.

It took Tocqueville some time to get started on the first volume of *Democracy in America,* but he began in earnest in late 1833 and the book was published by 1835. It was a great success and made him famous. The irony here is that one of the classic works on democracy in general, and American democracy in particular, was written by a French aristocrat. He launched a political career while putting the finishing touches on volume two of *Democracy,* which appeared in 1840. This volume was more sociological (Aron, 1965) than the first, which was clearly about politics, particularly the American political system and how it compared to other political systems, especially the French

the clear line of development in French social theory from Saint-Simon and Comte to the crucially important Durkheim. Tocqueville has long been seen as a political scientist, not a sociologist, and furthermore many have not perceived the existence of a social theory in his work (e.g., Seidman, 1983:306). However, not only is there a social theory in his work, but it is one that deserves a much more significant place in the history of social theory not only in France but in the rest of the world.

system. (In general, Tocqueville was very favorably disposed to the American system, although he had reservations about democracy more generally.) Volume two was not well received, perhaps because of this shift in orientation, as well as the book's more abstract nature.

Tocqueville continued in politics and, even though he was an aristocrat, was comparatively liberal in many of his views. Of this, he said:

> People ascribe to me alternatively aristocratic and democratic prejudices. If I had been born in another period, or in another country, I might have had either one or the other. But my birth, as it happened, made it easy for me to guard against both. I came into the world at the end of a long revolution, which, after destroying ancient institutions, created none that could last. When I entered life, aristocracy was dead and democracy was yet unborn. My instinct, therefore, could not lead me blindly either to the one or the other.
> (Tocqueville, cited in Nisbet, 1976–1977:61).

It is because of this ambivalence that Nisbet (1976–1977:65) argues that unlike the development of Marxism flowing from Marx's intellectual certainty, "at no time has there been, or is there likely to be, anything called Tocquevilleism."

Tocqueville lived through the Revolution of 1848 and the abdication of the king. However, he opposed the military coup staged by Louis Napoleon, spent a few days in jail, and saw, as a result, the end of his political career (he had become minister of foreign affairs but was fired by Louis Napoleon). He never accepted the dictatorship of Napoleon III and grew increasingly critical of the political direction taken by France. As a way of critiquing the France of his day, Tocqueville decided to write about the French Revolution of 1789 (although he believed it continued through the first half of the nineteenth century and to his day) in his other well-known book, *The Old Regime and the Revolutions,* which was published in 1856. The book focused on French despotism but continued the concerns of *Democracy in America* with the relationship between freedom, equality, and democracy. Unlike the second volume of *Democracy in America, Old Regime* was well received and quite successful. It made Tocqueville the "grand old man" of the liberal movement of the day in France.

Tocqueville died at age 53 on April 16, 1859 (Janara, 2011; Mancini, 1994; Zunz and Kahan, 2002). One can gain a great deal of insight into the man and his thinking though *The Recollections of Alexis de Tocqueville* (Tocqueville, 1893/1959), his posthumously published memoirs of the Revolution of 1848 and his role in it.

Tocqueville is best known for the legendary and highly influential *Democracy in America* (1835/1840/1969), especially the first volume, which deals, in a very laudatory way, with the early American democratic system and came to be seen as an early contribution to the development of "political science." However, in the later volumes of that work, as well as in later works, Tocqueville clearly develops a broad social theory that deserves a place in the canon of social theory.

Three interrelated issues lie at the heart of Tocqueville's theory. As a product of the Enlightenment, he is first and foremost a great supporter of, and advocate for, *freedom*. However, he is much more critical of *equality,* which he sees as tending to produce mediocrity in comparison to the higher-quality outcomes associated with the aristocrats (he himself was an aristocrat) of a prior, more inegalitarian, era. More important, equality and mediocrity are also linked to what most concerns him, and that is the growth of *centralization,* especially in the government, and the threat centralized government poses to freedom. In his view, it was the inequality of the prior age, the power of the aristocrats, that acted to keep government centralization in check. How-ever, with the demise of aristocrats, and the rise of greater equality, there are no groups capable of countering the ever-present tendency toward centralization. The mass of largely equal people are too "servile" to oppose this trend. Furthermore, Tocqueville links equality to "individualism" (an important concept that he claimed to "invent" and for which he is credited), and the resulting individualists are far less interested in the well-being of the larger "community" than were the aristocrats who preceded them.

It is for this reason that Tocqueville is critical of democracy and especially socialism. Democracy's commitment to freedom was ultimately threatened by its par-allel commitment to equality and its tendency toward centralized government. Of course, from Tocqueville's point of view the situation would be far worse in socialism because its far greater commitment to equality, and the much greater likelihood of government centralization, posed a far greater threat to freedom. The latter view is quite prescient given what transpired in the Soviet Union and other societies that operated, at least in name, under the banner of socialism.

Thus, the strength of Tocqueville's theory lies in the interrelated ideas of free-dom, equality, and especially centralization. His "grand narrative" on the increasing control of central governments anticipates other theories including Weber's work on bureaucracy and especially the more contemporary work of Michel Foucault on "gov-ernmentality" and its gradual spread, increasing subtlety, and propensity to invade even the "soul" of the people controlled by it. There is a very profound social theory in Tocqueville's work, but it had no influence on the theories and theorists to be discussed in the remainder of this section on French social theory. Its influence was largely restricted to the development of political science and to work on American democracy and the French Revolution (Tocqueville, 1856/1983). There are certainly sociologists (and other social scientists) who recognized his importance, especially those interested in the relationship between individualism and community (Bellah et al., 1985; Nisbet, 1953; Putnam, 2001; Riesman, 1950), but to this day Tocqueville's theories have not been accorded the place they deserve in social theory in general, and even in French social theory (Gane, 2003).

Claude Henri Saint-Simon (1760–1825)

Saint-Simon was older than Auguste Comte (see next page), and in fact Comte, in his early years, served as Saint-Simon's secretary and disciple. There is a very strong similarity between the ideas of these two thinkers, yet a bitter debate developed between them that led to their eventual split (Pickering, 1993; K. Thompson, 1975).

The most interesting aspect of Saint-Simon was his significance to the development of *both* conservative (like Comte's) and radical Marxian theory. On the conservative side, Saint-Simon wanted to preserve society as it was, but he did not seek a return to life as it had been in the Middle Ages, as did Bonald and Maistre. In addition, he was a *positivist* (Durkheim, 1928/1962:142), which meant that he believed that the study of social phenomena should employ the same scientific techniques that were used in the natural sciences. On the radical side, Saint-Simon saw the need for socialist reforms, especially the centralized planning of the economic system. But Saint-Simon did not go nearly as far as Marx did later. Although he, like Marx, saw the capitalists superseding the feudal nobility, he felt it inconceivable that the working class would come to replace the capitalists. Many of Saint-Simon's ideas are found in Comte's work, but Comte developed them in a more systematic fashion (Pickering, 1997).

Auguste Comte (1798–1857)

Comte was the first to use the term *sociology* (Pickering, 2011; J. Turner, 2001).[4] He had an enormous influence on later sociological theorists (especially Herbert Spencer and Emile Durkheim). And he believed that the study of sociology should be scientific, just as many classical theorists did and most contemporary sociologists do (Lenzer, 1975).

Comte was greatly disturbed by the anarchy that pervaded French society and was critical of those thinkers who had spawned both the Enlightenment and the French Revolution. He developed his scientific view, "positivism," or "positive philosophy," to combat what he considered to be the negative and destructive philosophy of the Enlightenment. Comte was in line with, and influenced by, the French counterrevolutionary Catholics (especially Bonald and Maistre). However, his work can be set apart from theirs on at least two grounds. First, he did not think it possible to return to the Middle Ages; advances in science and industry made that impossible. Second, he developed a much more sophisticated theoretical system than his predecessors, one that was adequate to shape a good portion of early sociology.

Comte developed *social physics,* or what in 1839 he called *sociology* (Pickering, 2011). The use of the term *social physics* made it clear that Comte sought to model sociology after the "hard sciences." This new science, which in his view would ultimately become *the* dominant science, was to be concerned with both social statics (existing social structures) and social dynamics (social change). Although both involved the search for laws of social life, he felt that social dynamics was more important than social statics. This focus on change reflected his interest in social reform, particularly reform of the ills created by the French Revolution and the Enlightenment. Comte did not urge revolutionary change, because he felt the natural evolution of society would make things better. Reforms were needed only to assist the process a bit.

---

[4] While he recognizes that Comte created the label "sociology," Eriksson (1993) has challenged the idea that Comte is the progenitor of modern, scientific sociology. Rather, Eriksson sees people like Adam Smith, and more generally the Scottish Moralists as the true source of modern sociology. See also L. Hill (1996) on the importance of Adam Ferguson, Ullmann-Margalit (1997) on Ferguson and Adam Smith, and Rundell (2001).

AUGUSTE COMTE

A Biographical Sketch

Auguste Comte was born in Montpelier, France, on January 19, 1798 (Pickering, 1993:7; Wernick, 2005a; Orenstein, 2007). His parents were middle class, and his father eventually rose to the position of official local agent for the tax collector. Although a precocious student, Comte never received a college-level degree. He and his whole class were dismissed from the Ecole Polytechnique for their rebelliousness and their political ideas. This expulsion had an adverse effect on Comte's academic career. In 1817 he became secretary (and "adopted son" [Manuel, 1962:251]) to Claude Henri Saint-Simon, a philosopher forty years Comte's senior. They worked closely together for several years, and Comte acknowledged his great debt to Saint-Simon: "I certainly owe a great deal intellectually to Saint-Simon . . . he contributed powerfully to launching me in the philosophic direction that I clearly created for myself today and which I will follow without hesitation all my life" (Durkheim, 1928/1962:144). But in 1824 they had a falling-out because Comte believed that Saint-Simon wanted to omit Comte's name from one of his contributions. Comte later wrote of his relationship with Saint-Simon as "catastrophic" (Pickering, 1993:238) and described him as a "depraved juggler" (Durkheim, 1928/1962:144). In 1852, Comte said of Saint-Simon, "I owed nothing to this personage" (Pickering, 1993:240).

Heilbron (1995) describes Comte as short (perhaps 5 feet, 2 inches), a bit cross-eyed, and very insecure in social situations, especially ones involving women. He was also alienated from society as a whole. These facts may help account for the fact that Comte married Caroline Massin (the marriage lasted from 1825 to 1842). She was an illegitimate child whom Comte later called a "prostitute," although that label has been questioned recently (Pickering, 1997:37). Comte's personal insecurities stood in contrast to his great security about his own intellectual capacities, and it appears that his self-esteem was well founded:

> Comte's prodigious memory is famous. Endowed with a photographic memory he could recite backwards the words of any page he had read but once. His powers of concentration were such that he could sketch out an entire

This leads us to the cornerstone of Comte's approach—his evolutionary theory, or the *law of the three stages*. The theory proposes that there are three intellectual stages through which the world has gone throughout its history. According to Comte, not only does the world go through this process, but groups, societies, sciences, individuals, and even minds go through the same three stages. The *theological stage* is book without putting pen to paper. His lectures were all delivered without notes. When he sat down to write out his books he wrote everything from memory.

(Schweber, 1991:134)

In 1826, Comte concocted a scheme by which he would present a series of seventy-two public lectures (to be held in his apartment) on his philosophy. The course drew a distinguished audience, but it was halted after three lectures when Comte suffered a nervous breakdown. He continued to suffer from mental problems, and once in 1827 he tried (unsuccessfully) to commit suicide by throwing himself into the Seine River.

Although he could not get a regular position at the Ecole Polytechnique, Comte did get a minor position as a teaching assistant there in 1832. In 1837, Comte was given the additional post of admissions examiner, and this, for the first time, gave him an adequate income (he had often been economically dependent on his family until this time). During this period, Comte worked on the six-volume work for which he is best known, *Cours de Philosophie Positive,* which was finally published in its entirety in 1842 (the first volume had been published in 1830). In that work Comte outlined his view that sociology was the ultimate science. He also attacked the Ecole Polytechnique, and the result was that in 1844 his assistantship there was not renewed. By 1851 he had completed the four-volume *Systeme de Politique Positive,* which had a more practical intent, offering a grand plan for the reorganization of society.

Heilbron argues that a major break took place in Comte's life in 1838 and it was then that he lost hope that anyone would take his work on science in general, and sociology in particular, seriously. It was also at that point that he embarked on his life of "cerebral hygiene"; that is, Comte began to avoid reading the work of other people, with the result that he became hopelessly out of touch with recent intellectual developments. It was after 1838 that he began developing his bizarre ideas about reforming society that found expression in *Systeme de Politique Positive.* Comte came to fancy himself as the high priest of a new religion of humanity; he believed in a world that eventually would be led by sociologist-priests. (Comte had been strongly influenced by his Catholic background.) Interestingly, in spite of such outrageous ideas, Comte eventually developed a considerable following in France, as well as in a number of other countries.

Auguste Comte died on September 5, 1857.

the first, and it characterized the world prior to 1300. During this period, the major idea system emphasized the belief that supernatural powers and religious figures, modeled after humankind, are at the root of everything. In particular, the social and physical world is seen as produced by God. The second stage is the *metaphysical* stage, which occurred roughly between 1300 and 1800. This era was characterized by the belief that abstract forces like "nature," rather than personalized gods, explain virtually everything. Finally, in 1800 the world entered the *positivistic* stage, characterized by belief in science. People now tended to give up the search for absolute causes (God or nature) and concentrated instead on observation of the social and physical world in the search for the laws governing them.

It is clear that in his theory of the world Comte focused on intellectual factors. Indeed, he argued that intellectual disorder is the cause of social disorder. The disorder stemmed from earlier idea systems (theological and metaphysical) that continued to exist in the positivistic (scientific) age. Only when positivism gained total control would social upheavals cease. Because this was an evolutionary process, there was no need to foment social upheaval and revolution. Positivism would come, although perhaps not as quickly as some would like. Here Comte's social reformism and his sociology coincide. Sociology could expedite the arrival of positivism and hence bring order to the social world. Above all, Comte did not want to seem to be espousing revolution. There was, in his view, enough disorder in the world. In any case, from Comte's point of view, it was intellectual change that was needed, and so there was little reason for social and political revolution.

We have already encountered several of Comte's positions that were to be of great significance to the development of classical sociology—his basic conservatism, reformism, and scientism and his evolutionary view of the world. Several other aspects of his work deserve mention because they also were to play a major role in the development of sociological theory. For example, his sociology does not focus on the individual but rather takes as its basic unit of analysis larger entities such as the family. He also urged that we look at both social structure and social change. Of great importance to later sociological theory, especially the work of Spencer and Parsons, is Comte's stress on the systematic character of society—the links among and between the various components of society. He also accorded great importance to the role of consensus in society. He saw little merit in the idea that society is characterized by inevitable conflict between workers and capitalists. In addition, Comte emphasized the need to engage in abstract theorizing and to go out and do sociological research. He urged that sociologists use observation, experimentation, and comparative historical analysis. Finally, Comte believed that sociology ultimately would become the dominant scientific force in the world because of its distinctive ability to interpret social laws and to develop reforms aimed at patching up problems within the system.

Comte was in the forefront of the development of positivistic sociology (Bryant, 1985; Halfpenny, 1982). To Jonathan Turner, Comte's positivism emphasized that "the social universe is amenable to the development of abstract laws that can be tested through the careful collection of data," and "these abstract laws will denote the basic and generic properties of the social universe and they will specify their 'natural relations'" (1985:24). As we will see, a number of classical theorists (especially Spencer and Durkheim) shared Comte's interest in the discovery of the laws of social life. While positivism remains important in contemporary sociology, it has come under attack from a number of quarters (Morrow, 1994).

Even though Comte lacked a solid academic base on which to build a school of Comtian sociological theory, he nevertheless laid a basis for the development of a significant stream of sociological theory. But his long-term significance is dwarfed by that of his successor in French sociology and the inheritor of a number of its ideas, Emile Durkheim. (For a debate over the canonization of Durkheim, as well as other classical theorists discussed in this chapter, see D. Parker, 1997; Mouzelis, 1997.)

Emile Durkheim (1858–1917)

Durkheim's relation to the Enlightenment was much more ambiguous than Comte's. Durkheim has been seen as an inheritor of the Enlightenment tradition because of his emphasis on science and social reformism. However, he also has been seen as the inheritor of the conservative tradition, especially as it was manifested in Comte's work. But whereas Comte had remained outside of academia (as had Tocqueville), Durkheim developed an increasingly solid academic base as his career progressed. Durkheim legitimized sociology in France, and his work ultimately became a dominant force in the development of sociology in general and of sociological theory in particular (Rawls, 2007; R. Jones, 2000; Milbrandt and Pearce, 2011).

Durkheim was politically liberal, but he took a more conservative position intellectually. Like Comte and the Catholic counterrevolutionaries, Durkheim feared and hated social disorder. His work was informed by the disorders produced by the general social changes discussed earlier in this chapter, as well as by others (such as industrial strikes, disruption of the ruling class, church-state discord, the rise of political anti-Semitism) more specific to the France of Durkheim's time (Karady, 1983). In fact, most of his work was devoted to the study of social order. His view was that social disorders are not a necessary part of the modern world and could be reduced by social reforms. Whereas Marx saw the problems of the modern world as inherent in society, Durkheim (along with most other classical theorists) did not. As a result, Marx's ideas on the need for social revolution stood in sharp contrast to the reformism of Durkheim and the others. As classical sociological theory developed, it was the Durkheimian interest in order and reform that came to dominate, while the Marxian position was eclipsed.

Social Facts

Durkheim developed a distinctive conception of the subject matter of sociology and then tested it in an empirical study. In *The Rules of Sociological Method* (1895/1982), Durkheim argued that it is the special task of sociology to study what he called *social facts* (Nielsen, 2005a, 2007a). He conceived of social facts as forces (Takla and Pope, 1985) and structures that are external to, and coercive of, the individual. The study of these large-scale structures and forces—for example, institutionalized law and shared moral beliefs—and their impact on people became the concern of many later sociological theorists (Parsons, for example). In *Suicide* (1897/1951), Durkheim reasoned that if he could link such an individual behavior as suicide to social causes (social facts), he would have made a persuasive case for the importance of the discipline of sociology. But Durkheim did not examine why individual *A* or *B* committed suicide; rather, he was interested in the causes of differences in suicide rates among groups, regions, countries, and different categories of people (for example, married and single). His basic argument was that it was the nature of, and changes in, social facts that led to differences in suicide rates. For example, a war or an economic depression would create a collective mood of depression that would in turn lead to increases in suicide rates. More will be said on this subject in Chapter 3, but the key point is that Durkheim developed a distinctive view of sociology and sought to demonstrate its usefulness in a scientific study of suicide.

In *The Rules of Sociological Method* (1895/1982), Durkheim differentiated between two types of social facts—material and nonmaterial. Although he dealt with both in the course of his work, his main focus was on *nonmaterial social facts* (for example, culture, social institutions) rather than *material social facts* (for example, bureaucracy, law). This concern for nonmaterial social facts was already clear in his earliest major work, *The Division of Labor in Society* (1893/1964). His focus there was a comparative analysis of what held society together in the primitive and modern cases. He concluded that earlier societies were held together primarily by nonmaterial social facts, specifically, a strongly held common morality, or what he called a strong *collective conscience*. However, because of the complexities of modern society, there had been a decline in the strength of the collective conscience. The primary bond in the modern world was an intricate division of labor, which tied people to others in dependency relationships. However, Durkheim felt that the modern division of labor brought with it several "pathologies"; it was, in other words, an inadequate method of holding society together. Given his conservative sociology, Durkheim did not feel that revolution was needed to solve these problems. Rather, he suggested a variety of reforms that could "patch up" the modern system and keep it functioning. Although he recognized that there was no going back to the age when a powerful collective conscience predominated, he did feel that the common morality could be strengthened in modern society and that people thereby could cope better with the pathologies that they were experiencing.

Religion

In his later work, nonmaterial social facts occupied an even more central position. In fact, he came to focus on perhaps the ultimate form of a nonmaterial social fact—religion—in his last major work, *The Elementary Forms of Religious Life* (1912/1965). Durkheim examined primitive society in order to find the roots of religion. He believed that he would be better able to find those roots in the comparative simplicity of primitive society than in the complexity of the modern world. What he found, he felt, was that the source of religion was society itself. Society comes to define certain things as religious and others as profane. Specifically, in the case he studied, the clan was the source of a primitive kind of religion, *totemism*, in which things like plants and animals are deified. Totemism, in turn, was seen as a specific type of nonmaterial social fact, a form of the collective conscience. In the end, Durkheim came to argue that society and religion (or, more generally, the collective conscience) were one and the same. Religion was the way society expressed itself in the form of a nonmaterial social fact. In a sense, then, Durkheim came to deify society and its major products. Clearly, in deifying society, Durkheim took a highly conservative stance: one would not want to overturn a deity *or* its societal source.

Because he identified society with God, Durkheim was not inclined to urge social revolution. Instead, he was a social reformer seeking ways of improving the functioning of society. In these and other ways, Durkheim was clearly in line with French conservative sociology. The fact that he avoided many of its excesses helped make him the most significant figure in French sociology.

These books and other important works helped carve out a distinctive domain for sociology in the academic world of turn-of-the-century France, and they earned Durkheim the leading position in that growing field. In 1898, Durkheim set up a scholarly journal devoted to sociology, *L'année sociologique* (Besnard, 1983). It became a powerful force in the development and spread of sociological ideas. Durkheim was intent on fostering the growth of sociology, and he used his journal as a focal point for the development of a group of disciples. They later would extend his ideas and carry them to many other locales and into the study of other aspects of the social world (for example, sociology of law and sociology of the city) (Besnard, 1983:1). By 1910, Durkheim had established a strong center of sociology in France, and the academic institutionalization of sociology was well under way in that nation (Heilbron, 1995).

The Development of German Sociology

Whereas the early history of French sociology is a fairly coherent story of the progression from the Enlightenment and the French Revolution to the conservative reaction and to the increasingly important sociological ideas of Tocqueville, Saint-Simon, Comte, and Durkheim, German sociology was fragmented from the beginning. A split developed between Marx (and his supporters), who remained on the edge of sociology, and the early giants of mainstream German sociology, Max Weber and Georg Simmel.[5] However, although Marxian theory itself was deemed unacceptable, its ideas found their way in a variety of positive and negative ways into mainstream German sociology.

The Roots and Nature of the Theories of Karl Marx (1818–1883)

The dominant intellectual influence on Karl Marx was the German philosopher G.W.F. Hegel (1770–1831).

Hegel

According to Terence Ball, "it is difficult for us to appreciate the degree to which Hegel dominated German thought in the second quarter of the nineteenth century. It was largely within the framework of his philosophy that educated Germans—including the young Marx—discussed history, politics and culture" (1991:25). Marx's education at the University of Berlin was shaped by Hegel's ideas as well as by the split that developed

---

[5] For an argument against this and the view of continuity between Marxian and mainstream sociology, see Seidman (1983).

among Hegel's followers after his death. The "Old Hegelians" continued to subscribe to the master's ideas, while the "Young Hegelians," although still working in the Hegelian tradition, were critical of many facets of his philosophical system.

Two concepts represent the essence of Hegel's philosophy—the dialectic and idealism (Beamish, 2007a; Hegel, 1807/1967, 1821/1967). The *dialectic* is both a way of thinking and an image of the world. On the one hand, it is a way of thinking that stresses the importance of processes, relations, dynamics, conflicts, and contradictions—a dynamic rather than a static way of thinking about the world. On the other hand, it is a view that the world is made up not of static structures but of processes, relationships, dynamics, conflicts, and contradictions. Although the dialectic generally is associated with Hegel, it certainly predates him in philosophy. Marx, trained in the Hegelian tradition, accepted the significance of the dialectic. However, he was critical of some aspects of the way Hegel used it. For example, Hegel tended to apply the dialectic only to ideas, whereas Marx felt that it applied as well to more material aspects of life, for example, the economy.

Hegel is also associated with the philosophy of *idealism* (Kleiner, 2005), which emphasizes the importance of the mind and mental products rather than the material world. It is the social definition of the physical and material worlds that matters most, not those worlds themselves. In its extreme form, idealism asserts that *only* the mind and psychological constructs exist. Some idealists believed that their mental processes would remain the same even if the physical and social worlds no longer existed. Idealists emphasize not only mental processes but also the ideas produced by these processes. Hegel paid a great deal of attention to the development of such ideas, especially to what he referred to as the "spirit" of society.

In fact, Hegel offered a kind of evolutionary theory of the world in idealistic terms. At first, people were endowed only with the ability to acquire a sensory understanding of the world around them. They could understand things like the sight, smell, and feel of the social and physical world. Later, people developed the ability to be conscious of, to understand, themselves. With self-knowledge and self-understanding, people began to understand that they could become more than they were. In terms of Hegel's dialectical approach, a contradiction developed between what people were and what they felt they could be. The resolution of this contradiction lay in the development of an individual's awareness of his or her place in the larger spirit of society. Individuals come to realize that their ultimate fulfillment lies in the development and the expansion of the spirit of society as a whole. Thus, in Hegel's scheme, individuals evolve from an understanding of things to an understanding of self to an understanding of their place in the larger scheme of things.

Hegel, then, offered a general theory of the evolution of the world. It is a subjective theory in which change is held to occur at the level of consciousness. However, that change occurs largely beyond the control of actors. Actors are reduced to little more than vessels swept along by the inevitable evolution of consciousness.

Feuerbach

Ludwig Feuerbach (1804–1872) was an important bridge between Hegel and Marx (Staples, 2007). As a Young Hegelian, Feuerbach was critical of Hegel for, among other things, his excessive emphasis on consciousness and the spirit of society. Feuerbach's adoption of a materialist philosophy led him to argue that what was needed was to move from Hegel's subjective idealism to a focus not on ideas but on the material reality of real human beings. In his critique of Hegel, Feuerbach focused on religion. To Feuerbach, God is simply a projection by people of their human essence onto an impersonal force. People set God over and above themselves, with the result that they become alienated from God and project a series of positive characteristics onto God (that he is perfect, almighty, and holy), while they reduce themselves to being imperfect, powerless, and sinful. Feuerbach argued that this kind of religion must be overcome and that its defeat could be aided by a materialist philosophy in which people (not religion) became their own highest object, ends in themselves. Real people, not abstract ideas like religion, are deified by a materialist philosophy.

Marx, Hegel, and Feuerbach

Marx was simultaneously influenced by, and critical of, *both* Hegel and Feuerbach. Marx, following Feuerbach, was critical of Hegel's adherence to an idealist philosophy. Marx took this position not only because of his adoption of a materialist orientation but also because of his interest in practical activities. Social facts like wealth and the state are treated by Hegel as ideas rather than as real, material entities. Even when he examined a seemingly material process like labor, Hegel was looking only at abstract mental labor. This is very different from Marx's interest in the labor of real, sentient people. Thus Hegel was looking at the wrong issues as far as Marx was concerned. In addition, Marx felt that Hegel's idealism led to a very conservative political orientation. To Hegel, the process of evolution was occurring beyond the control of people and their activities. In any case, in that people seemed to be moving toward greater consciousness of the world as it could be, there seemed no need for any revolutionary change; the process was already moving in the "desired" direction. Whatever problems did exist lay in consciousness, and the answer therefore seemed to lie in changing thinking.

Marx took a very different position, arguing that the problems of modern life can be traced to real, material sources (for example, the structures of capitalism) and that the solutions, therefore, can be found only in the overturning of those structures by the collective action of large numbers of people (Marx and Engels, 1845/1956:254). Whereas Hegel "stood the world on its head" (that is, focused on consciousness, not the real material world), Marx firmly embedded his dialectic in a material base.

Marx applauded Feuerbach's critique of Hegel on a number of counts (for example, its materialism and its rejection of the abstractness of Hegel's theory), but he was far from fully satisfied with Feuerbach's position (Thomson, 1994). For one thing, Feuerbach focused on the religious world, whereas Marx believed that it was the entire social world, and the economy in particular, that had to be analyzed. Although Marx accepted Feuerbach's materialism, he felt that Feuerbach had gone too far in focusing onesidedly, nondialectically, on the material world. Feuerbach failed to include the most important of Hegel's contributions, the dialectic, in his materialist orientation, particularly the relationship between people and the material world. Finally, Marx argued that Feuerbach, like most philosophers, failed to emphasize *praxis*—practical activity—in particular, revolutionary activity (Wortmann, 2007). As Marx put it, "The philosophers have only *interpreted* the world, in various ways; the point, however, is to *change* it" (cited in Tucker, 1970:109).

Marx extracted what he considered to be the two most important elements from these two thinkers—Hegel's dialectic and Feuerbach's materialism—and fused them into his own distinctive orientation, *dialectical materialism,*[6] which focuses on dialectical relationships within the material world.

Political Economy

Marx's materialism and his consequent focus on the economic sector led him rather naturally to the work of a group of *political economists* (for example, Adam Smith and David Ricardo) (Howard and King, 2005). Marx was very attracted to a number of their positions. He lauded their basic premise that labor was the source of all wealth. This ultimately led Marx to his *labor theory of value,* in which he argued that the profit of the capitalist was based on the exploitation of the laborer. Capitalists performed the rather simple trick of paying the workers less than they deserved, because they received less pay than the value of what they actually produced in a work period. This *surplus value,* which was retained and reinvested by the capitalist, was the basis of the entire capitalist system. The capitalist system grew by continually increasing the level of exploitation of the workers (and therefore the amount of surplus value) and investing the profits for the expansion of the system.

Marx also was affected by the political economists' depiction of the horrors of the capitalist system and the exploitation of the workers. However, whereas they depicted the evils of capitalism, Marx criticized the political economists for seeing these evils as inevitable components of capitalism. Marx deplored their general acceptance of capitalism and the way they urged people to work for economic success within it. He also was critical of the political economists for failing to see the inherent conflict between capitalists and laborers and for denying the need for a radical change in the economic order. Such conservative economics was hard for Marx to accept, given his commitment to a radical change from capitalism to socialism.

Marx and Sociology

Marx was not a sociologist and did not consider himself one. Although his work is too broad to be encompassed by the term *sociology,* there is a sociological theory to be found in Marx's work. From the beginning, there were those who were heavily influenced by Marx, and there has been a continuous strand of Marxian sociology, primarily in Europe. But for the majority of early sociologists, his work was a negative force, something against which to shape their sociology. Until very recently, sociological theory, especially in America, has been characterized by either hostility to or ignorance of Marxian theory. This has, as we will see in Chapter 6, changed dramatically, but the negative reaction to Marx's work was a major force in the shaping of much of sociological theory (Gurney, 1981).

---

[6] First used by Joseph Dietzgen in 1887, the term was made central by Georgi Plekhanov in 1891 (Beamish, 2007a). Although Marx certainly operated from the perspective of dialectical materialism, he never used the concept.

The basic reason for this rejection of Marx was ideological. Many of the early sociological theorists were inheritors of the conservative reaction to the disruptions of the Enlightenment and the French Revolution. Marx's radical ideas and the radical social changes he foretold and sought to bring to life were clearly feared and hated by such thinkers. Marx was dismissed as an ideologist. It was argued that he was not a serious sociological theorist. However, ideology per se could not have been the real reason for the rejection of Marx, because the work of Comte, Durkheim, and other conservative thinkers also was heavily ideological. It was the nature of the ideology, not the existence of ideology as such, that put off many sociological theorists. They were ready and eager to buy conservative ideology wrapped in a cloak of sociological theory, but not the radical ideology offered by Marx and his followers.

There were, of course, other reasons why Marx was not accepted by many early theorists. He seemed to be more an economist than a sociologist. Although the early sociologists would certainly admit the importance of the economy, they would also argue that it was only one of a number of components of social life.

Another reason for the early rejection of Marx was the nature of his interests. Whereas the early sociologists were reacting to the disorder created by the Enlightenment, the French Revolution, and later the Industrial Revolution, Marx was not upset by these disorders—or by disorder in general. Rather, what interested and concerned Marx most was the oppressiveness of the capitalist system that was emerging out of the Industrial Revolution. Marx wanted to develop a theory that explained this oppressiveness and that would help overthrow that system. Marx's interest was in revolution, which stood in contrast to the conservative concern for reform and orderly change.

Another difference worth noting is the difference in philosophical roots between Marxian and conservative sociological theory. Most of the conservative theorists were heavily influenced by the philosophy of Immanuel Kant. Among other things, this led them to think in linear, cause-and-effect terms. That is, they tended to argue that a change in A (say, the change in ideas during the Enlightenment) leads to a change in B (say, the political changes of the French Revolution). In contrast, Marx was most heavily influenced, as we have seen, by Hegel, who thought in dialectical rather than cause-and-effect terms. Among other things, the dialectic attunes us to the ongoing reciprocal effects of social forces. Thus, a dialectician would reconceptualize the example discussed above as a continual, ongoing interplay of ideas and politics.

Marx's Theory

To oversimplify enormously (see Chapter 2 for a much more detailed discussion), Marx offered a theory of capitalist society based on his image of the basic nature of human beings. Marx believed that people are basically productive; that is, in order to survive, people need to work in, and with, nature. In so doing, they produce the food, clothing, tools, shelter, and other necessities that permit them to live. Their productivity is a perfectly natural way by which they express basic creative impulses. Furthermore, these impulses are expressed in concert with other people; in other words, people are inherently social. They need to work together to produce what they need to survive.

Throughout history this natural process has been subverted, at first by the mean conditions of primitive society and later by a variety of structural arrangements erected by societies in the course of history. In various ways, these structures interfered with the natural productive process. However, it is in capitalist society that this breakdown is most acute; the breakdown in the natural productive process reaches its culmination in capitalism.

Basically capitalism is a structure (or, more accurately, a series of structures) that erects barriers between an individual and the production process, the products of that process, and other people; ultimately, it even divides the individual himself or herself. This is the basic meaning of the concept of *alienation:* it is the breakdown of the natural interconnection among people and what they produce. Alienation occurs because capitalism has evolved into a two-class system in which a few capitalists own the production process, the products, and the labor time of those who work for them. Instead of naturally producing for themselves, people produce unnaturally in capitalist society for a small group of capitalists. Intellectually, Marx was very concerned with the structures of capitalism and their oppressive impact on actors. Politically, he was led to an interest in emancipating people from the oppressive structures of capitalism.

Marx actually spent very little time dreaming about what a utopian socialist state would look like (Lovell, 1992). He was more concerned with helping to bring about the demise of capitalism. He believed that the contradictions and conflicts within capitalism would lead dialectically to its ultimate collapse, but he did not think that the process was inevitable. People had to act at the appropriate times and in the appropriate ways for socialism to come into being. The capitalists had great resources at their disposal to forestall the coming of socialism, but they could be overcome by the concerted action of a class-conscious proletariat. What would the proletariat create in the process? What is socialism? Most basically, it is a society in which, for the first time, people could approach Marx's ideal image of productivity. With the aid of modern technology, people could interact harmoniously with nature and other people to create what they needed to survive. To put it another way, in socialist society, people would no longer be alienated.

The Roots and Nature of the Theories of
Max Weber (1864–1920) and Georg Simmel (1858–1918)

Although Marx and his followers in the late nineteenth and early twentieth centuries remained outside mainstream German sociology, to a considerable extent early German sociology can be seen as developing in opposition to Marxian theory.

Weber and Marx

Albert Salomon, for example, claimed that a large part of the theory of the early giant of German sociology, Max Weber, developed "in a long and intense debate with the ghost of Marx" (1945:596). This is probably an exaggeration, but in many ways Marxian theory did play a negative role in Weberian theory. In other ways, however, Weber was working within the Marxian tradition, trying to "round out" Marx's theory. Also, there were many inputs into Weberian theory other than Marxian theory

(Burger, 1976). We can clarify a good deal about the sources of German sociology by outlining each of these views of the relationship between Marx and Weber (Antonio and Glassman, 1985; Schroeter, 1985). It should be borne in mind that Weber was not intimately familiar with Marx's work (much of it was not published until after Weber's death) and that Weber was reacting more to the work of the Marxists than to Marx's work itself (Antonio, 1985:29; B. Turner, 1981:19–20).

Weber *did* tend to view Marx and the Marxists of his day as economic determinists who offered single-cause theories of social life. That is, Marxian theory was seen as tracing all historical developments to economic bases and viewing all contemporaneous structures as erected on an economic base. Although this is not true of Marx's own theory (as we will see in Chapter 2), it was the position of many later Marxists.

One of the examples of economic determinism that seemed to rankle Weber most was the view that ideas are simply the reflections of material (especially economic) interests, that material interests determine ideology. From this point of view, Weber was supposed to have "turned Marx on his head" (much as Marx had inverted Hegel). Instead of focusing on economic factors and their effect on ideas, Weber devoted much of his attention to ideas and their effect on the economy. Rather than seeing ideas as simple reflections of economic factors, Weber saw them as fairly autonomous forces capable of profoundly affecting the economic world. Weber certainly devoted a lot of attention to ideas, particularly systems of religious ideas, and he was especially concerned with the impact of religious ideas on the economy. In *The Protestant Ethic and the Spirit of Capitalism* (1904–1905/1958), he was concerned with Protestantism, mainly as a system of ideas, and its impact on the rise of another system of ideas, the "spirit of capitalism," and ultimately on a capitalist economic system. Weber had a similar interest in other world religions, looking at how their nature might have obstructed the development of capitalism in their respective societies. On the basis of this kind of work, some scholars came to the conclusion that Weber developed his ideas in opposition to those of Marx.

A second view of Weber's relationship to Marx, as mentioned earlier, is that he did not so much oppose Marx as try to round out Marx's theoretical perspective. Here Weber is seen as working more within the Marxian tradition than in opposition to it. His work on religion, interpreted from this point of view, was simply an effort to show that not only do material factors affect ideas but ideas themselves affect material structures.

A good example of the view that Weber was engaged in a process of rounding out Marxian theory is in the area of stratification theory. In this work on stratification, Marx focused on social *class,* the economic dimension of stratification. Although Weber accepted the importance of this factor, he argued that other dimensions of stratification were also important. He argued that the notion of social stratification should be extended to include stratification on the basis of prestige (*status*) and *power.* The inclusion of these other dimensions does not constitute a refutation of Marx but is simply an extension of his ideas.

Both of the views outlined above accept the importance of Marxian theory for Weber. There are elements of truth in both positions; at some points Weber was working in opposition to Marx, while at other points he was extending Marx's ideas. However, a third view of this issue may best characterize the relationship between Marx and Weber. In this view, Marx is simply seen as only one of many influences on Weber's thought.

Other Influences on Weber

We can identify a number of sources of Weberian theory, including German historians, philosophers, economists, and political theorists. Among those who influenced Weber, the philosopher Immanuel Kant (1724–1804) stands out above all the others. But we must not overlook the impact of Friedrich Nietzsche (1844–1900) (Antonio, 2001)—especially his emphasis on the hero—on Weber's work on the need for individuals to stand up to the impact of bureaucracies and other structures of modern society.

The influence of Immanuel Kant on Weber and on German sociology generally shows that German sociology and Marxism grew from different philosophical roots. As we have seen, it was Hegel, not Kant, who was the important philosophical influence on Marxian theory. Whereas Hegel's philosophy led Marx and the Marxists to look for relations, conflicts, and contradictions, Kantian philosophy led at least some German sociologists to take a more static perspective. To Kant the world was a buzzing confusion of events that could never be known directly. The world could be known only through thought processes that filter, select, and categorize these events. The content of the real world was differentiated by Kant from the forms through which that content can be comprehended. The emphasis on these forms gave the work of those sociologists within the Kantian tradition a more static quality than that of the Marxists within the Hegelian tradition.

Weber's Theory

Whereas Karl Marx offered basically a theory of capitalism, Weber's work was fundamentally a theory of the process of rationalization (Brubaker, 1984; Kalberg, 1980, 1990, 1994, 2011). Weber was interested in the general issue of why institutions in the Western world had grown progressively more rational while powerful barriers seemed to prevent a similar development in the rest of the world.

Although rationality is used in many different ways in Weber's work, what interests us here is a process involving one of four types identified by Kalberg (1980, 1990, 1994; see also Brubaker, 1984; D. Levine, 1981a), *formal rationality*. Formal rationality involves, as was usually the case with Weber, a concern for the actor making choices of means and ends. However, in this case, that choice is made in reference to universally applied rules, regulations, and laws. These, in turn, are derived from various large-scale structures, especially bureaucracies and the economy. Weber developed his theories in the context of a large number of comparative historical studies of the West, China, India, and many other regions of the world. In those studies, he sought to delineate the factors that helped bring about or impede the development of rationalization.

Weber saw the bureaucracy (and the historical process of bureaucratization) as the classic example of rationalization, but rationalization is perhaps best illustrated today by the fast-food restaurant (Ritzer, 2013). The fast-food restaurant is a formally rational system in which people (both workers and customers) are led to seek the most rational means to ends. The drive-through window, for example, is a rational means by which workers can dispense, and customers can obtain, food quickly and efficiently. Speed and efficiency are dictated by the fast-food restaurants and the rules and regulations by which they operate.

Weber embedded his discussion of the process of bureaucratization in a broader discussion of the political institution. He differentiated among three types of authority systems—traditional, charismatic, and rational-legal. Only in the modern Western world can a rational-legal authority system develop, and only within that system does one find the full-scale development of the modern bureaucracy. The rest of the world remains dominated by traditional or charismatic authority systems, which generally impede the development of a rational-legal authority system and modern bureaucracies. Briefly, *traditional* authority stems from a long-lasting system of beliefs. An example would be a leader who comes to power because his or her family or clan has always provided the group's leadership. A *charismatic* leader derives his or her authority from extraordinary abilities or characteristics, or more likely simply from the belief on the part of followers that the leader has such traits. Although these two types of authority are of historical importance, Weber believed that the trend in the West, and ultimately in the rest of the world, is toward systems of *rational-legal* authority (Bunzel, 2007). In such systems, authority is derived from rules legally and rationally enacted. Thus, the president of the United States derives his authority ultimately from the laws of society. The evolution of rational-legal authority, with its accompanying bureaucracies, is only one part of Weber's general argument on the rationalization of the Western world.

Weber also did detailed and sophisticated analyses of the rationalization of such phenomena as religion, law, the city, and even music. But we can illustrate Weber's mode of thinking with one other example—the rationalization of the economic institution. This discussion is couched in Weber's broader analysis of the relationship between religion and capitalism. In a wide-ranging historical study, Weber sought to understand why a rational economic system (capitalism) had developed in the West and why it had failed to develop in the rest of the world. Weber accorded a central role to religion in this process. At one level, he was engaged in a dialogue with the Marxists in an effort to show that, contrary to what many Marxists of the day believed, religion was not merely an epiphenomenon. Instead, it had played a key role in the rise of capitalism in the West and in its failure to develop elsewhere in the world. Weber argued that it was a distinctively rational religious system (Calvinism) that played the central role in the rise of capitalism in the West. In contrast, in the other parts of the world that he studied, Weber found more irrational religious systems (for example, Confucianism, Taoism, Hinduism), which helped inhibit the development of a rational economic system. However, in the end, one gets the feeling that these religions provided only temporary barriers, for the economic systems—indeed, the entire social structure—of these societies ultimately would become rationalized.

Although rationalization lies at the heart of Weberian theory, it is far from all there is to the theory. But this is not the place to go into that rich body of material.

Instead, let us return to the development of sociological theory. A key issue in that development is this: Why did Weber's theory prove more attractive to later sociological theorists than Marxian theory?

The Acceptance of Weber's Theory

One reason is that Weber proved to be more acceptable politically. Instead of espousing Marxian radicalism, Weber was more of a liberal on some issues and a conservative on others (for example, the role of the state). Although he was a severe critic of many aspects of modern capitalist society and came to many of the same critical conclusions as did Marx, he was not one to propose radical solutions to problems (Heins, 1993). In fact, he felt that the radical reforms offered by many Marxists and other socialists would do more harm than good.

Later sociological theorists, especially Americans, saw their society under attack by Marxian theory. Largely conservative in orientation, they cast about for theoretical alternatives to Marxism. One of those who proved attractive was Max Weber. (Durkheim and Vilfredo Pareto were others.) After all, rationalization affected not only capitalist but also socialist societies. Indeed, from Weber's point of view, rationalization constituted an even greater problem in socialist than in capitalist societies.

Also in Weber's favor was the form in which he presented his judgments. He spent most of his life doing detailed historical studies, and his political conclusions were often made within the context of his research. Thus they usually sounded very scientific and academic. Marx, although he did much serious research, also wrote a good deal of explicitly polemical material. Even his more academic work is laced with acid political judgments. For example, in *Capital* (1867/1967), he described capitalists as "vampires" and "werewolves." Weber's more academic style helped make him more acceptable to later sociologists.

Another reason for the greater acceptability of Weber was that he operated in a philosophical tradition that also helped shape the work of later sociologists. That is, Weber operated in the Kantian tradition, which meant, as we have seen, that he tended to think in cause-and-effect terms. This kind of thinking was more acceptable to later sociologists, who were largely unfamiliar and uncomfortable with the dialectical logic that informed Marx's work.

Finally, Weber appeared to offer a much more rounded approach to the social world than did Marx. Whereas Marx appeared to be almost totally preoccupied with the economy, Weber was interested in a wide range of social phenomena. This diversity of focus seemed to give later sociologists more to work with than the apparently more single-minded concerns of Marx.

Weber produced most of his major works in the late 1800s and early 1900s. Early in his career Weber was identified more as a historian who was concerned with sociological issues, but in the early 1900s his focus grew more and more sociological. Indeed, he became the dominant sociologist of his time in Germany. In 1910, he founded (with, among others, Georg Simmel, whom we discuss next) the German Sociological Society (Glatzer, 1998). His home in Heidelberg was an intellectual center not only for sociologists but for scholars from many fields. Although his work was broadly influential in Germany, it was to become even more influential in the

United States, especially after Talcott Parsons introduced Weber's ideas (and those of other European theorists, especially Durkheim) to a large American audience. Although Marx's ideas did not have a significant positive effect on American sociological theorists until the 1960s, Weber was already highly influential by the late 1930s.

Simmel's Theory

Georg Simmel was Weber's contemporary and a cofounder of the German Sociological Society. Simmel was a somewhat atypical sociological theorist (Frisby, 1981; D. Levine, Carter, and Gorman, 1976a, 1976b). For one thing, he had an immediate and profound effect on the development of American sociological theory, whereas Marx and Weber were largely ignored for a number of years. Simmel's work helped shape the development of one of the early centers of American sociology—the University of Chicago—and its major theory, symbolic interactionism (Jaworski, 1995, 1997). The Chicago school and symbolic interactionism came, as we will see, to dominate American sociology in the 1920s and early 1930s (Bulmer, 1984). Simmel's ideas were influential at Chicago mainly because the dominant figures in the early years of Chicago, Albion Small and Robert Park, had been exposed to Simmel's theories in Berlin in the late 1800s. Park attended Simmel's lectures in 1899 and 1900, and Small carried on an extensive correspondence with Simmel during the 1890s. They were instrumental in bringing Simmel's ideas to students and faculty at Chicago, in translating some of his work, and in bringing it to the attention of a large-scale American audience (Frisby, 1984:29).

Another atypical aspect of Simmel's work is his "level" of analysis, or at least that level for which he became best known in America. Whereas Weber and Marx were preoccupied with large-scale issues like the rationalization of society and a capitalist economy, Simmel was best known for his work on smaller-scale issues, especially individual action and interaction. He became famous early for his thinking, derived from Kantian philosophy, on *forms* of interaction (for example, conflict) and *types* of interactants (for example, the stranger). Basically, Simmel saw that understanding interaction among people was one of the major tasks of sociology. However, it was impossible to study the massive number of interactions in social life without some conceptual tools. This is where forms of interaction and types of interactants came in. Simmel felt that he could isolate a limited number of forms of interaction that could be found in a large number of social settings. Thus equipped, one could analyze and understand these different interaction settings. The development of a limited number of types of interactants could be similarly useful in explaining interaction settings. This work had a profound effect on symbolic interactionism, which, as the name suggests, was focally concerned with interaction. One of the ironies, however, is that Simmel also was concerned with large-scale issues similar to those that obsessed Marx and Weber. However, this work was much less influential than his work on interaction, although there are contemporary signs of a growing interest in the large-scale aspects of Simmel's sociology.

It was partly Simmel's style in his work on interaction that made him accessible to early American sociological theorists. Although he wrote heavy tomes like those of Weber and Marx, he also wrote a set of deceptively simple essays on such interesting topics as poverty, the prostitute, the miser and the spendthrift, and the stranger. The brevity of such essays and the high interest level of the material made the dissemination of Simmel's ideas much easier. Unfortunately, the essays had the negative effect of obscuring Simmel's more massive works (for example, *Philosophy of Money*, translated in 1978; see Poggi, 1993), which were potentially as significant to sociology. Nevertheless, it was partly through the short and clever essays that Simmel had a much more significant effect on early American sociological theory than either Marx or Weber did.

We should not leave Simmel without saying something about *Philosophy of Money* (1907/1978), because its English translation made Simmel's work attractive to a whole new set of theorists interested in culture and society. Although a macro orientation is clearer in *Philosophy of Money*, it always existed in Simmel's work. For example, it is clear in his famous work on the dyad and the triad. Simmel thought that some crucial sociological developments take place when a two-person group (or *dyad*) is transformed into a *triad* by the addition of a third party. Social possibilities emerge that simply could not exist in a dyad. For example, in a triad, one of the members can become an arbitrator or mediator of the differences between the other two. More important, two of the members can band together and dominate the other member. This represents on a small scale what can happen with the emergence of large-scale structures that become separate from individuals and begin to dominate them.

This theme lies at the base of *Philosophy of Money*. Simmel was concerned primarily with the emergence in the modern world of a money economy that becomes separate from the individual and predominant. This theme, in turn, is part of an even broader and more pervasive one in Simmel's work: the domination of the culture as a whole over the individual. As Simmel saw it, in the modern world, the larger culture and all its various components (including the money economy) expand, and as they expand, the importance of the individual decreases. Thus, for example, as the industrial technology associated with a modern economy expands and grows more sophisticated, the skills and abilities of the individual worker grow progressively less important. In the end, the worker is confronted with an industrial machine over which he or she can exert little, if any, control. More generally, Simmel thought that in the modern world, the expansion of the larger culture leads to the growing insignificance of the individual.

Although sociologists have become increasingly attuned to the broader implications of Simmel's work, his early influence was primarily through his studies of small-scale social phenomena, such as the forms of interaction and types of interactants.

The Origins of British Sociology

We have been examining the development of sociology in France (Comte, Durkheim) and Germany (Marx, Weber, and Simmel). We turn now to the parallel development of sociology in England. As we will see, continental European ideas had their impact on early British sociology, but more important were native influences.

SIGMUND FREUD

A Biographical Sketch

Another leading figure in German social science in the late 1800s and early 1900s was Sigmund Freud. Although he was not a sociologist, Freud influenced the work of many sociologists (for example, Talcott Parsons and Norbert Elias) and continues to be of relevance to social theorists (Chodorow, 1990; Craib, 1994; A. Elliott, 1992, 2004; A. Elliott and Frosh, 1995; Kaye, 1991, 2003; Kurzweil, 1995; Movahedi, 2007).

Sigmund Freud was born in the Austro-Hungarian city of Freiberg on May 6, 1856. In 1859, his family moved to Vienna, and in 1873, Freud entered the medical school at the University of Vienna. Freud was more interested in science than in medicine and took a position in a physiology laboratory. He completed his degree in medicine, and after leaving the laboratory in 1882, he worked in a hospital and then set up a private medical practice with a specialty in nervous diseases.

Freud at first used hypnosis in an effort to deal with a type of neurosis known as hysteria. He had learned the technique in Paris from Jean Martin Charcot in 1885. Later he adopted a technique, pioneered by a fellow Viennese physician, Joseph Breuer, in which hysterical symptoms disappeared when the patient talked through the circumstances in which the symptoms first arose. By 1895, Freud had published a book with Breuer with a series of revolutionary implications: that the causes of neuroses like hysteria were psychological (not, as had been believed, physiological) and that the therapy involved talking through the original causes. Thus was born the practical and theoretical field of psychoanalysis. Freud began to part company with Breuer as he came to see sexual factors, or more generally the libido, at the root of neuroses. Over the next several years, Freud refined his therapeutic techniques and wrote a great deal about his new ideas.

By 1902, Freud began to gather a number of disciples around him, and they met weekly at his house. By 1903 or 1904, others (like Carl Jung) began to use Freud's ideas in their psychiatric practices. In 1908, the first Psychoanalytic Congress was held, and the next year a periodical for disseminating psychoanalytic knowledge was formed. As quickly as it had formed, the new field of psychoanalysis became splintered as Freud broke with people like Jung and they went off to develop their own ideas and found their own groups. World War I slowed the development of psychoanalysis, but psychoanalysis expanded and developed greatly in the 1920s. With the rise of Nazism, the center of psychoanalysis shifted to the United States, where it remains to this day. But Freud remained in Vienna until the Nazis took over in 1938, despite the fact that he was Jewish and the Nazis had burned his books as early as 1933. On June 4, 1938, only after a ransom had been paid and President Roosevelt had interceded, Sigmund Freud left Vienna. Freud had suffered from cancer of the jaw since 1923, and he died in London on September 23, 1939.

Political Economy, Ameliorism, and Social Evolution

Philip Abrams (1968) contended that British sociology was shaped in the nineteenth century by three often conflicting sources—political economy, ameliorism, and social evolution.[7] Thus when the Sociological Society of London was founded in 1903, there were strong differences over the definition of *sociology*. However, there were few who doubted the view that sociology could be a science. It was the differences that gave British sociology its distinctive character, and we will look at each of them briefly.

Political Economy

We have already touched on *political economy,* which was a theory of industrial and capitalist society traceable in part to the work of Adam Smith (1723–1790).[8] As we saw, political economy had a profound effect on Karl Marx. Marx studied political economy closely, and he was critical of it. But that was not the direction taken by British economists and sociologists. They tended to accept Smith's idea that there was an "invisible hand" that shaped the market for labor and goods. The market was seen as an independent reality that stood above individuals and controlled their behavior. The British sociologists, like the political economists and unlike Marx, saw the market as a positive force, as a source of order, harmony, and integration in society. Because they saw the market, and more generally society, in a positive light, the task of the sociologist was not to criticize society but simply to gather data on the laws by which it operated. The goal was to provide the government with the facts it needed to understand the way the system worked and to direct its workings wisely.

The emphasis was on facts, but which facts? Whereas Marx, Weber, Durkheim, and Comte looked to the structures of society for their basic facts, the British thinkers tended to focus on the individuals who made up those structures. In dealing with large-scale structures, they tended to collect individual-level data and then combine them to form a collective portrait. In the mid-1800s it was the statisticians who dominated British social science, and this kind of data collection was deemed to be the major task of sociology. The objective was the accumulation of "pure" facts without theorizing or philosophizing. These empirical sociologists were detached from the concerns of social theorists. Instead of general theorizing, the "emphasis settled on the business of producing more exact indicators, better methods of classification and data collection, improved life tables, higher levels of comparability between discrete bodies of data, and the like" (Abrams, 1968:18).

It was almost in spite of themselves that these statistically oriented sociologists came to see some limitations in their approach. A few began to feel the need for broader theorizing. To them, a problem such as poverty pointed to failings in the market system as well as in the society as a whole. But most, focused as they were on individuals, did not question the larger system; they turned instead to more detailed

---

[7] For later developments in British sociology, see Abrams et al. (1981).
[8] Smith is usually included as a leading member of the Scottish Enlightenment (Chitnis, 1976; Strydom, 2005) and as one of the Scottish Moralists (L. Schneider, 1967:xi), who were establishing a basis for sociology.

field studies and to the development of more complicated and more exact statistical techniques. To them, the source of the problem had to lie in inadequate research methods, not in the system as a whole. As Philip Abrams noted, "Focusing persistently on the distribution of individual circumstances, the statisticians found it hard to break through to a perception of poverty as a product of social structure. . . . They did not and probably could not achieve the concept of structural victimization" (1968:27). In addition to their theoretical and methodological commitments to the study of individuals, the statisticians worked too closely with government policy makers to arrive at the conclusion that the larger political and economic system was the problem.

Ameliorism

Related to, but separable from, political economy was the second defining characteristic of British sociology—*ameliorism,* or a desire to solve social problems by reforming individuals. Although British scholars began to recognize that there were problems in society (for example, poverty), they still believed in that society and wanted to preserve it. They desired to forestall violence and revolution and to reform the system so that it could continue essentially as it was. Above all, they wanted to prevent the coming of a socialist society. Thus, like French sociology and some branches of German sociology, British sociology was conservatively oriented.

Because the British sociologists could not, or would not, trace the source of problems such as poverty to the society as a whole, the source had to lie within the individuals themselves. This was an early form of what William Ryan (1971) later called "blaming the victim." Much attention was devoted to a long series of individual problems—"ignorance, spiritual destitution, impurity, bad sanitation, pauperism, crime, and intemperance—above all intemperance" (Abrams, 1968:39). Clearly, there was a tendency to look for a simple cause for all social ills, and the one that suggested itself before all others was alcoholism. What made this perfect to the ameliorist was that this was an individual pathology, not a social pathology. The ameliorists lacked a theory of social structure, a theory of the social causes of such individual problems.

Social Evolution

But a stronger sense of social structure was lurking below the surface of British sociology, and it burst through in the latter part of the nineteenth century with the growth of interest in social evolution (Maryanski, 2005; Sanderson, 2001). One important influence was the work of Auguste Comte, part of which had been translated into English in the 1850s by Harriet Martineau (Hoecker-Drysdale, 2011). Although Comte's work did not inspire immediate interest, by the last quarter of the century, a number of thinkers had been attracted to it and to its concern for the larger structures of society, its scientific (positivistic) orientation, its comparative orientation, and its evolutionary theory. However, a number of British thinkers sharpened their own conception of the world in opposition to some of the excesses of Comtian theory (for example, the tendency to elevate sociology to the status of a religion).

In Abrams's view, the real importance of Comte lay in his providing one of the bases on which opposition could be mounted against the "oppressive genius of Herbert

Spencer" (Abrams, 1968:58). In both a positive and a negative sense, Spencer was a dominant figure in British sociological theory, especially evolutionary theory (Francis, 2007, 2011; J. Turner, 2000, 2007a).

Herbert Spencer (1820–1903)

In attempting to understand Spencer's ideas (Haines, 2005; J. Turner, 2005), it is useful to compare and contrast them with Comtian theory.

Spencer and Comte

Spencer is often categorized with Comte in terms of their influence on the development of sociological theory (J. Turner, 2001), but there are some important differences between them. For example, it is less easy to categorize Spencer as a conservative. In fact, in his early years, Spencer is better seen as a political liberal, and he retained elements of liberalism throughout his life. However, it is also true that Spencer grew more conservative during the course of his life and that his basic influence, as was true of Comte, was conservative.

One of his liberal views, which coexisted rather uncomfortably with his conservatism, was his acceptance of a laissez-faire doctrine: he felt that the state should not intervene in individual affairs except in the rather passive function of protecting people. This meant that Spencer, unlike Comte, was not interested in social reforms; he wanted social life to evolve free of external control.[9]

This difference points to Spencer as a *social Darwinist* (G. Jones, 1980; Weiler, 2007a). As such, he held the evolutionary view that the world was growing progressively better. Therefore, it should be left alone; outside interference could only worsen the situation. He adopted the view that social institutions, like plants and animals, adapted progressively and positively to their social environment. He also accepted the Darwinian view that a process of natural selection, "survival of the fittest," occurred in the social world. That is, if unimpeded by external intervention, people who were "fit" would survive and proliferate whereas the "unfit" eventually would die out. (Interestingly, it was Spencer who coined the phrase "survival of the fittest" several years before Charles Darwin's work on natural selection.) Another difference with Comte was that Spencer emphasized the individual, whereas Comte focused on larger units such as the family.

Comte and Spencer shared with Durkheim and others a commitment to a science of sociology (Haines, 1992), which was a very attractive perspective to early theorists. Another influence of Spencer's work, shared with both Comte and Durkheim, was his tendency to see society as an *organism*. In this, Spencer borrowed his perspective and concepts from biology. He was concerned with the overall structure of society, the interrelationship of the *parts* of society, and the *functions* of the parts for each other as well as for the system as a whole.

Most important, Spencer, like Comte, had an evolutionary conception of historical development (Maryanski, 2005). However, Spencer was critical of Comte's

---

[9] This said, Mark Francis (2011) argues that contemporary interpreters of Spencer have overemphasized his commitment to laissez-faire capitalism. Referring to the work of Thomas Leonard (2009), Francis says that "references to Spencer as a prophet of *laissez-faire* capitalism were also very scarce before the second half of the twentieth century" (2011:168).

evolutionary theory on several grounds. Specifically, he rejected Comte's law of the three stages. He argued that Comte was content to deal with evolution in the realm of ideas, in terms of intellectual development. Spencer, however, sought to develop an evolutionary theory in the real, material world.

Evolutionary Theory
It is possible to identify at least two major evolutionary perspectives in Spencer's work (Haines, 1988; Perrin, 1976).

The first of these theories relates primarily to the increasing size of society. Society grows through both the multiplication of individuals and the union of groups (compounding). The increasing size of society brings with it larger and more differentiated social structures, as well as the increasing differentiation of the functions they perform. In addition to their growth in size, societies evolve through compounding, that is, by unifying more and more adjoining groups. Thus, Spencer talks of the evolutionary movement from simple to compound, doubly-compound, and trebly-compound societies.

Spencer also offers a theory of evolution from *militant* to *industrial* societies. Earlier, militant societies are defined by being structured for offensive and defensive warfare. While Spencer was critical of warfare, he felt that in an earlier stage it was functional in bringing societies together (for example, through military conquest) and in creating the larger aggregates of people necessary for the development of industrial society. However, with the emergence of industrial society, warfare ceases to be functional and serves to impede further evolution. Industrial society is based on friendship, altruism, elaborate specialization, recognition for achievements rather than the characteristics one is born with, and voluntary cooperation among highly disciplined individuals. Such a society is held together by voluntary contractual relations and, more important, by a strong common morality. The government's role is restricted and focuses only on what people ought not to do. Obviously, modern industrial societies are less warlike than their militant predecessors. Although Spencer sees a general evolution in the direction of industrial societies, he also recognizes that it is possible that there will be periodic regressions to warfare and more militant societies.

In his ethical and political writings, Spencer offered other ideas on the evolution of society. For one thing, he saw society as progressing toward an ideal, or perfect, moral state. For another, he argued that the fittest societies survive and that unfit societies should be permitted to die off. The result of this process is adaptive upgrading for the world as a whole.

Thus Spencer offered a rich and complicated set of ideas on social evolution. His ideas first enjoyed great success, then were rejected for many years, and more recently have been revived with the rise of neoevolutionary sociological theories (Buttel, 1990).

The Reaction against Spencer in Britain
Despite his emphasis on the individual, Spencer was best known for his large-scale theory of social evolution. In this, he stood in stark contrast to the sociology that preceded him in Britain. However, the reaction against Spencer was based more on the threat that his idea of survival of the fittest posed to the ameliorism so dear to most early British sociologists. Although Spencer later repudiated some of his more

HERBERT SPENCER

A Biographical Sketch

Herbert Spencer was born in Derby, England, on April 27, 1820. He was not schooled in the arts and humanities, but rather in technical and utilitarian matters. In 1837 he began work as a civil engineer for a railway, an occupation he held until 1846. During this period, Spencer continued to study on his own and began to publish scientific and political works.

In 1848 Spencer was appointed an editor of *The Economist,* and his intellectual ideas began to solidify. By 1850, he had completed his first major work, *Social Statics.* During the writing of this work, Spencer first began to experience insomnia, and over the years his mental and physical problems mounted. He was to suffer a series of nervous breakdowns throughout the rest of his life.

In 1853 Spencer received an inheritance that allowed him to quit his job and live for the rest of his life as a gentleman scholar. He never earned a university degree or held an academic position. As he grew more isolated, and physical and mental illness mounted, Spencer's productivity as a scholar increased. Eventually, Spencer began to achieve not only fame within England but also an international reputation. As Richard Hofstadter put it: "In the three decades after the Civil War it was impossible to be active in any field of intellectual work without mastering Spencer" (1959:33). Among his supporters was the important industrialist Andrew Carnegie, who wrote the following to Spencer during the latter's fatal illness of 1903:

> Dear Master Teacher . . . you come to me every day in thought, and the everlasting "why" intrudes—Why lies he? Why must he go? . . . The world jogs on unconscious of its greatest mind. . . . But it will wake some day to its teachings and decree Spencer's place is with the greatest.
>
> (Carnegie, cited in Peel, 1971:2)

outrageous ideas, he did argue for a survival-of-the-fittest philosophy and against government intervention and social reform:

> Fostering the good-for-nothing at the expense of the good, is an extreme cruelty. It is a deliberate stirring-up of miseries for future generations. There is no greater curse to posterity than that of bequeathing to them an increasing population of imbeciles and idlers and criminals. . . . The whole effort of nature is to get rid of such, to clear the world of them, and make room for better. . . . If they are not sufficiently complete to live, they die, and it is best they should die.
>
> (Spencer, cited in Abrams, 1968:74)

Such sentiments were clearly at odds with the ameliorative orientation of the British reformer-sociologists.

But that was not to be Spencer's fate.

One of Spencer's most interesting characteristics, one that was ultimately to be the cause of his intellectual undoing, was his unwillingness to read the work of other people. In this, he resembled another early giant of sociology, Auguste Comte, who practiced "cerebral hygiene." Of the need to read the works of others, Spencer said: "All my life I have been a thinker and not a reader, being able to say with Hobbes that 'if I had read as much as other men I would have known as little'" (Wiltshire, 1978:67). A friend asked Spencer's opinion of a book, and "his reply was that on looking into the book he saw that its fundamental assumption was erroneous, and therefore did not care to read it" (Wiltshire, 1978:67). One author wrote of Spencer's "incomprehensible way of absorbing knowledge through the powers of his skin . . . he never seemed to read books" (Wiltshire, 1978:67).

If he didn't read the work of other scholars, where, then, did Spencer's ideas and insights come from? According to Spencer, they emerged involuntarily and intuitively from his mind. He said that his ideas emerged "little by little, in unobtrusive ways, without conscious intention or appreciable effort" (Wiltshire, 1978:66). Such intuition was deemed by Spencer to be far more effective than careful study and thought: "A solution reached in the way described is more likely to be true than one reached in the pursuance of a determined effort [which] causes perversion of thought" (Wiltshire, 1978:66).

Spencer suffered because of his unwillingness to read seriously the works of other people. In fact, if he read other work, it was often only to find confirmation for his own, independently created ideas. He ignored those ideas that did not agree with his. Thus, his contemporary, Charles Darwin, said of Spencer: "If he had trained himself to observe more, even at the expense of . . . some loss of thinking power, he would have been a wonderful man" (Wiltshire, 1978:70). Spencer's disregard for the rules of scholarship led him to a series of outrageous ideas and unsubstantiated assertions about the evolution of the world. For these reasons, sociologists in the twentieth century came to reject Spencer's work and to substitute for it careful scholarship and empirical research.

Spencer died on December 8, 1903.

The Key Figure in Early Italian Sociology

We close this sketch of early, primarily conservative, European sociological theory with a brief mention of one Italian sociologist, Vilfredo Pareto (1848–1923). Pareto was influential in his time, but his contemporary relevance is minimal (for one exception, see Powers, 1986). There was a brief outburst of interest in Pareto's (1935) work in the 1930s, when the major American theorist, Talcott Parsons, devoted as much attention to him as he gave to Weber and Durkheim. However, in recent years, except for a few of his major concepts, Pareto also has receded in importance and contemporary relevance (Femia, 1995).

Zeitlin argued that Pareto developed his "major ideas as a refutation of Marx" (1996:171). In fact, Pareto was rejecting not only Marx but also a good portion of

Enlightenment philosophy. For example, whereas the Enlightenment philosophers emphasized rationality, Pareto emphasized the role of nonrational factors such as human instincts (Mozetič and Weiler, 2007). This emphasis also was tied to his rejection of Marxian theory. That is, because nonrational, instinctual factors were so important and so unchanging, it was unrealistic to hope to achieve dramatic social changes with an economic revolution.

Pareto also developed a theory of social change that stood in stark contrast to Marxian theory. Whereas Marx's theory focused on the role of the masses, Pareto offered an elite theory of social change, which held that society inevitably is dominated by a small elite that operates on the basis of enlightened self-interest (Adams, 2005). It rules over the masses of people, who are dominated by nonrational forces. Because they lack rational capacities, the masses, in Pareto's system, are unlikely to be a revolutionary force. Social change occurs when the elite begins to degenerate and is replaced by a new elite derived from the nongoverning elite or higher elements of the masses. Once the new elite is in power, the process begins anew. Thus, we have a cyclical theory of social change instead of the directional theories offered by Marx, Comte, Spencer, and others. In addition, Pareto's theory of change largely ignores the plight of the masses. Elites come and go, but the lot of the masses remains the same.

This theory, however, was not Pareto's lasting contribution to sociology. That lay in his scientific conception of sociology and the social world: "My wish is to construct a system of sociology on the model of celestial mechanics [astronomy], physics, chemistry" (cited in Hook, 1965:57). Briefly, Pareto conceived of society as a system in equilibrium, a whole consisting of interdependent parts. A change in one part was seen as leading to changes in other parts of the system. Pareto's systemic conception of society was the most important reason Parsons devoted so much attention to Pareto's work in his 1937 book, *The Structure of Social Action,* and it was Pareto's most important influence on Parsons's thinking. Fused with similar views held by those who had an organic image of society (Comte, Durkheim, and Spencer, for example), Pareto's theory played a central role in the development of Parsons's theory and, more generally, in structural functionalism.

Although few modern sociologists now read Pareto's work, it can be seen as a rejection of the Enlightenment and of Marxism and as offering an elite theory of social change that stands in opposition to the Marxian perspective.

Turn-of-the-Century Developments in European Marxism

While many nineteenth-century sociologists were developing their theories in opposition to Marx, there was a simultaneous effort by a number of Marxists to clarify and extend Marxian theory (Beilharz, 2005f; Steinmetz, 2007). Between roughly 1875 and 1925, there was little overlap between Marxism and sociology. (Weber is an exception to this.) The two schools of thought were developing in parallel fashion with little or no interchange between them.

After the death of Marx, Marxian theory was first dominated by those who saw in his theory scientific and economic determinism (Bakker, 2007a). Wallerstein calls this the era of "orthodox Marxism" (1986:1301). Friedrich Engels, Marx's benefactor and collaborator, lived on after Marx's death and can be seen as the first exponent of such a perspective. Basically, this view was that Marx's scientific theory had uncovered the economic laws that ruled the capitalist world. Such laws pointed to the inevitable collapse of the capitalist system. Early Marxian thinkers, like Karl Kautsky, sought to gain a better understanding of the operation of these laws. There were several problems with this perspective. For one thing, it seemed to rule out political action, a cornerstone of Marx's position. That is, there seemed no need for individuals, especially workers, to do anything. In that the system was inevitably crumbling, all they had to do was sit back and wait for its demise. On a theoretical level, deterministic Marxism seemed to rule out the dialectical relationship between individuals and larger social structures.

These problems led to a reaction among Marxian theorists and to the development of *"Hegelian Marxism"* in the early 1900s. The Hegelian Marxists refused to reduce Marxism to a scientific theory that ignored individual thought and action. They are labeled Hegelian Marxists because they sought to combine Hegel's interest in consciousness (which some, including the author of this text, view Marx as sharing) with the determinists' interest in the economic structures of society. The Hegelian theorists were significant for both theoretical and practical reasons. Theoretically, they reinstated the importance of the individual, consciousness, and the relationship between thought and action. Practically, they emphasized the importance of individual action in bringing about a social revolution.

The major exponent of this point of view was Georg Lukács (Fischer, 1984; Markus, 2005). According to Martin Jay, Lukács was "the founding father of Western Marxism" and his work *History and Class Consciousness* (1922/1968) is "generally acknowledged as the charter document of Hegelian Marxism" (1984:84). Lukács had begun in the early 1900s to integrate Marxism with sociology (in particular, Weberian and Simmelian theory). This integration was soon to accelerate with the development of critical theory in the 1920s and 1930s.

Summary

This chapter sketches the early history of sociological theory. The first section deals with the various social forces involved in the development of sociological theory. Although there were many such influences, we focus on how political revolution, the Industrial Revolution, and the rise of capitalism, socialism, feminism, urbanization, religious change, and the growth of science affected sociological theory. The second part of the chapter examines the influence of intellectual forces on the rise of sociological theory in various countries. We begin with France and the role played by the Enlightenment, stressing the conservative and romantic reaction to it. It is out of this interplay that French sociological theory developed. In this context, we examine the major figures in the early years of French sociology—Alexis de Tocqueville, Claude Henri Saint-Simon, Auguste Comte, and Emile Durkheim.

Next we turn to Germany and the role played by Karl Marx in the development of sociology in that country. We discuss the parallel development of Marxian theory and sociological theory and the ways in which Marxian theory influenced sociology, both positively and negatively. We begin with the roots of Marxian theory in Hegelianism, materialism, and political economy. Marx's theory itself is touched upon briefly. The discussion then shifts to the roots of German sociology. Max Weber's work is examined in order to show the diverse sources of German sociology. Also discussed are some of the reasons why Weber's theory proved more acceptable to later sociologists than did Marx's ideas. This section closes with a brief discussion of Georg Simmel's work.

The rise of sociological theory in Britain is considered next. The major sources of British sociology were political economy, ameliorism, and social evolution. In this context, we touch on the work of Herbert Spencer as well as on some of the controversy that surrounded it.

This chapter closes with a brief discussion of Italian sociological theory, in particular the work of Vilfredo Pareto, and the turn-of-the-century developments in European Marxian theory, primarily economic determinism and Hegelian Marxism.

Karl Marx

Chapter Outline

Introduction

Marx began his most famous work, *The Manifesto of the Communist Party* (Marx and Engels 1848/1948), with the following line: "There is a spectre haunting Europe, the spectre of communism." It might be said that the same ghost is haunting our understanding of Marx. It is difficult to separate the ideas of Marx from the political movements that they inspired. Nevertheless, as Tom Rockmore (2002:96) tells us, we must try "to free Marx from Marxism."

For many, Marx has become more of an icon than a thinker deserving of serious study. The symbolism of his name tends to muddle understanding of his ideas. Marx is the only theorist we will study who has had political movements and social systems named after him. He is probably the only theorist your friends and family have strong opinions about. He is often criticized, as well as praised, by people who have never actually read his work. Even among his followers, Marx's ideas frequently are reduced to slogans such as "the opium of the people" and "the dictatorship of the proletariat," but the role of these slogans in Marx's encompassing theory often is ignored.

There are many reasons for this lack of understanding of Marx's social theory, the main one being that Marx never really completed his social theory. He planned, early in his career, to publish separate works on economics, law, morals, politics, and

43

so forth, and then "in a special work, to present them once again as a connected whole, to show the relationship between the parts" (Marx, 1932/1964:280). He never did this final work and never even completed his separate work on economics. Instead, much of his time was taken up by study, journalism, political activity, and a series of minor intellectual and political arguments with friends and adversaries.

In addition, although Marx could write clear and inspiring prose, especially in his political tracts, he often preferred a vocabulary that relied on complex philosophical traditions, and he made these terms even more difficult to understand by implicitly redefining them for his own use. Vilfredo Pareto made the classic critique of Marx by comparing his words to a fable about bats. When someone said they were birds, the bats would cry, "No, we are mice." When someone said they were mice, they protested that they were birds. Whatever interpretation one makes of Marx, others can offer alternative interpretations. For example, some stress Marx's early work on human potential and tend to discount his political economy (see, for example, Ollman, 1976; Wallimann, 1981; Wartenberg, 1982). Others stress Marx's later work on the economic structures of society and see that work as distinct from his early, largely philosophical work on human nature (see Althusser, 1969; Gandy, 1979; McMurty, 1978).[1] A recent interpreter of Marx made the following comment, which applies equally to this chapter: "Virtually every paragraph in this chapter could be accompanied by three concise paragraphs describing why other readers of Marx, erudite and influential, think that this paragraph is wrong, in emphasis or substance" (R. Miller, 1991:105). And, of course, the differing interpretations have political consequences, making any disagreement extremely contentious.[2]

Despite these problems, Marx's theories have produced one of sociology's most productive and significant research programs. When Marx died in 1883, the eleven mourners at his funeral seemed to belie what Engels said in his eulogy: "His name and work will endure through the ages." Nevertheless, Engels seems to have been right. His ideas have been so influential that even one of his critics admitted that, in a sense, "we are all Marxists now" (P. Singer, 1980:1). As Hannah Arendt (2002:274) wrote, if Marx seems to be forgotten, it is not "because Marx's thought and the methods he introduced have been abandoned, but rather because they have become so axiomatic that their origin is no longer remembered."

It is for these reasons that a return to Marx has proven so productive to those working in sociology. Thinking about Marx helps to clarify what sociology and, indeed, our society have taken for granted. Rediscoveries and reinterpretations of Marx have often renewed sociology and opened up a fresh perspective on such issues as alienation, globalization, and the environment (Foster, 2000).

Despite differing interpretations, there is general agreement that Marx's main interest was in the historical basis of inequality, especially the unique form that it takes under capitalism. However, Marx's approach is different from many of the theories that we will examine. For Marx, a theory about how society works would be partial, because

---

[1] The approach here is based on the premise that there is no discontinuity or contradiction between Marx's early work on human potential and his later work on the structures of capitalist society—that his early ideas continue, at least implicitly, in his later work even though these ideas were certainly modified by his study of the economic structures of capitalism.
[2] In Joseph Stalin's Soviet Union, there was no problem about the "correct" interpretation of Marx. Stalin himself provided the interpretation and brutally eliminated all those, such as Leon Trotsky, who disagreed.

what he mainly sought was a theory about how to change society. Marx's theory, then, is an analysis of inequality under capitalism and how to change it.

As capitalism has come to dominate the globe and the most significant communist alternatives have disappeared, some might argue that Marx's theories have lost their relevance. However, once we realize that Marx provides an analysis of capitalism, we can see that his theories are more relevant now than ever (McLennan, 2001:43). Marx provides a diagnosis of capitalism that is able to reveal its tendencies to crises, point out its perennial inequalities, and, if nothing else, demand that capitalism live up to its own promises. The example of Marx makes an important point about theory. Even when their particular predictions are disproved—even though the proletariat revolution that Marx believed to be imminent did not come about—theories still hold a value as an alternative to our current society. Theories may not tell us what will happen, but they can argue for what should happen and help us develop a plan for carrying out the change that the theory envisions or for resisting the change that the theory predicts.

The Dialectic

Vladimir Lenin (1972:180) said that no one can fully understand Marx's work without a prior understanding of the German philosopher G.W.F. Hegel. We can only hope that this is not true, because Hegel was one of the most purposefully difficult philosophers ever to have written. Nevertheless, we must understand some of Hegel in order to appreciate the central Marxian conception of the dialectic.

The idea of a dialectical philosophy had been around for centuries (Gadamer, 1989). Its basic idea is the centrality of contradiction. While most philosophies, and indeed common sense, treat contradictions as mistakes, a dialectical philosophy believes that contradictions exist in reality and that the most appropriate way to understand reality is to study the development of those contradictions. Hegel used the idea of contradiction to understand historical change. According to Hegel, historical change has been driven by the contradictory understandings that are the essence of reality, by our attempts to resolve the contradictions, and by the new contradictions that develop.

Marx also accepted the centrality of contradictions to historical change. We see this in such well-known formulations as the "contradictions of capitalism" and "class contradictions." However, unlike Hegel, Marx did not believe that these contradictions could be worked out in our understanding, that is, in our minds. Instead, for Marx these are real, existing contradictions (Wilde, 1991:277). For Marx, such contradictions are resolved not by the philosopher sitting in an armchair but by a life-and-death struggle that changes the social world. This was a crucial transformation because it allowed Marx to move the dialectic out of the realm of philosophy and into the realm of a study of social relations grounded in the material world. It is this focus that makes Marx's work so relevant to sociology, even though the dialectical approach is very different from the mode of thinking used by most sociologists. The dialectic leads to an interest in the conflicts and contradictions among various levels of social reality, rather than to the more traditional sociological interest in the ways these various levels mesh neatly into a cohesive whole.

For example, one of the contradictions within capitalism is the relationship between the workers and the capitalists who own the factories and other means of production with which the work is done. The capitalist must exploit the workers in order to make a profit from the workers' labor. The workers, in contradiction to the capitalists, want to keep at least some of the profit for themselves. Marx believed that this contradiction was at the heart of capitalism, and that it would grow worse as capitalists drove more and more people to become workers by forcing small firms out of business and as competition between the capitalists forced them to further exploit the workers to make a profit. As capitalism expands, the number of workers exploited, as well as the degree of exploitation, increases. This contradiction can be resolved not through philosophy but only through social change. The tendency for the level of exploitation to escalate leads to more and more resistance by the workers. Resistance begets more exploitation and oppression, and the likely result is a confrontation between the two classes (Boswell and Dixon, 1993).

Dialectical Method

Marx's focus on real, existing contradictions led to a particular method for studying social phenomena that has also come to be called "dialectical" (T. Ball, 1991; Friedrichs, 1972; Ollman, 1976; L. Schneider, 1971; Starosta, 2008).

Fact and Value

In dialectical analysis, social values are not separable from social facts. Many sociologists believe that their values can and must be separated from their study of facts about the social world. The dialectical thinker believes that it is not only impossible to keep values out of the study of the social world but also undesirable, because to do so would produce a dispassionate, inhuman sociology that has little to offer to people in search of answers to the problems they confront. Facts and values are inevitably intertwined, with the result that the study of social phenomena is value-laden. Thus to Marx it was impossible and, even if possible, undesirable to be dispassionate in his analysis of capitalist society. But Marx's emotional involvement in what he was studying did not mean that his observations were inaccurate. It could even be argued that Marx's passionate views on these issues gave him unparalleled insight into the nature of capitalist society. A less passionate student might have delved less deeply into the dynamics of the system. In fact, research into the work of scientists indicates that the idea of a dispassionate scientist is largely a myth and that the very best scientists are the ones who are most passionate about, and committed to, their ideas (Mitroff, 1974).

Reciprocal Relations

The dialectical method of analysis does not see a simple, one-way, cause-and-effect relationship among the various parts of the social world. For the dialectical thinker, social influences never simply flow in one direction as they often do for cause-and-effect thinkers. To the dialectician, one factor may have an effect on another, but it is just as likely that the latter will have a simultaneous effect on the former. For example, the increasing exploitation of the workers by the capitalist may cause the workers to become increasingly dissatisfied and more militant, but the increasing militancy of the proletariat may well cause the capitalists to react by becoming even more exploitative in order to crush the resistance of the workers. This kind of thinking does not mean that the dialectician never considers causal relationships in the social world. It does mean that when dialectical thinkers talk about causality, they are always attuned to reciprocal relationships among social factors as well as to the dialectical totality of social life in which they are embedded.

Past, Present, Future

Dialecticians are interested not only in the relationships of social phenomena in the contemporary world but also in the relationship of those contemporary realities to both past (Bauman, 1976:81) and future social phenomena. This has two distinct implications for a dialectical sociology. First, it means that dialectical sociologists are concerned with studying the historical roots of the contemporary world as Marx (1857–1858/1964) did in his study of the sources of modern capitalism. In fact, dialectical thinkers are very critical of modern sociology for its failure to do much historical research. A good example of Marx's thinking in this regard is found in the following famous quotation from *The Eighteenth Brumaire of Louis Bonaparte:*

> Men make their own history, but they do not make it just as they please; they do not make it under circumstances chosen by themselves, but under circumstances directly encountered from the past. The tradition of all the dead generations weighs like a nightmare on the brain of the living.
>
> (Marx, 1852/1970:15)

Second, many dialectical thinkers are attuned to current social trends in order to understand the possible future directions of society. This interest in future possibilities is one of the main reasons dialectical sociology is inherently political. It is interested in encouraging practical activities that would bring new possibilities into existence. However, dialecticians believe that the nature of this future world can be discerned only through a careful study of the contemporary world. It is their view that the sources of the future exist in the present.

No Inevitabilities

The dialectical view of the relationship between the present and the future need not imply that the future is determined by the present. Terence Ball (1991) describes Marx as a "political possibilist" rather than a "historical inevitabilist." Because social phenomena are constantly acting and reacting, the social world defies a simple, deterministic model. The future may be based on some contemporary model, but not inevitably.[3] Marx's historical studies showed him that people make choices but that these choices are limited. For instance, Marx believed that society was engaged in a class struggle and that people could choose to participate either in "the revolutionary reconstitution

---

[3] Marx did, however, occasionally discuss the inevitability of socialism.

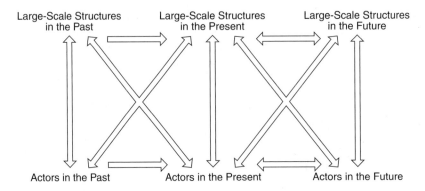

FIGURE 2.1   *Schematic Representation of a Sociologically Relevant Dialectic*

of society at large, or in the common ruin of the contending classes" (Marx and Engels 1848/1948). Marx hoped and believed that the future was to be found in communism, but he did not believe that the workers could simply wait passively for it to arrive. Communism would come only through their choices and struggles.

This disinclination to think deterministically is what makes the best-known model of the dialectic—thesis, antithesis, synthesis—inadequate for sociological use. This simple model implies that a social phenomenon will inevitably spawn an opposing form and that the clash between the two will inevitably lead to a new, synthetic social form. But in the real world, there are no inevitabilities. Furthermore, social phenomena are not easily divided into the simple thesis, antithesis, and synthesis categories adopted by some Marxists. The dialectician is interested in the study of real relationships rather than grand abstractions. It is this disinclination to deal in grand abstractions that led Marx away from Hegel and would lead him today to reject such a great oversimplification of the dialectic as thesis, antithesis, synthesis.

Actors and Structures

Dialectical thinkers are also interested in the dynamic relationship between actors and social structures. Marx was certainly attuned to the ongoing interplay among the major levels of social analysis. The heart of Marx's thought lies in the relationship between people and the large-scale structures they create (Lefebvre, 1968:8). On the one hand, these large-scale structures help people fulfill themselves; on the other, they represent a grave threat to humanity. But the dialectical method is even more complex than this, because, as we have already seen, the dialectician considers past, present, and future circumstances—both actors and structures. Figure 2.1 is a simplified schematic representation of this enormously complex and sophisticated perspective.

Human Potential

A good portion of this chapter will be devoted to a discussion of Marx's macrosociology, in particular his analysis of the macrostructures of capitalism. But before we can analyze these topics, we need to begin with Marx's thoughts on the more microsociological aspects of social reality. Marx built his critical analysis of the contradictions of capitalist society on his premises about human potential, its relation to labor, and its potential for alienation under capitalism. He believed that there was a real contradiction between our human potential and the way that we must work in capitalist society.

Marx (1850/1964:64) wrote in an early work that human beings are an "ensemble of social relations." He indicates by this that our human potential is intertwined with our specific social relations and our institutional context. Therefore, human nature is not a static thing but varies historically and socially. To understand human potential, we need to understand social history, because human nature is shaped by the same dialectical contradictions that Marx believed shapes the history of society.

For Marx, a conception of human potential that does not take social and historical factors into account is wrong, but to take them into account is not the same as being without a conception of human nature. It simply complicates this conception. For Marx, there is a human potential in general, but what is more important is the way it is "modified in each historical epoch" (Marx, 1842/1977:609). When speaking of our general human potential, Marx often used the term *species being*. By this he meant the potentials and powers that are uniquely human and that distinguish humans from other species.

Some Marxists, such as Louis Althusser (1969:229), have contended that the mature Marx did not believe in human nature. There are certainly reasons to downplay human nature for someone interested in changing society. Ideas about human nature— such as our "natural" greed, our "natural" tendency to violence, our "natural" gender differences—have often been used to argue against any social change. Such conceptions of human nature are innately conservative. If our problems are due to human nature, we had better learn to just adapt instead of trying to change things.

Nevertheless, there is much evidence that Marx did have a notion of human nature (Geras, 1983). Indeed, it makes little sense to say there is no human nature. Even if we are like a blank chalkboard, the chalkboard must be made out of something and must have a nature such that chalk marks can show up on it. Some conception of human nature is part of any sociological theory. Our concept of human nature dictates how society can be sustained and how it can be changed, but most important for Marx's theory, it suggests how society *should* be changed. The real question is not whether we have a human nature, but what kind of nature it is— unchanging or open to historical processes (the use of the idea of human potential here indicates that we think it is open):

> Unless we confront the idea, however dangerous, of our human nature and species being and get some understanding of them, we cannot know what it is we might be alienated from or what emancipation might mean. Nor can we determine which of our "slumbering powers" must be awakened to achieve emancipatory goals. A working definition of human nature, however tentative and insecure, is a necessary step in the search for real as opposed to fantastic alternatives. A conversation about our "species being" is desperately called for.
>
> (D. Harvey, 2000:207)

KARL MARX

A Biographical Sketch

Karl Marx was born in Trier, Prussia, on May 5, 1818 (Beilharz, 2005e). His father, a lawyer, provided the family with a fairly typical middle-class existence. Both parents were from rabbinical families, but for business reasons the father had converted to Lutheranism when Karl was very young. In 1841 Marx received his doctorate in philosophy from the University of Berlin, a school heavily influenced by Hegel and the Young Hegelians, supportive, yet critical, of their master. Marx's doctorate was a dry philosophical treatise, but it did anticipate many of his later ideas. After graduation he became a writer for a liberal-radical newspaper and within ten months had become its editor in chief. However, because of its political positions, the paper was closed shortly thereafter by the government. The early essays published in this period began to reflect a number of the positions that would guide Marx throughout his life. They were liberally sprinkled with democratic principles, humanism, and youthful idealism. He rejected the abstractness of Hegelian philosophy, the naive dreaming of utopian communists, and those activists who were urging what he considered to be premature political action. In rejecting these activists, Marx laid the groundwork for his own life's work:

> Practical attempts, even by the masses, can be answered with a cannon as soon as they become dangerous, but ideas that have overcome our intellect and conquered our conviction, ideas to which reason has riveted our conscience, are chains from which one cannot break loose without breaking one's heart; they are demons that one can only overcome by submitting to them.
>
> (Marx, 1842/1977:20)

Marx married in 1843 and soon thereafter was forced to leave Germany for the more liberal atmosphere of Paris. There he continued to grapple with the ideas of Hegel and his supporters, but he also encountered two new sets of ideas—French socialism and English political economy. It was the unique way in which he combined Hegelianism, socialism, and political economy that shaped his intellectual orientation. Also of great importance at this point was his meeting the man who was to become his lifelong friend, benefactor, and collaborator—Friedrich Engels (Carver, 1983). The son of a textile manufacturer, Engels had become a socialist critical of the conditions facing the working class. Much of Marx's compassion for the misery of the working class came from his exposure to Engels and his ideas. In 1844 Engels and Marx had a lengthy conversation in a famous café in Paris and laid the groundwork for a lifelong association. Of that conversation Engels said, "Our complete agreement in all theoretical fields became obvious . . . and our joint work dates from that time" (McLellan, 1973:131). In the following year, Engels published a notable work, *The Condition of the Working Class in England*. During this period Marx wrote a number of abstruse works (many unpublished in his lifetime), including *The Holy Family* (1845/1956) and

The German Ideology (1845–1846/1970) (both coauthored with Engels), but he also produced *The Economic and Philosophic Manuscripts of 1844* (1932/1964), which better foreshadowed his increasing preoccupation with the economic domain.

While Marx and Engels shared a theoretical orientation, there were many differences between the two men. Marx tended to be theoretical, a disorderly intellectual, and very oriented to his family. Engels was a practical thinker, a neat and tidy businessman, and a person who did not believe in the institution of the family. In spite of their differences, Marx and Engels forged a close union in which they collaborated on books and articles and worked together in radical organizations, and Engels even helped support Marx throughout the rest of his life so that Marx could devote himself to his intellectual and political endeavors.

In spite of the close association of the names of Marx and Engels, Engels made it clear that he was the junior partner:

> Marx could very well have done without me. What Marx accomplished I would not have achieved. Marx stood higher, saw farther, and took a wider and quicker view than the rest of us. Marx was a genius.
>
> (Engels, cited in McLellan, 1973:131–132)

In fact, many believe that Engels failed to understand many of the subtleties of Marx's work (C. Smith, 1997). After Marx's death, Engels became the leading spokesperson for Marxian theory and in various ways distorted and oversimplified it, although he remained faithful to the political perspective he had forged with Marx.

Because some of his writings had upset the Prussian government, the French government (at the request of the Prussians) expelled Marx in 1845, and he moved to Brussels. His radicalism was growing, and he had become an active member of the international revolutionary movement. He also associated with the Communist League and was asked to write a document (with Engels) expounding its aims and beliefs. The result was the *Communist Manifesto* of 1848 (1848/1948), a work that was characterized by ringing political slogans (for example, "Working men of all countries, unite!").

In 1849 Marx moved to London, and, in light of the failure of the political revolutions of 1848, he began to withdraw from active revolutionary activity and to move into more serious and detailed research on the workings of the capitalist system. In 1852, he began his famous studies in the British Museum of the working conditions in capitalism. These studies ultimately resulted in the three volumes of *Capital,* the first of which was published in 1867; the other two were published posthumously. He lived in poverty during these years, barely managing to survive on a small income from his writings and the support of Engels. In 1864 Marx became reinvolved in political activity by joining the International, an international movement of workers. He soon gained preeminence within the movement and devoted a number of years to it. He began to gain fame both as a leader of the International and as the author of *Capital.* But the disintegration of the International by 1876, the failure of various revolutionary movements, and personal illness took their toll on Marx. His wife died in 1881, a daughter in 1882, and Marx himself on March 14, 1883.

Labor

For Marx, species being and human potential are intimately related to labor:

> Labour is, in the first place, a process in which both man and Nature participate, and in which man of his own accord starts, regulates, and controls the material reactions between himself and Nature . . . . By thus acting on the external world and changing it, he at the same time changes his own nature. He develops his slumbering powers and compels them to act in obedience to his sway . . . . We presuppose labour in a form that stamps it as exclusively human. A spider conducts operations that resemble those of a weaver and a bee puts to shame many an architect in the construction of her cells. But what distinguishes the worst architect from the best of bees is this, that the architect raises his structure in imagination before he erects it in reality. At the end of every labour process we get a result that existed in the imagination of the labourer at its commencement. He not only effects a change of form in the material on which he works, but he also realizes a purpose.
>
> (Marx, 1867/1967:177–178)

We see in that quotation many important parts of Marx's view of the relation between labor and human nature. First, what distinguishes us from other animals—our species being—is that our labor creates something in reality that previously existed only in our imagination. Our production reflects our purpose. Marx calls this process in which we create external objects out of our internal thoughts *objectification*. Second, this labor is material (Sayers, 2007). It works with the more material aspects of nature (e.g., raising fruits and vegetables, cutting down trees for wood) in order to satisfy our material needs. Finally, Marx believed that this labor does not just transform the material aspects of nature but also transforms us, including our needs, our consciousness, and our human nature. Labor is thus at the same time (1) the objectification of our purpose, (2) the establishment of an essential relation between human need and the material objects of our need, and (3) the transformation of our human nature.

Marx's use of the term *labor* is not restricted to economic activities; it encompasses all productive actions that transform the material aspects of nature in accordance with our purpose. Whatever is created through this free purposive activity is both an expression of our human nature and a transformation of it.

As we will see below, the process of labor has been changed under capitalism, making it difficult for us to understand Marx's conception, but we get close to Marx's concept when we think of the creative activity of an artist. Artwork is a representation of the thought of the artist. In Marx's terms, artwork is an objectivation of the artist. However, it is also true that the process of creating the art changes the artist. Through the process of producing the art, the artist's ideas about the art change, or the artist may become aware of a new vision that needs objectivation. In addition, the completed artwork can take on a new meaning for the artist and transform the artist's conceptions of that particular work or of art in general.

Labor, even artistic labor, is in response to a need, and the transformation that labor entails also transforms our needs. The satisfaction of our needs can lead to the creation of new needs (Marx and Engels, 1845–1846/1970:43). For example, the production of cars to satisfy our need for long-distance transportation led to a new need for highways. Even more significantly, although few people thought they needed cars when cars were first invented, now most people feel that they need them. A similar change has occurred with the computer. Whereas a generation ago few thought they needed a personal computer, now many people need one, as well as all of the software and peripherals that go with it.

We labor in response to our needs, but the labor itself transforms our needs, which can lead to new forms of productive activity. According to Marx, this transformation of our needs through labor is the engine of human history.

> Not only do the objective conditions change in the act of production . . . but the producers change, too, in that they bring out new qualities in themselves, develop themselves in production, transform themselves, develop new powers and ideas, new modes of intercourse, new needs and new language.
>
> (Marx, 1857–1858/1974:494).

Labor, for Marx, is the development of our truly human powers and potentials. By transforming material reality to fit our purpose, we also transform ourselves. Furthermore, labor is a social activity. Work involves others, directly in joint productions, or because others provide us with the necessary tools or raw materials for our work, or because they enjoy the fruits of our labor. Labor does not transform only the individual human; it also transforms society. Indeed, for Marx, the emergence of a human as an individual depends on a society. Marx wrote, "Man is in the most literal sense of the word a *zoon politikon,* not only a social animal, but an animal which can develop into an individual only in society" (1857–1858/1964:84). In addition, Marx tells us that this transformation includes even our consciousness: "Consciousness is, therefore, from the very beginning a social product, and remains so as long as men exist at all" (Marx and Engels, 1845–1846/1970:51). Consequently, the transformation of the individual through labor and the transformation of society are not separable.

Alienation

Although Marx believed that there is an inherent relation between labor and human nature, he thought that this relation is perverted by capitalism. He calls this perverted relation *alienation* (Beilharz, 2005a; Cooper, 1991; Meisenhelder, 1991). The present discussion of Marx's concept of human nature and of alienation is derived mainly from Marx's early work. In his later work on the nature of capitalist society, he shied away from such a heavily philosophical term as *alienation,* yet alienation remained one of his main concerns (Barbalet, 1983:95).

Marx analyzed the peculiar form that our relation to our own labor has taken under capitalism. We no longer see our labor as an expression of our purpose. There is no objectivation. Instead, we labor in accordance with the purpose of the capitalist who hires and pays us. Rather than being an end in itself—an expression of human capabilities—labor in capitalism is reduced to being a means to an end: earning money (Marx, 1932/1964:173). Because our labor is not our own, it no longer transforms us. Instead we are alienated from our labor and therefore alienated from our true human nature.

Although it is the individual who feels alienated in capitalist society, Marx's basic analytic concern was with the structures of capitalism that cause this alienation (Israel, 1971). Marx uses the concept of alienation to reveal the devastating effect of capitalist production on human beings and on society. Of crucial significance here is the two-class system in which capitalists employ workers (and thereby own workers' labor time) and capitalists own the means of production (tools and raw materials) as well as the ultimate products. To survive, workers are forced to sell their labor time to capitalists. These structures, especially the division of labor, are the sociological basis of alienation.

> First, the fact that labor is external to the worker, i.e., it does not belong to his essential being; that in his work, therefore, he does not affirm himself but denies himself, does not feel content but unhappy, does not develop freely his physical and mental energy but mortifies his body and ruins his mind. The worker therefore only feels himself outside his work, and in his work feels outside himself. He is at home when he is not working, and when he is working he is not at home. His labor therefore is not voluntary, but coerced; it is forced labor. It is therefore not the satisfaction of a need; it is merely a means to satisfy needs external to it.
>
> (Marx, 1850/1964:72)

As a result, people feel freely active only in their animal functions—eating, drinking, procreating. In the essentially human process of labor, they no longer feel themselves to be anything but animals. What is animal becomes human, and what is human becomes animal. Certainly eating, drinking, procreating, and so on are human functions, but when separated from the sphere of all other human activity and turned into sole and ultimate ends, they become animal functions.

Alienation can be seen as having four basic components.

1. Workers in capitalist society are alienated from their *productive activity.* They do not produce objects according to their own ideas or to directly satisfy their own needs. Instead, workers work for capitalists, who pay them a subsistence wage in return for the right to use them in any way they see fit. Because productive activity belongs to the capitalists, and because they decide what is to be done with it, we can say that workers are alienated from that activity. Furthermore, many workers who perform highly specialized tasks have little sense of their role in the total production process. For example, automobile assembly-line workers who tighten a few bolts on an engine may have little feel for how their labor contributes to the production of the entire car. They do not objectivate their ideas, and they are not transformed by the labor in any meaningful way. Instead of being a process that is satisfying in and of itself, productive activity in capitalism is reduced, Marx argued, to an often boring and stultifying means to the fulfillment of the only end that really matters in capitalism: earning enough money to survive.

2. Workers in capitalist society are alienated not only from productive activities but also from the object of those activities—the *product.* The product of their labor belongs not to the workers but to the capitalists, who may use it in any way they wish because it is the capitalists' private property. Marx (1932/1964:117) tells us, "Private property is thus the product, the result, the necessary consequence of alienated labour." The capitalist will use his or her ownership in order to sell the product for a profit.

If workers wish to own the product of their own labor, they must buy it like anyone else. No matter how desperate the workers' needs, they cannot use the products of their own labor to satisfy their needs. Even workers in a bakery can starve if they don't have the money to buy the bread that they make. Because of this peculiar relation, things that we buy—that are made by others—seem to us to be more an expression of ourselves than do the things we make at our jobs. People's personalities are judged more by the cars they drive, the clothes they wear, the gadgets they use—none of which they have made—than by what they actually produce in their daily work, which appears to be an arbitrary and accidental means for making money in order to buy things.

3. Workers in capitalist society are alienated from their *fellow workers*. Marx's assumption was that people basically need and want to work cooperatively in order to appropriate from nature what they require to survive. But in capitalism this cooperation is disrupted, and people, often strangers, are forced to work side by side for the capitalist. Even if the workers on the assembly line are close friends, the nature of the technology makes for a great deal of isolation. Here is the way one worker describes his social situation on the assembly line:

> You can work next to a guy for months without even knowing his name. One thing, you're too busy to talk. Can't hear. . . . You have to holler in his ear. They got these little guys coming around in white shirts and if they see you runnin' your mouth, they say, "This guy needs more work." Man, he's got no time to talk.
> (Terkel, 1974:165)

Of course, much the same is true in the newest version of the assembly line: the office cubicle. But in this social situation, workers experience something worse than simple isolation. Workers often are forced into outright competition, and sometimes conflict, with one another. To extract maximum productivity and to prevent the development of cooperative relationships, the capitalist pits one worker against another to see who can produce more, work more quickly, or please the boss more. The workers who succeed are given a few extra rewards; those who fail are discarded. In either case, considerable hostility is generated among the workers toward their peers. This is useful to the capitalists because it tends to deflect hostility that otherwise would be aimed at them. The isolation and the interpersonal hostility tend to alienate workers in capitalism from their fellow workers.

4. Workers in capitalist society are alienated from their own *human potential*. Instead of being a source of transformation and fulfillment of our human nature, the workplace is where we feel least human, least ourselves. Individuals perform less and less like human beings as they are reduced in their work to functioning like machines. Even smiles and greetings are programmed and scripted. Consciousness is numbed and, ultimately, destroyed as relations with other humans and with nature are progressively controlled. The result is a mass of people unable to express their essential human qualities, a mass of alienated workers.

Alienation is an example of the sort of contradiction that Marx's dialectical approach focused on. There is a real contradiction between human nature, which is defined and transformed by labor, and the actual social conditions of labor under capitalism. What Marx wanted to stress is that this contradiction cannot be resolved merely in thought. We are not any less alienated because we identify with our employer or with the things that our wages can purchase. Indeed, these things are a symptom of our alienation, which can be resolved only through real social change.

The Structures of Capitalist Society

In Europe in Marx's time, industrialization was increasing. People were being forced to leave agricultural and artisan trades and to work in factories where conditions were often harsh. By the 1840s, when Marx was entering his most productive period, Europe was experiencing a widespread sense of social crisis (Seigel, 1978:106). In 1848 a series of revolts swept across Europe (soon after the publication of Marx and Engel's *Communist Manifesto*). The effects of industrialization and the political implications of industrialization were especially apparent in the mostly rural states collectively referred to as Germany.

At the beginning of the nineteenth century, cheap manufactured goods from England and France began to force out of business the less efficient manufacturers in Germany. In response, the political leaders of the German states imposed capitalism on their still mainly feudal societies. The resulting poverty, dislocation, and alienation were particularly evident because of the rapidity of the change.

Marx's analysis of alienation was a response to the economic, social, and political changes that Marx saw going on around him. He did not view alienation as a philosophical problem. He wanted to understand what changes would be needed to create a society in which human potential could be adequately expressed. Marx's important insight was that the capitalist economic system is the primary cause of alienation. Marx's work on human nature and alienation led him to a critique of capitalist society and to a political program oriented to overcoming the structures of capitalism so that people could express their essential humanity (Mészáros, 1970).

Capitalism is an economic system in which great numbers of workers who own little produce commodities for the profit of small numbers of capitalists who own all of the following: the commodities, the means of producing the commodities, and the labor time of the workers, which they purchase through wages (H. Wolf, 2005b). One of Marx's central insights is that capitalism is much more than an economic system. It is also a system of power. The secret of capitalism is that political powers have been transformed into economic relations (Wood, 1995). Capitalists seldom need to use brute force. Capitalists are able to coerce workers through their power to dismiss workers and close plants. Capitalism, therefore, is not simply an economic system; it is also a political system, a mode of exercising power, and a process for exploiting workers.

In a capitalist system, the economy seems to be a natural force. People are laid off, wages are reduced, and factories are closed because of "the economy." We do not see these events as the outcomes of social or political decisions. Links between human suffering and the economic structures are deemed irrelevant or trivial.

For example, you might read in the newspaper that the Federal Reserve Board of the United States has raised interest rates. A reason often given for this action is that the economy is "overheated," which is to say that there is the possibility of inflation. Raising interest rates does indeed "cool off" the economy. How does it do so? It puts some people out of work. As a result, workers become afraid to demand higher wages, which might get passed on as higher prices, which might lead to additional interest-rate increases and to still more workers losing their jobs. Thus, inflation is averted. By raising interest rates, the Federal Reserve Board adopts a policy that helps capitalists and hurts workers. This decision, however, usually is presented as a purely economic one. Marx would say that it is a political decision that favors capitalists at the expense of workers.

Marx's aim is to make the social and political structures of the economy clearer by revealing "the economic law of motion of modern society" (quoted in Ollman, 1976:168). Furthermore, Marx intends to reveal the internal contradictions that he hopes will inevitably transform capitalism.

Commodities

The basis of all of Marx's work on social structures, and the place in which that work is most clearly tied to his views on human potential, is his analysis of commodities, or products of labor intended primarily for exchange. As Georg Lukács (1922/1968:83) put it, "The problem of commodities is . . . the central, structural problem of capitalist society." By starting with the commodity, Marx is able to reveal the nature of capitalism.

Marx's view of the commodity was rooted in his materialist orientation, with its focus on the productive activities of actors. As we saw earlier, it was Marx's view that in their interactions with nature and with other actors, people produce the objects that they need in order to survive. These objects are produced for personal use or for use by others in the immediate environment. Such uses are what Marx called the commodity's *use value.* However, in capitalism this process takes on a new and dangerous form. Instead of producing for themselves or for their immediate associates, the actors produce for someone else (the capitalist). The products have *exchange value;* that is, instead of being used immediately, they are exchanged in the market for money or for other objects.

Use value is connected to the intimate relation between human needs and the actual objects that can satisfy those needs. It is difficult to compare the use values of different things. Bread has the use value of satisfying hunger; shoes have the use value of protecting our feet. It is difficult to say that one has more use value than the other. They are *qualitatively* different. Furthermore, use value is tied to the physical properties of a commodity. Shoes cannot satisfy our hunger and bread cannot protect our feet because they are physically different kinds of objects. In the process of exchange, however, different commodities are compared to one another. One pair of shoes can be exchanged for six loaves of bread. Or if the medium of exchange is money, as is common, a pair of shoes can be worth six times as much money as a loaf of bread. Exchange values are *quantitatively* different. One can say that a pair of shoes has more exchange value than a loaf of bread. Furthermore, exchange value is separate from the physical property of the commodity. Only things that can be eaten can have the use value of satisfying hunger, but any type of thing can have the exchange value of a dollar.

Fetishism of Commodities

Commodities are the products of human labor, but they can become separated from the needs and purposes of their creators. Because exchange value floats free from the actual commodity and seems to exist in a realm separate from any human use, we are led to believe that these objects and the market for them have independent existences. In fully developed capitalism, this belief becomes reality as the objects and their markets actually become real, independent phenomena. The commodity takes on an independent, almost mystical external reality (Marx, 1867/1967:35). Marx called this process the *fetishism of commodities* (Dant, 1996; Sherlock, 1997). Marx did not mean that commodities take on sexual meanings, for he wrote before Freud gave the term *fetish* this twist. Marx was alluding to the ways in which the practitioners of some religions, such as the Zunis, carve figures and then worship them. By fetish, Marx meant a thing that we ourselves make and then worship as if it were a god.

In capitalism, the products that we make, their values, and the economy that consists of our exchanges all seem to take on lives of their own, separate from any human needs or decisions. Even our own labor—the thing that, according to Marx, makes us truly human—becomes a commodity that is bought and sold. Our labor acquires an exchange value that is separate from us. It is turned into an abstract thing and used by the capitalist to make the objects that come to dominate us. Hence, commodities are the source of the alienation discussed above. Even the labor of self-employed commodity producers is alienated, because they must produce for the market instead of to achieve their own purposes and satisfy their own needs.

Thus, the economy takes on a function that Marx believed only actors could perform: the production of value. For Marx, the true value of a thing comes from the fact that labor produces it and someone needs it. A commodity's true value represents human social relations. In contrast, in capitalism, Marx tells us, "A definite social relation between men . . . assumes, in their eyes, the fantastic form of a relation between things" (1867/1967:72). Granting reality to commodities and to the market, the individual in capitalism progressively loses control over them. A commodity, therefore, is "a mysterious thing, simply because in it the social character of men's labor appears to them as an objective character stamped upon the product of that labor: because the relations of the producers to the sum total of their own labor is presented to them as a social relation, existing not between themselves, but between the products of their labor" (Marx, 1867/1967:72).

Think, for example, of the cup of coffee that you might have bought before sitting down to read this text. In that simple transaction, you entered into a relationship with hundreds of others: the waitperson, the owner of the coffee shop, the people working at the roaster, the importer, the truck driver, dockworkers, all the people on the ship that brought the beans, the coffee plantation owner, the pickers, and so on. In addition, you supported a particular trading relation between countries, a particular form of government in the grower's country that has been historically shaped by the coffee trade, a particular relation between the plantation owner and the worker, and many other social relations. You did all this by exchanging money for a cup of coffee. In the relation between those objects—money and coffee—lies hidden all those social relations.

Marx's discussion of commodities and their fetishism takes us from the level of the individual actor to the level of large-scale social structures. The fetishism of commodities imparts to the economy an independent, objective reality that is external to, and coercive of, the actor. Looked at in this way, the fetishism of commodities is translated into the concept of *reification* (Lukács, 1922/1968; Sherlock, 1997). Reification can be thought of as "thingification," or the process of coming to believe that humanly created social forms are natural, universal, and absolute things. As a result of reification, social forms do acquire those characteristics. The concept of reification implies that people believe that social structures are beyond their control and unchangeable. Reification occurs when this belief becomes a self-fulfilling prophecy. Then structures actually do acquire the character people endowed them with. People become mesmerized by the seeming objectivity and authority of the economy. People lose their jobs, make career choices, or move across the country because of the economy. According to Marx, however, the economy is not an objective, natural thing. It is a form of domination, and decisions about interest rates and layoffs are political decisions that tend to benefit one group over another.

People reify the whole range of social relationships and social structures. Just as people reify commodities and other economic phenomena (for example, the division of labor [Rattansi, 1982; Wallimann, 1981]), they also reify religious (Barbalet, 1983:147), political, and organizational structures. Marx made a similar point in reference to the state: "And out of this very contradiction between the individual and . . . the community the latter takes an independent form as the State, divorced from the real interests of individual and community" (cited in Bender, 1970:176). Capitalism is made up of particular types of social relations that tend to take forms that appear to be and eventually are independent of the actual people involved. As Moishe Postone (1993:4) tells us, "The result is a new, increasingly abstract form of social domination—one that subjects people to impersonal structural imperatives and constraints that cannot be adequately grasped in terms of concrete domination (e.g., personal or group domination)."

Capital, Capitalists, and the Proletariat

Marx found the heart of capitalist society within the commodity. A society dominated by objects whose main value is exchange produces certain categories of people. The two main types that concerned Marx were the proletariat and the capitalist. Let us start with the proletariat.

Workers who sell their labor and do not own their own means of production are members of the proletariat. They do not own their own tools or their factories. Marx (1867/1967:714–715) believed that proletarians would eventually lose their own skills as they increasingly serviced machines that had their skills built into them. Because members of the proletariat produce only for exchange, they are also consumers. Because they don't have the means to produce for their own needs, they must use their wages to buy what they need. Consequently, proletarians are completely dependent on their wages in order to live. This makes the proletariat dependent on those who pay the wages.

Those who pay the wages are the capitalists. Capitalists are those who own the means of production. Before we can fully understand capitalists, we must first understand capital itself (H. Wolf, 2005a). Capital is money that produces more money, capital is money that is invested rather than being used to satisfy human needs or desires. This distinction becomes clearer when we look at what Marx considered to be "the starting-point of capital" (1867/1967:146): the *circulation of commodities*. Marx discussed two types of circulation of commodities. One type of circulation is characteristic of capital: Money → Commodities → (a larger sum of) Money (M_1-C-M_2). The other type is not: Commodities → Money → Commodities (C_1-M-C_2).

In a noncapitalist circulation of commodities, the circuit C_1-M-C_2 predominates. An example of C_1-M-C_2 would be a fisherman who sells his catch (C_1) and then uses the money (M) to buy bread (C_2). The primary goal of exchange in noncapitalist circulation is a commodity that one can use and enjoy.

In a capitalist circulation of commodities (M_1-C-M_2), the primary goal is to produce more money. Commodities are purchased in order to generate profit, not necessarily for use. In the capitalist circuit, referred to by Marx as "buying in order to sell" (1867/1967:147), the individual actor buys a commodity with money and in turn exchanges the commodity for presumably more money. For example, a store owner would buy (M_1) the fish (C) in order to sell them for more money (M_2). To further increase profits, the store owner might buy the boat and fishing equipment and pay the fisherman a wage. The goal of this circuit is not the consumption of the use value, as it is in the simple circulation of commodities. The goal is more money. The particular properties of the commodity used to make money are irrelevant. The commodity can be fish or it can be labor. Also, the real needs and desires of human beings are irrelevant; all that matters is what will produce more money.

Capital is money that produces more money, but Marx tells us it is more than that: it is also a particular social relation. Money becomes capital only because of a social relation between, on the one hand, the proletariat, which does the work and must purchase the product, and, on the other hand, those who have invested the money. The capacity of capital to generate profit appears "as a power endowed by Nature— a productive power that is immanent in Capital" (1867/1967:333); but, according to Marx, it is a relation of power. Capital cannot increase except by exploiting those who actually do the work. The workers are exploited by a system, and the irony is that the system is produced through the workers' own labor. The capitalist system is the social structure that emerges from that exploitive relationship.

Capitalists are those who live off the profit of capital. They are the beneficiaries of the proletariat's exploitation. Within the idea of capital is contained a social relation between those who own the means of production and those whose wage labor is exploited.

Exploitation

For Marx, exploitation and domination reflect more than an accidentally unequal distribution of wealth and power. *Exploitation* is a necessary part of the capitalist economy. All societies have exploitation, but what is peculiar in capitalism is that the exploitation is accomplished by the impersonal and "objective" economic system. It seems to be less a matter of power and more a matter of economists' charts and figures. Furthermore, the coercion is rarely naked force and is instead the worker's own needs, which can now be satisfied only through wage labor. Dripping irony, Marx describes the freedom of this wage labor:

> For the conversion of his money into capital . . . the owner of money must meet in the market with the free labourer, free in the double sense, that as a free man he can dispose of his labour-power as his own commodity, and that on the other hand he has no other commodity for sale, is short of everything necessary for the realization of his labour-power.
>
> (Marx, 1867/1967:169)

Workers appear to be "free laborers," entering into free contracts with capitalists. But Marx believed that the workers must accept the terms the capitalists offer them, because the workers can no longer produce for their own needs. This is especially true because capitalism usually creates what Marx referred to as a *reserve army* of the unemployed. If a worker does not want to do a job at the wage the capitalist offers, someone else in the reserve army of the unemployed will. This, for example, is what Barbara Ehrenreich discovered is the purpose of many of the want ads for low-paying jobs:

> Only later will I realize that the want ads are not a reliable measure of the actual jobs available at any particular time. They are . . . the employers' insurance policy against the relentless turnover of the low-wage workforce. Most of the big hotels run ads almost continually if only to build a supply of applicants to replace the current workers as they drift away or are fired.
>
> (Ehrenreich, 2001:15)

The capitalists pay the workers less than the value that the workers produce and keep the rest for themselves. This *practice* leads us to Marx's central concept of *surplus value,* which is defined as the difference between the value of the product when it is sold and the value of the elements consumed in the formation of that product (including the worker's labor). The capitalists can use this profit for private consumption, but doing so would not lead to the expansion of capitalism. Rather, capitalists expand their enterprises by converting profit into a base for the creation of still more surplus value.

It should be stressed that surplus value is not simply an economic concept. Surplus value, like capital, is a particular social relation and a form of domination, because labor is the real source of surplus value. "The rate of surplus-value is therefore an exact expression for the degree of exploitation of labor-power by capital, or of the laborer by the capitalist" (Marx, 1867/1967:218). This observation points to one of Marx's more colorful metaphors: "Capital is dead labor, that, vampire-like, only lives by sucking living labor, and lives the more, the more labor it sucks" (1867/1967:233).

Marx (1857–1858/1974:414) makes one other important point about capital: "Capital exists and can only exist as many capitals." What he means is that capitalism is always driven by incessant competition. Capitalists may seem to be in control, but even they are driven by the constant competition between capitals. The capitalist is driven to make more profit in order to accumulate and invest more capital. The capitalist who does not do this will be outcompeted by others who do. "As such, he shares with the miser an absolute drive towards self-enrichment. But what appears in the miser as the mania of an individual is in the capitalist the effect of a social mechanism in which he is merely a cog" (Marx, 1867/1967:739).

The desire for more profit and more surplus value for expansion pushes capitalism toward what Marx called the *general law of capitalist accumulation.* Capitalists seek to exploit workers as much as possible: "The constant tendency of capital is to force the cost of labor back towards . . . zero" (Marx, 1867/1967:600). Marx basically argued that the structure and the ethos of capitalism push capitalists in the direction of the accumulation of more and more capital. Given Marx's view that labor is the source of value, capitalists are led to intensify the exploitation of the proletariat, thereby driving class conflict.

Class Conflict

Marx often used the term *class* in his writings, but he never systematically defined what he meant (So and Suwarsono, 1990:35). He usually is taken to have meant a group of people in similar situations with respect to their control of the means of production. This, however, is not a complete description of the way Marx used the term. *Class,* for Marx, was always defined in terms of its potential for conflict. Individuals form a class insofar as they are in a common conflict with others over the surplus value. In capitalism there is an inherent conflict of interest between those who hire wage laborers and those whose labor is turned into surplus value. It is this inherent conflict that produces classes (Ollman, 1976).

Because class is defined by the potential for conflict, it is a theoretical and historically variant concept. A theory about where potential conflict exists in a society is required before identifying a class.[4] Richard Miller (1991:99) tells us that "there is no rule that could, in principle, be used to sort out people in a society into classes without studying the actual interactions among economic processes on the one hand and between political and cultural processes on the other."

For Marx, a class truly exists only when people become aware of their conflicting relation to other classes. Without this awareness, they only constitute what Marx called a class *in itself.* When they become aware of the conflict, they become a true class, a class *for itself.*

In capitalism, Marx's analysis discovered two primary classes: bourgeoisie and proletariat.[5] Bourgeoisie is Marx's name for capitalists in the modern economy. The bourgeoisie owns the means of production and employs wage labor. The conflict between the bourgeoisie and the proletariat is another example of a real material contradiction. This contradiction grows out of the previously mentioned contradiction between labor and capitalism. None of these contradictions can be resolved except by changing the capitalist structure. In fact, until that change occurs, the contradiction will only become worse. Society will be increasingly polarized into these two great opposing classes.

---

[4] Marx did acknowledge that class conflict often is affected by other forms of stratification, such as ethnic, racial, gender, and religious; however, he did not accept that these could be primary.

[5] Although his theoretical work looked mainly at these two classes, his historical studies examined a number of different class formations. Most significant are the petty bourgeois—small shopkeepers employing at most a few workers—and the lumpenproletariat—the proletariat who readily sell out to the capitalists. For Marx, these other classes can be understood only in terms of the primary relationship between bourgeoisie and proletariat.

Competition with megastores and franchise chains will shut down many small, independent businesses; mechanization will replace skilled artisans; and even some capitalists will be squeezed out through attempts to establish monopolies, for example, by means of mergers. All these displaced people will be forced down into the ranks of the proletariat. Marx called this inevitable increase in the proletariat *proletarianization.*

In addition, because capitalists have already reduced the workers to laboring machines performing a series of simple operations, mechanization becomes increasingly easy. As mechanization proceeds, more and more people are put out of work and fall from the proletariat into the industrial reserve army. In the end, Marx foresaw a situation in which society would be characterized by a tiny number of exploitative capitalists and a huge mass of proletarians and members of the industrial reserve army. By reducing so many people to this condition, capitalism creates the masses that will lead to its own overthrow. The increased centralization of factory work, as well as the shared suffering, increases the possibility of an organized resistance to capitalism. Furthermore, the international linking of factories and markets encourages workers to be aware of more than their own local interests. This awareness is likely to lead to revolution.

The capitalists, of course, seek to forestall this revolution. For example, they sponsor colonial adventures with the objective of shifting at least some of the burden of exploitation from the home front to the colonies. However, in Marx's view (1867/1967:10), these efforts are doomed to failure because the capitalist is as much controlled by the laws of the capitalist economy as are the workers. Capitalists are under competitive pressure from one another, forcing each to try to reduce labor costs and intensify exploitation—even though this intensified exploitation will increase the likelihood of revolution and therefore contribute to the capitalists' demise. Even good-hearted capitalists will be forced to further exploit their workers in order to compete: "The law of capitalist accumulation, metamorphosed by economists into pretended law of nature, in reality merely states that the very nature of accumulation excludes every diminution in the degree of exploitation" (Marx, 1867/1967:582).

Though not a Marxist, Robert Reich, a former U.S. secretary of labor, echoes Marx's analysis that it is not the evil of individual capitalists but the capitalist system itself that explains the increasing layoffs in America and the movement of manufacturing to take advantage of cheaper overseas labor:

> It's tempting to conclude from all this that enterprises are becoming colder-hearted, and executives more ruthless—and to blame it on an ethic of unbridled greed that seems to have taken hold in recent years and appears to be increasing. But this conclusion would be inaccurate. The underlying cause isn't a change in the American character. It is to be found in the increasing ease by which buyers and investors can get better deals, and the competitive pressure this imposes on all enterprises.
>
> (Reich, 2000:71)

Whether they want to or not, capitalists must move their factories where labor is cheaper; they must exploit workers. A capitalist who does not will not be able to compete with capitalists who do.

Marx usually did not blame individual members of the bourgeoisie for their actions; he saw these actions as largely determined by the logic of the capitalist system. This is consistent with his view that actors in capitalism generally are devoid of creative independence.[6] However, the developmental process inherent in capitalism provides the conditions necessary for the ultimate reemergence of such creative action and, with it, the overthrow of the capitalist system. The logic of the capitalist system is forcing the capitalists to produce more exploited proletarians, and these are the very people who will bring an end to capitalism through their revolt. "What the bourgeoisie, therefore, produces, is, above all, its own gravediggers" (Marx and Engels, 1848/1948).

It is not only the ultimate proletariat revolution that Marx sees as caused by the underlying contradictions of capitalism, but also many of the various personal and social crises that beset modern society. On the personal side, we have already discussed some of the facets of the alienation that Marx believed was at the root of the feeling of meaninglessness in so many people's lives. At the economic level, Marx predicted a series of booms and depressions as capitalists overproduced or laid off workers in their attempts to increase their profits. At the political level, Marx predicted the increasing inability of a civil society to discuss and solve social problems. Instead we would see the growth of a state whose only purposes are the protection of the capitalists' private property and an occasional brutal intervention when economic coercion by the capitalists fails.

Capitalism as a Good Thing

Despite his focus on the inevitable crises of capitalism and his portrayal of it as a system of domination and exploitation, Marx saw capitalism as primarily a good thing. Certainly, Marx did not want to return to the traditional values of precapitalism. Past generations were just as exploited; the only difference is that the old exploitation was not veiled behind an economic system. The birth of capitalism opened up new possibilities for the freedom of the workers. Notwithstanding its exploitation, the capitalist system provides the possibility for freedom from the traditions that bound all previous societies. Even if the worker is not yet truly free, the promise is there. Similarly, as the most powerful economic system ever developed, capitalism holds the promise of freedom from hunger and from other forms of material deprivation. It was from the viewpoint of these promises that Marx criticized capitalism.

In addition, Marx believed that capitalism is the root cause of the defining characteristics of the modern age. Modernity's constant change and propensity to challenge all accepted traditions are driven by the inherent competition of capitalism, which pushes capitalists to continuously revolutionize the means of production and transform society:

> Constant revolutionizing of production, uninterrupted disturbance of all social conditions, everlasting uncertainty and agitation distinguish the bourgeois epoch from all earlier ones. All fixed, fast-frozen relations, with their train of ancient and venerable prejudices and opinions, are swept away, all new-formed ones become antiquated before they can ossify. All that is solid melts into air, all that is holy is profaned, and man is at last compelled to face with sober senses, his real conditions of life, and his relations with his kind.
>
> (Marx and Engels, 1848/1948:11)

---

[6] Marx might be seen as an exception to his own theory. He does acknowledge that it is possible for some individuals among the bourgeoisie to lay aside their class characteristics and adopt a communist consciousness (Marx and Engels, 1845–1846/1970:69).

Capitalism has been a truly revolutionary force. It has created a global society; it has introduced unrelenting technological change; it has overthrown the traditional world. But now, Marx believed, it must be overthrown. Capitalism's role is finished, and it is time for the new stage of communism to begin.

Materialist Conception of History

Marx was able to criticize capitalism from the perspective of its future because of his belief that history would follow a predictable course. This belief was based on his materialist conception of history (often simply shortened to the term *historical materialism* [Vandenberghe, 2005]). The general claim of Marx's historical materialism is that the way in which people provide for their material needs determines or, in general, conditions the relations that people have with each other, their social institutions, and even their prevalent ideas.[7]

Because of the importance of the way in which people provide for their material needs, this, along with the resultant economic relations, is often referred to as the *base*. Noneconomic relations, other social institutions, and prevalent ideas are referred to as the *superstructure*. It should be noted that Marx's view of history does not envision a straightforward trend in which the superstructure simply comes into line with the base. Human history is set into motion by the attempt to satisfy needs, but as noted above, these needs themselves are historically changing. Consequently, advances in the satisfaction of needs tend to produce more needs so that human needs are both the motivating foundation and the result of the economic base.

The following quotation is one of Marx's best summaries of his materialist conception of history:

> In the social production which men carry on they enter into definite relations that are indispensable and independent of their will. These relations of production correspond to a definite stage of development of their material forces of production. The totality of these relations of production constitutes the economic structure of society, which is the real foundation on top of which arises a legal and political superstructure to which correspond definite forms of social consciousness. At a certain stage of their development, the material forces of production in society come in conflict with the existing relations of production or—what is but a legal expression of the same thing—with the property relations within which they had been at work before. From forms of development of the forces of production these relations turn into their fetters. Then occurs a period of social revolution. With the change of the economic foundation the entire immense superstructure is more or less rapidly transformed.
>
> (Marx, 1859/1970:20–21)

---

[7] Antonio (2011:119–120) distinguishes between a hard and a soft material determinism. "Although hard determinist passages exist in Marx's texts, he suggested much more often a complex, historically contingent materialism, which ought not to be reduced to 'technological determinism' (i.e., social change arises from technical change) or to 'reflection theory' (i.e., ideas are mere emanations of material reality)."

The place to start in that quotation is with the "material forces of production." These are the actual tools, machinery, factories, and so forth used to satisfy human needs. The "relations of production" are the kinds of associations that people have with each other in satisfying their needs.

Marx's theory holds that a society will tend to adopt the system of social relations that best facilitates the employment and development of its productive powers. Therefore, the relations of production correspond to the state of the material forces of production. For example, certain stages of low technology correspond to social relations characterized by a few large landowners and a large number of serfs who work the land in return for a share of the produce. The higher technology of capitalism corresponds to a few capitalists who are able to invest in the expensive machinery and factories and a large number of wage workers. As Marx succinctly, if somewhat simplistically, puts it, "the hand-mill gives you society with the feudal lord; the steam-mill society with the capitalist" (Marx, 1847/1963:95). Marx adds that these relations between people also can be expressed as property relations: the capitalist owns the means of production, and the wage laborer does not.

Capitalist economies foster unique relations between people and create certain expectations, obligations, and duties. For example, wage laborers must show a certain deference to capitalists if they want to keep their jobs. For Marx, what was important about these relations of production was their propensity to class conflict, but it is also possible to see the effect of the relations of production in family and personal relations. The socialization necessary to produce the "good" male worker also produces a certain type of husband. Similarly, early capitalism's requirement that the man leave the home to work all day led to a definition of the mother as the primary caretaker of the children. Hence, changes in the forces of production led to deep changes in the family structure. These changes too can be seen as relations of production.

Marx is never quite clear about where the relations of production leave off and the superstructure starts. However, he clearly felt that some relations and forms of "social consciousness" play only a supporting role in the material means of production. Marx predicted that although these elements of the superstructure are not directly involved, they tend to take a form that will support the relations of production.

Marx's view of history was a dynamic one, and he therefore believed that the forces of production will change to better provide for material needs. For example, this is what happened with the advent of capitalism, when technological changes made factories possible. However, before capitalism could actually occur, there had to be changes in society, changes in the relations of production. Factories, capitalists, and wage laborers were not compatible with feudal relations. The feudal lords, who derived their wealth solely from the ownership of land and who felt a moral obligation to provide for their serfs, had to be replaced by capitalists who derived their wealth from capital and who felt no moral obligation to wage laborers. Similarly, the serf's feeling of personal loyalty to the lord had to be replaced by proletarians' willingness to sell their labor to whoever will pay. The old relations of production were in conflict with the new forces of production.

A revolution is often required to change the relations of production. The main source of revolution is the material contradiction between the forces of production and the relations of production. However, revolution also results from another contradiction: between exploiters and the exploited. According to Marx, this contradiction, which has always existed, leads to revolutionary change when the exploited line up in support of a change in the relations of production that favors changes occurring in the forces of production. Marx did not believe that all workers' revolts could be effective, only those in support of a change in the forces of production. An effective revolution, according to Marx, will cause the supporting relations, institutions, and prevalent ideas to change so that they validate the new relations of production.

Cultural Aspects of Capitalist Society

In addition to his focus on the material structures of capitalism, Marx also theorized about its cultural aspects.

Ideology

Not only do the existing relations of production tend to prevent changes necessary for the development of the forces of production, but similarly, the supporting relations, institutions, and, in particular, prevalent ideas also tend to prevent these changes. Marx called prevalent ideas that perform this function *ideologies*. As with many terms, Marx is not always precise in his use of the word *ideology*. He seems to use it to indicate two related sorts of ideas.

First, *ideology* refers to ideas that naturally emerge out of everyday life in capitalism but, because of the nature of capitalism, reflect reality in an inverted manner (Larrain, 1979). To explain this meaning of the term, Marx used the metaphor of a camera obscura, which employs an optical quirk to show a real image reflected upside down. This is the type of ideology represented by the fetishism of commodities or by money. Even though we know that money is nothing but a piece of paper that has value only because of underlying social relations, in our daily lives we treat money as though it had inherent value. Instead of our seeing that we give money its value, it often seems that money gives us our value.

This first type of ideology is vulnerable to disruption because it is based on underlying material contradictions. Human value is not really dependent on money, and we often meet people who are living proof of that contradiction. In fact, it is at this level that we usually become aware of the material contradictions that Marx believed will drive capitalism to the next phase. We become aware, for example, that the economy is not an objective, independent system, but a political sphere. We become aware that our labor is not just another commodity and that its sale for wages produces alienation. Or if we don't become aware of the underlying truth, we at least become aware of the disruption because of a blatantly political move in the economic system or our own feeling of alienation. It is in addressing these disruptions that Marx's second use of *ideology* is relevant.

When disruptions occur and the underlying material contradictions are revealed, or are in danger of being revealed, the second type of ideology will emerge. Here Marx uses the term *ideology* to refer to systems of ruling ideas that attempt once again to hide the contradictions that are at the heart of the capitalist system. In most cases, they do this in one of three ways: (1) They lead to the creation of subsystems of ideas—a religion, a philosophy, a literature, a legal system—that makes the contradictions appear to be coherent. (2) They explain away those experiences that reveal the contradictions, usually as personal problems or individual idiosyncrasies. Or (3) they present the capitalist contradiction as really being a contradiction in human nature and therefore one that cannot be fixed by social change.

In general, members of the ruling class create this second type of ideology. For example, Marx refers to bourgeois economists who present the commodity form as natural and universal. Or he criticizes bourgeois philosophers, such as Hegel, for pretending that material contradictions can be resolved by changing how we think. However, even the proletariat can create this type of ideology. People who have given up the hope of actually changing society need such ideologies. But no matter who creates them, these ideologies always benefit the ruling class by hiding the contradictions that would lead to social change.

Freedom, Equality, and Ideology

For an example of ideology, we will look at Marx's ideas about the bourgeois conception of equality and freedom. According to Marx, our particular ideas of equality and freedom emerge out of capitalism. Although we take our belief in freedom and equality to be an obvious thing, any historical study will demonstrate that it is not. Most societies would have considered the idea that all people are essentially equal as absurd. For most cultures throughout history, slavery seemed quite natural. Now, under capitalism, we believe quite the opposite: inequality is absurd, and slavery is unnatural.

Marx thought that this change in our ideas could be traced to the everyday practices of capitalism. The act of exchange, which is the basis of capitalism, presupposes the equality of the people in the exchange, just as it presupposes the equality of the commodities in the exchange. For the commodities, the particular qualitative differences of their use values are hidden by their exchange value. In other words, apples and oranges are made equal by reducing them to their monetary value. The same thing happens to the differences between the people involved in the exchange. Most exchanges in advanced capitalism involve people who never meet and don't know each other. We don't care who grew the apples and oranges we buy. This anonymity and indifference constitutes a kind of equality.

Furthermore, freedom is assumed in this exchange, since any of the partners to the exchange are presumed to be free to exchange or not as they see fit. The very idea of capitalist exchange means that commodities are not taken by force but are freely traded. This is also true of the exchange of labor time for wages. It is assumed that the worker or the employer is free to enter into the exchange and free to terminate it. Marx (1857–1858/1974:245) concludes that "equality and freedom are not only respected in exchange which is based on exchange values, but the exchange of exchange values is the real productive basis of all equality and freedom." Nevertheless, Marx believed that capitalist practices result in an inverted view of freedom. It seems that we are free; but in fact, it is capital that is free and we who are enslaved.

According to Marx, freedom is the ability to have control over your own labor and its products. Although individuals may seem free under capitalism, they are not. Under previous social forms, people were directly dominated by others and so were aware of their unfreedom. Under capitalism, people are dominated by capitalist relations that seem objective and natural and therefore are not perceived as a form of domination. Marx (1857–1858/1974:652) decries "the insipidity of the view that free competition is the ultimate development of human freedom. . . . This kind of individual freedom is therefore at the same time the most complete suspension of all individual freedom, and the most complete subjugation of individuality under social conditions which assume the form of objective powers."

Because the capitalist owns the means of production, the exchange of wages for labor time cannot be free. The proletariat must work in order to live, but the capitalist has the choice to hire others from the reserve army of labor, or to mechanize, or to let the factory sit idle until the workers become desperate enough to "freely" accept the capitalist's wages. The worker is neither free nor equal to the capitalist.

Hence, we see that the first level of the ideology of freedom and equality emerges from the practices of exchange in capitalism, but that our ideas are inverted and do not represent real freedom and equality. It is capital that is freely and equally exchanged; it is capital that is accepted without prejudice; it is capital that is able to do as it wishes, not us. This first type of ideology is easily disrupted, and our awareness of this disruption drives capitalism to the next phase. Despite the ideology of equality and freedom, few workers feel equal to their employers; few feel free in their jobs. This is why the second type of ideology is necessary. These disruptions somehow must be explained away or made to look inevitable.

This is especially true with the ideology of equality and freedom, because these ideas are among the most threatening to capitalism. They are another example of how capitalism creates its own gravediggers. Older forms of unfreedom and inequality were clearly tied to people, and there was hope, therefore, of becoming free and equal by changing the hearts of the people who oppressed us. When we become aware of the source of unfreedom and inequality under capitalism, we begin to realize that capitalism itself must be changed. Ideologies therefore must be created to protect the capitalist system, and one way in which they do this is by portraying inequality as equality and unfreedom as freedom.

Marx believed that the capitalist system is inherently unequal. The capitalists automatically benefit more from the capitalist system, while the workers are automatically disadvantaged. Under capitalism, those who own the means of production, those with capital, make money from their money. Under capitalism, capital begets more capital—that is, investments give a return—and as we saw above, Marx believed that this was derived from the exploitation of the workers. Not only are the workers automatically exploited, they also bear the burden of unemployment due to technological changes, geographical shifts, and other economic dislocations, all of which benefit the capitalist. The rule of capitalism is reflected in the common saying that the rich get richer while the poor get poorer. Constantly increasing inequality is built into the capitalist system.

Any attempt toward a more equal society must take into account this automatic propensity of the capitalist system to increased inequality. Nevertheless, attempts to make the capitalist system more equal often are portrayed as forms of inequality. From the Marxist viewpoint these attempts would be the second form of ideology. For example, ideologues promote a "flat tax" that taxes the rich and the poor at the same rate. They argue that because the rate is the same for rich and poor, it is equal.

They ignore the fact that a graduated tax rate may be just compensation for the built-in inequality of capitalism. They create an ideology by portraying the obvious inequalities of the capitalist system as inevitable or as being due to the laziness of the poor. In this way, inequality is portrayed as equality, and the freedom of the rich to keep the fruits of exploitation trumps the freedom of the workers.

We see in this example not only the two types of ideology but also another instance of how Marx thought that capitalism is a good thing. The ideas of freedom and equality emerge from capitalism itself, and it is these ideas that drive us toward the dissolution of capitalism, toward communism.

Religion

Marx also sees religion as an ideology. He famously refers to religion as the opiate of the people, but it is worthwhile to look at the entire quotation:

> Religious distress is at the same time the expression of real distress and also the protest against real distress. Religion is the sigh of the oppressed creature, the heart of a heartless world, just as it is the spirit of spiritless conditions. It is the opium of the people.

(Marx, 1843/1970)

Marx believed that religion, like all ideology, reflects a truth but that this truth is inverted. Because people cannot see that their distress and oppression are produced by the capitalist system, their distress and oppression are given a religious form. Marx clearly says that he is not against religion per se, but against a system that requires the illusions of religion.

This religious form is vulnerable to disruption and therefore is always liable to become the basis of a revolutionary movement. We do indeed see that religious movements have often been in the forefront of opposition to capitalism (for example, liberation theology). Nevertheless, Marx felt that religion is especially amenable to becoming the second form of ideology by portraying the injustice of capitalism as a test for the faithful and pushing any revolutionary change off into the afterlife. In this way, the cry of the oppressed is used to further oppression.

Marx's Economics: A Case Study

This chapter is devoted to an analysis of Marx's sociology, but of course it is his economics for which he is far better known. Although we have touched on a number of aspects of Marx's economics, we have not dealt with it in a coherent fashion. In this section, we look at Marx's economics, not as economics per se but rather as an exemplification of his sociological theory (Mazlish, 1984).[8] There is much more to Marxian economics, but this is the most relevant way to deal with it in a book devoted to sociological theory.

---

[8] *One* way of looking at Marx's economic theory (for example, the labor theory of value) is as a specific application of his more general sociological theory. This stands in contrast to G. A. Cohen's (1978) work, in which his overriding concern is the underlying *economic* theory in Marx's work. Although Cohen sees the "economic" and the "social" as being interchangeable in Marx's work, he clearly implies that Marx's economic theory is the more general.

A starting point for Marxian economics is in the concepts, previously touched on, of use value and exchange value. People have always created use values; that is, they have always produced things that directly satisfy their wants. A *use value* is defined qualitatively; that is, something either is or is not useful. An *exchange value*, however, is defined quantitatively, not qualitatively. It is defined by the amount of labor needed to appropriate useful qualities. Whereas use values are produced to satisfy one's own needs, exchange values are produced to be exchanged for values of another use. Whereas the production of use values is a natural human expression, the existence of exchange values sets in motion a process by which humanity is distorted. The entire edifice of capitalism, including commodities, the market, money, and so forth, is erected on the basis of exchange values.

To Marx, the basic source of any value was the amount of socially necessary labor-time needed to produce an article under the normal conditions of production and with the average degree of skill and intensity of the time. This is the well-known *labor theory of value*. Although it is clear that labor lies at the base of use value, this fact grows progressively less clear as we move to exchange values, commodities, the market, and capitalism. To put it another way, "The determination of the magnitude of value by labor-time is therefore a secret, hidden under the apparent fluctuations in relative values of commodities" (Marx, 1867/1967:75). Labor, as the source of all value, is a secret in capitalism that allows the capitalists to exploit the workers.

According to Peter Worsley, Marx "put at the heart of his sociology—as no other sociology does—the theme of exploitation" (1982:115). The capitalists pay the workers *less* than the value the workers produce and keep the rest for themselves. The workers are not aware of this exploitation, and often, neither are the capitalists. The capitalists believe that this extra value is derived from their own cleverness, their capital investment, their manipulation of the market, and so on. Marx stated that "so long as trade is good, the capitalist is too much absorbed in money grubbing to take notice of this gratuitous gift of labor" (1867/1967:207). In sum, Marx said:

> The capitalist does not know that the normal price of labor also includes a definite quantity of unpaid labor, and that this very unpaid labor is the normal source of his gain. The category, surplus labor-time, does not exist at all for him, since it is included in the normal working-day, which he thinks he has paid for in the day's wages.
>
> (Marx, 1867/1967:550)

This leads us to Marx's central concept of *surplus value*. This is defined as the difference between the value of the product when it is sold and the value of the elements consumed in the formation of that product. Although means of production (raw materials and tools, the value of which comes from the labor involved in extracting or producing them) are consumed in the production process, it is labor that is the real source of surplus value. "The rate of surplus-value is therefore an exact expression for the degree of exploitation of labor-power by capital, or of the laborer by the capitalist" (Marx, 1867/1967:218). This points to one of Marx's more colorful metaphors: "Capital is dead labor, that, vampire-like, only lives by sucking living labor, and lives the more, the more labor it sucks" (1867/1967:233).

The surplus derived from this process is used by the capitalists to pay for such things as rent to landowners and interest to banks. But the most important derivation from it is profit. The capitalists can use this profit for private consumption, but that would not lead to the expansion of capitalism. Rather, they expand their enterprise by converting it into a base for the creation of still more surplus value.

The desire for more profit and more surplus value for expansion pushes capitalism toward what Marx called the *general law of capitalist accumulation*. The capitalists seek to exploit workers as much as possible: "The constant tendency of capital is to force the cost of labor back towards . . . zero" (Marx, 1867/1967:600). Marx basically argued that the structure and the ethos of capitalism push the capitalists in the direction of the accumulation of more and more capital. In order to do this, given Marx's view that labor is the source of value, the capitalists are led to intensify the exploitation of the proletariat. Ultimately, however, increased exploitation yields fewer and fewer gains; an upper limit of exploitation is reached. In addition, as this limit is approached, the government is forced by pressure from the working class to place restrictions on the actions of capitalists (for example, laws limiting the length of the workday). As a result of these restrictions, the capitalists must look for other devices, and a major one is the substitution of machines for people. This substitution is made relatively easy, because the capitalists already have reduced the workers to laboring machines performing a series of simple operations. This shift to capital-intensive production is, paradoxically, a cause of the declining rate of profit since it is labor (not machines) that is the ultimate source of profit.

As mechanization proceeds, more and more people are put out of work and fall from the proletariat to the "industrial reserve army." At the same time, heightening competition and the burgeoning costs of technology lead to a progressive decline in the number of capitalists. In the end, Marx foresaw a situation in which society would be characterized by a tiny number of exploitative capitalists and a huge mass of proletarians and members of the industrial reserve army. In these extreme circumstances, capitalism would be most vulnerable to revolution. As Marx put it, the expropriation of the masses by the capitalists would be replaced by "the expropriation of a few usurpers by the mass of people" (1867/1967:764). The capitalists, of course, seek to forestall their demise. For example, they sponsor colonial adventures with the objective of shifting at least some of the burden of exploitation from the home front to the colonies. However, in Marx's view these efforts are ultimately doomed to failure, and the capitalists will face rebellion at home and abroad.

The key point about the general law of capitalist accumulation is the degree to which actors, both capitalist and proletarian, are impelled by the structure and ethos of capitalism to do what they do. Marx usually did not blame individual capitalists for their actions; he saw these actions as largely determined by the logic of the capitalist system. This is consistent with his view that actors in capitalism generally are devoid of creative independence. However, the developmental process inherent in capitalism provides the conditions necessary for the ultimate reemergence of such creative action and, with it, the overthrow of the capitalist system.

Communism

Marx often wrote as though changes in the mode of production were inevitable, as in the quotation about the hand-mill giving you feudalism and the steam-mill giving you capitalism. Unless one wishes to find reasons for rejecting Marx's theories, it is probably best to interpret Marx's historical materialism as motivated by a desire to identify some predictable trends and to use these trends to discover the points where political action could be most effective. This is certainly the way that Marx used his theories in his concrete political and economic studies, such as *Class Struggles in France* (1850) and *The Eighteenth Brumaire of Louis Bonaparte* (1869). The truth of historical materialism, then, does not depend on the inevitability of its historical predictions, but on whether a focus on the way that we satisfy our material needs is the best way to reveal the opportunities for effective political intervention.

If the goal of Marx's materialist view of history was to predict those points where political action could be most effective, then it is his view of what changes will lead to the next stage that is most important. Marx thought that capitalism had developed its productive powers so that it was ready to enter a new mode of production, which he called *communism*. Most of his analysis dwelt on conflicts in the present that will lead to this new economic form.

Despite the importance to Marx of the future communist society, he spent surprisingly little time depicting what this world would be like. He refused to write "recipes for the kitchens of the future" (Marx, cited in T. Ball, 1991:139). The era in which Marx wrote was filled with talk of revolutions and new forms of society—of communism, socialism, anarchy, and many more now forgotten. Charismatic political leaders appeared on the historical stage and stirred audiences with their speeches. Marx, however, was intellectually opposed to painting utopian visions of the future. To Marx, the most important task was the critical analysis of contemporary capitalist society. He believed that such criticism would help bring down capitalism and create the conditions for the rise of a new socialist world. There would be time to construct communist society once capitalism was overcome. In general, however, Marx believed that communism would involve taking decisions about what is to be produced away from the reified economy that runs in the interests of the few capitalists and putting in its place some sort of social decision making that would allow the needs of the many to be taken into account.

Criticisms

Five problems in Marx's theory need to be discussed. The first is the problem of communism as it came to exist. The failure of communist societies and their turn to a more capitalistically oriented economy raise questions about the role of Marxian theory within sociology (Antonio, 2011; Aronson, 1995; Hudelson, 1993; Manuel, 1992). Marx's ideas seem to have been tried and to have failed. At one time, almost one-third of the world's population lived under states inspired by the ideas of Marx. Many of those formerly Marxist states have become capitalist, and even those (except perhaps for Cuba) that still claim to be Marxist manifest nothing but a highly bureaucratized form of capitalism.

Against this criticism, it could be argued that those states never truly followed Marxist precepts, and that it is unfair for critics to blame Marx for every misuse of his theory. However, those making the criticism claim that Marx himself insisted that Marxist theory should not be split from its actually existing practice. As Alvin Gouldner (1970:3) writes, "Having set out to change the world, rather than produce one more interpretation of it, Marxist theory must ultimately be weighed on the scales of history." If Marxism never works out in practice, then, for Marx, the theory would be useless at best and ideological at worst. Furthermore, it seems clear that Marx's lack of a theory regarding the problems of state bureaucracy has contributed to the failures of actually existing communism. Had he developed a complete theory of state bureaucracy, it is conceivable that Marx might have preferred the evils of capitalism.

The second problem is often referred to as the *missing emancipatory subject.* Critics say that although Marx's theory places the proletariat at the heart of the social change leading to communism, the proletariat has rarely assumed this leading position and often is among the groups that are most opposed to communism. This problem is compounded by the fact that intellectuals—for example, academic sociologists—have leapt into the gap left by the proletariat and substituted intellectual activity for class struggle. In addition, the intellectuals' disappointment at the proletariat's conservativism is transformed into a theory that emphasizes the role of ideology much more strongly than Marx did and that tends to see the "heroes" of the future revolution as manipulated dupes.

The third problem is the *missing dimension of gender.* One of the main points of Marx's theory is that labor becomes a commodity under capitalism, yet it is a historical fact that the commodifying of labor has happened less to women than to men. To a large degree, men's paid labor still depends on the *unpaid* labor of women, especially the all-important rearing of the next generation of workers. Sayer (1991) points out that the missing dimension of gender not only leaves a hole in Marx's analysis but also affects his primary argument that capitalism is defined by its growing dependence on wage labor, because the growth of wage labor has been dependent on the unpaid labor of women. Patriarchy may be an essential foundation for the emergence of capitalism, but Marx simply ignores it.

The fourth problem is that Marx saw the economy as driven almost solely by production, and he ignored the role of consumption. The focus on production led him to predict that concerns for efficiency and cost cutting would lead to proletarianization, increasing alienation, and deepening class conflict. It could be argued, however, that the central role of consumption in the modern economy encourages some creativity and entrepreneurship and that these provide at least some wage labor jobs that are not alienating. People who create new video games or direct movies or perform popular music are less alienated from their work, even though they are firmly entrenched in a capitalist system. Although there are only a few such jobs, their existence gives hope to the alienated masses, who can anticipate that they, or at least their children, might someday work in interesting and creative jobs.

Finally, some might point to Marx's uncritical acceptance of Western conceptions of progress as a problem. Marx believed that the engine of history is humanity's always improving exploitation of nature for its material needs. In addition, Marx thought that the essence of human nature is our ability to shape nature to our purposes. It may be that these assumptions are a root cause of many of our current and future ecological crises.

Summary

Marx presents a complex and still relevant analysis of the historical basis of inequality in capitalism and how to change it. Marx's theories are open to many interpretations, but this chapter tries to present an interpretation that makes his theories consistent with his actual historical studies.

The chapter begins with a discussion of the dialectical approach that Marx derived from Hegel and that shapes all of Marx's work. The important point here is that Marx believed that society is structured around contradictions that can be resolved only through actual social change. One of the primary contradictions that Marx looked at was between human potential (nature) and the conditions for labor in capitalism. For Marx, human nature is intimately tied to labor, which both expresses and transforms human potential. Under capitalism, our labor is sold as a commodity, and the commodifying of our labor leads to alienation from our productive activity, from the objects that we make, from our fellow workers, and even from ourselves.

Next the chapter presents Marx's analysis of capitalist society. We begin with the central concept of commodities and then look at the contradiction between their use value and their exchange value. In capitalism, the exchange value of commodities tends to predominate over their actual usefulness in satisfying human needs; therefore, commodities begin to appear to be separate from human labor and from human need and eventually appear to have power over humans. Marx called this the fetishism of commodities. This fetishism is a form of reification, and it affects more than just commodities; in particular, it affects the economic system, which begins to seem like an objective, nonpolitical force that determines our lives. Because of this reification we don't see that the very idea of capital contains a contradictory social relation between those who profit from their investments and those whose actual labor provides the surplus value that constitutes profit. In other words, the ability of capital to generate profit rests on the exploitation of the proletariat. This underlying contradiction leads to class conflict between the proletariat and bourgeoisie, which eventually will result in revolution because proletarianization will swell the ranks of the proletariat. This section concludes by stressing that despite his criticisms of capitalism, Marx believed that capitalism has been good and that his criticisms of it are from the perspective of its potential future.

Marx felt that he was able to take the view from capitalism's potential future because of his materialist conception of history. By focusing on the forces of production, Marx was able to predict historical trends that allowed him to identify where political action could be effective. Political action and even revolution are necessary because relations of production and ideology hold back the necessary development of the forces of production. In Marx's view these changes eventually will lead to a communist society.

We also offer a discussion of some of the most important nonmaterial (cultural) aspects of Marx's theory—especially ideology and religion—as well as some of his famous ideas on economics, especially the labor theory of value.

The chapter ends with some criticisms of Marx's theories. Despite their significance, these criticisms have contributed to the strength of the Marxist approach, even where the strengthening of some Marxist approaches has meant abandoning some of Marx's most strongly held positions.

Emile Durkheim

Chapter Outline
Introduction
Social Facts
The Division of Labor in Society
Suicide
The Elementary Forms of Religious Life
Moral Education and Social Reform
Criticisms

Introduction

There are two main themes in the work of Emile Durkheim. The first is the priority of the social over the individual, and the second is the idea that society can be studied scientifically. Because both of these themes continue to be controversial, Durkheim is still relevant today.

We live in a society that tends to see everything as attributable to individuals, even clearly social problems such as racism, pollution, and economic recessions. Durkheim approaches things from the opposite perspective, stressing the social dimension of all human phenomena. However, even some who recognize the importance of society tend to see it as an amorphous entity that can be intuitively understood but never scientifically studied. Here again, Durkheim provides the opposing approach. For Durkheim, society is made up of "social facts," which exceed our intuitive understanding and must be investigated through observations and measurements. These ideas are so central to sociology that Durkheim is often seen as the "father" of sociology (Gouldner, 1958). To found sociology as a discipline was indeed one of Durkheim's primary goals.

Durkheim (1900/1973:3) believed that sociology, as an idea, was born in France in the nineteenth century. He wanted to turn this idea into a discipline, a well-defined field of study. He recognized the roots of sociology in the ancient philosophers—such as Plato and Aristotle—and more proximate sources in French philosophers such as Montesquieu and Condorcet. However, in Durkheim's (1900/1973:6) view, previous philosophers did not go far enough because they did not try to create an entirely new discipline.

Although the term *sociology* had been coined some years earlier by Auguste Comte, there was no field of sociology per se in late-nineteenth-century universities. There were no schools, departments, or even professors of sociology. There were a few thinkers who were dealing with ideas that were in one way or another sociological, but there was as yet no disciplinary "home" for sociology. Indeed, there was strong opposition from existing disciplines to the founding of such a field. The most significant opposition came from psychology and philosophy, two fields that claimed already to cover the domain sought by sociology. The dilemma for Durkheim, given his aspirations for sociology, was how to create for it a separate and identifiable niche.

To separate it from philosophy, Durkheim argued that sociology should be oriented toward empirical research. This seems simple enough, but the situation was complicated by Durkheim's belief that sociology was also threatened by a philosophical school within sociology itself. In his view, the two other major figures of the epoch who thought of themselves as sociologists, Comte and Herbert Spencer, were far more interested in philosophizing, in abstract theorizing, than they were in studying the social world empirically. If the field continued in the direction set by Comte and Spencer, Durkheim felt, it would become nothing more than a branch of philosophy. As a result, he found it necessary to attack both Comte and Spencer (Durkheim, 1895/1982:19–20) for relying on preconceived ideas of social phenomena instead of actually studying the real world. Thus Comte was said to be guilty of assuming theoretically that the social world was evolving in the direction of an increasingly perfect society, rather than engaging in the hard, rigorous, and basic work of actually studying the changing nature of various societies. Similarly, Spencer was accused of assuming harmony in society rather than studying whether harmony actually existed.

Social Facts

In order to help sociology move away from philosophy and to give it a clear and separate identity, Durkheim (1895/1982) proposed that the distinctive subject matter of sociology should be the study of social facts (see M. Gane, 1988; Gilbert, 1994; Nielsen, 2005a, 2007a; and the special edition of *Sociological Perspectives* [1995]). Briefly, *social facts* are the social structures and cultural norms and values that are external to, and coercive of, actors. Students, for example, are constrained by such social structures as the university bureaucracy as well as the norms and values of American society, which place great importance on a college education. Similar social facts constrain people in all areas of social life.

Crucial in separating sociology from philosophy is the idea that social facts are to be treated as "things" (S. Jones, 1996) and studied empirically. This means that we must study social facts by acquiring data from outside of our own minds through observation and experimentation. The empirical study of social facts as things sets Durkheimian sociology apart from more philosophical approaches.[1]

---

[1] For a critique of Durkheim's attempt to separate sociology from philosophy, see Boudon (1995).

A social fact is every way of acting, fixed or not, capable of exercising on the individual an external constraint; or again, every way of acting which is general throughout a given society, while at the same time existing in its own right independent of its individual manifestations.

(Durkheim, 1895/1982:13)

Note that Durkheim gave two ways of defining a social fact so that sociology is distinguished from psychology. First, a social fact is experienced as an external constraint rather than an internal drive; second, it is general throughout the society and is not attached to any particular individual.

Durkheim argued that social facts cannot be reduced to individuals, but must be studied as their own reality. Durkheim referred to social facts with the Latin term *sui generis,* which means "unique." He used this term to claim that social facts have their own unique character that is not reducible to individual consciousness. To allow that social facts could be explained by reference to individuals would be to reduce sociology to psychology. Instead, social facts can be explained only by other social facts. We will study some examples of this type of explanation below, where Durkheim explains the division of labor and even the rate of suicide with other social facts rather than individual intentions. To summarize, social facts can be empirically studied, are external to the individual, are coercive of the individual, and are explained by other social facts.

Durkheim himself gave several examples of social facts, including legal rules, moral obligations, and social conventions. He also refers to language as a social fact, and it provides an easily understood example. First, language is a "thing" that must be studied empirically. One cannot simply philosophize about the logical rules of language. Certainly, all languages have some logical rules regarding grammar, pronunciation, spelling, and so forth; however, all languages also have important exceptions to these logical rules (Quine, 1972). What follows the rules and what are exceptions must be discovered empirically by studying actual language use, especially since language use changes over time in ways that are not completely predictable.

Second, language is external to the individual. Although individuals use a language, language is not defined or created by the individual. The fact that individuals adapt language to their own use indicates that language is first external to the individual and in need of adaptation for individual use. Indeed, some philosophers (Kripke, 1982; Wittgenstein, 1953) have argued that there cannot be such a thing as a private language. A collection of words with only private meanings would not qualify as a language because it could not perform the basic function of a language: communication. Language is, by definition, social and therefore external to any particular individual.

Third, language is coercive of the individual. The language that we use makes some things extremely difficult to say. For example, people in lifelong relationships with same-sex partners have a very difficult time referring to each other. Should they call each other "partners"—leading people into thinking they are in business together— "significant others," "lovers," "spouses," "special friends"? Each seems to have its disadvantages. Language is part of the system of social facts that makes life with a same-sex partner difficult even if every individual should be personally accepting of same-sex relationships.

Finally, changes in language can be explained only by other social facts and never by one individual's intentions. Even in those rare instances where a change in language can be traced to an individual, the actual explanation for the change is the social facts that have made society open to this change. For example, the most changeable part of language is slang, which almost always originates in a marginal social group. We may assume that an individual first originates a slang term, but which individual is irrelevant. It is the fact of the marginal social group that truly explains the history and function of the slang.

Some sociologists feel that Durkheim took an "extremist" position (Karady, 1983:79–80) in limiting sociology to the study of social facts. This position has limited at least some branches of sociology to the present day. Furthermore, Durkheim seemed to artificially sever sociology from neighboring fields. As Lemert (1994a:91) puts it, "Because he defined sociology so exclusively in relation to its own facts, Durkheim cut it off from the other sciences of man." Nevertheless, whatever its subsequent drawbacks, Durkheim's idea of social facts both established sociology as an independent field of study and provided one of the most convincing arguments for studying society as it is before we decide what it should be.

Material and Nonmaterial Social Facts

Durkheim differentiated between two broad types of social facts—material and nonmaterial. *Material social facts,* such as styles of architecture, forms of technology, and legal codes, are the easier to understand of the two because they are directly observable. Clearly, such things as laws are external to individuals and coercive over them. More importantly, these material social facts often express a far larger and more powerful realm of moral forces that are at least equally external to individuals and coercive over them. These are nonmaterial social facts.

The bulk of Durkheim's studies, and the heart of his sociology, lies in the study of nonmaterial social facts. Durkheim said: "Not all social consciousness achieves . . . externalization and materialization" (1897/1951:315). What sociologists now call norms and values, or more generally culture (Alexander, 1988), are good examples of what Durkheim meant by *nonmaterial social facts.* But this idea creates a problem: How can nonmaterial social facts like norms and values be external to the actor? Where could they be found except in the minds of actors? And if they are in the minds of actors, are they not internal rather than external?

Durkheim recognized that nonmaterial social facts are, to a certain extent, found in the minds of individuals. However, it was his belief that when people begin to interact in complex ways, their interactions will "obey laws all their own" (Durkheim, 1912/1965:471). Individuals are still necessary as a kind of substrate for the nonmaterial social facts, but the particular form and content will be determined by the complex interactions and not by the individuals. Hence, Durkheim could write in the same work first that "Social things are actualized only through men; they are the product of human activity" (1895/1982:17) and second that "Society is not a mere sum of individuals" (1895/1982:103). Despite the fact that society is made up only of human beings and contains no immaterial "spiritual" substance, it can be understood only through studying the interactions rather than the individuals. The interactions, even when nonmaterial, have their own levels of reality. This has been called "relational realism" (Alpert, 1939).

Durkheim saw social facts along a continuum of materiality (Lukes, 1972:9–10). The sociologist usually begins a study by focusing on material social facts, which are empirically accessible, in order to understand nonmaterial social facts, which are the real focus of his work. The most material are such things as population size and density, channels of communication, and housing arrangements (Andrews, 1993). Durkheim called these facts *morphological,* and they figure most importantly in his first book, *The Division of Labor in Society* (1893/1964). At another level are structural components (a bureaucracy, for example), which are a mixture of morphological components (the density of people in a building and their lines of communication) and nonmaterial social facts (such as the bureaucratic norms).

Types of Nonmaterial Social Facts

Since nonmaterial social facts are so important to Durkheim, we will examine four different types—morality, collective conscience, collective representations, and social currents—before considering how Durkheim used these types in his studies.

Morality

Durkheim was a sociologist of morality in the broadest sense of the word (R. T. Hall, 1987; Mestrovic, 1988; Varga, 2006). Studying him reminds us that a concern with morality was at the foundation of sociology as a discipline. Durkheim's view of morality had two aspects. First, Durkheim was convinced that morality is a social fact, in other words, that morality can be empirically studied, is external to the individual, is coercive of the individual, and is explained by other social facts. This means that morality is not something that one can philosophize about, but something that one has to study as an empirical phenomenon. This is particularly true because morality is intimately related to the social structure. To understand the morality of any particular institution, you have to *first study* how the institution is constituted, how it came to assume its present form, what its place is in the overall structure of society, how the various institutional obligations are related to the social good, and so forth.

Second, Durkheim was a sociologist of morality because his studies were driven by his concern about the moral "health" of modern society. Much of Durkheim's sociology can be seen as a by-product of his concern with moral issues. Indeed, one of Durkheim's associates wrote in a review of his life's work that "one will fail to understand his works if one does not take account of the fact that morality was their center and object" (Davy, trans. in R. T. Hall, 1987:5).

This second point needs more explanation if we are to understand Durkheim's perspective. It was not that Durkheim thought that society had become, or was in danger of becoming, immoral. That was simply impossible because morality was, for Durkheim (1925/1961:59), identified with society. Therefore, society could not be immoral, but it could certainly lose its moral force if the collective interest of society became nothing but the sum of self-interests. Only to the extent that morality was a social fact could it impose an obligation on individuals that superseded their self-interest. Consequently, Durkheim believed that society needs a strong common morality. What the morality should be was of less interest to him.

Durkheim's great concern with morality was related to his curious definition of *freedom*. In Durkheim's view, people were in danger of a "pathological" loosening of moral bonds. These moral bonds were important to Durkheim, for without them the individual would be enslaved by ever-expanding and insatiable passions. People would be impelled by their passions into a mad search for gratification, but each new gratification would lead only to more and more needs. According to Durkheim, the one thing that every human will always want is "more." And, of course, that is the one thing we ultimately cannot have. If society does not limit us, we will become slaves to the pursuit of more. Consequently, Durkheim held the seemingly paradoxical view that the individual needs morality and external control in order to be free. This view of the insatiable desire at the core of every human is central to his sociology.

Collective Conscience

Durkheim attempted to deal with his interest in common morality in various ways and with different concepts. In his early efforts to deal with this issue, Durkheim developed the idea of the *collective conscience*. In French, the word *conscience* means both "consciousness" and "moral conscience." Durkheim characterized the collective conscience in the following way:

> The totality of beliefs and sentiments common to average citizens of the same society forms a determinate system which has its own life; one may call it the collective or common conscience. . . . It is, thus, an entirely different thing from particular consciences, although it can be realized only through them.
>
> (Durkheim, 1893/1964:79–80)

Several points are worth underscoring in this definition. First, it is clear that Durkheim thought of the collective conscience as occurring throughout a given society when he wrote of the "totality" of people's beliefs and sentiments. Second, Durkheim clearly conceived of the collective conscience as being independent and capable of determining other social facts. It is not just a reflection of a material base as Marx sometimes suggested. Finally, although he held such views of the collective conscience, Durkheim also wrote of its being "realized" through individual consciousness.

Collective conscience refers to the general structure of shared understandings, norms, and beliefs. It is therefore an all-embracing and amorphous concept. As we will see below, Durkheim employed this concept to argue that "primitive" societies had a stronger collective conscience—that is, more shared understandings, norms, and beliefs—than modern societies.

Collective Representations

Because collective conscience is such a broad and amorphous idea, it is impossible to study directly and must be approached through related material social facts. (For example, we will look at Durkheim's use of the legal system to say something about the collective conscience.) Durkheim's dissatisfaction with this limitation led him to use the collective conscience less in his later work in favor of the much more specific concept of *collective representations* (Nemedi, 1995; Schmaus, 1994). The French word *représentation* literally means "idea." Durkheim used the term to refer to both a collective concept and a social "force." Examples of collective representations are religious symbols, myths, and popular legends. All of these are ways in which society reflects on itself (Durkheim, 1895/1982:40). They represent collective beliefs, norms, and values, and they motivate us to conform to these collective claims.

Collective representations also cannot be reduced to individuals because they emerge out of social interactions, but they can be studied more directly than collective conscience because they are more likely to be connected to material symbols such as flags, icons, and pictures or connected to practices such as rituals. Therefore, the sociologist can begin to study how certain collective representations fit well together, or have an affinity, and others do not. As an example, we can look at a sociological study that shows how representations of Abraham Lincoln have changed in response to other social facts.

> Between the turn of the century and 1945, Lincoln, like other heroic presidents, was idealized. Prints showed him holding Theodore Roosevelt's hand and pointing him in the right direction, or hovering in ethereal splendor behind Woodrow Wilson as he contemplated matters of war and peace, or placing his reassuring hand on Franklin Roosevelt's shoulder. Cartoons showed admirers looking up to his statue or portrait. Neoclassical statues depicted him larger than life; state portraits enveloped him in the majesty of presidential power; "grand style" history painting showed him altering the fate of the nation. By the 1960s, however, traditional pictures had disappeared and been replaced by a new kind of representation on billboards, posters, cartoons, and magazine covers. Here Lincoln is shown wearing a party hat and blowing a whistle to mark a bank's anniversary; there he is playing a saxophone to announce a rock concert; elsewhere he is depicted arm in arm with a seductive Marilyn Monroe, or sitting upon his Lincoln Memorial chair of state grasping a can of beer, or wearing sunglasses and looking "cool," or exchanging Valentine cards with George Washington to signify that Valentine's Day had displaced their own traditional birthday celebrations. Post-1960s commemorative iconography articulates the diminishing of Lincoln's dignity.
>
> (B. Schwartz, 1998:73)

Abraham Lincoln functions in American society as a collective representation in that his various representations allow a people to think about themselves as Americans—as either American patriots or American consumers. His image is also a force that motivates us to perform a patriotic duty or to buy a greeting card. A study of this representation allows us to better understand changes in American society.

Social Currents

Most of the examples of social facts that Durkheim refers to are associated with social organizations. However, he made it clear that there are social facts "which do not present themselves in this already crystallized form" (1895/1982:52). Durkheim called these *social currents*. He gave as examples "the great waves of enthusiasm, indignation, and pity" that are produced in public gatherings (Durkheim, 1895/1982:52–53). Although social currents are less concrete than other social facts, they are nevertheless social facts because they cannot be reduced to the individual. We are swept along by such social currents, and this has a coercive power over us even if we become aware of it only when we struggle against the common feelings.

It is possible for these nonmaterial and ephemeral social facts to affect even the strongest institutions. Ramet (1991), for example, reports that the social currents that are potentially created among a crowd at a rock concert were looked at as a threat by Eastern European communist governments and, indeed, contributed to their downfall. Rock concerts were places for the emergence and dissemination of "cultural standards, fashions, and behavioral syndromes independent of party control" (Ramet, 1991:216). In particular, members of the audience were likely to see an expression of their alienation in the concert. Their own feelings were thereby affirmed, strengthened, and given new social and political meanings. In other words, political leaders were afraid of rock concerts because of the potential for the depressing individual *feelings* of alienation to be transformed into the motivating *social fact* of alienation. This provides another example of how social facts are related to but different from individual feelings and intentions.

Given the emphasis on norms, values, and culture in contemporary sociology, we have little difficulty accepting Durkheim's interest in nonmaterial social facts. However, the concept of social currents does cause us a few problems. Particularly troublesome is the idea of a set of independent social currents "coursing" through the social world as if they were somehow suspended in a social void. This problem has led many to criticize Durkheim for having a group-mind orientation (Pope, 1976:192–194). (Such an idea was prevalent in the late 1800s and early 1900s, especially in the work of Franklin H. Giddings [Chriss, 2006].) Those who accuse Durkheim of having such a perspective argue that he accorded nonmaterial social facts an autonomous existence, separate from actors. But cultural phenomena cannot float by themselves in a social void, and Durkheim was well aware of this.

> But how are we to conceive of this social consciousness? Is it a simple and transcendent being, soaring above society? . . . It is certain that experience shows us nothing of the sort. The collective mind [*l'esprit collectif*] is only a composite of individual minds. But the latter are not mechanically juxtaposed and closed off from one another. They are in perpetual interaction through the exchange of symbols; they interpenetrate one another. They group themselves according to their natural affinities; they coordinate and systematize themselves. In this way is formed an entirely new psychological being, one without equal in the world. The consciousness with which it is endowed is infinitely more intense and more vast than those which resonate within it. For it is "a consciousness of consciousnesses" [*une conscience de consciences*]. Within it, we find condensed at once all the vitality of the present and of the past.
>
> (Durkheim, 1885/1978:103)

Social currents can be viewed as sets of meanings that are shared by the members of a collectivity. As such, they cannot be explained in terms of the mind of any given individual. Individuals certainly contribute to social currents, but by becoming social something new develops through their interactions. Social currents can only be explained intersubjectively, that is, in terms of the *interactions* between individuals. They exist at the level of interactions, not at the level of individuals. These collective "moods," or social currents, vary from one collectivity to another, with the result that there is variation in the rate of certain behaviors, including, as we will see below, something as seemingly individualistic as suicide.

In fact, there are very strong similarities between Durkheim's theory of social facts and current theories about the relation between the brain and the mind (Sawyer, 2002). Both theories use the idea that complex, constantly changing systems will begin to display new properties that "cannot be predicted from a full and complete description of the component units of the system" (Sawyer, 2002:228). Even though modern philosophy assumes that the mind is nothing but brain functions, the argument is that the complexity of the interconnections in the brain creates a new level of reality, the mind, that is not explainable in terms of individual neurons. This was precisely Durkheim's argument: that the complexity and intensity of interactions between individuals cause a new level of reality to emerge that cannot be explained in terms of the individuals. Hence, it could be argued that Durkheim had a very modern conception of nonmaterial social facts that encompasses norms, values, culture, and a variety of shared social-psychological phenomena (Emirbayer, 1996).

The Division of Labor in Society

The Division of Labor in Society (Durkheim, 1893/1964; Gibbs, 2003) has been called sociology's first classic (Tiryakian, 1994). In this work, Durkheim traced the development of the modern relation between individuals and society. In particular, Durkheim wanted to use his new science of sociology to examine what many at the time had come to see as the modern crisis of morality. The preface to the first edition begins, "This book is above all an attempt to treat the facts of moral life according to the methods of the positive sciences."

In France in Durkheim's day, there was a widespread feeling of moral crisis. The French Revolution had ushered in a focus on the rights of the individual that often expressed itself as an attack on traditional authority and religious beliefs. This trend continued even after the fall of the revolutionary government. By the mid-nineteenth century, many people felt that social order was threatened because people thought only about themselves and not about society. In the less than 100 years between the French Revolution and Durkheim's maturity, France went through three monarchies, two empires, and three republics. These regimes produced fourteen constitutions. The feeling of moral crisis was brought to a head by Prussia's crushing defeat of France in 1870, which included the annexation of Durkheim's birthplace by Prussia. This was followed by the short-lived and violent revolution known as the Paris Commune.[2] Both the defeat and the subsequent revolt were blamed on the problem of rampant individualism.

---

[2] Before its bloody repression, Marx saw the Paris Commune as the harbinger of the proletariat revolution.

August Comte argued that many of these events could be traced to the increasing division of labor. In simpler societies, people do basically the same thing, such as farming, and they share common experiences and consequently have common values. In modern society, in contrast, everyone has a different job. When different people are assigned various specialized tasks, they no longer share common experiences. This diversity undermines the shared moral beliefs that are necessary for a society. Consequently, people will not sacrifice in times of social need. Comte proposed that sociology create a new pseudo-religion that would reinstate social cohesion. To a large degree, *The Division of Labor in Society* can be seen as a refutation of Comte's analysis (Gouldner, 1962). Durkheim argues that the division of labor does not represent the disappearance of social morality so much as a new kind of social morality.

The thesis of *The Division of Labor* is that modern society is not held together by the similarities between people who do basically similar things. Instead, it is the division of labor itself that pulls people together by forcing them to be dependent on each other. It may seem that the division of labor is an economic necessity that corrodes the feeling of solidarity, but Durkheim (1893/1964:17) argued that "the economic services that it can render are insignificant compared with the moral effect that it produces and its true function is to create between two or more people a feeling of solidarity."

Mechanical and Organic Solidarity

The change in the division of labor has had enormous implications for the structure of society. Durkheim was most interested in the changed way in which social solidarity is produced, in other words, the changed way in which society is held together and how its members see themselves as part of a whole. To capture this difference, Durkheim referred to two types of solidarity—mechanical and organic. A society characterized by *mechanical* solidarity is unified because all people are generalists. The bond among people is that they are all engaged in similar activities and have similar responsibilities. In contrast, a society characterized by *organic* solidarity is held together by the differences among people, by the fact that all have different tasks and responsibilities.[3]

Because people in modern society perform a relatively narrow range of tasks, they need many other people in order to survive. The primitive family headed by father-hunter and mother–food gatherer is practically self-sufficient, but the modern family needs the grocer, baker, butcher, auto mechanic, teacher, police officer, and so forth. These people, in turn, need the kinds of services that others provide in order to live in the modern world. Modern society, in Durkheim's view, is thus held together by the specialization of people and their need for the services of many others. This specialization includes not only that of individuals but also of groups, structures, and institutions.

---

[3] For a comparison with Spencer's evolutionary theory, see Perrin (1995).

EMILE DURKHEIM

A Biographical Sketch

Emile Durkheim was born on April 15, 1858, in Epinal, France. He was descended from a long line of rabbis and studied to be a rabbi, but by the time he was in his teens, he had largely disavowed his heritage (Strenski, 1997:4). From that time on, his lifelong interest in religion was more academic than theological (Mestrovic, 1988). He was dissatisfied not only with his religious training but also with his general education and its emphasis on literary and esthetic matters. He longed for schooling in scientific methods and in the moral principles needed to guide social life. He rejected a traditional academic career in philosophy and sought instead to acquire the scientific training needed to contribute to the moral guidance of society. Although he was interested in scientific sociology, there was no field of sociology at that time, so between 1882 and 1887 he taught philosophy in a number of provincial schools in the Paris area.

His appetite for science was whetted further by a trip to Germany, where he was exposed to the scientific psychology being pioneered by Wilhelm Wundt (Durkheim, 1887/1993). In the years immediately after his visit to Germany, Durkheim published a good deal, basing his work, in part, on his experiences there (R. Jones, 1994). These publications helped him gain a position in the department of philosophy at the University of Bordeaux in 1887 (Pearce, 2005). There Durkheim offered the first course in social science in a French university. This was a particularly impressive accomplishment, because only a decade earlier, a furor had erupted in a French university after the mention of Auguste Comte in a student dissertation. Durkheim's main responsibility, however, was teaching courses in education to schoolteachers, and his most important course was in the area of moral education. His goal was to communicate a moral system to the educators, who he hoped would then pass the system on to young people in an effort to help reverse the moral degeneration he saw around him in French society.

The years that followed were characterized by a series of personal successes for Durkheim. In 1893 he published his French doctoral thesis, *The Division of Labor in Society,* as well as his Latin thesis on Montesquieu (Durkheim, 1892/1997; W. Miller, 1993). His major methodological statement, *The Rules of Sociological Method,* appeared in 1895, followed (in 1897) by his empirical application of those methods in the study *Suicide.* By 1896 he had become a full professor at Bordeaux. In 1902 he was summoned to the famous French university the Sorbonne, and in 1906 he was named professor of the science of education, a title that was changed in 1913 to professor of the science of education and sociology. The other of his most famous works, *The Elementary Forms of Religious Life,* was published in 1912.

Durkheim is most often thought of today as a political conservative, and his influence within sociology certainly has been a conservative one. But in his time, he was considered a liberal, and this was exemplified by the active public role he played in the defense of Alfred Dreyfus, the Jewish army captain whose court-martial for treason was felt by many to be anti-Semitic (Farrell, 1997).

Durkheim was deeply offended by the Dreyfus affair, particularly its anti-Semitism (Goldberg, 2008). But Durkheim did not attribute this anti-Semitism to racism among the French people. Characteristically, he saw it as a symptom of the moral sickness confronting French society as a whole (Birnbaum and Todd, 1995). He said:

> When society undergoes suffering, it feels the need to find someone whom it can hold responsible for its sickness, on whom it can avenge its misfortunes: and those against whom public opinion already discriminates are naturally designated for this role. These are the pariahs who serve as expiatory victims. What confirms me in this interpretation is the way in which the result of Dreyfus's trial was greeted in 1894. There was a surge of joy in the boulevards. People celebrated as a triumph what should have been a cause for public mourning. At least they knew whom to blame for the economic troubles and moral distress in which they lived. The trouble came from the Jews. The charge had been officially proved. By this very fact alone, things already seemed to be getting better and people felt consoled.
>
> (Lukes, 1972:345)

Thus, Durkheim's interest in the Dreyfus affair stemmed from his deep and lifelong interest in morality and the moral crisis confronting modern society.

To Durkheim, the answer to the Dreyfus affair and crises like it lay in ending the moral disorder in society. Because that could not be done quickly or easily, Durkheim suggested more specific actions such as severe repression of those who incite hatred of others and government efforts to show the public how it is being misled. He urged people to "have the courage to proclaim aloud what they think, and to unite together in order to achieve victory in the struggle against public madness" (Lukes, 1972:347).

Durkheim's (1928/1962) interest in socialism is also taken as evidence against the idea that he was a conservative, but his kind of socialism was very different from the kind that interested Marx and his followers (Milbrandt and Pearce, 2011). In fact, Durkheim labeled Marxism as a set of "disputable and out-of-date hypotheses" (Lukes, 1972:323). To Durkheim, socialism represented a movement aimed at the moral regeneration of society through scientific morality, and he was not interested in short-term political methods or the economic aspects of socialism. He did not see the proletariat as the salvation of society, and he was greatly opposed to agitation or violence. Socialism for Durkheim was very different from what we usually think of as socialism; it simply represented a system in which the moral principles discovered by scientific sociology were to be applied.

Durkheim, as we will see throughout this book, had a profound influence on the development of sociology, but his influence was not restricted to it (Halls, 1996). Much of his impact on other fields came through the journal *L'année sociologique*, which he founded in 1898. An intellectual circle arose around the journal with Durkheim at its center. Through it, he and his ideas influenced such fields as anthropology, history (especially the "Annales school" [Nielsen, 2005b]), linguistics, and—somewhat ironically, considering his early attacks on the field—psychology.

Durkheim died on November 15, 1917, a celebrated figure in French intellectual circles, but it was not until over twenty years later, with the publication of Talcott Parsons's *The Structure of Social Action* (1937), that his work became a significant influence on American sociology.

TABLE 3.1

The Four Dimensions of the Collective Conscience

Solidarity	Volume	Intensity	Rigidity	Content
Mechanical	Entire society	High	High	Religious
Organic	Particular groups	Low	Low	Moral individualism

Durkheim argued that primitive societies have a stronger collective conscience, that is, more shared understandings, norms, and beliefs. The increasing division of labor has caused a diminution of the collective conscience. The collective conscience is of much less significance in a society with organic solidarity than it is in a society with mechanical solidarity. People in modern society are more likely to be held together by the division of labor and the resulting need for the functions performed by others than they are by a shared and powerful collective conscience. Nevertheless, even organic societies have a collective consciousness, albeit in a weaker form that allows for more individual differences.

Anthony Giddens (1972) points out that the collective conscience in the two types of society can be differentiated on four dimensions—volume, intensity, rigidity, and content (see Table 3.1). *Volume* refers to the number of people enveloped by the collective conscience; *intensity,* to how deeply the individuals feel about it; *rigidity,* to how clearly it is defined; and *content,* to the form that the collective conscience takes in the two types of society. In a society characterized by mechanical solidarity, the collective conscience covers virtually the entire society and all its members; it is believed in with great intensity; it is extremely rigid; and its content is highly religious in character. In a society with organic solidarity, the collective conscience is limited to particular groups; it is adhered to with much less intensity; it is not very rigid; and its content is the elevation of the importance of the individual to a moral precept.

Dynamic Density

The division of labor was a material social fact to Durkheim because it is a pattern of interactions in the social world. As indicated above, social facts must be explained by other social facts. Durkheim believed that the cause of the transition from mechanical to organic solidarity was dynamic density. This concept refers to the number of people in a society and the amount of interaction that occurs among them. More people means an increase in the competition for scarce resources, and more interaction means a more intense struggle for survival among the basically similar components of society.

The problems associated with dynamic density usually are resolved through differentiation and, ultimately, the emergence of new forms of social organization. The rise of the division of labor allows people to complement, rather than conflict with, one another. Furthermore, the increased division of labor makes for greater efficiency, with the result that resources increase, making the competition over them more peaceful.

This points to one final difference between mechanical and organic solidarity. In societies with organic solidarity, less competition and more differentiation allow people to cooperate more and to all be supported by the same resource base. Therefore, difference allows for even closer bonds between people than does similarity. Thus, in a society characterized by organic solidarity, there are both more solidarity and more individuality than there are in a society characterized by mechanical solidarity (Rueschemeyer, 1994). Individuality, then, is not the opposite of close social bonds but a requirement for them (Muller, 1994).

Repressive and Restitutive Law

The division of labor and dynamic density are material social facts, but Durkheim's main interest was in the forms of solidarity, which are nonmaterial social facts. Durkheim felt that it was difficult to study nonmaterial social facts directly, especially something as pervasive as a collective conscience. In order to study nonmaterial social facts scientifically, the sociologist should examine material social facts that reflect the nature of, and changes in, nonmaterial social facts. In *The Division of Labor in Society,* Durkheim chose to study the differences between law in societies with mechanical solidarity and law in societies with organic solidarity (Cotterrell, 1999).

Durkheim argued that a society with mechanical solidarity is characterized by *repressive law.* Because people are very similar in this type of society, and because they tend to believe very strongly in a common morality, any offense against their shared value system is likely to be of significance to most individuals. Since everyone feels the offense and believes deeply in the common morality, a wrongdoer is likely to be punished severely for any action that offends the collective moral system. Theft might lead to the cutting off of the offender's hands; blaspheming might result in the removal of one's tongue. Even minor offenses against the moral system are likely to be met with severe punishment.

In contrast, a society with organic solidarity is characterized by *restitutive law,* which requires offenders to make restitution for their crimes. In such societies, offenses are more likely to be seen as committed against a particular individual or segment of society than against the moral system itself. Because there is a weak common morality, most people do not react emotionally to a breach of the law. Instead of being severely punished for every offense against the collective morality, offenders in an organic society are likely to be asked to make restitution to those who have been harmed by their actions. Although some repressive law continues to exist in a society with organic solidarity (for example, the death penalty), restitutive law predominates, especially for minor offenses.

In summary, Durkheim argues in *The Division of Labor* that the form of moral solidarity has changed in modern society, not disappeared. We have a new form of solidarity that allows for more interdependence and closer, less competitive relations and that produces a new form of law based on restitution. However, this book was far from a celebration of modern society. Durkheim argued that this new form of solidarity is prone to certain kinds of social pathologies.

Normal and Pathological

Perhaps the most controversial of Durkheim's claims was that the sociologist is able to distinguish between healthy and pathological societies. After using this idea in *The Division of Labor,* Durkheim wrote another book, *The Rules of Sociological Method* (1895/1982), in which, among other things, he attempted to refine and defend this idea. He claimed that a healthy society can be recognized because the sociologist will find similar conditions in other societies in similar stages. If a society departs from what is normally found, it is probably pathological.

This idea was attacked at the time, and there are few sociologists today who subscribe to it. Even Durkheim, when he wrote the "Preface to the Second Edition" of *The Rules,* no longer attempted to defend it: "It seems pointless for us to revert to the other controversies that this book has given rise to, for they do not touch upon anything essential. The general orientation of the method does not depend upon the procedures preferred to classify social types or distinguish the normal from the pathological" (1895/1982:45).

Nevertheless, there is one interesting idea that Durkheim derived from this argument: the idea that crime is normal (P. Smith, 2008) rather than pathological. He argued that since crime is found in every society, it must be normal and provide a useful function. Crime, he claimed, helps societies define and delineate their collective conscience: "Imagine a community of saints in an exemplary and perfect monastery. In it crime as such will be unknown, but faults that appear venial to the ordinary person will arouse the same scandal as does normal crime in ordinary consciences. If therefore that community has the power to judge and punish, it will term such acts criminal and deal with them as such" (1895/1982:100).

In *The Division of Labor,* he used the idea of pathology to criticize some of the "abnormal" forms the division of labor takes in modern society. He identified three abnormal forms: (1) the anomic division of labor, (2) the forced division of labor, and (3) the poorly coordinated division of labor. Durkheim maintained that the moral crises of modernity that Comte and others had identified with the division of labor were really caused by these abnormal forms.

The *anomic division of labor* refers to the lack of regulation in a society that celebrates isolated individuality and refrains from telling people what they should do. Durkheim further develops this concept of *anomie* in his work on suicide, discussed later. In both works, he uses the term to refer to social conditions in which humans lack sufficient moral restraint (Bar-Haim, 1997; Hilbert, 1986). For Durkheim, modern society is always prone to anomie, but it comes to the fore in times of social and economic crises.

Without the strong common morality of mechanical solidarity, people might not have a clear concept of what is and what is not proper and acceptable behavior. Even though the division of labor is a source of cohesion in modern society, it cannot entirely make up for the weakening of the common morality. Individuals can become isolated and be cut adrift in their highly specialized activities. They can more easily cease to feel a common bond with those who work and live around them. This gives rise to anomie. Organic solidarity is prone to this particular "pathology," but it is important to remember that Durkheim saw this as an abnormal situation. The modern division of labor has the capacity to promote increased moral interactions rather than reducing people to isolated and meaningless tasks and positions.

While Durkheim believed that people needed rules and regulation to tell them what to do, his second abnormal form pointed to a kind of rule that could lead to conflict and isolation and therefore increase anomie. He called this the *forced division of labor.* This second pathology refers to the fact that outdated norms and expectations can force individuals, groups, and classes into positions for which they are ill suited. Traditions, economic power, or status can determine who performs what jobs regardless of talent and qualification. It is here that Durkheim comes closest to a Marxist position:

> If one class in society is obliged, in order to live, to take any price for its services, while another class can pass over this situation, because of the resources already at its disposal, resources that, however, are not necessarily the result of some social superiority, the latter group has an unjust advantage over the former with respect to the law.
>
> (Durkheim, 1895/1982:319)

Finally, the third form of abnormal division of labor is evident when the specialized functions performed by different people are *poorly coordinated.* Again Durkheim makes the point that organic solidarity flows from the interdependence of people. If people's specializations do not result in increased interdependence but simply in isolation, the division of labor will not result in social solidarity.

Justice

For the division of labor to function as a moral and socially solidifying force in modern society, anomie, the forced division of labor, and the improper coordination of specialization must be addressed. Modern societies are no longer held together by shared experiences and common beliefs. Instead, they are held together through their very differences, so long as those differences are allowed to develop in a way that promotes interdependence. Key to this for Durkheim is social justice:

> The task of the most advanced societies is, then, a work of justice. . . . Just as the idea of lower societies was to create or maintain as intense a common life as possible, in which the individual was absorbed, so our ideal is to make social relations always more equitable, so as to assure the free development of all our socially useful forces.
>
> (Durkheim, 1893/1964:387)

Morality, social solidarity, justice—these were big themes for a first book in a fledgling field. Durkheim was to return to these ideas again in his work, but never again would he look at them in terms of society as a whole. He predicted in his second book, *The Rules of Sociological Method* (1895/1982:184), that sociology itself would succumb to the division of labor and break down into a collection of specialties. Whether this has led to an increased interdependence and an organic solidarity in sociology is still an open question.

Suicide

It has been suggested that Durkheim's study of suicide is the paradigmatic example of how a sociologist should connect theory and research (Merton, 1968). Indeed, Durkheim makes it clear in the "Preface" that he intended this study not only to contribute to the understanding of a particular social problem, but also to serve as an example of his new sociological method. (For a series of appraisals of *Suicide* nearly 100 years after its publication, see Lester, 1994.)

Durkheim chose to study suicide because it is a relatively concrete and specific phenomenon for which there were comparatively good data available. However, Durkheim's most important reason for studying suicide was to prove the power of the new science of sociology. Suicide is generally considered to be one of the most private and personal acts. Durkheim believed that if he could show that sociology had a role to play in explaining such a seemingly individualistic act as suicide, it would be relatively easy to extend sociology's domain to phenomena that are much more readily seen as open to sociological analysis.

As a sociologist, Durkheim was not concerned with studying why any specific individual committed suicide (for a critique of this, see Berk, 2006). That was to be left to the psychologists. Instead, Durkheim was interested in explaining differences in *suicide rates;* that is, he was interested in why one group had a higher rate of suicide than did another. Psychological or biological factors may explain why a particular individual in a group commits suicide, but Durkheim assumed that only social facts could explain why one group had a higher rate of suicide than did another. (For a critique of this approach and an argument for the need to include cultural and psychological factors in the study of suicide, see Hamlin and Brym, 2006.)

Durkheim proposed two related ways of evaluating suicide rates. One way is to compare different societies or other types of collectivities. Another way is to look at the changes in the suicide rate in the same collectivity over time. In either case, cross-culturally or historically, the logic of the argument is essentially the same. If there is variation in suicide rates from one group to another or from one time period to another, Durkheim believed that the difference would be the consequence of variations in sociological factors, in particular, social currents. Durkheim acknowledged that individuals may have reasons for committing suicide, but these reasons are not the real cause: "They may be said to indicate the individual's weak points, where the outside current bearing the impulse to self-destruction most easily finds introduction. But they are no part of this current itself, and consequently cannot help us to understand it" (1897/1951:151).

Durkheim began *Suicide* by testing and rejecting a series of alternative ideas about the causes of suicide. Among these are individual psychopathology, alcoholism, race, heredity, and climate. Not all of Durkheim's arguments are convincing (see, for example, Skog, 1991, for an examination of Durkheim's argument against alcoholism). However, what is important is his method of empirically dismissing what he considered extraneous factors so that he could get to what he thought of as the most important causal variables.

In addition, Durkheim examined and rejected the imitation theory associated with one of his contemporaries, the French social psychologist Gabriel Tarde (1843–1904). The theory of imitation argues that people commit suicide (and engage in a wide range of other actions) because they are imitating the actions of others. This social-psychological approach was the most important competitor to Durkheim's focus on social facts. As a result, Durkheim took great pains to discredit it. For example, Durkheim reasoned that if imitation were truly important, we should find that nations that border on a country with a high suicide rate would themselves have high rates, but an examination of the data showed that no such relationship existed. Durkheim admitted that some individual suicides may be the result of imitation, but it is such a minor factor that it has no significant effect on the overall suicide rate.

Durkheim concluded that the critical factors in differences in suicide rates were to be found in differences at the level of social facts. Different groups have different collective sentiments,[4] which produce different social currents. It is these social currents that affect individual decisions about suicide. In other words, changes in the collective sentiments lead to changes in social currents, which, in turn, lead to changes in suicide rates.

The Four Types of Suicide

Durkheim's theory of suicide can be seen more clearly if we examine the relation between the types of suicide and his two underlying social facts—integration and regulation (Pope, 1976). Integration refers to the strength of the attachment that we have to society. Regulation refers to the degree of external constraint on people. For Durkheim, the two social currents are continuous variables, and suicide rates go up when either of these currents is too low or too high. We therefore have four types of suicide (see Table 3.2). If integration is high, Durkheim calls that type of suicide altruistic. Low integration results in an increase in egoistic suicides. Fatalistic suicide is associated with high regulation, and anomic suicide with low regulation.

Egoistic Suicide

High rates of *egoistic suicide* (Berk, 2006) are likely to be found in societies or groups in which the individual is not well integrated into the larger social unit. This lack of integration leads to a feeling that the individual is not part of society, but this also means that society is not part of the individual. Durkheim believed that the best parts of a human being—our morality, values, and sense of purpose—come from society. An integrated society provides us with these things, as well as a general feeling of moral support to get us through the daily small indignities and trivial disappointments. Without this, we are liable to commit suicide at the smallest frustration.

---

[4] Durkheim is moving away from using the term *collective conscience* in this work, but he has not fully developed the idea of collective representations. We see no substantial difference between his use of *collective sentiments* in *Suicide* and his use of *collective conscience* in *The Division of Labor.*

TABLE 3.2

The Four Types of Suicide

Integration	Low	Egoistic suicide
	High	Altruistic suicide
Regulation	Low	Anomic suicide
	High	Fatalistic suicide

The lack of social integration produces distinctive social currents, and these currents cause differences in suicide rates. For example, Durkheim talked of societal disintegration leading to "currents of depression and disillusionment" (1897/1951:214). Politics is dominated by a sense of futility, morality is seen as an individual choice, and popular philosophies stress the meaninglessness of life. In contrast, strongly integrated groups discourage suicide. The protective, enveloping social currents produced by integrated societies prevent the widespread occurrence of egoistic suicide by, among other things, providing people with a sense of the broader meaning of their lives. Here is the way Durkheim puts it regarding religious groups:

> Religion protects man against the desire for self-destruction. . . . What constitutes religion is the existence of a certain number of beliefs and practices common to all the faithful, traditional and thus obligatory. The more numerous and strong these collective states of mind are, the stronger the integration of the religious community, also the greater its preservative value.
>
> (Durkheim, 1897/1951:170)

However, Durkheim demonstrated that not all religions provide the same degree of protection from suicide. Protestant religions with their emphasis on individual faith over church community and their lack of communal rituals tend to provide less protection. His principal point is that it is not the particular beliefs of the religion that are important, but the degree of integration.

Durkheim's statistics also showed that suicide rates go up for those who are unmarried and therefore less integrated into a family, whereas the rates go down in times of national political crises such as wars and revolutions, when social causes and revolutionary or nationalist fervor give people's lives greater meaning. He argues that the only thing that all of these have in common is the increased feeling of integration.

Interestingly, Durkheim affirms the importance of social forces even in the case of egoistic suicide, where the individual might be thought to be free of social constraints. Actors are never free of the force of the collectivity: "However individualized a man may be, there is always something collective remaining—the very depression and melancholy resulting from this same exaggerated individualism. He effects communion through sadness when he no longer has anything else with which to achieve it" (Durkheim, 1897/1951:214). The case of egoistic suicide indicates that in even the most individualistic, most private of acts, social facts are the key determinant.

Altruistic Suicide

The second type of suicide discussed by Durkheim is altruistic suicide. Whereas egoistic suicide is more likely to occur when social integration is too weak, *altruistic suicide* is more likely to occur when "social integration is too strong" (Durkheim, 1897/1951:217). The individual is literally forced into committing suicide.

One notorious example of altruistic suicide was the mass suicide of the followers of the Reverend Jim Jones in Jonestown, Guyana, in 1978. They knowingly took a poisoned drink and in some cases had their children drink it as well. They clearly were committing suicide because they were so tightly integrated into the society of Jones's fanatical followers. Durkheim notes that this is also the explanation for those who seek to be martyrs (Durkheim, 1897/1951:225), as in the terrorist attack of September 11, 2001. More generally, those who commit altruistic suicide do so because they feel that it is their duty to do so. Durkheim argued that this is particularly likely in the military, where the degree of integration is so strong that an individual will feel that he or she has disgraced the entire group by the most trivial of failures.

Whereas higher rates of egoistic suicide stem from "incurable weariness and sad depression," the increased likelihood of altruistic suicide "springs from hope, for it depends on the belief in beautiful perspectives beyond this life" (Durkheim, 1897/1951:225). When integration is low, people will commit suicide because they have no greater good to sustain them. When integration is high, they commit suicide in the name of that greater good.

Anomic Suicide

The third major form of suicide discussed by Durkheim is *anomic suicide,* which is more likely to occur when the regulative powers of society are disrupted. Such disruptions are likely to leave individuals dissatisfied because there is little control over their passions, which are free to run wild in an insatiable race for gratification. Rates of anomic suicide are likely to rise whether the nature of the disruption is positive (for example, an economic boom) or negative (an economic depression). Either type of disruption renders the collectivity temporarily incapable of exercising its authority over individuals. Such changes put people in new situations in which the old norms no longer apply but new ones have yet to develop. Periods of disruption unleash currents of anomie—moods of rootlessness and normlessness—and these currents lead to an increase in rates of anomic suicide. This is relatively easy to envisage in the case of an economic depression. The closing of a factory because of a depression may lead to the loss of a job, with the result that the individual is cut adrift from the regulative effect that both the company and the job may have had. Being cut off from these structures or others (for example, family, religion, and state) can leave an individual highly vulnerable to the effects of currents of anomie.

Somewhat more difficult to imagine is the effect of an economic boom. In this case, Durkheim argued that sudden success leads individuals away from the traditional structures in which they are embedded. It may lead individuals to quit their jobs, move to a new community, perhaps even find a new spouse. All these changes disrupt the regulative effect of extant structures and leave the individual in boom periods vulnerable to anomic social currents. In such a condition, people's activity is released from regulation, and even their dreams are no longer restrained. People in an economic boom seem to have limitless prospects, and "reality seems valueless by comparison with the dreams of fevered imaginations" (Durkheim, 1897/1951:256).

The increases in rates of anomic suicide during periods of deregulation of social life are consistent with Durkheim's views on the pernicious effect of individual passions when freed of external constraint. People thus freed will become slaves to their passions and as a result, in Durkheim's view, commit a wide range of destructive acts, including killing themselves.

Fatalistic Suicide

There is a little-mentioned fourth type of suicide—fatalistic—that Durkheim discussed only in a footnote in *Suicide* (Acevedo, 2005; Besnard, 1993). Whereas anomic suicide is more likely to occur in situations in which regulation is too weak, *fatalistic suicide* is more likely to occur when regulation is excessive. Durkheim (1897/1951:276) described those who are more likely to commit fatalistic suicide as "persons with futures pitilessly blocked and passions violently choked by oppressive discipline." The classic example is the slave who takes his own life because of the hopelessness associated with the oppressive regulation of his every action. Too much regulation—oppression—unleashes currents of melancholy that, in turn, cause a rise in the rate of fatalistic suicide.

Durkheim argued that social currents cause changes in the rates of suicides. Individual suicides are affected by these underlying currents of egoism, altruism, anomie, and fatalism. This proved, for Durkheim, that these currents are more than just the sum of individuals, but are *sui generis* forces, because they dominate the decisions of individuals. Without this assumption, the stability of the suicide rate for any particular society could not be explained.

Suicide Rates and Social Reform

Durkheim concludes his study of suicide with an examination of what reforms could be undertaken to prevent it. Most attempts to prevent suicide have failed because it has been seen as an individual problem. For Durkheim, attempts to directly convince individuals not to commit suicide are futile, since its real causes are in society.

Of course, the first question to be asked is whether suicide should be prevented or whether it counts among those social phenomena that Durkheim would call normal because of its widespread prevalence. This is an especially important question for Durkheim because his theory says that suicides result from social currents that, in a less exaggerated form, are good for society. We would not want to stop all economic booms because they lead to anomic suicides, nor would we stop valuing individuality because it leads to egoistic suicide. Similarly, altruistic suicide results from our virtuous tendency to sacrifice ourselves for the community. The pursuit of progress, the belief in the individual, and the spirit of sacrifice all have their place in society, and cannot exist without generating some suicides.

Durkheim admits that some suicide is normal, but he argues that modern society has seen a pathological increase in both egoistic and anomic suicides. Here his position can be traced back to *The Division of Labor,* where he argued that the anomie of modern culture is due to the abnormal way in which labor is divided so that it leads to isolation rather than interdependence. What is needed, then, is a way to preserve the benefits of modernity without unduly increasing suicides—a way of balancing these social currents. In our society, Durkheim believes, these currents are out of balance. In particular, social regulation and integration are too low, leading to an abnormal rate of anomic and egoistic suicides.

Many of the existing institutions for connecting the individual and society have failed, and Durkheim sees little hope of their success. The modern state is too distant from the individual to influence his or her life with enough force and continuity. The church cannot exert its integrating effect without at the same time repressing freedom of thought. Even the family, possibly the most integrative institution in modern society, will fail in this task because it is subject to the same corrosive conditions that are increasing suicide.

Instead, what Durkheim suggests is the need of a different institution based on occupational groups. We will discuss these occupational associations more below, but what is important here is that Durkheim proposes a social solution to a social problem.

The Elementary Forms of Religious Life

Early and Late Durkheimian Theory

Before we go on to Durkheim's last great sociological work, *The Elementary Forms of Religious Life* (1912/1965), we should say some things about the way in which his ideas were received into American sociology. As we said, Durkheim is seen as the "father" of modern sociology, but, unlike biological paternity, the parentage of disciplines is not susceptible to DNA tests and therefore must be seen as a social construction. To a large degree, Durkheim was awarded his status of "father" by one of America's greatest theorists, Talcott Parsons (1937), and this has influenced subsequent views of Durkheim.

Parsons presented Durkheim as undergoing a theoretical change between *Suicide* and *The Elementary Forms.* He believed that the early Durkheim was primarily a positivist who tried to apply the methods of the natural sciences to the study of society, while the later Durkheim was an idealist who traced social changes to changes in collective ideas. Even though Parsons (1975) later admitted that this division was "overdone," it has made its way into many sociologists' understanding of Durkheim. For the most part, sociologists tend to find an early or a late Durkheim they agree with and emphasize that aspect of his work.

There is some truth to this periodization of Durkheim, but it seems to be more a matter of his focus than any great theoretical shift. Durkheim always believed that social forces were akin to natural forces and always believed that collective ideas shaped social practices as well as vice versa. However, there is no doubt that after *Suicide,* the question of religion became of overriding importance in Durkheim's sociological theory. It would be wrong to see this as a form of idealism. In fact, we see in the text that Durkheim was actually worried that he would be seen as too materialistic since he assumed that religious beliefs are dependent upon such concrete social practices as rituals.

In addition, Durkheim, in his later period, more directly addressed how individuals internalize social structures. Durkheim's often overly zealous arguments for sociology and against psychology have led many to argue that he had little to offer on how social facts affected the consciousnesses of human actors (Lukes, 1972:228). This was particularly true in his early work, where he dealt with the link between social facts and individual consciousness in only a vague and cursory way. Nevertheless, Durkheim's ultimate goal was to explain how individual humans are shaped by social facts. We see his clear announcement of that intent in regard to *The Elementary Forms of Religious Life:* "In general, we hold that sociology has not completely achieved its task so long as it has not penetrated into the mind . . . of the individual in order to relate the institutions it seeks to explain to their psychological conditions. . . . Man is for us less a point of departure than a point of arrival" (Durkheim, cited in Lukes, 1972:498–499). As we will see in what follows, he proposed a theory of ritual and effervescence that addressed the link between social facts and human consciousness, as did his work on moral education.

Theory of Religion—The Sacred and the Profane

Raymond Aron (1965:45) said of *The Elementary Forms of Religious Life* that it was Durkheim's most important, most profound, and most original work. Randall Collins and Michael Makowsky (1998:107) call it "perhaps the greatest single book of the twentieth century." In this book, Durkheim put forward both a sociology of religion and a theory of knowledge. His sociology of religion consisted of an attempt to identify the enduring essence of religion through an analysis of its most primitive forms. His theory of knowledge attempted to connect the fundamental categories of human thought to their social origins. It was Durkheim's great genius to propose a sociological connection between these two disparate puzzles. Put briefly, he found the enduring essence of religion in the setting apart of the *sacred* from all that is profane (Edwards, 2007). This sacred is created through rituals that transform the moral power of society into religious symbols that bind individuals to the group. Durkheim's most daring argument is that this moral bond becomes a cognitive bond because the categories for understanding, such as classification, time, space, and causation, are also derived from religious rituals.

Let us start with Durkheim's theory of religion. Society (through individuals) creates religion by defining certain phenomena as sacred and others as profane. Those aspects of social reality that are defined as *sacred*—that is, that are set apart from the everyday—form the essence of religion. The rest are defined as *profane*—the commonplace, the utilitarian, the mundane aspects of life. On the one hand, the sacred brings out an attitude of reverence, awe, and obligation. On the other hand, it is the attitude accorded to these phenomena that transforms them from profane to sacred. The question for Durkheim was, What is the source of this reverence, awe, and obligation?

Here he proposed to both retain the essential truth of religion while revealing its sociological reality.[5] Durkheim refused to believe that all religion is nothing but an illusion. Such a pervasive social phenomenon must have some truth. However, that truth need not be precisely that which is believed by the participants. Indeed, as a strict agnostic, Durkheim could not believe that anything supernatural was the source of these religious feelings. There really is a superior moral power that inspires believers, but it is society and not God. Durkheim argued that religion symbolically embodies society itself. Religion is the system of symbols by means of which society becomes conscious of itself. This was the only way that he could explain why every society has had religious beliefs but each has had different beliefs.

Society is a power that is greater than we are. It transcends us, demands our sacrifices, suppresses our selfish tendencies, and fills us with energy. Society, according to Durkheim, exercises these powers through representations. In God, he sees "only society transfigured and symbolically expressed" (Durkheim, 1906/1974:52). Thus society is the source of the sacred.

Beliefs, Rituals, and Church

The differentiation between the sacred and the profane and the elevation of some aspects of social life to the sacred level are necessary but not sufficient conditions for the development of religion. Three other conditions are needed. First, there must be the development of a set of religious beliefs. These *beliefs* are "the representations which express the nature of sacred things and the relations which they sustain, either with each other or with profane things" (Durkheim, 1912/1965:56). Second, a set of religious *rituals* is necessary. These are "the rules of conduct which prescribe how a man should comport himself in the presence of these sacred objects" (Durkheim, 1912/1965:56). Finally, a religion requires a *church,* or a single overarching moral community. The interrelationships among the sacred, beliefs, rituals, and church led Durkheim to the following definition of a religion: "A religion is a unified system of beliefs and practices which unite into one single moral community called a Church, all those who adhere to them" (1912/1965:62).

Rituals and the church are important to Durkheim's theory of religion because they connect the representations of the social to individual practices. Durkheim often assumes that social currents are simply absorbed by individuals through some sort of contagion, but here he spells out how such a process might work. Individuals learn about the sacred and its associated beliefs through participating in rituals and in the community of the church. As we will see below, this is also how individuals learn the categories of understanding (Rawls, 1996). Furthermore, rituals and the church keep social representations from dissipating and losing their force by dramatically reenacting the collective memory of the group. Finally, they reconnect individuals to the social, a source of greater energy that inspires them when they return to their mundane pursuits.

---

[5] Other sociologies of religion, for example, by Marx, Weber, and Simmel, saw religions as false explanations of natural phenomena (B. Turner, 1991).

Why Primitive?

Although the research reported in *The Elementary Forms* was not Durkheim's own, he felt it necessary, given his commitment to empirical science, to embed his thinking on religion in published data. The major sources of his data were studies of a clan-based Australian tribe, the Arunta, who, for Durkheim, represented primitive culture. Although today we are very skeptical of the idea that some cultures are more primitive than others, Durkheim wanted to study religion within a "primitive" culture for several reasons. First, he believed that it is much easier to gain insight into the essential nature of religion in a primitive culture because the ideological systems of primitive religions are less well developed than are those of modern religions, with the result that there is less obfuscation. Religious forms in primitive society could be "shown in all their nudity," and it would require "only the slightest effort to lay them open" (Durkheim, 1912/1965:18). In addition, whereas religion in modern society takes diverse forms, in primitive society there is "intellectual and moral conformity" (Durkheim, 1912/1965:18). This makes it easier to relate the common beliefs to the common social structures.

Durkheim studied primitive religion only in order to shed light on religion in modern society. Religion in a nonmodern society is an all-encompassing collective conscience. But as society grows more specialized, religion comes to occupy an increasingly narrow domain. It becomes simply one of a number of collective representations. Although it expresses some collective sentiments, other institutions (for example, law and science) come to express other aspects of the collective morality. Durkheim recognized that religion per se comes to occupy an ever narrower domain, but he also contended that most, if not all, of the various collective representations of modern society have their origin in the all-encompassing religion of primitive society.

Totemism

Because Durkheim believed that society is the source of religion, he was particularly interested in totemism among the Australian Arunta. *Totemism* is a religious system in which certain things, particularly animals and plants, come to be regarded as sacred and as emblems of the clan. Durkheim viewed totemism as the simplest, most primitive form of religion, and he believed it to be associated with a similarly simple form of social organization, the clan.

Durkheim argued that the totem is nothing but the representation of the clan itself. Individuals who experience the heightened energy of social force in a gathering of the clan seek some explanation for this state. Durkheim believed that the gathering itself was the real cause, but even today, people are reluctant to attribute this power to social forces. Instead, the clan member mistakenly attributes the energy he or she feels to the symbols of the clan. The totems are the material representations of the nonmaterial force that is at their base, and that nonmaterial force is none other than society. Totemism, and more generally religion, are derived from the collective morality and become impersonal forces. They are not simply a series of mythical animals, plants, personalities, spirits, or gods.

As a study of primitive religion, the specifics of Durkheim's interpretation have been questioned (Hiatt, 1996). However, even if totemism is not the most primitive religion, it was certainly the best vehicle to develop Durkheim's new theory linking together religion, knowledge, and society.

Although a society may have a large number of totems, Durkheim did not view these totems as representing a series of separate, fragmentary beliefs about specific animals or plants. Instead, he saw them as an interrelated set of ideas that give the society a more or less complete representation of the world. In totemism, three classes of things are connected: the totemic symbol, the animal or plant, and the members of the clan. As such, totemism provides a way to classify natural objects that reflects the social organization of the tribe. Hence, Durkheim was able to argue that the ability to classify nature into cognitive categories is derived from religious and ultimately social experiences. Later, society may develop better ways to classify nature and its symbols, for example, into scientific genera and species, but the basic idea of classification comes from social experiences. He expanded on this idea that the social world grounds our mental categories in his earlier essay with his nephew Marcel Mauss:

> Society was not simply a model which classificatory thought followed; it was its own divisions which served as divisions for the system of classification. The first logical categories were social categories; the first classes of things were classes of men. . . . It was because men were grouped, and thought of themselves in the form of groups, that in their ideas they grouped other things, and in the beginning the two modes of grouping were merged to the point of being indistinct.
>
> (Durkheim and Mauss, 1903/1963:82–83)

Sociology of Knowledge

Whereas the early Durkheim was concerned with differentiating sociology from philosophy, he now wanted to show that sociology could answer the most intractable philosophical questions. Philosophy had proposed two general models for how humans are able to develop concepts from their sense impressions. One, called *empiricism,* contends that our concepts are just generalizations from our sense impressions. The problem with this philosophy is that we seem to need some initial concepts such as space, time, and categories even to begin to group sense impressions together so that we can generalize from them. Consequently, another school of philosophy, *apriorism,* contends that we must be born with some initial categories of understanding. For Durkheim, this was really no explanation at all. How is it that we are born with these particular categories? How are they transmitted to each new generation? These are questions that Durkheim felt the philosophers could not answer. Instead, philosophers usually imply some sort of transcendental source. In other words, their philosophy has a religious character, and we already know what Durkheim thinks is the ultimate source of religion.

Durkheim contended that human knowledge is not a product of experience alone, nor are we just born with certain mental categories that are applied to experience. Instead our categories are social creations. They are collective representations. Marx had already proposed a sociology of knowledge, but his was purely in the negative sense. Ideology was the distortion of our knowledge by social forces. In that sense, it was a theory of false knowledge. Durkheim offers a much more powerful sociology of knowledge that explains our "true" knowledge in terms of social forces.

Categories of Understanding

The Elementary Forms presents an argument for the social origin of six fundamental categories that some philosophers had identified as essential to human understanding: time, space, classification, force, causality, and totality. *Time* comes from the rhythms of social life. The category of *space* develops from the division of space occupied by society. We've already discussed how in totemism *classification* is tied to the human group. *Force* is derived from experiences with social forces. Imitative rituals are the origin of the concept of *causality*. Finally, society itself is the representation of *totality* (Nielsen, 1999). These descriptions are necessarily brief, but the important point is that the fundamental categories that allow us to transform our sense impressions into abstract concepts are derived from social experiences, in particular experiences of religious rituals. In these rituals, the bodily involvement of participants in the ritual's sounds and movements creates feelings that give rise to the categories of understanding (Rawls, 2001).

Even if our abstract concepts are based on social experiences, this does not mean that our thoughts are determined by society. Remember that social facts acquire laws of development and association of their own, and they are not reducible to their source. Although social facts emerge out of other social facts, their subsequent development is autonomous. Consequently, even though these concepts have a religious source, they can develop into nonreligious systems. In fact, this is exactly what Durkheim sees as having happened with science. Rather than being opposed to religion, science has developed out of religion.

Despite their autonomous development, some categories are universal and necessary. This is the case because these categories develop in order to facilitate social interaction. Without them, all contact between individual minds would be impossible, and social life would cease. This explains why they are universal to humanity, because everywhere human beings have lived in societies. This also explains why they are necessary.

> Hence society cannot leave the categories up to the free choice of individuals without abandoning itself. To live, it requires not only a minimum moral consensus but also a minimum logical consensus that it cannot do without either. Thus, in order to prevent dissidence, society weighs on its members with all its authority. Does a mind seek to free itself from these norms of all thought? Society no longer considers this a human mind in the full sense, and treats it accordingly.
>
> (Durkheim, 1912/1965:16)

Collective Effervescence

Nevertheless, there are times when even the most fundamental moral and cognitive categories can change or be created anew. Durkheim calls this *collective effervescence*

(Ono, 1996; Tiryakian, 1995). The notion of collective effervescence is not well spelled out in any of Durkheim's works. He seemed to have in mind, in a general sense, the great moments in history when a collectivity is able to achieve a new and heightened level of collective exaltation that in turn can lead to great changes in the structure of society. The Reformation and the Renaissance would be examples of historical periods when collective effervescence had a marked effect on the structure of society. As described later, effervescence is possible even in a classroom. It was during such a period of collective effervescence that the clan members created totemism. Collective effervescences are the decisive formative moments in social development. They are social facts at their birth.

To summarize Durkheim's theory of religion, society is the source of religion, the concept of God, and ultimately everything that is sacred (as opposed to profane). In a very real sense, then, we can argue that the sacred, God, and society are one and the same. Durkheim believed that this is fairly clear-cut in primitive society and that it remains true today, even though the relationship is greatly obscured by the complexities of modern society. To summarize Durkheim's sociology of knowledge, he claimed that concepts and even our most fundamental categories are collective representations that society produces, at least initially, through religious rituals. Religion is what connects society and the individual, because it is through sacred rituals that social categories become the basis for individual concepts.

Moral Education and Social Reform

Durkheim did not consider himself to be political and indeed avoided most partisan politics as not compatible with scientific objectivity. Nevertheless, as we've seen, most of his writings dealt with social issues, and, unlike some who see themselves as objective scientists today, he was not shy about suggesting specific social reforms, in particular regarding education and occupational associations. Mike Gane (2001:79) writes that Durkheim "believed the role of social science was to provide guidance for specific kinds of social intervention."

Durkheim saw problems in modern society as temporary aberrations and not as inherent difficulties (Fenton, 1984:45). Therefore, he believed in social reform. In taking this position, he stood in opposition to both the conservatives and the radicals of his day. Conservatives saw no hope in modern society and sought instead the restoration of the monarchy or of the political power of the Roman Catholic Church. Radicals like the socialists of Durkheim's time agreed that the world could not be reformed, but they hoped that a revolution would bring into existence socialism or communism.

Both Durkheim's programs for reform and his reformist approach were due to his belief that society is the source of any morality. His reform programs were dictated by the fact that society needs to be able to produce moral direction for the individual. To the extent that society is losing that capacity, it must be reformed. His reformist approach was dictated by the fact that the source for any reform has to be the actually existing society. It does no good to formulate reform programs from the viewpoint of an abstract morality. The program must be generated by that society's social forces and not from some philosopher's, or even sociologist's, ethical system. "Ideals cannot be legislated into existence; they must be understood, loved and striven for by the body whose duty it is to realize them" (Durkheim, 1938/1977:38).

Morality

Durkheim offered courses and gave public lectures on moral education and the sociology of morals. And he intended, had he lived long enough, to culminate his oeuvre with a comprehensive presentation of his science of morals. The connection that Durkheim saw between sociology and morality has not until recently been appreciated by most sociologists:

> It is not a coincidence, it seems to me, that the new emphasis on Durkheim should be in the areas of morality, philosophy, and intellectual milieu; it is indicative of a growing reflective need of sociology for ontological problems, those which relate professional concerns to the socio-historical situation of the profession. Whereas only a decade or so ago many sociologists might have been embarrassed if not vexed to discuss "ethics" and "morality," the increasing amorality and immorality of the public and private sectors of our society may be tacitly leading or forcing us back to fundamental inquiries, such as the moral basis of modern society, ideal and actual. This was a central theoretical and existential concern of Durkheim.
>
> (Tiryakian, 1974:769)

As we have said, Durkheim was centrally concerned with morality, but it is not easy to classify his theory of morality according to the typical categories. On the one hand, he was a moral relativist who believed that ethical rules do and should change in response to other social facts. On the other hand, he was a traditionalist because he did not believe that one could simply create a new morality. Any new morality could only grow out of our collective moral traditions. He insisted that one must "see in morality itself a fact the nature of which one must investigate attentively, I would even say respectfully, before daring to modify" (Durkheim, cited in Bellah, 1973:xv). Durkheim's sociological theory of morality cuts across most of the positions concerning morality today and offers the possibility of a fresh perspective on contemporary debates over such issues as traditional families and the moral content of popular culture.

Morality, for Durkheim, has three components. First, morality involves discipline, that is, a sense of authority that resists idiosyncratic impulses. Second, morality involves attachment to society because society is the source of our morality. Third, it involves autonomy, a sense of individual responsibility for our actions.

Discipline

Durkheim usually discussed *discipline* in terms of constraint upon one's egoistic impulses. Such constraint is necessary because individual interests and group interests are not the same and may, at least in the short term, be in conflict. Discipline confronts one with one's moral duty, which, for Durkheim, is one's duty to society. As discussed above, this social discipline also makes the individual happier because it limits his or her limitless desires and therefore provides the only chance of happiness for a being who otherwise would always want more.

Attachment

But Durkheim did not see morality as simply a matter of constraint. His second element in morality is *attachment* to social groups—the warm, voluntary, positive aspect of group commitment—not out of external duty but out of willing attachment.

> It is society that we consider the most important part of ourselves. From this point of view, one can readily see how it can become the thing to which we are bound. In fact, we could not disengage ourselves from society without cutting ourselves off from ourselves. Between it and us there is the strongest and most intimate connection, since it is a part of our own being, since in a sense it constitutes what is best in us. . . . Consequently, . . . when we hold to ourselves, we hold to something other than ourselves. . . . Thus, just as morality limits and constrains us, in response to the requirements of our nature, so in requiring our commitment and subordination to the group does it compel us to realize ourselves.
>
> (Durkheim, 1925/1961:71–72)

These two elements of morality—discipline and attachment—complement and support each other because they are both just different aspects of society. The former is society seen as making demands on us, and the latter is society seen as part of us.

Autonomy

The third element of morality is *autonomy*. Here Durkheim follows Kant's philosophical definition and sees it as a rationally grounded impulse of the will, with the sociological twist that the rational grounding is ultimately social.

Durkheim's focus on society as the source of morality has led many to assume that his ideal actor is one who is almost wholly controlled from without—a total conformist. However, Durkheim did not subscribe to such an extreme view of the actor: "Conformity must not be pushed to the point where it completely subjugates the intellect. Thus it does not follow from a belief in the need for discipline that it must be blind and slavish" (cited in Giddens, 1972:113).

Autonomy comes to full force in modernity only with the decline of the myths and symbols that previous moral systems used to demand discipline and encourage attachment. Durkheim believed that now that these myths have passed away, only scientific understanding can provide the foundation for moral autonomy. In particular, modern morality should be based on the relation between individuals and society as revealed by Durkheim's new science of sociology. The only way for this sociological understanding to become a true morality is through education.

Moral Education

Durkheim's most consistent attempts to reform society in order to enable a modern morality were directed at education (Dill, 2007). *Education* was defined by Durkheim as the process by which the individual acquires the physical, intellectual, and, most important to Durkheim, moral tools needed to function in society (Durkheim, 1922/1956:71). As Lukes (1972:359) reports, Durkheim had always believed "that the relation of the science of sociology to education was that of theory to practice." In 1902, he was given the powerful position of head of the Sorbonne's education department. "It is scarcely an exaggeration to say that every young mind in Paris, in the decade prior to World War I, came directly or indirectly under his influence" (Gerstein, 1983:239).

Before Durkheim began to reform education there had been two approaches. One saw education as an extension of the church, and the other saw education as the unfolding of the natural individual. In contrast, Durkheim argued that education should help children develop a moral attitude toward society. He believed that the schools were practically the only existing institution that could provide a social foundation for modern morality.

For Durkheim, the classroom is a small society, and he concluded that its collective effervescence could be made powerful enough to inculcate a moral attitude. The classroom could provide the rich collective milieu necessary for reproducing collective representations (Durkheim, 1925/1961:229). This would allow education to present and reproduce all three elements of morality.

First, it would provide individuals with the discipline they need to restrain the passions that threaten to engulf them. Second, education could develop in the students a sense of devotion to society and to its moral system. Most important is education's role in the development of autonomy, in which discipline is "freely desired," and the attachment to society is by virtue of "enlightened assent" (Durkheim, 1925/1961:120).

> For to teach morality is neither to preach nor to indoctrinate; it is to explain. If we refuse the child all explanation of this sort, if we do not try to help him understand the reasons for the rules he should abide by, we would be condemning him to an incomplete and inferior morality.
>
> (Durkheim, 1925/1961:120–121)

Occupational Associations

As discussed, the primary problem that Durkheim saw in modern society was the lack of integration and regulation. Even though the cult of the individual provided a collective representation, Durkheim believed that there was a lack of social organizations that people could feel part of and that could tell people what they should and should not do. The modern state is too distant to influence most individuals. The church tends to integrate people by repressing freedom of thought. And the family is too particular and does not integrate individuals into society as a whole. As we've seen, the schools provided an excellent milieu for children. For adults, Durkheim proposed another institution: the *occupational association.*

Genuine moral commitments require a concrete group tied to the basic organizing principle of modern society, the division of labor. Durkheim proposed the development of occupational associations. All the workers, managers, and owners involved in a particular industry should join together in an association that would be both professional and social. Durkheim did not believe that there was a basic conflict of interest among the owners, managers, and workers within an industry. In this, of course, he took a position diametrically opposed to that of Marx, who saw an essential conflict of interest between the owners and the workers. Durkheim believed that any such conflict occurred only because the various people involved lacked a common morality, which was traceable to the lack of an integrative structure. He suggested that the structure that was needed to provide this integrative morality was the occupational association, which would encompass "all the agents of the same industry united and organized into a single group" (Durkheim, 1893/1964:5). Such an organization was deemed to be superior to such organizations as labor unions and employer associations, which in Durkheim's view served only to intensify the differences between owners, managers, and workers. Involved in a common organization, people in these categories would recognize their common interests as well as their common need for an integrative moral system. That moral system, with its derived rules and laws, would serve to counteract the tendency toward atomization in modern society as well as help stop the decline in the significance of collective morality.

Criticisms

As mentioned earlier, Durkheim's reception into American sociology was strongly influenced by Talcott Parsons, who presented Durkheim as both a functionalist and a positivist. Although these labels don't fairly characterize Durkheim's position, a number of criticisms have been directed at his ideas on the basis of these characterizations. Since the sociology student is bound to come across these criticisms they are briefly addressed here.

Functionalism and Positivism

Durkheim's focus on macro-level social facts was one of the reasons his work played a central role in the development of structural functionalism, which has a similar, macro-level orientation (see Chapter 7). However, whether Durkheim himself was a functionalist is open to debate and depends upon how one defines functionalism. Functionalism can be defined in two different ways, a weak sense and a strong sense. When Kingsley Davis (1959) said that all sociologists are functionalists, he referred to the weak sense: that functionalism is an approach that attempts "to relate the parts of society to the whole, and to relate one part to another." A stronger definition of functionalism is given by Jonathan H. Turner and A. Z. Maryanski (1988), who define it as an approach that is based on seeing society as analogous to a biological organism and attempts to explain particular social structures in terms of the needs of society as a whole.

In this second sense, Durkheim was only an occasional and, one might say, accidental functionalist. Durkheim was not absolutely opposed to drawing analogies between biological organisms and social structures (Lehmann, 1993a:15), but he did not believe that sociologists can infer sociological laws by analogy with biology. Durkheim (1898/1974:1) called such inferences "worthless."

Durkheim urged that we distinguish functions from the historical causes of social facts. The historical study is primary because social needs cannot simply call structures into existence. Certainly, Durkheim's initial hypothesis was always that enduring social facts probably perform some sort of function, but he recognized that some social facts are historical accidents. Furthermore, we see in Durkheim no attempt to predefine the needs of society. Instead, the needs of a particular society can be established only by studying that society. Consequently, any functionalist approach must be preceded by a historical study.

Despite this theoretical injunction, it must be admitted that Durkheim did sometimes slip into functional analysis (J. Turner and Maryanski, 1988:111–112). Consequently, there are many places where one can fairly criticize Durkheim for assuming that societies as a whole have needs and that social structures automatically emerge to respond to these needs.

Durkheim also is often criticized for being a positivist, and indeed, he used the term to describe himself. However, as Robert Hall notes, the meaning of the term has changed:

> The term "positive" was needed to distinguish the new approach from those of the philosophers who had taken to calling their ethical theories "scientific" and who used this term to indicate the dialectical reasoning they employed. In an age in which one could still speak of the "science" of metaphysics, the term "positive" simply indicated an empirical approach.
>
> (Hall, 1987:137)

Today, positivism refers to the belief that social phenomena should be studied with the same methods as the natural sciences, and it is likely that Durkheim would accept this. However, it has also come to mean a focus on invariant laws (S. Turner, 1993), and we find little of that in Durkheim. Social facts were, for Durkheim, autonomous from their substrate, but also autonomous in their relation to other social facts. Each social fact required historical investigation, and none could be predicted on the basis of invariant laws.

Other Criticisms

There are some other problems with Durkheim's theory that need to be discussed. The first has to do with the crucial idea of a social fact. It is not at all clear that social facts can be approached in the objective manner that Durkheim recommends. Even such seemingly objective evidence for these social facts as a suicide rate can be seen as an accumulation of interpretations. In other words, whether a particular death is a suicide depends upon ascertaining the intention of a dead person (J. Douglas, 1967). This may be especially difficult in such cases as drug overdoses. In addition, the interpretation may be biased in a systemic manner so that, for example, deaths among those of high status may be less likely to be interpreted as suicides, even if the body is found clutching the fatal gun. Social facts and the evidence for them should always be approached as interpretations, and even the sociologist's own use of the social fact should be seen as such.

There are also some problems with Durkheim's view of the individual. Despite having made a number of crucial assumptions about human nature, Durkheim denied that he had done so. He argued that he did not begin by postulating a certain conception of human nature in order to deduce a sociology from it. Instead, he said that it was from sociology that he sought an increasing understanding of human nature. However, Durkheim may have been less than honest with his readers, and perhaps even with himself.

One of Durkheim's assumptions about human nature—one that we have already encountered—may be viewed as the basis of his entire sociology. That assumption is that people are impelled by their passions into a mad search for gratification that always leads to a need for more. If these passions are unrestrained, they multiply to the point where the individual is enslaved by them and they become a threat to the individual as well as to society. It can be argued that Durkheim's entire theoretical edifice, especially his emphasis on collective morality, was erected on this basic assumption about people's passions. However, Durkheim provides no evidence for this assumption, and indeed, his own theories would suggest that such an insatiable subject may be a creation of social structures rather than the other way around.

In addition, Durkheim failed to give consciousness an active role in the social process. He treated the actor and the actor's mental processes as secondary factors or, more commonly, as dependent variables to be explained by the independent and decisive variables—social facts. Individuals are, in general, controlled by social forces in his theories; they do not actively control those forces. Autonomy, for Durkheim, meant nothing more than freely accepting those social forces. However, even if we accept that consciousness and some mental processes are types of social facts, there is no reason to suppose that they cannot develop the same autonomy that Durkheim recognized in other social facts. Just as science has developed its own autonomous rules, making its religious roots almost unrecognizable, couldn't consciousness do the same?

The final set of criticisms to be discussed here has to do with the centrality of morality in Durkheim's sociology. All sociologists are driven by moral concerns, but for Durkheim, morality was more than just the driving force behind sociology; it was also its ultimate goal. Durkheim believed that the sociological study of morality would produce a science of morality. As Everett White (1961:xx) wrote, "To say that the moral is an inevitable aspect of the social—is a far cry from asserting, as Durkheim does, that there can be a science of morality."

Furthermore, even without the fantasy of a science of morality, a sociology that attempts to determine what *should be done* from what *now exists* is inherently conservative. This conservatism is the most frequently cited criticism of Durkheim (Milbrandt and Pearce, 2011; Pearce, 1989). This is often attributed to his functionalism and positivism, but it is more correctly traced to the connection that he sees between morality and sociology. Whatever value there is in the scientific study of morality, it cannot relieve us of making moral choices. Indeed, it is likely that such study will make moral choice more difficult even as it makes us more flexible and responsive to changing social situations.

We should note, however, that Durkheim is not alone in having failed to work out the proper relation between morality and sociology. This problem disturbs modern sociology at least as much as it does Durkheim's theories. In an increasingly pluralistic culture, it is clear that we cannot just accept our moral traditions. For one thing, it is impossible to say whose moral traditions we should accept. It is equally clear, thanks in part to Durkheim's insight, that we cannot just create a new morality that is separate from our moral traditions. A new morality must emerge, and it must emerge from our moral traditions, but what role sociology can and should play in this is a question that appears to be both unanswerable and unavoidable.

Summary

The two main themes in Durkheim's sociology were the priority of the social over the individual and the idea that society can be studied scientifically. These themes led to his concept of social facts. Social facts can be empirically studied, are external to the individual, are coercive of the individual, and are explained by other social facts. Durkheim differentiated between two basic types of social facts—material and nonmaterial. The most important focus for Durkheim was on nonmaterial social facts. He dealt with a number of them, including morality, collective conscience, collective representations, and social currents.

Durkheim's first major work was *The Division of Labor in Society,* in which he argued that the collective conscience of societies with mechanical solidarity had been replaced by a new organic solidarity based on mutual interdependence in a society organized by a division of labor. He investigated the difference between mechanical and organic solidarity through an analysis of their different legal systems. He argued that mechanical solidarity is associated with repressive laws while organic solidarity is associated with legal systems based on restitution.

Durkheim's next book, a study of suicide, is a good illustration of the significance of nonmaterial social facts in his work. In his basic causal model, changes in nonmaterial social facts ultimately cause differences in suicide rates. Durkheim differentiated among four types of suicide—egoistic, altruistic, anomic, and fatalistic—and showed how each is affected by different changes in social currents. The study of suicide was taken by Durkheim and his supporters as evidence that sociology has a legitimate place in the social sciences. After all, it was argued, if sociology could explain so individualistic an act as suicide, it certainly could be used to explain other, less individual aspects of social life.

In his last major work, *The Elementary Forms of Religious Life,* Durkheim focused on another aspect of culture: religion. In his analysis of primitive religion, Durkheim sought to show the roots of religion in the social structure of society. It is society that defines certain things as sacred and others as profane. Durkheim demonstrated the social sources of religion in his analysis of primitive totemism and its roots in the social structure of the clan. Durkheim concluded that religion and society are one and the same, two manifestations of the same general process. He also presented a sociology of knowledge in this work. He claimed that concepts and even our most fundamental mental categories are collective representations that society produces, at least initially, through religious rituals.

Although Durkheim was against any radical change, his central concern with morality led him to propose two reforms in society that he hoped would lead to a stronger collective morality. For children, he successfully implemented a new program for moral education in France that focused on teaching children discipline, attachment to society, and autonomy. For adults, he proposed occupational associations to restore collective morality and to cope with some of the curable pathologies of the modern division of labor.

The chapter concludes with some criticisms of Durkheim's theories. There are serious problems with his basic idea of the social fact, with his assumptions about human nature, and with his sociology of morality.

Max Weber

Chapter Outline
Methodology
Substantive Sociology
Criticisms

Max Weber (1864–1920) is probably the best known and most influential figure in sociological theory (Burger, 1993; R. Collins, 1985; Kalberg, 2011; Sica, 2001; Whimster, 2001, 2005).[1] Weber's work is so varied and subject to so many interpretations that it has influenced a wide array of sociological theories. It certainly had an influence on structural functionalism, especially through the work of Talcott Parsons. It has also come to be seen as important to the conflict tradition (R. Collins, 1975, 1990) and to critical theory, which was shaped almost as much by Weber's ideas as it was by Marx's orientation, as well as to Jurgen Habermas, the major inheritor of the critical-theory tradition (Outhwaite, 1994). Symbolic interactionists have been affected by Weber's ideas on *verstehen,* as well as by other of Weber's ideas. Alfred Schutz was powerfully affected by Weber's work on meanings and motives, and he, in turn, played a crucial role in the development of ethnomethodology (see Chapter 10). Recently, rational choice theorists have acknowledged their debt to Weber (Norkus, 2000). Weber was and is a widely influential theorist.

This chapter begins with a discussion of Weber's (1903–1917/1949) ideas on the methodology of the social sciences, which remain remarkably relevant and fruitful even today (Bruun, 2007; Ringer, 1997:171). A clear understanding of these ideas is necessary in dealing with Weber's substantive and theoretical ideas. Weber was opposed to pure abstract theorizing. Instead, his theoretical ideas are embedded in his empirical, usually historical, research. Weber's methodology shaped his research, and the combination of the two lies at the base of his theoretical orientation.

---

[1] For a time, his position was threatened by the increase in interest in the work of Karl Marx, who was already much better known to those in other fields and to the general public. But with the demise of world communism, Weber's position of preeminence seems secure once again.

Methodology

History and Sociology

Even though Weber was a student of, and took his first academic job in, law, his early career was dominated by an interest in history. As Weber moved more in the direction of the relatively new field of sociology, he sought to clarify its relationship to the established field of history. Although Weber felt that each field needed the other, his view was that the task of sociology was to provide a needed "service" to history (G. Roth, 1976:307). In Weber's words, sociology performed only a "preliminary, quite modest task" (cited in R. Frank, 1976:21). Weber explained the difference between sociology and history: "Sociology seeks to formulate type concepts and generalized uniformities of empirical processes. This distinguishes it from history, which is oriented to the causal analysis and explanation of individual actions, structures, and personalities possessing cultural significance" (1921/1968:19). Despite this seemingly clear-cut differentiation, in his own work Weber was able to combine the two. His sociology was oriented to the development of clear concepts so that he could perform a causal analysis of historical phenomena. Weber defined his ideal procedure as "the sure imputation of individual concrete events occurring in historical reality *to concrete, historically* given causes through the study of precise empirical data which have been selected from specific points of view" (1903–1917/1949:69). We can think of Weber as a historical sociologist.

Weber's thinking on sociology was profoundly shaped by a series of intellectual debates (*Methodenstreit*) raging in Germany during his time. The most important of these debates was over the issue of the relationship between history and science. At the poles in this debate were those (the positivists [Halfpenny, 2005]) who thought that history was composed of general (*nomothetic*) laws and those (the subjectivists) who reduced history to idiosyncratic (*idiographic*) actions and events. (The positivists thought that history could be like a natural science; the subjectivists saw the two as radically different.) For example, a nomothetic thinker would generalize about social revolutions, whereas an idiographic analyst would focus on the specific events leading up to the American Revolution. Weber rejected both extremes and in the process developed a distinctive way of dealing with historical sociology. In Weber's view, history is composed of unique empirical events; there can be no generalizations at the empirical level. Sociologists must, therefore, separate the empirical world from the conceptual universe that they construct. The concepts never completely capture the empirical world, but they can be used as heuristic tools for gaining a better understanding of reality. With these concepts, sociologists can develop generalizations, but these generalizations are not history and must not be confused with empirical events.

Although Weber was clearly in favor of generalizing, he also rejected historians who sought to reduce history to a simple set of laws: "For the knowledge of historical phenomena in their concreteness, the most general laws, because they are devoid of content, are also the least valuable" (1903–1917/1949:80). For example, Weber rejected one historian (Wilhelm Roscher) who took as his task the search for the laws

MAX WEBER

A Biographical Sketch

Max Weber was born in Erfurt, Germany, on April 21, 1864, into a decidedly middle-class family (Radkau, 2009). Important differences between his parents had a profound effect upon both his intellectual orientation and his psychological development. His father was a bureaucrat who rose to a relatively important political position. He was clearly a part of the political establishment and as a result eschewed any activity or idealism that would require personal sacrifice or threaten his position within the system. In addition, the senior Weber was a man who enjoyed earthly pleasures, and in this and many other ways he stood in sharp contrast to his wife. Max Weber's mother was a devout Calvinist, a woman who sought to lead an ascetic life largely devoid of the pleasures craved by her husband. Her concerns were more otherworldly; she was disturbed by the imperfections that were signs that she was not destined for salvation. These deep differences between the parents led to marital tension, and both the differences and the tension had an immense impact on Weber.

Because it was impossible to emulate both parents, Weber was presented with a clear choice as a child (Marianne Weber, 1975:62). He first seemed to opt for his father's orientation to life, but later he drew closer to his mother's approach. Whatever the choice, the tension produced by the need to choose between such polar opposites negatively affected Max Weber's psyche.

At age 18, Max Weber left home for a short time to attend the University of Heidelberg. Weber had already demonstrated intellectual precocity, but on a social level he entered Heidelberg shy and underdeveloped. However, that quickly changed after he gravitated toward his father's way of life and joined his father's old dueling fraternity. There he developed socially, at least in part because of the huge quantities of beer he consumed with his peers. In addition, he proudly displayed the dueling scars that were the trademark of such fraternities. Weber not only manifested his identity with his father's way of life in these ways but also chose, at least for the time being, his father's career—the law.

After three terms, Weber left Heidelberg for military service, and in 1884 he returned to Berlin and to his parents' home to take courses at the University of Berlin. He remained there for most of the next eight years as he completed his studies, earned his Ph.D., became a lawyer (see Turner and Factor, 1994, for a discussion of the impact of legal thinking on Weber's theorizing), and started teaching at the University of Berlin. In the process, his interests shifted more

of the historical evolution of a people and who believed that all peoples went through a typical sequence of stages (1903–1906/1975). As Weber put it, "The reduction of empirical reality . . . to 'laws' is meaningless" (1903–1917/1949:80). In other terms: "A systematic science of culture . . . would be senseless in itself" (Weber, 1903–1917/1949:84).

toward his lifelong concerns—economics, history, and sociology. During his eight years in Berlin, Weber was financially dependent on his father, a circumstance he progressively grew to dislike. At the same time, he moved closer to his mother's values, and his antipathy to his father increased. He adopted an ascetic life and plunged deeply into his work. For example, during one semester as a student, his work habits were described as follows: "He continues the rigid work discipline, regulates his life by the clock, divides the daily routine into exact sections for the various subjects, saves in his way, by feeding himself evenings in his room with a pound of raw chopped beef and four fried eggs" (Mitzman, 1969/1971:48; Marianne Weber, 1975:105). Thus Weber, following his mother, had become ascetic and diligent, a compulsive worker—in contemporary terms a "workaholic."

This compulsion for work led in 1896 to a position as professor of economics at Heidelberg. But in 1897, when Weber's academic career was blossoming, his father died following a violent argument between them. Shortly thereafter Weber began to manifest symptoms that were to culminate in a nervous breakdown. Often unable to sleep or to work, Weber spent the next six or seven years in near-total collapse. After a long hiatus, some of his powers began to return in 1903, but it was not until 1904, when he delivered (in the United States) his first lecture in six and a half years, that Weber was able to begin to return to active academic life. In 1904 and 1905, he published one of his best-known works, *The Protestant Ethic and the Spirit of Capitalism*. In this work, Weber announced the ascendance of his mother's religion on an academic level. Weber devoted much of his time to the study of religion, though he was not personally religious.

Although he continued to be plagued by psychological problems, after 1904 Weber was able to function, indeed to produce some of his most important work. In these years, Weber published his studies of the world's religions in world-historical perspective (for example, China, India, and ancient Judaism). At the time of his death (June 14, 1920), he was working on his most important work, *Economy and Society* (1921/1968). Although this book was published, and subsequently translated into many languages, it was unfinished.

In addition to producing voluminous writings in this period, Weber undertook a number of other activities. He helped found the German Sociological Society in 1910. His home became a center for a wide range of intellectuals, including sociologists such as Georg Simmel, Robert Michels, and his brother Alfred Weber, as well as the philosopher and literary critic Georg Lukács (Scaff, 1989:186–222). In addition, Max Weber was active politically and wrote essays on the issues of the day.

There was a tension in Weber's life and, more important, in his work between the bureaucratic mind, as represented by his father, and his mother's religiosity. This unresolved tension permeates Weber's work as it permeated his personal life.

This view is reflected in various specific historical studies. For example, in his study of ancient civilizations, Weber admitted that although in some respects earlier times were precursors of things to come, "the long and continuous history of Mediterranean-European civilization does not show either closed cycles or linear progress. Sometimes phenomena of ancient civilizations have disappeared entirely and then come to light again in an entirely new context" (1896–1906/1976:366).

In rejecting these opposing views of German historical scholarship, Weber fashioned his own perspective, which constituted a fusion of the two orientations. Weber felt that history (that is, historical sociology) was appropriately concerned with both individuality *and* generality. The unification was accomplished through the development and utilization of general concepts (what are later called "ideal types") in the study of particular individuals, events, or societies. These general concepts are to be used "to identify and define the individuality of each development, the characteristics which made the one conclude in a manner so different from that of the other. Thus done, one can then determine the causes which led to the differences" (Weber, 1896–1906/1976:385). In doing this kind of causal analysis, Weber rejected, at least at a conscious level, the idea of searching for a single causal agent throughout history.[2] He instead used his conceptual arsenal to rank the various factors involved in a given historical case in terms of their causal significance (G. Roth, 1971).

Weber's views on historical sociology were shaped in part by the availability of, and his commitment to the study of, empirical historical data. His was the first generation of scholars to have available reliable data on historical phenomena from many parts of the world (MacRae, 1974). Weber was more inclined to immerse himself in these historical data than he was to dream up abstract generalizations about the basic thrust of history. Although this led him to some important insights, it also created serious problems in understanding his work; he often got so involved in historical detail that he lost sight of the basic reasons for the historical study. In addition, the sweep of his historical studies encompassed so many epochs and so many societies that he could do little more than make rough generalizations (G. Roth, 1971). Despite these problems, Weber's commitment to the scientific study of empirical phenomena made him attractive to the developing discipline of sociology in the United States.

In sum, Weber believed that history is composed of an inexhaustible array of specific phenomena. To study these phenomena, it was necessary to develop a variety of concepts designed to be useful for research on the real world. As a general rule, although Weber (as we will see) did not adhere to it strictly and neither do most sociologists and historians, the task of sociology was to develop these concepts, which history was to use in causal analyses of specific historical phenomena. In this way, Weber sought to combine the specific and the general in an effort to develop a science that did justice to the complex nature of social life.

Verstehen

Weber felt that sociologists had an advantage over natural scientists. That advantage resided in the sociologist's ability to *understand* social phenomena, whereas the natural scientist could not gain a similar understanding of the behavior of an atom

---

[2] Ironically, Weber did seem (as we will see later in this chapter) to argue in his substantive work that there was such a causal agent in society—rationalization.

or a chemical compound. The German word for understanding is *verstehen* (Soeffner, 2005). Weber's special use of the term *verstehen* in his historical research is one of his best-known and most controversial contributions to the methodology of contemporary sociology. As we clarify what Weber meant by *verstehen*, we will also underscore some of the problems involved in his conceptualization of it. The controversy surrounding the concept of *verstehen*, as well as some of the problems involved in interpreting what Weber meant, grows out of a general problem with Weber's methodological thoughts. As Thomas Burger argued, Weber was neither very sophisticated nor very consistent in his methodological pronouncements (1976; see also Hekman, 1983:26). He tended to be careless and imprecise because he felt that he was simply repeating ideas that were well known in his day among German historians. Furthermore, as pointed out above, Weber did not think too highly of methodological reflections.

Weber's thoughts on *verstehen* were relatively common among German historians of his day and were derived from a field known as *hermeneutics* (R. Brown, 2005; M. Martin, 2000; Pressler and Dasilva, 1996). Hermeneutics was a special approach to the understanding and interpretation of published writings. Its goal was to understand the thinking of the author as well as the basic structure of the text. Weber and others (for example, Wilhelm Dilthey) sought to extend this idea from the understanding of texts to the understanding of social life:

> Once we have realized that the historical method is nothing more or less than the
> classical method of interpretation applied to overt action instead of to texts, a
> method aiming at identifying a human design, a "meaning" behind observable
> events, we shall have no difficulty in accepting that it can be just as well applied to
> human interaction as to individual actors. From this point of view all history is
> interaction, which has to be interpreted in terms of the rival plans of various actors.
>
> (Lachman, 1971:20)

In other words, Weber sought to use the tools of hermeneutics to understand actors, interaction, and indeed all of human history.[3]

One common misconception about *verstehen* is that it is simply the use of "intuition" by the researcher. Thus many critics see it as a "soft," irrational, subjective research methodology. However, Weber categorically rejected the idea that *verstehen* involved simply intuition, sympathetic participation, or empathy (1903–1917/1949). To him, *verstehen* involved doing systematic and rigorous research rather than simply getting a "feeling" for a text or social phenomenon. In other words, for Weber (1921/1968) *verstehen* was a rational procedure of study.

The key question in interpreting Weber's concept of *verstehen* is whether he thought that it was most appropriately applied to the subjective states of individual actors or to the subjective aspects of large-scale units of analysis (for example, culture). As we will see, Weber's focus on the cultural and social-structural contexts of action leads us to the view that *verstehen* is a tool for macro-level analysis.

---

[3] Hermeneutics has become a major intellectual concern in recent years, especially in the work of Martin Heidegger, Hans-Georg Gadamer, and Jurgen Habermas (Bleicher, 1980). For a strong argument in favor of using hermeneutics today, see Sica (1986), and for an appreciation of Weber's hermeneutics, see Oliver (1983).

Causality

Another aspect of Weber's methodology was his commitment to the study of causality (Ringer, 1997:75). Weber was inclined to see the study of the causes of social phenomena as being within the domain of history, not sociology. Yet to the degree that history and sociology cannot be clearly separated—and they certainly are not clearly separated in Weber's substantive work—the issue of causality is relevant to sociology. Causality is also important because it is, as we will see, another place in which Weber sought to combine nomothetic and idiographic approaches.

By *causality* Weber (1921/1968) simply meant the probability that an event will be followed or accompanied by another event. It was not, in his view, enough to look for historical constants, repetitions, analogies, and parallels, as many historians are content to do. Instead, the researcher has to look at the reasons for, as well as the meanings of, historical changes (G. Roth, 1971). Although Weber can be seen as having a one-way causal model—in contrast to Marx's dialectical mode of reasoning—in his substantive sociology he was always attuned to the interrelationships among the economy, society, polity, organization, social stratification, religion, and so forth (G. Roth, 1968). Thus, Weber operates with a multicausal approach in which "*hosts* of interactive influences are very often effective causal factors" (Kalberg, 1994:13).

Weber was quite clear on the issue of multiple causality in his study of the relationship between Protestantism and the spirit of capitalism. Although he is sometimes interpreted differently, Weber (1904–1905/1958) simply argued that the Protestant ethic was *one of* the causal factors in the rise of the modern spirit of capitalism. He labeled as "foolish" the idea that Protestantism was the sole cause. Similarly foolish, in Weber's view, was the idea that capitalism could have arisen "only" as a result of the Protestant Reformation; other factors could have led to the same result. Here is the way Weber made his point:

> We shall as far as possible clarify the manner and the general *direction in which . . .* the religious movements have influenced the development of material culture. Only when this has been determined with reasonable accuracy can the attempt be made to estimate to what extent the historical development of modern culture can be attributed to those *religious forces and to what extent to others.*
>
> (Weber, 1904–1905/1958:91–92; italics added)

In *The Protestant Ethic and the Spirit of Capitalism,* as well as in most of the rest of his historical work, Weber was interested in the question of causality, but he did not operate with a simple one-way model; he was always attuned to the interrelationships among a number of social factors.

The critical thing to remember about Weber's thinking on causality is his belief that because we can have a special understanding of social life (*verstehen*), the causal knowledge of the social sciences is different from the causal knowledge of the natural sciences. As Weber put it: " 'Meaningfully' interpretable human conduct ('action') is identifiable by reference to 'valuations' and meanings. For this reason, our criteria for *causal* explanation have a unique kind of satisfaction in the 'historical' explanation of such an 'entity' " (1903–1906/1975:185). Thus the causal knowledge of the social scientist is different from the causal knowledge of the natural scientist.

Weber's thoughts on causality were intimately related to his efforts to come to grips with the conflict between nomothetic and idiographic knowledge. Those who subscribe to a nomothetic point of view would argue that there is a necessary relationship among social phenomena, whereas the supporters of an idiographic perspective would be inclined to see only random relationships among these entities. As usual, Weber took a middle position, epitomized in his concept of "adequate causality." The notion of *adequate causality* adopts the view that the best we can do in sociology is make probabilistic statements about the relationship between social phenomena; that is, if x occurs, then it is *probable* that y will occur. The goal is to "estimate the *degree* to which a certain effect is 'favored' by certain 'conditions'" (Weber, 1903–1917/1949:183).

Ideal Types

The ideal type is one of Weber's best-known contributions to contemporary sociology (Drysdale, 1996; Hekman, 1983; Lindbekk, 1992; McKinney, 1966; Zijderveld, 2005). As we have seen, Weber believed it was the responsibility of sociologists to develop conceptual tools, which could be used later by historians and sociologists. The most important such conceptual tool was the ideal type:

> An ideal type is formed by the one-sided *accentuation* of one or more points of view and by the synthesis of a great many diffuse, discrete, more or less present and occasionally absent *concrete individual* phenomena, which are arranged according to those one-sidedly emphasized viewpoints into a unified *analytical* construct . . . In its conceptual purity, this mental construct . . . cannot be found empirically anywhere in reality.
>
> (Weber, 1903–1917/1949:90)

In spite of this definition, Weber was not totally consistent in the way he used the ideal type. To grasp what the concept means initially, we will have to overlook some of the inconsistencies. At its most basic level, an *ideal type* is a concept constructed by a social scientist, on the basis of his or her interests and theoretical orientation, to capture the essential features of some social phenomenon.

The most important thing about ideal types is that they are heuristic devices; they are to be useful and helpful in doing empirical research and in understanding a specific aspect of the social world (or a "historical individual"). As Lachman said, an ideal type is "essentially a measuring rod" (1971:26), or in Kalberg's terms, a "yardstick" (1994:87). Here is the way Weber put it: "Its function is the comparison with empirical reality in order to establish its divergences or similarities, to describe them with the *most unambiguously intelligible concepts,* and to understand and explain them causally" (1903–1917/1949:43). Ideal types are heuristic devices to be used in the study of slices of historical reality. For example, social scientists would construct an ideal-typical bureaucracy on the basis of their immersion in historical data. This ideal type can then be compared to actual bureaucracies. The researcher looks for divergences in the real case from the exaggerated ideal type. Next, the social scientist must look for the causes of the deviations. Some typical reasons for these divergences are:

1. Actions of bureaucrats that are motivated by *misinformation.*
2. *Strategic errors,* primarily by the bureaucratic leaders.

3. *Logical fallacies* undergirding the actions of leaders and followers.
4. Decisions made in the bureaucracy on the basis of *emotion.*
5. *Any irrationality* in the action of bureaucratic leaders and followers.

To take another example, an ideal-typical military battle delineates the principal components of such a battle—opposing armies, opposing strategies, materiel at the disposal of each, disputed land ("no-man's land"), supply and support forces, command centers, and leadership qualities. Actual battles may not have all these elements, and that is one thing a researcher wants to know. The basic point is that the elements of any particular military battle may be compared with the elements identified in the ideal type.

The elements of an ideal type (such as the components of the ideal-typical military battle) are not to be thrown together arbitrarily; they are combined on the basis of their compatibility. As Hekman puts it, "Ideal types are not the product of the whim or fancy of a social scientist, but are logically constructed concepts" (1983:32). (However, they can and should reflect the interests of the social scientist.)

In Weber's view, the ideal type was to be derived inductively from the real world of social history. Weber did not believe that it was enough to offer a carefully defined set of concepts, especially if they were deductively derived from an abstract theory. The concepts had to be empirically adequate (G. Roth, 1971). Thus, in order to produce ideal types, researchers had first to immerse themselves in historical reality and then derive the types from that reality.

In line with Weber's efforts to find a middle ground between nomothetic and idiographic knowledge, he argued that ideal types should be neither too general nor too specific. For example, in the case of religion he would reject ideal types of the history of religion in general, but he would also be critical of ideal types of very specific phenomena, such as an individual's religious experience. Rather, ideal types are developed of intermediate phenomena such as Calvinism, Pietism, Methodism, and Baptism (Weber, 1904–1905/1958).

Although ideal types are to be derived from the real world, they are not to be mirror images of that world. Rather, they are to be one-sided exaggerations (based on the researcher's interests) of the essence of what goes on in the real world. In Weber's view, the more exaggerated the ideal type, the more useful it will be for historical research.

The use of the word *ideal* or *utopia* should not be construed to mean that the concept being described is in any sense the best of all possible worlds. As used by Weber, the term meant that the form described in the concept was rarely, if ever, found in the real world. In fact, Weber argued that the ideal type need not be positive or correct; it can just as easily be negative or even morally repugnant (1903–1917/1949).

Ideal types should make sense in themselves, the meaning of their components should be compatible, and they should aid us in making sense of the real world. Although we have come to think of ideal types as describing static entities, Weber believed that they could describe either static or dynamic entities. Thus we can have an ideal type of a structure, such as a bureaucracy, or of a social development, such as bureaucratization.

Ideal types also are not developed once and for all. Because society is constantly changing, and the interests of social scientists are as well, it is necessary to develop new typologies to fit the changing reality. This is in line with Weber's view that there can be no timeless concepts in the social sciences (G. Roth, 1968).

Although we have presented a relatively unambiguous image of the ideal type, there are contradictions in the way Weber defined the concept. In addition, in his own substantive work, Weber used the ideal type in ways that differed from the ways he said it was to be used. As Burger noted, "The ideal types presented in *Economy and Society* are a mixture of definitions, classification, and specific hypotheses seemingly too divergent to be reconcilable with Weber's statements" (1976:118). Although she disagrees with Burger on Weber's inconsistency in defining ideal types, Hekman (1983:38–59) also recognizes that Weber offers several varieties of ideal types:

1. *Historical ideal types.* These relate to phenomena found in some particular historical epoch (for example, the modern capitalistic marketplace).
2. *General sociological ideal types.* These relate to phenomena that cut across a number of historical periods and societies (for example, bureaucracy).
3. *Action ideal types.* These are pure types of action based on the motivations of the actor (for example, affectual action).
4. *Structural ideal types.* These are forms taken by the causes and consequences of social action (for example, traditional domination).

Clearly Weber developed an array of varieties of ideal types, and some of the richness in his work stems from their diversity, although common to them all is their mode of construction.

Kalberg (1994) argues that while the heuristic use of ideal types in empirical research is important, it should not be forgotten that they also play a key *theoretical* role in Weber's work. Although Weber rejects the idea of theoretical laws, he does use ideal types in various ways to create theoretical models. Thus, ideal types constitute the theoretical building blocks for the construction of a variety of theoretical models (for example, the routinization of charisma and the rationalization of society— both of which are discussed later in this chapter), and these models are then used to analyze specific historical developments.

Values

Modern sociological thinking in America on the role of values in the social sciences has been shaped to a large degree by an interpretation, often simplistic and erroneous, of Weber's notion of *value-free* sociology (Hennis, 1994; McFalls, 2007). A common perception of Weber's view is that social scientists should *not* let their personal values influence their scientific research in any way. As we will see, Weber's work on values is far more complicated and should not be reduced to the simplistic notion that values should be kept out of sociology (Tribe, 1989:3).

Values and Teaching

Weber (1903–1917/1949) was most clear about the need for teachers to control their personal values in the classroom. From his point of view, academicians have a perfect right to express their personal values freely in speeches, in the press, and so forth, but the academic lecture hall is different. Weber was opposed to those teachers who preached "their evaluations on ultimate questions 'in the name of science' in governmentally privileged lecture halls in which they are neither controlled, checked by discussion, nor subject to contradiction. . . . The lecture hall should be held separate from the arena of public discussion" (1903–1917/1949:4). The most important difference between a public speech and an academic lecture lies in the nature of the audience. A crowd watching a public speaker has chosen to be there and can leave at any time. But students, if they want to succeed, have little choice but to listen attentively to their professor's value-laden positions. There is little ambiguity in this aspect of Weber's position on value-freedom. The academician is to express "facts," not personal values, in the classroom. Although teachers may be tempted to insert values because they make a course more interesting, teachers should be wary of employing values, because such values will "weaken the students' taste for sober empirical analysis" (Weber, 1903–1917/1949:9). The only question is whether it is realistic to think that professors could eliminate most values from their presentations. Weber could adopt this position because he believed it possible to separate fact and value. However, Marx would disagree because in his view fact and value are intertwined, dialectically interrelated.

Values and Research

Weber's position on the place of values in social research is far more ambiguous. Weber did believe in the ability to separate fact from value, and this view could be extended to the research world: "Investigator and teacher should keep unconditionally separate the establishment of empirical facts . . . and *his* own personal evaluations, i.e., his evaluation of these facts as satisfactory or unsatisfactory" (1903–1917/1949:11). He often differentiated between existential knowledge of what is and normative knowledge of what ought to be (Weber, 1903–1917/1949). For example, on the founding of the German Sociological Society, he said: "The Association rejects, in principle and definitely, all propaganda for action-oriented ideas from its midst." Instead, the association was pointed in the direction of the study of "what is, why something is the way it is, for what historical and social reasons" (G. Roth, 1968:5).

However, several facts point in a different direction and show that despite the evidence described, Weber did not operate with the simplistic view that values should be totally eliminated from social research. While, as we will see, Weber perceived a role for values in a specific aspect of the research process, he thought that they should be kept out of the actual collection of research data. By this Weber meant that we should employ the regular procedures of scientific investigation, such as accurate observation and systematic comparison.

Values are to be restricted to the time before social research begins. They should shape the selection of what we choose to study. Weber's (1903–1917/1949:21) ideas on the role of values prior to social research are captured in his concept of *value-relevance*. As with many of Weber's methodological concepts, value-relevance is derived from the work of the German historicist Heinrich Rickert, for whom it involved "a selection of those parts of empirical reality which for human beings embody one or several of those general cultural values which are held by people in the society in which the scientific observers live" (Burger, 1976:36). In historical research, this would mean that the choice of objects to study would be made on the basis of what is considered important in the particular society in which the researchers live. That is, they choose what to study of the past on the basis of the contemporary value system. In his specific case, Weber wrote of value-relevance from the "standpoint of the interests of the modern European" (1903–1917/1949:30). For example, bureaucracy was a very important part of the German society of Weber's time, and he chose, as a result, to study that phenomenon (or the lack of it) in various historical settings.

Thus, to Weber, value judgments are not to be withdrawn completely from scientific discourse. Although Weber was opposed to confusing fact and value, he did not believe that values should be excised from the social sciences: "An *attitude of moral indifference* has no connection with *scientific* 'objectivity'" (1903–1917/1949:60). He was prepared to admit that values have a certain place, though he warned researchers to be careful about the role of values: "It should be constantly made clear . . . exactly at which point the scientific investigator becomes silent and the evaluating and acting person begins to speak" (Weber, 1903–1917/1949:60). When expressing value positions, sociological researchers must always keep themselves and their audiences aware of those positions.

There is a gap between what Weber said and what he actually did. Weber was not afraid to express a value judgment, even in the midst of the analysis of historical data. For example, he said that the Roman state suffered from a convulsive sickness of its social body. It can be argued that in Weber's actual work values not only were a basic device for selecting subjects to study but also were involved in the acquisition of meaningful knowledge of the social world. Gary Abraham (1992) has made the point that Weber's work, especially his views on Judaism as a world religion, was distorted by his values. In his sociology of religion (discussed later in this chapter), Weber termed the Jews "pariah people." Weber traced this position of outsider more to the desire of Jews to segregate themselves than to their exclusion by the rest of society. Thus Weber, accepting the general view of the day, argued that Jews would need to surrender Judaism in order to be assimilated into German society. Abraham argues that this sort of bias affected not only Weber's ideas on Judaism, but his work in general. This casts further doubt on Weber as a "value-free" sociologist, as well as on the conventional view of Weber as a liberal thinker. As Abraham says, "Max Weber was probably as close to tolerant liberalism as majority Germany could offer at the time" (1992:22). Weber was more of a nationalist supporting the assimilation of minority groups than he was a classical liberal favoring pluralism, and those values had a profound effect on his work (G. Roth, 2000).

Most American sociologists regard Weber as an exponent of value-free sociology. The truth is that most American sociologists themselves subscribe to the idea of value-freedom, and they find it useful to invoke Weber's name in support of their position. As we have seen, however, Weber's work is studded with values.

One other aspect of Weber's work on values worth noting is his ideas on the role of the social sciences in helping people make choices among various ultimate value positions. Basically, Weber's view is that there is *no* way of scientifically choosing among alternative value positions. Thus, social scientists cannot presume to make such choices for people. "The social sciences, which are strictly empirical sciences, are the least fitted to presume to save the individual the difficulty of making a choice" (Weber, 1903–1917/1949:19). The social scientist can derive certain factual conclusions from social research, but this research cannot tell people what they "ought" to do. Empirical research can help people choose an adequate means to an end, but it cannot help them choose that end as opposed to other ends. Weber says, "It can never be the task of an empirical science to provide binding norms and ideals from which directions for immediate practical activity can be derived" (1903–1917/1949:52).

Substantive Sociology

We turn now to Weber's substantive sociology. We begin, as did Weber in his monumental *Economy and Society,* at the levels of action and interaction, but we will soon encounter the basic paradox in Weber's work: despite his seeming commitment to a sociology of small-scale processes, his work is primarily at the large-scale levels of the social world. (Many Weberians would disagree with this portrayal of paradox in Weber's work. Kalberg [1994], for example, argues that Weber offers a more fully integrated micro-macro, or agency-structure, theory.)

What Is Sociology?

In articulating his view on sociology, Weber often took a stance against the large-scale evolutionary sociology, the organicism, that was preeminent in the field at the time. For example, Weber said: "I became one [a sociologist] in order to put an end to collectivist notions. In other words, sociology, too, can only be practiced by proceeding from the action of one or more, few or many, individuals, that means, by employing a strictly 'individualist' method" (G. Roth, 1976:306). Despite his stated adherence to an "individualist" method, Weber was forced to admit that it is impossible to eliminate totally collective ideas from sociology.[4] But even when he admitted the significance of collective concepts, Weber ultimately reduced them to patterns and regularities of individual action: "For the subjective interpretation of action in sociological work these collectivities must be treated as *solely* the resultants and modes of organization of the particular acts of individual persons, since these alone can be treated as agents in a course of subjectively understandable action" (1921/1968:13).

At the individual level, Weber was deeply concerned with meaning, and the way in which it was formed. There seems little doubt that Weber believed in, and intended to undertake, a microsociology. But is that, in fact, what he did? Guenther Roth, one of Weber's foremost interpreters, provides us with an unequivocal answer in his

---

[4] In fact, Weber's ideal types *are* collective concepts.

description of the overall thrust of *Economy and Society:* "the first strictly *empirical comparison of social structure* and normative order in *world-historical* depth" (1968: xxvii). Mary Fulbrook directly addresses the discontinuity in Weber's work:

> Weber's overt emphasis on the importance of [individual] meanings and motives in causal explanation of social action does not correspond adequately with the true mode of explanation involved in his comparative-historical studies of the world religions. Rather, the ultimate level of causal explanation in Weber's substantive writings is that of the social-structural conditions under which certain forms of meaning and motivation can achieve historical efficacy.
>
> (Fulbrook, 1978:71)

Lars Udehn (1981) has cast light on this problem in interpreting Weber's work by distinguishing between Weber's methodology and his substantive concerns and recognizing that there is a conflict or tension between them. In Udehn's view, Weber uses an "individualist and subjectivist methodology" (1981:131). In terms of the latter, Weber is interested in what individuals do and why they do it (their subjective motives). In the former, Weber is interested in reducing collectivities to the actions of individuals. However, in most of his substantive sociology (as we will see), Weber focuses on large-scale structure (such as bureaucracy or capitalism) and is not focally concerned with what individuals do or why they do it.[5] Such structures are not reduced by Weber to the actions of individuals, and the actions of those in them are determined by the structures, not by their motives. There is little doubt that there is an enormous contradiction in Weber's work, and it will concern us through much of this chapter.

With this as background, we are now ready for Weber's definition of *sociology:* "Sociology . . . is a *science* concerning itself with the *interpretive understanding* of *social action* and thereby with a *causal* explanation of its course and consequences" (1921/1968:4). Among the themes discussed earlier that are mentioned or implied in this definition are the following:

Sociology should be a science.
Sociology should be concerned with causality. (Here, apparently, Weber was
     combining sociology and history.)
Sociology should utilize interpretive understanding (*verstehen*).

We are now ready for what Weber meant by social action.

Social Action

Weber's entire sociology, if we accept his words at face value, was based on his conception of social action (S. Turner, 1983). He differentiated between action and purely reactive behavior. The concept of behavior is reserved, then as now, for automatic behavior that involves no thought processes. A stimulus is presented and behavior occurs, with little intervening between stimulus and response. Such behavior was

---

[5] Udehn argues that one exception is Weber's analysis of the behavior of leaders.

not of interest in Weber's sociology. He was concerned with action that clearly involved the intervention of thought processes (and the resulting meaningful action) between the occurrence of a stimulus and the ultimate response. To put it slightly differently, action was said to occur when individuals attached subjective meanings to their action. To Weber, the task of sociological analysis involved "the interpretation of action in terms of its subjective meaning" (1921/1968:8). A good, and more specific, example of Weber's thinking on action is found in his discussion of *economic action,* which he defined as "*a conscious, primary* orientation to economic consideration . . . for what matters is not the objective necessity of making economic provision, but the belief that it is necessary" (1921/1968:64).

In embedding his analysis in mental processes and the resulting meaningful action, Weber (1921/1968) was careful to point out that it is erroneous to regard psychology as the foundation of the sociological interpretation of action. Weber seemed to be making essentially the same point made by Durkheim in discussing at least some nonmaterial social facts. That is, sociologists are interested in mental processes, but this is not the same as psychologists' interest in the mind, personality, and so forth.

Although Weber implied that he had a great concern with mental processes, he actually spent little time on them. Hans Gerth and C. Wright Mills called attention to Weber's lack of concern with mental processes: "Weber sees in the concept of personality a much abused notion referring to a profoundly irrational center of creativity, a center before which analytical inquiry comes to a halt" (1958:55). Schutz (1932/1967) was quite correct when he pointed out that although Weber's work on mental processes is suggestive, it is hardly the basis for a systematic microsociology. But it was the suggestiveness of Weber's work that made him relevant to those who developed theories of individuals and their behavior—symbolic interactionism, phenomenology, and so forth.

In his action theory, Weber's clear intent was to focus on individuals and patterns and regularities of action and not on the collectivity. "Action in the sense of subjectively understandable orientation of behavior exists only as the behavior of one or more *individual* human beings" (Weber, 1921/1968:13). Weber was prepared to admit that for some purposes we may have to treat collectivities as individuals, "but for the subjective interpretation of action in sociological work these collectivities must be treated as *solely* the resultants and modes of organization of the particular acts of individual persons, since these alone can be treated as agents in a course of subjectively understandable action" (1921/1968:13). It would seem that Weber could hardly be more explicit: the sociology of action is ultimately concerned with individuals, *not* collectivities.

Weber utilized his ideal-type methodology to clarify the meaning of *action* by identifying four basic types of action. Not only is this typology significant for understanding what Weber meant by action, but it is also, in part, the basis for Weber's concern with larger social structures and institutions. Of greatest importance is Weber's differentiation between the two basic types of rational action. The first is *means-ends rationality,* or action that is "determined by expectations as to the behavior of objects in the environment and of other human beings; these expectations are used as 'conditions' or 'means' for the attainment of the actor's own rationally pursued and calculated ends" (Weber, 1921/1968:24). The second is *value rationality*, or action that is "determined by a conscious belief in the value for its own sake of some ethical, aesthetic, religious, or other form of behavior, independently of its prospects for success" (Weber, 1921/1968:24–25). *Affectual* action (which was of little concern to Weber) is determined by the emotional state of the actor. *Traditional* action (which was of far greater concern to Weber) is determined by the actor's habitual and customary ways of behaving.

It should be noted that although Weber differentiated four ideal-typical forms of action, he was well aware that any given action usually involves a combination of all four ideal types of action. In addition, Weber argued that sociologists have a much better chance of understanding action of the more rational variety than they do of understanding action dominated by affect or tradition.

We turn now to Weber's thoughts on social stratification, or his famous ideas on class, status, and party (or power). His analysis of stratification is one area in which Weber does operate, at least at first, as an action theorist.

Class, Status, and Party

One important aspect of this analysis is that Weber refused to reduce stratification to economic factors (or class, in Weber's terms) but saw it as multidimensional. Thus, society is stratified on the bases of economics, status, and power. One resulting implication is that people can rank high on one or two of these dimensions of stratification and low on the other (or others), permitting a far more sophisticated analysis of social stratification than is possible when stratification is simply reduced (as it was by some Marxists) to variations in one's economic situation.

Starting with class, Weber adhered to his action orientation by arguing that a class is not a community. Rather, a class is a group of people whose shared situation is a possible, and sometimes frequent, basis for action by the group (K. Smith, 2007). Weber contends that a "class situation" exists when three conditions are met:

(1) A number of people have in common a specific causal component of their life chances, insofar as (2) this component is represented exclusively by economic interests in the possession of goods and opportunities for income, and (3) is represented under the conditions of the commodity or labor markets. This is "class situation."

(Weber, 1921/1968:927)

The concept of "class" refers to any group of people found in the same class situation. Thus a class is *not* a community but merely a group of people in the same economic, or market, situation.

In contrast to class, status does normally refer to communities; status groups are ordinarily communities, albeit rather amorphous ones. "Status situation" is defined by Weber as "every typical component of the life of men that is determined by a specific, positive or negative, social estimation of *honor*" (1921/1968:932). As a general rule, status is associated with a style of life. (Status relates to consumption of goods produced, whereas class relates to economic production.) Those at the top of the status hierarchy have a different lifestyle than do those at the bottom. In this case, lifestyle, or status, is related to class situation. But class and status are not necessarily linked to one another: "Money and an entrepreneurial position are not in themselves status qualifications, although they may lead to them; and the lack of property is not in itself a status disqualification, although this may be a reason for it" (Weber, 1921/1968:306). There is a complex set of relationships between class and status, and it is made even more complicated when we add the dimension of party.

While classes exist in the economic order and status groups in the social order, parties can be found in the political order. To Weber, parties "are always *structures struggling for domination*" (cited in Gerth and Mills, 1958:195; italics added). Thus, parties are the most organized elements of Weber's stratification system. Weber thinks of parties very broadly as including not only those that exist in the state but also those that may exist in a social club. Parties usually, but not always, represent class or status groups. Whatever they represent, parties are oriented to the attainment of power.

While Weber remained close to his action approach in his ideas on social stratification, these ideas already indicate a movement in the direction of macro-level communities and structures. In most of his other work, Weber focused on such large-scale units of analysis. Not that Weber lost sight of the action; the actor simply moved from being the focus of his concern to being largely a dependent variable determined by a variety of large-scale forces. For example, as we will see, Weber believed that individual Calvinists are impelled to act in various ways by the norms, values, and beliefs of their religion, but his focus was not on the individual but on the collective forces that impel the actor.

Structures of Authority

Weber's sociological interest in the structures of authority was motivated, at least in part, by his political interests (Eliaeson, 2000). Weber was no political radical; in fact, he was often called the "bourgeois Marx" to reflect the similarities in the intellectual interests of Marx and Weber as well as their very different political orientations. Although Weber was almost as critical of modern capitalism as Marx was, he did not advocate revolution. He wanted to change society gradually, not overthrow it. He had little faith in the ability of the masses to create a "better" society. But Weber also saw little hope in the middle classes, which he felt were dominated by shortsighted, petty bureaucrats. Weber was critical of authoritarian political leaders like Bismarck. Nevertheless, for Weber the hope—if indeed he had any hope—lay with the great political leaders rather than with the masses or the bureaucrats. Along with his faith in political leaders went his unswerving nationalism. He placed the nation above all else: "The vital interests of the nation stand, of course, above democracy and parliamentarianism" (Weber, 1921/1968:1383). Weber preferred democracy as a political form not because he believed in the masses but because it offered maximum dynamism and the best milieu to generate political leaders (Mommsen, 1974). Weber noted that authority structures exist in every social institution, and his political views were related to his analysis of these structures in all settings. Of course, they were most relevant to his views on the polity.

Weber began his analysis of authority structures in a way that was consistent with his assumptions about the nature of action. He defined *domination* as the "probability that certain specific commands (or all commands) will be obeyed by a given group of persons" (Weber, 1921/1968:212). Domination can have a variety of bases, legitimate as well as illegitimate, but what mainly interested Weber were the legitimate forms of domination, or what he called *authority* (Leggewie, 2005). What concerned Weber, and what played a central role in much of his sociology, were the three bases on which authority is made legitimate to followers—rational, traditional, and charismatic. In defining these three bases, Weber remained fairly close to his ideas on individual action, but he rapidly moved to the large-scale structures of authority.

Authority legitimized on *rational* grounds rests "on a belief in the legality of enacted rules and the right of those elevated to authority under such rules to issue commands" (Weber, 1921/1968:215). Authority legitimized on *traditional* grounds is based on "an established belief in the sanctity of immemorial traditions and the legitimacy of those exercising authority under them" (Weber, 1921/1968:215). Finally, authority legitimized by *charisma*[6] rests on the devotion of followers to the exceptional sanctity, exemplary character, heroism, or special powers (for example, the ability to work miracles) of leaders, as well as on the normative order sanctioned by them. All these modes of legitimizing authority clearly imply individual actors, thought processes (beliefs), and actions. But from this point, Weber, in his thinking about authority, did move quite far from an individual action base, as we will see when we discuss the authority structures erected on the basis of these types of legitimacy.

Rational-Legal Authority

Rational-legal authority can take a variety of structural forms, but the form that most interested Weber was *bureaucracy,* which he considered "the purest type of exercise of legal authority" (1921/1968:220).

Ideal-Typical Bureaucracy   Weber depicted bureaucracies in ideal-typical terms:

> From a purely technical point of view, a bureaucracy is capable of attaining the highest degree of efficiency, and is in this sense formally the most rational known means of exercising authority over human beings. It is superior to any other form in precision, in stability, in the stringency of its discipline, and in its reliability. It thus makes possible a particularly high degree of calculability of results for the heads of the organization and for those acting in relation to it. It is finally superior both in intensive efficiency and in the scope of its operations and is formally capable of application to all kinds of administrative tasks.
>
> (Weber, 1921/1968:223)

Despite his discussion of the positive characteristics of bureaucracies, here and elsewhere in his work, there is a fundamental ambivalence in his attitude toward them. Although he detailed their advantages, he was well aware of their problems. Weber expressed various reservations about bureaucratic organizations. For example,

---

[6] The term *charisma* is used in Weber's work in a variety of other ways and contexts as well; see Miyahara (1983).

he was cognizant of the "red tape" that often makes dealing with bureaucracies so trying and so difficult. His major fear, however, was that the rationalization that dominates all aspects of bureaucratic life was a threat to individual liberty. As Weber put it:

> No machinery in the world functions so precisely as this apparatus of men and, moreover, so cheaply. . . . Rational calculation . . . reduces every worker to a cog in this bureaucratic machine and, seeing himself in this light, he will merely ask how to transform himself into a somewhat bigger cog. . . . The passion for bureaucratization drives us to despair.

> (Weber, 1921/1968:liii)

Weber was appalled by the effects of bureaucratization and, more generally, of the rationalization of the world of which bureaucratization is but one component, but he saw no way out. He described bureaucracies as "escape proof," "practically unshatterable," and among the hardest institutions to destroy once they are established. Along the same lines, he felt that individual bureaucrats could not "squirm out" of the bureaucracy once they were "harnessed" in it (for a less ominous view of bureaucratization, see Klagge, 1997). Weber concluded that "the future belongs to bureaucratization" (1921/1968:1401), and time has borne out his prediction.

Weber would say that his depiction of the advantages of bureaucracy is part of his ideal-typical image of the way it operates. The ideal-typical bureaucracy is a purposeful exaggeration of the rational characteristics of bureaucracies. Such an exaggerated model is useful for heuristic purposes and for studies of organizations in the real world, but it is not to be mistaken for a realistic depiction of the way bureaucracies actually operate.

Weber distinguished the ideal-typical bureaucracy from the ideal-typical bureaucrat. He conceived of bureaucracies as structures and of bureaucrats as positions within those structures. He did *not,* as his action orientation might lead us to expect, offer a social psychology of organizations or of the individuals who inhabit those bureaucracies (as modern symbolic interactionists might).

The ideal-typical bureaucracy is a type of organization. Its basic units are offices organized in a hierarchical manner with rules, functions, written documents, and means of compulsion. All these are, to varying degrees, large-scale structures that represent the thrust of Weber's thinking. He could, after all, have constructed an ideal-typical bureaucracy that focused on the thoughts and actions of individuals within the bureaucracy. There is a whole school of thought in the study of organizations that focuses precisely on this level rather than on the structures of bureaucracies (see, for example, Blankenship, 1977).

The following are the major characteristics of the ideal-typical bureaucracy:

1. It consists of a continuous organization of official functions (offices) bound by rules.
2. Each office has a specified sphere of competence. The office carries with it a set of obligations to perform various functions, the authority to carry out these functions, and the means of compulsion required to do the job.
3. The offices are organized into a hierarchical system.

4. The offices may carry with them technical qualifications that require that the participants obtain suitable training.
5. The staff that fills these offices does not own the means of production associated with them;[7] staff members are provided with the use of those things that they need to do the job.
6. The incumbent is not allowed to appropriate the position; it always remains part of the organization.
7. Administrative acts, decisions, and rules are formulated and recorded in writing.

Any Alternatives?   A bureaucracy is one of the rational structures that is playing an ever-increasing role in modern society, but one may wonder whether there is any alternative to the bureaucratic structure. Weber's clear and unequivocal answer was that there is no possible alternative: "The needs of mass administration make it today completely indispensable. The choice is only between bureaucracy and dilettantism in the field of administration" (1921/1968:223).

Although we might admit that bureaucracy is an intrinsic part of modern capitalism, we might ask whether a socialist society might be different. Is it possible to create a socialist society without bureaucracies and bureaucrats? Once again, Weber was unequivocal: "When those subject to bureaucratic control seek to escape the influence of existing bureaucratic apparatus, this is normally possible only by creating an organization of their own which is equally subject to the process of bureaucratization" (1921/1968:224). In fact, Weber believed that in the case of socialism we would see an increase, not a decrease, in bureaucratization. If socialism were to achieve a level of efficiency comparable to capitalism, "it would mean a tremendous increase in the importance of professional bureaucrats" (Weber, 1921/1968:224). In capitalism, at least the owners are not bureaucrats and therefore would be able to restrain the bureaucrats, but in socialism, even the top-level leaders would be bureaucrats. Weber thus believed that even with its problems "capitalism presented the best chances for the preservation of individual freedom and creative leadership in a bureaucratic world" (Mommsen, 1974:xv). We are once again at a key theme in Weber's work: his view that there is really no hope for a better world. Socialists can, in Weber's view, only make things worse by expanding the degree of bureaucratization in society. Weber noted: "Not summer's bloom lies ahead of us, but rather a polar night of icy darkness and hardness, no matter which group may triumph externally now" (cited in Gerth and Mills, 1958:128).

Any Hope?   A ray of hope in Weber's work—and it is a small one—is that professionals who stand outside the bureaucratic system can control it to some degree. In this category, Weber included professional politicians, scientists, intellectuals (Sadri, 1992), and even capitalists, as well as the supreme heads of the bureaucracies. For example, Weber said that politicians "must be the countervailing force against bureaucratic domination" (1921/1968:1417). His famous essay "Politics as a Vocation" is

---

[7] Here and elsewhere in his work Weber adopts a Marxian interest in the means of production. This is paralleled by his concern with alienation, not only in the economic sector but throughout social life (science, politics, and so forth).

basically a plea for the development of political leaders with a calling to oppose the rule of bureaucracies and of bureaucrats. But in the end these appear to be rather feeble hopes. In fact, a good case can be made that these professionals are simply another aspect of the rationalization process and that their development serves only to accelerate that process (Nass, 1986; Ritzer, 1975c; Ritzer and Walczak, 1988).

In Weber's "'Churches' and 'Sects' in North America: An Ecclesiastical Socio-Political Sketch" (1906/1985), Colin Loader and Jeffrey Alexander (1985) see a fore-runner of Weber's thoughts on the hope provided by an ethic of responsibility in the face of the expansion of bureaucratization. American sects such as the Quakers prac-tice an ethic of responsibility by combining rationality and larger values. Rogers Brubaker defines the *ethic of responsibility* as "the passionate commitment to ultimate values with the dispassionate analysis of alternative means of pursuing them" (1984:108). He contrasts this to the *ethic of conviction,* in which a rational choice of means is foregone and the actor orients "his action to the realization of some absolute value or unconditional demand" (1984:106; for a somewhat different view, see N. Gane, 1997). The ethic of conviction often involves a withdrawal from the rational world, whereas the ethic of responsibility involves a struggle within that world for greater humanness. The ethic of responsibility provides at least a modicum of hope in the face of the onslaught of rationalization and bureaucratization.

Traditional Authority

Whereas rational-legal authority stems from the legitimacy of a rational-legal system, traditional authority is based on a claim by the leaders, and a belief on the part of the followers, that there is virtue in the sanctity of age-old rules and powers. The leader in such a system is not a superior but a personal master. The administrative staff, if any, consists not of officials but mainly of personal retainers. In Weber's words, "Per-sonal loyalty, not the official's impersonal duty, determines the relations of the admin-istrative staff to the master" (1921/1968:227). Although the bureaucratic staff owes its allegiance and obedience to enacted rules and to the leader, who acts in their name, the staff of the traditional leader obeys because the leader carries the weight of tradition—he or she has been chosen for that position in the traditional manner.

Weber was interested in the staff of the traditional leader and how it measured up to the ideal-typical bureaucratic staff. He concluded that it was lacking on a num-ber of counts. The traditional staff lacks offices with clearly defined spheres of com-petence that are subject to impersonal rules. It also does not have a rational ordering of relations of superiority and inferiority; it lacks a clear hierarchy. There is no regu-lar system of appointment and promotion on the basis of free contracts. Technical training is not a regular requirement for obtaining a position or an appointment. Appointments do not carry with them fixed salaries paid in money.

Weber also used his ideal-type methodology to analyze historically the different forms of traditional authority. He differentiated between two very early forms of traditional authority. A *gerontocracy* involves rule by elders, whereas *primary patri-archalism* involves leaders who inherit their positions. Both of these forms have a supreme chief but lack an administrative staff. A more modern form is *patrimonialism,* which is traditional domination with an administration and a military force that are purely personal instruments of the master (Andrew Eisenberg, 1998). Still more modern is *feudalism,* which limits the discretion of the master through the development of more routinized, even contractual, relationships between leader and subordinate. This restraint, in turn, leads to more stabilized power positions than exist in patrimonialism. All four of these forms may be seen as structural variations of traditional authority, and all of them differ significantly from rational-legal authority.

Weber saw structures of traditional authority, in any form, as barriers to the development of rationality. This is our first encounter with an overriding theme in Weber's work—factors that facilitate or impede the development of (formal) rationality. Over and over we find Weber concerned, as he was here, with the structural factors conducive to rationality in the Western world and the structural and cultural impediments to the development of a similar rationality throughout the rest of the world. In this specific case, Weber argued that the structures and practices of traditional authority constitute a barrier to the rise of rational economic structures—in particular, capitalism—as well as to various other components of a rational society. Even patrimonialism—a more modern form of traditionalism—while permitting the development of certain forms of "primitive" capitalism, does not allow for the rise of the highly rational type of capitalism characteristic of the modern West.

Charismatic Authority

Charisma is a concept that has come to be used very broadly (Adair-Toteff, 2005; Oakes, 1997; S. Turner, 2003; Werbner and Basu, 1998). The news media and the general public are quick to point to a politician, a movie star, or a rock musician as a charismatic individual. By this they most often mean that the person in question is endowed with extraordinary qualities. The concept of charisma plays an important role in the work of Max Weber, but his conception of it was very different from that held by most laypeople today. Although Weber did not deny that a charismatic leader may have outstanding characteristics, his sense of charisma was more dependent on the group of disciples and the way that they *define* the charismatic leader (D. N. Smith, 1998). To put Weber's position bluntly, if the disciples define a leader as charismatic, then he or she is likely to be a charismatic leader irrespective of whether he or she actually possesses any outstanding traits. A charismatic leader, then, can be someone who is quite ordinary. What is crucial is the process by which such a leader is set apart from ordinary people and treated as if endowed with supernatural, superhuman, or at least exceptional powers or qualities that are not accessible to the ordinary person (Miyahara, 1983).

Charisma and Revolution   To Weber, charisma was a revolutionary force, one of the most important revolutionary forces in the social world. Whereas traditional authority clearly is inherently conservative, the rise of a charismatic leader may well pose a threat to that system (as well as to a rational-legal system) and lead to a dramatic change in that system. What distinguishes charisma as a revolutionary force is that it leads to changes in the minds of actors; it causes a "subjective or internal reorientation." Such changes may lead to "a radical alteration of the central attitudes and direction of action with a completely new orientation of all attitudes toward different problems of the world" (Weber, 1921/1968:245). Although Weber was here addressing changes in the thoughts and actions of individuals, such changes are clearly reduced to the status of dependent variables. Weber focused on changes in the structure of authority, that is, the rise of charismatic authority. When such a new authority structure emerges, it is likely to change people's thoughts and actions dramatically.

The other major revolutionary force in Weber's theoretical system, and the one with which he was much more concerned, is (formal) rationality. Whereas charisma is an internal revolutionary force that changes the minds of actors, Weber saw (formal) rationality as an external revolutionary force changing the structures of society first and then ultimately the thoughts and actions of individuals. There is more to be said about rationality as a revolutionary force later, but this closes the discussion of charisma as a revolutionary factor because Weber had very little to say about it. Weber was interested in the revolutionary character of charisma as well as its structure and the necessity that its basic character be transformed and routinized in order for it to survive as a system of authority.

Charismatic Organizations and the Routinization of Charisma   In his analysis of charisma, Weber began, as he did with traditional authority, with the ideal-typical bureaucracy. He sought to determine to what degree the structure of charismatic authority, with its disciples and staff, differs from the bureaucratic system. Compared to that of the ideal-typical bureaucracy, the staff of the charismatic leader is lacking on virtually all counts. The staff members are not technically trained but are chosen instead for their possession of charismatic qualities or, at least, of qualities similar to those possessed by the charismatic leader. The offices they occupy form no clear hierarchy. Their work does not constitute a career, and there are no promotions, clear appointments, or dismissals. The charismatic leader is free to intervene whenever he or she feels that the staff cannot handle a situation. The organization has no formal rules, no established administrative organs, and no precedents to guide new judgments. In these and other ways, Weber found the staff of the charismatic leader to be "greatly inferior" to the staff in a bureaucratic form of organization.

Weber's interest in the organization behind the charismatic leader and the staff that inhabits it led him to the question of what happens to charismatic authority when the leader dies. After all, a charismatic system is inherently fragile; it would seem to be able to survive only as long as the charismatic leader lives. But is it possible for such an organization to live after the leader dies? The answer to this question is of the greatest consequence to the staff members of the charismatic leader, for they are likely to live on after the leader dies. They are also likely to have a vested interest in the continued existence of the organization: if the organization ceases to exist, they are out of work. Thus the challenge for the staff is to create a situation in which charisma in some adulterated form persists even after the leader's death. It is a difficult struggle because, for Weber, charisma is by its nature unstable; it exists in its pure form only as long as the charismatic leader lives.

In order to cope with the departure of the charismatic leader, the staff (as well as the followers) may adopt a variety of strategies to create a more lasting organization. The staff may search for a new charismatic leader, but even if the search is successful, the new leader is unlikely to have the same aura as his or her predecessor. A set of rules also may be developed that allows the group to identify future charismatic leaders. But such rules rapidly become tradition, and what was charismatic leadership is on the way toward becoming traditional authority. In any case, the nature of leadership is radically changed as the purely personal character of charisma is eliminated. Still another technique is to allow the charismatic leader to designate his or her successor and thereby to transfer charisma symbolically to the next in line. Again it is questionable whether this is ever very successful or whether it can be successful in the long run. Another strategy is having the staff designate a successor and having its choice accepted by the larger community. The staff could also create ritual tests, with the new charismatic leader being the one who successfully undergoes the tests. However, all these efforts are doomed to failure. In the long run, charisma cannot be routinized and still be charisma; it must be transformed into either traditional or rational-legal authority (or into some sort of institutionalized charisma like the Catholic Church).

Indeed, we find a basic theory of history in Weber's work. If successful, charisma almost immediately moves in the direction of routinization. But once routinized, charisma is en route to becoming either traditional or rational-legal authority. Once it achieves one of those states, the stage is set for the cycle to begin all over again. However, despite a general adherence to a cyclical theory, Weber believed that a basic change has occurred in the modern world and that we are more and more likely to see charisma routinized in the direction of rational-legal authority. Furthermore, he saw rational systems of authority as stronger and as increasingly impervious to charismatic movements. The modern, rationalized world may well mean the death of charisma as a significant revolutionary force (Seligman, 1993). Weber contended that rationality—not charisma—is the most irresistible and important revolutionary force in the modern world.

Types of Authority and the "Real World"

In this section, the three types of authority are discussed as ideal types, but Weber was well aware that in the real world, any specific form of authority involves a combination of all three. Thus we can think of Franklin D. Roosevelt as a president of the United States who ruled on all three bases. He was elected president in accordance with a series of rational-legal principles. By the time he was elected president for the fourth time, a good part of this rule had traditional elements. Finally, many disciples and followers regarded him as a charismatic leader (McCann, 1997).

Although the three forms of authority are presented here as parallel structures, in the real world there is constant tension and, sometimes, conflict among them. The charismatic leader is a constant threat to the other forms of authority. Once in power, the charismatic leader must address the threat posed to him or her by the other two forms. Even if charismatic authority is successfully routinized, there then arises the problem of maintaining its dynamism and its original revolutionary qualities. Then there is the conflict produced by the constant development of rational-legal authority and the threat it poses to the continued existence of the other forms. If Weber was right, however, we might face a future in which the tension among the three forms of authority is eliminated, a world of the uncontested hegemony of the rational-legal system. This is the "iron cage" of a totally rationalized society that worried Weber so much. In such a society, the only hope lies with isolated charismatic individuals who manage somehow to avoid the coercive power of society. But a small number of isolated individuals hardly represent a significant hope in the face of an increasingly powerful bureaucratic machine.

Rationalization

There has been a growing realization in recent years that rationalization lies at the heart of Weber's substantive sociology (Brubaker, 1984; R. Collins, 1980; Eisen, 1978; Kalberg, 1980, 1990, 2011; D. Levine, 1981a; Ritzer, 2013; Scaff, 1989, 2005; Schluchter, 1981; Sica, 1988). As Kalberg put it, "It *is* the case that Weber's interest in a broad and overarching theme—the 'specific and peculiar "rationalism" of Western culture' and its unique origins and development—stands at the center of his sociology" (1994:18). However, it is difficult to extract a clear definition of *rationalization* from Weber's work.[8] In fact, Weber operated with a number of different definitions of the term, and he often failed to specify which definition he was using in a particular discussion (Brubaker, 1984:1). As we saw earlier, Weber did define *rationality;* indeed, he differentiated between two types—means–ends and value rationality. However, these concepts refer to types of *action*. They are the basis of, but not coterminous with, Weber's larger-scale sense of rationalization. Weber is interested in far more than fragmented action orientations; his main concern is with regularities and patterns of action within civilizations, institutions, organizations, strata, classes, and groups. Donald Levine (1981a) argues that Weber is interested in "objectified" rationality, that is, action that is in accord with some process of external systematization. Stephen Kalberg (1980) performs a useful service by identifying four basic types of ("objective") rationality in Weber's work. (Levine offers a very similar differentiation.) These types of rationality were "the basic heuristic tools [Weber] employed to scrutinize the historical fates of rationalization as sociocultural processes" (Kalberg, 1980:1172; for an application, see Takayama, 1998).

Types of Rationality

The first type is *practical rationality,* which is defined by Kalberg as "every way of life that views and judges worldly activity in relation to the individual's purely pragmatic and egoistic interests" (1980:1151). People who practice practical rationality accept given realities and merely calculate the most expedient ways of dealing with the difficulties that they present. This type of rationality arose with the severing of the bonds of primitive magic, and it exists trans-civilizationally and trans-historically; that is, it is not restricted to the modern Occident. This type of rationality stands in opposition to anything that threatens to transcend everyday routine. It leads people to

---

[8] It might be argued that there is no single definition because the various forms of rationality are so different from one another that they preclude such a definition. We would like to thank Jere Cohen for this point.

distrust all impractical values, either religious or secular-utopian, as well as the theoretical rationality of the intellectuals, the type of rationality to which we now turn.

Theoretical rationality involves a cognitive effort to master reality through increasingly abstract concepts rather than through action. It involves such abstract cognitive processes as logical deduction, induction, attribution of causality, and the like. This type of rationality was accomplished early in history by sorcerers and ritualistic priests and later by philosophers, judges, and scientists. Unlike practical rationality, theoretical rationality leads the actor to transcend daily realities in a quest to understand the world as a meaningful cosmos. Like practical rationality, it is trans-civilizational and trans-historical. The effect of intellectual rationality on action is limited. In that it involves cognitive processes, it need not affect action taken, and it has the potential to introduce new patterns of action only indirectly.

Substantive rationality (like practical rationality but *not* theoretical rationality) directly orders action into patterns through clusters of values. Substantive rationality involves a choice of means to ends within the context of a system of values. One value system is no more (substantively) rational than another. Thus, this type of rationality also exists trans-civilizationally and trans-historically, wherever consistent value postulates exist.

Finally, and most important from Kalberg's point of view, is *formal rationality,* which involves means–ends calculation (Cockerham, Abel, and Luschen, 1993). But whereas in practical rationality this calculation occurs in reference to pragmatic self-interests, in formal rationality it occurs with reference to "universally applied rules, laws, and regulations." As Brubaker puts it, "Common to the rationality of industrial capitalism, formalistic law and bureaucratic administration is its objectified, institutionalized, supra-individual form; in each sphere, rationality is embodied in the social structure and confronts individuals as something external to them" (1984:9). Weber makes this quite clear in the specific case of bureaucratic rationalization:

> Bureaucratic rationalization . . . revolutionizes with *technical means,* in principle,
> as does every economic reorganization, "from without": It *first* changes the material
> and social orders, and *through* them the people, by changing the conditions of
> adaptation, and perhaps the opportunities for adaptation, through a rational
> determination of means and ends.
>
>   (Weber, 1921/1968:1116)

Although all the other types of rationality are trans-civilizational and epoch-transcending, formal rationality arose only in the West with the coming of industrialization. The universally applied rules, laws, and regulations that characterize formal rationality in the West are found particularly in the economic, legal, and scientific institutions, as well as in the bureaucratic form of domination. Thus, we have already encountered formal rationality in our discussion of rational-legal authority and the bureaucracy.

An Overarching Theory?

Although Weber had a complex, multifaceted sense of rationalization, he used it most powerfully and meaningfully in his image of the modern Western world, especially in the capitalistic economy (R. Collins, 1980; Weber, 1927/1981) and bureaucratic organizations (I. Cohen, 1981:xxxi; Weber, 1921/1968:956–1005), as an iron cage (Mitzman, 1969/1971; Tiryakian, 1981) of formally rational structures. Weber described capitalism and bureaucracies as "two great rationalizing forces" (1921/1968:698).[9] In fact, Weber saw capitalism and bureaucracies as being derived from the same basic sources (especially innerworldly asceticism), involving similarly rational and methodical action, and reinforcing one another and in the process furthering the rationalization of the Occident.[10] In Weber's (1921/1968:227, 994) view, the only real rival to the bureaucrat in technical expertise and factual knowledge was the capitalist.

However, if we take Weber at his word, it is difficult to argue that he had an overarching theory of rationalization. He rejected the idea of "general evolutionary sequence" (Weber, 1927/1981:34). He was critical of thinkers like Hegel and Marx, who he felt offered general, teleological theories of society. In his own work, he tended to shy away from studies of, or proclamations about, whole societies. Instead, he tended to focus, in turn, on social structures and institutions such as bureaucracy, stratification, law, the city, religion, the polity, and the economy. Lacking a sense of the whole, he was unlikely to make global generalizations, especially about future directions. Furthermore, the rationalization process that Weber described in one social structure or institution was usually quite different from the rationalization of another structure or institution. As Weber put it, the process of rationalization assumes "unusually varied forms" (1922–1923/1958:293; see also Weber, 1921/1958:30; 1904–1905/1958:78), and "the history of rationalism shows a development which by no means follows parallel lines in the various departments of life" (1904–1905/1958:77; see also Brubaker, 1984:9; Kalberg, 1980:1147). Weber also looked at many things other than rationalization in his various comparative-historical studies (Kalberg, 1994).

This being said, it is clear that Weber does have a deep concern for the overarching effect of the formal rationalization of the economy and bureaucracies on the Western world (Brubaker, 1984). For example, in *Economy and Society,* Weber says:

> This whole process of rationalization in the factory as elsewhere, and especially in the bureaucratic state machine, parallels the centralization of the material implements of organization in the hands of the master. Thus, discipline inexorably takes over ever larger areas as the satisfaction of political and economic needs is increasingly rationalized. This universal phenomenon more and more restricts the importance of charisma and of individually differentiated conduct.
>
> (Weber, 1921/1968:1156)

Formal rationalization will be our main, but certainly not only, concern in this section.

---

[9] In the 1920 introduction to *The Protestant Ethic and the Spirit of Capitalism,* Weber focused on "a specially trained organization of officials" (bureaucracy) in his discussion of rationalization, but he also mentioned capitalism in the same context as "the most fateful force in our modern life."

[10] Of course, these are not completely distinct because large capitalistic enterprises are one of the places in which we find bureaucracies (Weber, 1922–1923/1958:299). However, Weber also sees the possibility that bureaucracies can stand in opposition to, can impede, capitalism.

Formal and Substantive Rationality

Various efforts have been made to delineate the basic characteristics of formal rationality. In Ritzer's view, formal rationality may be defined in terms of six basic characteristics (Ritzer, 1983, 2013): (1) Formally rational structures and institutions emphasize *calculability,* or those things that can be counted or quantified. (2) There is a focus on *efficiency,* on finding the best means to a given end. (3) There is great concern with ensuring *predictability,* or that things operate in the same way from one time or place to another. (4) A formally rational system progressively reduces human technology and ultimately *replaces human technology with nonhuman technology.* Nonhuman technologies (such as computerized systems) are viewed as more calculable, more efficient, and more predictable than human technologies. (5) Formally rational systems seek to gain *control* over an array of uncertainties, especially the uncertainties posed by human beings who work in, or are served by, them. (6) Rational systems tend to have a series of *irrational consequences* for the people involved with them and for the systems themselves, as well as for the larger society (Sica, 1988). One of the irrationalities of rationality, from Weber's point of view, is that the world tends to become less enchanted, less magical, and ultimately less meaningful to people (MacKinnon, 2001; Ritzer, 2010a; M. Schneider, 1993).[11]

Formal rationality stands in contrast to all the other types of rationality but is especially in conflict with substantive rationality (Brubaker, 1984:4). Kalberg argues that Weber believed that the conflict between these two types of rationality played "a particularly fateful role in the unfolding of rationalization processes in the West" (1980:1157).

In addition to differentiating among the four types of rationality, Kalberg deals with their capacity to introduce methodical ways of life. Practical rationality lacks this ability because it involves reactions to situations rather than efforts to order them. Theoretical rationality is cognitive and therefore has a highly limited ability to suppress practical rationality and seems to be more of an end product than a producer. To Weber, substantive rationality is the *only* type with the "potential to introduce methodical ways of life" (Kalberg, 1980:1165). Thus, in the West, a particular substantive rationality with an emphasis on a methodical way of life—Calvinism— subjugated practical rationality and led to the development of formal rationality.

Weber's fear was that substantive rationality was becoming less significant than the other types of rationality, especially formal rationality, in the West. Thus practitioners of formal rationality, like the bureaucrat and the capitalist, were coming to dominate the West, and the type that "embodied Western civilization's highest ideals: the autonomous and free individual whose actions were given continuity by their reference to ultimate values" (Kalberg, 1980:1176) was fading away (for an alternative view on this, see Titunik, 1997).

---

[11] However, Mark Schneider argues that Weber overstated the case and that in spite of rationalization, parts of the world continue to be enchanted: "Enchantment, we suggest, is part of our normal condition, and far from having fled with the rise of science [one of Weber's rationalized systems], it continues to exist (though often unrecognized) wherever our capacity to explain the world's behavior is slim, that is, where neither science nor practical knowledge seem of much utility" (1993:x). Ritzer (2010a) argues that disenchanted realms will try to find ways to, at least, temporarily be reenchanted. This is particularly true of consumer-driven economic systems that depend on enchanted consumers.

Rationalization in Various Social Settings

Although the differences among Weber's four types of rationalization have been emphasized here, there are a number of commonalities among them. Thus, as we move from setting to setting, we, like Weber, focus sometimes on rationalization in general and at other times on the specific types of rationalization.

Economy   Engerman (2000:258) argues that, although this is rarely cited, "Weber laid out much of the methodological underpinning to what is conventionally called neoclassical economics." This includes the ideal type, methodological individualism, and, most important, rationality and rationalization. The most systematic presentation of Weber's thoughts on the rationalization of the economic institution is to be found in his *General Economic History*. Weber's concern is with the development of the rational capitalistic economy in the Occident, which is a specific example of a rational economy defined as a "functional organization oriented to money-prices which originate in the interest-struggles of men in the *market*" (Weber, 1915/1958:331). Although there is a general evolutionary trend, Weber, as always, is careful to point out that there are various sources of capitalism, alternative routes to it, and a range of results emanating from it (Swedberg, 1998). In fact, in the course of rejecting the socialistic theory of evolutionary change, Weber rejects the whole idea of a "general evolutionary sequence" (1927/1981:34).

Weber begins by depicting various irrational and traditional forms, such as the household, clan, village, and manorial economies. For example, the lord of the manor in feudalism was described by Weber as being traditionalistic, "too lacking in initiative to build up a business enterprise in a large scale into which the peasants would have fitted as a labor force" (1927/1981:72). However, by the twelfth and thirteenth centuries in the Occident, feudalism began to break down as the peasants and the land were freed from control by the lord and a money economy was introduced. With this breakdown, the manorial system "showed a strong tendency to develop in a capitalistic direction" (Weber, 1927/1981:79).

At the same time, in the Middle Ages, cities were beginning to develop. Weber focuses on the largely urban development of industry involved in the transformation of raw materials. Especially important to Weber is the development of such industrial production beyond the immediate needs of the house community. Notable here is the rise of free craftsmen in the cities. They developed in the Middle Ages in the Occident because, for one thing, this society had developed consumptive needs greater than those of any other. In general, there were larger markets and more purchasers, and the peasantry had greater purchasing power. On the other side, forces operated against the major alternative to craftsmen—slaves. Slavery was found to be too unprofitable and too unstable, and it was made increasingly more unstable by the growth of the towns that offered freedom to the slaves.

In the Occident, along with free craftsmen came the development of the *guild,* defined by Weber as "an organization of craft workers specialized in accordance with the type of occupation . . . [with] internal regulation of work and monopolization against outsiders" (1927/1981:136). Freedom of association was also characteristic of the guilds. But although rational in many senses, guilds also had traditional, anticapitalistic aspects. For example, one master was not supposed to have more capital than another, and this requirement was a barrier to the development of large capitalistic organizations.

As the Middle Ages came to a close, the guilds began to disintegrate. This disintegration was crucial because the traditional guilds stood in the way of technological advance. With the dissolution of the guild system came the rise of the domestic system of production, especially the "putting out" system in the textile industry. In such a system, production was decentralized, with much of it taking place within the homes of the workers. Although domestic systems were found throughout the world, it was only in the Occident that the owners controlled the means of production (for example, tools, raw materials) and provided them to the workers in exchange for the right to dispose of the product. Whereas a fully developed domestic system developed in the West, it was impeded in other parts of the world by such barriers as the clan system (China), the caste system (India), traditionalism, and the lack of free workers.

Next, Weber details the development of the workshop (a central work setting without advanced machinery) and then the emergence of the factory in the fourteenth through sixteenth centuries. In Weber's view, the factory did not arise out of craft work or the domestic system, but alongside them. Similarly, the factory was not called into existence by advances in machinery; the two developments were correlated with each other. The factory was characterized by free labor that performed specialized and coordinated activities, ownership of the means of production by the entrepreneur, the fixed capital of the entrepreneur, and the system of accounting that is indispensable to such capitalization. Such a factory was, in Weber's view, a capitalistic organization. In addition to the development of the factory, Weber details the rise of other components of a modern capitalistic economy, such as advanced machinery, transportation systems, money, banking, interest, bookkeeping systems, and so on.

What most clearly defines modern rational capitalistic enterprises for Weber is their calculability, which is best represented in their reliance on modern bookkeeping. Isolated calculable enterprises existed in the past in the Occident as well as in other societies. However, an entire society is considered capitalistic only when the everyday requirements of the population are supplied by capitalistic methods and enterprises. Such a society is found only in the Occident, and there only since the mid-nineteenth century.

The development of a capitalistic system hinged on a variety of developments within the economy as well as within the larger society. Within the economy, some of the prerequisites included a free market with large and steady demand, a money economy, inexpensive and rational technologies, a free labor force, a disciplined labor force, rational capital-accounting techniques, and the commercialization of economic life involving the use of shares, stocks, and the like. Many of the economic prerequisites were found only in the Occident. Outside the economy, Weber identified a variety of needed developments, such as a modern state with "professional administration, specialized officialdom, and law based on the concept of citizenship" (1927/1981:313), rational law "made by jurists and rationally interpreted and applied" (1927/1981:313), cities, and modern science and technology. To these Weber adds a factor that will concern us in the next section: "a rational ethic for the conduct of life . . . a religious basis for the ordering of life which consistently followed out must lead to explicit rationalism" (1927/1981:313–314). Like the economic prerequisites, these noneconomic presuppositions occurred together only in the Occident. The basic point is that a rational economy is dependent upon a variety of noneconomic forces throughout the rest of society in order to develop.

Religion   Although we will focus on the rationalization of religion in this section, Weber spent much time analyzing the degree to which early, more primitive religions—and religions in much of the world—acted as impediments to the rise of rationality. Weber noted that "the sacred is the uniquely unalterable" (1921/1968:406). Despite this view, religion in the West did prove to be alterable; it was amenable to rationalization, and it did play a key role in the rationalization of other sectors of society (Kalberg, 1990).

Early religion was composed of a bewildering array of gods, but with rationalization, a clear and coherent set of gods (a pantheon) emerged. Early religions had household gods, kin-group gods, local political gods, and occupational and vocational gods. We get the clear feeling that Weber did believe that a cultural force of (theoretical) rationality impelled the emergence of this set of gods: "*Reason favored the primacy of universal gods; and every consistent crystallization of a pantheon followed systematic rational principles*" (1921/1968:417). A pantheon of gods was not the only aspect of the rationalization of religion discussed by Weber. He also considered the delimitation of the jurisdiction of gods, monotheism, and the anthropomorphization of gods as part of this development. Although the pressure for rationalization exists in many of the world's religions, in areas outside the Western world, the barriers to rationalization more than counterbalance the pressures for rationalization.

Although Weber had a cultural conception of rationalization, he did not view it simply as a force "out there" that impels people to act. He did not have a group-mind concept. In religion, rationalization is tied to concrete groups of people, in particular to priests. Specifically, the professionally trained priesthood is the carrier[12] and the expediter of rationalization. In this, priests stand in contrast to magicians, who support a more irrational religious system. The greater rationality of the priesthood is traceable to several factors. Members go through a systematic training program, whereas the training of magicians is unsystematic. Also, priests are fairly highly specialized, whereas magicians tend to be unspecialized. Finally, priests possess a systematic set of religious concepts, and this, too, sets them apart from magicians. We can say that priests are both the products and the expediters of the process of rationalization.

The priesthood is not the only group that plays a key role in rationalization. Prophets and a laity are also important in the process. Prophets can be distinguished from priests by their personal calling, their emotional preaching, their proclamation of a doctrine, and the fact that they tend to be unpopular and to work alone. The key

---

[12] For a general discussion of the role of carriers in Weber's work, see Kalberg (1994:58–62).

role of the prophet is the mobilization of the laity, because there would be no religion without a group of followers. Unlike priests, prophets do not tend to the needs of a congregation. Weber differentiated between two types of prophets: ethical and exemplary. *Ethical prophets* (Muhammad, Jesus Christ, and the Old Testament prophets) believe that they have received a commission directly from God and demand obedience from followers as an ethical duty. *Exemplary prophets* (Buddha is a model) demonstrate to others by personal example the way to religious salvation. In either case, successful prophets are able to attract large numbers of followers, and it is this mass, along with the priests, that forms the heart of religion. Prophets are likely at first to attract a personal following, but it is necessary that that group be transformed into a permanent congregation. Once such a laity has been formed, major strides have been made in the direction of the rationalization of religion.

Prophets play a key initial role, but once a congregation is formed, they are no longer needed. In fact, because they are largely irrational, they represent a barrier to that rationalization of religion. A conflict develops between priests and prophets, but it is a conflict that must be won in the long run by the more rational priesthood. In their conflict, the priests are aided by the rationalization proceeding in the rest of society. As the secular world becomes more and more literate and bureaucratized, the task of educating the masses falls increasingly to the priests, whose literacy gives them a tremendous advantage over the prophets. In addition, while the prophets tend to do the preaching, the priests take over the task of day-to-day pastoral care. Although preaching is important during extraordinary times, pastoral care, or the daily religious cultivation of the laity, is an important instrument in the growing power of the priesthood. It was the church in the Western world that combined a rationalized pastoral character with an ethical religion to form a peculiarly influential and rational form of religion. This rationalized religion proved particularly well suited to winning converts among the urban middle class, and it was there that it played a key role in the rationalization of economic life as well as all other sectors of life.

Law   As with his analysis of religion, Weber began his treatment of law with the primitive, which he saw as highly irrational. Primitive law was a rather undifferentiated system of norms. For example, no distinction was made between a civil wrong (a tort) and a crime. Thus cases involving differences over a piece of land and homicide were likely to be handled, and offenders punished, in much the same way. In addition, primitive law tended to lack any official machinery. Vengeance dominated reactions to a crime, and law was generally free from procedural formality or rules. Leaders, especially, were virtually unrestrained in what they could do to followers. From this early irrational period, Weber traced a direct line of development to a formalized legal procedure. And as was usual in Weber's thinking, it is only in the West that a rational, systematic theory of law is held to have developed.

Weber traced several stages in the development of a more rational legal system (Shamir, 1993). An early stage involves charismatic legal revelation through law prophets. Then there is the empirical creation and founding of law by honorary legal officials. Later there is the imposition of law by secular or theocratic powers. Finally, in the most modern case, we have the systematic elaboration of law and professionalized administration of justice by persons who have received their legal training formally and systematically.

In law, as in religion, Weber placed great weight on the process of professionalization: the legal profession is crucial to the rationalization of Western law. There are certainly other factors (for example, the influence of Roman law), but the legal profession was central to his thinking: "Formally elaborated law constituting a complex of maxims consciously applied in decisions has never come into existence without the decisive cooperation of trained specialists" (Weber, 1921/1968:775). Although Weber was aware that there was a series of external pressures—especially from the rationalizing economy—impelling law toward rationalization, his view was that the most important force was the internal factor of the professionalization of the legal profession (1921/1968:776).

Weber differentiated between two types of legal training but saw only one as contributing to the development of rational law. The first is *craft training,* in which apprentices learn from masters, primarily during the actual practice of law. This kind of training produces a formalistic type of law dominated by precedents. The goal is not the creation of a comprehensive, rational system of law but, instead, the production of practically useful precedents for dealing with recurring situations. Because these precedents are tied to specific issues in the real world, a general, rational, and systematic body of law cannot emerge.

In contrast, *academic legal training* laid the groundwork for the rational law of the West. In this system, law is taught in special schools where the emphasis is placed on legal theory and science—in other words, where legal phenomena are given rational and systematic treatment. The legal concepts produced have the character of abstract norms. Interpretation of these laws occurs in a rigorously formal and logical manner. They are general, in contrast to the specific, precedent-bound laws produced in the case of craft training.

Academic legal training leads to the development of a rational legal system with a number of characteristics, including the following:

1. Every concrete legal decision involves the application of abstract legal propositions to concrete situations.
2. It must be possible in every concrete case to derive the decision logically from abstract legal propositions.
3. Law must tend to be a gapless system of legal propositions or at least be treated as one.
4. The gapless legal system should be applicable to all social actions.

Weber seemed to adopt the view that history has seen law evolve from a cultural system of norms to a more structured system of formal laws. In general, actors are increasingly constrained by a more and more rational legal system. Although this is true, Weber was too good a sociologist to lose sight completely of the independent significance of the actor. For one thing, Weber (1921/1968:754–755) saw actors as crucial in the emergence of, and change in, law. However, the most important aspect of Weber's work in this area—for the purposes of this discussion—is the degree to which law is regarded as part of the general process of rationalization throughout the West.

Polity   The rationalization of the political system is intimately linked to the rationalization of law and, ultimately, to the rationalization of all elements of the social system. For example, Weber argued that the more rational the political structure becomes, the more likely it is to eliminate systematically the irrational elements within the law. A rational polity cannot function with an irrational legal system, and vice versa. Weber did not believe that political leaders follow a conscious policy of rationalizing the law; rather, they are impelled in that direction by the demands of their own increasingly rational means of administration. Once again, Weber took the position that actors are being impelled by structural (the state) and cultural (rationalization) forces.

Weber defined the *polity* as "a community whose social action is aimed at subordinating to orderly domination by the participants a territory and the conduct of the persons within it, through readiness to resort to physical force, including normally force of arms" (1921/1968:901). This type of polity has existed neither everywhere nor always. It does not exist as a separate entity where the task of armed defense against enemies is assigned to the household, the neighborhood association, an economic group, and so forth. Although Weber clearly viewed the polity as a social structure, he was more careful to link his thinking here to his individual action orientations. In his view, modern political associations rest on the prestige bestowed upon them by their members.

As was his usual strategy, Weber went back to the primitive case in order to trace the development of the polity. He made it clear that violent social action is primordial. However, the monopolization and rational ordering of legitimate violence did not exist in early societies but evolved over the centuries. Not only is rational control over violence lacking in primitive society, but other basic functions of the modern state either are totally absent or are not ordered in a rational manner. Included here would be functions like legislation, police, justice, administration, and the military. The development of the polity in the West involves the progressive differentiation and elaboration of these functions. But the most important step is their subordination under a single, dominant, rationally ordered state.

The City   Weber was also interested in the rise of the city in the West. The city provided an alternative to the feudal order and a setting in which modern capitalism and, more generally, rationality could develop. He defined a city as having the following characteristics:

1. It is a relatively closed settlement.
2. It is relatively large.
3. It possesses a marketplace.
4. It has partial political autonomy.

Although many cities in many societies had these characteristics, Western cities developed a peculiarly rational character with, among other things, a rationally organized marketplace and political structure.

Weber looked at various other societies in order to determine why they did not develop the rational form of the city. He concluded that barriers like the traditional community in China and the caste system in India impeded the rise of such a city. But in the West, a number of rationalizing forces coalesced to create the modern city. For example, the development of a city requires a relatively rational economy. But, of course, the converse is also true: the development of a rational economy requires the modern city.

Art Forms   To give a sense of the breadth of Weber's thinking, a few words are needed about his work on the rationalization of various art forms. For example, Weber (1921/1958) viewed music in the West as having developed in a peculiarly rational direction. Musical creativity is reduced to routine procedures based on comprehensive principles. Music in the Western world has undergone a "transformation of the process of musical production into a calculable affair operating with known means, effective instruments, and understandable rules" (Weber, 1921/1958:li). Although the process of rationalization engenders tension in all the institutions in which it occurs, that tension is nowhere more noticeable than in music. After all, music is supposed to be an arena of expressive flexibility, but it is being progressively reduced to a rational, and ultimately mathematical, system.

Weber (1904–1905/1958) sees a similar development in other art forms. For example, in painting, Weber emphasizes "the rational utilization of lines and spatial perspective—which the Renaissance created for us" (1904–1905/1958:15). In architecture, "the rational use of the Gothic vault as a means of distributing pressure and of roofing spaces of all forms, and above all as the constructive principle of great monumental buildings and the foundation of a *style* extending to sculpture and painting, such as that created by our Middle Ages, does not occur elsewhere [in the world]" (Weber, 1904–1905/1958:15).

We have now spent a number of pages examining Weber's ideas on rationalization in various aspects of social life. Although nowhere does Weber explicitly say so, it is reasonable to argue that he adopted the view that changes in the cultural level of rationality are leading to changes in the structures as well as in the individual thoughts and actions of the modern world. The rationalization process is not left to float alone above concrete phenomena but is embedded in various social structures and in the thoughts and actions of individuals. To put it slightly differently, the key point is that the cultural system of rationality occupies a position of causal priority in Weber's work. This can be illustrated in still another way by looking at Weber's work on the relationship between religion and economics—more specifically, the relationship between religion and the development, or lack of development, of a capitalist economy.

Religion and the Rise of Capitalism

Weber spent much of his life studying religion—this in spite of, or perhaps because of, his being areligious, or, as he once described himself, "religiously unmusical" (Gerth and Mills, 1958:25). One of his overriding concerns was the relationship among a variety of the world's religions and the development only in the West of a capitalist economic system (Schlucter, 1996). It is clear that the vast bulk of this work is done at the social-structural and cultural levels; the thoughts and actions of

Calvinists, Buddhists, Confucians, Jews, Muslims (Nafassi, 1998; B. Turner, 1974), and others are held to be affected by changes in social structures and social institutions. Weber was interested primarily in the systems of ideas of the world's religions, in the "spirit" of capitalism, and in rationalization as a modern system of norms and values. He was also very interested in the structures of the world's religions, the various structural components of the societies in which they exist that serve to facilitate or impede rationalization, and the structural aspects of capitalism and the rest of the modern world.

Weber's work on religion and capitalism involved an enormous body of cross-cultural historical research; here, as elsewhere, he did comparative-historical sociology (Kalberg, 1997). Freund (1968:213) summarized the complicated interrelationships involved in this research:

1. Economic forces influenced Protestantism.
2. Economic forces influenced religions other than Protestantism (for example, Hinduism, Confucianism, and Taoism).
3. Religious idea systems influenced individual thoughts and actions—in particular, economic thoughts and actions.
4. Religious idea systems have been influential throughout the world.
5. Religious idea systems (particularly Protestantism) have had the unique effect in the West of helping to rationalize the economic sector and virtually every other institution.

To this we can add:

6. Religious idea systems in the non-Western world have created overwhelming structural barriers to rationalization.

By according the religious factor great importance, Weber appeared to be simultaneously building on and criticizing his image of Marx's work. Weber, like Marx, operated with a complicated model of the interrelationship of primarily large-scale systems: "Weber's sociology is related to Marx's thought in the common attempt to grasp the interrelations of institutional orders making up a social structure: In Weber's work, military and religious, political and juridical institutional systems are functionally related to the economic order in a variety of ways" (Gerth and Mills, 1958:49). In fact, Weber's affinities with Marx are even greater than is often recognized. Although Weber, especially early in his career, gave primacy to religious ideas, he later came to see that material forces, not idea systems, are of greater importance (Kalberg, 1985:61). As Weber said, "Not ideas, but material and ideal interests, directly govern men's conduct. Yet very frequently the 'world images' that have been created by 'ideas' have, like switchmen, determined the tracks along which action has been pushed by the dynamic of interest" (cited in Gerth and Mills, 1958:280).

Paths to Salvation

In analyzing the relationship between the world's religions and the economy, Weber (1921/1963) developed a typology of the paths of salvation. *Asceticism* is the first broad type of religiosity, and it combines an orientation toward action with the commitment of believers to denying themselves the pleasures of the world. Ascetic religions are divided into two subtypes. *Otherworldly asceticism* involves a set of norms and values that command the followers not to work within the secular world and to fight against its temptations (Kalberg, 2001). Of greater interest to Weber, because it encompasses Calvinism, was *innerworldly asceticism*. Such a religion does not reject the world; instead, it actively urges its members to work within the world so that they can find salvation, or at least signs of it. The distinctive goal here is the strict, methodical control of the members' patterns of life, thought, and action. Members are urged to reject everything unethical, esthetic, or dependent on their emotional reactions to the secular world. Innerworldly ascetics are motivated to systematize their own conduct.

Whereas both types of asceticism involve some type of action and self-denial, *mysticism* involves contemplation, emotion, and inaction. Weber subdivided mysticism in the same way as asceticism. *World-rejecting mysticism* involves total flight from the world. *Innerworldly mysticism* leads to contemplative efforts to understand the meaning of the world, but these efforts are doomed to failure, because the world is viewed as being beyond individual comprehension. In any case, both types of mysticism and world-rejecting asceticism can be seen as idea systems that inhibit the development of capitalism and rationality. In contrast, innerworldly asceticism is the system of norms and values that contributed to the development of these phenomena in the West.

The Protestant Ethic and the Spirit of Capitalism   In Max Weber's best-known work, *The Protestant Ethic and the Spirit of Capitalism* (1904–1905/1958), he traced the impact of ascetic Protestantism—primarily Calvinism—on the rise of the spirit of capitalism (Breiner, 2005; H. Jones, 1997). This work is but a small part of a larger body of scholarship that traces the relationship between religion and modern capitalism throughout much of the world.

Weber, especially later in his work, made it clear that his most general interest was in the rise of the distinctive rationality of the West. Capitalism, with its rational organization of free labor, its open market, and its rational bookkeeping system, is only one component of that developing system. He directly linked it to the parallel development of rationalized science, law, politics, art, architecture, literature, universities, and the polity.

Weber did not directly link the idea system of the Protestant ethic to the structures of the capitalist system; instead, he was content to link the Protestant ethic to another system of ideas, the "spirit of capitalism." In other words, two systems of ideas are directly linked in this work. Although links of the capitalist economic system to the material world are certainly implied and indicated, they were not Weber's primary concern. Thus, *The Protestant Ethic* is not about the rise of modern capitalism but is about the origin of a peculiar spirit that eventually made modern rational capitalism (some form of capitalism had existed since early times) expand and come to dominate the economy.

Weber began by examining and rejecting alternative explanations of why capitalism arose in the West in the sixteenth and seventeenth centuries (for an alternative view on this, see R. Collins, 1997a). To those who contended that capitalism arose because the material conditions were right at that time, Weber retorted that material conditions were also ripe at other times and capitalism did not arise. Weber also rejected the psychological theory that the development of capitalism was due simply to the acquisitive instinct. In his view, such an instinct always has existed, yet it did not produce capitalism in other situations.

Evidence for Weber's views on the significance of Protestantism was found in an examination of countries with mixed religious systems. In looking at these countries, he discovered that the leaders of the economic system—business leaders, owners of capital, high-grade skilled labor, and more advanced technically and commercially trained personnel—were all overwhelmingly Protestant. This suggested that Protestantism was a significant cause in the choice of these occupations and, conversely, that other religions (for example, Roman Catholicism) failed to produce idea systems that impelled individuals into these vocations.

In Weber's view, the spirit of capitalism is not defined simply by economic greed; it is in many ways the exact opposite. It is a moral and ethical system, an ethos, that among other things stresses economic success. In fact, it was the turning of profit making into an ethos that was critical in the West. In other societies, the pursuit of profit was seen as an individual act motivated at least in part by greed. Thus it was viewed by many as morally suspect. However, Protestantism succeeded in turning the pursuit of profit into a moral crusade. It was the backing of the moral system that led to the unprecedented expansion of profit seeking and, ultimately, to the capitalist system. On a theoretical level, by stressing that he was dealing with the relationship between one ethos (Protestantism) and another (the spirit of capitalism), Weber was able to keep his analysis primarily at the level of systems of ideas.

The spirit of capitalism can be seen as a normative system that involves a number of interrelated ideas. For example, its goal is to instill an "attitude which seeks profit rationally and systematically" (Weber, 1904–1905/1958:64). In addition, it preaches an avoidance of life's pleasures: "Seest thou a man diligent in business? He shall stand before kings" (Weber, 1904–1905/1958:53). Also included in the spirit of capitalism are ideas such as "time is money," "be industrious," "be frugal," "be punctual," "be fair," and "earning money is a legitimate end in itself." Above all, there is the idea that it is people's duty to increase their wealth ceaselessly. This takes the spirit of capitalism out of the realm of individual ambition and into the category of an ethical imperative. Although Weber admitted that a type of capitalism (for example, adventurer capitalism) existed in China, India, Babylon, and the classical world and during the Middle Ages, it was different from Western capitalism, primarily because it lacked "this particular ethos" (1904–1905/1958:52).

Weber was interested not simply in describing this ethical system but also in explaining its derivations. He thought that Protestantism, particularly Calvinism, was crucial to the rise of the spirit of capitalism. Calvinism is no longer necessary to the continuation of that economic system. In fact, in many senses modern capitalism, given its secularity, stands in opposition to Calvinism and to religion in general. Capitalism today has become a real entity that combines norms, values, market, money, and laws. It has become, in Durkheim's terms, a social fact that is external to, and coercive of, the individual. As Weber put it:

> Capitalism is today an immense cosmos into which the individual is born, and which presents itself to him, at least as an individual, as an unalterable order of things in which he must live. It forces the individual, in so far as he is involved in the system of market relationships, to conform to capitalist rules of action.
>
> (Weber, 1904–1905/1958:54)

Another crucial point here is that Calvinists did not consciously seek to create a capitalist system. In Weber's view, capitalism was an *unanticipated consequence* (Cherkaoui, 2007) of the Protestant ethic. The concept of unanticipated consequences has broad significance in Weber's work, for he believed that what individuals and groups intend by their actions often leads to a set of consequences that are at variance with their intentions. Although Weber did not explain this point, it seems that it is related to his theoretical view that people create social structures but those structures soon take on a life of their own, over which the creators have little or no control. Because people lack control over them, structures are free to develop in a variety of totally unanticipated directions. Weber's line of thinking led Arthur Mitzman (1970) to argue that Weber created a sociology of reification. Reified social structures are free to move in unanticipated directions, as both Marx and Weber showed in their analyses of capitalism.

Calvinism and the Spirit of Capitalism   Calvinism was the version of Protestantism that interested Weber most. One feature of Calvinism was the idea that only a small number of people are chosen for salvation. In addition, Calvinism entailed the idea of predestination; people were predestined to be either among the saved or among the damned. There was nothing that the individual or the religion as a whole could do to affect that fate. Yet the idea of predestination left people uncertain about whether they were among the saved. To reduce this uncertainty, the Calvinists developed the idea that *signs* could be used as indicators of whether a person was saved. People were urged to work hard, because if they were diligent, they would uncover the signs of salvation, which were to be found in economic success. In sum, the Calvinist was urged to engage in intense, worldly activity and to become a "man of vocation."

However, isolated actions were not enough. Calvinism, as an ethic, required self-control and a systematized style of life that involved an integrated round of activities, particularly business activities. This stood in contrast to the Christian ideal of the Middle Ages, in which individuals simply engaged in isolated acts as the occasion arose in order to atone for particular sins and to increase their chances of salvation. "The God of Calvinism demanded of his believers not single good works, but a life of good works combined into a unified system" (Weber, 1904–1905/1958:117). Calvinism produced an ethical system and ultimately a group of people who were nascent capitalists. Calvinism "has the highest ethical appreciation of the sober, middle-class, self-made man" (Weber, 1904–1905/1958:163). Weber neatly summarized his own position on Calvinism and its relationship to capitalism as follows:

> The religious valuation of restless, continuous, systematic work in a worldly
> calling, as the highest means of asceticism, and at the same time the surest and
> most evident proof of rebirth and genuine faith, must have been the most powerful
> conceivable lever for the expansion of . . . the spirit of capitalism.
>
> (Weber, 1904–1905/1958:172)

In addition to its general link to the spirit of capitalism, Calvinism had some more specific links. First, as already mentioned, capitalists could ruthlessly pursue their economic interests and feel that such pursuit was not merely self-interest but was, in fact, their ethical duty. This not only permitted unprecedented mercilessness in business but also silenced potential critics, who could not simply reduce these actions to self-interest. Second, Calvinism provided the rising capitalist "with sober, conscientious and unusually industrious workmen who clung to their work as to a life purpose willed by god" (Weber, 1904–1905/1958:117). With such a workforce, the nascent capitalist could raise the level of exploitation to unprecedented heights. Third, Calvinism legitimized an unequal stratification system by giving the capitalist the "comforting assurances that the unequal distribution of the goods of this world was a special dispensation of Divine Providence" (Weber, 1904–1905/1958:117).

Weber also had reservations about the capitalist system, as he did about all aspects of the rationalized world. For example, he pointed out that capitalism tends to produce "specialists without spirit, sensualists without heart; this nullity imagines that it has attained a level of civilization never before achieved" (Weber, 1904–1905/1958:182).

Although in *The Protestant Ethic* Weber focused on the effect of Calvinism on the spirit of capitalism, he was well aware that social and economic conditions have a reciprocal impact on religion. He chose not to deal with such relationships in this book, but he made it clear that his goal was not to substitute a one-sided spiritualist interpretation for the one-sided materialist explanation that he attributed to Marxists. (The same is true of much of the rest of his work, including his essays on the Russian Revolution; see Wells and Baehr, 1995:22.) As Kalberg (1996) has pointed out, *The Protestant Ethic* raises a wide number of issues that go to the heart of contemporary sociological theory.

If Calvinism was one of the causal factors in the rise of capitalism in the West, then the question arises: Why didn't capitalism arise in other societies? In his effort to answer this question, Weber dealt with spiritual and material barriers to the rise of capitalism. Let us look briefly at Weber's analysis of those barriers in two societies—China and India.

Religion and Capitalism in China

One crucial assumption that allowed Weber to make legitimate the comparison between the West and China is that both had the prerequisites for the development of capitalism. In China, there was a tradition of intense acquisitiveness and unscrupulous competition. There was great industry and an enormous capacity for work in the populace. Powerful guilds existed. The population was expanding. And there was a steady growth in precious metals. With these and other material prerequisites, why didn't capitalism arise in China? As has been pointed out before, Weber's general answer was that social, structural, and religious barriers in China prevented the development of capitalism. This is not to say that capitalism was entirely absent in China (Love, 2000). There were moneylenders and purveyors who sought high rates of profit. But a market, as well as various other components of a rational capitalistic system, was absent. In Weber's view, the rudimentary capitalism of China "pointed in a direction opposite to the development of rational economic corporate enterprises" (1916/1964:86).

Structural Barriers   Weber listed several structural barriers to the rise of capitalism in China. First, there was the structure of the typical Chinese community. It was held together by rigid kinship bonds in the form of sibs. The sibs were ruled by elders, who made them bastions of traditionalism. The sibs were self-contained entities, and there was little dealing with other sibs. This encouraged small, encapsulated landholdings and a household-based, rather than a market, economy. The extensive partitioning of the land prevented major technological developments, because economies of scale were impossible. Agricultural production remained in the hands of peasants, industrial production in the hands of small-scale artisans. Modern cities, which were to become the centers of Western capitalism, were inhibited in their development because the people retained their allegiance to the sibs. Because of the sibs' autonomy, the central government was never able to govern these units effectively or to mold them into a unified whole.

The structure of the Chinese state was a second barrier to the rise of capitalism. The state was largely patrimonial and governed by tradition, prerogative, and favoritism. In Weber's view, a rational and calculable system of administration and law enforcement, which was necessary for industrial development, did not exist. There were very few formal laws covering commerce, there was no central court, and legal formalism was rejected. This irrational type of administrative structure was a barrier to the rise of capitalism, as Weber made clear: "Capital investment in industry is far too sensitive to such irrational rule and too dependent upon the possibility of calculating the steady and rational operation of the state machinery to emerge within an administration of this type" (1916/1964:103). In addition to its general structure, a number of more specific components of the state acted against the development of capitalism. For example, the officials of the bureaucratic administration had vested material interests that made them oppose capitalism. Officials often bought offices primarily to make a profit, and this kind of orientation did not necessarily make for a high degree of efficiency.

A third structural barrier to the rise of capitalism was the nature of the Chinese language. In Weber's view, it militated against rationality by making systematic thought difficult. It remained largely in the realm of the "pictorial" and the "descriptive." Logical thinking was also inhibited because intellectual thought remained largely in the form of parables, and this hardly was the basis for the development of a cumulative body of knowledge.

Although there were other structural barriers to the rise of capitalism (for example, a country without wars or overseas trade), a key factor was the lack of the required "mentality," the lack of the needed idea system. Weber looked at the two dominant systems of religious ideas in China—Confucianism and Taoism—and the characteristics of both that militated against the development of a spirit of capitalism.

Confucianism   A central characteristic of Confucian thinking was its emphasis on a literary education as a prerequisite for office and for social status. To acquire a position in the ruling strata, a person had to be a member of the literati. Movement up the hierarchy was based on a system of ideas that tested literary knowledge, not the technical knowledge needed to conduct the office in question. What was valued and tested was whether the individual's mind was steeped in culture and whether it was characterized by ways of thought suitable to a cultured man. In Weber's terms, Confucianism encouraged "a highly bookish literary education." The literati produced by this system came to see the actual work of administration as beneath them, mere tasks to be delegated to subordinates. Instead, the literati aspired to clever puns, euphemisms, and allusions to classical quotations—a purely literary kind of intellectuality. With this kind of orientation, it is easy to see why the literati were unconcerned with the state of the economy or with economic activities. The worldview of the Confucians ultimately grew to be the policy of the state. As a result, the Chinese state came to be only minimally involved in rationally influencing the economy and the rest of society. The Confucians maintained their influence by having the constitution decree that only they could serve as officials, and competitors to Confucians (for example, the bourgeoisie, prophets, and priests) were blocked from serving in the government. In fact, if the emperor dared to deviate from this rule, he was thought to be toying with disaster and his potential downfall.

Many other components of Confucianism militated against capitalism. It was basically an ethic of adjustment to the world and to its order and its conventions. Rather than viewing material success and wealth as a sign of salvation as the Calvinist did, the Confucian simply was led to accept things as they were. In fact, there was no idea of salvation in Confucianism, and this lack of tension between religion and the world also acted to inhibit the rise of capitalism. The snobbish Confucian was urged to reject thrift, because it was something that commoners practiced. In contrast to the Puritan work ethic, it was not regarded as proper for a Confucian gentleman to work, although wealth was prized. Active engagement in a profitable enterprise was regarded as morally dubious and unbecoming to a Confucian's station. The acceptable goal for such a gentleman was a good position, not high profits. The ethic emphasized the abilities of a gentleman rather than the highly specialized skills that could have proved useful to a developing capitalist system. In sum, Weber contended that Confucianism became a relentless canonization of tradition.

Taoism   Weber perceived Taoism as a mystical Chinese religion in which the supreme good was deemed to be a psychic state, a state of mind, and not a state of grace to be obtained by conduct in the real world. As a result, Taoists did not operate in a rational way to affect the external world. Taoism was essentially traditional, and one of its basic tenets was "Do not introduce innovations" (Weber, 1916/1964:203).

Such an idea system was unlikely to produce any major changes, let alone one as far-reaching as capitalism.

One trait common to Taoism and Confucianism is that neither produced enough tension, or conflict, among the members to motivate them to much innovative action in this world:

> Neither in its official state cult nor in its Taoist aspect could Chinese religiosity produce sufficiently strong motives for a religiously oriented life for the individual such as the Puritan method represents. Both forms of religion lacked even the traces of the Satanic force or evil against which [the] pious Chinese might have struggled for his salvation.
>
> (Weber, 1916/1964:206)

As was true of Confucianism, there was no inherent force in Taoism to impel actors to change the world or, more specifically, to build a capitalist system.

Religion and Capitalism in India

For our purposes, a very brief discussion of Weber's (1916–1917/1958) thinking on the relationship between religion and capitalism in India will suffice. The argument, though not its details, parallels the Chinese case. For example, Weber discussed the structural barriers of the caste system (Gellner, 1982:534). Among other things, the caste system erected overwhelming barriers to social mobility, and it tended to regulate even the most minute aspects of people's lives. The idea system of the Brahmans had a number of components. For example, Brahmans were expected to avoid vulgar occupations and to observe elegance in manners and proprieties in conduct. Indifference to the world's mundane affairs was the crowning idea of Brahman religiosity. The Brahmans also emphasized a highly literary kind of education. Although there certainly were important differences between Brahmans and Confucians, the ethos of each presented overwhelming barriers to the rise of capitalism.

The Hindu religion posed similar ideational barriers. Its key idea was reincarnation. To the Hindu, a person is born into the caste that he or she deserves by virtue of behavior in a past life. Through faithful adherence to the ritual of caste, the Hindu gains merit for the next life. Hinduism, unlike Calvinism, was traditional in the sense that salvation was to be achieved by faithfully following the rules; innovation, particularly in the economic sphere, could not lead to a higher caste in the next life. Activity in this world was not important, because the world was seen as a transient abode and an impediment to the spiritual quest. In these and other ways, the idea system associated with Hinduism failed to produce the kind of people who could create a capitalist economic system and, more generally, a rationally ordered society.

Criticisms

There have been numerous criticisms of Weber. We will examine four of the most important. The first criticism has to do with Weber's *verstehen* method. Weber was caught between two problems in regard to *verstehen*. On the one hand, it could not simply mean a subjective intuition because this would not be scientific. On the other hand, the sociologist could not just proclaim the "objective" meaning of the social phenomenon. Weber declared that his method fell between these two choices, but he never fully explained how (Herva, 1988). The deficiencies in his methodology are not always apparent from the reading of Weber's insightful analysis based on his own interpretations. But they become perfectly clear when sociologists try to apply his method to their own research or, even more so, when they attempt to teach *verstehen* to others. Clearly, the method involves systemic and rigorous research, but the magic of turning that research into Weber's illuminating insights eludes us. This has led some (Abel, 1948) to relegate *verstehen* to a heuristic operation of discovery that precedes the real scientific work of sociology. Others have suggested that *verstehen* needs to be seen as itself a social process and that our understanding of others always proceeds out of a dialogue (Shields, 1996).

The second criticism is that Weber lacks a fully theorized macrosociology. We have already spent some time exploring the contradiction between Weber's individualistic method and his focus on large-scale social structures and world-historical norms. In Weber's method, class is reduced to a collection of people in the same economic situation. Political structure is reduced to the acceptance of domination because of subjectively perceived legitimacy in terms of rationality, charisma, or traditions. Weber certainly recognizes that class and political structures have effects on people—not to mention such macrophenomena as religion and rationalization—but he has no way to theorize these effects except as a collection of unintended consequences. He has no theory of how these work as systems behind the back of individuals and, in some cases, even to determine the intention of actors (B. Turner, 1981).

The third criticism of Weber is that he lacks a critical theory. In other words, others have said that Weber's theory cannot be used to point out opportunities for constructive change. This criticism can be demonstrated through examining Weber's theory of rationalization.

Weber used the term *rationalization* in a number of ways, but he was primarily concerned with two types. One concerns the development of bureaucracy and its legal form of authority (see pp. 129–132). The other refers to the subjective changes in attitude that he called formal rationality (see p. 137). In the confluence of bureaucracy and formal rationality we see what Weber described as unintended consequences. The creation of bureaucracy and the adaptation of formal rationality end up undermining the very purposes that the rationalization was meant to serve. This is what we have called the irrational consequences of rationality. Weber's famous iron cage is one of these irrational consequences. Bureaucracy and formal rationality were initially developed because of their efficiency, predictability, calculability, and control in achieving a given goal (for example, to help the poor). But as rationalization proceeds, the original goal tends to be forgotten, and the organization increasingly devotes itself to efficiency, predictability, calculability, and control for their own sakes. For example, welfare bureaucracies measure their success by their efficiency in "dealing" with clients, even their efficiency in getting them off welfare, regardless of whether doing so actually serves the original goal of helping the poor to better their situations.

In some of his most-quoted passages, Weber implies that this process is inevitable, as for example in his metaphor of the iron cage. However, as argued above, it would be wrong to see this as a general evolutionary sequence of inevitable rationalization. Johannes Weiss (1987) maintains that rationalization is inevitable only to the extent that we want it to be so. It is simply that our world is so complex that it is difficult to conceive of accomplishing any significant task without the efficiency, calculability, predictability, and control of rationalization—even if it inevitably ends in its own peculiar irrationality. We may dream of a world without bureaucracies, but "the real question is whether—with due regard to the obligations of intellectual honesty—we seriously strive to attain it or ever could" (Weiss, 1987:162).

Many people prefer to ignore their own complicity and to see rationalization as something that is imposed on them. Indeed, one of the most cited criticisms of Weber is that he did not provide a strategy for opposing this rationalization (Marcuse, 1971). Since we work in bureaucracies (universities), deal with them every day, and will complain when they are not efficient or predictable enough, we are not in a position to make such a strong criticism of Weber. Nevertheless, part of the reason for our complicity is the lack of fully developed alternatives to an increasingly bureaucratized world. Consequently, it is quite fair to criticize Weber for not offering such an alternative, and it is right for those who follow Weber to work at providing a theory of an alternative.

The final criticism is of the unremitting pessimism of Weber's sociology. We can see from Weber's sociological method that he firmly believed in the centrality of individual meaning; however, his substantive work on rationalization and domination indicated that we are trapped in an increasingly meaningless and disenchanted world. It could be said that anyone who still feels optimistic about our culture after reading the closing pages of *The Protestant Ethic* simply hasn't understood them. This alone is not a criticism of Weber. It is shortsighted to criticize someone who points out your cage, if in fact you are in one. Nevertheless, not only did Weber not attempt to provide us with alternatives, he seems to have missed the fact that some of the unintended consequences may be beneficial.

Summary

Max Weber has had a more powerful positive impact on a wide range of sociological theories than any other sociological theorist. This influence is traceable to the sophistication, complexity, and sometimes even confusion of Weberian theory. Despite its problems, Weber's work represents a remarkable fusion of historical research and sociological theorizing.

This chapter opens with a discussion of the theoretical roots and methodological orientations of Weberian theory. Weber, over the course of his career, moved progressively toward a fusion of history and sociology, that is, toward the development of a historical sociology. One of his most critical methodological concepts is *verstehen*. Although this is often interpreted as a tool to be used to analyze individual consciousness, in Weber's hands it was more often a scientific tool to analyze structural and institutional constraints on actors. Other aspects of Weber's methodology, including his propensity to think in terms of causality and to employ ideal types, are discussed. In addition, we examine his analysis of the relationship between values and sociology.

The heart of Weberian sociology lies in substantive sociology, not in methodological statements. Although Weber based his theories on his thoughts about social action and social relationships, his main interest was the large-scale structures and institutions of society. We examine especially his analysis of the three structures of authority—rational-legal, traditional, and charismatic. In the context of rational-legal authority, we deal with his famous ideal-typical bureaucracy and show how he used that tool to analyze traditional and charismatic authority. Of particular interest is Weber's work on charisma. Not only did he have a clear sense of it as a structure of authority, he was also interested in the processes by which such a structure is produced.

Although his work on social structures—such as authority—is important, it is at the cultural level, in his work on the rationalization of the world, that Weber's most important insights lie. Weber articulated the idea that the world is becoming increasingly dominated by norms and values of rationalization. In this context, we discuss Weber's work on the economy, religion, law, the polity, the city, and art forms. Weber argued that rationalization was sweeping across all these institutions in the West, whereas there were major barriers to this process in the rest of the world.

Weber's thoughts on rationalization and various other issues are illustrated in his work on the relationship between religion and capitalism. At one level, this is a series of studies of the relationship between ideas (religious ideas) and the development of the spirit of capitalism and, ultimately, capitalism itself. At another level, it is a study of how the West developed a distinctively rational religious system (Calvinism) that played a key role in the rise of a rational economic system (capitalism). Weber also studied other societies, in which he found religious systems (for example, Confucianism, Taoism, and Hinduism) that inhibit the growth of a rational economic system. It is this kind of majestic sweep over the history of many sectors of the world that helps give Weberian theory its enduring significance.

Georg Simmel

Chapter Outline

Primary Concerns

Individual Consciousness

Social Interaction ("Association")

Social Structures

Objective Culture

The Philosophy of Money

Secrecy: A Case Study in Simmel's Sociology

Criticisms

The impact of the ideas of Georg Simmel (1858–1918) on American sociological theory, as well as sociological theory in general, differs markedly from that of the three theorists discussed in the preceding three chapters of this book (see Dahme, 1990; Featherstone, 1991; Helle, 2005; Kaern, Phillips, and Cohen, 1990; for a good overview of the secondary literature on Simmel, see Frisby, 1994; Nedelmann, 2001; Scaff, 2011). Marx, Durkheim, and Weber, despite their later significance, had relatively little influence on American theory in the early twentieth century. Simmel was much better known to the early American sociologists (Jaworski, 1997). Simmel was eclipsed by Marx, Durkheim, and Weber, although he is far more influential today than classical thinkers such as Comte and Spencer. In recent years we have seen an increase in Simmel's impact on sociological theory (Aronowitz, 1994; D. Levine, 1985, 1989, 1997; Scaff, 2011) as a result of the growing influence of one of his most important works, *The Philosophy of Money* (for an analysis of this work, see Poggi, 1993), as well as the linking of his ideas to one of the most important developments in social thought—postmodern social theory (Weinstein and Weinstein, 1993, 1998).

Primary Concerns

Here we will focus on Simmel's contributions to sociological theory. Simmel, however, was primarily a philosopher, and many of his publications dealt with philosophical issues (for example, ethics) and with other philosophers (for example, Kant).

With the exception of his contribution to the primarily macroscopic conflict theory (Coser, 1956; Simmel, 1908/1955), Georg Simmel is best known as a microsociologist who played a significant role in the development of small-group research (Caplow, 1968), symbolic interactionism, and exchange theory. All of Simmel's contributions in these areas reflect his belief that sociologists should study primarily forms and types of social interaction. Robert Nisbet presents this view of Simmel's contribution to sociology:

> It is the *microsociological* character of Simmel's work that may always give him an edge in timeliness over the other pioneers. He did not disdain the small and the intimate elements of human association, nor did he ever lose sight of the primacy of human beings, of concrete individuals, in his analysis of institutions.
>
> (Nisbet, 1959:480)

David Frisby makes a similar point: "The grounding of sociology in some psychological categories may be one reason why Simmel's sociology has proved attractive not merely to the interactionist but also to social psychology" (1984:57; see also Frisby, 1992:20–41). However, it is often forgotten that Simmel's microsociological work on the forms of interaction is embedded in a broader theory of the relations between individuals and the larger society.

Levels and Areas of Concern

Simmel had a much more complicated and sophisticated theory of social reality than he commonly is given credit for in contemporary American sociology. Tom Bottomore and David Frisby (1978) argue that there are four basic levels of concern in Simmel's work. First are his microscopic assumptions about the psychological components of social life. Second, on a slightly larger scale, is his interest in the sociological components of interpersonal relationships. Third, and most macroscopic, is his work on the structure of, and changes in, the social and cultural "spirit" of his times. Not only did Simmel operate with this image of a three-tiered social reality, he adopted the principle of *emergence* (Sawyer, 2005), the idea that the higher levels emerge out of the lower levels: "Further development replaces the immediacy of interacting forces with the creation of higher supra-individual formations, which appear as independent representatives of these forces and absorb and mediate the relations between individuals" (1907/1978:174). He also said, "If society is to be an autonomous object of an independent science, then it can only be so through the fact that, out of the sum of the individual elements that constitute it, a new entity emerges; otherwise all problems of social science would only be those of individual psychology" (Simmel, cited in Frisby, 1984:56–57). Overarching these three tiers is a fourth that involves ultimate metaphysical principles of life. These eternal truths affect all of Simmel's work and, as we will see, lead to his image of the future direction of the world.

This concern with multiple levels of social reality is reflected in Simmel's definition of three separable problem "areas" in sociology in "The Problem Areas of Sociology" (1917/1950). The first he described as "pure" sociology. In this area, psychological variables are combined with forms of interactions. Although Simmel clearly assumed that actors have creative mental abilities, he gave little explicit attention to this aspect of social reality. His most microscopic work is with the *forms* that interaction takes as well as with the *types* of people who engage in interaction (Korllos, 1994). The forms include subordination, superordination, exchange, conflict, and sociability. In his work

GEORG SIMMEL

A Biographical Sketch

Georg Simmel was born in the heart of Berlin on March 1, 1858. He studied a wide range of subjects at the University of Berlin. However, his first effort to produce a dissertation was rejected, and one of his professors remarked, "We would do him a great service if we do not encourage him further in this direction" (Frisby, 1984:23). Despite this, Simmel persevered and received his doctorate in philosophy in 1881. He remained at the university in a teaching capacity until 1914, although he occupied a relatively unimportant position as *Privatdozent* from 1885 to 1900. In the latter position, Simmel served as an unpaid lecturer whose livelihood was dependent on student fees. Despite his marginality, Simmel did rather well in this position, largely because he was an excellent lecturer and attracted large numbers of (paying) students (Frisby, 1981:17; Salomon, 1963/1997). His style was so popular that even cultured members of Berlin society were drawn to his lectures, which became public events (Leck, 2000).

Simmel's marginality is paralleled by the fact that he was a somewhat contradictory and therefore bewildering person:

> If we put together the testimonials left by relatives, friends, students, contemporaries, we find a number of sometimes contradictory indications concerning Georg Simmel. He is depicted by some as being tall and slender, by others as being short and as bearing a forlorn expression. His appearance is reported to be unattractive, typically Jewish, but also intensely intellectual and noble. He is reported to be hard-working, but also humorous and overarticulate as a lecturer. Finally we hear that he was intellectually brilliant [Lukács, 1991:145], friendly, well-disposed—but also that *inside* he was irrational, opaque, and wild.
>
> (Schnabel, cited in Poggi, 1993:55)

Simmel wrote innumerable articles ("The Metropolis and Mental Life" [1903/1971]) and books (*The Philosophy of Money* [1907/1978]). He was well known in German academic circles and even had an international following, especially in the United States, where his work was of great significance in the

on types, he differentiated between positions in the interactional structure, such as "competitor" and "coquette," and orientations to the world, such as "miser," "spendthrift," "stranger," and "adventurer." At the intermediate level is Simmel's "general" sociology, dealing with the social and cultural products of human history. Here Simmel manifested his larger-scale interests in the group, the structure and history of societies birth of sociology. Finally, in 1900, Simmel received official recognition, a purely honorary title at the University of Berlin, which did not give him full academic status. Simmel tried to obtain many academic positions, but he failed in spite of the support of such scholars as Max Weber.

One of the reasons for Simmel's failure was that he was a Jew in a nineteenth-century Germany rife with anti-Semitism (Birnbaum, 2008; Kasler, 1985). Thus, in a report on Simmel written to a minister of education, Simmel was described as "an Israelite through and through, in his external appearance, in his bearing and in his mode of thought" (Frisby, 1981:25). Another reason was the kind of work that he did. Many of his articles appeared in newspapers and magazines; they were written for an audience more general than simply academic sociologists (Rammstedt, 1991). In addition, because he did not hold a regular academic appointment, he was forced to earn his living through public lectures. Simmel's audience, both for his writings and for his lectures, was more the intellectual public than professional sociologists, and this tended to lead to derisive judgments from fellow professionals. For example, one of his contemporaries damned him because "his influence remained . . . upon the general atmosphere and affected, above all, the higher levels of journalism" (Troeltsch, cited in Frisby, 1981:13). Simmel's personal failures can also be linked to the low esteem that German academicians of that day had for sociology.

In 1914 Simmel finally obtained a regular academic appointment at a minor university (Strasbourg), but he once again felt estranged. On the one hand, he regretted leaving his audience of Berlin intellectuals. Thus his wife wrote to Max Weber's wife: "Georg has taken leave of the auditorium very badly. . . . The students were very affectionate and sympathetic. . . . It was a departure at the full height of life" (Frisby, 1981:29). On the other hand, Simmel did not feel a part of the life of his new university. Thus, he wrote to Mrs. Weber: "There is hardly anything to report from us. We live . . . a cloistered, closed-off, indifferent, desolate external existence. Academic activity is 0, the people . . . alien and inwardly hostile" (Frisby, 1981:32).

World War I started soon after Simmel's appointment at Strasbourg; lecture halls were turned into military hospitals, and students went off to war. Thus, Simmel remained a marginal figure in German academia until his death in 1918. He never did have a normal academic career. Nevertheless, Simmel attracted a large academic following in his day, and his fame as a scholar has, if anything, grown over the years.

and cultures. Finally, in Simmel's "philosophical" sociology, he dealt with his views on the basic nature, and inevitable fate, of humankind. Throughout this chapter, we will touch on all these levels and sociologies. We will find that although Simmel sometimes separated the different levels and sociologies, he more often integrated them into a broader totality.

Dialectical Thinking

Simmel's way of dealing with the interrelationships among three basic levels of social reality (leaving out his fourth, metaphysical, level) gave his sociology a dialectical character reminiscent of Marx's sociology (D. Levine, 1991b:109). A dialectical approach, as we saw earlier, is multicausal and multidirectional, integrates fact and value, rejects the idea that there are hard-and-fast dividing lines between social phenomena, focuses on social relations (B. Turner, 1986), looks not only at the present but also at the past and the future, and is deeply concerned with both conflicts and contradictions.

In spite of the similarities between Marx and Simmel in their use of a dialectical approach, there are important differences between them. Of greatest importance is the fact that they focused on very different aspects of the social world and offered very different images of the future of the world. Instead of Marx's revolutionary optimism, Simmel had a view of the future closer to Weber's image of an "iron cage" from which there is no escape (for more on the intellectual relationship between Simmel and Weber, see Scaff, 1989:121–151).

Simmel manifested his commitment to the dialectic in various ways (Featherstone, 1991:7). For one thing, Simmel's sociology was always concerned with relationships (Lichtblau and Ritter, 1991), especially interaction (*association*). More generally, Simmel was a "methodological relationist" (Ritzer and Gindoff, 1992) operating with the "principle that everything interacts in some way with everything else" (Simmel, cited in Frisby, 1992:9). Overall he was ever attuned to dualisms, conflicts, and contradictions in whatever realm of the social world he happened to be working on (Sellerberg, 1994). Donald Levine states that this perspective reflects Simmel's belief that *"the world can best be understood in terms of conflicts and contrasts between opposed categories"* (1971:xxxv). Rather than try to deal with this mode of thinking throughout Simmel's work, we will illustrate it from his work on one of his forms of interaction—fashion. Simmel used a similar mode of dialectical thinking in most of his essays on social forms and social types, but this discussion of fashion amply illustrates his method of dealing with these phenomena. We will also deal with the dialectic in Simmel's thoughts on subjective-objective culture and the concepts of "more-life" and "more-than-life."

Fashion

In one of his typically fascinating and dualistic essays, Simmel (1904/1971; Gronow, 1997; Nedelmann, 1990) illustrated the contradictions in fashion in a variety of ways. On the one hand, fashion is a form of social relationship that allows those who wish to conform to the demands of the group to do so. On the other hand, fashion also provides the norm from which those who wish to be individualistic can deviate. Fashion involves a historical process as well: at the initial stage, everyone accepts what is fashionable; inevitably, individuals deviate from this; and finally, in the process of deviation, they may adopt a whole new view of what is in fashion. Fashion is also dialectical in the sense that the success and spread of any given fashion lead to its eventual failure. That is, the distinctiveness of something leads to its being considered fashionable; however, as large numbers of people come to accept it, it ceases to be distinctive and hence it loses its attractiveness. Still another duality involves the role of the leader of a fashion movement. Such a person leads the group, paradoxically, by *following* the fashion better than anyone else, that is, by adopting it more determinedly. Finally, Simmel argued that not only does following what is in fashion involve dualities, so does the effort on the part of some people to be out of fashion. Unfashionable people view those who follow a fashion as being imitators and themselves as mavericks, but Simmel argued that the latter are simply engaging in an inverse form of imitation. Individuals may avoid what is in fashion because they are afraid that they, like their peers, will lose their individuality, but in Simmel's view, such a fear is hardly a sign of great personal strength and independence. In sum, Simmel noted that in fashion "all . . . leading antithetical tendencies . . . are represented in one way or another" (1904/1971:317).

Simmel's dialectical thinking can be seen at a more general level as well. As we will see throughout this chapter, he was most interested in the conflicts and contradictions that exist between the individual and the larger social and cultural structures that individuals construct. These structures ultimately come to have a life of their own, over which the individual can exert little or no control.

Individual (Subjective) Culture and Objective Culture

People are influenced, and in Simmel's view threatened, by social structures and, more important for Simmel, by their cultural products. Simmel distinguished between individual culture and objective culture. *Objective culture* refers to those things that people produce (art, science, philosophy, and so on). *Individual (subjective) culture* is the capacity of the actor to produce, absorb, and control the elements of objective culture. In an ideal sense, individual culture shapes, and is shaped by, objective culture. The problem is that objective culture comes to have a life of its own. As Simmel put it, "They [the elements of culture] acquire fixed identities, a logic and lawfulness of their own; this new rigidity inevitably places them at a distance from the spiritual dynamic which created them and which makes them independent" (1921/1968:11). The existence of these cultural products creates a contradiction with the actors who created them because it is an example of

> the deep estrangement or animosity which exists between organic and creative processes of the soul and its contents and products: the vibrating, restless life of the creative soul; which develops toward the infinite contrasts with its fixed and ideally unchanging product and its uncanny feedback effect, which arrests and indeed rigidifies this liveliness. Frequently it appears as if creative movement of the soul was dying from its own product.
>
> (Simmel, 1921/1968:42)

As K. Peter Etzkorn said, "In Simmel's dialectic, man is always in danger of being slain by those objects of his own creation which have lost their organic human coefficient" (1968:2).

More-Life and More-Than-Life

Another area of Simmel's thinking, his philosophical sociology, is an even more general manifestation of his dialectical thinking. In discussing the emergence of social and cultural structures, Simmel took a position very similar to some of Marx's ideas.

Marx used the concept of the fetishism of commodities to illustrate the separation between people and their products. For Marx, this separation reached its apex in capitalism, could be overcome only in the future socialist society, and thus was a specific historical phenomenon. But for Simmel this separation is inherent in the nature of human life. In philosophical terms, there is an inherent and inevitable contradiction between "more-life" and "more-than-life" (Oakes, 1984:6; Weingartner, 1959).

The issue of more-life and more-than-life is central in Simmel's essay "The Transcendent Character of Life" (1918/1971). As the title suggests and as Simmel makes clear, *"Transcendence is immanent in life"* (1918/1971:361). People possess a doubly transcendent capability. First, because of their restless, creative capacities (more-life), people are able to transcend themselves. Second, this transcendent, creative ability makes it possible for people to constantly produce sets of objects that transcend them. The objective existence of these phenomena (more-than-life) comes to stand in irreconcilable opposition to the creative forces (more-life) that produced the objects in the first place. In other words, social life "creates and sets free from itself something that is not life but 'which has its own significance and follows its own law'" (Weingartner, citing Simmel, 1959:53). Life is found in the unity, and the conflict, between the two. As Simmel concludes, "Life finds its essence, its process, in being more-life and more-than-life" (1918/1971:374).

Thus, because of his metaphysical conceptions, Simmel came to an image of the world far closer to Weber's than to Marx's. Simmel, like Weber, saw the world as becoming an iron cage of objective culture from which people have progressively less chance of escape. We will have more to say about a number of these issues in the following sections, which deal with Simmel's thoughts on the major components of social reality.

Individual Consciousness

At the individual level, Simmel focused on forms of association and paid relatively little attention to the issue of individual consciousness (for at least one exception, a discussion of memory, see Jedlowski, 1990), which was rarely dealt with directly in his work. Still, Simmel clearly operated with a sense that human beings possess creative consciousness. As Frisby put it, the bases of social life to Simmel were "conscious individuals or groups of individuals who interact with one another for a variety of motives, purposes, and interests" (1984:61). This interest in creativity is manifest in Simmel's discussion of the diverse forms of interaction, the ability of actors to create social structures, as well as the disastrous effects those structures have on the creativity of individuals.

All of Simmel's discussions of the forms of interaction imply that actors must be consciously oriented to one another. Thus, for example, interaction in a stratified system requires that superordinates and subordinates orient themselves to each other. The interaction would cease and the stratification system would collapse if a process of mutual orientation did not exist. The same is true of all other forms of interaction.

Consciousness plays other roles in Simmel's work. For example, although Simmel believed that social (and cultural) structures come to have a life of their own, he realized that people must conceptualize such structures in order for them to have an effect on the people. Simmel stated that society is not simply "out there" but is also "'my representation'—something dependent on the activity of consciousness" (1908/1959a:339).

Simmel also had a sense of individual conscience and of the fact that the norms and values of society become internalized in individual consciousness. The existence of norms and values both internally and externally

> explains the dual character of the moral command: that on the one hand, it
> confronts us as an impersonal order to which we simply have to submit, but that,
> on the other, no external power, but only our most private and internal impulses,
> imposes it upon us. At any rate, here is one of the cases where the individual,
> within his own consciousness, repeats the relationships which exist between him,
> as a total personality, and the group.
>
> (Simmel, 1908/1950a:254)

This very modern conception of internalization is a relatively undeveloped assumption in Simmel's work.

In addition, Simmel had a conception of people's ability to confront themselves mentally, to set themselves apart from their own actions, that is very similar to the views of George Herbert Mead and the symbolic interactionists (Simmel, 1918/1971:364; see also Simmel, 1907/1978:64). The actor can take in external stimuli, assess them, try out different courses of action, and then decide what to do. Because of these mental capacities, the actor is not simply enslaved by external forces. But there is a paradox in Simmel's conception of the actor's mental capacities. The mind can keep people from being enslaved by external stimuli, but it also has the capacity to reify social reality, to create the very objects that come to enslave it. As Simmel said, "Our mind has a remarkable ability to think of contents as being independent of the act of thinking" (1907/1978:65). Thus, although their intelligence enables people to avoid being enslaved by the same external stimuli that constrain lower animals, it also creates the structures and institutions that constrain their thoughts and actions.

Although we can find manifestations of Simmel's concern with consciousness in various places in his work, he did very little more than assume its existence. Raymond Aron clearly makes this point: "He [Simmel] must know the laws of behavior . . . of human reaction. But he does not try to discover or to explain what goes on in the mind itself" (1965:5–6).

Social Interaction ("Association")

Georg Simmel is best known in contemporary sociology for his contributions to our understanding of the patterns, or forms, of social interaction. He expressed his interest in this level of social reality in this way:

> We are dealing here with microscopic-molecular processes within human material,
> so to speak. These processes are the actual occurrences that are concatenated or
> hypostatized into those macrocosmic, solid units and systems. That people look at
> one another and are jealous of one another; that they exchange letters or have dinner

together; that apart from all tangible interests they strike one another as pleasant or unpleasant; that gratitude for altruistic acts makes for inseparable union; that one asks another to point out a certain street; that people dress and adorn themselves for each other—these are a few casually chosen illustrations from the whole range of relations that play between one person and another. They may be momentary or permanent, conscious or unconscious, ephemeral or of grave consequence, but they incessantly tie men together. At each moment such threads are spun, dropped, taken up again, displaced by others, interwoven with others. These interactions among the atoms of society are accessible only to psychological microscopy.

(Simmel, 1908/1959b:327–328)

Simmel made clear here that one of his primary interests was interaction (association) among conscious actors and that his intent was to look at a wide range of interactions that may seem trivial at some times but crucially important at others. His was not a Durkheimian expression of interest in social facts but a declaration of a smaller-scale focus for sociology.

Because Simmel sometimes took an exaggerated position on the importance of interaction in his sociology, many have lost sight of his insights into the larger-scale aspects of social reality. At times, for example, he equated society with interaction: "Society . . . is only the synthesis or the general term for the totality of these specific interactions. . . . 'Society' is identical with the sum total of these relations" (Simmel, 1907/1978:175). Such statements may be taken as a reaffirmation of his interest in interaction, but as we will see, in his general and philosophical sociologies, Simmel held a much larger-scale conception of society as well as culture.

Interaction: Forms and Types

One of Simmel's dominant concerns was the *form* rather than the *content* of social interaction. This concern stemmed from Simmel's identification with the Kantian tradition in philosophy, in which much is made of the difference between form and content. Simmel's position here, however, was quite simple. From Simmel's point of view, the real world is composed of innumerable events, actions, interactions, and so forth. To cope with this maze of reality (the "contents"), people order it by imposing patterns, or forms, on it. Thus, instead of a bewildering array of specific events, the actor is confronted with a limited number of forms. In Simmel's view, the sociologist's task is to do precisely what the layperson does, that is, impose a limited number of forms on social reality, on interaction in particular, so that it may be better analyzed. This methodology generally involves extracting commonalities that are found in a wide array of specific interactions. For example, the superordination and subordination forms of interaction are found in a wide range of settings, "in the state as well as in a religious community, in a band of conspirators as in an economic association, in art school as in a family" (Simmel, 1908/1959b:317). Donald Levine, one of Simmel's foremost contemporary analysts, describes Simmel's method of doing formal interactional sociology in this way: "His method is to select some bounded, finite phenomenon from the world of flux; to examine the multiplicity of elements which compose it; and to ascertain the cause of their coherence by disclosing its form. Secondarily, he investigates the origins of this form and its structural implications" (1971:xxxi). More specifically, Levine points out that "forms are the patterns exhibited by the associations" of people (1981b:65).[1]

Simmel's interest in the forms of social interaction has been subjected to various criticisms. For example, he has been accused of imposing order where there is none and of producing a series of unrelated studies that in the end really impose no better order on the complexities of social reality than does the layperson. Some of these criticisms are valid only if we focus on Simmel's concern with forms of interaction, his formal sociology, and ignore the other types of sociology he practiced.

However, there are a number of ways to defend Simmel's approach to formal sociology. First, it is close to reality, as reflected by the innumerable real-life examples employed by Simmel. Second, it does not impose arbitrary and rigid categories on social reality but tries instead to allow the forms to flow from social reality. Third, Simmel's approach does not employ a general theoretical schema into which all aspects of the social world are forced. He thus avoided the reification of a theoretical schema that plagues a theorist like Talcott Parsons. Finally, formal sociology militates against the poorly conceptualized empiricism that is characteristic of much of sociology. Simmel certainly used empirical "data," but they are subordinated to his effort to impose some order on the bewildering world of social reality.

Social Geometry

In Simmel's formal sociology, one sees most clearly his effort to develop a "geometry" of social relations. Two of the geometric coefficients that interested him are numbers and distance (others are position, valence, self-involvement, and symmetry [Levine, 1981b]).

Numbers   Simmel's interest in the impact of numbers of people on the quality of interaction can be seen in his discussion of the difference between a dyad and a triad.

Dyad and Triad.   For Simmel (1950) there was a crucial difference between the *dyad* (two-person group) and the *triad* (three-person group). The addition of a third person causes a radical and fundamental change. Increasing the membership beyond three has nowhere near the same impact as does adding a third member. Unlike all other groups, the dyad does not achieve a meaning beyond the two individuals involved. There is no independent group structure in a dyad; there is nothing more to the group than the two separable individuals. Thus, each member of a dyad retains a high level of individuality. The individual is not lowered to the level of the group. This is not the case in a triad. A triad does have the possibility of obtaining a meaning beyond the individuals involved. There is likely to be more to a triad than the individuals involved. It is likely to develop an independent group structure. As a result, there is

---

[1] In the specific case of interaction, contents are the *"drives, purposes and ideas which lead people to associate* with one another" (Levine, 1981b:65).

a greater threat to the individuality of the members. A triad can have a general leveling effect on the members.

With the addition of a third party to the group, a number of new social roles become possible. For example, the third party can take the role of arbitrator or mediator in disputes within the group. Then the third party can use disputes between the other two for his or her own gain or become an object of competition between the other two parties. The third member also can intentionally foster conflict between the other two parties in order to gain superiority (divide and rule). A stratification system and an authority structure then can emerge. The movement from dyad to triad is essential to the development of social structures that can become separate from, and dominant over, individuals. Such a possibility does not exist in a dyad.

The process that is begun in the transition from a dyad to a triad continues as larger and larger groups and, ultimately, societies emerge. In these large social structures, the individual, increasingly separated from the structure of society, grows more and more alone, isolated, and segmented. This results finally in a dialectical relationship between individuals and social structures: "According to Simmel, the socialized individual always remains in a dual relation toward society: he is incorporated within it and yet stands against it. . . . The individual is determined, yet determining; acted upon, yet self-actuating" (Coser, 1965:11). The contradiction here is that "society allows the emergence of individuality and autonomy, but it also impedes it" (Coser, 1965:11).

Group Size.   At a more general level, there is Simmel's (1908/1971a) ambivalent attitude toward the impact of group *size.* On the one hand, he took the position that the increase in the size of a group or society increases individual freedom. A small group or society is likely to control the individual completely. However, in a larger society, the individual is likely to be involved in a number of groups, each of which controls only a small portion of his or her total personality. In other words, "*Individuality in being and action generally increases to the degree that the social circle encompassing the individual expands*" (Simmel, 1908/1971a:252). However, Simmel took the view that large societies create a set of problems that ultimately threaten individual freedom. For example, he saw the masses as likely to be dominated by one idea, the simplest idea. The physical proximity of a mass makes people suggestible and more likely to follow simplistic ideas, to engage in mindless, emotional actions.

Perhaps most important, in terms of Simmel's interest in forms of interaction, is that increasing size and differentiation tend to loosen the bonds between individuals and leave in their place much more distant, impersonal, and segmental relationships. Paradoxically, the large group that frees the individual simultaneously threatens that individuality. Also paradoxical is Simmel's belief that one way for individuals to cope with the threat of the mass society is to immerse themselves in small groups such as the family.

Distance   Another of Simmel's concerns in social geometry was *distance.* Levine offers a good summation of Simmel's views on the role of distance in social relationships:

"The properties of forms and the meanings of things are a function of the relative distances between individuals and other individuals or things" (1971:xxxiv). This concern with distance is manifest in various places in Simmel's work. We will discuss it in two different contexts—in Simmel's massive *The Philosophy of Money* and in one of his cleverest essays, "The Stranger."

In *The Philosophy of Money* (1907/1978), Simmel enunciated some general principles about value—and about what makes things valuable—that served as the basis for his analysis of money. Because we deal with this work in detail later in this chapter, we discuss this issue only briefly here. The essential point is that the value of something is determined by its distance from the actor. It is not valuable if it is either too close and too easy to obtain or too distant and too difficult to obtain. Objects that are attainable, but only with great effort, are the most valuable.

Distance also plays a central role in Simmel's "The Stranger" (1908/1971b; McVeigh and Sikkink, 2005; Tabboni, 1995), an essay on a type of actor who is neither too close nor too far. If he (or she) were too close, he would no longer be a stranger, but if he were too far, he would cease to have any contact with the group. The interaction that the stranger engages in with the group members involves a combination of closeness and distance. The peculiar distance of the stranger from the group allows him to have a series of unusual interaction patterns with the members. For example, the stranger can be more objective in his relationships with the group members. Because he is a stranger, other group members feel more comfortable expressing confidences to him. In these and other ways, a pattern of coordination and consistent interaction emerges between the stranger and the other group members. The stranger becomes an organic member of the group. But Simmel not only considered the stranger a social type, he considered strangeness a form of social interaction. A degree of strangeness, involving a combination of nearness and remoteness, enters into all social relationships, even the most intimate. Thus we can examine a wide range of specific interactions in order to discover the degree of strangeness found in each.

Although geometric dimensions enter a number of Simmel's types and forms, there is much more to them than simply geometry. The types and forms are constructs that Simmel used to gain a greater understanding of a wide range of interaction patterns.

Social Types

We have already encountered one of Simmel's types, the stranger; others include the miser, the spendthrift, the adventurer, and the nobleman. To illustrate his mode of thinking in this area, we will focus on one of his types, the poor.

The Poor As is typical of types in Simmel's work, the *poor* were defined in terms of social relationships, as being aided by other people or at least having the right to that aid. Here Simmel quite clearly did not hold the view that *poverty* is defined by a quantity, or rather a lack of quantity, of money.

Although Simmel focused on the poor in terms of characteristic relationships and interaction patterns, he also used the occasion of his essay "The Poor" (1908/1971c) to develop a wide range of interesting insights into the poor and poverty. It was characteristic of Simmel to offer a profusion of insights in every essay. Indeed, this is one of his great claims to fame. For example, Simmel argued that a reciprocal set of rights and obligations defines the relationship between the needy and the givers. The needy have the right to receive aid, and this right makes receiving aid less painful. Conversely, the giver has the obligation to give to the needy. Simmel also took the functionalist position that aid to the poor by society helps support the system. Society requires aid to the poor "so that the poor will not become active and dangerous enemies of society, so as to make their reduced energies more productive, and so as to prevent the degeneration of their progeny" (Simmel, 1908/1971c:154). Thus, aid to the poor is for the sake of society, not so much for the poor per se. The state plays a key role here, and, as Simmel saw it, the treatment of the poor grows increasingly impersonal as the mechanism for giving aid becomes more bureaucratized.

Simmel also had a relativistic view of poverty; that is, the poor are not simply those who stand at the bottom of society. From his point of view, poverty is found in *all* social strata. This concept foreshadowed the later sociological concept of *relative deprivation*. If people who are members of the upper classes have less than their peers do, they are likely to feel poor in comparison to them. Therefore, government programs aimed at eradicating poverty can never succeed. Even if those at the bottom are elevated, many people throughout the stratification system will still feel poor in comparison to their peers.

Social Forms

As with social types, Simmel looked at a wide range of social forms, including exchange, conflict, prostitution, and sociability. We can illustrate Simmel's (1908/1971d) work on social forms through his discussion of domination, that is, superordination and subordination.

Superordination and Subordination   Superordination and subordination have a reciprocal relationship. The leader does not want to determine completely the thoughts and actions of others. Rather, the leader expects the subordinate to react either positively or negatively. Neither this nor any other form of interaction can exist without mutual relationships. Even in the most oppressive form of domination, subordinates have at least some degree of personal freedom.

To most people, superordination involves an effort to eliminate completely the independence of subordinates, but Simmel argued that a social relationship would cease to exist if this were the case.

Simmel asserted that one can be subordinated to an individual, a group, or an objective force. Leadership by a single individual generally leads to a tightly knit group either in support of or in opposition to the leader. Even when opposition arises in such a group, discord can be resolved more easily when the parties stand under the same higher power. Subordination under a plurality can have very uneven effects. On the one hand, the objectivity of rule by a plurality may make for greater unity in the group than does the more arbitrary rule of an individual. On the other hand, hostility is likely to be engendered among subordinates if they do not get the personal attention of a leader.

Simmel found subordination under an objective principle to be most offensive, perhaps because human relationships and social interactions are eliminated. People feel they are determined by an impersonal law that they have no ability to affect. Simmel saw subordination to an individual as freer and more spontaneous: "Subordination under a person has an element of freedom and dignity in comparison with which all obedience to laws has something mechanical and passive" (1908/1971d:115). Even worse is subordination to objects (for example, icons), which Simmel found a "humiliatingly harsh and unconditional kind of subordination" (1908/1971d:115). Because the individual is dominated by a thing, "he himself psychologically sinks to the category of mere thing" (Simmel, 1908/1971d:117).

Social Forms and Simmel's Larger Problematic   Guy Oakes (1984) linked Simmel's discussion of forms to his basic problematic, the growing gap between objective and subjective culture. He begins with the position that in "Simmel's view, the discovery of objectivity—the independence of things from the condition of their subjective or psychological genesis—was the greatest achievement in the cultural history of the West" (Oakes, 1984:3). One of the ways in which Simmel addresses this objectivity is in his discussion of forms, but although such formalization and objectification are necessary and desirable, they can come to be quite undesirable:

> On the one hand, forms are necessary conditions for the expression and the realization of the energies and interests of life. On the other hand, these forms become increasingly detached and remote from life. When this happens, a conflict develops between the process of life and the configurations in which it is expressed. Ultimately, this conflict threatens to nullify the relationship between life and form, and thus to destroy the conditions under which the process of life can be realized in autonomous structures.
>
> (Oakes, 1984:4)

Social Structures

Simmel said relatively little directly about the large-scale structures of society. In fact, at times, given his focus on patterns of interaction, he denied the existence of that level of social reality. A good example of this is found in his effort to define *society,* where he rejected the realist position exemplified by Emile Durkheim that society is a real, material entity. Lewis Coser notes, "He did not see society as a thing or an organism" (1965:5). Simmel was also uncomfortable with the nominalist conception that society is nothing more than a collection of isolated individuals. He adopted an intermediate position, conceiving of society as a set of interactions (Spykman, 1925/1966:88). "*Society* is merely the name for a number of individuals connected by 'interaction'" (Simmel, cited in Coser, 1965:5).

Although Simmel enunciated this interactionist position, in much of his work he operated as a realist, as if society were a real material structure. There is, then, a basic contradiction in Simmel's work on the social-structural level. Simmel noted, "Society transcends the individual and lives its own life which follows its own laws. It, too, confronts the individual with a historical, imperative firmness" (1908/1950a:258). Coser catches the essence of this aspect of Simmel's thought: "The larger superindividual structures—the state, the clan, the family, the city, or the trade union—turn out to be but crystallizations of this interaction, even though they may attain autonomy and permanency and confront the individual as if they were alien powers" (1965:5). Rudolph Heberle makes essentially the same point: "One can scarcely escape the impression that Simmel views society as an interplay of structural factors, in which the human beings appear as passive objects rather than as live and willing actors" (1965:117).

The resolution of this paradox lies in the difference between Simmel's formal sociology, in which he tended to adhere to an interactionist view of society, and his historical and philosophical sociologies, in which he was much more inclined to see society as an independent, coercive social structure. In the latter sociologies, he saw society as part of the broader process of the development of objective culture, which worried him. Although objective culture is best seen as part of the cultural realm, Simmel included the growth of large-scale social structures as part of this process. That Simmel related the growth of social structures to the spread of objective culture is clear in this statement: "The increasing objectification of our culture, whose phenomena consist more and more of impersonal elements and less and less absorb the subjective totality of the individual . . . also involves sociological structures" (1908/1950b:318). In addition to clarifying the relationship between society and objective culture, this statement leads to Simmel's thoughts on the cultural level of social reality.

Objective Culture

One of the main focuses of Simmel's historical and philosophical sociology is the cultural level of social reality, or what he called the "objective culture." In Simmel's view, people produce culture, but because of their ability to reify social reality, the cultural world and the social world come to have lives of their own, lives that come increasingly to dominate the actors who created, and daily re-create, them. "The cultural objects become more and more linked to each other in a self-contained world which has increasingly fewer contacts with the [individual] subjective psyche and its desires and sensibilities" (Coser, 1965:22). Although people always retain the capacity to create and re-create culture, the long-term trend of history is for culture to exert a more and more coercive force on the actor.

> The preponderance of objective over [individual] subjective culture that developed during the nineteenth century . . . this discrepancy seems to widen steadily. Every day and from all sides, the wealth of objective culture increases, but the individual mind can enrich the forms and content of its own development only by distancing itself still further from that culture and developing its own at a much slower pace.
>
> (Simmel, 1907/1978:449)

In various places in his work, Simmel identified a number of components of the objective culture, for example, tools, means of transport, products of science, technology, arts, language, the intellectual sphere, conventional wisdom, religious dogma, philosophical systems, legal systems, moral codes, and ideals (for example, the "fatherland"). The objective culture grows and expands in various ways. First, its absolute size grows with increasing modernization. This can be seen most obviously in the case of scientific knowledge, which is expanding exponentially, although this is just as true of most other aspects of the cultural realm. Second, the number of different components of the cultural realm also grows. Finally, and perhaps most important, the various elements of the cultural world become more and more intertwined in an ever more powerful, self-contained world that is increasingly beyond the control of the actors (Oakes, 1984:12). Simmel not only was interested in describing the growth of objective culture but also was greatly disturbed by it: "Simmel was impressed—if not depressed—by the bewildering number and variety of human products which in the contemporary world surround and unceasingly impinge upon the individual" (Weingartner, 1959:33).

What worried Simmel most was the threat to individual culture posed by the growth of objective culture. Simmel's personal sympathies were with a world dominated by individual culture, but he saw the possibility of such a world as more and more unlikely. It is this that Simmel described as the "tragedy of culture." Simmel's specific analysis of the growth of objective culture over individual subjective culture is simply one example of a general principle that dominates all of life: "The total value of something increases to the same extent as the value of its individual parts declines" (1907/1978:199).

We can relate Simmel's general argument about objective culture to his more basic analysis of forms of interaction. In one of his best-known essays, "The Metropolis and Mental Life" (1903/1971), Simmel analyzed the forms of interaction that take place in the modern city (Vidler, 1991). He saw the modern metropolis as the "genuine arena" of the growth of objective culture and the decline of individual culture. It is the scene of the predominance of the money economy, and money, as Simmel often made clear, has a profound effect on the nature of human relationships. The widespread use of money leads to an emphasis on calculability and rationality in all spheres of life. Thus genuine human relationships decline, and social relationships tend to be dominated by a blasé and reserved attitude. Whereas the small town was characterized by greater feeling and emotionality, the modern city is characterized by a shallow intellectuality that matches the calculability needed by a money economy. The city is also the center of the division of labor, and, as we have seen, specialization plays a central role in the production of an ever-expanding objective culture, with a corresponding decline in individual culture. The city is a "frightful leveler," in which virtually everyone is reduced to emphasizing unfeeling calculability. It is more and more difficult to maintain individuality in the face of the expansion of objective culture (Lohmann and Wilkes, 1996).

It should be pointed out that in his essay on the city (as well as in many other places in his work) Simmel also discussed the liberating effect of this modern development. For example, he emphasized the fact that people are freer in the modern city than in the tight social confines of the small town. More is said about Simmel's thoughts on the liberating impact of modernity at the close of the following section, devoted to Simmel's book *The Philosophy of Money*.

First, it is necessary to indicate that one of the many ironies of Simmel's influence on the development of sociology is that his microanalytic work is used, but its broader implications are ignored almost totally. Take the example of Simmel's work on exchange relationships. He saw exchange as the "purest and most developed kind" of interaction (Simmel, 1907/1978:82). Although all forms of interaction involve some sacrifice, it occurs most clearly in exchange relationships. Simmel thought of all social exchanges as involving "profit and loss." Such an orientation was crucial to Simmel's microsociological work and specifically to the development of his largely micro-oriented exchange theory. However, his thoughts on exchange are also expressed in his broader work on money. To Simmel, money is the purest form of exchange. In contrast to a barter economy, where the cycle ends when one object has been exchanged for another, an economy based on money allows for an endless series of exchanges. This possibility is crucial for Simmel because it provides the basis for the widespread development of social structures and objective culture. Consequently, money as a form of exchange represented for Simmel one of the root causes of the alienation of people in a modern reified social structure.

In his treatment of the city and exchange, one can see the elegance of Simmel's thinking as he related small-scale sociological forms of exchange to the development of modern society in its totality. Although this link can be found in his specific essays (especially Simmel, 1991), it is clearest in *The Philosophy of Money*.

The Philosophy of Money

The Philosophy of Money (1907/1978) illustrates well the breadth and sophistication of Simmel's thinking (Deflem, 2003). It demonstrates conclusively that Simmel deserves at least as much recognition for his general theory as for his essays on microsociology, many of which can be seen as specific manifestations of his general theory.

Although the title makes it clear that Simmel's focus is money, his interest in that phenomenon is embedded in a set of his broader theoretical and philosophical concerns. For example, as we have already seen, Simmel was interested in the broad issue of value, and money can be seen as simply a specific form of value. At another level, Simmel was interested not in money per se but in its impact on such a wide range of phenomena as the "inner world" of actors and the objective culture as a whole. At still another level, he treated money as a specific phenomenon linked with a variety of other components of life, including "exchange, ownership, greed, extravagance, cynicism, individual freedom, the style of life, culture, the value of the personality, etc." (Siegfried Kracauer, cited in Bottomore and Frisby, 1978:7). Finally, and most generally, Simmel saw money as a specific component of life capable of helping us understand the totality of life. As Tom Bottomore and David Frisby put it, Simmel sought no less than to extract "the totality of the spirit of the age from his analysis of money" (1978:7).

The Philosophy of Money has much in common with the work of Karl Marx. Like Marx, Simmel focused on capitalism and the problems created by a money economy. Despite this common ground, however, the differences are overwhelming. For example, Simmel saw the economic problems of his time as simply a specific manifestation of a more general cultural problem, the alienation of objective from subjective culture (Poggi, 1993). To Marx these problems are specific to capitalism, but to Simmel they are part of a universal tragedy—the increasing powerlessness of the individual in the face of the growth of objective culture. Whereas Marx's analysis is historically specific, Simmel's analysis seeks to extract timeless truths from the flux of human history. As Frisby says, "In his *The Philosophy of Money* . . . [w]hat is missing . . . is a historical sociology of money relationships" (1984:58). This difference in their analyses is related to a crucial political difference between Simmel and Marx. Because Marx saw economic problems as time-bound, the product of capitalist society, he believed that eventually they could be solved. Simmel, however, saw the basic problems as inherent in human life and held out no hope for future improvement. In fact, Simmel believed that socialism, instead of improving the situation, would heighten the kinds of problems discussed in *The Philosophy of Money*. Despite some substantive similarities to Marxian theory, Simmel's thought is far closer to that of Weber and his "iron cage" in terms of his image of both the modern world and its future.

The Philosophy of Money begins with a discussion of the general forms of money and value. Later the discussion moves to the impact of money on the "inner world" of actors and on culture in general. Because the argument is so complex, it is only highlighted here.

Money and Value

One of Simmel's initial concerns in the work, as we discussed briefly earlier, is the relationship between money and value (Kamolnick, 2001). In general, he argued that people create value by making objects, separating themselves from those objects, and then seeking to overcome the "distance, obstacles, difficulties" (Simmel, 1907/1978:66). The greater the difficulty of obtaining an object, the greater its value. However, difficulty of attainment has a "lower and an upper limit" (Simmel, 1907/1978:72). The general principle is that the value of things comes from the ability of people to distance themselves properly from objects. Things that are too close, too easily obtained, are not very valuable. Some exertion is needed for something to be considered valuable. Conversely, things that are too far, too difficult, or nearly impossible to obtain are also not very valuable. Things that defy most, if not all, of our efforts to obtain them cease to be valuable to us. Those things that are most valuable are neither too distant nor too close. Among the factors involved in the distance of an object from an actor are the time it takes to obtain it, its scarcity, the difficulties involved in acquiring it, and the need to give up other things in order to acquire it. People try to place themselves at a proper distance from objects, which must be attainable, but not too easily.

In this general context of value, Simmel discussed money. In the economic realm, money serves both to create distance from objects and to provide the means to overcome it. The money value attached to objects in a modern economy places them at a distance from us; we cannot obtain them without money of our own. The difficulty in obtaining the money and therefore the objects makes them valuable to us. At the same time, once we obtain enough money, we are able to overcome the distance between ourselves and the objects. Money thus performs the interesting function of creating distance between people and objects and then providing the means to overcome that distance.

Money, Reification, and Rationalization

In the process of creating value, money also provides the basis for the development of the market, the modern economy, and ultimately modern (capitalistic) society (Poggi, 1996). Money provides the means by which these entities acquire a life of their own that is external to, and coercive of, the actor. This stands in contrast to earlier societies in which barter or trade could not lead to the reified world that is the distinctive product of a money economy. Money permits this development in various ways. For example, Simmel argued that money allows for "long-range calculations, large-scale enterprises and long-term credits" (1907/1978:125). Later, Simmel said that "money has . . . developed . . . the most objective practices, the most logical, purely mathematical norms, the absolute freedom from everything personal" (1907/1978:128). He saw this process of reification as only part of the more general process by which the mind embodies and symbolizes itself in objects. These embodiments, these symbolic structures, become reified and come to exert a controlling force on actors.

Not only does money help create a reified social world, it also contributes to the increasing rationalization of that social world (Deutschmann, 1996; B. Turner, 1986). This is another of the concerns that Simmel shared with Weber (D. Levine, 2000). A money economy fosters an emphasis on quantitative rather than qualitative factors. Simmel stated:

> It would be easy to multiply the examples that illustrate the growing preponderance of the category of quantity over that of quality, or more precisely the tendency to dissolve quality into quantity, to remove the elements more and more from quality, to grant them only specific forms of motion and to interpret everything that is specifically, individually, and qualitatively determined as the more or less, the bigger or smaller, the wider or narrower, the more or less frequent of those colourless elements and awarenesses that are only accessible to numerical determination—even though this tendency may never absolutely attain its goal by mortal means. . . .
>
> Thus, one of the major tendencies of life—the reduction of quality to quantity—achieves its highest and uniquely perfect representation in money. Here, too, money is the pinnacle of a cultural historical series of developments which unambiguously determines its direction.
>
> (Simmel, 1907/1978:278–280)

Less obviously, money contributes to rationalization by increasing the importance of intellectuality in the modern world (B. Turner, 1986; Deutschmann, 1996). On the one hand, the development of a money economy presupposes a significant expansion of mental processes. As an example, Simmel pointed to the complicated mental processes that are required by such money transactions as covering bank notes with cash reserves. On the other hand, a money economy contributes to a considerable change in the norms and values of society; it aids in the "fundamental reorientation of culture towards intellectuality" (Simmel, 1907/1978:152). In part because of a money economy, intellect has come to be considered the most valuable of our mental energies.

Simmel saw the significance of the individual declining as money transactions become an increasingly important part of society and as reified structures expand. This is part of his general argument on the decline of individual subjective culture in the face of the expansion of objective culture (the "tragedy of culture"):

> The rapid circulation of money induces habits of spending and acquisition; it makes a specific quantity of money psychologically less significant and valuable, while money in general becomes increasingly important because money matters now affect the individual more vitally than they do in a less agitated style of life. We are confronted here with a very common phenomenon; namely, that the total value of something increases to the same extent as the value of its individual parts declines. For example, the size and significance of a social group often becomes greater the less highly the lives and interests of its individual members are valued; the objective culture, the diversity and liveliness of its content attain their highest point through a division of labour that often condemns the individual representative and participant in this culture to a monotonous specialization, narrowness, and stunted growth. The whole becomes more perfect and harmonious, the less the individual is a harmonious being.
>
> (Simmel, 1907/1978:199)

Jorge Arditi (1996) has put this issue in slightly different terms. Arditi recognizes the theme of increasing rationalization in Simmel's work, but argues that it must be seen in the context of Simmel's thinking on the nonrational. "According to Simmel, the nonrational is a primary, essential element of 'life,' an integral aspect of our humanity. Its gradual eclipse in the expanses of a modern, highly rationalized world implies, then, an unquestionable impoverishment of being" (Arditi, 1996:95). One example of the nonrational is love (others are emotions and faith), and it is nonrational because, among other things, it is impractical, is the opposite of intellectual experience, does not necessarily have real value, is impulsive, nothing social or cultural intervenes between lover and beloved, and it springs " 'from the completely *nonrational* depths of life' " (Simmel, in Arditi, 1996:96). With increasing rationalization, we begin to lose the nonrational and with it "we lose . . . the most meaningful of our human attributes: our authenticity" (Arditi, 1996:103). This loss of authenticity, of the nonrational, is a real human tragedy.

In some senses, it may be difficult to see how money can take on the central role that it does in modern society. On the surface, it appears that money is simply a means to a variety of ends or, in Simmel's words, "the purest form of the tool" (1907/1978:210). However, money has come to be the most extreme example of a means that has become an end in itself:

> Never has an object that owes its value exclusively to its quality as a means, to its convertibility into more definite values, so thoroughly and unreservedly developed into a psychological value absolute, into a completely engrossing final purpose governing our practical consciousness. This ultimate craving for money must increase to the extent that money takes on the quality of a pure means. For this implies that the range of objects made available to money grows continuously, that

things submit more and more defencelessly to the power of money, that money itself becomes more and more lacking in quality yet thereby at the same time becomes powerful in relation to the quality of things.

(Simmel, 1907/1978:232)

Negative Effects

A society in which money becomes an end in itself, indeed the ultimate end, has a number of negative effects on individuals (Beilharz, 1996), two of the most interesting of which are the increase in cynicism and the increase in a blasé attitude. Cynicism is induced when both the highest and the lowest aspects of social life are for sale, reduced to a common denominator—money. Thus we can "buy" beauty or truth or intelligence almost as easily as we can buy cornflakes or underarm deodorant. This leveling of everything to a common denominator leads to the cynical attitude that everything has its price, that anything can be bought or sold in the market. A money economy also induces a blasé attitude, "all things as being of an equally dull and grey hue, as not worth getting excited about" (Simmel, 1907/1978:256). The blasé person has lost completely the ability to make value differentiations among the ultimate objects of purchase. Put slightly differently, money is the absolute enemy of esthetics, reducing everything to formlessness, to purely quantitative phenomena.

Another negative effect of a money economy is the increasingly impersonal relations among people. Instead of dealing with individuals with their own personalities, we are increasingly likely to deal solely with positions—the delivery person, the baker, and so forth—regardless of who occupies those positions. In the modern division of labor characteristic of a money economy, we have the paradoxical situation that while we grow more dependent on other positions for our survival, we know less about the people who occupy those positions. The specific individual who fills a given position becomes progressively insignificant. Personalities tend to disappear behind positions that demand only a small part of them. Because so little is demanded of them, many individuals can fill the same position equally well. People thus become interchangeable parts.

A related issue is the impact of the money economy on individual freedom. A money economy leads to an increase in individual enslavement. The individual in the modern world becomes atomized and isolated. No longer embedded within a group, the individual stands alone in the face of an ever-expanding and increasingly coercive objective culture. The individual in the modern world is thus enslaved by a massive objective culture.

Another impact of the money economy is the reduction of all human values to dollar terms, "the tendency to reduce the value of man to a monetary expression" (Simmel, 1907/1978:356). For example, Simmel offers the case in primitive society of atonement for a murder by a money payment. But his best example is the exchange of sex for money. The expansion of prostitution is traceable in part to the growth of the money economy.

Some of Simmel's most interesting insights lie in his thoughts on the impact of money on people's styles of life. For example, a society dominated by a money economy tends to reduce everything to a string of causal connections that can be comprehended intellectually, not emotionally. Related to this is what Simmel called the "calculating character" of life in the modern world. The specific form of intellectuality that is peculiarly suited to a money economy is a mathematical mode of thinking. This, in turn, is related to the tendency to emphasize quantitative rather than qualitative factors in the social world. Simmel concluded that "the lives of many people are absorbed by such evaluating, weighing, calculating, and reducing of qualitative values to quantitative ones" (1907/1978:444).

The key to Simmel's discussion of money's impact on style of life is in the growth of objective culture at the expense of individual culture. The gap between the two grows larger at an accelerating rate:

> This discrepancy seems to widen steadily. Every day and from all sides, the wealth of objective culture increases, but the individual mind can enrich the forms and contents of its own development only by distancing itself still further from that culture and developing its own at a much slower pace.
>
> (Simmel, 1907/1978:449)

The Tragedy of Culture

The major cause of this increasing disparity is the increasing division of labor in modern society (Oakes, 1984:19). Increased specialization leads to an improved ability to create the various components of the cultural world. But at the same time, the highly specialized individual loses a sense of the total culture and loses the ability to control it. As objective culture grows, individual culture atrophies. One of the examples of this is that language in its totality has clearly expanded enormously, yet the linguistic abilities of given individuals seem to be declining. Similarly, with the growth of technology and machinery, the abilities of the individual worker and the skills required have declined dramatically. Finally, although there has been an enormous expansion of the intellectual sphere, fewer and fewer individuals seem to deserve the label "intellectual." Highly specialized individuals are confronted with an increasingly closed and interconnected world of products over which they have little or no control. A mechanical world devoid of spirituality comes to dominate individuals, and their lifestyles are affected in various ways. Acts of production come to be meaningless exercises in which individuals do not see their roles in the overall process or in the production of the final product. Relationships among people are highly specialized and impersonal. Consumption becomes little more than the devouring of one meaningless product after another.

The massive expansion of objective culture has had a dramatic effect upon the rhythm of life. In general, the unevenness that was characteristic of earlier epochs has been leveled and replaced in modern society by a much more consistent pattern of living. Examples of this leveling of modern culture abound.

In times past, food consumption was cyclical and often very uncertain. What foods were consumed and when they were available depended on the harvest. Today, with improved methods of preservation and transportation, we can consume virtually any food at any time. Furthermore, the ability to preserve and store huge quantities of food has helped offset disruptions caused by bad harvests, natural catastrophes, and so forth.

In communication the infrequent and unpredictable mail coach has been replaced by the telegraph, telephone, daily mail service, fax machines, cell phones, and e-mail, which make communication available at all times.

In an earlier time, night and day gave life a natural rhythm. Now, with artificial lighting, the natural rhythm has been altered greatly. Many activities formerly restricted to daylight hours can now be performed at night as well.

Intellectual stimulation, which formerly was restricted to an occasional conversation or a rare book, is now available at all times because of the ready availability of books and magazines. In this realm, as in all the others, the situation has grown even more pronounced since Simmel's time. With radio, television, videotape and DVD players and recorders, and home computers, the availability and possibilities of intellectual stimulation have grown far beyond anything Simmel could have imagined.

There are positive elements to all this, of course. For example, people have much more freedom because they are less restricted by the natural rhythm of life. But in spite of the human gains, problems arise because all these developments are at the level of objective culture and are integral parts of the process by which objective culture grows and further impoverishes individual culture.

In the end, money has come to be the symbol of, and a major factor in, the development of a relativistic mode of existence. Money allows us to reduce the most disparate phenomena to numbers of dollars, and this allows them to be compared to each other. In other words, money allows us to relativize *everything*. Our relativistic way of life stands in contrast to earlier methods of living in which people believed in a number of eternal verities. A money economy destroys such eternal truths. The gains to people in terms of increased freedom from absolute ideas are far outweighed by the costs. The alienation endemic to the expanding objective culture of a modern money economy is a far greater threat to people, in Simmel's eyes, than the evils of absolutism. Perhaps Simmel would not wish us to return to an earlier, simpler time, but he certainly would warn us to be wary of the seductive dangers associated with the growth of a money economy and objective culture in the modern world.

While we have focused most of our attention on the negative effects of the modern money economy, such an economy also has its liberating aspects (Beilharz, 1996; D. Levine, 1981b, 1991b; Poggi, 1993). First, it allows us to deal with many more people in a much-expanded marketplace. Second, our obligations to one another are highly limited (to specific services or products) rather than all-encompassing. Third, the money economy allows people to find gratifications that were unavailable in earlier economic systems. Fourth, people have greater freedom in such an environment to develop their individuality to a fuller extent. Fifth, people are better able to maintain and protect their subjective center because they are involved only in very limited relationships. Sixth, the separation of the worker from the means of production, as Simmel points out, allows the individual some freedom from those productive forces. Finally, money helps people grow increasingly free of the constraints of their social groups. For example, in a barter economy people are largely controlled by their groups, but in the modern economic world such constraints are loosened, with the result that people are freer to make their own economic deals. However, while Simmel is careful to point out a variety of liberating effects of the money economy, and of modernity in general, in our view the heart of his work lies in his discussion of the problems associated with modernity, especially the "tragedy of culture."

Secrecy: A Case Study in Simmel's Sociology

The Philosophy of Money demonstrates that Simmel has a theoretical scope that rivals that of Marx, Weber, and Durkheim, but it remains an atypical example of his work. A more characteristic type of Simmelian scholarship is his work on a specific form of interaction—secrecy. *Secrecy* is defined as the condition in which one person has the intention of hiding something while the other person is seeking to reveal that which is being hidden.

Simmel begins with the basic fact that people must know some things about other people in order to interact with them. For instance, we must know with whom we are dealing (for example, a friend, a relative, a shopkeeper). We may come to know a great deal about other people, but we can never know them absolutely. That is, we can never know all the thoughts, moods, and so on, of other people. However, we do form some sort of unitary conception of other people and out of the bits and pieces that we know about them, we form a fairly coherent mental picture of the people with whom we interact. Simmel sees a dialectical relationship between interaction (being) and the mental picture we have of others (conceiving): "Our relationships thus develop upon the basis of reciprocal knowledge, and this knowledge upon the basis of actual relations. Both are inextricably interwoven" (1906/1950:309).

In all aspects of our lives we acquire not only truth but also ignorance and error. However, it is in the interaction with other people that ignorance and error acquire a distinctive character. This relates to the inner lives of the people with whom we interact. People, in contrast to any other object of knowledge, have the capacity to *intentionally* reveal the truth about themselves *or* to lie and conceal such information.

The fact is that even if people wanted to reveal all (and they almost always do not), they could not do so because so much information "would drive everybody into the insane asylum" (Simmel, 1906/1950:312). Thus, people must select the things that they report to others. From the point of view of Simmel's concern with quantitative issues, we report only "fragments" of our inner lives to others. Furthermore, we choose which fragments to reveal and which to conceal. Thus, in all interaction, we reveal only a part of ourselves, and which part we opt to show depends on how we select and arrange the fragments we choose to reveal.

This brings us to the *lie,* a form of interaction in which the liar *intentionally* hides the truth from others. In the lie, it is not just that others are left with an erroneous conception but also that the error is traceable to the fact that the liar intended that the others be deceived.

Simmel discusses the lie in terms of *social geometry*, specifically his ideas on distance. For example, in Simmel's view, we can better accept and come to terms with the lies of those who are distant from us. Thus, we have little difficulty learning that the politicians who habituate Washington, D.C., frequently lie to us. In contrast, "If the persons closest to us lie, life becomes unbearable" (Simmel, 1906/1950:313). The lie of a spouse, lover, or child has a far more devastating impact on us than does the lie of a government official whom we know only through the television screen.

More generally, all everyday communication combines elements known to both parties with facts known to only one or the other. It is the existence of the latter that leads to "distanceness" in all social relationships. Indeed, Simmel argues that social relationships require both elements that are known to the interactants *and* elements that are unknown to one party or the other. In other words, even the most intimate relationships require both nearness and distance, reciprocal knowledge and mutual concealment. Thus, secrecy is an integral part of all social relationships, although a relationship may be destroyed if the secret becomes known to the person from whom it was being kept.

Secrecy is linked to the size of society. In small groups, it is difficult to develop secrets: "Everybody is too close to everybody else and his circumstances, and frequency and intimacy of contact involve too many temptations to revelation" (Simmel, 1906/1950:335). Furthermore, in small groups, secrets are not even needed because everyone is much like everyone else. In large groups, in contrast, secrets can more easily develop and are much more needed because there are important differences among people.

At the most macroscopic level, secrecy not only is a form of interaction (which, as we have seen, affects many other forms) but also can come to characterize a group in its entirety. Unlike the secret possessed by a single individual, the secret in a *secret society* is shared by all the members and determines the reciprocal relations among them. As with the individual case, however, the secret of the secret society cannot be hidden forever. In such a society there is constant tension caused by the fact that the secret can be uncovered, or revealed, thereby eliminating the entire basis for the existence of the secret society.

Secrecy and Social Relationships

Simmel examines various forms of social relationships from the point of view of reciprocal knowledge and secrecy. For example, we all are involved in a range of interest groups in which we interact with other people on a very limited basis. The total personalities of these people are irrelevant to our specific concerns. Thus, in the university the student is concerned with what the professor says and does in the classroom and not with all aspects of the professor's life and personality. Linking this distinction to his ideas on the larger society, Simmel argues that the increasing objectification of culture brings with it more and more limited-interest groups and the kinds of relationships associated with them. Such relationships require less and less of the subjective totality of the individual (individual culture) than do associations in premodern societies.

In the impersonal relationships characteristic of modern objectified society, *confidence,* as a form of interaction, becomes increasingly important. To Simmel "confidence is intermediate between knowledge and ignorance about a man"

(1906/1950:318). In premodern societies people are much more likely to know a great deal about the people they deal with. But in the modern world we do not, and cannot, have a great deal of knowledge about most of the people with whom we have associations. Thus, students do not know a great deal about their professors (and vice versa), but they must have the confidence that their professors will show up at the appointed times and talk about what they are supposed to discuss.

Another form of social relationship is *acquaintanceship*. We know our acquaintances, but we do not have intimate knowledge of them: "One knows of the other only what he is toward the outside, either in the purely social-representative sense, or in the sense of that which he shows us" (Simmel, 1906/1950:320). Thus, there is far more secretiveness among acquaintances than there is among intimates.

Under the heading "acquaintanceship," Simmel discusses another form of association—*discretion*. We are discrete with our acquaintances, staying "away from the knowledge of all the other does not expressly reveal to us. It [discretion] does not refer to anything particular which we are not permitted to know, but to a quite general reserve in regard to the total personality" (Simmel, 1906/1950:321). In spite of being discrete, we often come to know more about other people than they reveal to us voluntarily. More specifically, we often come to learn things that others would prefer we do not know. Simmel offers a very Freudian example of how we learn such things: "To the man with the psychologically fine ear, people innumerable times betray their most secret thoughts and qualities, not only *although,* but often *because,* they anxiously try to guard them" (1906/1950:323–324). In fact, Simmel argues that human interaction is dependent on both discretion *and* the fact that we often come to know more than we are supposed to know.

Turning to another form of association, *friendship,* Simmel contradicts the assumption that friendship is based on total intimacy, full reciprocal knowledge. The lack of full intimacy is especially true of friendships in modern, differentiated society: "Modern man, possibly, has too much to hide to sustain a friendship in the ancient sense" (Simmel, 1906/1950:326). Thus, we have a series of differentiated friendships based on such things as common intellectual pursuits, religion, and shared experiences. There is a very limited kind of intimacy in such friendships and thus a good deal of secrecy. However, in spite of these limitations, friendship still involves some intimacy:

> But the relation which is thus restricted and surrounded by discretions, may yet stem from the center of the total personality. It may yet be reached by the sap of the ultimate roots of the personality, even though it feeds only part of the person's periphery. In its idea, it involves the same affective depth and the same readiness for sacrifice, which less differentiated epochs and persons connect only with a common *total* sphere of life, for which reservations and discretion constitute no problem.
> (Simmel, 1906/1950:326)

Then there is what is usually thought of as the most intimate, least secret form of association—*marriage*. Simmel argues that there is a temptation in marriage to reveal all to the partner, to have no secrets. However, in his view, doing this would be a mistake. For one thing, all social relationships require "a certain proportion of truth and error," and thus it would be impossible to remove all error from a social relationship (Simmel, 1906/1950:329). More specifically, complete self-revelation (assuming such a thing is even possible) would make a marriage matter-of-fact and remove all possibility of the unexpected. Finally, most of us have limited internal resources, and every revelation reduces the (secret) treasures that we have to offer to others. Only those few individuals with a great storehouse of personal accomplishments can afford numerous revelations to a marriage partner. All others are left denuded (and uninteresting) by excessive self-revelation.

Other Thoughts on Secrecy

Next, Simmel turns to an analysis of the functions, the positive consequences, of secrecy. Simmel sees the secret as "one of man's greatest achievements . . . the secret produces an immense enlargement of life: numerous contents of life cannot even emerge in the presence of full publicity. The secret offers, so to speak, the possibility of a second world alongside the manifest world" (1906/1950:330). More specifically in terms of its functionality, the secret, especially if it is shared by a number of people, makes for a strong "we feeling" among those who know the secret. High status is also associated with the secret; there is something mysterious about superordinate positions and superior achievements.

Human interaction in general is shaped by secrecy and its logical opposite, *betrayal*. The secret is always accompanied dialectically by the possibility that it can be discovered. Betrayal can come from two sources. Externally, another person can discover our secret, while internally there is always the possibility that we will reveal our secret to others. "The secret puts a barrier between men but, at the same time, it creates the tempting challenge to break through it, by gossip or confession. . . . Out of the counterplay of these two interests, in concealing and revealing, spring nuances and fates of human interaction that permeate it in its entirety" (Simmel, 1906/1950:334).

Simmel links his ideas on the lie to his views on the larger society of the modern world. To Simmel, the modern world is much more dependent on honesty than earlier societies were. For one thing, the modern economy is increasingly a credit economy, and credit is dependent on people's willingness to repay what they promise. For another, in modern science, researchers are dependent on the results of many studies that they cannot examine in minute detail. Those studies are produced by innumerable scientists whom the researchers are unlikely to know personally. Thus, the modern scientist is dependent on the honesty of all other scientists. Simmel concludes: "Under modern conditions, the lie, therefore, becomes something much more devastating than it was earlier, something which questions the very foundations of our life" (1906/1950:313).

More generally, Simmel connects secrecy to his thoughts on the social structure of modern society. On the one hand, a highly differentiated society permits and requires a high degree of secrecy. On the other hand, and dialectically, the secret serves to intensify such differentiation.

Simmel associates the secret with the modern money economy. Money makes possible a level of secrecy that was unattainable previously. First, money's "compressibility" makes it possible to make others rich by simply slipping them checks without anyone else noticing the act. Second, the abstractness and the qualityless character of money make it possible to hide "transactions, acquisitions, and changes in ownership" that could not be hidden if more tangible objects were exchanged (Simmel, 1906/1950:335). Third, money can be invested in very distant things, thereby making the transaction invisible to those in the immediate environment.

Simmel also sees that in the modern world, public matters, such as those relating to politics, have tended to lose their secrecy and inaccessibility. In contrast, private affairs are much more secret than they are in premodern societies. Here Simmel ties his thoughts on secrecy to those on the modern city by arguing that "modern life has developed, in the midst of metropolitan crowdedness, a technique for making and keeping private matters secret" (Simmel, 1906/1950:337). Overall, "what is public becomes even more public, and what is private becomes even more private" (Simmel, 1906/1950:337).

Thus, Simmel's work on secrecy illustrates many aspects of his theoretical orientation.

Criticisms

We have already discussed some criticisms of Simmel's particular ideas—for example, that his emphasis on forms imposes order where none exists (see p. 167) and that he seems to contradict himself by viewing social structures, on the one hand, as simply a form of interaction and, on the other hand, as coercive and independent of interactions (see p. 171). In addition, we have explored the difference between Marx and Simmel on alienation, which suggests the primary Marxist criticism of Simmel. This criticism is that Simmel does not suggest a way out of the tragedy of culture, because he considers alienation to be inherent to the human condition. For Simmel, the disjuncture between objective and subjective culture is as much a part of our "species being" as labor is to Marx. Therefore, whereas Marx believes that alienation will be swept away with the coming of socialism, Simmel has no such political hope.

Undoubtedly, the most frequently cited criticism of Simmel is the fragmentary nature of his work. Simmel is accused of having no coherent theoretical approach, but instead a set of fragmentary or "impressionistic" (Frisby, 1981) approaches. It certainly is true that Simmel focused on forms and types of association, but that is hardly the sort of theoretical unity that we see in the other founders of sociology. Indeed, one of Simmel's most enthusiastic living supporters in American sociology, Donald Levine (Levine, Ellwood, and Gorman, 1976a:814), admits that "although literate American sociologists today could be expected to produce a coherent statement of the theoretical frameworks and principal themes of Marx, Durkheim, and Weber, few would be able to do the same for Simmel." Further, Levine (Levine, Ellwood, and Gorman, 1976b:1128) admits that it is not the obtuseness of modern interpreters but "the character of Simmel's work itself: the scatter of topics, the failure to integrate related materials, the paucity of coherent general statements, and the cavalier attitude toward academic tradition." Although Levine attempts to present the core of Simmel's unique approach, he must admit that "in spite of these achievements of Simmelian scholarship, there remains for the reader the undeniable experience of Simmel as an unsystematic writer. Indeed, although many have found his work powerfully stimulating, virtually no one knows how to practice as a full-blown proponent of Simmelian social science" (Levine 1997:200).

Despite the fact that there are few Simmelians, Simmel has often been recognized as an "innovator of ideas and theoretical lead" (Tenbruck, 1959:61). This really is exactly what Simmel intended.

> I know that I shall die without spiritual heirs (and that is good). The estate I leave is like cash distributed among many heirs, each of whom puts his share to use in some trade that is compatible with his nature but which can no longer be recognized as coming from that estate.
>
> (Simmel in Frisby, 1984:150)

Consequently, Simmel has often been regarded as a natural resource of insights to be mined for empirical hypothesis rather than as a coherent framework for theoretical analysis.

Nevertheless, its potential for positivistic hypothesis is not a satisfactory answer to the objection that Simmel's work is fragmentary. If these are the terms by which Simmel is measured, he most certainly must be judged a failure whose ideas are saved only because of the work of his more scientific successors. This was, in fact, Durkheim's (1979:328) assessment of Simmel's work. We, however, agree more with Nisbet's (1959:481) assessment that there is, in Simmel's work, "a larger element of irreducible humanism and . . . it will always be possible to derive something of importance from him directly that cannot be absorbed by the impersonal propositions of science."

It is important for students to directly encounter the original writings of all the classical theorists, even if only in translation. The power and humor of Marx's language evaporate in summaries of his theories. The broad strokes of any précis obscure Durkheim's carefully detailed arguments. The optimistic faith in scholarship that lies behind Weber's pessimistic conclusions is missed. But the importance of a firsthand encounter with Simmel is especially great. There simply is no substitute for picking up one of Simmel's essays and being taught to look anew at fashion (1904/1971) or flirting (1984) or the stranger (1908/1971b) or secrecy (1906/1950).

Summary

The work of Georg Simmel has been influential in American sociological theory for many years. The focus of this influence seems to be shifting from microsociology to a general sociological theory. Simmel's microsociology is embedded in a broad dialectical theory that interrelates the cultural and individual levels. This chapter identifies four basic levels of concern in Simmel's work: psychological, interactional, structural and institutional, and the ultimate metaphysics of life.

Simmel operated with a dialectical orientation, although it is not as well articulated as that of Karl Marx. The chapter illustrates Simmel's dialectical concerns in various ways. It deals with the way they are manifested in forms of interaction—specifically, fashion. Simmel also was interested in the conflicts between the individual and social structures, but his greatest concern was the conflicts that develop between individual culture and objective culture. He perceived a general process by which objective culture expands and individual culture becomes increasingly impoverished in the face of this expansion. Simmel saw this conflict, in turn, as part of a broader philosophical conflict between more-life and more-than-life.

The bulk of this chapter is devoted to Simmel's thoughts on each of the four levels of social reality. Although he has many useful assumptions about consciousness, he did comparatively little with them. He had much more to offer on forms of inter-action and types of interactants. In this formal sociology, we see Simmel's great interest in social geometry, for example, numbers of people. In this context, we exam-ine Simmel's work on the crucial transition from a dyad to a triad. With the addition of one person, we move from a dyad to a triad and with it the possibility of the development of large-scale structures that can become separate from, and dominant over, individuals. This creates the possibility of conflict and contradiction between the individual and the larger society. In his social geometry, Simmel was also concerned with the issue of distance, as in, for example, his essay on the "stranger," including "strangeness" in social life. Simmel's interest in social types is illustrated in a discus-sion of the poor, and his thoughts on social forms are illustrated in a discussion of domination, that is, superordination and subordination.

At the macro level, Simmel had comparatively little to say about social structures. In fact, at times he seemed to manifest a disturbing tendency to reduce social struc-tures to little more than interaction patterns. Simmel's real interest at the macro level was objective culture. He was interested in the expansion of this culture and in its destructive effects on individuals (the "tragedy of culture"). This general concern is manifest in a variety of his specific essays, for example, those on the city and exchange.

In *The Philosophy of Money* Simmel's discussion progressed from money to value to the problems of modern society and, ultimately, to the problems of life in general. Of particular concern is Simmel's interest in the tragedy of culture as part of a broader set of apprehensions about culture. Finally, the discussion of Simmel's work on secrecy is intended to illustrate the full range of his theoretical ideas. The discus-sion of his work on money, as well as his ideas on secrecy, demonstrates that Simmel has a far more elegant and sophisticated theoretical orientation than he is usually given credit for by those who are familiar with only his thoughts on micro-level phenomena.

Modern Sociological Theory: The Major Schools

C   H   A   P   T   E   R   **6**

A Historical Sketch of Sociological Theory: The Later Years

Chapter Outline

Early American Sociological Theory
Women in Early Sociology
W.E.B. Du Bois and Race Theory
Sociological Theory to Midcentury
Sociological Theory from Midcentury
Late-Twentieth-Century Developments in Sociological Theory
Theories of Modernity and Postmodernity
Social Theory in the Twenty-First Century

It is difficult to give a precise date for the founding of sociology in the United States. A course in social problems was taught at Oberlin as early as 1858, Comte's term *sociology* was used by George Fitzhugh in 1854, and William Graham Sumner taught social science courses at Yale beginning in 1873. During the 1880s, courses specifically bearing the title "Sociology" began to appear. The first department with *sociology* in its name was founded at the University of Kansas in 1889. In 1892, Albion Small moved to the University of Chicago and set up the new department of sociology. The Chicago department became the first important center of American sociology in general and of sociological theory in particular (Matthews, 1977).

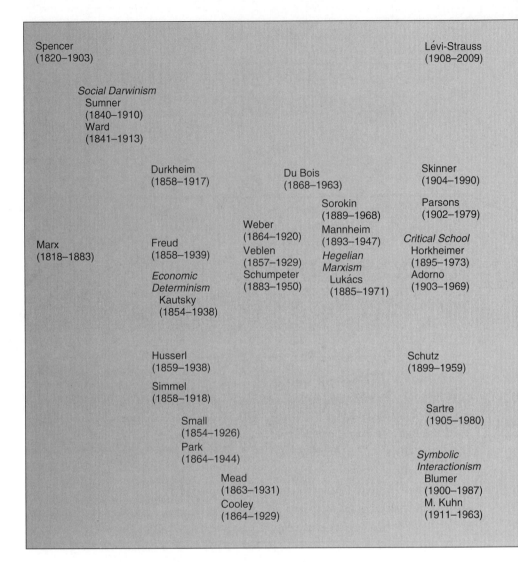

FIGURE 6.1   *Sociological Theory: The Later Years*

Early American Sociological Theory

Politics

Schwendinger and Schwendinger (1974) argue that the early American sociologists are best described as political liberals and not, as was true of most early European theorists, as conservatives. The liberalism characteristic of early American sociology had two basic elements. First, it operated with a belief in the freedom and welfare of the individual. In this belief, it was influenced far more by Spencer's orientation than by Comte's more collective position. Second, many sociologists associated with this

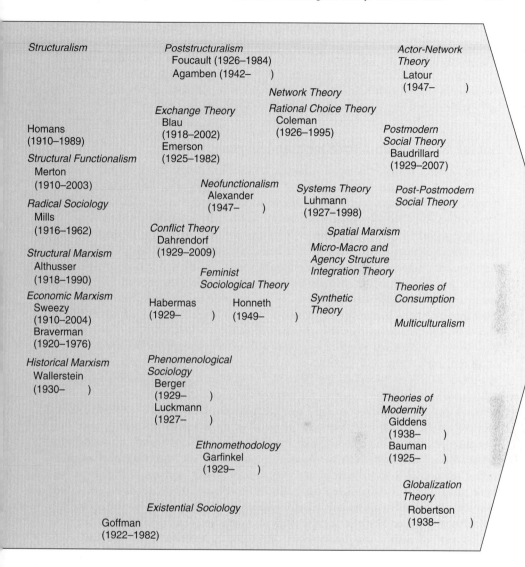

Structuralism

Poststructuralism
Foucault (1926–1984)
Agamben (1942–   )

Actor-Network
Theory
Latour
(1947–   )

Network Theory

Exchange Theory
Blau
(1918–2002)
Emerson
(1925–1982)

Rational Choice Theory
Coleman
(1926–1995)

Homans
(1910–1989)

Structural Functionalism
Merton
(1910–2003)

Postmodern
Social Theory
Baudrillard
(1929–2007)

Radical Sociology
Mills
(1916–1962)

Neofunctionalism
Alexander
(1947–   )

Systems Theory
Luhmann
(1927–1998)

Post-Postmodern
Social Theory

Conflict Theory
Dahrendorf
(1929–2009)

Spatial Marxism

Structural Marxism
Althusser
(1918–1990)

Micro-Macro and
Agency Structure
Integration Theory

Feminist
Sociological Theory

Economic Marxism
Sweezy
(1910–2004)
Braverman
(1920–1976)

Habermas
(1929–   )

Honneth
(1949–   )

Synthetic
Theory

Theories of
Consumption

Multiculturalism

Historical Marxism
Wallerstein
(1930–   )

Phenomenological
Sociology
Berger
(1929–   )
Luckmann
(1927–   )

Theories of
Modernity
Giddens
(1938–   )
Bauman
(1925–   )

Ethnomethodology
Garfinkel
(1929–   )

Existential Sociology
Goffman
(1922–1982)

Globalization
Theory
Robertson
(1938–   )

orientation adopted an evolutionary view of social progress (W. Fine, 1979). However, they were split over how best to bring about this progress. Some argued that steps should be taken by the government to aid social reform, whereas others pushed a laissez-faire doctrine, arguing that the various components of society should be left to solve their own problems.

Liberalism, taken to its extreme, comes very close to conservatism. The belief in social progress—in reform or a laissez-faire doctrine—and the belief in the importance of the individual both lead to positions supportive of the system as a whole. The overriding belief is that the social system works or can be reformed to work. There is little criticism of the system as a whole; in the American case this means, in particular, that there is little questioning of capitalism. Instead of imminent class struggle, the early sociologists saw a future of class harmony and class cooperation. Ultimately this meant that early American sociological theory helped rationalize exploitation, domestic and international imperialism, and social inequality (Schwendinger and Schwendinger, 1974). In the end, the political liberalism of the early sociologists had enormously conservative implications.

Social Change and Intellectual Currents

In their analyses of the founding of American sociological theory, Roscoe Hinkle (1980) and Ellsworth Fuhrman (1980) outline several basic contexts from which that body of theory emerged. Of utmost importance are the social changes that occurred in American society after the Civil War (Bramson, 1961). In Chapter 1, we discussed an array of factors involved in the development of European sociological theory; several of those factors (such as industrialization and urbanization) were also intimately involved in the development of theory in America. In Fuhrman's view, the early American sociologists saw the positive possibilities of industrialization, but they also were well aware of its dangers. Although these early sociologists were attracted to the ideas generated by the labor movement and socialist groups about dealing with the dangers of industrialization, they were not in favor of radically overhauling society.

Arthur Vidich and Stanford Lyman (1985) make a strong case for the influence of Christianity, especially Protestantism, on the founding of American sociology. American sociologists retained the Protestant interest in saving the world and merely substituted one language (science) for another (religion). "From 1854, when the first works in sociology appeared in the United States, until the outbreak of World War I, sociology was a moral and intellectual response to the problems of American life and thought, institutions, and creeds" (Vidich and Lyman, 1985:1). Sociologists sought to define, study, and help solve these social problems. While the clergyman worked within religion to help improve it and people's lot within it, the sociologist did the same thing within society. Given their religious roots, and the religious parallels, the vast majority of sociologists did not challenge the basic legitimacy of society.

Another major factor in the founding of American sociology discussed by both Hinkle and Fuhrman is the simultaneous emergence in America, in the late 1800s, of academic professions (including sociology) and the modern university system. In Europe, in contrast, the university system was already well established *before* the emergence of sociology. Although sociology had a difficult time becoming established in Europe, it had easier going in the more fluid setting of the new American university system.

Another characteristic of early American sociology (as well as other social science disciplines) was its turn away from a historical perspective and in the direction of a positivistic, or "scientistic," orientation. As Dorothy Ross puts it, "The desire to achieve universalistic abstraction and quantitative methods turned American social scientists away from interpretive models available in history and cultural anthropology, and from the generalizing and interpretive model offered by Max Weber" (1991:473). Instead of interpreting long-term historical changes, sociology had turned in the direction of scientifically studying short-term processes.

Still another factor was the impact of established European theory on American sociological theory. European theorists largely created sociological theory, and the Americans were able to rely on this groundwork. The Europeans most important to the Americans were Spencer and Comte. Simmel was of some importance in the early years, but the influence of Durkheim, Weber, and Marx was not to have a dramatic effect for a number of years. The history of Herbert Spencer's ideas provides an interesting and informative illustration of the impact of early European theory on American sociology.

Herbert Spencer's Influence on Sociology

Why were Spencer's ideas so much more influential in the early years of American sociology than those of Comte, Durkheim, Marx, and Weber? Hofstadter (1959) offered several explanations. To take the easiest first, Spencer wrote in English, whereas the others did not. In addition, Spencer wrote in nontechnical terms, making his work broadly accessible. Indeed, some have argued that the lack of technicality is traceable to Spencer's *not* being a very sophisticated scholar. But there are other, more important reasons for Spencer's broad appeal. He offered a scientific orientation that was attractive to an audience that was becoming enamored of science and its technological products. He offered a comprehensive theory that seemed to deal with the entire sweep of human history. The breadth of his ideas, as well as the voluminous work he produced, allowed his theory to be many different things to many different people. Finally, and perhaps most important, his theory was soothing and reassuring to a society undergoing the wrenching process of industrialization—society was, according to Spencer, steadily moving in the direction of greater and greater progress.

Spencer's most famous American disciple was William Graham Sumner, who accepted and expanded upon many of Spencer's Social Darwinist ideas. Spencer also influenced other early American sociologists, among them Lester Ward, Charles Horton Cooley, E. A. Ross, and Robert Park.

By the 1930s, however, Spencer was in eclipse in the intellectual world in general, as well as in sociology. His Social Darwinist, laissez-faire ideas seemed ridiculous in the light of massive social problems, a world war, and a major economic depression. In 1937 Talcott Parsons announced Spencer's intellectual death for sociology when he echoed the historian Crane Brinton's words of a few years earlier, "Who now reads Spencer?" Today Spencer is of little more than historical interest, but his ideas *were* important in shaping early American sociological theory. Let us look briefly at the work of two American theorists who were influenced, at least in part, by Spencer's work.

William Graham Sumner (1840–1910)   William Graham Sumner was the person who taught the first course in the United States that could be called sociology (Delaney, 2005b). Sumner contended that he had begun teaching sociology "years before any such attempt was made at any other university in the world" (Curtis, 1981:63).

Sumner was the major exponent of Social Darwinism in the United States, although he appeared to change his view late in life (Delaney, 2005b; Dickens, 2005;

N. Smith, 1979; Weiler, 2007a, 2007b). The following exchange between Sumner and one of his students illustrates his "liberal" views on the need for individual freedom and his position against government interference:

> "Professor, don't you believe in any government aid to industries?"
>
> "No! It's root, hog, or die."
>
> "Yes, but hasn't the hog got a right to root?"
>
> "There are no rights. The world owes nobody a living."
>
> "You believe then, Professor, in only one system, the contract-competitive system?"
>
> "That's the only sound economic system. All others are fallacies."
>
> "Well, suppose some professor of political economy came along and took your job away from you. Wouldn't you be sore?"
>
> "Any other professor is welcome to try. If he gets my job, it is my fault. My business is to teach the subject so well that no one can take the job away from me."
>
> (Phelps, cited in Hofstadter, 1959:54)

Sumner basically adopted a survival-of-the-fittest approach to the social world. Like Spencer, he saw people struggling against their environment, and the fittest were those who would be successful. Thus Sumner was a supporter of human aggressiveness and competitiveness. Those who succeeded deserved it, and those who did not succeed deserved to fail. Again like Spencer, Sumner was opposed to efforts, especially government efforts, to aid those who had failed. In his view such intervention operated against the natural selection that, among people as among lower animals, allowed the fit to survive and the unfit to perish. As Sumner put it, "If we do not like the survival of the fittest, we have only one possible alternative, and that is survival of the unfittest" (Curtis, 1981:84). This theoretical system fit in well with the development of capitalism because it provided theoretical legitimacy for the existence of great differences in wealth and power.

Sumner is of little more than historical interest for two main reasons. First, his orientation and Social Darwinism in general have come to be regarded as little more than a crude legitimation of competitive capitalism and the status quo. Second, he failed to establish a solid enough base at Yale to build a school of sociology with many disciples. That kind of success was to occur some years later at the University of Chicago (Heyl and Heyl, 1976). In spite of success in his time, "Sumner is remembered by few today" (Curtis, 1981:146).

Lester F. Ward (1841–1913)   Lester Ward had an unusual career in that he spent most of it as a paleontologist working for the federal government. During that time, Ward read Spencer and Comte and developed a strong interest in sociology. He published a number of works in the late 1800s and early 1900s in which he expounded his sociological theory. As a result of the fame that this work achieved, in 1906 Ward was elected the first president of the American Sociological Society. It was only then that he took his first academic position, at Brown University, a position that he held until his death (M. Hill, 2007).

Ward, like Sumner, accepted the idea that people had evolved from lower forms to their present status. He believed that early society was characterized by its simplicity and its moral poverty, whereas modern society was more complex, was happier, and offered greater freedom. One task of sociology, *pure sociology,* was to study the basic laws of social change and social structure. But Ward was not content simply to have sociologists study social life. He believed that sociology should have a practical side; there should also be an *applied sociology.* This applied sociology involved the conscious use of scientific knowledge to attain a better society. Thus, Ward was not an extreme Social Darwinist; he believed in the need for and importance of social reform.

Although of historical importance, Sumner and Ward have not been of long-term significance to sociological theory. However, now we turn, first briefly to a theorist of the time, Thorstein Veblen, who has been of long-term significance and whose influence today in sociology is increasing. Then we will look at a group of theorists, especially Mead, and a school, the Chicago school, that came to dominate sociology in America. The Chicago school was unusual in the history of sociology in that it was one of the few (the Durkheimian school in Paris was another) "collective intellectual enterprises of an integrated kind" in the history of sociology (Bulmer, 1984:1). The tradition begun at the University of Chicago is of continuing importance to sociology and its theoretical (and empirical) status.

Thorstein Veblen (1857–1929)

Veblen, who was not a sociologist but mainly held positions in economics departments and even in economics was a marginal figure, nonetheless produced a body of social theory that is of enduring significance to those in a number of disciplines, including sociology (McCormick, 2011; Powers, 2005b). The central problem for Veblen was the clash between "business" and "industry." By business, Veblen meant the owners, leaders, "captains" of industry who focused on the profits of their own companies but, to keep prices and profits high, often engaged in efforts to limit production. In so doing they obstructed the operation of the industrial system and adversely affected society as a whole (through higher rates of unemployment, for example), which is best served by the unimpeded operation of industry. Thus, business leaders were the source of many problems within society, which, Veblen felt, should be led by people (e.g., engineers) who understood the industrial system and its operation and were interested in the general welfare.

Most of Veblen's importance today is traceable to his book *The Theory of the Leisure Class* (1899/1994; Varul, 2007). Veblen is critical of the leisure class (which is closely tied to business) for its role in fostering wasteful consumption. To impress the rest of society, the leisure class engaged in both "conspicuous leisure" (the nonproductive use of time) and "conspicuous consumption" (spending more money on goods than they are worth). People in all other social classes are influenced by this example and seek, directly and indirectly, to emulate the leisure class. The result is a society characterized by the waste of time and money. What is of utmost importance about this work is that unlike most other sociological works of the time (as well as most of Veblen's other works), *The Theory of the Leisure Class* focuses on consumption rather than production. Thus, it anticipated the current shift in social theory away from a focus on production and toward a focus on consumption (Ritzer, 2010a; Ritzer, Goodman, and Wiedenhoft, 2001; Slater, 1997; also a journal—*Journal of Consumer Culture*—began publication in 2001).

A Biographical Sketch

Thorstein Veblen was born in rural Wisconsin on July 30, 1857. His parents were poor farmers of Norwegian origin (Dorfman, 1966). Thorstein was the sixth of twelve children. He was able to escape the farm and at the age of 17 began studying at Carleton College in Northfield, Minnesota. Early in his schooling he demonstrated both the bitterness and the sense of humor that were to characterize his later work. He met his future first wife, niece of the president of Carleton College, at the school (they eventually married in 1888). Veblen graduated in 1880 and obtained a teaching position, but the school soon closed and he went east to study philosophy at Johns Hopkins University. However, he failed to obtain a scholarship and moved on to Yale in the hopes of finding economic support for his studies. He managed to get by economically and obtained his Ph.D. from Yale in 1884 (one of his teachers was an early giant of sociology, William Graham Sumner). However, in spite of strong letters of recommendation, he was unable to obtain a university position because, at least in part, of his agnosticism, his lack (at the time) of a professional reputation, and the fact that he was perceived as an immigrant lacking the polish needed to hold a university post. He was idle for the next few years (he attributed this idleness to ill health), but by 1891 he returned to his studies, this time focusing more on the social sciences at Cornell University. With the help of one of his professors of economics (A. Laurence Laughlin) who was moving to the University of Chicago, Veblen was able to become a fellow at that university in 1892. He did much of the editorial work associated with *The Journal of Political Economy*, one of the many new academic journals created during this period at Chicago. Veblen was a marginal figure at Chicago, but he did teach some courses and, more important, used the *Journal of Political Economy* as an outlet for his writings. His work also began to appear in other outlets, including *The American Journal of Sociology*, another of the University of Chicago's new journals.

In 1899 he published his first and what became his best-known book, *The Theory of the Leisure Class,* but his position at Chicago remained tenuous. In fact, when he asked for a customary raise of a few hundred dollars, the university president made it clear that he would not be displeased if Veblen left the university. However, the book received a great deal of attention, and Veblen was eventually promoted to the position of assistant professor. Although some students found his teaching inspiring, most found it abysmal. One of his Chicago students said that he was "'an exceedingly queer fish . . . Very commonly with his cheek in hand, or in some such position, he talked in a low, placid monotone, in itself a most uninteresting delivery and manner of conducting the class'" (Dorfman, 1966:248–249). It was not unusual for him to begin a course with a large number of students who had heard of his growing fame, but for the class to dwindle to a few diehards by the end of the semester.

Veblen's days at Chicago were numbered for various reasons, including the fact that his marriage was crumbling and he offended Victorian sentiments with affairs with other women. In 1906 Veblen took an associate professorship at Stanford University. Unlike the situation at Chicago, he taught mainly undergraduates at Stanford, and many of them were put off by his appearance (one said he looked like a "tramp") and his boring teaching style. What did Veblen in once again was his womanizing, which forced him to resign from Stanford in 1909 under circumstances that made it difficult for him to find another academic position. But with help of a colleague and friend who was the head of the department of economics at the University of Missouri, Veblen was able to obtain a position there in 1911. He also obtained a divorce in that year, and in 1914 married a divorcee and former student.

Veblen's appointment at Missouri was at a lower rank (lecturer) and paid less than the position at Stanford. In addition, he hated the then-small town, Columbia, Missouri, that was the home of the university (he reportedly called it a "woodpecker hole of a town" and the state a "rotten stump" [Dorfman, 1966:306]). However, it was during his stay at Missouri that another of his best-known books, *The Instinct of Workmanship and the State of the Industrial Arts* appeared (1914).

Veblen's stormy academic career took another turn in 1917 when he moved to Washington, D.C., to work with a group commissioned by President Woodrow Wilson to analyze possible peace settlements for World War I. After working for the U.S. Food Administration for a short time, Veblen moved to New York City as one of the editors of a magazine, *The Dial*. The magazine shifted its orientation, and within a year Veblen lost his editorial position. However, in the interim he had become connected with the New School for Social Research. His pay there was comparatively high (a good portion of it contributed by one of his former students at Chicago), and because he lived frugally, the great critic of American business began investing his money, at first in raisin vineyards in California and later in the stock market.

Veblen returned to California in 1926, and by the next year he was living in a town shack in northern California. His economic situation became a disaster as he lost the money he had invested in the raisin industry and his stocks became worthless. He continued to earn $500 to $600 a year from royalties, and his former Chicago student continued to send him $500 a year.

Veblen was, to put it mildly, an unusual man. For example, he often could sit for hours and contribute little or nothing to a conversation going on around him. His friends and admirers made it possible for him to become president of the American Economic Association, but he declined the offer. The following vignette offered by a bookseller gives a bit more sense of this complex man:

> a man used to appear every six or eight weeks quite regularly, an ascetic, mysterious person . . . with a gentle air. He wore his hair long . . . I used to try to interest him in economics . . . I even once tried to get him to begin with *The Theory of the Leisure Class*. I explained to him what a brilliant port of entry it is to social consciousness . . . He listened attentively to all I said and melted like a snow drop through the door. One day he ordered a volume of Latin hymns. "I shall have to take your name because we will order this expressly for you," I told him. "We shall not have an audience for such a book as this again in a long time, I am afraid." "My name is Thorstein Veblen," he breathed rather than said.
>
> (cited in Tilman, 1992:9–10)

Thorstein Veblen died on August 3, 1929, just before the Great Depression that many felt his work anticipated (Powers, 2005b).

JOSEPH SCHUMPETER

A Biographical Sketch

Born and educated in Austria-Hungary, Joseph Schumpeter's life was filled with a mixture of success, paradox, and tragedy. He received his Ph.D. in 1906 from the University of Vienna and, after practicing law in Egypt for a year, earned early success as a promising young economist. However, his academic career was interrupted by World War I. He served as Minister of Finance in Austria's only socialist government between World War I and World War II, and later became president of a bank. The bank collapsed in 1924 when the Vienna stock market crashed, bankrupting Schumpeter. In spite of this personal disaster, Schumpeter gained invaluable practical insight into capitalism and its ever-present "gales." He took a position at the University of Bonn (Germany) in 1925 but began visiting Harvard in the late 1920s, and with the rise of Nazism in Germany, he moved to Harvard on a permanent basis in 1932. He taught there until his death in 1950.

Schumpeter carried himself in an aristocratic manner with much time and effort devoted to his appearance and dress (he told the wife of one colleague that it took him an hour to get dressed in the morning) (Allen, 1991a:134). He also liked to tell his students that as a young man he had three ambitions in life: to be the world's greatest economist, the world's greatest horseman, and the world's greatest lover (Swedberg, 1991:12). But despite all of his bravado and his escapades, Schumpeter's personal life was also filled with tragedy. It appears that Schumpeter had two great loves in his life. The first was his mother, who doted on him and took great pains to ensure that he had a proper upbringing even to the point of marrying a minor noble to ensure that Schumpeter could attend the best schools (Allen, 1991a:18). The other was his second wife, whom Schumpeter married in 1925. In June 1926 Schumpeter's mother died; in August of the same year so, too, did his wife and son during childbirth. Although Schumpeter was able to recover from these tragedies, he often characterized his life as one of peace but not joy (Allen 1991a). In the fall of 1926 he began recopying his dead wife's diary, eventually inserting his own comments and contemporary thoughts into it. Schumpeter also began to elevate his dead wife and mother into his own personal deities from whom he would ask for advice and protection (Allen, 1991a:225–229).

Known primarily as an economist, Schumpeter was a multidisciplinary thinker who "knew that law, mathematics, and history mattered mightily, as did the newer fields of *sociology*, psychology, and political science" (McCraw, 2007:55; italics added; see also Dahms, 2011a). Integrating insights from various disciplines, and focusing on the big economic issues of his day, Schumpeter, like many of the other theorists dealt with in this book, "was following a long European tradition aimed at constructing *grand social theory*" (McCraw, 2007:156).

Joseph Schumpeter (1883–1950)

Like Veblen, Joseph Schumpeter was an economist, not a sociologist, but he has come to be seen as a significant figure in sociology, especially economic sociology (Dahms, 2011a; Swedberg, 1991). He is best known for his work on the nature of capitalism, especially the process of "creative destruction" that, in his view, lies at the heart of the capitalist system (Schumpeter, 1976). Creation, or innovation, is central to capitalism, but it cannot occur without the destruction of older or out-of-date elements that could impede the new ones or the capitalist system more generally. This is a dynamic theory of capitalism and exists as part of Schumpeter's highly dynamic economic theory. He contrasts his approach to the more static theories (e.g., supply and demand) that he sees as dominant in the field of economics and of which he is highly critical.

The Chicago School[1]

The department of sociology at the University of Chicago was founded in 1892 by Albion Small (J. Williams, 2007). Small's intellectual work is of less contemporary significance than is the key role he played in the institutionalization of sociology in the United States (Faris, 1970; Matthews, 1977). He was instrumental in creating a department at Chicago that was to become the center of the discipline in the United States for many years. Small collaborated on the first textbook in sociology in 1894. In 1895 he founded the *American Journal of Sociology,* a journal that to this day is a dominant force in the discipline. In 1905, Small cofounded the American Sociological Society, *the* major professional association of American sociologists to this day (Rhoades, 1981). (The embarrassment caused by the initials of the American Sociological Society, ASS, led to a name change in 1959 to the American Sociological Association—ASA.)

Early Chicago Sociology

The early Chicago department had several distinctive characteristics. For one thing, it had a strong connection with religion. Some members were ministers themselves, and others were sons of ministers. Small, for example, believed that "the ultimate goal of sociology must be essentially Christian" (Matthews, 1977:95). This opinion led to a view that sociology must be interested in social reform, and this view was combined with a belief that sociology should be scientific.[2] Scientific sociology with an objective of social amelioration was to be practiced in the burgeoning city of Chicago, which was beset by the positive and negative effects of urbanization and industrialization.

W. I. Thomas (1863–1947)   In 1895, W. I. Thomas became a fellow at the Chicago department, where he wrote his dissertation in 1896 (T. McCarthy, 2005). Thomas's lasting significance was in his emphasis on the need to do scientific research on

---

[1] See Bulmer (1985) for a discussion of what defines a school and why we can speak of the "Chicago school." Tiryakian (1979, 1986) also deals with schools in general, and the Chicago school in particular, and emphasizes the role played by charismatic leaders as well as methodological innovations. For a discussion of this school within the broader context of developments in American sociological theory, see Hinkle (1994).

[2] As we will see, however, the Chicago school's conception of science was to become too "soft," at least in the eyes of the positivists who later came to dominate sociology.

sociological issues (Lodge, 1986). Although he championed this position for many years, its major statement came in 1918 with the publication of *The Polish Peasant in Europe and America,* which Thomas coauthored with Florian Znaniecki (Halas, 2005; Stebbins, 2007a, 2007b; Wiley, 2007). Martin Bulmer sees it as a landmark study because it moved sociology away from "abstract theory and library research and toward the study of the empirical world utilizing a theoretical framework" (1984:45). Norbert Wiley sees *The Polish Peasant* as crucial to the founding of sociology in the sense of "clarifying the unique intellectual space into which this discipline alone could see and explore" (1986:20). The book was the product of eight years of research in both Europe and the United States and was primarily a study of social disorganization among Polish migrants. The data were of little lasting importance. However, the methodology was significant. It involved a variety of data sources, including autobiographical material, paid writings, family letters, newspaper files, public documents, and institutional letters.

Although *The Polish Peasant* was primarily a macrosociological study of social institutions, over the course of his career Thomas gravitated toward a microscopic, social-psychological orientation. He is best known for the following social-psychological statement (made in a book coauthored by Dorothy Thomas): "If men define situations as real, they are real in their consequences" (Thomas and Thomas, 1928:572). The emphasis was on the importance of what people think and how this affects what they do. This microscopic, social-psychological focus stood in contrast to the macroscopic, social-structural and social-cultural perspectives of such European scholars as Marx, Weber, and Durkheim. It was to become one of the defining characteristics of Chicago's theoretical product—symbolic interactionism (Rock, 1979:5).

Robert Park (1864–1944)   Another figure of significance at Chicago was Robert Park (Shils, 1996). Park had come to Chicago as a part-time instructor in 1914 and quickly worked his way into a central role in the department. Park's importance in the development of sociology lay in several areas. First, he became the dominant figure in the Chicago department, which, in turn, dominated sociology into the 1930s. Second, Park had studied in Europe and was instrumental in bringing continental European thinkers to the attention of Chicago sociologists. Park had taken courses with Simmel, and Simmel's ideas, particularly his focus on action and interaction, were instrumental in the development of the Chicago school's theoretical orientation (Rock, 1979:36–48). Third, prior to becoming a sociologist, Park had been a reporter, and that experience gave him a sense of the importance of urban problems and of the need to go out into the field to collect data through personal observation (Lindner, 1996; Strauss, 1996). Out of this emerged the Chicago school's substantive interest in urban ecology (Gaziano, 1996; Maines, Bridger, and Ulmer, 1996; Perry, Abbott, and Hutter, 1997). Fourth, Park played a key role in guiding graduate students and helping develop "a cumulative program of graduate research" (Bulmer, 1984:13). Finally, in 1921, Park and Ernest W. Burgess published the first truly important sociology textbook, *Introduction to the Science of Sociology.* It was to be an influential book for many years and was particularly notable for its commitments to science, research, and the study of a wide range of social phenomena.

Beginning in the late 1920s and early 1930s, Park began to spend less time in Chicago. Finally, his lifelong interest in race relations (he had been secretary to Booker T. Washington before becoming a sociologist) led him to take a position at Fisk University (a black university) in 1934. Although the decline of the Chicago department was not caused solely or even chiefly by Park's departure, its status began to wane in the 1930s. But before we can deal with the decline of Chicago sociology and the rise of other departments and theories, we need to return to the early days of the school and the two figures whose work was to be of the most lasting theoretical significance—Charles Horton Cooley and, most important, George Herbert Mead.[3]

Charles Horton Cooley (1864–1929)   The association of Cooley with the Chicago school is interesting in that he spent his career at the University of Michigan. But Cooley's theoretical perspective was in line with the theory of symbolic interactionism that was to become Chicago's most important product (Jacobs, 2006; Sandstrom and Kleinman, 2005; Schubert, 2005, 2007).

Cooley received his Ph.D. from the University of Michigan in 1894. He had developed a strong interest in sociology, but there was as yet no department of sociology at Michigan. As a result, the questions for his Ph.D. examination came from Columbia University, where sociology had been taught since 1889 under the leadership of Franklin Giddings. Cooley began his teaching career at Michigan in 1892 before completion of his doctorate.

Although Cooley theorized about large-scale phenomena such as social classes, social structures, and social institutions, he is remembered today mainly for his insights into the social-psychological aspects of social life (Schubert, 2005, 2007). His work in this area is in line with that of George Herbert Mead, although Mead was to have a deeper and more lasting effect on sociology than Cooley had. Cooley had an interest in consciousness, but he refused (as did Mead) to separate consciousness from the social context. This is best exemplified by a concept of his that survives to this day—the *looking-glass self*. By this concept, Cooley understood that people possess consciousness and that it is shaped in continuing social interaction.

A second basic concept that illustrates Cooley's social-psychological interests, and is also of continuing interest and importance, is that of the primary group. *Primary groups* are intimate, face-to-face groups that play a key role in linking the actor to the larger society. Especially crucial are the primary groups of the young—mainly the family and the peer group. Within these groups, the individual grows into a social being. It is basically within the primary group that the looking-glass self emerges and that the ego-centered child learns to take others into account and, thereby, to become a contributing member of society.

Both Cooley (Winterer, 1994) and Mead rejected a *behavioristic* view of human beings, the view that people blindly and unconsciously respond to external stimuli. They believed that people had consciousness, a self, and that it was the responsibility of the sociologist to study this aspect of social reality. Cooley urged sociologists to try to put

---

[3] There were many other significant figures associated with the Chicago school, including Everett Hughes (Chapoulie, 1996; Strauss, 1996).

ROBERT PARK

A Biographical Sketch

Robert Park did not follow the typical career route of an academic sociologist—college, graduate school, professorship. Instead, he had a varied career before he became a sociologist late in life. Despite his late start, Park had a profound effect on sociology in general and on theory in particular. Park's varied experiences gave him an unusual orientation to life, and this view helped shape the Chicago school, symbolic interactionism, and, ultimately, a good portion of sociology.

Park was born in Harveyville, Pennsylvania, on February 14, 1864 (Matthews, 1977). As a student at the University of Michigan, he was exposed to a number of great thinkers, such as John Dewey. Although he was excited by ideas, Park felt a strong need to work in the real world. As Park said, "I made up my mind to go in for experience for its own sake, to gather into my soul . . . 'all the joys and sorrows of the world' " (1927/1973:253). Upon graduation, he began a career as a journalist, which gave him this real-world opportunity. He particularly liked to explore ("hunting down gambling houses and opium dens" [Park, 1927/1973:254]). He wrote about city life in vivid detail. He would go into the field, observe and analyze, and finally write up his observations. In fact, he was already doing essentially the kind of research ("scientific reporting") that came to be one of the hallmarks of Chicago sociology—that is, urban ethnology using participant observation techniques (Lindner, 1996).

Although the accurate description of social life remained one of his passions, Park grew dissatisfied with newspaper work because it did not fulfill his familial or, more important, his intellectual needs. Furthermore, it did not seem to contribute to the improvement of the world, and Park had a deep interest in social reform. In 1898, at age 34, Park left newspaper work and enrolled in the

themselves in the place of the actors they were studying, to use the method of *sympathetic introspection,* in order to analyze consciousness. By analyzing what they as actors might do in various circumstances, sociologists could understand the meanings and motives that are at the base of social behavior. The method of sympathetic introspection seemed to many to be very unscientific. In this area, among others, Mead's work represents an advance over Cooley's. Nevertheless, there is a great deal of similarity in the interests of the two men, not the least of which is their shared view that sociology should focus on such social-psychological phenomena as consciousness, action, and interaction.

George Herbert Mead (1863–1931)   The most important thinker associated with the Chicago school and symbolic interactionism was not a sociologist but a philosopher, philosophy department at Harvard. He remained there for a year but then decided to move to Germany, at that time the heart of the world's intellectual life. In Berlin he encountered Georg Simmel, whose work was to have a profound influence on Park's sociology. In fact, Simmel's lectures were the *only* formal sociological training that Park received. As Park said, "I got most of my knowledge about society and human nature from my own observations" (1927/1973:257). In 1904, Park completed his doctoral dissertation at the University of Heidelberg. Characteristically, he was dissatisfied with his dissertation: "All I had to show was that little book and I was ashamed of it" (Matthews, 1977:57). He refused a summer teaching job at the University of Chicago and turned away from academe as he had earlier turned away from newspaper work.

His need to contribute to social betterment led him to become secretary and chief publicity officer for the Congo Reform Association, which was set up to help alleviate the brutality and exploitation then taking place in the Belgian Congo. During this period, he met Booker T. Washington, and he was attracted to the cause of improving the lot of black Americans. He became Washington's secretary and played a key role in the activities of the Tuskegee Institute. In 1912 he met W. I. Thomas, the Chicago sociologist, who was lecturing at Tuskegee. Thomas invited him to give a course on "the Negro in America" to a small group of graduate students at Chicago, and Park did so in 1914. The course was successful, and he gave it again the next year to an audience twice as large. At this time he joined the American Sociological Society, and only a decade later he became its president. Park gradually worked his way into a full-time appointment at Chicago, although he did not get a full professorship until 1923, when he was 59 years old. Over the approximately two decades that he was affiliated with the University of Chicago, he played a key role in shaping the intellectual orientation of the sociology department.

Park remained peripatetic even after his retirement from Chicago in the early 1930s. He taught courses and oversaw research at Fisk University until he was nearly 80 years old. He traveled extensively. He died on February 7, 1944, one week before his 80th birthday.

George Herbert Mead.[4] Mead started teaching philosophy at the University of Chicago in 1894, and he taught there until his death in 1931 (Chriss, 2005b; G. Cook, 1993). He is something of a paradox, given his central importance in the history of sociological theory, both because he taught philosophy, not sociology, and because he published comparatively little during his lifetime. The paradox is, in part, resolved by two facts. First, Mead taught courses in social psychology in the philosophy department, and they were taken by many graduate students in sociology. His ideas had a profound effect on a number of them. These students combined Mead's ideas with those they were getting in the sociology department from people such as Park and Thomas.

---

[4] For a dissenting view, see J. Lewis and Smith (1980).

Although at the time there was no theory known as symbolic interactionism, it was created by students out of these various inputs. Thus Mead had a deep, personal impact on the people who were later to develop symbolic interactionism. Second, these students put together their notes on Mead's courses and published a posthumous volume under his name. The work, *Mind, Self and Society* (Mead, 1934/1962), moved his ideas from the realm of oral to that of written tradition. Widely read to this day, this volume forms the main intellectual pillar of symbolic interactionism.

We deal with Mead's ideas in Chapter 9, but it is necessary at this point to underscore a few points in order to situate him historically. Mead's ideas need to be seen in the context of psychological behaviorism. Mead was quite favorably impressed with this orientation and accepted many of its tenets. He adopted its focus on the actor and his behavior. He regarded as sensible the behaviorists' concern with the rewards and costs involved in the behaviors of the actors. What troubled Mead was that behaviorism did not seem to go far enough. That is, it excluded consciousness from serious consideration, arguing that it was not amenable to scientific study. Mead vehemently disagreed and sought to extend the principles of behaviorism to an analysis of the mind. In so doing, Mead enunciated a focus similar to that of Cooley. But whereas Cooley's position seemed unscientific, Mead promised a more scientific conception of consciousness by extending the highly scientific principles and methods of psychological behaviorism.

Mead offered American sociology a social-psychological theory that stood in stark contrast to the primarily societal theories offered by most of the major European theorists (Shalin, 2011). The most important exception was Simmel. Thus symbolic interactionism was developed, in large part, out of Simmel's (Low, 2008) interest in action and interaction and Mead's interest in consciousness. However, such a focus led to a weakness in Mead's work, as well as in symbolic interactionism in general, at the societal and cultural levels.

The Waning of Chicago Sociology

Chicago sociology reached its peak in the 1920s, but by the 1930s, with the death of Mead and the departure of Park, the department had begun to lose its position of central importance in American sociology (Cortese, 1995). Fred Matthews (1977; see also Bulmer, 1984) pinpoints several reasons for the decline of Chicago sociology, two of which seem of utmost importance.

First, the discipline had grown increasingly preoccupied with being scientific—that is, using sophisticated methods and employing statistical analysis. However, the Chicago school was viewed as emphasizing descriptive, ethnographic studies (Prus, 1996), often focusing on their subjects' personal orientations (in Thomas's terms, their "definitions of the situation"). Park progressively came to despise statistics (he called it "parlor magic") because it seemed to prohibit the analysis of subjectivity, the idiosyncratic, and the peculiar. The fact that important work in quantitative methods was done at Chicago (Bulmer, 1984:151–189) tended to be ignored in the face of its overwhelming association with qualitative methods.

Second, more and more individuals outside Chicago grew increasingly resentful of Chicago's dominance of both the American Sociological Society and the *American*

Journal of Sociology. The Eastern Sociological Society was founded in 1930, and eastern sociologists became more vocal about the dominance of the Midwest in general and Chicago in particular (Wiley, 1979:63). By 1935, the revolt against Chicago had led to a non-Chicago secretary of the association and the establishment of a new official journal, the *American Sociological Review* (Lengermann, 1979). According to Wiley, "the Chicago school had fallen like a mighty oak" (1979:63). This signaled the growth of other power centers, most notably Harvard and the Ivy League in general. Symbolic interactionism was largely an indeterminate, oral tradition and as such eventually lost ground to more explicit and codified theoretical systems such as the structural functionalism associated with the Ivy League (Rock, 1979:12).

Though it would never again be the center of American sociology, the Chicago school remained a force into the 1950s. Herbert Blumer (1900–1987) was a significant figure in the department until his departure for Berkeley in 1952 (Blumer, 1969a; Maines, 2005). He was a major exponent of the theoretical approach developed at Chicago out of the work of Mead, Cooley, Simmel, Park, Thomas, and others. In fact, it was Blumer who coined the phrase *symbolic interactionism* in 1937. Blumer played a key role in keeping this tradition alive through his teaching at Chicago and wrote a number of essays that were instrumental in keeping symbolic interactionism vital into the 1950s. Whatever the state of the Chicago school, the Chicago tradition has remained alive to this day with major exponents dispersed throughout the country and the world (Sandstrom, Martin, and Fine, 2001).

Women in Early Sociology

Simultaneously with the developments at the University of Chicago described in the previous section, even sometimes in concert with them, and at the same time that Durkheim, Weber, and Simmel were creating a European sociology, and sometimes in concert with them as well, a group of women who formed a broad and surprisingly connected network of social reformers were also developing pioneering sociological theories. These women included Jane Addams (1860–1935), Charlotte Perkins Gilman (1860–1935), Anna Julia Cooper (1858–1964), Ida Wells-Barnett (1862–1931), Marianne Weber (1870–1954), and Beatrice Potter Webb (1858–1943). With the possible exception of Cooper, they can all be connected through their relationship to Jane Addams. That they are not today known or recognized in conventional histories of the discipline as sociologists or sociological theorists is a chilling testimony to the power of gender politics within the discipline of sociology and to sociology's essentially unreflective and uncritical interpretation of its own practices. Although the sociological theory of each of these women is a product of individual theoretical effort, when they are read collectively, they represent a coherent and complementary statement of early feminist sociological theory.

The chief hallmarks of their theories, hallmarks that may in part account for their being passed over in the development of professional sociology, include (1) an emphasis on women's experience and women's lives and works being equal in importance to men's; (2) an awareness that they spoke from a situated and embodied standpoint and therefore, for the most part, not with the tone of imperious objectivity that male sociological theory would come to associate with authoritative theory making (Lemert, 2000); (3) the idea that the purpose of sociology and sociological theory is social reform—that is, the end is to improve people's lives through knowledge; and (4) the claim that the chief problem for amelioration in their time was inequality. What distinguishes these early women most from each other is the nature of and the remedy for the inequality on which they focused—gender, race, or class, or the intersection of these factors. But all these women translated their views into social and political activism that helped shape and change the North Atlantic societies in which they lived, and this activism was as much a part of their sense of practicing sociology as creating theory was. They believed in social science research as part of both their theoretical and activist enactments of sociology and were highly creative innovators of social science method.

As the developing discipline of sociology marginalized these women as sociologists and sociological theorists, it often incorporated their research methods into its own practices, while using their activism as an excuse to define these women as "not sociologists." Thus they are remembered as social activists and social workers rather than sociologists. Their heritage is a sociological theory that is a call to action as well as to thought.

W.E.B. Du Bois and Race Theory[5]

Although W.E.B. Du Bois (1868–1963) taught in a sociology department (Atlanta University) for a considerable amount of time, he usually is not thought of as a sociologist, let alone as a theorist. He is far better known as a public intellectual and for his founding and leadership roles in various civil rights organizations, including the National Association for the Advancement of Colored People (NAACP). However, there is powerful sociology in many of his writings, and there are a number of abstract ideas that can be seen as theory, even though Du Bois (like Marx) was loath to distinguish between theory and practice. That is, he was uninterested in theory in itself, but rather developed abstract ideas in the service of advancing the cause of civil rights, primarily for African Americans.

Within sociology, Du Bois's reputation has been based to a large degree on his empirical study *The Philadelphia Negro* (1899/1996). This study of the seventh ward in Philadelphia was conducted single-handedly by Du Bois, and although he employed a multitude of methods, it is best known as a pioneering ethnography. Over his long career, Du Bois wrote an unbelievable number of books, articles, and editorials, but few would be immediately obvious as "theory." However, there is theory in his work, especially in his several unique autobiographical efforts (the best known of which is *The Souls of Black Folk* [Du Bois, 1903/1996]) that allowed him to develop interesting theoretical ideas in the context of reflections on his own life. Overarching all was his interest in the "race idea," which he considered the "the central thought of all history" (Du Bois, 1897/1995:21), and the "color line," which he saw as drawn across not only the United States but across much of the world. One of his best-known theoretical

---

[5] We will discuss a more specific and contemporary version of race theory—critical theories of race and racism—at the close of this chapter and in greater detail in Chapter 17.

ideas is the *veil,* which creates a clear separation, or barrier, between African Americans and whites. The imagery is *not* of a wall but rather of a thin, porous material through which each race can see the other, but which nonetheless serves to separate the races. Another key theoretical idea is *double-consciousness,* a sense of "two-ness," or a feeling among African Americans of seeing and measuring themselves through others' eyes. There is not a full-fledged theory of society in Du Bois's work, but there is a series of theoretical ideas about race and race relations in the United States and the world. With the rise of multicultural (and feminist) theories in recent years, Du Bois's focus on race and his view of the world from the African American perspective have attracted a large number of new admirers and, more important, thinkers who are building on his pioneering ideas, perspectives, and commitments.

Sociological Theory to Midcentury

The Rise of Harvard, the Ivy League, and Structural Functionalism

We can trace the rise of sociology at Harvard from the arrival of Pitirim Sorokin in 1930 (Avino, 2006; Jeffries, 2005; Johnston, 1995). When Sorokin arrived at Harvard, there was no sociology department, but by the end of his first year one had been organized, and he had been appointed its head. Sorokin was a sociological theorist and continued to publish into the 1960s, but his work is surprisingly little cited today. Although some disagree (e.g., Tiryakian, 2007b), the dominant view is that his theorizing has not stood the test of time very well. Sorokin's long-term significance may well have been in the creation of the Harvard sociology department and the hiring of Talcott Parsons (who had been an instructor of economics at Harvard) for the position of instructor in sociology. Parsons became *the* dominant figure in American sociology for introducing European theorists to an American audience, for his own sociological theories, and for his many students who became major sociological theorists.

Talcott Parsons (1902–1979)

Although Parsons published some early essays, his major contribution in the early years was his influence on graduate students, many of whom became notable sociological theorists themselves. The most famous was Robert Merton, who received his Ph.D. in 1936 and soon became a major theorist and the heart of Parsonsian-style theorizing at Columbia University. In the same year (1936), Kingsley Davis received his Ph.D., and he, along with Wilbert Moore (who received his Harvard degree in 1940), wrote one of the central works in structural-functional theory, the theory that was to become the major product of Parsons and the Parsonsians. But Parsons's influence was not restricted to the 1930s. Remarkably, he produced graduate students of great influence well into the 1960s.

The pivotal year for Parsons and for American sociological theory was 1937, the year in which he published *The Structure of Social Action.* This book was of significance to sociological theory in America for four main reasons. First, it

W.E.B. Du Bois

A Biographical Sketch

William Edward Burghardt Du Bois was born on February 23, 1868, in Great Barrington, Massachusetts (D. Lewis, 1993; P. Taylor, 2011). Compared to the vast majority of blacks of his day, Du Bois had a comparatively advantaged upbringing that led to college at Fisk University and later to a Ph.D. from Harvard University with a stop along the way at the University of Berlin. At Harvard and in Germany, Du Bois came into contact with some of the great thinkers of his day, including philosophers William James and Josiah Royce, as well as the great social theorist Max Weber.

Du Bois took his first job teaching Greek and Latin at a black college (Wilberforce). He notes that "the institution would have no sociology, even though I offered to teach it on my own time" (Du Bois, 1968:189). Du Bois moved on in the fall of 1896 when he was offered a position as assistant instructor at the University of Pennsylvania to do research on blacks in Philadelphia. That research led to the publication of one of the classic works of early sociology, *The Philadelphia Negro* (1899/1996). When that project was completed, Du Bois moved (he never had a regular faculty position at Pennsylvania, and that, like many other things in his lifetime, rankled him) to Atlanta University, where he taught sociology from 1897 to 1910 and was responsible for a number of research reports on various aspects of Negro life in America. It was also in this period that he authored the first and most important of his autobiographical memoirs, *The Souls of Black Folk* (1903/1996). This was a highly literary and deeply personal work that also made a series of general theoretical points and contributed greatly to the understanding of black Americans and of race relations. Du Bois published a number of such autobiographical works during the course of his life, including *Darkwater: Voices from within the Veil* (1920/1999), *Dusk of Dawn: An Essay toward an Autobiography of a Race Concept* (1940/1968), and *The Autobiography of W.E.B. Du Bois: A Soliloquy on Viewing My Life from the Last Decade of Its First Century* (1968). Of *Dusk of Dawn,* Du Bois (1968:2) says, "I have written then what is meant to be not so much my autobiography as the autobiography of a concept of race, elucidated, magnified and doubtless distorted in the thoughts and deeds that were mine." (Du Bois was not lacking in self-esteem and has often been criticized for his outsized ego.)

While at Atlanta University, Du Bois became more publicly and politically engaged. In 1905 he called for and attended a meeting near Buffalo, New York, that led to the formation of the Niagara Movement, an interracial civil rights organization interested in such things as the "abolition of all caste distinctions based simply on race and color" (Du Bois, 1968:249). This formed the basis of the similarly interracial National Association for the Advancement of Colored People (NAACP), which came into existence in 1910, and Du Bois became its director of publications and research. He founded the NAACP's magazine, *The Crisis,* and in its pages authored many essays on a wide range of issues relating to the state of the

Negro in America. Du Bois took this new position because it offered him a platform for the widespread dissemination of his ideas (he was solely responsible for the editorial opinions of *The Crisis*). In addition, his position at Atlanta University had become untenable because of his conflict with the then very popular and powerful Booker T. Washington, who was regarded by most white leaders and politicians as the spokesman for black America. Du Bois came to view Washington as far too conservative and much too willing to subordinate Negroes to whites in general and specifically within the white-dominated economy, where they were to be trained for, and satisfied with, manual work.

For the next half century Du Bois was a tireless writer and activist on behalf of Negro and other racial causes (D. Lewis, 2000). He attended and participated in meetings throughout the United States and much of the world on Negroes in particular, and all "colored" races in general. He took positions on many of the pressing issues of the day, almost always from the vantage point of Negroes and other minorities. For example, he had views on which presidential candidates Negroes should support, whether the United States should enter World Wars I and II, and whether Negroes should support those wars and participate in them.

By the early 1930s the Great Depression had begun to wreak havoc on the circulation of *The Crisis,* and Du Bois lost control to young dissidents within the NAACP. He returned to Atlanta University and scholarly work and, among other things, authored *Black Reconstruction in America, 1860–1880* (1935/1998). His tenure lasted a little more than a decade, and in 1944 Du Bois (then 76) was forcibly retired by the university. Under pressure, the NAACP invited him back as an ornamental figure, but Du Bois refused to play that role or to act his age and was dismissed in 1948. His ideas and work grew increasingly radical over the ensuing nearly two decades of his life. He joined and participated in various peace organizations and eventually was indicted by a grand jury in 1951 for failing to register as an agent of a foreign power in the peace movement.

Early in his life Du Bois had hope in America in general and, more specifically, believed that it could solve its racial problems peacefully within the context of a capitalist society. Over the years he lost faith in capitalists and capitalism and grew more supportive of socialism. Eventually, he grew more radical in his views and drifted toward communism. He was quite impressed with the advances communism brought to the Soviet Union and China. In the end, he joined the Communist Party. Toward the very end of his long life, Du Bois seemed to give up hope in the United States and moved to the African nation of Ghana. Du Bois became a citizen of Ghana and died there on August 27, 1963, the day before Martin Luther King Jr. delivered his "I have a dream" speech on the Mall in Washington, D.C. Du Bois was 95.

While wide-scale recognition of Du Bois as an important theorist may be relatively recent, he has long been influential within the black community. For example, on his becoming chairman of the board of the NAACP, Julian Bond said: "I think for people of my age and generation, this [a picture in his home of a young Bond holding Du Bois's hand] was a normal experience—not to have Du Bois in your home, but to have his name in your home, to know about him in your home. . . . This was table conversation for us" (cited in Lemert, 2000:346).

served to introduce grand European theorizing to a large American audience. The bulk of the book was devoted to Durkheim, Weber, and Pareto. His interpretations of these theorists shaped their images in American sociology for many years. Second, Parsons devoted almost no attention to Marx or to Simmel (D. Levine, 1991a). As a result, Marxian theory continued to be largely excluded from legitimate sociology.

Third, *The Structure of Social Action* made the case for sociological theorizing as a legitimate and significant sociological activity. The theorizing that has taken place in the United States since then owes a deep debt to Parsons's work (Lidz, 2011b).

Finally, Parsons argued for specific sociological theories that were to have a profound influence on sociology. At first, Parsons was thought of, and thought of himself, as an action theorist (Joas, 1996). He seemed to focus on actors and their thoughts and actions. But by the close of his 1937 work and increasingly in his later work, Parsons sounded more like a structural-functional theorist focusing on large-scale social and cultural systems. Although Parsons argued that there was no contradiction between these theories, he became best known as a structural functionalist, and he was the primary exponent of this theory, which gained dominance within sociology and maintained that position until the 1960s. Parsons's theoretical strength, and that of structural functionalism, lay in delineating the relationships among large-scale social structures and institutions (see Chapter 7).

Parsons's major statements on his structural-functional theory came in the early 1950s in several works, most notably *The Social System* (1951) (Barber, 1994). In that work and others, Parsons tended to concentrate on the structures of society and their relationship to each other. Those structures were seen as mutually supportive and tending toward a dynamic equilibrium. The emphasis was on how order was maintained among the various elements of society (Wrong, 1994). Change was seen as an orderly process, and Parsons (1966, 1971) ultimately came to adopt a neoevolutionary view of social change. Parsons was concerned not only with the social system per se but also with its relationship to the other *action systems,* especially the cultural and personality systems. But his basic view on intersystemic relations was essentially the same as his view of intrasystemic relations; that is, that they were defined by cohesion, consensus, and order. In other words, the various *social structures* performed a variety of positive *functions* for each other.

It is clear, then, why Parsons came to be defined primarily as a *structural functionalist.* As his fame grew, so did the strength of structural-functional theory in the United States. His work lay at the core of this theory, but his students and disciples also concentrated on extending both the theory and its dominance in the United States.

Although Parsons played a number of important and positive roles in the history of sociological theory in the United States, his work also had negative consequences (Holton, 2001). First, he offered interpretations of European theorists that seemed to reflect his own theoretical orientation more than theirs. Many American sociologists were initially exposed to erroneous interpretations of the European masters. Second, as already pointed out, early in his career Parsons largely ignored Marx, which resulted in Marx's ideas being on the periphery of sociology for many years. Third, his own theory as it developed over the years had a number of serious weaknesses. However, Parsons's preeminence in American sociology served for many years to mute or overwhelm the critics. Not until much later did the weaknesses of Parsons's theory, and of structural functionalism in general, receive a full airing.

But returning to the early 1930s and other developments at Harvard, we can gain a good deal of insight into the development of the Harvard department by looking at it through an account of its other major figure, George Homans.

George Homans (1910–1989)

A wealthy Bostonian, George Homans received his bachelor's degree from Harvard in 1932 (Homans, 1962, 1984; see also Bell, 1992). As a result of the Great Depression, he was unemployed but certainly not penniless. In the fall of 1932, L. J. Henderson, a physiologist, was offering a course in the theories of Vilfredo Pareto, and Homans was invited to attend; he accepted. (Parsons also attended the Pareto seminars.) Homans's description of why he was drawn to and taken with Pareto says much about why American sociological theory was so highly conservative, so anti-Marxist:

> I took to Pareto because he made clear to me what I was already prepared to believe. . . . Someone has said that much modern sociology is an effort to answer the arguments of the revolutionaries. As a Republican Bostonian who had not rejected his comparatively wealthy family, I felt during the thirties that I was under personal attack, above all from the Marxists. I was ready to believe Pareto because he provided me with a defense.
>
> (Homans, 1962:4)

Homans's exposure to Pareto led to a book, *An Introduction to Pareto* (coauthored with Charles Curtis), published in 1934. The publication of this book made Homans a sociologist even though Pareto's work was virtually the only sociology he had read up to that point.

In 1934, Homans was named a junior fellow at Harvard, a program started to avoid the problems associated with the Ph.D. program. In fact, Homans never did earn a Ph.D., even though he became one of the major sociological figures of his day. Homans was a junior fellow until 1939, and in those years he absorbed more and more sociology. In 1939, Homans was affiliated with the sociology department, but the connection was broken by the war.

By the time Homans had returned from the war, the department of social relations had been founded by Parsons at Harvard, and Homans joined it. Although Homans respected some aspects of Parsons's work, he was highly critical of Parsons's style of theorizing. A long-running exchange began between the two men that later manifested itself publicly in the pages of many books and journals. Basically, Homans argued that Parsons's theory was not a theory at all but rather a vast system of intellectual categories into which most aspects of the social world fit. Further, Homans believed that theory should be built from the ground up on the basis of careful observations of the social world. Parsons's theory, however, started on the general theoretical level and worked its way down to the empirical level.

In his own work, Homans amassed a large number of empirical observations over the years, but it was only in the 1950s that he hit upon a satisfactory theoretical approach with which to analyze those data. That theory was psychological behaviorism, as it was best expressed in the ideas of his colleague at Harvard, the psychologist B. F. Skinner. On the basis of this perspective, Homans developed his exchange theory. We will pick up the story of this theoretical development later in this chapter. The crucial point here is that Harvard and its major theoretical product, structural functionalism, became preeminent in sociology in the late 1930s, replacing the Chicago school and symbolic interactionism.

Developments in Marxian Theory

From the early 1900s to the 1930s, Marxian theory continued to develop largely independently of mainstream sociological theory. At least partially the exception to this was the emergence of the critical, or Frankfurt, school out of the earlier Hegelian Marxism.

The idea of a school for the development of Marxian theory was the product of Felix J. Weil. The Institute of Social Research was officially founded in Frankfurt, Germany, on February 3, 1923 (Jay, 1973; Wheatland, 2009; Wiggershaus, 1994). Over the years, a number of the most famous thinkers in Marxian theory were associated with the critical school—Max Horkheimer (Schulz, 2007a), Theodor Adorno (Schulz, 2007b), Erich Fromm (N. McLaughlin, 2007), Herbert Marcuse (Dandaneau, 2007a), and, more recently, Jurgen Habermas and Axel Honneth.

The institute functioned in Germany until 1934, but by then things were growing increasingly uncomfortable under the Nazi regime. The Nazis had little use for the Marxian ideas that dominated the institute, and their hostility was heightened because many of those associated with it were Jewish. In 1934 Horkheimer, as head of the institute, came to New York to discuss its status with the president of Columbia University. Much to Horkheimer's surprise, he was invited to affiliate the institute with the university, and he was even offered a building on campus. And so *a* center of Marxian theory moved to *the* center of the capitalist world. The institute stayed there until the end of the war, but after the war pressure mounted to return it to Germany. In 1949, Horkheimer did return to Germany, and he brought the institute with him. Although the institute itself moved to Germany, many of the figures associated with it took independent career directions.

It is important to underscore a few of the most important aspects of critical theory (Calhoun and Karaganis, 2001). In its early years, those associated with the institute tended to be fairly traditional Marxists, devoting a good portion of their attention to the economic domain. But around 1930, a major change took place as this group of thinkers began to shift its attention from the economy to the cultural system especially the "culture industry" (Lash and Lury, 2007), which it came to see as the major force in modern capitalist society. This was consistent with, but an extension of, the position taken earlier by Hegelian Marxists such as Georg Lukács. To help them understand the cultural domain, the critical theorists were attracted to the work of Max Weber. The effort to combine Marx and Weber and thereby create

"Weberian Marxism"[6] (Dahms, 1997; Lowy, 1996) gave the critical school some of its distinctive orientations and served in later years to make it more legitimate to sociologists who began to grow interested in Marxian theory.

A second major step taken by at least some members of the critical school was to employ the rigorous social-scientific techniques developed by American sociologists to research issues of interest to Marxists. This, like the adoption of Weberian theory, made the critical school more acceptable to mainstream sociologists.

Third, critical theorists made an effort to integrate individually oriented Freudian theory with the societal- and cultural-level insights of Marx and Weber. This seemed to many sociologists to represent a more inclusive theory than that offered by either Marx or Weber alone. If nothing else, the effort to combine such disparate theories proved stimulating to sociologists and many other intellectuals.

The critical school has done much useful work since the 1920s, and a significant amount of it is of relevance to sociologists. However, the critical school had to await the late 1960s before it was "discovered" by large numbers of American theorists.

Karl Mannheim and the Sociology of Knowledge

Brief mention should be made at this point of the work of Karl Mannheim (1893–1947) (Kettler and Meja, 1995; Loader, 2011; Ruef, 2007). Born in Hungary, Mannheim was forced to move first to Germany and later to England. He was influenced by the work of Marx on ideology, as well as that of Weber, Simmel, and the neo-Marxist Georg Lukács. Also of significance is his thinking on rationality, which tends to pick up themes developed in Weber's work on this topic but deals with them in a far more concise and a much clearer manner (Ritzer, 1998).

He is best known, however, as the founder of an area of sociology, called the sociology of knowledge, that continues to be important to this day (E. McCarthy, 1996, 2007; Stehr, 2001). Mannheim, of course, built on the work of many predecessors, most notably Karl Marx (although Mannheim was far from being a Marxist). Basically, the sociology of knowledge involves the systematic study of knowledge, ideas, or intellectual phenomena in general. To Mannheim, knowledge is determined by social existence. For example, Mannheim seeks to relate the ideas of a group to that group's position in the social structure. Marx did this by relating ideas to social classes, but Mannheim extends this perspective by linking ideas to a variety of different positions within society (for example, differences between generations).

In addition to playing a major role in creating the sociology of knowledge, Mannheim is perhaps best known for his distinction between two idea systems—*ideology* and *utopia* (B. Turner, 1995). An ideology is an idea system that seeks to conceal and conserve the present by interpreting it from the point of view of the past. A utopia, in contrast, is a system of ideas that seeks to transcend the present by focusing on the future. Conflict between ideologies and utopias is an ever-present reality in society (Mannheim, 1931/1936).

---

[6] This label fits some critical theorists better than others, and it also applies to a wide range of other thinkers (Agger, 1998).

Sociological Theory from Midcentury

Structural Functionalism: Peak and Decline

The 1940s and 1950s were paradoxically the years of greatest dominance and the beginnings of the decline of structural functionalism. In those years, Parsons produced his major statements that clearly reflected his shift from action theory to structural functionalism. Parsons's students had fanned out across the country and occupied dominant positions in many of the major sociology departments (for example, Columbia and Cornell). These students were producing works of their own that were widely recognized contributions to structural-functional theory.

However, just as it was gaining theoretical hegemony, structural functionalism came under attack, and the attacks mounted until they reached a climax in the 1960s and 1970s. There was an attack by C. Wright Mills on Parsons in 1959, and other major criticisms were mounted by David Lockwood (1956), Alvin Gouldner (1959/1967, 1970; Chriss, 2005a), and Irving Horowitz (1962/1967). In the 1950s, these attacks were seen as little more than "guerrilla raids," but as sociology moved into the 1960s, the dominance of structural functionalism was clearly in jeopardy.

George Huaco (1986) linked the rise and decline of structural functionalism to the position of American society in the world order. As America rose to world dominance after 1945, structural functionalism achieved hegemony within sociology. Structural functionalism supported America's dominant position in the world in two ways. First, the structural-functional view that "every pattern has consequences which contribute to the preservation and survival of the larger system" was "nothing less than a celebration of the United States and its world hegemony" (Huaco, 1986:52). Second, the structural-functional emphasis on equilibrium (the best social change is no change) meshed well with the interests of the United States, then "the wealthiest and most powerful empire in the world." The decline of U.S. world dominance in the 1970s coincided with structural functionalism's loss of its preeminent position in sociological theory.

Radical Sociology in America: C. Wright Mills

As we have seen, although Marxian theory was largely ignored or reviled by mainstream American sociologists, there were exceptions, the most notable of which is C. Wright Mills (1916–1962). Mills is noteworthy for his almost single-handed effort to keep a Marxian tradition alive in sociological theory. Modern Marxian sociologists have far outstripped Mills in theoretical sophistication, but they owe him a deep debt nonetheless for the personal and professional activities that helped set the stage for their own work (Alt, 1985–1986). Mills was not a Marxist, and he did not read Marx until the mid-1950s. Even then he was restricted to the few available English translations because he could not read German. Because Mills had published most of his major works by then, his work was not informed by a very sophisticated Marxian theory.

Mills published two major works that reflected his radical politics as well as his weaknesses in Marxian theory. The first was *White Collar* (1951), an acid critique of the status of a growing occupational category, white-collar workers. The second was *The Power Elite* (1956), a book that sought to show how America was dominated by a small group of businessmen, politicians, and military leaders (Zweigenhaft and Domhoff, 2006). Sandwiched in between was his most theoretically sophisticated work, *Character and Social Structure* (Gerth and Mills, 1953), coauthored with Hans Gerth (N. Gerth, 1993).

Mills's radicalism put him on the periphery of American sociology. He was the object of much criticism, and he, in turn, became a severe critic of sociology. The critical attitude culminated in *The Sociological Imagination* (1959). Of particular note is Mills's severe criticism of Talcott Parsons and his practice of grand theory.

Mills died in 1962, an outcast in sociology. However, before the decade was out, both radical sociology and Marxian theory (Levine, 2005) would begin to make important inroads into the discipline.

The Development of Conflict Theory

Another precursor to a true union of Marxism and sociological theory was the development of a conflict-theory alternative to structural functionalism. As we have just seen, structural functionalism had no sooner gained leadership in sociological theory than it came under increasing attack. The attack was multifaceted: structural functionalism was accused of such things as being politically conservative, unable to deal with social change because of its focus on static structures, and incapable of adequately analyzing social conflict.

One of the results of this criticism was an effort on the part of a number of sociologists to overcome the problems of structural functionalism by integrating a concern for structure with an interest in conflict. This work constituted the development of *conflict theory* as an alternative to structural-functional theory. Unfortunately, it often seemed little more than a mirror image of structural functionalism with little intellectual integrity of its own.

The first effort of note was Lewis Coser's (1956) book on the functions of social conflict (Delaney, 2005a; Jaworski, 1991). This work clearly tried to deal with social conflict from within the framework of a structural-functional view of the world. Although it is useful to look at the functions of conflict, there is much more to the study of conflict than an analysis of its positive functions.

The biggest problem with most of conflict theory was that it lacked what it needed most—a sound basis in Marxian theory. After all, Marxian theory was well developed outside of sociology and should have provided a base on which to develop a sophisticated sociological theory of conflict. The one exception here is the work of Ralf Dahrendorf (1929–2009).

Dahrendorf was a European scholar who was well versed in Marxian theory. He sought to embed his conflict theory in the Marxian tradition. Dahrendorf's major work, *Class and Class Conflict in Industrial Society* (1959), was the most influential piece in conflict theory, but that was largely because it sounded so much like structural functionalism that it was palatable to mainstream sociologists. That is, Dahrendorf operated at the same level of analysis as the structural functionalists (structures and

C. WRIGHT MILLS

A Biographical Sketch

C. Wright Mills was born on August 28, 1916, in Waco, Texas (Dandaneau, 2007b; Domhoff, 2005; Hayden, 2006). He came from a conventional middle-class background: His father was an insurance broker, and his mother was a housewife. He attended the University of Texas and by 1939 had obtained both a bachelor's degree and a master's degree. He was quite an unusual student who, by the time he left Texas, already had published articles in the two major sociology journals. Mills did his doctoral work at, and received a Ph.D. from, the University of Wisconsin (Scimecca, 1977). He took his first job at the University of Maryland but spent the bulk of his career, from 1945 until his death, at Columbia University.

Mills was a man in a hurry (Horowitz, 1983). By the time he died at forty-five from his fourth heart attack, Mills had made a number of important contributions to sociology.

One of the most striking things about C. Wright Mills was his combativeness; he seemed to be constantly at war (Furm, 2007). He had a tumultuous personal life, characterized by many affairs, three marriages, and a child from each marriage. He had an equally tumultuous professional life. He seemed to have fought with and against everyone and everything. As a graduate student at Wisconsin, he took on a number of his professors. Later, in one of his early essays, he engaged in a thinly disguised critique of the ex-chairman of the

institutions) and looked at many of the same issues. (In other words, structural functionalism and conflict theory are part of the same paradigm; see the Appendix.) Dahrendorf recognized that although aspects of the social system could fit together rather neatly, there also could be considerable conflict and tension among them.

In the end, conflict theory should be seen as little more than a transitional development in the history of sociological theory. It failed because it did not go far enough in the direction of Marxian theory. It was still too early in the 1950s and 1960s for American sociology to accept a full-fledged Marxian approach. But conflict theory was helpful in setting the stage for the beginning of that acceptance by the late 1960s.

The Birth of Exchange Theory

Another important theoretical development in the 1950s was the rise of exchange theory (Molm, 2001). The major figure in this development is George Homans, a sociologist whom we left earlier, just as he was being drawn to B. F. Skinner's

Wisconsin department. He called the senior theorist at Wisconsin, Howard Becker, a "real fool" (Horowitz, 1983). He eventually came into conflict with his coauthor, Hans Gerth, who called Mills "an excellent operator, whippersnapper, promising young man on the make, and Texas cowboy á la ride and shoot" (Horowitz, 1983:72). As a professor at Columbia, Mills was isolated and estranged from his colleagues. Said one of his Columbia colleagues:

> There was no estrangement between Wright and me. We began estranged. Indeed, at the memorial services or meeting that was organized at Columbia University at his death, I seemed to be the only person who could not say: 'I used to be his friend, but we became somewhat distant.' It was rather the reverse.
>
> (cited in Horowitz, 1983:83)

Mills was an outsider, and he knew it: "I am an outlander, not only regionally, but down deep and for good" (Horowitz, 1983:84). In *The Sociological Imagination* (1959), Mills challenged not only the dominant theorist of his day, Talcott Parsons, but also the dominant methodologist, Paul Lazarsfeld, who also happened to be a colleague at Columbia.

Mills, of course, was at odds not only with people; he was also at odds with American society and challenged it on a variety of fronts. But perhaps most telling is the fact that when Mills visited the Soviet Union and was honored as a major critic of American society, he took the occasion to attack censorship in the Soviet Union with a toast to an early Soviet leader who had been purged and murdered by the Stalinists: "To the day when the complete works of Leon Trotsky are published in the Soviet Union!" (Tilman, 1984:8)

C. Wright Mills died in Nyack, New York, on March 20, 1962.

psychological behaviorism. Skinner's behaviorism is a major source of Homans's, and sociology's, exchange theory.

At first, Homans did not see how Skinner's propositions, developed to help explain the behavior of pigeons, might be useful for understanding human social behavior. But as Homans looked further at data from sociological studies of small groups and anthropological studies of primitive societies, he began to see that Skinner's behaviorism was applicable and that it provided a theoretical alternative to Parsonsian-style structural functionalism. This realization led in 1961 to Homans's book *Social Behavior: Its Elementary Forms*. This work represented the birth of exchange theory as an important perspective in sociology.

Homans's basic view was that the heart of sociology lies in the study of individual behavior and interaction. He was little interested in consciousness or in the various kinds of large-scale structures and institutions that were of concern to most sociologists. His main interest was instead in the reinforcement patterns, the history of rewards and costs, that lead people to do what they do. Basically, Homans argued that people continue to do what they have found to be rewarding in the past. Conversely, they cease doing what has proved to be costly in the past. To understand behavior, we need to understand an individual's history of rewards and costs. Thus, the focus of sociology should be not on consciousness or on social structures and institutions but rather on patterns of reinforcement.

As its name suggests, exchange theory is concerned not only with individual behavior but also with interaction between people involving an exchange of rewards and costs. The premise is that interactions are likely to continue when there is an exchange of rewards. Conversely, interactions that are costly to one or both parties are much less likely to continue.

Another major statement in exchange theory is Peter Blau's *Exchange and Power in Social Life,* published in 1964. Blau basically adopted Homans's perspective, but there was an important difference. Whereas Homans was content to deal mainly with elementary forms of social behavior, Blau wanted to integrate this with exchange at the structural and cultural levels, beginning with exchanges among actors but quickly moving on to the larger structures that emerge out of this exchange. He ended by dealing with exchanges among large-scale structures.

Although he was eclipsed for many years by Homans and Blau, Richard Emerson (1981) has emerged as a central figure in exchange theory (Cook and Whitmeyer, 2011). He is noted particularly for his effort to develop a more integrated micro-macro approach to exchange theory. Exchange theory has now developed into a significant strand of sociological theory, and it continues to attract new adherents and to take new directions (Cook, O'Brien, and Kollock, 1990; Szmatka and Mazur, 1996).

Dramaturgical Analysis: The Work of Erving Goffman

Erving Goffman (1922–1982) is often thought of as the last major thinker associated with the original Chicago school (Scheff, 2006; Smith, 2006; Travers, 1992; Tseelon, 1992); Fine and Manning (2000) see him as arguably the most influential twentieth-century American sociologist. Between the 1950s and the 1970s, Goffman published a series of books and essays that gave birth to dramaturgical analysis as a variant of symbolic interactionism. Although Goffman shifted his attention in his later years, he remained best known for his *dramaturgical theory* (Alieva, 2008; P. Manning, 2005a, 2007).

Goffman's best-known statement of dramaturgical theory, *Presentation of Self in Everyday Life,* was published in 1959. To put it simply, Goffman saw much in common between theatrical performances and the kinds of "acts" we all put on in our day-to-day actions and interactions. Interaction is seen as very fragile, maintained by social performances. Poor performances or disruptions are seen as great threats to social interaction just as they are to theatrical performances.

Goffman went quite far in his analogy between the stage and social interaction. In all social interaction there is a *front region,* which is the parallel of the stage front in a theatrical performance. Actors both on the stage and in social life are seen as being interested in appearances, wearing costumes, and using props. Furthermore, in both there is a *back region,* a place to which the actors can retire to prepare themselves for their performance. Backstage or offstage, in theater terms, the actors can shed their roles and be themselves.

Dramaturgical analysis is clearly consistent with its symbolic-interactionist roots. It has a focus on actors, action, and interaction. Working in the same arena as traditional symbolic interactionism, Goffman found a brilliant metaphor in the theater to shed new light on small-scale social processes (P. Manning, 1991, 1992).

The Development of Sociologies of Everyday Life

The 1960s and 1970s witnessed a boom (Ritzer, 1975a, 1975b) in several theoretical perspectives that can be lumped together under the heading of sociologies of everyday life (J. Douglas, 1980; Fontana, 2005; Schutte, 2007; Weigert, 1981).

Phenomenological Sociology and the Work of Alfred Schutz (1899–1959)

The philosophy of phenomenology (Srubar, 2005), with its focus on consciousness, has a long history, but the effort to develop a sociological variant of phenomenology (Ferguson, 2001) can be traced to the publication of Alfred Schutz's *The Phenomenology of the Social World* in Germany in 1932 (Dreher, 2011; J. Hall, 2007; Prendergast, 2005a; Rogers, 2000). Schutz was focally concerned with the way in which people grasp the consciousness of others while they live within their own stream of consciousness. Schutz also used intersubjectivity in a larger sense to mean a concern with the social world, especially the social nature of knowledge.

Much of Schutz's work focuses on an aspect of the social world called the *life-world,* or the world of everyday life. This is an intersubjective world in which people both create social reality and are constrained by the preexisting social and cultural structures created by their predecessors. Although much of the life-world is shared, there are also private (biographically articulated) aspects of that world. Within the life-world, Schutz differentiated between intimate face-to-face relationships ("we-relations") and distant and impersonal relationships ("they-relations"). While face-to-face relations are of great importance in the life-world, it is far easier for the sociologist to study more impersonal relations scientifically. Although Schutz turned away from consciousness and toward the intersubjective life-world, he did offer insights into consciousness, especially in his thoughts on meaning and people's motives.

Overall, Schutz was concerned with the dialectical relationship between the way people construct social reality and the obdurate social and cultural reality that they inherit from those who preceded them in the social world.

Ethnomethodology

Although there are important differences between them, ethnomethodology and phenomenology are often seen as closely aligned (Langsdorf, 1995). One of the major reasons for this association is that the creator of this theoretical perspective, Harold Garfinkel, was a student of Alfred Schutz at the New School. Interestingly, Garfinkel previously had studied under Talcott Parsons, and it was the fusion of Parsonsian and Schutzian ideas that helped give ethnomethodology its distinctive orientation.

Basically, *ethnomethodology* is the study of "the body of common-sense knowledge and the range of procedures and considerations [the methods] by means of which the ordinary members of society make sense of, find their way about in, and act on the circumstances in which they find themselves" (Heritage, 1984:4). Writers in this tradition are heavily tilted in the direction of the study of everyday life (Sharrock, 2001). Whereas phenomenological sociologists tend to focus on what people think, ethnomethodologists are more concerned with what people actually do. Thus, ethnomethodologists devote a lot of attention to the detailed study of conversations. Such mundane concerns stand in stark contrast to the interest of many mainstream sociologists in such abstractions as bureaucracies, capitalism, the division of labor, and the social system. Ethnomethodologists might be interested in the way a sense of these structures is created in everyday life; they are not interested in such structures as phenomena in themselves.

In the last few pages, we have dealt with several micro theories—exchange theory, phenomenological sociology, and ethnomethodology. Although the last two theories share a sense of a thoughtful and creative actor, such a view is not held by exchange theorists. Nevertheless, all three theories have a primarily micro orientation to actors and their actions and behavior. In the 1970s, such theories grew in strength in sociology and threatened to replace more macro-oriented theories (such as structural functionalism, conflict theory, and neo-Marxian theories) as the dominant theories in sociology (Knorr-Cetina, 1981; Ritzer, 1985).

The Rise and Fall (?) of Marxian Sociology

In the late 1960s, Marxian theory finally began to make significant inroads into American sociological theory (Cerullo, 1994). An increasing number of sociologists turned to Marx's original work, as well as to that of many Marxists, for insights that would be useful in the development of a Marxian sociology. At first this simply meant that American theorists were finally reading Marx seriously, but later there emerged many significant pieces of Marxian scholarship by American sociologists.

American theorists were particularly attracted to the work of the critical school, especially because of its fusion of Marxian and Weberian theory (Calhoun and Karaganis, 2001). Many of the works have been translated into English, and a number of scholars have written books about the critical school (for example, Jay, 1973; Kellner, 1993).

Along with an increase in interest came institutional support for such an orientation. Several journals devoted considerable attention to Marxian sociological theory, including *Theory and Society, Telos,* and *Marxist Studies.* A section on Marxist sociology was created in the American Sociological Association in 1977. Not only did the first generation of critical theorists become well known in America, but second-generation thinkers, especially Jurgen Habermas, and even third-generation theorists such as Axel Honneth, received wide recognition.

Of considerable importance was the development of significant pieces of American sociology done from a Marxian point of view. One very significant strand is a group of sociologists doing historical sociology from a Marxian perspective (for example, Skocpol, 1979; Wallerstein, 1974/2011, 1980/2011, 1989/2011; 2011a). Another is a group analyzing the economic realm from a sociological perspective (for example, Baran and Sweezy, 1966; Braverman, 1974; Burawoy, 1979). Still others are doing fairly traditional empirical sociology, but work that is informed by a strong sense of Marxian theory (Kohn, 1976, for example). A relatively recent and promising development is spatial Marxism. A number of important social thinkers (D. Harvey, 2000; Lefebvre, 1974/1991; Soja, 1989) have been examining social geography from a Marxian perspective.

However, with the disintegration of the Soviet Union and the fall of Marxist regimes around the world, Marxian theory fell on hard times in the 1990s. Some people remain unreconstructed Marxists; others have been forced to develop modified versions of Marxian theory (see the discussion below of the post-Marxists; there is also a journal entitled *Rethinking Marxism*). Still others have come to the conclusion that Marxian theory must be abandoned. Representative of the latter position is Ronald Aronson's book *After Marxism* (1995). The very first line of the book tells the story: "Marxism is over, and we are on our own" (Aronson, 1995:1). This from an avowed Marxist! While Aronson recognizes that some will continue to work with Marxian theory, he cautions that they must recognize that it is no longer part of the larger Marxian project of social transformation. That is, Marxian theory is no longer related, as Marx intended, to a program aimed at changing the basis of society; it is theory without practice. One-time Marxists are on their own in the sense that they can no longer rely on the Marxian project but rather must grapple with modern society with their "own powers and energies" (Aronson, 1995:4).

Aronson is among the more extreme critics of Marxism from within the Marxian camp. Others recognize the difficulties, but seek in various ways to adapt some variety of Marxian theory to contemporary realities (Brugger, 1995; Kellner, 1995). Nevertheless, larger social changes have posed a grave challenge for Marxian theorists, who are desperately seeking to adapt to these changes in a variety of ways. Whatever else can be said, the "glory days" of Marxian social theory appear to be over. Marxian social theorists of various types will survive, but they are not likely to approach the status and power of their predecessors in the recent history of sociology.

While neo-Marxian theory will never achieve the status it once had, it is undergoing a mini-renaissance (e.g., Hardt and Negri, 2000) in light of globalization, perceptions that the rich nations are growing richer and the poor are growing poorer (Stiglitz, 2002), and the resulting worldwide protests against these disparities and other abuses. There are many who believe that globalization has served to open the entire world, perhaps for the first time, to unbridled capitalism and the excesses that Marxists believe inevitably accompany it (Ritzer, 2004). If that is the case, and if the excesses continue and even accelerate, we will see a resurgence of interest in Marxian theory, this time applied to a truly global capitalist economy.

The Challenge of Feminist Theory

Beginning in the late 1970s, precisely at the moment when Marxian sociology gained significant acceptance from American sociologists, a new theoretical outsider issued a challenge to established sociological theories—and even to Marxian sociology itself. This brand of radical social thought is contemporary feminist theory (Rogers, 2001).

In Western societies, one can trace the record of critical feminist writings back almost 500 years, and there has been an organized political movement by and for women for more than 150 years. In America in 1920, the movement finally won the right for women to vote, fifty-five years after that right had been constitutionally extended to all men. Exhausted and to a degree satiated by victory, the American women's movement over the next thirty years weakened in both size and vigor, only to spring back to life, fully reawakened, in the 1960s. Three factors helped create this new wave of feminist activism: (1) the general climate of critical thinking that characterized the period; (2) the anger of women activists who flocked to the antiwar, civil rights, and student movements only to encounter the sexist attitudes of the liberal and radical men in those movements (Densimore, 1973; Evans, 1980; Morgan, 1970; Shreve, 1989); and (3) women's experience of prejudice and discrimination as they moved in ever-larger numbers into wage work and higher education (Bookman and Morgen, 1988; Garland, 1988). For these reasons, particularly the last one, the women's movement continued into the twenty-first century, even though the activism of many other 1960s movements faded. Moreover, during these years activism by and for women became an international phenomenon, drawing in women from many societies. Feminist writing has now entered its "third wave" in the writings of women who will spend most of their adult lives in the twenty-first century (C. Bailey, 1997; Orr, 1997). The most significant recent change in the women's movement has been the emergence among activist women of both a feminist and an antifeminist movement Fraser 1989).

A major feature of this international women's movement has been an explosively growing new literature on women that makes visible all aspects of women's hitherto unconsidered lives and experiences. This literature, which is popularly referred to as *women's studies,* is the work of an international and interdisciplinary community of writers, located both within and outside universities and writing for both the general public and specialized academic audiences. Feminist scholars have launched a probing, multifaceted critique that makes visible the complexity of the system that subordinates women.

Feminist theory is the theoretical strand running through this literature: sometimes implicit in writings on such substantive issues as work or rape or popular culture; sometimes centrally and explicitly presented, as in the analyses of motherhood; and increasingly the sole, systematic project of a piece of writing. Of this recent spate of wholly theoretical writing, certain statements have been particularly salient to sociology because they are directed to sociologists by people well versed in sociological theory. Journals such as *Signs, Hypatia, Feminist Studies, Sociological Inquiry,* and *Gender & Society* bring feminist theory to the attention of sociologists; however, there is hardly a sociological journal that could not be called pro-feminist.

Feminist theory looks at the world from the vantage points of women, with an eye to discovering the significant but unacknowledged ways in which the activities of women—subordinated by gender and variously affected by other stratificational practices, such as class, race, age, enforced heterosexuality, and geosocial inequality—help create our world. This viewpoint dramatically reworks our understanding of social life. From this base, feminist theorists have begun to challenge sociological theory, especially its classical statements and early research.

Structuralism and Poststructuralism

One development that we have said little about up to this point is the impact of *structuralism* (Lemert, 1990). We can get a preliminary feeling for structuralism by delineating the basic differences that exist among those who support a structuralist perspective. There are those who focus on what they call the "deep structures of the mind." It is their view that these unconscious structures lead people to think and act as they do. The work of the psychoanalyst Sigmund Freud might be seen as an example of this orientation. Then there are structuralists who focus on the invisible larger structures of society and see them as determinants of the actions of people as well as of society in general. Marx is sometimes thought of as someone who practiced such a brand of structuralism, with his focus on the unseen economic structure of capitalist society. Still another group sees structures as the models they construct of the social world. Finally, a number of structuralists are concerned with the dialectical relationship between individuals and social structures. They see a link between the structures of the mind and the structures of society. The anthropologist Claude Lèvi-Strauss is most often associated with this view.

As structuralism grew within sociology, outside sociology a movement was developing beyond the early premises of structuralism: *poststructuralism* (Lemert, 1990; McCormick, 2007). The major representative of poststructuralism is Michel Foucault (Dean, 2001; J. Miller, 1993); another is Giorgio Agamben. In his early work, Foucault focused on structures, but he later moved beyond structures to focus on power and the linkage between knowledge and power. More generally, poststructuralists accept the importance of structure but go beyond it to encompass a wide range of other concerns.

Poststructuralism is important not only in itself but also because it often is seen as a precursor to postmodern social theory (to be discussed later in this chapter). In fact, it is difficult, if not impossible, to draw a clear line between poststructuralism and postmodern social theory. Thus Foucault, a poststructuralist, is often seen as a postmodernist, while Jean Baudrillard (1972/1981), who usually is labeled a postmodernist, certainly did work that is poststructuralist in character.

Late-Twentieth-Century Developments in Sociological Theory

While many of the developments discussed in the preceding pages continued to be important in the late twentieth century, in this section we will deal with three broad movements—micro-macro integration, agency-structure integration, and theoretical syntheses—that were of utmost importance in that era and are to this day.

Micro-Macro Integration

A good deal of recent work in American sociological theory has been concerned with the linkage between micro and macro theories and levels of analysis (Barnes, 2001; Berk, 2006; J. Ryan, 2005a). Ritzer (1990a) argued that micro-macro linkage emerged as the central problematic in American sociological theory in the 1980s, and it continued to be of focal concern in the 1990s. The contribution of European sociologist Norbert Elias (1939/1994) is an important precursor to contemporary American work on the micro-macro linkage and aids our understanding of the relationship between micro-level manners and the macro-level state (Kilminster and Mennell, 2011; Van Krieken, 2001).

There are a number of examples of efforts to link micro-macro levels of analysis and/or theories. Ritzer (1979, 1981a) sought to develop a sociological paradigm that integrates micro and macro levels in both their objective and their subjective forms. Thus, there are four major levels of social analysis that must be dealt with in an integrated manner—macro subjectivity, macro objectivity, micro subjectivity, and micro objectivity. Jeffrey Alexander (1982–1983) created a "multidimensional sociology" which deals, at least in part, with a model of levels of analysis that closely resembles Ritzer's model. James Coleman (1986) concentrated on the micro-to-macro problem, while Allen Liska (1990) extended Coleman's approach to deal with the macro-to-micro problem as well. Coleman (1990) extended his micro-to-macro model and developed a much more elaborate theory of the micro-macro relationship based on a rational choice approach derived from economics (see the following section on agency-structure integration).

Agency-Structure Integration

Paralleling the growth in interest in the United States in micro-macro integration has been a concern in Europe for agency-structure integration (J. Ryan, 2005b; Sztompka, 1994). Just as Ritzer saw the micro-macro issue as the central problem in American theory, Margaret Archer (1988) saw the agency-structure topic as the basic concern in European social theory. While there are many similarities between the micro-macro and agency-structure literatures (Ritzer and Gindoff, 1992, 1994), there are also substantial differences. For example, although agents are usually micro-level actors, collectivities such as labor unions can also be agents. And while structures are usually macro-level phenomena, we also find structures at the micro level. Thus, we must be careful in equating these two bodies of work and must take much care when trying to interrelate them.

There are several major efforts in contemporary European social theory that can be included under the heading of agency-structure integration. The first is Anthony Giddens's (1984; Stones, 2005b) structuration theory. Giddens's approach sees agency and structure as a "duality." That is, they cannot be separated from one another: agency is implicated in structure, and structure is involved in agency. Giddens refuses to see structure as simply constraining (as, for example, does Durkheim), but instead sees structure as both constraining and enabling. Margaret Archer (1982) rejects the idea that agency and structure can be viewed as a duality, but instead sees them as a dualism. That is, agency and structure can and should be separated. In distinguishing them, we become better able to analyze their relationship to one another. Archer (1988) is also notable for extending the agency-structure literature to a concern for the relationship between culture and agency and for developing a more general agency-structure theory (Archer, 1995).

While both Giddens and Archer are British, another major contemporary figure involved in the agency-structure literature is Pierre Bourdieu from France (Bourdieu, 1977; Bourdieu and Wacquant, 1992; Swartz, 1997). In Bourdieu's work, the agency-structure issue translates into a concern for the relationship between habitus and field (Eisenberg, 2007). *Habitus* is an internalized mental, or cognitive, structure through which people deal with the social world. The habitus both produces, and is produced by, the society. The *field* is a network of relations among objective positions. The structure of the field serves to constrain agents, whether they are individuals or collectivities. Overall, Bourdieu is concerned with the relationship between habitus and field. The field conditions the habitus, and the habitus constitutes the field. Thus, there is a dialectical relationship between habitus and field.

The final major theorist of the agency-structure linkage is the German social thinker Jurgen Habermas. We have already mentioned Habermas as a significant contemporary contributor to critical theory. Habermas (1987a) has also dealt with the agency-structure issue under the heading of "the colonization of the life-world." The life-world is a micro world where people interact and communicate. The system has its roots in the life-world, but it ultimately comes to develop its own structural characteristics. As these structures grow in independence and power, they come to exert more and more control over the life-world. In the modern world, the system has come to "colonize" the life-world—that is, to exert control over it.

The theorists discussed in this section are not only the leading theorists on the agency-structure issue, they were arguably (especially Bourdieu, Giddens, and Habermas) the leading theorists in the last quarter of the twentieth century, and their work continues to shape the discipline. While Bourdieu has died, Giddens and Habermas continue to write and comment on issues such as globalization and the environment. Perhaps the most influential contemporary theorist, Michel Foucault (to be discussed below), was French. After a long period of dominance by American theorists (Mead, Parsons, Merton, Homans, and others), the center of social theory seems to be returning to its birthplace—Europe. Furthermore, Nedelmann and Sztompka argued that with the end of the Cold War and the fall of communism, we were about to "witness another Golden Era of European Sociology" (1993:1). This seems to be supported by the fact that today the works that catch the attention of large numbers of the world's theorists are European. Further to this, 1998 saw the establishment of a new major social theory journal entitled the *European Journal of Social Theory*.

Theoretical Syntheses

The movements toward micro-macro and agency-structure integration began in the 1980s, and both continued to be strong in the 1990s. They set the stage for the broader movement toward theoretical syntheses, which began at about the beginning of the 1990s. Reba Lewis (1991) has suggested that sociology's problem (assuming it has a problem) may be the result of excessive fragmentation and that the movement toward greater integration may enhance the status of the discipline. What is involved here is a wide-ranging effort to synthesize two or more different theories (for example, structural functionalism and symbolic interactionism). Such efforts have occurred throughout the history of sociological theory (Holmwood and Stewart, 1994). However, there are two distinctive aspects of the recent synthetic work in sociological theory. First, it is very widespread and not restricted to isolated attempts at synthesis. Second, the goal is generally a relatively narrow synthesis of theoretical ideas, not the development of a grand synthetic theory that encompasses all of sociological theory. These synthetic works are occurring within and among many of the theories discussed in this chapter.

Then there are efforts to bring perspectives from outside sociology into sociological theory. For example, under the title "social and political thought" there are numerous research programs that attempt to draw together political and social theory. Indeed, one of the founding principles of the aforementioned, newly established, *European Journal of Social Theory* is "to overcome the divide between social and political theory with respect to the reinterpretation of the classics and the demands of the present situation" (Delanty, 1998:1; see also B. Turner, 2009). The implication is that adequate analysis of the contemporary world situation requires interdisciplinary perspectives. Major contemporary social theory journals such as *Theory, Culture & Society* as well as *Body & Society* also embrace interdisciplinary perspectives. There also have been works oriented to bringing biological ideas into sociology in an effort to create sociobiology (Crippen, 1994; Maryanski and Turner, 1992) and more recently affect theory (Clough, 2008; Gregg and Seigworth, 2010; Massumi, 2002). Rational choice theory is based in economics, but it has made inroads into a number of fields, including sociology (Coleman, 1990; Heckathorn, 2005). Systems theory has its roots in the hard sciences, but in the late twentieth century Niklas Luhmann (1984/1995) made a powerful effort to develop a system theory that could be applied to the social world.

Theories of Modernity and Postmodernity

Toward the end of the twentieth century, social theorists[7] were increasingly interested in the question of whether society (as well as theories about it) has undergone a dramatic transformation. On one side is a group of theorists (for example, Jurgen Habermas, Zygmunt Bauman, and Anthony Giddens) who believe that we continue to live in a society that still can best be described as modern and about which we can theorize in much the same way that social thinkers have long contemplated society. On the other side is a group of thinkers (for example, Jean Baudrillard, Jean-François Lyotard, and Fredric Jameson) who contend that society has changed so dramatically that we now live in a qualitatively different, postmodern society. Furthermore, they argue that this new society needs to be thought about in new and different ways. The debate between modernists and postmodernists was heated, and led to numerous theoretical developments that continue to influence the field.

The Defenders of Modernity

All the great classical sociological theorists (Marx, Weber, Durkheim, and Simmel) were concerned, in one way or another, with the modern world and its advantages

---

[7] The term *social theorist* rather than *sociological theorist* is used here to reflect the fact that many contributors to the recent literature are not sociologists, although they are theorizing about the social world.

and disadvantages (Sica, 2005). Of course, the last of these (Weber) died in 1920, and the world has changed dramatically since then. Although contemporary theorists recognize these dramatic changes, there are some who believe that there is more continuity than discontinuity between the world today and the world that existed around the last *fin de siècle*.

Mestrovic (1998:2) has labeled Anthony Giddens "the high priest of modernity." Giddens (1990, 1991, 1992) uses terms such as "radical," "high," or "late" modernity to describe society today and to indicate that while it is not the same society as the one described by the classical theorists, it is continuous with that society. Giddens sees modernity today as a "juggernaut" that is, at least to some degree, out of control. Ulrich Beck (1992, 2005a; Ekberg, 2007; Jensen and Blok, 2008; Then, 2007) contends that whereas the classical stage of modernity was associated with industrial society, the emerging new modernity is best described as a "risk society." Whereas the central dilemma in classical modernity was wealth and how it ought to be distributed, the central problem in new modernity is the prevention, minimization, and channeling of risk (from, for example, a nuclear accident). Jurgen Habermas (1981, 1987b) sees modernity as an "unfinished project." That is, the central issue in the modern world continues, as it was in Weber's day, to be rationality. The utopian goal is still the maximization of the rationality of both the "system" and the "life-world." Charles Taylor (1989, 2004, 2007) argues that contemporary selves and societies are emerging out of cultural frameworks and moral ideals developed across the modern era. This said, contemporary Western society experiences malaise (or as Durkheim termed it, anomie) because we are largely unaware of the role that the modern cultural frameworks play in our lives. From this perspective, postmodern theories that explicitly reject modern cultural frameworks only deepen contemporary malaise. Social theory, from Taylor's perspective, should instead help us to better understand the relation of the present moment to the broader culture of modernity. Ritzer (2013) sees rationality as the key process in the world today. However, he picks up on Weber's focus on the problem of the increase in formal rationality and the danger of an "iron cage" of rationality. Weber focused on the bureaucracy. Today Ritzer sees the paradigm of this process as the fast-food restaurant, and describes the increase in formal rationality as the McDonaldization of society. Zygmunt Bauman (2000, 2003, 2005, 2006, 2007b, 2010, 2011, 2012), has produced a series of basically modern analyses of what he calls the "liquid" world.

The Proponents of Postmodernity

Postmodernism was hot (Crook, 2001; Kellner, 1989a; Ritzer, 1997; Ritzer and Goodman, 2001). And even though few would now call themselves postmodernists, postmodernism has had a major impact on social theory. We need to differentiate, at least initially, between postmodernity and postmodern social theory (Best and Kellner, 1991). *Postmodernity* is a historical epoch that is supposed to have succeeded the modern era, or modernity. *Postmodern social theory* is a way of thinking about postmodernity; the world is so different that it requires entirely new ways of thinking. Postmodernists would tend to reject the theoretical perspectives outlined in the previous section, as well as the ways in which the thinkers involved created their theories.

There are probably as many portrayals of postmodernity as there are postmodern social theorists. To simplify things, we will summarize some of the key elements of a depiction offered by one of the most prominent postmodernists, Fredric Jameson (1984, 1991). First, postmodernity is a depthless, superficial world; it is a world of simulation (for example, a jungle cruise at Disneyland rather than the real thing). Second, it is a world that is lacking in affect and emotion. Third, there is a loss of a sense of one's place in history; it is hard to distinguish past, present, and future. Fourth, instead of the explosive, expanding, productive technologies of modernity (for example, automobile assembly lines), postmodern society is dominated by implosive, flattening, reproductive technologies (television, for example). In these and other ways, postmodern society is very different from modern society.

Such a different world requires a different way of thinking. Rosenau (1992; Ritzer, 1997) defines the postmodern mode of thought in terms of the things that it opposes, largely characteristics of the modern way of thinking. First, postmodernists reject the kind of grand narratives that characterize much of classical sociological theory. Instead, postmodernists prefer more limited explanations, or even no explanations at all. Second, there is a rejection of the tendency to put boundaries between disciplines—to engage in something called sociological (or social) theory that is distinct from, say, philosophical thinking or even novelistic storytelling. Third, postmodernists are often more interested in shocking or startling the reader than they are in engaging in careful, reasoned academic discourse. Finally, instead of looking for the core of society (say, rationality or capitalistic exploitation), postmodernists are more inclined to focus on more peripheral aspects of society.

Although postmodern theory has reached its peak and now is in decline, it continues to exert a powerful impact on theory. On the one hand, new contributions to the theory continue to appear (for example, Powell and Owen, 2008). On the other hand, it is very difficult to theorize these days without taking into account postmodern theory, especially its critiques of modern theorizing and its analyses of the contemporary world.

Social Theory in the Twenty-First Century

The debates surrounding theoretical integration and then modernism and postmodernism, while still relevant, have for the most part faded without clear resolution. This has left social theory, at the beginning of the twenty-first century, struggling for renewed identity (B. Turner, 2009). The major theoretical perspectives outlined in this review and detailed throughout this book will remain relevant and continue to grow. Theory will always ground itself in relationship to its history and the debates that history has entailed. This said, it is worth considering where theory is now and where it might be going. To this end, in this section we describe a number of thematic areas that are particularly relevant to social theory at the beginning of the twenty-first century: identity, consumption, globalization, and science and technology. As we will see, each of these areas has given rise to a variety of theoretical perspectives that are pushing social theory in new directions.

Theories of Identity

A central area of theoretical examination in recent years has been around the theme of identity. There are at least two ways that sociologists have understood the concept of identity. The first is associated with social psychology, where identity refers to individual self-conceptions produced by one's position within a social structure (Vryan, 2007). Though not unrelated, the second is concerned with the social processes that lead to the construction of identity categories: gender, race, (dis)ability, and sexuality, among others. While social psychological perspectives on identity remain an important influence in social theory, the current moment has witnessed a tremendous upsurge in the study of the social processes surrounding identity construction.

This focus on identity construction is often framed by concepts such as citizenship, human rights, and social justice (B. Turner, 1993, 2009). These all describe the intersection of identity and the state. Historically, theorists of citizenship distinguished between *civic citizenship* (the right, for example, to freedom of worship), *political citizenship* (the right to participate in political decision making), and *social citizenship* (the right to state protection and social welfare) (Delanty, 2005). Recently, theorists have added the concepts of *cultural citizenship* (the right to recognition of one's cultural background and practices) and *biological citizenship* (the right to have one's biological well-being protected and supported) (Petryna, 2002; Rose and Novas, 2005). All of these citizenship categories are created through social and political processes. Moreover, one's identity in relationship to state and society has a tremendous impact not only on one's sense of self, but more generally one's capacity to exist. On the latter point, recent theorists have been particularly concerned with the state's capacity to make decisions about life and death; that is, through war and other means of violence, to exclude some people from protection under the law and entitlement to human rights (Agamben, 1995/1998; Butler, 2004b).

Of particular importance is the way in which marginalized identities are constructed and managed. It is, of course, marginalized identities that suffer the most painful and debilitating forms of social stigma, exclusion, and violence. Concern over these issues has given rise to "multicultural social theory" (Lemert, 2001; Rogers, 1996a). Multicultural theory was foreshadowed by the emergence of feminist sociological theory in the 1970s. The feminists argued that sociological theory had been largely closed to women's voices, and in the ensuing years many minority groups echoed the feminists' concerns. In fact, minority women (for example, African Americans and Latinas) began to argue that feminist theory was restricted to white, middle-class females and had to be more receptive to many other voices. Today, feminist theory has become far more diverse, as has sociological theory.

Multicultural theory has taken a series of diverse forms. Examples include Afrocentric theory (Asante, 1996), Appalachian studies (Banks, Billings, and Tice, 1996), Native American theory (Buffalohead, 1996), and even theories of masculinity (Connell, 1996; Kimmel, 1996). Among the things that characterize multicultural theory are the following:

- Multicultural theories reject universalistic theories that tend to support those in power; multicultural theories seek to empower those who lack clout.

- Multicultural theory seeks to be inclusive, to offer theory on behalf of many disempowered groups.
- Multicultural theorists are not value-free; they often theorize on behalf of those without power and work in the social world to change social structure, culture, and the prospects for individuals.
- Multicultural theorists seek to disrupt not only the social world but also the intellectual world; they seek to make it far more open and diverse.
- There is no effort to draw a clear line between theory and other types of narratives.
- There is ordinarily a critical edge to multicultural theory; it is both self-critical and critical of other theories and, most important, of the social world.
- Multicultural theorists recognize that their work is limited by the particular historical, social, and cultural context in which they happen to live (Rogers, 1996b:11–16).

Two of the most important of today's multicultural theories are *critical theories of race and racism (CTRR)* and *queer theory*.

Sociologists and other social scientists have been making significant contributions to theories of racism at least since W.E.B. Du Bois's work early in the twentieth century. Such theorizing received an important impetus in recent years from the development of "critical race theory" largely in the field of law (Delgado and Stefancic, 2001). That theory was a result of the growing recognition that the momentum of the civil rights movement of the 1960s had been lost and what was needed was not only a revival of social activism but also new ways of theorizing race. Most importantly, critical race theory shows that racism is not simply a matter of individual or personal prejudice but rather that racism is built into the structure of society, in particular, the law. At the same time critical race theorists draw attention to the way that the concept of race is constructed and deployed in social life.

Critical theories of race and racism (CTRR) are rooted much more in the social sciences, including sociology, than is critical race theory. Thus, CTRR deal with such cutting-edge issues in theory as the relationship between race and racism and agency structure, science and technology, political economy, and globalization (including how race and racism relates to nation-states, nationalism, colonialism, neocolonialism, decolonization, imperialism, and empire). CTRR have a much broader, even global, focus than critical race theory. CTRR are also open to a much wider array of classical and contemporary theories as they apply to race, and they adopt a much broader macrostructural and macrocultural approach, especially one that focuses on power. A general conclusion to be derived from CTRR is that "race matters" and continues to matter not only in the legal system but throughout the structures and institutions of society (West, 1994). For example, Bonilla-Silva (2003) is critical of the view that racism today is of little more than historical interest. Rather, he sees color blindness as a smoke screen that allows white Americans to continue to perpetuate racial discrimination. Also in tune with CTRR is Bonilla-Silva's proposal for a variety of practical steps to deal with this new form of racism. Another distinctive characteristic of CTRR is their effort to show that race also matters globally (Winant, 2001).

Queer theory grew out of a series of key publications, academic conferences, political organizations, and published texts largely during the early 1990s. Its theoretical roots lie in a number of fields including feminist studies, literary criticism, and, most notably, social constructionism and poststructuralism. Queer theory also has political sources, notably in the larger project of queer politics and of groups such as ACT UP and Queer Nation. Academically, queer theory has strong early roots in the works of Michel Foucault, Judith Butler, Eve Kosofsky Sedgwick, and Teresa de Lauretis.

Queer theory involves a range of intellectual ideas rooted in the contention that identities are not fixed and stable and do not determine who we are. Rather, identities are seen as historically and socially constructed processes that are both fluid and contested. Further, these identities need not be gay or lesbian. In fact, queer theory does not seek to explain homosexual or heterosexual identities by themselves, but rather approaches the homosexual/heterosexual divide as a figure of knowledge and power that orders desires, behaviors, social institutions, and social relations. Thus, although queer theory does take sexuality as one of its central concerns, it is a much broader intellectual project than gay and lesbian, or even sexuality, studies. Indeed, queer theory is a theory of social life more generally: all social institutions and identities are structured through sexual identifications and performances.

Theories of Consumption

Coming of age during the Industrial Revolution and animated by its problems and prospects, sociological theory has long had a "productivist bias." That is, theories have tended to focus on industry, industrial organizations, work, and workers. This bias is most obvious in Marxian and neo-Marxian theory, but it is found in many other theories, such as Durkheim's thinking on the division of labor, Weber's work on the rise of capitalism in the West and the failure to develop it in other parts of the world, Simmel's analysis of the tragedy of culture produced by the proliferation of human products, the interest of the Chicago school in work, and the concern in conflict theory with relations between employers and employees, leaders and followers, and so on. Much less attention has been devoted to consumption and the consumer. There are exceptions such as Thorstein Veblen's (1899/1994) famous work on "conspicuous consumption" and Simmel's thinking on money (1907/1978) and fashion (1904/1971), but for the most part, social theorists have had far less to say about consumption than about production.

Postmodern social theory has tended to define postmodern society as a consumer society, with the result that consumption plays a central role in that theory (Venkatesh, 2007). Most notable is Jean Baudrillard's (1970/1998) *The Consumer Society*. Lipovetsky's (1987/1994) post-postmodern work on fashion is reflective of the growing interest in and out of postmodern social theory in consumption. Since consumption is likely to continue to grow in importance, especially in the West, and production is likely to decline, it is safe to assume that we will see a dramatic increase in theoretical (and empirical) work on consumption (Ritzer, Goodman, and Wiedenhoft, 2001; for an overview of extant theories of consumption, see Slater, 1997, 2005).

To take one example, we are witnessing something of an outpouring of theoretically based work on the settings in which we consume, such as *Consuming Places* (Urry, 1995), *Enchanting a Disenchanted World: Continuity and Change in the Cathedrals of Consumption* (Ritzer, 2010a), and *Shelf Life: Supermarkets and the Changing Cultures of Consumption* (Humphery, 1998). We are likely to see much more work on such settings, as well as on consumers, consumer goods, and the process of consumption. A very new direction in this domain is work on *prosumers*, those who simultaneously produce and consume, especially on the Internet and Web 2.0 (for example, blogs, Facebook) (Ritzer, 2009; Ritzer, Dean, and Jurgenson, 2012).

Theories of Globalization

Although there have been other important developments in theory in the early twenty-first century, it seems clear that *the* most important developments are in theories of globalization (W. Robinson, 2007). Theorizing globalization is nothing new. In fact, it could be argued that although classical theorists such as Marx and Weber lacked the term, they devoted much attention to theorizing globalization. Similarly, many theories (e.g., modernization, dependency, and world-system theory) and theorists (e.g., Alex Inkeles, Andre Gunder Frank, and Immanuel Wallerstein) were theorizing about globalization in different terms and under other theoretical rubrics. Precursors to theorizing about globalization go back to the 1980s (and even before; see Moore, 1966; Nettl and Robertson, 1968) and began to gain momentum in the 1990s (Albrow, 1996; Albrow and King, 1990; Appadurai, 1996; Bauman, 1998; Garcia Canclini, 1995; Meyer, Boli, and Ramirez, 1997; Robertson, 1992). Such theorizing has really taken off in the twenty-first century (Beck, 2000, 2005b; Giddens, 2000; Hardt and Negri, 2000, 2004; Ritzer, 2004, 2007c, 2010b; Rosenau, 2003). Theorizing globalization has become so important that we devote an entire chapter (15) to it.

Theories of globalization can be categorized under three main headings—economic, political, and cultural theories. Economic theories, undoubtedly the best known, can be broadly divided into two categories: theories that celebrate the neoliberal global economic market (e.g., T. Friedman, 2000, 2005; see Antonio, 2007a, for a critique of Friedman's celebration of the neoliberal market) and theories, often from a Marxian perspective (Collier, 2011; Hardt and Negri, 2000, 2004; W. Robinson, 2004; Sklair, 1992), that are critical of it.

In political theory, one position is represented by the liberal approach (derived from the classical work of John Locke, Adam Smith, and others) (MacPherson, 1962), especially in the form of neoliberal thinking (J. Campbell and Pederson, 2001) (often called the "Washington consensus" [Williamson, 1990, 1997]), which favors political systems that support and defend the free market. On the other side are thinkers more on the left (e.g., Hardt and Negri, 2000, 2004; D. Harvey, 2005) who are critical of this view.

A central issue in political theory is the continued viability of the nation-state. On one side are those who see the nation-state as dead or dying in an era of globalization, or at least changing dramatically (Cerny, 2010). On the other side of this issue are defenders of the continued importance of the nation-state. At least one of them

(J. Rosenberg, 2005) has gone so far as to argue that globalization theory has already come and gone as a result of the continued existence, even reassertion, of the nation-state (e.g., France and the Netherlands vetoing the EU constitution in 2005; the importance of various EU nations, especially Germany, in the ongoing euro crisis).

Although economic and political issues are of great importance, it is cultural issues and cultural theories that have attracted the most attention in sociology. We can divide cultural theories into three broad approaches (Pieterse, 2004). The first is *cultural differentialism*, in which the argument is made that among cultures there are deep and largely impervious differences that are unaffected or are affected only superficially by globalization (Huntington, 1996). Second, the proponents of *cultural convergence* argue that although important differences remain among cultures, there is also convergence, increasing homogeneity, across cultures (Boli and Lechner, 2005; DiMaggio and Powell, 1983; Meyer et al., 1997; Ritzer, 2004, 2007c, 2013). Third, there is *cultural hybridization*, in which it is contended that the global and the local interpenetrate to create unique indigenous realities that can be seen as "glocalization" (Robertson, 1992, 2001), "hybridization" (Garcia Canclini, 1995), and "creolization" (Hannerz, 1987). Much of the sociological thinking on globalization has been concerned with the issue, implied above, of the degree to which globalization is leading to homogenization or to heterogenization.

It seems clear that the various theories of globalization, as well as later variants of it that will come to the fore in the coming years, will continue to dominate new developments in sociological theory. However, other developments are worth watching.

Theories of Science, Technology, and Society

Another area of recent theoretical growth is captured under the term *science and technology studies* (also referred to as science, technology, and society studies and science studies; see Hess, 1997 for discussion of these differences). Some theorists in this field prefer to use the term *technoscience* to indicate the fusion of scientific knowledge with practical interventions into everyday life (Erikson and Webster, 2011).

This field studies how science and technology impacts social, cultural, and personal life. The field is quite diverse, often leading to very different ideas about how science and society are interrelated. For example, early theorists of science and society (such as Robert Merton) treated science as just one more social institution. Contemporary theorists tend to see science and society as more deeply intertwined and many have adopted a social constructionist perspective (see Erikson and Webster, 2011), meaning that science does not neutrally describe reality, but actually structures social life and generates meanings and ideals. Donna Haraway (1991; Wirth-Cauchon, 2011) has argued that we now live in a technoscientific society that has turned people into cyborgs. The interest here is in the constitutive relationship, both positive and negative, between humans and technology, and more recently humans and animals (see Haraway, 2008). Many contemporary theories of science also focus on the interrelationship among capitalism, politics, and technoscience. This has led to the widespread use (see Collier, 2011) of terms like Michel Foucault's *biopolitics* (the manipulation and control of populations through biological knowledge) and *biocapital* (the economic value produced through technoscientific research).

In terms of contributions to social theory more generally, actor-network theory is likely the most important perspective in science and technology studies. On one hand, it is part of the broad and increasing interest in networks of various kinds (e.g., Castells, 1996; Mizruchi, 2005). But on the other hand, it has a variety of unique orientations (Latour, 2007), not the least of which is its notion of the *actant*, which involves a number of obvious inclusions such as human agents but also includes a wide variety of nonhuman actors such as the Internet, ATMs, and telephone answering machines. This is in line with the move in the social world toward, and increasing scholarly interest in, the *posthuman* (Franklin, 2007) and the *postsocial* (Knorr-Cetina, 2001, 2005, 2007; Mayall, 2007). That is, we are increasingly involved in networks that encompass both human and nonhuman components, and in their relationships with the latter, humans are clearly in a posthuman and postsocial world.

The study of science and technology has also led theorists to a more interdisciplinary engagement with the findings of the natural sciences. Historically, the most important of these perspectives is sociobiology, which draws on evolutionary theory to make claims about the biological basis of human behavior (F. Nielsen, 1994). Systems theorists such as Niklas Luhmann (1982, 1997/2012) and Kenneth Bailey (1994) draw on research in cybernetics, biological science, and cognitive psychology, among others. Most recently, theorists in the area of *affect theory* combine research in the life sciences with postmodern and poststructuralist ideas (Clough, 2008; Gregg and Seigworth, 2010; Massumi, 2002). This emerging theoretical perspective takes a critical view of mainstream science but nevertheless respects nature or matter as a force in itself, independent of culture and society. The problem for affect theory is to understand how biology and society mutually influence each other.

We are now at the close of the chapter reviewing developments in contemporary theory, but we certainly have not reached the end of theory development. Some of the theories discussed in this chapter will increase in importance (CTRR) while others (neofunctionalism) will experience a decline. One thing seems sure—the landscape of social theory is likely to be dotted with more theories, none of them likely to gain hegemony in the field. Postmodernists have criticized the idea of "totalizations," or overarching theoretical frameworks. It seems unlikely that social theory will come to be dominated by a single totalization. Rather, we are likely to see a field with a proliferating number of perspectives that have some supporters and that help us understand part of the social world. Sociological theory will not be a simple world to understand and to use, but it will be an exciting world that offers a plethora of old and new ideas.

Summary

This chapter picks up where Chapter 1 left off and deals with the history of sociological theory since the beginning of the twentieth century. We begin with the early history of American sociological theory, which was characterized by its liberalism, by its interest in social Darwinism, and consequently by the influence of Herbert Spencer.

In this context, the work of the two early sociological theorists, Sumner and Ward, is discussed. However, they did not leave a lasting imprint on American sociological theory. In contrast, the Chicago school, as embodied in the work of people such as Small, Park, Thomas, Cooley, and especially Mead, did leave a strong mark on sociological theory, especially on symbolic interactionism.

While the Chicago school was still predominant, a different form of sociological theory began to develop at Harvard. Pitirim Sorokin played a key role in the founding of sociology at Harvard, but it was Talcott Parsons who was to lead Harvard to a position of preeminence in American theory, replacing Chicago's symbolic interactionism. Parsons was important not only for legitimizing "grand theory" in the United States and for introducing European theorists to an American audience but also for his role in the development of action theory and, more important, structural functionalism. In the 1940s and 1950s, structural functionalism was furthered by the disintegration of the Chicago school that began in the 1930s and was largely complete by the 1950s.

The major development in Marxian theory in the early years of the twentieth century was the creation of the Frankfurt, or critical, school. This Hegelianized form of Marxism also showed the influence of sociologists like Weber and of the psychoanalyst Sigmund Freud. Marxism did not gain a widespread following among sociologists in the early part of the century.

Structural functionalism's dominance within American theory in midcentury was rather short-lived. Although traceable to a much earlier date, phenomenological sociology, especially the work of Alfred Schutz, began to attract significant attention in the 1960s. Marxian theory was still largely excluded from American theory, but C. Wright Mills kept a radical tradition alive in America in the 1940s and 1950s. Mills also was one of the leaders of the attacks on structural functionalism, attacks that mounted in intensity in the 1950s and 1960s. In light of some of these attacks, a conflict-theory alternative to structural functionalism emerged in that period. Although influenced by Marxian theory, conflict theory suffered from an inadequate integration of Marxism. Still another alternative born in the 1950s was exchange theory, which continues to attract a small but steady number of followers. Although symbolic interactionism lost some of its steam, the work of Erving Goffman on dramaturgical analysis in this period gained a following.

Important developments took place in other sociologies of everyday life (symbolic interactionism can be included under this heading) in the 1960s and 1970s, including some increase in interest in phenomenological sociology and, more important, an outburst of work in ethnomethodology. During this period Marxian theories of various types came into their own in sociology, although those theories were seriously compromised by the fall of the Soviet Union and other communist regimes in the late 1980s and early 1990s. Also of note during this period was the growing importance of structuralism and then poststructuralism, especially in the work of Michel Foucault. Of overwhelming significance was the explosion of interest in feminist theory, an outpouring of work that continues apace as we move through the twenty-first century.

In addition to those just mentioned, three other notable developments occurred in the 1980s and continued into the 1990s. First was the rise in interest in the United

States in the micro-macro link. Second was the parallel increase in attention in Europe to the relationship between agency and structure. Third was the growth, especially in the 1990s, of a wide range of synthetic efforts. Finally, there was considerable interest in a series of theories of modernity and postmodernity in the latter twentieth and early twenty-first centuries.

The chapter concludes with a discussion of several thematic areas that have occupied social theorists in the twenty-first century. The theme of identity has led to significant growth in multicultural theories, in particular critical theories of race and racism (CTRR) and queer theory. We can also expect increasing interest in consumption and in theorizing about it. This relates to postmodern theory (consumer society is closely associated with postmodern society), reflects changes in society from an emphasis on production to consumption, as well as a reaction against the productivist bias that has dominated sociological theory since its inception. Perhaps the most dramatic growth is taking place, and is likely to continue to take place, in the theories of globalization. Recent theory is also concerned with the role that science and technology, or technoscience, play in the constitution of society. Major theories in this area are actor-network theory and affect theory.

Structural Functionalism, Systems Theory, and Conflict Theory

Chapter Outline

Structural Functionalism

Systems Theory

Conflict Theory

Structural functionalism, especially in the work of Talcott Parsons, Robert Merton, and their students and followers, was for many years *the* dominant sociological theory. However, in the last three decades it has declined dramatically in importance (Chriss, 1995) and, in at least some senses, has receded into the recent history of sociological theory. This decline is reflected in Colomy's (1990a) description of structural functionalism as a theoretical "tradition." This said, some contemporary thinkers find useful tools for sociological analysis in Parsons's work and continue to provide both historical and theoretical analyses (Gerhardt, 2011; Lidz, 2011a, 2011b). In addition, over the years various scholars have attempted to revise or extend structural functionalism. In the 1980s, Jeffrey Alexander turned to Parsons's work in order to develop a neofunctionalist sociology (Abrahamson, 2001; Alexander and Colomy, 1990a; Nielsen, 2007b), though he has since turned to the development of what he calls *cultural sociology* (Alexander, 2003). More recently, the systems theory developed by German sociologist Niklas Luhmann has been described as a version of structural functionalism. Though Luhmann's work is not widely known in the United States, internationally he is recognized as one of the most important contemporary sociological theorists (Stichweh, 2011). For this reason, following the discussion of structural functionalism, we describe Luhmann's systems theory.

For many years, the major alternative to structural functionalism was conflict theory. We will discuss Ralf Dahrendorf's traditional version of conflict theory, as well as a more recent integrative and synthetic effort by Randall Collins.

Before turning to the specifics of structural functionalism, systems theory, and conflict theory, we need, following Thomas Bernard (1983), to place these theories in the broader context of the debate between consensus theories (one of which is structural functionalism) and conflict theories (one of which is the sociological conflict theory that will be discussed in this chapter). *Consensus theories* see shared norms and values as fundamental to society, focus on social order based on tacit agreements, and view social change as occurring in a slow and orderly fashion. In contrast, *conflict theories* emphasize the dominance of some social groups by others, see social order as based on manipulation and control by dominant groups, and view social change as occurring rapidly and in a disorderly fashion as subordinate groups overthrow dominant groups.

Although these criteria broadly define the essential differences between the sociological theories of structural functionalism and conflict theory, Bernard's view is that the disagreement is far broader and has "been a recurring debate that has taken a variety of different forms throughout the history of Western thought" (1983:6). Bernard traced the debate back to ancient Greece (and the differences between Plato [consensus] and Aristotle [conflict]) and through the history of philosophy. Later, in sociology, the debate was joined by (the conflict theorist is listed first) Marx and Comte, Simmel and Durkheim, and Dahrendorf and Parsons. We already have examined briefly the ideas of the first two pairs of sociologists (although, as we have seen, their work is far broader than is implied by the label "conflict" or "consensus" theorist); in this chapter we examine Dahrendorf's conflict theory and Parsons's consensus theory, among others.

Although we emphasize the differences between structural functionalism and conflict theory, we should not forget that they have important similarities. In fact, Bernard argues that "the areas of agreement among them are more extensive than the areas of disagreement" (1983:214). For example, they are both macro-level theories focally concerned with large-scale social structures and social institutions. As a result, in Ritzer's (1980) terms, both theories exist within the same sociological ("social facts") paradigm (see the Appendix).

Structural Functionalism

Robert Nisbet argued that structural functionalism was "without any doubt, the single most significant body of theory in the social sciences in the present [twentieth] century" (cited in J. Turner and Maryanski, 1979:xi). Kingsley Davis (1959) took the position that structural functionalism was, for all intents and purposes, synonymous with sociology. Alvin Gouldner (1970) implicitly took a similar position when he attacked Western sociology largely through a critical analysis of the structural-functional theories of Talcott Parsons.

Despite its undoubted hegemony in the two decades after World War II, structural functionalism has declined in importance as a sociological theory. Even Wilbert Moore, a man who was intimately associated with this theory, argued that it had "become an embarrassment in contemporary theoretical sociology" (1978:321). Two observers even stated: "Thus, functionalism as an explanatory theory is, we feel, 'dead' and continued efforts to use functionalism as a theoretical explanation should be abandoned in favor of more promising theoretical perspectives" (J. Turner and Maryanski, 1979:141).[1] Nicholas Demerath and Richard Peterson (1967) took a more positive view, arguing that structural functionalism is not a passing fad. However, they

---

[1] Despite this statement, Jonathan Turner and Alexandra Maryanski (1979) are willing to argue that functionalism can continue to be useful as a method.

admitted that it is likely to evolve into another sociological theory, just as this theory itself evolved out of the earlier organicism.

In structural functionalism, the terms *structural* and *functional* need not be used in conjunction, although they typically are conjoined. We could study the structures of society without being concerned with their functions (or consequences) for other structures. Similarly, we could examine the functions of a variety of social processes that may not take a structural form. Still, the concern for both elements characterizes structural functionalism. Although structural functionalism takes various forms (Abrahamson, 1978), *societal functionalism* is the dominant approach among sociological structural functionalists (Sztompka, 1974) and as such will be the focus of this chapter. The primary concern of societal functionalism is the large-scale social structures and institutions of society, their interrelationships, and their constraining effects on actors.

The Functional Theory of Stratification and Its Critics

The functional theory of stratification as articulated by Kingsley Davis and Wilbert Moore (1945) is perhaps the best-known single piece of work in structural-functional theory. Davis and Moore made it clear that they regarded social stratification as both universal and necessary. They argued that no society is ever unstratified, or totally classless. Stratification is, in their view, a *functional* necessity. All societies need such a system, and this need brings into existence a system of stratification.[2] They also viewed a stratification system as a structure, pointing out that stratification refers not to the individuals in the stratification system but rather to a system of positions. They focused on how certain positions come to carry with them different degrees of prestige, not on how individuals come to occupy certain positions.

Given this focus, the major functional issue is how a society motivates and places people in their "proper" positions in the stratification system. This is reducible to two problems. First, how does a society instill in the "proper" individuals the desire to fill certain positions? Second, once people are in the right positions, how does society then instill in them the desire to fulfill the requirements of those positions?

Proper social placement in society is a problem for three basic reasons. First, some positions are more pleasant to occupy than others. Second, some positions are more important to the survival of society than others. Third, different social positions require different abilities and talents.

Although these issues apply to all social positions, Davis and Moore were concerned with the functionally more important positions in society. The positions that rank high within the stratification system are presumed to be those that are *less* pleasant to occupy but *more* important to the survival of society and that require the greatest ability and talent. In addition, society must attach sufficient rewards to these positions so that enough people will seek to occupy them and the individuals who do come to occupy them will work diligently. For example, in order to ensure that society

---

[2] This is an example of a teleological argument. We will have occasion to discuss this issue later in the chapter, but for now we can define a *teleological argument* as one that sees the social world as having purposes, or goals, that bring needed structures or events into being. In this case society "needs" stratification, and so it brings such a system into existence.

TALCOTT PARSONS

A Biographical Sketch

Talcott Parsons was born in 1902 in Colorado Springs, Colorado. He came from a religious and intellectual background; his father was a Congregational minister, a professor, and ultimately the president of a small college. Parsons got an undergraduate degree from Amherst College in 1924 and set out to do graduate work at the London School of Economics. In the next year, he moved on to Heidelberg, Germany. Max Weber had spent a large portion of his career at Heidelberg, and although he had died five years before Parsons arrived, Weber's influence survived and his widow continued to hold meetings in her home, meetings that Parsons attended. Parsons was greatly affected by Weber's work and ultimately wrote his doctoral thesis at Heidelberg, dealing, in part, with Weber's work (Lidz, 2007).

Parsons became an instructor at Harvard in 1927, and although he switched departments several times, Parsons remained at Harvard until his death in 1979. His career progress was not rapid; he did not obtain a tenured position until 1939. Two years previously, he had published *The Structure of Social Action,* a book that not only introduced major sociological theorists such as Weber to large numbers of sociologists but also laid the groundwork for Parsons's own developing theory.

After that, Parsons made rapid academic progress. He was made chairman of the Harvard sociology department in 1944 and two years later set up and chaired the innovative department of social relations, which included not only sociologists but a variety of other social scientists. By 1949 he had been elected president of the American Sociological Association. In the 1950s and into the 1960s, with the publication of such books as *The Social System* (1951), Parsons became the dominant figure in American sociology.

However, in the late 1960s, Parsons came under attack from the emerging radical wing of American sociology. Parsons was seen as a political conservative, and his theory was considered highly conservative and little more than an elaborate categorization scheme. But in the 1980s, there was a resurgence in interest in Parsonsian theory not only in the United States but around the world (Alexander, 1982–1983; Buxton, 1985; Camic, 1990; Holton and Turner, 1986; Sciulli and Gerstein, 1985). Holton and Turner have perhaps gone the farthest, arguing that "Parsons' work . . . represents a more powerful contribution to sociological theory

has enough doctors, they must receive rewards like great prestige, a high salary, and sufficient leisure. Davis and Moore implied that we could not expect people to undertake the "burdensome" and "expensive" process of medical education if we did not offer such rewards. The implication seems to be that people at the top must receive the rewards that they do. If they did not, those positions would remain understaffed than that of Marx, Weber, Durkheim or any of their contemporary followers" (1986:13). Furthermore, Parsons's ideas influenced not only conservative thinkers but neo-Marxian theorists as well, especially Jurgen Habermas.

Upon Parsons's death, a number of his former students, themselves sociologists of considerable note, reflected on his theory, as well as on the man behind the theory (for a more recent, and highly personal, reminiscence, see Fox, 1997). In their musings, these sociologists offered some interesting insights into Parsons and his work. The few glimpses of Parsons reproduced here do not add up to a coherent picture, but they offer some provocative glimpses of the man and his work.

Robert Merton was one of his students when Parsons was just beginning his teaching career at Harvard. Merton, who became a noted theorist in his own right, makes it clear that graduate students came to Harvard in those years to study not with Parsons but rather with Pitirim Sorokin, the senior member of the department, who was to become Parsons's archenemy (Zafirovski, 2001):

> Of the very first generation of graduate students coming to Harvard . . . precisely none came to study with Talcott. They could scarcely have done so for the simplest of reasons: in 1931, he had no public identity whatever as a sociologist.
>
> Although we students came to study with the renowned Sorokin, a subset of us stayed to work with the unknown Parsons.
>
> (Merton, 1980:69)

Merton's reflections on Parsons's first course in theory are interesting too, especially because the material provided the basis for one of the most influential theory books in the history of sociology:

> Long before Talcott Parsons became one of the Grand Old Men of world sociology, he was for an early few of us its Grand Young Man. This began with his first course in theory. . . . [It] would provide him with the core of his masterwork, *The Structure of Social Action* which . . . did not appear in print until five years after its first oral publication.
>
> (Merton, 1980:69–70)

Although all would not share Merton's positive evaluation of Parsons, they would acknowledge the following:

> The death of Talcott Parsons marks the end of an era in sociology. When [a new era] does begin . . . it will surely be fortified by the great tradition of sociological thought which he has left to us.
>
> (Merton, 1980:71)

or unfilled and society would crumble. The converse was implied by Davis and Moore but was not discussed. That is, low-ranking positions in the stratification system are presumed to be *more* pleasant and *less* important and to require less ability and talent. Also, society has less need to be sure that individuals occupy these positions and perform their duties with diligence.

Davis and Moore did not argue that a society consciously develops a stratification system in order to be sure that the high-level positions are filled, and filled adequately. Rather, they made it clear that stratification is an "unconsciously evolved device." However, it is a device that every society does, and *must,* develop if it is to survive.

The structural-functional theory of stratification has been subject to much criticism since its publication in 1945 (see Tumin, 1953, for the first important criticism; Huaco, 1966, for a good summary of the main criticisms to that date; and P. McLaughlin, 2001, for a philosophical overview).

One basic criticism is that the functional theory of stratification simply perpetuates the privileged position of those people who already have power, prestige, and money. It does this by arguing that such people deserve their rewards; indeed, they need to be offered such rewards for the good of society.

The functional theory also can be criticized for assuming that simply because a stratified social structure existed in the past, it must continue to exist in the future. It is possible that future societies will be organized in other, nonstratified ways.

In addition, it has been argued that the idea of functional positions varying in their importance to society is difficult to support. Are garbage collectors really any less important to the survival of society than advertising executives? Despite the lower pay and prestige of the garbage collectors, they actually may be *more* important to the survival of the society. Even in cases where it could be said that one position serves a more important function for society, the greater rewards do not necessarily accrue to the more important position. Nurses may be much more important to society than movie stars are, but nurses have far less power, prestige, and income than movie stars have.

Is there really a scarcity of people capable of filling high-level positions? In fact, many people are prevented from obtaining the training they need to achieve prestigious positions even though they have the ability. In the medical profession, for example, there is a persistent effort to limit the number of practicing doctors. In general, many able people never get a chance to show that they can handle high-ranking positions even though there is a clear need for them and their contributions. Those in high-ranking positions have a vested interest in keeping their own numbers small and their power and income high.

Finally, it can be argued that we do not have to offer people power, prestige, and income to get them to want to occupy high-level positions. People can be equally motivated by the satisfaction of doing a job well or by the opportunity to be of service to others.

Talcott Parsons's Structural Functionalism

Over the course of his life, Talcott Parsons did a great deal of theoretical work (Holmwood, 1996; Lidz, 2011b; Münch, 2005). There are important differences between his early work and his later work. In this section we deal with his later, structural-functional theorizing. We begin this discussion of Parsons's structural functionalism with the four functional imperatives for all "action" systems, his famous

AGIL scheme. After this discussion of the four functions, we will turn to an analysis of Parsons's ideas on structures and systems.

AGIL

A *function* is "a complex of activities directed towards meeting a need or needs of the system" (Rocher, 1975:40; R. Stryker, 2007). Using this definition, Parsons believes that there are four functional imperatives that are necessary for (characteristic of) all systems—adaptation (A), goal attainment (G), integration (I), and latency (L), or pattern maintenance. Together, these four functional imperatives are known as the AGIL scheme. In order to survive, a system must perform these four functions:

1. *Adaptation:* A system must cope with external situational exigencies. It must adapt to its environment and adapt the environment to its needs.
2. *Goal attainment:* A system must define and achieve its primary goals.
3. *Integration:* A system must regulate the interrelationship of its component parts. It also must manage the relationship among the other three functional imperatives (A, G, L).
4. *Latency (pattern maintenance):* A system must furnish, maintain, and renew both the motivation of individuals and the cultural patterns that create and sustain that motivation.

Parsons designed the AGIL scheme to be used at *all* levels in his theoretical system (for one example, see Paulsen and Feldman, 1995). In the discussion below on the four action systems, we will illustrate how Parsons uses AGIL.

The *behavioral organism* is the action system that handles the adaptation function by adjusting to and transforming the external world. The *personality system* performs the goal-attainment function by defining system goals and mobilizing resources to attain them. The *social system* copes with the integration function by controlling its component parts. Finally, the *cultural system* performs the latency function by providing actors with the norms and values that motivate them for action. Figure 7.1 summarizes the structure of the action system in terms of the AGIL schema.

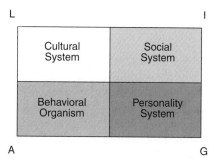

FIGURE 7.1   *Structure of the General Action System*

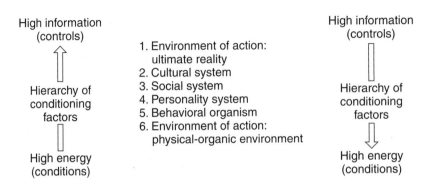

FIGURE 7.2 *Parsons's Action Schema*

The Action System

We are now ready to discuss the overall shape of Parsons's action system. Figure 7.2 outlines Parsons's schema.

It is obvious that Parsons had a clear notion of "levels" of social analysis as well as their interrelationship. The hierarchical arrangement is clear, and the levels are integrated in Parsons's system in two ways. First, each of the lower levels provides the conditions, the energy, needed for the higher levels. Second, the higher levels control those below them in the hierarchy.

In terms of the environments of the action system, the lowest level, the physical and organic environment, involves the nonsymbolic aspects of the human body, its anatomy and physiology. The highest level, ultimate reality, has, as Jackson Toby suggests, "a metaphysical flavor," but Toby also argues that Parsons "is not referring to the supernatural so much as to the universal tendency for societies to address symbolically the uncertainties, concerns, and tragedies of human existence that challenge the meaningfulness of social organization" (1977:3).

The heart of Parsons's work is found in his four action systems, and ultimately the action systems were conceived to address the problem of order (Schwanenberg, 1971). According to Parsons (1937) the problem of order—what prevents a social war or all against all—was not satisfactorily answered by philosophers. Parsons found his answer to the problem of order in structural functionalism, which operates in his view with the following set of assumptions:

1.   Systems have the property of order and interdependence of parts.
2.   Systems tend toward self-maintaining order, or equilibrium.[3]
3.   The system may be static or involved in an ordered process of change.
4.   The nature of one part of the system has an impact on the form that the other parts can take.
5.   Systems maintain boundaries with their environments.

---

[3] Most often, to Parsons, the problem of order related to the issue of why action was nonrandom or patterned. The issue of equilibrium was a more empirical question to Parsons. Nonetheless, Parsons himself often conflated the issues of order and equilibrium.

6.   Allocation and integration are two fundamental processes necessary for a given state of equilibrium of a system.
7.   Systems tend toward self-maintenance involving the maintenance of boundaries and of the relationships of parts to the whole, control of environmental variations, and control of tendencies to change the system from within.

These assumptions led Parsons to make the analysis of the *ordered* structure of society his first priority. In so doing, he did little with the issue of social change, at least until later in his career:

> We feel that it is uneconomical to describe changes in systems of variables before the variables themselves have been isolated and described; therefore, we have chosen to begin by studying particular combinations of variables and to move toward description of how these combinations change only when a firm foundation for such has been laid.
>
> (Parsons and Shils, 1951:6)

Parsons was so heavily criticized for his static orientation that he devoted more and more attention to change; in fact, as we will see, he eventually focused on the evolution of societies. However, in the view of most observers, even his work on social change tended to be highly static and structured.

In reading about the four action systems, the reader should keep in mind that they do not exist in the real world but are, rather, analytical tools for analyzing the real world.

Social System   Parsons's conception of the social system begins at the micro level with interaction between ego and alter ego, defined as the most elementary form of the social system. He spent little time analyzing this level, although he did argue that features of this interaction system are present in the more complex forms taken by the social system. Parsons defined a *social system* thus:

> A social system consists in a plurality of individual actors *interacting* with each other in a situation which has at least a physical or environmental aspect, actors who are motivated in terms of a tendency to the "optimization of gratification" and whose relation to their situations, including each other, is defined and mediated in terms of a system of culturally structured and shared symbols.
>
> (Parsons, 1951:5–6)

This definition seeks to define a social system in terms of many of the key concepts in Parsons's work—actors, interaction, environment, optimization of gratification, and culture.

Despite his commitment to viewing the social system as a system of interaction, Parsons did not take interaction as his fundamental unit in the study of the social system. Rather, he used the *status-role* complex as the basic unit of the system. This is neither an aspect of actors nor an aspect of interaction but rather a *structural* component of the social system. *Status* refers to a structural position within the social system, and *role* is what the actor does in such a position, seen in the context of its functional significance for the larger system. The actor is viewed not in terms of thoughts and actions but instead (at least in terms of position in the social system) as nothing more than a bundle of statuses and roles.

In his analysis of the social system, Parsons was interested primarily in its structural components. In addition to a concern with the status-role, Parsons (1966:11) was interested in such large-scale components of social systems as collectivities, norms, and values. In his analysis of the social system, however, Parsons was not simply a structuralist but also a functionalist. He thus delineated a number of the functional prerequisites of a social system. First, social systems must be structured so that they operate compatibly with other systems. Second, to survive, the social system must have the requisite support from other systems. Third, the system must meet a significant proportion of the needs of its actors. Fourth, the system must elicit adequate participation from its members. Fifth, it must have at least a minimum of control over potentially disruptive behavior. Sixth, if conflict becomes sufficiently disruptive, it must be controlled. Finally, a social system requires a language in order to survive.

It is clear in Parsons's discussion of the functional prerequisites of the social system that his focus was large-scale systems and their relationship to one another (societal functionalism). Even when he talked about actors, it was from the point of view of the system. Also, the discussion reflects Parsons's concern with the maintenance of order within the social system.

Actors and the Social System   However, Parsons did not completely ignore the issue of the relationship between actors and social structures in his discussion of the social system. In fact, he called the integration of value patterns and need-dispositions "the fundamental dynamic theorem of sociology" (Parsons, 1951:42). Given his central concern with the social system, of key importance in this integration are the processes of internalization and socialization. That is, Parsons was interested in the ways in which the norms and values of a system are transferred to the actors within the system. In a successful socialization process these norms and values are internalized; that is, they become part of the actors' "consciences." As a result, in pursuing their own interests, the actors are in fact serving the interests of the system as a whole. As Parsons put it, "The combination of value-orientation patterns which is acquired [by the actor in socialization] *must in a very important degree be a function of the fundamental role structure and dominant values of the social system*" (1951:227).

In general, Parsons assumed that actors usually are passive recipients in the socialization process.[4] Children learn not only how to act but also the norms and values, the morality, of society. Socialization is conceptualized as a conservative process in which need-dispositions (which are themselves largely molded by society) bind children to the social system, and it provides the means by which the need-dispositions can be satisfied. There is little or no room for creativity; the need for gratification ties children to the system as it exists. Parsons sees socialization as a lifelong experience. Because the norms and values inculcated in childhood tend to be very general, they do not prepare children for the various specific situations they

---

[4] This is a controversial interpretation of Parsons's work with which many disagree. François Bourricaud, for example, talks of "the dialectics of socialization" (1981:108) in Parsons's work and not of passive recipients of socialization.

encounter in adulthood. Thus socialization must be supplemented throughout the life cycle with a series of more specific socializing experiences. Despite this need later in life, the norms and values learned in childhood tend to be stable and, with a little gentle reinforcement, tend to remain in force throughout life.

Despite the conformity induced by lifelong socialization, there is a wide range of individual variation in the system. The question is: Why is this normally not a major problem for the social system, given its need for order? For one thing, a number of social control mechanisms can be employed to induce conformity. However, as far as Parsons was concerned, social control is strictly a second line of defense. A system runs best when social control is used only sparingly. For another thing, the system must be able to tolerate some variation, some deviance. A flexible social system is stronger than a brittle one that accepts no deviation. Finally, the social system should provide a wide range of role opportunities that allow different personalities to express themselves without threatening the integrity of the system.

Socialization and social control are the main mechanisms that allow the social system to maintain its equilibrium. Modest amounts of individuality and deviance are accommodated, but more extreme forms must be met by reequilibrating mechanisms. Thus, social order is built into the structure of Parsons's social system:

> Without deliberate planning on anyone's part there have developed in our type of social system, and correspondingly in others, mechanisms which, within limits, are capable of forestalling and reversing the deep-lying tendencies for deviance to get into the vicious circle phase which puts it beyond the control of ordinary approval-disapproval and reward-punishment sanctions.
>
> (Parsons, 1951:319)

Again, Parsons's main interest was the system as a whole rather than the actor in the system—how the system controls the actor, not how the actor creates and maintains the system. This reflects Parsons's commitment on this issue to a structural-functional orientation.

Society   Although the idea of a social system encompasses all types of collectivities, one specific and particularly important social system is *society,* "a relatively self-sufficient collectivity the members of which are able to satisfy all their individual and collective needs and to live entirely within its framework" (Rocher, 1975:60).[5] As a structural functionalist, Parsons distinguished among four structures, or subsystems, in society in terms of the functions (AGIL) they perform (see Figure 7.3). The *economy* is the subsystem that performs the function for society of adapting to the environment through labor, production, and allocation. Through such work, the economy adapts the environment to society's needs, and it helps society adapt to these external realities. The *polity* (or political system) performs the function of goal attainment by pursuing societal objectives and mobilizing actors and resources to that end. The *fiduciary system* (for example, in the schools, the family) handles the latency function by transmitting culture (norms and values) to actors and allowing it to be internalized by them. Finally, the integration

---

[5] Barnard Barber (1993, 1994) argues that while there is considerable terminological confusion in Parsons's work, the idea of a social system should be restricted to inclusive, total systems like societies.

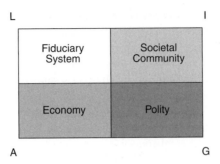

FIGURE 7.3   *Society, Its Subsystems, and the Functional Imperatives*

function is performed by the *societal community* (for example, the law), which coordinates the various components of society (Parsons and Platt, 1973).

As important as the structures of the social system were to Parsons, the cultural system was more important. In fact, as we saw earlier, the cultural system stood at the top of Parsons's action system, and Parsons (1966) labeled himself a "cultural determinist."[6]

Cultural System   Parsons conceived of culture as the major force binding the various elements of the social world, or, in his terms, the action system. Culture mediates interaction among actors and integrates the personality and the social systems. Culture has the peculiar capacity to become, at least in part, a component of the other systems. Thus, in the social system culture is embodied in norms and values, and in the personality system it is internalized by the actor. But the cultural system is not simply a part of other systems; it also has a separate existence in the form of the social stock of knowledge, symbols, and ideas. These aspects of the cultural system are available to the social and personality systems, but they do not become part of them (Morse, 1961:105; Parsons and Shils, 1951:6).

Parsons defined the cultural system, as he did his other systems, in terms of its relationship to the other action systems. Thus *culture* is seen as a patterned, ordered system of symbols that are objects of orientation to actors, internalized aspects of the personality system, and institutionalized patterns (Parsons, 1990) in the social system. Because it is largely symbolic and subjective, culture is transmitted readily from one system to another. Culture can move from one social system to another through diffusion and from one personality system to another through learning and socialization. However, the symbolic (subjective) character of culture also gives it another characteristic, the ability to control Parsons's other action systems. This is one of the reasons Parsons came to view himself as a cultural determinist.

However, if the cultural system is preeminent in Parsonian theory, we must question whether he offers a genuinely integrative theory. As pointed out in the

---

[6] Interestingly Alexander and Smith (2001:139) describe Parsons as "insufficiently cultural," lacking a "thick description" of culture.

Appendix, a truly integrative theory gives rough equivalency to all major levels of analysis. Cultural determinism, indeed any kind of determinism, is highly suspect from the point of view of an integrated sociology. (For a more integrated conception of Parsons's work, see Camic, 1990.) This problem is exacerbated when we look at the personality system and see how weakly it is developed in Parsons's work.

Personality System The personality system is controlled not only by the cultural system but also by the social system. That is not to say that Parsons did not accord some independence to the personality system:

> My view will be that, while the main content of the structure of the personality is derived from social systems and culture through socialization, the personality becomes an independent system through its relations to its own organism and through the uniqueness of its own life experience; it is not a mere epiphenomenon.
>
> (Parsons, 1970:82)

We get the feeling here that Parsons is protesting too much. If the personality system is not an epiphenomenon, it is certainly reduced to a secondary or dependent status in his theoretical system.

The *personality* is defined as the organized system of orientation and motivation of action of the individual actor. The basic component of the personality is the "need-disposition." Parsons and Shils defined *need-dispositions* as the "most significant units of motivation of action" (1951:113). They differentiated need-dispositions from drives, which are innate tendencies—"physiological energy that makes action possible" (Parsons and Shils, 1951:111). In other words, drives are better seen as part of the biological organism. Need-dispositions are then defined as "these same tendencies when they are not innate but acquired through the process of action itself" (Parsons and Shils, 1951:111). In other words, need-dispositions are drives that are shaped by the social setting.

Need-dispositions impel actors to accept or reject objects presented in the environment or to seek out new objects if the ones that are available do not adequately satisfy need-dispositions. Parsons differentiated among three basic types of need-dispositions. The first type impels actors to seek love, approval, and so forth, from their social relationships. The second type includes internalized values that lead actors to observe various cultural standards. Finally, there are the role expectations that lead actors to give and get appropriate responses.

This presents a very passive image of actors. They seem to be impelled by drives, dominated by the culture, or, more usually, shaped by a combination of drives and culture (that is, by need-dispositions). A passive personality system is clearly a weak link in an integrated theory, and Parsons seemed to be aware of that. On various occasions, he tried to endow the personality with some creativity. For example, he said: "We do not mean . . . to imply that a person's values are entirely 'internalized culture' or mere adherence to rules and laws. The person makes creative modifications as he internalizes culture; but the novel aspect is not the culture aspect" (Parsons and Shils, 1951:72). Despite claims such as these, the dominant impression that emerges from Parsons's work is one of a passive personality system.

Parsons's emphasis on need-dispositions creates other problems. Because it leaves out so many other important aspects of personality, his system becomes a largely impoverished one. Alfred Baldwin, a psychologist, makes precisely this point:

> It seems fair to say that Parsons fails in his theory to provide the personality with a reasonable set of properties or mechanisms aside from need-dispositions, and gets himself into trouble by not endowing the personality with enough characteristics and enough different kinds of mechanisms for it to be able to function.
>
> (A. Baldwin, 1961:186)

Baldwin makes another telling point about Parsons's personality system, arguing that even when Parsons analyzed the personality system, he was really not focally interested in it: "Even when he is writing chapters on personality structure, Parsons spends many more pages talking about social systems than he does about personality" (1961:180). This is reflected in the various ways Parsons linked the personality to the social system. First, actors must learn to see themselves in a way that fits with the place they occupy in society (Parsons and Shils, 1951:147). Second, role expectations are attached to each of the roles occupied by individual actors. Then there is the learning of self-discipline, internalization of value orientations, identification, and so forth. All these forces point toward the integration of the personality system with the social system, which Parsons emphasized. However, he also pointed out the possible malintegration, which is a problem for the system that needs to be overcome.

Another aspect of Parsons's work—his interest in internalization as the personality system's side of the socialization process—reflects the passivity of the personality system. Parsons (1970:2) derived this interest from Durkheim's work on internalization, as well as from Freud's work, primarily that on the superego. In emphasizing internalization and the superego, Parsons once again manifested his conception of the personality system as passive and externally controlled.

Although Parsons was willing to talk about the subjective aspects of personality in his early work, he progressively abandoned that perspective. In so doing, he limited his possible insights into the personality system. Parsons at one point stated clearly that he was shifting his attention away from the internal meanings that the actions of people may have: "The organization of observational data in terms of the theory of action is quite possible and fruitful in modified behavioristic terms, and such formulation avoids many of the difficult questions of introspection or empathy" (Parsons and Shils, 1951:64).

Behavioral Organism   Though he included the behavioral organism as one of the four action systems, Parsons had very little to say about it. It is included because it is the source of energy for the rest of the systems. Although it is based on genetic constitution, its organization is affected by the processes of conditioning and learning that occur during the individual's life.[7] The behavioral organism is clearly a residual system in Parsons's work, but at the minimum Parsons is to be lauded for including it as a part of his sociology, if for no other reason than that he anticipated interest in sociobiology, the sociology of the body (B. Turner, 1985), and work on the intersection between the life sciences and social theory (Capra, 2005; Fraser et al., 2005, 2006).

---

[7] Because of this social element, in his later work Parsons dropped the word *organism* and labeled this the "behavioral system" (1975:104).

Change and Dynamism in Parsonsian Theory

Parsons's work with conceptual tools such as the four action systems and the functional imperatives led to the accusation that he offered a structural theory that was unable to deal with social change. Parsons had long been sensitive to this charge, arguing that although a study of change was necessary, it must be preceded by a study of structure. But by the 1960s he could resist the attacks no longer and made a major shift in his work to the study of social change,[8] particularly the study of social evolution (Parsons, 1977:50).

Evolutionary Theory   Parsons's (1966) general orientation to the study of social change was shaped by biology. To deal with this process, Parsons developed what he called "a paradigm of evolutionary change."

The first component of that paradigm is the process of *differentiation*. Parsons assumed that any society is composed of a series of subsystems that differ in both their *structure* and their *functional* significance for the larger society. As society evolves, new subsystems are differentiated. This is not enough, however; they also must be more adaptive than earlier subsystems. Thus, the essential aspect of Parsons's evolutionary paradigm was the idea of *adaptive upgrading*. Parsons described this process:

> If differentiation is to yield a balanced, more evolved system, each newly differentiated substructure . . . must have increased adaptive capacity for performing its *primary* function, as compared to the performance of *that* function in the previous, more diffuse structure. . . . We may call this process the *adaptive upgrading* aspect of the evolutionary change cycle.
>
> (Parsons, 1966:22)

This is a highly positive model of social change (although Parsons certainly had a sense of its darker side). It assumes that as society evolves, it grows generally better able to cope with its problems. In contrast, in Marxian theory social change leads to the eventual destruction of capitalist society. For this reason, among others, Parsons often is thought of as a very conservative sociological theorist.

Next, Parsons argued that the process of differentiation leads to a new set of problems of *integration* for society. As subsystems proliferate, the society is confronted with new problems in coordinating the operations of these units.

A society undergoing evolution must move from a system of ascription to one of achievement. A wider array of skills and abilities is needed to handle the more diffuse subsystems. The generalized abilities of people must be freed from their ascriptive bonds so that they can be utilized by society. Most generally, this means that groups formerly excluded from contributing to the system must be freed for inclusion as full members of the society.

Finally, the *value* system of the society as a whole must undergo change as social structures and functions grow increasingly differentiated. However, since the new system is more diverse, it is harder for the value system to encompass it. Thus a more differentiated society requires a value system that is "couched at a higher level of generality in order to legitimize the wider variety of goals and functions of its

---

[8] To be fair, we must report that Parsons had done some earlier work on social change (see Parsons, 1942, 1947; see also Alexander, 1981; Baum and Lechner, 1981).

subunits" (Parsons, 1966:23). However, this process of generalization of values often does not proceed smoothly as it meets resistance from groups committed to their own narrow value systems.

Evolution proceeds through a variety of cycles, but no general process affects all societies equally. Some societies may foster evolution, whereas others may "be so beset with internal conflicts or other handicaps" that they impede the process of evolution, or they may even "deteriorate" (Parsons, 1966:23). What most interested Parsons were those societies in which developmental "breakthroughs" occur, since he believed that once they occurred, the process of evolution would follow his general evolutionary model.

Although Parsons conceived of evolution as occurring in stages, he was careful to avoid a unilinear evolutionary theory: "We do not conceive societal evolution to be either a continuous or a simple linear process, but we can distinguish between broad levels of advancement without overlooking the considerable variability found in each" (1966:26). Making it clear that he was simplifying matters, Parsons distinguished three broad evolutionary stages—primitive, intermediate, and modern. Characteristically, he differentiated among these stages primarily on the basis of cultural dimensions. The crucial development in the transition from primitive to intermediate is the development of language, primarily written language. The key development in the shift from intermediate to modern is "the institutionalized codes of normative order," or law (Parsons, 1966:26).

Parsons next proceeded to analyze a series of specific societies in the context of the evolution from primitive to modern society. One particular point is worth underscoring here: Parsons turned to evolutionary theory, at least in part, because he was accused of being unable to deal with social change. However, his analysis of evolution is *not* in terms of process; rather, it is an attempt to "order structural types and relate them sequentially" (Parsons, 1966:111). This is comparative *structural* analysis, not really a study of the processes of social change. Thus, even when he was supposed to be looking at change, Parsons remained committed to the study of structures and functions.

Generalized Media of Interchange   One of the ways in which Parsons introduces some dynamism, some fluidity (Alexander, 1983:115), into his theoretical system is through his ideas on the generalized media of interchange within and among the four action systems (especially within the social system) discussed above (Treviño, 2005). The model for the generalized media of interchange is money, which operates as such a medium within the economy. But instead of focusing on material phenomena such as money, Parsons focuses on *symbolic* media of exchange. Even when Parsons does discuss money as a medium of interchange within the social system, he focuses on its symbolic rather than its material qualities. In addition to money, and more clearly symbolic, are other generalized media of interchange—political power, influence, and value commitments. Parsons makes it quite clear why he is focusing on symbolic media of interchange: "The introduction of a theory of media into the kind of structural perspective I have in mind goes far, it seems to me, to refute the frequent allegations that this type of structural analysis is inherently plagued with a static bias, which makes it impossible to do justice to dynamic problems" (1975:98–99).

Symbolic media of interchange have the capacity, like money, to be created and to circulate in the larger society. Thus, within the social system, those in the political system are able to create political power. More important, they can expend that power, thereby allowing it to circulate freely in, and have influence over, the social system. Through such an expenditure of power, leaders presumably strengthen the political system as well as the society as a whole. More generally, it is the generalized media that circulate between the four action systems and within the structures of each of those systems. It is their existence and movement that give dynamism to Parsons's largely structural analyses.

As Alexander (1983:115) points out, generalized media of interchange lend dynamism to Parsons's theory in another sense. They allow for the existence of "media entrepreneurs" (for example, politicians) who do not simply accept the system of exchange as it is. That is, they can be creative and resourceful and in this way alter not only the quantity of the generalized media but also the manner and direction in which the media flow.

Robert Merton's Structural Functionalism

Although Talcott Parsons is the most important structural-functional theorist, his student Robert Merton authored some of the most important statements on structural functionalism in sociology (Crothers, 2011; Sztompka, 2000; Tiryakian, 1991). Merton criticized some of the more extreme and indefensible aspects of structural functionalism. But equally important, his new conceptual insights helped give structural functionalism a continuing usefulness (Jasso, 2000).

Although both Merton and Parsons are associated with structural functionalism, there are important differences between them. For one thing, while Parsons advocated the creation of grand, overarching theories, Merton favored more limited, middle-range theories. For another, Merton was more favorable toward Marxian theories than Parsons was. In fact, Merton and some of his students (especially Alvin Gouldner) can be seen as having pushed structural functionalism more to the left politically.

A Structural-Functional Model

Merton criticized what he saw as the three basic postulates of functional analysis as it was developed by anthropologists such as Malinowski and Radcliffe-Brown. The first is the postulate of the functional unity of society. This postulate holds that all standardized social and cultural beliefs and practices are functional for society as a whole as well as for individuals in society. This view implies that the various parts of a social system must show a high level of integration. However, Merton maintained that although it may be true of small, primitive societies, this generalization cannot be extended to larger, more complex societies.

Universal functionalism is the second postulate that he rejects. That is, it is argued that *all* standardized social and cultural forms and structures have positive functions. Merton argued that this contradicts what we find in the real world. It is clear that not every structure, custom, idea, belief, and so forth, has positive functions. For example, rabid nationalism can be highly dysfunctional in a world of proliferating nuclear arms.

ROBERT K. MERTON

*An Autobiographical Sketch**

It is easy enough to identify the principal teachers, both close at hand and at a distance, who taught me most. During my graduate studies, they were: P. A. Sorokin, who oriented me more widely to European social thought and with whom, unlike some other students of the time, I never broke although I could not follow him in the directions of inquiry he began to pursue in the late 1930s; the then quite young Talcott Parsons, engaged in thinking through the ideas which first culminated in his magisterial *Structure of Social Action;* the biochemist and sometime sociologist L. J. Henderson, who taught me something about the disciplined investigation of what is first entertained as an interesting idea; the economic historian E. F. Gay, who taught me about the workings of economic development as reconstructible from archival sources; and, quite consequentially, the then dean of the history of science, George Sarton, who allowed me to work under his guidance for several years in his famed (not to say, hallowed) workshop in the Widener Library of Harvard. Beyond these teachers with whom I studied directly, I learned most from two sociologists: Emile Durkheim, above all others, and Georg Simmel, who could teach me only through the powerful works they left behind, and from that sociologically sensitive humanist, Gilbert Murray. During the latter period of my life, I learned most from my colleague, Paul F. Lazarsfeld, who probably had no idea of how much he taught me during our uncountable conversations and collaborations during more than a third of a century.

Looking back over my work through the years, I find more of a pattern in it than I had supposed was there. For almost from the beginning of my own work, after those apprenticeship years as a graduate student, I was determined to follow my intellectual interests as they evolved rather than pursue a predetermined lifelong plan. I chose to adopt the practice of my master-at-a-distance, Durkheim, rather than the practice of my master-at-close-range, Sarton. Durkheim repeatedly changed the subjects he chose to investigate. Starting with his study of the social division of labor, he examined methods of sociological inquiry and then turned successively to the seemingly unrelated subjects of suicide, religion, moral education, and socialism, all the while developing a theoretical orientation which, to his mind, could be effectively developed by attending to such varied aspects of life in society. Sarton had proceeded quite the other way: in his earliest years as a scholar, he had worked out a program of research in the history of science that was to culminate in his monumental five-volume *Introduction* [sic] to the *History of Science* (which carried the story through to the close of the fourteenth century!).

The first of these patterns seemed more suitable for me. I wanted and still want to advance sociological theories of social structure and cultural change that will help us understand how social institutions and the character of life in society come to be as they are. That concern with theoretical sociology has led me to avoid the kind of subject specialization that has become (and, in my opinion, has for the most part rightly become) the order of the day in sociology, as in other evolving disciplines. For my purposes, study of a variety of sociological subjects was essential.

In that variety, only one special field—the sociology of science—has persistently engaged my interest. During the 1930s, I devoted myself almost entirely to the social contexts of science and technology, especially in seventeenth-century England, and focused on the unanticipated consequences of purposive social action. As my theoretical interests broadened, I turned, during the 1940s and afterward, to studies of the social sources of nonconforming and deviant behavior, of the workings of bureaucracy, mass persuasion, and communication in modern complex society, and to the role of the intellectual, both within bureaucracies and outside them. In the 1950s, I centered on developing a sociological theory of basic units of social structure: the role-set and status-set and the role models people select not only for emulation but also as a source of values adopted as a basis for self-appraisal (this latter being "the theory of reference groups"). I also undertook, with George Reader and Patricia Kendall, the first large-scale sociological study of medical education, aiming to find out how, all apart from explicit plan, different kinds of physicians are socialized in the same schools of medicine, this being linked with the distinctive character of professions as a type of occupational activity. In the 1960s and 1970s, I returned to an intensive study of the social structure of science and its interaction with cognitive structure, these two decades being the time in which the sociology of science finally came of age, with what's past being only prologue. Throughout these studies, my primary orientation was toward the connections between sociological theory, methods of inquiry, and substantive empirical research.

I group these developing interests by decades only for convenience. Of course, they did not neatly come and go in accord with such conventional divisions of the calendar. Nor did all of them go, after the first period of intensive work on them. I am at work on a volume centered on the unanticipated consequences of purposive social action, thus following up a paper first published almost half a century ago and intermittently developed since. Another volume in the stocks, entitled *The Self-Fulfilling Prophecy,* follows out in a half-dozen spheres of social life the workings of this pattern as first noted in my paper by the same title, a mere third of a century ago. And should time, patience, and capacity allow, there remains the summation of work on the analysis of social structure, with special reference to status-sets, role-sets, and structural contexts on the structural side, and manifest and latent functions, dysfunctions, functional alternatives, and social mechanisms on the functional side.

Mortality being the rule and painfully slow composition being my practice, there seems small point in looking beyond this series of works in progress.

[For more on Merton, see Johnston, 2007; Schultz, 1995; and Sztompka, 2005. Robert Merton died on February 23, 2003.]

The third postulate that he rejects is the postulate of indispensability. The argument here is that all standardized aspects of society not only have positive functions but also represent indispensable parts of the working whole. This postulate leads to the idea that all structures and functions are functionally necessary for society. No other structures and functions could work quite as well as those that are currently found within society. Merton's criticism, following Parsons, was that we must at least be willing to admit that there are various structural and functional alternatives to be found within society.

Merton's position was that all these functional postulates rely on nonempirical assertions based on abstract, theoretical systems. At a minimum, it is the responsibility of the sociologist to examine each empirically. Merton's belief that empirical tests, not theoretical assertions, are crucial to functional analysis led him to develop his "paradigm" of functional analysis as a guide to the integration of theory and research.

Merton made it clear from the outset that structural-functional analysis focuses on groups, organizations, societies, and cultures. He stated that any object that can be subjected to structural-functional analysis must "represent a standardized (that is, patterned and repetitive) item" (Merton, 1949/1968:104). He had in mind such things as "social roles, institutional patterns, social processes, cultural patterns, culturally patterned emotions, social norms, group organization, social structure, devices for social control, etc." (Merton, 1949/1968:104).

Early structural functionalists tended to focus almost entirely on the *functions* of one social structure or institution for another. However, in Merton's view, early analysts tended to confuse the subjective motives of individuals with the functions of structures or institutions. The focus of the structural functionalist should be on social functions rather than on individual motives. *Functions,* according to Merton, are defined as "those observed consequences which make for the adaptation or adjustment of a given system" (1949/1968:105). However, there is a clear ideological bias when one focuses only on adaptation or adjustment, for they are always positive consequences. It is important to note that one social fact can have negative consequences for another social fact. To rectify this serious omission in early structural functionalism, Merton developed the idea of a *dysfunction.* Just as structures or institutions could contribute to the maintenance of other parts of the social system, they also could have negative consequences for them. Slavery in the southern United States, for example, clearly had positive consequences for white southerners, such as supplying cheap labor, support for the cotton economy, and social status. It also had dysfunctions, such as making southerners overly dependent on an agrarian economy and therefore unprepared for industrialization. The lingering disparity between the North and the South in industrialization can be traced, at least in part, to the dysfunctions of the institution of slavery in the South.

Merton also posited the idea of *nonfunctions,* which he defined as consequences that are simply irrelevant to the system under consideration. Included here might be social forms that are "survivals" from earlier historical times. Although they may have had positive or negative consequences in the past, they have no significant effect on contemporary society. One example, although a few might disagree, is the Women's Christian Temperance Movement.

To help answer the question of whether positive functions outweigh dysfunctions, or vice versa, Merton developed the concept of *net balance.* However, we never can simply add up positive functions and dysfunctions and objectively determine which outweighs the other, because the issues are so complex and are based on so much subjective judgment that they cannot be calculated and weighed easily. The usefulness of Merton's concept comes from the way it orients the sociologist to the question of relative significance. To return to the example of slavery, the question becomes whether, on balance, slavery was more functional or dysfunctional to the South. Still, this question is too broad and obscures a number of issues (for example, that slavery was functional for groups such as white slaveholders).

To cope with problems like these, Merton added the idea that there must be *levels of functional analysis.* Functionalists had generally restricted themselves to analysis of the society as a whole, but Merton made it clear that analysis also could be done on an organization, institution, or group. Returning to the issue of the functions of slavery for the South, it would be necessary to differentiate several levels of analysis and ask about the functions and dysfunctions of slavery for black families, white families, black political organizations, white political organizations, and so forth. In terms of net balance, slavery was probably more functional for certain social units and more dysfunctional for other social units. Addressing the issue at these more specific levels helps in analyzing the functionality of slavery for the South as a whole.

Merton also introduced the concepts of *manifest* and *latent* functions. These two terms have also been important additions to functional analysis.[9] In simple terms, *manifest functions* are those that are intended, whereas *latent functions* are unintended. The manifest function of slavery, for example, was to increase the economic productivity of the South, but it had the latent function of providing a vast underclass that served to increase the social status of southern whites, both rich and poor. This idea is related to another of Merton's concepts—*unanticipated consequences.* Actions have both intended and unintended consequences. Although everyone is aware of the intended consequences, sociological analysis is required to uncover the unintended consequences; indeed, to some this is the very essence of sociology. Peter Berger (1963) has called this "debunking," or looking beyond stated intentions to real effects.

Merton made it clear that unanticipated consequences and latent functions are not the same. A latent function is one type of unanticipated consequence, one that is functional for the designated system. But there are two other types of unanticipated consequences: "those that are dysfunctional for a designated system, and these comprise the latent dysfunctions," and "those which are irrelevant to the system which they affect neither functionally or dysfunctionally . . . non-functional consequences" (Merton, 1949/1968:105).

As further clarification of functional theory, Merton pointed out that a structure may be dysfunctional for the system as a whole yet may continue to exist. One might make a good case that discrimination against blacks, females, and other minority groups is dysfunctional for American society, yet it continues to exist because it is functional for a part of the social system; for example, discrimination against females

---

[9] Colin Campbell (1982) has criticized Merton's distinction between manifest and latent functions. Among other things, he points out that Merton is vague about these terms and uses them in various ways (for example, as intended versus actual consequences and as surface meanings versus underlying realities). More important, he feels that Merton (like Parsons) never adequately integrated action theory and structural functionalism. The result is that we have an uncomfortable mixture of the intentionality ("manifest") of action theory and the structural consequences ("functions") of structural functionalism. Because of these and other confusions, Campbell believes, Merton's distinction between manifest and latent functions is little used in contemporary sociology.

is generally functional for males. However, these forms of discrimination are not without some dysfunctions, even for the group for which they are functional. Males do suffer from their discrimination against females; similarly, whites are hurt by their discriminatory behavior toward blacks. One could argue that these forms of discrimination adversely affect those who discriminate by keeping vast numbers of people underproductive and by increasing the likelihood of social conflict.

Merton contended that not all structures are indispensable to the workings of the social system. Some parts of our social system *can* be eliminated. This helps functional theory overcome another of its conservative biases. By recognizing that some structures are expendable, functionalism opens the way for meaningful social change. Our society, for example, could continue to exist (and even be improved) by the elimination of discrimination against various minority groups.

Merton's clarifications are of great utility to sociologists (for example, Gans, 1972, 1994) who wish to perform structural-functional analyses.

Social Structure and Anomie

Before leaving this section, we must devote some attention to one of the best-known contributions to structural functionalism, indeed to all of sociology (Adler and Laufer, 1995; Menard, 1995; Merton, 1995)—Merton's (1968) analysis of the relationship between culture, structure, and anomie. Merton defines *culture* as "that organized set of *normative values* governing behavior which is common to members of a designated society or group" and *social structure* as "that organized set of *social relationships* in which members of the society or group are variously implicated" (1968:216; italics added). Anomie occurs "when there is an acute disjunction between the cultural norms and goals and the socially structured capacities of members of the group to act in accord with them" (Merton, 1968:216). That is, because of their position in the social structure of society, some people are unable to act in accord with normative values. The culture calls for some type of behavior that the social structure prevents from occurring.

For example, in American society, the culture places great emphasis on material success. However, by their position within the social structure, many people are prevented from achieving such success. If one is born into the lower socioeconomic classes and as a result is able to acquire, at best, only a high school degree, one's chances of achieving economic success in the generally accepted way (for example, through succeeding in the conventional work world) are slim or nonexistent. Under such circumstances (and they are widespread in contemporary American society) anomie can be said to exist, and as a result, there is a tendency toward deviant behavior. In this context, deviance often takes the form of alternative, unacceptable, and sometimes illegal means of achieving economic success. Thus, becoming a drug dealer or a prostitute in order to achieve economic success is an example of deviance generated by the disjunction between cultural values and social-structural means of attaining those values. This is one way in which the structural functionalist would seek to explain crime and deviance.

Thus, in this example of structural functionalism, Merton is looking at social (and cultural) structures, but he is not focally concerned with the functions of those structures. Rather, consistent with his functional paradigm, he is mainly concerned with dysfunctions, in this case anomie. More specifically, as we have seen, Merton links anomie with deviance and thereby is arguing that disjunctions between culture and structure have the dysfunctional consequence of leading to deviance within society.

It is worth noting that implied in Merton's work on anomie is a critical attitude toward social stratification (for example, for blocking the means of some to socially desirable goals). Thus, while Davis and Moore wrote approvingly of a stratified society, Merton's work indicates that structural functionalists can be critical of social stratification.

The Major Criticisms

No single sociological theory in the history of the discipline has been the focus of as much interest as structural functionalism. By the 1960s, however, criticisms of the theory had increased dramatically, and ultimately they became more prevalent than praise. Mark Abrahamson depicted this situation quite vividly: "Thus, metaphorically, functionalism has ambled along like a giant elephant, ignoring the stings of gnats, even as the swarm of attackers takes its toll" (1978:37).

Substantive Criticisms

One major criticism is that structural functionalism does not deal adequately with history—that it is inherently ahistorical. In fact, structural functionalism was developed, at least in part, in reaction to the historical evolutionary approach of certain anthropologists. In its early years in particular, structural functionalism went too far in its criticism of evolutionary theory and came to focus on either contemporary or abstract societies. However, structural functionalism need not be ahistorical (J. Turner and Maryanski, 1979). In fact, Parsons's (1966, 1971) work on social change, as we have seen, reflects the ability of structural functionalists to deal with change if they so wish.

Structural functionalists also are attacked for being unable to deal effectively with the *process* of social change (Abrahamson, 1978; P. Cohen, 1968; Mills, 1959; J. Turner and Maryanski, 1979).[10] Whereas the preceding criticism deals with the seeming inability of structural functionalism to deal with the past, this one is concerned with the parallel incapacity of the approach to deal with the contemporary process of social change. Percy Cohen (1968) sees the problem as lying in structural-functional theory, in which all the elements of a society are seen as reinforcing one another as well as the system as a whole. This makes it difficult to see how these elements can also contribute to change. While Cohen sees the problem as inherent in the theory, Turner and Maryanski believe, again, that the problem lies with the practitioners and not with the theory.

Perhaps the most often voiced criticism of structural functionalism is that it is unable to deal effectively with conflict (Abrahamson, 1978; P. Cohen, 1968; Gouldner, 1970; Horowitz, 1962/1967; Mills, 1959; J. Turner and Maryanski, 1979).[11] This criticism takes a variety of forms. Alvin Gouldner argues that Parsons, as the main

---

[10] However, there are some important works on social change by structural functionalists (C. Johnson, 1966; Smelser, 1959, 1962).
[11] Again, there are important exceptions—see Coser (1956, 1967), Goode (1960), and Merton (1975).

representative of structural functionalism, tended to overemphasize harmonious relationships. Irving Louis Horowitz contends that structural functionalists tend to see conflict as necessarily destructive and as occurring outside the framework of society. The issue once again is whether this is inherent in the theory or in the way practitioners have interpreted and used it (P. Cohen, 1968; J. Turner and Maryanski, 1979).

The overall criticisms that structural functionalism is unable to deal with history, change, and conflict have led many (for example, P. Cohen, 1968; Gouldner, 1970) to argue that structural functionalism has a conservative bias. It may indeed be true that there is a conservative bias in structural functionalism that is attributable not only to what it ignores (change, history, conflict) but also to what it chooses to focus on. For one thing, structural functionalists have tended to focus on culture, norms, and values (P. Cohen, 1968; Lockwood, 1956; Mills, 1959). People are seen as constrained by cultural and social forces. As Gouldner says, to emphasize his criticism of structural functionalism, "Human beings are as much engaged in using social systems as in being used by them" (1970:220).

Related to their cultural focus is the tendency of structural functionalists to mistake the legitimizations employed by elites in society for social reality (Gouldner, 1970; Harré, 2002; Horowitz, 1962/1967; Mills, 1959). The normative system is interpreted as reflective of the society as a whole, when it may in fact be better viewed as an ideological system promulgated by, and existing for, the elite members of the society.

These substantive criticisms point in two basic directions. First, it seems clear that structural functionalism has a rather narrow focus that prevents it from addressing a number of important issues and aspects of the social world. Second, its focus tends to give it a very conservative flavor; structural functionalism has operated in support of the status quo and the dominant elites (Huaco, 1986).

Methodological and Logical Criticisms

One of the often expressed criticisms (see, for example, Abrahamson, 1978; Mills, 1959) is that structural functionalism is basically vague, unclear, and ambiguous. Part of the ambiguity is traceable to the fact that structural functionalists choose to deal with abstract social systems instead of real societies.

A related criticism is that although no single grand scheme ever can be used to analyze all societies throughout history (Mills, 1959), structural functionalists have been motivated by the belief that there is a single theory or at least a set of conceptual categories that could be used to do this. Many critics regard this grand theory as an illusion, believing that the best sociology can hope for is more historically specific, "middle-range" (Merton, 1968) theories.

Among the other specific methodological criticisms is the issue of whether there are adequate methods to study the questions of concern to structural functionalists. Percy Cohen (1968), for instance, wonders what tools can be used to study the contribution of one part of a system to the system as a whole. Another methodological criticism is that structural functionalism makes comparative analysis difficult. If the assumption is that a part of a system makes sense only in the context of the social system in which it exists, how can we compare it with a similar part in another system? Cohen asks, for example: If the English family makes sense only in the context of English society, how can we compare it to the French family?

Teleology and Tautology Percy Cohen (1968) and Jonathan Turner and A. Z. Maryanski (1979) see teleology and tautology as the two most important logical problems confronting structural functionalism. Some tend to see teleology as an inherent problem (Abrahamson, 1978; P. Cohen, 1968), but it's likely that Turner and Maryanski (1979) are correct when they argue that the problem with structural functionalism is not teleology per se, but *illegitimate* teleology. In this context, *teleology* is defined as the view that society (or other social structures) has purposes or goals. In order to achieve these goals, society creates, or causes to be created, specific social structures and social institutions. Turner and Maryanski do not see this view as necessarily illegitimate; in fact, they argue that social theory *should* take into account the teleological relationship between society and its component parts.

The problem, according to Turner and Maryanski, is the extension of teleology to unacceptable lengths. An illegitimate teleology is one that implies "that purpose or end states guide human affairs when such is not the case" (J. Turner and Maryanski, 1979:118). For example, it is illegitimate to assume that because society needs procreation and socialization it will create the family institution. A variety of alternative structures could meet these needs; society does not "need" to create the family. The structural functionalist must define and document the various ways in which the goals do, in fact, lead to the creation of specific substructures. It also would be useful to be able to show why other substructures could not meet the same needs. A legitimate teleology would be able to define and demonstrate *empirically* and *theoretically* the links between society's goals and the various substructures that exist within society. An illegitimate teleology would be satisfied with a blind assertion that a link between a societal end and a specific substructure must exist.

The other major criticism of the logic of structural functionalism is that it is tautological. A *tautological* argument is one in which the conclusion merely makes explicit what is implicit in the premise or is simply a restatement of the premise. In structural functionalism, this circular reasoning often takes the form of defining the whole in terms of its parts and then defining the parts in terms of the whole. Thus, it would be argued that a social system is defined by the relationship among its component parts and that the component parts of the system are defined by their place in the larger social system. Because each is defined in terms of the other, neither the social system nor its parts are in fact defined at all. We really learn nothing about either the system or its parts.

Systems Theory[12]

Though there are a number of sociologists who have worked in the area of systems theory (see, for example, Bailey, 1990, 1994, 1997, 2001; Ball, 1978; Buckley, 1967), the most prominent is Niklas Luhmann (1927–1998) (Nollman, 2005a; Rogowski, 2007, Stichweh, 2011). Luhmann (1982, 1984/1995, 1987, 1997/2012) developed a

---

[12] This is an adaptation of a section that was originally co-authored by Douglas Goodman and Matthias Junge.

sociological approach that combined elements of Parsons's structural functionalism with general systems theory. General systems theory is an interdisciplinary research area that traces its roots to the 1960s (Bailey, 2005). It draws on fields such as biology, cognitive psychology, organizational theory, computer science and information theory (cybernetics), phenomenology (Paul, 2001) and sociology (among others). It assumes that phenomena as diverse as biological organisms, ecosystems, human cognition, and information processing can all be treated as systems that operate according to a shared set of principles. Recently, systems theory has been taken up by scholars in the human sciences who are interested in fusing insights from the natural sciences with poststructuralist thought (Rasch, 2000; Wolfe, 2000). Luhmann has served as a bridge between these two presumably distinct scholarly fields.

Luhmann saw Parsons's later ideas as the only general theory complex enough to form the basis for a new sociological approach that could incorporate the latest findings in biological and cybernetic systems. Like Parsons, Luhmann studied social systems as functionally differentiated units. However in his reliance on systems theory, Luhmann presents a much more dynamic conception of social systems, their formation and evolution. In particular, Luhmann moves beyond Parsons in two ways. First, Luhmann adds the concept of *self-reference*. Self-reference is society's ability to take itself as an object of analysis and action. According to Luhmann, self-reference is central to our understanding of society as a system. Societies are systems insofar as they work on themselves. Second, Luhmann relies upon the concept of *contingency*. Contingency refers to the idea that social systems do not possess universal and everlasting structures and functions. Instead, system organization is a limited-term accomplishment. Systems change and evolve as demanded by their relationships with an external environment. As a result, Parsons cannot adequately analyze modern society as it is because he does not see that it could be otherwise. To take one example from Parsons's work, the AGIL scheme should not be seen as a fact, but instead as a model of possibilities. The AGIL scheme shows that the adaptive and the goal attainment subsystems can be related in various ways; therefore the aim of analysis should be to understand why the system produced a particular relationship between these two subsystems at any given time. Luhmann addresses these two problems in Parsons's work by developing a theory that takes self-reference as central to systems and that focuses on contingency, the fact that things could be different.

As a sociologist, Luhmann's most important contribution to systems theory is his analysis of social systems. In this review, we describe three concepts that are of central importance to Luhmann's analysis of the social system: the distinction between the system and environment, autopoiesis, and differentiation. In brief, the theory argues that social systems bring themselves into existence when they differentiate themselves from their surrounding environment and then generate further divisions within themselves.

System and Environment

The key to understanding what Luhmann means by a system can be found in the distinction between a system and its environment. Every system is situated in an environment and a system is separated from its environment by a boundary. An example of a boundary is the distinction between a human body and the world around it. The human body is a system situated in an environment that contains, among other things, other people and objects. Another example of a boundary is the distinction between a nation-state, such as the United States, and the surrounding nation-states to which it relates. The United States is the system and the collection of other nations is the environment for that system.

Central to Luhmann's definition of system is the concept of *complexity*. The world is complex, meaning that it is filled with numerous incalculable possibilities for action and interaction. In fact, the world is so complex that unless human beings find ways to manage complexity they will be overwhelmed by the world. With this in mind, Luhmann says that systems, in particular social systems, emerge when they are able to reduce the complexity of the world. This reduction of complexity—making the world simpler than it actually is—creates the distinction between a system and its environment. The system is always less complex than its environment. In other words, by putting up boundaries, by ignoring parts of the environment, the system carves out a unique place for itself in the environment. For example, while a country such as the United States might be concerned with the foreign policy of a nation like China, it is not necessarily concerned with the way that art is made and produced in China. The United States reduces the complexity of its environment by focusing on some aspects of the environment (foreign policy) and not others (art production).

Another way that Luhmann deals with this is to say that the system *selects* the components of its environment with which it will relate. It chooses to interact with Chinese foreign policy rather than the field of art production. In so doing the system defines its limits and boundaries. This kind of selection has implications for the system. By ignoring parts of the environment it may put itself at *risk* (1986/1989, 1991). Events may occur in parts of the environment that the system has ignored and that later will threaten its functionality. This said, what should also be clear is that the system is attuned to such environmental risks and when risks become too much of a threat, a system can reorganize itself. To use an evolutionary language, the system is able to adapt to changes in its environment.

Autopoiesis

Luhmann is best known for his thinking on *autopoiesis*.[13] He borrows the concept from the biologists Humberto Maturana and Francisco Varela (1980). Autopoiesis has been used to refer to a diversity of systems from biological cells to the entire world system and Luhmann uses it to refer to systems such as the economy (1988), the political system, the legal system (1993), the scientific system (1990), and bureaucracies, among others. The word is derived from classical Greek: "poiesis" refers to the act of making, and "auto" refers to the self. As such, autopoiesis means that systems are self-making or, more broadly, self-generating, or self-organizing. There is no superentity outside of a system that determines the development and evolution of a system. In other words, the system is ultimately responsible for its own organization

---

[13] On the significance of this concept, see Zinn (2007b) and K. Bailey (1998).

and development. In the previous discussion, we have described the most basic sense in which systems are autopoietic. They come into existence when they make a distinction between themselves and their environment. The system in effect creates itself when it draws a boundary between itself and the rest of the world.

Luhmann's focus on autopoiesis implies a number of related features of social systems. As self-making entities social systems are *self-referential* (Esposito, 1996). Another way of saying this is that systems are self-monitoring; they operate on the basis of feedback mechanisms. The system creates structures, and then the system constantly "checks in" on itself and its structures to ensure that they are functioning properly. Other theorists, such as Harold Garfinkel (Chapter 10) and Anthony Giddens (Chapter 13) call this self-monitoring feature *reflexivity*. So systems generate structures, and they develop mechanisms by which they can monitor structures. Luhmann also says that systems create the *elements* that make up the system. Elements are the building blocks of a system. For example, many social systems distinguish between institutions such as religion and politics. These institutions are made up of various elements. In religious institutions, elements include things like sacred objects, rituals, and belief systems. Each of these elements is required for the continued existence of the religious institution.

Finally, Luhmann says that autopoietic systems are closed systems. This means that there is no direct connection between a system and its environment. Instead, a system deals with its representations of the environment. Even though this sounds like a difficult idea, it is no more than an extension of what we have already said about systems theory. Systems are always less complex than their environment. However, the simplification of complexity is not immediately given to the system. It does not just happen that a system becomes simpler than its environment. Instead there must be some kind of mechanism through which simplification is achieved. When talking about social systems, the mechanisms by which environments are made less complex are representational or communicational. In words, images, thoughts, diagrams, symbols, and so on, the system re-presents, or presents differently, to itself an otherwise overwhelmingly complex environment. In short, the system brings itself into existence when it paints a simplified picture of the environment, or what matters in the environment, for itself.

The important point in all of this is not only that the system generates its own structures and elements. In addition, autopoesis means that the system must constantly create and re-create itself. This is what distinguishes Luhmann from previous structural-functional scholars like Talcott Parsons. These earlier functionalists took for granted the existence of social structures; certain kinds of structures were universal and ever-present. But Luhmann argues that the makeup of an autopoietic system is never given or guaranteed. It must constantly be created. This is very similar to the ethnomethodological idea (see Chapter 10) that social life is an ongoing accomplishment of its members. In their actions and activities people, and on a larger scale social systems, are constantly making up the structures within which they live. On the one hand, this means that the creation of a social system is an extraordinary and, Luhmann even suggests, unlikely achievement. On the other hand, this means that social systems are also quite adaptive. Since they are always making their structures and elements, they can also remake these elements in ways that respond to changes and demands of the environment.

Differentiation

From what we have already said it should be clear that differentiation is a key concept in Luhmann's systems theory. Luhmann argues that differentiation is the principal feature of modern society. It is the means by which a system deals with the complexity of its environment (Rasch, 2000; Vanderstraeten, 2005). Luhmann defines differentiation as the "replication, within a system of the difference between a system and its environment" (Luhmann, 1982:230). The system comes into existence when it is able to describe the difference between itself and its environment and then organize itself around that distinction. For our purposes we can say that differentiation refers to the process by which systems make distinctions.

In Luhmann's theory there are two basic kinds of distinctions, two general forms of differentiation. The first is the distinction between the system and its environment. The second is the distinctions that a system makes within itself, internal distinctions. In other words, once a system has distinguished itself from its environment it proceeds to develop subsystems. Over time, systems can become increasingly complex, meaning that they are characterized by a growing number of internal distinctions. This growth in internal complexity makes a system incredibly rich and dynamic.

Perhaps the most practical aspect of Luhmann's social systems theory is his description of the different forms of internal differentiation. There are at least four ways that social systems are divided and organized—segmentation, stratification, center-periphery, and functional differentiation.

Segmentary Differentiation

Segmentary differentiation divides parts of the system on the basis of the need to fulfill identical functions over and over. For instance, an automobile manufacturer has functionally similar factories for the production of cars at many different locations. Every location is organized in much the same way; each has the same structure and fulfills the same function—producing cars.

Stratificatory Differentiation

Stratificatory differentiation is a vertical differentiation according to rank or status. This kind of differentiation is hierarchical. Every rank fulfills a particular and distinct function in the system. In the automobile firm, we find different ranks. The manager of the new department of international relations occupies the top rank within the hierarchy of that department. The manager has the function of using power to direct the operations of that department. A variety of lower-ranking workers within the department handle a variety of specific functions (e.g., word processing).

Center-Periphery Differentiation

The third type of differentiation, *center-periphery differentiation*, is a link between segmentary and stratificatory differentiation. It refers to a component within the system that coordinates relations between elements in the periphery with those in the center. For instance, some automobile firms have built factories in other countries; nevertheless, the headquarters of the company remains the center, ruling and, to some extent, controlling the peripheral factories.

Differentiations of Functional Systems

Functional differentiation is the most complex form of differentiation and the form that dominates modern society. Every function within a system is ascribed to a particular unit. For instance, an automobile manufacturer has functionally differentiated departments such as production, administration, accounting, planning, and personnel.

Functional differentiation is more flexible than stratificatory differentiation, but, if one system fails to fulfill its task, the whole system will have great trouble surviving. However, as long as each unit fulfills its function, the different units can attain a high degree of independence. In fact, functionally differentiated systems are a complex mixture of interdependence and independence. For instance, although the planning division is dependent upon the accounting division for economic data, as long as the figures are accurate, the planning division can be blissfully ignorant of exactly how the accountants produced the data.

This indicates a further difference between the forms of differentiation. In the case of segmentary differentiation, if a segment fails to fulfill its function (e.g., one of the automobile manufacturer's factories cannot produce cars because of a labor strike), it does not threaten the system. However, in the case of the more complex forms of differentiation such as functional differentiation, failure will cause a problem for the social system, possibly leading to its breakdown. On the one hand, the growth of complexity increases the abilities of a system to deal with its environment. On the other hand, complexity increases the risk of a system breakdown if a function is not properly fulfilled. In most cases, this increased vulnerability is a necessary price to pay for the increase in possible relations between different subsystems. Having more types of possible relations between the subsystems means more variation to use to select structural responses to changes in the environment.

Conflict Theory

Conflict theory can be seen as a development that took place, at least in part, in reaction to structural functionalism and as a result of many of the criticisms discussed earlier. However, it should be noted that conflict theory has various other roots, such as Marxian and Weberian theory and Simmel's work on social conflict (Sanderson, 2007; J. Turner, 2005). In the 1950s and 1960s, conflict theory provided an alternative to structural functionalism, but it was superseded by a variety of neo-Marxian theories (see Chapter 8). Indeed, one of the major contributions of conflict theory was the way it laid the groundwork for theories more faithful to Marx's work, theories that came to attract a wide audience in sociology. The basic problem with conflict theory is that it never succeeded in divorcing itself sufficiently from its structural-functional roots. It was more a kind of structural functionalism turned on its head than a truly critical theory of society.

The Work of Ralf Dahrendorf

Like functionalists, conflict theorists are oriented toward the study of social structures and institutions. In the main, this theory is little more than a series of contentions that are often the direct opposites of functionalist positions. This antithesis is best exemplified by the work of Ralf Dahrendorf (1958, 1959; see also Strasser and Nollman, 2005), in which the tenets of conflict and functional theory are juxtaposed. To the functionalists, society is static or, at best, in a state of moving equilibrium, but to Dahrendorf and the conflict theorists, every society at every point is subject to processes of change. Where functionalists emphasize the orderliness of society, conflict theorists see dissension and conflict at every point in the social system. Functionalists (or at least early functionalists) argue that every element in society contributes to stability; the exponents of conflict theory see many societal elements as contributing to disintegration and change.

Functionalists tend to see society as being held together informally by norms, values, and a common morality. Conflict theorists see whatever order there is in society as stemming from the coercion of some members by those at the top. Where functionalists focus on the cohesion created by shared societal values, conflict theorists emphasize the role of power in maintaining order in society.

Dahrendorf (1959, 1968) is the major exponent of the position that society has two faces (conflict and consensus) and that sociological theory therefore should be divided into two parts, conflict theory and consensus theory. Consensus theorists should examine value integration in society, and conflict theorists should examine conflicts of interest and the coercion that holds society together in the face of these stresses. Dahrendorf recognized that society could not exist without both conflict and consensus, which are prerequisites for each other. Thus, we cannot have conflict unless there is some prior consensus. For example, French housewives are highly unlikely to conflict with Chilean chess players because there is no contact between them, no prior integration to serve as a basis for a conflict. Conversely, conflict can lead to consensus and integration. An example is the alliance between the United States and Japan that developed after World War II.

Despite the interrelationship between consensus and conflict, Dahrendorf was not optimistic about developing a single sociological theory encompassing both processes: "It seems at least conceivable that unification of theory is not feasible at a point which has puzzled thinkers ever since the beginning of Western philosophy" (1959:164). Eschewing a singular theory, Dahrendorf set out to construct a conflict theory of society.[14]

Dahrendorf began with, and was heavily influenced by, structural functionalism. He noted that to the functionalist, the social system is held together by voluntary cooperation or general consensus or both. However, to the conflict (or coercion) theorist, society is held together by "enforced constraint"; thus, some positions in society are delegated power and authority over others. This fact of social life led Dahrendorf to his central thesis that the differential distribution of authority "invariably becomes the determining factor of systematic social conflicts" (1959:165).

Authority

Dahrendorf concentrated on larger social structures.[15] Central to his thesis is the idea that various positions within society have different amounts of authority. Authority does not reside in individuals but in positions. Dahrendorf was interested not only in

---

[14] Dahrendorf called conflict and coercion "the ugly face of society" (1959:164). We can ponder whether a person who regards them as "ugly" can develop an adequate theory of conflict and coercion.

[15] In his other work, Dahrendorf (1968) continued to focus on social facts (for example, positions and roles), but he also manifested a concern for the dangers of reification endemic to such an approach.

the structure of these positions but also in the conflict among them: "The *structural* origin of such conflicts must be sought in the arrangement of social roles endowed with expectations of domination or subjection" (1959:165; italics added). The first task of conflict analysis, to Dahrendorf, was to identify various authority roles within society. In addition to making the case for the study of large-scale structures such as authority roles, Dahrendorf was opposed to those who focus on the individual level. For example, he was critical of those who focus on the psychological or behavioral characteristics of the individuals who occupy such positions. He went so far as to say that those who adopted such an approach were not sociologists.

The authority attached to positions is the key element in Dahrendorf's analysis. Authority always implies both superordination and subordination. Those who occupy positions of authority are expected to control subordinates; that is, they dominate because of the expectations of those who surround them, not because of their own psychological characteristics. Like authority, these expectations are attached to positions, not people. Authority is not a generalized social phenomenon; those who are subject to control, as well as permissible spheres of control, are specified in society. Finally, because authority is legitimate, sanctions can be brought to bear against those who do not comply.

Authority is not a constant as far as Dahrendorf was concerned, because authority resides in positions, not in persons. Thus, a person of authority in one setting does not necessarily hold a position of authority in another setting. Similarly, a person in a subordinate position in one group may be in a superordinate position in another. This follows from Dahrendorf's argument that society is composed of a number of units that he called *imperatively coordinated associations*. These may be seen as associations of people controlled by a hierarchy of authority positions. Since society contains many such associations, an individual can occupy a position of authority in one and a subordinate position in another.

Authority within each association is dichotomous; thus two, and only two, conflict groups can be formed within any association. Those in positions of authority and those in positions of subordination hold certain interests that are "contradictory in substance and direction." Here we encounter another key term in Dahrendorf's theory of conflict—*interests*. Groups on top and at the bottom are defined by common interests. Dahrendorf continued to be firm in his thinking that even these interests, which sound so psychological, are basically large-scale phenomena:

> For purposes of the sociological analysis of conflict groups and group conflicts, it is necessary to assume certain *structurally generated* orientations of the actions of incumbents of defined *positions*. By analogy to conscious ("subjective") orientations of action, it appears justifiable to describe these as interests. . . . The assumption of "objective" interests associated with social positions has *no psychological implications* or ramifications; it belongs to the level of sociological analysis proper.
>
> (Dahrendorf, 1959:175; italics added)

Within every association, those in dominant positions seek to maintain the status quo while those in subordinate positions seek change. A conflict of interest within any association is at least latent at all times, which means that the legitimacy of authority is *always* precarious. This conflict of interest need not be conscious in order for superordinates or subordinates to act. The interests of superordinates and subordinates are objective in the sense that they are reflected in the expectations (roles) attached to positions. Individuals do not have to internalize these expectations or even be conscious of them in order to act in accord with them. If they occupy given positions, they will behave in the expected manner. Individuals are "adjusted" or "adapted" to their roles when they contribute to conflict between superordinates and subordinates. Dahrendorf called these unconscious role expectations *latent interests. Manifest interests* are latent interests that have become conscious. Dahrendorf saw the analysis of the connection between latent and manifest interests as a major task of conflict theory. Nevertheless, actors need not be conscious of their interests in order to act in accord with them.

Groups, Conflict, and Change

Next, Dahrendorf distinguished three broad types of groups. The first is the *quasi group,* or "aggregates of incumbents of positions with identical role interests" (Dahrendorf, 1959:180). These are the recruiting grounds for the second type of group—*the interest group.* Dahrendorf described the two groups:

> Common modes of behavior are characteristic of *interest groups* recruited from larger quasi-groups. Interest groups are groups in the strict sense of the sociological term; and they are the real agents of group conflict. They have a structure, a form of organization, a program or goal, and a personnel of members.
>
> (Dahrendorf, 1959:180)

Out of all the many interest groups emerge *conflict groups,* or those that actually engage in group conflict.

Dahrendorf felt that the concepts of latent and manifest interests, of quasi groups, interest groups, and conflict groups, were basic to an explanation of social conflict. Under *ideal* conditions no other variables would be needed. However, because conditions are never ideal, many different factors do intervene in the process. Dahrendorf mentioned technical conditions such as adequate personnel, political conditions such as the overall political climate, and social conditions such as the existence of communication links. The way people are recruited into the quasi group was another social condition important to Dahrendorf. He felt that if the recruitment is random and is determined by chance, an interest group, and ultimately a conflict group, is unlikely to emerge. In contrast to Marx, Dahrendorf did not feel that the *lumpenproletariat*[16] would ultimately form a conflict group, because people are recruited to it by chance. However, when recruitment to quasi groups is structurally determined, these groups provide fertile recruiting grounds for interest groups and, in some cases, conflict groups.

The final aspect of Dahrendorf's conflict theory is the relationship of conflict to change. Here Dahrendorf recognized the importance of Lewis Coser's work (see the next section), which focused on the functions of conflict in maintaining the

---

[16] This is Marx's term for the mass of people at the bottom of the economic system, those who stand below even the proletariat.

status quo. Dahrendorf felt, however, that the conservative function of conflict is only one part of social reality; conflict also leads to change and development.

Briefly, Dahrendorf argued that once conflict groups emerge, they engage in actions that lead to changes in social structure. When the conflict is intense, the changes that occur are radical. When it is accompanied by violence, structural change will be sudden. Whatever the nature of conflict, sociologists must be attuned to the relationship between conflict and change as well as that between conflict and the status quo.

The Major Criticisms and Efforts to Deal with Them

Conflict theory has been criticized on a variety of grounds. For example, it has been attacked for ignoring order and stability, whereas structural functionalism has been criticized for ignoring conflict and change. Conflict theory has also been criticized for being ideologically radical, whereas functionalism was criticized for its conservative ideology. In comparison to structural functionalism, conflict theory is rather underdeveloped. It is not nearly as sophisticated as functionalism, perhaps because it is a more derivative theory.

Dahrendorf's conflict theory has been subjected to a number of critical analyses (for example, Hazelrigg, 1972; J. Turner, 1973; Weingart, 1969), including some critical reflections by Dahrendorf (1968) himself. First, Dahrendorf's model is not as clear a reflection of Marxian ideas as he claimed. Second, as has been noted, conflict theory has more in common with structural functionalism than with Marxian theory. Dahrendorf's emphasis on such things as systems (imperatively coordinated associations), positions, and roles links him directly to structural functionalism. As a result, his theory suffers from many of the same inadequacies as structural functionalism. For example, conflict seems to emerge mysteriously from legitimate systems (just as it does in structural functionalism). Further, conflict theory seems to suffer from many of the same conceptual and logical problems (for example, vague concepts, tautologies) as structural functionalism (J. Turner, 1975, 1982). Finally, like structural functionalism, conflict theory is almost wholly macroscopic and as a result has little to offer to our understanding of individual thought and action.

Both functionalism and Dahrendorf's conflict theory are inadequate because each is itself useful for explaining only a *portion* of social life. Sociology must be able to explain order as well as conflict, structure as well as change. This has motivated several efforts to reconcile conflict and functional theory. Although none has been totally satisfactory, these efforts suggest at least some agreement among sociologists that what is needed is a theory explaining *both* consensus and dissension.

The criticisms of conflict theory and structural functionalism, as well as the inherent limitations in each, led to many efforts to cope with the problems by reconciling or integrating the two theories (K. Bailey, 1997; Chapin, 1994; Himes, 1966; van den Berghe, 1963). The assumption was that some combination of the two theories would be more powerful than either one alone. The best known of these works was Lewis Coser's *The Functions of Social Conflict* (1956).

The early seminal work on the functions of social conflict was done by Georg Simmel, but it has been expanded by Coser (Delaney, 2005a; Jaworski, 1991), who argued that conflict may serve to solidify a loosely structured group. In a society that seems to be disintegrating, conflict with another society may restore the integrative core. The cohesiveness of Israeli Jews might be attributed, at least in part, to the long-standing conflict with the Arab nations in the Middle East. The possible end of the conflict might well exacerbate underlying strains in Israeli society. Conflict as an agent for solidifying a society is an idea that has long been recognized by propagandists, who may construct an enemy where none exists or seek to fan antagonisms toward an inactive opponent.

Conflict with one group may serve to produce cohesion by leading to a series of alliances with other groups. For example, conflict with the Arabs has led to an alliance between the United States and Israel. Lessening of the Israeli-Arab conflict might weaken the bonds between Israel and the United States.

Within a society, conflict can bring some ordinarily isolated individuals into an active role. The protests over the Vietnam War motivated many young people to take vigorous roles in American political life for the first time. With the end of that conflict, a more apathetic spirit emerged again among American youth.

Conflict also serves a communication function. Prior to conflict, groups may be unsure of their adversary's position, but as a result of conflict, positions and boundaries between groups often become clarified. Individuals therefore are better able to decide on a proper course of action in relation to their adversary. Conflict also allows the parties to get a better idea of their relative strengths and may well increase the possibility of rapprochement, or peaceful accommodation.

From a theoretical perspective, it is possible to wed functionalism and conflict theory by looking at the functions of social conflict. Still, it must be recognized that conflict also has dysfunctions.

While a number of theorists sought to integrate conflict theory with structural functionalism, others wanted no part of conflict theory (or structural functionalism). For example, the Marxist Andrè Gunder Frank (1966/1974) rejected conflict theory because it represented an inadequate form of Marxian theory. Although conflict theory has some Marxian elements, it is not the true heir of Marx's original theory. In the next chapter we examine an array of theories that are more legitimate heirs. Before we do, however, we must deal with a more successfully integrative type of conflict theory.

A More Integrative Conflict Theory

Randall Collins's *Conflict Sociology* (1975; Rossel and Collins, 2001) moved in a much more micro-oriented direction than the macro conflict theory of Dahrendorf and others. Collins says of his early work, "My own main contribution to conflict theory . . . was to add a micro level to these macro-level theories. I especially tried to show that stratification and organization are grounded in the interactions of everyday life" (1990:72).[17]

---

[17] Collins also stresses that conflict theory, more than other sociological theories, has been open to the integration of the findings of empirical research.

Collins made it clear that his focus on conflict would not be ideological; that is, he did not begin with the political view that conflict is either good or bad. Rather, he claimed, he chose conflict as a focus on the realistic ground that conflict is a—perhaps *the*—central process in social life.

Unlike others who started, and stayed, at the societal level, Collins approached conflict from an individual point of view because his theoretical roots lie in phenomenology and ethnomethodology. Despite his preference for individual-level and small-scale theories, Collins was aware that "sociology cannot be successful on the microlevel alone" (1975:11); conflict theory cannot do without the societal level of analysis. However, whereas most conflict theorists believed that social structures are external to, and coercive of, the actor, Collins saw social structures as inseparable from the actors who construct them and whose interaction patterns are their essence. Collins was inclined to see social structures as interaction patterns rather than as external and coercive entities. In addition, whereas most conflict theorists saw the actor as constrained by external forces, Collins viewed the actor as constantly creating and re-creating social organization.

Collins saw Marxian theory as the "starting point" for conflict theory, but it is, in his view, laden with problems. For one thing, he saw it (like structural functionalism) as heavily ideological, a characteristic he wanted to avoid. For another, he tended to see Marx's orientation as reducible to an analysis of the economic domain, although this is an unwarranted criticism of Marx's theory. Actually, although Collins invoked Marx frequently, his conflict theory shows relatively little Marxian influence. It is far more influenced by Weber, Durkheim, and above all phenomenology and ethnomethodology.

Social Stratification

Collins chose to focus on social stratification because it is an institution that touches so many features of life, including "wealth, politics, careers, families, clubs, communities, lifestyles" (1975:49). In Collins's view, the great theories of stratification are "failures." He criticized Marxian theory as "a monocausal explanation for a multicausal world" (R. Collins, 1975:49). He viewed Weber's theory as little more than an "anti-system" with which to view the features of the two great theories. Weber's work was of some use to Collins, but "the efforts of phenomenological sociology to ground all concepts in the observables of every life" (R. Collins, 1975:53) were the most important to him because his major focus in the study of social stratification was small-scale, not large-scale. In his view, social stratification, like all other social structures, is reducible to people in everyday life encountering each other in patterned ways.

Despite his ultimate commitment to a microsociology of stratification, Collins began (even though he had some reservations about them) with the large-scale theories of Marx and Weber as underpinnings for his work. He started with Marxian principles, arguing that they, "with certain modifications, provide the basis for a conflict theory of stratification" (R. Collins, 1975:58).

First, Collins contended that it was Marx's view that the material conditions involved in earning a living in modern society are the major determinants of a person's lifestyle. The basis of earning a living for Marx is a person's relationship to private property. Those who own or control property are able to earn their livings in a much more satisfactory way than are those who do not and who must sell their labor time to gain access to the means of production.

Second, from a Marxian perspective, material conditions affect not only how individuals earn a living but also the nature of social groups in the different social classes. The dominant social class is better able to develop more coherent social groups, tied together by intricate communication networks, than is the subordinate social class.

Finally, Collins argued that Marx also pointed out the vast differences among the social classes in their access to, and control over, the cultural system. That is, the upper social classes are able to develop highly articulated symbol and ideological systems, systems that they often are able to impose on the lower social classes. The lower social classes have less-developed symbol systems, many of which are likely to have been imposed on them by those in power.

Collins viewed Weber as working within and developing further Marx's theory of stratification. For one thing, Weber was said to have recognized the existence of different forms of conflict that lead to a multifaceted stratification system (for example, class, status, and power). For another, Weber developed the theory of organizations to a high degree, which Collins saw as still another arena of conflict of interest. Weber was also important to Collins for his emphasis on the state as the agency that controls the means of violence, which shifted attention from conflict over the economy (means of production) to conflict over the state. Finally, Weber was recognized by Collins for his understanding of the social arena of emotional products, particularly religion. Conflict clearly can occur in this arena, and these emotional products, like other products, can be used as weapons in social conflict.

A Conflict Theory of Stratification   With this background, Collins turned to his own conflict approach to stratification, which has more in common with phenomenological and ethnomethodological theories than with Marxian or Weberian theory. Collins opened with several assumptions. People are seen as inherently sociable but also as particularly conflict-prone in their social relations. Conflict is likely to occur in social relations because "violent coercion" can always be used by one person or many people in an interaction setting. Collins believed that people seek to maximize their "subjective status" and that their ability to do this depends on their resources as well as the resources of those with whom they are dealing. He saw people as self-interested; thus, clashes are possible because sets of interests may be inherently antagonistic.

This conflict approach to stratification can be reduced to three basic principles. First, Collins believed that people live in self-constructed subjective worlds. Second, other people may have the power to affect, or even control, an individual's subjective experience. Third, other people frequently try to control the individual, who opposes them. The result is likely to be interpersonal conflict.

On the basis of this approach, Collins developed five principles of conflict analysis that he applied to social stratification, although he believed that they could be applied to any area of social life. First, Collins believed that conflict theory must focus on real life rather than on abstract formulations. This belief seems to reflect a preference for a Marxian-style material analysis over the abstraction of structural functionalism. Collins urged us to think of people as animals whose actions, motivated by self-interest, can be seen as maneuvers to obtain various advantages so that they can achieve satisfaction and avoid dissatisfaction. However, unlike exchange and rational choice theorists, Collins did not see people as wholly rational. He recognized that they are vulnerable to emotional appeals in their efforts to find satisfaction.

Second, Collins believed that a conflict theory of stratification must examine the material arrangements that affect interaction. Although the actors are likely to be affected by material factors such as "the physical places, the modes of communication, the supply of weapons, devices for staging one's public impression, tools, goods" (R. Collins, 1975:60), not all actors are affected in the same way. A major variable is the resources that the different actors possess. Actors with considerable material resources can resist or even modify these material constraints, whereas those with fewer resources are more likely to have their thoughts and actions determined by their material setting.

Third, Collins argued that in a situation of inequality, those groups that control resources are likely to try to exploit those that lack resources. He was careful to point out that such exploitation need not involve conscious calculation on the part of those who gain from the situation; rather, the exploiters are merely pursuing what they perceive to be their best interests. In the process they may be taking advantage of those who lack resources.

Fourth, Collins wanted the conflict theorist to look at such cultural phenomena as beliefs and ideals from the point of view of interests, resources, and power. It is likely that those groups with resources and, therefore, power can impose their idea systems on the entire society; those without resources have an idea system imposed on them.

Finally, Collins made a firm commitment to the scientific study of stratification and every other aspect of the social world. Thus, he prescribed several things: Sociologists should not simply theorize about stratification but should study it empirically, if possible, in a comparative way. Hypotheses should be formulated and tested empirically through comparative studies. Last, the sociologist should look for the causes of social phenomena, particularly the multiple causes of any form of social behavior.

This kind of scientific commitment led Collins to develop a wide array of propositions about the relationship between conflict and various specific aspects of social life. We can present only a few here, but they should allow readers to get a feel for Collins's type of conflict sociology.

> **1.0** Experiences of giving and taking orders are the main determinants of individual outlooks and behaviors.
>
> **1.1** The more one gives orders, the more he is proud, self-assured, formal, and identifies with organizational ideals in whose names he justifies the orders.
>
> **1.2** The more one takes orders, the more he is subservient, fatalistic, alienated from organizational ideals, externally conforming, distrustful of others, concerned with extrinsic rewards, and amoral.
>
> (R. Collins, 1975:73–74)

Among other things, these propositions all reflect Collins's commitment to the *scientific study* of the small-scale social manifestations of social conflicts.

Other Social Domains

Collins was not content to deal with conflict within the stratification system but sought to extend it to various other social domains. For example, he extended his analysis of stratification to relationships between the sexes as well as among age groups. He took the view that the family is an arena of sexual conflict, in which males have been the victors, with the result that women are dominated by men and are subject to various kinds of unequal treatment. Similarly, he saw the relationship between age groups—in particular, between young and old—as one of conflict. This idea contrasts with the view of structural functionalists, who saw harmonious socialization and internalization in this relationship. Collins looked at the resources possessed by the various age groups. Adults have a variety of resources, including experience, size, strength, and the ability to satisfy the physical needs of the young. In contrast, one of the few resources young children have is physical attractiveness. This means that young children are likely to be dominated by adults. However, as children mature, they acquire more resources and are better able to resist, with the result of increasing social conflict between the generations.

Collins also looked at formal organizations from a conflict perspective. He saw them as networks of interpersonal influences and as the arenas in which conflicting interests are played out. In short, "Organizations are arenas for struggle" (R. Collins, 1975:295). Collins again couched his argument in propositional form. For example, he argued that "coercion leads to strong efforts to avoid being coerced" (R. Collins, 1975:298). In contrast, he felt that the offering of rewards is a preferable strategy: "Control by material rewards leads to compliance to the extent that rewards are directly linked to the desired behavior" (R. Collins, 1975:299). These propositions and others all point to Collins's commitment to a scientific, largely micro-oriented study of conflict.

In sum, Collins is, like Dahrendorf, not a true exponent of Marxian conflict theory, although for different reasons. Although Collins used Marx as a starting point, Weber, Durkheim, and particularly ethnomethodology were much more important influences on his work. Collins's small-scale orientation is a helpful beginning toward the development of a more integrated conflict theory. However, despite his stated intentions of integrating large- and small-scale theory, he did not accomplish that task fully.

Summary

Not too many years ago, structural functionalism was *the* dominant theory in sociology. Conflict theory was its major challenger and was the likely alternative to replace it in that position. However, dramatic changes have taken place in recent years. Both theories have been the subject of intense criticism, whereas a series of alternative theories (to be discussed throughout the rest of this book) have developed that have attracted ever greater interest and ever larger followings.

Although several varieties of structural functionalism exist, the focus here is on societal functionalism and its large-scale focus, its concern with interrelationships at the societal level and with the constraining effects of social structures and institutions on actors. Structural functionalists developed a series of large-scale concerns in social systems, subsystems, relationships among subsystems and systems, equilibrium, and orderly change.

We examine three bodies of work by structural functionalists (Davis and Moore, Parsons, and Merton). Davis and Moore, in one of the best-known and most criticized pieces in the history of sociology, examined social stratification as a social system and the various positive functions it performs. We also discuss in some detail Talcott Parsons's structural-functional theory and his ideas on the four functional imperatives of all action systems—adaptation, goal attainment, integration, and latency (AGIL). We also analyze his structural-functional approach to the four action systems—the social system, cultural system, personality system, and behavioral organism. Finally, we deal with his structural-functional approach to dynamism and social change—his evolutionary theory and his ideas on the generalized media of interchange.

Merton's effort to develop a "paradigm" for functional analysis is the most important single piece in modern structural functionalism. Merton began by criticizing some of the more naive positions of structural functionalism. He then sought to develop a more adequate model of structural-functional analysis. On one point Merton agreed with his predecessors—the need to focus on large-scale social phenomena. But, Merton argued, in addition to focusing on positive functions, structural functionalism should be concerned with dysfunctions and even nonfunctions. Given these additions, Merton urged that analysts concern themselves with the net balance of functions and dysfunctions. Further, he argued, in performing structural-functional analysis, we must move away from global analyses and specify the *levels* on which we are working. Merton also added the idea that structural functionalists should be concerned not only with manifest (intended) but also with latent (unintended) functions. This section concludes with a discussion of Merton's application of his functional paradigm to the issue of the relationship of social structure and culture to anomie and deviance.

Next, we discuss the numerous criticisms of structural functionalism that have succeeded in damaging its credibility and popularity. We discuss the criticisms that structural functionalism is ahistorical, unable to deal with conflict and change, highly conservative, preoccupied with societal constraints on actors, accepting of elite legitimations, teleological, and tautological.

We then discuss what many consider to be the most recent version of structural functionalism—Niklas Luhmann's systems theory. Though Luhmann's theory extends far beyond the assumptions of Parsons's original formulation, systems theory begins with the attempt to study society as a set of functionally differentiated units. Beyond this, systems theory combines insights from biology, cognitive psychology, organizational theory, and sociology, among others. Luhmann sees society as an autopoetic (self-making) system that brings itself into existence when it distinguishes between system and environment. It is within this initial distinction that further functional differentiations can be made.

The last part of this chapter is devoted to the major alternative to structural functionalism in the 1950s and 1960s—conflict theory. The best-known work in this tradition is by Ralf Dahrendorf, who, although he consciously tried to follow the Marxian tradition, is best seen as having inverted structural functionalism. Dahrendorf looked at change rather than equilibrium, conflict rather than order, how the parts of society contribute to change rather than to stability, and conflict and coercion rather than normative constraint. Dahrendorf offered a large-scale theory of conflict that parallels the structural functionalist's large-scale theory of order. His focus on authority, positions, imperatively coordinated associations, interests, quasi groups, interest groups, and conflict groups reflects this orientation. Dahrendorf's theory suffers from some of the same problems as structural functionalism; in addition, it represents a rather impoverished effort to incorporate Marxian theory. Dahrendorf also can be criticized for being satisfied with alternative theories of order and conflict rather than seeking a theoretical integration of the two.

The chapter concludes with a discussion of Randall Collins's effort to develop a more integrative conflict theory, especially one that integrates micro and macro concerns

Varieties of Neo-Marxian Theory

Chapter Outline

Economic Determinism

Hegelian Marxism

Critical Theory

Neo-Marxian Economic Sociology

Historically Oriented Marxism

Neo-Marxian Spatial Analysis

Post-Marxist Theory

In this chapter we deal with a variety of theories that are better reflections of Marx's ideas than are the conflict theories discussed at the close of the preceding chapter. Although each of the theories discussed here is derived from Marx's theory, there are many important differences among them.

Economic Determinism

Marx often sounded like an economic determinist; that is, he seemed to consider the economic system of paramount importance and to argue that it determined all other sectors of society—politics, religion, idea systems, and so forth. Although Marx did see the economic sector as preeminent, at least in capitalist society, as a dialectician he could not have taken a deterministic position, because the dialectic is characterized by the notion that there is continual feedback and mutual interaction among the various sectors of society. Politics, religion, and so on cannot be reduced to epiphenomena determined by the economy because they affect the economy just as they are affected by it. Despite the nature of the dialectic, Marx still is interpreted as an economic determinist. Although some aspects of Marx's work would lead to this conclusion, adopting it means ignoring the overall dialectical thrust of his theory.

Agger (1978) argued that economic determinism reached its peak as an interpretation of Marxian theory during the period of the Second Communist International, between 1889 and 1914. This historical period often is seen as the apex of early market capitalism, and its booms and busts led to many predictions about its imminent demise. Those Marxists who believed in economic determinism saw the breakdown of capitalism as inevitable. In their view, Marxism was capable of producing a scientific theory of this breakdown (as well as other aspects of capitalist society) with the predictive reliability of the physical and natural sciences. All an analyst had to do was examine the structures of capitalism, especially the economic structures. Built into those structures was a series of processes that inevitably would bring down capitalism, and so it was up to the economic determinist to discover how these processes worked.

Friedrich Engels, Marx's collaborator and benefactor, led the way in this interpretation of Marxian theory, as did Karl Kautsky and Eduard Bernstein. Kautsky, for example, discussed the inevitable decline of capitalism as

> unavoidable in the sense that the inventors improve technic and the capitalists in their desire for profit revolutionize the whole economic life, as it is also inevitable that the workers aim for shorter hours of labor and higher wages, that they organize themselves, that they fight the capitalist class and its state, as it is inevitable that they aim for the conquest of political power and the overthrow of capitalist rule. Socialism is inevitable because the class struggle and the victory of the proletariat is inevitable.
>
> (Kautsky, cited in Agger, 1978:94)

The imagery here is of actors impelled by the structures of capitalism into taking a series of actions.

It was this imagery that led to the major criticism of scientifically oriented economic determinism—that it was untrue to the dialectical thrust of Marx's theory. Specifically, the theory seemed to short-circuit the dialectic by making individual thought and action insignificant. The economic structures of capitalism that determined individual thought and action were the crucial element. This interpretation also led to political quietism and therefore was inconsistent with Marx's thinking (Guilhot, 2002). Why should individuals act if the capitalist system was going to crumble under its own structural contradictions? Clearly, given Marx's desire to integrate theory and practice, a perspective that omits action and even reduces it to insignificance would not be in the tradition of his thinking.

Hegelian Marxism

As a result of the criticisms just discussed, economic determinism began to fade in importance, and a number of theorists developed other varieties of Marxian theory. One group of Marxists returned to the Hegelian roots of Marx's theory in search of a subjective orientation to complement the strength of the early Marxists at the objective, material level. The early Hegelian Marxists sought to restore the dialectic between the subjective and the objective aspects of social life. Their interest in subjective factors laid the basis for the later development of critical theory, which came to focus almost exclusively on subjective factors. A number of thinkers (for example, Karl Korsch) could be taken as illustrative of Hegelian Marxism, but we will focus on the work of one who has gained great prominence, Georg Lukács (Aronowitz, 2007; Markus, 2005), especially his book *History and Class Consciousness* (1922/1968). We also pay brief attention to the ideas of Antonio Gramsci.

Georg Lukács

The attention of Marxian scholars of the early twentieth century was limited mainly to Marx's later, largely economic works, such as *Capital* (1867/1967). The early work, especially *The Economic and Philosophic Manuscripts of 1844* (1932/1964), which was more heavily influenced by Hegelian subjectivism, was largely unknown to Marxian thinkers. The rediscovery of the *Manuscripts* and their publication in 1932 was a major turning point. However, by the 1920s Lukács already had written his major work, in which he emphasized the subjective side of Marxian theory. As Martin Jay puts it, "*History and Class Consciousness* anticipated in several fundamental ways the philosophical implications of Marx's *1844 Manuscripts,* whose publication it antedated by almost a decade" (1984:102). Lukács's major contribution to Marxian theory lies in his work on two major ideas—reification (Dahms, 1998) and class consciousness.

Reification

Lukács made it clear from the beginning that he was not totally rejecting the work of the economic Marxists on reification, but simply seeking to broaden and extend their ideas. Lukács commenced with the Marxian concept of commodities, which he characterized as "the central, structural problem of capitalist society" (1922/1968:83). A *commodity* is at base a relation among people that, they come to believe, takes on the character of a thing and develops an objective form. People in their interaction with nature in capitalist society produce various products, or commodities (for example, bread, automobiles, motion pictures). However, people tend to lose sight of the fact that they produce these commodities and give them their value. Value comes to be seen as being produced by a market that is independent of the actors. The *fetishism of commodities* is the process by which commodities and the market for them are granted independent objective existence by the actors in capitalist society. Marx's concept of the fetishism of commodities was the basis for Lukács's concept of reification.

The crucial difference between the fetishism of commodities and reification lies in the extensiveness of the two concepts. Whereas the former is restricted to the economic institution, the latter is applied by Lukács to all of society—the state, the law, *and* the economic sector. The same dynamic applies in all sectors of capitalist society: people come to believe that social structures have a life of their own, and as a result the structures do come to have an objective character. Lukács delineated this process:

> Man in capitalist society confronts a reality "made" by himself (as a class) which appears to him to be a natural phenomenon alien to himself; he is wholly at the mercy of its "laws"; his activity is confined to the exploitation of the inexorable fulfillment of certain individual laws for his own (egoistic) interests. But even while "acting" he remains, in the nature of the case, the object and not the subject of events.
>
> (Lukács, 1922/1968:135)

In developing his ideas on reification, Lukács integrated insights from Weber and Simmel. However, because reification was embedded in Marxian theory, it was seen as a problem limited to capitalism and not, as it was to Weber and Simmel, the inevitable fate of humankind.

Class and False Consciousness

Class consciousness refers to the belief systems shared by those who occupy the same class position within society. Lukács made it clear that class consciousness is neither the sum nor the average of individual consciousnesses; rather, it is a property of a group of people who share a similar place in the productive system. This view leads to a focus on the class consciousness of the bourgeoisie and especially of the proletariat. In Lukács's work, there is a clear link between objective economic position, class consciousness, and the "real, psychological thoughts of men about their lives" (1922/1968:51).

The concept of class consciousness necessarily implies, at least in capitalism, the prior state of *false consciousness.* That is, classes in capitalism generally do not have a clear sense of their true class interests (Kalekin-Fishman, 2008). For example, until the revolutionary stage, members of the proletariat do not fully realize the nature and extent of their exploitation in capitalism. The falsity of class consciousness is derived from the class's position within the economic structure of society: "Class consciousness implies a class-conditioned *unconsciousness* of one's own socio-historical and economic condition. . . . The 'falseness,' the illusion implicit in this situation, is in no sense arbitrary" (Lukács, 1922/1968:52; Starks and Junisbai, 2007). Most social classes throughout history have been unable to overcome false consciousness and thereby achieve class consciousness. The structural position of the proletariat within capitalism, however, gives it the unique ability to achieve class consciousness.

The ability to achieve class consciousness is peculiar to capitalist societies. In precapitalist societies, a variety of factors prevented the development of class consciousness. For one thing, the state, independent of the economy, affected social strata; for another, status (prestige) consciousness tended to mask class (economic) consciousness. As a result, Lukács concluded, "There is therefore no possible position within such a society from which the economic basis of all social relations could be made conscious" (1922/1968:57). In contrast, the economic base of capitalism is clearer and simpler. People may not be conscious of its effects, but they are at least unconsciously aware of them. As a result, "class consciousness arrived at the point where *it could become conscious*" (Lukács, 1922/1968:59). At this stage, society turns into an ideological battleground in which those who seek to conceal the class character of society are pitted against those who seek to expose it.

Lukács compared the various classes in capitalism on the issue of class consciousness. He argued that the petty bourgeoisie and the peasants cannot develop class consciousness because of the ambiguity of their structural position within capitalism. Because these two classes represent vestiges of society in the feudal era, they are not able to develop a clear sense of the nature of capitalism. The bourgeoisie can develop class consciousness, but at best it understands the development of capitalism as something external, subject to objective laws, that it can experience only passively.

The proletariat has the capacity to develop true class consciousness, and as it does, the bourgeoisie is thrown on the defensive. Lukács refused to see the proletariat as simply driven by external forces but viewed it instead as an active creator of its own fate. In the confrontation between the bourgeoisie and the proletariat, the former class has all the intellectual and organizational weapons, whereas all the latter has, at least at first, is the ability to see society for what it is. As the battle proceeds, the proletariat moves from being a "class in itself," that is, a structurally created entity, to a "class for itself," a class conscious of its position and mission (Bottero, 2007). In other words, "the class struggle must be raised from the level of economic necessity to the level of conscious aim and effective class consciousness" (Lukács, 1922/1968:76). When the struggle reaches this point, the proletariat is capable of the action that can overthrow the capitalist system.

Lukács had a rich sociological theory, although it is embedded in Marxian terms. He was concerned with the dialectical relationship among the structures (primarily economic) of capitalism, the idea systems (especially class consciousness), individual thought, and, ultimately, individual action. His theoretical perspective provides an important bridge between the economic determinists and more modern Marxists.

Antonio Gramsci

The Italian Marxist Antonio Gramsci also played a key role in the transition from economic determinism to more modern Marxian positions (Beilharz, 2005b; Davidson, 2007; Salamini, 1981). Gramsci was critical of Marxists who are "deterministic, fatalistic and mechanistic" (1971:336). In fact, he wrote an essay entitled "The Revolution against '*Capital*'" (Gramsci, 1917/1977) in which he celebrated "the resurrection of political will against the economic determinism of those who reduced Marxism to the historical laws of Marx's best-known work [*Capital*]" (Jay, 1984:155). Although he recognized that there were historical regularities, he rejected the idea of automatic or inevitable historical developments. Thus, the masses had to act in order to bring about a social revolution. But to act, the masses had to become conscious of their situation and the nature of the system in which they lived. Thus, although Gramsci recognized the importance of structural factors, especially the economy, he did not believe that these structural factors led the masses to revolt. The masses needed to develop a revolutionary ideology, but they could not do that on their own. Gramsci operated with a rather elitist conception in which ideas were generated by intellectuals and then extended to the masses and put into practice by them. The masses could not generate such ideas, and they could experience them, once in existence, only on faith. The masses could not become self-conscious on their own; they needed the help of social elites. However, once the masses had been influenced by these ideas, they would take the actions that lead to social revolution. Gramsci, like Lukács, focused on collective ideas rather than on social structures like the economy, and both operated within traditional Marxian theory.

Gramsci's central concept, one that reflects his Hegelianism, is hegemony (for a contemporary use of the concept of hegemony, see the discussion of the work of Laclau and Mouffe later in this chapter; Abrahamsen, 1997). According to Gramsci, "the essential ingredient of the most modern philosophy of praxis [the linking of thought and action] is the historical-philosophical concept of 'hegemony'" (1932/1975:235). *Hegemony* is defined by Gramsci as cultural leadership exercised by the ruling class. He contrasts hegemony to coercion that is "exercised by legislative or executive powers, or expressed through police intervention" (Gramsci, 1932/1975:235). Whereas economic Marxists tended to emphasize the economy and the coercive aspects of state domination, Gramsci emphasized "'hegemony' and cultural leadership" (1932/1975:235). In an analysis of capitalism, Gramsci wanted to know how some intellectuals, working on behalf of the capitalists, achieved cultural leadership and the assent of the masses.

Not only does the concept of hegemony help us understand domination within capitalism, but it also serves to orient Gramsci's thoughts on revolution. That is, through revolution, it is not enough to gain control of the economy and the state apparatus; it is also necessary to gain cultural leadership over the rest of society. It is here that Gramsci sees a key role for communist intellectuals and a communist party.

We turn now to critical theory, which grew out of the work of Hegelian Marxists such as Lukács and Gramsci and has moved even farther from the traditional Marxian roots of economic determinism.

Critical Theory

Critical theory is the product of a group of German neo-Marxists who were dissatisfied with the state of Marxian theory (J. Bernstein, 1995; Kellner, 1993, 2005c; for a broader view of critical theory, see Agger, 1998), particularly its tendency toward economic determinism. The organization associated with critical theory, the Institute of Social Research, was officially founded in Frankfurt, Germany, on February 23, 1923 (Wheatland, 2009; Wiggershaus, 1994). Critical theory has spread beyond the confines of the Frankfurt school (Calhoun and Karaganis, 2001; Kellner, 2005c; Langman, 2007; *Telos,* 1989–1990). Critical theory was and is largely a European orientation, although its influence in American sociology has grown (Marcus, 1999; van den Berg, 1980).

The Major Critiques of Social and Intellectual Life

Critical theory is composed largely of criticisms of various aspects of social and intellectual life, but its ultimate goal is to reveal more accurately the nature of society (Bleich, 1977).

Criticisms of Marxian Theory

Critical theory takes as its starting point a critique of Marxian theories. The critical theorists are most disturbed by the economic determinists—the mechanistic, or mechanical, Marxists (Antonio, 1981; Schroyer, 1973; Sewart, 1978). Some (for example, Habermas, 1971) criticize the determinism implicit in parts of Marx's original work, but most focus their criticisms on the neo-Marxists, primarily because they had interpreted Marx's work too mechanistically. The critical theorists do not say that economic determinists were wrong in focusing on the economic realm but that they should have been concerned with other aspects of social life as well. As we will see, the critical school seeks to rectify this imbalance by focusing its attention on the cultural realm (Fuery and Mansfield, 2000; Schroyer, 1973:33). In addition to attacking other Marxian theories, the critical school critiqued societies, such as the former Soviet Union, built ostensibly on Marxian theory (Marcuse, 1958).

Criticisms of Positivism

Critical theorists also focus on the philosophical underpinnings of scientific inquiry, especially positivism (Bottomore, 1984; Fuller, 2007a; Halfpenny, 2001, 2005; Morrow, 1994). The criticism of positivism is related, at least in part, to the criticism of economic determinism, because some of those who were determinists accepted part or all of the positivistic theory of knowledge. Positivism is depicted as accepting the idea that a single scientific method is applicable to all fields of study. It takes the physical sciences as the standard of certainty and exactness for all disciplines. Positivists believe that knowledge is inherently neutral. They feel that they can keep human values out of their work. This belief, in turn, leads to the view that science is not in the position of advocating any specific form of social action. (See Chapter 1 for more discussion of positivism.)

Positivism is opposed by the critical school on various grounds (Sewart, 1978). For one thing, positivism tends to reify the social world and see it as a natural process. The critical theorists prefer to focus on human activity as well as on the ways in which such activity affects larger social structures. In short, positivism loses sight of the actors (Habermas, 1971), reducing them to passive entities determined by "natural forces." Given their belief in the distinctiveness of the actor, the critical theorists would not accept the idea that the general laws of science can be applied without question to human action. Positivism is assailed for being content to judge the adequacy of means toward given ends and for not making a similar judgment about ends. This critique leads to the view that positivism is inherently conservative, incapable of challenging the existing system. As Martin Jay says of positivism, "The result was the absolutizing of 'facts' and the reification of the existing order" (1973:62). Positivism leads the actor and the social scientist to passivity. Few Marxists of any type would support a perspective that does not relate theory and practice. Despite these criticisms of positivism, some Marxists (for example, some structuralists, analytic Marxists) espouse positivism, and Marx himself was often guilty of being overly positivistic (Habermas, 1971).

Criticisms of Sociology

Sociology is attacked for its "scientism," that is, for making the scientific method an end in itself. In addition, sociology is accused of accepting the status quo. The critical school maintains that sociology does not seriously criticize society or seek to transcend the contemporary social structure. Sociology, the critical school contends, has surrendered its obligation to help people oppressed by contemporary society.

Members of this school are critical of sociologists' focus on society as a whole rather than on individuals in society; sociologists are accused of ignoring the interaction of the individual and society. Although most sociological perspectives are *not* guilty of ignoring this interaction, this view is a cornerstone of the critical school's attacks on sociologists. Because they ignore the individual, sociologists are seen as being unable to say anything meaningful about political changes that could lead to a "just and humane society" (Frankfurt Institute for Social Research, 1973:46). As Zoltan Tar put it, sociology becomes "an integral part of the existing society instead of being a means of critique and a ferment of renewal" (1977:x).

Critique of Modern Society

Most of the critical school's work is aimed at a critique of modern society and a variety of its components. Whereas much of early Marxian theory aimed specifically at the economy, the critical school shifted its orientation to the cultural level in light of what it considers the realities of modern capitalist society. That is, the locus of domination in the modern world shifted from the economy to the cultural realm. Still, the critical school retains its interest in domination,[1] although in the modern world it is likely to be domination by cultural rather than economic elements. The critical school thus seeks to focus on the cultural repression of the individual in modern society.

The critical thinkers have been shaped not only by Marxian theory but also by Weberian theory, as reflected in their focus on rationality as the dominant development in the modern world. In fact, supporters of this approach often are labeled "Weberian Marxists" (Dahms, 1997; Lowy, 1996). As Trent Schroyer (1970) made clear, the view of the critical school is that in modern society the repression produced by rationality has replaced economic exploitation as the dominant social problem. The critical school clearly has adopted Weber's differentiation between *formal rationality* and *substantive rationality,* or what the critical theorists think of as *reason.* To the critical theorists, formal rationality is concerned unreflectively with the question of the most effective means for achieving any given purpose (Tar, 1977). This is viewed as "technocratic thinking," in which the objective is to serve the forces of domination, not to emancipate people from domination. The goal is simply to find the most efficient means to whatever ends are defined as important by those in power. Technocratic thinking is contrasted to reason, which is, in the minds of critical theorists, the hope for society. Reason involves the assessment of means in terms of the ultimate human values of justice, peace, and happiness. Critical theorists identified Nazism in general, and its concentration camps more specifically, as examples of formal rationality in mortal combat with reason. Thus, as George Friedman puts it, "Auschwitz was a rational place, but it was not a reasonable one" (1981:15; see also Chapter 14 and the discussion of Bauman, 1989).

Despite the seeming rationality of modern life, the critical school views the modern world as rife with irrationality (Crook, 1995). This idea can be labeled the "irrationality of rationality" or, more specifically, the irrationality of formal rationality. In Herbert Marcuse's view, although it appears to be the embodiment of rationality, "this society is irrational as a whole" (1964:ix; see also Farganis, 1975). It is irrational that the rational world is destructive of individuals and their needs and abilities, that peace is maintained through a constant threat of war, and that despite the existence

---

[1] This is made abundantly clear by Trent Schroyer (1973), who entitled his book on the critical school *The Critique of Domination.*

of sufficient means, people remain impoverished, repressed, exploited, and unable to fulfill themselves.

The critical school focuses primarily on one form of formal rationality—modern technology (Feenberg, 1996). Marcuse (1964), for example, was a severe critic of modern technology, at least as it is employed in capitalism. He saw technology in modern capitalist society as leading to totalitarianism. In fact, he viewed it as leading to new, more effective, and even more "pleasant" methods of external control over individuals. The prime example is the use of television to socialize and pacify the population (other examples are mass sport, and pervasive exploitation of sex). Marcuse rejected the idea that technology is neutral in the modern world and saw it instead as a means to dominate people. It is effective because it is made to seem neutral when it is in fact enslaving. It serves to suppress individuality. The actor's inner freedom has been "invaded and whittled down" by modern technology. The result is what Marcuse called "one-dimensional society," in which individuals lose the ability to think critically and negatively about society. Marcuse did not see technology per se as the enemy, but rather technology as it is employed in modern capitalist society: "Technology, no matter how 'pure,' sustains and streamlines the continuum of domination. This fatal link can be cut only by a revolution which makes technology and technique subservient to the needs and goals of free men" (1969:56). Marcuse retained Marx's original view that technology is not inherently a problem and that it can be used to develop a "better" society.

Critique of Culture

The critical theorists level significant criticisms at what they call the "culture industry" (Kellner and Lewis, 2007), the rationalized, bureaucratized structures (for example, the television networks) that control modern culture. Interest in the culture industry reflects their concern with the Marxian concept of "superstructure" rather than with the economic base (Beamish, 2007e). The *culture industry,* producing what is conventionally called "mass culture," is defined as the "administered . . . nonspontaneous, reified, phony culture rather than the real thing" (Jay, 1973:216).[2] Two things worry the critical thinkers most about this industry. First, they are concerned about its falseness. They think of it as a prepackaged set of ideas mass-produced and disseminated to the masses by the media. Second, the critical theorists are disturbed by its pacifying, repressive, and stupefying effect on people (D. Cook, 1996; G. Friedman, 1981; Tar, 1977:83; Zipes, 1994).

Douglas Kellner (1990) has self-consciously offered a critical theory of television. While he embeds his work in the cultural concerns of the Frankfurt school, Kellner draws on other Marxian traditions to present a more rounded conception of the television industry. He critiques the critical school because it "neglects detailed analysis of the political economy of the media, conceptualizing mass culture merely as an instrument of capitalist ideology" (Kellner, 1990:14). Thus, in addition to looking at television as part of the culture industry, Kellner connects it to both corporate capitalism and the

---

[2] In recent work (Garnham, 2007), this has been broadened to the idea of "culture industries" to include various "industries" (entertainment, knowledge, etc.) as well as the fact that there are differences among them.

political system. Furthermore, Kellner does not see television as monolithic or as controlled by coherent corporate forces but rather as a "highly conflictual mass medium in which competing economic, political, social and cultural forces intersect" (1990:14). Thus, while working within the tradition of critical theory, Kellner rejects the view that capitalism is a totally administered world. Nevertheless, Kellner sees television as a threat to democracy, individuality, and freedom and offers suggestions (for example, more democratic accountability, greater citizen access and participation, greater diversity on television) to deal with the threat. Thus, Kellner goes beyond a mere critique to offer proposals for dealing with the dangers posed by television.

The critical school is also interested in and critical of what it calls the "knowledge industry," which refers to entities concerned with knowledge production (for example, universities and research institutes) that have become autonomous structures in our society. Their autonomy has allowed them to extend themselves beyond their original mandate (Schroyer, 1970). They have become oppressive structures interested in expanding their influence throughout society.

Marx's critical analysis of capitalism led him to have hope for the future, but many critical theorists have come to a position of despair and hopelessness. They see the problems of the modern world not as specific to capitalism but as endemic to a rationalized world. They see the future, in Weberian terms, as an "iron cage" of increasingly rational structures from which hope for escape lessens all the time.

Much of critical theory (like the bulk of Marx's original formulation) is in the form of critical analyses. Even though the critical theorists also have a number of positive interests, one of the basic criticisms made of critical theory is that it offers more criticisms than it does positive contributions. This incessant negativity galls many scholars, and for this reason they feel that critical theory has little to offer to sociological theory.

The Major Contributions

Subjectivity

The great contribution of the critical school has been its effort to reorient Marxian theory in a subjective direction. Although this constitutes a critique of Marx's materialism and his dogged focus on economic structures, it also represents a strong contribution to our understanding of the subjective elements of social life at both the individual and the cultural levels.

The Hegelian roots of Marxian theory are the major source of interest in subjectivity. Many of the critical thinkers see themselves as returning to those roots, as expressed in Marx's early works. In doing so, they are following up on the work of the early-twentieth-century Marxian revisionists, such as Georg Lukács, who sought not to focus on subjectivity but simply to integrate such an interest with the traditional Marxian concern with objective structures (Agger, 1978). Lukács did not seek a fundamental restructuring of Marxian theory, although the later critical theorists do have this broader and more ambitious objective.

We begin with the critical school's interest in culture. As pointed out above, the critical school has shifted to a concern with the cultural "superstructure" rather than with the economic "base." One factor motivating this shift is that the critical school feels that Marxists have overemphasized economic structures and that this emphasis has served to overwhelm their interest in the other aspects of social reality, especially the culture. In addition to this factor, a series of external changes in society point to such a shift (Agger, 1978). In particular, the prosperity of the post–World War II period in America *seems* to have led to a disappearance of internal economic contradictions in general and class conflict in particular. False consciousness *seems* to be nearly universal: all social classes, including the working class, appear to be beneficiaries and ardent supporters of the capitalist system. In addition, the former Soviet Union, despite its socialist economy, was at least as oppressive as capitalist society. Because the two societies had different economies, the critical thinkers had to look elsewhere for the major source of oppression. What they looked toward initially was culture.

To the previously discussed aspects of the Frankfurt school's concerns— rationality, the culture industry, and the knowledge industry—can be added another set of concerns, the most notable of which is an interest in ideology. By *ideology* the critical theorists mean the idea systems, often false and obfuscating, produced by societal elites. All these specific aspects of the superstructure and the critical school's orientation to them can be subsumed under the heading "critique of domination" (Agger, 1978; Schroyer, 1973). This interest in domination was at first stimulated by fascism in the 1930s and 1940s, but it has shifted to a concern with domination in capitalist society. The modern world has reached a stage of unsurpassed domination of individuals. In fact, the control is so complete that it no longer requires deliberate actions on the part of the leaders. The control pervades all aspects of the cultural world and, more important, is internalized in the actor. In effect, actors have come to dominate themselves in the name of the larger social structure. Domination has reached a complete stage where it no longer appears to be domination at all. Because domination is no longer perceived as personally damaging and alienating, it often seems as if the world is the way it is supposed to be. It is no longer clear to actors what the world *ought* to be like. Thus, the pessimism of the critical thinkers is buttressed because they no longer can see how rational analysis can help alter the situation.

One of the critical school's concerns at the cultural level is with what Habermas (1975) called *legitimations*. These can be defined as systems of ideas generated by the political system, and theoretically by any other system, to support the existence of the system. They are designed to "mystify" the political system, to make it unclear exactly what is happening.

In addition to such cultural interests, the critical school is concerned with actors and their consciousness and what happens to them in the modern world. The consciousness of the masses came to be controlled by external forces (such as the culture industry). As a result, the masses failed to develop a revolutionary consciousness. Unfortunately, the critical theorists, like most Marxists and most sociologists, often fail to differentiate clearly between individual consciousness and culture or specify the many links between them. In much of their work, they move freely back and forth between consciousness and culture with little or no sense that they are changing levels.

Of great importance here is the effort by critical theorists, most notably Marcuse (1969), to integrate Freud's insights at the level of consciousness (and unconsciousness) into the critical theorists' interpretation of the culture. Critical theorists derive three things from Freud's work: (1) a psychological structure to work with in developing their theories, (2) a sense of psychopathology that allows them to understand both the negative impact of modern society and the failure to develop revolutionary consciousness, and (3) the possibilities of psychic liberation (G. Friedman, 1981). One of the benefits of this interest in individual consciousness is that it offers a useful corrective to the pessimism of the critical school and its focus on cultural constraints. Although people are controlled, imbued with false needs, and anesthetized, in Freudian terms they also are endowed with a libido (broadly conceived as sexual energy), which provides the basic source of energy for creative action oriented toward the overthrow of the major forms of domination.

Dialectics

The second main positive focus of critical theory is an interest in dialectics (this idea is critiqued from the viewpoint of analytical Marxism later in this chapter). At the most general level, a dialectical approach means a focus on the social *totality*.[3] "No partial aspect of social life and no isolated phenomenon may be comprehended unless it is related to the historical whole, to the social structure conceived as a global entity" (Connerton, 1976:12). This approach involves rejection of a focus on any *specific* aspect of social life, especially the economic system, outside of its broader context. This approach also entails a concern with the interrelation of the various levels of social reality—most important, individual consciousness, the cultural superstructure, and the economic structure. Dialectics also carries with it a methodological prescription: One component of social life cannot be studied in isolation from the rest.

This idea has both diachronic and synchronic components. A *synchronic* view leads us to be concerned with the interrelationship of components of society within a contemporary totality. A *diachronic* view carries with it a concern for the historical roots of today's society as well as for where it might be going in the future (Bauman, 1976). The domination of people by social and cultural structures—the "one-dimensional" society, to use Marcuse's phrase—is the result of a specific historical development and is not a universal characteristic of humankind. This historical perspective counteracts the commonsense view that emerges in capitalism that the system is a natural and inevitable phenomenon. In the view of the critical theorists (and other Marxists), people have come to see society as "second nature"; it is "perceived by commonsensical wisdom as an alien, uncompromising, demanding and high-handed power—exactly like non-human nature. To abide by the rules of reason, to behave rationally, to achieve success, to be free, man now had to accommodate himself to the 'second nature'" (Bauman, 1976:6).

In particular, in his critique of positivism, Theodor Adorno (1966/1973) developed *negative dialectics*. In the spirit of Marx, Adorno emphasizes the interplay of social ideas and material forces. However, unlike Marx, Adorno does not try to

---

[3] Jay (1984) sees "totality" as the heart of Marxian theory in general, not just of critical theory. However, this idea is rejected by postmodern Marxists (see the discussion later in this chapter).

develop new propositions, new statements of fact. Instead, the goal of negative dialectics is to demonstrate the contingency of social science knowledge, in particular its relationship to modern capitalism. In doing this, negative dialectics also tries to avoid "identity thinking" (Dahms, 2011b). Identity thinking is a facet of positivism, and of all modern thought, that Adorno does not want to reproduce in critical theory. Dahms describes it like this:

> Identity thinking corresponds to the control function of thought, as a kind of
> thinking that collapses the potential complexity of a concept (in the Hegelian sense
> of *Begriff*) into the simplicity of a term, attaches this seemingly unambiguous
> problematic term to an object, and posits that all the dimensions of an object can
> be adequately expressed on the basis of this term (575).

In other words, much like contemporary postmodern thought (see Chapter 16), negative dialectics emphasizes the ever-changing complexity of social life over reductive accounts of social life.

The critical theorists also are oriented to thinking about the future, but following Marx's lead, they refuse to be utopian; rather, they focus on criticizing and changing contemporary society (Alway, 1995a). However, instead of directing their attention to society's economic structure as Marx had done, they concentrate on its cultural superstructure. Their dialectical approach commits them to work in the real world. They are not satisfied with seeking truth in scientific laboratories. The ultimate test of their ideas is the degree to which they are accepted and used in practice. This process they call *authentication,* which occurs when the people who have been the victims of distorted communication take up the ideas of critical theory and use them to free themselves from that system (Bauman, 1976:104). Thus we arrive at another aspect of the concerns of the critical thinkers—the *liberation* of humankind (Marcuse, 1964:222).

In more abstract terms, critical thinkers can be said to be preoccupied with the interplay and relationship between theory and practice. The view of the Frankfurt school was that the two have been severed in capitalist society (Schroyer, 1973:28). That is, theorizing is done by one group, which is delegated, or more likely takes, that right, whereas practice is relegated to another, less powerful group. In many cases, the theorist's work is uninformed by what went on in the real world, leading to an impoverished and largely irrelevant body of Marxian and sociological theory. The point is to unify theory and practice so as to restore the relationship between them. Theory thus would be informed by practice, whereas practice would be shaped by theory. In the process, both theory and practice would be enriched.

Despite this avowed goal, most of critical theory has failed abysmally to integrate theory and practice. In fact, one of the most often voiced criticisms of critical theory is that it usually is written in such a way that it is totally inaccessible to the mass of people. Furthermore, in its commitment to studying culture and superstructure, critical theory addresses a number of very esoteric topics and has little to say about the pragmatic, day-to-day concerns of most people.

Knowledge and Human Interests   One of the best-known dialectical concerns of the critical school is Jurgen Habermas's (1970, 1971) interest in the relationship between knowledge and human interests—an example of a broader dialectical concern with the relationship between subjective and objective factors. But Habermas has been careful to point out that subjective and objective factors cannot be dealt with in isolation from one another. To him, knowledge systems exist at the objective level whereas human interests are more subjective phenomena.

Habermas differentiated among three knowledge systems and their corresponding interests. The interests that lie behind and guide each system of knowledge are generally unknown to laypeople, and it is the task of the critical theorists to uncover them. The first type of knowledge is *analytic science,* or *classical positivistic scientific systems.* In Habermas's view, the underlying interest of such a knowledge system is technical prediction and control, which can be applied to the environment, other societies, or people within society. In Habermas's view, analytic science lends itself quite easily to enhancing oppressive control. The second type of knowledge system is *humanistic knowledge,* and its interest lies in *understanding* the world. It operates from the general view that understanding our past generally helps us understand what is transpiring today. It has a practical interest in mutual and self-understanding. It is neither oppressive nor liberating. The third type is *critical knowledge,* which Habermas, and the Frankfurt school in general, espoused. The interest attached to this type of knowledge is *human emancipation.* It was hoped that the critical knowledge generated by Habermas and others would raise the self-consciousness of the masses (through mechanisms articulated by the Freudians) and lead to a social movement that would result in the hoped-for emancipation.

Criticisms of Critical Theory

A number of criticisms have been leveled at critical theory (Bottomore, 1984). First, critical theory has been accused of being largely ahistorical, of examining a variety of events without paying much attention to their historical and comparative contexts (for example, Nazism in the 1930s, anti-Semitism in the 1940s, student revolts in the 1960s). This is a damning criticism of any Marxian theory, which should be inherently historical and comparative. Second, the critical school, as we have seen already, generally has ignored the economy. Finally, and relatedly, critical theorists have tended to argue that the working class has disappeared as a revolutionary force, a position decidedly in opposition to traditional Marxian analysis.

Criticisms such as these led traditional Marxists such as Bottomore to conclude, "The Frankfurt School, in its original form, and as a school of Marxism or sociology, is dead" (1984:76). Similar sentiments have been expressed by Greisman, who labels critical theory "the paradigm that failed" (1986:273). If it is dead as a distinctive school, that is because many of its basic ideas have found their way into Marxism, neo-Marxian sociology, and even mainstream sociology. Thus, as Bottomore himself concludes in the case of Habermas, the critical school has undergone a rapprochement with Marxism and sociology, and "at the same time some of the distinctive ideas of the Frankfurt School are conserved and developed" (1984:76).

The Ideas of Jurgen Habermas

Although critical theory *may* be on the decline, Jurgen Habermas[4] and his theories are very much alive (J. Bernstein, 1995; R. Brown and Goodman, 2001; Outhwaite, 1994). We touched on a few of his ideas earlier in this chapter, but here we present a more detailed look at his theory (still other aspects of his thinking are covered in Chapters 13 and 14).

Differences with Marx

Habermas contends that his goal has been "to develop a theoretical program that I understand as a reconstruction of historical materialism" (1979:95). Habermas takes Marx's starting point (human potential, species-being, "sensuous human activity") as his own. However, Habermas (1971) argues that Marx failed to distinguish between two analytically distinct components of species-being—work (or labor, purposive-rational action) and social (or symbolic) interaction (or communicative action). In Habermas's view, Marx tended to ignore the latter and to reduce it to work. As Habermas put it, the problem in Marx's work is the "*reduction of the self-generative act of the human species to labor*" (1971:42). Thus, Habermas says: "I take as my starting point the fundamental distinction between *work* and *interaction*" (1970:91). Throughout his writings, Habermas's work is informed by this distinction, although he is most prone to use the terms *purposive-rational action* (work) and *communicative action* (interaction).

Under the heading "purposive-rational action," Habermas distinguishes between instrumental action and strategic action. Both involve the calculated pursuit of self-interest. *Instrumental action* involves a single actor rationally calculating the best means to a given goal. *Strategic action* involves two or more individuals coordinating purposive-rational action in the pursuit of a goal. The objective of *both* instrumental and strategic action is instrumental mastery.

Habermas is most interested in *communicative action,* in which

> the actions of the agents involved are coordinated not through egocentric calculations of success but through acts of *reaching understanding*. In communicative action participants are not primarily oriented to their own successes; they pursue their individual goals under the condition that they can *harmonize* their plans of action on the basis of *common situation definitions*.
>
> (Habermas, 1984:286; italics added)

Whereas the end of purposive-rational action is to achieve a goal, the objective of communicative action is to achieve communicative understanding (Stryker, 1998).

Clearly, there is an important speech component in communicative action. However, such action is broader than that encompassing "speech acts or equivalent nonverbal expressions" (Habermas, 1984:278).

Habermas's key point of departure from Marx is to argue that communicative action, *not* purposive-rational action (work), is the most distinctive and most pervasive human phenomenon. It (not work) is the foundation of all sociocultural life as well as all the human sciences. Whereas Marx was led to focus on work, Habermas is led to focus on communication.

---

[4] Habermas began as Theodor Adorno's research assistant in 1955 (Wiggershaus, 1994:537).

Not only did Marx focus on work, he took free and creative work (species-being) as his baseline for critically analyzing work in various historical epochs, especially capitalism. Habermas, too, adopts a baseline, but in the realm of communicative rather than in that of purposive-rational action. Habermas's baseline is undistorted communication, communication without compulsion. With this baseline, Habermas is able to critically analyze distorted communication. Habermas is concerned with those social structures that distort communication, just as Marx examined the structural sources of the distortion of work. Although they have different baselines, both Habermas and Marx *have* baselines, and these permit them to escape relativism and render judgments about various historical phenomena. Habermas is critical of those theorists, especially Weber and previous critical theorists, for their lack of such a baseline and their lapse into relativism.

There is still another parallel between Marx and Habermas and their baselines. For both, these baselines represent not only their analytical starting points but also their political objectives. That is, whereas for Marx the goal was a communist society in which undistorted work (species-being) would exist for the first time, for Habermas the political goal is a society of undistorted communication (communicative action). In terms of immediate goals, Marx seeks the elimination of (capitalist) barriers to undistorted work and Habermas is interested in the elimination of barriers to free communication.

Here Habermas (1973; see also Habermas, 1994:101), like other critical theorists, draws on Freud and sees many parallels between what psychoanalysts do at the individual level and what he thinks needs to be done at the societal level. Habermas sees psychoanalysis as a theory of distorted communication and as being preoccupied with allowing individuals to communicate in an undistorted way. The psychoanalyst seeks to find the sources of distortions in individual communication, that is, repressed blocks to communication. Through reflection, the psychoanalyst attempts to help the individual overcome these blocks. Similarly, through *therapeutic critique,* "a form of argumentation that serves to clarify systematic self-deception" (Habermas, 1984:21), the critical theorist attempts to aid people in general to overcome social barriers to undistorted communication. There is, then, an analogy (many critics think an illegitimate analogy) between psychoanalysis and critical theory. The psychoanalyst aids the patient in much the same way that the social critic helps those unable to communicate adequately to become "undisabled" (Habermas, 1994:112).

As for Marx, the basis of Habermas's ideal future society exists in the contemporary world. That is, for Marx elements of species-being are found in work in capitalist society. For Habermas, elements of undistorted communication are found in every act of contemporary communication.

Rationalization

This brings us to the central issue of rationalization in Habermas's work. Here Habermas is influenced not only by Marx's work but by Weber's as well. Most prior work, in Habermas's view, has focused on the rationalization of purposive-rational action, which has led to a growth of productive forces and an increase in technological control over life (Habermas, 1970). This form of rationalization, as it was to Weber and Marx, is a major, perhaps *the* major, problem in the modern world. However, the problem is rationalization of purposive-rational action, *not* rationalization in general. In fact, for Habermas, the antidote to the problem of the rationalization of purposive-rational action lies in the rationalization of communicative action. The rationalization of communicative action leads to communication free from domination, free and open communication. Rationalization here involves emancipation, *"removing restrictions on communication"* (Habermas, 1970:118; see also Habermas, 1979). This is where Habermas's previously mentioned work on *legitimations* and, more generally, *ideology* fits in. That is, these are two of the main causes of distorted communication, causes that must be eliminated if we are to have free and open communication.

At the level of social norms, such rationalization would involve decreases in normative repressiveness and rigidity leading to increases in individual flexibility and reflectivity. The development of this new, less-restrictive or nonrestrictive normative system lies at the heart of Habermas's theory of social evolution. Instead of a new productive system, rationalization for Habermas (1979) leads to a new, less-distorting normative system. Although he regards it as a misunderstanding of his position, many have accused Habermas of cutting his Marxian roots in this shift from the material level to the normative level.

The end point of this evolution for Habermas is a rational society (Delanty, 1997). *Rationality* here means removal of the barriers that distort communication, but more generally it means a communication system in which ideas are openly presented and defended against criticism; unconstrained agreement develops during argumentation. To understand this better, we need more details of Habermas's communication theory.

Communication

Habermas distinguishes between the previously discussed communicative action and discourse. Whereas communicative action occurs in everyday life, *discourse* is

> that form of communication that is removed from contexts of experience and action and whose structure assures us: that the bracketed validity claims of assertions, recommendations, or warnings are the exclusive object of discussion; that participants, themes, and contributions are not restricted except with reference to the goal of testing the validity claims in questions; that no force except that of the better argument is exercised; and that all motives except that of the cooperative search for truth are excluded.
>
> (Habermas, 1975:107–108)

In the theoretical world of discourse, but also hidden and underlying the world of communicative actions, is the "ideal speech situation," in which force or power does not determine which arguments win out; instead the better argument emerges victorious. The weight of evidence and argumentation determine what is considered valid or true. The arguments that emerge from such a discourse (and that the participants agree on) are true (Hesse, 1995). Thus Habermas adopts a consensus theory of truth (rather than a copy [or "reality"] theory of truth [Outhwaite, 1994:41]). This truth is part of all communication, and its full expression is the goal of Habermas's evolutionary theory. As Thomas McCarthy says, "The idea of truth points ultimately to a form of interaction that is free from all distorting influences. The 'good and true life' that is the goal of critical theory is inherent in the notion of truth; it is anticipated in every act of speech" (1982:308).

Consensus arises theoretically in discourse (and pretheoretically in communicative action) when four types of validity claims are raised and recognized by interactants. First, the speaker's utterances are seen as understandable, comprehensible. Second, the propositions offered by the speaker are true; that is, the speaker is offering reliable knowledge. Third, the speaker is being truthful (veracious) and sincere in offering the propositions; the speaker is reliable. Fourth, it is right and proper for the speaker to utter such propositions; he or she has the normative basis to do so. Consensus arises when all these validity claims are raised and accepted; it breaks down when one or more are questioned. Returning to an earlier point, there are forces in the modern world that distort this process, prevent the emergence of a consensus, and would have to be overcome for Habermas's ideal society to come about (Morris, 2001).

Critical Theory Today: The Work of Axel Honneth

While Habermas is the most prominent of today's social thinkers, he is not alone in struggling to develop a critical theory that is better adapted to contemporary realities (see, for example, the various essays in Wexler, 1991; Antonio and Kellner, 1994). Castells (1996) has made the case for the need for a critical theory of the new "information society." To illustrate these continuing efforts, a brief discussion follows of the work of Axel Honneth, especially on the struggle for recognition.

The Ideas of Axel Honneth

A student of Jurgen Habermas, Axel Honneth (b. 1949) is the current director of the Frankfurt Institute of Social Research. With Habermas now in retirement, Honneth has emerged as today's leading critical theorist. To achieve that status, he has developed a theoretical position that builds on, but critiques, the work of the critical school as well as that of Habermas in particular (Honneth, 1985/1991, 1990/1995, 1992/1994, 2000/2007, 2008).

Honneth's critique of his predecessors, as well as his own theoretical perspective, is based on his fundamental views on the requirements of a critical theory. For one thing, it must be based on and emerge from practical critiques that exist in the everyday world. As Honneth (1990/1995:xii) puts it, the explanation of a social phenomenon must be done "in such a way that a practical dimension of critique emerges as a constitutive requirement for critical understanding." For another, a critical theory must have an interest in emancipating people from the domination and oppression that they experience in the real world. That is, in line with the traditional Marxian perspective, critical theory must have an integrative interest in both theory *and* practice. It must seek the "determination of the driving forces of society which locates in the historical process itself the impetus both to critique as well as to overcoming established forms of domination" (Honneth, 1990/1995:xii). That is, the emancipatory interest of critical theory lies within (is immanent within) society itself.

The basic problem with classic critical theory, especially that of Horkheimer and Adorno, is that its totally administered view of the capitalist world led to negativism; it left no hope for practical critique and emancipatory possibilities in the everyday world and in critical theory itself. Of critical theory, Honneth (1990/1995:xii) said that it supposed a "closed circle between capitalist domination and cultural manipulation, that there could remain within the social reality of their time no space for a zone of moral-practical critique." This leads him to the conclusion that the key problem for critical theory today, and therefore for him, is how to come "to grips with the structure of social domination as well as with identifying the social resources for its practical transformation" (Honneth, 1990/1995:xiii).

In this context, Honneth sees Habermas's communication theory as a step forward because it offered us a way of dealing with, and getting at, the everyday life-world. In that world there exists "in the form of the normative expectations of interaction—a layer of moral experiences . . . which would serve as the point of reference for an immanent, yet transcending moment of critique" (Honneth, 1990/1995:xiii). But in the end, Honneth did not find that Habermas's work went far enough, especially in the direction of getting at moral reactions and feelings as they exist in everyday life. Thus Honneth seeks to build upon Habermas, but to go farther and in a different direction than that taken by Habermas.

While Habermas is concerned with communication, Honneth comes to focus on the recognition of identity claims made by individuals and collectivities. Consistent with critical theory, he wants to deal with the violence committed against those claims for recognition and the injuries and pathologies that result for the claimants. Individuals and groups come to engage in political resistance not because of some abstract moral principles but because of the "experience of violence to intuitively presupposed conceptions of justice" (Honneth, 1900/1995:xiv). That is, they feel that they deserve recognition. When they do not get it, their sense of fair play is upset, and they come to resist those who are seen as being unfair to them. And "it is principally violence to individual or collective claims to social recognition within the lifeworld which will be experienced as moral injustice" (Honneth, 1990/1995:xv). Critical theorists, including Honneth, must look to the everyday social world for their moral reference points. It is the everyday world that provides "social criticism with a moral foothold" (Honneth, 1990/1995:xv).

At the heart of Honneth's work is an idea—"the struggle for recognition"—derived from Hegel. Honneth finds Hegel's ideas attractive, not only for their focus on recognition but also because they connect morality to the moral sentiments of people, as well as indicating the way that feelings about a lack of recognition can lead to social action and social conflict. People feel that it is normative for them to receive recognition, and when it is not forthcoming, especially repeatedly, they feel that they have not gotten the respect they deserve.

Historically people often have felt that they did not get the recognition they deserved and it is possible, even likely, that there is an increasing crisis of recognition in contemporary society. For example, it is difficult to get recognition for one's work (especially for women; see Honneth, 2000/2007:75–77; Rossler, 2007). More generally, there has been a decline in the ability of various institutions (for example, family, work) to create the kinds of recognition people need.

More specifically, and also following Hegel, people are seen as needing three forms of recognition from others. First is *love*, or caring for a person's needs and emotions. People gain self-confidence when they receive such recognition. Second is *respect* for a person's moral and legal dignity, and this leads to self-respect. Finally, there is *esteem* for a person's social achievements, and this leads to self-esteem (Van den Brink and Owen, 2007b). These forms of recognition are acquired and maintained intersubjectively (a perspective derived from Mead). That is, in order to relate to themselves in these ways (and have self-confidence, self-respect, and self-esteem), people must receive recognition from others. Ultimately, "[r]elations of recognition are a necessary condition of our moral subjectivity and agency" (Van den Brink and Owen, 2007b:4–5). It is only with adequate recognition that people can realize their full autonomy as human beings.

Disrespect (Honneth, 2000/2007) occurs when people do not receive the recognition they feel they deserve, and this adversely affects their ability to form appropriate identities. Feelings of a lack of respect are not unverifiable feelings but are based on a normative standard that people deserve certain forms of recognition; most generally, they deserve love, respect, and esteem. Conflict and resistance are likely to result when they do not get the recognition the normative system says they should. The existence of such a normative standard not only lies at the base of such actions, but it allows outsiders (including critical theorists) to utilize established norms to evaluate those actions, and the concrete claims for recognition on which those actions are based. That is, Honneth offers us an Archimedean point from which to evaluate claims for recognition; our judgments of the legitimacy of those claims need not be arbitrary.

There are at least four major criticisms of Honneth's critical theory. First, some critics question the placement of recognition at the heart of a social and ethical theory: Is recognition as important as Honneth suggests? Is it as important as work and labor in Marx's theory or communication in Habermas's theory? In an ongoing debate Nancy Fraser has criticized Honneth for emphasizing recognition over the equally important economic problem of redistribution (Fraser & Honneth, 2003). Second, there are doubts about the kind of monistic theory created by Honneth: Is recognition all that matters? Third, some question whether there are three bases of recognition: Why not more or less? Finally, it is hard to discern the operations of power in Honneth's theory.

Later Developments in Cultural Critique

Kellner and Lewis (2007) see the Frankfurt school as part of a tradition of work that involves "cultural critique," which, in turn, is part of the "cultural turn" and cultural studies (McGuigan, 2005; Storey, 2007). At the center of this tradition lies the Frankfurt school, but it is predated by work by Kant, Nietzsche, Marx, and Freud (among others) and is succeeded by later work, especially that associated with the "Birmingham school."

As the name suggests, the Birmingham school, or the Centre for Contemporary Cultural Studies, was associated with the University of Birmingham in the United Kingdom (Barker, 2007). Founded in 1964, it remained in existence until 1988. Created by Richard Hoggart, the center gained its greatest fame and coherence as a center of cultural studies under the leadership of Stuart Hall (Rojek, 2003, 2005).

In contrast to the literary tradition in England, which privileged and valued high art and the elite classes, the Birmingham school valued and focused on popular culture, its products, and the lower classes with which they are associated. Furthermore, popular culture was seen as the arena in which hegemonic ideas operated as mechanisms of social control, were consented to, and, most important from a Marxian perspective, were resisted by the lower classes. Concepts like hegemonic ideas, consent, and resistance clearly aligned the Birminghan school with Marxian theory, especially the theories of Antonio Gramsci (although structuralism and semiotics influenced at least some of its work). An ideological struggle was in existence, and as "organic intellectuals" (thinkers who were, at least theoretically, part of the working class) it was the responsibility (if not always fulfilled) of the Birmingham scholars to be part of popular culture and help those associated with it wage a counter-hegemonic ideological battle against those in power. They also saw as their role the debunking and demystification of dominant texts with their abundant ideologies and myths that served the interests of elites. They were not disinterested social scientists but rather "populists" who sided with the "people" against the power elite (McGuigan, 2002, 2005). Thus, like the critical theorists, those associated with the Birmingham school moved away from economic determinism and a base-superstructure perspective and toward an emphasis on the superstructure, especially culture (as well as the nation-state), which was seen as relatively autonomous of the economic base.

At that level of culture, the focus was on ideology and hegemony and on the ways that power and control manifested itself and was resisted. This meant a concern, on the one hand, with how the media expressed ideologies of the dominant groups and how working-class youth reproduced their subordinate position and, on the other hand, with how working-class youth resisted that position and the ideology of the dominant groups through such things as dress and style (for example, the "skinheads"). Relatedly, the Birmingham school was interested in analyzing a variety of texts (reflecting the influence of structuralism and semiotics; see Chapter 16)—films, advertisements, soap operas, news broadcasts—in order to show how they were hegemonic products and how their meanings were not fixed but rather were produced in various, sometimes antithetical or oppositional, ways by the audience. Again, this was a reflection of the school's dual concern with hegemony and resistance.

The power of the lower classes to redefine culture in antithetical and oppositional ways was related to a major difference between the Birmingham school and the Frankfurt school. The latter saw culture as debased by the culture industry; the former saw that as an elitist perspective. The Birmingham school had a much more positive view of culture, especially as it was interpreted and produced by the lower classes.

Neo-Marxian Economic Sociology

Many neo-Marxists (for example, critical theorists) have made relatively few comments on the economic institution, at least in part as a reaction against the excesses of the economic determinists. However, these reactions have set in motion a series of counterreactions. In this section we deal with the work of some of the Marxists who have returned to a focus on the economic realm. Their work constitutes an effort to adapt Marxian theory to the realities of modern capitalist society (Lash and Urry, 1987; Mészáros, 1995).

We deal with two bodies of work in this section. The first focuses on the broad issue of capital and labor. The second comprises the narrower, and more contemporary, work on the transition from Fordism to post-Fordism.

Capital and Labor

Marx's original insights into economic structures and processes were based on his analysis of the capitalism of his time—what we can think of as competitive capitalism. Capitalist industries were comparatively small, with the result that no single industry, or small group of industries, could gain complete and uncontested control over a market. Much of Marx's economic work was based on the premise, accurate for his time, that capitalism is a competitive system. To be sure, Marx foresaw the possibility of future monopolies, but he commented only briefly on them. Many later Marxian theorists continued to operate as if capitalism remained much as it had been in Marx's time.

Monopoly Capital

It is in this context that we must examine the work of Paul Baran and Paul Sweezy (1966; Toscano, 2007b). They began with a criticism of Marxian social science for repeating familiar formulations and failing to explain important recent developments in capitalistic society. They accused Marxian theory of stagnating because it continued to rest on the assumption of a competitive economy. A modern Marxian theory must, in their view, recognize that competitive capitalism largely has been replaced by monopoly capitalism.

In *monopoly capitalism*, one or a few capitalists control a given sector of the economy. Clearly, there is far less competition in monopoly capitalism than in competitive capitalism. In competitive capitalism, organizations competed on a price basis; that is, capitalists tried to sell more goods by offering lower prices. In monopoly capitalism, firms no longer have to compete in this way because one or a few firms control a market; competition shifts to the sales domain. Advertising, packaging, and other methods of appealing to potential consumers are the main areas of competition.

The movement from price to sales competition is part of another process characteristic of monopoly capitalism—*progressive rationalization*. Price competition comes to be seen as highly irrational. That is, from the monopoly capitalist's point of view, offering lower and lower prices can lead only to chaos in the marketplace, to say nothing of lower profits and perhaps even bankruptcy. Sales competition, in contrast, is not a cutthroat system; in fact, it even provides work for the advertising industry. Furthermore, prices can be kept high, with the costs of the sales and promotion simply added to the price. Thus sales competition is also far less risky than price competition.

Another crucial aspect of monopoly capitalism is the rise of the giant corporation, with a few large corporations controlling most sectors of the economy. In competitive capitalism, the organization was controlled almost single-handedly by an entrepreneur. The modern corporation is owned by a large number of stockholders, but a few large stockholders own most of the stock. Although stockholders "own" the corporation, managers exercise the actual day-to-day control. The managers are crucial in monopoly capitalism, whereas the entrepreneurs were central in competitive capitalism. Managers have considerable power, which they seek to maintain. They even seek financial independence for their firms by trying, as much as possible, to generate whatever funds they need internally rather than relying on external sources of funding.

Baran and Sweezy commented extensively on the central position of the corporate manager in modern capitalist society. Managers are viewed as a highly rational group oriented to maximizing the profits of the organization. Therefore, they are not inclined to take the risks that were characteristic of the early entrepreneurs. They have a longer time perspective than the entrepreneurs did. Whereas the early capitalist was interested in maximizing profits in the short run, modern managers are aware that such efforts may well lead to chaotic price competition that might adversely affect the long-term profitability of the firm. The manager will thus forgo *some* profits in the short run to maximize long-term profitability.

Baran and Sweezy have been criticized on various grounds. For example, they overemphasize the rationality of managers. Herbert Simon (1957), for example, would argue that managers are more interested in finding (and are only able to find) minimally satisfactory solutions than they are in finding the most rational and most profitable solutions. Another issue is whether managers are, in fact, the pivotal figures in modern capitalism. Many would argue that it is the large stockholders who really control the capitalistic system.

Labor and Monopoly Capital

Harry Braverman (1974) considered the labor process and the exploitation of the worker the heart of Marxian theory. He intended not only to update Marx's interest in manual workers but also to examine what has happened to white-collar and service workers.

Toward the goal of extending Marx's analysis, Braverman argued that the concept "working class" does not describe a specific group of people or occupations but is rather an expression of a process of buying and selling labor power. In modern capitalism, virtually no one owns the means of production; therefore, the many, including most white-collar and service workers, are forced to sell their labor power to the few who do. In his view, capitalist control and exploitation, as well as the derivative processes of mechanization and rationalization, are being extended to white-collar and service occupations.

Managerial Control   Braverman recognized economic exploitation, which was Marx's focus, but concentrated on the issue of *control*. He asked the question: How do the capitalists control the labor power they employ? One answer is that they exercise such control through managers. In fact, Braverman defined *management* as *"a labor process conducted for the purpose of control within the corporation"* (1974:267).

Braverman concentrated on the more impersonal means employed by managers to control workers. One of his central concerns was the utilization of specialization to control workers. Here he carefully differentiated between the division of labor in society as a whole and specialization of work within the organization. All known societies have had a division of labor (for example, between men and women, farmers and artisans, and so forth), but the specialization of work within the organization is a special development of capitalism. Braverman believed that the division of labor at the societal level may enhance the individual, whereas specialization in the workplace has the disastrous effect of subdividing human capabilities: "The subdivision of the individual, when carried on without regard to human capabilities and needs, is a crime against the person and against humanity" (1974:73).

Specialization in the workplace involves the continual division and subdivision of tasks or operations into minute and highly specialized activities, each of which is then likely to be assigned to a *different* worker. This process constitutes the creation of what Braverman calls "detail workers." Out of the range of abilities any individual possesses, capitalists select a small number that the worker is to use on the job. As Braverman put it, the capitalist first breaks down the work process and then "dismembers the worker as well" (1974:78) by requiring the worker to use only a small proportion of his or her skills and abilities. In Braverman's terms, the worker "never voluntarily converts himself into a lifelong detail worker. This is the contribution of the capitalist" (1974:78).

Why does the capitalist do this? First, it increases the control of management. It is easier to control a worker doing a specified task than it is to control one employing a wide range of skills. Second, it increases productivity. That is, a group of workers performing highly specialized tasks can produce more than can the same number of craftspeople, each of whom has all the skills and performs all the production activities. For instance, workers on an automobile assembly line produce more cars than would a corresponding number of skilled craftspeople, each of whom produces his or her own car. Third, specialization allows the capitalist to pay the least for the labor power needed. Instead of highly paid, skilled craftspeople, the capitalist can employ lower-paid, unskilled workers. Following the logic of capitalism, employers seek to progressively cheapen the labor of workers, and this results in a virtually undifferentiated mass of what Braverman called "simple labor."

Specialization is not a sufficient means of control for capitalists and the managers in their employ. Another important means is scientific technique, including such efforts as scientific management, which is an attempt to apply science to the control of labor on the behalf of management. To Braverman, scientific management is the science of "how best to control alienated labor" (1974:90). Scientific management is found in a series of stages aimed at the control of labor—gathering many workers in one workshop, dictating the length of the workday, supervising workers directly to ensure diligence, enforcing rules against distractions (for example, talking), and setting minimum acceptable production levels. Overall scientific management contributed to control through *"the dictation to the worker of the precise manner in which work is to be performed"* (Braverman, 1974:90). For example, Braverman discussed F. W. Taylor's (Kanigel, 1997) early work on the shoveling of coal, which led him to develop rules about the kind of shovel to use, the way to stand, the angle at which the shovel should enter the coal pile, and how much coal to pick up in each motion. In other words, Taylor developed methods that ensured almost total control over the labor process. Workers were to be left with as few independent decisions as possible; thus, a separation of the mental and the manual was accomplished. Management used its monopoly over work-related knowledge to control each step of the labor process. In the end, the work itself was left without any meaningful skill, content, or knowledge. Craftsmanship was utterly destroyed.

Braverman also saw machinery as a means of control over workers. Modern machinery comes into existence "when the tool and/or the work are given a fixed motion path by the structure of the machine itself" (Braverman, 1974:188). The skill is built into the machine rather than being left for the worker to acquire. Instead of controlling the work process, workers come to be controlled by the machine. Furthermore, it is far easier for management to control machines than to control workers.

Braverman argued that through mechanisms such as the specialization of work, scientific management, and machines, management has been able to extend its control over its manual workers. Although this is a useful insight, especially the emphasis on control, Braverman's distinctive contribution has been his effort to extend this kind of analysis to sectors of the labor force that were not included in Marx's original analysis of the labor process. Braverman argued that white-collar and service workers are now being subjected to the same processes of control that were used on manual workers in the nineteenth century (Schmutz, 1996).

One of Braverman's examples is white-collar clerical workers. At one time such workers were considered to be a group distinguished from manual workers by such things as their dress, skills, training, and career prospects (Lockwood, 1956). However, today both groups are being subjected to the same means of control. Thus it has become more difficult to differentiate between the factory and the modern factorylike office, as the workers in the latter are progressively proletarianized. For one thing, the work of the clerical worker has grown more and more specialized. This means, among other things, that the mental and manual aspects of office work have been separated. Office managers, engineers, and technicians now perform the mental work, whereas the "line" clerical workers do little more than manual tasks such as keypunching. As a result, the level of skills needed for these jobs has been lowered, and the jobs require little or no special training.

Scientific management also is seen as invading the office. Clerical tasks have been scientifically studied and, as a result of that research, have been simplified, routinized, and standardized. Finally, mechanization has made significant inroads into the office, primarily through the computer and computer-related equipment.

By applying these mechanisms to clerical work, managers find it much easier to control such workers. It is unlikely that such control mechanisms are as strong and effective in the office as they are in the factory; still, the trend is toward the development of the white-collar "factory."[5]

---

[5] It is important to note that Braverman's book was written before the boom in computer technology in the office, especially the widespread use of the word processor. It may be that such technology, requiring greater skill and training than do older office technologies, will increase worker autonomy (Zuboff, 1988).

Several obvious criticisms can be leveled at Braverman. For one thing, he probably has overestimated the degree of similarity between manual work and clerical work. For another, his preoccupation with control has led him to devote relatively little attention to the dynamics of economic exploitation in capitalism. Nonetheless, he has enriched our understanding of the labor process in modern capitalist society (Foster, 1994; Meiksins, 1994).

Other Work on Labor and Capital

The issue of control is even more central to Richard Edwards (1979). To Edwards, control lies at the heart of the twentieth-century transformation of the workplace. Following Marx, Edwards sees the workplace, both past and present, as an arena of class conflict, in his terms a "contested terrain." Within this arena, dramatic changes have taken place in the way in which those at the top control those at the bottom. In nineteenth-century competitive capitalism, "simple" control was used, in which "bosses exercised power personally, intervening in the labor process often to exhort workers, bully and threaten them, reward good performance, hire and fire on the spot, favor loyal employees, and generally act as despots, benevolent or otherwise" (Edwards, 1979:19). Although this system of control continues in many small businesses, it has proved too crude for modern, large-scale organizations. In such organizations, simple control has tended to be replaced by impersonal and more sophisticated technical and bureaucratic control. Modern workers can be controlled by the technologies with which they work. The classic example of this is the automobile assembly line, in which the workers' actions are determined by the incessant demands of the line. Another example is the modern computer, which can keep careful track of how much work an employee does and how many mistakes he or she makes. Modern workers also are controlled by the impersonal rules of bureaucracies rather than the personal control of supervisors. Capitalism is changing constantly and with it the means by which workers are controlled.

Also of note is the work of Michael Burawoy (1979) and its interest in why workers in a capitalist system work so hard. He rejects Marx's explanation that such hard work is a result of coercion. The advent of labor unions and other changes largely eliminated the arbitrary power of management. "Coercion alone could no longer explain what workers did once they arrived on the shop floor" (Burawoy, 1979:xii). To Burawoy, workers, at least in part, consent to work hard in the capitalist system, and at least part of that consent is produced in the workplace.

We can illustrate Burawoy's approach with one aspect of his research, the games that workers play on the job and, more generally, the informal practices that they develop. Most analysts see these as workers' efforts to reduce alienation and other job-related discontent. In addition, they usually have been seen as social mechanisms that workers develop to oppose management. In contrast, Burawoy concludes that these games "are usually neither independent nor in opposition to management" (1979:80). In fact, "management, at least at the lower levels, actually participates not only in the organization of the game but in the enforcement of its rules" (1979:80). Rather than challenging management, the organization, or, ultimately, the capitalist system, these games actually support them. For one thing, playing the game creates consent among the workers about the rules on which the game is based and, more generally, about the system of social relations (owner-manager-worker) that defines the rules of the game. For another, because managers and workers both are involved in the game, the system of antagonistic social relations to which the game was supposed to respond is obscured.

Burawoy argues that such methods of generating active cooperation and consent are far more effective in getting workers to cooperate in the pursuit of profit than is coercion (such as firing those who do not cooperate). In the end, Burawoy believes that games and other informal practices are all methods of getting workers to accept the system and of eliciting their contributions to ever higher profits.

Fordism and Post-Fordism

One of the most recent concerns of economically oriented Marxists is the issue of whether we have witnessed, or are witnessing, a transition from "Fordism" to "post-Fordism" (A. Amin, 1994; Kiely, 1998; Wiedenhoft, 2005). This concern is related to the broader issue of whether we have undergone a transition from a modern to a postmodern society (Gartman, 1998). We will discuss this larger issue in general (Chapter 16), as well as the way in which it is addressed by contemporary Marxian theorists (later in this chapter). In general, *Fordism* is associated with the modern era, while *post-Fordism* is linked to the more recent, postmodern epoch. (The Marxian interest in Fordism is not new; Gramsci [1971] published an essay on it in 1931.)

Fordism, of course, refers to the ideas, principles, and systems spawned by Henry Ford. Ford generally is credited with the development of the modern mass-production system, primarily through the creation of the automobile assembly line. The following characteristics may be associated with Fordism:

- The mass production of homogeneous products.
- The use of inflexible technologies such as the assembly line.
- The adoption of standardized work routines (Taylorism).
- Increases in productivity derived from "economies of scale as well as the deskilling, intensification and homogenization of labor" (Clarke, 1990:73).
- The resulting rise of the mass worker and bureaucratized unions.
- The negotiation by unions of uniform wages tied to increases in profits and productivity.
- The growth of a market for the homogenized products of mass-production industries and the resulting homogenization of consumption patterns.
- A rise in wages, caused by unionization, leading to a growing demand for the increasing supply of mass-produced products.
- A market for products that is governed by Keynesian macroeconomic policies and a market for labor that is handled by collective bargaining overseen by the state.
- Mass educational institutions providing the mass workers required by industry (Clarke, 1990:73).

While Fordism grew throughout the twentieth century, especially in the United States, it reached its peak and began to decline in the 1970s, especially after the oil crisis of 1973 and the subsequent decline of the American automobile industry and the rise of its Japanese counterpart. As a result, it is argued that we are witnessing the decline of Fordism and the rise of post-Fordism, characterized by the following:

- A decline of interest in mass products is accompanied by a growth of interest in more specialized products, especially those high in style and quality.
- More specialized products require shorter production runs, resulting in smaller and more productive systems.
- More flexible production is made profitable by the advent of new technologies.
- New technologies require that workers, in turn, have more diverse skills and better training, more responsibility and greater autonomy.
- Production must be controlled through more flexible systems.
- Huge, inflexible bureaucracies need to be altered dramatically in order to operate more flexibly.
- Bureaucratized unions (and political parties) no longer adequately represent the interests of the new, highly differentiated labor force.
- Decentralized collective bargaining replaces centralized negotiations.
- The workers become more differentiated as people and require more differentiated commodities, lifestyles, and cultural outlets.
- The centralized welfare state no longer can meet the needs (for example, health, welfare, education) of a diverse population, and differentiated, more flexible institutions are required (Clarke, 1990:73–74).

If one needed to sum up the shift from Fordism to post-Fordism, it would be described as the transition from homogeneity to heterogeneity. There are two general issues involved here. First, has a transition from Fordism to post-Fordism actually occurred (Pelaez and Holloway, 1990)? Second, does post-Fordism hold out the hope of solving the problems associated with Fordism?

First, of course, there has been *no* clear historical break between Fordism and post-Fordism (S. Hall, 1988). Even if we are willing to acknowledge that elements of post-Fordism have emerged in the modern world, it is equally clear that elements of Fordism persist and show no signs of disappearing. For example, something we might call "McDonaldism," a phenomenon that has many things in common with Fordism, is growing at an astounding pace in contemporary society. On the basis of the model of the fast-food restaurant, more and more sectors of society are coming to utilize the principles of McDonaldism (Ritzer, 2013). McDonaldism shares many characteristics with Fordism—homogeneous products, rigid technologies, standardized work routines, deskilling, homogenization of labor (and customer), the mass worker, homogenization of consumption, and so on. Thus, Fordism is alive and well in the modern world, although it has been transmogrified into McDonaldism. Furthermore, classic Fordism—for example, in the form of the assembly line—retains a significant presence in the American economy.

Second, even if we accept the idea that post-Fordism is with us, does it represent a solution to the problems of modern capitalist society? Some neo-Marxists (and many supporters of the capitalist system [Womack, Jones, and Roos, 1990]) hold out great hope for it: "Post-Fordism is mainly an expression of hope that future capitalist development will be the salvation of social democracy" (Clarke, 1990:75). However, this is merely a hope, and in any case, there is already evidence that post-Fordism may not be the nirvana hoped for by some observers.

The Japanese model (tarnished by the precipitous decline of Japanese industry in the 1990s) is widely believed to be the basis of post-Fordism. However, research on Japanese industry (Satoshi, 1982) and on American industries utilizing Japanese management techniques (Parker and Slaughter, 1990) indicates that there are great problems with these systems and that they may even serve to *heighten* the level of exploitation of the worker. Parker and Slaughter label the Japanese system as it is employed in the United States (and it is probably worse in Japan) "management by stress": "The goal is to stretch the system like a rubber band on the point of breaking" (1990:33). Among other things, work is speeded up even further than on traditional American assembly lines, putting enormous strain on the workers, who need to labor heroically just to keep up with the line. More generally, Levidow describes the new, post-Fordist workers as "relentlessly pressurized to increase their productivity, often in return for lower real wages—be they factory workers, homeworkers in the rag trade, privatized service workers or even polytechnic lecturers" (1990:59). Thus, it may well be that rather than representing a solution to the problems of capitalism, post-Fordism may simply be merely a new, more insidious phase in the heightening of the exploitation of workers by capitalists.

Historically Oriented Marxism

Marxists oriented toward historical research argue that they are being true to the Marxian concern for historicity. The most notable of Marx's historical research was his study of precapitalist economic formations (1857–1858/1964). There has been a good deal of subsequent historical work from a Marxian perspective (for example, S. Amin, 1977; Dobb, 1964; Hobsbawm, 1965). In this section, we deal with a body of work that reflects a historical orientation—Immanuel Wallerstein's (1974/2011, 1980/2011, 1989/2011, 1992, 1995, 2011a; Chase-Dunn, 2001, 2005a; Chase-Dunn and Inoue, 2011) research on the modern world-system (Chase-Dunn, 2005b).

The Modern World-System

Wallerstein chose a unit of analysis unlike the units used by most Marxian thinkers. He did not look at workers, classes, or even states because he found most of these too narrow for his purposes. Instead, he looked at a broad economic entity with a division of labor that is not circumscribed by political or cultural boundaries. He found that unit in his concept of the *world-system,* which is a largely self-contained social system with a set of boundaries and a definable life span; that is, it does not last forever. It is composed internally of a variety of social structures and member groups. However, Wallerstein was not inclined to define the system in terms of a consensus that holds it together. Rather, he saw the system as held together by a variety of forces that are in inherent tension. These forces always have the potential for tearing the system apart.

IMMANUEL WALLERSTEIN

A Biographical Sketch

Although Immanuel Wallerstein achieved recognition in the 1960s as an expert on Africa, his most important contribution to sociology is his book *The Modern World-System* (1974/2011). That book was an instant success. It has received worldwide recognition and has been translated into ten languages and Braille.

Born on September 28, 1930, Wallerstein received all his degrees from Columbia University, including a doctorate in 1959. He next assumed a position on the faculty at Columbia; after many years there and a five-year stint at McGill University in Montreal, Wallerstein became, in 1976, distinguished professor of sociology at the State University of New York at Binghamton.

Wallerstein was awarded the prestigious Sorokin Award for the first volume of *The Modern World-System* in 1975. Since that time, he has continued to work on the topic and has produced a number of articles as well as three additional volumes, in which he takes his analysis of the world-system up to 1914.

In fact, in many ways the attention this analysis has attracted and will continue to attract is more important than the body of work itself. The concept of the world-system has become the focus of thought and research in sociology, an accomplishment to which few scholars can lay claim. Many of the sociologists now doing research and theorizing about the world-system are critical of Wallerstein in one way or another, but they all clearly recognize the important role he played in the genesis of their ideas (Chase-Dunn, 2005a).

Although the concept of the world-system is an important contribution, at least as significant has been the role Wallerstein played in the revival of theoretically informed historical research. The most important work in the early years of sociology, by people such as Marx, Weber, and Durkheim, was largely of this variety. However, in more recent years, most sociologists have turned away from doing this kind of research and toward using ahistorical methods such as questionnaires and interviews. These methods are quicker and easier to use than historical methods, and the data produced are easier to analyze with a computer. Use of such methods tends to require a narrow range of technical knowledge rather than a wide range of historically oriented knowledge. Furthermore, theory plays a comparatively minor role in research utilizing questionnaires and interviews. Wallerstein has been in the forefront of those involved in a revival of interest in historical research with a strong theoretical base.

Wallerstein argued that thus far we have had only two types of world-systems. One is the world empire, of which ancient Rome is an example. The other is the modern capitalist world-economy. A world empire is based on political (and military) domination, whereas a capitalist world-economy relies on economic domination. A capitalist world-economy is seen as more stable than a world empire for several reasons. For one thing, it has a broader base because it encompasses many states. For another, it has a built-in process of economic stabilization. The separate political entities within the capitalist world-economy absorb whatever losses occur, while economic gain is distributed to private hands. Wallerstein foresaw the *possibility* of still a third world-system, a *socialist world government*. Whereas the capitalist world-economy separates the political sector from the economic sector, a socialist world-economy would reintegrate them.

The *core* geographical area dominates the capitalist world-economy and exploits the rest of the system. The *periphery* consists of those areas that provide raw materials to the core and are heavily exploited by it. The *semiperiphery* is a residual category that encompasses a set of regions somewhere between the exploiting and the exploited. The key point is that to Wallerstein the international division of exploitation is defined not by state borders but by the economic division of labor in the world.

In the first volume on the world-system, Wallerstein (1974/2011) dealt with the origin of the world-system roughly between the years 1450 and 1640. The significance of this development was the shift from political (and thus military) to economic dominance. Wallerstein saw economics as a far more efficient and less primitive means of domination than politics. Political structures are very cumbersome, whereas economic exploitation "makes it possible to increase the flow of the surplus from the lower strata to the upper strata, from the periphery to the center, from the majority to the minority" (Wallerstein, 1974/2011:15–16). In the modern era, capitalism provided a basis for the growth and development of a world-economy; this has been accomplished without the aid of a unified political structure. Capitalism can be seen as an economic alternative to political domination. It is better able to produce economic surpluses than are the more primitive techniques employed in political exploitation.

Wallerstein argued that three things were necessary for the rise of the capitalist world-economy out of the "ruins" of feudalism: geographical expansion through exploration and colonization, development of different methods of labor control for zones (for example, core, periphery) of the world-economy, and the development of strong states that were to become the core states of the emerging capitalist world-economy. Let us look at each of these in turn.

Geographical Expansion

Wallerstein argued that geographical expansion by nations is a prerequisite for the other two stages. Portugal took the lead in overseas exploration, and other European nations followed. Wallerstein was wary of talking about specific countries or about Europe in general terms. He preferred to see overseas expansion as caused by a group of people acting in their immediate interests. Elite groups, such as nobles, needed overseas expansion for various reasons. For one thing, they were confronted with a nascent class war brought on by the crumbling of the feudal economy. The slave trade provided them with a tractable labor force on which to build the capitalist economy. The expansion also provided them with various commodities needed to develop it— gold bullion, food, and raw materials of various types.

Worldwide Division of Labor

Once the world had undergone geographical expansion, it was prepared for the next stage, the development of a worldwide division of labor. In the sixteenth century, capitalism replaced statism as the major mode of dominating the world, but capitalism did not develop uniformly around the world. In fact, Wallerstein argued, the solidarity of the capitalist system ultimately was based on its unequal development. Given his Marxian orientation, Wallerstein did not think of this as a consensual equilibrium but rather as one that was laden with conflict from the beginning. Different parts of the capitalist world-system came to specialize in specific functions—breeding labor power, growing food, providing raw materials, and organizing industry. Furthermore, different areas came to specialize in producing particular types of workers. For example, Africa produced slaves; western and southern Europe had many peasant tenant-farmers; western Europe was also the center of wage workers, the ruling classes, and other skilled and supervisory personnel.

More generally, each of the three parts of the international division of labor tended to differ in terms of mode of labor control. The core had free labor, the periphery was characterized by forced labor, and the semiperiphery was the heart of share-cropping. In fact, Wallerstein argued that the key to capitalism lies in a core dominated by a free labor market for skilled workers and a coercive labor market for less-skilled workers in peripheral areas. Such a combination is the essence of capitalism. If a free labor market should develop throughout the world, we would have socialism.

Some regions of the world begin with small initial advantages, which are used as the basis for developing greater advantages later on. The core area in the sixteenth century, primarily western Europe, rapidly extended its advantages as towns flourished, industries developed, and merchants became important. It also moved to extend its domain by developing a wider variety of activities. At the same time, each of its activities became more specialized in order to produce more efficiently. In contrast, the periphery stagnated and moved more toward what Wallerstein called a "monoculture," or an undifferentiated, single-focus society.

Development of Core States

The third stage of the development of the world-system involved the political sector and how various economic groups used state structures to protect and advance their interests. Absolute monarchies arose in western Europe at about the same time that capitalism developed. From the sixteenth to the eighteenth centuries, the states were the central economic actors in Europe, although the center later shifted to economic enterprises. The strong states in the core areas played a key role in the development of capitalism and ultimately provided the economic base for their own demise. The European states strengthened themselves in the sixteenth century by, among other things, developing and enlarging bureaucratic systems and creating a monopoly of force in society, primarily by developing armies and legitimizing their activities so that they were assured of internal stability. Whereas the states of the core zone developed strong political systems, the periphery developed correspondingly weak states.

Later Developments

In *The Modern World-System II,* Wallerstein (1980/2011) picked up the story of the consolidation of the world-economy between 1600 and 1750. This was not a period of significant expansion of the European world-economy, but there were a number of significant changes within that system. For example, Wallerstein discussed the rise and subsequent decline in the core of the Netherlands. Later, he analyzed the conflict between two core states, England and France, as well as the ultimate victory of England. In the periphery, Wallerstein's detailed descriptions include the cyclical fortunes of Hispanic America. In the semiperiphery we witness, among other things, the decline of Spain and the rise of Sweden.

In *The Modern World System III*, Wallerstein (1989/2011) brings his historical analysis up to the 1840s. Wallerstein looks at three great developments during the period from 1730 to the 1840s—the Industrial Revolution (primarily in England), the French Revolution, and the independence of the once-European colonies in America. In his view, none of these were fundamental challenges to the world capitalist system; instead, they represented its "further consolidation and entrenchment" (Wallerstein, 1989/2011:256).

Wallerstein continues the story of the struggle between England and France for dominance of the core. Whereas the world-economy had been stagnant during the prior period of analysis, it was now expanding, and Great Britain was able to industrialize more rapidly and come to dominate large-scale industries. This shift in domination to England occurred in spite of the fact that in the eighteenth century France had dominated in the industrial realm. The French Revolution played an important role in the development of the world capitalist system, especially by helping to bring the lingering cultural vestiges of feudalism to an end and by aligning the cultural-ideological system with economic and political realities (see discussion of Volume IV below). However, the revolution served to inhibit the industrial development of France, as did the ensuing Napoleonic rules and wars. By the end of this period, "Britain was finally truly hegemonic in the world-system" (Wallerstein, 1989/2011:122).

The period between 1750 and 1850 was marked by the incorporation of vast new zones (the subcontinent of India, the Ottoman and Russian empires, and West Africa) into the periphery of the world-economy. These zones had been part of what Wallerstein calls the "external area" of the world-system and thus had been linked to, but were not in, that system. *External zones* are those from which the capitalist world-economy wanted goods but which were able to resist the reciprocal importation of manufactured goods from the core nations. As a result of the incorporation of these external zones, countries adjacent to the once-external nations also were drawn into the world-system. Thus, the incorporation of India contributed to China's becoming part of the periphery. By the end of the nineteenth century and the beginning of the twentieth, the pace of incorporation had quickened, and "the entire globe, even those regions that had never been part even of the external area of the capitalist world-economy were pulled inside" (Wallerstein, 1989/2011:129).

The pressure for incorporation into the world-economy comes not from the nations being incorporated but "rather from the need of the world-economy to expand its boundaries, a need which was itself the outcome of pressures internal to the world-economy" (Wallerstein, 1989/2011:129). Furthermore, the process of incorporation is not an abrupt process but one that occurs gradually.

Reflecting his Marxian focus on economics, Wallerstein (1989/2011:170) argues that becoming part of the world-economy "necessarily" means that the political structures of the involved nations must become part of the interstate system. Thus, states in incorporated zones must transform themselves into part of that interstate political system, be replaced by new political forms willing to accept this role, or be taken over by states that already are part of that political system. The states that emerge at the end of the process of incorporation not only must be part of the interstate system but also must be strong enough to protect their economies from external interference. However, they must not be too strong; that is, they must not become powerful enough to be able to refuse to act in accord with the dictates of the capitalist world-economy.

Finally, Wallerstein examines the decolonization of the Americas between 1750 and 1850. That is, he details the fact that the Americas freed themselves from the control of Great Britain, France, Spain, and Portugal. That decolonization, especially in the United States, was, of course, to have great consequences for later developments in the world capitalist system.

Most recently, Wallerstein (2011a) has published volume IV of *The Modern World-System*, subtitled *Centrist Liberalism Triumphant*. This volume covers a period between 1789 and 1914. In contrast to previous volumes that described the emergence of the economic and political structures of the capitalist world-economy, this volume describes the emergence of the ideology of the capitalist world-economy. Before the nineteenth century there was a "disjuncture between the political economy of the world-system and its discursive rhetoric" (2011a:277). The implication is that to consolidate these earlier structural gains the world-system also required a legitimating ideology. Wallerstein calls this ideology a *geoculture:* "by geoculture, we mean values that are widely shared throughout the world-system, both explicitly and latently" (2011a:277). The argument of volume IV is that by the middle of the nineteenth century *centrist liberalism* emerges as the geoculture of the modern world-system.

Coming out of the French Revolution, it was not clear that centrist liberalism would succeed as the geoculture of world capitalism. For the first half of the nineteenth century, centrist liberalism was opposed by the socialism of the left and the conservatism of the right. Each of these viewpoints offered a distinct interpretation of the meaning of the French Revolution, a unique view of the "historical subject" of modernity, and different ideas about the relationship of the state to this historical subject. Yet: "Behind this façade of intense opposition to liberalism one finds as a core component of the demands of all these regimes the same faith in progress via productivity that has been the gospel of liberals" (2011a:18). Even though strains of conservatism and socialism remain active, this commonality led all positions to gravitate toward centrist liberalism.

Wallerstein shows how liberalism becomes part of the world-system by detailing the emergence of three modern social institutions: the liberal state, modern citizenship, and the social sciences. Contrary to the laissez-faire ideology usually associated with liberalism, Wallerstein (echoing Karl Polanyi) shows that centrist liberalism requires the creation of a strong state. The priority of the liberal state is not to provide for a laissez-faire marketplace, but rather to ensure economic growth in general. While this might involve free market legislation, it could also involve legislation unrelated to the creation of a free market. For example, the liberal state was also involved in the creation of social welfare programs. Social amelioration policies were thought to contribute to economic productivity, but more importantly, the programs served the political purpose of the "taming of the dangerous classes" (2011a:140). This drew radical socialism into the project of liberalism, eliminating it as a serious ideological threat.

Concerning citizenship, the concepts of equality and democratic collective governance were "the centerpiece of liberal ideology" (2011a:217). The problem was that universal suffrage also threatened the power of the elites who were creating the liberal state. As a result, the inclusive conception of citizenship was accompanied by a set of exclusions intended to limit the number of "active" citizens (i.e., those permitted to participate in collective governance). Among others, women and racialized groups were categorized as "passive" citizens. They could benefit from the protections of the liberal state but could not participate in its governance. In this system of inclusion-exclusion "the nineteenth century saw the creation of our entire contemporary conceptual apparatus of identities" that would become the basis for the major nineteenth- and twentieth-century social movements (2011a:217).

Finally, Wallerstein treats the emergence of the historical social sciences: history, economics, sociology, and political science. These played a central role in both legitimating the liberal state and contributing to its operation. While these disciplines have sought to portray themselves as neutral and objective sciences, they are firmly allied with the tasks of liberalism and thus have been central to the development of the geoculture of the world economic-system.

Volume IV of *The Modern World-System* only takes us to 1914 and therefore leaves some important developments in the last 100 years untouched. As such, Wallerstein indicates that there are at least two volumes forthcoming. These will describe the emergence of the United States as the most recent global hegemon, and then detail the structural crisis of capitalism that brings us into the present moment and beyond.

World-System Theory Today

Marxists have criticized the world-system perspective for its failure to emphasize relations between social classes adequately (Bergeson, 1984). From their point of view, Wallerstein focuses on the wrong issue. To Marxists the key is not the core–periphery international division of labor but rather class relationships *within* given societies. Bergeson seeks to reconcile these positions by arguing that there are strengths and weaknesses on both sides. His middle-ground position is that core–periphery relations are not only unequal exchange relations but also global *class* relations. His key point is that core–periphery relations *are* important, not only as exchange relations, as Wallerstein argues, but also, and more importantly, as power-dependence relationships, that is, class relationships.

This said, world-systems theory has become one of the most influential forms of contemporary neo-Marxian analysis. In recent years, world-system theorists have pushed the theory forward to deal with the world today and in the coming years (Chase-Dunn, 2001; Wallerstein, 1992, 1999, 2011b) as well as backward to before the modern era (Chase-Dunn and Hall, 1994). Its influence has, in part, to do with its overlap with research in the area of globalization theory (see Chapter 15).

In particular, world-system theorists have produced a number of analyses of the capitalist world-economy in light of the global economic crisis that began in 2008 (Silver and Arrighi, 2011; Wallerstein, 2011b). These analyses generally conclude that the capitalist world-economy is in the midst of a long-term decline, and that the ongoing crisis signals the end of the capitalist world-economy. Wallerstein puts it most strongly: "The question is no longer, how will the capitalist system mend itself and renew its forward thrust? The question is, what will replace this system? What order will be chosen out of this chaos?" (2011b:84).

Over the last 400 years capitalism has suffered numerous crises. These, as most Marxists point out, are built into the very structure of capitalism. Capitalism has been able to survive these crises by expanding the world-system and seeking new sources of profit abroad (as described above). However, there are good reasons to think that capitalism may not be able to survive this most recent crisis. For example, drawing on complex systems and chaos theory, Wallerstein (2011b) says that each economic crisis moves the capitalist world-system away from a state of equilibrium. The world-economy restabilizes only after the system is modified into a new configuration of core, periphery, and semiperiphery relations. However, each successive crisis also moves the system further away from equilibrium. The system is increasingly characterized by massive unpredictable fluctuations to the point where it can no longer return to a stable state. The current crisis has brought the capitalist world-economy to a state where it can no longer return to equilibrium.

In less abstract terms, capitalists find it increasingly difficult to save on production costs in the three key areas of personnel, inputs to production, and taxation:

> Capitalism is no longer viable not simply because it involves much oppression for
> the majority of the world's population but because it no longer offers capitalists the
> opportunity to achieve their principal objective, the endless accumulation of capital.
> The game is no longer worth the candle—something that is becoming more evident
> to capitalists themselves.

(2011b:84)

Add to this the fact that the capitalist world-economy is destroying the environment and has nearly exhausted its energy supplies, and capitalism has no more wiggle-room. From Wallerstein's perspective, the only question left is: What follows the collapse of capitalism? He suggests two alternatives. First, the current system could be replaced by one that is even more "hierarchical, exploitative, and polarizing" than the present system (2011b:85). Second, we could collectively choose "a system that is relatively democratic and relatively egalitarian" (2011b:85). Even though this latter kind of system has never existed, Wallerstein suggests that, historically, we are in the best position ever to realize its possibilities.[6]

Neo-Marxian Spatial Analysis

Categorization of neo-Marxian theories, indeed all theories, is somewhat arbitrary. That is made clear here by the fact that the work on world-systems discussed in the previous section under the heading "Neo-Marxian Economic Sociology" also could be discussed in this section. For example, the idea of the world-system is, among other things, inherently spatial, concerned with the global differentiation of the world-economy. Work on the world-system is part of a broader body of work that involves a number of notable contributions by neo-Marxian theorists to our understanding of space and its role in the social world. And this is only part of a broader resurgence of interest in space in sociology (Gieryn, 2000) and social theory. In this section we deal with several of the leading contributions to this area in which neo-Marxists have been in the forefront.[7]

A starting point for the growth in interest in space in neo-Marxian theory (and elsewhere) is the work of Michel Foucault (see Chapter 16), who pointed out that many theories, but especially Marxian theories, had privileged time over space: "This devaluation of space that has prevailed for generations. . . . Space was treated as the dead, the fixed, the undialectical, the immobile. Time, on the contrary, was richness, fecundity, life, dialectic" (Foucault, 1980b:70). The implication is that space should, along with time, be given its due and treated as rich, fecund, alive, and dialectical. While the focus may have been on time (and history) in the past, Foucault (1986:22) contends, "The present epoch will perhaps be above all the epoch of space." In fact, as we will see in Chapter 16, Foucault offers a number of important insights into space in his discussion of such topics as the "carceral archipelago" and the Panopticon.

The Production of Space

The pathbreaking work in the neo-Marxian theory of space is Henri Lefebvre's (1974/1991) *The Production of Space* (see also Faist, 2005; Goonewardena, 2011; Kurasawa, 2005). According to Lefebvre, social theorists have not sufficiently theorized the nature of space and its relationship to social life. They have primarily treated space as a neutral backdrop to the more important events that occurred *in* space. To these older theorists, space was a place in which things happened, but space in itself did not have meaning or significance. Marxists, in particular, focused on the production of things in space (for example, the means of production such as factories) rather

---

[6] For a thorough analysis of the causes as well as implications of the 2008 economic crisis see Calhoun and Derluguian's (2011) invaluable three-volume collection, which includes analyses from world-system theorists and other perspectives.
[7] Reflective of categorization problems is the fact that at least one major contribution to the theory of space that can be seen as neo-Marxian—Fredric Jameson's (1984, 1991) work on "hyperspace"—is discussed elsewhere in this book under the heading "Postmodern Social Theory" (see Chapter 16). Furthermore, additional important contributions on space have emanated from still other theoretical roots and are discussed at yet other points in this book. For example, Anthony Giddens's very important ideas on space (and time), distanciation, and so on, are discussed in Chapter 14.

than the production of space itself. Marxian theory needs to broaden its concerns from (industrial) production to the production of space.

As a Marxist, Lefebvre is particularly interested in the way that capitalism shapes the spaces in which people live. To better understand the capitalist domination of space, Lefebvre provides a history of the ways in which space has been shaped by human societies. Early pastoral and agricultural societies did not dominate space. They lived quite close to nature and Lefebvre suggests that these early societies were dominated by the spaces and forces of nature. They lived in response to the demands placed on them by their immediate geography. This starts to change with the development of what Lefebvre calls absolute space. *Absolute space* is shaped by religious and political concerns. These spaces are built in places like mountaintops and caves. Examples include Greek temples and Christian tombs and cemeteries. On the surface, Lefebvre says, these spaces seem to draw their power from nature. For example, the ancient Greek temple is built in a natural setting and is constructed to reflect natural geometrical principles of order and symmetry. Similarly, the Christian cemetery is built in a natural setting and puts us into contact with the natural force of death. Ultimately, however, these spaces dominate nature. They are, after all, built spaces and built spaces necessarily impose their order on the natural world that they displace. In addition, the elites who control these spaces use their symbolic power to dominate human populations.

The next kind of space is called *historical space*. This kind of space starts to be produced in early modern Europe. Even though Lefebvre spends relatively little time discussing historical space, it is an important bridge between absolute space and the abstract space of the present moment. Historical space is secular. It breaks with the religious connection to nature found in absolute space. Historical space is produced as separate nations vie with one another for power and the accumulation of wealth. This space is produced with human interests in mind, rather than nature or religion. Ultimately historical space gives way to abstract space.

Abstract space is the kind of space produced within the modern, industrial, capitalist society. Abstract space involves the total domination of nature and society. In order to ensure as much profit as possible, the capitalist, working alongside the state, tries to exert as much control over space as possible. Indeed, for Lefebvre the control of space is essential to the growth of capitalism. This kind of control requires that the capitalist take an abstract view of space. Within a capitalist society professions like urban planning and architecture serve the purpose of producing abstract *representations of space*. The abstract representations treat space as a series of problems to be analyzed and solved. They treat space more like a mathematical grid than a place in which people live their lives. Indeed, instead of seeing space from the perspective of the person who uses space, planners seek to maximize the efficient and profitable use of space: How can space be most efficiently used? How can space be organized to benefit the growth of the economy? From this view, it is not only the factory that generates profit, but also the bus routes, railway lines, and highways that provide routes into the factory for workers and raw materials and out of the factory for finished products. The city, the country, and ultimately the planet is treated as a monolithic problem in spatial management.

As should be clear, the production of abstract space has implications for the everyday experience of space. Abstract space controls the way that people use and move through space and in so doing it also determines the way that people experience and live their lives. For example, North American cities designed in the latter half of the twentieth century were organized around the interests of the automobile industry. City planners chose to build highways and intricate road systems that stretched into suburbs, rather than planning walkable cities like those found in Europe. People who live in the former kinds of cities are likely to experience the city through the lens of high-speed traffic and congestion. They will spend many hours commuting to and from work in single-passenger cars and their homes in the suburbs will become the self-enclosed center of their existence.

This said, as a good Marxian theorist, Lefebvre emphasizes that abstract space is also full of contradictions that will ultimately bring about its demise. For example, one of the consequences of capitalism is a clear and growing distinction between the rich and the poor. Spatially, this inequality has been realized through the development of wealthy suburbs and gated communities. Gated communities are designed to defend the property of the wealthy against intrusions by the poor who live in low-income neighborhoods and slums. If inequality continues to grow (as Marxists predict), then we can also expect to see further spatial divisions between rich and poor. Although, until the present, scholars have only commented on the inequalities made apparent through these spaces, Lefebvre suggests that recognition of these kinds of contradictions will eventually produce challenges to these spatial divisions and the emergence of a new kind of space.

This brings us to Lefebvre's concept of *differential space*. While abstract space seeks to control and homogenize everyone and everything, differential space accentuates difference and freedom from control. While abstract space breaks up the natural unity that exists in the world, differential space restores that unity. Differential space allows for the use of space that is not imagined through the principles of abstraction and calculation. A differential space would be one in which space is produced from the perspective of those who live within it rather than from the perspective of the system of capitalism. It would also, Lefebvre suggests, bring people closer to the power of natural spaces that have for so long been dominated by human interests. Indeed, differential space is revolutionary and transformative because it allows room for tension, difference, and unique forms of human spatial expression to thrive. In contrast to abstract space, then, differential space is a dynamic space that is accountable and responsive to the variety of people who live in that space.

Within the context of Marxian theory then, Lefebvre's analysis of space is important for two reasons. First, it offers a new focus of analysis and critique. Our attention should shift from the capitalist production of wealth through the means of production, to the way that capitalism shapes the total space of contemporary society. The forces of capital, in other words, are not only found in factories and financial exchange centers but they also organize the spaces of everyday life. Second, Lefebvre conducts this analysis in order to motivate social change. We live in a world in which the state, the capitalist, and the bourgeoisie dominate space. It is a closed, sterile world, one that is being emptied out of contents (e.g., highways are replacing and destroying local communities). Lefebvre argues that we need instead a world in which people work with others to produce the kinds of spaces that they need to survive and prosper. They would not try to dominate space, but rather would modify natural space to serve their collective needs. Thus, Lefebvre's goal is the production of space that is a product and reflection of human beings rather than abstract systems. It would be planet-wide space that would serve as the basis for transforming everyday life. Needless to say, state and private ownership of the means of production would wither away under such a system.

Trialectics

Edward Soja (1989) was heavily influenced by both Foucault and Lefebvre. For example, like Foucault he critiques the focus on time (and history) as creating "carceral historicism" and a "temporal prisonhouse" (Soja, 1989:1). He seeks to integrate the study of space and geography with that of time. Lefebvre has had a profound influence on Soja's thinking, but Soja is critical of some aspects of his work and seeks to go beyond it in various ways.

Perhaps the core of Soja's (1996, 2000) theoretical contribution to our understanding of space is his notion of *trialectics*. Obviously, Soja is building, and expanding, on the Marxian (and Hegelian) notion of dialectics. However, a more immediate source is Lefebvre's work. Soja uses Lefebvre's work to theorize what he calls *cityspace*, or "the city as a historical-social-spatial phenomenon, but *with its intrinsic spatiality highlighted* for interpretive and explanatory purposes" (Soja, 2000:8). This definition highlights one of Soja's basic premises; that is, while he privileges space, he insists on including in his analysis history (or time more generally) and social relations. While the move toward including space in social analyses is to be encouraged, it should not be done to the detriment of the analysis of history and time. Furthermore, the inclusion of social relations sets Soja's perspective squarely in the tradition of the sociological and social theories dealt with throughout this book.

The Firstspace perspective is basically a materialist orientation that is consistent with the approach most often taken by geographers in the study of the city. Here is the way Soja (2000:10) describes a Firstspace approach: "cityspace can be studied as a set of materialized 'social practices' that work together to produce and reproduce the concrete forms and specific patternings of urbanism as a way of life. Here cityspace is physically and empirically perceived as form and process, as measurable and mappable configurations and practices of urban life." A Firstspace approach focuses on objective phenomena and emphasizes "things in space."

In contrast, a Secondspace approach tends to be more subjective and to focus on "thoughts about space." In a Secondspace perspective, "cityspace becomes more of a mental or ideational field, conceptualized in imagery, reflexive thought, and symbolic representation, a *conceived* space of the imagination, or . . . urban imaginary" (Soja, 2000:11). Examples of a Secondspace perspective include the mental maps we all carry with us, visions of an urban utopia, and more formal methods for obtaining and conveying information about the geography of the city.

Soja seeks to subsume both of the above in Thirdspace, which is viewed as

> another way of thinking about the social production of human spatiality that
> incorporates both Firstspace and Secondspace perspectives while at the same time
> opening up the scope and complexity of the geographical or spatial imagination.
> In this alternative or "third" perspective, the spatial specificity of urbanism is
> investigated as fully *lived space,* a simultaneously real-and-imagined, actual-and-
> virtual, locus of structured individual and collective experience and agency.
>
> (Soja, 2000:11)

This is a highly complex view of cityspace. Because of its great complexity and because much is hidden and perhaps unknowable, the best we can do is to explore cityspace selectively "through its intrinsic spatial, social, and historical dimensions, its interrelated spatiality, sociality, and historicality" (Soja, 2000:12). Throughout his career, Soja's favorite cityspace has been Los Angeles, and he returns to it over and over to analyze it from various perspectives, including his own integrative sense of Thirdspace.

Spaces of Hope

We began this section with the point that the categorization of theories is somewhat arbitrary. In fact, the work of Edward Soja fits as much into a category—postmodern Marxian theory—we will discuss below as it does into neo-Marxian spatial analyses. The same is true of the work of the thinker we discuss next—David Harvey—and, in fact, we discuss his work not only under this heading but also under that of postmodern Marxian theory.

In fact, Harvey has produced analyses of space under a variety of guises as his work has undergone several twists and turns over the years. In reflecting on his early work, Harvey thought of himself as lax scientifically, but he underwent a first change of orientation in the late 1960s and declared himself a positivist guided by the scientific method and, as a result, oriented toward quantification, the development of theories, the discovery of laws, and the like (Harvey, 1969). However, within a few years Harvey (1973) had undergone another paradigm change and rejected his earlier commitment to positivism. He now favored materialist theory with a powerful debt to the work of Karl Marx.

While, as we will see later, Harvey flirted with postmodern theory and certainly was influenced by it in many ways, he has retained his commitment to Marxian theory, and this is clear in one of his more recent books, *Spaces of Hope* (Harvey, 2000). One aspect of Harvey's argument that is particularly relevant to this discussion of neo-Marxian theory is his analysis and critique of the geographical arguments made in the *Communist Manifesto.* Harvey sees the idea of the "spatial fix" as central to the *Manifesto.* That is, the need to create ever-higher profits means that capitalist firms must, among other things, continually seek new geographical areas (and markets) to exploit and find more thorough ways of exploiting the areas in which they already operate. While such geographical arguments occupy an important place in the *Manifesto,* they characteristically are subordinated in a "rhetorical mode that in the last instance privileges time and history over space and geography" (Harvey, 2000:24).

Harvey (2000:31) begins by acknowledging the strengths of the *Manifesto* and its recognition that "geographical reorderings and restructurings, spatial strategies and geopolitical elements, uneven geographical developments, and the like, are vital aspects to the accumulation of capital and the dynamics of class struggle, both historically and today." However, the arguments made in the *Manifesto* on space (and other matters) are severely limited, and Harvey sets out to strengthen them and bring them up to date.

For example, Harvey argues that Marx and Engels operate with a simplistic differentiation between civilized-barbarian and more generally core–periphery areas of the world. Relatedly, the *Manifesto* operates with a diffusionist model, with capitalism seen as spreading from civilized to barbarian areas, from core to periphery. Although Harvey acknowledges that there are instances of such diffusion, there are others, both historically and contemporaneously, in which internal developments within peripheral nations lead to the insertion of their labor power and commodities into the global marketplace.

More important, Harvey (2000:34) argues that "one of the biggest absences in the *Manifesto* is its lack of attention to the territorial organization of the world in general and of capitalism in particular." Thus, the recognition that the state was the executive arm of the bourgeoisie needs to be buttressed by recognition that "the state had to be territorially defined, organized, and administered" (Harvey, 2000:34). For example, loosely connected provinces had to be brought together to form the nation. However, territories do not remain set in stone once they have been transformed into states. All sorts of things alter territorial configurations, including revolutions in transportation and communication, "uneven dynamics of class struggle," and "uneven resource endowments." Furthermore, "[f]lows of commodities, capital, labor, and information always render boundaries porous" (Harvey, 2000:35). Thus, territories continually are being redefined and reorganized, with the result that any model that envisions a final formation of the state on a territorial basis is overly simplistic. The implication is that we need to be attuned continuously to territorial changes in a world dominated by capitalism.

Another of the spatial arguments in the *Manifesto* is that the concentration of capitalism (for example, factories in the cities) leads to the concentration of the proletariat, which formerly was scattered throughout the countryside. Instead of conflict between isolated workers and capitalists, it becomes more likely that a collectivity of workers will confront capitalists, who are themselves now more likely to be organized into a collectivity. Thus, in Harvey's (2000:36) words, "the production of spatial struggle is not neutral with respect to class struggle." However, there is much more to be said about the relationship between space and class struggle, and this is amply demonstrated in the more recent history of capitalism. For example, capitalists in the late nineteenth century dispersed factories from the cities to the suburbs in an effort to limit the concentration of workers and their power. And in the late twentieth century we witnessed the dispersal of factories to remote areas of the world in a further effort to weaken the proletariat and strengthen the capitalists.

Harvey also points out that the *Manifesto* tended to focus on the *urban* proletariat and thereby largely ignored rural areas, as well as agricultural workers and peasants. Of course, the latter groups over the years have proved to be very active in revolutionary movements. Furthermore, Marx and Engels tended to homogenize the world's workers, to argue that they have no country and that national differences are disappearing in the development of a homogeneous proletariat. Harvey notes that not only do national differences persist, but capitalism itself produces national (and other) differences among workers, "sometimes by feeding off ancient cultural distinctions, gender relations, ethnic predilections, and religious beliefs" (Harvey, 2000:40). In addition, labor plays a role here in sustaining spatial distinctions by, for example, mobilizing "through territorial forms of organization, building place-bound loyalties *en route*" (Harvey, 2000:40). Finally, Harvey notes the famous call in the *Manifesto* for workers of the world to unite and argues that given the increasingly global character of capitalism, such an exhortation is more relevant and more important than ever.

This is only a small part of a highly varied argument made by Harvey, but what does he mean by "spaces of hope"? First, he wishes to counter what he perceives to be a pervasive pessimism among today's scholars. Second, he wants to acknowledge the existence of "spaces of political struggle," and therefore hope, in society. Finally, he describes a utopian space of the future that offers hope to those concerned about the oppressiveness of today's spaces.

Thus, in these and many other ways, Harvey builds on Marx's (and in this case Engels's) limited insights into space and capitalism to develop a richer and more contemporary perspective on their relationship to each other. In that sense, what Harvey is doing here is an almost paradigmatic example of neo-Marxian theory.

Post-Marxist Theory

Since the 1980s, dramatic changes have taken place in neo-Marxian theory (Aronson, 1995; Grossberg and Nelson, 1988; Jay, 1988). The most recent varieties of neo-Marxian theory are rejecting many of the basic premises of Marx's original theory as well as those of the neo-Marxian theories discussed earlier in this chapter. Hence, these new approaches have come to be thought of as post-Marxist theories (Beilharz, 2005d; Dandaneau, 1992; Wright, 1987). While these theories reject the basic elements of Marxian theory, they still have sufficient affinities with it for them to be considered part of neo-Marxian theory. Post-Marxist theories are discussed here because they often involve the synthesis of Marxian theories with other theories, ideas, methods, and so on. How can we account for these dramatic changes in neo-Marxian theory? Two sets of factors are involved, one external to theory and involving changes in the social world and the other internal to theory itself (P. Anderson, 1984; Ritzer, 1991a).

First, and external to Marxian theory, was the end of the Cold War (Halliday, 1990) and the collapse of world communism. The Soviet Union is gone, and Russia has moved toward a market economy that resembles, at least in part, a capitalist economy (Piccone, 1990; Zaslavsky, 1988). Eastern Europe has shifted, often even more rapidly than Russia, in the direction of a capitalist-style economy (Kaldor, 1990). China clings to communism, but capitalism flourishes throughout that nation. Thus, the failure of communism on a worldwide scale made it necessary for Marxists to reconsider and reconstruct their theories (Burawoy, 1990; Aronson, 1995).

These changes in the world were related to a second set of changes, internal to theory itself, the series of intellectual changes that, in turn, affected neo-Marxian theory (P. Anderson, 1990a, 1990b). New theoretical currents such as poststructuralism and post-modernism (see Chapter 16) had a profound impact on neo-Marxian theory. In addition, a movement known as *analytical Marxism* gained ground; it was premised on the belief that Marxian theories needed to employ the same methods as those used by any other scientific enterprise. This approach led to reinterpretations of Marx in more conventional intellectual terms, efforts to apply rational choice theory to Marxian issues, and attempts to study Marxian topics by utilizing the methods and techniques of positivistic science. As Mayer puts it more specifically, "Increased humility toward the conventional norms of science coincides with diminished piety toward Marxist theory itself" (1994:296).

Thus, a combination of social and intellectual changes dramatically altered the landscape of neo-Marxian theory in the 1990s. While the theories discussed earlier remain important, much of the energy in neo-Marxian theory as we enter the twenty-first century is focused on the theories to be discussed in this section.

Analytical Marxism

Here is the way one of the leaders of analytical Marxism, John Roemer (1986a:1), defines it:

> During the past decade, what now appears as a new species in social theory has been forming: analytically sophisticated Marxism. Its practitioners are largely inspired by Marxian questions, which they pursue with contemporary tools of logic, mathematics and model building. Their methodological posture is conventional. These writers are, self-consciously, products of both the Marxian and neo-Marxian traditions.

Thus, analytical Marxists bring mainstream, "state-of-the-art" methods of analytical philosophy and social science to bear on Marxian substantive issues (Mayer, 1994:22). Analytical Marxism is discussed in this chapter because it "explicitly proposes to synthesize *non-Marxist* methods and Marxist theory" (Veneziani, 2008; Weldes, 1989:371).

Analytical Marxism adopts a nondogmatic approach to Marx's theory. It does not blindly and unthinkingly support Marx's theory, it does not deny historical facts in order to support Marx's theory, and it does not totally reject Marx's theory as fundamentally wrong. Rather, it views Marx's theory as a form of nineteenth-century social science with great power and with a valid core but also with substantial weaknesses. It rejects the idea that there is a distinctive Marxian methodology and criticizes those who think that such a methodology exists and is valid:

> I do not think there is a specific form of Marxist logic or explanation. Too often, obscurantism protects itself behind a yoga of special terms and privileged logic. The yoga of Marxism is "dialectics." Dialectical logic is based on several propositions which may have a certain inductive appeal, but are far from being rules of inference: that things turn into their opposites, and quantity turns into quality. In Marxian social science, dialectics is often used to justify a lazy kind of teleological reasoning. Developments occur because they must in order for history to be played out as it was intended.
>
> (Roemer, 1986b:191)

Analytical Marxists also reject the idea that fact and value cannot be separated, that they are dialectically related. They seek, following the canons of mainstream philosophic and social-scientific thinking, to separate fact and value and to deal with facts dispassionately through theoretical, conceptual, and empirical analysis.

One might ask why analytical Marxism should be called Marxist. Roemer, in reply to this question, says, "I am not sure that it should" (1986a:2). However, he does offer several reasons why we can consider it a neo-Marxian theory. First, it deals with traditional Marxian topics such as exploitation and class. Second, it continues to regard socialism as preferable to capitalism. Third, it seeks to understand and explain the problems associated with capitalism. However, while it is Marxist in these senses, it also "borrows willingly and easily from other viewpoints" (Roemer, 1986a:7).

Three varieties of analytical Marxism will be discussed, at least briefly, in this section. First, we will discuss the effort to reanalyze Marx's work by utilizing mainstream intellectual tools, especially those found in functional analysis. Second, we will deal with rational choice and game-theoretic Marxism. Finally, we will touch on Erik Olin Wright's empirical Marxism.

One of the key documents in analytical Marxism is G. A. Cohen's *Karl Marx's Theory of History: A Defence* (1978). Instead of interpreting Marx as an exotic dialectician, Cohen argues that he employs the much more prosaic functional form of explanation in his work. That is, he treats Marx as a functional rather than a dialectical thinker. The nature of the explanation is functional, in Cohen's view, because "the character of what is explained is determined by its effect on what explains it" (1978/1986:221). He offers the following examples of functional explanation in Marx's work:

- Relations of production *correspond* to productive forces.
- The legal and political superstructure *rises* on a real foundation.
- The social, political, and intellectual process *is conditioned* by the mode of production of material life.
- Consciousness *is determined* by social being.

In each of these examples, the second concept *explains* the first concept. Thus, in the case of the last example, the character of consciousness is explained by its effect on, more specifically its propensity to sustain, social being.

Cohen takes pains to differentiate functional thinking from the sociological variety of (structural) functionalism discussed in Chapter 7. Cohen sees (structural) functionalism as composed of three theses. First, all elements of the social world are interconnected. Second, all components of society reinforce one another, as well as the society as a whole. Third, each aspect of society is the way it is because of its contribution to the larger society. These theses are objectionable to Marxists for a variety of reasons, especially because of their conservatism. However, the functional explanations mentioned previously can be employed by Marxists without their accepting any of the tenets of functionalism. Thus, functional explanation is not necessarily conservative; indeed, it can be quite revolutionary.

A second key area of analytical Marxism is shaped by neoclassical economics, especially rational choice theory and game theory (see Chapter 11 for a discussion of the use of rational choice theory in mainstream sociological theory). Historically, the only microsocial component of Marxism theory was provided by critical theorists in their use of Freud. Through rational choice theory, analytic Marxists add an alternative microdimension to Marxist theory. Roemer argues that "Marxian analysis requires micro-foundations," especially those provided by rational choice and game theory, and "the arsenal of modelling techniques developed by neoclassical economics" (1986b:192). This emphasis on the microfoundations also serves as a critique of structural Marxists. John Elster says that Marx *was*, in fact, concerned with actors, their goals, their intentions, and their rational choices: "Capitalist entrepreneurs are *agents* in the genuinely active sense. They cannot be reduced to mere place-holders in the capitalist system of production" (1985:13). Rational choice Marxism focuses on these rational agents (capitalist and proletariats) and their interrelationships.

Elster (1982, 1986), then, believes that Marxian theory ought to make greater use of game theory, a variant of rational choice theory. Game theory, like other types of rational choice theory, assumes that actors are rational and seek to maximize their gains (Macy and Van de Rijt, 2007). Although it recognizes structural constraints, it does not suggest that they completely determine actors' choices. What is distinctive about game theory as a type of rational choice theory is that it permits the analyst to go beyond the rational choices of a single actor and deal with the interdependence of the decisions and actions of a number of actors. Elster (1982) identifies three interdependencies among actors involved in a game. First, the reward for each actor depends on the choices made by all the actors. Second, the reward for each actor depends on the reward for all. Finally, the choice made by each actor depends on the choices made by all. The analysis of "games" (such as the famous "prisoner's dilemma" game, in which actors end up worse off if they follow their own self-interest than if they sacrifice those interests) helps explain the strategies of the various actors and the emergence of such collectivities as social class.

Also drawing on rational choice theories, Roemer (1982) has been in the forefront of the development of an approach toward exploitation (for a critique, see J. Schwartz, 1995). Roemer has moved away from thinking of exploitation as occurring at the point of production (and therefore from the highly dubious labor theory of value) and toward thinking of exploitation as relating to coercion associated with differential ownership of property. As Mayer puts it, "exploitation can arise from unequal possession of productive resources even without a coercive production process" (1994:62). Among other things, this perspective allows us to conceive of exploitation in socialist as well as capitalist societies. This view of exploitation relates to rational choice theory in the sense, for example, that those whose exploitation arises from the unequal distribution of property can join social movements designed to redistribute property more equally. This kind of orientation also allows analytical Marxism to retain its ethical and political goals while buying into a mainstream orientation such as rational choice theory. That is, while analytic Marxism has drawn on neoclassical economics, it remains different from the latter. For example, it retains an interest in collective action for changing society and accepts the idea that capitalism is an unjust system.

Finally, the leading figure associated with the importation and application of rigorous methods to the empirical study of Marxian concepts is Erik Olin Wright (1985; Burawoy and Wright, 2001). Wright explicitly associates himself with analytical Marxism in general and the work of John Roemer in particular. Wright's work involves three basic components: first, the clarification of basic Marxian concepts such as class; second, empirical studies of those concepts; third, the development of a more coherent theory based on those concepts (especially class).

In his book *Classes* (1985), Wright seeks to answer the question posed by Marx but never answered by him: "What constitutes class?" He makes it clear that his answer will be true to Marx's original theoretical agenda. However, it will not be the same as the answer Marx might have offered, because since Marx's day there have been over 100 years of both theoretical work and history. In this spirit, one of Wright's best-known conceptual contributions is the idea of "contradictory locations within class relations" (Wright, 1985:43). His basic premise is that a given position need not, as is commonly assumed, be located within a given class; it may be in more than one class simultaneously. Thus, a position may be simultaneously proletarian and bourgeois. For example, managers are bourgeois in the sense that they supervise subordinates, but they are also proletarian in that they are supervised by others. The idea of contradictory class locations is derived through careful conceptual analysis and then is studied empirically (see Gubbay, 1997, for a critique of Wright's approach to social class).

Postmodern Marxian Theory

Marxian theory has been profoundly affected by theoretical developments in structuralism, poststructuralism (P. Anderson, 1984:33), and, of particular interest here, postmodernism (Landry, 2000; E. Wood and Foster, 1997; see Chapter 16).

Hegemony and Radical Democracy
A major representative work of postmodern Marxism is Ernesto Laclau and Chantal Mouffe's *Hegemony and Socialist Strategy* (1985). In Ellen Wood's view, this work, accepting the focus on linguistics, texts, and discourse in postmodernism, detaches ideology from its material base and ultimately dissolves "the social altogether into ideology or 'discourse'" (1986:47). The concept of hegemony, which is of central importance to Laclau and Mouffe, was developed by Gramsci to focus on cultural leadership rather than on the coercive effect of state domination. This shift in focus, of course, leads us away from the traditional Marxian concern with the material world and in the direction of ideas and discourse. As Wood puts it, "In short, the Laclau-Mouffe argument is that there *are* no such things as material interests but only discursively constructed *ideas* about them" (1986:61).

In addition to substituting ideas for material interests, Laclau and Mouffe displace the proletariat from its privileged position at the center of Marxian theory. As Wood argues, Laclau and Mouffe are part of a movement involved in the "declassing of the socialist project" (1986:4). Laclau and Mouffe put the issue of class in subjective, discursive terms. The social world is characterized by diverse positions and antagonisms. As a result, it is impossible to come up with the kind of "unified discourse" that Marx envisioned surrounding the proletariat. The universal discourse of the proletariat "has been replaced by a polyphony of voices, each of which constructs its own irreducible discursive identity" (Laclau and Mouffe, 1985:191). Thus, instead of focusing on the single discourse of the proletariat, Marxian theorists are urged to focus on a multitude of diverse discourses emanating from a wide range of dispossessed voices, such as those of women, blacks, ecologists, immigrants, and consumers, among others. Marxian theory has, as a result, been *decentered* and *detotalized* because it no longer focuses only on the proletariat and no longer sees the problems of the proletariat as *the* problem in society.

Having rejected a focus on material factors and a focal concern for the proletariat, Laclau and Mouffe proceed to reject, as the goal of Marxian theory, communism involving the emancipation of the proletariat. Alternatively, they propose a system labeled "radical democracy." Instead of focusing, as the political right does, on individual democratic rights, they propose to "create a new hegemony, which will be the outcome of the articulation of the greatest number of democratic struggles" (Mouffe, 1988:41). What is needed in this new hegemony is a "hegemony of democratic values, and this requires a multiplication of democratic practices, institutionalizing them into even more diverse social relations" (Mouffe, 1988:41). Radical democracy seeks to bring together under a broad umbrella a wide range of democratic struggles—antiracist, antisexist, anticapitalist, antiexploitation of nature (Eder, 1990), and many others. Thus, this is a "radical and plural democracy" (Laclau, 1990:27). The struggle of one group must not be waged at the expense of the others; all democratic struggles must be seen as equivalent struggles. Thus, it is necessary to bring these struggles together by modifying their identity so that the groups see themselves as part of the larger struggle for radical democracy. As Laclau and Mouffe argue:

> The alternative of the Left should consist of locating itself fully in the field of the democratic revolution and expanding the chains of equivalents between different struggles against oppression. *The task of the Left therefore cannot be to renounce liberal-democratic ideology, but on the contrary, to deepen and expand it in the direction of a radical and plural democracy.* . . . It is not in the abandonment of the democratic terrain but, on the contrary, in the extension of the field of democratic struggles to the whole of civil society and the state, that the possibility resides for a hegemonic strategy of the Left.
>
> (Laclau and Mouffe, 1985:176)

While radical democracy retains the objective of the abolition of capitalism, it recognizes that such abolition will not eliminate the other inequalities within society. Dealing with all social inequalities requires a far broader movement than that anticipated by traditional Marxists.

Continuities and Time-Space Compression

Another Marxian foray into postmodernist theory (see Chapter 16 for a discussion of yet another, the work of Fredric Jameson) is David Harvey's *The Condition of Postmodernity* (1989). Although Harvey sees much that is of merit in postmodern thinking, he sees serious weaknesses in it from a Marxian viewpoint. Postmodernist theory is accused of overemphasizing the problems of the modern world and underemphasizing its material achievements. Most important, it seems to accept postmodernity and its associated problems rather than suggesting ways of overcoming these difficulties: "The rhetoric of postmodernism is dangerous for it avoids confronting the realities of political economy and the circumstances of global power" (Harvey, 1989:117). What postmodernist theory needs to confront is the source of its ideas—the political and economic transformation of early twenty-first-century capitalism.

Central to the political economic system is control over markets and the labor process (these two arenas involve the issue of *accumulation* in capitalism). While the postwar period between 1945 and 1973 was characterized by an inflexible process of accumulation, since 1973 we have moved to a more flexible process. Harvey associates the earlier period with Fordism (as well as Keynesian economics) and the later period with post-Fordism (for a critique of this, see Gartman, 1998), but we need not discuss these issues here because they already have been covered in this chapter. While Fordism is inflexible, Harvey sees post-Fordism as associated with flexible accumulation resting "on flexibility with respect to labour processes, labour markets, products, and patterns of consumption. It is characterized by the emergence of entirely new sectors of production, new ways of providing financial services, new markets, and, above all, greatly intensified rates of commercial, technological, and organizational innovation" (1989:147).

Although Harvey sees great changes, and argues that it is these changes that lie at the base of postmodern thinking, he believes that there are many *continuities* between the Fordist and post-Fordist eras. His major conclusion is that while "there has certainly been a sea-change in the surface appearance of capitalism since 1973 . . . the underlying logic of capitalist accumulation and its crisis tendencies remain the same" (Harvey, 1989:189).

Central to Harvey's approach is the idea of time-space compression. He believes that modernism served to compress both time and space and that that process has accelerated in the postmodern era, leading to "an intense phase of time-space compression that has a disorienting and disruptive impact upon political-economic practices, the balance of class power, as well as upon cultural and social life" (Harvey, 1989:284). But this time-space compression is *not* essentially different from earlier epochs in capitalism: "We have, in short, witnessed another fierce round in that process of annihilation of space through time that has always lain at the center of capitalism's dynamic" (Harvey, 1989:293). To give an example of the annihilation of space through time, cheeses once available only in France now are sold throughout the United States because of rapid, low-cost transportation. Or, in the 1991 war with Iraq, television transported us instantaneously from air raids in Baghdad to "scud" attacks on Tel Aviv to military briefings in Riyadh.

Thus, to Harvey, postmodernism is *not* discontinuous with modernism; they are reflections of the same underlying capitalist dynamic.[8] Both modernism and postmodernism, Fordism and post-Fordism, coexist in today's world. The emphasis on Fordism and post-Fordism will "vary from time to time and place to place, depending on which configuration is profitable and which is not" (Harvey, 1989:344). Such a viewpoint serves to bring the issue of postmodernity under the umbrella of neo-Marxian theory, although it is, in turn, modified by developments in postmodern thinking.

Finally, Harvey discerns changes and cracks in postmodernity, indicating that we already may be moving into a new era, an era that neo-Marxian theory must be prepared to theorize, perhaps by integrating still other idea systems.

After Marxism

There are innumerable post-Marxist positions (Beilharz, 2005d) that *could* be discussed in this section, but we close with one of the more extreme positions.

The title of Ronald Aronson's (1995) book, *After Marxism,* tells much of the story. Aronson, a self-avowed Marxist, makes it clear that Marxism is over and that Marxist theorists are now on their own in dealing with the social world and its problems. This position is based on the idea that the "Marxian project" involved the integration of theory and practice. Although some Marxists may continue to buy into parts of Marxian theory, the Marxian project of the transformation from capitalism to socialism is dead, because it clearly has failed in its objectives. It is history, not Aronson, that has rendered the judgment that the Marxian project has failed. Thus, those Marxists who continue to buy into the theory are destroying the dialectical whole of theory and practice that constituted the Marxian project. This splintering is disastrous because what gave Marxism its compelling power is the fact that it represented "a single coherent theoretical and practical project" (Aronson, 1995:52).

But how can the Marxian project be over if capitalism continues to exist and may, with the death of communism, be more powerful than ever? In fact, Aronson recognizes that there are a variety of arguments to be made on behalf of the idea that Marxism is still relevant. For example, he recognizes that most people around the world are worse off today than they were at the dawn of capitalism and that in spite of a number of changes, the fundamental exploitative structure of capitalism is unaltered. In spite of such realities, Aronson argues that a variety of transformations must lead us to the conclusion that crucial aspects of Marxian theory are obsolete:

- The working class has *not* become increasingly impoverished.
- The class structure has *not* simplified to two polarized classes (bourgeoisie and proletariat).
- Because of the transformation of manufacturing processes, the number of industrial workers has declined, the working class has become more fragmented, and their consciousness of their situation has eroded.

---

[8] Bauman (1990) contends that capitalism and socialism are simply mirror images of modernity.

- The overall shrinkage of the working class has led to a decline in its strength, its class consciousness, and its ability to engage in class struggle.
- Workers are increasingly less likely to identify themselves as workers; they have multiple and competing identities, and so being a worker is now just one of many identities.

While Marxism is over as far as Aronson is concerned, he argues that we should not regret its existence, even with the excesses (for example, Stalinism) that were committed in its name. Marxism

> gave hope, it made sense of the world; it gave direction and meaning to many and countless lives. As the twentieth century's greatest call to arms, it inspired millions to stand up and fight, to believe that humans could one day shape their lives and their world to meet their needs.
>
> (Aronson, 1995:85)

In addition to the failures of Marxism in the real world, Aronson traces the demise of Marxism to problems within the theory itself. Those problems he traces to the fact that Marx's original theory was created during the early days of the modern world and, as a result, contains an uncomfortable mixture of modern and premodern ideas. This problem has plagued Marxian theory throughout its history. For example, the premodern, prophetic belief in emancipation coexisted with a modern belief in science and the search for facts: "Beneath its veneer of science, such dogmatic prophecy reveals its deeper and premodern kinship with religious anticipations of a world redeemed by a divine power beyond our control" (Aronson, 1995:97). To take one other example, Marxism tended to emphasize objective processes and to deemphasize subjective processes.

Aronson begins one of his chapters with the following provocative statement: "Feminism destroyed Marxism" (1995:124). He quickly makes it clear that feminism did not accomplish this feat on its own. However, feminism did contribute to the destruction of Marxism by demanding a theory that focuses on the "oppression of women *as women*" (Aronson, 1995:126). This focus clearly undermined Marxian theory, which purported to offer a theory applicable to all human beings. Feminism also set the stage for the development of other groups demanding that theories focus on their specific plight rather than on the universal problems of humanity.

Aronson describes post-Marxist theories like the analytical Marxism discussed earlier as Marxism without Marxism. That is, they are pure theories, lacking in practice, and therefore, in his view, should not be called Marxism:

> They may claim the name, as does analytical Marxism, but they do so as so many Marxisms without Marxism. They have become so transformed, so limited, so narrowly theoretical that even when their words and commitments ring true they only invoke Marxism's aura, but no more. However evocative, the ideas cannot conjure the fading reality.
>
> (Aronson, 1995:149)

Such Marxian theories will survive, but they will occupy a far humbler place in the world. They will represent just one theoretical voice in a sea of such voices.

Given all this, Aronson concludes that critical analysts of the modern world are on their own without a Marxian project to build upon. However, this is a mixed blessing. While the Marxian project had enormous strengths, it was also an albatross around the necks of critical analysts. Should former Marxists search for a new Marx? Or a new Marxian project? In light of developments in society and in theory, Aronson feels that the answer to these questions is no, because we have moved "beyond the possibility of the kind of holism, integration, coherence and confidence that Marxism embodied" (1995:168). Thus, for example, instead of a single radical movement, what we must seek today is a radical coalition of groups and ideas. The goal of such a coalition is the emancipation of modernity from its explosive inner tensions and its various forms of oppressiveness.

One problem facing such a new radical movement is that it can no longer hope to be driven by a compelling vision of some future utopia. Yet it must have some sort of emotional cement to hold it together and keep it moving ahead. The movement must have a moral base, a sense of what is right and what is wrong. It also must have hope, albeit a far more modest hope than that which characterized the Marxian project. Although modest, such hopes are less likely to lead to the profound disenchantment that characterized the Marxian project when it failed to achieve its social objectives.

Criticisms of Post-Marxism

Many Marxian theorists are unhappy with post-Marxist developments (for example, Burawoy, 1990; E. Wood, 1986; E. Wood and Foster, 1997). Burawoy, for instance, attacks the analytical Marxists for eliminating the issue of history and for making a fetish of clarity and rigor. Weldes criticizes analytical Marxism for allowing itself to be colonized by mainstream economics, adopting a purely "technical, problem-solving approach," becoming increasingly academic and less political, and growing more conservative (1989:354). Ellen Wood picks up on the political issue and criticizes analytical Marxism (as well as postmodern Marxism) for its political quietism and its "cynical defeatism, where every radical programme of change is doomed to failure" (1989:88). Even supporters of one branch of analytical Marxism, the rigorous empirical study of Marxian ideas, have been critical of their brethren in rational choice theory, who, mistakenly in their view, adopt a position of methodological individualism (A. Levine, Sober, and Wright, 1987).

The work of Laclau and Mouffe has come under particularly heavy attack. For example, Allen Hunter criticizes them for their overall commitment to idealism and, more specifically, for situating "themselves at the extreme end of discourse analysis, viewing *everything* as discourse" (1988:892). Similarly, Geras (1987) attacks Laclau and Mouffe for their idealism, but he also sees them as profligate, dissolute, illogical, and obscurantist. The tenor of Laclau and Mouffe's reply to Geras is caught by its title "Post-Marxism without Apologies" (1987). Burawoy attacks Laclau and Mouffe for getting "lost in the web of history where everything is important and explanation is therefore impossible" (1990:790).

Finally, in contrast to Aronson, Burawoy believes that Marxism remains useful in understanding capitalism's dynamics and contradictions (see also E. Wood, 1995).

Thus, with the demise of communism and the ascendancy of worldwide capitalism, "Marxism will . . . , once more, come into its own" (Burawoy, 1990:792). More recently, and in light of developments in the 1990s, Wood and Foster (1997:67) argue that Marxism is more necessary than ever because "humanity is more and more connected in the global dimensions of exploitation and oppression."

Summary

In this chapter we examine a wide range of approaches that can be categorized as neo-Marxian sociological theories. All of them take Marx's work as their point of departure, but they often go in very different directions. Although these diverse developments give neo-Marxian theory considerable vitality, they also create at least some unnecessary and largely dysfunctional differentiation and controversy. Thus, one task for the modern Marxian sociological theorist is to integrate this broad array of theories while recognizing the value of various specific pieces of work.

The first neo-Marxian theory historically, but the least important at present, especially to the sociologically oriented thinker, is economic determinism. It was against this limited view of Marxian theory that other varieties developed. Hegelian Marxism, especially in the work of Georg Lukács, was one such reaction. This approach sought to overcome the limitations in economic determinism by returning to the subjective, Hegelian roots of Marxian theory. Hegelian Marxism is also of little contemporary relevance; its significance lies largely in its impact on later neo-Marxian theories.

The critical school, which was the inheritor of the tradition of Hegelian Marxism, *is* of contemporary importance to sociology. The great contributions of the critical theorists (Marcuse, Habermas, Honneth, and so forth) are the insights offered into culture, consciousness, and their interrelationships. These theorists have enhanced our understanding of cultural phenomena such as instrumental rationality, the "culture industry," the "knowledge industry," communicative action, domination, and legitimations. To this they add a concern with consciousness, primarily in the form of an integration of Freudian theory in their work. However, critical theory has gone too far in its efforts to compensate for the limitations of economic determinism; it needs to reintegrate a concern for economics, indeed, for large-scale social forces in general.

Also discussed in this context is the work of the Birmingham school, which had a much more positive view of culture, especially as it emerged from the lower classes.

Next this chapter offers discussions of two lines of work in neo-Marxian economic sociology. The first deals with the relationship between capital and labor, especially in the works of Baran and Sweezy and of Braverman. The second is concerned with the transition from Fordism to post-Fordism. Both sets of work represent efforts to return to some of the traditional economic concerns of Marxian sociology. This work is significant for its effort to update Marxian economic sociology by taking into account the emerging realities of contemporary capitalist society.

Another concern is historically oriented Marxism, specifically the work of Immanuel Wallerstein and his supporters on the modern world-system. Then there is a discussion of those neo-Marxists who focus on spatial issues. The chapter closes with a section devoted to what, in light of the demise of communism, have come to be called post-Marxist theories. Included under this heading are several types of analytical Marxism and postmodern Marxian theory. Also included in this section is a discussion of an example of the kind of position taken by Marxists who have been forced to give up on the Marxian project in light of developments in the world.

Symbolic Interactionism

Chapter Outline

The Major Historical Roots
The Ideas of George Herbert Mead
Symbolic Interactionism: The Basic Principles
The Self and the Work of Erving Goffman
The Sociology of Emotions
Criticisms
The Future of Symbolic Interactionism

Symbolic interactionism (Sandstrom and Kleinman, 2005) offers a wide range of interesting and important ideas, and a number of major thinkers have been associated with the approach, including George Herbert Mead, Charles Horton Cooley, W. I. Thomas, Herbert Blumer, and Erving Goffman.

The Major Historical Roots

We begin our discussion of symbolic interactionism with Mead (Shalin, 2011). The two most significant intellectual roots of Mead's work in particular, and of symbolic interactionism in general, are the philosophy of pragmatism (D. Elliot, 2007) and psychological behaviorism (Joas, 1985; Rock, 1979).

Pragmatism

Pragmatism is a wide-ranging philosophical position[1] from which we can identify several aspects that influenced Mead's developing sociological orientation (Charon, 2000; Joas, 1993). First, to pragmatists true reality does not exist "out there" in the real world; it "is actively created as we act in and toward the world" (Hewitt and Shulman, 2011:6; see also Shalin, 1986). Second, people remember and base their knowledge of the world on what has proved useful to them. They are likely to alter what no longer "works." Third, people define the social and physical "objects" that

---

[1] See Joas (1996) for an effort to develop a theory of creative action based, at least in part, on pragmatism.

they encounter in the world according to their use for them. Finally, if we want to understand actors, we must base that understanding on what people actually do in the world. Three points are critical for symbolic interactionism: (1) a focus on the inter action between the actor and the world, (2) a view of both the actor and the world as dynamic processes and not static structures, and (3) the great importance attributed to the actor's ability to interpret the social world.

The last point is most pronounced in the work of the philosophical pragmatist John Dewey (Jacobs, 2007b; Sjoberg et al., 1997). Dewey did not conceive of the mind as a thing or a structure but rather as a thinking process that involves a series of stages. These stages include defining objects in the social world, outlining possible modes of conduct, imagining the consequences of alternative courses of action, eliminating unlikely possibilities, and finally selecting the optimal mode of action (Sheldon Stryker, 1980). This focus on the thinking process was enormously influential in the development of symbolic interactionism.

In fact, David Lewis and Richard Smith argue that Dewey (along with William James; see Musolf, 1994) was more influential in the development of symbolic interactionism than was Mead. They go so far as to say that "Mead's work was peripheral to the mainstream of early Chicago sociology" (Lewis and Smith, 1980:xix). In making this argument, they distinguish between two branches of pragmatism— "philosophical realism" (associated with Mead) and "nominalist pragmatism" (associated with Dewey and James). In their view, symbolic interactionism was influenced more by the nominalist approach and was even inconsistent with philo-sophical realism. The nominalist position is that although macro-level phenomena exist, they do not have "independent and determining effects upon the consciousness of and behavior of individuals" (Lewis and Smith, 1980:24). More positively, this view "conceives of the individuals themselves as existentially free agents who accept, reject, modify, or otherwise 'define' the community's norms, roles, beliefs, and so forth, according to their own personal interests and plans of the moment" (Lewis and Smith, 1980:24). In contrast, to social realists the emphasis is on society and how it constitutes and controls individual mental processes. Rather than being free agents, actors and their cognitions and behaviors are controlled by the larger community.[2]

Given this distinction, Mead fits better into the realist camp and therefore did not mesh well with the nominalist direction taken by symbolic interactionism. The key figure in the latter development is Herbert Blumer, who, while claiming to operate with a Meadian approach, was in fact better thought of as a nominalist. Theoretically, Lewis and Smith catch the essence of their differences:

> Blumer . . . moved completely toward psychical interactionism. . . . Unlike the Meadian social behaviorist, the psychical interactionist holds that the meanings of symbols are not universal and objective; rather meanings are individual and subjective in that they are "attached" to the symbols by the receiver according to however he or she chooses to "interpret" them.
>
> (Lewis and Smith, 1980:172)

---

[2] For a criticism of the distinctions made here, see D. Miller (1982b, 1985).

Behaviorism

Buttressing the Lewis and Smith interpretation of Mead is the fact that Mead was influenced by psychological behaviorism (J. C. Baldwin, 1986, 1988a, 1988b; Mandes, 2007), a perspective that also led him in a realist and an empirical direction. In fact, Mead called his basic concern *social behaviorism* to differentiate it from the *radical behaviorism* of John B. Watson (who was one of Mead's students).

Radical behaviorists of Watson's persuasion (K. Buckley, 1989) were concerned with the *observable* behaviors of individuals. Their focus was on the stimuli that elicited the responses, or behaviors, in question. They either denied or were disinclined to attribute much importance to the covert mental process that occurred between the time a stimulus was applied and the time a response was emitted. Mead recognized the importance of observable behavior, but he also felt that there were *covert* aspects of behavior that the radical behaviorists had ignored. But because he accepted the empiricism that was basic to behaviorism, Mead did not simply want to philosophize about these covert phenomena. Rather, he sought to extend the empirical science of behaviorism to them—that is, to what goes on between stimulus and response. Bernard Meltzer summarized Mead's position:

> For Mead, the unit of study is "the act," which comprises both overt and covert aspects of human action. Within the act, all the separated categories of the traditional, orthodox psychologies find a place. Attention, perception, imagination, reasoning, emotion, and so forth, are seen as parts of the act . . . the act, then, encompasses the total process involved in human activity.
>
> (Meltzer, 1964/1978:23)

Mead and the radical behaviorists also differed in their views on the relationship between human and animal behavior. Whereas radical behaviorists tended to see no difference between humans and animals, Mead argued that there was a significant, qualitative difference. The key to this difference was seen as the human possession of mental capacities that allowed people to use language between stimulus and response in order to decide how to respond.

Mead simultaneously demonstrated his debt to Watsonian behaviorism and dissociated himself from it. Mead made this clear when he said, on the one hand, that "we shall approach this latter field [social psychology] from a behavioristic point of view." On the other hand, Mead criticized Watson's position when he said, "The behaviorism which we shall make use of is *more adequate* than that of which Watson makes use" (1934/1962:2; italics added).

Charles Morris, in his introduction to *Mind, Self and Society,* enumerated three basic differences between Mead and Watson. First, Mead considered Watson's exclusive focus on behavior simplistic. In effect, he accused Watson of wrenching behavior out of its broader social context. Mead wanted to deal with behavior as a small part of the broader social world.

Second, Mead accused Watson of an unwillingness to extend behaviorism into mental processes. Watson had no sense of the actor's consciousness and mental processes, as Mead made vividly clear: "John B. Watson's attitude was that of the Queen in *Alice in Wonderland*—'Off with their heads!'—there were no such things. There was no . . .

consciousness" (1934/1962:2–3). Mead contrasted his perspective with Watson's: "It is behavioristic, but unlike Watsonian behaviorism it recognizes the parts of the act which do not come to external observation" (1934/1962:8). More concretely, Mead saw his mission as extending the principles of Watsonian behaviorism to include mental processes.

Finally, because Watson rejected the mind, Mead saw him as having a passive image of the actor as puppet. Mead, on the other hand, subscribed to a much more dynamic and creative image of the actor, and it was this that made him attractive to later symbolic interactionists.

Pragmatism and behaviorism, especially in the theories of Dewey and Mead, were transmitted to many graduate students at the University of Chicago, primarily in the 1920s. These students, among them Herbert Blumer, established symbolic interactionism. Of course, other important theorists influenced these students, the most important of whom was Georg Simmel (see Chapter 5). Simmel's interest in forms of action and interaction was both compatible with and an extension of Meadian theory.

Between Reductionism and Sociologism

Blumer coined the term *symbolic interactionism* in 1937 and wrote several essays that were instrumental in its development (Morrione, 2007). Whereas Mead sought to differentiate the nascent symbolic interactionism from behaviorism, Blumer saw symbolic interactionism as being embattled on two fronts. First was the reductionist behaviorism that had worried Mead. To this was added the serious threat from larger-scale sociologistic theories, especially structural functionalism. To Blumer, behaviorism and structural functionalism both tended to focus on factors (for example, external stimuli and norms) that cause human behavior. As far as Blumer was concerned, both theories ignored the crucial process by which actors endow the forces acting on them and their own behaviors with meaning (Morrione, 1988).

To Blumer, behaviorists, with their emphasis on the impact of external stimuli on individual behavior, were clearly psychological reductionists. In addition to behaviorism, several other types of psychological reductionism troubled Blumer. For example, he criticized those who seek to explain human action by relying on conventional notions of the concept of "attitude" (Blumer, 1955/1969:94). In his view, most of those who use the concept think of an attitude as an "already organized tendency" within the actor; they tend to think of actions as being impelled by attitudes. In Blumer's view, this is very mechanistic thinking; what is important is not the attitude as an internalized tendency "but the defining process through which the actor comes to forge his act" (Blumer, 1955/1969:97). Blumer also singled out for criticism those who focus on conscious and unconscious motives. He was particularly irked by their view that actors are impelled by independent, mentalistic impulses over which they are supposed to have no control. Freudian theory, which sees actors as impelled by forces such as the id or libido, is an example of the kind of psychological theory to which Blumer was opposed. In short, Blumer was opposed to any psychological theory that ignores the process by which actors construct meaning—the fact that actors have selves and relate to themselves.

Blumer also was opposed to sociologistic theories (especially structural functionalism) that view individual behavior as being determined by large-scale external forces. In this category Blumer included theories that focus on such social-structural and social-cultural factors as "'social system,' 'social structure,' 'culture,' 'status position,' 'social role,' 'custom,' 'institution,' 'collective representation,' 'social situation,' 'social norm,' and 'values'" (Blumer, 1962/1969:83). Both sociologistic theories and psychological theories ignore the importance of meaning and the social construction of reality:

> In both such typical psychological and sociological explanations the meanings of things for the human beings who are acting are either bypassed or swallowed up in the factors used to account for their behavior. If one declares that the given kinds of behavior are the result of the particular factors regarded as producing them, there is no need to concern oneself with the meaning of the things towards which human beings act.
>
> (Blumer, 1969b:3)

The Ideas of George Herbert Mead

Mead is the most important thinker in the history of symbolic interactionism (Chriss, 2005b; Joas, 2001), and his book *Mind, Self and Society* is the most important single work in that tradition.

The Priority of the Social

In his review of *Mind, Self and Society,* Ellsworth Faris argued that "not mind and then society; but society first and then minds arising within that society . . . would probably have been [Mead's] preference" (cited in D. Miller, 1982a:2). Faris's inversion of the title of this book reflects the widely acknowledged fact, recognized by Mead himself, that society, or more broadly the social, is accorded priority in Mead's analysis.

In Mead's view, traditional social psychology began with the psychology of the individual in an effort to explain social experience; in contrast, Mead always gives priority to the social world in understanding social experience. Mead explains his focus in this way:

> We are not, in social psychology, building up the behavior of the social group in terms of the behavior of separate individuals composing it; rather, we are *starting out with a given social whole* of complex group activity, into which we analyze (as elements) the behavior of each of the separate individuals composing it. . . . We attempt, that is, to explain the conduct of the social group, rather than to account for the organized conduct of the social group in terms of the conduct of the separate individuals belonging to it. For social psychology, the *whole (society) is prior to the part (the individual),* not the part to the whole; and the part is explained in terms of the whole, not the whole in terms of the part or parts.
>
> (Mead, 1934/1962:7; italics added)

To Mead, the social whole precedes the individual mind both logically and temporally. A thinking, self-conscious individual is, as we will see later, logically impossible in Mead's theory without a prior social group. The social group comes first, and it leads to the development of self-conscious mental states.

The Act

Mead considers the act to be the most "primitive unit" in his theory (1982:27). In analyzing the act, Mead comes closest to the behaviorist's approach and focuses on stimulus and response. However, even here the stimulus does not elicit an automatic, unthinking response from the human actor. As Mead says, "We conceive of the stimulus as an occasion or opportunity for the act, not as a compulsion or a mandate" (1982:28). Mead (1938/1972) identified four basic and interrelated stages in the act (Schmitt and Schmitt, 1996). Both lower animals and humans act, and Mead is interested in the similarities, and especially the differences, between the two.[3]

The first stage is that of the *impulse*, which involves an "immediate sensuous stimulation" and the actor's reaction to the stimulation, the need to do something about it. Hunger is a good example of an impulse. The actor (both nonhuman and human) may respond immediately and unthinkingly to the impulse, but more likely the human actor will think about the appropriate response (for example, eat now or later). The second stage of the act is *perception*, in which the actor searches for and reacts to stimuli that relate to the impulse, in this case hunger as well as the various means available to satisfy it. People have the capacity to sense or perceive stimuli through hearing, smell, taste, and so on. Perception involves incoming stimuli, as well as the mental images they create. People do not simply respond immediately to external stimuli but rather think about and assess them through mental imagery. Mead refuses to separate people from the objects that they perceive. It is the act of perceiving an object that makes it an object to a person; perception and object cannot be separated from (are dialectically related to) one another.

The third stage is *manipulation*. Once the impulse has manifested itself and the object has been perceived, the next step is manipulating the object or, more generally, taking action with regard to it. In addition to their mental advantages, people have another advantage over lower animals. People have hands (with opposable thumbs) that allow them to manipulate objects far more subtly than can lower animals. The manipulation phase constitutes, for Mead, an important temporary pause in the process so that a response is not manifested immediately. A hungry human being sees a mushroom, but before eating it, he or she is likely to pick it up first, examine it, and perhaps check in a guidebook to see whether that particular variety is edible. The pause afforded by handling the object allows humans to contemplate various responses. On the basis of these deliberations, the actor may decide to eat the mushroom (or not), and this constitutes the last phase of the act, *consummation*, or more generally the taking of action that satisfies the original impulse. Both humans and lower animals may consume the mushroom, but the human is less likely to eat a bad mushroom because of his or her ability to manipulate the mushroom and to think (and read) about the implications of eating it.

For ease of discussion, the four stages of the act have been separated from one another in sequential order, but Mead sees a dialectical relationship among the

---

[3] For a critique of Mead's thinking on the differences between humans and lower animals, see Alger and Alger (1997).

GEORGE HERBERT MEAD

A Biographical Sketch

Most of the important theorists discussed throughout this book achieved their greatest recognition in their lifetimes for their published work. George Herbert Mead, however, was at least as important, at least during his lifetime, for his teaching as for his writing. His words had a powerful impact on many people who were to become important sociologists in the twentieth century. As one of his students said, "Conversation was his best medium; writing was a poor second" (T. V. Smith, 1931:369). Let us have another of his students, himself a well-known sociologist—Leonard Cottrell— describe what Mead was like as a teacher:

> For me, the course with Professor Mead was a unique and unforgettable experience. . . . Professor Mead was a large, amiable-looking man who wore a magnificent mustache and a Vandyke beard. He characteristically had a benign, rather shy smile matched with a twinkle in his eyes as if he were enjoying a secret joke he was playing on the audience. . . .
>
> As he lectured—always without notes—Professor Mead would manipulate the piece of chalk and watch it intently. . . . When he made a particularly subtle point in his lecture he would glance up and throw a shy, almost apologetic smile over our heads—never looking directly at anyone. His lecture flowed and we soon learned that questions or comments from the class were not welcome. Indeed, when someone was bold enough to raise a question there was a murmur of disapproval from the students. They objected to any interruption of the golden flow. . . .
>
> His expectations of students were modest. He never gave exams. The main task for each of us students was to write as learned a paper as one could. These Professor Mead read with great care, and what he thought of your paper was your grade in the course. One might suppose that students would read materials for the paper rather than attend his lectures but that was not the case. Students always came. They couldn't get enough of Mead.
>
> (Cottrell, 1980:49–50)

Mead had enormous difficulty writing, and this troubled him a great deal. "'I am vastly depressed by my inability to write what I want to'" (cited in G. Cook, 1993:xiii). However, over the years many of Mead's ideas came to be published, especially in *Mind, Self and Society* (a book based on students' notes from a course

four stages. John C. Baldwin expresses this idea in the following way: "Although the four parts of the act sometimes *appear* to be linked in linear order, they actually interpenetrate to form one organic process: Facets of each part are present at all times from the beginning of the act to the end, such that each part affects the other" taught by Mead). This book and others of Mead's works had a powerful influence on the development of contemporary sociology, especially symbolic interactionism.

Born in South Hadley, Massachusetts, on February 27, 1863, Mead was trained mainly in philosophy and its application to social psychology. He received a bachelor's degree from Oberlin College (where his father was a professor) in 1883, and after a few years as a secondary-school teacher, surveyor for railroad companies, and private tutor, Mead began graduate study at Harvard in 1887. After a few years of study at Harvard, as well as at the universities of Leipzig and Berlin, Mead was offered an instructorship at the University of Michigan in 1891. It is interesting to note that Mead *never* received any graduate degrees. In 1894, at the invitation of John Dewey, he moved to the University of Chicago and remained there for the rest of his life.

As Mead makes clear in the following excerpt from a letter, he was heavily influenced by Dewey: "'Mr. Dewey is a man of not only great originality and profound thought but the most appreciative thinker I ever met. I have gained more from him than from any one man I ever met'" (cited in G. Cook, 1993:32). This was especially true of Mead's early work at Chicago, and he even followed Dewey into educational theory (Dewey left Chicago in 1904). However, Mead's thinking quickly diverged from Dewey's and led him in the direction of his famous social psychological theories of mind, self, and society. He began teaching a course on social psychology in 1900. In 1916–1917 it was transformed into an advanced course (the stenographic student notes from the 1928 course became the basis of *Mind, Self and Society*) that followed a course in elementary social psychology that was taught after 1919 by Ellsworth Faris of the sociology department. It was through this course that Mead had such a powerful influence on students in sociology (as well as psychology and education).

In addition to his scholarly pursuits, Mead became involved in social reform. He believed that science could be used to deal with social problems. For example, he was heavily involved as a fund raiser and policy maker at the University of Chicago Settlement House, which had been inspired by Jane Addams's Hull House. Perhaps most important, he played a key role in social research conducted by the settlement house.

Although eligible for retirement in 1928, he continued to teach at the invitation of the university and in the summer of 1930 became chair of the philosophy department. Unfortunately, he became embroiled in a bitter conflict between the department and the president of the university. This led in early 1931 to a letter of resignation from Mead written from his hospital bed. He was released from the hospital in late April, but died from heart failure the following day. Of him, John Dewey said he was "'the most original mind in philosophy in the America of the last generations'" (G. Cook, 1993:194).

(1986:55–56). Thus, the later stages of the act may lead to the emergence of earlier stages. For example, manipulating food may lead the individual to the impulse of hunger and the perception that the individual is hungry and that food is available to satisfy the need.

Gestures

The act involves only one person, but the *social act* involves two or more persons. The *gesture* is in Mead's view the basic mechanism in the social act and in the social process more generally. As he defines them, "gestures are movements of the first organism which act as specific stimuli calling forth the (socially) appropriate responses of the second organism" (Mead, 1934/1962:14; see also Mead, 1959:187). Both lower animals and humans are capable of gestures in the sense that the action of one individual mindlessly and automatically elicits a reaction by another individual. The following is Mead's famous example of a dog fight in terms of gestures:

> The act of each dog becomes the stimulus to the other dog for his response. . . . The very fact that the dog is ready to attack another becomes a stimulus to the other dog to change his own position or his own attitude. He has no sooner done this than the change of attitude in the second dog in turn causes the first dog to change his attitude.
>
> (Mead, 1934/1962:42–43)

Mead labels what is taking place in this situation a "conversation of gestures." One dog's gesture automatically elicits a gesture from the second; there are no thought processes taking place on the part of the dogs.

Humans sometimes engage in mindless conversations of gestures. Mead gives as examples many of the actions and reactions that take place in boxing and fencing matches, when one combatant adjusts "instinctively" to the actions of the second. Mead labels such unconscious actions "nonsignificant" gestures; what distinguishes humans is their ability to employ "significant" gestures, or those that require thought on the part of the actor before a reaction.

The vocal gesture is particularly important in the development of significant gestures. However, not all vocal gestures are significant. The bark of one dog to another is not significant; even some human vocal gestures (for example, a mindless grunt) may not be significant. However, it is the development of vocal gestures, especially in the form of language, that is the most important factor in making possible the distinctive development of human life: "The specialization of the human animal within this field of the gesture has been responsible, ultimately, for the origin and growth of present human society and knowledge, with all the control over nature and over the human environment which science makes possible" (Mead, 1934/1962:14).

This development is related to a distinctive characteristic of the vocal gesture. When we make a physical gesture, such as a facial grimace, we cannot see what we are doing (unless we happen to be looking in the mirror). In contrast, when we utter a vocal gesture, we hear ourselves just as others do. One result is that the vocal gesture can affect the speaker in much the same way that it affects the listeners. Another is that we are far better able to stop ourselves in vocal gestures than we are able to stop ourselves in physical gestures. In other words, we have far better control over vocal gestures than physical ones. This ability to control oneself and one's reactions is critical, as we will see, to the other distinctive capabilities of humans. More generally, "it has been the vocal gesture that has preeminently provided the medium of social organization in human society" (Mead, 1959:188).

Significant Symbols

A significant symbol is a kind of gesture, one which only humans can make. Gestures become *significant symbols* when they arouse in the individual who is making them the same kind of response (it need not be identical) they are supposed to elicit from those to whom the gestures are addressed. Only when we have significant symbols can we truly have communication; communication in the full sense of the term is not possible among ants, bees, and so on. Physical gestures can be significant symbols, but as we have seen, they are not ideally suited to be significant symbols because people cannot easily see or hear their own physical gestures. Thus, it is vocal utterances that are most likely to become significant symbols, although not all vocalizations are such symbols. The set of vocal gestures most likely to become significant symbols is *language:* "a symbol which answers to a meaning in that experience of the first individual and which also calls out the meaning in the second individual. Where the gesture reaches that situation it has become what we call 'language.' It is now a significant symbol and it signifies a certain meaning" (Mead, 1934/1962:46). In a conversation of gestures, only the gestures themselves are communicated. However, with language the gestures and their meanings are communicated.

One of the things that language, or significant symbols more generally, does is call out the same response in the individual who is speaking that it does in others. The word *dog* or *cat* elicits the same mental image in the person uttering the word that it does in those to whom it is addressed. Another effect of language is that it stimulates the person speaking as it does others. The person yelling "fire" in a crowded theater is at least as motivated to leave the theater as are those to whom the shout is addressed. Thus, significant symbols allow people to be the stimulators of their own actions.

Adopting his pragmatist orientation, Mead also looks at the "functions" of gestures in general and of significant symbols in particular. The function of the gesture "is to make adjustment possible among the individuals implicated in any given social act with reference to the object or objects with which that act is concerned" (Mead, 1934/1962:46). Thus, an involuntary facial grimace may be made in order to prevent a child from going too close to the edge of a precipice and thereby prevent him or her from being in a potentially dangerous situation. While the nonsignificant gesture works, the "significant symbol affords far greater facilities for such adjustment and readjustment than does the nonsignificant gesture, because it calls out in the individual making it the same attitude toward it . . . and enables him to adjust his subsequent behavior to theirs in the light of that attitude" (Mead, 1934/1962:46). For example, in communicating our displeasure to others, an angry verbal rebuke works far better than does contorted body language. This is because the person who is using significant symbols (speech) can imagine the various ways that the child would respond to the rebuke. The speaker is prepared, then, to defend or explain the basis for the rebuke with the expectation that the child can learn the reason behind the words. This rich form of interaction cannot proceed if the person is merely responding to the child through unconscious body language.

Another very important function of significant symbols is that they contribute to the emergence of the mind and mental processes. It is only through significant symbols, especially language, that human *thinking* is possible (lower animals cannot think, in Mead's terms). Mead defines *thinking* as "simply an internalized or implicit conversation of the individual with himself by means of such gestures" (1934/1962:47). Even more strongly, Mead argues: "Thinking is the same as talking to other people" (1982:155). In other words, thinking involves talking to oneself Thus, we can see clearly here how Mead defines thinking in behaviorist terms. Conversations involve behavior (talking), and that behavior also occurs within the individual; when it does, thinking is taking place. This is not a mentalistic definition of thinking; it is decidedly behavioristic.

Significant symbols also make possible *symbolic interaction.* That is, people can interact with one another not just through gestures but also through significant symbols. This ability, of course, makes a world of difference and makes possible much more complex interaction patterns and forms of social organization than would be possible through gestures alone.

The significant symbol obviously plays a central role in Mead's thinking. In fact, David Miller (1982a:10–11) accords the significant symbol *the* central role in Mead's theory.

Mind

The mind, which is defined by Mead as a process and not a thing, as an inner conversation with one's self, is not found within the individual; it is not intracranial but is a social phenomenon (Franks, 2007). It arises and develops within the social process and is an integral part of that process. The social process precedes the mind; it is not, as many believe, a product of the mind. Thus, the mind, too, is defined functionally rather than substantively. Given these similarities to ideas such as consciousness, is there anything distinctive about the mind? We already have seen that humans have the peculiar capacity to call out in themselves the response they are seeking to elicit from others. A distinctive characteristic of the mind is the ability of the individual "to call out in himself not simply a single response of the other but the response, so to speak, of the community as a whole. That is what gives to an individual what we term 'mind.' To do anything now means a certain organized response; and if one has in himself that response, he has what we term 'mind'" (Mead, 1934/1962:267). Thus, the mind can be distinguished from other like-sounding concepts in Mead's work by its ability to respond to the overall community and put forth an organized response.

Mead also looks at the mind in another, pragmatic way. That is, the mind involves thought processes oriented toward problem solving. The real world is rife with problems, and it is the function of the mind to try to solve those problems and permit people to operate more effectively in the world.

Self

Much of Mead's thinking in general, and especially on the mind, involves his ideas on the critically important concept of the *self* (Schwalbe, 2005). For Mead the self is defined as a process. This means that the child is not born with a self, but that it emerges over time. People acquire selves when they are able to take themselves as objects. That is, they are able to act on and respond to themselves as they would to any other object in their environment. The self, then, has the ability to both act as a subject (a source of action) and to take itself as an object.

As is true of all of Mead's major concepts, what should be clear is that selves do not precede society. Rather, they are a product of social processes, in particular the process of communication among human beings. In contrast to many psychological theories that treat the self as an entity that exists inside of the person, Mead embeds the self in social experience and social processes. In this way, Mead seeks to give a behavioristic sense of the self: "But it is where one does respond to that which he addresses to another and where that response of his own becomes a part of his conduct, where he not only hears himself but responds to himself, talks and replies to himself as truly as the other person replies to him, that we have *behavior* in which the individuals become objects to themselves" (1934/1962:139; italics added). The self, then, is simply another aspect of the overall social process of which the individual is a part. This said, once a self has developed, it is possible for it to continue to exist without social contact. Thus, Robinson Crusoe developed a self while he was in civilization, and he continued to have it when he was living alone on what he thought for a while was a deserted island. In other words, he continued to have the ability to take himself as an object.

The general mechanism for the development of the self is reflexivity, or the ability to put ourselves unconsciously into others' places and to act as they act. As a result, people are able to examine themselves as others would examine them. As Mead says:

> It is by means of reflexiveness—the turning-back of the experience of the individual upon himself—that the whole social process is thus brought into the experience of the individuals involved in it; it is by such means, which enable the individual to take the attitude of the other toward himself, that the individual is able consciously to adjust himself to that process, and to modify the resultant process in any given social act in terms of his adjustment to it.
>
> (Mead, 1934/1962:134)

The self also allows people to take part in their conversations with others. That is, one is aware of what one is saying and as a result is able to monitor what is being said and to determine what is going to be said next.

In order to have selves, individuals must be able to get "outside themselves" so that they can evaluate themselves, so that they can become objects to themselves. To do this, people basically put themselves in the same experiential field as they put everyone else.

Indeed, one of the most counterintuitive, and sociologically important, assumptions of Mead's theory of self is that people cannot experience themselves directly. They can do so only indirectly by putting themselves in the position of others and viewing themselves from that standpoint. The standpoint from which one views one's self can be that of a particular individual or that of the social group as a whole. As Mead puts it, most generally, "It is only by taking the roles of others that we have been able to come back to ourselves" (1959:184–185). The implication is that even in their most private moments people bear the mark of their relationships with others. Selves are deeply social in their makeup and character.

Child Development

Mead is very interested in the genesis of the self. He sees the conversation of gestures as the background for the self, but it does not involve a self because in such a conversation the people are not taking themselves as objects. Mead traces the genesis of the self through two stages[4] in childhood development.

Play Stage   The first stage is the *play stage;* it is during this stage that children learn to take the attitude of particular others to themselves (Vail, 2007b). Although lower animals also play, only human beings "play at being someone else" (Aboulafia, 1986:9). Mead gives the example of a child playing "at being a mother, at being a teacher, at being a policeman." In playing these roles the child prompts itself with the same stimuli that would prompt action in these other people (Mead, 1934/1962:150). As a result of such play, the child learns to become both subject and object and begins to become able to build a self. However, it is a limited self because the child can take only the roles of distinct and separate others. Children may play at being "mommy" and "daddy" and in the process develop the ability to evaluate themselves as their parents, and other specific individuals, do. However, they lack a more general and organized sense of themselves.

Game Stage   It is the next stage, the *game stage,* that is required if a person is to develop a self in the full sense of the term (Vail, 2007c). Whereas in the play stage the child takes the role of discrete others, in the game stage the child must take the role of everyone else involved in the game. Furthermore, these different roles must have a definite relationship to one another. In illustrating the game stage, Mead gives his famous example of a baseball (or, as he calls it, "ball nine") game:

> But in a game where a number of individuals are involved, then the child taking
> one role must be ready to take the role of everyone else. If he gets in a ball nine
> he must have the responses of each position involved in his own position. He must
> know what everyone else is going to do in order to carry out his own play. He has
> to take all of these roles. They do not all have to be present in consciousness at the
> same time, but at some moments he has to have three or four individuals present in
> his own attitude, such as the one who is going to throw the ball, the one who is
> going to catch it, and so on. These responses must be, in some degree, present in
> his own make-up. In the game, then, there is a set of responses of such others so
> organized that the attitude of one calls out the appropriate attitudes of the other.
>
> (Mead, 1934/1962:151)

In the play stage, children are not organized wholes because they play at a series of discrete roles. As a result, in Mead's view they lack definite personalities. However, in the game stage,[5] such organization begins and a definite personality starts to emerge. Children begin to become able to function in organized groups and, most important, to determine what they will do within a specific group.

---

[4] A first, preparatory stage involving mimicry is implied (Vail, 2007a) in Mead's work.
[5] Although Mead uses the term *games,* it is clear, as Aboulafia (1986:198) points out, that he means any system of organized responses (for example, the family).

Generalized Other

The game stage yields one of Mead's (1959:87) best-known concepts, the *generalized other* (Vail, 2007d). The generalized other is the attitude of the entire community or, in the example of the baseball game, the attitude of the entire team. The ability to take the role of the generalized other is essential to the self: "Only in so far as he takes the attitudes of the organized social group to which he belongs toward the organized, co-operative social activity or set of such activities in which that group is engaged, does he develop a complete self" (Mead, 1934/1962:155). It is also crucial that people be able to evaluate themselves from the point of view of the generalized other and not merely from the viewpoint of discrete others. Taking the role of the generalized other, rather than that of discrete others, allows for the possibility of abstract thinking and objectivity (Mead, 1959:190). Here is the way Mead describes the full development of the self:

> So the self reaches its full development by organizing these individual attitudes of others into the organized social or group attitudes, and by thus becoming an individual reflection of the general systematic pattern of social or group behavior in which it and others are involved—a pattern which enters as a whole into the individual's experience in terms of these organized group attitudes which, through the mechanism of the central nervous system, he takes toward himself, just as he takes the individual attitudes of others.

> (Mead, 1934/1962:158)

In other words, to have a self, one must be a member of a community and be directed by the attitudes common to the community. While play requires only pieces of selves, the game requires a coherent self.

Not only is taking the role of the generalized other essential to the self, it also is crucial for the development of organized group activities. A group requires that individuals direct their activities in accord with the attitudes of the generalized other. The generalized other also represents Mead's familiar propensity to give priority to the social, because it is through the generalized other that the group influences the behavior of individuals.

Mead also looks at the self from a pragmatic point of view. At the individual level, the self allows the individual to be a more efficient member of the larger society. Because of the self, people are more likely to do what is expected of them in a given situation. Because people often try to live up to group expectations, they are more likely to avoid the inefficiencies that come from failing to do what the group expects. Furthermore, the self allows for greater coordination in society as a whole. Because individuals can be counted on to do what is expected of them, the group can operate more effectively.

The preceding, as well as the overall discussion of the self, might lead us to believe that Mead's actors are little more than conformists and that there is little individuality, since everyone is busy conforming to the expectations of the generalized other. But Mead is clear that each self is different from all the others. Selves share a common structure, but each self receives unique biographical articulation. In addition, it is clear that there is not simply one grand generalized other but that there are many generalized others in society, because there are many groups in society. People therefore have multiple generalized others and, as a result, multiple selves. Each person's unique set of selves makes him or her different from everyone else. Furthermore, people need not accept the community as it is; they can reform things and seek to make them better. We are able to change the community because of our capacity to think.

Mead identifies two aspects, or phases, of the self, which he labels the "I" and the "me" (for a critique of this distinction, see Athens, 1995). As Mead puts it, "The self is essentially a social process going on with these two distinguishable phases" (1934/1962:178). It is important to bear in mind that the "I" and the "me" are processes within the larger process of the self; they are not "things."

"I" and "Me"

The "I" is the immediate response of an individual to others. It is the incalculable, unpredictable, and creative aspect of the self. People do not know in advance what the action of the "I" will be: "But what that response will be he does not know and nobody else knows. Perhaps he will make a brilliant play or an error. The response to that situation as it appears in his immediate experience is uncertain" (Mead, 1934/1962:175). We are never totally aware of the "I," and through it we surprise ourselves with our actions. We know the "I" only after the act has been carried out. Thus, we know the "I" only in our memories. Mead lays great stress on the "I" for four reasons. First, it is a key source of novelty in the social process. Second, Mead believes that it is in the "I" that our most important values are located. Third, the "I" constitutes something that we all seek—the realization of the self. It is the "I" that permits us to develop a "definite personality." Finally, Mead sees an evolutionary process in history in which people in primitive societies are dominated more by the "me" while in modern societies there is a greater component of the "I."

The "I" gives Mead's theoretical system some much-needed dynamism and creativity. Without it, Mead's actors would be totally dominated by external and internal controls. With it, Mead is able to deal with the changes brought about not only by the great figures in history (for example, Einstein) but also by individuals on a day-to-day basis. It is the "I" that makes these changes possible. Since every personality is a mix of "I" and "me," the great historical figures are seen as having a larger proportion of "I" than most others have. But in day-to-day situations, anyone's "I" may assert itself and lead to change in the social situation. Uniqueness is also brought into Mead's system through the biographical articulation of each individual's "I" and "me." That is, the specific exigencies of each person's life give him or her a unique mix of "I" and "me."

The "I" reacts against the "me," which is the "organized set of attitudes of others which one himself assumes" (Mead, 1934/1962:175). In other words, the "me" is the adoption of the generalized other. In contrast to the "I," people are conscious of the "me"; the "me" involves conscious responsibility. As Mead says, "The 'me' is a conventional, habitual individual" (1934/1962:197). Conformists are dominated by the "me," although everyone—whatever his or her degree of conformity—has, and must have, a substantial "me." It is through the "me" that society dominates the individual. Indeed, Mead defines the idea of *social control* as the dominance of the expression of the "me" over the expression of the "I." Later in *Mind, Self and Society,* Mead elaborates on his ideas on social control:

Social control, as operating in terms of self-criticism, exerts itself so intimately and extensively over individual behavior or conduct, serving to integrate the individual and his actions with reference to the organized social process of experience and behavior in which he is implicated. . . . Social control over individual behavior or conduct operates by virtue of the social origin and basis of such [self-] criticism. That is to say, self-criticism is essentially social criticism, and behavior controlled socially. Hence social control, so far from tending to crush out the human individual or to obliterate his self-conscious individuality, is, on the contrary, actually constitutive of and inextricably associated with that individuality.

(Mead, 1934/1962:255)

Mead also looks at the "I" and the "me" in pragmatic terms. The "me" allows the individual to live comfortably in the social world, while the "I" makes change in society possible. Society gets enough conformity to allow it to function, and it gets a steady infusion of new developments to prevent it from stagnating. The "I" and the "me" are thus part of the whole social process and allow both individuals and society to function more effectively.

Society

At the most general level, Mead uses the term *society* to mean the ongoing social process that precedes both the mind and the self. Given its importance in shaping the mind and self, society is clearly of central importance to Mead. At another level, society to Mead represents the organized set of responses that are taken over by the individual in the form of the "me." Thus, in this sense individuals carry society around with them, giving them the ability, through self-criticism, to control themselves. Mead also deals with the evolution of society. But Mead has relatively little to say explicitly about society, in spite of its centrality in his theoretical system. His most important contributions lie in his thoughts on mind and self. Even John C. Baldwin, who sees a much more societal (macro) component in Mead's thinking, is forced to admit: "The macro components of Mead's theoretical system are not as well developed as the micro" (1986:123).

At a more specific societal level Mead does have a number of things to say about social *institutions*. Mead broadly defines an *institution* as the "common response in the community" or "the life habits of the community" (1934/1962:261, 264; see also Mead, 1936:376). More specifically, he says that "the whole community acts toward the individual under certain circumstances in an identical way . . . there is an identical response on the part of the whole community under these conditions. We call that the formation of the institution" (Mead, 1934/1962:167). We carry this organized set of attitudes around with us, and they serve to control our actions, largely through the "me."

Education is the process by which the common habits of the community (the institution) are "internalized" in the actor. This is an essential process because, in Mead's view, people neither have selves nor are genuine members of the community until they can respond to themselves as the larger community does. To do this, people must have internalized the common attitudes of the community.

But again Mead is careful to point out that institutions need not destroy individuality or stifle creativity. Mead recognizes that there are "oppressive, stereotyped, and ultra-conservative social institutions—like the church—which by their more or less rigid and inflexible unprogressiveness crush or blot out individuality" (1934/1962:262). However, he is quick to add: "There is no necessary or inevitable reason why social institutions should be oppressive or rigidly conservative, or why they should not rather be, as many are, flexible and progressive, fostering individuality rather than discouraging it" (Mead, 1934/1962:262). To Mead, institutions should define what people ought to do only in a very broad and general sense and should allow plenty of room for individuality and creativity. Mead here demonstrates a very modern conception of social institutions as both constraining individuals *and* enabling them to be creative individuals (see Giddens, 1984). Mead was distinct from the other classical theorists in emphasizing the enabling character of society—arguably disregarding society's constraining power (Athens, 2002).

What Mead lacks in his analysis of society in general, and institutions in particular,[6] is a true macro sense of them in the way that theorists such as Marx, Weber, and Durkheim dealt with this level of analysis. This is true in spite of the fact that Mead does have a notion of *emergence* (Sawyer, 2005, 2007) in the sense that the whole is seen as more than the sum of its parts. More specifically, "Emergence involves a reorganization, but the reorganization brings in something that was not there before. The first time oxygen and hydrogen come together, water appears. Now water is a combination of hydrogen and oxygen, but water was not there before in the separate elements" (Mead, 1934/1962:198). However, Mead is much more prone to apply the idea of emergence to consciousness than to apply it to the larger society. That is, mind and self are seen as emergent from the social process. Moreover, Mead is inclined to use the term *emergence* merely to mean the coming into existence of something new or novel (D. Miller, 1973:41).

Symbolic Interactionism: The Basic Principles

The heart of this chapter is a discussion of the basic principles of symbolic interaction theory. Although we try to characterize the theory in general terms, this is not easy to do, for as Paul Rock says, it has a "deliberately constructed vagueness" and a "resistance to systematisation" (1979:18–19). There are significant differences within symbolic interactionism, some of which are discussed as we proceed.

Some symbolic interactionists (Blumer, 1969a; Manis and Meltzer, 1978; A. Rose, 1962; Snow, 2001) have tried to enumerate the basic principles of the theory. These principles include the following:

1. Human beings, unlike lower animals, are endowed with the capacity for thought.
2. The capacity for thought is shaped by social interaction.

---

[6] There are at least two places where Mead offers a more macro sense of society. At one point he defines *social institutions* as "organized forms of group or social activity" (Mead, 1934/1962:261). Earlier, in an argument reminiscent of Comte, he offers a view of the family as the fundamental unit within society and as the base of such larger units as the clan and the state.

3. In social interaction people learn the meanings and the symbols that allow them to exercise their distinctively human capacity for thought.
4. Meanings and symbols allow people to carry on distinctively human action and interaction.
5. People are able to modify or alter the meanings and symbols that they use in action and interaction on the basis of their interpretation of the situation.
6. People are able to make these modifications and alterations because, in part, of their ability to interact with themselves, which allows them to examine possible courses of action, assess their relative advantages and disadvantages, and then choose one.
7. The intertwined patterns of action and interaction make up groups and societies.

Capacity for Thought

The crucial assumption that human beings possess the ability to think differentiates symbolic interactionism from its behaviorist roots. This assumption also provides the basis for the entire theoretical orientation of symbolic interactionism. Bernard Meltzer, James Petras, and Larry Reynolds stated that the assumption of the human capacity for thought is one of the major contributions of early symbolic interactionists, such as James, Dewey, Thomas, Cooley, and of course, Mead: "Individuals in human society were not seen as units that are motivated by external or internal forces beyond their control, or within the confines of a more or less fixed structure. Rather, they were viewed as reflective or interacting units which comprise the societal entity" (1975:42). The ability to think enables people to act reflectively rather than just behave unreflectively. People must often construct and guide what they do, rather than just release it.

The ability to think is embedded in the mind, but the symbolic interactionists have a somewhat unusual conception of the mind as originating in the socialization of consciousness. They distinguish it from the physiological brain. People must have brains in order to develop minds, but a brain does not inevitably produce a mind, as is clear in the case of lower animals (Troyer, 1946). Also, symbolic interactionists do not conceive of the mind as a thing, a physical structure, but rather as a continuing process. It is a process that is itself part of the larger process of stimulus and response. The mind is related to virtually every other aspect of symbolic interactionism, including socialization, meanings, symbols, the self, interaction, and even society.

Thinking and Interaction

People possess only a general capacity for thought. This capacity must be shaped and refined in the process of social interaction. Such a view leads the symbolic interactionist to focus on a specific form of social interaction—*socialization.* The human ability to think is developed early in childhood socialization and is refined during adult socialization. Symbolic interactionists have a view of the socialization process that is different from that of most other sociologists. To symbolic interactionists, conventional sociologists are likely to see socialization as simply a process by which people learn the things that they need to survive in society (for instance, culture, role expectations). To the symbolic interactionists, socialization is a more dynamic process that allows people to develop the ability to think, to develop in distinctively human ways. Furthermore, socialization is not simply a one-way process in which the actor receives information, but is a dynamic process in which the actor shapes and adapts the information to his or her own needs (Manis and Meltzer, 1978:6).

Symbolic interactionists are, of course, interested not simply in socialization but in interaction in general, which is of "vital importance in its own right" (Blumer, 1969b:8). *Interaction* is the process in which the ability to think is both developed and expressed. All types of interaction, not just interaction during socialization, refine our ability to think. Beyond that, thinking shapes the interaction process. In most interaction, actors must take account of others and decide if and how to fit their activities to others. However, not all interaction involves thinking. The differentiation made by Blumer (following Mead) between two basic forms of social interaction is relevant here. The first, nonsymbolic interaction—Mead's conversation of gestures—does not involve thinking. The second, symbolic interaction, does require mental processes.

The importance of thinking to symbolic interactionists is reflected in their views on *objects*. Blumer differentiates among three types of objects: *physical objects,* such as a chair or a tree; *social objects,* such as a student or a mother; and *abstract objects,* such as an idea or a moral principle. Objects are seen simply as things "out there" in the real world; what is of greatest significance is the way they are defined by actors. The latter leads to the relativistic view that different objects have different meanings for different individuals: "A tree will be a different object to a botanist, a lumberman, a poet, and a home gardener" (Blumer, 1969b:11).

Individuals learn the meanings of objects during the socialization process. Most of us learn a common set of meanings, but in many cases, as with the tree mentioned above, we have different definitions of the same objects. Although this definitional view can be taken to an extreme, symbolic interactionists need not deny the existence of objects in the real world. All they need do is point out the crucial nature of the definition of those objects as well as the possibility that actors may have different definitions of the same object. As Herbert Blumer said: "The nature of an object . . . consists of the meaning that it has for the person for whom it is an object" (1969b:11).

Learning Meanings and Symbols

Symbolic interactionists, following Mead, tend to accord causal significance to social interaction. Thus, meaning stems not from solitary mental processes but from interaction. This focus derives from Mead's pragmatism: he focused on human action and interaction, not on isolated mental processes. Symbolic interactionists have in general continued in this direction. Among other things, the central concern is not how people mentally create meanings and symbols but how they learn them during interaction in general and socialization in particular.

People learn symbols as well as meanings in social interaction. Whereas people respond to signs unthinkingly, they respond to symbols in a thoughtful manner. Signs stand for themselves (for example, the gestures of angry dogs or water to a person dying of thirst). "*Symbols are social objects used to represent* (or 'stand in for,' 'take the place of') whatever people agree they shall represent" (Charon, 1998:47). Not all social objects stand for other things, but those that do are symbols. Words, physical artifacts, and physical actions (for example, the word *boat*, a cross or a Star of David, and a clenched fist) all can be symbols. People often use symbols to communicate something about themselves: they drive Rolls-Royces, for instance, to communicate a certain style of life.

Symbolic interactionists conceive of language as a vast system of symbols. Words are symbols because they are used to stand for things. Words make all other symbols possible. Acts, objects, and other words exist and have meaning only because they have been and can be described through the use of words.

Symbols are crucial in allowing people to act in distinctively human ways. Because of the symbol, the human being "does not respond passively to a reality that imposes itself but actively creates and re-creates the world acted in" (Charon, 1998:69). In addition to this general utility, symbols in general and language in particular have a number of specific functions for the actor.

First, symbols enable people to deal with the material and social world by allowing them to name, categorize, and remember the objects they encounter there. In this way, people are able to order a world that otherwise would be confusing. Language allows people to name, categorize, and especially remember much more efficiently than they could with other kinds of symbols, such as pictorial images.

Second, symbols improve people's ability to perceive the environment. Instead of being flooded by a mass of indistinguishable stimuli, the actor can be alerted to some parts of the environment rather than others.

Third, symbols improve the ability to think. Although a set of pictorial symbols would allow a limited ability to think, language greatly expands this ability. Thinking, in these terms, can be conceived of as symbolic interaction with one's self.

Fourth, symbols greatly increase the ability to solve various problems. Lower animals must use trial-and-error, but human beings can think through symbolically a variety of alternative actions before actually taking one. This ability reduces the chance of making costly mistakes.

Fifth, the use of symbols allows actors to transcend time, space, and even their own persons. Through the use of symbols, actors can imagine what it was like to live in the past or what it might be like to live in the future. In addition, actors can transcend their own persons symbolically and imagine what the world is like from another person's point of view. This is the well-known symbolic-interactionist concept of *taking the role of the other* (D. Miller, 1981).

Sixth, symbols allow us to imagine a metaphysical reality, such as heaven or hell. Seventh, and most generally, symbols allow people to avoid being enslaved by their environment. They can be active rather than passive—that is, self-directed in what they do.

Action and Interaction

Symbolic interactionists' primary concern is with the impact of meanings and symbols on human action and interaction. Here it is useful to employ Mead's differentiation between covert and overt behavior. *Covert behavior* is the thinking process, involving symbols and meanings. *Overt behavior* is the actual behavior performed by an actor. Some overt behavior does not involve covert behavior (habitual behavior or mindless responses to external stimuli). However, most human action involves both kinds. Covert behavior is of greatest concern to symbolic interactionists, whereas overt behavior is of greatest concern to exchange theorists or to traditional behaviorists in general.

Meanings and symbols give human social action (which involves a single actor) and social interaction (which involves two or more actors engaged in mutual social action) distinctive characteristics. Social action is that in which the individuals are acting with others in mind. In other words, in undertaking an action, people simultaneously try to gauge its impact on the other actors involved. Although they often engage in mindless, habitual behavior, people have the capacity to engage in social action.

In the process of social interaction, people symbolically communicate meanings to the others involved. The others interpret those symbols and orient their responding action on the basis of their interpretation. In other words, in social interaction, actors engage in a process of mutual influence. Christopher (2001) refers to this dynamic social interaction as a "dance" that partners engage in.

Making Choices

Partly because of the ability to handle meanings and symbols, people, unlike lower animals, can make choices in the actions in which they engage. People need not accept the meanings and symbols that are imposed on them from without. On the basis of their own interpretation of the situation, "humans are capable of forming new meanings and new lines of meaning" (Manis and Meltzer, 1978:7). Thus, to the symbolic interactionist, actors have at least some autonomy. They are not simply constrained or determined; they are capable of making unique and independent choices. Furthermore, they are able to develop a life that has a unique style (Perinbanayagam, 1985:53).

W. I. Thomas and Dorothy Thomas were instrumental in underscoring this creative capacity in their concept of *definition of the situation:* "If men define situations as real, they are real in their consequences" (Thomas and Thomas, 1928:572). The Thomases knew that most of our definitions of situations have been provided for us by society. In fact, they emphasized this point, identifying especially the family and the community as sources of our social definitions. However, the Thomases' position is distinctive for its emphasis on the possibility of "spontaneous" individual definitions of situations, which allow people to alter and modify meanings and symbols.

Groups and Societies

Symbolic interactionists are generally highly critical of the tendency of other sociologists to focus on macro structures. As Paul Rock says, "Interactionism discards most macrosociological thought as an unsure and overambitious metaphysics . . . not accessible to intelligent examination" (1979:238). Dmitri Shalin points to "interaction-ist criticism aimed at the classical view of social order as external, atemporal, deter-minate at any given moment and resistant to change" (1986:14). Rock also says, "Whilst it [symbolic interactionism] does not wholly shun the idea of social structure, its stress upon activity and process relegates structural metaphors to a most minor place" (1979:50).

Blumer is in the forefront of those who are critical of this "sociological determinism [in which] the social action of people is treated as an outward flow or expression of forces playing on them rather than as acts which are built up by people through their interpretation of the situations in which they are placed" (1962/1969:84).[7] To Blumer, society is not made up of macro structures. The essence of society is to be found in actors and action: "Human society is to be seen as consisting of acting people, and the life of the society is to be seen as consisting of their actions" (Blumer, 1962/1969:85). Human society is action; group life is a "complex of ongoing activity." However, soci-ety is not made up of an array of isolated acts. There is collective action as well, which involves "individuals fitting their lines of action to one another . . . participants making indications to one another, not merely each to himself" (Blumer, 1969b:16). This gives rise to what Mead called the *social act* and Blumer calls *joint action.*

Blumer accepted the idea of emergence—that large-scale structures emerge from micro processes (Morrione, 1988). According to Maines, "The key to understanding Blumer's treatment of large-scale organizations rests on his conception of joint action" (1988:46). A joint action is not simply the sum total of individual acts—it comes to have a character of its own. A joint action thus is not external to or coercive of actors and their actions; rather, it is created by actors and their actions.

From this discussion one gets the sense that the joint act is almost totally flexible—that is, that society can become almost anything the actors want it to be. However, Blumer was not prepared to go as far as that. He argued that each instance of joint action must be formed anew, but he did recognize that joint action is likely to have a "well-established and repetitive form" (Blumer, 1969b:17). Not only does most joint action recur in patterns, but Blumer also was willing to admit that such action is guided by systems of preestablished meanings, such as culture and social order.

It would appear that Blumer admitted that there are large-scale structures and that they are important. Here Blumer followed Mead (1934/1962), who admitted that such structures are very important. However, such structures have an extremely limited role in symbolic interactionism. For one thing, Blumer most often argued that large-scale structures are little more than "frameworks" within which the really important aspects of social life, action and interaction, take place (1962/1969:87). Large-scale structures do set the conditions and limitations on human action, but they do not determine it. In his view, people do not act within the context of structures such as society; rather, they act in situations. Large-scale structures are important in that they shape the situations in which individuals act and supply to actors the fixed set of symbols that enable them to act.

---

[7] Although they recognize that Blumer takes this view, Wood and Wardell (1983) argue that Mead did *not* have an "astructural bias." See also Joas (1981).

Even when Blumer discussed such preestablished patterns, he hastened to make it clear that "areas of unprescribed conduct are just as natural, indigenous, and recurrent in human group life as those areas covered by preestablished and faithfully followed prescriptions of joint action" (1969b:18). Not only are there many unprescribed areas, but even in prescribed areas joint action has to be created and re-created consistently. Actors are guided by generally accepted meanings in this creation and re-creation, but they are not determined by them. They may accept them as is, but they also can make minor and even major alterations in them. In Blumer's words, "It is the social process in group life that creates and upholds the rules, not the rules that create and uphold group life" (1969b:19).

Sheldon Stryker was not satisfied with Blumer's treatment of the relationship between micro-process and macro-structures and he enunciated a more ambitious integrative goal for symbolic interactionism: "A satisfactory theoretical framework must bridge social structure and person, must be able to move from the level of the person to that of large-scale social structure and back again. . . . There must exist a conceptual framework facilitating movement across the levels of organization and person" (1980:53). (Perinbanayagam articulated a similar goal for symbolic interactionism: "the existence of structure *and* meaning, self *and* others, the dialectic of being and emergence, leading to a dialectical interactionism" [1985:xv].) Stryker embedded his orientation in Meadian symbolic interactionism but sought to extend it to the societal level, primarily through the use of role theory:

> This version begins with Mead, but goes beyond Mead to introduce role theoretic concepts and principles, in order to adequately deal with the reciprocal impact of social person and social structure. The nexus in this reciprocal impact is interaction. It is in the context of the social process—the ongoing patterns of interaction joining individual actors—that social structure operates to constrain the conceptions of self, the definitions of the situation, and the behavioral opportunities and repertoires that bound and guide the interaction that takes place.
>
> (Sheldon Stryker, 1980:52)

Stryker developed his orientation in terms of eight general principles:

1. Human action is dependent on a named and classified world in which the names and classifications have meaning for actors. People learn through interaction with others how to classify the world, as well as how they are expected to behave toward it.
2. Among the most important things that people learn are the symbols used to designate social *positions*. A critical point here is that Stryker conceived of positions in structural terms: "the relatively stable, morphological components of social structure" (Stryker, 1980:54). Stryker also accorded *roles* central importance, conceiving of them as the shared behavioral expectations attached to social positions.
3. Stryker also recognized the importance of larger social structures, although he was inclined, like other symbolic interactionists, to conceive of them in terms of organized patterns of behavior. In addition, his discussion treated social

structure as simply the "framework" within which people act. Within these structures, people name one another, that is, recognize one another as occupants of positions. In so doing, people evoke reciprocal expectations of what each is expected to do.

4. Furthermore, in acting in this context, people name not only each other but also themselves; that is, they apply positional designations to themselves. These self-designations become part of the self, internalized expectations with regard to their own behavior.

5. When interacting, people define the situation by applying names to it, to other participants, to themselves, and to particular features of the situation. These definitions are then used by the actors to organize their behavior.

6. Social behavior is not determined by social meanings, although it is constrained by them. Stryker is a strong believer in the idea of *role making*. People do not simply take roles; rather, they take an active, creative orientation to their roles.

7. Social structures also serve to limit the degree to which roles are "made" rather than just "taken" (D. Martin and Wilson, 2005). Some structures permit more creativity than others do.

8. The possibilities of role making make various social changes possible. Changes can occur in social definitions—in names, symbols, and classifications—and in the possibilities for interaction. The cumulative effect of these changes can be alterations in the larger social structures.

Although Stryker offered a useful beginning toward a more adequate symbolic interactionism, his work has a number of limitations. The most notable is that he said little about larger social structures per se. Stryker saw the need to integrate these larger structures in his work, but he recognized that a "full-fledged development of how such incorporation could proceed is beyond the scope of the present work" (1980:69). Stryker saw only a limited future role for large-scale structural variables in symbolic interactionism. He hoped ultimately to incorporate structural factors such as class, status, and power as variables constraining interaction, but he was disinclined to see symbolic interactionism deal with the interrelationships among these structural variables. Presumably, this kind of issue is to be left to other theories that focus more on large-scale social phenomena.

The Self and the Work of Erving Goffman

The self is a concept of enormous importance to symbolic interactionists (Bruder, 1998). In fact, Rock argues that the self "constitutes the very hub of the interactionists' intellectual scheme. All other sociological processes and events revolve around that hub, taking from it their analytic meaning and organization" (1979:102). Though the work of Erving Goffman cannot be reduced to his theories of the self (Smith, 2011), it is clear that one of his most important contributions to sociology is his theory of self. In what follows we place Goffman's theory of the self in the context of other symbolic interactionist theories of self as well as Goffman's more general theories.

ERVING GOFFMAN

A Biographical Sketch

Erving Goffman died in 1982 at the peak of his fame. He had long been regarded as a "cult" figure in sociological theory. That status was achieved in spite of the fact that he had been a professor in the prestigious sociology department at the University of California, Berkeley, and later held an endowed chair at the Ivy League's University of Pennsylvania (Manning, 2005b; G. Smith, 2007, 2011).

By the 1980s he had emerged as a centrally important theorist. In fact, he had been elected president of the American Sociological Association in the year he died but was unable to give his presidential address because of advanced illness. Given Goffman's maverick status, Randall Collins says of his address: "Everyone wondered what he would do for his Presidential address: a straight, traditional presentation seemed unthinkable for Goffman with his reputation as an iconoclast . . . we got a far more dramatic message: Presidential address cancelled, Goffman dying. It was an appropriately Goffmanian way to go out" (1986b:112).

Goffman was born in Alberta, Canada, on June 11, 1922 (S. Williams, 1986). He earned his advanced degrees from the University of Chicago and is most often thought of as a member of the Chicago school and as a symbolic interactionist. However, when he was asked shortly before his death whether he was a symbolic interactionist, he replied that the label was too vague to allow him to put himself in that category (Manning, 1992). In fact, it is hard to squeeze his work into any single category. In creating his theoretical perspective, Goffman drew on many sources and created a distinctive orientation.

The Self

In attempting to understand the concept of the self beyond its initial Meadian formulation, we must first understand the idea of the *looking-glass self* developed by Charles Horton Cooley (Franks and Gecas, 1992). Cooley defined this concept as

> a somewhat definite imagination of how one's self—that is, any idea he appropriates—appears in a particular mind, and the kind of self-feeling one has is determined by the attitude toward this attributed to that other mind. . . . So in imagination we perceive in another's mind some thought of our appearance, manners, aims, deeds, character, friends, and so on, and are variously affected by it.

> (Cooley, 1902/1964:169)

The idea of a looking-glass self can be broken down into three components. First, we imagine how we appear to others. Second, we imagine what their judgment of that appearance must be. Third, we develop some self-feeling, such as pride or mortification, as a result of our imagining others' judgments.

Collins (1986b; Williams, 1986) links Goffman more to social anthropology than to symbolic interactionism. As an undergraduate at the University of Toronto, Goffman had studied with an anthropologist, and at Chicago "his main contacts were not with Symbolic Interactionists, but with W. Lloyd Warner [an anthropologist]" (Collins, 1986b:109). In Collins's view, an examination of the citations in Goffman's early work indicates that he was influenced by social anthropologists and rarely cited symbolic interactionists, and when he did, it was to be critical of them. However, Goffman was influenced by the descriptive studies produced at Chicago and integrated their outlook with that of social anthropology to produce his distinctive perspective. Thus, whereas a symbolic interactionist would look at how people create or negotiate their self-images, Goffman was concerned with how "society . . . forces people to present a certain image of themselves . . . because it forces us to switch back and forth between many complicated roles, is also making us always somewhat untruthful, inconsistent, and dishonorable" (Collins, 1986a:107).

Despite the distinctiveness of his perspective, Goffman had a powerful influence on symbolic interactionism. In addition, it could be argued that he had a hand in shaping another sociology of everyday life, ethnomethodology. In fact, Collins sees Goffman as a key figure in the formation not only of ethnomethodology, but of conversation analysis as well: "It was Goffman who pioneered the close empirical study of everyday life, although he had done it with his bare eyes, before the days of tape recorders and video recorders" (1986b:111). (See Chapter 11 for a discussion of the relationship between ethnomethodology and conversation analysis.) In fact, a number of important ethnomethodologists (Sacks, Schegloff) studied with Goffman at Berkeley and not with the founder of ethnomethodology, Harold Garfinkel.

Given their influence on symbolic interactionism, structuralism, and ethnomethodology, Goffman's theories are likely to be influential for a long time.

Cooley's concept of the looking-glass self and Mead's concept of the self were important in the development of the modern symbolic-interactionist conception of the self. Blumer defined the *self* in extremely simple terms: "Nothing esoteric is meant by this expression [self]. It means merely that a human being can be an object of his own action . . . he acts toward himself and guides himself in his actions toward others on the basis of the kind of object he is to himself" (1969b:12). The self is a process, not a thing (Perinbanayagam, 1985). As Blumer made clear, the self helps human beings to act rather than simply respond to external stimuli:

> The process [interpretation] has two distinct steps. First, the actor indicates to himself the things toward which he is acting; he has to point out in himself the things that have meaning. . . . This interaction with himself is something other than an interplay of psychological elements; it is an instance of the person engaging in a process of communicating with himself. . . . Second, by virtue of this process of communicating with himself, interpretation becomes a matter of handling meanings.

The actor selects, checks, suspends, regroups, and transforms the meanings in the light of the situation in which he is placed and the direction of his action.

(Blumer, 1969b:5)

Although this description of interpretation underscores the part played by the self in the process of choosing how to act, Blumer has really not gone much beyond the early formulations of Cooley and Mead.

Goffman, however, significantly extends interactionist conceptions of the self in his book *Presentation of Self in Everyday Life* (1959; Dowd, 1996; Schwalbe, 1993; Travers, 1992; Tseelon, 1992). Goffman's conception of the self is deeply indebted to Mead's ideas, in particular his discussion of the tension between the "I," the spontaneous self, and the "me," social constraints within the self. This tension is mirrored in Goffman's work on what he called the "crucial discrepancy between our all-too-human selves and our socialized selves" (1959:56). The tension results from the difference between what people expect us to do and what we may want to do spontaneously. We are confronted with the demand to do what is expected of us; moreover, we are not supposed to waver. As Goffman put it, "We must not be subject to ups and downs" (1959:56). In order to maintain a stable self-image, people perform for their social audiences. As a result of this interest in performance, Goffman focused on *dramaturgy*, or a view of social life as a series of dramatic performances akin to those performed on the stage.

Dramaturgy   Goffman's sense of the self was shaped by his dramaturgical approach (Alieva, 2008). To Goffman (as to Mead and most other symbolic interactionists), the self is

not an organic thing that has a specific location. . . . In analyzing the self then we are drawn from its possessor, from the person who will profit or lose most by it, for he and his body merely provide the peg on which something of collaborative manufacture will be hung for a time. . . . The means of producing and maintaining selves do not reside inside the peg.

(Goffman, 1959:252–253)

Goffman perceived the self not as a possession of the actor but rather as the product of the dramatic interaction between actor and audience. The self "is a dramatic effect arising . . . from a scene that is presented" (Goffman, 1959:253). Because the self is a product of dramatic interaction, it is vulnerable to disruption during the performance (Misztal, 2001). Goffman's dramaturgy is concerned with the processes by which such disturbances are prevented or dealt with. Although the bulk of his discussion focuses on these dramaturgical contingencies, Goffman pointed out that most performances are successful. The result is that in ordinary circumstances a firm self is accorded to performers, and it "appears" to emanate from the performer.

Goffman assumed that when individuals interact, they want to present a certain sense of self that will be accepted by others. However, even as they present that self, actors are aware that members of the audience can disturb their performance. For that reason actors are attuned to the need to control the audience, especially those elements of it that might be disruptive. The actors hope that the sense of self that they present to the audience will be strong enough for the audience to define the actors as the actors want them to. The actors also hope that this will cause the audience to act voluntarily as the actors want them to. Goffman characterized this central interest as "impression management." It involves techniques actors use to maintain certain impressions in the face of problems they are likely to encounter and methods they use to cope with these problems.

Following this theatrical analogy, Goffman spoke of a front stage. The *front* is that part of the performance that generally functions in rather fixed and general ways to define the situation for those who observe the performance. Within the front stage, Goffman further differentiated between the setting and the personal front. The *setting* refers to the physical scene that ordinarily must be there if the actors are to perform. Without it, the actors usually cannot perform. For example, a surgeon generally requires an operating room, a taxi driver a cab, and an ice skater ice. The *personal front* consists of those items of expressive equipment that the audience identifies with the performers and expects them to carry with them into the setting. A surgeon, for instance, is expected to dress in a medical gown, have certain instruments, and so on.

Goffman then subdivided the personal front into appearance and manner. *Appearance* includes those items that tell us the performer's social status (for instance, the surgeon's medical gown). *Manner* tells the audience what sort of role the performer expects to play in the situation (for example, the use of physical mannerisms, demeanor). A brusque manner and a meek manner indicate quite different kinds of performances. In general, we expect appearance and manner to be consistent.

Although Goffman approached the front and other aspects of his system as a symbolic interactionist, he did discuss their structural character. For example, he argued that fronts tend to become institutionalized, and so "collective representations" arise about what is to go on in a certain front. Very often when actors take on established roles, they find particular fronts already established for such performances. The result, Goffman argued, is that fronts tend to be selected, not created. This idea conveys a much more structural image than we would receive from most symbolic interactionists.

Despite such a structural view, Goffman's most interesting insights lie in the domain of interaction. He argued that because people generally[8] try to present an idealized picture of themselves in their front-stage performances, inevitably they feel that they must hide things in their performances. First, actors may want to conceal secret pleasures (for instance, drinking alcohol) engaged in prior to the performance or in past lives (for instance, as drug addicts) that are incompatible with their performance. Second, actors may want to conceal errors that have been made in the preparation of the performance as well as steps that have been taken to correct these errors. For example, a taxi driver may seek to hide the fact that he started in the wrong direction. Third, actors may find it necessary to show only end products and to conceal the process involved in producing them. For example, professors may spend several hours preparing a lecture, but they may want to act as if they have always known the material. Fourth, it may be necessary for actors to conceal from

---

[8] But not always—see Ungar (1984) on self-mockery as a way of presenting the self.

the audience that "dirty work" was involved in the making of the end products. Dirty work may include tasks that "were physically unclean, semi-legal, cruel, and degrading in other ways" (Goffman, 1959:44). Fifth, in giving a certain performance, actors may have to let other standards slide. Finally, actors probably find it necessary to hide any insults, humiliations, or deals made so that the performance could go on. Generally, actors have a vested interest in hiding all such facts from their audience.

Another aspect of dramaturgy in the front stage is that actors often try to convey the impression that they are closer to the audience than they actually are. For example, actors may try to foster the impression that the performance in which they are engaged at the moment is their only performance or at least their most important one. To do this, actors have to be sure that their audiences are segregated so that the falsity of the performance is not discovered. Even if it is discovered, Goffman argued, the audiences themselves may try to cope with the falsity so as not to shatter their idealized image of the actor. This reveals the interactional character of performances. A successful performance depends on the involvement of all the parties. Another example of this kind of impression management is an actor's attempt to convey the idea that there is something unique about this performance as well as his or her relationship to the audience. The audience, too, wants to feel that it is the recipient of a unique performance.

Actors try to make sure that all the parts of any performance blend together. In some cases, a single discordant aspect can disrupt a performance. However, performances vary in the amount of consistency required. A slip by a priest on a sacred occasion would be terribly disruptive, but if a taxi driver made one wrong turn, it would not be likely to damage the overall performance greatly.

Another technique employed by performers is *mystification*. Actors often tend to mystify their performances by restricting the contact between themselves and the audience. By generating "social distance" between themselves and the audience, they try to create a sense of awe in the audience. This, in turn, keeps the audience from questioning the performance. Again Goffman pointed out that the audience is involved in this process and often itself seeks to maintain the credibility of the performance by keeping its distance from the performer.

This leads us to Goffman's interest in teams. To Goffman, as a symbolic interactionist, a focus on individual actors obscured important facts about interaction. Goffman's basic unit of analysis was thus not the individual but the team. A *team* is any set of individuals who cooperate in staging a single routine. Thus, the preceding discussion of the relationship between the performer and audience is really about teams.[9] Each member is reliant on the others, because all can disrupt the performance and all are aware that they are putting on an act. Goffman concluded that a team is a kind of "secret society."

Goffman also discussed a *back stage* where facts suppressed in the front or various kinds of informal actions may appear. A back stage is usually adjacent to the

---

[9] A performer and the audience are one kind of team, but Goffman also talked of a group of performers as one team and the audience as another. Interestingly, Goffman argued that a team also can be a single individual. His logic, following classic symbolic interactionism, was that an individual can be his or her own audience—can *imagine* an audience to be present.

front stage, but it is also cut off from it. Performers can reliably expect no members of their front audience to appear in the back. Furthermore, they engage in various types of impression management to make sure of this. A performance is likely to become difficult when actors are unable to prevent the audience from entering the back stage. There is also a third, residual domain, the *outside,* which is neither front nor back.

No area is *always* one of these three domains. Also, a given area can occupy all three domains at different times. A professor's office is front stage when a student visits, back stage when the student leaves, and outside when the professor is at a university basketball game.

Impression Management   In general, *impression management* (P. Manning, 2005c) is oriented to guarding against a series of unexpected actions, such as unintended gestures, inopportune intrusions, and faux pas, as well as intended actions, such as making a scene. Goffman was interested in the various methods of dealing with such problems. First, there is a set of methods involving actions aimed at producing dramaturgical loyalty by, for example, fostering high in-group loyalty, preventing team members from identifying with the audience, and changing audiences periodically so that they do not become too knowledgeable about the performers. Second, Goffman suggested various forms of dramaturgical discipline, such as having the presence of mind to avoid slips, maintaining self-control, and managing the facial expressions and verbal tone of one's performance. Third, he identified various types of dramaturgical circumspection, such as determining in advance how a performance should go, planning for emergencies, selecting loyal teammates, selecting good audiences, being involved in small teams where dissension is less likely, making only brief appearances, preventing audience access to private information, and settling on a complete agenda to prevent unforeseen occurrences.

The audience also has a stake in successful impression management by the actor or team of actors. The audience often acts to save the show through such devices as giving great interest and attention to it, avoiding emotional outbursts, not noticing slips, and giving special consideration to a neophyte performer.

Manning points not only to the centrality of the self but also to Goffman's *cynical* view of people in this work:

> The overall tenor of *The Presentation of Self* is to a world in which people,
> whether individually or in groups, pursue their own ends in cynical disregard for
> others. . . . The view here is of the individual as a set of performance masks
> hiding a manipulative and cynical self.
>
> (P. Manning, 1992:44)

Manning puts forth a "two selves thesis" to describe this aspect of Goffman's thinking; that is, people have both a performance self and a hidden, cynical self.

Role Distance   Goffman (1961) was interested in the degree to which an individual embraces a given role. In his view, because of the large number of roles, few people get completely involved in any given role. *Role distance* deals with the degree to which individuals separate themselves from the roles they are in (Butera, 2008). For example, if older children ride on a merry-go-round, they are likely to be aware that they are really too old to enjoy such an experience. One way of coping with this feeling is to demonstrate distance from the role by doing it in a careless, lackadaisical way by performing seemingly dangerous acts while on the merry-go-round. In performing such acts, the older children are really explaining to the audience that they are not as immersed in the activity as small children might be or that if they are, it is because of the special things they are doing.

One of Goffman's key insights is that role distance is a function of one's social status. High-status people often manifest role distance for reasons other than those of people in low-status positions. For example, a high-status surgeon may manifest role distance in the operating room to relieve the tension of the operating team. People in low-status positions usually manifest more defensiveness in exhibiting role distance. For instance, people who clean toilets may do so in a lackadaisical and uninterested manner. They may be trying to tell their audience that they are too good for such work.

Stigma   Goffman (1963) was interested in the gap between what a person ought to be, *"virtual social identity,"* and what a person actually is, *"actual social identity."* Anyone who has a gap between these two identities is stigmatized. *Stigma* focuses on the dramaturgical interaction between stigmatized people and normals. The nature of that interaction depends on which of the two types of stigma an individual has. In the case of *discredited* stigma, the actor assumes that the differences are known by the audience members or are evident to them (for example, a paraplegic or someone who has lost a limb). A *discreditable* stigma is one in which the differences are neither known by audience members nor perceivable by them (for example, a person who has had a colostomy or a homosexual passing as straight). For someone with a discredited stigma, the basic dramaturgical problem is managing the tension produced by the fact that people know of the problem. For someone with a discreditable stigma, the dramaturgical problem is managing information so that the problem remains unknown to the audience. (For a discussion of how the homeless deal with stigma, see Anderson, Snow, and Cress, 1994.)

Most of the text of Goffman's *Stigma* is devoted to people with obvious, often grotesque stigmas (for instance, the loss of a nose). However, as the book unfolds, the reader realizes that Goffman is really saying that we are all stigmatized at some time or other or in one setting or another. His examples include the Jew "passing" in a predominantly Christian community, the fat person in a group of people of normal weight, and the individual who has lied about his past and must be constantly sure that the audience does not learn of this deception.

Frame Analysis   In *Frame Analysis* (1974), Goffman moved away from his classic symbolic-interactionist roots and toward the study of the small-scale structures of social life (for a study employing the idea of frames, see McLean, 1998). Although he still felt that people define situations in the sense meant by W. I. Thomas, he now thought that such definitions were less important: "Defining situations as real certainly has consequences, but these may contribute very marginally to the events in progress" (Goffman, 1974:1). Furthermore, even when people define situations, they do not ordinarily create those definitions. Action is defined more by mechanical adherence to rules than through an active, creative, and negotiated process. Goffman enunciated his goal: "to try to isolate some of the basic frameworks of understanding available in our society for making sense out of events and to analyze the special vulnerabilities to which these frames of reference are subject" (1974:10).

Goffman looked beyond and behind everyday situations in a search for the structures that invisibly govern them. These are "'schemata of interpretation' that enable individuals 'to locate, perceive, identify, and label' occurrences within their life space and the world at large (Chambliss, 2005). By rendering events or occurrences meaningful, frames function to organize experience and guide action, whether individual or collective" (Snow, 1986:464). Frames are principles of organization that define our experiences. They are assumptions about what we are seeing in the social world. Without frames, our world would be little more than a number of chaotic individual and unrelated events and facts. Gonos provided other structural characteristics of frames:

> From Goffman's analyses of particular framed activities, we can derive certain principal characteristics of frames. A frame is not conceived as a loose, somewhat accidental amalgamation of elements put together over a short time-span. Rather, it is constituted of a set number of essential components, having a definite arrangement and stable relations. These components are not gathered from here and there, as are the elements of a situation, but are always found together as a system. The standard components cohere and are complete. . . . Other less essential elements are present in any empirical instance and lend some of their character to the whole. . . . In all this, frames are very close in conception to "structures."
>
> (Gonos, 1977:860)

To Gonos, frames are largely rules or laws that fix interaction. The rules are usually unconscious and ordinarily nonnegotiable. Among the rules identified by Gonos are those that define "how signs are to be 'interpreted,' how outward indications are to be related to 'selves,' and what 'experience' will accompany activity" (1980:160). Gonos concludes, "Goffman's problematic thus promotes the study not of observable interaction of 'everyday life' as such, but its eternal structure and ideology; not of situations, but of their frames" (1980:160).

One can grant frames the status of preexisting structures, especially in the larger culture, but it is also the case that interpretive, constructionist (P. Berger and Luckmann, 1967; Swatos, 2007) work is required by actors in relationship to frames. Actors must decide which frame among others is the one to be used in a given situation. Frames themselves may be transformed by actors as the need arises. Frames also may change over time rather than remaining static. This is especially the case when successful social movements arise that contest extant frames or succeed in replacing them with different ones.

According to Snow (2007), frames perform three functions in interpretive work. First, they *focus attention* on our surroundings by highlighting what is relevant or irrelevant, what is "in-frame" and what is "out-of-frame." Second, they act as *articulation mechanisms* by linking the various highlighted elements, so that a "story" is told about them, so that one set of meanings rather than another is conveyed. Third, they serve a *transformative function* through the reconstitution of the way some things are seen in relation to other things or to the actor. Snow (2007:1778–1786) concludes that "it is arguable that they [frames] are fundamental to interpretation, so much so that few, if any, utterances could be meaningfully understood apart from the way they are framed."

Philip Manning (1992:119) gives the following examples of how different frames applied to the same set of events serve to give those same events very different meaning. For example, what are we to make of the sight of a woman putting two watches in her pocket and leaving a shop without paying? Seen through the frame of a store detective, this appears to be a clear case of shoplifting. However, the legal frame leads her lawyer to see this as the act of an absentminded woman who was out shopping for gifts for her daughters.

Another change that Manning argues is clear in *Frame Analysis,* and that was foreshadowed in other works by Goffman, is a shift away from the cynical view of life that lay at the heart of *Presentation of Self in Everyday Life.* In fact, on the first page of *Frame Analysis,* Goffman says, "All the world is not a stage— certainly the theater isn't entirely" (1974:1). Goffman clearly came to recognize the limitations of the theater as a metaphor for everyday life. While still useful in some ways, this metaphor conceals some aspects of life just as it illuminates others. One of the things that is concealed is the importance of ritual in everyday life. Here is the way Manning describes one of the roles played by ritual in everyday life:

> For Goffman, ritual is essential because it maintains our confidence in basic social relationships. It provides others with opportunities to affirm the legitimacy of our position in the social structure while obliging us to do the same. Ritual is a placement mechanism in which, for the most part, social inferiors affirm the higher positions of their superiors. The degree of ritual in a society reflects the legitimacy of its social structure, because the ritual respect paid to individuals is also a sign of respect for the roles they occupy.
>
> (P. Manning, 1992:133)

More generally, we can say that rituals are one of the key mechanisms by which everyday life, and the social world in general, are made orderly and given solidity.

Goffman's interest in rituals brought him close to the later work of Emile Durkheim, especially *The Elementary Forms of Religious Life* (1912/1965). More generally, in accord with Durkheim's sense of social facts, Goffman came to focus on rules and see them as external constraints on social behavior. However, rules are generally only partial, indeterminate guides to conduct. Furthermore, even though people are constrained, such constraint does not rule out the possibility of individual variation, even imaginative use by individuals of those rules. As Philip Manning puts it, "For the most part, Goffman assumed that rules are primarily constraints. . . . However, at other times Goffman emphasized the limitations of the Durkheimian idea that rules are constraints governing behavior, and argued instead that we frequently ignore or abuse rules intended to limit our actions" (1992:158). In fact, in line with modern thinking, to Goffman rules could be both constraints and resources to be used by people in social interaction.

The Sociology of Emotions

Since the 1970s the sociology of emotions has become a major area of inquiry within sociology and sociological theory (Kemper, 1990; Turner and Stets, 2005). This field includes contributions from sociologists of culture, evolutionary sociologists, structural theorists, and microsociological theorists in traditions as diverse as exchange theory, conversation analysis, and symbolic interactionism. Indeed, Turner and Stets (2005) claim that the study of emotions is at the forefront of contemporary microsociology.

What Is Emotion?

Arlie Hochschild (1983/2003), one of the founding figures in the sociology of emotion, argues that in the last century there have been two major models of emotion. The *organismic model* is exemplified in the work of Charles Darwin, William James, and Sigmund Freud. This model treats emotion as largely biological and argues that some emotions are universally shared. For example, in their review of the emotions literature Turner and Stets (2005) identify fear, anger, happiness, and sadness as universal primary emotions. In the organismic model emotion is guided by instinct and its basic character remains unshaped by social factors. Happiness, for example, is independent of the culture or social context in which it is expressed. This is related to another assumption, namely, that emotion is passive. It cannot be managed or worked on by the people who experience emotions.

The *interactional model* is exemplified in the work of John Dewey, Hans Gerth and C. Wright Mills, and Erving Goffman. Though, as Hochschild points out, interactionists agree that some component of emotion is biological, they argue that "social factors enter not simply before and after but interactively during the experience of emotion" (1983/2003:221). This means that people do not passively respond to emotion but actively engage with emotion as it is expressed. This also allows for the idea that the experience and expression of emotion varies according to cultural rules and social context.

Clearly symbolic interactionist work on emotion shares features of Hochschild's interactional model. Many of the early symbolic interactionists address emotions at least to some extent. Mead, for example, dedicates several passages of *Mind, Self and Society* to the relationship between emotion and symbols. He points out that most vocal gestures have an emotional character. However, unlike symbols, the emotional component of vocal gestures does not arouse the same response in us as it does in others. When people express anger at others they do not feel other people's experience of that anger. This said, Mead argues that there are some kinds of human expressions that are intended to arouse the same emotional experience in others. Poetry, for example, uses symbols in order to evoke the same emotional response in both poet and audience. Charles Cooley's theory of the looking-glass self also includes an emotional component. Recall that Cooley's theory of self-development unfolds in three phases (see previous discussion under Goffman). In the third phase, after a person recognizes that others view him or her in a certain way, the person develops a self-feeling, in particular a feeling of pride or shame. Goffman (1967) also touched on the problem of emotion when he argued that people engage in self-presentation, in part, to avoid the feelings of embarrassment that accompany failed performances.

In these earlier theories, though, emotion is treated as less important to social interaction than symbol and language exchange. In this sense, symbolic interactionism has exhibited a *cognitive bias* and overemphasized the role that symbol use and thought (the internalization of symbol use) play in shaping self and social reality. In what follows we focus on two theorists who have been central in the development of the sociology of emotions: Thomas Scheff and Arlie Hochschild. Both theorists treat emotion as central to social interaction and social organization more generally.

Shame: The Social Emotion

Thomas Scheff (2003) combines the work of Charles Cooley, Erving Goffman, and psychoanalytic theorist Helen Lewis to create a particularly dynamic theory of emotion. Scheff argues that it is important to theorize the nature of specific emotions. Implied in this is that different emotions enter into social interaction in different ways. Scheff has focused on the emotions of pride and, in particular, shame because, he says, these are the most important emotions for understanding social interaction.

Indeed, in one essay Scheff nominates shame as the "premiere social emotion" (2003:39).[10] This implies a distinction between emotions that are fully social and those that can be accounted for by individual and biological factors. Fear, for example, is not primarily social because it signals a threat to the body (2003:256). It can thus be experienced irrespective of other people. Shame, on the other hand, always depends upon judgments passed by other persons and is therefore a social emotion. Scheff defines shame in the following way:

> By shame I mean a large family of emotions that includes many cognates and variants, most notably embarrassment, humiliation, and related feelings such as shyness that involve reactions to rejection or feelings of failure or inadequacy. What unites all these cognates is that they involve the feeling of a *threat to the social bond.*

> (2000:96–97)

As the quotation indicates, shame is important because it mediates the social bond. In particular Scheff describes three ways that shame does this. First, it functions as a "moral gyroscope" forcing people not just to recognize, but also to feel their social transgressions (2003:254). Second, it most often arises when a relationship is in trouble, thus signaling a need to restore the social bond. Third, it regulates the expression of all other emotions. We are unlikely to express love, fear, and anger if we anticipate that these emotions will lead to feelings of shame.

The strength of Scheff's theory is its attention to the intricacy of microsocial emotional exchanges. Like Mead he assumes that people are in a continuous state of self-assessment—shifting back and forth between the perspectives of the I and the Me.

---

[10] Scheff is not alone in this claim. As noted, both Cooley and Goffman treat shame as a central social emotion. The psychologist Sylvan Tomkins, one of the inspirations for an emerging area of social theory called "affect theory" (Sedgwick and Frank, 1995; see Chapter 17), also identifies shame as one of the most important emotions.

He develops this concept by drawing on the work of another American pragmatist, Charles Sanders Peirce. Scheff (1997) insists that when in interaction, on a moment-to-moment basis we shift between observing other people's external behavior and imagining other people's inner experiences, both symbolic and emotional. In this process it is possible to approximate interpersonal understanding, which he also calls *attunement*. People become attuned to one another's cognitive and emotional states. The achievement of attunement is one way in which the social bond is secured. The more people feel like they understand one another the tighter the social bond. The discussion of attunement and the social bond is important because it connects Scheff's microsociological theory of emotion to macrosociological problems. He argues that if we understand the nature of the social bond, then we can also begin to understand how societies more broadly are held together. In other words, in the tradition of Emile Durkheim, the study of emotion is the study of the glue that holds society together.

Tied to the process of attunement are feelings of pride and shame. In social interaction people not only seek intersubjective understanding, but also this understanding is suffused with feelings of pride or shame. Interaction is not simply driven by the exchange of symbols but, more importantly, there is an underlying "exchange of feelings"—a back and forth movement between pride and shame, which often and unwittingly guides the interactive process (1997:100, 102). Drawing on Goffman (1967), Scheff calls this the *deference-emotion system*. Each exchange, each sentence, each intonation of the voice brings with it acts of deference. In some cases deference is granted. The individual is treated with respect and experiences feelings of pride. In other cases deference is withheld. The person is judged inadequate and experiences feelings of shame.

The Invisibility of Shame

This said, Scheff argues that when it comes to the acknowledgement of shame we are faced with a paradox. Feelings of shame and pride attend every moment of interaction. Yet, he points out, people are largely unaware of shame feelings. Shame is ever-present, directing interaction, but invisible. This is part of a larger argument in which Scheff (1997, 2006) claims that in the contemporary Western world most people are unaware of the central role that emotions in general, and shame in particular, play in their social-relational lives. This is due to a shift toward value systems that overemphasize the virtues of self-sustaining individualism. It is difficult for Western people to conceive of shame because it reveals that self-feelings come to us through other people. In a culture that prizes self-containment, the feeling of shame demonstrates our utter dependency and vulnerability before others.

Here Scheff's theory parallels Norbert Elias's (1939/1994) analysis of the history of manners (see Chapter 13). Elias shows that in the transition from medieval to modern Western society the tolerance for embarrassing and shameful acts has declined. Where, for example, picking one's nose in public was at one time inconsequential, within the modern age it became an occasion for embarrassment and shame. At the same time the awareness of these shame feelings has declined, so that while one may be embarrassed about picking one's nose in public one will not be able and willing to openly discuss that embarrassment. Not only are shameful acts hidden, but the fact that they are hidden is denied. This *double denial of emotion*, shame about shame, ensures the invisibility of shame and allows the efficient and rational coordination of everyday social life.

The problem with the denial of shame is that it can lead to pathological shame and other destructive emotions. This is where Scheff (1997) incorporates psychoanalytic arguments. The essential idea is that when shame is denied, or in psychoanalytic terms repressed, it has a negative impact on self and others and ultimately threatens the social bond. For example, when shame is denied, people can become caught in what Helen Lewis (1971) calls a *feeling trap*. Shame finds no outward expression but rather cycles inward. When it is turned inward, people begin to feel shame about their shame. Returning to Goffman's deference-emotion concept, Scheff says that people can also become caught in *interpersonal feeling traps*. This happens when one person starts to feel ashamed of another person's shame. In turn, this increases the first person's shame, further deepening the feeling trap. Because of the cultural taboo against shame, all of this remains unspoken and individuals become incapable of moving beyond the shame that characterizes both the interpersonal relationship and the intrapersonal relation of self to self.

Furthermore, this shame can turn into outwardly expressed humiliation and anger. People who are ashamed of themselves do not admit the shame but rather strike out against others, another attack on the social bond. When the denial of shame becomes a central component of a society, as it has become in the West, the social order in general is threatened. Thus, Scheff's theory of emotion is not only aimed at restoring psychological and interpersonal relationship, but also at understanding the origins of macrosocial chaos and conflict (see, for example, his analysis of the emotional roots of Franco-German relations from 1871 to 1945; Scheff, 1997).

Emotion Management and Emotion Work

We have already mentioned the ideas of Arlie Hochschild in the introduction to this discussion. She works in the interactionist tradition but takes one step beyond it to introduce the *emotion management* perspective. In this theory, Hochschild offers a microsociological theory of emotion, informed by the work of Goffman and the theater director Constantin Stanislavski. However, she also places these microsocial processes within the context of larger social structures. In particular she brings a Marxian and feminist dimension to her analysis of emotion management.

Drawing on Goffman, Hochschild argues that emotions are not stored inside of people but rather they are dependent upon emotion management, or as she also calls it *emotion work*. In its most basic form emotion is biological. However, this is only the raw material on which human agents go to work. Hochschild likens emotion and feeling to other human senses:

> Emotion, I suggest, is a biologically given sense, and our most important one. Like other senses—hearing, touch, and smell—it is a means by which we know about our relation to the world, and is therefore crucial for the survival of human beings in group life. Emotion is unique among the senses, however, because it is related not only to an orientation toward action but also to an orientation toward cognition.
>
> (1983/2003:229)

Emotion is given by biology but it is not determined by biology. Rather it is modified through cognition (or thought). In symbolic interactionist theory cognition is a product of culturally constructed significant symbols. Therefore, it is by manipulating symbols, through various kinds of acting (a la Goffman), that people are able to modify emotions.

Hochschild extends Goffman's ideas by distinguishing between *surface acting* and *deep acting*. To say that emotions are a product of acting implies that emotions are performed. However, they can be performed in two different ways. In surface acting the person manipulates surface appearances such as facial expression and tone of voice in order to convey an emotional expression to others. The politician, for example, smiles and warmly shakes a supporter's hands in order to communicate appreciation. Referring to the ideas of Stanislavski, Hochschild says that in this kind of performance "the body, not the soul, is the main tool of the trade" (1983/2003:37). Goffman is regarded as the master theorist of surface acting and in fact a criticism of his work is that he reduced all of human behavior to strategic and cynical forms of surface acting.

Hochschild, on the other hand, develops the notion of deep acting through reflection on Stanislavski's technique of method acting. Stanislavski wanted his actors to not only communicate emotion through the surface of the body but through the "soul" as well. In deep acting the performance of emotions comes from living through them. A deep actor does not simply perform the emotion but actually experiences the emotions as part of the performance. Emotions are conjured up and performed, but this is done with depth.

Hochschild argues that in everyday life people engage in a similar kind of deep acting. Since emotions are not instinctually produced, each time that a person enters into a new situation he or she must generate the emotion appropriate to the setting. According to Hochschild the technique involves the following:

- A person recognizes that she or he is expected to feel a particular way in a situation.
- The person then creates the conditions under which that emotion could emerge.
- To create these conditions the person conjures up an *emotion memory.*
- An emotion memory is a autobiographical episode that carries within it strong feelings.
- The person then acts "as if" the feeling contained in the memory was relevant to the present moment.
- This allows the person to deeply feel the emotion appropriate to the situation.

Hochschild gives numerous examples of how this works in everyday life. A person is not as strongly affected by a friend's mental breakdown as would be expected, so he recalls a similar episode from his own past and uses that emotion member to better sympathize with his friend. A young Catholic woman works hard to feel love for a man in order to justify having slept with him. In this procedure there is an intense use of memory and imagination in order to bring the body into alignment with the expectations of the moment.

This said, emotion work does not only involve a person's relationship with her or his own emotion memory. Hochschild identifies the numerous ways in which people use their immediate setting to conjure up deep feeling. For example, people may rely upon "stage props" to better help conjure up an emotion memory. Or they may rely upon friends and family—members of their performance team, to use Goffman's term—to help them feel the right emotion. Alternately people might leave a particularly evocative setting in order to suppress an unwanted emotion. Here we see that emotion work is not only used to *evoke* particular emotions but also to *suppress* particular emotions. If, for example, an individual starts to feel inappropriate joy at a failure of a friend or classmate, she might imagine a similar failure from her own past. If this emotion work is successful she will suppress the emotion of joy and evoke the more appropriate emotion of sympathy.

Two things should be clear from this summary. First, even though Hochschild argues that surface acting is an insufficient concept to understand the experience of emotion in everyday life, she still sees emotion as something that is created by the actor in interaction with self and others. Second, much of the deep acting in which we engage is automatic, quick, and private. Therefore it is not immediately recognizable as something created through emotion work. That is, even though Hochschild's description of emotion work might seem quite complex, most of us have made this kind of emotion work a habitual part of our everyday interaction. Indeed, we generally only come to recognize the hard work of creating emotion when our feelings are at odds with the feeling rules that pervade a situation.

Feeling Rules

Emotion management varies historically, culturally, and cross-situationally. In other words, different situations are accompanied by what Hochschild calls *feeling rules*. Feeling rules are culturally determined standards for emotion management. For example, Lyn Lofland (1985) describes the way that expressions of grief at the death of a loved one have changed over historical time. Feeling rules lay out the *extent, direction* and *duration* of feeling in a particular situation. Extent refers to how strongly a particular emotion should be felt. Should I be very happy at the birth of my friend's child or a little bit happy? Direction refers to the kind of emotion appropriate to a situation. Can I feel sad at the birth of my friend's child? Duration refers to the length of time that a particular feeling can be felt. Can I feel happy for my friend for days, weeks, months, a year?

More specifically, feeling rules enter the microsituation as a set of rules for interpersonal exchange. Hochschild likens emotional exchange to gift-giving. The important point is that gift-giving is governed by cultural rules. Like the well-given gift, the appropriate exchange of feeling ensures the viability of the social bond. In everyday life, then, we expect to receive certain feelings from others and to give back certain feelings to others: "feeling rules set out what is owed in gestures of exchange between people" (1983/2003:76).[11] These rules also bear upon the previous discussion of surface acting and deep acting. Hochschild says that people are quite good at recognizing the

---

[11] Candace Clark (1987) further develops this idea with her concepts of sympathy biography and sympathy credit.

difference between surface and deep acting. In some situations, where the feeling rules allow, we can exchange feelings through surface acting. We fully expect that the politician's expression of warmth for a supporter is, at least in part, a surface performance. We are usually content if they merely put in the effort to keep up this performance. In other cases, such as a love affair, emotional exchange will require deep acting. If a person feels that his lover is only going through the motions, rather than conjuring real feeling, this will generally be considered an inadequate exchange of feeling.

Commercialization of Feeling

A central theme in Hochschild's work is the effect of capitalism on emotion management. Where in the past feeling rules were organically produced within the realm of everyday life, increasingly feeling rules are determined by the machinations of capitalism. She calls the process by which our private and unconscious emotion work is overtaken by corporations and organizations the *transmutation of emotional systems*. The private emotional system of previous eras is replaced by an increasingly public and corporate emotion system. A brief review of Hochschild's research on this process also demonstrates various ways in which we can conceive the relationship between the microsocial management of emotion and macrosocial structures.

Hochschild (1983/2003) first examined the commercialization of emotion in her famous book-length study of airline stewardesses, *The Managed Heart*. Studying economic production in the eighteenth and nineteenth centuries, Karl Marx argued that economic value was produced through manual labor. In contrast, in contemporary America economic value is increasingly produced through service work. A large component of service work involves *emotional labor*. For example, in the airline industry flight attendants are expected to keep up a smile and maintain a happy face despite long hours and often challenging customers. The emotional atmosphere that the flight attendant creates within the airplane cabin is one component of the product sold by the airline. Indeed, as Hochschild's work reveals, industry managers provide flight attendants with specific instructions on the kinds of feelings they are to project to customers and the techniques they can use to generate these feelings. Where manual labor exerted a toll on the body, service work exerts a toll on the emotional system. At one level, of course, this kind of emotional labor can be viewed as surface acting and the individual can maintain some role-distance from the performance. However, Hochschild worries that the increasing preponderance of corporately managed emotion work may impact our capacity to feel and detect deeper forms of emotional expression in other areas of our lives.

Hochschild (1997, 2003) has further developed these ideas in her research on the relationship between work and home in American families. In her study of a company that she calls Amerco, Hochschild noticed a perplexing shift in the relationship between home and work. Where traditionally people viewed the family home as a warm and welcoming place of respite and recuperation, increasingly the home is viewed as a place of tension. Instead the workplace has come to be viewed as a place of respite: "family life had become like 'work' and work had become more like 'home'" (2003:198). She argues that the reason for this shift has been a transformation in the *emotional culture* of corporate America. In explaining this concept, Hochschild draws on Anthony Giddens's structuration theory (see Chapter 13). Individual emotions are not unilaterally determined by an overarching corporate structure, rather institutions work with individuals to create an environment that is conducive to the promotion of feelings of comfort and happiness. More specifically: "An emotional culture is a set of rituals, beliefs about feelings, and rules governing feeling that induce emotional focus and even a sense of the 'sacred'" (203). Like the flight attendants who are expected to create an atmosphere of safety and comfort in the airline cabin, many contemporary American corporations have been able to generate an emotional culture that is viewed as welcoming and sacred, an alternative to the increasingly troubled and desacralized space of the family home.

Hochschild offers one further conceptual innovation in her examination of *care work*. Here she connects the emotional systems described in her earlier theoretical work with recent research on global social systems. She defines care in this way:

> by the term 'care' I refer to an emotional bond, usually mutual, between the caregiver and cared-for, a bond in which the caregiver feels responsible for others' well-being and does mental, emotional, and physical work in the course of fulfilling that responsibility.

> (2003:214)

Care work involves tasks that, in America, have been performed historically by women: maintaining the family home, caring for children, nursing the elderly. However, as more middle-class American families become dual-income families, care work has been outsourced: nannies, nurses, and homecare workers are hired to care for children and the elderly. Unable to secure a living wage in their home countries, many of these care workers are imported through global networks. In particular many care workers are women from Third World countries. They leave their own families and children behind in order to care for the children of middle-class American families. Hearkening back to her early Marxist theories of emotional labor, with this example in hand, Hochschild argues that feelings have become "distributable resources" (2003:191). Where in previous eras capitalism extracted gold and other forms of capital wealth from the Third World, in the contemporary moment capitalism extracts love and care from the Third World.

Though Hochschild does not explicitly offer a theory that connects the global system to the microsocial practice of emotion management, it is clear that these emerging social structures reach deeply into the emotional lives and emotion work of people around the world.

Criticisms

Having analyzed the ideas of symbolic interactionism, particularly those of Mead, Blumer, Goffman, and the sociologists of emotion, we will now enumerate some of the major criticisms of this perspective.

The first criticism is that the mainstream of symbolic interactionism has too readily given up on conventional scientific techniques. Eugene Weinstein and Judith Tanur expressed this point well: "Just because the contents of consciousness are qualitative, does not mean that their exterior expression cannot be coded, classified, even counted" (1976:105). Science and subjectivism are *not* mutually exclusive. Though we have not examined it here, it is important to note that, beginning with the work of Manford Kuhn (1964), symbolic interactionists from what is called the Iowa School have attempted to develop what they consider a more scientific version of interactionism (Miller, 2011).

Second, Manford Kuhn (1964), William Kolb (1944), Bernard Meltzer, James Petras, and Larry Reynolds (1975), and many others have criticized the vagueness of essential Meadian concepts such as mind, self, I, and me. Most generally, Kuhn (1964) spoke of the ambiguities and contradictions in Mead's theory. Beyond Meadian theory, they have criticized many of the basic symbolic-interactionist concepts for being confused and imprecise and therefore incapable of providing a firm basis for theory and research. Because these concepts are imprecise, it is difficult, if not impossible, to operationalize them; the result is that testable propositions cannot be generated (Sheldon Stryker, 1980).

The third major criticism of symbolic interactionism has been of its tendency to downplay or ignore large-scale social structures. This criticism has been expressed in various ways. For example, Weinstein and Tanur argued that symbolic interactionism ignores the connectedness of outcomes to each other: "*It is the aggregated outcomes that form the linkages among episodes of interaction that are the concern of sociology qua sociology. . . .* The concept of social structure is necessary to deal with the incredible density and complexity of relations through which episodes of interaction are interconnected" (1976:106). Sheldon Stryker argued that the micro focus of symbolic interactionism serves "to minimize or deny the facts of social structure and the impact of the macro-organizational features of society on behavior" (1980:146).

Somewhat less predictable is the fourth criticism, that symbolic interactionism is not sufficiently microscopic, that it ignores the importance of factors such as the unconscious and emotions (Meltzer, Petras, and Reynolds, 1975; Sheldon Stryker, 1980). Similarly, symbolic interactionism has been criticized for ignoring psychological factors such as needs, motives, intentions, and aspirations. In their effort to deny that there are immutable forces impelling the actor to act, symbolic interactionists have focused instead on meanings, symbols, action, and interaction. They ignore psychological factors that might impel the actor, an action that parallels their neglect of the larger societal constraints on the actor. In both cases, symbolic interactionists are accused of making a "fetish" out of everyday life (Meltzer, Petras, and Reynolds, 1975:85). This focus on everyday life, in turn, leads to a marked overemphasis on the immediate situation and an "obsessive concern with the transient, episodic, and fleeting" (Meltzer, Petras, and Reynolds, 1975:85).

The Future of Symbolic Interactionism

Gary Fine (1993) offered an interesting portrait of symbolic interactionism in the 1990s. His fundamental point is that symbolic interactionism has changed dramatically in recent years. First, it has undergone considerable *fragmentation* since its heyday at the University of Chicago in the 1920s and 1930s. A great diversity of work is now included under the broad heading of symbolic interactionism. Second, symbolic interactionism has undergone *expansion* and has extended far beyond its traditional concern with micro relations (S. Harris, 2001). Third, symbolic interactionism has *incorporated* ideas from many other theoretical perspectives (Feather, 2000). This is illustrated in our discussion of the sociology of emotions. Scheff, for example, draws on the work of Cooley, Mead, and Goffman but has also made use of psychoanalytic ideas. So too, Hochschild, while starting with Goffman, uses the writing of Stanislavski as well as Marx's macrosociological theories. In addition, the ideas of symbolic interactionists have, in turn, been *adopted* by sociologists who are focally committed to other theoretical perspectives. Finally, symbolic interactionists are deeply involved in some of the major issues confronting sociological theory in the late twentieth and early twenty-first centuries. This includes concerns with micro-macro and agency-structure integration, studies of the relationship between selfhood and the Internet (see special issue of *Symbolic Interaction,* 2010), and a recent concern with the contributions that symbolic interactionism can make to the field of globalization studies (Knorr-Cetina, 2009).

Thus, lines dividing symbolic interactionism and other sociological theories have blurred considerably (Maines, 2001). While symbolic interactionism will survive, it is increasingly unclear what it means to be a symbolic interactionist (and every other type of sociological theorist, for that matter). Here is the way Fine puts it:

> Predicting the future is dangerous, but it is evident that the label symbolic interaction will abide. . . . Yet, we will find more intermarriage, more interchange, and more interaction. Symbolic interaction will serve as a label of convenience for the future, but will it serve as a label of thought?
>
> (G. Fine, 1993:81–82)

Summary

This chapter begins with a brief discussion of the roots of symbolic interactionism in philosophical pragmatism (the work of John Dewey) and psychological behaviorism (the work of John B. Watson). Out of the confluence of pragmatism, behaviorism, and other influences, such as Simmelian sociology, symbolic interactionism developed at the University of Chicago in the 1920s.

The symbolic interactionism that developed stood in contrast to the psychological reductionism of behaviorism and the structural determinism of more macro-oriented sociological theories such as structural functionalism. Its distinctive orientation was toward the mental capacities of actors and their relationship to action and interaction. All this was conceived in terms of process; there was a disinclination to see the actor impelled by either internal psychological states or large-scale structural forces.

The single most important theory in symbolic interactionism is that of George Herbert Mead. Substantively, Mead's theory accorded primacy and priority to the social world. That is, it is out of the social world that consciousness, the mind, the self, and so on, emerge. The most basic unit in his social theory is the act, which includes four dialectically related stages—impulse, perception, manipulation, and consummation. A *social* act involves two or more persons, and the basic mechanism of the social act is the gesture. While lower animals and humans are capable of having a conversation of gestures, only humans can communicate the conscious meaning of their gestures. Humans are peculiarly able to create vocal gestures, and this leads to the distinctive human ability to develop and use significant symbols. Significant symbols lead to the development of language and the distinctive capacity of humans to communicate, in the full sense of the term, with one another. Significant symbols also make possible thinking, as well as symbolic interaction.

Mead looks at an array of mental processes as part of the larger social process, including reflective intelligence, consciousness, mental images, meaning, and, most generally, the mind. Humans have the distinctive capacity to carry on an inner conversation with themselves. All the mental processes are, in Mead's view, lodged not in the brain but rather in the social process.

The self is the ability to take oneself as an object. Again, the self arises within the social process. The general mechanism of the self is the ability of people to put themselves in the place of others, to act as others act and to see themselves as others see them. Mead traces the genesis of the self through the play and game stages of childhood. Especially important in the latter stage is the emergence of the generalized other. The ability to view oneself from the point of view of the community is essential to the emergence of the self as well as of organized group activities. The self also has two phases—the "I," which is the unpredictable and creative aspect of the self, and the "me," which is the organized set of attitudes of others assumed by the actor. Social control is manifest through the "me," while the "I" is the source of innovation in society.

Mead has relatively little to say about society, which he views most generally as the ongoing social processes that precede mind and self. Mead largely lacks a macro sense of society. Institutions are defined as little more than collective habits.

Symbolic interactionism may be summarized by the following basic principles:

1. Human beings, unlike lower animals, are endowed with a capacity for thought.
2. The capacity for thought is shaped by social interaction.
3. In social interaction, people learn the meanings and symbols that allow them to exercise their distinctively human capacity for thought.
4. Meanings and symbols allow people to carry on distinctively human action and interaction.
5. People are able to modify or alter the meanings and symbols they use in action and interaction on the basis of their interpretation of the situation.
6. People are able to make these modifications and alterations because, in part, of their ability to interact with themselves, which allows them to examine possible courses of action, assess their relative advantages and disadvantages, and then choose one.
7. The intertwined patterns of action and interaction make up groups and societies.

In the context of these general principles, we seek to clarify the nature of the work of several important thinkers in the symbolic-interactionist tradition, including Charles Horton Cooley, Herbert Blumer, and, most important, Erving Goffman.

We present in detail Goffman's dramaturgical analysis of the self and his related works on role distance, stigma, and frame analysis. However, we also note that Goffman's work on frames has exaggerated a tendency in his earlier work and moved further in the direction of a structuralist analysis. We also introduce one of the most important areas of recent symbolic interactionist theory: the sociology of emotions. We present theories developed by two of the founding figures in emotions research. Thomas Scheff argues that shame is the most important social emotion and drawing on both symbolic interactionism and psychoanalysis, he develops a theory of self and social order that places shame at its center. Arlie Hochschild combines her interest in emotion with theories developed by the theater director Constantin Stanislavski and Karl Marx. This leads to the concepts of deep acting, emotion work, and emotion labor.

We conclude with some of the major criticisms of symbolic interactionism, as well as one image of symbolic interactionism's future.

Ethnomethodology

Chapter Outline

Defining Ethnomethodology
The Diversification of Ethnomethodology
Some Early Examples
Conversation Analysis
Studies of Institutions
Criticisms of Traditional Sociology
Stresses and Strains in Ethnomethodology
Synthesis and Integration

Given its Greek roots, the term *ethnomethodology* literally means the "methods" that people use on a daily basis to accomplish their everyday lives. To put it slightly differently, the world is seen as an ongoing practical accomplishment. People are viewed as rational, but they use "practical reasoning," not formal logic, in accomplishing their everyday lives.

Defining Ethnomethodology

We begin with the definition of *ethnomethodology* offered in Chapter 6: the study of "the body of common-sense knowledge and the range of procedures and considerations by means of which the ordinary members of society make sense of, find their way about in, and act on the circumstances in which they find themselves" (Heritage, 1984:4; Linstead, 2006).

We can gain further insight into the nature of ethnomethodology by examining efforts by its founder, Harold Garfinkel (1988, 1991, 2002), to define it. Like Durkheim, Garfinkel considers "social facts" to be the fundamental sociological phenomenon (Hilbert, 2005). However, Garfinkel's social facts are very different from Durkheim's social facts. For Durkheim, social facts are external to and coercive of individuals. Those who adopt such a focus tend to see actors as constrained or determined by social structures and institutions and able to exercise little or no independent judgment. In the acerbic terms of the ethnomethodologists, such sociologists tended to treat actors like "judgmental dopes."

In contrast, ethnomethodology treats the objectivity of social facts as the accomplishment of members (a definition of "members" follows shortly)—as a product of

HAROLD GARFINKEL

*A Biographical Sketch**

Like many who came of age during the Depression and later World War II, Harold Garfinkel took a convoluted path into sociology. Garfinkel was born in Newark, New Jersey, on October 29, 1917 and died on April 21, 2011 (Maynard, 2011). His father was a small businessman who sold household goods on the installment plan to immigrant families. While his father was eager for him to learn a trade, Harold wanted to go to college. He did go into his father's business but also began taking business courses at the then-unaccredited University of Newark. Because the courses tended to be taught by graduate students from Columbia, they were both high in quality and, because the students lacked practical experience, highly theoretical. His later theoretical orientation and his specific orientation to "accounts" are traceable, at least in part, to these courses in general, and particularly to an accounting course on the "theory of accounts." "'How do you make the columns and figures accountable [to superiors]?' was the big question according to Garfinkel" (Rawls, 2011:104). Also of importance was the fact that Garfinkel encountered other Jewish students at Newark who were taking courses in sociology and were later to become social scientists.

Graduating in 1939, Garfinkel spent a summer in a Quaker work camp in rural Georgia. There he learned that the University of North Carolina had a sociology program that was also oriented to the furtherance of public works projects like the one in which he was involved. Admitted to the program with a fellowship, Garfinkel chose Guy Johnson as his thesis adviser and Johnson's interest in race relations led Garfinkel to do his master's thesis on interracial homicide. He also was exposed to a wide range of social theory, most notably the works of phenomenologists and the recently published (in 1937) *The Structure of Social Action,* by Talcott Parsons. Although the vast majority of graduate students at North Carolina at that time were drawn toward statistics and "scientific sociology," Garfinkel was attracted to theory, especially Florian Znaniecki's now almost forgotten work on social action and the importance of the actor's point of view. These interests were evidenced also by Garfinkel's work during wartime. He was drafted into the Air Force in 1942.

> [Garfinkel] was given the task of training troops in tank warfare on a golf course on Miami Beach in the complete absence of tanks. Garfinkel had only

members' methodological activities. Garfinkel, in his inimitable and nearly impenetrable style, describes the focus of ethnomethodology as follows:

> For ethnomethodology the objective reality of social facts, in that, and just how, it is every society's locally, endogenously produced, naturally organized, reflexively accountable, ongoing, practical achievement, being everywhere, always, only, exactly and entirely, members' work, with no time out, and with no possibility of

pictures of tanks from *Life* magazine. The real tanks were all in combat. The man who would insist on concrete empirical detail *in lieu* of theorized accounts was teaching real troops who were about to enter live combat to fight against only imagined tanks in situations where things like the proximity of the troops to the imagined tank could make the difference between life and death. The impact of this on the development of his views can only be imagined. He had to train troops to throw explosives into the tracks of imaginary tanks; to keep imaginary tanks from seeing them by directing fire at imaginary tank ports. This task posed in a new and very concrete way the problems of the adequate description of action and accountability that Garfinkel had taken up at North Carolina as theoretical issues.

(Rawls, 2011)

When the war ended, Garfinkel proceeded to Harvard and studied with Talcott Parsons. Parsons stressed the importance of abstract categories and generalizations, but Garfinkel was interested in detailed description. When Garfinkel achieved prominence in the discipline, this became a focal debate within sociology. However, he soon became more interested in the empirical demonstration of the importance of his theoretical orientation than in debating it in the abstract. While still a student at Harvard, Garfinkel taught for two years at Princeton and, after obtaining his doctorate, moved on to Ohio State, where he had a two-year position in a "soft money" project studying leadership on airplanes and submarines. That research was cut short by reductions in funding, but Garfinkel then joined a project researching juries in Wichita, Kansas. In preparing for a talk on the project at the 1954 American Sociological Association meetings, Garfinkel came up with the term *ethnomethodology* to describe what fascinated him about jury deliberations and social life more generally.

In the fall of 1954 Garfinkel took a position at UCLA, a position he held until he retired in 1987. From the beginning, he used the term *ethnomethodology* in his seminars. A number of notable students were taken by Garfinkel's approach and disseminated it around the United States and eventually the world. Most notable were a group of sociologists, especially Harvey Sacks, Emmanuel Schegloff, and Gail Jefferson, who, inspired by Garfinkel's approach, developed what is, at least at the moment, the most important variety of ethnomethodology—conversation analysis.

* This biographical sketch is based on Anne Rawls, "Harold Garfinkel," in George Ritzer and Jeffrey Stepnisky, eds. *The Wiley-Blackwell Companion to Major Social Theorists: Volume II—Contemporary Social Theorists* (Malden, MA, and Oxford, England: Wiley-Blackwell). See also Maynard and Kardash (2007) and Rawls (2005b).

evasion, hiding out, passing, postponement, or buy-outs, is *thereby* sociology's fundamental phenomenon.

(Garfinkel, 1991:11)

To put it another way, ethnomethodology is concerned with the organization of everyday life, or as Garfinkel (1988:104) describes it, "immortal, ordinary society." In Pollner's terms, this is "the extraordinary organization of the ordinary" (1987:xvii).

Ethnomethodology is certainly not a macrosociology in the sense intended by Durkheim with his concept of a social fact, but its adherents do not see it as a micro-sociology either. Thus, while ethnomethodologists refuse to treat actors as judgmental dopes, they do not believe that people are "almost endlessly reflexive, self-conscious and calculative" (Heritage, 1984:118). Rather, following Alfred Schutz, they recognize that most often action is routine and relatively unreflective. Hilbert (1992) argues that ethnomethodologists do not focus on actors or individuals, but rather on "members." However, members are viewed not as individuals, but rather "strictly and solely, [as] membership activities—the artful practices whereby they produce what are *for them* large-scale organization structure and small-scale interactional or personal structure" (Hilbert, 1992:193). In sum, ethnomethodologists are interested in *neither* micro structures nor macro structures; they are concerned with the artful practices that produce *both* types of structures. Thus, what Garfinkel and the ethnomethodologists have sought is a new way of getting at the traditional concern of sociology with objective structures, both micro and macro (Maynard and Clayman, 1991).

One of Garfinkel's key points about ethnomethods is that they are "reflexively accountable." *Accounts* are the ways in which actors explain (describe, criticize, and idealize) specific situations (Bittner, 1973; Orbuch, 1997). *Accounting* is the process by which people offer accounts in order to make sense of the world. Ethnomethod-ologists devote a lot of attention to analyzing people's accounts, as well as to the ways in which accounts are offered and accepted (or rejected) by others. This is one of the reasons that ethnomethodologists are preoccupied with analyzing conversations. To take an example, when a student explains to her professor why she failed to take an examination, she is offering an account. The student is trying to make sense out of an event for her professor. Ethnomethodologists are interested in the nature of that account but more generally in the *accounting practices* (Sharrock and Anderson, 1986) by which the student offers the account and the professor accepts or rejects it. In analyzing accounts, ethnomethodologists adopt a stance of "ethnomethodological indifference." That is, they do not judge the nature of the accounts but rather analyze them in terms of how they are used in practical action. They are concerned with the accounts as well as the methods needed by both speaker and listener to proffer, under-stand, and accept or reject accounts (for more on this, see Young, 1997).

Extending the idea of accounts, ethnomethodologists take great pains to point out that sociologists, like everyone else, offer accounts. Thus, reports of sociological studies can be seen as accounts and analyzed in the same way that all other accounts can be studied. This perspective on sociology serves to disenchant the work of soci-ologists, indeed all scientists. A good deal of sociology (indeed all sciences) involves commonsense interpretations. Ethnomethodologists can study the accounts of the sociologist in the same way that they can study the accounts of the layperson. Thus, the everyday practices of sociologists and all scientists come under the scrutiny of the ethnomethodologist.

We can say that accounts are reflexive in the sense that they enter into the constitution of the state of affairs they make observable and are intended to deal with. Thus, in trying to describe what people are doing, we alter the nature of what they are doing. This is as true for sociologists as it is for laypeople. In studying and reporting on social life, sociologists are, in the process, changing what they are studying. That is, subjects alter their behavior as a result of being the subject of scrutiny and in response to descriptions of that behavior (for a similar idea, see the discussion of Giddens's "double hermeneutic" in Chapter 13).

The Diversification of Ethnomethodology

Ethnomethodology was "invented" by Garfinkel beginning in the late 1940s, but it was first systematized with the publication of his *Studies in Ethnomethodology* in 1967. Over the years, ethnomethodology has grown enormously and expanded in a number of different directions (Lynch and Sharrock, 2003). Only a decade after the publication of *Studies in Ethnomethodology,* Don Zimmerman concluded that there already were several varieties of ethnomethodology. As Zimmerman put it, ethnomethodology encompassed "a number of more or less distinct and sometimes incompatible lines of inquiry" (1978:6). Ten years later, Paul Atkinson (1988) underscored the lack of coherence in ethnomethodology and argued further that at least some ethnomethodologists had strayed too far from the underlying premises of the approach. Thus, while it is a very vibrant type of sociological theory, ethnomethodology has experienced some increasing "growing pains" in recent years. It is safe to say that ethnomethodology, its diversity, and its problems are likely to proliferate in the coming years. After all, the subject matter of ethnomethodology is the infinite variety of everyday life. As a result, there will be many more studies, more diversification, and further "growing pains."

Studies of Institutional Settings

Maynard and Clayman (1991) describe a number of varieties of work in ethnomethodology, but two stand out from our point of view.[1] The first type is ethnomethodological *studies of institutional settings.* Early ethnomethodological studies carried on by Garfinkel and his associates (which are discussed below) took place in casual, noninstitutionalized settings such as the home. Later, there was a move toward studying everyday practices in a wide variety of institutional settings—courtrooms, medical settings (Ten Have, 1995), police departments—and studies of this type have been increasing since the early 1990s (Perakyla, 2007). The goal of such studies is an understanding of the way people perform their official tasks and, in the process, constitute the institution in which the tasks take place.

Conventional sociological studies of such institutional settings focus on their structure, formal rules, and official procedures to explain what people do within them. To the ethnomethodologists, such external constraints are inadequate for explaining what really goes on in these institutions. People are not determined by these external

---

[1] Another body of ethnomethodological work deals with the *study of science,* particularly in fields such as mathematics, astronomy, biology, and optics (for example, Lynch, 1985, 1993). In common with the rest of ethnomethodology, studies in this area concentrate on the commonsense procedures, the practical reasoning employed by scientists even in some of the greatest discoveries in the history of mathematics and science. The focus is on the work that scientists do as well as the conversations in which they engage. The ethnomethodologist is concerned with the "workbench practices" employed by scientists on a day-to-day basis.

forces; rather, they use them to accomplish their tasks and create the institution in which they exist. People employ their practical procedures not only to make their daily lives but also to manufacture the institutions' products. For example, the crime rates compiled by the police department are not merely the result of officials' following clearly defined rules in their production. Rather, officials utilize a range of commonsense procedures to decide, for example, whether victims should be classified as homicides. Thus, such rates are based on the interpretive work of professionals, and this kind of record keeping is a practical activity worthy of study in its own right.

Conversation Analysis

The second variety of ethnomethodology is *conversation analysis* (Rawls, 2005a; Schegloff, 2001).[2] The goal of conversation analysis is "the detailed understanding of the fundamental structures of conversational interaction" (Zimmerman, 1988:429). Conversation is defined in terms that are in line with the basic elements of the ethnomethodological perspective: "Conversation is an *interactional activity* exhibiting *stable, orderly* properties that are the analyzable *achievements* of the conversants" (Zimmerman, 1988:406; italics added). Although there are rules and procedures for conversations, they do not determine what is said but instead are used to "accomplish" a conversation. The focus of conversational analysis is the constraints on what is said that are internal to the conversation itself and not external forces that constrain talk. Conversations are seen as internally, sequentially ordered.

Zimmerman details five basic working principles of conversation analysis. First, conversation analysis requires the collection and analysis of highly detailed data on conversations. These data include not only words but also "the hesitations, cut-offs, restarts, silences, breathing noises, throat clearings, sniffles, laughter, and laughterlike noises, prosody, and the like, not to mention the 'nonverbal' behaviors available on video records that are usually closely integrated with the stream of activity captured on the audiotape" (Zimmerman, 1988:413). All these things are part of most conversations, and they are seen as methodic devices in the making of a conversation by the actors involved (Lynch, 1999).

Second, even the finest detail of a conversation must be presumed to be an orderly accomplishment. Such minute aspects of a conversation are not ordered just by the ethnomethodologist; they are first "ordered by the methodical activities of the social actors themselves" (Zimmerman, 1988:415).

Third, interaction in general and conversation in particular have stable, orderly properties that are the achievements of the actors involved. In looking at conversations, ethnomethodologists treat them as if they were autonomous, separable from the cognitive processes of the actors as well as the larger context in which they take place.

Fourth, "the fundamental framework of conversation is sequential organization" (Zimmerman, 1988:422). Finally, and relatedly, "the course of conversational interaction

---

[2] While we are treating conversation analysis as a variety of ethnomethodology, it should be noted that conversation analysis has distinctive roots in the work of Harvey Sacks (who was a student of Erving Goffman, not Harold Garfinkel; see Jacobsen, 2007) and has over the years developed a distinctive set of interests.

is managed on a turn-by-turn or local basis" (Zimmerman, 1988:423). Here Zimmerman invokes Heritage's (1984) distinction between "context-shaped" and "context-renewing" conversation. Conversations are context-shaped in the sense that what is said at any given moment is shaped by the preceding sequential context of the conversation. Conversations are context-shaping in that what is being said in the present turn becomes part of the context for future turns.

Methodologically, conversation analysts are led to study conversations in naturally occurring situations, often using audiotape or videotape. This method allows information to flow from the everyday world rather than being imposed on it by the researcher. The researcher can examine and reexamine an actual conversation in minute detail instead of relying on his or her notes. This technique also allows the researcher to do highly detailed analyses of conversations.

Conversation analysis is based on the assumption that conversations are the bedrock of other forms of interpersonal relations (David Gibson, 2000). They are the most pervasive form of interaction, and a conversation "consists of the fullest matrix of socially organized communicative practices and procedures" (Heritage and Atkinson, 1984:13).

We have tried to give a general sense of ethnomethodology in the preceding pages. However, the heart of ethnomethodology lies not in its theoretical statements but in its empirical studies. What we know theoretically is derived from those studies. Thus, we turn now to a series of those studies in the hope of giving the reader a better feel for ethnomethodology.

Some Early Examples

We begin with some of the early research in ethnomethodology that gained for it much early notoriety. While some of the early methods are rarely, if ever, used today, they tell us a good deal about ethnomethodological research.

Breaching Experiments

In breaching experiments (Jansen, 2008), social reality is violated in order to shed light on the methods by which people construct social reality. The assumption behind this research is not only that the methodical production of social life occurs all the time but also that the participants are unaware that they are engaging in such actions. The objective of the breaching experiment is to disrupt normal procedures so that the process by which the everyday world is constructed or reconstructed can be observed and studied. In his work, Garfinkel (1967) offered a number of examples of breaching experiments, most of which were undertaken by his students in casual settings to illustrate the basic principles of ethnomethodology.

Lynch (1991:15) offers the following example (Figure 10.1) of breaching, derived from earlier work by Garfinkel (1963): This, of course, is a game of tic-tac-toe. The well-known rules allow participants in the game to place a mark *within* each of the cells, but the rules have been breached in this case and a mark has been placed *between* two cells. If this breach were to occur in a real game of tic-tac-toe, the other player

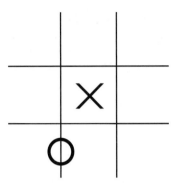

FIGURE 10.1 *Breaching in Tic-Tac-Toe*

SOURCE: Michael Lynch, 1991. "Pictures of Nothing? Visual Constructs in Social Theory." *Sociological Theory* 9:15.

(player 2) would probably insist on a correct placement. If such a placement did not occur, player 2 would try to explain why player 1 had taken such an extraordinary action. The actions of player 2 would be studied by the ethnomethodologist to see how the everyday world of tic-tac-toe is reconstructed.

To take one other example, Garfinkel asked his students to spend between fifteen minutes and an hour in their homes imagining that they were boarders and then acting on the basis of that assumption. "They were instructed to conduct themselves in a circumspect and polite fashion. They were to avoid getting personal, to use formal address, to speak only when spoken to" (Garfinkel, 1967:47). In the vast majority of cases, family members were dumbfounded by such behavior: "Reports were filled with accounts of astonishment, bewilderment, shock, anxiety, embarrassment, and anger, and with charges by various family members that the student was mean, inconsiderate, selfish, nasty, or impolite" (Garfinkel, 1967:47). These reactions indicate how important it is that people act in accord with the commonsense assumptions about how they are supposed to behave.

What most interested Garfinkel was how the family members sought in commonsense ways to cope with such a breach. They demanded explanations from the students for their behavior. In their questions, they often implied an explanation of the aberrant behavior:

"Did you get fired?"
"Are you sick?"
"Are you out of your mind or are you just stupid?"

(Garfinkel, 1967:47)

Family members also sought to explain the behaviors to themselves in terms of previously understood motives. For example, a student was thought to be behaving oddly because she was working too hard or had had a fight with her fiancé. Such explanations are important to participants—the other family members, in this case—because the explanations help them feel that under normal circumstances interaction would occur as it always had.

If the student did not acknowledge the validity of such explanations, family members were likely to withdraw and to seek to isolate, denounce, or retaliate against the culprit. Deep emotions were aroused because the effort to restore order through explanation was rejected by the student. The other family members felt that more intense statements and actions were necessary to restore the equilibrium:

> "Don't bother with him, he's in one of his moods again."
> "Why must you always create friction in our family harmony?"
> "I don't want any more of *that* out of *you* and if you can't treat your mother decently you'd better move out!"
>
> (Garfinkel, 1967:48)

In the end, the students explained the experiment to their families, and in most situations, harmony was restored. However, in some instances hard feelings lingered.

Breaching experiments are undertaken to illustrate the way people order their everyday lives. These experiments reveal the resilience of social reality, since the subjects (or victims) move quickly to normalize the breach—that is, to render the situation accountable in familiar terms. It is assumed that the way people handle these breaches tells us much about how they handle their everyday lives (Handel, 1982). Although these experiments seem innocent enough, they often lead to highly emotional reactions. These extreme reactions reflect how important it is to people to engage in routine, commonsense activities. The reactions to breaches are sometimes so extreme that Hugh Mehan and Houston Wood have cautioned about their use: *"Interested persons are strongly advised not to undertake any new breaching studies"* (1975:113).

Accomplishing Gender

It seems incontrovertible that one's gender—male or female—is biologically based. People are seen as simply manifesting the behaviors that are an outgrowth of their biological makeup. People usually are not thought of as *accomplishing* their gender. In contrast, sexiness is clearly an accomplishment; people need to speak and act in certain ways in order to be seen as sexy. However, it generally is assumed that one does not have to do or say *anything* to be seen as a man or a woman. Ethnomethodology has investigated the issue of gender, with some very unusual results (Stokoe, 2006).

The ethnomethodological view is traceable to one of Harold Garfinkel's (1967) now classic demonstrations of the utility of this orientation. In the 1950s Garfinkel met a person named Agnes, who seemed unquestionably a woman.[3] Not only did she have the figure of a woman, but it was virtually a "perfect" figure with an ideal set of measurements. She also had a pretty face, a good complexion, no facial hair, and plucked eyebrows—and she wore lipstick. This was clearly a woman, or was it? Garfinkel discovered that Agnes had not always appeared to be a woman. In fact, at the time he met her, Agnes was trying, eventually successfully, to convince physicians that she needed an operation to remove her male genitalia and create a vagina.

---

[3] For an interesting debate over Garfinkel's interpretation of Agnes, see Denzin (1990a, 1991), Hilbert (1991), Lynch and Bogen (1991), and Maynard (1991).

Agnes was defined as a male at birth. In fact, she was by all accounts a boy until she was 16 years of age. At that age, sensing something was awry, Agnes ran away from home and started to dress like a girl. She soon discovered that dressing like a woman was not enough; she had to *learn to act* like (to "pass" as) a woman if she was to be accepted as one. She did learn the accepted practices and as a result came to be defined, and to define herself, as a woman. Garfinkel was interested in the passing practices that allowed Agnes to function like a woman in society. The more general point here is that we are not simply born men or women; we all also learn and routinely use the commonplace practices that allow us to pass as men or women. It is only in learning these practices that we come to be, in a sociological sense, a man or a woman. Thus, even a category like gender, which is thought to be an ascribed status, can be understood as an accomplishment of a set of situated practices.

Conversation Analysis

We now turn to what has become the major type of research within ethnomethodology—conversation analysis. The goal of conversation analysis is to study the taken-for-granted ways in which conversation is organized. Conversation analysts are concerned with the relationships among utterances in a conversation rather than in the relationships between speakers and hearers (Sharrock and Anderson, 1986:68).

Telephone Conversations: Identification and Recognition

Emanuel A. Schegloff (1979) viewed his examination of the way in which telephone conversations are opened as part of a larger effort to understand the orderly character of social interaction:

> The work in which my colleagues and I have been engaged is concerned with . . . *detecting* and *describing* the *orderly* phenomena of which conversation and interaction are composed, and an interest in depicting the *systematic organizations* by reference to which those phenomena are produced.
>
> (Schegloff, 1979:24, italics added)

This interest extends to various orderly phenomena within interaction, such as the organization of turn taking in conversations and the ways in which people seek to repair breaches in normal conversational procedure. In addition, there is interest in the overall structure of a conversation, including openings, closings, and regularly recurring internal sequences.

In this context Schegloff looked at the opening of a phone conversation, which he defined as "a place where the type of conversation being opened can be proffered, displayed, accepted, rejected, modified—in short, incipiently constituted by the parties to it" (1979:25). Although the talk one hears on the phone is no different from that in face-to-face conversations, the participants lack visual contact. Schegloff focused on one element of phone conversations not found in face-to-face conversations: the sequence by which parties who have no visual contact identify and recognize each other.

Schegloff found that telephone openings are often quite straightforward and standardized:

A. Hello?
B. Shar'n?
A. Hi!

(Schegloff, 1979:52)

But some openings "look and sound idiosyncratic—almost virtuoso performances" (Schegloff, 1979:68):

A. Hello.
B. Hello Margie?
A. Yes.
B. hhh We do painting, antiquing,
A. is that right.
B. eh, hh—hhh
A. hnh, hnh, hnh
B. nhh, hnh, hnh! hh
A. hh
B. keep people's pa'r tools
A. y(hhh)! hnh, hnh
B. I'm sorry about that—that—I din' see that.

(adapted from Schegloff, 1979:68)

Although such openings may be different from the usual openings, they are not without their organization. They are "engendered by a systemic sequential organization adapted and fitted by the parties to some particular circumstances" (Schegloff, 1979:68). For example, the preceding conversation is almost incomprehensible until we understand that *B* is calling to apologize for keeping some borrowed power tools too long. *B* makes a joke out of it by building it into a list (painting, antiquing), and it is only at the end, when both are laughing, that the apology comes.

Schegloff's conclusion was that even very idiosyncratic cases are to be examined "to extract from their local particularities the formal organization into which their particularities are infused" (Schegloff, 1979:71).

Initiating Laughter

Gail Jefferson (1979; see also Jefferson, 1984) looked at the question of how one knows when to laugh in the course of a conversation. The lay view is that laughter is a totally free event in the course of a conversation or interaction. However, Jefferson found that several basic structural characteristics of an utterance are designed to induce the other party to laugh. The first is the placement, by the speaker, of a laugh at the end of his utterance:

Dan. I thought that was pretty out of sight. Did you hear me say you're a junkie . . . heh, heh Dolly. heh, heh, heh.

(adapted from Jefferson, 1979:80)

The second device reported by Jefferson is within-speech laughter—for example, in mid-sentence:

A. You know I didn't . . . you know
B. Hell, *you* know I'm on ret (haha);
A. ehh, yeh, ha ha.

(adapted from Jefferson, 1979:83)

Jefferson (1979:83) concluded from these examples that the occurrence of laughter is more organized than we realize.

Jefferson was interested not only in the decision to laugh but also in the declining of an invitation to laugh. She found that silence after an invitation is not enough, that a clear signal is required indicating refusal of the invitation. If, for example, someone refuses to laugh, a strategy would be to commence, just after the onset of the speaker's laugh, a serious pursuit of the topic.

Phillip Glenn (1989) has examined the initiation of shared laughter in a multiparty conversation. Glenn argues that whereas in two-party interactions the speaker ordinarily laughs first, in multiparty interactions someone other than the speaker usually provides the first laugh. In a two-party interaction, the speaker is virtually forced to laugh at his or her own material because there is only one other person present who can perform that function. However, in a multiparty interaction, the fact that there are many other people who can laugh first means that the speaker can better afford the risk of not taking the initiative of being the first to laugh.

Generating Applause

John Heritage and David Greatbatch (1986) have studied the rhetoric of British political speeches (derived from a body of work developed by J. Maxwell Atkinson [1984a, 1984b]) and uncovered basic devices by which speakers generate applause from their audiences. They argue that applause is generated by "statements that are verbally constructed (a) to *emphasize* and thus highlight their contents against a surrounding background of speech materials and (b) to *project a clear completion point* for the message in question" (Heritage and Greatbatch, 1986:116). Emphasis tells the audience that applause is appropriate, and advance notice of a clear completion point allows the audience to begin applauding more or less in unison. In their analysis of British political speeches, Heritage and Greatbatch uncovered seven basic rhetorical devices:

1. *Contrast:* For example, a politician might argue: "Too much is spent on war . . . too little is spent on peace." Such a statement generates applause because, for emphasis, the same point is made first in negative terms and then in positive terms. The audience also is able to anticipate when to applaud by matching the unfolding of the second half of the statement with the already completed first half.
2. *List:* A list of political issues, especially the often used three-part list, provides emphasis as well as a completion point that can be anticipated by the audience.

3. *Puzzle solution:* Here the politician first poses a puzzle for the audience and then offers a solution. This double presentation of the issue provides emphasis, and the audience can anticipate the completion of the statement at the end of the solution.
4. *Headline—punch line:* Here the politician proposes to make a statement and then makes it.
5. *Combination:* This involves use of two or more of the devices just listed.
6. *Position taking:* This involves an initial description of a state of affairs that the speaker would be expected to feel strongly about. However, at first it is presented nonevaluatively. Only at the end does the speaker offer his or her own position.
7. *Pursuit:* This occurs when an audience fails to respond to a particular message. The speaker may actively pursue applause by, for example, restating the central point.

In the political party conferences studied by Heritage and Greatbatch, these seven devices accounted for slightly more than two-thirds of the total applause. Of the seven, *contrast* (accounting for almost a quarter of applause events) was by far the most commonly applauded format. The speaker's manner of delivering the message ("intonation, timing, and gesture") also is important (Heritage and Greatbatch, 1986:143). Finally, Heritage and Greatbatch note that the seven devices are not restricted to political speech making, but also are found in advertising slogans, newspaper editorials, scientific texts, and so forth. In fact, they conclude that these devices have their roots and are found in everyday, natural, conversational interaction. The implication is that we all use these devices daily to generate positive reactions from those with whom we interact.

Booing

In a later and parallel piece of research, Steven Clayman (1993) studied booing as an expression of disapproval in the context of public speaking. While applause allows the audience to affiliate with the speaker, booing is an act of disaffiliation.

There are two fundamental ways in which responses such as applause and booing begin—as a result of independent individual decision making and as a product of the mutual monitoring of the behavior of members of an audience. Previous research has demonstrated that individual decision making predominates in the onset of applause. Because the decision is made largely alone, applause occurs almost immediately after a popular remark is made. Also consistent with individual decision making is the fact that applause occurs in a burst that reaches its peak in the first second or two. Further, as demonstrated in the preceding section, a series of well-known devices are employed by speakers to lead audience members to the decision to applaud and then to the applause itself.

Booing, however, is a result more of mutual monitoring than of individual decision making. There is usually a significant time lag between the utterance of the objectionable words and the onset of booing. If booing were the result of a number of individuals making independent decisions, it would occur about as quickly as applause does. The time lag tends to indicate that audience members are monitoring the behavior of others before deciding whether booing is appropriate. In addition, the onset of booing often is preceded by displays by the audience.

For example, the audience may engage in incipient displays of its disaffiliation[4] from the speaker through "a variety of vocalizations—whispering or talking among themselves, talking, shouting, or jeering at the speaker . . . the resulting sound can be characterized as a 'murmur,' 'buzz,' or 'roar'" (Clayman, 1993:117). Audience members monitor these sounds; they indicate to the members that the audience is predisposed to disapprove of the utterance in question. A given audience member feels freer to boo because she has reason to believe that she will not be alone and therefore suffer the disapproval of other audience members.

Of course, one might ask where the incipient displays come from, if not from independent decision making. Clayman believes that some degree of independent decision making is involved here. Individual decision making occurs in the case of incipient displays because the resulting behaviors (for example, private whispering with neighbors, self-talk [for example, "yikes"]) are more private and less likely to be disapproved of by the rest of the audience than is booing. Thus, there is little or no need to monitor the audience in order to determine the appropriateness of such behaviors.

Clayman concludes that collectively produced applause and booing are very much like individually produced agreement and disagreement in everyday behavior. In both cases, "Agreements tend to be produced promptly, in an unqualified manner, and are treated as requiring no special explanation or account. Disagreements, by contrast, typically are delayed, qualified, and accountable" (Clayman, 1993:125). This similarity leads to the conclusion that applause and booing may be explained by general interactional principles that cut across all sectors of life and not just by the organizational and institutional structures and norms involved in public speaking. Those "general principles of human conduct" are part of the interaction order that "is a species of social institution in its own right, one that predates and is constitutive of most other societal institutions, and possesses its own indigenous organizational properties and conventional practices" (Clayman, 1993:127). In other words, the fundamental principles being uncovered by conversation analysts allow us to understand positive (applause) and negative (booing) responses to public speeches.

The Interactive Emergence of Sentences and Stories

Charles Goodwin (1979) challenged the traditional linguistic assumption that sentences can be examined in isolation from the process of interaction in which they occur. His view was that "sentences emerge with conversation" (Goodwin, 1979:97). The fact is that the "speaker can reconstruct the meaning of his sentence *as he is producing it* in order to maintain its appropriateness to its recipient of the moment" (Goodwin, 1979:98; italics added).

---

[4] Booing is also likely to occur after displays of affiliation such as applause, but a different process is involved and we will not deal with it here.

Speakers pay acute attention to listeners as they are speaking. As the listeners react verbally, facially, or with body language, the speaker—on the basis of those reactions—adjusts the sentence as it is emerging. The reactions allow the speaker to decide whether his or her point is being made and, if not, to alter the structure of the sentence. Goodwin described some of the alterations that took place in a particular sentence sequence: "the unfolding meaning of John's sentence is reconstructed twice, a new segment is added to it, and another is deleted prior to its production but replaced with a different segment" (1979:112). In other words, sentences are the products of collaborative processes.

Mandelbaum (1989) examined the interactive emergence of stories. Her key point is that the audience is not passive, as is conventionally assumed, but rather can be seen as the "co-author" of the story. Paralleling Goodwin's analysis of the interactive emergence of sentences, Mandelbaum shows that the audience members have resources that allow them to work with the author to alter a story while the storytelling is in process. The audience participates by allowing the suspension of turn-by-turn talk so that the storyteller may dominate the conversation. The audience members also help the story along by displaying their understanding through the use of expressions such as "uh huh" and "mm hm." The audience may also "repair" some problem in the story, thereby permitting it to proceed more smoothly. Most important for the purposes of this discussion, the audience may intervene in the story and cause it to move off in a new direction. Thus, in a very real sense, stories, like sentences and conversations in general, are interactional products.

Integration of Talk and Nonvocal Activities

Conversation analysts have focused on talk, and other ethnomethodologists on nonvocal activities. Some researchers use videotapes and films to analyze the integration of vocal and nonvocal activities. Charles Goodwin (1984), for example, examined a videotape of a dinner party involving two couples. One issue in the relationship between vocal and nonvocal activities is the body posture of a person (in this case Ann) who tells a story at the party:

> Ann clasps her hands together, places both elbows on the table, and leans forward while gazing toward her addressed recipient, Beth. With this posture the speaker displays full orientation toward her addressed recipient, complete engagement in telling her story, and lack of involvement in any activities other than conversation. The posture appears to . . . constitute a visual display that a telling is in progress.
>
> (C. Goodwin, 1984:228)

More generally, Goodwin concludes, "Ann's telling is thus made visible not only in her talk but also in the way in which she organizes her body and activities during the telling" (1984:229).

Another nonvocal activity examined by Goodwin is the gaze, which he relates to talk:

> When a speaker gazes at a recipient that recipient should be gazing at him. When speakers gaze at nongazing recipients, and thus locate violations of the rule, they frequently produce phrasal breaks such as restarts and pauses, in their talk.

These phrasal breaks both orient to the event as a violation by locating the talk in progress at that point as impaired in some fashion and provide a remedy by functioning as requests for the gaze of the hearer. Thus just after phrasal breaks nongazing recipients frequently begin to move their gaze to the speaker.

(C. Goodwin, 1984:230)

Body posture and gaze are only two of many nonvocal activities that are intimately related to vocal activities.

Doing Shyness (and Self-Confidence)

We tend to think of shyness and self-confidence as psychological traits, but Philip Manning and George Ray (1993) have attempted to show that they are things that we "do" as we are managing conversational encounters. There are a range of typical procedures that we all use to get acquainted with those we do not know, and the shy and the self-confident modify these procedures, albeit in different ways, in order to deal with social situations distinctively. Thus, the shy and the self-confident employ different conversational strategies.

Manning and Ray conducted a laboratory study with college students involving videotaping and transcribing the interaction of ten shy and ten self-confident dyads. While we all engage in "setting-talk"—that is, talk about our immediate environment— shy people do this much more than do those who are self-confident. Take the following example:

A. (nervous laughter) A microphone
B. We're being tape recorded
A. I know probably
B. Huh
A. Okay
B. I guess they're going to observe how nervous we are (laughs)
A. I know

(Manning and Ray, 1993:182)

Manning and Ray found that shy participants were more than two and a half times as likely to engage in setting-talk at the beginning of a conversation than were those who are self-confident. Further, those who are shy were eight times more likely to return to setting-talk later, whenever the conversation flagged. Manning and Ray conclude, "We believe that shy participants used setting-talk as a 'safe' topic, comparable to discussions about the weather. By contrast . . . self-confident participants viewed setting-talk as a dead end to be avoided" (1993:183). Instead, those high in self-confidence were more likely to exchange names and move immediately into the introduction of a topic for conversation (a "pretopical sequence"). While shy participants tend to reject these pretopical sequences, those who are self-confident are likely to respond to them, and in depth.

One key issue is whether these and other differences in conversation are symptoms of underlying psychological differences or whether shyness and self-confidence *are* the different conversational procedures. Needless to say, Manning and Ray (1993:189), adopting the ethnomethodological perspective, tend to prefer the latter view.

Studies of Institutions

As pointed out earlier in this chapter, a number of ethnomethodologists have become interested in the study of conversation and interaction in various social institutions. In this section we examine a few examples of this kind of work.

Job Interviews

Some ethnomethodologists have turned their attention to the work world. For example, Button (1987) has looked at the job interview. Not surprisingly, he sees the interview as a sequential, turn-taking conversation and as the "situated practical accomplishment of the parties to that setting" (Button, 1987:160). One issue addressed in this study involves the things that interviewers can do, after an answer has been given, to move on to something else, thereby preventing the interviewee from returning to, and perhaps correcting, his or her answer. First, the interviewer may indicate that the interview as a whole is over. Second, the interviewer may ask another question that moves the discussion in a different direction. Third, the interviewer may assess the answer given in such a way that the interviewee is precluded from returning to it.

Button wonders what it is that makes a job interview an interview. He argues that it is not the sign on the door or the gathering together of people. Rather, it is "what those people do, and how they structure and organize their interactions with one another, that achieves for some social settings its characterizability as an interview. This integrally involves the way in which the participants organize their speech exchange with one another" (Button, 1987:170). Thus it is the nature of the interaction, of the conversation, that defines a job interview.

Executive Negotiations

Anderson, Hughes, and Sharrock (1987) have examined the nature of negotiations among business executives. One of their findings about such negotiations is how reasonable, detached, and impersonal they are:

> Everything is carried out in a considered, measured, reasonable way. No personal animus is involved or intended in their maneuverings. It is simply what they do; part of their working day. . . . Animosities, disagreements and disputes are always contained, in hand, controlled. If a deal cannot be made this time, so be it.
>
> (Anderson, Hughes, and Sharrock, 1987:155)

This kind of interaction tells us a great deal about the business world.

Interestingly, Anderson, Hughes, and Sharrock go on to argue that what takes place in the business world is no different from what takes place in everyday life. In most of our social relationships we behave the way the business executives described above behaved. "Business life does not take place in a sealed compartment, set off from the rest of social life. It is continuous with and interwoven with it" (Anderson, Hughes, and Sharrock, 1987:155).

Calls to Emergency Centers

Whalen and Zimmerman (1987) have examined telephone calls to emergency communications centers. The context of such calls leads to a reduction of the opening of telephone conversations. In normal telephone conversations we usually find summons-answer, identification-recognition, greeting, and "howareyou" sequences. In emergency calls, however, the opening sequences are reduced and recognitions, greetings, and "howareyous" are routinely absent.

Another interesting aspect of emergency phone calls is that certain opening events that would be ignored in a normal conversation are treated quite seriously:

> . . . those situations in which caller hangs up after dispatcher answers, or there is silence on the line or sounds such as dogs barking, arguing and screaming in the background, or a smoke alarm ringing. Despite the lack of direct conversational engagement on the line, dispatchers initially treat these events as possible indicators of a need for assistance, and thus as functional or *virtual* requests.
>
> (Whalen and Zimmerman, 1987:178)

The peculiar nature of the emergency telephone conversation leads to these and other adaptations to the structure of the normal conversation.

In a related study, Whalen, Zimmerman, and Whalen (1988) looked at a specific emergency telephone conversation that failed, leading to the delayed dispatch of an ambulance and the death of a woman. The media tended to blame the dispatcher for this incident, but Whalen, Zimmerman, and Whalen trace the problem to the nature of the specific emergency phone conversation:

> Our investigation revealed that the participants had rather different understandings of what was happening and different expectations of what was supposed to happen in this conversation. Over the course of the interaction the talk of both caller and nurse-dispatcher (and her supervisor) operated to extend and deepen this misalignment. This misalignment contributed in a fundamental way to a dispute that contaminated and transformed the participants' activity.
>
> (Whalen, Zimmerman, and Whalen, 1988:358)

Thus, it was the nature of the specific conversation, not the abilities of the dispatcher, that "caused" the mishap.

Dispute Resolution in Mediation Hearings

Angela Garcia (1991) analyzed conflict resolution in a California program designed to mediate a variety of disputes—between landlord and tenant, over small sums of money, and among family members or friends. Her ultimate goal is to compare institutional conflict resolution with that which takes place in ordinary conversations. Garcia's key point is that institutional mediation makes conflict resolution easier by eliminating processes that lead to escalating levels of strife in ordinary conversation. Further, when arguments do occur in mediation, procedures exist that do not exist in ordinary conversation that make termination of the conflict possible.

Garcia begins with the familiar concern of conversation analysts with turn taking. Mediation stipulates who is allowed to speak at any given time and what form responses may take. For example, complainants speak first and may not be interrupted by disputants during their presentations. These constraints on interruptions greatly restrict the amount of conflict in mediated disputes. In contrast, the ability to interrupt in normal conversations greatly escalates the likelihood and amount of conflict. Also reducing the possibility of conflict is the fact that disputants must ask the mediator's permission to speak or to use sanctions. The request may be denied, and even if it isn't, the fact that a request has been made serves to mitigate the possibility of direct conflict between disputants. Another key factor in reducing the possibility of conflict is the fact that disputants address their remarks to the mediator rather than to each other. During periods when an issue is under joint discussion, the mediator, not the participants, controls both the topic and who participates by asking disputants directed questions. The mediator therefore serves as both a buffer and a controller and in both roles operates to limit the possibility of conflict.

The mediator seeks especially to limit the possibility of direct and adjacent accusations and denials by the disputants. Such "cross talk" is highly likely to lead to conflict, and mediators seek to prevent it from occurring and are quick to act once it begins. To halt cross talk, the mediator may try to change topics, redirect a question, or sanction the disputants.

In sum, "in mediation, the adjacent and directly addressed oppositional utterances that constitute argument do not occur" (A. Garcia, 1991:827). Garcia summarizes her conclusions by offering four characteristics of mediation that allow disputants to reduce or eliminate arguments while at the same time saving face:

1. Accusations and denials are not adjacent to one another in the turn-taking system of a mediated dispute, thereby reducing the possibility of escalation into an argument.
2. Denials are made not directly to accusations, but to queries by the mediator. Because they are separated from responses, denials are less likely to provoke disputational responses.
3. Because there is a delay between accusation and response, disputants are permitted not to respond to certain accusations without their lack of response implying that they are guilty of those accusations. The delay allows the disputant to "bypass some accusations, focus on the more important accusations, or ignore accusations she or he cannot credibly deny" (A. Garcia, 1991:830). The result is that there generally end up being fewer issues on the table about which arguments can occur.
4. Accusations and denials are mitigated by the mediation system. For example, the agent being accused may be referred to implicitly rather than explicitly, that agent may be referred to collectively as "we" with the result that the complainant is including himself as the blamed party, or the accusations themselves can be downgraded by the use of words and phrases such as "I would imagine" and "maybe."

Unlike Clayman in his study of booing, Garcia does not argue that the structure of interaction in mediation is similar to the interactional organization of everyday life. In fact, her point is that they are very different interactional orders. However, like

Clayman and other conversation analysts, Garcia (1991:833) does see the key to understanding what goes on in interaction, specifically in this case in mediation, in "the interactional order of mediation itself," rather than in the social or normative structure of mediation.

Greatbatch and Dingwall (1997) examined divorce mediation sessions conducted in ten agencies in England. In contrast to Garcia's study, disputants do talk directly to one another and often become involved in arguments. Given this, Greatbatch and Dingwall are interested in the ways in which such arguments are exited. While mediators can take various actions, the focus in this study is on things that the disputants can do to exit an argument, such as one party passing on the opportunity to speak and leaving only the other party talking, taking the initiative and addressing the mediator rather than the other disputant, announcing that one is withdrawing from the argument, and offering conciliatory accounts (e.g., "I'm to blame"). Nevertheless, in most instances in the British case disputants do not talk directly to one another; they do address mediators. Perhaps of greater importance than the specific differences between the two studies is the fact that Greatbatch and Dingwall (1997:164) also take issue with Garcia's argument that what takes place in such settings is not similar to everyday life: "The deescalatory practices described here are not unique to mediation; they are generic speaking practices deriving from ordinary conversation." In other words, the things that disputants do to exit arguments are similar to the ways in which we extricate ourselves from arguments on a daily basis.

Criticisms of Traditional Sociology

Ethnomethodologists criticize traditional sociologists for several reasons.

Separated from the Social

Sociologists are critiqued for imposing *their* sense of social reality on the social world (Mehan and Wood, 1975). They believe that sociology has not been attentive enough to, or respectful enough of, the everyday world that should be its ultimate source of knowledge (Sharrock and Anderson, 1986). More extremely, sociology has rendered the most essential aspects of the social world (ethnomethods) unavailable and focuses instead on a constructed world that conceals everyday practices. Enamored of their own view of the social world, sociologists have tended not to share the same social reality as those they study. As Mehan and Wood put it, "In attempting to do a social *science,* sociology has become alienated from the social" (1975:63).

Within this general orientation, Mehan and Wood (see also Sharrock and Anderson, 1986) leveled a number of specific criticisms at sociology. The concepts used by sociologists are said to distort the social world, to destroy its ebb and flow. Further distortion is caused by sociology's reliance on scientific techniques and statistical analyses of data. Statistics simply do not usually do justice to the elegance and sophistication of the real world. The coding techniques used by sociologists when they translate human behavior into their preconceived categories distort the social world. Furthermore, the seeming simplicity of the codes conceals the complicated and distorting work involved in turning aspects of the social world into the sociologist's preconceived categories. Sociologists also are seen as tending to accept unquestioningly a respondent's description of a phenomenon rather than looking at the phenomenon itself. Thus, a description of a social setting is taken to *be* that setting rather than one conception of that setting. Finally, Mehan and Wood argued that sociologists are prone to offer abstractions of the social world that are increasingly removed from the reality of everyday life.

Confusing Topic and Resource

Taking a slightly different approach, Don Zimmerman and Melvin Pollner (1970) argued that conventional sociology has suffered from a confusion of *topic* and *resource*. That is, the everyday social world is a resource for the favorite topics of sociology, but it is rarely a topic in its own right. This can be illustrated in a variety of ways. For example, Roy Turner (1970; see also Sharrock and Anderson, 1986) argued that sociologists usually look at everyday speech not as a topic in itself but as a resource with which to study hidden realities such as norms, values, attitudes, and so on. However, instead of being a resource, everyday speech can be seen as one of the ways in which the business of social life is carried on—a topic in itself. Matthew Speier (1970) argued that when sociologists look at childhood socialization, they look not at the processes themselves but at a series of abstract "stages" generalized from those processes. Speier argued that *"socialization is the acquisition of interactional competencies"* (1970:189). Thus, the ethnomethodologist must look at the way these competencies are acquired and used in the everyday reality of the real world.

Another analysis of childhood socialization, by Robert W. Mackay (1974), is even more useful as a critique of traditional sociology and the confusion of topic and resource. Mackay contrasted the "normative" approach of traditional sociology with the interpretive approach of ethnomethodology. The normative approach is seen as arguing that socialization is merely a series of stages in which "complete" adults teach "incomplete" children the ways of society. Mackay viewed this as a "gloss" that ignores the reality that socialization involves an interaction between children and adults. Children are not passive, incomplete receptacles; rather, they are active participants in the socialization process because they have the ability to reason, invent, and acquire knowledge. Socialization is a two-sided process. Mackay believed that the ethnomethodological orientation "restores the interaction between adults and children based on interpretive competencies as the phenomenon of study" (1974:183).

Zimmerman and Pollner (1970) cited other examples of the confusion of topic and resource. For example, they argued that sociologists normally explain action in bureaucracies by the rules, norms, and values of the organization. However, had they looked at organizations as topics, they would have seen that actors often simply make it *appear* through their actions that those actions can be explained by the rules. It is not the rules but the actors' *use* of the rules that should be the topic of sociological research. Zimmerman and Pollner then cited the example of a code of behavior among prison convicts. Whereas traditional sociology would look at the ways in which actors are constrained by a convict code, ethnomethodologists would examine how the convicts use the code as an explanatory and persuasive device.

Don Zimmerman and Lawrence Wieder offered the following generalization on the confusion of topic and resource:

> The ethnomethodologist is not concerned with providing causal explanations of observably regular, patterned, repetitive actions by some kind of analysis of the actor's point of view. He *is* concerned with how members of society go about the task of *seeing, describing,* and *explaining* order in the world in which they live.
>
> (Zimmerman and Wieder, 1970:289)

Social order is not a reality in itself to the ethnomethodologist but an accomplishment of social actors.

Stresses and Strains in Ethnomethodology

Although ethnomethodology has made enormous strides in sociology and has demonstrated, especially in the area of conversation analysis, some capacity to cumulate knowledge of the world of everyday life, there are some problems worth noting.

First, while ethnomethodology is far more accepted today than it was a decade or two ago, it is still regarded with considerable suspicion by many sociologists (Pollner, 1991). They view it as focusing on trivial matters and ignoring the crucially important issues confronting society today. The ethnomethodologists' response is that they *are* dealing with the crucial issues because it is everyday life that matters most. Paul Atkinson sums up the situation: "Ethnomethodology continues to be greeted with mixtures of incomprehension and hostility in some quarters, but it is unquestionably a force to be reckoned with when it comes to the theory, methods, and empirical conduct of sociological inquiry" (1988:442).

Second, there are those (for example, Atkinson, 1988) who believe that ethnomethodology has lost sight of its phenomenological roots and its concern for conscious, cognitive processes (exceptions are Cicourel [1974] and Coulter [1983], although Coulter is inclined to embed cognition within the everyday world). Instead of focusing on such conscious processes, ethnomethodologists, especially conversation analysts, have come to focus on the "structural properties of the talk itself" (Atkinson, 1988:449). Ignored in the process are motives and the internal motivations for action. In Atkinson's view, ethnomethodology has grown "unduly restricted" and has come to be "behaviorist and empiricist" (1988:441). In moving in this direction, ethnomethodology is seen as having gone back on some of its basic principles, including its desire not to treat the actor as a judgmental dope:

> Garfinkel's early inspiration was to reject the judgmental dope image in order to focus attention on the skillful and artful, methodical work put into the production of social order. In the intervening years, however, some versions of ethnomethodology have returned to the judgmental dope as their model actor. Intentionality and meaning have been all but eliminated.
>
> (Atkinson, 1988:449)

Third, some ethnomethodologists have worried about the link between the concerns in their work (for example, conversations) and the larger social structure. This concern exists even though, as we discussed earlier in the chapter and will return to toward the end, ethnomethodologists tend to see themselves as bridging the micro-macro divide. For example, some years ago, Zimmerman viewed cross-fertilization with macrosociology as "an open question, and an intriguing possibility" (1978:12). Later, Pollner urged ethnomethodology to "return to sociology to understand those [taken-for-granted] practices in their larger social context . . . mundane reason in terms of structural and historical processes. Mundane reason, it is suggested is not simply the product of local work of mundane reasoners, for it is also shaped by longer term and larger scale dynamics" (1987:xvi). Some such cross-fertilization has been undertaken by people like Giddens (1984), who has integrated ethnomethodological ideas into his structuration theory. More generally, Boden (1990; see the next section) has outlined what ethnomethodology has to offer to the issue of the relationship between structure and agency. She argues that the findings of ethnomethodological studies are relevant not only to micro structures but to macro structures as well. There is hope that institutional studies will shed more light on the macro structure and its relationship to micro-level phenomena.

Fourth, and from within the field, Pollner (1991) has criticized ethnomethodology for losing sight of its original radical reflexivity. Radical reflexivity leads to the view that all social activity is accomplished, including the activities of ethnomethodologists. However, ethnomethodology has come to be more accepted by mainstream sociologists. As Pollner puts it, "Ethnomethodology is settling down in the suburbs of sociology" (1991:370). As they have come to be more accepted, ethnomethodologists have tended to lose sight of the need to analyze their own work. As a result, in Pollner's view, ethnomethodology is in danger of losing its self-analytical and critical edge and becoming just another establishment theoretical specialty.

Finally, it should be noted that although they are discussed under the same heading, there is a growing uneasiness in the relationship between ethnomethodology and conversation analysis (Lynch, 1993:203–264). As mentioned earlier, they have somewhat different roots. More important, in recent years it is conversation analysis that has made the greatest headway in sociology as a whole. Its tendency to study conversations empirically makes it quite acceptable to the discipline's mainstream. The tension between the two is likely to increase if conversation analysis continues to settle into the mainstream while ethnomethodological studies of institutions remain more on the periphery.

Synthesis and Integration

Even ethnomethodology, one of the most determinedly microextremist perspectives in sociological theory, has shown some signs of openness to synthesis and integration. For example, ethnomethodology seems to be expanding into domains that appear to be more in line with mainstream sociology. Good examples are Heritage and Greatbatch's (1986) analysis of the methods used to generate applause from audiences and Clayman's (1993) study of booing. Typologies developed by such ethnomethodologists seem little different from the kinds of typologies employed by various other types of sociological theorists.

However, ethnomethodology remains embattled and insecure and thus, in some ways, seems to run counter to the trend toward theoretical synthesis. Seemingly rejecting the idea of synthesis, Garfinkel sees ethnomethodology as an "incommensurably alternate sociology" (1988:108). Boden (1990) finds it necessary to make a strong, albeit somewhat self-conscious, case *for* ethnomethodology and conversation analysis. It is certainly true, as Boden suggests, that ethnomethodology has widened and deepened its support in sociology. However, one wonders whether it, or any other sociological theory for that matter, is, as Boden contends, "here to stay." In any case, such an argument contradicts the idea that theoretical boundaries are weakening and new synthetic perspectives are emerging. It may be that ethnomethodology is still too new and too insecure to consider an erosion of its boundaries.

Nevertheless, much of Boden's (1990) essay deals with synthetic efforts *within* ethnomethodology, especially regarding integrative issues such as the relationship between agency and structure, the embeddedness of action, and fleeting events within the course of history. Boden also deals with the extent to which an array of European and American theorists have begun to integrate ethnomethodology and conversation analysis into their orientations. Unfortunately, what is lacking is a discussion of the degree to which ethnomethodologists are integrating the ideas of other sociological theories into their perspective. Ethnomethodologists seem quite willing to have other theorists integrate ethnomethodological perspectives, but they seem far less eager to reciprocate.

Ethnomethodology and the Micro-Macro Order

Hilbert (1990) deals with the relationship between ethnomethodology and the micro-macro order. As we saw earlier, Hilbert rejects the conventional idea that ethnomethodology is a microsociology, but it is not, in his view, to be seen as a macrosociology either. Rather, Hilbert argues that ethnomethodology "transcends" the micro-macro issue because it is concerned "with social practices [membership practices] which are the methods of producing *both* microstructure and macrostructure as well as any presumed 'linkage' between these two" (1990:794).

Hilbert, somewhat erroneously (see Chapter 13), reduces the micro-macro linkage issue to a set of structural concerns. That is, it involves a focus on micro structures, macro structures, and the linkage between them. In Hilbert's view, ethnomethodologists are "indifferent" to structures *at any level.* Instead of being concerned with either micro or macro structures, ethnomethodologists are interested in the membership practices, the "ethnomethods," "the artful production," of structure in general. That is, ethnomethodologists are interested in the "methods of producing, maintaining, sustaining, and reproducing social structure by and for the membership, whether oriented to large scale institutional (macro) structure or smaller, more intimate (micro) structure" (Hilbert, 1990:799).

Hilbert offers what he calls the "radical thesis" of ethnomethodology, which serves to transcend the issue of micro-macro linkage:

> The empirical phenomena that conversation analysts witness but which members
> cannot possibly know about, and . . . the structural phenomena that members orient

to and take for granted but which nevertheless are nonempirical and unavailable for social science are (in a subtle way) . . . *the same phenomena.*

(Hilbert, 1990.801)

In other words, to the ethnomethodologist there is no distinction to be made between micro and macro structures because they are generated simultaneously. However, neither ethnomethodologists nor any other sociological theorists have offered the ultimate solution to the micro-macro issue. Hilbert's effort is marred by his reduction of this issue to a concern for the linkage of micro and macro *structures.* As we will see in Chapter 13, there is far more to this issue than such a linkage. Nevertheless, the ethnomethodologists do offer an interesting, indeed radical, approach to this question, dissolving it and arguing that the micro and the macro are the same thing! Certainly one way to deal with the micro-macro issue is to refuse to separate the two levels, seeing them instead as part of the same general process.

Summary

This chapter is devoted to a very distinctive kind of sociology and sociological theory—ethnomethodology. Ethnomethodology is the study of the everyday practices used by the ordinary members of society in order to deal with their day-to-day lives. People are seen as accomplishing their everyday lives through a variety of artful practices. Over the years, ethnomethodology has grown increasingly diverse. However, the two main varieties of ethnomethodology are institutional studies and conversation analysis.

We examine several early examples of ethnomethodology, including "breaching experiments," as well as Garfinkel's famous study of Agnes and the ways in which "she" accomplished being a female (even though she was actually a he). The bulk of the chapter is devoted to a discussion of the heart of ethnomethodology—studies of conversations and institutions. Included in the discussion of studies of conversations are reviews of work on such things as how people know when it is appropriate to laugh, applaud, and boo. We also discuss several institutional studies, including one that deals with the way disputes are resolved in mediation hearings.

Ethnomethodologists tend to be highly critical of mainstream sociology. For example, mainstream sociologists are seen as imposing their sense of social reality on people rather than studying what people actually do. Sociologists distort the social world in various ways by imposing their concepts, utilizing statistics, and so on. Sociologists also are accused of confusing topic and resource—that is, using the everyday world as a resource rather than as a topic in its own right.

There are a variety of stresses and strains within ethnomethodology, including its continued exclusion from the mainstream of sociology, the accusation that it has lost sight of cognitive processes, the inability to deal adequately with social structures, the loss of its original radical quality, and the tension between ethnomethodologists and conversation analysts. The chapter closes with a discussion of some work within ethnomethodology on integration and synthesis. However, there are those who regard ethnomethodology as incompatible with other sociological theories.

Exchange, Network, and Rational Choice Theories

Chapter Outline

Exchange Theory
Network Theory
Network Exchange Theory
Rational Choice Theory

In this chapter we focus on three related theories—exchange theory, rational choice theory, and network theory. Rational choice theory was one of the intellectual influences that shaped the development of exchange theory, especially its tendency to assume a rational actor. However, while contemporary exchange theory continues to demonstrate the influence of rational choice theory, it has been affected by other intellectual currents and has gone off in a series of unique directions (Willer and Emanuelson, 2008). Thus, contemporary exchange and rational choice theories are far from coterminous. One fundamental difference is that rational choice theorists focus on individual decision making, whereas the basic unit of analysis to exchange theorists is the social relationship. Recently, exchange theorists have been devoting more attention to networks of social relationships, and this focus tends to connect them with network theory itself. Network theory has much in common with rational choice theory, although it rejects the assumption of the rationality of human actors (Mizruchi, 1994). Overall, and unlike the theories discussed in the preceding two chapters, these theories share a positivistic orientation.

Exchange Theory

We begin, following Molm and Cook (1995; Cook and Rice, 2001, 2005; Lovaglia, 2007), with an overview of the history of the development of exchange theory, beginning with its roots in behaviorism.

Behaviorism

Behaviorism is best known in psychology, but in sociology it had both direct effects on behavioral sociology (Baldwin and Baldwin, 1986; Bushell and Burgess, 1969) and indirect effects, especially on exchange theory (Molm, 2005a). The behavioral sociologist is concerned with the relationship between the effects of an actor's behavior on the environment and its impact on the actor's later behavior. This relationship is basic to *operant conditioning,* or the learning process by which "behavior is modified by its consequences" (Baldwin and Baldwin, 1986:6). One might almost think of this behavior, at least initially in the infant, as a random behavior. The environment in which the behavior exists, whether social or physical, is affected by the behavior and in turn "acts" back in various ways. That reaction—positive, negative, or neutral—affects the actor's later behavior. If the reaction has been rewarding to the actor, the same behavior is likely to be emitted in the future in similar situations. If the reaction has been painful or punishing, the behavior is less likely to occur in the future. The behavioral sociologist is interested in the relationship between the *history* of environmental reactions or consequences and the nature of present behavior. Past consequences of a given behavior govern its present state. By knowing what elicited a certain behavior in the past, we can predict whether an actor will produce the same behavior in the present situation.

Of great interest to behaviorists are rewards (or reinforcers) and costs (or punishments). Rewards are defined by their ability to strengthen (that is, reinforce) behavior, while costs reduce the likelihood of behavior. As we will see, behaviorism in general, and the ideas of rewards and costs in particular, had a powerful impact on early exchange theory.

Rational Choice Theory

The basic principles of rational choice theory are derived from neoclassical economics (as well as utilitarianism and game theory; Levi et al., 1990; Lindenberg, 2001; Simpson, 2007). Based on a variety of different models, Debra Friedman and Michael Hechter (1988) have put together what they describe as a "skeletal" model of rational choice theory.

The focus in rational choice theory is on actors. Actors are seen as being purposive, or as having intentionality. That is, actors have ends or goals toward which their actions are aimed. Actors also are seen as having preferences (or values, utilities). Rational choice theory is not concerned with what these preferences, or their sources, are. Of importance is the fact that action is undertaken to achieve objectives that are consistent with an actor's preference hierarchy.

Although rational choice theory starts with actors' purposes or intentions, it must take into consideration at least two major constraints on action. The first is the scarcity of resources. Actors have different resources as well as differential access to other resources. For those with lots of resources, the achievement of ends may be relatively easy. However, for those with few, if any, resources, the attainment of ends may be difficult or impossible.

Related to scarcity of resources is the idea of *opportunity costs* (D. Friedman and Hechter, 1988:202). In pursuing a given end, actors must keep an eye on the costs of forgoing their next-most-attractive action. An actor may choose not to pursue the most highly valued end if her resources are negligible, if as a result the chances of achieving that end are slim, and if in striving to achieve that end she jeopardizes her chances of achieving her next-most-valued end. Actors are seen as trying to maximize

George Caspar Homans

An Autobiographical Sketch

How I became a sociologist, which was largely a matter of accident, I have described in other publications. [For a full autobiography, see Homans, 1984.] My sustained work in sociology began with my association, beginning in 1933, with Professors Lawrence Henderson and Elton Mayo at the Harvard Business School. Henderson, a biochemist, was studying the physiological characteristics of industrial work; Mayo, a psychologist, the human factors. Mayo was then and later the director of the famous researches at the Hawthorne Plant of the Western Electric Company in Chicago.

I took part in a course of readings and discussions under Mayo's direction. Among other books, Mayo asked his students to read several books by prominent social anthropologists, particularly Malinowski, Radcliffe-Brown, and Firth. Mayo wanted us to read these books so that we should understand how in aboriginal, in contrast to modern, societies social rituals supported productive work.

I became interested in them for a wholly different reason. In those days the cultural anthropologists were intellectually dominant, and friends of mine in this group, such as Clyde Kluckhohn, insisted that every culture was unique. Instead I began to perceive from my reading that certain institutions of aboriginal societies repeated themselves in places so far separated in time and space that the societies could not have borrowed them from one another. Cultures were not unique and, what was more, their similarities could only be explained on the assumption that human nature was the same the world over. Members of the human species working in similar circumstances had independently created the similar institutions. This was not a popular view at the time. I am not sure it is now.

By this time I had also been exposed to a number of concrete or "field" studies of small human groups both modern and aboriginal. When I was called to active duty in the Navy in World War II, I reflected on this material during long watches at sea. Quite suddenly, I conceived that a number of these studies might be described in concepts common to them all. In a few days I had sketched out such a conceptual scheme.

Back at Harvard with a tenured position after the war, I began working on a book, later entitled *The Human Group* (1950), which was intended to apply my conceptual scheme to the studies in question. In the course of this work it occurred to me that a conceptual scheme was useful only as the starting point

their benefits,[1] and that goal may involve assessing the relationship between the chances of achieving a primary end and what that achievement does for the chances of attaining the second-most-valuable objective.

---

[1] Although contemporary rational choice theorists recognize that there are limits on the desire and ability to maximize (Heckathorn, 1997).

of a science. What was next required were propositions relating the concepts to one another. In *The Human Group,* I stated a number of such propositions, which seemed to hold good for the groups I had chosen.

I had long known Professor Talcott Parsons and was now closely associated with him in the Department of Social Relations. The sociological profession looked upon him as its leading theorist. I decided that what he called theories were only conceptual schemes, and that a theory was not a theory unless it contained at least a few propositions. I became confident that this view was correct by reading several books on the philosophy of science.

Nor was it enough that a theory should contain propositions. A theory of a phenomenon was an explanation of it. Explanation consisted in showing that one or more propositions of a low order of generality followed in logic from more general propositions applied to what were variously called given or boundary conditions or parameters. I stated my position on this issue in my little book *The Nature of Social Science* (1967).

I then asked myself what general propositions I could use in this way to explain the empirical propositions I had stated in *The Human Group* and other propositions brought to my attention by later reading of field and experimental studies in social psychology. The general propositions would have to meet only one condition: in accordance with my original insight, they should apply to individual human beings as members of a species.

Such propositions were already at hand—luckily, for I could not have invented them for myself. They were the propositions of behavioral psychology as stated by my old friend B. F. Skinner and others. They held good of persons both when acting alone in the physical environment and when in interaction with other persons. In the two editions of my book *Social Behavior* (1961 and revised in 1974), I used these propositions to try to explain how, under appropriate given conditions, relatively enduring social structures could arise from, and be maintained by, the actions of individuals, who need not have intended to create the structures. This I conceive to be the central intellectual problem of sociology.

Once the structures have been created, they have further effects on the behavior of persons who take part in them or come into contact with them. But these further effects are explained by the same propositions as those used to explain the creation and maintenance of the structures in the first place. The structures only provide new given conditions to which the propositions are to be applied. My sociology remains fundamentally individualistic and not collectivistic.

[George Homans died in 1989. See Bell, 1992, for a biographical sketch of Homans. See also Fararo, 2007; Molm, 2005b.]

A second source of constraints on individual action is social institutions. As Friedman and Hechter put it, an individual typically will

find his or her actions checked from birth to death by familial and school rules; laws and ordinances; firm policies; churches, synagogues and mosques; and hospitals and funeral parlors. By restricting the feasible set of courses of action available to individuals, enforceable rules of the game—including norms, laws, agendas, and voting rules—systematically affect social outcomes.

(D. Friedman and Hechter, 1988:202)

These institutional constraints provide both positive and negative sanctions that serve to encourage certain actions and discourage others.

Friedman and Hechter enumerate two other ideas that they see as basic to rational choice theory. The first is an aggregation mechanism, or the process by which "the separate individual actions are combined to produce the social outcome" (D. Friedman and Hechter, 1988:203). The second is the importance of information in making rational choices. At one time, it was assumed that actors had perfect, or at least sufficient, information to make purposive choices among the alternative courses of action open to them. However, there is a growing recognition that the quantity or quality of available information is highly variable and that that variability has a profound effect on actors' choices (Heckathorn, 1997).

At least in its early formation, exchange theory was affected by a rudimentary theory of rationality. Later in this chapter, when we deal with rational choice theory itself, we will discuss some of the greater complexity associated with it.

The Exchange Theory of George Homans

The heart of George Homans's exchange theory lies in a set of fundamental propositions. Although some of his propositions deal with at least two interacting individuals, Homans was careful to point out that these propositions are based on psychological principles. According to Homans, they are psychological for two reasons. First, "they are usually stated and empirically tested by persons who call themselves psychologists" (Homans, 1967:39–40). Second, and more important, they are psychological because of the level at which they deal with the individual in society: "They are propositions about the behavior of individual human beings, rather than propositions about groups or societies as such; and *the behavior of men, as men,* is generally considered the province of psychology" (Homans, 1967:40; italics added). As a result of this position, Homans admitted to being "what has been called—and it is a horrid phrase—a psychological reductionist" (1974:12). Reductionism to Homans is "the process of showing how the propositions of one named science [in this case, sociology] follow in logic from the more general propositions of another named science [in this case, psychology]" (1984:338).

Although Homans made the case for psychological principles, he did not think of individuals as isolated. He recognized that people are social and spend a considerable portion of their time interacting with other people. He attempted to explain social behavior with psychological principles: "What the position [Homans's] does assume is that the general propositions of psychology, which are propositions about the effects on human behavior of the results thereof, do not change when the results come from other men rather than from the physical environment" (Homans, 1967:59). Homans did not deny the Durkheimian position that something new emerges from interaction. Instead, he argued that those emergent properties can be explained by psychological principles; there is no need for new sociological propositions to explain social facts. He used the basic sociological concept of a norm as illustration:

> The great example of a social fact is a social norm, and the norms of the groups to which they belong certainly constrain towards conformity the behavior of many more individuals. The question is not that of the existence of constraint, but of its explanation. . . . The norm does not constrain automatically: individuals conform, when they do so, because they perceive it is to their net advantage to conform, and it is psychology that deals with the effect on behavior of perceived advantage.
>
> (Homans, 1967:60)

Homans detailed a program to "bring men back in[to]" sociology, but he also tried to develop a theory that focuses on psychology, people, and the "elementary forms of social life." According to Homans, this theory "envisages social *behavior* as an exchange of activity, tangible or intangible, and more or less rewarding or costly, between at least two persons" (1961:13; italics added).

For example, Homans sought to explain the development of power-driven machinery in the textile industry, and thereby the Industrial Revolution, through the psychological principle that people are likely to act in such a way as to increase their rewards. More generally, in his version of exchange theory, he sought to explain elementary social behavior in terms of rewards and costs. He was motivated in part by the structural-functional theories of his acknowledged "colleague and friend" Talcott Parsons. He argued that such theories "possess every virtue except that of explaining anything" (Homans, 1961:10). To Homans, the structural functionalists did little more than create conceptual categories and schemes. Homans admitted that a scientific sociology needs such categories, but sociology "also needs a set of general propositions about the relations among the categories, for without such propositions explanation is impossible. No explanation without propositions!" (1974:10). Homans, therefore, set for himself the task of developing those propositions that focus on the psychological level; these form the groundwork of exchange theory.

In *Social Behavior: Its Elementary Forms* (1961, 1974),[2] Homans acknowledged that his exchange theory is derived from both behavioral psychology and elementary economics (rational choice theory). In fact, Homans (1984) regrets that his theory was labeled "exchange theory" because he sees it as a behavioral psychology applied to specific situations. Homans began with a discussion of the exemplar of the behaviorist paradigm, B. F. Skinner, in particular of Skinner's study of pigeons:[3]

> Suppose, then, that a fresh or naïve pigeon is in its cage in the laboratory. One of the items in its inborn repertory of behavior which it uses to explore its environment is the peck. As the pigeon wanders around the cage pecking away, it happens to hit a round red target, at which point the waiting psychologists or, it may be, an automatic machine feeds it grain. The evidence is that the probability

---

[2] In the following discussion we move back and forth between the two editions of Homans's book. We do not restrict ourselves to the revised edition because many aspects of the first edition more clearly reflect Homans's position. In the preface to the revised edition, Homans said that although it was a thorough revision, he had not "altered the substance of the underlying argument" (Homans, 1974:v). Thus we feel safe in dealing simultaneously with both volumes.

[3] Skinner also studied other species, including humans.

of the pigeon's emitting the behavior again—the probability, that is, of its not just pecking but pecking on the target—has increased. In Skinner's language the pigeon's behavior in pecking the target is an *operant;* the operant has been *reinforced;* grain is the *reinforcer;* and the pigeon has undergone *operant conditioning.* Should we prefer our language to be ordinary English, we may say that the pigeon has learned to peck the target by being rewarded for doing so.

(Homans, 1961:18)

Skinner was interested in this instance in pigeons; Homans's concern was humans. According to Homans, Skinner's pigeons are not engaged in a true exchange relationship with the psychologist. The pigeon is engaged in a one-sided exchange relationship, whereas human exchanges are at least two-sided. The pigeon is being reinforced by the grain, but the psychologist is not truly being reinforced by the pecks of the pigeon. The pigeon is carrying on the same sort of relationship with the psychologist that it would have with the physical environment. Because there is no reciprocity, Homans defined this as *individual behavior.* Homans seemed to relegate the study of this sort of behavior to the psychologist, whereas he urged the sociologist to study social behavior "where the activity of each of at least two animals reinforces (or punishes) the activity of the other, and where accordingly each influences the other" (1961:30). However, it is significant that, according to Homans, *no new propositions* are needed to explain social behavior as opposed to individual behavior. The laws of individual behavior as developed by Skinner in his study of pigeons explain social behavior as long as we take into account the complications of mutual reinforcement. Homans admitted that he might ultimately have to go beyond the principles derived by Skinner, but only reluctantly.

In his theoretical work, Homans restricted himself to everyday social interaction. It is clear, however, that he believed that a sociology built on his principles ultimately would be able to explain all social behavior. Here is the case Homans used to exemplify the kind of exchange relationship he was interested in:

Suppose that two men are doing paperwork jobs in an office. According to the office rules, each should do his job by himself, or, if he needs help, he should consult the supervisor. One of the men, whom we shall call Person, is not skillful at the work and would get it done better and faster if he got help from time to time. In spite of the rules he is reluctant to go to the supervisor, for to confess his incompetence might hurt his chances for promotion. Instead he seeks out the other man, whom we shall call Other for short, and asks him for help. Other is more experienced at the work than is Person; he can do his work well and quickly and be left with time to spare, and he has reason to suppose that the supervisor will not go out of his way to look for a breach of rules. Other gives Person help and in return Person gives Other thanks and expressions of approval. The two men have exchanged help and approval.

(Homans, 1961:31–32)

Focusing on this sort of situation, and basing his ideas on Skinner's findings, Homans developed several propositions.

The Success Proposition

For all actions taken by persons, the more often a particular action of a person is rewarded, the more likely the person is to perform that action.

(Homans, 1974:16)

In terms of Homans's Person–Other example in an office situation, this proposition means that a person is more likely to ask others for advice if he or she has been rewarded in the past with useful advice. Furthermore, the more often a person received useful advice in the past, the more often he or she will request more advice. Similarly, the other person will be more willing to give advice and give it more frequently if he or she often has been rewarded with approval in the past. Generally, behavior in accord with the success proposition involves three stages: first, a person's action; next, a rewarded result; and finally, a repetition of the original action or at minimum one similar in at least some respects.

Homans specified a number of things about the success proposition. First, although it is generally true that increasingly frequent rewards lead to increasingly frequent actions, this reciprocation cannot go on indefinitely. At some point individuals simply cannot act that way as frequently. Second, the shorter the interval is between behavior and reward, the more likely a person is to repeat the behavior. Conversely, long intervals between behavior and reward lower the likelihood of repeat behavior. Finally, it was Homans's view that intermittent rewards are more likely to elicit repeat behavior than regular rewards are. Regular rewards lead to boredom and satiation, whereas rewards at irregular intervals (as in gambling) are very likely to elicit repeat behaviors.

The Stimulus Proposition

> If in the past the occurrence of a particular stimulus, or set of stimuli, has been
> the occasion on which a person's action has been rewarded, then the more
> similar the present stimuli are to the past ones, the more likely the person is to
> perform the action, or some similar action.
>
> (Homans, 1974:23)

Again we look at Homans's office example: If, in the past, Person and Other found the giving and getting of advice rewarding, they are likely to engage in similar actions in similar situations in the future. Homans offered an even more down-to-earth example: "A fisherman who has cast his line into a dark pool and has caught a fish becomes more apt to fish in dark pools again" (1974:23).

Homans was interested in the process of *generalization,* that is, the tendency to extend behavior to similar circumstances. In the fishing example, one aspect of generalization would be to move from fishing in dark pools to fishing in any pool with any degree of shadiness. Similarly, success in catching fish is likely to lead from one kind of fishing to another (for instance, freshwater to saltwater) or even from fishing to hunting. However, the process of *discrimination* is also of importance. That is, the actor may fish only under the specific circumstances that proved successful in the past. For one thing, if the conditions under which success occurred were too complicated, similar conditions may not stimulate behavior. If the crucial stimulus occurs too long before behavior is required, it may not actually stimulate that behavior. An actor can become oversensitized to stimuli, especially if they are very valuable to the actor. In fact, the actor could respond to irrelevant stimuli, at least until the situation is corrected by repeated failures. All this is affected by the individual's alertness or attentiveness to stimuli.

The Value Proposition

The more valuable to a person is the result of his action, the more likely he is to
perform the action.

(Homans, 1974:25)

In the office example, if the rewards each offers to the other are considered valuable,
the actors are more likely to perform the desired behaviors than they are if the rewards
are not valuable. At this point, Homans introduced the concepts of rewards and punishments. Rewards are actions with positive values; an increase in rewards is more likely
to elicit the desired behavior. Punishments are actions with negative values; an increase
in punishment means that the actor is less likely to manifest undesired behaviors.
Homans found punishments to be an inefficient means of getting people to change their
behavior, because people may react in undesirable ways to punishment. It is preferable
simply not to reward undesirable behavior; then such behavior eventually becomes
extinguished. Rewards are clearly to be preferred, but they may be in short supply.
Homans did make it clear that his is not simply a hedonistic theory; rewards can be
either materialistic (for example, money) or altruistic (helping others).

The Deprivation-Satiation Proposition

The more often in the recent past a person has received a particular reward, the
less valuable any further unit of that reward becomes for him.

(Homans, 1974:29)

In the office, Person and Other may reward each other so often for giving and getting
advice that the rewards cease to be valuable to them. Time is crucial here; people
are less likely to become satiated if particular rewards are stretched over a long period
of time.

At this point, Homans defined two other critical concepts: cost and profit. The
cost of any behavior is defined as the rewards lost in forgoing alternative lines of
action. *Profit* in social exchange is seen as the greater number of rewards gained over
costs incurred. The latter led Homans to recast the deprivation-satiation proposition
as "the greater the profit a person receives as a result of his action, the more likely
he is to perform the action" (1974:31).

The Aggression-Approval Propositions

Proposition A: When a person's action does not receive the reward he expected, or
receives punishment he did not expect, he will be angry; he becomes more likely
to perform aggressive behavior, and the results of such behavior become more
valuable to him.

(Homans, 1974:37)

In the office case, if Person does not get the advice he or she expected and Other
does not receive the praise he or she anticipated, both are likely to be angry.[4] We are

---

[4] Although Homans still called this the "law of distributive justice" in the revised later edition, he developed the concept
more extensively in the first edition. *Distributive justice* refers to whether the rewards and costs are distributed fairly among
the individuals involved. In fact, Homans originally stated it as a proposition: "The more to a man's disadvantage the rule
of distributive justice fails of realization, the more likely he is to display the emotional behavior we call anger" (1961:75).

surprised to find the concepts of frustration and anger in Homans's work because they would seem to refer to mental states. In fact, Homans admitted as much: "When a person does not get what he expected, he is said to be frustrated. A purist in behaviorism would not refer to the expectation at all, because the word seems to refer . . . to a state of mind" (1974:31). Homans went on to argue that frustration of such expectations need *not* refer "only" to an internal state. It also can refer to "wholly external events," observable not just by Person but also by outsiders.

Proposition A on aggression-approval refers only to negative emotions, whereas Proposition B deals with more positive emotions:

> *Proposition B:* When a person's action receives the reward he expected, especially a greater reward than he expected, or does not receive punishment he expected, he will be pleased; he becomes more likely to perform approving behavior, and the results of such behavior become more valuable to him.
>
> (Homans, 1974:39)

For example, in the office, when Person gets the advice that he or she expects and Other gets the praise that he or she expects, both are pleased and are more likely to get or give advice. Advice and praise become more valuable to each one.

The Rationality Proposition

> In choosing between alternative actions, a person will choose that one for which, as perceived by him at the time, the value, V, of the result, multiplied by the probability, p, of getting the result, is the greater.
>
> (Homans, 1974:43)

While the earlier propositions rely heavily on behaviorism, the rationality proposition demonstrates most clearly the influence of rational choice theory on Homans's approach. In economic terms, actors who act in accord with the rationality proposition are maximizing their utilities.

Basically, people examine and make calculations about the various alternative actions open to them. They compare the amount of rewards associated with each course of action. They also calculate the likelihood that they actually will receive the rewards. Highly valued rewards will be devalued if the actors think it unlikely that they will obtain them. In contrast, lesser-valued rewards will be enhanced if they are seen as highly attainable. Thus, there is an interaction between the value of the reward and the likelihood of attainment. The most desirable rewards are those that are *both* very valuable *and* highly attainable. The least desirable rewards are those that are not very valuable and are unlikely to be attained.

Homans relates the rationality proposition to the success, stimulus, and value propositions. The rationality proposition tells us that whether people will perform an action depends on their perceptions of the probability of success. But what determines this perception? Homans argues that perceptions of whether chances of success are high or low are shaped by past successes and the similarity of the present situation to past successful situations. The rationality proposition also does not tell us why an actor values one reward more than another; for this we need the value proposition. In these ways, Homans links his rationality principle to his more behavioristic propositions.

PETER M. BLAU

A Biographical Sketch

Peter Blau was born in Vienna, Austria, on February 7, 1918. He emigrated to the United States in 1939 and became a United States citizen in 1943. In 1942 he received his bachelor's degree from the relatively little known Elmhurst College in Elmhurst, Illinois. His schooling was interrupted by World War II, and he served in the United States Army and was awarded the Bronze Star. After the war, he returned to school and completed his education, receiving his Ph.D. from Columbia University in 1952 (Bienenstock, 2005).

Blau first received wide recognition in sociology for his contributions to the study of formal organizations. His empirical studies of organizations as well as his textbooks on formal organizations are still widely cited in that subfield, and he continued to be a regular contributor to it until his death in 2002. He was also noted for a book he coauthored with Otis Dudley Duncan, *The American Occupational Structure* (1967), which won the prestigious Sorokin Award from the American Sociological Association in 1968. That work constitutes a very important contribution to the sociological study of social stratification.

Although he is well known for a range of work, what interests us here is Blau's contribution to sociological theory. What is distinctive about it is that Blau made important contributions to two distinct theoretical orientations. His 1964 book *Exchange and Power in Social Life* is a major component of contemporary exchange theory. Blau's chief contribution there was to take the primarily small-scale exchange theory and try to apply it to larger-scale issues. Although it has some notable weaknesses, it constitutes an important effort to theoretically integrate large- and small-scale sociological issues. Blau was also in the forefront of structural theory. During his term as president of the American Sociological Association (1973–1974), he made this the theme of the annual meeting of the association. He published a number of books and articles designed to clarify and extend structural theory. Among his later works in this area are *Structural Contexts of Opportunities* (1994) and the second edition of *Crosscutting Social Circles* (Blau and Schwartz, 1997).

Peter Blau died on March 12, 2002.

In the end, Homans's theory can be condensed to a view of the actor as a rational profit seeker. However, Homans's theory was weak on mental states (Abrahamsson, 1970; Mitchell, 1978) and large-scale structures (Ekeh, 1974). For example, on consciousness Homans admitted the need for a "more fully developed psychology" (1974:45).

Despite such weaknesses, Homans remained a behaviorist who worked resolutely at the level of individual behavior. He argued that large-scale structures can be understood if we adequately understand elementary social behavior. He contended that exchange processes are "identical" at the individual and societal levels, although he granted that at the societal level, "the way the fundamental processes are combined is more complex" (Homans, 1974:358).

Peter Blau's Exchange Theory

Peter Blau's (1964) goal was "an understanding of social structure on the basis of an analysis of the social processes that govern the relations between individuals and groups. The basic question . . . is how social life becomes organized into increasingly complex structures of associations among men" (1964:2). Blau's intention was to go beyond Homans's concern with elementary forms of social life and into an analysis of complex structures: "The main sociological purpose of studying processes of face-to-face interaction is to lay the foundation for an understanding of the social structures that evolve and the emergent social forces that characterize their development" (1964:13).[5]

Blau focused on the process of exchange, which, in his view, directs much of human behavior and underlies relationships among individuals as well as among groups. In effect, Blau envisioned a four-stage sequence leading from interpersonal exchange to social structure to social change:

Step 1: Personal exchange transactions between people give rise to . . .
Step 2: Differentiation of status and power, which leads to . . .
Step 3: Legitimization and organization, which sow the seeds of . . .
Step 4: Opposition and change

Micro to Macro

On the individual level, Blau and Homans were interested in similar processes. However, Blau's concept of social exchange is limited to actions that are contingent, that depend, on rewarding reactions from others—actions that cease when expected reactions are not forthcoming. People are attracted to each other for a variety of reasons that induce them to establish social associations. Once initial ties are forged, the rewards that they provide to each other serve to maintain and enhance the bonds. The opposite situation is also possible: with insufficient rewards, an association will weaken or break. Rewards that are exchanged can be either intrinsic (for instance, love, affection, respect) or extrinsic (for instance, money, physical labor). The parties cannot always reward each other equally; when there is inequality in the exchange, a difference of power will emerge within an association.

When one party needs something from another but has nothing comparable to offer in return, four alternatives are available. First, people can force other people to help them. Second, they can find another source to obtain what they need. Third, they

---

[5] It is interesting to note that Blau (1987) no longer accepts the idea of building macro theory on a micro base.

can attempt to get along without what they need from the others. Finally, and most important, they can subordinate themselves to the others, thereby giving the others "generalized credit" in their relationship; the others then can draw on this credit when they want them to do something. (This last alternative is, of course, the essential characteristic of power.)

Up to this point, Blau's position is similar to Homans's position, but Blau extended his theory to the level of social facts. He noted, for example, that we cannot analyze processes of social interaction apart from the social structure that surrounds them. Social structure emerges from social interaction, but once this occurs, social structures have a separate existence that affects the process of interaction.

Social interaction exists first within social groups. People are attracted to a group when they feel that the relationships offer more rewards than those from other groups. Because they are attracted to the group, they want to be accepted. To be accepted, they must offer group members rewards. This involves impressing the group members by showing them that associating with the new people will be rewarding. The relationship with the group members will be solidified when the newcomers have impressed the group—when members have received the rewards they expected. Newcomers' efforts to impress group members generally lead to group cohesion, but competition and, ultimately, social differentiation can occur when too many people actively seek to impress each other with their abilities to reward.

The paradox here is that although group members with the ability to impress can be attractive associates, their impressive characteristics also can arouse fears of dependence in other group members and cause them to acknowledge their attraction only reluctantly. In the early stages of group formation, competition for social recognition among group members actually acts as a screening test for potential leaders of the group. Those best able to reward are most likely to end up in leadership positions. Those group members with less ability to reward want to continue to receive the rewards offered by the potential leaders, and this usually more than compensates for their fears of becoming dependent on them. Ultimately, those individuals with the greater ability to reward emerge as leaders, and the group is differentiated.

The inevitable differentiation of the group into leaders and followers creates a renewed need for integration. Once they have acknowledged the leader's status, followers have an even greater need for integration. Earlier, followers flaunted their most impressive qualities. Now, to achieve integration with fellow followers, they display their weaknesses. This is, in effect, a public declaration that they no longer want to be leaders. This self-deprecation leads to sympathy and social acceptance from the other also-rans. The leader (or leaders) also engages in some self-deprecation at this point to improve overall group integration. By admitting that subordinates are superior in some areas, the leader reduces the pain associated with subordination and demonstrates that he or she does not seek control over every area of group life. These types of forces serve to reintegrate the group despite its new, differentiated status.

All this is reminiscent of Homans's discussion of exchange theory. Blau, however, moved to the societal level and differentiated between two types of social organization. Exchange theorists and behavioral sociologists also recognize the emergence of social organization, but there is, as we will see, a basic difference between Blau and "purer" social behaviorists on this issue. The first type, in which Blau recognized the emergent properties of social groups, emerges from the processes of exchange and competition discussed earlier. The second type of social organization is not emergent but is explicitly established to achieve specified objectives—for example, manufacturing goods that can be sold for a profit, participating in bowling tournaments, engaging in collective bargaining, and winning political victories. In discussing these two types of organization, Blau clearly moved beyond the "elementary forms of social behavior" that are typically of interest to social behaviorists.

In addition to being concerned with these organizations, Blau was interested in the subgroups within them. For example, he argued that leadership and opposition groups are found in both types of organization. In the first type, these two groups emerge out of the process of interaction. In the second, leadership and opposition groups are built into the structure of the organization. In either case, differentiation between the groups is inevitable and lays the groundwork for opposition and conflict within the organization between leaders and followers.

Having moved beyond Homans's elementary forms of behavior and into complex social structures, Blau knew that he must adapt exchange theory to the societal level. Blau recognized the essential difference between small groups and large collectivities, whereas Homans minimized this difference in his effort to explain all social behavior in terms of basic psychological principles.

> The complex social structures that characterize large collectives differ fundamentally from the simpler structures of small groups. A structure of social relations develops in a small group in the course of social interaction among its members. Since there is no direct social interaction among most members of a large community or entire society, some other mechanism must mediate the structure of social relations among them.
>
> (Blau, 1964:253)

This statement requires scrutiny. On the one hand, Blau clearly ruled out social behaviorism as an adequate paradigm for dealing with complex social structures (see the Appendix). On the other hand, he ruled out the social-definitionist paradigm because he argued that social interaction and the social definitions that accompany it do not occur directly in a large-scale organization. Thus, starting from the social-behavior paradigm, Blau aligned himself with the social-facts paradigm in dealing with more complex social structures.

Norms and Values

For Blau, the mechanisms that mediate among the complex social structures are the norms and values (the value consensus) that exist within society:

> Commonly agreed upon values and norms serve as media of social life and as mediating links for social transactions. They make indirect social exchange possible, and they govern the processes of social integration and differentiation in complex social structures as well as the development of social organization and reorganization in them.
>
> (Blau, 1964:255)

Other mechanisms mediate among social structures, but Blau focused on value consensus. Looking first at social norms, Blau argued that they substitute indirect exchange for direct exchange. One member conforms to the group norm and receives approval for that conformity and implicit approval for the fact that conformity contributes to the group's maintenance and stability. In other words, the group or collectivity engages in an exchange relationship with the individual. This is in contrast to Homans's simpler notion, which focused on interpersonal exchange. Blau offered a number of examples of collectivity-individual exchanges replacing individual-individual exchanges:

> Staff officials do not assist line officials in their work in exchange for rewards received from them, but furnishing this assistance is the official obligation of staff members, and in return for discharging these obligations they receive financial rewards from the company.
>
> Organized philanthropy provides another example of indirect social exchange. In contrast to the old-fashioned lady bountiful who brought her baskets to the poor and received their gratitude and appreciation, there is no direct contact and no exchange between individual donors and recipients in contemporary organized charity. Wealthy businessmen and members of the upper class make philanthropic contributions to conform with the normative expectations that prevail in their social class and to earn the social approval of their peers, not in order to earn the gratitude of the individuals who benefit from their charity.
>
> (Blau, 1964:260)

The concept of the norm in Blau's formulation moves Blau to the level of exchange between individual and collectivity, but the concept of values moves him to the largest-scale societal level and to the analysis of the relationship *among collectivities.* Blau said:

> Common values of various types can be conceived of as media of social transactions that expand the compass of social interaction and the structure of social relations through social space and time. Consensus on social values serves as the basis for extending the range of social transactions beyond the limits of direct social contacts and for perpetuating social structures beyond the life span of human beings. Value standards can be considered media of social life in two senses of the term; the value context is the medium that molds the form of social relationships; and common values are the mediating links for social associations and transactions on a broad scale.
>
> (Blau, 1964:263–264)

For example, *particularistic* values are the media of integration and solidarity. These values serve to unite the members of a group around such things as patriotism or the good of the school or the company. These are seen as similar at the collective level to sentiments of personal attraction that unite individuals on a face-to-face basis. However, they extend integrative bonds beyond mere personal attraction. Particularistic values also differentiate the in-group from the out-group, thereby enhancing their unifying function.

Blau's analysis carries us far from Homans's version of exchange theory. The individual and individual behavior, paramount for Homans, have almost disappeared in Blau's conception. Taking the place of the individual are a wide variety of *social facts.* For example, Blau discussed groups, organizations, collectivities, societies, norms, and values. Blau's analysis is concerned with what holds large-scale social units together and what tears them apart, clearly traditional concerns of the social factist.

Although Blau argued that he was simply extending exchange theory to the societal level, in so doing he twisted exchange theory beyond recognition. He was even forced to admit that processes at the societal level are fundamentally different from those at the individual level. In his effort to extend exchange theory, Blau managed only to transform it into another macro-level theory. Blau seemed to recognize that exchange theory is concerned primarily with face-to-face relations. As a result, it needs to be complemented by other theoretical orientations that focus mainly on macro structures. Blau (1987, 1994) came to recognize this explicitly, and his later work focuses on macro-level, structural phenomena.

The Work of Richard Emerson and His Disciples

In 1962 Richard Emerson published an important paper on power-dependence relations, but it was two related essays written in 1972 (Emerson, 1972a, 1972b) that "marked the beginning of a new stage in the development of social exchange theory" (Cook and Whitmeyer, 2011; Molm and Cook, 1995:215). Molm and Cook see three basic factors as the impetus for this new body of work. First, Emerson was interested in exchange theory as a broader framework for his earlier interest in power dependence. It seemed clear to Emerson that power was central to the exchange theory perspective. Second, Emerson felt that he could use behaviorism (operant psychology) as the base of his exchange theory but avoid some of the problems that had affected Homans. For one thing, Homans and other exchange theorists had been accused of assuming an overly rational image of human beings, but Emerson felt he could use behaviorism without assuming a rational actor. For another, Emerson believed he could avoid the problem of tautology that ensnared Homans:

> Homans predicted individual exchange behavior from the reinforcement provided by another actor, but behavioral responses and reinforcement do not have independent meaning in operant psychology. A reinforcer is, by definition, a stimulus consequence that increases or maintains response frequency.
>
> (Molm and Cook, 1995:214)

In addition, Emerson felt he could avoid the charge of reductionism (one that Homans reveled in) by being able to develop an exchange perspective capable of explaining macro-level phenomena. Third, unlike Blau, who resorted to an explanation reliant on normative phenomena, Emerson wanted to deal with social structure and social change by using "social relations and social networks as building blocks that spanned different levels of analysis" (Molm and Cook, 1995:215). In addition, the actors in Emerson's system could be either individuals or larger corporate structures (albeit structures working through agents). Thus, Emerson used the principles of operant psychology to develop a theory of social structure.

In the two essays published in 1972, Emerson developed the basis of his integrative exchange theory. In the first of those essays (1972a) Emerson dealt with the psychological basis for social exchange, while in the second (1972b) he turned to macro-level and exchange relations and network structures. Later, Emerson made the

RICHARD EMERSON

*A Biographical Sketch**

Richard Emerson was born in Salt Lake City, Utah, in 1925. Raised near mountains, he never seemed to stray too far from rivers, mountain peaks, and glaciers. One of his most prized personal accomplishments was his participation in the successful ascent of Mt. Everest in 1963. Aspects of this experience are captured in his publication "Everest Traverse" in the December 1963 edition of the *Sierra Club Annual Bulletin* and in an article published in *Sociometry* in 1966. He received a grant from the National Science Foundation to study group performance under prolonged stress on this climb. That project earned him the Hubbard Medal, presented to him by President Kennedy on behalf of the National Geographic Society in July 1963 (Cook, 2005).

His love of mountains and the rural social life of the mountain villages of Pakistan became a constant source of sociological inspiration for Richard Emerson during his career. His studies of interpersonal behavior, group performance, power, and social influence were often driven by his close personal encounters with expedition teams for which the intensity of cooperation and competition were exacerbated by environmental stress.

After World War II and a tour of duty with the Army in Western Europe, he completed his B.A. in 1950 at the University of Utah and then went on to earn an M.A. (1952) and a Ph.D. (1955) from the University of Minnesota, where his major field was sociology and his minor field was psychology. His doctoral dissertation was titled "The Determinants of Influence in Face to Face Groups."

micro-macro linkage more explicit: "I am attempting to extend exchange theory and research from *micro* to more *macro* levels of analysis through the study of *exchange network structures*" (cited in Cook, 1987:212). As Karen Cook (Whitmeyer, 2005a), Emerson's most important disciple, points out, it is the idea of exchange network structures that is central to the micro-macro linkage: "The use of the notion, exchange networks, allows for the development of theory that bridges the conceptual gap between isolated individuals or dyads and larger aggregates or collections of individuals (e.g., formal groups or associations, organizations, neighborhoods, political parties, etc.)" (1987:219).[6]

Both Emerson and Cook accept and begin with the basic, micro-level premises of exchange theory. Emerson, for example, says, "The exchange approach takes as its first focus of attention the benefits people obtain from, and contribute to, the process of social interaction" (1981:31). More specifically, Emerson accepts behavioristic

---

[6] Emerson and Cook (as well as Blau) are not the only ones to have developed integrative exchange theories. See also Uehara (1990) and Willer, Markovsky, and Patton (1989).

Emerson's first academic post was at the University of Cincinnati (1955–1964). Upon leaving Cincinnati Emerson wrote, "A recurring theme in my work was crystallized in the article on power-dependence relations. However, this theory is clearly a springboard for the future rather than a summary of the past. I have rather specific plans for both theoretical and empirical extensions into stratification and community power structure." He was still engaged in this work when he died unexpectedly in December 1982. His work on power-dependence relations (1962) is now a citation classic and has influenced much current work on power in American sociology.

Two other pieces have been highly influential. These are his two chapters on social exchange theory which were written in 1967 and subsequently published in 1972. This work was completed at the University of Washington, where he joined the faculty in 1965. He was drawn to the Northwest, I am sure, by the lure of the Olympics and Cascades.

Emerson's influence on sociological theory crystallized while he was at the University of Washington, where he collaborated with Karen Cook for a ten-year period (1972–1982) on the empirical development of social exchange theory. They carried out a program of research in the first computerized laboratory for conducting research of this type in the United States. This work was funded by three successive grants from the National Science Foundation.

Emerson is remembered by former colleagues and students as a "thinker." This aspect of his personality is best captured in a quote from an article he wrote in 1960 in Robert Bowen's book *The New Professors:* "So, what is there of value in the academic (that is, 'nonpractical, removed-from-life') study of a topic? People ask this question, too. Such questions are difficult to answer because those who ask have never climbed a mountain and have no interest in a topic. I say they are far removed from life."

*This biographical sketch was written by Karen Cook.

principles as his starting point. Emerson (1981:33) outlines three core assumptions of exchange theory:

1. People for whom events are beneficial tend to act "rationally," and so such events occur.
2. Because people eventually become satiated with behavioral events, such events come to be of diminishing utility.
3. The benefits that people obtain through social processes are dependent on the benefits that they are able to provide in exchange, giving exchange theory "its focus [on] the flow of *benefits through social interaction.*"

All this is quite familiar, but Emerson begins to point behavioristically oriented exchange theory in a different direction at the close of his first, micro-oriented 1972 essay: "Our main purpose in this chapter is to incorporate operant principles into a framework which can handle more complex situations than operant psychology confronts" (1972a:48).

This theme opens the second 1972 essay: "The purpose of this essay is to begin construction of a theory of social exchange in which *social structure* is taken as the dependent variable" (Emerson, 1972b:58). Whereas in the first 1972 essay Emerson was concerned with a single actor involved in an exchange relation with his or her environment (for example, a person fishing in a lake), in the second essay he turns to social-exchange relationships as well as to exchange networks.

The actors in Emerson's macro-level exchange theory can be either individuals or collectivities. Emerson is concerned with the exchange relationship among actors. An *exchange network* has the following components (Cook et al., 1983:277):

1. There is a set of either individual or collective actors.
2. Valued resources are distributed among the actors.
3. There is a set of exchange opportunities among all the actors in the network.
4. Some exchange opportunities have developed into actually used exchange relations.
5. Exchange relations are connected to one another in a single network structure.

In sum: "An 'exchange network' is a specific social structure formed by two or more connected exchange relations between actors" (Cook et al., 1983:277).

The idea of an exchange network links exchange between two actors (dyadic exchange) to more macro-level phenomena (Yamagishi, Gillmore, and Cook, 1988:835).

Each exchange relation is embedded within a larger exchange network consisting of sets of connected exchange relations. By connected, it is meant that the exchange in one relationship affects the exchange in another.

Thus, we may say that two dyadic-exchange relations, *A-B* and *A-C*, form a minimal network (*A-B-C*) when exchange in one affects exchange in the other. It is *not* enough for *A, B,* and *C* to have a common membership for an exchange network to develop; there must be a relationship between exchanges in *A-B* and *B-C*. For example, Abe may exchange information with Bill about office politics and Bill may exchange services with Cathy, but that alone would not make them an exchange network unless Abe's information positively or negatively affected Bill's exchange of services with Cathy.

An important distinction is that between positive and negative exchange connections (Emerson, 1972b). Connections are positive when the exchange in one positively affects the exchange in another (for example, the information that Abe gives Bill helps Bill provide services for Cathy), negative when one serves to inhibit the exchange in the other (Abe might tell Bill some gossip about Cathy that interferes with Bill and Cathy's relationship), or mixed.

Power-Dependence

Emerson defined *power* as "the level of potential cost which one actor can induce another to 'accept,'" while *dependence* involves "the level of potential cost an actor will accept within a relation" (1972b:64). These definitions lead to Emerson's power-dependence theory (Molm, 2007), which Yamagishi, Gillmore, and Cook summarize in the following way: "The power of one party over another in an exchange relation is an inverse function of his or her dependence on the other party" (1988:837; Whitmeyer, 2005b).

Unequal power and dependency lead to imbalances in relationships, but over time these move toward a more balanced power-dependence relationship.

Molm and Cook (1995) regard dependence as the critical concept in Emerson's work. As Molm puts it, "The actors' *dependencies* on each other are the major structural determinants of their interaction and of their power over each other" (1988:109). Here is the way Emerson originally dealt with the issue: "The dependence of actor A upon actor B is (1) directly proportional to A's *motivational investment* in goals mediated by B, and (2) inversely proportional to the *availability* of those goals to A outside of the A-B relation" (1962:32). Thus, a sense of dependence is linked to Emerson's definition of power: "the power of A over B is equal to, and based upon, the dependence of B upon A" (1962:33). There is balance in the relationship between A and B when the dependence of A on B equals the dependence of B on A. Where there is an imbalance in the dependencies, the actor with less dependence has an advantage in terms of power. Thus, power is a potential built into the structure of the *relationship* between A and B. Power also can be used to acquire rewards from the relationship. Even in balanced relationships, power exists, albeit in a kind of equilibrium.

Power-dependence studies have focused on positive outcomes—the ability to reward others. However, in a series of studies, Molm (1988, 1989, 1994, 1997; Peterson, 2005) has emphasized the role of negative outcomes—punishment power—in power-dependence relationships. That is, power can be derived from both the ability to reward and the ability to punish others. In general, Molm has found that punishment power is weaker than reward power, in part because acts of punishment are likely to elicit negative reactions. This means that the risk of escalating negative reactions is an important part of punishment power. The element of risk leads to the conclusion that punishment power is used more strategically than is reward power (Molm, 2001).

However, in one study, Molm (1994) has suggested that the relative weakness and associated risk of punishment power may arise because it is not widely used, not because it is inherently less effective than reward power. Molm, Quist, and Wisely (1994) found that the use of punishment power is more likely to be perceived as fair when it is used by those who also have the power to reward but that it is likely to be perceived as unfair and therefore a weak reinforcer when partners are expecting rewards.

A More Integrative Exchange Theory

Cook, O'Brien, and Kollock (1990) define exchange theory in inherently integrative terms as being concerned with exchanges at various levels of analysis, including those among interconnected individuals, corporations, and nation-states. They identify two strands of work in the history of exchange—one at the micro level, focusing on social behavior as exchange, and the other at the more macro level, viewing social structure as exchange. They see the strength of exchange theory in micro-macro integration because "it includes within a single theoretical framework propositions that apply to individual actors as well as to the macro level (or systemic level) and it attempts to formulate explicitly the consequences of changes at one level for other levels of analysis" (Cook, O'Brien, and Kollock, 1990:175).

Cook, O'Brien, and Kollock identify three contemporary trends, all of which point toward a more integrative exchange theory. The first is the increasing use of field research focusing on more macroscopic issues, which can complement the traditional use of the laboratory experiment to study microscopic issues. Second, they note the shift in substantive work away from a focus on dyads and toward larger networks of exchange. Third, and most important, is the ongoing effort, discussed further below, to synthesize exchange theory and structural sociologies, especially network theory.

Along the way, Cook, O'Brien, and Kollock discuss the gains to be made from integrating insights from a variety of other micro theories. Decision theory offers "a better understanding of the way actors make choices relevant to transactions" (Cook, O'Brien, and Kollock, 1990:168). More generally, cognitive science (which includes cognitive anthropology and artificial intelligence) sheds "more light on the way in which actors perceive, process, and retrieve information" (Cook, O'Brien, and Kollock, 1990:168). Symbolic interactionism offers knowledge about how actors signal their intentions to one another, and this is important in the development of trust and commitment in exchange relationships. Most generally, they see their synthetic version of exchange theory as being well equipped to deal with the centrally important issue of the agency-structure relationship. In their view, "Exchange theory is one of a limited number of theoretical orientations in the social sciences that explicitly conceptualize purposeful actors in relation to structures" (Cook, O'Brien, and Kollock, 1990:172).

There are a number of recent examples of efforts by exchange theorists to synthesize their approach with other theoretical orientations. For example, Yamagishi and Cook (1993) have sought to integrate exchange theory with social dilemma theory (Yamagishi, 1995), a variant of rational choice theory. The social dilemma approach is derived from the famous dyadic concept of the prisoner's dilemma and the research on it: "A social dilemma is defined as a situation involving a particular type of incentive structure, such that (1) if all group members cooperate, all gain, whereas (2) for each individual it is more beneficial not to cooperate" (Yamagishi and Cook, 1993:236; Yamagishi, 2005). Without going into the details of their study, Yamagishi and Cook find that the nature of the exchange relationship and structure affects the way people deal with social dilemmas.

In another effort, Hegtvedt, Thompson, and Cook (1993) sought to integrate exchange theory with one approach that deals with cognitive processes: attribution theory. The integration with this theory gives exchange theory a mechanism to deal with the way people perceive and make attributions, and exchange theory compensates for the weakness in attribution theory in dealing with "the social structural antecedents and the behavioral consequences of attribution" (Hegtvedt, Thompson, and Cook, 1993:100). Thus, for example, the authors found support for the hypotheses that perceived power is related to one's structural power position and that those "who perceive themselves to have greater power are more likely to attribute their exchange outcomes to personal actions or interactions" (Hegtvedt, Thompson, and Cook, 1993:104). Although not fully supportive of the authors' hypotheses, this study points to the importance of studying the relationship between social structure, cognitive processes (perception and attribution), and behavior.

An important proposal was made by Meeker (1971) that would disconnect exchange theory from its reliance on rational choice theory and allow its integration with a variety of micro theories of agency. Meeker suggested that rationality be looked at as one type of exchange rule and that exchanges could be based on other exchange rules, such as altruism, competition, reciprocity, and status consistency.

In recent years, exchange theory has begun to move in a variety of new directions (Molm, 2001). First, there is increasing attention to the risk and uncertainty involved in exchange relationships (Kollock, 1994). For example, one actor may provide valuable outcomes for the other without receiving anything of value in return. Second, an interest in risk leads to a concern for trust in exchange relations. The issue is: Can one actor trust another to reciprocate when valued outcomes have been provided? Third, there is the related issue of actors reducing risk and increasing trust by developing a set of mutual commitments to one another (Molm, 1997). This, in turn, is linked to a fourth issue—increasing attention to affect and emotions in a theory that has been dominated by a focus on self-interested actors. Fifth, while much of recent exchange theory has focused on structure, there is increasing interest in fleshing out the nature and role of the actor in exchange relationships. In terms of issues in need of greater attention, Molm argues that exchange theory has tended to focus on exchange structures but needs to do more with change, or exchange dynamics. Finally, the new direction that has seen most attention in recent years has been the integration of exchange theory with network theory. We will come back to this network exchange theory after we have discussed network theory.

Network Theory

Network analysts (for example, Mizruchi, 2005; Wasserman and Faust, 1994; Wellman and Berkowitz, 1988/1997; Harrison White, 1992) take pains to differentiate their approach from what Ronald Burt calls "atomistic" and "normative" sociological approaches (Burt, 1982; see also Granovetter, 1985). Atomistic sociological orientations focus on actors making decisions in isolation from other actors. More generally, they focus on the "personal attributes" of actors (Wellman, 1983). Atomistic approaches are rejected because they are too microscopic and ignore relationships among actors. As Barry Wellman puts it, "Accounting for individual motives is a job better left to psychologists" (1983:163). This, of course, constitutes a rejection of a number of sociological theories that are in one way or another deeply concerned with motives.

In the view of network theorists, normative approaches focus on culture and the socialization process through which norms and values are internalized in actors. In the normative orientation, what holds people together are sets of shared ideas. Network theorists reject such a view and argue that one should focus on the objective pattern of ties linking the members of society (Mizruchi, 1994). Here is how Wellman articulates this view:

> Network analysts want to study regularities in how people and collectivities behave rather than regularities in beliefs about how they ought to behave. Hence network analysts try to avoid normative explanations of social behavior. They dismiss as non-structural any explanation that treats social process as the sum of individual actors' personal attributes and internalized norms.
>
> (Wellman, 1983:162)

Basic Concerns and Principles

Having made clear what it is not, network theory then clarifies its major concern—social relationships, or the objective pattern of ties linking the members (individual and collective) of society (Burt, 1992). Let us look at how Wellman articulates this focus:

> Network analysts start with the simple, but powerful, notion that the primary business of sociologists is to study social structure. . . . The most direct way to study a social structure is to analyze the pattern of ties linking its members. Network analysts search for deep structures—regular network patterns beneath the often complex surface of social systems. . . . Actors and their behavior are seen as constrained by these structures. Thus, the focus is not on voluntaristic actors, but on structural constraint.
>
> (Wellman, 1983:156–157)

One distinctive aspect of network theory is that it focuses on a wide range of micro to macro structures. That is, to network theory the actors may be people (Wellman and Wortley, 1990), but they also may be groups, corporations (W. Baker, 1990; Clawson, Neustadtl, and Bearden, 1986; Mizruchi and Koenig, 1986), and societies. Links occur at the large-scale, social-structural level as well as at more microscopic levels. Mark Granovetter describes such micro-level links as action "embedded" in "the concrete personal relations and structures (or 'networks') of such relations" (1985:490). Basic to any of these links is the idea that any "actor" (individual or collective) may have differential access to valued resources (wealth, power, information). The result is that structured systems tend to be stratified, with some components dependent on others.

One key aspect of network analysis is that it tends to move sociologists away from the study of social groups and social categories and toward the study of ties among and between actors that are not "sufficiently bounded and densely knit to be termed groups" (Wellman, 1983:169). A good example of this is Granovetter's (1973, 1983, 2005; Tindall and Malinick, 2007) work on "the strength of weak ties." Granovetter differentiates between "strong ties," for example, links between people and their close friends, and "weak ties," for example, links between people and mere acquaintances. Sociologists have tended to focus on people with strong ties or social groups. They have tended to regard strong ties as crucial, whereas weak ties have been thought of as being of little sociological importance. Granovetter's contribution is to make it clear that weak ties can be very important. For example, weak ties between two actors can serve as a bridge between two groups with strong internal ties. Without such a weak tie, the two groups might be totally isolated. This isolation, in turn, could lead to a more fragmented social system. An individual without weak ties would find himself or herself isolated in a tightly knit group and would lack information about what is going on in other groups as well as in the larger society. Weak ties therefore prevent isolation and allow individuals to be better integrated into the larger society. Although Granovetter emphasizes the importance of weak ties, he hastens to make it clear "that strong ties can also have value" (1983:209; see Bian, 1997). For example, people with strong ties have greater motivation to help one another and are more readily available to one another.

Network theory is relatively new and undeveloped. As Burt says, "There is currently a loose federation of approaches referenced as network analysis" (1982:20). But it is growing, as evidenced by the number of papers and books being published from a network perspective and the fact that there is a journal (*Social Networks*) devoted to it. Although it may be a loose conglomeration of work, network theory does seem to rest on a coherent set of principles (Wellman, 1983).

First, ties among actors usually are symmetrical in both content and intensity. Actors supply each other with different things, and they do this with greater or lesser intensity. Second, the ties among individuals must be analyzed within the context of the structure of larger networks. Third, the structuring of social ties leads to various kinds of nonrandom networks. On the one hand, networks are transitive: if there is a tie between A and B and between B and C, there is likely to be a tie between A and C. The result is that there is more likely to be a network involving A, B, and C. On the other hand, there are limits to how many links can exist and how intense they can be. The result is that network clusters with distinct boundaries separating one cluster from another are also likely to develop. Fourth, the existence of clusters leads to the fact that there can be cross-linkages between clusters as well as between individuals. Fifth, there are asymmetric ties among elements in a system, with the result that scarce resources are differentially distributed. Finally, the unequal distribution of scarce resources leads to both collaboration and competition. Some groups band together to acquire scarce resources collaboratively, whereas others compete and conflict over resources. Thus, network theory has a dynamic quality (Rosenthal et al., 1985), with the structure of the system changing with shifting patterns of coalition and conflict.

To take one example, Mizruchi (1990) is interested in the issue of the cohesion of corporations and its relationship to power. He argues that historically cohesion has been defined in two different ways. The first, or subjective view, is that "cohesion is a function of group members' feelings of identification with the group, in particular their feeling that their individual interests are bound up with the interests of the group" (Mizruchi, 1990:21). The emphasis here is on the normative system, and cohesion is produced either by the internalization of the normative system or by group pressure. The second, or objective, view is that "solidarity can be viewed as an objective, observable process independent of the sentiments of individuals" (Mizruchi, 1990:22). Needless to say, given his alignment with network theory, Mizruchi comes down on the side of the objective approach to cohesion.

Mizruchi sees similarity of behavior as a result not only of cohesion but also of what he calls *structural equivalence:* "Structurally equivalent actors are those with identical relations with other actors in the social structure" (1990:25). Thus, structural equivalence exists among, say, corporations, even though there may be no communication among them. They behave in the same way because they stand in the same relationship to some other entity in the social structure. Mizruchi concludes that structural equivalence plays at least as strong a role as cohesion in explaining similarity of behavior. Mizruchi accords great importance to structural equivalence, which, after all, implies a network of social relations.

A More Integrative Network Theory

Ronald Burt (1982) has been in the forefront of network theorists who have sought to develop an integrated approach instead of another form of structural determinism. Burt begins by articulating a schism within action theory between the "atomistic" and "normative" orientations. The atomistic orientation "assumes that alternative actions are evaluated independently by separate actors so that evaluations are made without reference to other actors," whereas the "normative perspective is defined by separate actors within a system having interdependent interests as social norms generated by actors socializing one another" (Burt, 1982:5).

Burt develops a perspective that "circumvents the schism between atomistic and normative action," one that "is less a synthesis of the existing two perspectives on action than it is a third view intellectually bridging the two views" (1982:8). Although he admittedly borrows from the other two perspectives, Burt develops what he calls a *structural perspective* that differs from the other two "in the criterion for the postulate of marginal evaluation. The criterion assumed by the proposed structural perspective is an actor's status/role-set as generated by the division of labor. An actor evaluates the utility of alternative actions partly in regard to his personal conditions and partly in regard to the conditions of others" (1982:8). He sees his approach as a logical extension of the atomistic approach and an "empirically accurate restriction" on normative theory.

Figure 11.1 depicts Burt's structural theory of action. According to Burt's description of the premise of a structural theory of action, "actors are purposive under social structural constraints" (1982:9; see also Mizruchi, 1994). In his view:

> Actors find themselves in a social structure. That social structure defines their
> social similarities, which in turn pattern their perceptions of the advantages to be
> had by taking each of several alternative actions. At the same time, social structure
> differentially constrains actors in their ability to take actions. Actions eventually
> taken are therefore a joint function of actors pursuing their interests to the limit
> of their ability where both interests and ability are patterned by social structure.
> Finally, actions taken under social structural constraint can modify social structure
> itself, and these modifications have the potential to create new constraints to be
> faced by actors within the structure.
>
> (Burt, 1982:9)

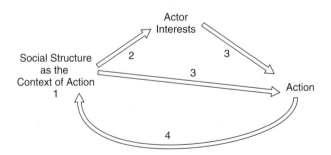

FIGURE 11.1 *Ronald Burt's Integrative Model*

Network Exchange Theory

Network exchange theory (Markovsky, 2005) combines social exchange theory and network analysis. The combination is assumed to preserve the advantages of both theories while remedying their deficiencies. On the one hand, network analysis has the advantage of being able to build complex representations of social interactions from simple, diagrammable models of social relations, but Cook and Whitmeyer (1992:123) argue that it has a deficient conception of exactly what the relation is. On the other hand, social exchange theory has the advantage of a simple model of actors who make choices based on possible benefits, but it is deficient because it sees social structures mainly as an outcome of individual choices rather than a determinant of those choices. To put it more simply, network theory has a strong model of structure (networks of relations) but a vague model of what the relations consist of, whereas exchange theory has a strong model of the relations between actors (exchanges) but a weak model of the social structures within which they operate. Social exchange theory's model of the actor exchanging in order to increase benefits provides the content that network analysis is lacking, and network analysis provides the model of social structure as an independent variable that exchange theory is lacking.

The fundamental idea behind network exchange theory is that any social exchange occurs in the context of larger networks of social exchanges. What is being exchanged is less important in this approach than the various sizes, shapes, and connections of the networks within which these exchanges occur. Like social exchange, network exchange theory focuses primarily on the issue of power. A basic premise is that the more opportunities an actor has for exchange, the greater the actor's power is. It is assumed that these opportunities for exchange are directly related to the structure of the network. As a result of their position in the network, actors vary in their opportunities to exchange benefits and therefore in their ability to control or accumulate benefits.

Emerson (1972a, 1972b) initiated the research on social exchange networks when he concluded that social exchange theory was limited by its focus on two-person, or dyadic, exchange relations. By treating those relations as interconnected, Emerson moved toward seeing exchange as being embedded in larger network structures. Emerson's (1972b:58) original intent was to develop "a theory of social exchange in which social structure is taken as the dependent variable." However, his research soon demonstrated that social structure also could be an independent variable; in other words, not only was structure determined by exchange relations, exchange relations were determined by social structures.

Yamagishi, Gillmore, and Cook (1988) went further by linking exchange theory and network theory. They argued that power is central to exchange theory but that power cannot be studied meaningfully in the dyad. Rather, power "is fundamentally a social structural phenomenon" (Yamagishi, Gillmore, and Cook, 1988:834). A fully adequate theory must combine an analysis of exchange relations with an analysis of the linkages between exchange relations. To do this, they built on Emerson's idea of positively and negatively linked exchanges to generate predictions about the distribution of power in networks.

In a subsequent article, Cook and Whitmeyer (1992) more rigorously examined the possibility of combining exchange theory and network analysis. They looked at the compatibilities between the two approaches' views of actors and their views of structure. They concluded that the two theories' views of actors were essentially the same, because virtually all exchange theories explicitly and most network analyses implicitly assume that actors are rationally pursuing the maximization of their self-interest in whatever way they define it. They also noted a great deal of similarity in the two approaches' view of structure. The main difference is that exchange theory sees the social relations that constitute the structure only in terms of actual exchanges, whereas network analysis is inclined to include any kind of relation, whether exchange is believed to occur or not.

It is this difference in their definitions of a relation that constitutes the essential difference between an exchange network (Friedkin, 2005) and the kind of network of interest to network analysis. Network exchange theorists are interested only in relations of exchange, whereas network theorists are interested in many types of relations. As an example, many network studies focus on "centrality." This might mean the advantage of being linked to many different people. According to network exchange theorists, just being "linked" is not enough; the relations must be ones of exchange. Thus, in the earlier example of Abe, Bill, and Cathy, Bill is "central," according to network exchange, only if Abe and Bill as well as Bill and Cathy have some sort of exchange and, in addition, one dyad's exchanges have some sort of effect on the other's exchanges. In contrast, for network analysis, it is enough if they are linked, and the precise nature of the link is irrelevant.

Structural Power

One of the reasons for linking exchange theory and network analysis was to be able to move beyond an analysis of power within dyadic relations and be able to analyze the distribution of power in the network as a whole. This has become one of the most important topics in contemporary network exchange theory. In one of the first attempts to look at the distribution of power in a network, Cook and her colleagues (1983) developed a theory of "vulnerability." They argued that the determination of the power of a position is based on the amount of dependence of the entire structure on that position. In their view, this systemwide dependence is a function of both the structural centrality of the position and the nature of power-dependence relationships. In other words, vulnerability involves the networkwide dependence on a particular structural position.

Another important attempt to look at the distribution of power in networks was developed by Markovsky, Willer, and their colleagues (Markovsky, Willer, and Patton, 1988; Willer and Patton, 1987). This approach has become so influential that it usually goes by the name of *network exchange theory* (Markovsky, 2005), often abbreviated as NET. The theory assumes that power is determined by the structure of the network, in particular the availability of alternative connections among actors. The theory uses a graph-theoretical power index (GPI) based on counting alternative network paths and a resistance model based on actors' expectations about outcomes to predict relative power in networks.

Strong and Weak Power Structures

NET distinguishes between two types of networks—strong and weak power—based on whether actors can be excluded from exchanges. Strong power networks include some actors who must be excluded (low power actors) and other actors who cannot be excluded (high power actors). For example, in a company, the decision about whom to promote to a higher position can be looked at as an exchange. The higher position is exchanged for the work done for the boss who can grant the higher position. If we assume that there is only one boss and there are many competitors for the position, we would have a strong power network. The boss cannot be excluded from the exchange, whereas all but one of the competitors must be. The theory predicts that high power actors in strong power networks will obtain virtually all the available resources. In this case, the competitors will be motivated to provide whatever work the boss demands. However, if we introduce another boss into the network who also can promote a competitor, the theory predicts that both bosses would have much less power because the competitors for the promotion would now have an alternative for exchange.

The introduction of a second boss would make this a weak power structure. In weak power structures, all positions are vulnerable to exclusions. The presence of Boss 2 means that Boss 1 can be excluded from the exchange. Competitors therefore can perform services for a boss who will promote them while demanding the least amount of work in exchange. In weak power networks, positions may have different possibilities for exclusion. Let us say that there are twenty competitors for the promotion and only two bosses. This makes a given competitor more likely to be excluded than a given boss. The theory predicts that positions less likely to be excluded (bosses) benefit proportionally more than do positions more likely to be excluded (competitors).

One of the great advantages of linking exchange theory to network analysis is the expanded view of agency. Network analysis has tended to downplay agency and concentrate on descriptions of the properties of given structures. Exchange theory has a model of a rational self-interested agent, but this model has disregarded the power of agents to change structure to enhance their bargaining positions. Leik (1992) has used network exchange theory to examine actor's "strategic manipulation of network linkages." This suggests that low power positions, such as the competitors for the promotion, may seek out other sources of promotion in order to enhance their position, while "high power actors prefer to isolate those dependent on them" (Leik, 1992:316).

One other, more ambiguous characteristic of network exchange theory should be mentioned: its propensity for laboratory experiments. Most of the theory's developments have been driven by experiments with test subjects in controlled laboratory conditions. It is, of course, a great advantage to be able to test theories under controlled conditions, and the rarity of this situation in sociology is often a source of embarrassment. However, in order to isolate relevant characteristics, these laboratory conditions have been extremely artificial. Even in laboratories, the theory's predictions are obviated if subjects are allowed to know the unequal effects of their exchanges because normative considerations interfere (Molm, 2001:264). This means that experimental results must be interpreted carefully when applied to social interactions outside the laboratory. Furthermore, the artificial conditions of the laboratory can encourage an artificial theory. As Willer (1999:289) points out, "When an established experimental paradigm governs what will and will not be investigated, theory development becomes one-sided and research focuses on issues that have no importance or no known importance outside the laboratory." As an example Willer cites the intense interest in weak power networks. "No one has studied weak power networks in the field. Therefore, their empirical significance, even their empirical existence, is not known" (Willer, 1999:290).

Rational Choice Theory

Although it influenced the development of exchange theory, rational choice theory was generally marginal to mainstream sociological theory (Hechter and Kanazawa, 1997). It is largely through the efforts of one man, James S. Coleman, that rational choice theory has become one of the "hot" theories in contemporary sociology (Heckathorn, 2005; Chriss, 1995; Lindenberg, 2000; Tilly, 1997). For one thing, in 1989 Coleman founded a journal, *Rationality and Society,* devoted to the dissemination of work from a rational choice perspective. For another, Coleman (1990) published an enormously influential book, *Foundations of Social Theory,* based on this perspective. Finally, Coleman became president of the American Sociological Association in 1992 and used that forum to push rational choice theory and to present an address entitled "The Rational Reconstruction of Society" (Coleman, 1993b).

Since we have outlined the basic tenets of rational choice theory, it would be useful to begin with Coleman's (1989) introductory comments to the first issue of *Rationality and Society.* The journal was to be interdisciplinary because rational choice theory (or, as Coleman calls it, "the paradigm of rational action" [1989:5]) is the only theory with the possibility of producing paradigmatic integration. Coleman does not hesitate to argue that the approach operates from a base in methodological individualism and to use rational choice theory as the micro-level base for the explanation of macro-level phenomena. Even more interesting is what Coleman's approach does not find "congenial":

> work that is methodologically holistic, floating at the system level without recourse to the actors whose actions generate that system . . . the view of action as purely expressive, the view of action as irrational, and also the view of action as something wholly caused by outside forces without the intermediation of intention or purpose. It excludes that empirical work widely carried out in social science in which individual behavior is "explained" by certain factors or determinants without any model of action whatsoever.

> (Coleman, 1989:6)

Thus, a large portion of work in sociology is excluded from the pages of *Rationality and Society.* Not to be excluded, however, are macro-level concerns and their linkage to rational action. Beyond such academic concerns, Coleman wants work done from a rational choice perspective to have practical relevance to our changing social world. For example, Heckathorn and Broadhead (1996) have examined the issue of public policies aimed at AIDS prevention from a rational choice perspective.

Foundations of Social Theory

Coleman argues that sociology should focus on social systems but that such macro phenomena must be explained by factors internal to them, prototypically individuals. He favors working at this level for several reasons, including the fact that data usually are gathered at the individual level and then aggregated or composed to yield the system level. Among the other reasons for favoring a focus on the individual level is that this is where "interventions" ordinarily are made to create social changes. As we will see, central to Coleman's perspective is the idea that social theory is not merely an academic exercise but should affect the social world through such "interventions."

Given his focus on the individual, Coleman recognizes that he is a method-ological individualist, although he sees his particular perspective as a "special variant" of that orientation. His view is special in the sense that it accepts the idea of emer-gence and that while it focuses on factors internal to the system, those factors are not necessarily individual actions and orientations. That is, micro-level phenomena other than individuals can be the focus of his analysis.

Coleman's rational choice orientation is clear in his basic idea that "persons act purposively toward a goal, with the goal (and thus the actions) shaped by values or preferences" (1990:13). But Coleman (1990:14) then goes on to argue that for most theoretical purposes, he will need a more precise conceptualization of the rational actor derived from economics, one that sees the actors choosing those actions that will maximize utility, or the satisfaction of their needs and wants.

There are two key elements in his theory—actors and resources. Resources are those things over which actors have control and in which they have some interest. Given these two elements, Coleman details how their interaction leads to the system level:

> A minimal basis for a social system of action is two actors, each having control
> over resources of interest to the other. It is each one's interest in resources under
> the other's control that leads the two, as purposive actors, to engage in actions that
> involve each other . . . a system of action. . . . It is this structure, together with
> the fact that the actors are purposive, each having the goal of maximizing the
> realization of his interests, that gives the interdependence, or systemic character, to
> their actions.
>
> (Coleman, 1990:29)

Although he has faith in rational choice theory, Coleman does not believe that this perspective, at least as yet, has all the answers. But it is clear that he believes that it can move in that direction, since he argues that the "success of a social theory based on rationality lies in successively diminishing that domain of social activity that cannot be accounted for by the theory" (Coleman, 1990:18).

Coleman recognizes that in the real world people do not always behave rationally, but he feels that this makes little difference in his theory: "My implicit assumption is that the theoretical predictions made here will be substantively the same whether the

JAMES S. COLEMAN

A Biographical Sketch

James S. Coleman had a remarkably varied career in sociology; the label "theorist" is only one of several that can be applied to him. He received his Ph.D. from Columbia University in 1955 (on the importance of the Columbia "school" to his work, see Swedberg, 1996), and a year later he began his academic career as an assistant professor at the University of Chicago (to which he returned in 1973, after a fourteen-year stay at Johns Hopkins University, and where he remained until his death). In the same year that he began teaching at Chicago, Coleman was the junior author (with Seymour Martin Lipset and Martin A. Trow) of one of the landmark studies in the history of industrial sociology, if not sociology as a whole, *Union Democracy* (1956). (Coleman's doctoral dissertation at Columbia, directed by Lipset, dealt with some of the issues examined in *Union Democracy*.) Coleman then turned his attention to research on youth and education, the culmination of which was a landmark federal government report (it came to be widely known as the "Coleman Report") that helped lead to the highly controversial policy of busing as a method for achieving racial equality in American schools. It is through this work that Coleman has had a greater practical impact than any other American sociologist. Next, Coleman turned his attention from the practical world to the rarefied atmosphere of mathematical sociology (especially *Introduction to Mathematical Sociology* [1964] and *The Mathematics of Collective Action* [1973]; see Jasso, 2011 for a review of the theoretical relevance of this work). In later years, Coleman turned to sociological theory, especially rational choice theory, in the publication of the book *Foundations of Social Theory* (1990) and the founding in 1989 of the journal *Rationality and Society*. The body of work mentioned here reflects almost unbelievable diversity, and it does not even begin to scratch the surface of the 28 books and 301 articles listed on Coleman's résumé.

Coleman received a B.S. from Purdue University in 1949 and worked as a chemist for Eastman Kodak before he entered the famous department of sociology at Columbia University in 1951. One key influence on Coleman was the theorist Robert Merton (see Chapter 7), especially his lectures on Durkheim and the social determinants of individual behavior. Another influence was the famous methodologist Paul Lazarsfeld, from whom Coleman derived his lifelong interest in quantitative methods and mathematical sociology. The third important influence was Seymour Martin Lipset, whose research team Coleman joined, thereby ultimately participating in the production of the landmark study *Union Democracy*. Thus, Coleman's graduate training gave him a powerful introduction to theory, methods, and their linkage in empirical research. This was, and is, the model for all aspiring sociologists.

On the basis of these experiences, Coleman described his "vision" for sociology when he left graduate school and embarked on his professional career:

> Sociology . . . should have the social system (whether a small system or a large one) as its unit of analysis, rather than the individual; but it should use quantitative methods, leaving behind the unsystematic techniques which lend themselves to investigator bias, fail to lend themselves to replication, and often lack an explanatory or causation focus. Why did I, and other students at Columbia at the time, have this vision? I believe it was the unique combination of Robert K. Merton and Paul Lazarsfeld.
>
> (Coleman, 1994:30–31)

Looking back from the vantage point of the mid-1990s, Coleman found that his approach had changed, but not as much as he had assumed. For example, with respect to his work on social simulation games at Johns Hopkins in the 1960s he said that they "led me to change my theoretical orientation from one in which properties of the system are not only determinants of action (à la Emile Durkheim's Suicide study), to one in which they are also consequences of actions sometimes intended, sometimes unintended" (Coleman, 1994:33). Thus, Coleman needed a theory of action, and he chose, in common with most economists,

> the simplest such foundation, that of rational, or if you prefer, purposive action. The most formidable task of sociology is the development of a theory that will move from the micro level of action to the macro level of norms, social values, status distribution, and social conflict.
>
> (Coleman, 1994:33)

It is this interest that explains why Coleman was drawn to economics:

> What distinguishes economics from the other social sciences is not its use of "rational choice" but its use of a mode of analysis that allows moving between the level of individual action and the level of system functioning. By making two assumptions, that persons act rationally and that markets are perfect with full communication, economic analysis is able to link the macro level of system functioning with the micro level of individual actions.
>
> (Coleman, 1994:32)

Another aspect of Coleman's vision for sociology, consistent with his early work on schools, is that it be applicable to social policy. Of theory he said, "One of the criteria for judging work in social theory is its potential usefulness for informing social policy" (Coleman, 1994:33). Few sociologists would disagree with Coleman's goal of linking theory, methods, and social policy, although many would disagree with at least some of the ways in which Coleman chose to link them. Whether or not they agree with the specifics, future sociologists will continue to be challenged by the need to do a better job of linking these three key aspects of sociological practice, and at least some of them will find in the work of James Coleman a useful model.

James Coleman died on March 25, 1995 (J. Clark, 1996; Lindenberg, 2005; Marsden, 2007).

actors act precisely according to rationality as commonly conceived or deviate in the ways that have been observed" (1990:506; Inbar, 1996).

Given his orientation to individual rational action, it follows that Coleman's focus in terms of the micro-macro issue is the micro-to-macro linkage, or how the combination of individual actions brings about the behavior of the system. Although he accords priority to this issue, Coleman also is interested in the macro-to-micro linkage, or how the system constrains the orientations of actors. Finally, he evinces an interest in the micro-micro aspect of the relationship, or the impact of individual actions on other individual actions.

In spite of this seeming balance, there are at least three major weaknesses in Coleman's approach. First, he accords overwhelming priority to the micro-to-macro issue, thereby giving short shrift to the other relationships. Second, he ignores the macro-macro issue. Finally, his causal arrows go in only one direction; in other words, he ignores the dialectical relationship among and between micro and macro phenomena.

Utilizing his rational choice approach, Coleman explains a series of macro-level phenomena. His basic position is that theorists need to keep their conceptions of the actor constant and generate from those micro-constants various images of macro-level phenomena. In this way, differences in macro phenomena can be traced to different structures of relations at the macro level and not to variations at the micro level.

A key step in the micro-to-macro movement is the granting of the authority and rights possessed by one individual to another. This action tends to lead to the subordination of one actor to another. More important, it creates the most basic macro phenomenon—an acting unit consisting of two people, rather than two independent actors. The resulting structure functions independently of the actors. Instead of maximizing his or her own interests, in this instance an actor seeks to realize the interests of another actor, or of the independent collective unit. Not only is this a different social reality, it is one that "has special deficiencies and generates special problems" (Coleman, 1990:145). Given his applied orientation, Coleman is interested in the diagnosis and solution of these problems.

Collective Behavior

One example of Coleman's approach to dealing with macro phenomena is the case of collective behavior (Zablocki, 1996). He chooses to deal with collective behavior because its often disorderly and unstable character is thought to be hard to analyze from a rational choice perspective. But Coleman's view is that rational choice theory can explain all types of macro phenomena, not just those that are orderly and stable. What is involved in moving from the rational actor to "the wild and turbulent systemic functioning called collective behavior is a simple (and rational) transfer of control over one's actions to another actor . . . made unilaterally, not as part of an exchange" (Coleman, 1990:198).

Why do people unilaterally transfer control over their actions to others? The answer, from a rational choice perspective, is that they do this in an attempt to maximize their utility. Normally, individual maximization involves a balancing of control among several actors, and this produces equilibrium within society. However, in the case of collective behavior, because there is a unilateral transfer of control, individual maximization does not necessarily lead to system equilibrium. Instead, there is the disequilibrium characteristic of collective behavior.

Norms

Another macro-level phenomenon that comes under Coleman's scrutiny is norms. Most sociologists take norms as given and invoke them to explain individual behavior, but they do not explain why and how norms come into existence. Coleman wonders how, in a group of rational actors, norms can emerge and be maintained. Coleman argues that norms are initiated and maintained by some people who see benefits resulting from the observation of norms and harm stemming from the violation of those norms. People are willing to give up some control over their own behavior, but in the process they gain some control (through norms) over the behavior of others. Coleman summarizes his position on norms:

> The central element of this explanation . . . is the giving up of partial rights of
> control over one's own action and the receiving of partial rights of control over the
> actions of others, that is, the emergence of a norm. The end result is that control . . .
> which was held by each alone, becomes widely distributed over the whole set of
> actors, who exercise that control.

> (Coleman, 1990:292)

Once again, people are seen as maximizing their utility by partially surrendering rights of control over themselves and gaining partial control over others. Because the transfer of control is not unilateral, there is equilibrium in the case of norms.

But there are also circumstances in which norms act to the advantage of some people and the disadvantage of others. In some cases, actors surrender the right to control their own actions to those who initiate and maintain the norms. Such norms become effective when a consensus emerges that some people have the right to control (through norms) the actions of other people. Furthermore, the effectiveness of norms depends on the ability to enforce that consensus. It is consensus and enforcement that prevent the kind of disequilibrium characteristic of collective behavior.

Coleman recognizes that norms become interrelated, but he sees such a macro issue as beyond the scope of his work on the foundations of social systems. However, he is willing to take on the micro issue of the internalization of norms. He recognizes that in discussing internalization he is entering "waters that are treacherous for a theory grounded in rational choice" (Coleman, 1990:292). He sees the internalization of norms as the establishment of an internal sanctioning system; people sanction themselves when they violate a norm. Coleman looks at this in terms of the idea of one actor or set of actors endeavoring to control others by having norms internalized in them. Thus, it is in the interests of one set of actors to have another set internalize norms and be controlled by them. He feels that this is rational "when such attempts can be effective at reasonable cost" (Coleman, 1990:294).

Coleman looks at norms from the point of view of the three key elements of his theory—micro to macro, purposive action at the micro level, and macro to micro. Norms are macro-level phenomena that come into existence on the basis of micro-level purposive action. Once in existence, norms, through sanctions or the threat of sanctions, affect the actions of individuals. Certain actions may be encouraged, while others are discouraged.

The Corporate Actor

With the case of norms, Coleman has moved to the macro level, and he continues his analysis at this level in a discussion of the corporate actor (J. Clark, 1996). Within such a collectivity, actors may not act in terms of their self-interest but must act in the interest of the collectivity.

There are various rules and mechanisms for moving from individual choice to collective (social) choice. The simplest is the case of voting and the procedures for tabulating the individual votes and coming up with a collective decision. This is the micro-to-macro dimension, whereas such things as the slate of candidates proposed by the collectivity involve the macro-to-micro linkage.

Coleman argues that both corporate actors and human actors have purposes. Furthermore, within a corporate structure such as an organization, human actors may pursue purposes of their own that are at variance with corporate purposes. This conflict of interest helps us understand the sources of revolts against corporate authority. The micro-to-macro linkage here involves the ways in which people divest authority from the corporate structure and vest legitimacy in those engaged in the revolt. But there is also a macro-to-micro linkage in that certain macro-level conditions lead people to such acts of divestment and investment.

As a rational choice theorist, Coleman starts with the individual and with the idea that all rights and resources exist at this level. The interests of individuals determine the course of events. However, this is untrue, especially in modern society, where "a large fraction of rights and resources, and therefore sovereignty, may reside in corporate actors" (Coleman, 1990:531). In the modern world corporate actors have taken on increasing importance. The corporate actor may act to the benefit or the harm of the individual. How are we to judge the corporate actor in this regard? Coleman contends that "only by starting conceptually from a point where all sovereignty rests with individual persons is it possible to see just how well their ultimate interests are realized by any existing social system. The postulate that individual persons are sovereign provides a way in which sociologists may evaluate the functioning of social systems" (1990:531–532).

To Coleman, the key social change has been the emergence of corporate actors to complement "natural person" actors. Both may be considered actors because they have "control over resources and events, interests in resources and events, and the capability of taking actions to realize those interests through that control" (Coleman, 1990:542). Of course, there have always been corporate actors, but the old ones, such as the family, are steadily being replaced by new, purposively constructed, freestanding corporate actors. The existence of these new corporate actors raises the issue of how to ensure their social responsibility. Coleman suggests that we can do this by instituting internal reforms or by changing the external structure, such as the laws affecting such corporate actors or the agencies that regulate them.

Coleman differentiates between primordial structures based on the family, such as neighborhoods and religious groups, and purposive structures, such as economic organizations and the government. He sees a progressive "unbundling" of the activities that once were tied together within the family. The primordial structures are "unraveling" as their functions are being dispersed and being taken over by a range of corporate actors. Coleman is concerned about this unraveling as well as about the fact that we are now forced to deal with positions in purposive structures rather than with the people who populated primordial structures. He thus concludes that the goal of his work is "providing the foundation for constructing a viable social structure, as the primordial structure on which persons have depended vanishes" (Coleman, 1990:652).

Coleman is critical of most of social theory for adopting a view that he labels *homo sociologicus.* This perspective emphasizes the socialization process and the close fit between the individual and society. Therefore, *homo sociologicus* is unable to deal with the freedom of individuals to act as they will in spite of the constraints placed upon them. Furthermore, this perspective lacks the ability to evaluate the actions of the social system. In contrast, *homo economicus,* in Coleman's view, possesses all these capacities. In addition, Coleman attacks traditional social theory for doing little more than chanting old theoretical mantras and for being irrelevant to the changes taking place in society and incapable of helping us know where society is headed. Sociological theory (as well as sociological research) must have a purpose, a role in the functioning of society. Coleman is in favor of social theory that is interested not just in knowledge for the sake of knowledge but also in "a search for knowledge for the reconstruction of society" (1990:651).

Coleman's views on social theory are closely linked to his views on the changing nature of society. The passing of primordial structures and their replacement by purposive structures have left a series of voids that have not been filled adequately by the new social organizations. Social theory and the social sciences more generally are made necessary by the need to reconstruct a new society (Coleman, 1993a, 1993b; Bulmer, 1996). The goal is not to destroy purposive structures but rather to realize the opportunities and avoid the problems of such structures. The new society requires a new social science. The linkages among institutional areas have changed, and as a result the social sciences must be willing to cut across traditional disciplinary boundaries.

Criticisms

Needless to say, rational choice theory in general (Goldfield and Gilbert, 1997; D. Green and Shapiro, 1994; Imber, 1997) has come under heavy fire in sociology. In fact, as Heckathorn (1997:15) points out, there is a kind of "hysteria" in some quarters of sociology about rational choice theory. James Coleman's work has been attacked from many quarters (Alexander, 1992; Rambo, 1995). For example, Tilly (1997:83) offers the following basic criticisms of Coleman's theory:

1. Neglected to specify causal mechanisms.
2. Promoted an incomplete and therefore misleading psychological reductionism.
3. Advocated a form of general theory—rational choice analysis—that has for some time been enticing social scientists into blind alleys, where they have wandered aimlessly, falling victim to local thugs and confidence men selling various brands of individual reductionism.

More generally, some researchers have found rational choice theory wanting (Weakliem and Heath, 1994), but the vast majority of the criticisms have come from supporters of alternative positions within sociology (Wrong, 1997). For example, given his macro-structural position, Blau (1997) argues that sociology should focus on macro-level phenomena, and as a result, the explanation of individual behavior that is the metier of rational choice theory falls outside the bounds of sociology.

Rational choice theory has been criticized from many quarters for being overly ambitious, for seeking to replace all other theoretical perspectives. Thus, Donald Green and Ian Shapiro (1994:203) argue that rational choice theory would do well "to probe the limits of what rational choice can explain" and to "relinquish the . . . tendency to ignore, absorb, or discredit competing theoretical accounts."

From a feminist point of view, England and Kilbourne (1990) have criticized the assumption of selfishness in rational choice theory; from their perspective selfishness-altruism should be considered as a variable. The assumption of selfishness represents a masculine bias. They recognize that rejecting this assumption, and looking at it as a variable, would reduce the "deductive determinacy" of rational choice theory, but they think the benefits of such a more realistic, less-biased theoretical orientation outweigh the costs.

From a symbolic-interactionist perspective, Denzin (1990b; see also Chapter 9 of this book) offers just the critique one might expect from such a diametrically opposed theoretical orientation:

> Rational choice theory . . . fails to offer a convincing answer to the question: How is society possible? . . . its ideal norms of rationality do not fit everyday life and the norms of rationality and emotionality that organize the actual activities of interacting individuals.
>
>   Rational choice theory has limited utility for contemporary social theory. Its scheme of group life and its picture of the human being, of action, interaction, the self, gender, emotionality, power, language, the political economy of everyday life, and of history, are woefully narrow and completely inadequate *for interpretive purposes.*
>   (Denzin, 1990a:182–183; italics added)

Most of those operating from a broadly interpretive perspective would accept Denzin's strong criticisms of rational choice theory.

In addition to general criticisms, rational choice theory has been attacked for underplaying or ignoring things such as culture (Fararo, 1996) and chance events (G. Hill, 1997).

Finally, although many other criticisms could be delineated, we might mention Smelser's (1992) argument that like many other theoretical perspectives, rational choice theory has degenerated as a result of internal evolution or responses to external criticisms. Thus, rational choice theory has become tautological and invulnerable to falsifiability, and most important, it has developed the "capacity to explain everything and hence nothing" (Smelser, 1992:400).

Rational choice theory has many supporters (Hedstrom and Swedberg, 1996). We will see many efforts to legitimize it further as a sociological theory and even more attempts to apply and extend the theory. We also are likely to see a further escalation of the criticisms leveled at rational choice theory.

Summary

This chapter deals with three interrelated theories that, among other things, share a positivistic orientation. Modern exchange theory has evolved out of a series of intellectual influences, especially behaviorism and rational choice theory. The founder of modern exchange theory is George Homans. His reductionistic, determinedly micro-oriented exchange theory is summarized in a small number of propositions. Blau sought to extend exchange theory to the macro level, primarily by emphasizing the importance of norms. Much of the contemporary work in exchange theory has been influenced by Richard Emerson's more structural effort to develop an integrative, micro-macro approach to exchange. Emerson's disciples, and others, are busy extending his theoretical perspective into a variety of new domains.

One of Emerson's concerns is with networks, a concern also of those associated with network theory. Although there are many overlaps between exchange theory and network theory, many network theorists operate outside an exchange framework. Network theory is distinguished by its focus on the objective pattern of ties within and between micro and macro levels of social reality.

Network exchange theory combines social exchange theory and network analysis in order to focus on the distribution of power in a network of exchange. It looks at the way in which the structures themselves can be said to be strong or weak.

Thanks largely to the efforts of James Coleman, rational choice theory, which had played a role in the development of exchange theory, has come into its own as a theoretical perspective. Utilizing a few basic principles derived largely from economics, rational choice theory purports to be able to deal with micro- and macro-level issues, as well as the role played by micro-level factors in the formation of macro-level phenomena. The number of supporters of rational choice theory is increasing in sociology, but so is the resistance to it by those who support other theoretical perspectives.

Contemporary Feminist Theory

Patricia Madoo Lengermann
The George Washington University

Gillian Niebrugge
American University

Chapter Outline

Feminism's Basic Questions

Historical Framing: Feminism, Sociology, and Gender

Varieties of Contemporary Feminist Theory

Feminist Sociological Theorizing

Feminist theory is a generalized, wide-ranging system of ideas about social life and human experience developed from a woman-centered perspective. Feminist theory is woman-centered—or women-centered—in two ways. First, the starting point of all its investigation is the situation (or the situations) and experiences of women in society. Second, it seeks to describe the social world from the distinctive vantage points of women. Feminist theory differs from most sociological theories in that it is the work of an interdisciplinary and international community of scholars, artists, and activists.[1] Feminist sociologists seek to broaden and deepen sociology by reworking disciplinary knowledge to take account of discoveries being made by this interdisciplinary community.

The chapter begins with an outline of the basic questions guiding feminist scholarship, followed by a brief history of the relation between feminism and sociology. It then describes the various types of contemporary feminist theory, emphasizing the contributions of sociologists to those theories. It concludes with an integrated statement of the feminist sociological thinking developing out of these various theoretical traditions.

Feminism's Basic Questions

The impetus for contemporary feminist theory begins in a deceptively simple question: *"And what about the women?"* In other words, where are the women in any situation being investigated? If they are not present, why? If they are present, what

---

[1] This chapter draws primarily on the English-language contribution to this international effort.

exactly are they doing? How do they experience the situation? What do they contribute to it? What does it mean to them?

In response to this question, feminist scholarship has produced some generalizable answers. Women are present in most social situations. Where they are not, it is not because they lack ability or interest but because there have been deliberate efforts to exclude them. Where they have been present, women have played roles very different from the popular conception of them (as, for example, passive wives and mothers). Indeed, as wives and as mothers and in a series of other roles, women, along with men, have actively created the situations being studied. Yet though women are actively present in most social situations, scholars, publics, and social actors themselves, both male and female, have been blind to their presence. Moreover, women's roles in most social situations, though essential, have been different from, less privileged than, and subordinate to the roles of men. Their invisibility is only one indicator of this inequality.

Feminism's second basic question is: *"Why is all this as it is?"* In answering this question, feminist theory has produced a general social theory with broad implications for sociology. One of feminist sociological theory's major contributions to answering this question has been the development of the concept of *gender.* Beginning in the 1970s, feminist theorists made it possible for people to see the distinctions between (a) biologically determined attributes associated with male and female and (b) the socially learned behaviors associated with masculinity and femininity. They did so by designating the latter as "gender."[2] The essential qualities of gender remain a point of theoretical debate in feminism, and these debates offer one way to distinguish among some of the varieties of feminist theory. But a starting point of agreement among nearly all varieties of feminist theory is an understanding of gender as a social construction, something not emanating from nature but created by people as part of the processes of group life.

As the circle of feminists exploring these questions became more inclusive of people of diverse backgrounds both in the United States and internationally, feminist theorists raised a third question: *"And what about the differences among women?"* The answers to this question lead to a general conclusion that the invisibility, inequality, and role differences in relation to men that generally characterize women's lives are profoundly affected by a woman's social location—that is, by her class, race, age, affectional preference, marital status, religion, ethnicity, and global location.

The fourth question for all feminists is: *"How can we change and improve the social world so as to make it a more just place for all people?"* This commitment to social transformation in the interest of justice is the distinctive characteristic of critical social theory, as Patricia Hill Collins (1998:xiv) explains, "Critical social theory encompasses bodies of knowledge . . . that actively grapple with the central questions

---

[2] The word *gender* has origins as early as the fourteenth century when it was used interchangeably with *sex* but especially in discussion of grammar (whether a noun is understood as masculine or feminine). *Gender* is used occasionally in early sociology articles of the 1900s but in a sense interchangeable with *sex.* The first feminist sociological conceptualization of the distinction between biologically determined attributes and socially learned behaviors was made by Charlotte Perkins Gilman in her 1898 classic *Women and Economics*, where she created the concept of *excessive sex distinction* to refer to what we now mean by *gender.*

facing groups of people differently placed in specific political, social, and historic contexts characterized by injustice." This commitment is practiced in sociology by feminism, Marxism, neo-Marxism, and social theories being developed by racial and ethnic minorities and in postcolonial societies. But today, after more than five decades of activism and genuine material gains, feminist social theorists are confronting the question emerging from a record of victories and defeats: *"How—and why—does gender inequality persist in the modern world?"* (Ridgeway, 2011).

But feminist theory is not just about women, nor is its major project the creation of a middle-range theory of gender relations. Rather, the appropriate parallel for feminism's major theoretical achievement is to one of Marx's epistemological accomplishments. Marx showed that the knowledge people had of society, what they assumed to be an absolute and universal statement about reality, in fact reflected the experience of those who economically and politically ruled the world; he effectively demonstrated that one also could view the world from the vantage point of the world's workers. This insight relativized ruling-class knowledge and, in allowing us to juxtapose that knowledge with knowledge gained from the workers' perspective, vastly expanded our ability to analyze social reality. More than a century after Marx's death we are still assimilating the implications of this discovery.

Feminism's basic theoretical questions have similarly produced a revolutionary switch in our understanding of the world: what we have taken as universal and absolute knowledge of the world is, in fact, knowledge derived from the experiences of a powerful section of society, men as "masters." That knowledge is relativized if we rediscover the world from the vantage point of a hitherto invisible, unacknowledged "underside": women, who in subordinated but indispensable "serving" roles have worked to sustain and re-create the society we live in. This discovery raises questions about everything we thought we knew about society, and its implications constitute the essence of contemporary feminist theory's significance for sociological theory.

Feminist theory deconstructs established systems of knowledge by showing their masculinist bias and the gender politics framing and informing them. To say that knowledge is "deconstructed" is to say that we discover what was hitherto hidden behind the presentation of the knowledge as established, singular, and natural— namely, that that presentation is a construction resting on social, relational, and power arrangements. But feminism itself has become the subject of relativizing and deconstructionist pressures from within its own theoretical boundaries. The first and more powerful of these pressures comes from women confronting the white, privileged-class, heterosexual status of many leading feminists—that is, from women of color, women in postcolonial societies, working-class women, and lesbians. These women, speaking from "margin to center" (hooks, 1984), show that there are many differently situated women, and that there are many women-centered knowledge systems that oppose both established, male-stream knowledge claims and any hegemonic feminist claims about a unitary woman's standpoint. The second deconstructionist pressure within feminism comes from a growing postmodernist literature that raises questions about gender as an undifferentiated concept and about the individual self as a stable locus of consciousness and personhood from which gender and the world are experienced. The potential impact of these questions falls primarily on feminist epistemology—its system for making truth claims—and is explored more fully below.

Historical Framing: Feminism, Sociology, and Gender

Feminism and sociology share a long-standing relationship, originating in feminists turning to sociology to help answer feminism's foundational questions.

The feminist perspective is an enduring feature in Western history. Wherever women are subordinated—and they have been subordinated almost always and everywhere—they have recognized and protested that situation (Lerner, 1993). In the Western world, published works of protest appeared as a thin but persistent trickle from the 1630s to about 1780. Since then feminist writing has been a significant collective effort, growing in both the number of its participants and the scope of its critique as numerous intellectual histories have shown (Cott, 1977; Donovan, 1985; Giddings, 1984; Lerner, 1993; Rossi, 1974; Spender, 1982, 1983; Tong, 2009).

Feminist writing is linked to feminist social activism, which has varied in intensity over the last two hundred years; high points occur in the liberationist "moments" of modern Western history. In U.S. history, major periods of feminist mobilization frequently are understood as "waves." First Wave feminism began in the 1830s as an offshoot of the antislavery movement and focused on women's struggle for political rights, especially the vote. It is marked by two key dates—1848, when the first women's rights convention was held at Seneca Falls, New York, and 1920, when the Nineteenth Amendment gave women the right to vote. Second Wave feminism (ca. 1960–1990) worked to translate these basic political rights into economic and social equality and to reconceptualize relations between men and women with the concept of gender. The term *Third Wave feminism* is used to describe the critical responses of various groups—women of color, lesbians, working-class women, women in the global South as well as women who will live their adult lives in the twenty-first century—to the arguments of Second Wave feminism (Feree, 2009).

Women, most of whom were feminist in their understandings, were active in the development of sociology as both a discipline and a profession from its beginnings. Feminist ideas of the First Wave were abroad in the world in the 1830s when Auguste Comte coined the term *sociology* and feminist Harriet Martineau (1802–1876) was asked to edit a proposed journal in sociology. Martineau is an important player in the history of sociology whose work has only been recovered under the impact of Second Wave feminism (Deegan, 1991; Hill, 1989; Hoecker-Drysdale, 1994; Lengermann and Niebrugge, 1998; Niebrugge, Lengermann, and Dickerson, 2010) and whose contribution undergirds the claim that women were "present at the creation" of sociology (Lengermann and Niebrugge, 1998).

Sociology's development into an organized discipline in its "classic generation"— the period marked by white male thinkers who did significant work from 1890 to 1920 (e.g., Emile Durkheim [1858–1917] and Max Weber [1862–1920]) overlapped with the increasing activism of First Wave feminism. Feminists Jane Addams, Charlotte Perkins Gilman, Florence Kelley, and Marianne Weber played important roles in the development of sociology, creating theory, inventing research methods, publishing in sociological journals, belonging to sociological associations, and holding offices in professional associations—and directly or indirectly speaking from the standpoint of women. U.S. women of color Anna Julia Cooper and Ida B. Wells-Barnett, though barred by racist practices from full participation in the organization of sociology, developed both social theory and a powerful practice of sociological critique and activism. Gilman is particularly significant in the history of feminist contributions to sociology, providing the first conceptualization of what will become the idea of gender in her concept of excessive sex distinction, which she defines as socially maintained differences between men and women that go beyond the differences dictated by biological reproduction (Lengermann and Niebrugge, 2013). But repeatedly the achievements of these women have been erased from the history of sociology by a male-dominated professional elite (Delamont, 2003; Skeggs, 2008; for a detailed examination of this process see Lengermann and Niebrugge, 1998).

Between 1920 and 1960 feminist thinking and activism ebbed, partly due to a sense of anomie produced by its victory in getting the vote, partly in response to social crises—World War I and its aftermath, the Great Depression, World War II and its aftermath, and the Cold War of the 1950s. Women sociologists were left without a framework for critique of their professional marginalization. They worked as isolated individuals for a foothold in the male-dominated university. Even so these women sociologists did research on women's lives and worked to conceptualize gender within the prevailing framework of "sex roles" in work such as Helen Mayer Hacker's "Women as a Minority Group" (1951) and Mirra Komarovsky's "Cultural Contradictions of Sex Roles" (1946).

Beginning in the 1960s, as a second wave of feminist activism energized feminist thinking, women in sociology drew strength to confront the organization of their profession and to (re-)establish a feminist perspective in the discipline (Feree, Khan, and Morimoto, 2007; Niebrugge, Lengermann, and Dickinson, 2010). Key to their success was the leadership of individual women like Alice Rossi, the establishment of the Women's Caucus within the American Sociological Association, and then in 1971 of a separate feminist organization, Sociologists for Women in Society (SWS), which in 1987 undertook the financially daring launch of a new journal, *Gender & Society,* under the editorship of Judith Lorber. These moves brought women a feminist base from which to speak to the profession and a feminist publication from which to introduce ideas to the discipline.

The effects of Second Wave feminism continue to this day in sociology. Women have moved into the profession in unprecedented numbers, as students, teachers, and scholars; the majority of undergraduate majors and about half of Ph.D. recipients are now women (England, 2010; Stacey and Thorne, 1996). Women hold office in the discipline's professional associations in percentages greater than their overall presence in the discipline (Rosenfeld, Cunningham, and Schmidt, 1997).

Central to this Second Wave triumph has been establishing gender as a core concept in sociology (Feree, Khan, and Morimoto, 2007; Finlay, 2007; Tarrant, 2006).

Gender, which is broadly understood as a social construction for classifying people and behaviors in terms of "man" and "woman," "masculine" and "feminine," is now an almost unavoidable variable in research studies—a variable whose presence implies a normative commitment to some standard of gender equality or the possibility that findings of inequality may be explained by practices of gender discrimination. The emphasis on gender vastly expanded the reach of feminist understandings to clearly include men as well as women, and the community of feminist scholars, though still primarily female, now includes important work by male feminists (Brickell, 2005; Connell, 1995; Diamond, 1992; Hearn, 2004; M. Hill, 1989; A. Johnson, 1997; Kimmel, 1996, 2002; Messner, 1997; Schwalbe, 1996; Trexler, 1995; Wedgwood, 2009).

Yet there remains a recurring unease about the relationship between feminism and sociology, an unease classically framed by Stacey and Thorne in their 1985 essay "The Missing Feminist Revolution in Sociology" and revisited subsequently (Alway, 1995b; Chafetz, 1997; Stacey and Thorne, 1996; Thistle, 2000; Wharton, 2006; C. Williams, 2006). A "feminist revolution in sociology" presumably would mean reworking sociology's content, concepts, and practices to take account of the perspectives and experiences of women. This effort has been far from wholesale or systematic. For instance, within the sociological theory community, feminists constitute a distinct and active theory group, intermittently acknowledged but unassimilated, whose ideas have not yet radically affected the dominant conceptual frameworks of the discipline.

The concern with gender has focused the energy of much feminist scholarship in sociology. But it may also have moved that energy away from two original primary concerns of feminist theory—the liberation of women and, as a means to that end, an articulation of the world in terms of women's experience. The study of gender is certainly not antithetical to these projects but neither is it coterminous with them. This chapter attempts to take account of the enormous developments around the concept of gender while at the same time remembering that feminist theory is not the same thing as the sociology of gender, an awareness that may help explain recent developments in feminist theorizing such as the growth of intersectionality theory and the resurgence of sexual difference theory, as well as the persistence of materialist or socialist feminism.

Varieties of Contemporary Feminist Theory

In this section we present a typology of contemporary feminist theories that guide feminist sociological theorizing.[3] Our typology is organized around answers to feminism's most basic question. *And what about the women?* Essentially there have been

---

[3] Several other classificatory systems already exist, for example, those developed by Chafetz (1988); Clough (1994); Glennon (1979); Jaggar (1983); Jaggar and Rothenberg (1984); Kirk and Okazawa-Rey (1998); Lengermann and Wallace (1985); Snitow, Stansell, and Thompson (1983); Sokoloff (1980); Tong (1998). Readers might turn to these works for balance or amplification of the ideal type presented here. In combination, these efforts have generated a long list of types of feminist theory, including black feminism, conservatism, expressionism, ecofeminism, existentialism, global instrumentalism, lesbian feminism, liberalism, Marxism, polarism, psychoanalytic feminism, radicalism, separatism, socialism, and synthesism. Our own typology attempts to include most of these theories, though not always as identified by these specific labels.

five answers to that question (see Table 12.1). The first of these can be framed in terms of *gender difference*—women's location in, and experience of, most situations is *different* from that of the men in those situations. The second is that of *gender inequality*—women's location in most situations is not only different from but also less privileged than or *unequal* to that of men. The third is that of *gender oppression*—that is, a direct power relationship between men and women through which women are restrained, subordinated, molded, used, and abused by men. The fourth is that

TABLE 12.1

Overview of Varieties of Feminist Theory

Basic varieties of feminist theory— answers to the descriptive question "What about the women?"	Distinctions within theories—answers to the explanatory question, "Why is all this as it is?"
Gender difference	
Women's location in, and experience of, most situations is *different* from that of men in the situation.	Cultural feminism Sexual difference theories Sociological theories • Institutional • Interactional
Gender inequality	
Women's location in most situations is not only different from but also less privileged than or *unequal* to that of men.	Liberal feminism
Gender oppression	
Women are *oppressed,* not just different from or unequal to, but actively restrained, subordinated, molded, and used and abused by men.	Psychoanalytic feminism Radical feminism
Structural oppression	
Women's experience of difference, inequality, and oppression varies by their social location within capitalism, patriarchy, and racism.	Socialist feminism Intersectionality theory
Interrogating gender	
What is really to be understood by the category "woman"? How is it produced and maintained?	Postmodernist feminism

women's experience of difference, inequality, and oppression varies according to their location within societies' arrangements of *structural oppression*—class, race, ethnicity, age, affectional preference, marital status, and global location. The fifth, a major focus in Third Wave feminism, questions the concept of woman so central to other theoretical positions, asking what implications flow from assuming the concept "woman" as a given in social analysis.

Within these basic categories we can distinguish among theories in terms of their differing answers to the second or explanatory question, "Why is all this as it is?"

This typology provides one way to pattern the general body of contemporary feminist theory, created within and outside sociology. It also helps to pattern the expanding literature in the sociology of gender. The focus in the sociology of gender on the relationship of men and women is not equivalent to a feminist theory that presents a critical woman-centered patterning of human experience (Alsop, Fitzsimons, and Lennon, 2002; Chafetz, 2004), but some sociologists who begin from a sociology-of-gender standpoint have produced works of significance for feminist theory, and many sociologists are directly involved in producing feminist theory.

This typology also needs to be read with the following cautions in mind: that it outlines theoretical positions, not the location of specific theorists, who over the course of a career may write from several of these positions, and that feminist theory and feminist sociological theory are dynamic enterprises that change over time. At the current moment, this typology is located within the following intellectual trends: (1) a steady movement toward synthesis, toward critically assessing how elements of these various theories may be combined; (2) a shift from women's oppression to oppressive practices and structures that affect both men and women; (3) tension between interpretations that emphasize culture and meaning and those that emphasize the material consequence of powers; (4) and finally, the fact that feminist theory is coming to be practiced as part of what Thomas Kuhn has called "normal science," that is, its assumptions are taken for granted as a starting point for empirical research.

Gender Difference

Theories of gender difference, among the oldest of feminist theories, are currently experiencing a resurgence of interest and elaboration. Although historically the concept of "difference" has been at the center of several theoretical debates in feminism, we use it here to refer to theories that describe, explain, and trace the implications of the ways in which men and women are or are not the same in behavior and experience. All theories of gender difference have to confront the problem of what usually is termed "the essentialist argument": the thesis that the fundamental differences between men and women are immutable. That immutability usually is seen as traceable to three factors: (1) biology, (2) social institutional needs for men and women to fill different roles, most especially but not exclusively in the family, and (3) the existential or phenomenological need of human beings to produce an "Other" as part of the act of self-definition. There has been some interest in sociobiology by feminist scholars, most notably Alice Rossi (1977, 1983), who have explored the thesis that human biology determines many social differences between men and women. A continuation of this feminist interest in the interaction of biology and sociocultural processes is also to be found in recent statements on *new (or neo-) materialism* (Ahmed, 2008; Davis, 2009; Hird, 2004). But overall the feminist response to sociobiology has been oppositional (Chancer and McCaughey, 2008; Palmer, 2001; Risman, 2001). Theories of gender difference important in feminist theory today issue from a range of locations: the women's movement, psychology, existential and phenomenological philosophy, sociology, and postmodernism.

Cultural Feminism

Cultural feminism is unique among theories analyzed here in that it is less focused on explaining the origins of difference and more on exploring—and even celebrating—the social value of women's distinctive ways of being, that is, of the ways in which women are different from men. This approach has allowed cultural feminism to sidestep rather than resolve problems posed by the essentialist thesis.

The essentialist argument of immutable gender difference first was used against women in male patriarchal discourse to claim that women were inferior to men and that this natural inferiority explained their social subordination. But that argument was reversed by some First Wave feminists who created a theory of cultural feminism, which extols the positive aspects of what is seen as "the female character" or "feminine personality." Theorists such as Margaret Fuller, Frances Willard, Jane Addams, and Charlotte Perkins Gilman were proponents of a cultural feminism that argued that in the governing of the state, society needed such women's virtues as cooperation, caring, pacifism, and nonviolence in the settlement of conflicts (Deegan and Hill, 1998; Donovan, 1985; Lengermann and Niebrugge-Brantley, 1998). This tradition has continued to the present day in arguments about women's distinctive standards for ethical judgment (Day, 2000; Gilligan, 1982; Held, 1993), about a mode of "caring attention" in women's consciousness (Fisher, 1995; Reiger, 1999; Ruddick, 1980), about a female style of communication (M. Crawford, 1995; Tannen, 1990, 1993, 1994), about women's capacity for openness to emotional experience (Beutel and Marini, 1995; Mirowsky and Ross, 1995), and about women's lower levels of aggressive behavior and greater capacity for creating peaceful coexistence (Forcey, 2001; Ruddick, 1994; Wilson and Musick, 1997).

The theme from cultural feminism most current in contemporary literature is that developed from Carol Gilligan's argument that women operate out of a different method of moral reasoning than men. Gilligan contrasts these two ethical styles as "the ethic of care," which is seen as female and focuses on achieving outcomes where all parties feel that their needs are noticed and responded to, and the "ethic of justice," which is seen as male and focuses on protecting the equal rights of all parties (Gilligan and Attanucci, 1988). Although much research is concerned with whether there are gender differences in people's appeal to these two ethics, the more lasting influence of this research lies in the idea that an ethic of care is a moral position in the world (Orme, 2002; Reitz-Pustejovsky, 2002; F. Robinson, 2001). Despite criticism (Alcoff, 1988; Alolo, 2006), cultural feminism has wide popular appeal because it suggests that women's ways of being and knowing may be a healthier template for producing a just society than those of an androcentric culture.

Theories of Sexual Difference

Theories of sexual difference are having a resurgence in feminist discourse (e.g., Khanna, 2010; Mortensen, 2006; Zerilli, 2005). "Sexual difference" is a term for a range of philosophical explorations—existential, phenomenological, Lacanian—of the question of the constitution of humans as sexed beings, that is, as personalities that both conform to and resist cultural or symbolic representations of the masculine and feminine. Sexual difference theories stand in marked contrast to sociobiology and cultural feminism, which basically accept "difference" as a fact of life. Sexual difference theories understand difference not as a fact but as a process that masculine culture both creates and uses to constitute itself. That culture, at best, pushes women's experience and ways of knowing themselves to the very margins of conceptual framing and, in its most intense form, creates a construct of the woman as "the Other," an objectified being who is assigned traits that represent the opposite of the agentic, subject male. Feminist sexual difference theorists explore what these processes may tell about the possibilities for women's freedom and human emancipation.

In its classic form, sexual difference theory arose in France as a feminist response to ideas in male-created (and male-centered) philosophy, literature, and psychoanalysis (Egeland, 2006). Its earliest representation is Simone de Beauvoir's analysis in *The Second Sex* (1949/1957), a feminist existentialism she creates as part of the larger project of existentialism, of which she was a part with Jean-Paul Sartre. Existentialism argues that, unlike all other things in the world, human beings are distinguished by the fact that their "essence" (what they truly are) follows their "existence"—that is, people are free to (or "condemned to") create themselves. For the individual, the "other" person both confirms one's existence and limits one's freedom—by looking at one, "fixing" one, as an object with a history. The great challenge for each individual is to assume the responsibilities of freedom, which means rejecting the need for the other's confirmation of self. It is against this background that De Beauvoir declares, "One is not born a woman, one becomes one." But for women, this existential journey is more difficult—as it is for members of racial minorities, lower classes, nonmainstream religions—because the dominant, in woman's case the male, has attempted to define woman's essence by stereotyping women and denying them the freedom to choose what they will become. Women can pursue their own project of freedom only by overcoming the oppression by men who attempt to make them into a perpetual Other who exists only to recognize a master. This, however, requires that women discover who they are in terms of their own acts of definition.

De Beauvoir's call for women to reject their status in masculine culture as the existential Other has been reworked and elaborated by a later group of French feminists, including Hélène Cixous, Luce Irigaray, Julia Kristeva, and Monique Wittig, who draw on the work of Jacques Lacan, Jacques Derrida, and Ferdinand de Saussure to build an argument that the quality of Otherness that shapes all women's experience is located in the realm of the symbolic, most especially, language. This point derives from two arguments in Lacanian psychoanalysis: one, following de Saussure, sees language and the symbolic constituted out of differences—words have no positive or absolute meaning but only an oppositional meaning in relation to other words—a second, revising Freud, postulates that within the unconscious there is no symbol of sexual difference but only the phallus as the signifier of sex; masculinity and femininity arise as positions around the phallus—which for Lacan exists in all three "registers," the imaginary, the symbolic, and the real. Sexual difference is based in the different ways in which women and men relate to a language based in the symbolism and fantasies of male power (E. Purcell, 2011). These theorists seek women's emancipation, both personal and collective, by tapping alternative preverbal experience, particularly of the mother as powerful, for a new symbolic possibility in which to anchor women's language, writing, and semiotics.

The recent return to these theories of sexual difference, largely but not solely by European feminists, may be seen as an attempt to chart a new course between the static images of gender as a social construction, and the overly fluid conceptualization of gender as performance, notably in ethnomethodology's "doing" gender theory (see next section) and postmodern performativity theories (see postmodern feminism below). These latest theories of sexual difference offer the realm of the symbolic as a basis for feminist analysis (e.g., Pollock, 2010). They analyze the experiences of women as they live in a world of phallocentric meanings in which they are inevitably marginalized, tracing both the costs to women and their covert efforts to tap their own experience for meaning (Mortensen, 2006). Recent writings in this tradition also call for a collective effort by women to construct their own world of meaning, and from this base to begin to repattern the world made by men; most especially women are urged to collectively discover and make political claims that can confirm their identity as women and perhaps reform the social world (Zerilli, 2005).

Sociological Theories: Institutional and Interactionist

Institutional

This theory posits that gender differences result from the different roles that women and men come to play within various institutional settings. A major determinant of difference is seen to be the sexual division of labor that links women to the functions of wife, mother, and household worker; to the private sphere of home and family; and thus to a lifelong series of events and experiences very different from those of men. Women's roles as mothers and wives in producing and reproducing a female personality and culture have been analyzed by theorists as diverse as J. Bernard (1981, 1972/1982), Chodorow (1978), M. Johnson (1989), and Risman and Ferree (1995). The central motif for this line of thinking is the sexual division of labor in the family. Repeated experience in these settings is pictured as carrying over into other institutions and producing differences between women and men in political behavior (e.g., the gender gap in voting), in choice of careers (e.g., the caring professions as female), in styles of corporate management, and in possibilities for advancement (e.g., the mommy track). Institutional placement theories have not been disproved so much as subsumed under deeper questions of how routine activities produce permanent features of the gendered personality. Institutional placement theories have been subject to two criticisms. First, they do not account for the persistence of gender difference when men and women occupy the same institutional position (though some feminist theorists argue that men and women can never occupy the same institutional position precisely because of the persistence of gender as a separate structure) (Kan, Sullivan, and Gershuny, 2011). Second, many sociologists see institutional theories as presenting too static and deterministic a model of gender differences in personality and action.

Interactionist

The most currently elaborated sociological understanding of the origins of gender difference comes from ethnomethodology's analysis of gender as an *accomplishment.* Ethnomethodology (see Chapter 10) posits that institutions, culture, and stratificational systems are maintained by the ongoing activities of individuals in interaction. When this idea is applied to gender, it produces the understanding that "people do gender"—or what is called in shorthand "doing gender."

West and Zimmerman's 1987 article "Doing Gender," the now classic statement of this position, is perhaps the most cited work in recent feminist sociological theory. Its starting point is in distinguishing among sex, sex category, and gender. A baby is born with some configuration of biological sex (which may be more or less clear). On the basis of what the adults attending to the birth interpret as its sex, the baby is assigned to a sex category. After that assignment, everyone around the child and the child itself over time begin to do gender, to act in ways considered appropriate to the sex category designation. The question of how everyone knows what is appropriate is resolved in ethonomethodology by the principle of *accountability:* People do not just act in any way they choose; people in interactions hold other people "accountable" for behaving in ways that are expected or useful or understandable. That is, people "manage conduct in anticipation of how others might describe it on a particular occasion" (Fenstermaker and West, 2002:212). Thus, gender is constantly being produced by people in interaction with each other as a way of making sense of and letting the world work.

For instance, using the "right" public restroom is a way of avoiding all sorts of potential embarrassments. It is a method of getting through the day hassle-free, and it is one so taken for granted that the person doing it hardly considers it doing gender. Ways of hugging, laughing, complaining—conveying the whole range of human emotions—are deeply gendered and are situationally enacted by people as they attempt to communicate with other people. Indeed, one question that emerges from the doing-gender perspective is whether it is possible *not* to do gender.

The current appeal of this approach reflects not only its abstract theoretical validity but also its suitability to a moment in U.S. history in which many people see men and women being more alike than different or at least having a great deal in common. The ethnomethodological insight gives a common origin to all gender experience in the movement from sex to sex category to gender: men and women both experience this and both are caught up in the activities of doing gender.

But although the elemental understanding of "doing" holds constant for women and men, West and Fenstermaker (1995, 2002) and West and Zimmerman (1987) recognize that a part of the substance of the doing in gender is "doing difference"— acting to make distinctions, to distinguish oneself as masculine not feminine or, conversely, as feminine not masculine. These acts of distinction are repeated from situation to situation to maintain gender identity. These theorists have further expanded their analysis of "doing" to other expressions of difference, notably race and class. The social mechanism that produces all this doing of gender difference is the operation of accountability in terms of sex category.

A major criticism of this approach is that it is not clear where the standards for accountability come from, for its emphasis on individual agency overlooks the fact that people in individual interactions do for the most part produce remarkably similar behaviors when doing gender (e.g., Maldonado, 1995; Weber, 1995). Another recurring concern is that much of the discussion and research that has built on the "doing gender" thesis uncritically focuses on interactional reproductions of gender inequality, failing to pursue the feminist project of "undoing" such patterns (Deutsch, 2007; Risman, 2009; Thorne, 1995). Another criticism is the failure of the approach to address the corporality or embodiment of those doing gender difference (R. Connell, 2009; Messerschmidt 2009). Dorothy Smith (2009) has advanced another critique: that "doing" oversimplifies and homogenizes the differences between gender, race, and class. Yet as any literature search will show, the thesis of doing gender difference continues to inspire teachers, researchers, and theorists in an expanding project of tracing its ramifications, including an expansion to the life experience of transpeople (C. Connell, 2010). "Doing gender" as a theory has also gained additional attention through its resonance with the postmodernist thesis of philosopher Judith Butler that gender is a "performance" (see "Feminism and Postmodernism" below).

Gender Inequality

Four themes characterize feminist theorizing of gender inequality. Men and women are situated in society not only differently but also unequally. Women get less of the material resources, social status, power, and opportunities for self-actualization than do men who share their social location—be it a location based on class, race, occupation, ethnicity, religion, education, nationality, or any intersection of these factors. This inequality results from the organization of society, for although individual human beings vary in their profile of potentials and traits, no significant pattern of natural variation distinguishes the sexes. All human beings are characterized by an intrinsic need for self-actualization and by a fundamental malleability that lets them adapt to the constraints or opportunities of their situations. To say that there is gender inequality is to claim that women are situationally less empowered than men to realize the need they share with men for self-actualization. All inequality theories assume that both women and men will respond fairly easily to more egalitarian social structures and situations. In this belief, theorists of gender inequality contrast with the theorists of gender difference, who present a picture of social life in which gender differences are, whatever their cause, more durable, more penetrative of personality, and less easily changed.

Liberal Feminism

The major expression of gender inequality theory is liberal feminism, which argues that women may claim equality with men on the basis of an essential human capacity for reasoned moral agency, that gender inequality is the result of a sexist patterning of the division of labor, and that gender equality can be produced by transforming the division of labor through the repatterning of key institutions—law, work, family, education, and media (Bem, 1993; Friedan, 1963; Lorber, 1994; Pateman, 1999; A. Rossi, 1964; Schaeffer, 2001).

Historically, these claims were first politically articulated in the Declaration of Sentiments drafted at Seneca Falls, New York, in 1848 with the express purpose of paralleling and expanding the Declaration of Independence to include women. It opens with the revisionist line "We hold these truths to be self-evident, that all men *and women* are created equal" [italics added] and concludes with a call for women to do whatever is required to gain equal rights with men. The radical nature of this foundational document is that it conceptualizes the woman not in the context of home and family but as an autonomous individual with rights in her own person (DuBois, 1973/1995). In so doing, it articulates the case on which all liberal feminism rests, the beliefs that (1) all human beings have certain essential features—capacities for reason, moral agency, and self-actualization—(2) the exercise of these capacities can be secured through legal recognition of universal rights, (3) the inequalities between men and women assigned by sex are social constructions having no basis in "nature," and (4) social change for equality can be produced by an organized appeal to a reasonable public and the use of the state.

Contemporary liberal feminism has expanded to include a global feminism that confronts racism in North Atlantic societies and works for "the human rights of women" everywhere, promoting in its foundational organizational documents such as the National Organization for Women's Statement of Purpose (1966) and the Beijing Declaration (1996) a theory of human equality as a right that the state—local, national, international—must respect.

Second Wave liberal feminism has focused on translating political rights won by the First Wave into economic equality for women. Feminist sociology has contributed theory and research to this project, explicating the barriers to achieving that equality by analyzing the gender division of labor, an ideology and practice that separates the world into public and private spheres. Men have privileged access to the public sphere, which allocates the major rewards of social life—money, power, status, freedom, opportunities for growth and self-worth. Women are assigned primary responsibility for the private sphere, the world of domesticity, where largely unpaid labor reproduces the world's workers day after day. The two spheres constantly interact in the lives of women (more than they do for men), and both spheres are still shaped by patriarchal ideology and sexism.

In a series of now classic works (Acker, 1990; Bernard, 1972/1982; Hochschild, 1989) liberal feminist sociologists develop three primary insights about the public-private patterning of social life: one, the dynamics of the private world limit women's agency and, thus, their participation in the public sphere; two, the public sphere itself is organized around assumptions about gender that keep women at a disadvantage; and three, negotiating the interface of private and public is perhaps the most formidable and enduring of the barriers to women's economic equality.

Jessie Bernard's *The Future of Marriage* (1972/1982) offers a model of marriage as, simultaneously, a cultural system of beliefs and ideals, an institutional arrangement of roles and norms, and a complex of interactional experiences for individual women and men. Culturally, marriage is idealized as the destiny and source of fulfillment for women; a mixed blessing of domesticity, responsibility, and constraint for men; and in American society as a whole, an essentially egalitarian association between husband and wife. Institutionally, marriage empowers the role of husband with authority and with the freedom—indeed, the obligation—to move beyond the domestic setting; it meshes the idea of male authority with sexual prowess and male power; and it mandates that wives be compliant, dependent, self-emptying, and essentially centered on the activities and demands of the isolated domestic household.

Experientially, then, there are two marriages in any institutional marriage: the man's marriage, in which the husband holds to the belief of being constrained and burdened, while experiencing what the norms dictate—authority, independence, and a right to domestic, emotional, and sexual service by the wife; and the woman's marriage, in which the wife affirms the cultural belief of fulfillment, while experiencing normatively mandated powerlessness and dependence, an obligation to provide domestic, emotional, and sexual services, and a gradual "dwindling away" of the independent young person she was before marriage. Bernard offered data on measurements of human stress to support her claims, data showing that *married* women, whatever their claims to fulfillment, and *unmarried* men, whatever their claims to freedom, rank high on all stress indicators. Recent studies have suggested Bernard's analysis still holds for many marriages (Dempsey, 2002; Steil, 1997) but that other couples are achieving, through dedicated effort, the liberal feminist ideal of egalitarian marriage (Graf and C. Schwartz, 2011; P. Schwartz, 1994).

Joan Acker (1990) addresses the pervasive assumption that organizations are gender neutral, positing instead the existence of "the gendered substructure of organizations," the existence of which we need to understand for at least five reasons:

> First, the gender segregation of work, including divisions between paid and unpaid work, is partly created through organizational practices. Second, and related to gender segregation, income and status inequality between women and men is also partly created in organizational processes; . . . Third, organizations are one arena in which widely disseminated cultural images of gender are invented and reproduced. Fourth, some aspects of individual gender identity, perhaps particularly masculinity, are also products of organizational processes and pressures. Fifth, an important feminist project is to make large-scale organizations more democratic and more supportive of humane goals.
>
> (Acker, 1990:140)

Acker illustrates her argument by unmasking the gender substructure behind the seemingly gender-neutral task of "job evaluation." While the focus on "the job" as the unit of analysis suggests gender neutrality, it obscures the gender job segregation characteristic of organizational structure. Job evaluation is done in terms of what Acker describes as "organizational logic"—"an assumption of congruence among responsibility, complexity and hierarchical position"—which also seems gender neutral. But because women hold jobs at the bottom of the hierarchy, their jobs, according to organizational logic, cannot be viewed as involving responsibility and complexity—even when delegated to them by a supervisor.

Acker's analysis has been pathbreaking, offering a model of the gendering of organizational processes and the study of concepts like "the gender subtext," "the ideal worker," "the ideal worker norm," and "inequality regimes," and providing a frame for studying the policy of "comparable worth" (Kelly, Ammons, Chermack, and Moen 2010; Sayce, 2012; Schneidhofer, Schiffinger, and Mayrhofer, 2012).

In *The Second Shift* (1989) Arlie Hochschild demonstrates the unequal terms on which women who are both wives and mothers enter the public sphere; she does this by conceptualizing the work of the private sphere as "a second shift," that is, an hours-long round of daily duties that must be done by these women and are largely non-negotiable. Drawing on interviews with couples who both work in the public paid economy, Hochschild paints a picture of women's double day—the work of the office followed by the work of the home—and the emotional and physical toll this schedule exacts: "These women talked about sleep the way a hungry person talks about food" (1989:10).

Hochschild's work has permeated popular understandings of women's experience and has led to ongoing investigations of how women and men "juggle work and family" (e.g., Gimenez-Nadal and Sevilla-Sanz, 2011; Latshaw, 2011; Milkie, Raley, and Bianchi, 2009). In *The Time Bind* (1997), Hochschild probes more deeply the problem of balancing work and family in dual-income households, the stress of not having time to meet the responsibilities of work and home. She explores the effects of companies offering family-friendly policies, discovering that workers underutilize these policies because they feel that in a corporate culture that equates hours on the job—"face time"—with commitment to the work, they may be viewed as less serious players, risking job loss. Many workers, both women and men, also develop a preference for being at work because of the linearity of demands and clearer rewards system than they can experience in the unstructured, unending, intangibly rewarded work of the home.

Building on such studies, liberal feminist sociologists have moved to the project of defining gender as a structure (Ferree, Lorber, and Hess, 1999; Lorber, 1994; Martin, 2004; Risman, 2004). Risman (2004:432) contrasts this approach with past analyses that have explained gender in terms of other social structures (such as those of institutional placement discussed above under "Gender Difference"). Instead she describes gender as a complex structure patterning human behavior at three levels—individual, cultural/interactional, and institutional. From this perspective, gender is seen as "a socially constructed stratification system" (Risman, 2004:430) that produces a gendered division of labor, the organizational lens of public and private spheres, and a culture permeated by sexist ideology.

Most recently, feminist sociologists have begun to seek answers for the persistence of gender inequality despite the gains of the last fifty years (England, 2010; Ridgeway, 2011).

Ridgeway (2011) explains the persistence of gender inequality with the concept of gender frames. Frames are culturally shared ideas that offer a simplified categorizing schema by which people can adjust their behaviors to others. Ridgeway places gender frames in the larger social context of people's needs to coordinate activity—and to do so often fairly quickly—by placing other actors in a few general categories such as gender, race, and age. They then respond to those actors in terms of traits assumed to belong to the category. She sees these frames as being slower to change than the organizational arrangements, like work and education, of society. Thus, frames permeate new interactional settings with old understandings—an idea Ridgeway tests by looking at gender in Silicon Valley IT startup work settings, contrasting these with more traditional biotech firms. She argues that if frame analysis is correct, effects of conventional gender beliefs will be stronger in the IT firms, despite an identity based in informality and innovation, because men are "framed" as stronger in engineering and math skills; on the other hand, in the life sciences, there is less gender framing of ability and therefore more possibility for women to work equally with men.

Reviewing the data on women's gains in education and employment, England (2010) nevertheless concludes that feminists may be facing "a stalled revolution." For women's gains have not affected all women equally, have not produced a major reconfiguration of the culture that devalues traditional female activity and jobs, nor produced a new script for negotiating heterosexual intimacy. England argues that this slowing down of the movement toward full gender equality reflects the interaction of three widely held beliefs: that every individual has a right to upward mobility through personal effort; that there are, nevertheless, essential differences between men and women; and that what men do has more intrinsic value than what women do. Thus, the revolution has stalled because (1) men see no upward mobility in moving to traditionally female careers; (2) the acceptance of essentialist beliefs by both women and men fundamentally shapes how they do dating, courtship, and marriage; and (3) women accepting the essentialist belief prefer to pursue traditionally female careers (the choice of blue-collar women) unless their experience of mobility is blocked, as it is for middle-class daughters aspiring to move up from the position of mother in traditional women's careers.

There have been a variety of responses to England's analysis (Crawley, 2011; Graf and Schwartz 2011; Latshaw, 2011; Reskin, 2011). This growing concern with the pace of change produces among liberal feminists a perhaps moderate convergence with or at least interest in theories of difference.

Gender Oppression

Theories of gender oppression describe women's situation as the consequence of a direct power relationship between men and women in which men have fundamental and concrete interests in controlling, using, and oppressing women—that is, in the practice of domination. By *domination,* oppression theorists mean any relationship in which one party (individual or collective), the *dominant,* succeeds in making the other party (individual or collective), the *subordinate,* an instrument of the dominant's will. Instrumentality, by definition, is understood as involving the denial of the suborbinate's independent subjectivity (Lengermann and Niebrugge-Brantley, 1995). Women's situation, for theorists of gender oppression, is centrally that of being dominated and oppressed by men. This pattern of gender oppression is incorporated in the deepest and most pervasive ways into society's organization, a basic arrangement of domination most commonly called *patriarchy,* in which society is organized to privilege men in all aspects of social life. Patriarchy is not the unintended and secondary consequence of some other set of factors—be it biology or socialization or sex roles or the class system. It is a primary power arrangement sustained by strong and deliberate intention. Indeed, to theorists of gender oppression, gender differences and gender inequality are by-products of patriarchy.

We review here two major variants of gender oppression theory: psychoanalytic feminism and radical feminism.

Psychoanalytic Feminism[4]

Psychoanalytic feminism attempts to explain patriarchy by reformulating the theories of Freud and his intellectual heirs (J. Benjamin, 1988, 1996, 1998; Chodorow, 1978, 1990, 1994, 1999; Langford, 1999). These theories map and emphasize the emotional dynamics of personality, emotions often deeply buried in the subconscious or unconscious areas of the psyche; they also highlight the importance of infancy and early childhood in the patterning of these emotions. In attempting to use Freud's theories, however, feminists have to undertake a fundamental reworking of his conclusions in order to reject his gender-specific conclusions, which are sexist and patriarchal.

Like all oppression theorists, psychoanalytic theorists see patriarchy as a system in which men subjugate women, a universally pervasive system, durable over time and space, and steadfastly maintained in the face of occasional challenge. Distinctive to psychoanalytic feminism, however, is the view that this system is one that all men, in their individual daily actions, work to create and sustain. Women resist only occasionally but more often either acquiesce in or actively work for their own subordination. The puzzle that psychoanalytical feminists set out to solve is why men everywhere bring such unremitting energy to the task of sustaining patriarchy and why there is an absence of countervailing energy on the part of women.

Psychoanalytic feminists discount the argument that a cognitive calculus of practical benefits is sufficient for male support for patriarchy. Cognitive mobilization does not seem a sufficient source for the intense energy that men invest in patriarchy, especially because, in light of the human capacity to debate and second-guess, men may not always and everywhere be certain that patriarchy is of unqualified value to them. Moreover, an argument anchored in the cognitive pursuit of self-interest would suggest that women would as energetically mobilize against patriarchy. Instead, these theorists look to those aspects of the psyche so effectively mapped by the Freudians: the zone of human emotions, of half-recognized or unrecognized desires and fears, and of neurosis and pathology. Here they find a clinically proven source of motivational energy and debilitation, one springing from psychic structures too deep to be recognized or monitored by individual consciousness.

In searching for the energic underpinnings of patriarchy, psychoanalytical feminists turn their analytic lens on the socioemotional environment in which the

---

[4]European feminists' use of Lacanian psychoanalytic theory was discussed under "Theories of Equal Difference" above; this section takes up another strand of psychoanalytic theory—object relations theory—and its use by American feminists.

personality of the young child takes form and to two facets of early childhood development: (1) the assumption that human beings grow into mature people by learning to balance a never-resolved tension between *individuation,* the desire for freedom of action, and *recognition,* the desire for confirmation by another; and (2) the observable fact that in all societies infants and children experience their earliest and most crucial development in a close, uninterrupted, intimate relationship with a woman, their mother or mother substitute. As infants and young children, for considerable periods lacking even language as a tool for understanding experience, individuals experience their earliest phases of personality development as an ongoing turbulence of primitive emotions: fear, love, hate, pleasure, rage, loss, desire. The emotional consequences of these early experiences stay with people always as potent but often unconscious "feeling memories." Central to that experiential residue is a cluster of deeply ambivalent feelings for the woman/mother/caregiver: need, dependence, love, possessiveness, but also fear and rage over her ability to thwart one's will. Children's relationship to the father/man is much more occasional, secondary, and emotionally uncluttered.

From this beginning, the male child, growing up in a culture that positively values maleness and devalues femaleness and increasingly aware of his own male identity, attempts to achieve an awkwardly rapid separation of identity from the woman/mother—an emotional separation that is partial, and costly in its consequences. In adulthood the emotional carryover from early childhood toward women—need, love, hate, possessiveness—energizes the man's quest for a woman of his own who meets his emotional needs yet is dependent on and controlled by him—that is, he has an urge to dominate and finds recognition of the other difficult. The female child, bearing the same feelings toward the woman/mother, discovers her own female identity in a culture that devalues women. She grows up with deeply mixed positive and negative feelings about herself and about the woman/mother and in that ambivalence dissipates much of her potential for mobilized resistance to her social subordination (Oliver, 2006). She seeks to resolve her emotional carryover in adulthood by emphasizing her capacities for according recognition—often submissively with males in acts of sexual attraction and mutually with females in acts of kinship maintenance and friendship. And rather than seeking mother substitutes, she re-creates the early infant-woman relationship by becoming a mother.

Psychoanalytical feminist theorists have extended their analyses beyond individual personality to Western culture: emphases in Western science on a distinct separation between "man" and "nature" (Jaggar and Bordo, 1989; Keller, 1985); motifs in popular culture (J. Benjamin, 1985, 1988; Chancer, 1992; Zannetino, 2008), the organizational practices of professional groups (Ford and Harding, 2008), of service providers (Varley, 2008), and of masculinity's engagement with feminism in women's studies (Landreau, 2011). Two pathologies result from the tension between recognition and individuation—the overindividuated dominator, who "recognizes" the other only through acts of control, and the underindividuated subordinate, who relinquishes independent action to find identity only as a mirror of the dominator (Zosky, 1999).

Psychoanalytical feminists, then, explain women's oppression in terms of men's deep emotional need to control women, a drive arising from ambivalence toward the women who reared them. Women either lack these neuroses or are subject to complementary neuroses, but in either case they are left psychically without an equivalent source of energy to resist domination. Clinical psychiatric evidence supports the thesis that these neuroses are widespread in Western societies, as does recent work in cross-cultural psychology (Haaken, 2008). But these theories, in drawing a straight line from human emotions to female oppression, fail to explore the intermediate social arrangements that link emotion to oppression and fail to suggest possible lines of variation in emotions, social arrangements, or oppression produced by the variable of class, nationality, and ethnicity. Moreover, psychoanalytic feminist theory suggests very few strategies for change, except perhaps that we restructure our child-rearing practices.

Radical Feminism

Radical feminism is based on two emotionally charged central beliefs: (1) that women are of absolute positive value as women, a belief asserted against what they claim to be the universal devaluing of women, and (2) that women are everywhere oppressed— often violently—by the system of patriarchy (Bunch, 1987; Chesler, 1994; Daly, 1973; C. Douglas, 1990; Dworkin, 1989; Echols, 1989; Frye, 1983; Hunnicutt, 2009; MacKinnon, 1989, 1993; Rhodes, 2005; Rich, 1976, 1980). With passion and militance similar to the "black power" cry of African American mobilization and the "witnessing" by Jewish survivors of the Holocaust, radical feminists elaborate a theory of social organization, gender oppression, and strategies for change.

Radical feminists see in every institution and in society's most basic stratificational arrangements systems of domination and subordination, the most fundamental of which is patriarchy. Patriarchy is historically the first structure of domination and submission and continues as the most pervasive and basic societal model of domination (Lerner, 1986). Through participation in patriarchy, men learn how to hold other human beings in contempt and to control them. Within patriarchy men see and women learn what subordination looks like. Patriarchy creates guilt and repression, sadism and masochism, manipulation and deception, all of which drive men and women to other forms of tyranny. Patriarchy, to radical feminists, is the least noticed yet the most significant structure of social inequality.

Central to this analysis is the image of patriarchy as violence practiced by men and by male-dominated organizations against women. Violence may not always take the form of overt physical cruelty. It can be hidden in more complex practices of exploitation and control: in denial of basic economic resources (Klasnic, 2011); in standards of fashion and beauty (B. Thompson, 1994; N. Wolf, 1991); in tyrannical ideals of motherhood, monogamy, chastity, and heterosexuality (Rich, 1976, 1980); in sexual harassment in the workplace (MacKinnon, 1979; L. Roth, 1999); in the practices of gynecology, obstetrics, and psychotherapy; and in unpaid household drudgery and underpaid wage work. Violence exists whenever one group controls in its own interests the life chances, environments, actions, and perceptions of another group, as men do to women.

But the theme of violence as overt physical cruelty lies at the heart of radical feminism's linking of patriarchy to violence: sexual abuse and rape (Bart and Moran, 1993; Buchwald, Fletcher, and Roth, 1993; Mardorossian, 2002; Martin, Vieratis, and Britto, 2006;

Scully, 1990), enforced prostitution (Barry, 1979, 1993), spouse abuse and murder (Caputi, 1989; Hammer, 2002), sadism in pornography (Russell, 1998), the historical and cross-cultural practices of witch burning, the stoning to death of adulteresses, the persecution of lesbians, female infanticide, Chinese foot-binding, the abuse of widows, and the practice of clitoridectomy.

Once patriarchy is in place, economic, ideological, legal, and emotional power resources can be marshaled to sustain it. But physical violence always remains its fundamental resource, and in both interpersonal and intergroup relations that violence is used to protect patriarchy from women's individual and collective resistance. Men also have a deep interest in controlling women because women are a uniquely effective means of satisfying male sexual desire, producing progeny, doing sustained and heavy labor, being ornaments that enhance male status and power, having companionship and emotional support, and reinforcing the male's sense of central social significance. These useful functions mean that men everywhere seek to keep women compliant. But differing social circumstances give different rank orders to these functions and therefore lead to cross-cultural variations in the patterning of patriarchy.

How is patriarchy to be defeated? Radicals hold that this defeat must begin with a basic reworking of women's consciousness so that each woman recognizes her own value and strength (Villalon, 2010); rejects patriarchal pressures to see herself as weak, dependent, and second-class (Blackstone, Uggen and McLaughlin, 2009); and works in unity with other women, regardless of differences among them, to establish a broad-based sisterhood of trust, support, appreciation, and mutual defense (Chasteen, 2001; McCaughey, 1997; Whitehead, 2007). With this sisterhood in place, two strategies suggest themselves: a critical confrontation with any facet of patriarchal domination whenever it is encountered and a degree of separatism as women withdraw into women-run businesses, households, communities, centers of artistic creativity, and lesbian love relationships. Lesbian feminism, as a major strand in radical feminism, is the practice and belief that "erotic and/or emotional commitment to women is part of resistance to patriarchal domination" (Phelan, 1994; Rudy, 2001; Taylor and Rupp, 1993).

A theoretical evaluation of radical feminism should note that it incorporates arguments made by both socialist and psychoanalytical feminists about the reasons for women's subordination yet moves beyond those theories. Similarly, it takes recent analyses from liberal feminist analyses of gender as a multilevel structure to show how the coercive control of women is achieved (Andersen, 2009). Radical feminists, moreover, have done significant research to support their thesis that patriarchy ultimately rests on the practice of violence against women. They have a reasonable though perhaps incomplete program for change. They may, however, be faulted for their exclusive focus on patriarchy, a focus that simplifies the realities of social organization and social inequality.

Structural Oppression

Structural oppression theories, like gender oppression theories, recognize that oppression results from the fact that some groups of people derive direct benefits from controlling, using, and subjugating other groups of people. Structural oppression theorists analyze how interests in domination are enacted through social structure, here understood as those recurring and routinized large-scale arrangements of social relations that arise out of history and are always arrangements of power. These theorists focus on the structures of patriarchy, capitalism, racism, and heterosexism, and they locate enactments of domination and experiences of oppression in the interplay of these structures, that is, in the way they mutually reinforce each other. Structural oppression theorists do not absolve or deny the agency of individual dominants, but they examine how that agency is the product of structural arrangements. In this section we look at two types of structural oppression theory: socialist feminism and intersectionality theory.

Socialist Feminism

The theoretical project of socialist feminism develops around three goals: (1) to achieve a critique of the distinctive yet interrelated oppressions of patriarchy and capitalism from a standpoint in women's experience, (2) to develop explicit and adequate methods for social analysis out of an expanded understanding of historical materialism, and (3) to incorporate an understanding of the significance of ideas into a materialist analysis of the determination of human affairs. Socialist feminists have set themselves the formal project of achieving both a synthesis of and a theoretical step beyond other feminist theories, most specifically Marxian and radical feminist thought (Acker, 2008; Eisenstein, 1979; Fraser, 1989, 1997; Fraser and Bedford, 2008; Gimenez, 2005; Hartsock, 1983; Hennessey and Ingraham, 1997; Jackson, 2001; MacKinnon, 1989; Dorothy Smith, 1979, 1987, 1990a, 1990b, 1999a, 1999b, 2000, 2004a, 2009; Vogel, 1995).

Radical feminism, as discussed above, is a critique of patriarchy. Marxian feminism, described here, has traditionally brought together Marxian class analysis and feminist social protest. But this amalgam—portrayed as an uneasy marriage (Hartmann, 1981; Shelton and Agger, 1993)—often produced not an intensified theory of gender oppression but a more muted statement of gender inequality as women's concerns were grafted onto, rather than made equal partners in, the critique of class oppression. While pure Marxian feminism is a relatively dormant theory in contemporary American feminism, it remains important as an influence on socialist feminism. Its foundation was laid by Marx and Engels (see Chapter 2). Their major concern was social class oppression, but they occasionally turned their attention to gender oppression, most famously in *The Origins of the Family, Private Property, and the State* (written by Engels in 1884 from extensive notes made by Marx in the year immediately preceding his death in 1883). We briefly summarize this book because it gives a good introduction to the classic Marxian theory of gender oppression and to the method of historical materialism.

The major argument of *The Origins* is that woman's subordination results not from her biology, which is presumably immutable, but from social relations that have a clear and traceable history and that presumably can be changed. In the context of nineteenth-century thinking about gender, this was a radical, indeed a feminist, argument. The relational basis for women's subordination lies in the family, an institution

DOROTHY E. SMITH

A Biographical Sketch

Dorothy E. Smith explains that her sociological theory derives from her life experiences as a woman, particularly as a woman moving between two worlds—the male-dominated academic sphere and the female-centered life of the single parent. Remembering herself at Berkeley in the early 1960s studying for a doctorate in sociology while single-parenting, Smith reflects that her life seems to have been framed by what she sees as "not so much . . . a career as a series of contingencies, of accidents" (1979:151). This theme of contingency is one of many personal experiences that have led Smith to challenge sociological orthodoxy such as the image of the purposive actor engaged in linear pursuits of projects.

Whether they occurred by accident or design, the following events appear to the outsider as significant stages in Smith's development. She was born into a multigenerational family of independent and activist women in 1926 in Great Britain (Smythe, 2009); she earned her bachelor's degree in sociology from the University of London in 1955 and her Ph.D. in sociology from the University of California at Berkeley in 1963. During this period, she had "the experience of marriage, of immigration [to Canada] closely following marriage, of the arrival of children, of the departure of a husband rather early one morning, of the jobs that became available" (Smith, 1979:151). Of these events, Smith stresses, they "were moments in which I had in fact little choice and certainly little foreknowledge." The jobs that became available included research sociologist at Berkeley; lecturer in sociology at Berkeley; lecturer in sociology at the University of Essex, Colchester, England; associate professor and then professor in the department of sociology at the University of British Columbia; and professor of sociology in education at the Ontario Institute for Studies in Education, Toronto.

Smith has written on a wide variety of topics, all connected by a concern with "bifurcation," sometimes as a central theme and sometimes as a motif. Smith sees the experience of bifurcation manifesting itself in the separation between social-scientific description and people's lived experience, between

aptly named from the Latin word for *servant,* because the family as it exists in complex societies is overwhelmingly a system in which men command women's services. Although the ideology of contemporary societies treats family as a fundamental and universal feature of social life, Engels and Marx use archaeological and anthropological evidence to show that the family is a fairly recent relational invention, that for much of prehistory men and women lived in kin structures in which women enjoyed relative autonomy primarily because they had an independent economic base as gatherers, crafters, storers, and distributors of essential materials. The factor that destroyed women's lived experience and the patriarchal ideal types they are given for describing that experience, between the micro-world and the macro-world structures that dictate micro experience, and, especially, between the micro world of the oppressed and the micro world of the dominants whose actions create the macro structures of oppression. The concretization of these themes can be seen in a selective review of the titles of some of Smith's works. In 1987 Smith produced her most extensive and integrated treatment of these themes in what has become a landmark in feminist sociology, *The Everyday World as Problematic* (1987). She followed this with *The Conceptual Practices of Power* (1990a), *Texts, Facts and Femininity* (1990b), *Writing the Social* (1999b), and *Institutional Ethnography: A Sociology for People* (2004b).

What Smith is producing for feminist sociologists, and indeed for all sociologists interested in the theoretical frontiers of the profession, is a sociology that integrates neo-Marxian concerns with the structures of domination and phenomenological insights into the variety of subjective and micro-interactional worlds. Smith sees these various everyday life-worlds as shaped by macro structures that are themselves shaped by the historical specifics of economic demand. What Smith wishes to avoid, in developing this line of reasoning, is a vision of the world in which the oppressors are consistently interpreted as individual actors making rational decisions on the basis of self-interest. Smith sees that self-interest itself is structurally situated, but she believes that these structures can become known only by beginning with the outcome at hand, that is, by exploring the everyday worlds of situated individuals. Smith is concerned that much social science serves to obfuscate rather than clarify the structures that produce these worlds because much social science begins with an assumption that the structures are already known and can be known separately from the everyday life-worlds. Her recent work extends her project of a sociology for women to a sociology for people that explores macro structures as organizers of everyday/everynight worlds. She is particularly interested in analyzing text-based organization and text-mediated social relations in people's everyday local practices (Smith, 2006). Here her work offers a sociological alternative to feminist postmodernism. The implications of Smith's work for sociological theory form the basis for much of this chapter. An important contemporary review of her career is given in Marie L. Campbell and Marjorie L. DeVault (2011).

this type of social system, producing what Engels calls "the world historic defeat of the female sex" (Engels, 1884/1970:87), was an economic one, specifically the replacement of hunting and gathering by herding and farming economies in which men's resources of strength, mobility, and a technology derived from their earlier hunting roles gave them a systematic advantage over women. This period saw the invention of the concept of *property*, the idea and reality of a male class claiming as its own the communal resources for economic production. In these new economies, men as property owners needed both a compliant labor force—be it of slaves, captives, women-wives, children—and heirs who would serve as a means of preserving and passing on property. Thus emerged the first *familia,* a master and his slave-servants, wife-servants, children-servants. Since then, the exploitation of labor has developed into increasingly complex structures of domination, most particularly class relations, and the family has evolved along with historical transformations of economic and property systems into an embedded and dependent institution, reflecting all the injustices of the economy and consistently enforcing the subordination of women. Engels and Marx conclude that only with the destruction of property rights through class revolution will women attain freedom of social, political, economic, and personal action.

Locating the origin of patriarchy in the emergence of property relations subsumes women's oppression under the general framework of Marxian class analysis. "Property"—understood not as personal possessions but as ownership of the resources necessary for social production (the means of production)—is the basis of class division because it creates a situation in which some groups are able to claim that they own the means of production while other groups work to do the producing. Marxian analysis focuses particularly on how this class division works out under capitalism, the economic system of modern societies. The distinctive feature of capitalism is that the class that owns the means of production—the capitalists—operates on a logic of continuous capital accumulation; *capital* is wealth (money and other assets), which can be used to generate the material infrastructure of economic production. Unlike other forms of economic organization in which people may seek to exchange either goods or money for more goods, capitalists seek to exchange goods in order to amass wealth. The mechanism by which capitalists turn goods into wealth is surplus value; surplus value is the difference between the compensation given to workers for their production and the value of the goods they produce; this surplus value is appropriated by the capitalist, who uses it to enhance his own lifestyle and power and, above all, to reinvest in the ongoing process of capital accumulation and expansion.

Socialist feminists accept the Marxian analysis of capitalism's class relations as an explication of one major structure of oppression. But they reject the Marxian analysis of patriarchy as a by-product of the same economic production. Instead they endorse the radical feminist argument that patriarchy, while interacting with economic conditions, is an independent structure of oppression.

Socialist feminism sets out to bring together these dual knowledges—knowledge of oppression under capitalism and of oppression under patriarchy—into a unified explanation of all forms of social oppression. One term used to try to unify these two oppressions is *capitalist patriarchy* (Eisenstein, 1979; Hartmann, 1979; A. Kuhn and Wolpe, 1978). But the term perhaps more widely used is *domination,* defined above (under "Gender Oppression") as a relationship in which one party, *the dominant,* succeeds in making the other party, *the subordinate,* an instrument of the dominant's will, refusing to recognize the subordinate's independent subjectivity. Socialist feminism's explanations of oppression present domination as a large-scale structural arrangement, a power relation between categories of social actors that is reproduced by the willful and intentional actions of individual actors. Women are central to socialist feminism as the primary topic for analysis, and as the essential vantage point on domination in all its forms. But these theorists are concerned with all experiences of oppression, both by women and by men. They also explore how some women, them-selves oppressed, actively participate in the oppression of other women, for example, privileged-class women in American society who oppress poor women (Eisenstein, 1994; Hochschild, 2000).

Socialist feminists use historical materialism as their analytical method (Hennessey and Ingraham, 1997). *Historical materialism,* a basic principle in Marxian social theory, is the claim that the material conditions of human life, including the activities and relationships that produce those conditions, are the key factors that pat-tern human experience, personality, ideas, and social arrangements; that those condi-tions change over time because of dynamics immanent within them; and that history is a record of the changes in the material conditions of a group's life and of the cor-relative changes in experiences, personality, ideas, and social arrangements. Historical materialists hold that any effort at social analysis must trace in historically concrete detail the specifics of a group's material conditions and the links between those con-ditions and the experiences, personalities, events, ideas, and social arrangements char-acteristic of the group. In linking historical materialism to their focus on domination, socialist feminists attempt to realize their goal of a theory that probes the broadest of human social arrangements, domination, yet remains firmly committed to precise, historically concrete analyses of the material and social arrangements that frame particular situations of domination.

The use of historical materialism by socialist feminism shows the school's indebtedness to Marxian thought. But in their use of this method, socialist feminists move beyond the Marxians in three crucial ways: their redefinition of *material conditions,* their reevaluation of the significance of ideology, and their focus on domination. First, they broaden the concept of the *material conditions* to include not only the Marxian concept of economic production for the market but other conditions that create and sustain human life: sexuality, involvement in procreation, and child rearing; the unpaid, invisible round of domestic tasks; emotional care; and the production of knowledge. In *all* these life-sustaining activities, exploitative arrangements profit some and impoverish others. An analysis of the historical trans-formation of all production and exploitation is essential to a theory of domination (McDowell, 2008).

The second point of difference between Marxian historical materialism and the historical materialism of socialist feminism is the latter perspective's emphasis on what some Marxians might dismiss as consciousness, motivation, ideas, social defini-tions of the situation, knowledge, texts, ideology, the will to act in one's interests or acquiesce to the interests of others.[5] To socialist feminists all these factors deeply affect human personality, human action, and the structures of domination that are realized through that action. Moreover, these aspects of human subjectivity are produced by social structures that are inextricably intertwined with, and are as elabo-rate and powerful as, those that produce economic goods. Within all these structures, too, exploitative arrangements enrich and empower some while impoverishing and

---

[5]Admittedly some neo-Marxians, notably the critical theorists, have reevaluated the explanatory significance of ideology (see Chapter 8).

immobilizing others. Historical materialist analysis of the processes that pattern human subjectivity is vital to a theory of domination.

Third unlike the object of analysis theorists for whom class inequality is Marxian, socialist feminists focus on the complex intertwining of a wide range of social inequalities. They develop a portrait of social organization in which the public structures of economy, polity, and ideology interact with the intimate, private processes of human reproduction, domesticity, sexuality, and subjectivity to sustain a multifaceted system of domination, the workings of which are discernible both as impersonal social patterns and as the more varied subtleties of interpersonal relationships. To analyze this system, socialist feminists shuttle between mapping large-scale systems of domination and situationally specific, detailed exploration of the mundane daily experiences of oppressed people. Their strategy for change rests in this process of discovery, in which they attempt to involve the oppressed groups that they study and through which they hope that both individuals and groups, in large and small ways, will learn to act in pursuit of their collective emancipation.

Within this general theoretical framing, socialist feminist analysis has distinct emphases. First, *materialist feminism* situates gender relations within the structure of the contemporary capitalist system, particularly as that system is now operating globally. The interest of materialist feminists is in the implications of global capitalism for women's lives and in the ways in which women's labor contributes to the expanding wealth of capitalism. Within global capitalism, women as wage earners are more poorly paid than men because patriarchal ideology assigns them a lower social status. Because patriarchy assigns them the responsibility for the home, they are structurally more precariously positioned in wage-sector employment than men are and thus are more difficult to organize. These two factors make them an easy source of profit for the capitalist class. Further, capitalism depends on the unpaid production of women whose work as housewives, wives, and mothers subsidizes and disguises the real costs of reproducing and maintaining the workforce. And women's work as consumers of goods and services for the household becomes a major source of capitalist profit making (J. L. Collins, 2002; Hennessey and Ingraham, 1997; Ingraham, 2008; N. Rose, 1995; Vogel, 1995).

A second emphasis given most form by Dorothy Smith and her students is on the *relations of ruling,* the processes by which capitalist patriarchal domination is enacted through an interdependent system of control that includes not only the economy but the state and the privileged professions (including social science). The dynamics of this arrangement of control are explored through a focus on women's daily activities and experiences in the routine maintenance of daily life. The relations of ruling are revealed as pervading and controlling women's daily production via "texts," extralocal, generalized requirements that seek to pattern and appropriate their labor—texts like health insurance forms, the school calendar, advertisements about the ideal home and the ideal female body (M. Campbell and Manicom, 1995; Currie, 1997, 1999; Widerberg, 2008).

Socialist feminists' program for change calls for global solidarity among women to combat the abuses capitalism works in their lives, in the lives of their communities, and in the environment. Indeed, eco-feminism is a major current trend in socialist feminism (Dordoy and Mellor, 2000; Goldman and Schurman, 2000; Kirk, 1997). They call on the feminist community to be ever vigilant about the dangers of their own co-optation into a privileged intelligentsia that serves capitalist interests. Their project is to mobilize people to use the state as a means for the effective redistribution of societal resources through the provision of an extensive safety net of public services such as publicly supported education, health care, transportation, child care, and housing; a progressive tax structure that reduces the wide disparities of income between rich and poor; and the guarantee of a living wage to all members of the community. They believe that this mobilization will be effective only if people become aware of and caring about the life conditions of others as well as their own. The feminist social scientist's duty is to make visible the material inequalities that shape people's lives.

At this moment there is a curious hiatus in socialist feminist theory in the United States. Its main North American theorist, Dorothy E. Smith (see box), continues to inspire many dissertations and some articles, but they most frequently draw on her work in "institutional ethnography" or epistemological questions in sociology (Hart and MacKinnon, 2010). But socialist feminist theorizing in other parts of the world remains vital. In some cases its basic tenets offer a framework for feminist theorizing as in Branka Galic's 2011 consideration of the importance of gendered work in modern capitalist societies, like Croatia. Jesook Song (2010) places the search for "a room of one's own" by unmarried South Korean women in the context of the interface of capitalism and patriarchy, showing how on the one hand, young women in their twenties and thirties find it hard to secure loans because of a bias toward heterosexuality and marriage in the finance industry; but on the other hand, she points out that the desire for this autonomy serves to reinforce a "neo-liberal" understanding of the individual in the labor market. Anne-Meike Fechter (2010) asks of global corporate capitalism the question, "Where are the women?" Instead of looking at women as low-paid, exploited labor in global capitalism, she looks at the unexplored lives of the wives of privileged-class expatriate corporate leaders, linking their lives to early phases of capitalism expansion, that is, to the wives of imperial colonial officials. In both cases, she sees women who perform the emotional work of sustaining their husbands and at the same time are made to function ideologically as emblems of all that is troubling in capitalist global expansion. Catherine Hakim (2010) revisions Bourdieu's concept of kinds of capital to argue that women have cultivated greater "erotic capital" assets than men and to suggest that many restrictions placed on their use of those assets by the capitalist-patriarchy need to be understood not in terms of morality but of economic control of scarce resources.

Intersectionality Theory

The central issue for intersectionality theory is the understanding that women experience oppression in varying configurations and in varying degrees of intensity (Andersen, 2005; Anzaldúa, 1990; Anzaldúa and Keating, 2002; P. Collins, 1990, 1998, 1999, 2000, 2001, 2004, 2012; Crenshaw, 1991; E. Glenn, 1999; Lorde, 1984; Misra, 2012; Smith, 2009; Yuval-Davis, 2012). The explanation for that variation is that while all women potentially experience oppression on the basis of gender, women

PATRICIA HILL COLLINS

A Biographical Sketch

Patricia Hill Collins was born in 1948. By her own report, she grew up in a supportive and extended black working-class family located in a black community in Philadelphia; she moved from this secure base daily to attend an academically demanding public high school for girls, and then, more permanently, to earn her bachelor's degree at Brandeis University in 1969 and her M.A.T. at Harvard in 1970. During the 1970s she worked as a curriculum specialist in schools in Boston, Pittsburgh, Hartford, New York, and Washington, D.C. She returned to Brandeis to earn her Ph.D. in sociology in 1984. She spent much of her career in higher education at the University of Cincinnati, where she held a dual appointment as Charles Phelps Taft Professor of Sociology and as Professor of African-American Studies. Currently, she is Distinguished University Professor at the University of Maryland. She was president of the American Sociological Association in 2009—the first African American woman elected to this position.

Collins writes that her experiences of educational success were permeated by the counterexperience of being "the 'first,' or 'one of the few,' or the 'only' African-American and/or woman and/or working-class person in my schools, communities, and work settings" (1990:xi). In these situations, she found herself judged as being less than others who came from different backgrounds, and she learned that educational success seemed to demand that she distance herself

are, nevertheless, differentially oppressed by the varied intersections of other arrangements of social inequality. These *vectors of oppression and privilege* (or, in Patricia Hill Collins's phrase, "the matrix of domination" [1990]) include not only gender but also class, race, global location, sexual preference, and age. The variation of these intersections qualitatively alters the experience of being a woman—and this alteration, this diversity, must be taken into account in theorizing the experiences of "women." The argument in intersectionality theory is that it is intersection itself that produces a particular experience of oppression, and one cannot arrive at an adequate explanation by using an additive strategy of gender, plus race, plus class, plus sexuality (Andersen, 2005). Crenshawe, for example, shows that black women frequently experience discrimination in employment because they are *black women,* but courts routinely refuse to recognize this discrimination—unless it can be shown to be a case of what is considered general discrimination, "sex discrimination" (read "also white women"), or "race discrimination" (read "also black men"). In characterizing these as vectors of oppression *and* privilege, we wish to suggest a fundamental insight of intersectionality theories—that the privilege exercised by some women and men turns from her black working-class background. This created in her a tension that produced "a loss of voice."

Her response to these tensions has been to formulate an alternative understanding of social theory and an alternative way of doing theory. This project led her to discover the theoretical voice of her community and to reclaim her own voice by situating it in that community. It culminated in *Black Feminist Thought* (1990), a landmark text in feminist and social theory that received both the Jessie Bernard Award and the C. Wright Mills Award. *Black Feminist Thought* presents social theory as the understandings of a specific group, black women; to this end, Collins draws on a wide range of voices, some famous, others obscure. What she presents is a community-based social theory that articulates that group's understanding of its oppression by intersections of race, gender, and class—and its historical struggle against that oppression. In this work, Collins uncovers the distinctive epistemology by which black women assess truth and validity; she also argues convincingly for a feminist standpoint epistemology. In both practice and theory she has pursued her theory of intersectionality, helping to organize the ASA section Race, Gender, Class; editing, with Margaret Andersen, the essay collection *Race, Class and Gender* (1992); and authoring a multiplicity of articles in a wide range of journals.

In *Fighting Words: Black Women and the Search for Justice* (1998) Collins continued her project of redefining social theory not as the province and practice of an elite intellectual group but as the understandings variously situated groups have achieved about the social world. In *Black Sexual Politics: African Americans, Gender and the New Racism* (2004), Collins expands the reach of her intersectionality theory to the analysis of the varied experiences of oppression of black women and black men, tracing the consequences of these experiences for the relation between black women and men.

on the oppression of other women and men. Theories of intersectionality at their core understand these arrangements of inequality as hierarchical structures based in unjust power relations. The theme of injustice signals the consistent critical focus of this analysis.

Intersectionality theory recognizes the fundamental link between ideology and power that allows dominants to control subordinates by creating a politics in which difference becomes a conceptual tool for justifying arrangements of oppression. In social practice, dominants use differences among people to justify oppressive practices by translating difference into models of inferiority/superiority; people are socialized to relate to difference not as a source of diversity, interest, and cultural wealth but evaluatively in terms of "better" or "worse." As Lorde (1984:115) argues, this "institutional rejection of difference is an absolute necessity in a profit economy which needs outsiders as surplus people." These ideologies operate in part by creating *"a mythical norm"* against which people evaluate others and themselves; in United States society this norm is "white, thin, male, young, heterosexual, Christian, and financially secure" (Lorde, 1984:116). This norm not only allows dominants to control social production (both paid and unpaid), but also becomes part of individual subjectivity—an internalized rejection of difference that can operate to make people devalue themselves, reject people from different groups, and create criteria within their own group for excluding, punishing, or marginalizing group members. Anzaldúa describes this last practice as "Othering," an act of definition done within a subordinated group to establish that a group member is unacceptable, an "other," by some criterion; this definitional activity, she points out, erodes the potential for coalition and resistance.

The intersection of vectors of oppression and privilege creates variations in both the forms and the intensity of people's experience of oppression. Much of the writing and research done out of an intersectionality perspective presents the concrete reality of people's lives as those lives are shaped by the intersections of these vectors. The most-studied intersections by feminists are of gender and race (Dill, 1994; S. Hill and Sprague, 1999; Tester, 2008), gender and class (P. Cohen, 1998; Foner, 1994; Gregson and Lowe, 1994; Wrigley, 1995), and race, gender, and class (Andersen and Collins, 1992; Edin and Lein, 1997; Edin and Kefalas, 2005; Lareau, 2003). Other analyses include gender and age (D. Gibson, 1996; Lopata, 1996), gender and global location (Desai, 2007; Purkayastha, 2012; Reddock, 2000), and gender and sexual preference (Mullins, 2005; Nagel, 2003; Schilt, 2008). In the most recent writings out of this perspective, intersectionality theory has also been applied to the circumstances of subordinate men (P. Collins, 2004; Edin and Kefalas, 2005; Shows and Gerstel, 2009; Lamont, 2000).

In response to their material circumstances, people create interpretations and strategies for surviving and resisting the persistent exercise of unjust power. One part of the project of intersectionality theory is to give voice to the group knowledges worked out in specific life experiences created by historical intersections of inequality and to develop various feminist expressions of these knowledges—for example, black feminist thought or Chicana feminism or postcolonial understandings (Chilisa and Ntseane, 2010; P. Collins, 1990; Cordova et al., 1990; James and Busia, 1993).

Intersectionality theory develops a critique of work done in Second Wave (and First Wave) feminism as work reflecting the experience and concerns of white privileged-class feminists in North Atlantic societies. Some of this work of critique is paralleled by work done in postmodernism—but this parallelism should not be overstated. Intersectionality theory is one of the oldest traditions in feminism, at least in the United States, going back, for example, to Sojourner Truth's "Aint I a Woman" speech at the Akron Women's Rights Convention of 1852 (Zerai, 2000). This critique has produced questions about what we mean by categories such as "woman," "gender," "race," and "sisterhood"—questions that are essentially political in intent, and not, as in postmodernism, philosophical (Chopra, 2004; hooks, 1984; Kaminsky, 1994; Mohanty, 1991). There has recently been a comment on Collins, arguing that black men often share the ideas described as "Black feminist thought" (Harnois, 2012). It has focused on the diversity of experience in such seeming universals as "mothering" and "family" and has reinterpreted theoretical works like the sociological-psychoanalytic studies of Chodorow and Benjamin (Dickerson, 1995; E. Glenn, Chang, and Forcey, 1993; Mahoney and Yngvesson,

1992; Segura and Pierce, 1993). This critique has prompted a repositioning of the understandings of "whiteness" by white feminists who seek to understand whiteness as a construction, the ways whiteness results in privilege, what they can actively do to reduce racism, and how they can contribute to producing a more inclusive feminist analysis (Alcoff, 1998; Chodorow, 1994; Frankenberg, 1993; Rowe, 2000; Ward, 1994; Yancy, 2000).

Intersectionality as a concept has been widely embraced in feminist sociology and it becomes increasingly hard to imagine a study that does not acknowledge its basic premise. Two central concerns have arisen amid this widespread recognition of its validity. One, which seems tentatively resolved, is the issue of how to allow for the analytical principle and empirical fact of diversity among women while at the same time holding to the valuational and political position that women share a distinctive standpoint. The resolution of this issue seems to lie in a return to one of the fundamental points of feminist theory, the concept of standpoint. Explaining standpoint, Collins (1998:224–225) proposes that it is the view of the world shared by a group characterized by a "heterogeneous commonality"; "shared," Collins refers, as Marx suggests, to "'circumstances directly encountered, given, and transmitted from the past.'" Thus, Collins concludes that a group's standpoint is constituted not out of some essentialism but out of a recognition that its members, in this case women, have common experiences and interests. While vectors of oppression and privilege—race, class, gender, age, global location, sexual preference—intersect in all people's lives, these theorists argue that the way they intersect markedly affects the degree to which a which a common standpoint is affirmed.

The second issue, which is proving much harder to resolve, is how to operationalize the concept of intersectionality so that one can empirically observe and discuss the interplay of multiple vectors of oppression and/or privilege in people's experiences and actions rather than pursuing an additive process that talks first about the effects of gender, then adds race, then class. The additive process is rejected as fundamentally false to the lived experience, individuals' empirical reality. But how then do these various vectors coexist in people's lives? In balance? In hierarchy? In shifting schema of ascendency? Intersectionality theorists warn that while it is both conceptually and methodologically fairly easy to locate the experience of intersection and of standpoint in individuals, this reductionism is theoretically and politically dangerous if it blinds scholars to the historical structures of unequal power that have produced the individual experience and thus obscure the need for political change.

Among numerous sociological engagements with this problem (Ken, 2008; Weber, 2009; Weldon, 2006), Choo and Ferree (2010) provide an overview both of what is currently happening in intersectionality research and a program for what needs to happen. They argue that intersectionality can be conceptualized in three ways. One, it can take as its project inclusion, bringing in and privileging marginalized voices, moving them in hooks's phrase "from margin to center." Two, it can try to capture the process of intersectionality, that is, the way that different vectors coming together in individual lives vary in their effects on action and perhaps change the exact nature of the vectors themselves; this approach calls for comparisons, the need to find actors differently located in terms of the matrix of domination but in similar situations.

The third approach is to try to look at the ways in which intersecting structures and institutions create and reproduce what they call "systemic intersectionality"; that approach challenges the researcher to forego the vision of a "main effect"—like class—and to see the various hierarchical power arrangements of a society in interaction, producing the intersections that variously frame people lives. They here reference Walby (2009), who takes as a model for intersectionality study "the feedback loops of modern computational dynamics and complexity theories of environment-system interactions in the biological sciences to reconceptualize interaction effects as inherent in the nature of the process of stratification themselves."

In developing an agenda for change, intersectionality theory turns to the knowledge of oppressed people and their long-held evaluative principles of faith and justice (P. Collins, 1990, 1998, 2012; hooks, 1990; Lorde, 1984; Misra, 2012). The theory argues for the need to bear witness, to protest, and to organize for change within the context of the oppressed community, for only within community can one keep faith in the eventual triumph of justice—a justice understood not in the narrow framing of legal rationality but as the working-out within social institutions and social relations of the principles of fairness to and concern for others and oneself.

Feminism and Postmodernism

Postmodernist theory has affected feminist theory in general in two important ways. First, it has radically challenged the central question of all feminist theory, *"And what about the women?"* by developing a philosophic argument about what the category "women" really means, an argument that extends to challenge the concept of gender. Second, postmodernism has provided feminist theory with "an oppositional epistemology," a strategy for questioning the claims to truth advanced by any given theory. It has done the latter most effectively through its creation of a rich and provocative language to be used in challenging the taken-for-granted assumptions that it argues were constituted by modernity. The most important thinker in a feminist postmodern theory is philosopher Judith Butler; she and other feminist postmodernists draw on the work of Michel Foucault and Jacques Derrida, among other poststructuralist and postmodernist thinkers (see Chapter 16).

Postmodernist theory begins with the observation that people no longer live under conditions of modernity but live now in "postmodernity." This postmodern world is produced by the interplay of four major changes: (1) an expansive stage in global capitalism; (2) the weakening of centralized state power (with the collapse of the old imperial systems, the fragmentation of the communist bloc, and the rise of ethnic politics within nation-states); (3) the patterning of life by an increasingly powerful and penetrative technology that controls production and promotes consumerism; and (4) the development of liberationist social movements based not in class but in other forms of identity—nationalism, race, gender, sexual orientation, ethnicity, religion, and environmentalism. These changes, as feminist philosopher Susan Bordo explains, were brought about by people worldwide engaged in political practice and asking a new set of questions: *"Whose* truth? *Whose* nature? *Whose* version of reason? *Whose* history? *Whose* tradition?" (Bordo, 1990:136–137).

These questions led postmodernists to reject the basic principle of modernist epistemology—that humans can, by the exercise of pure reason, arrive at a complete and objective knowledge of the world, a knowledge that is a representation of reality, "a mirror of nature." They argue that this modernist principle gives rise to a number of epistemological errors—the *god-eye* view that locates the observer outside the world being observed; the *grand narrative* that holistically explains that world; *foundationalism* that identifies certain rules of analysis as always appropriate; *universalism* that asserts that there are discoverable principles that everywhere govern the world; *essentialism* that claims that people are constituted by core and unchanging qualities; *representation* that presumes that one's statement about the world can accurately reflect the world. Postmodernism questions the existence both of "reason" as a universal, essential quality of the human mind and of the "reasoning subject" as a consistent, unified configuration of consciousness. Postmodernists portray the knowledge-making process as one of multiple representations of experience created by differently located discourse groups in which the establishment of any hegemonic knowledge-claim results from an effective exercise of power. They have produced a powerful set of practices and vocabulary for *interrogating* the modernist claim of definitive statements. They suggest alternative epistemological practices such as *decentering,* which moves the understandings of nonprivileged groups to the center of discourse and knowledge; *deconstruction,* which shows how concepts, posed as accurate representations of the world, are historically constructed and contain contradictions; and a focus on *difference,* which explores any knowledge construct not only for what it says but for what it erases or marginalizes, particularly through the application of modernist *binary logic* of "either/or."

A major substantive contribution of postmodernist theory to general feminist theory has been its questioning of the primary category of feminist theory: woman (or women). The classic statement of this questioning has been Judith Butler's 1990 *Gender Trouble.* Butler questioned *woman, gender,* and whether there is, as popularly presumed, a coherent relation among *sex, gender,* and *sexuality*—and she situated her argument directly in the political context of the women's movement, warning that "The premature insistence on a stable subject of feminism, understood as a seamless category of women, inevitably generates multiple refusals to accept the category. These domains of exclusion reveal the coercive and regulatory consequences of that construction, even when the construction has been elaborated for emancipatory purposes. Indeed, the fragmentation within feminism and the paradoxical opposition to feminism from 'women' whom feminism claims to represent suggest the necessary limits of identity politics" (Butler, 1990:4); this warning helped focus a range of Third Wave feminist concerns with the Second Wave position that was seemingly anchored in the concept of woman as a possible if not a seamless category.

For Butler, the category of woman arises out of the process that produces gender, a process she names "performativity." Her definition of *performativity,* a work in progress, has its origins in speech-act theory, where a performative is "that discursive practice that brings into being or enacts that which it names and so marks the constitutive or productive power of discourse" (Butler, 1995:134). (A classic example of a performative, drawn from speech-act philosopher J. L. Austin, occurs when a judge or minister says, "I now pronounce you man and wife.") Butler sees gender arising as people perform it in interaction with each other—by performing gender, they create it. Butler later elaborates how this occurs in *Bodies That Matter* (1993) using Jacques Derrida's principle of *iterability* to explain how these repeated performances lead to a sense of gender and woman and man. Iterability is the capacity of signs or symbols to be repeated in different situations—for example, "I love you," "You're looking great," "You wanna go out?" This repetition both confers consistency to performance and allows for some possibility of variation in the meaning and outcome. But people are not free to choose their performances. Drawing on Foucault, Butler sets performativity in the context of discourse or "regulative discourse." For Foucault, a discourse is a composite of ideas, actions, beliefs, and attitudes that systematically relate and construct the worlds and the subjects about which they speak. Gender performance then is subject to regulative discourses that vary across history and culture but that control what one is able to do to act as a man or a woman. Because of performativity, subject to iterability and regulative discourse, gender is experienced as a core identity that everyone shares. The assignment of sex to an individual, in terms of two binary opposites, is a performance, subject to regulative discourse that specifies what can be taken into account in making this assignment and reproduced through iterability. But an alternative understanding, Butler says, is that "In the place of an original identification which serves as a determining cause, gender identity might be reconceived as a personal/cultural history of received meanings subject to a set of imitative practices which refer laterally to other imitations and which, jointly, construct the illusion of a primary and interior gendered self or parody the mechanism of that construction" (Butler, 1990:138). In Butler's thinking, people do not begin life with an internal identity as man or woman; rather they get hold of certain understandings of man and woman depending on their personal biographies and their location in history, and the regulatory discourses that constitute them. These meanings suggest ways of acting, and as the person looks around, she or he can see other people engaged in similar ways of acting. Thus, gender is created as people imitate other people trying to act in accord with culturally given ideas about masculinity and femininity. These ideas so effectively bring into being what they name that people take as real the idea of a core gendered self. But Butler (1990:25) argues, playing off Nietzsche, that "There is no gender identity behind the expressions of gender; that identity is performatively constituted by the very 'expressions' that are said to be its results." Key to those expressions in a society governed by a sociocultural history that privileges heterosexuality as natural is the need to establish oneself as different from the other gender in order to participate in the ongoing imitation that is heterosexuality.

Butler's work constitutes the major contribution of postmodern feminism, but other scholars have adapted ideas from Michel Foucault (Oksala, 2011) to the project of women's liberation, most especially his insights about power, power/knowledge, and body. Illustrative of feminist adaptations are studies by Bartky (1992) and Bordo (1993) that turn on Foucault's insights into the body as the principal site for the exercise of power in modern societies, his ability to present a nonessentialist but very material body that is historically constructed by discourses at a given moment in time.

Bartsky looks at women's "self-imposed" exercise and dieting regimes and Bordo at women's eating disorders, both of which are seen as examples of bodies being created out of regulative discourses or power/knowledge regimes that say this is what can be done at this moment in the production of femininity.

But the feminist relation to postmodernism is also marked by unease. Many feminists see postmodernism as exclusive in aspiration and therefore antithetical to the feminist project of inclusion (Benhabib, 1998). Evidence for this unease includes postmodernism's arcane vocabulary, its location in the academy rather than in political struggle, and its nonreflexive grasp for hegemonic status in that academic discourse. Many feminists also question the "innocence" of the postmodernist challenge, wondering whether it is truly liberationist or is part of a politics of knowledge in which a privileged academic class responds to the challenges of marginalized persons with a technically complex argument to the effect that no location for speech can claim authority. Hartsock (1990:169) has made the classic statement of this concern: "Somehow it seems highly suspicious that it is at the precise moment when so many groups have been engaged in . . . redefinitions of the marginalized Others that suspicions emerge about the nature of the 'subject,' about the possibilities for a general theory which can describe the world, about historical 'progress.'" Another source of unease is that the postmodernist emphasis on an infinite regress of deconstruction and difference leads people away from collective, liberationist politics and toward a radical individualism that may conclude that "'because every . . . one of us is different and special, it follows that every problem or crisis is exclusively our own, or, conversely, your problem—not mine'" (P. Collins, 1998:150; Jordan, 1992). Above all, the postmodernist turn takes feminist scholars away from the materiality of inequality, injustice, and oppression and toward a neo-idealist posture that sees the world as "discourse," "representation," and "text." In severing the link to material inequality, postmodernism may be moving feminism away from its commitment to progressive change—the foundational project of any critical social theory.

Feminist Sociological Theorizing

This section presents a synthesis of ideas implicit or explicit in the varieties of feminist theory described above in order to develop a statement of some fundamental principles of feminist *sociological* theorizing. We identify four distinctive features of this effect: its sociology of knowledge, its model of society, its patterning of social interaction, and its focus on a subjective level of social experience. Our synthesis draws on classic statements by theorists writing out of a variety of disciplines, including sociology. The major influences are Andersen, 2005; J. Benjamin, 1988; Bordo, 1993; Butler, 1990, 1993; Chodorow, 1978; P. Collins, 1990, 1998, 2004; England, 2010; Fenstermaker and West, 2002; Gilligan, 1982; Heilbrun, 1988; Hennessey and Ingraham, 1997; Ingraham, 1999; Lorde, 1984; MacKinnon, 1989; Rich, 1976, 1980; Ridgeway, 2011; Dorothy Smith, 1989, 1990a, 1990b, 1999a, 1999b, 2004a, 2009; and West and Fenstermaker, 1993.

A Feminist Sociology of Knowledge

A feminist sociology of knowledge sees everything that people label "knowledge of the world" as having four characteristics: (1) it is always created from the standpoint of embodied actors situated in groups that are differentially located in social structure; (2) it is, thus, always partial and interested, never total and objective; (3) it is produced in and varies among groups and, to some degree, among actors within groups; and (4) it is always affected by power relations—whether formulated from the standpoint of dominant or subordinate groups. This understanding of knowledge has been named "feminist standpoint epistemology" (Harding, 1986). Feminist sociological theorizing begins with a sociology of knowledge because feminists attempt to describe, analyze, and change the world from the standpoint of women and because, working from women's subordinated position in social relations, feminist sociological theorists see that knowledge production is part of the system of power governing all production in society. Feminist sociological theory attempts to alter the balance of power within sociological discourse—and within social theory—by establishing the standpoint of women in particular, and of oppressed people more broadly, as standpoints from which social knowledge is constructed.

In attempting to do sociology from the standpoint of women, feminist socio-logical theorists have to consider what constitutes a standpoint of women. A stand-point is the product of a social collectivity with a sufficient history and commonality of circumstance to develop a shared knowledge of social relations. Feminists, starting where Marx left off, have identified three crucial collectivities—owners, workers, *and women*—whose distinctive relationships to the processes of social production and reproduction constitute them as standpoint groups. Historically women under patriar-chy, whatever their class and race, have been assigned to the tasks of social reproduc-tion (childbearing, child rearing, housekeeping, food preparation, care of the ill and dependent, emotional and sexual service). Yet any solidarity of women as a "class" in patriarchal production is fractured by other class configurations, including eco-nomic class and race class. While women's shared and historical relation to social reproduction in circumstances of subordination is the basis for the feminist claim of "the standpoint of women," in the daily workings of social power the intersection of gender inequality with race inequality, class inequality, geosocial inequality, and inequalities based on sexuality and age produces a complex system of unequally empowered standpoint groups relating through shifting arrangements of coalition and opposition. These intersectionalities are now an integral part of the feminist descrip-tion and analysis of women's standpoint.

This understanding of knowledge as the product of different standpoint groups presents feminist sociological theorists with the problem of how to produce a feminist sociological account that is both acceptable to sociologists and useful to feminism's emancipatory project. At least four strategies are used. One is asserting the validity of "webbed accounts," that is, accounts woven together by reporting all the various actors' or standpoint groups' knowledges of an experience and describing the situa-tions, including the dynamics of power, out of which the actors or groups came to create these versions (Haraway, 1988). A second strategy is that of privileging the accounts or standpoints of the less empowered actors or groups because a major factor in unequal power relations is that dominants' views are given both more credence and more circulation. The privileging of the standpoints of the disempowered is a part of the feminist emancipatory project, but it also produces an important corrective to mainstream sociological theories by changing the angle of vision from which social processes are understood. A third strategy requires the feminist theorist to be reflexive about and able to give an account of the stages through which she or he moves from knowledge of an individual's or group's standpoint to the generalizations of a socio-logical account, for that translation is an act of power (P. Collins, 1990, 1998; Dorothy Smith, 1990a). A fourth strategy is for the social theorist to identify the particular location from which she or he speaks and thus to identify her or his partiality (in all meanings of that word) and its effect on the theory constructed.

In keeping with the fourth strategy, we should declare the standpoint from which we create the theoretical synthesis presented here. We write from the relatively privi-leged class position of academic social scientists living in the contemporary United States, but also as women located within a particular intersection of vectors of oppres-sion and privilege that makes us subject to experiences of racism, ageism, and hetero-sexism. We also write out of family heritages of membership in historically constituted standpoint groups shaped by poverty and by colonial status. This intermingling of cur-rent status and family history shapes both our interests and our values. The synthesis we present here reflects oppression theories' concept of a just society as one that empowers all people to claim as a fundamental right (not a begrudged concession or a reward) a fair share of social goods—from the material essentials of food, clothing, shelter, health care, and education, to an absence of fear of violence, to a positive valuation of self in the particularities of one's group and individual identity.

The Macro-Social Order

In this and the next two sections we operate within the established sociological con-ventions of vocabulary and conceptualization by organizing our presentation around the categories of *macro-social, micro-social,* and *subjectivity*—although much of feminist sociological theory poses a fundamental critique of those categories.

Feminist sociology's view of the macro-social order begins by expanding the Marxian concept of economic production into a much more general concept of social production, that is, the production of all human social life. Along with the production of commodities for the market, social production for feminists also includes arrange-ments such as the organization of housework, which produce the essential commodi-ties and services of the household; sexuality, which pattern and satisfy human desire; intimacy, which pattern and satisfy human emotional needs for acceptance, approval, love, and self-esteem; state and religion, which create the rules and laws of a com-munity; and politics, mass media, and academic discourse, which establish institution-alized, public definitions of the situation.

Thus framed and expanded, the Marxian model of intergroup relations remains visible in a feminist model of social organization. Each of these various types of social production is based on an arrangement by which some actors, controlling the resources crucial to that activity, act as dominants, or "masters," who dictate and profit from the circumstances of production. Within each productive sector, production rests on the work of subordinates, or "servants," whose energies create the world ordered into being by their masters and whose exploitation denies them the rewards and satisfactions produced by their work. Through feminist theory, we see, more vividly than through Marxian theory, the intimate association between masters and servants that may lie at the heart of production and the indispensability of the servant's work in creating and sustaining everything necessary to human social life. In intimate relations of exploitation, domination may be expressed not as coercion but as paternalism, "the combination of positive feelings toward the group with discriminatory intentions toward the group." Paternalism masks for both parties but does not transform a relationship of domination and subordination (Jackman, 1994:11). Social production occurs through a multidimensional structure of domination and exploitation that organizes class, gender, race, sex, power, and knowledge into overlapping hierarchies of intimately associated masters and workers.

This model of stratification in social production offers a direct critique of the structural-functionalist vision of a society composed of a system of separate institutions and distinct, though interrelated, roles. Feminist theory claims that this image is not generalizable but that it depicts the experiences and vantage points of society's dominants—white, male, upper-class, and adult. Feminist research shows that women and other nondominants do not experience social life as a movement among compartmentalized roles. Instead, they are involved in a balancing of roles, a merging of role-associated interests and orientations, and, through this merging, in a weaving together of social institutions. Indeed, one indicator of the dominant group's control over the situations of production may be that its members can achieve purposive role compartmentalization. But feminist sociology stresses that this condition depends on the subordinate services of actors who cannot compartmentalize their lives and actions. Indeed, were these subordinate actors to compartmentalize similarly, the whole system of production in complex industrialized societies would collapse. In contrast to the structural-functional model, the feminist model emphasizes that the role-merging experience of women may be generalizable to the experience of many other subordinate "servant" groups whose work produces the fine-grained texture of daily life. The understandings that such subordinated groups have of the organization of social life may be very different from the understanding depicted in structural-functionalist theory; even the identification of key institutional spheres may differ. Yet their vantage point springs from situations necessary to society as it is currently organized and from work that makes possible the masters' secure sense of an institutionally compartmentalized world.

Further, feminism emphasizes the centrality of ideological domination to the structure of social domination. Ideology is an intricate web of beliefs about reality and social life that is institutionalized as public knowledge and disseminated throughout society so effectively that it becomes taken-for-granted knowledge for all social groups. Thus, what feminists see as "public knowledge of social reality" is not an overarching culture, a consensually created social product, but a reflection of the interests and experiences of society's dominants and one crucial index of their power in society. What distinguishes this view from traditional Marxian analysis is that for feminists ideological control is a basic process in domination, and the hierarchical control of discourse and knowledge is a key element in societal domination.

Central to feminist concerns about the macro-social order is the macro-structural patterning of gender as a structure. It is on this structure that oppression is founded. Feminist theorists argue that women's bodies constitute an essential resource in social production and reproduction and therefore become a site of exploitation and control. Gender oppression is reproduced by an ideological system of institutionalized knowledge that reflects the interests and experiences of men. Among other things, this gender ideology identifies men as the bearers of sociocultural authority and allocates to the male role the right to dominate and to the female role the obligation to serve in all dimensions of social production. Gender ideology constructs women as objects of male desire whose social value is determined by their fabrication of an appropriately molded body. Gender ideology also systematically flattens and distorts women's productive activities by (1) trivializing some of them, for example, housework; (2) idealizing to the point of unrecognizability other activities, for example, mothering; and (3) making invisible yet other crucial work, for example, women's multiple and vital contributions to the production of marketplace commodities. These ideological processes may be generalizable to the macro-structural production of all social subordination.

Capitalism and patriarchy, although analytically separate forms of domination, reinforce each other in numerous ways. For example, the organization of production into public and private spheres and the gendering of those spheres benefit both systems of domination. Capitalism benefits in that women's labor in the private sphere reproduces the worker at no cost to capital; further, their responsibility for the private sphere makes women a marginal but always co-optable source of cheap labor, driving wages down generally. At the same time patriarchy benefits from this exploitation of the woman worker because it sustains her dependence on men. Women's difficult entry into the public sphere ensures that what "good" employment may be available there will go first to men. Women's experiences of sexual harassment on the job and of being hassled in public places are not incidental and insignificant micro events but examples of a power relation in which patriarchy helps police the borders for capital. This division is further complicated by the "race-ing" and "age-ing" as well as the gendering of public and private.

The Micro-Social Order

At the micro-interactional level, feminist sociology (like some microsociological perspectives) focuses on how individuals take account of each other as they pursue objective projects or intersubjective meanings. Feminist sociological theory argues that the conventional models of interaction (social behaviorist and social definitionist—see the Appendix) may depict how equals in macro-structural, power-conferring categories create meanings and negotiate relationships in the pursuit of joint projects or how structural dominants experience interaction with both equals and subordinates. But feminist theory suggests that when structural unequals interact there are many other qualities to their association than those suggested by the conventional models: that action is responsive rather than purposive, that there is a continuous enactment of power differentials, that the meaning of many activities is obscured or invisible, that access is not always open to those settings in which shared meanings are most likely to be created. This analysis offers an additional dimension to the sociology of gender literature on doing gender and to the postmodernist conception of gender as performativity. What may be a near constant in all interactive situations in addition to doing gender and doing difference is doing power. People in interaction are adjusting their actions not only in anticipation of other people's responses or in the work of imitation of others' imitations but also in terms of a calculus of who can finally get their way by what means.

Most mainstream microsociology presents a model of purposive human beings setting their own goals and pursuing them in linear courses of action in which they (individually or collectively) strive to link means to ends. In contrast, feminist research shows, first, that women's lives have a quality of incidentalism, as women find themselves caught up in agendas that shift and change with the vagaries of marriage, husbands' courses of action, children's unpredictable impact on life plans, divorce, widowhood, and the precariousness of most women's wage-sector occupations. Second, in their daily activities, women find themselves not so much pursuing goals in linear sequences but responding continuously to the needs and demands of others. This theme has been developed from analysis of the emotional and relational symbiosis between mothers and daughters, through descriptions of intensely relational female play groups, to analyses of women in their typical occupations as teachers, nurses, secretaries, receptionists, and office helpers and accounts of women in their roles as wives, mothers, and community and kin coordinators. In calling women's activities "responsive," we are not describing women as passively reactive. Instead, we are drawing a picture of beings who are oriented not so much to their own goals as to the tasks of monitoring, coordinating, facilitating, and moderating the wishes, actions, and demands of others. In place of microsociology's conventional model of purposeful actors, then, feminist research presents a model of actors who are in their daily lives responsively located at the center of a web of others' actions and who in the long term find themselves located in one or another of these situations by forces that they can neither predict nor control.

Conventional micro-social theory assumes that the pressures in interactive situations toward collaboration and meaning construction are so great that actors, bracketing considerations of the macro structure, orient toward each other on an assumption of equality. Feminist research on interactions between women and men contradicts this idea, showing that these social interactions are pervasively patterned by influences from their macro-structural context. In their daily activities, women are affected by the fact that they are structurally subordinate to the men with whom they interact in casual associations, courtship, marriage, family, and wage work. Any interpersonal equality or dominance that women as individuals may achieve is effectively offset, within the interactive process itself, by these structural patterns—of which the most pervasive is the institution of gender. The macro-structural patterning of gender inequality is intricately woven through the interactions between women and men and affects not only its broad division of labor, in who sets and who implements projects, but also its processual details, which repeatedly show the enactment of authority and deference in seating and seating-standing arrangements, forms of address and conversation, eye contact, and the control of space and time. This assumption of inequality as a feature in interactive situations is intensified and complicated when factors of race and class are included in the feminist analytical frame.

Social definitionists assume that one of the major ongoing projects in social interaction is the construction of shared meanings. Actors, seeing each other in activity and interaction, form shared understandings through communication and achieve a common vantage point on their experiences. Feminists argue that this assumption must be qualified by the fact that micro interactions are embedded in and permeated by the macro structures of power and ideology. These structures pattern the meanings assigned to activities in interaction. Men as dominants in interaction with women are more likely to assign to women's activity meanings drawn from the macro structure of gender ideology than either to enter the situation with an attitude of open inquiry or to draw on any other macro-level typing for interpreting women's activity. Women, immersed in the same ideological interpretation of their experiences, stand at a point of dialectical tension, balancing this ideology against the actuality of their lives. A great diversity of meanings develops out of this tension. Social definitionists assume that actors, relating and communicating intimately and over long periods of time, create a common vantage point or system of shared understanding. Feminists' research on what may be the most intimate, long-term, male-female association—marriage— shows that, for all the reasons reported above, marriage partners remain strangers to each other and inhabit separate worlds of meaning. This "stranger-ness" may be greater for the dominant man, in the interests of effective control, than for the subordinate woman who must monitor the dominant's meanings (Dorothy Smith, 1979).

A democratic ethos shapes both social-definitionist and social-behaviorist descriptions of interaction. Conventional models imply that people have considerable equality of opportunity and freedom of choice in moving in and out of interactional settings. Feminist research shows that the interactions in which women are most free to create with others meanings that depict their life experiences are those that occur when they are in relationship and communication with similarly situated women. Moreover, these associations can be deeply attractive to women because of the practical, emotional, and meaning-affirming support they provide. Women, however, are not freely empowered to locate in these settings. Law, interactional domination, and ideology restrict and demean this associational choice so that, insidiously, even women become suspicious of its attractions. Under these circumstances, the association becomes not a free and open choice but a subterranean, circumscribed, and publicly invisible arena for relationship and meaning.

Finally, a feminist analysis of interactional practices may emphasize differences between men and women explainable in terms of deep psychic structures. Male training rewards individuation and the repudiation of the female so that the male understands at an early age that his claim to male privilege involves his distancing from female behaviors. Similarly, the female learns early that one of the duties of women— to men and to each other—is to recognize the subjectivity of the other through interactional gestures such as paying attention, commenting on actions done, and using gestures to indicate approval and awareness. These behaviors permeate and explain not only interactions across gender but interactions within same-gender groups. Women are repeatedly shown as enacting more responsiveness to the other and engaging in more ongoing monitoring of the other's needs and desires. Men are more inclined to feel both the right and the duty to compartmentalize in order to attain individual projects and to view their responsiveness to other as an act of generosity, not a part of expected interactional behavior.

Subjectivity

Most sociological theories subsume the subjective level of social experience under micro-social action (micro subjectivity) or as "culture" or "ideology" at the macro level (macro subjectivity) (see Chapter 13 and the Appendix). Feminist sociology, however, insists that the actor's individual interpretation of goals and relationships must be looked at as a distinct level. This insistence, like so much of feminist sociology, grows out of the study of women's lives and seems applicable to the lives of subordinates in general. Women as subordinates are particularly aware of the distinctiveness of their subjective experience precisely because their own experience so often runs counter to prevailing cultural and micro-interactionally established definitions. When sociologists do look at the subjective level of experience, usually as part of the micro-social order, they focus on four major issues: (1) role taking and knowledge of the other, (2) the process of the internalization of community norms, (3) the nature of the self as social actor, and (4) the nature of the consciousness of everyday life. This section explores the feminist thesis on each of these issues.

The conventional sociological model of subjectivity (as presented to us in the theories of Mead [see Chapter 9] and Schutz) assumes that in the course of role taking, the social actor learns to see the self through the eyes of others deemed more or less the same as the actor. But feminist sociology shows that women are socialized to see themselves through the eyes of men. Even when significant others are women, they have been so socialized that they too take the male view of self and of other women. Women's experience of learning to role-take is shaped by the fact that they must, in a way men need not, learn to take the role of the genuine *other*, not just a social other who is taken to be much like oneself. The other for women is the male and is alien. The other for men is, first and foremost, men who are like them in a quality that the culture considers of transcendent importance: gender. Feminist theory emphasizes that this formula is complicated by the intersection of the vectors of oppression and privilege within individual lives.

Role taking usually is seen as culminating in the internalization of community norms via the social actor's learning to take the role of "the generalized other," a construct that the actor mentally creates out of the amalgam of macro- and micro-level experiences that form her or his social life. The use of the singular *other* indicates that microsociologists usually envision this imagined generalized other as a cohesive, coherent, singular expression of expectations. But feminists argue that in a male-dominated patriarchal culture, the generalized other represents a set of male-dominated community norms that force the woman to picture herself as "less than" or "unequal to" men. To the degree that a woman succeeds in formulating a sense of generalized other that accurately reflects the dominant perceptions of the community, she may have damaged her own possibilities for self-esteem and self-exploration. Feminist theory calls into question the existence of a unified generalized other for the majority of people. The subordinate has to pivot between a world governed by a dominant generalized other, or meaning system, and locations in "home groups" that offer alternative understandings and generalized others. The awareness of the possibility of multiple generalized others is essential to understanding the potential complexity of having or being a self.

Microsociologists describe the social actor as picturing the everyday world as something to be mastered according to one's particular interests. Feminist sociologists argue that women may find themselves so limited by their status as women that the idea of projecting their own plans onto the world becomes meaningless in all but theory. Further, women may not experience the life-world as something to be mastered according to their own particular interests. They may be socialized to experience that life-world as a place in which one balances a variety of actors' interests. Women may not have the same experience of control of particular spheres of space, free from outside interference. Similarly, their sense of time rarely can follow the simple pattern of first things first because they have as a life project the balancing of the interests and projects of others. Thus, women may experience planning and actions as acts of concern for a variety of interests, their own and others; may act in projects of cooperation rather than mastery; and may evaluate their ongoing experiences of role balancing not as role conflicts but as a more appropriate response to social life than role compartmentalization.

Feminist sociologists have critically evaluated the thesis of a unified consciousness of everyday life that traditional microsociologists usually assume. Feminist sociologists stress that for women the most pervasive feature of the cognitive style of everyday life is that of a "bifurcated consciousness," developing along "a line of fault" between their own personal, lived, and reflected-on experience and the established types available in the social stock of knowledge to describe that experience (Dorothy Smith, 1979, 1987). Everyday life itself thus divides into two realities for subordinates: the reality of actual, lived, reflected-on experience and the reality of social typifications. Often aware of the way that their own experience differs from that of the culturally dominant males with whom they interact, women may be less likely to assume a shared subjectivity. As biological and social beings whose activities are not perfectly regulated by patriarchal time, they are more aware of the demarcation between time as lived experience and time as a social mandate. A feminist sociology of subjectivity perhaps would begin here: How do people survive when their own experience does not fit the established social typifications of that experience? We know already that some do so by avoiding acts of sustained reflection; some by cultivating their own series of personal types to make sense of their experience; some by seeking community with others who share this bifurcated reality; and some by denying the validity of their own experience.

What we have generalized here for women's subjectivity may be true for the subjectivity of all subordinates. (1) Their experience of role taking is complicated by their awareness that they must learn the expectations of an other who by virtue of differences in power is alien. (2) They must relate not to a generalized other but to many generalized others in both the culture of the powerful and the various subcultures of the less empowered and the disempowered. (3) They do not experience themselves as purposive social actors who can chart their own course through life—although they may be constantly told that they can do so, especially within the American ethos. (4) Most pervasively, they live daily with a bifurcated consciousness, a sense of the line of fault between their own lived experiences and what the dominant culture tells them is the social reality.

Everything in this discussion has assumed a unified subject, that is, an individual woman or man with an ongoing, consistent consciousness and a sense of self. The unified subject is important to feminist theory because it is that subject who experiences pain and oppression, makes value judgments, and resists or accepts the world in place—the unified subject is the primary agent of social change. Yet our discussion of subjectivity also raises questions about how unified this subject is; there are the problems of a subject whose generalized other is truly "other" or "alien," who experiences not *a* generalized other but many generalized others, whose consciousness is bifurcated, and whose self in its capacities for development and change may be viewed more as a process than as a product. All these tendencies toward an understanding of the self as fragmented rather than as unified are inherent in feminist theorizing of the self—indeed, they are at the heart of feminist ideas about resistance and change. This sense of fragmentation is much intensified in postmodernist feminist critiques (discussed earlier in this chapter), a theoretical position that raises questions about the very possibility of "a unified subject or consciousness." If a self, any self, is subject to change from day to day or even moment to moment, if we can speak of "being not myself," then on what basis do we posit a self? Yet feminist critics of postmodernism respond by beginning in the experience of women in daily life, who when they say "I was not myself" or "I have not been myself" assume a stable self from which they have departed and, further, by those very statements, some self that knows of the departure.

Summary

Feminist theory develops a system of ideas about human life that features women as objects and subjects, doers and knowers. Feminism has a history as long as women's subordination—and women have been subordinated almost always and everywhere. Until the late 1700s feminist writing survived as a thin but persistent trickle of protest; from that time to the present, feminist writing has become a growing tide of critical work. While the production of feminist theory has typically expanded and contracted with societal swings between reform and retrenchment, the contemporary stage of feminist scholarship shows a self-sustaining expansion despite new conservative societal trends.

Although feminist theoretical production has occurred in the same time frame as the development of sociology, feminist theory remained on the margins of sociology, ignored by the central male formulators of the discipline until the 1970s. Since the 1970s, a growing presence of women in sociology and the momentum of the women's movement have established feminist theory as a new sociological paradigm that inspires much sociological scholarship and research.

Feminist scholarship is guided by four basic questions: *And what about the women? Why is women's situation as it is? How can we change and improve the social world?* and *What about differences among women?* Answers to these questions produce the varieties of feminist theory. This chapter patterns this variety to show four major groupings of feminist theory. Theories of gender difference see women's situation as different from men's, explaining this difference in terms of two distinct and enduring ways of being, male and female, or institutional roles and social interaction, or ontological constructions of woman as "other." Theories of gender inequality, notably by liberal feminists, emphasize women's claim to a fundamental right of equality and describe the unequal opportunity structures created by sexism. Gender oppression theories include feminist psychoanalytic theory and radical feminism. The former explains the oppression of women in terms of psychoanalytic descriptions of the male psychic drive to dominate; the latter, in terms of men's ability and willingness to use violence to subjugate women. Structural oppression theories include socialist feminism and intersectionality theory; socialist feminism describes oppression as arising from a patriarchal and a capitalist attempt to control social production and reproduction; intersectionality theories trace the consequences of class, race, gender, affectional preference, and global location for lived experience, group standpoints, and relations among women.

Feminist theory offers five key propositions as a basis for the revision of standard sociological theories. First, the practice of sociological theory must be based in a sociology of knowledge that recognizes the partiality of all knowledge, the knower as embodied and socially located, and the function of power in effecting what becomes knowledge. Second, macro social structures are based in processes controlled by dominants acting in their own interests and executed by subordinates whose work is made largely invisible and undervalued even to themselves by dominant ideology. Thus, dominants appropriate and control the productive work of society, including not only economic production but also women's work of social reproduction. Third, micro-interactional processes in society are enactments of these dominant-subordinate power arrangements, enactments very differently interpreted by powerful actors and subordinate actors. Fourth, these conditions create in women's subjectivity a bifurcated consciousness along the line of fault caused by the juxtaposition of patriarchal ideology and women's experience of the actualities of their lives. Fifth, what has been said for women may be applicable to all subordinate peoples in some parallel, though not identical, form.

Integrative Sociological Theory

Micro-Macro and Agency-Structure Integration

Chapter Outline

Micro-Macro Integration

Agency-Structure Integration

Agency-Structure and Micro-Macro Linkages: Fundamental Differences

In this chapter we deal with two important developments in late twentieth-century sociological theory. Our first concern is a dramatic development that occurred largely in the United States in the 1980s (although, as we will see, it had important precursors) and continues to this day. That development is the growth of interest in the issue of the *micro-macro linkage* (Barnes, 2001; J. Turner, 2007b; Turner and Boyns, 2001). Then we will deal with a parallel development that occurred largely in European sociological theory—the rise in interest in the *relationship between agency and structure*. As we will see, there are important similarities *and* crucial differences between the American micro-macro literature and the European work on agency and structure. The micro-macro and agency-structure literatures themselves can be seen as synthetic developments and thus as parts of the broad movement toward theoretical synthesis that has gripped many of the perspectives discussed throughout Part Two of this book.

Micro-Macro Integration

Micro-Macro Extremism

Until recently, *one* of the major divisions in contemporary American sociological theory was the conflict between extreme *microscopic* and *macroscopic*[1] theories (and theorists) and, perhaps more important, between those who have *interpreted* sociological theories in these ways (Archer, 1982). Such extreme theories and interpretations of theories have tended to heighten the image of a great chasm between micro and macro theories and, more generally, the image of conflict and disorder (Gouldner, 1970; Wardell and Turner, 1986; Wiley, 1985) in sociological theory.

Although it is possible to interpret (and many have) the classic sociological theorists discussed in Part One of this book (Marx, Durkheim, Weber, Simmel) as either micro or macro extremists, the most defensible perspective, or at least the one that will orient this chapter, is that they were most generally concerned with the micro-macro linkage (Moscovici, 1993). Marx can be seen as being interested in the coercive and alienating effect of capitalist society on individual workers (and capitalists). Weber may be viewed as being focally concerned with the plight of the individual within the iron cage of a formally rational society. Simmel was interested primarily in the relationship between objective (macro) culture and subjective (or individual, micro) culture. Even Durkheim was concerned with the effect of macro-level social facts on individuals and individual behavior (for example, suicide). If we accept these characterizations of the classic sociological theorists, it appears that much of the last century of American sociological theory has involved a loss of concern for this linkage and the dominance of micro and macro extremists—that is, the preeminence of theorists and theories that accord overwhelming power and significance to either the micro or the macro level. Thus, the theories discussed in Part Two of this book tended toward micro or macro extremism. On the macro-extreme side were structural functionalism, conflict theory, and some varieties of neo-Marxian theory (especially economic determinism). On the micro-extreme end were symbolic interactionism, ethnomethodology, exchange, and rational choice theory.

Among the most notable of the twentieth-century macro-extreme theories are Parsons's (1966) "cultural determinism"[2]; Dahrendorf's (1959) conflict theory, with its focus on imperatively coordinated associations; and Peter Blau's macrostructuralism, epitomized by his proud announcement, "I am a structural determinist" (1977:x). Macrostructural extremism comes from other sources as well (Rubinstein, 1986), including network theorists such as White, Boorman, and Breiger (1976), ecologists such as Duncan and Schnore (1959), and structuralists such as Mayhew (1980). Few take a more extreme position than Mayhew, who says such things as, "In structural sociology the unit of analysis is always the social network, *never the individual*" (1980:349).

---

[1] Although the use of the terms *micro* and *macro* might suggest that we are dealing with a dichotomy, always keep in mind that there is a *continuum* ranging from the micro end to the macro end (see the Appendix).

[2] Even as sympathetic an observer as Jeffrey Alexander (1987a:296) admits Parsons's "own collectivist bias"; see also Coleman (1986:1310). However, although Parsons's greatest influence was in collectivistic theory, it is also possible to find within his work a strong micro-macro integrative theory.

On the micro-extreme side we can point to a good portion of symbolic interactionism and the work of Blumer (1969a), who often seemed to have structural functionalism in mind as he positioned symbolic interactionism as a sociological theory seemingly single-mindedly concerned with micro-level phenomena (see Chapter 9 for a very different interpretation of Blumer's perspective). An even clearer case of micro extremism is exchange theory and George Homans (1974), who sought an alternative to structural functionalism and found it in the extreme micro orientation of Skinnerian behaviorism. Then there is ethnomethodology and its concern for the everyday practices of actors. Garfinkel (1967) was put off by the macro foci of structural functionalism and its tendency to turn actors into "judgmental dopes." Scheff (2007) makes a more general case for "microsociology."

The Movement toward Micro-Macro Integration

Although micro-macro extremism characterized much of twentieth-century sociological theory, it became possible, beginning mainly in the 1980s, to discern a movement, largely in American sociology, away from micro-macro extremism and toward a broad consensus that *the* focus, instead, should be on *the integration (or synthesis, linkage) of micro and macro theories and/or levels of social analysis.* This approach represents quite a change from that of the 1970s, when Kemeny argued: "So little attention is given to this distinction that the terms 'micro' and 'macro' are not commonly even indexed in sociological works" (1976:731). It could be argued that at least in this sense American sociological theorists have rediscovered the theoretical project of the early masters.

While developments in the 1980s and 1990s were particularly dramatic, isolated earlier works directly addressed the micro-macro linkage. For example, in the mid-1960s Helmut Wagner (1964) dealt with the relationship between small-scale and large-scale theories. At the end of the decade Walter Wallace (1969) examined the micro-macro continuum, but it occupied a secondary role in his analysis and was included as merely one of the "complications" of his basic taxonomy of sociological theory. In the mid-1970s Kemeny (1976) called for greater attention to the micro-macro distinction as well as to the ways in which micro and macro relate to each other.

However, it was in the 1980s that we witnessed a flowering of work on the micro-macro linkage issue. Randall Collins argued that work on this topic "promises to be a significant area of theoretical advance for some time to come" (1986a:1350). In their introduction to a two-volume set of books, one devoted to macro theory (Eisenstadt and Helle, 1985a) and the other to micro theory (Helle and Eisenstadt, 1985), Eisenstadt and Helle concluded that "the confrontation between micro- and macro-theory belong[s] to the past" (1985b:3). Similarly, Münch and Smelser, in their conclusion to the anthology *The Micro-Macro Link* (Alexander et al., 1987), asserted: "Those who have argued polemically that one level is more fundamental than the other . . . must be regarded as in error. Virtually every contributor to this volume has correctly insisted on the mutual interrelations between micro and macro levels" (1987:385).

There are two major strands of work on micro-macro integration. Some theorists focus on integrating micro and macro *theories,* whereas others are concerned with developing a theory that deals with the linkage between micro and macro *levels* (Alford and Friedland, 1985; Edel, 1959) of social analysis. Above, for example, we quoted

Eisenstadt and Helle (1985b:3), who concluded that the confrontation between micro and macro *theories* was behind us, while Münch and Smelser (1987:385) came to a similar conclusion about the need to choose between emphasizing micro or macro *levels*. There are important differences between trying to integrate macro (for example, structural functionalism) and micro (for example, symbolic interactionism) theories and attempting to develop a theory that can deal with the relationship between macro (for example, social-structure) and micro (for example, personality) levels of social analysis (for an example of the latter, see Summers-Effler, 2002).[3]

Given this general introduction, we turn now to some examples of micro-macro integration. At a number of places throughout Part Two of this book, we dealt with efforts to integrate micro and macro *theories.* All the examples that follow focus on integrating micro and macro *levels of social analysis.*

Examples of Micro-Macro Integration

Integrated Sociological Paradigm

This section begins with George Ritzer's (1979, 1981a) effort at micro-macro integration. The discussion here will be relatively brief, because the integrated sociological paradigm also is discussed in the Appendix. In this section the focus is on what the integrated paradigm has to say about the issue of micro-macro linkage.

It should be noted that Ritzer's thinking on the integrated paradigm in general, and more specifically on micro-macro linkage, was shaped by the work of a number of predecessors, especially that of Abraham Edel (1959) and Georges Gurvitch (1964; see also Bosserman, 1968). Gurvitch operates with the belief that the social world can be studied in terms of five "horizontal," or micro-macro, levels (Smelser [1997] identifies four), presented in ascending order from micro to macro: forms of sociality, groupings, social class, social structure, and global structures. To complement this hierarchy, Gurvitch also offers ten "vertical," or "depth," levels, beginning with the most objective social phenomena (for example, ecological factors, organizations) and ending with the most subjective social phenomena (collective ideas and values, the collective mind). Gurvitch crosscuts his horizontal and vertical dimensions in order to produce numerous levels of social analysis.

Ritzer's work on the integrated sociological paradigm was motivated, in part, by the need to build upon Gurvitch's insights but to produce a more parsimonious model. It begins with the micro-macro continuum (Gurvitch's horizontal levels), ranging from individual thought and action to world-systems (see the Appendix, Figure A.1). To this continuum is added an objective-subjective continuum (Gurvitch's vertical levels), ranging from material phenomena such as individual action and bureaucratic structures to nonmaterial phenomena such as consciousness and norms and values (see the Appendix, Figure A.2). Like Gurvitch, Ritzer crosscuts these two continua, but in this case the result is a far more manageable four, rather than many, levels of social analysis. Figure 13.1 depicts Ritzer's major levels of social analysis.

---

[3] As well as with meso-level phenomena (Ulmer, 2007).

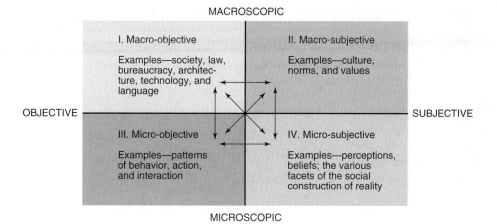

FIGURE 13.1   *Ritzer's Major Levels of Social Analysis*
Note that this is a "snapshot" in time. It is embedded in an ongoing historical process.

In terms of the micro-macro issue, Ritzer's view is that it cannot be dealt with apart from the objective-subjective continuum. All micro and macro social phenomena are also either objective or subjective. Thus, the conclusion is that there are four major levels of social analysis and that sociologists must focus on the dialectical interrelationship among these levels. The macro-objective level involves large-scale material realities such as society, bureaucracy, and technology. The macro-subjective level encompasses large-scale nonmaterial phenomena such as norms and values. At the micro levels, micro objectivity involves small-scale objective entities such as patterns of action and interaction, whereas micro subjectivity is concerned with the small-scale mental processes by which people construct social reality. Each of these four levels is important in itself, but of utmost importance is the dialectical relationship among and between them.

Ritzer has employed an integrative micro-macro approach in *Expressing America: A Critique of the Global Credit Card Society* (1995; see also R. Manning, 2000). Specifically, he used C. Wright Mills's (1959) ideas on the relationship between micro-level *personal troubles* and macro-level *public issues* to analyze the problems created by credit cards. Personal troubles are those problems that affect an individual and those people immediately around him or her. Public issues tend to be those that affect large numbers of people, perhaps society as a whole.

Ritzer examines a wide range of personal troubles and public issues associated with credit cards. This argument, and an integrated approach to the micro-macro linkage, can be illustrated by following this discussion of the issue of consumer debt. At the macro level, aggregate consumer debt has become a public issue because a large and growing number of people are increasingly indebted to credit card companies. A by-product of this growing consumer debt is an increase in delinquencies and bankruptcies. Also at the macro level, and a public issue, is the role played by the

JEFFREY C. ALEXANDER

An Autobiographical Sketch

Since my earliest days as an intellectual I have been pre-occupied with the problems of social action and social order and with the possibilities of developing approaches to these problems that avoid the extremes of one-dimensional thought. I have always been convinced that tense dichotomies, while vital as ideological currents in a democratic society, can be overcome in the theoretical realm.

My theoretical concerns first took form during the late 1960s and early 1970s, when I participated in the student protest movements as an undergraduate at Harvard College and as a graduate student at the University of California, Berkeley. New Left Marxism represented a sophisticated effort to overcome the economism of vulgar Marxism, as it tried to reinsert the actor into history. Because it described how material structures are interpenetrated with culture, personality, and everyday life, New Left Marxism—which for better or worse we largely taught ourselves—provided my first important training in the path to theoretical synthesis, which has marked my intellectual career.

In the early 1970s, I became dissatisfied with New Left Marxism, in part for political and empirical reasons. The New Left's turn toward sectarianism and violence frightened and depressed me, whereas the Watergate crisis demonstrated America's capacity for self-criticism. I decided that capitalist democratic societies provided opportunities for inclusion, pluralism, and reform that could not be envisioned even within the New Left version of Marxian thought.

Yet there were also more abstract theoretical reasons for leaving the Marxian approach to synthesis behind. As I more fully engaged classical and contemporary theory, I realized that this synthesis was achieved more by hyphenating—psychoanalytic-Marxism, cultural-Marxism, phenomenological-Marxism—than by opening up the central categories of action and order. In fact, the neo-Marxist categories of consciousness, action, community, and culture were black boxes. This recognition led me to the traditions that supplied the theoretical resources upon which New Left Marxism had drawn. I was fortunate in this graduate student effort to be guided by Robert Bellah and Neil Smelser, whose ideas about culture, social structure, and sociological theory made an indelible impression upon me and continue to be intellectual resources today.

In *Theoretical Logic in Sociology* (1982–1983), I published the results of this effort. The idea for this multivolume work began germinating in 1972, after an extraordinary encounter with Talcott Parsons's masterpiece, *The Structure of*

Social Action, allowed me to see my problems with Marxism in a new way. Later, under the supervision of Bellah, Smelser, and Leo Lowenthal, I worked through classical and contemporary theory with this new framework in mind.

My ambition in *Theoretical Logic* was to show that Durkheim and Weber supplied extensive theories of the culture that Marx had neglected and that Weber actually developed the first real sociological synthesis. I concluded, however, that Durkheim ultimately moved in an idealistic direction and that Weber developed a mechanistic view of modern society. I suggested that Parsons's work should be seen as a masterly modern effort at synthesis rather than as theory in the functionalist mode. Yet Parsons, too, failed to pursue synthesis in a truly determined way, allowing his theory to become overly formal and normatively based.

In *Twenty Lectures: Sociological Theory since World War II* (1987b), I argued that the divisions in post-Parsonsian sociology—between conflict and order theories, micro and macro approaches, structural and cultural views—were not fruitful. These groupings obscured basic social processes, like the continuing play of order and conflict and the dichotomized dimensions of society, that are always intertwined.

My response to this dead end has been to return to the original concerns of Parsons (Alexander and Colomy, 1990a) and to the earlier classics.

Yet, in trying to push theory into a new, "post-Parsonsian" phase, I have also tried to go beyond classical and modern theory. My encounters with the powerful group of phenomenologists in my home department at UCLA, particularly those with Harold Garfinkel, were an important stimulus. In "Action and Its Environments" (1987a), which I still regard as my most important piece of theoretical work, I laid out the framework for a new articulation of the micro-macro link.

I have also concentrated on developing a new cultural theory. An early reading of Clifford Geertz convinced me that traditional social-science approaches to culture are too limited. Since that time, my approach has been powerfully affected by semiotics, hermeneutics, and poststructuralist thought. Incorporating theories from outside of sociology, I have tried to theorize the manifold ways in which social structure is permeated by symbolic codes and meanings.

I believe this movement toward theoretical synthesis is being pushed forward by events in the world at large. In the postcommunist world, it seems important to develop models that help us understand our complex and inclusive, yet very fragile, democracies. I would like to believe, despite a great deal of evidence to the contrary, that progress is possible not only in society but in sociology as well. It is only through a multidimensional and synthetic view of society that such progress can be achieved.

[For more on Alexander, see Colomy, 2005.]

government in encouraging consumer debt through its tendency to accumulate debt. More important is the role played by the credit card firms in encouraging people to go into debt by doing everything they can to get as many credit cards into as many hands as possible. There is, for example, the increasing tendency for people to receive notices in the mail that they are eligible for preapproved credit cards. People can easily acquire a large number of credit cards with a huge collective credit limit. Perhaps the most reprehensible activities of the credit card firms involve their efforts to get cards into the hands of college and high school students. They are endeavoring to "hook" young people on a life of credit and indebtedness. Such activities are clearly a public issue and are causing personal troubles for untold numbers of people.

Millions of people have gotten themselves into debt, sometimes irretrievably, as a result of the abuse of credit cards. People build up huge balances, sometimes surviving by taking cash advances on one card to make minimum payments on other cards. Overwhelmed, many people become delinquent and sometimes are forced to declare bankruptcy. As a result, some people spend years, in some cases the rest of their lives, trying to pay off old debts and restore their ability to get credit. Even if it does not go this far, many people are working long hours just to pay the interest on their credit card debt and are able to make only a small, if any, dent in their credit balances. Thus, one could say they are indentured for life to the credit card companies.

The kinds of personal troubles described here, when aggregated, create public issues for society. And as we saw previously, public issues such as the policies and procedures of the credit card firms (for example, offering preapproved cards and recruiting students) help create personal troubles. Thus, there is a dialectical relationship between personal troubles and public issues, with each exacerbating the other. More generally, this example of credit cards illustrates the applicability of an integrated micro-macro approach to a pressing social problem.

Multidimensional Sociology

Jeffrey Alexander has offered what he calls a "new 'theoretical logic' for sociology" (1982:xv). That new logic affects "sociological thought at every level of the intellectual continuum" (Alexander, 1982:65). In this spirit, Alexander offers what he terms a *multidimensional sociology*. Although *multidimensionality* has several meanings in his work, the most relevant here is Alexander's multidimensional sense of levels of social analysis.

We can begin with what Alexander (following Parsons) terms the *problem of order*. Alexander suggests that the micro-macro continuum ("an 'individual' or 'collective' level of analysis" [1982:93]) is involved in the way order is created in society. At the macro end of the continuum, order is externally created and is collectivist in nature; that is, order is produced by collective phenomena. At the micro end, order is derived from internalized forces and is individualistic in nature; that is, order stems from individual negotiation.

To the problem of order is added, in a classic Parsonsian position, the *problem of action*. Action involves a materialist-idealist continuum that parallels the objective-subjective continuum employed in Ritzer's integrated sociological paradigm. At the material end, action is described as instrumental, rational, and conditional. At the

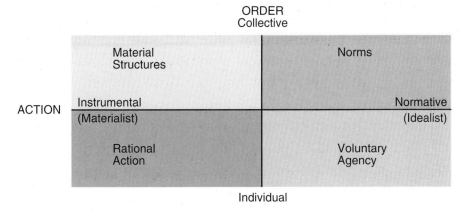

FIGURE 13.2   *Alexander's Integrative Model*

nonmaterial pole, action is normative, nonrational, and affective. When we crosscut Alexander's order and action continua, we come up with four levels of social analysis that strongly resemble the four levels that Ritzer employs (see Figure 13.2).

Although the terminology is slightly different, there are few if any differences between the models offered by Alexander and Ritzer. The major difference lies in the way they relate the four levels. Whereas Ritzer wants to focus on the dialectical relationship among all four levels, Alexander seeks to grant priority to one of the levels.

Alexander believes that according privilege to the micro levels is "a theoretical mistake" (1987a:295). He is highly critical of all theories, such as symbolic interactionism, that begin at the individual-normative level with nonrational voluntary agency and build toward the macro levels. From his point of view, the problem with these theories is that while maintaining notions of individual freedom and voluntarism, they are unable to deal with the unique (*sui generis*) character of collective phenomena. Alexander is also critical of theories, such as exchange theory, that start at the individual-instrumental level and move toward macro-level structures such as the economy. Such theories are also unable to handle macro-level phenomena adequately. Thus, Alexander is critical of all theories that have their origins at the micro levels and seek to explain macro-level phenomena from that base.

At the macro level, Alexander is critical of collective-instrumental theories (for example, economic and structural determinism) that emphasize coercive order and eliminate individual freedom. Basically, the problem is that such theories do not allow for individual agency.

Although he expressed an interest in focusing on the relationships among all four of his levels, Alexander's sympathies (not surprisingly, given his Parsonsian and structural-functionalist roots) lay with the collective-normative level and theories that begin at that level. As he put it, "The hope for combining collective order and individual voluntarism lies with the normative, rather than the rationalist tradition" (Alexander, 1982:108). Central to this belief is his view that such an orientation is preferable because the sources of order are internalized (in the conscience) rather than externalized, as is the case with the collective-instrumental orientation. This focus on the internalization of norms allows for *both* order and voluntary agency.

Overall, Alexander argues that any individual, or micro, perspective is to be rejected because it ends with "randomness and complete unpredictability" rather than order (1985:27). Thus, "the general framework for social theory can be derived *only* from a collectivist perspective" (1985:28; italics added). And between the two collectivist perspectives, Alexander subscribes to the collective-normative position.

Thus, to Alexander social theorists must choose either a collectivist (macro) or an individualist (micro) perspective. If they choose a collectivist position, they can incorporate only a "relatively small" element of individual negotiation. If, however, they choose an individualist theory, they are doomed to the "individualist dilemma" of trying to sneak into theory supraindividual phenomena to deal with the randomness inherent in their theory. This dilemma can be resolved only "if the formal adherence to individualism is abandoned" (Alexander, 1985:27).

Thus, although Alexander employs four levels of analysis that closely resemble those utilized by Ritzer, there is an important difference in the two models. Alexander accords priority to collective-normative theories and to a focus on norms in social life. Ritzer refuses to accord priority to any level and argues for the need to examine the dialectical relationship among and between all four levels. Alexander ends up giving inordinate significance to macro (subjective) phenomena, and as a result, his contribution to the development of a theory of micro-macro integration is highly limited. In a later work, Alexander said, "I believe theorists falsely generalize from a single variable to the immediate reconstruction of the whole" (1987a:314). It can be argued that Alexander is one of these theorists because he seeks to falsely generalize from the collective-normative level to the rest of the social world.

While not directly addressing Alexander's work, Giddens (1984) came to the similar conclusion that *all* work derived from the Parsonian distinction between action and order inevitably ends up weak at the micro levels, especially on "the knowledgeability of social actors, as constitutive in part of social practices. I [Giddens] do not think that any standpoint which is heavily indebted to Parsons can cope satisfactorily with this issue at the very core of social theory" (1984:xxxvii).

However, it should be noted that Alexander has articulated a more truly integrative perspective, one that defines *micro* and *macro* in terms of each other. Here is the way he expresses this perspective: "The collective environments of action simultaneously inspire and confine it. If I have conceptualized action correctly, these environments will be seen as its products; if I can conceptualize the environments correctly, action will be seen as their end result" (Alexander, 1987a:303). It appears that Alexander has a more complex, dialectical sense of the micro-macro nexus, one that is more similar to Ritzer's integrated sociological paradigm than his earlier model.

The Micro Foundations of Macrosociology

In an essay entitled "On the Microfoundations of Macrosociology," Randall Collins (1981a; see also 1981b) has offered a highly reductionistic orientation toward the micro-macro link question (for a critique, see Ritzer, 1985). In fact, despite the inherently integrative title of his essay, Collins labels his approach "radical microsociology." Collins's focus, the focus of radical microsociology, is what he calls "interaction ritual chains," or bundles of "individual chains of interactional experience, crisscrossing each other in space as they flow along in time" (1981a:998). In focusing on interaction ritual chains, Collins seeks to avoid what he considers to be even more reductionistic concerns with individual behavior and consciousness. Collins raises the level of analysis to interaction, chains of interaction, and the "marketplace" for such interaction. Collins thus rejects the extreme micro levels of thought and action (behavior) and is critical of the theories (such as phenomenology and exchange theory) that focus on these levels.

Collins also seeks to distance himself from macro theories and their concerns with macro-level phenomena. For example, he is critical of structural functionalists and their concern with macro-objective (structure) and macro-subjective (norms) phenomena. In fact, he goes so far as to say that "the terminology of norms ought to be dropped from sociological theory" (Collins, 1981a:991). He has a similarly negative attitude toward concepts associated with conflict theory, arguing, for example, that there are no "inherent objective" entities such as property and authority; there are only "varying senses that people feel at particular places and times of how strong these enforcing coalitions are" (Collins, 1981a:997). His point is that only people do anything; structures, organizations, classes, and societies "never *do* anything. Any causal explanation must ultimately come down to the actions of real individuals" (Collins, 1975:12).

Collins seeks to show how "all macrophenomena" can be translated "into combinations of micro events" (1981a:985). Specifically, he argues that social structures may be translated empirically into "patterns of repetitive micro interaction" (Collins, 1981a:985). Thus, in the end, Collins seeks *not* an integrated approach but the predominance of micro theory and micro-level phenomena (for a similar critique, see Giddens, 1984). As Collins puts it, "The effort coherently to reconstitute macro sociology upon radically empirical micro foundations is the crucial step toward a more successful sociological science" (1981b:82).

We can contrast Collins's orientation to that of Karin Knorr-Cetina (1981). Although she, too, accords great importance to the interactional domain, Knorr-Cetina grants a greater role to both consciousness and macro-level phenomena in her work. Although Knorr-Cetina, like Collins, makes the case for a radical reconstruction of macro theory on a microsociological base, she also is willing to consider the much less radical course of simply integrating microsociological results into macro-social theory. In addition, she seems to take the position that the ultimate goal of microsociological research is a better understanding of the larger society, its structure, and its institutions:

> I . . . believe in the seeming paradox that it is through micro-social approaches that we will learn most about the macro order, for it is these approaches which through their unashamed empiricism afford us a glimpse of the reality about which we speak. Certainly, we will not get a grasp of whatever is the whole of the matter by a microscopic recording of face-to-face interaction. However, it may be enough to begin with if we—for the first time—hear the macro order tick.
>
> (Knorr-Cetina, 1981:41–42)

RANDALL COLLINS

An Autobiographical Sketch

I started becoming a sociologist at an early age. My father was working for military intelligence at the end of World War II and then joined the State Department as a foreign service officer. One of my earliest memories is of arriving in Berlin to join him in the summer of 1945. My sisters and I couldn't play in the park because there was live ammunition everywhere, and one day Russian soldiers came into our backyard to dig up a corpse. This gave me a sense that conflict is important and violence always possible.

My father's subsequent tours of duty took us to the Soviet Union, back to Germany (then under American military occupation), to Spain, and South America. In between foreign assignments we would live in the States, so I went back and forth between being an ordinary American kid and being a privileged foreign visitor. I think this resulted in a certain amount of detachment in viewing social relationships. As I got older the diplomatic life looked less dramatic and more like an endless round of formal etiquette in which people never talked about the important politics going on; the split between backstage secrecy and front-stage ceremonial made me ready to appreciate Erving Goffman.

When I was too old to accompany my parents abroad, I was sent to a prep school in New England. This taught me another great sociological reality: the existence of stratification. Many of the other students came from families in the Social Register, and it began to dawn on me that my father was not in the same social class as the ambassadors and undersecretaries of state whose children I sometimes met.

I went on to Harvard, where I changed my major half a dozen times. I studied literature and tried being a playwright and novelist. I went from mathematics to philosophy; I read Freud and planned to become a psychiatrist. I finally majored in social relations, which covered sociology, social psychology, and anthropology. Taking courses from Talcott Parsons settled me onto a path. He covered virtually everything, from the micro to the macro and across the

Thus, it seems clear that Knorr-Cetina takes a far more balanced position on the relationship between the macro and micro levels than does Collins.

An even more integrative position is taken by Aaron Cicourel (1981): "Neither micro nor macro structures are self-contained levels of analysis; they *interact* with each other at all times despite the convenience and sometimes the dubious luxury of only examining one or the other level of analysis" (Cicourel, 1981:54). There is an implied criticism of Collins here, but Cicourel adopts another position that can be seen as a more direct critique of the kind of position adopted by Collins: "The issue is not simply one of dismissing one level of analysis or another, but showing how range of world history. What I got from him was not so much his own theory but rather the ideal of what sociology could do. He also provided me with some important pieces of cultural capital: that Weber was less concerned with the Protestant Ethic than he was with comparing the dynamics of all the world religions and that Durkheim asked the key question when he tried to uncover the precontractual basis of social order.

I thought I wanted to become a psychologist and went to Stanford, but a year of implanting electrodes in rats' brains convinced me that sociology was a better place to study human beings. I switched universities and arrived in Berkeley in the summer of 1964, just in time to join the civil rights movement. By the time the free speech movement emerged on campus in the fall, we were veterans of sit-ins, and being arrested for another cause felt emotionally energizing when one could do it in solidarity with hundreds of others. I was analyzing the sociology of conflict at the same time that we were experiencing it. As the Vietnam War and the racial conflicts at home escalated, the opposition movement began to repudiate its nonviolent principles; many of us became disillusioned and turned to the cultural lifestyle of the hippie dropouts. If you didn't lose your sociological consciousness, it could be illuminating. I studied Erving Goffman along with Herbert Blumer (both of them Berkeley professors at the time) and began to see how all aspects of society—conflict, stratification, and all the rest—are constructed out of the interaction rituals of our everyday lives.

I never set out to be a professor, but by now I have taught in many universities. I tried to put everything together into one book, *Conflict Sociology* (1975), but it turned out I had to write another, *The Credential Society* (1979), to explain the inflationary status system in which we are all enmeshed. Taking my own analysis seriously, I quit the academic world and for a while made a living by writing a novel and textbooks. Eventually, attracted by some interesting colleagues, I got back into teaching. Our field is learning some tremendous things, from a new picture of world history down through the micro details of social emotions. One of the most important influences for me is my second wife, Judith McConnell. She organized women lawyers to break down discriminatory barriers in the legal profession, and now I am learning from her about the backstage politics of the higher judiciary. In sociology and in society, there is plenty yet to be done.

[See also Li, 2005.]

they must be integrated if we are not to be convinced about one level to the exclusion of the other by conveniently ignoring competing frameworks for research and theory" (1981:76). To his credit, Cicourel understands not only the importance of linking macro and micro levels but also the fact that that link needs to take place ontologically, theoretically, and methodologically.

Collins continued to subscribe to his micro-reductionistic position for some time. For example, in a later work Collins argued: "Macrostructure consists of nothing more than large numbers of microencounters, repeated (or sometimes changing over time and across space)" (1987:195). He concluded, unashamedly: "This may sound as if I am giving a great deal of prominence to the micro. That is true" (Collins, 1987:195). However, it is worth noting that just one year later Collins (1988a) was willing to give the macro level greater significance. This approach led to a more balanced conception of the micro-macro relationship: "The micro-macro translation shows that everything macro is composed out of micro. Conversely, anything micro is part of the composition of macro; it exists in a macro context . . . it is possible to pursue the micro-macro connection fruitfully in either direction" (Collins, 1988a:244). The latter contention implies a more dialectical approach to the micro-macro relationship. Yet Collins (1988a:244), like Coleman (1986, 1987), subscribes to the view that the "big challenge" in sociology is showing "how micro affects macro." Thus, while Collins has shown some growth in his micro-macro theory, it continues to be a highly limited approach.

Back to the Future: Norbert Elias's Figurational Sociology

We have now discussed some of the major recent American efforts at micro-macro integration. However, there is a European theorist, Norbert Elias, whose work is best discussed under this heading. (For a nice selection of his work, see Mennell and Goudsblom, 1998). Elias was involved in an effort to overcome the micro-macro distinction, and more generally to surmount the tendency of sociologists to distinguish between individuals and society (Dunning, 1986:5; Mennell, 1992; Rundell, 2005). Elias's major work was done in the 1930s, but it has only recently begun to receive the recognition it deserves (Kilminster and Mennell, 2011; Dennis Smith, 2001; Van Krieken, 1998, 2001).

In order to help achieve his integrative goal, Elias proposed the concept of *figuration* (Kasperson and Gabriel, 2008; Mennell, 2005a), an idea which

> makes it possible to resist the socially conditioned pressure to split and polarize our conception of mankind, which has repeatedly prevented us from thinking of people as individuals *at the same time* as thinking of them as societies. . . . The concept of figuration therefore serves as a simple conceptual tool to loosen this social constraint to speak and think as if "the individual" and "society" were antagonistic as well as different.
>
> (Elias, 1978:129–130; italics added)

Figurations can be seen, above all, as processes. In fact, later in his life Elias came to prefer the term *process sociology* to describe his work (Mennell, 1992:252). Figurations are social processes involving the "interweaving" of people. They are *not* structures that are external to and coercive of relationships between people; they *are* those interrelationships. Individuals are seen as open and interdependent; figurations are made up of such individuals. Power is central to social figurations, which are, as a result, constantly in flux:

> At the core of changing figurations—indeed the very hub of the figuration process—is a fluctuating, tensile equilibrium, a balance of power moving to and fro, inclining first to one side and then to the other. This kind of fluctuating balance of power is a structural characteristic of the flow of every figuration.
>
> (Elias, 1978:131)

Figurations emerge and develop, but in largely unseen and unplanned ways.

Central to this discussion is the fact that the idea of a figuration applies at both the micro and the macro levels and to every social phenomenon between those two poles. The concept

> can be applied to relatively small groups just as well as to societies made up of thousands or millions of interdependent people. Teachers and pupils in a class, doctors and patients in a therapeutic group, regular customers at a pub, children at a nursery school—they all make up relatively comprehensible figurations with each other. But the inhabitants of a village, a city or a nation also form figurations, although in this instance the figurations cannot be perceived directly because the *chains of interdependence* which link people together are longer and more differentiated.
>
> (Elias, 1978:131; italics added)

Thus, Elias refuses to deal with the relationship between "individual" and "society" but focuses on "the relationship between people perceived as individuals and people perceived as societies" (Elias, 1986:23). In other words, both individuals and societies (and every social phenomenon in between) involve people—human relationships. The idea of "chains of interdependence" underscored in the extract above is as good an image as any of what Elias means by figurations and what constitutes the focus of his sociology: "How and why people are bound together to form specific dynamic figurations is one of the central questions, perhaps even *the* central question, of sociology" (1969/1983:208).

Elias's notion of figuration is linked to the idea that individuals are open to, and interrelated with, other individuals. He argues that most sociologists operate with a sense of *homo clausus,* that is, "an image of single human beings each of whom is ultimately absolutely independent of all others—an individual-in-himself" (Elias, 1969/1983:143). Such an image does not lend itself to a theory of figurations; an image of open, interdependent actors is needed for figurational sociology.

The History of Manners

If Weber can be seen as being concerned with the rationalization of the West, Elias's focal interest is on the *civilization* of the Occident (Bogner, Baker, and Kilminster, 1992; for an application of his ideas to another part of the world—Singapore—see Stauth, 1997). By the way, Elias is not arguing that there is something inherently good, or better, about civilization as it occurs in the West, or anywhere else for that matter. Nor is he arguing that civilization is inherently bad, although he does recognize that various difficulties have arisen in Western civilization. More generally, Elias (1968/1994:188) is not arguing that to be more civilized is to be better, or conversely that to be less civilized is worse. In saying that people have become more civilized, we are not necessarily saying that they have become better (or worse); we are simply stating a sociological fact. Thus, Elias is concerned with the sociological study of what he calls the "sociogenesis" of civilization in the West (as we will see shortly).

Specifically, Elias is interested in the gradual changes (Elias, 1997) that took place in the behavior and psychological makeup of people in the West. It is an

NORBERT ELIAS

A Biographical Sketch

Norbert Elias had an interesting and instructive career. He produced his most important work in the 1930s, but it was largely ignored at the time and for many years thereafter. However, late in his life Elias and his work were "discovered," especially in England and the Netherlands. Today, Elias's reputation is growing, and his work is receiving increasing attention and recognition throughout the world (Dennis Smith, 2001). Elias lived until he was 93 (he died in 1990), long enough to bask belatedly in long-delayed recognition of the significance of his work.

Elias was born in Breslau, Germany, in 1897 (Mennell, 1992). His father was a small manufacturer, and the family lived a comfortable existence. The home was apparently a loving one, and it imbued Elias with a self-confidence that was to stand him in good stead later when his work was not recognized:

> I put that down to the great feeling of security I had as a child . . . I have a basic feeling of great security, a feeling that in the end things will turn out for the best, and I attribute that to an enormous emotional security which my parents gave me as an only child.
>
> I knew very early on what I wanted to do; I wanted to go to university, and I wanted to do research. I knew that from when I was young, and I have done it, even though sometimes it seemed impossible . . . I had great confidence that in the end my work would be recognized as a valuable contribution to knowledge about humanity.
>
> (Elias, cited in Mennell, 1992:6–7)

Elias served in the German army in World War I and returned after the war to study philosophy and medicine at the University of Breslau. Although he progressed quite far in his medical studies, he eventually dropped them in favor of the study of philosophy. His work in medicine gave him a sense of the interconnections among the various parts of the human body, and that view shaped his orientation to human interconnections—his concern for figurations. Elias received his Ph.D. in January 1924; only then did he go to Heidelberg to learn sociology.

Elias received no pay at Heidelberg, but he did become actively involved in sociology circles at the university. Max Weber had died in 1920, but a salon headed by his wife, Marianne, was active, and Elias became involved in it. He also associated with Max Weber's brother, Alfred, who held a chair in sociology at the university, as well as with Karl Mannheim (described by Elias [1994:34] as "unquestionably brilliant"), who was slightly ahead of Elias in terms of career progress. In fact, Elias became Mannheim's friend and unpaid, unofficial assistant.

When Mannheim was offered a position at the University of Frankfurt in 1930, Elias went with him as his paid and official assistant (on the relationship between the two men and their work, see Kilminster, 1993).

Adolf Hitler came to power in February 1933, and soon after, Elias, like many other Jewish scholars (including Mannheim), went into exile, at first in Paris and later in London (it is believed that Elias's mother died in a concentration camp in 1941). It was in London that he did most of the work on *The Civilizing Process,* which was published in German in 1939. There was no market in Germany then for books written by a Jew, and Elias never received a penny of royalties from that edition. In addition, the book received scant recognition in other parts of the world.

Both during the war and for almost a decade after it, Elias bounced around with no secure employment and remained marginal to British academic circles. However, in 1954 Elias was offered two academic positions, and he accepted the one at Leicester. Thus, Elias *began* his formal academic career at the age of 57! Elias's career blossomed at Leicester, and a number of important publications followed. However, Elias was disappointed with his tenure at Leicester because he failed in his effort to institutionalize a developmental approach that could stand as an alternative to the kinds of static approaches (of Talcott Parsons and others) that were then preeminent in sociology. He was also disappointed that few students adopted his approach; he continued to be a voice in the wilderness, even at Leicester, where the students tended to regard him as an eccentric "voice from the past" (Mennell, 1992:22). Reflective of this feeling of being on the outside is a recurrent dream reported by Elias during those years in which a voice on the telephone repeats, "'Can you speak louder? I can't hear you'" (Mennell, 1992:23). It is interesting to note that throughout his years at Leicester *none* of his books was translated into English and few English sociologists of the day were fluent in German.

However, in continental Europe, especially in the Netherlands and Germany, Elias's work began to be rediscovered in the 1950s and 1960s. In the 1970s Elias began to receive not only academic but public recognition in Europe. Throughout the rest of his life Elias received a number of significant awards, an honorary doctorate, a *Festschrift* in his honor, and a special double issue of *Theory, Culture and Society* devoted to his work.

Interestingly, while Elias has now received wide recognition in sociology (including inclusion in this text), his work has received that recognition during a period in which sociology is growing *less* receptive to his kind of work. That is, the rise of postmodern thinking has led sociologists to question any grand narrative, and Elias's major work, *The Civilizing Process,* is, if nothing else, a grand narrative in the old style (Dennis Smith, 1999). That is, it is concerned with the long-term historical development (admittedly with ebbs and flows) of civilization in the West. The growth of postmodern thinking threatens to limit interest in Elias's work just as it is beginning to receive wide attention.

analysis of these changes that is his concern in *The History of Manners,* the first volume of *The Civilizing Process* (1939/1978). In the second volume of *The Civilizing Process, Power and Civility* (1939/1982), Elias turns to the societal changes that accompany, and are closely related to, these behavioral and psychological changes. Overall, Elias is concerned with "the connections between changes in the structure of society and changes in the structure of behavior and psychical makeup" (1939/1994:xv).

In his study of the history of manners, Elias is interested in the gradual, historical transformation of a variety of very mundane behaviors in the direction of what we would now call civilized behavior (although there are also periods of "decivilization"; see Elias, 1995; Mennell, 2005b). Although he begins with the Middle Ages, Elias makes it clear that there is not, and cannot be, such a thing as a starting (or ending) point for the development of civilization: "Nothing is more fruitless, when dealing with long-term social processes, than to attempt to locate an absolute beginning" (Elias, 1969/1983:232). That is, civilizing processes can be traced back to ancient times, continue to this day, and will continue into the future. Civilization is an ongoing developmental process that Elias is picking up, for convenience, in the Middle Ages. He is interested in tracing such things as changes in what embarrasses us, our increasing sensitivity, how we've grown increasingly observant of others, and our sharpened understanding of others. However, the best way of gaining an understanding of what Elias is doing is not through abstractions but through a discussion of some of his concrete examples.

Behavior at the Table   Elias's most basic point is that the threshold of embarrassment has gradually advanced. What people did at the table with little or no embarrassment in the thirteenth century would cause much mortification in the nineteenth century. What is regarded as distasteful is over time increasingly likely to be *"removed behind the scenes of social life"* (Elias, 1939/1994:99).

For example, a thirteenth-century poem warned, "A number of people gnaw on a bone and then put it back in the dish—this is a serious offense" (Elias, 1939/1994:68). Another thirteenth-century volume warns, "It is not decent to poke your fingers into your ears or eyes, as some people do, or to pick your nose while eating" (Elias, 1939/1994:71). Clearly, the implication of these warnings is that many people at that time engaged in such behaviors and that it generally caused them, or those around them, no embarrassment. There was a perceived need for such admonitions because people did not know that such behavior was "uncivilized." As time goes by there is less and less need to warn people about such things as picking one's nose while eating. Thus, a late-sixteenth-century document says, "Nothing is more improper than to lick your fingers, to touch the meats and put them into your mouth with your hand, to stir sauce with your fingers, or to dip bread into it with your fork and then suck it" (Elias, 1939/1994:79). Of course, there *are* things, picking one's nose, for example, more improper than licking one's fingers, but by this time civilization has progressed to the point where it is widely recognized that such behaviors are uncivilized. With nose picking safely behind the scenes, society found other, less egregious behaviors that it defined as uncivilized.

Natural Functions

A similar trend is found in the performance of natural functions. A fourteenth-century book used by schoolchildren, among others, found it necessary to offer advice on the expelling of wind:

> To contract an illness: Listen to the old maxim about the sound of wind. If it can be purged without a noise that is best. But it is better that it be emitted with a noise than it be held back. . . .
>
>   . . . The sound of farting, especially of those who stand on elevated ground, is horrible. One should make sacrifices with the buttocks pressed firmly together . . .
>
>   . . . let a cough hide the explosive sound . . . Follow the law of Chiliades: Replace farts with coughs.
>
> (Elias, 1939/1994:106)

Here we see things being discussed openly that by the nineteenth century (and certainly today) it was no longer necessary to mention because it had come to be well known that the behaviors in question were uncivilized. Further, we are likely to be startled by such a discussion, which offends our contemporary sense of propriety. But all this reflects the process of civilization and the movement of the "frontier of embarrassment" (Elias, 1939/1994:107). Things that could be discussed openly have over time progressively moved beyond that frontier. The fact that we are startled by reading advice on farting reflects the fact that the frontier today is very different from what it was in the fourteenth century.

Elias relates this change in the notion of the appropriate way to expel wind to changes in social figurations, especially in the French court. More people were living in closer proximity and in more permanent interdependence. Therefore, there was a greater need to regulate people's impulses and to get them to practice greater restraint. The control over impulses that began in the higher echelons of the court eventually was transmitted to those of lower social status. The need to extend these restraints was made necessary by further figurational changes, especially people of different statuses moving closer together, becoming more interdependent, and by the decreasing rigidity of the stratification system, which made it easier for those of lower status to interact with those of higher status. As a result, to put it baldly, there was increasingly just as much need for the lower classes to control their wind (and many other behaviors) as there was for the upper classes. At the same time, those from the upper classes needed to control their wind in the presence not only of peers but of social inferiors as well.

Elias sums up his discussion of such natural functions:

> Society is gradually beginning to suppress the positive pleasure component in certain functions more and more strongly by the arousal of anxiety; or, more exactly, it is rendering this pleasure 'private' and 'secret' (i.e. suppressing it within the individual), while fostering the negatively charged affects—displeasure, revulsion, distaste—as the only feelings customary in society.
>
> (Elias, 1939/1994:117)

Blowing One's Nose   A similar process is seen in the restraints on blowing one's nose. For example, a fifteenth-century document warned, "Do not blow your nose with the same hand that you use to hold the meat" (Elias, 1939/1994:118). Or, in the sixteenth century, the reader is informed, "Nor is it seemly, after wiping your nose, to spread out your handkerchief and peer into it as if pearls and rubies might have fallen out of your head" (Elias, 1939/1994:119). However, by the late eighteenth century these kinds of details are avoided in sources of advice: "Every voluntary movement of the nose . . . is impolite and puerile. To put your fingers into your nose is a revolting impropriety. . . . You should observe, in blowing your nose, all the rules of propriety and cleanliness" (Elias, 1939/1994:121). As Elias says, "The 'conspiracy of silence' is spreading" (1939/1994:121). That is, things that could be discussed openly a century or two before are now discussed more discreetly, or not at all. The "shame frontier" as it relates to blowing one's nose, and many other things, has progressed. Shame has come to be attached to things (for example, blowing one's nose, farting) that in the past were not considered shameful. More and more walls are being erected between people so that things that formerly could be done in the presence of others are now hidden from view.

Sexual Relations   Elias describes the same general trend in sexual relations. In the Middle Ages it was common for many people, including men and women, to spend the night together in the same room. And it was not uncommon for them to sleep naked. However, over time, it came to be viewed as increasingly shameful to show oneself naked in the presence of the opposite sex. As an example of "uncivilized" sexual behavior, Elias describes the following wedding customs beginning in the Middle Ages:

> The procession into the bridal chamber was led by the best man. The bride was undressed by the bridesmaids; she had to take off all finery. The bridal bed had to be mounted in the presence of witnesses if the marriage was to be valid. They were "laid together." "Once in bed you are rightly wed," the saying went. In the later Middle Ages this custom gradually changed to the extent that the couple was allowed to lie on the bed in their clothes. . . . Even in the absolutist society of France, bride and bridegroom were taken to bed by the guests, undressed, and given their nightdress.
>
> (Elias, 1939/1994:145–146)

Clearly, this changed further over time with the advance of civilization. Today, everything that occurs in the wedding bed is concealed, taking place behind the scenes and out of the sight of all observers. More generally, sexual life has been taken out of the larger society and enclosed within the nuclear family.

Overall, in the *History of Manners* Elias is concerned with changes in the way individuals think, act, and interact. He sometimes speaks of this, in general, as a change in "personality structure," but Elias seems to be describing more than changes in personality; he also is describing changes in the way people act and interact. Taken together, it could be argued that the *History of Manners* focuses largely on micro-level concerns. However, two factors militate against such an interpretation. First, Elias often deals in *The History of Manners* with concomitant macro-level changes (in the court, for example), and he argues that "the structures of personality and of society evolve in indissoluble interrelationship" (1968/1994:188). Second, *The History of*

Manners is written with the awareness that *Power and Civility,* dealing focally with these more macro-level changes, is to accompany it. Nonetheless, even though Elias wishes to avoid the micro-macro dichotomy, *The Civilizing Process* consists of two separate volumes, the first focally concerned with micro issues and the second interested mainly in macro questions.

Power and Civility

If self-constraint is the key to the civilizing process, then what Elias is concerned with in *Power and Civility* are the changes in social constraint that are associated with this rise in self-restraint. However, Elias, despite his later overt rejection of the micro-macro distinction, seems to announce that in *Power and Civility* he is dealing with another, more "macroscopic" level of analysis:

> *This basic tissue resulting from the many single plans and actions of men can give rise to changes and patterns that no individual person has planned or created. From this interdependence of people arises an order sui generis, an order more compelling and stronger than the will and reason of the individual people composing it.* It is this order of interweaving human impulses and strivings, this social order, which determines the course of historical change; it underlies the civilizing process.

> (Elias, 1939/1982:230)

These are strong, almost Durkheimian words, depicting a unique (*sui generis*) and compelling reality that "determines the course of historical change." In spite of Elias's later rhetoric about the need to overcome the micro-macro distinction, such a position is not, in the main, supported by *Power and Civility,* which tends at times to deal with the effect, sometimes the determining effect, of macro structures on micro-level phenomena. (However, we hasten to add that Elias often says that he is merely interested in the covariation of macro and micro phenomena, or the connection between "specific changes in the structure of human relations and the corresponding changes in the structure of the personality" [1939/1982:231].)

Reflective of his difficulties in dealing with micro and macro in an integrated way is the fact that Elias distinguishes between *psychogenetic* and *sociogenetic* investigations. In a psychogenetic investigation, one focuses on individual psychology, whereas sociogenetic investigations have a larger radius and a longer-range perspective, focusing on "the overall structure, not only of a single state society but of the social field formed by a specific group of interdependent societies, and of the sequential order of its evolution" (Elias, 1939/1982:287–288).

Lengthening Interdependency Chains   What is the macro-structural change that is of such great importance to the process of civilization? It can be described as the lengthening of "interdependency chains":

> From the earliest period of the history of the Occident to the present, social functions have become more and more differentiated under the pressure of competition. The more differentiated they become, the larger grows the number of functions and thus of people on whom the individual constantly depends in all

> his actions, from the simplest and most commonplace to the more complex and
> uncommon. As more and more people must attune their conduct to that of others,
> the web of actions must be organized more and more strictly and accurately, if
> each individual action is to fulfil its social function. The individual is compelled
> to regulate his conduct in an increasingly differentiated, more even and stable
> manner . . . the more complex and stable control of conduct is increasingly
> instilled in the individual from his earliest years as an automatism, a self-
> compulsion that he cannot resist even if he consciously wishes to.
>
> (Elias, 1939/1982:232–233)

The result of all this is "the lengthening of the chains of social action and interdependence," which is what contributes to the corresponding need for individuals to
moderate their emotions by developing the "habit of connecting events in terms of
chains of cause and effect" (Elias, 1939/1982:236).

Thus, to Elias, the increasing differentiation of social functions plays a key role
in the civilization process. In addition to, and in conjunction with, this differentiation
is the importance of what Elias calls "a total reorganization of the social fabric"
(1939/1982:234). Here he is describing the historical process that witnessed the
emergence of increasingly stable central organs of society that monopolize the means
of physical force and of taxation. Crucial to this development is the emergence of a
king with absolute status, as well as of the court society (especially in France and
during the reign of Louis XIV, although the courts of Europe came to be closely
linked). What Elias calls a "royal mechanism" is operating here—kings are able to
emerge in a specific figuration where competing functional groups are ambivalent
(they were characterized by both mutual dependency and hostility) and power is
evenly distributed between them, thus prohibiting a decisive conflict or a decisive
compromise. As Elias puts it, "Not by chance, not whenever a strong ruling personality is born, but when a specific social structure provides the opportunity, does the
central organ attain that optimal power which usually finds expression in strong
autocracy" (1939/1982:174). In other words, a king emerges when the appropriate
figuration is in place.

The king's court took on special importance for Elias because it was here that
changes took place that eventually affected the whole of society. In contrast to the
warrior, whose short chains of dependence made it relatively easy for him to engage
in violent behavior, the court noble, with much longer chains of dependence on many
other nobles, found it necessary to be increasingly sensitive to others. The noble also
found it increasingly difficult to give free play to his emotions through violence or
any other action. The noble was further limited by the fact that the king was gaining
increasing control over the means of violence. "The monopolization of physical violence, the concentration of arms and armed men under one authority . . . forces
unarmed men in the pacified social spaces to restrain their own violence through
foresight or reflection; in other words it imposes on people a greater or lesser degree
of self-control" (Elias, 1939/1982:239). The monopoly of violence is intimately
related to the ability of the king to monopolize taxation, because taxes are what allow
the king to pay for control over the means of violence (Elias, 1939/1982:208). In fact,
Elias describes a situation that involves the interplay of these two monopolies: "The

financial means thus flowing into this central authority maintains its monopoly of military force, while this in turn maintains the monopoly of taxation" (1939/1982:104). In addition, the increase in the king's income is accompanied by a reduction of the nobility's, and this disparity serves to enhance further the power of the king (Elias, 1969/1983:155).

The nobles play a key role in the civilization process because changes that take place among this elite group are gradually disseminated throughout society:

> It is in this courtly society that the basic stock of models of conduct is formed which then, fused with others and modified in accordance with the position of the groups carrying them, spread, with the compulsion to exercise foresight, to ever-wider circles of functions. Their special situation makes the people of courtly society, more than any other Western group affected by this movement, specialists in the elaboration and moulding of social conduct.
>
> (Elias, 1939/1982:258)

Furthermore, these changes that started in the West began to spread through many other parts of the world.

The rise of the king and the court and the transition from warrior to courtier (or the "courtization" of the warrior) represent for Elias a key "spurt" in the civilizing process. This idea of "spurts" is central to Elias's theory of social change; he does not view change as a smooth, unilinear process, but rather one with much stopping and starting—much to-and-fro movement.

Although Elias gives great importance to the rise of the court,[4] the ultimate cause of the decisive changes that ensued was the change in the entire social figuration of the time. That is, the key was the changes in various relationships among groups (for example, between warriors and nobles), as well as changes in the relationships among individuals in those groups. Furthermore, this figuration was constraining on nobles and king alike: "Princes and aristocratic groups are apt to appear as people leading a free and unconstrained life. Here . . . it emerged very clearly to what constraints upper classes, and not least their most powerful member, the absolute monarch, are subjected" (Elias, 1969/1983:266).

From the dominance of the king and his nobles there is gradual movement toward a state. In other words, once a private monopoly (by the king) of arms and taxes is in place, the ground is set for the public monopoly of those resources—that is, the emergence of the state. There is a direct link between the growth of the king and later the state as controlling agencies in society and the development of a parallel controlling agency within the individual. Together, they begin to wield unprecedented power over the individual's ability to act on his or her emotions. It is not that before this time people totally lacked self-control, but self-control grew more continuous and stable, affecting more and more aspects of people's lives. Elias's argument is very close to Durkheim's when he contends that with the longer chains of interdependence, "the individual learns to control himself more steadily; he is now less a prisoner of his passions" (1939/1982:241).

---

[4] For an interesting study of the court, the bourgeoisie, and their impact on Mozart, see Elias (1993).

An interesting aspect of Elias's argument is that he recognizes that this control over passions is not an unmitigated good. Life has grown less dangerous, but it has also become less pleasurable. Unable to express their emotions directly, people need to find other outlets, such as in their dreams or through books. In addition, what were external struggles may come to be internalized as, in Freudian terms, battles between the id and the superego. (Elias's thinking on the individual was heavily influenced by Freudian theory.) Thus, while the greater control over passions brings a welcome reduction in violence, it also brings with it increasing boredom and restlessness.

The longer dependency chains are associated not only with greater affective control but with increasing sensitivity to others and to the self. Furthermore, people's judgments become more finely shaded and nuanced, making them better able to judge and control both themselves and others. Before the rise of the court society, people had to protect themselves from violence and death. Afterward, as this danger receded, people could afford to grow more sensitive to far more subtle threats and actions. This greater sensitivity is a key aspect of the civilizing process and a key contributor to its further development.

Agency-Structure Integration

Paralleling the growth in interest in American sociological theory in the micro-macro issue has been an increase in interest among European theorists in the relationship between agency and structure. In fact, this interest is so intense that Fuller (1998) has called it a "craze." For example, Margaret Archer has contended that "the problem of structure and agency has rightly come to be seen as the basic issue in modern social theory" (1988:ix). In fact, she argues that dealing with this linkage (as well as a series of other linkages implied by it) has become the "acid test" of a general social theory and the "central problem" in theory (Archer, 1988:x). Earlier, Dawe went even further than Archer: *"Here, then, is the problematic around which the entire history of sociological analysis could be written: the problematic of human agency"* (1978:379). Implied in Dawe's concern with agency is also an interest in social structure as well as the constant tension between them.[5]

At a superficial level the micro-macro and agency-structure issues sound similar, and they often are treated as if they resembled one another greatly. However, there are other ways to think of both agency-structure and micro-macro issues that make the significant differences between these two conceptualizations quite clear.

Although *agency* generally refers to micro-level, individual human actors,[6] it also can refer to (macro) collectivities that act. For example, Burns sees human agents as including "individuals as well as organized groups, organizations and nations" (1986:9). Touraine (1977) focuses on social classes as actors. If we accept such collectivities as agents, we cannot equate agency and micro-level phenomena. In addition, although *structure* usually refers to large-scale social structures, it also can refer to micro

---

[5] In fact, agency often is used in such a way as to include a concern for structure (Abrams, 1982:xiii).

[6] A variety of contemporary theorists, especially those associated with poststructuralism and postmodernism, have questioned and even rejected the idea of human agency. See, for example, M. Jones (1996).

structures such as those involved in human interaction. Giddens's definition of *systems* (which is closer to the usual meaning of *structure* than is his own concept of structure) implies both types of structures, because it involves "reproduced relations between actors or collectivities" (1979:66). Thus, both *agency* and *structure* can refer to either micro-level or macro-level phenomena or to both.

Turning to the micro-macro distinction, *micro* often refers to the kind of conscious, creative actor of concern to many agency theorists, but it also can refer to a more mindless "behaver" of interest to behaviorists, exchange theorists, and rational choice theorists. Similarly, the term *macro* can refer not only to large-scale social structures but also to the cultures of collectivities. Thus, *micro* may or may not refer to "agents," and *macro* may or may not refer to "structures."

When we look closely at the micro-macro and agency-structure schemas, we find that there are substantial differences between them.

Major Examples of Agency-Structure Integration

Structuration Theory

One of the best-known and most articulated efforts to integrate agency and structure is Anthony Giddens's structuration theory (Bryant and Jary, 2011; I. Cohen, 1989, 2005; Craib, 1992; Held and Thompson, 1989). Giddens goes so far as to say, "Every research investigation in the social sciences or history is involved in relating action [often used synonymously with *agency*] to structure . . . there is no sense in which structure 'determines' action or vice versa" (1984:219).

Although Giddens is not a Marxist, there is a powerful Marxian influence in his work, and he even sees *The Constitution of Society* as an extended reflection on Marx's inherently integrative dictum: "Men make history, but they do not make it just as they please; they do not make it under circumstances chosen by themselves, but under circumstances directly encountered, given, and transmitted from the past" (Marx, 1869/1963:15).[7]

Marx's theory is but one of many theoretical inputs into structuration theory. At one time or another, Giddens has analyzed and critiqued most major theoretical orientations and derived a range of useful ideas from many of them. Structuration theory is extraordinarily eclectic; in fact, Craib (1992:20–31) outlines nine major inputs into Giddens's thinking.

Giddens surveys a wide range of theories that begin with either the individual/ agent (for example, symbolic interactionism) or the society/structure (for example, structural functionalism) and rejects both of these polar alternatives. Rather, Giddens argues that we must begin with "recurrent social practices" (1989:252). Giving slightly more detail, he argues: "The basic domain of the study of the social sciences, according to the theory of structuration, is neither the experience of the individual actor, nor the existence of any form of social totality, but social practices ordered across time and space" (Giddens, 1984:2).

---

[7] It is appropriate to accord Marx such a central place in structuration theory and, more generally, in theories that integrate agency and structure. As Ritzer has written elsewhere, Marx's work is the best "exemplar for an integrated sociological paradigm" (Ritzer, 1981a:232).

At its core Giddens's structuration theory, with its focus on social practices, is a theory of the relationship between agency and structure. According to Richard J. Bernstein, "the very heart of the theory of structuration" is "intended to illuminate the duality and dialectical interplay of agency and structure" (1989:23). Thus, agency and structure cannot be conceived of apart from one another; they are two sides of the same coin. In Giddens's terms, they are a duality. All social action involves structure, and all structure involves social action. Agency and structure are inextricably interwoven in ongoing human activity or practice.

As pointed out earlier, Giddens's analytical starting point is human practices, but he insists that they be seen as recursive. That is, activities are "not brought into being by social actors but are continually recreated by them via the very means whereby they express themselves as actors. In and through their activities agents produce the conditions that make these activities possible" (Giddens, 1984:2). Thus, activities are not produced by consciousness, by the social construction of reality, nor are they produced by social structure. Rather, in expressing themselves as actors, people are engaging in practice, and it is through that practice that both consciousness and structure are produced. Focusing on the recursive character of structure, Held and Thompson argue that "structure is reproduced in and through the succession of situated practices which are organized by it" (1989:7). The same thing can be said about consciousness. Giddens is concerned with consciousness, or reflexivity. However, in being reflexive, the human actor not only is self-conscious but also is engaged in the monitoring of the ongoing flow of activities and structural conditions. Bernstein argues that "agency itself is reflexively and recursively implicated in social structures" (1989:23). Most generally, it can be argued that Giddens is concerned with the dialectical process in which practice, structure, and consciousness are produced. Thus, Giddens deals with the agency-structure issue in a historical, processual, and dynamic way.

Not only are social actors reflexive, so are the social researchers who are studying them. This idea leads Giddens to his well-known ideas on the "double hermeneutic." Both social actors and sociologists use language. Actors use language to account for what they do, and sociologists, in turn, use language to account for the actions of social actors. Thus, we need to be concerned with the relationship between lay and scientific language. We particularly need to be aware of the fact that the social scientist's understanding of the social world may have an impact on the understandings of the actors being studied. In that way, social researchers can alter the world they are studying and thus come up with distorted findings and conclusions.

Elements of Structuration Theory   Let us discuss some of the major components of Giddens's structuration theory, starting with his thoughts on agents, who, as we have seen, continuously monitor their own thoughts and activities as well as their physical and social contexts. In their search for a sense of security, actors rationalize their world. By rationalization Giddens means the development of routines that not only give actors a sense of security but enable them to deal efficiently with their social lives. Actors also have motivations to act, and these motivations involve the wants and desires that prompt action. Thus, while rationalization and reflexivity are continuously involved in action, motivations are more appropriately thought of as potentials for action.

Motivations provide overall plans for action, but most of our action, in Giddens's view, is not directly motivated. Although such action is not motivated and our motivations are generally unconscious, motivations play a significant role in human conduct.

Also within the realm of consciousness, Giddens makes a (permeable) distinction between discursive and practical consciousness. *Discursive consciousness* entails the ability to describe our actions in words. *Practical consciousness* involves actions that the actors take for granted, without being able to express in words what they are doing. It is the latter type of consciousness that is particularly important to structuration theory, reflecting a primary interest in what is done rather than what is said.

Given this focus on practical consciousness, we make a smooth transition from agents to agency, the things that agents actually *do:* "Agency concerns events of which an individual is a perpetrator. . . . Whatever happened would not have happened if that individual had not intervened" (Giddens, 1984:9). Thus, Giddens gives great (his critics say too much) weight to the importance of agency (Baber, 1991). Giddens takes great pains to separate agency from intentions because he wants to make the point that actions often end up being different from what was intended; in other words, intentional acts often have unintended consequences. The idea of unintended consequences plays a great role in Giddens's theory and is especially important in getting us from agency to the social-system level.

Consistent with his emphasis on agency, Giddens accords the agent great power. In other words, Giddens's agents have the ability to make a difference in the social world. Even more strongly, agents make no sense without power; that is, an actor ceases to be an agent if he or she loses the capacity to make a difference. Giddens certainly recognizes that there are constraints on actors, but this does not mean that actors have no choices and make no difference. To Giddens, power is logically prior to subjectivity because action involves power, or the ability to transform the situation. Thus, Giddens's structuration theory accords power to the actor and action and is in opposition to theories that are disinclined to such an orientation and instead grant great importance either to the intent of the actor (phenomenology) or to the external structure (structural functionalism).

The conceptual core of structuration theory lies in the ideas of structure, system, and duality of structure. *Structure* is defined as "the structuring properties [*rules and resources*] . . . the properties which make it possible for discernibly similar social practices to exist across varying spans of time and space and which lend them systemic form" (Giddens, 1984:17). Structure is made possible by the existence of rules and resources. Structures themselves do not exist in time and space. Rather, social phenomena have the capacity to become structured. Giddens contends that "structure only exists in and through the activities of human agents" (1989:256). Thus, Giddens offers a very unusual definition of *structure* that does not follow the Durkheimian pattern of viewing structures as external to and coercive of actors. He takes pains to avoid the impression that structure is "outside" or "external" to human action. "In my usage, structure is what gives form and shape to social life, but it is not *itself* that form and shape" (Giddens, 1989:256). As Held and Thompson put it, structure to Giddens is not a framework "like the girders of a building or the skeleton of a body" (1989:4).

Giddens does not deny the fact that structure can be constraining on action, but he feels that sociologists have exaggerated the importance of this constraint. Furthermore, they have failed to emphasize the fact that structure "is *always* both constraining *and* enabling" (Giddens, 1984:25, 163; italics added). Structures often allow agents to do things they would not otherwise be able to do. Although Giddens deemphasizes structural constraint, he does recognize that actors can lose control over the "structured properties of social systems" as they stretch away in time and space. However, he is careful to avoid Weberian iron-cage imagery and notes that such a loss of control is *not* inevitable.

The conventional sociological sense of structure is closer to Giddens's concept of social system (J. Thompson, 1989:60). Giddens defines *social systems* as reproduced social practices, or "reproduced relations between actors or collectivities organized as regular social practices" (1984:17, 25). Thus the idea of the social system is derived from Giddens's focal concern with practice. Social systems do *not* have structures, but they do exhibit structural properties. Structures do not themselves exist in time and space, but they are manifested in social systems in the form of reproduced practices. Although some social systems may be the product of intentional action, Giddens places greater emphasis on the fact that such systems are often the unanticipated consequences of human action. These unanticipated consequences may become unrecognized conditions of action and feed back into it. These conditions may elude efforts to bring them under control, but nevertheless actors continue their efforts to exert such control.

Thus structures are "instantiated" in social systems. In addition, they are also manifest in "memory traces orienting the conduct of knowledgeable human agents" (Giddens, 1984:17). As a result, rules and resources manifest themselves at both the macro level of social systems and the micro level of human consciousness.

We are now ready for the concept of *structuration,* which is premised on the idea that "[t]he constitution of agents and structures are not two independently given sets of phenomena, a dualism, but represent a duality . . . the structural properties of social systems are both medium and outcome of the practices they recursively organize," or "the moment of the production of action is also one of reproduction in the contexts of the day-to-day enactment of social life" (Giddens, 1984:25, 26). It is clear that structuration involves the dialectical relationship between structure and agency (Rachlin, 1991). Structure and agency are a duality; neither can exist without the other.

As has already been indicated, *time* and *space* are crucial variables in Giddens's theory. Both depend on whether other people are present temporally or spatially. The primordial condition is face-to-face interaction, in which others are present at the same time and in the same space. However, social systems extend in time and space, and so others may no longer be present. Such distancing in terms of time and space is made increasingly possible in the modern world by new forms of communication and transportation. Gregory (1989) argues that Giddens devotes more attention to time than to space. Underscoring the importance of space, Saunders contends that "any sociological analysis of *why* and *how* things happen will need to take account of *where* (and when) they happen" (1989:218). The central sociological issue of social order depends on how well social systems are integrated over time and across space. One of Giddens's most widely recognized achievements in social theory is his effort to bring the issues of time and space to the fore (Bryant and Jary, 2001b).

We end this section by bringing Giddens's very abstract structuration theory closer to reality by discussing the research program that can be derived from it. (For an overview of empirical research based on structuration theory see Bryant and Jary, 2001a.) First, instead of focusing on human societies, structuration theory would concentrate on "the orderings of institutions across time and space" (Giddens, 1989:300). (Institutions are viewed by Giddens as clusters of practices, and he identifies four of them—symbolic orders, political institutions, economic institutions, and law.) Second, there would be a focal concern for changes in institutions over time and space. Third, researchers would need to be sensitive to the ways in which the leaders of various institutions intrude on and alter social patterns. Fourth, structurationists would need to monitor, and be sensitive to, the impact of their findings on the social world. Most generally, Giddens is deeply concerned with the "shattering impact of modernity" (1989:301), and the structurationist should be concerned with the study of this pressing social problem.

There is much more to structuration theory than can be presented here; Giddens goes into great detail about the elements of the theory already outlined and discusses many others as well. Along the way he analyzes, integrates, and/or critiques a wide range of theoretical ideas. More recently, he has been devoting increasing attention to utilizing his theory for critical analysis of the modern world, including issues such as selfhood (1991), love and intimacy (1992), third way politics (1998), globalization (2000), and most recently, climate change (2009). (see Chapter 14). Unlike many others, Giddens has gone beyond a program statement for agency-structure integration; he has given a detailed analysis of its various elements and, more important, has focused on the nature of the interrelationship. What is most satisfying about Giddens's approach is the fact that his key concern, structuration, is defined in inherently integrative terms. The constitutions of agents and structures are not independent of one another; the properties of social systems are seen as both medium and outcome of the practices of actors, and those system properties recursively organize the practices of actors.

Layder, Ashton, and Sung (1991) have sought empirical evidence of Giddens's structuration theory in a study of the transition from school to work. Although they generally support his theoretical approach, their most important conclusion is that structure and agency are not as intertwined as Giddens suggests: "Thus we conclude that empirically structure and action are interdependent (and thus, deeply implicated in each other), *but partly autonomous and separable domains*" (Layder, Ashton, and Sung, 1991:461; italics added).

Criticisms   Ian Craib (1992) has offered the most systematic criticism of Giddens's structuration theory (for a more general critique, see Mestrovic, 1998). First, Craib argues that because Giddens focuses on social practices, his work lacks "ontological depth." That is, Giddens fails to get at the social structures that underlie the social world. Second, his effort at theoretical synthesis does not mesh well with the complexity of the social world. To deal with this complexity, instead of a single synthetic theory "we require a range of theories that might be quite incompatible" (Craib, 1992:178). The social world is also, in Craib's view, quite messy, and that messiness cannot be dealt with adequately by a single, conceptually neat approach like structuration theory. Giddens's approach also serves to limit the potential contributions that could be derived by employing the full range of sociological theories. In rejecting metatheories such as positivism and theories such as structural functionalism, Giddens is unable to derive useful ideas from them. Even when he does draw upon other theories, Giddens uses only some aspects of those theories, and as a result, he does not get all he can out of them. Third, since Giddens offers no base point from which he can operate, he lacks an adequate basis for critical analysis of modern society (see Chapter 14). As a result, his criticisms tend to have an ad hoc quality rather than emanating systematically from a coherent theoretical core. Fourth, Giddens's theory, in the end, seems quite fragmented. His eclecticism leads him to accumulate various theoretical bits and pieces that do not necessarily hold together well. Finally, it is difficult, if not impossible, to know exactly what Giddens is talking about (Mestrovic, 1998:207). Many times throughout his analysis, Craib indicates that he is unsure about, is guessing at, Giddens's meaning.

Given the number and severity of the criticisms, Craib asks, Why, then, deal with structuration theory at all? He offers two basic reasons. First, many of Giddens's ideas (for example, structures as both constraining and enabling) have become integral parts of contemporary sociology. Second, anyone working in social theory today needs to take into account, and respond to, Giddens's work. Craib closes with the faintest of praise for Giddens's work: "I find it difficult to conceive of any social theory that would not find *something* in his work on which to build. *For the time being,* at any rate, structuration theory will be the food at the centre of the plate" (1992:196; italics added).

Habitus and Field

Pierre Bourdieu's (1984a:483; Calhoun, 2011) theory was animated by the desire to overcome what Bourdieu considered to be the false opposition between objectivism and subjectivism, or in his words, the "absurd opposition between individual and society" (Bourdieu, 1990:31). As he put it, "the most steadfast (and, in my eyes, the most important) intention guiding my work has been to overcome the opposition between objectivism and subjectivism" (1989:15).

He placed Durkheim and his study of social facts (see Chapter 3) and the structuralism of Saussure, Lévi-Strauss, and the structural Marxists (see Chapter 16) within the objectivist camp. These perspectives are criticized for focusing on objective structures and ignoring the process of social construction by which actors perceive, think about, and construct these structures and then proceed to act on that basis. Objectivists ignore agency and the agent, whereas Bourdieu favored a position that is structuralist without losing sight of the agent. "My intention was to bring real-life actors back in who had vanished at the hands of Lévi-Strauss and other structuralists, especially Althusser" (Bourdieu, cited in Jenkins, 1992:18).

This goal moved Bourdieu (1980/1990:42) in the direction of a subjectivist position, one that during his days as a student was dominated by Sartre's existentialism.

In addition, Schutz's phenomenology, Blumer's symbolic interactionism, and Garfinkel's ethnomethodology are thought of as examples of subjectivism, focusing on the way agents think about, account for, or represent the social world while ignoring the objective structures in which those processes exist. Bourdieu saw these theories as concentrating on agency and ignoring structure.

Instead, Bourdieu focused on the dialectical relationship between objective structures and subjective phenomena:

> On the one hand, the objective structures . . . form the basis for . . . representations
> and constitute the structural constraints that bear upon interactions: but, on the
> other hand, these representations must also be taken into consideration, particularly
> if one wants to account for the daily struggles, individual and collective, which
> purport to transform or to preserve these structures.
>
> (Bourdieu, 1989:15)

To sidestep the objectivist-subjectivist dilemma, Bourdieu (1977:3) focused on *practice,* which he saw as the outcome of the dialectical relationship between structure and agency. Practices are not objectively determined, nor are they the product of free will. (Another reason for Bourdieu's focus on practice is that such a concern avoids the often irrelevant intellectualism that he associated with objectivism and subjectivism.)

Reflecting his interest in the dialectic between structure and the way people construct social reality, Bourdieu labeled his own orientation "constructivist structuralism," "structuralist constructivism," or "genetic structuralism." Here is the way Bourdieu defined genetic structuralism:

> The analysis of objective structures—those of different fields—is inseparable from
> the analysis of the genesis, within biological individuals, of the mental structures
> which are to some extent the product of the incorporation of social structures;
> inseparable, too, from the analysis of the genesis of these social structures themselves:
> the social space, and of the groups that occupy it, are the products of historical
> struggles (in which agents participate in accordance with their position in the
> social space and with the mental structures through which they apprehend
> this space).
>
> (Bourdieu, 1990:14)

He subscribed, at least in part, to a structuralist perspective, but it is one that is different from the structuralism of Saussure and Lévi-Strauss (as well as the structural Marxists). While they, in turn, focused on structures in language and culture, Bourdieu argued that structures also exist in the social world itself. Bourdieu saw "objective structures [as] independent of the consciousness and will of agents, which are capable of guiding and constraining their practices or their representations" (1989:14). He simultaneously adopted a constructivist position which allowed him to deal with the genesis of schemes of perception, thought, and action as well as that of social structures.

Bourdieu sought to bridge structuralism and constructivism, and succeeded to some degree, but there is a bias in his work in the direction of structuralism. It is for this reason that he (along with Foucault and others—see Chapter 16) is thought

PIERRE BOURDIEU

A Biographical Sketch

Born in a small rural town in southeast France in 1930, Bourdieu grew up in a lower-middle-class household (his father was a civil servant) (Jenkins, 2005a; Monnier, 2007). In the early 1950s he attended, and received a degree from, a prestigious teaching college in Paris, Ecole Normale Superieure. However, he refused to write a thesis, in part because he objected to the mediocre quality of his education and to the authoritarian structure of the school. He was put off by, and was active in the opposition against, the strong communist, especially Stalinist, orientation of the school.

Bourdieu taught briefly in a provincial school but was drafted in 1956 and spent two years in Algeria with the French Army. He wrote a book about his experiences and remained in Algeria for two years after his army tenure was over. He returned to France in 1960 and worked for a year as an assistant at the University of Paris. He attended the lectures of the anthropologist Lévi-Strauss at College de France and worked as an assistant to the sociologist Raymond Aron. Bourdieu moved to the University of Lille for three years and then returned to the powerful position of Director of Studies at L'Ecole Practique des Hautes Etudes in 1964.

In the succeeding years Bourdieu became a major figure in Parisian, French, and ultimately world intellectual circles. His work has had an impact on a number of different fields, including education, anthropology, and sociology. He gathered a group of disciples around him in the 1960s, and since then his followers have collaborated with him and made intellectual contributions of their own. In 1968 the Centre de Sociologie Européenne was founded, and Bourdieu was its director until his death. Associated with the center was a unique publishing venture, *Actes de la Recherche en Sciences Sociales,* that has been an important outlet for the work of Bourdieu and his supporters.

When Raymond Aron retired in 1981, the prestigious chair in sociology at College de France became open, and most of the leading French sociologists (for example, Raymond Boudon and Alain Touraine) were in competition for it. However, the chair was awarded to Bourdieu (Jenkins, 1992). In the time that followed, Bourdieu was, if anything, even more prolific than before, and his reputation continued to grow (for more on Bourdieu, see Swartz, 1997:15–51).

An interesting aspect of Bourdieu's work is the way in which his ideas were shaped in ongoing, sometimes explicit and sometimes implicit, dialogue with others. For example, many of his early ideas were formed in a dialogue with two of the leading scholars of the day during his years of training—Jean-Paul Sartre and Claude Lévi-Strauss. From the existentialism of Sartre, Bourdieu got a strong sense of actors as creators of their social worlds. However, Bourdieu felt that Sartre had gone too far and accorded the actors too much power and in the process ignored the structural constraints on them. Pulled in the direction of structure, Bourdieu naturally turned to the work of the preeminent structuralist, Lévi-Strauss. At first Bourdieu was strongly drawn to this orientation; in fact, he described himself for a time as a "'blissful structuralist'" (cited in Jenkins, 1992:17). However, some of his early research led him to the conclusion that structuralism was as limiting, albeit in a different direction, as existentialism. He objected to the fact that the structuralists saw themselves as privileged observers of people who are presumed to be controlled by structures of which they are unconscious. Bourdieu came to have little regard for a field that focused solely on such structural constraints, saying that sociology

> would perhaps not be worth an hour's trouble if it solely had as its end the intention of exposing the wires which activate the individuals it observes—if it forgot that it has to do with men, even those who, like puppets, play a game of which they do not know the rules—if, in short, it did not give itself the task of restoring to men the meaning of their actions.
>
> (Bourdieu, cited in Robbins, 1991:37)

Bourdieu defined one of his basic objectives in reaction to the excesses of structuralism: "'My intention was to bring real-life actors back in who had vanished at the hands of Lévi-Strauss and other structuralists . . . through being considered as epiphenomena of structures'" (cited in Jenkins, 1992:17–18). In other words, Bourdieu wanted to integrate at least a part of Sartre's existentialism with Lévi-Strauss's structuralism.

Bourdieu's thinking also was profoundly shaped by Marxian theory and the Marxists. As we have seen, as a student Bourdieu objected to some of the excesses of the Marxists, and he later rejected the ideas of structural Marxism. Although Bourdieu cannot be thought of as a Marxist, there are certainly ideas derived from Marxian theory that run through his work. Most notable is his emphasis on practice (praxis) and his desire to integrate theory and (research) practice in his sociology. (It could be said that instead of existentialism or structuralism, Bourdieu is doing "praxeology.") There is also a liberationist strand in his work in which he can be seen as being interested in freeing people from political and class domination. But, as was the case with Sartre and Lévi-Strauss, Bourdieu can best be seen as creating his ideas by using Marx and the Marxists as a point of departure.

There are traces of the influence of other theorists in his work, especially that of Weber and of the leading French sociological theorist, Emile Durkheim. However, Bourdieu resisted being labeled as a Marxian, Weberian, Durkheimian, or anything else. He regarded such labels as limiting, oversimplifying, and doing violence to his work. In a sense, Bourdieu developed his ideas in a critical dialogue that started while he was a student and continued throughout his life: "Everything that I have done in sociology and anthropology I have done as much against what I was taught as thanks to it" (Bourdieu, in Bourdieu and Wacquant, 1992:204). Bourdieu died January 3, 2002, at the age of 71.

of as a poststructuralist. There is more continuity in his work with structuralism than there is with constructivism. Unlike the approach of most others (for example, phenomenologists, symbolic interactionists), Bourdieu's constructivism ignores subjectivity and intentionality. He thought it important to include within his sociology the way people, on the basis of their position in social space, perceive and construct the social world. However, the perception and construction that take place in the social world are both animated and constrained by structures. This is well reflected in one of his own definitions of his theoretical perspective: "The analysis of objective structures . . . is inseparable from the analysis of the genesis, within biological individuals, of the mental structures which are to some extent the product of the incorporation of social structures; inseparable, too, from the analysis of the genesis of these social structures themselves" (Bourdieu, 1990:14). We can describe what he is interested in as the relationship "between social structures and mental structures" (Bourdieu, 1984a:471).

Thus some microsociologists would be uncomfortable with Bourdieu's perspective and would see it as little more than a more adequate structuralism. According to Wacquant, "Although the two moments of analysis are equally necessary, they are not equal: epistemological priority is granted objectivist rupture over subjectivist understanding" (1992:11). As Jenkins puts it, "In his sociological heart of hearts he [Bourdieu] is as committed to an objectivist view of the world as the majority of those whose work he so sternly dismisses" (1992:91). Or conversely, "At the end of the day, perhaps the most crucial weakness in Bourdieu's work is his inability to cope with subjectivity" (Jenkins, 1992:97). In fact, Bourdieu's one-time collaborators Luc Boltanski and Laurent Thevenot developed what has been called "French pragmatism" in order to correct the structuralist bias in Bourdieu's work (Boltanksi and Thevenot, 1991/2006).[8]

Yet there is a dynamic actor in Bourdieu's theory, an actor capable of "*intentionless invention* of regulated improvisation" (1977:79). The heart of Bourdieu's work, and of his effort to bridge subjectivism and objectivism, lies in his concepts of habitus and field (Aldridge, 1998), as well as their dialectical relationship to each other (Swartz, 1997). While habitus exist in the minds of actors, fields exist outside their minds. We will examine these two concepts in some detail over the next few pages.

Habitus   We begin with the concept for which Bourdieu is most famous—habitus (Jenkins, 2005b).[9] *Habitus* are the "mental, or cognitive structures" through which people deal with the social world. People are endowed with a series of internalized schemes through which they perceive, understand, appreciate, and evaluate the social world. It is through such schemes that people both produce their practices and perceive and evaluate them. Dialectically, habitus are "the product of the internalization of the structures" of the social world (Bourdieu, 1989:18). In fact, we can think of habitus as "internalized, 'embodied' social structures" (Bourdieu, 1984a:468). They are something like a "common sense" (Holton, 2000). They reflect objective divisions

---

[8] Silber (2003) describes the unique perspective that French pragmatism takes on the agency-structure debate.

[9] This idea was not created by Bourdieu but is, rather, a traditional philosophical idea that he resuscitated (Wacquant, 1989). The word *habitus* is used as both a plural and a singular noun.

in the class structure, such as age groups, genders, and social classes. A habitus is acquired as a result of long-term occupation of a position within the social world. Thus habitus varies depending on the nature of one's position in that world; not everyone has the same habitus. However, those who occupy the same position within the social world tend to have similar habitus. (To be fair to Bourdieu, we must report that he made statements such as that his work was guided "by the desire to reintroduce the agent's practice, his or her capacity for invention and improvisation" [Bourdieu, 1990:13].) In this sense, habitus also can be a collective phenomenon. The habitus allows people to make sense out of the social world, but the existence of a multitude of habitus means that the social world and its structures do not impose themselves uniformly on all actors.

The habitus available at any given time have been created over the course of collective history: "The habitus, the product of history, produces individual and collective practices, and hence history, in accordance with the schemes engendered by history" (Bourdieu, 1977:82). The habitus manifested in any given individual is acquired over the course of individual history and is a function of the particular point in social history in which it occurs. Habitus is both durable and transposable—that is, transferable from one field to another. However, it is possible for people to have an inappropriate habitus, to suffer from what Bourdieu called *hysteresis*. A good example is someone who is uprooted from an agrarian existence in a contemporary precapitalist society and put to work on Wall Street. The habitus acquired in a precapitalist society would not allow one to cope very well with life on Wall Street.

The habitus both produces and is produced by the social world. On the one hand, habitus is a "structuring structure"; that is, it is a structure that structures the social world. On the other hand, it is a "structured structure"; that is, it is a structure that is structured by the social world. In other terms, Bourdieu describes habitus as the *"dialectic of the internalization of externality and the externalization of internality"* (1977:72). Thus, habitus allowed Bourdieu to escape from having to choose between subjectivism and objectivism, to "escape from under the philosophy of the subject without doing away with the agent . . . as well as from under the philosophy of the structure but without forgetting to take into account the effects it wields upon and through the agent" (Bourdieu and Wacquant, 1992:121–122).

It is practice that mediates between habitus and the social world. On the one hand, it is through practice that the habitus is created; on the other hand, it is as a result of practice that the social world is created. Bourdieu expressed the mediating function of practice when he defined the habitus as "the system of structured and structuring dispositions which is constituted by practice and constantly aimed at practical . . . functions" (cited in Wacquant, 1989:42; see also Bourdieu, 1977:72). While practice tends to shape habitus, habitus, in turn, serves to both unify and generate practice.

Although habitus is an internalized structure that constrains thought and choice of action, it does *not* determine them (Myles, 1999). This lack of determinism is one of the main things that distinguishes Bourdieu's position from that of mainstream structuralists. The habitus merely "suggests" what people should think and what they should choose to do. People engage in a conscious deliberation of options, although this decision-making process reflects the operation of the habitus. The habitus provides the principles by which people make choices and choose the strategies that they will employ in the social world. As Bourdieu and Wacquant picturesquely put it, "people are not fools." However, people are not fully rational either (Bourdieu disdained rational choice theory); they act in a "reasonable" manner—they have practical sense. There is a logic to what people do; it is the "logic of practice" (Bourdieu, 1980/1990).

Robbins underscores the point that practical logic is "'polythetic'—that is to say that practical logic is capable of sustaining simultaneously a multiplicity of confused and logically (in terms of formal logic) contradictory meanings or theses because the overriding context of its operation is practical" (1991:112). This statement is important not only because it underscores the difference between practical logic and rationality (formal logic) but also because it reminds us of Bourdieu's "relationism." The latter is important in this context because it leads us to recognize that habitus is *not* an unchanging, fixed structure, but rather is adapted by individuals who are constantly changing in the face of the contradictory situations in which they find themselves.

The habitus functions "below the level of consciousness and language, beyond the reach of introspective scrutiny and control by the will" (Bourdieu, 1984a:466). Although we are not conscious of habitus and its operation, it manifests itself in our most practical activities, such as the way we eat, walk, talk, and even blow our noses. The habitus operates as a structure, but people do not simply respond mechanically to it or to external structures that are operating on them. Thus, in Bourdieu's approach we avoid the extremes of unpredictable novelty and total determinism.

Field We turn now to the "field," which Bourdieu thought of relationally rather than structurally. The *field* is a network of relations among the objective positions within it (Bourdieu and Wacquant, 1992:97). These relations exist apart from individual consciousness and will. They are *not* interactions or intersubjective ties among individuals. The occupants of positions may be either agents or institutions, and they are constrained by the structure of the field. There are a number of semiautonomous fields in the social world (for example, artistic [Bourdieu and Darbel, 1969/1990; Fowler, 1997], religious, higher education), all with their own specific logics and all generating among actors a belief about the things that are at stake in a field.

Bourdieu saw the field, by definition, as an arena of battle: "The field is also a field of struggles" (Bourdieu and Wacquant, 1992:101). It is the structure of the field that both "undergirds and guides the strategies whereby the occupants of these positions seek, individually or collectively, to safeguard or improve their position, and to impose the principle of hierarchization most favorable to their own products" (Bourdieu, cited in Wacquant, 1989:40). The field is a type of competitive marketplace in which various kinds of capital (economic, cultural, social, symbolic) are employed and deployed. However, it is the field of power (of politics) that is of the utmost importance; the hierarchy of power relationships within the political field serves to structure all the other fields.

Bourdieu laid out a three-step process for the analysis of a field. The first step, reflecting the primacy of the field of power, is to trace the relationship of any specific field to the political field. The second step is to map the objective structure of the relations among positions within the field. Finally, the analyst should seek to determine the nature of the habitus of the agents who occupy the various types of positions within the field.

The positions of various agents in the field are determined by the amount and relative weight of the capital they possess (Anheier, Gerhards, and Romo, 1995). Bourdieu even used military imagery to describe the field, calling it an arena of "strategic emplacements, fortresses to be defended and captured in a field of struggles" (1984a:244). It is capital that allows one to control one's own fate as well as the fate of others (on the negative aspects of capital, see Portes and Landolt, 1996). Bourdieu usually discussed four types of capital (for a discussion of a slightly different formulation of types of capital applied to the genesis of the state, see Bourdieu, 1994). This idea is, of course, drawn from the economic sphere (Guillory, 2000:32), and the meaning of *economic capital* is obvious. *Cultural capital* "comprises familiarity with and easy use of cultural forms institutionalized [e.g., through the university] at the apex of society's cultural hierarchy" (DiMaggio, 2005:167). *Social capital* consists of valued social relations between people. *Symbolic capital* stems from one's honor and prestige.

Occupants of positions within the field employ a variety of *strategies*. This idea shows, once again, that Bourdieu's actors have at least some freedom: "The habitus does not negate the possibility of *strategic* calculation on the part of agents" (Bourdieu, 1993:5; italics added). However, strategies do not refer "to the purposive and pre-planned pursuit of calculated goals . . . but to the active deployment of objectively oriented 'lines of action' that obey regularities and form coherent and socially intelligible patterns, even though they do not follow conscious rules or aim at the premeditated goals posited by a strategist" (Wacquant, 1992:25). It is via strategies that "the occupants of these positions seek, individually or collectively, to safeguard or improve their position and to impose the principle of hierarchization most favorable to their own products. The strategies of agents depend on their positions in the field" (Bourdieu and Wacquant, 1992:101).

Bourdieu saw the state as the site of the struggle over the monopoly of what he called *symbolic violence*. This is a "soft" form of violence—"violence which is exercised upon a social agent with his or her complicity" (Bourdieu and Wacquant, 1992:167). Symbolic violence is practiced indirectly, largely through cultural mechanisms, and stands in contrast to the more direct forms of social control that sociologists often focus on. The educational system is the major institution through which symbolic violence is practiced on people (Bourdieu and Passeron, 1970/1990; for an application of the idea of symbolic violence to the status of women, see Krais, 1993). The language, the meanings, the symbolic system of those in power are imposed on the rest of the population. This serves to buttress the position of those in power by, among other things, obscuring what they are doing from the rest of society and getting "the dominated [to] accept as legitimate their own condition of domination" (Swartz, 1997:89). More generally, Bourdieu (1996) saw the educational system as deeply implicated in reproducing existing power and class relations. It is in his ideas on symbolic violence that the political aspect of Bourdieu's work is clearest. That is, Bourdieu was interested in the emancipation of people from this violence and, more generally, from class and political domination (Postone, LiPuma, and Calhoun,

1993:6). Yet Bourdieu was no naive utopian; a better description of his position might be "reasoned utopianism" (Bourdieu and Wacquant, 1992:197).

In underscoring the importance of *both* habitus and field, Bourdieu rejected the split between methodological individualists and methodological holists and adopted a position that has been termed "methodological relationism" (Ritzer and Gindoff, 1992). That is, Bourdieu was focally concerned with the *relationship* between habitus and field. He saw this as operating in two main ways. On the one hand, the field *conditions* the habitus; on the other hand, the habitus *constitutes* the field as something that is meaningful, that has sense and value, and that is worth the investment of energy.

Applying Habitus and Field

Bourdieu did not simply seek to develop an abstract theoretical system; he also related it to a series of empirical concerns and thereby avoided the trap of pure intellectualism. We will illustrate the application of his theoretical approach in his empirical study *Distinction* (1984a), which examines the aesthetic preferences of different groups throughout society (for another application, see *Homo Academicus* [Bourdieu, 1984b]).

Distinction   In this work, Bourdieu attempted, among other things, to demonstrate that culture can be a legitimate object of scientific study.[10] He attempted to reintegrate culture in the sense of "high culture" (for example, preferences for classical music) with the anthropological sense of culture, which looks at all its forms, both high and low. More specifically, in this work Bourdieu linked taste for refined objects with taste for the most basic food flavors.

Because of structural invariants, especially field and habitus, the cultural preferences of the various groups within society (especially classes and fractions of classes) constitute coherent systems. Bourdieu was focally concerned with variations in aesthetic "taste," the acquired disposition to differentiate among the various cultural objects of aesthetic enjoyment and to appreciate them differentially. Taste is also practice that serves, among other things, to give an individual, as well as others, a sense of his or her place in the social order. Taste serves to unify those with similar preferences and to differentiate them from those with different tastes. That is, through the practical applications and implications of taste, people classify objects and thereby, in the process, classify themselves. We are able to categorize people by the tastes they manifest, for example, by their preferences for different types of music or movies. These practices, like all others, need to be seen in the context of all mutual relationships, that is, within the totality. Thus, seemingly isolated tastes for art or movies are related to preferences in food, sports, or hairstyles.

Two interrelated fields are involved in Bourdieu's study of taste—class relationships (especially within fractions of the dominant class) and cultural relationships (for a critique of this distinction, see Erickson, 1996). He saw these fields as a series of positions in which a variety of "games" are undertaken. The actions taken by the

---

[10] For a recent assessment of Bourdieu's relevance for cultural sociology see the special issue of *Cultural Sociology* (2011): "On the Shoulders of Pierre Bourdieu."

agents (individual or collective) who occupy specific positions are governed by the structure of the field, the nature of the positions, and the interests associated with them. However, it is also a game that involves self-positioning and the use of a wide range of strategies to allow one to excel at the game. Taste is an opportunity both to experience and to assert one's position within the field. But the field of social class has a profound effect on one's ability to play this game; those in the higher classes are far better able to have their tastes accepted and to oppose the tastes of those in the lower classes. Thus the world of cultural works is related to the hierarchical world of social class and is itself both hierarchical and hierarchizing.

Needless to say, Bourdieu also linked taste to his other major concept, habitus. Tastes are shaped far more by these deep-rooted and long-standing dispositions than they are by surface opinions and verbalizations. People's preferences for even such mundane aspects of culture as clothing, furniture, and cooking are shaped by the habitus. And it is these dispositions "that forge the unconscious unity of a class" (Bourdieu, 1984a:77). Bourdieu put this more colorfully later: "Taste is a matchmaker . . . through which a habitus confirms its affinity with other habitus" (1984a:243). Dialectically, of course, it is the structure of the class that shapes the habitus.

While both field and habitus were important to Bourdieu, it is their dialectical relationship that is of utmost importance and significance; field and habitus mutually define one another:

> The dispositions constituting the cultivated habitus are only formed, only function and are only valid in a *field,* in the relationship with a field . . . which is itself a 'field of possible forces,' a 'dynamic' situation in which forces are only manifested in their relationship with certain dispositions. This is why the same practices may receive opposite meanings and values in different fields, in different configurations, or in opposing sectors of the same field.
>
> (Bourdieu, 1984a:94; italics added)

Or, as Bourdieu put it, in more general terms: "There is a strong correlation between social positions and the dispositions of the agents who occupy them" (1984a:110). It is out of the relationship between habitus and field that practices, cultural practices in particular, are established.

Bourdieu saw culture as a kind of economy, or marketplace. In this marketplace people utilize cultural rather than economic capital. This capital is largely a result of people's social class origin and their educational experience. In the marketplace, people accrue more or less capital and either expend it to improve their position or lose it, thereby causing their position within the economy to deteriorate.

People pursue distinction in a range of cultural fields—the beverages they drink (Perrier or cola), the automobiles they drive (Mercedes Benz or Ford Escort), the newspapers they read (*The New York Times* or *USA Today*), and the resorts they visit (the French Riviera or Disney World). Relationships of distinction are objectively inscribed in these products and are reactivated each time they are appropriated. In Bourdieu's view, "The total field of these fields offers well-nigh inexhaustible possibilities for the pursuit of distinction" (1984a:227). The appropriation of certain cultural goods (for example, a Mercedes Benz) yields "profit," whereas that of others (an Escort) yields no gain, or even a "loss."

Bourdieu (1998a:9) took pains to make it clear that he was not simply arguing, following Thorstein Veblen's (1899/1994) famous theory of conspicuous consumption, that the "driving force of all human behavior was the search for distinction." Rather, he contended that his main point "is that to exist within a social space, to occupy a point or to be an individual within a social space, is to differ, to be different . . . being inscribed in the space in question, he or she . . . is endowed with categories of perception, with classificatory schemata, with a certain taste, which permits her to make differences, to discern, to distinguish" (Bourdieu, 1998a:9). Thus, for example, one who chooses to own a grand piano is different from one who opts for an accordion. That one choice (the piano) is worthy of distinction whereas the other (the accordion) is considered vulgar as a result of the dominance of one point of view and the symbolic violence practiced against those who adopt another viewpoint.

There is a dialectic between the nature of cultural products and tastes. Changes in cultural goods lead to alterations in taste, but changes in taste also are likely to result in transformations in cultural products. The structure of the field not only conditions the desires of the consumers of cultural goods but also structures what the producers create in order to satisfy those demands.

Changes in taste (and Bourdieu saw all fields temporally) result from the struggle between opposing forces in both the cultural (the supporters of old versus new fashions, for example) and the class (the dominant versus the dominated fractions within the dominant class) arenas. However, the heart of the struggle lies within the class system, and the cultural struggle between, for example, artists and intellectuals is a reflection of the interminable struggle between the different fractions of the dominant class to define culture, indeed the entire social world. It is oppositions within the class structure that condition oppositions in taste and in habitus. Although Bourdieu placed great importance on social class, he refused to reduce it to merely economic matters or to the relations of production but saw class as defined by habitus as well.

Bourdieu offered a distinctive theory of the relationship between agency and structure within the context of a concern for the dialectical relationship between habitus and field. His theory also is distinguished by its focus on practice (in the preceding case, aesthetic practices) and its refusal to engage in arid intellectualism. In that sense it represents a return to the Marxian concern for the relationship between theory and practice.

Concluding Thoughts   Bourdieu was one thinker (another is Garfinkel) who was considered a theorist but who rejected that label. He said that he was not "producing a general discourse on the social world" (Bourdieu and Wacquant, 1992:159). Bourdieu rejected pure theory that lacks an empirical base, but he also disdained pure empiricism performed in a theoretical vacuum. Rather, he saw himself engaged in research that was "inseparably empirical and theoretical . . . research without theory is blind, and theory without research is empty" (Bourdieu and Wacquant, 1992:160, 162).

Overall, we find ourselves in accord with Jenkins when he argues that "Bourdieu's intellectual project is longstanding, relatively coherent and cumulative. It amounts to nothing less than an attempt to construct a theory of social practice and society"

(1992:67). Calhoun sees Bourdieu as a critical theorist, which in this context is defined more broadly than simply those associated with the Frankfurt school. Calhoun defines critical theory as "the project of social theory that undertakes simultaneously critique of received categories, critique of theoretical practice, and critical substantive analysis of social life in terms of the possible, not just the actual" (1993a:63).

Although Bourdieu offered a theory, his theory does not have universal validity. For example, he said that there are "no transhistoric laws of the relations between fields" (Bourdieu and Wacquant, 1992:109). The nature of the actual relations between fields is always an empirical question. Similarly, the nature of habitus changes with altered historical circumstances: "Habitus . . . is a transcendental but a historical transcendental bound up with the structure and history of a field" (Bourdieu and Wacquant, 1992:189).

Practice theory

A common element in both Giddens's and Bourdieu's theory is the focus on practice. Though the term is not used in precisely the same way, in both cases the concept of practice is used to bridge the structure-agency gap. In fact, similar concepts can be found in the work of other theorists such as Foucault, Garfinkel, Latour, and Butler. It is linked to poststructuralism, structuration theory, ethnomethodology, actor-network theory (and science studies), and performativity theory. Indeed, as a result of this widespread attention, "practice theory" has become a perspective of growing theoretical importance (Biernacki, 2007; Reckwitz, 2007; Schatzki, 1996; Schatzki, Knorr-Cetina, and von Savigny, 2001; Turner, 1994).

What is practice? Above all, a focus on practice emphasizes the impact of "taken-for-granted, pre-theoretical assumptions on human conduct" (Biernacki, 2007:3607). Practice is a routinized way of acting, and those pretheoretical assumptions and routines affect how we act, especially how we manage our bodies, handle objects, treat subjects, describe things, and understand the world. Reckwitz (2002) seeks to clarify the abstract nature of practice and practice theory by focusing on its relationship to a number of core concepts.

The first is the *body*. Indeed, interest in the body is one of the central and defining characteristics of practice theory (and it is of increasing interest in sociology in general and in sociological theory in particular; see "affect theory" in Chapter 17 for a very different conception of the body). In many other theories the body is an epiphenomenon affected by, even controlled by, other phenomena (rational choices, norms, values). But for practice theory the body is the site of the social. In fact, practices are, at least in part, "routinized bodily performances" (Reckwitz, 2002:251). Practices are the result of training the body in a particular way. "A practice can be understood as the regular, skillful 'performance' of human bodies" (Reckwitz, 2002:251). This definition applies to obvious things such as using a golf club to drive a golf ball, but also to talking, reading, and writing.

Practice involves not only routinized bodily performances but also the *mind*, mental activities. To engage in practice entails the use of the body in various ways *and* engagement in mental activities—"certain routinized ways of understanding the world, of desiring something, of knowing something" (Reckwitz, 2002:251). Notice that while the focus here is on mental activities, they, like bodily activities, are routinized. Thus it is not that we consciously think through either what our bodies or minds will do; we simply act in a routinized manner. For example, playing tennis requires certain bodily movements that we perform routinely without thinking through each step to, say, hit a backhand or an overhead shot. But playing tennis also requires know-how about how the game is played, interpretation (of, for example, what it means when your opponent rushes the net), and aims (such as winning the point and the match). Playing tennis requires *both* routinized bodily and mental activities, as well as the interaction of the two.

Things are integral to practice and as necessary as bodily and mental activities. Practice often involves using things in particular ways. The use of things involves both bodily movements and mental activities. Thus, in tennis, one must be able to use a tennis racket in various ways depending on the nature of the shot required. No matter how good one's bodily and mental activities, one cannot play tennis without a racket. It is in the interaction of body, mind, and object that most practice exists. Overall, practice cannot occur in the absence of objects.

Knowledge also is required for practice to occur. More than just knowing various things, this knowledge also includes "ways of understanding, knowing how, ways of wanting and of feeling that are linked to each other within a practice" (Reckwitz, 2002:253). All of this knowledge is largely implicit. Thus, in playing tennis we know the rudiments of the game, we know how to hit certain shots and return various shots from our opponent, and we know that we want certain things (to win) and not other things (to be embarrassed) and that a certain level and type of emotional involvement (alert but not tense) is needed to do well. All of this knowledge is important, but in most cases it is employed routinely without thinking through all of the issues involved.

To practice theory, *discourse/language* is merely one practice among many practices. In contrast, many other similar perspectives (especially structuralism and semiotics; see Chapter 16)—all part of the "linguistic turn" in sociology—give discourse/language a privileged status. In those other perspectives, discursive practices are merely strings of signs. In practice theory, they are that, but they also are "bodily patterns, routinized mental activities—forms of understanding, know-how (here including grammar and pragmatic rules of use), and motivation—and above all objects (from sounds to computers) that are linked to each other" (Reckwitz, 2002:254–255). Thus, in practice theory, discourse/language involves not only signs but also all of the other key concerns of the theory.

In terms of *structure/process,* social structure is found in the routine nature of practice. Larger-scale social phenomena, from economic structures like corporations to intimate social relations, are structured by the routines that lie at the heart of social practices. Thus, structure (as well as process) does not exist "out there" in large-scale social phenomena, or in people's heads, but exists in the routine nature of action. Structure is *not,* say, an organization's structure as reflected in an organizational chart, or the structure of the brain; it is the routines of action.

This leads to a very distinctive view of the *agent/individual.* Many social theories, especially microtheories, focus on the agent/individual as, for example, self-interested (rational choice theory) or as controlled by norms and roles (structural functionalism). The focus in practice theory is on practice and *not* on agents. Agents exist, but they are best thought of as mind body combinations that constitute themselves and the world around them through social practices. Thus, the agent is neither autonomous (as in rational choice theory) nor a judgmental dope (as in structural functionalism), but rather "someone who understands the world and herself, who uses know-how and motivational knowledge, according to the particular practice" (Reckwitz, 2002:256). The key point here is that practice theory deemphasizes the importance of the agent and seeks to focus attention on the practices; it is those practices that are of central importance and *not* the agents who carry them out.

Colonization of the Life-World

We discussed Habermas's earlier ideas in Chapter 8, on neo-Marxian theory, in the section titled "Critical Theory." As we will see, Habermas's perspective can still be thought of, at least in part, as being a neo-Marxian orientation (McBride, 2000), but it has broadened considerably and is increasingly difficult to contain within that, or any other, theoretical category. Habermas's theory has grown and become more diverse as Habermas has addressed, and incorporated, the ideas of a wide range of sociological theorists, most recently and most notably those of George Herbert Mead, Talcott Parsons, Alfred Schutz, and Emile Durkheim. In spite of the difficulties involved in categorizing Habermas's innovative theoretical perspective, we will discuss his ideas about the "colonization of the life-world," under the heading "agency-structure issue." Habermas (1991:251) makes it clear that he is engaging in "paradigm combination"; that is, he is creating his agency-structure perspective by integrating ideas drawn from action theory and systems theory. It is, at least in part, in his thoughts on the life-world that Habermas deals with agency. Structure is dealt with primarily in Habermas's ideas on the social system, which, as we will see, is the force that is colonizing the life-world. What does Habermas mean by *life-world, system,* and *colonization?* We address these phenomena and their interrelationship, as well as other key ideas in Habermas's theorizing, in this section.

Before we get to these concepts, it should be made clear that Habermas's major focus continues to be on communicative action. Free and open communication remains both his theoretical baseline and his political objective. It also has the methodological function, much like Weber's ideal types, of allowing him to analyze variations from the model: "The construction of an unlimited and undistorted discourse can serve at most as a foil for setting off more glaringly the rather ambiguous developmental tendencies in modern society" (Habermas, 1987a:107). Indeed, his focal interest in the colonization of the life-world is in the ways in which that process is adversely affecting free communication.

Habermas also retains an interest in the Weberian process of rationalization, specifically the issue of the differential rationalization of life-world and system and the impact of this difference on the colonization of the former by the latter (for a somewhat counter view, see Bartos, 1996). In Weberian terms, the *system* is the domain of formal rationality, whereas the *life-world* is the site of substantive rationality. The *colonization of the life-world,* therefore, involves a restatement of the Weberian thesis that in the modern world, formal rationality is triumphing over substantive rationality and coming to dominate areas that formerly were defined by substantive rationality. Thus, while Habermas's theory has taken some interesting new turns, it retains its theoretical roots, especially in its Marxian and Weberian orientations.

The Life-World   This concept is derived from phenomenological sociology in general and, more specifically, the theories of Alfred Schutz (Bowring, 1996). But Habermas interprets the ideas of George Herbert Mead as also contributing to insights about the life-world. To Habermas, the life-world represents an internal perspective (whereas, as we will see, the system represents an external viewpoint): "Society is conceived from the perspective of the acting subject" (1987a:117). Thus, there is only one society; life-world and system are simply different ways of looking at it.

Habermas views the life-world and communicative action as "complementary" concepts. More specifically, communicative action can be seen as occurring within the life-world:

> The lifeworld is, so to speak, the transcendental site where speaker and hearer meet, where they reciprocally raise claims that their utterances fit the world . . . and where they can criticize and confirm those validity claims, settle their disagreements, and arrive at agreements.
>
> (Habermas, 1987a:126)

The life-world is a "context-forming background of processes of reaching understanding" through communicative action (Habermas, 1987a:204). It involves a wide range of unspoken presuppositions about mutual understanding that must exist and be mutually understood for communication to take place.

Habermas is concerned with the rationalization of the life-world, which involves, for one thing, increasingly rational communication in the life-world. He believes that the more rational the life-world becomes, the more likely it is that interaction will be controlled by "rationally motivated mutual understanding." Such understanding, or a rational method of achieving consensus, is based ultimately on the authority of the better argument.

Habermas sees the rationalization of the life-world as involving the progressive differentiation of its various elements. The life-world is composed of culture, society, and personality (note the influence of Parsons and his action systems). Each of these refers to interpretive patterns, or background assumptions, about culture and its effect on action, appropriate patterns of social relations (society), and what people are like (personality) and how they are supposed to behave. Engaging in communicative action and achieving understanding in terms of each of these themes lead to the reproduction of the life-world through the reinforcement of culture, the integration of society, and the formation of personality. While these components are closely intertwined in archaic societies, the rationalization of the life-world involves the "growing differentiation between culture, society and personality" (Habermas, 1987a:288).

System   While the life-world represents the viewpoint of acting subjects on society, system involves an external perspective that views society "from the observer's perspective of someone not involved" (Habermas, 1987a:117). In analyzing systems, we are attuned to the interconnection of actions, as well as the functional significance of actions and their contributions to the maintenance of the system. Each of the major components of the life-world (culture, society, personality) has corresponding elements in the system. Cultural reproduction, social integration, and personality formation take place at the system level.

The system has its roots in the life-world, but ultimately it comes to develop its own structural characteristics. Examples of such structures include the family, the judiciary, the state, and the economy. As these structures evolve, they grow more and more distant from the life-world. As in the life-world, rationalization at the system level involves progressive differentiation and greater complexity. These structures also grow more self-sufficient. As they grow in power, they exercise more and more steering capacity over the life-world. They come to have less and less to do with the process of achieving consensus and, in fact, limit the occurrence of that process in the life-world. In other words, these rational structures, instead of enhancing the capacity to communicate and reach understanding, threaten those processes through the exertion of external control over them.

Social Integration and System Integration   Given the preceding discussion of life-world and system, Habermas concludes: "*The fundamental problem of social theory is how to connect in a satisfactory way the two conceptual strategies indicated by the notions of 'system' and 'lifeworld'*" (1987a:151; italics added). Habermas labels those two conceptual strategies "social integration" and "system integration."

The perspective of *social integration* focuses on the life-world and the ways in which the action system is integrated through either normatively guaranteed or communicatively achieved consensus. Theorists who believe that society is integrated through social integration begin with communicative action and see society *as* the life-world. They adopt the internal perspective of the group members, and they employ a hermeneutic approach in order to be able to relate their understanding to that of the members of the life-world. The ongoing reproduction of society is seen as being a result of the actions undertaken by members of the life-world to maintain its symbolic structures. It also is seen only from their perspective. Thus, what is lost in this hermeneutic approach is the outsider's viewpoint as well as a sense of the reproductive processes that are occurring at the system level.

The perspective of *system integration* is focally concerned with the system and the way in which it is integrated through external control over individual decisions that are not subjectively coordinated. Those who adopt this perspective see society as a self-regulating system. They adopt the external perspective of the observer, but this perspective prohibits them from really getting at the structural patterns that can be understood only hermeneutically from the internal perspective of members of the life-world.

Thus, Habermas concludes that although each of these two broad perspectives has something to offer, both have serious limitations. On the basis of his critique of social and system integration, Habermas offers his alternative, which seeks to integrate these two theoretical orientations: he sees

> society as a system that has to fulfill conditions for the maintenance of sociocultural life-worlds. The formula-societies are *systematically stabilized* complexes of action of *socially integrated* groups. . . . [I] stand for the heuristic proposal that we view society as an entity that, in the course of social evolution, gets differentiated *both* as a *system* and a *lifeworld*.
>
> (Habermas, 1987a:151–152; italics added)

Having argued that he is interested in *both* system and life-world, Habermas makes it clear at the end of the above quotation that he is also concerned with the evolution of the two. Although both evolve in the direction of increasing rationalization, that rationalization takes different forms in life-world and system, and that differentiation is the basis of the colonization of the life-world.

Colonization   Crucial to the understanding of the idea of colonization is the fact that Habermas sees society as being composed of *both* life-world and system. Furthermore, while both concepts were closely intertwined in earlier history, today there is an increasing divergence between them; they have become "decoupled." Although both have undergone the process of rationalization, that process has taken different forms in the two settings. Although Habermas sees a dialectical relationship between system and life-world (they both limit and open up new possibilities for each other), his main concern is with the way in which system in the modern world has come to control the life-world. In other words, he is interested in the breakdown of the dialectic between system and life-world and the growing power of the former over the latter.[11]

Habermas contrasts the increasing rationality of system and life-world. The rationalization of the life-world involves growth in the rationality of communicative action. Furthermore, action that is oriented toward achieving mutual understanding is increasingly freed from normative constraint and relies more and more on everyday language. In other words, social integration is achieved more and more through the processes of consensus formation in language.

But the result of this is the fact that the demands on language grow and come to overwhelm its capacities. Delinguistified media (especially money in the economic system and power in the political system and its administrative apparatus)—having become differentiated in, and emanating from, the system—come to fill the void and replace, to at least some degree, everyday language. Instead of language coordinating action, it is money and power that perform that function. Life becomes monetarized and bureaucratized.

More generally, the increasingly complex system "unleashes system imperatives that burst the capacity of the lifeworld they instrumentalize" (Habermas, 1987a:155). Thus, Habermas writes of the "violence" exercised over the life-world by the system through the ways in which it restricts communication. This violence, in turn, produces

---

[11] However, Habermas also sees problems (domination, self-deception) *within* the life-world (Outhwaite, 1994:116).

"pathologies" within the life-world. Habermas embeds this development within a view of the history of the world:

> The far-reaching uncoupling of system and lifeworld was a necessary condition for the transition from the stratified class societies of European feudalism to the economic class societies of the early modern period; but the capitalist pattern of modernization is marked by a *deformation*, a reification of the symbolic structures of the lifeworld under the imperatives of subsystems differentiated out via money and power and rendered self-sufficient.
>
> (Habermas, 1987a:283; italics added)

It might be noted that by linking the deformities to capitalism, Habermas continues, at least in this sense, to operate within a neo-Marxian framework. However, when he looks at the modern world, Habermas is forced to abandon a Marxian approach (Sitton, 1996), because he concludes that the deformation of the life-world is "no longer localizable in any class-specific ways" (1987a:333). Given this limitation, and in line with his roots in critical theory, Habermas demonstrates that his work also is strongly influenced by Weberian theory. In fact, he argues that the distinction between life-world and system, along with the ultimate colonization of the life-world, allows us to see in a new light the Weberian thesis "of a modernity at variance with itself" (Habermas, 1987a:299). In Weber, this conflict exists primarily between substantive and formal rationality and the triumph in the West of the latter over the former. To Habermas, the rationalization of the system comes to triumph over the rationalization of the life-world, with the result that the life-world comes to be colonized by the system.

Habermas adds specificity to his thoughts on colonization by arguing that the main forces in the process are "formally organized domains of action" at the system level, such as the economy and the state. In traditional Marxian terms, Habermas sees modern society as subject to recurrent systemic crises. In seeking to deal with these crises, institutions such as the state and the economy undertake actions that adversely affect the life-world, leading to pathologies and crises within it. Basically, the life-world comes to be denuded by these systems, and communicative action comes to be less and less directed toward the achievement of consensus. Communication becomes increasingly rigidified, impoverished, and fragmented, and the life-world itself seems poised on the brink of dissolution. This assault on the life-world worries Habermas greatly, given his concern for the communicative action that takes place within it. However, no matter how extensive the colonization by the system, the life-world is "never completely husked away" (Habermas, 1987a:311).

If the essential problem in the modern world is the uncoupling of system and life-world and the domination of the life-world by the system, the solutions are clear-cut. On the one hand, life-world and system need to be recoupled. On the other hand, the dialectic between system and life-world needs to be reinstated so that instead of the latter being deformed by the former, the two become mutually enriching and enhancing. While the two were intertwined in primitive society, the rationalization process that has occurred in both system and life-world makes it possible that the future recoupling will produce a level of system, life-world, and their interrelationship unprecedented in human history.

Thus, once again, Habermas is back to his Marxian roots. Marx, of course, did not look back in history for the ideal state but saw it in the future in the form of communism and the full flowering of species-being. Habermas, too, does not look back to archaic societies where nonrationalized system and life-world were more unified but looks to a future state involving the far more satisfactory unification of rationalized system and life-world.

Habermas also reinterprets the Marxian theory of basic struggles within society. Marx, of course, emphasized the conflict between proletariat and capitalist and traced it to the exploitative character of the capitalist system. Habermas focuses not on exploitation but on colonization and sees many of the struggles of recent decades in this light. That is, he sees social movements such as those oriented to greater equality, increased self-realization, the preservation of the environment, and peace "as reactions to system assaults on the lifeworld. Despite the diversity of interests and political projects of these heterogeneous groups, they have resisted the colonization of the lifeworld" (Seidman, 1989:25). The hope for the future clearly lies in resistance to the encroachments on the life-world and in the creation of a world in which system and life-world are in harmony and serve to mutually enrich one another to a historically unprecedented degree.

Major Differences in the Agency-Structure Literature

As is the case with work on micro-macro integration in the United States, there are significant differences among Europeans working on the agency-structure issue. For example, there is considerable disagreement in the literature on the nature of the agent. Most of those working in this realm (for example, Giddens, Bourdieu) tend to treat the agent as an individual actor, but Touraine's "actionalist sociology" treats collectivities such as social classes as agents. In fact, Touraine defines *agency* as "an organization directly implementing one or more elements of the system of historical action and therefore intervening directly in the relations of social domination" (1977:459). A third, middle-ground position on this issue is taken by Burns and Flam (see also Crozier and Friedberg, 1980), who regard either individuals or collectivities as agents.

There is considerable disagreement even among those who focus on the individual actor as agent. For example, Bourdieu's agent, dominated by habitus, seems far more mechanical than Giddens's (or Habermas's) agent. Bourdieu's habitus involves "systems of durable, transposable *dispositions,* structuring structures, that is, as principles of the generation and structuring of practices and representations" (1977:72). The habitus is a source of strategies "without being the product of a genuine strategic intention" (Bourdieu, 1977:73). It is neither subjectivistic nor objectivistic but combines elements of both. It clearly rejects the idea of an actor with "the free and willful power to constitute" (Bourdieu, 1977:73). Giddens's agents may not have intentionality and free will either, but they have much more willful power than do Bourdieu's. Where Bourdieu's agents seem to be dominated by their habitus, by internal ("structuring") structures, the agents in Giddens's work are the perpetrators of action. They have at least some choice, at least the possibility of acting differently than they do. They have power, and they make a difference in their worlds (see also Lukes, 1977). Most important, they constitute (and are constituted by) structures. In contrast, in Bourdieu's work a sometimes seemingly disembodied habitus is involved in a dialectic with the external world.[12]

Similarly, there are marked disagreements among agency-structure theorists on precisely what they mean by structure.[13] Some adopt a specific structure as central, such as the organization in the work of Crozier and Friedberg and Touraine's relations of social domination as found in political institutions and organizations; others (for example, Burns, 1986:13) focus on an array of social structures, such as bureaucracy, the polity, the economy, and religion. Giddens offers a very idiosyncratic definition of *structure* ("recursively organized sets of rules and resources" [1984:25]) that is at odds with virtually every other definition in the literature (Layder, 1985). However, his definition of *systems* as reproduced social practices is very close to what many sociologists mean by structure. In addition to the differences among those working with structure, differences exist between these theorists and others.

The attempts at agency-structure linkage flow from a variety of very different theoretical directions. For example, within social theory Giddens seems to be animated by functionalism and structuralism versus phenomenology, existentialism, and ethnomethodology and, more generally, by new linguistic structuralism, semiotics, and hermeneutics (Archer, 1982). Bourdieu seeks to find a satisfactory alternative to subjectivism and objectivism in anthropological theory. Habermas seeks to synthesize ideas derived from Marx, Weber, critical theorists, Durkheim, Mead, Schutz, and Parsons.

There is a strain toward either the agency or the structural direction in Europe. Certainly Bourdieu is pulling strongly in the direction of structure, while Giddens has a more powerful sense of agency than do most other theorists of this genre (Layder, 1985:131). In spite of the existence of pulls in the directions of agency and structure, what is distinctive about the European work on agency and structure, compared with American micro-macro work, is a much stronger sense of the need to refuse to separate the two and to deal with them dialectically (for example, Giddens, Bourdieu, Habermas). In the American micro-macro literature, one parallel to the European efforts to deal with agency and structure dialectically is Ritzer's attempt to deal dialectically with the integration of the micro-macro and objective-subjective continua.

Dietz and Burns (1992) have made an effort to offer a view of agency and structure that reflects the strengths and weaknesses of earlier work. Four criteria must be met in order for agency to be attributed to a social actor. First, the actor must have power; the actor must be able to make a difference. Second, the actions undertaken by an agent must be intentional. Third, the actor must have some choice, some free play. The result is that observers can make only probabilistic statements about what actors may do. Finally, agents must be reflexive, monitoring the effects of their actions

---

[12] Although we are emphasizing the differences between Giddens and Bourdieu on agency, Giddens (1979:217) sees at least some similarities between the two perspectives.
[13] We are focusing here mainly on Europeans who deal with social structure and not those who see structure as hidden, underlying elements of culture.

and using that knowledge to modify the bases of action. Overall, agency is viewed as a continuum; all actors have agency to some degree, and no actor has full, unconstrained agency.

The other, structural side of the equation, from Dietz and Burns's point of view, consists of the constraints on agency. First, even if an agent can imagine certain actions, they simply may not be possible, given technological and physical realities. Second, structure (especially rules) makes certain actions seem necessary while others appear impossible. Finally, agency is limited by other agents who have sanctioning power, both positive and negative.

Agency-Structure and Micro-Macro Linkages: Fundamental Differences

One of the central differences between American and European theorists lies in their images of the actor. What is distinctive about American theory is the much greater influence of behaviorism as well as of exchange theory, which is derived, in part, from a behavioristic perspective. Thus, American theorists share the interest of (some) Europeans in conscious, creative action, but it is limited by a recognition of the importance of mindless behavior. This tendency to see the actor as behaving mindlessly is being enhanced now by the growing interest in rational choice theory in American sociology. The image here is of an actor more or less automatically choosing the most efficient means to ends.[14] The influence of rational choice theory in the United States promises to drive an even greater wedge between European and American conceptions of action and agency.

At the macro/structure level, Europeans have been inclined to focus on social structure. In cases where there has not been a single-minded focus on it, social structure has not been differentiated adequately from culture. (Indeed, this is the motivation behind Archer's [1988] work.) In contrast, there has been a much greater tendency in the United States to deal with *both* structure and culture in efforts aimed at micro-macro integration.

Another difference in the macro/structure issue stems from differences in theoretical influence in the United States and Europe. In the United States, the main influence on thinking on the macro/structure issue has been structural functionalism. The nature of that theory has led American theorists to focus on both large-scale social structures *and* culture. In Europe, the main influence has been structuralism, which has a much more wide-ranging sense of structures, extending all the way from micro structures of the mind to macro structures of society. Culture has been of far less importance to structuralists than to structural functionalists.

Another key difference is the fact that the micro-macro issue is subsumable under the broader issue of levels of analysis (Edel, 1959; Jaffee, 1998; Ritzer, 1981a, 1989; Wiley, 1988), whereas the concern for agency and structure is not. We can clearly think of the micro-macro linkage in terms of some sort of vertical hierarchy, with micro-level phenomena on the bottom, macro-level phenomena at the top, and

---

[14] DeVille (1989) sees such an actor as robotlike.

meso-level entities in between. The agency-structure linkage seems to have no clear connection to the levels-of-analysis issue, because both agency and structure can be found at any level of social analysis.

The agency-structure issue is much more firmly embedded in a historical, dynamic framework than is the micro-macro issue (Sztompka, 1991; again Elias is a clear exception, but of course he is European). In contrast, theorists who deal with micro-macro issues are more likely to depict them in static, hierarchical, ahistorical terms. Nevertheless, at least some of those who choose to depict the micro-macro relationship rather statically make it clear that they understand the dynamic character of the relationship: "The study of levels of social reality and their interrelationship is inherently a *dynamic* rather than a static approach to the social world. . . . A dynamic and historical orientation to the study of levels of the social world can be seen as integral parts of a more general *dialectical* approach" (Ritzer, 1981a:208; see also Wiley, 1988:260). Finally, morality is a central issue to agency-structure theorists but is largely ignored in the micro-macro literature. Agency-structure theory has much more powerful roots in, and a stronger orientation to, philosophy, including its great concern with moral issues. In contrast, micro-macro theory is largely indigenous to sociology and is oriented to the hard sciences as a reference group—areas where moral issues are of far less concern than they are in philosophy.

Summary

The focus in the first part of this chapter is micro-macro integration. This development represents a return to the concerns of the early giants of sociological theory and a move away from the theoretical extremism, either micro or macro, that characterized much of twentieth-century American sociological theory. Little attention was given to the micro-macro issue prior to the 1980s, but during that decade and through the 1990s interest in the topic exploded. The works came from both the micro and the macro extremes as well as various points between them. Some of this work focused on integrating micro and macro theories; the rest was concerned with the linkage between micro and macro levels of social analysis. In addition to this basic difference, there are important differences among those working on integrating theories and levels.

The heart of the first part of this chapter is a discussion of several major examples of work integrating micro and macro levels of social analysis. Two works, those by Alexander and Ritzer, develop very similar micro-macro models of the social world. Although there are important differences between these works, their similar images of the social world reflect considerable consensus among those seeking to link micro and macro levels of social analysis. Collins's effort at micro-macro integration is discussed and criticized for its micro reductionism—its tendency to reduce macro phenomena to micro phenomena.

The micro-macro section closes with a detailed examination of the work of one of the European precursors of American work on micro-macro integration—Norbert Elias. Of particular relevance are his thoughts on figurational sociology, as well as his historical-comparative study of the relationship between micro-level manners and macro-level changes in the court and the state.

The second part of this chapter deals with the largely European literature on the agency-structure linkage. This literature has a number of similarities to the American work on micro-macro integration, but there are a number of substantial differences.

Although a large number of contemporary European theorists are dealing with the agency-structure relationship, the bulk of the second part of this chapter is devoted to the work of three major examples of this type of theorizing. The first is Giddens's structuration theory. The core of Giddens's theory is his refusal to treat agents and structures apart from one another; they are seen as being mutually constitutive. We then turn to Bourdieu's theory, which focuses primarily on the relationship between habitus and field. As a recent development related to both Giddens's and Bourdieu's work on structure-agency we also discuss practice theory. Finally, we analyze Habermas's recent ideas on life-world and system and the colonization of the life-world by the system.

Following a discussion of these specific agency-structure works, we return to a more general treatment of this literature. We begin with a discussion of major differences in this literature, including differing views on the nature of the agent and structure. Another source of difference is the varying theoretical traditions on which these works are based. Some of these works strain in the direction of agency; others pull in the direction of structure.

The next issue is the similarities between the agency-structure and micro-macro literatures. Both literatures share an interest in integration and are wary of the excesses of micro/agency and macro/structural theories. There are, however, far more differences than similarities between these literatures. There are differences in their images of the actor, the ways in which structure is conceived, the theories from which their ideas are derived, the degree to which they may be subsumed under the idea of levels of analysis, the extent to which they are embedded in a historical, dynamic framework, and the degree to which they are concerned with moral issues.

From Modern to Postmodern Social Theory (and Beyond)

C   H   A   P   T   E   R   **14**

Contemporary Theories of Modernity

Chapter Outline
Classical Theorists on Modernity
The Juggernaut of Modernity
The Risk Society
The Holocaust and Liquid Modernity
Modernity's Unfinished Project
Self, Society, and Religion
Informationalism and the Network Society

There is a debate in sociology between those who see contemporary society as a modern world and those who argue that a substantial change has taken place in recent years and that we have moved into a new, postmodern world. Chapters 14 and 16 are devoted to these two theoretical positions. In this chapter we discuss the work of contemporary representatives of those who continue to see the world in modern terms. Chapter 16 offers an overview of the ideas of some of the most important postmodern theorists.

Classical Theorists on Modernity
Most of the classical sociologists were engaged in an analysis and critique of modern society. Such analysis is clear, for example, in the work of Marx, Weber, Durkheim, and Simmel. All were working at the point of the emergence and ascendancy of modernity. While all four were well aware of the advantages of modernity, what animated their work most was a critique of the problems posed by the modern world.

539

For Marx, of course, modernity was defined by the capitalist economy. Marx recognized the advances brought about by the transition from earlier societies to capitalism. However, in his work Marx restricted himself largely to a critique of that economic system and its deformities (alienation, exploitation, and so on).

To Weber, the most defining problem of the modern world was the expansion of formal rationality at the expense of the other types of rationality and the resulting emergence of the iron cage of rationality. People increasingly were being imprisoned in this iron cage and, as a result, were progressively unable to express some of their most human characteristics. Of course, Weber recognized the advantages of the advance of rationalization—for example, the advantages of the bureaucracy over earlier organizational forms—but he was most concerned with the problems posed by rationalization.

In Durkheim's view, modernity was defined by its organic solidarity and the weakening of the collective conscience. Although organic solidarity brought with it greater freedom and more productivity, it also posed a series of unique problems. For example, with such a weakening of the common morality, people tended to find themselves adrift meaninglessly in the modern world. In other words, they found themselves to be suffering from anomie.

Georg Simmel, the fourth of the classical theorists, will receive a more detailed treatment here, in large part because he has been described both as a modernist (Frisby, 1992) and as a postmodernist (Jaworski, 1997; Weinstein and Weinstein, 1993). Since he fits to some degree in both categories, Simmel represents an important bridge between this chapter and Chapter 16. We deal with the case for Simmel as a modernist here; in Chapter 16 we discuss the contention that he is a postmodernist.

Frisby accepts the point of view that "Simmel is the first sociologist of modernity" (1992:59). Simmel is seen as investigating modernity primarily in two major interrelated sites—the city and the money economy. The city is where modernity is concentrated or intensified, whereas the money economy involves the diffusion of modernity, its extension (Frisby, 1992:69).

Poggi (1993) picks up the theme of modernity as it relates to money, especially in Simmel's *The Philosophy of Money* (1907/1978). As Poggi sees it, three views of modernity are expressed in that work. The first is that modernization brings with it a series of advantages to human beings, especially the fact that they are able to express various potentialities that are unexpressed, concealed, and repressed in premodern society. In this sense, Simmel sees modernity "as an 'epiphany,' that is, as the express manifestation of powers intrinsic to the human species, but previously unrevealed" (Poggi, 1993:165). Second, Simmel deals with the powerful effect of money on modern society. Finally, there is Simmel's concentration on the adverse consequences of money for modernity, especially alienation. The issue of alienation brings us back to the central issue in Simmel's sociological theory in general, as well as in his sociology of modernity: the "tragedy of culture," the growing gap between objective and subjective culture, or as Simmel put it, "'the atrophy of individual culture and the hypertrophy of objective culture'" (cited in Frisby, 1992:69).

In Frisby's view, Simmel concentrates on the "experience" of modernity. The key elements of that experience—time, space, and contingent causality—are central aspects of at least some of the contemporary theories of modernity discussed in this chapter:

> The experience of modernity is viewed by Simmel as discontinuous of *time* as transitory, in which both the fleeting moment and the sense of presentness converge; *space* as the dialectic of distance and proximity . . . and *causality* as contingent, arbitrary and fortuitous.
>
> (Frisby, 1992:163–164)

Although it is certainly possible to view Simmel as a postmodernist, and as we will see in Chapter 16, he does seem to have more in common with postmodernists than do the other classical social theorists, the fact remains that it is at least equally appropriate to see him as a modernist. Almost certainly, the foci of much of his attention—especially the city and the money economy—are at the heart of modernity. Thus, even in the case of Simmel, and certainly in the cases of Marx, Weber, and Durkheim, it is best to think of these theorists as doing sociologies of modernity.

By 1920 all four of these classical sociological theorists were dead. As we move into the twenty-first century, it is obvious that the world is a very different place than it was in 1920. Although there is great disagreement over when the postmodern age began (assuming for the moment that it did), no one puts that date before 1920. The issue is whether the changes in the world since that time are modest and continuous with those associated with modernity or are so dramatic and discontinuous that the contemporary world is better described by a new term—postmodern. That issue informs the discussion in this chapter and Chapter 16.

In this chapter we examine the thoughts of several contemporary theorists (there are many others [for example, Lefebvre, 1962/1995; Touraine, 1995; P. Wagner, 1994; E. Wood, 1997] whose work we will not have space to deal with) who in various ways and to varying degrees see the contemporary world as still best described as modern.

The Juggernaut of Modernity

In an effort not only to be consistent with his structuration theory (see Chapter 13) but also to create an image to rival the images of classical thinkers such as Weber and his iron cage, Anthony Giddens (1990; see Mestrovic, 1998, for a bitter critique of Giddens's theory of modernity) has described the modern world (with its origins in seventeenth-century Europe) as a "juggernaut." More specifically, he is using this term to describe an advanced stage of modernity—radical, high, or late modernity. In so doing, Giddens is arguing against those who have contended that we have entered a postmodern age, although he holds out the possibility of some type of postmodernism in the future. However, while we still live in a modern age, in Giddens's view today's world is very different from the world of the classical sociological theorists.

Here is the way Giddens describes the juggernaut of modernity:

> a runaway engine of enormous power which, collectively as human beings, we can drive to some extent but which also threatens to rush out of our control and which could rend itself asunder. The juggernaut crushes those who resist it, and while it

ANTHONY GIDDENS

A Biographical Sketch

Anthony Giddens is Great Britain's most important contemporary social theorist and one of a handful of the world's most influential theorists (Stones, 2005a). Giddens was born on January 18, 1938 (Clark, Modgil, and Modgil, 1990). He studied at the University of Hull, the London School of Economics, and the University of London. Giddens was appointed lecturer at the University of Leicester in 1961. His early work was empirical and focused on the issue of suicide. By 1969 he had moved to the position of lecturer in sociology at the prestigious Cambridge University, as well as fellow of King's College. He engaged in cross-cultural work that led to the first of his books to achieve international fame, *The Class Structure of Advanced Societies* (1975). Over the next decade or so, Giddens published a number of important theoretical works. In those works he began a step-by-step process of building his own theoretical perspective, which has come to be known as structuration theory. Those years of work culminated in 1984 with the appearance of a book, *The Constitution of Society: Outline of the Theory of Structuration*, that constitutes the most important single statement of Giddens's theoretical perspective. In 1985 Giddens was appointed professor of sociology at the University of Cambridge.

Giddens has been a force in sociological theory for well over three decades. In addition, he has played a profound role in shaping contemporary British sociology. For one thing, he has served as a consulting editor for two publishing

sometimes seems to have a steady path, there are times when it veers away erratically in directions we cannot foresee. The ride is by no means wholly unpleasant or unrewarding; it can often be exhilarating and charged with hopeful anticipation. But, so long as the institutions of modernity endure, we shall never be able to control completely either the path or the pace of the journey. In turn, we shall never be able to feel entirely secure, because the terrain across which it runs is fraught with risks of high consequence.

(Giddens, 1990:139)

Modernity in the form of a juggernaut is extremely dynamic; it is a "'runaway world'" with great increases in the pace, scope, and profoundness of change over prior systems (Giddens, 1991:16). Giddens is quick to add that this juggernaut does not follow a single path. Furthermore, it is not of one piece but instead is made up of a number of conflicting and contradictory parts. Thus, Giddens is telling us that he is not offering an old-fashioned grand theory, or at least not a simple, unidirectional grand narrative.

The idea of a juggernaut fits nicely with structuration theory, especially with the importance in that theory of time and space. The image of a juggernaut is of something companies—Macmillan and Hutchinson. A large number of books have been produced under his editorship. More important, he was a cofounder of Polity Press, a publisher that has been both extremely active and influential, especially in sociological theory. Giddens also has published an American-style textbook, *Sociology*, that has been a worldwide success.

As a theorist, Giddens has been highly influential in the United States, as well as in many other parts of the world. Interestingly, his work often has been less well received in his home country of Great Britain than elsewhere. This lack of acceptance at home may be attributable, in part, to the fact that Giddens has succeeded in winning the worldwide theoretical following that many other British social theorists sought and failed to achieve. As Craib says, "Giddens has perhaps realized the fantasies of many of us who committed ourselves to sociology during the period of intense and exciting debate out of which structuration theory developed" (1992:12).

Giddens's career took a series of interesting turns in the 1990s (Bryant and Jary, 2011). Several years of therapy led to a greater interest in personal life and books such as *Modernity and Self-Identity* (1991) and *The Transformation of Intimacy* (1992). Therapy also gave him the confidence to take on a more public role and to become an adviser to British prime minister Tony Blair. In 1997 he became director of the highly prestigious London School of Economics (LSE). He strengthened the scholarly reputation of LSE as well as increased its voice in public discourse in Great Britain and around the world. More recently he has become involved in debates over globalization and climate change, publishing books such as *Runaway World* (2000) and *Politics of Climate Change* (2009). There is some feeling that all this had an adverse effect on Giddens's scholarly work (his most recent books lack the depth and sophistication of his earlier works), but he is clearly focused on being a force in public life.

that is moving along *through time* and *over physical space*. However, this image does not fit well with Giddens's emphasis on the power of the agent; the image of a juggernaut seems to accord this modern mechanism far more power than it accords the agents who steer it (Mestrovic, 1998:155). This problem is consistent with the more general criticism that there is a disjunction between the emphasis on agency in Giddens's purely theoretical work and the substantive historical analyses that "point to the dominance of system tendencies against our ability to change the world" (Craib, 1992:149).

Modernity and Its Consequences

Giddens defines modernity in terms of four basic institutions. The first is *capitalism*, characterized, familiarly, by commodity production, private ownership of capital, propertyless wage labor, and a class system derived from these characteristics. The second is *industrialism*, which involves the use of inanimate power sources and machinery to produce goods. Industrialism is not restricted to the workplace, and it affects an array of other settings, such as "transportation, communication and domestic life" (Giddens, 1990:56). While Giddens's first two characteristics of modernity are hardly novel, the third—*surveillance capacities*—is, although it owes a debt to the work of Michel Foucault (see Chapter 16). As Giddens defines it, "Surveillance refers to the supervision of the activities of subject populations [mainly but not exclusively] in the political sphere" (1990:58). The final institutional dimension of modernity is military power, or the *control of the means of violence,* including the industrialization of war. In addition, it should be noted that in his analysis of modernity, at least at the macro level, Giddens focuses on the *nation-state* (rather than the more conventional sociological focus on society), which he sees as radically different from the type of community characteristic of premodern society.

Modernity is given dynamism by three essential aspects of Giddens's structuration theory: distanciation, disembedding, and reflexivity. The first is *time and space separation,* or *distanciation* (although this process of increasing separation, like all aspects of Giddens's work, is not unilinear; it is dialectical). In premodern societies, time was always linked with space and the measurement of time was imprecise. With modernization, time was standardized and the close linkage between time and space was broken. In this sense, both time and space were "emptied" of content; no particular time or space was privileged; they became pure forms. In premodern societies, space was defined largely by physical presence and therefore by localized spaces. With the coming of modernity, space is progressively torn from place. Relationships with those who are physically absent and increasingly distant become more and more likely. To Giddens, place becomes increasingly "phantasmagoric"; that is, "locales are thoroughly penetrated by and shaped in terms of social influences quite distant from them . . . the 'visible form' of the locale conceals the distanciated relations which determine its nature" (Giddens, 1990:19).

Time and space distanciation is important to modernity for several reasons. First, it makes possible the growth of rationalized organizations such as bureaucracies and the nation-state, with their inherent dynamism (in comparison to premodern forms) and their ability to link local and global domains. Second, the modern world is positioned within a radical sense of world history, and it is able to draw upon that history to shape the present. Third, such distanciation is a major prerequisite for Giddens's second source of dynamism in modernity—disembedding.

As Giddens defines it, *disembedding* involves "the 'lifting out' of social relations from local contexts of interaction and their restructuring across indefinite spans of time-space" (1990:21). There are two types of disembedding mechanisms that play a key role in modern societies; both can be included under the heading "abstract systems." The first is *symbolic tokens,* the best known of which is money. Money allows for time-space distanciation—we are able to engage in transactions with others who are widely separated from us by time and/or space. The second is *expert systems,* defined as "systems of technical accomplishment or professional expertise that organize large areas of the material and social environments in which we live today" (Giddens, 1990:27). The most obvious expert systems involve professionals such as lawyers and physicians, but everyday phenomena such as our cars and homes are created and affected by expert systems. Expert systems provide guarantees (but not without risks) of performance across time and space.

Trust is very important in modern societies dominated by abstract systems and with great time-space distanciation. The need for trust is related to this distanciation: "We have no need to trust someone who is constantly in view and whose activities can be directly monitored" (Giddens, 1991:19). Trust becomes necessary when, as a result of increasing distanciation in terms of either time or place, we no longer have full information about social phenomena (Craib, 1992:99). Trust is defined "as confidence in the reliability of a person or systems, regarding a given set of outcomes or events, where that confidence expresses a faith in the probity or love of another, or in the correctness of abstract principles (technical knowledge)" (Giddens, 1990:34). Trust is of great importance not only in modern society in general, but also to the symbolic tokens and expert systems that serve to disembed life in the modern world. For example, in order for the money economy and the legal system to work, people must have trust in them.

The third dynamic characteristic of modernity is its *reflexivity*. Reflexivity is a fundamental feature of Giddens's structuration theory (as well as of human existence, in his view), but it takes on special meaning in modernity, where "social practices are constantly examined and reformed in the light of incoming information about those very practices, thus constitutively altering their character" (Giddens, 1990:38). Everything is open to reflection in the modern world, including reflection itself, leaving us with a pervasive sense of uncertainty. Furthermore, the problem of the double hermeneutic (see Chapter 13) recurs here because the reflection of experts on the social world tends to alter that world.

The disembedded character of modern life raises a number of distinctive issues. One is the need for trust in abstract systems in general, and expert systems in particular. In one of his more questionable metaphors, Giddens sees children as being "inoculated" with a "dosage" of trust during childhood socialization. This aspect of socialization serves to provide people with a "protective cocoon," which, as they mature into adulthood, helps give them a measure of ontological security and trust. This trust tends to be buttressed by the series of routines that we encounter on a day-to-day basis. However, there are new and dangerous risks associated with modernity that always threaten our trust and threaten to lead to pervasive ontological insecurity. As Giddens sees it, while the disembedding mechanisms have provided us with security in various areas, they also have created a distinctive "risk profile." Risk is global in intensity (nuclear war can kill us all) and in the expansion of contingent events that affect large numbers of people around the world (for example, changes in the worldwide division of labor). Then there are risks traceable to our efforts to manage our material environment. Risks also stem from the creation of institutional risk environments such as global investment markets. People are increasingly aware of risks, and religion and customs are increasingly less important as ways of believing that those risks can be transformed into certainties. A wide range of publics are now likely to know of the risks we face. Finally, there is a painful awareness that expert systems are limited in their ability to deal with these risks. It is these risks that give modernity the feeling of a runaway juggernaut and fill us with ontological insecurity.

What has happened? Why are we suffering the negative consequences of being aboard the juggernaut of modernity? Giddens suggests several reasons. The first is *design faults* in the modern world; those who designed elements of the modern world made mistakes. The second is *operator failure;* the problem is traceable not to the designers but to those who run the modern world. Giddens, however, gives prime importance to two other factors—*unintended consequences* and *reflexivity of social knowledge.* That is, the consequences of actions for a system can never be forecast fully, and new knowledge is continually sending systems off in new directions. For all these reasons, we cannot completely control the juggernaut, the modern world.

However, rather than giving up, Giddens suggests the seemingly paradoxical course of *utopian realism.* That is, he seeks a balance between utopian ideals and the realities of life in the modern world. He also accords importance to the role social movements can play in dealing with some of the risks of the modern world and pointing us toward a society in which those risks are ameliorated.

Giddens's (1994) effort to find a compromise political position is manifest in the title of one of his later books, *Beyond Left and Right: The Future of Radical Politics.* With extant political positions moribund, Giddens proposes a reconstituted "radical politics" based on utopian realism and oriented toward addressing the problems of poverty, environmental degradation, arbitrary power and force, and violence in social life. Giddens's political position involves an acceptance of at least some aspects of capitalism (e.g., markets) and rejection of many aspects of socialism (e.g., a revolutionary subject). Thus Giddens has chosen to walk a very narrow and difficult political tightrope.

Given his views on modernity, where does Giddens stand on postmodernity? For one thing, he rejects most, if not all, of the tenets we usually associate with postmodernism. For example, of the idea that systematic knowledge is impossible, Giddens says that such a view would lead us "to repudiate intellectual activity altogether" (1990:47). However, although he sees us as living in an era of high modernity, Giddens believes it is possible now to gain a glimpse of postmodernity. Such a world would, in his view, be characterized by a postscarcity system, increasingly multilayered democratization, demilitarization, and the humanization of technology. However, there are clearly no guarantees that the world will move in the direction of some, to say nothing of all, of these postmodern characteristics. Yet, reflexively, Giddens believes that in writing about such eventualities he (and others) can play a role in helping them come to pass.

Modernity and Identity

The Consequences of Modernity is a largely macro-oriented work, whereas *Modernity and Self-Identity* (Giddens, 1991) focuses more on the micro aspects of late modernity, especially the self. Although Giddens certainly sees the self as dialectically related to the institutions of modern society, most of his attention here is devoted to the micro end of the continuum. We, too, will focus on the micro issues, but we should not lose sight of the larger dialectic:

> Transformations in self-identity and globalisation . . . are the two poles of the
> dialectic of the local and the global in conditions of high modernity. Changes in
> intimate aspects of personal life . . . are directly tied to the establishment of social

connections of very wide scope . . . for the first time in human history, "self" and
"society" are interrelated in a global milieu.

                                                                    (Giddens, 1991:32)

As we have seen, Giddens defines the modern world as reflexive, and he argues
that the "reflexivity of modernity extends into the core of the self . . . the self becomes
a *reflexive project*" (1991:32). That is, the self comes to be something to be reflected
upon, altered, even molded. Not only does the individual become responsible for the
creation and maintenance of the self, but this responsibility is continuous and
all-pervasive. The self is a product both of self-exploration and of the development
of intimate social relationships. In the modern world, even the body gets "drawn into
the reflexive organisation of social life" (Giddens, 1991:98). We are responsible for
the design not only of our selves but also (and relatedly) that of our bodies. Central
to the reflexive creation and maintenance of the self are the appearance of the body
and its appropriate demeanor in a variety of settings and locales. The body is also
subject to a variety of "regimes" (for example, diet, exercise books, and cosmetic
surgery) that not only help individuals mold their bodies but also contribute to self-
reflexivity as well as to the reflexivity of modernity in general. The result, overall, is
an obsession with our bodies and our selves within the modern world.

The modern world brings with it the *"sequestration of experience,"* or the
"connected processes of concealment which set apart the routines of ordinary life from
the following phenomena: madness; criminality; sickness and death; sexuality; and
nature" (Giddens, 1991:149, 156). Sequestration occurs as a result of the growing role
of abstract systems in everyday life. This sequestration brings us greater ontological
security, but at the cost of the "exclusion of social life from fundamental existential
issues which raise central moral dilemmas for human beings" (Giddens, 1991:156).

While modernity is a double-edged sword, bringing both positive and negative
developments, Giddens perceives an underlying "looming threat of *personal
meaninglessness*" (1991:201). All sorts of meaningful things have been sequestered
from daily life; they have been repressed. However, dialectically, increasing self-
reflexivity leads to the increasing likelihood of the return of that which has been
repressed. Giddens sees us moving into a world in which "on a collective level and
in day-to-day life moral/existential questions thrust themselves back to centre-stage"
(1991:208). The world beyond modernity, for Giddens, is a world characterized by
"remoralization." Those key moral and existential issues that have been sequestered
will come to occupy center stage in a society that Giddens sees as being foreshadowed, and anticipated, in the self-reflexivity of the late modern age.

Modernity and Intimacy

Giddens picks up many of these themes in *The Transformation of Intimacy* (1992).
In this work he focuses on ongoing transformations of intimacy that show movement
toward another important concept in Giddens's thinking about the modern world—the
pure relationship, or "a situation where a social relation is entered into for its own
sake, for what can be derived by each person from a sustained association with
another; and which is continued only so far as it is thought by both parties to deliver

enough satisfactions for each individual to stay within it" (Giddens, 1992:58). In the case of intimacy, a pure relationship is characterized by emotional communication with self and other in a context of sexual and emotional equality. The democratization of intimate relationships can lead to the democratization not only of interpersonal relations in general but of the macro-institutional order as well. The changing nature of intimate relations, in which women ("the emotional revolutionaries of modernity" [Giddens, 1992:130]) have taken the lead and men have been "laggards," has revolutionary implications for society as a whole.

In the modern world intimacy and sexuality (and, as we have seen, much else) have been sequestered. However, while this sequestration was liberating in various senses from intimacy in traditional societies, it is also a form of repression. The reflexive effort to create purer intimate relationships must be carried out in a context separated from larger moral and ethical issues. However, this modern arrangement comes under pressure as people, especially women, attempt reflexive construction of themselves and others. Thus Giddens is arguing not for sexual liberation or pluralism but rather for a larger ethical and moral change, a change that he sees as already well under way in intimate relationships:

> We have no need to wait around for a sociopolitical revolution to further programmes of emancipation, nor would such a revolution help very much. Revolutionary processes are already well under way in the infrastructure of personal life. The transformation of intimacy presses for psychic as well as social change and such change, going "from the bottom up," could potentially ramify through other, more public, institutions.
>
> Sexual emancipation, I think, can be the medium of a wide-ranging emotional reorganisation of social life.
>
> (Giddens, 1992:181–182)

The Risk Society

We have already touched on the issue of risk in Giddens's work on modernity. As Giddens says,

> Modernity is a risk culture. I do not mean by this that social life is inherently more risky than it used to be; for most people that is not the case. Rather, the concept of risk becomes fundamental to the way both lay actors and technical specialists organise the social world. Modernity reduces the overall riskiness of certain areas and modes of life, yet at the same time introduces new risk parameters largely or completely unknown to previous eras.
>
> (Giddens, 1991:3–4)

Thus, Giddens (1991:28) describes as "quite accurate" the thesis of the work to be discussed in this section: Ulrich Beck's *Risk Society: Towards a New Modernity* (1992; Bora, 2007; Bronner, 1995; Then, 2007; Wilkinson, 2011).

In terms of this discussion, the subtitle of Beck's work is of great importance because it indicates that Beck, like Giddens, rejects the notion that we have moved into a postmodern age. Rather, in Beck's view we continue to exist in the modern world, albeit in a new form of modernity. The prior, "classical" stage of modernity was associated with industrial society, whereas the emerging new modernity and its technologies are associated with the risk society (N. Clark, 1997). Although we do not yet live in a risk society, we no longer live only in an industrial society; that is, the contemporary world has elements of both. In fact, the risk society can be seen as a type of industrial society, because many of those risks are traceable to industry. Beck offers the following overview of his perspective:

> *Just as modernization dissolved the structure of feudal society in the nineteenth century and produced the industrial society, modernization today is dissolving industrial society and another modernity is coming into being.* . . . The thesis of this book is: we are witnessing not the end but the beginning of modernity—that is, of a modernity *beyond* its classical industrial design.
>
> (Beck, 1992:10)

What, then, is this new modernity? And what is the risk society that accompanies it?

Beck labels the new, or better yet newly emerging, form *reflexive modernity* (Zinn, 2007a). A process of individualization has taken place in the West. That is, agents are becoming increasingly free of structural constraints and are, as a result, better able to reflexively create not only themselves but also the societies in which they live. For example, instead of being determined by their class situations, people operate more or less on their own. Left to their own devices, people have been forced to be more reflexive. Beck makes the case for the importance of reflexivity in the example of social relationships in such a world: "The newly formed social relationships and social networks now have to be individually chosen; social ties, too, are becoming *reflexive*, so that they have to be established, maintained, and constantly renewed by individuals" (1992:97).

Beck sees a break within modernity and a transition from classical industrial society to the risk society, which, while different from its predecessor, continues to have many of the characteristics of industrial society. The central issue in classical modernity was wealth and how it could be distributed more evenly. In advanced modernity the central issue is risk and how it can be prevented, minimized, or channeled. In classical modernity the ideal was equality, whereas in advanced modernity it is safety. In classical modernity people achieved solidarity in the search for the positive goal of equality, but in advanced modernity the attempt to achieve that solidarity is found in the search for the largely negative and defensive goal of being spared from dangers.

Creating the Risks

The risks are, to a large degree, being produced by the sources of wealth in modern society. Specifically, industry and its side effects are producing a wide range of hazardous, even deadly, consequences for society and, as a result of globalization (Featherstone, 1990; Robertson, 1992), for the world as a whole. Using the concepts of time and space, Beck makes the point that these modern risks are not restricted to place (a nuclear accident in one geographical locale could affect many other nations) or time (a nuclear accident could have genetic effects that might affect future generations).

While social class is central in industrial society and risk is fundamental to the risk society, risk and class are not unrelated. Says Beck,

> The history of risk distribution shows that, like wealth, risks adhere to the class pattern, only inversely: wealth accumulates at the top, risks at the bottom. To that extent, risks seem to *strengthen,* not to abolish, class society. Poverty attracts an unfortunate abundance of risks. By contrast, the wealthy (in income, power, or education) can purchase safety and freedom from risk.
>
> (Beck, 1992:35)

What is true for social classes is also true for nations. That is, to the degree that it is possible, risks are centered in poor nations, while the rich nations are able to push many risks as far away as possible. Further, the rich nations profit from the risks they produce by, for example, producing and selling technologies that help prevent risks from occurring or deal with their adverse effects once they do occur.

However, neither wealthy individuals nor the nations that produce risks are safe from risks. In this context, Beck discusses what he calls the "boomerang effect," whereby the side effects of risk "strike back even at the centers of their production. The agents of modernization themselves are emphatically caught in the maelstrom of hazards that they unleash and profit from" (1992:37).

Coping with the Risks

Although advanced modernization produces the risks, it also produces the reflexivity that allows it to question itself and the risks it produces. In fact, it is often the people themselves, the victims of the risks, who begin to reflect on those risks. They begin to observe and to collect data on the risks and their consequences for people. They become experts who come to question advanced modernity and its dangers. They do this, in part, because they can no longer rely on scientists to do it for them. Indeed, Beck is very hard on scientists for their role in the creation and maintenance of the risk society: "Science has become the *protector of a global contamination of people and nature.* In that respect, it is no exaggeration to say that in the way they deal with risks in many areas, the sciences *have squandered until further notice their historic reputation for rationality*" (1992:70).

In classical industrial society nature and society were separated, but in advanced industrial society nature and society are deeply intertwined. That is, changes in society often affect the natural environment, and those changes, in turn, affect society. Thus, according to Beck, today "nature *is* society and society is also '*nature*'" (1992:80). Thus nature has been politicized, with the result that natural scientists, like social scientists, have had their work politicized.

The traditional domain of politics, the government, is losing power because the major risks are emanating from what Beck calls "sub politics," for example, large companies, scientific laboratories, and the like. It is in the subpolitical system that "the structures of a new society are being implemented with regard to the ultimate goals of progress in knowledge, outside the parliamentary system, not in opposition to it, but simply ignoring it" (Beck, 1992:223). This is part of what he calls the "unbinding of politics," where politics is no longer left to the central government, but increasingly is becoming the province of various subgroups, as well as of individuals. These subgroups and individuals can be more reflexive and self-critical than a central government can, and they have the capability to reflect upon, to better deal with, the array of risks associated with advanced modernity. Thus, dialectically, advanced modernity has generated both unprecedented risks and unprecedented efforts to deal with those risks (Beck, 1996).

The Holocaust and Liquid Modernity

To Zygmunt Bauman (1989, 1991) the modern paradigm of formal rationality is the Holocaust, the systematic destruction of the Jews (and others) by the Nazis (Beilharz, 2005c, 2005d, 2011). As Bauman puts it, "Considered as a complex purposeful operation, the Holocaust may serve as a paradigm of modern bureaucratic rationality" (1989:149). To many it will seem obscene to discuss fast-food restaurants and the Holocaust in the same context. Yet there is a clear line in sociological thinking about modern rationality from the bureaucracy to the Holocaust and then to the fast-food restaurant. Weber's principles of rationality can be applied usefully and meaningfully to each. The perpetrators of the Holocaust employed the bureaucracy as one of their major tools. The conditions that made the Holocaust possible, especially the formally rational system, continue to exist today. Indeed, what the process of rationalization indicates is not only that formally rational systems persist, but that they are expanding dramatically. Thus, in Bauman's view, under the right set of circumstances the modern world would be ripe for an even greater abomination (if such a thing is possible) than the Holocaust.

A Product of Modernity

Rather than viewing the Holocaust, as most do, as an abnormal event, Bauman sees it as in many ways a "normal" aspect of the modern, rational world:

> The truth is that every "ingredient" of the Holocaust—all of those many things that rendered it possible—was normal; "normal" not in the sense of the familiar . . . but in the sense of being fully in keeping with everything we know about our civilization, its guiding spirit, its priorities, its immanent vision of the world.
>
> (Bauman, 1989:8)

Thus, the Holocaust, to Bauman, was a product of modernity and *not,* as most people view it, a result of the breakdown of modernity or a special route taken within it (Joas, 1998; Varcoe, 1998). In Weberian terms, there was an "elective affinity" between the Holocaust and modernity.

For example, the Holocaust involved the application of the basic principles of industrialization in general, and the factory system in particular, to the destruction of human beings:

> [Auschwitz] was also a mundane extension of the modern factory system. Rather than producing goods, the raw material was human beings and the end-product was death, so many units per day marked carefully on the manager's production charts.

The chimneys, the very symbol of the modern factory system, poured forth acrid smoke produced by burning human flesh. The brilliantly organized railroad grid of modern Europe carried a new kind of raw material to the factories. It did so in the same manner as with other cargo. . . . Engineers designed the crematoria; managers designed the system of bureaucracy that worked with a zest and efficiency. . . . What we witnessed was nothing less than a massive scheme of social engineering.

(Feingold, cited in Bauman, 1989:8)

What the Nazis succeeded in doing was to bring together the rational achievements of industry and the rational bureaucracy, and then bring both to bear on the objective of destroying people. Modernity, as embodied in these rational systems, was not a sufficient condition for the Holocaust, but it was clearly a necessary condition. Without modernity and rationality, "the Holocaust would be unthinkable" (Bauman, 1989:13).

The Role of Bureaucracy

The German bureaucracy did more than carry out the Holocaust; in a very real sense it created the Holocaust. The task of "getting rid of the Jews," as Hitler defined it, was picked up by the German bureaucrats, and as they resolved a series of day-to-day problems, extermination emerged as the best means to the end as it was defined by Hitler and his henchmen. Thus, Bauman argues that the Holocaust was not the result of irrationality, or premodern barbarity, but rather it was the product of the modern, rational bureaucracy. It was not crazed lunatics who created and managed the Holocaust, but highly rational and otherwise quite normal bureaucrats.

In fact, previous efforts, such as emotional and irrational pogroms, could not have accomplished the mass extermination that characterized the Holocaust. Such a mass extermination required a highly rationalized and bureaucratized operation. An irrational outburst such as a pogrom might kill some people, but it could never successfully carry on a mass extermination of the scale undertaken in the Holocaust. As Bauman puts it, "Rage and fury are pitiably primitive and inefficient tools of mass annihilation. They normally peter out before the job is done" (1989:90). In contrast, modern genocide as it was perpetrated by the Nazis had a seemingly rational purpose, the creation of a "better" society (unfortunately, to the Nazis, a better society was one that was free of "evil" Jews). And the Nazis and their bureaucrats went about achieving that goal in a cold and methodical manner.

Unlike most observers, Bauman does not see the bureaucracy as simply a neutral tool that can be propelled in any direction. Bauman sees the bureaucracy as "more like . . . loaded dice" (1989:104). While it can be used for either cruel or humane purposes, it is more likely to favor inhuman processes: "It is programmed to measure the optimum in such terms as would not distinguish between one human object and another, or between human and inhuman objects" (Bauman, 1989:104). And given its basic characteristics, the bureaucracy would see the inhuman task through to the end, and beyond. In addition to their normal operations, bureaucracies have a number of well-known incapacities, and they too fostered the Holocaust. For example, means often become ends in bureaucracies, and in this case the means, killing, often came to be the end.

Of course, the bureaucracy and its officials could not and did not create the Holocaust on their own; other factors were required. For one thing, there was the unquestioned control of the state apparatus with its monopoly of the means of violence over the rest of society. In other words, there were few if any countervailing power bases in Nazi Germany. And the state, of course, was controlled by Adolf Hitler, who had the ability to get the state to do his bidding. For another thing, there was a distinctly modern and rational form of anti-Semitism in which Jews were systematically set apart from the rest of society and portrayed as if they were preventing Germany from becoming a "perfect" society. To accomplish this goal, the Germans had to exterminate those who stood in the way of achieving a perfect society. German science (itself highly rationalized) was employed to help define the Jews as defective. Once they were defined as defective, and as a barrier to the perfect society, it followed that the only solution was their elimination. And once it was determined that they should be eliminated, the only important issue facing the bureaucrat was finding the most efficient way of bringing about this end.

Another factor here is that there is no place for moral considerations in modern structures such as bureaucracies. Whether it was right or wrong to exterminate the Jews was a nonissue. The absence of such moral concerns is another reason that the Holocaust is such a modern phenomenon.

The Holocaust and Rationalization

The Holocaust had all the characteristics of Weber's rationalization process (as well as of "McDonaldization"; see Chapter 15). There was certainly an emphasis on efficiency. For example, gas was determined to be a far more efficient method of killing large numbers of people than were bullets. The Holocaust had the predictability of an assembly line, with the long lines of trains snaking into the death camps, the long rows of people winding into the "showers," and the "production" of large stacks of bodies to be disposed of at the end of the process. It was calculable in the sense that the emphasis was on quantitative factors such as how many people could be killed and in how short a time.

> For railway managers, the only meaningful articulation of their object is in terms of tonnes per kilometre. They do not deal with humans, sheep, or barbed wire; they only deal with cargo, and this means an entity consisting entirely of measurements and devoid of quality. For most bureaucrats, even such a category as cargo would mean too strict a quality-bound restriction. They deal only with the financial effects of their actions. Their object is money.
>
> (Bauman, 1989:103)

There was certainly little attention paid to the quality of the life, or even of the death, of the Jews as they marched inexorably to the gas chambers. In another, quantitative sense, the Holocaust was the most extreme of mass exterminations:

> Like everything else done in the modern—rational, planned, scientifically informed, expert, efficiently managed, co-ordinated—way, the Holocaust left behind and put to shame all its alleged pre-modern equivalents, exposing them as primitive, wasteful and ineffective by comparison. Like everything else in our modern society, the Holocaust was an accomplishment in every respect superior. . . . It towers high above the past genocidal episodes.
>
> (Bauman, 1989:89)

Finally, the Holocaust used nonhuman technologies, such as the rules and regulations of the camps and the assembly-line operation of the ovens, to control both inmates and guards.

Of course, the characteristic of rationalization (and McDonaldization) that best fits the Holocaust is the irrationality of rationality, especially dehumanization. Here Bauman makes use of the idea of distanciation to make the point that the victims can be dehumanized because the bureaucrats making decisions about them have no personal contact with them. Furthermore, the victims are objects to be moved about and disposed of, numbers on a ledger; they are not human beings. In sum, "German bureaucratic machinery was put in the service of a goal incomprehensible in its irrationality" (Bauman, 1989:136).

One of Bauman's most interesting points is that the rational system put in place by the Nazis came to encompass the victims, the Jews. The ghetto was transformed into "an extension of the murdering machine" (Bauman, 1989:23). Thus,

> the leaders of the doomed communities performed most of the preliminary
> bureaucratic work the operation required (supplying the Nazis with the records and
> keeping the files on their prospective victims), supervised the productive and
> distributive activities needed to keep the victims alive until the time when the gas
> chambers were ready to receive them, policed the captive population so that law-
> and-order tasks did not stretch the ingenuity or resources of the captors, secured
> the smooth flow of the annihilation process by appointing the objects of its
> successive stages, delivered the selected objects to the sites from which they could
> be collected with a minimum of fuss, and mobilized the financial resources needed
> to pay for the last journey.
>
> (Bauman, 1989:118)

(This is similar to the idea that in a McDonaldized world, the customers become unpaid workers in the system, making their own salads, cleaning up after themselves, and so on.) In "ordinary genocide," the murderers and the murdered are separated from one another. The murderers are planning to do something terrible to their victims, with the result that the resistance of potential victims is likely. However, such resistance is far less likely when the victims are an integral part of a "system" created by the perpetrators.

In their actions, the Jews who cooperated with the Nazis were behaving rationally. They were doing what was necessary to, for example, keep themselves alive for another day or be selected as people deserving of special, more favorable treatment. They were even using rational tools, such as calculating that the sacrifice of a few would save the many, and that if they didn't cooperate many more would die. However, in the end, such actions were irrational in that they helped expedite the process of genocide and reduced the likelihood of resistance to it.

Modernity has prided itself on being civilized, on having safeguards in place so that something like the Holocaust could never occur. But it did occur; the safeguards were not sufficient to prevent it. Today, the forces of rationalization remain in place and are, if anything, stronger. And there is little to suggest that the safeguards needed to prevent rationalization from running amok are any stronger today than they were in the 1940s. As Bauman says, "None of the societal conditions that made Auschwitz possible has truly disappeared, and no effective measures have been undertaken to prevent . . . Auschwitz-like catastrophes" (1989:11). Necessary to prevent another Holocaust are a strong morality and pluralistic political forces. But there are likely to be times when a single power comes to predominate and there is little to lead us to believe that a strong enough moral system is in place to prevent another confluence of a powerful leader and an eager and willing bureaucracy.

Liquid Modernity

More recently, Bauman has articulated a new way of looking at modernity—"liquid modernity" (Atkinson, 2008; Binkley, 2008; Bryant, 2007; Jay, 2010)—that is informed by his earlier work on rationalization and the Holocaust. Basically, the latter involved what he came to call "solid" structures such as the bureaucracy and the concentration camp (see discussion of the work of Agamben in Chapter 16), structures that contained and restricted people in various ways and to varying degrees. However, in a series of books written in the twenty-first century, Bauman (2000, 2003, 2005, 2006, 2007a, 2010, 2011; Bauman & Lyon, 2012) describes a dramatic change in late modernity from such solidity to great liquidity. Basically, in early modernity the goal was to create and maintain that which was designed to be permanent (a human settlement and its settlers, a marriage), whereas in late modernity the goal becomes that which is temporary (human settlements that are more like caravan stops and the nomads who visit there, cohabitation). In early modernity, elites tended to be the most settled, entrenched in estates (perhaps with walls and guards) and engaged in lifelong careers often with lifetime employers, whereas the poor were forever on the move in search of work, greater security, and so on. Now, the situation is largely reversed as the elites seek to be as free as possible of encumbrances in order to be able to take advantages of the rapid changes taking place in the world, especially the economy. The poor, on the other hand, are largely stuck in a given place and are unable to take advantage of such changes; in fact, they are more likely to be victimized by changes in the economy and elsewhere (for example, from closed factories and lost jobs).

Bauman seeks to get at the essence of liquid modernity and its contrast to the earlier, more solid form of modernity in various ways. The earlier form can be seen as a Weberian "iron cage" (see Chapter 4); in late modernity the structures associated with such an iron cage are much more like a "light cloak" that can more easily be borne by people, especially elites on the move. Instead of the kind of solid prison dominated by the panopticon described by Foucault (see Chapter 16), we now live in a postpanopticon society characterized by much lighter forms of surveillance (for example, of our communications over the Internet). Education in early modernity involved learning all one would ever need to know early in life in school, whereas in late modernity education can take place anywhere and everywhere and is seen as a lifelong process needed to adapt to changing circumstances. Early modern society is dominated by producers and the material objects they produce in material structures (factories), whereas late modernity is characterized by consumers with their lightness and speed (Bauman, 2003:49; see also, Bauman, 2007b). In fact, according to Bauman (2005:9), "Liquid life is consuming life." While producers were oriented to creating that which would last, consumers want to buy that which has a short, limited life span. Innumerable other contrasts are made, or implied, by Bauman in his books on liquidity, but it is clear that he has produced a powerful new way of looking at the (late) modern world (we will have more to say about this in Chapter 15).

Modernity's Unfinished Project

Jurgen Habermas is arguably not only today's leading social theorist but also the leading defender of modernity and rationality in the face of the assault on those ideas by postmodernists (and others). According to Seidman:

> In contrast to many contemporary intellectuals who have opted for an anti- or postmodernist position, Habermas sees in the institutional orders of modernity structures of rationality. Whereas many intellectuals have become cynical about the emancipatory potential of modernity . . . Habermas continues to insist on the utopian potential of modernity. In a social context in which faith in the Enlightenment project of a good society promoted by reason sees a fading hope and spurned idol, Habermas remains one of its strongest defenders.
>
> (Seidman, 1989:2)

Habermas (1987b) sees modernity as an "unfinished project," implying that there is far more to be done in the modern world before we can begin thinking about the possibility of a postmodern world (Outhwaite, 2011; Scambler, 1996).

In Chapter 13 we covered a good portion of Habermas's thinking on modernity in our discussion of his ideas on system, life-world, and the colonization of the life-world by the system. Habermas (1986:96) can be seen as doing a "theory of the pathology of modernity" because he regards modernity as being at variance with itself. By this he means that the rationality (largely formal rationality) that has come to characterize social systems is different from, and in conflict with, the rationality that characterizes the life-world. Social systems have grown increasingly complex, differentiated, integrated, and characterized by instrumental reason. The life-world, too, has witnessed increasing differentiation and condensation (but of the knowledge bases and value spheres of truth, goodness, and beauty), secularization, and institutionalization of norms of reflexivity and criticism (Seidman, 1989:24). A rational society would be one in which both system and life-world were permitted to rationalize in their own way, following their own logics. The rationalization of system and life-world would lead to a society with material abundance and control over its environments as a result of rational systems and one of truth, goodness, and beauty stemming from a rational life-world. However, in the modern world, the system has come to dominate and colonize the life-world. The result is that while we may be enjoying the fruits of system rationalization, we are being deprived of the enrichment of life that would come from a life-world that was allowed to flourish. Many of the social movements that have arisen at the "borders" between life-world and system in the last few decades are traceable to a resistance against the colonization and impoverishment of the life-world.

In analyzing the way in which the system colonizes the life-world, Habermas sees himself in alignment with much of the history of social thought:

> The main strand of social theory—from Marx via Spencer and Durkheim to Simmel, Weber and Lukács—has to be understood as the answer to the entry of system-environment boundaries into society itself [Habermas's life-world], to the genesis of the "internal foreign country" . . . which has been understood as the hallmark of modernity.
>
> (Habermas, 1991:255–256; italics added)

In other words, the "hallmark of modernity" to Habermas, as well as to most of classical theory, has been, in Habermas's terms, the colonization of the life-world by the system.

What, then, for Habermas would constitute the completion of modernity's project? It seems clear that the final product would be a fully rational society in which both system and life-world rationality were allowed to express themselves fully without one destroying the other. We currently suffer from an impoverished life-world, and that problem must be overcome. However, the answer does not lie in the destruction of systems (especially the economic and administrative systems), because it is they that provide the material prerequisites needed to allow the life-world to rationalize.

One of the issues Habermas (1987b) deals with is the increasing problems confronted by the modern, bureaucratic, social welfare state. Many of those associated with such a state recognize the problems, but their solution is to deal with them at the system level by, for example, simply adding a new subsystem to deal with the problems. However, Habermas does not think the problems can be solved in this way. Rather, they must be solved in the relationship between system and life-world. First, "restraining barriers" must be put in place to reduce the impact of system on life-world. Second, "sensors" must be built in order to enhance the impact of life-world on system. Habermas concludes that contemporary problems cannot be solved "by systems learning to function better. Rather, impulses from the lifeworld must be able to enter into the self-steering of functional systems" (1987b:364). These would constitute important steps toward the creation of mutually enriching life-world and system. It is here that social movements enter the picture, because they represent the hope of a recoupling of system and life-world so that the two can rationalize to the highest possible degree.

Habermas sees little hope in the United States, which seems intent on buttressing system rationality at the cost of a continuing impoverishment of the life-world. However, Habermas does see hope in Europe, which has the possibility of putting "an end to the confused idea that the normative content of modernity that is stored in rationalized life worlds could be set free only by means of ever more complex systems" (1987b:366). Thus, Europe has the possibility of assimilating "in a decisive way the legacy of Occidental rationalism" (Habermas, 1987b:366). That legacy translates today into restraints on system rationality in order to allow life-world rationality to flourish to the extent that the two types of rationalities can coexist as equals within the modern world. Such a full partnership between system and life-world rationality would constitute the completion of modernity's project. Because we remain a long way from that goal, we are far from the end of modernity, let alone on the verge, or in the midst, of postmodernity.

JURGEN HABERMAS

A Biographical Sketch

Jurgen Habermas is arguably the most important social thinker in the world today. He was born in Düsseldorf, Germany, on June 18, 1929, and his family was middle class and rather traditional. Habermas's father was director of the Chamber of Commerce. In his early teens, during World War II, Habermas was profoundly affected by the war. The end of the war brought new hope and opportunities for many Germans, including Habermas. The fall of Nazism brought optimism about the future of Germany, but Habermas was disappointed in the lack of dramatic progress in the years immediately after the war. With the end of Nazism, all sorts of intellectual opportunities arose, and once-banned books became available to the young Habermas. They included Western and German literature, as well as tracts written by Marx and Engels. Between 1949 and 1954 Habermas studied a wide range of topics (for example, philosophy, psychology, German literature) in Göttingen, Zurich, and Bonn. However, none of the teachers at the schools at which Habermas studied were illustrious, and most were compromised by the fact that they either had supported the Nazis overtly or simply had continued to carry out their academic responsibilities under the Nazi regime. Habermas received his doctorate from the University of Bonn in 1954 and worked for two years as a journalist.

In 1956 Habermas arrived at the Institute for Social Research in Frankfurt and became associated with the Frankfurt school. Indeed, he became research assistant to one of the most illustrious members of that school, Theodor Adorno, as well as an associate of the Institute (Wiggershaus, 1994). Although the Frankfurt school often is thought of as highly coherent, that was not Habermas's view:

> For me there was never a consistent theory. Adorno wrote essays on the critique of culture and also gave seminars on Hegel. He presented a certain Marxist background—and that was it.
>
> (Habermas, cited in Wiggershaus, 1994:2)

While he was associated with the Institute for Social Research, Habermas demonstrated from the beginning an independent intellectual orientation. A 1957 article by Habermas got him into trouble with the leader of the Institute, Max Horkheimer. Habermas urged critical thought and practical action, but Horkheimer was afraid that such a position would jeopardize the publicly funded Institute. Horkheimer strongly recommended that Habermas be dismissed from the Institute. Horkheimer said of Habermas, "'He probably has a good, or even brilliant, career as a writer in front of him, but he would only cause the Institute immense damage'" (cited in Wiggershaus, 1994:555). The article eventually was published, but not under the auspices of the Institute and with virtually no reference to it. Eventually, Horkheimer enforced impossible conditions on Habermas's work and Habermas resigned.

In 1961 Habermas became a privatdocent and completed his "Habilitation" (a second dissertation required by German universities) at the University of Marburg. Having already published a number of notable works, Habermas was recommended for a professorship of philosophy at the University of Heidelberg even before he had completed his Habilitation. He remained at Heidelberg until 1964, when he moved on to the University of Frankfurt as a professor of philosophy and sociology. From 1971 to 1981 he was the director of the Max Planck Institute. He returned to the University of Frankfurt as a professor of philosophy, and in 1994 he became an emeritus professor at that institution. He has won a number of prestigious academic prizes and has been awarded honorary professorships at a number of universities.

For many years, Habermas was the world's leading neo-Marxist (Nollman, 2005b). However, over the years his work has broadened to involve many different theoretical inputs. Habermas continues to hold out hope for the future of the modern world. It is in this sense that Habermas writes of modernity's unfinished project. While Marx focused on work, Habermas is concerned mainly with communication, which he considers to be a more general process than is work. While Marx focused on the distorting effect of the structure of capitalist society on work, Habermas is concerned with the way the structure of modern society distorts communication. While Marx sought a future world involving full and creative labor, Habermas seeks a future society characterized by free and open communication. Thus, there are startling similarities between the theories of Marx and Habermas. Most generally, both are modernists who believed or believe that in their time modernity's project (creative and fulfilling work for Marx, open communication for Habermas) has not yet been completed. Yet both have had faith that in the future that project will be completed.

It is this commitment to modernism, along with his faith in the future, that sets Habermas apart from many leading contemporary thinkers, such as Jean Baudrillard and other postmodernists. While the latter are often driven to nihilism, Habermas continues to believe in his lifelong (and modernity's) project. Similarly, while other postmodernists (for example, Lyotard) reject the possibility of creating grand narratives, Habermas continues to work on and support what is perhaps the most notable grand theory in modern social theory. Much is at stake for Habermas in his battle with the postmodernists. If they win out, Habermas may come to be seen as the last great modernist thinker. If Habermas (and his supporters) emerge victorious, he may be viewed as the savior of the modernist project and of grand theory in the social sciences.

Habermas versus Postmodernists

Habermas makes a case not only for modernity but also against the postmodernists. Habermas offered some early criticisms in an essay, "Modernity versus Postmodernity" (1981), which has achieved wide recognition.[1] In that essay, Habermas raises the issue of whether, in light of the failures of the twentieth century, we "should try to hold on to the *intentions of the Enlightenment,* feeble as they may be, or should we declare the entire project of modernity a lost cause?" (1981:9). Habermas, of course, is not in favor of giving up on the Enlightenment project or, in other words, on modernity. Rather, he chooses to focus on the "mistakes" of those who do reject modernity. One of the latter's most important mistakes is their willingness to give up on science, especially a science of the life-world. The separation of science from the life-world, and the leaving of it to experts, would, if done in conjunction with the creation of other autonomous spheres, involve the surrender of "the project of modernity altogether" (Habermas, 1981:14). Habermas refuses to give up on the possibility of a rational, "scientific" understanding of the life-world as well as the possibility of the rationalization of that world.

Holub (1991) has offered an overview of Habermas's most important criticisms of the postmodernists. First, the postmodernists are equivocal about whether they are producing serious theory or literature. If we treat them as producing serious theory, their work becomes incomprehensible because of "their refusal to engage in the institutionally established vocabularies" (Holub, 1991:158). If we treat the work of the postmodernists as literature, "then their arguments forfeit all logical force" (Holub, 1991:158). In either case, it becomes almost impossible to critically analyze the work of the postmodernists seriously, because they can always claim that we do not understand their words or their literary endeavors.

Second, Habermas feels that the postmodernists are animated by normative sentiments but that what those sentiments are is concealed from the reader. Thus, the reader is unable to understand what postmodernists are really up to, why they are critiquing society, from their stated objectives. Furthermore, while they have hidden normative sentiments, the postmodernists overtly repudiate such sentiments. The lack of such overt sentiments prevents postmodernists from developing a self-conscious praxis aimed at overcoming the problems they find in the world. In contrast, the fact that Habermas's normative sentiments (free and open communication) are overt and clearly stated makes the source of his critiques of society clear, and it provides the base for political praxis.

Third, Habermas accuses postmodernism of being a totalizing perspective that fails "to differentiate phenomena and practices that occur within modern society" (Holub, 1991:159). For example, the view of the world as dominated by power and surveillance is not fine-grained enough to allow for meaningful analysis of the real sources of oppression in the modern world.

Finally, the postmodernists are accused of ignoring that which Habermas finds absolutely central—everyday life and its practices. This oversight constitutes a double

---

[1] There is a sense that in his later work Habermas has offered a softer and more fine-grained critique of the postmodernists (Peters, 1994).

loss for postmodernists. On the one hand, they are closed off from an important source for the development of normative standards. After all, the rational potential that exists in everyday life is an important source of Habermas's ideas on communicative ratio- nality (Cooke, 1994). On the other hand, the everyday world also constitutes the ultimate goal for work in the social sciences because it is there that theoretical ideas can have an impact on praxis.

Habermas (1994:107) offers a good summary of his views on modernity- postmodernity and a useful transition to Chapter 16 of this text, in which we deal with postmodern social theory: "The concept of modernity no longer comes with a promise of happiness. But despite all the talk of postmodernity, there are no visible rational alternatives to this form of life. What else is left for us, then, but at least to search out practical improvements *within* this form of life?"

Self, Society, and Religion

Charles Taylor (1989, 2004, 2007) is a philosopher whose work directly addresses problems in sociological theory. He is especially known for his writings on modernity. The central argument throughout Taylor's writings is that modern persons and societ- ies are shaped by moral orders. These moral orders are communicated through cultural frameworks or, as Taylor also calls them, grand narratives—the overarching stories that we tell about ourselves and our societies. While postmodernists argue that social theorists should deconstruct and dispense with grand narratives (see Chapter 16), Taylor says that we unavoidably live our lives through the meanings supplied in modern grand narratives. These narratives operate as deep background understandings that, often without our awareness, structure our lives. For Taylor, then, while members of modern Western societies[2] may disagree over the meaning and importance of these narratives, they cannot help but orient themselves within the "horizons of meaning" that they provide.

For example, the concept of equality has become a *moral good* (i.e., a moral ideal) in modern Western society. It shapes our understanding of social institutions such as politics, work, and romance. Giddens's concept of pure relationship, discussed earlier in this chapter, is an example of how contemporary romantic practices are shaped by ideals of equality. People may argue over whether or not a society has actually achieved equality (it is only recently that women have gained the political rights of equality, especially in the modern West), and some may contest the legiti- macy of the ideal of equality (as do some patriarchal worldviews). However, the point is that, despite one's views on equality, to live in contemporary Western society means that the problem of equality is an unavoidable concern and focus.

Thus, when Taylor talks about modern moral orientations he is talking about a set of ideals that have sunk deep into the makeup of social life and as such have become

---

[2] Throughout this section we refer to the modern West. Taylor has been quite explicit in his focus on Western or European modernity. He does not, however, believe that Western modernity is the only modernity, or that other parts of the world can be understood through the imaginaries and frameworks of the West. Indeed, in *Modern Social Imagi- naries* he describes Western modernity as only one of "multiple-modernities" (1994:1) and limits his work to understanding the modern West.

touchstones in the way that we think about ourselves. Taylor has examined the way that these modern narratives and moralities have framed three different areas of social life: selfhood (1989), the modern social imaginary (2004), and religion (2007).

Modernity and the Self

Like Giddens (1991), Taylor identifies selfhood as a central component of the modern order. In *Sources of the Self* (1989) he argues that the most important feature of selves is that they develop in relation to moral goods. Taylor breaks this down into several specific claims:

- "We are selves only in that certain issues matter for us. What I am as a self, my identity, is essentially defined in the way that things have significance for me" (1989:34).
- "We are only selves insofar as we move in a certain space of questions, as we seek and find an orientation to the good" (34).
- "One is a self only among other selves. A self can never be described without reference to those around it" (35).
- "There is no way we could be inducted into personhood except by being initiated into language" (35).

For Taylor, selves emerge in spaces of shared meaning, spaces of shared questions, and spaces of shared values. In addition, the last two points indicate that like symbolic interactionists (Chapter 9), ethnomethodologists (Chapter 10), postmodernists, and poststructuralists (Chapter 16), Taylor assumes that selves are relational and are constructed in language/symbol use. This is also captured in Taylor's idea that selves are narrative beings. Essentially, selfhood consists in the stories that people tell about their attempts to realize deep moral, culturally circumscribed ideals.

This leads to what Taylor calls the *malaise of modernity* (1991). Even though, according to Taylor, selfhood depends upon a grounding in shared narratives (stories that we, as a culture, tell about what it means to be a self), most contemporary people are disconnected from these narratives. We don't know the stories that make up our selves. Even worse, we don't know that selves are made up through shared stories in the first place. As a result, contemporary persons suffer existential disorientation, what Giddens (1991) calls ontological insecurity and what Durkheim called anomie (see Chapter 3). While the reasons for this disconnection are varied, basically it is because contemporary society promotes individualistic rather than relational and cultural views of selfhood.

For Taylor, the solution to this malaise is found in a renewed understanding of the cultural frames that make selfhood possible. He wants to show people how they are embedded in shared moralities and narratives. In this respect, Taylor treats selfhood as an ongoing cultural dialogue of which modern persons are a part. Presumably, awareness of and participation in this dialogue gives rise to a dynamic, rich, and better grounded understanding of self. To encourage this dialogue, Taylor (1989) describes the various *sources* of the self. We only have space to describe a few of the most important sources.

First, modern selves are defined through the ideals of self-mastery, rationality, and instrumentality. This kind of selfhood, first described in the writings of philosopher

John Locke, dovetails with the scientific worldview developed in the modern period. In later writings (2007:27), Taylor calls this the "buffered" self. In contrast to the premodern self that was connected to the cosmos and the power of the divine, this self retreats inward and finds personal power and a sense of worth through the quest for total and transparent self-knowledge and self-control. This ideal continues to operate into the present moment in, for example, psychotherapies that promote anger management and other techniques of self-discipline (for another perspective on the importance of discipline to modernity see Foucault, Chapter 16).

The other major source of selfhood is associated with eighteenth-century romanticism. This emerged in protest against the cool rationality of the buffered self. This selfhood praises spontaneity, emotion, and self-expression. It has led to a cultural ideal that Taylor calls "expressive" individualism and the pursuit of "authentic" selfhood (2007:473; see also Guignon, 2004). This is the very important modern idea that each person possesses a real, or authentic, self, and that one of the most valuable things that people can do with their lives is to discover and give expression to their "true" self. This kind of selfhood is expressed in slogans such as "live your dreams" and "seize the moment."

The ideal of authenticity is so central to the modern cultural framework that most people think of it as a natural fact, rather than a cultural good. Like the ideal of the buffered self, the ideal of authenticity remains alive in the contemporary moment in, for example, consumer advertising, new age psychotherapies, and artistic practice. In fact, Taylor identifies the artist as the contemporary person who most fully realizes the virtues of authenticity.

Modernity's Social Imaginary

Sources of the Self examines the frameworks that allow the development of modern selves. *Modern Social Imaginaries* (2004) considers the frameworks that allow the existence of the modern social order. Borrowing a term from Benedict Anderson (1983), Taylor argues that modernity is shaped by *social imaginaries*. The social imaginary is a set of ideas about society that is intertwined with everyday practice.[3] Social imaginaries have the following characteristics:

- They focus on the way that "ordinary" people, as opposed to intellectuals, "imagine" their social surroundings (2004:23).
- They are often "carried in images, stories, and legends" though they do not have to be explicitly acknowledged and described; they are part of the background understanding of everyday life (23).
- "They are shared by large groups of people, if not the whole society" (23).
- The social imaginary is "that common understanding that makes possible common practices and a widely shared sense of legitimacy" (23).

While social imaginaries originate in the work of philosophers and other social elites, over time, they become part of the taken-for-granted background knowledge of everyday life.

---

[3] Here Taylor's work shares similarities to both Giddens's structuration theory and Bourdieu's constructivist-structuralism (see Chapter 13). Like Giddens and Bourdieu, Taylor does not separate ideas from practices.

To delineate the unique elements of the modern social imaginary Taylor distinguishes it from the social imaginary of premodern Western society. Describing the premodern, Taylor emphasizes the concept of *hierarchical complementary:*

> Society was seen as made up of different orders. These needed and complemented each other, but this didn't mean that their relations were truly mutual, because they didn't exist on the same level. Rather, they formed a hierarchy in which some had greater dignity and value than others. An example of this is the often repeated medieval idealization of the society of three orders: . . . those who pray, those who fight, and those who work. It was clear that each needed the others, but there is no doubt that we have here a descending scale of dignity; some functions were in their essence higher than others. (11)

The premodern social imaginary, then, is organized around the idea that the world is composed of layers of different worth and value. This world does not serve human beings and their interests, but instead reflects religious and cosmic orders.

In the modern imaginary, all people are, at least in principle, of equal worth and value. From the 1600s forward, the modern West began to imagine itself as an order of "mutual benefit" (19). People are now thought of as self-enclosed individuals who enter into relations with one another of their own choosing. These relations between individuals bring with them the obligation of "mutual respect and service" which "is directed toward serving our ordinary goals: life, liberty, sustenance of self and family" (13). This is the beginning of the era in which the values of freedom, equality, dignity, and respect become part of the modern idea of the social.

The modern order of mutual benefit is realized in four institutions: the economy, the public sphere, the sovereign people, and fashion. First, *economy* is no longer equated with the management of the household (as it has been in previous eras) but is now thought of as an independent sphere that links people together in exchanges of goods and services. These exchanges bring about mutual benefit. This image is found, for example, in Adam Smith's famous metaphor of the invisible hand in which "our search for our own individual prosperity redounds to the general welfare" (Taylor, 2004:70). Despite challenges from Marxist and other critical perspectives, this component of the imaginary continues to exist in today's neoliberal economics (see Chapter 15) and the popular imagination more generally.

The next component of the modern social imaginary is the *public sphere* (see also Habermas, this chapter). Taylor defines the public sphere as

> a common space in which the members of a society are deemed to meet through a variety of media: print, electronic, and also face-to-face encounters; to discuss matters of common interest; and thus to be able to form a common mind about these. (2004:83)

In the public sphere people can imagine themselves simultaneously working and living alongside one another. They begin to live in what Taylor calls *secular time,* where together they build a society independent from the divine order.

The concept of the *sovereign people* is related to the public sphere. Here groups of people, formerly scattered across geographical space and subjected to despotic political rule, start to think of themselves as members of a nation—a group of people who share a common background and can organize and govern themselves. In this regard, the French revolution is an important historical event. When they deposed Louis XVI, the French people constituted themselves as a nation of citizens rather than subjects of monarchial rule.

Fashion is the most recent component of the imaginary to develop, but also of greatest significance to the present moment. The public sphere and the sovereign people are spaces of common action—people work together to create shared social and moral orders. The sphere of fashion, however, does not require shared action but only mutual recognition. Like the other spheres, fashion involves interpersonal exchange that generates benefit, but this operates largely through "mutual display" (2004:168). That is, other people do not serve as explicit interlocutors, but they act as "witnesses to the meaning of our action" (168). This kind of imaginary, as Georg Simmel also pointed out (see Chapter 5), emerges in urban spaces. This produces imaginaries that "hover between solitude and togetherness" (68).

Religion in a Secular Age

Taylor's most recent work examines the relationship between modernity and religion and in particular the process of *secularization* (the decline of religious belief and practice in modernity). According to Taylor most scholars think of secularization as an inevitable and automatic effect of modernity. With the decline of the Catholic Church in Europe, the development of science and technology, and the growth of humanist philosophy, the "death of God" seemed inevitable (Taylor, 2007:560). But Taylor challenges conventional scholarship and says that the real problem is to understand how *unbelief*—a particular moral stance—becomes possible in the first place: "why is it so hard to believe in God in (many milieu) of the modern West, while in 1500 it was virtually impossible not to?" (539).

As with his other work Taylor tries to understand religion through the cultural frameworks of modernity. There are two issues. First, what cultural frames make *unbelief* possible? Second, what form does religious belief take in the modern secular world, or, as Taylor calls it, in the *immanent frame*? The second question implies that even though religious belief undergoes significant transformation in modernity, it is by no means an inevitable conclusion that unbelief will win the day.

With respect to unbelief, Taylor views science, secularity, and atheism as forms of belief enabled by the immanent frame. In particular, he says people are attracted to unbelief because of an unacknowledged grand narrative that contains a powerful moral. This is a story about the progress of humanity in which the immaturity of religious belief is conquered by the maturity of science, reason, and atheism. Moreover, the refusal of religion is viewed as a heroic and courageous achievement in which the unbeliever forsakes the childish comforts of religion. Instead the unbeliever confronts the cold, hard reality of scientific truth. Describing a variant of this belief system Taylor says "the main virtue stressed here is the imaginative courage to face the void, and be energized by it to the creation of meaning" (2007:588–9). This narrative is articulated by scholars like Marx (who saw religion as an opiate of the masses) and Freud (who saw religion as a compensation for repressed childhood wishes).

The other theoretical puzzle is to understand what happens to belief in the modern West. Taylor describes three historical periods that led up to the present era: the *ancien regime* (premodern), the *age of mobilization* (early modernity), and the *age of authenticity* (1960s–present). The aspect of belief that Taylor finds common to all of these eras is a desire for connection with the transcendent. Religious belief lifts humans out of the sphere of exclusively human relations and gives them meaning through connection to some powerful outside force. In the *ancien regime* people are related to the transcendent through a preordained cosmic order. In the *age of mobilization,* religion becomes more closely associated with political and national projects and people begin to organize their religious lives through the relations of mutual obligation envisioned in the modern social imaginaries described above. In other words, religion is subsumed within modern social institutions and practices. God becomes a distant creator and humans are tasked with realizing his divine plan in their everyday activities (Weber's account of the relation between Calvinism and capitalism is an example of this; see Chapter 4).

Taylor argues that the *age of authenticity,* in which we now live, grows out of eighteenth-century romanticism. As noted in our discussion of *Sources of the Self,* romanticism gives expressive individualism and authentic selfhood a preeminent role in social life. This focus on the individual can lead to conflict with traditional forms of religious belief. The needs of the self come into conflict with the needs of the religious community. For some, this leads to a split with religion—a move toward unbelief and its supporting narratives. But this is not inevitable. Religious belief assumes new forms in the age of authenticity. In other words, people continue to seek meaning in a transcendent, extrahuman realm, but in new ways.

For example, in the age of authenticity religion is increasingly seen as a personal choice, and in order for belief to be authentic it must "speak to me." Taylor writes:

> Now if we don't accept the view that the human aspiration to religion will flag, and I do not, then where will the access lie to practice of and deeper engagement with religion? The answer is the various forms of spiritual practice to which each is drawn in his/her own spiritual life (2007:515).

One important consequence of this new form of belief is a general retreat, in the West, from institutionalized religions such as Christianity. This is not to say that religion has become a series of individualized personal practices. Taylor argues that the collective dimension of religion remains important. Indeed, as Durkheim (1912/1965) pointed out in *Elementary Forms of Religious Life* (see Chapter 3), a crucial component of religion is the experience of collective effervescence, or what Taylor calls the festive. Thus, Taylor concludes that while the new frame for religious practice is individualistic (living out the moral demands of expressive individualism), it is not necessarily individuating. People still seek others with whom to pursue their chosen belief in the transcendent.

Informationalism and the Network Society

One recent contribution to modern social theory is a trilogy authored by Manuel Castells (1996, 1997, 1998; Allan, 2007) with the overarching title *The Information Age: Economy, Society and Culture.* Castells (1996:4) articulates a position opposed to postmodern social theory, which he sees as indulging in "celebrating the end of history, and, to some extent, the end of Reason, giving up on our capacity to understand and make sense":

> The project informing this book swims against streams of destruction, and takes exception to various forms of intellectual nihilism, social skepticism, and political cynicism. I believe in rationality, and the possibility of calling upon reason . . . I believe in the chances of meaningful social action. . . . And, yes, I believe in spite of a long tradition of sometimes tragic intellectual errors, that observing, analyzing, and theorizing is a way of helping to build a different, better world.
>
> (Castells, 1996:4)

Castells examines the emergence of a new society, culture, and economy in light of the revolution, begun in the United States in the 1970s, in informational technology (television, computers, and so on). This revolution led, in turn, to a fundamental restructuring of the capitalist system beginning in the 1980s and to the emergence of what Castells calls "informational capitalism." Also emerging were "informational societies" (although there are important cultural and institutional differences among these societies). Both are based on "informationalism" ("a mode of development in which the main source of productivity is the qualitative capacity to optimize the combination and use of factors of production on the basis of knowledge and information" [Castells, 1998:7]). The spread of informationalism, especially informational capitalism, leads to the emergence of oppositional social movements based on self and identity ("the process by which a social actor recognizes itself and constructs meaning primarily on the basis of a given cultural attribute or set of attributes, to the exclusion of a broader reference to other social structures" [Castells, 1996:22]). Such movements bring about the contemporary equivalent of what Marxists call "class struggle." The hope against the spread of informational capitalism and the problems it causes (exploitation, exclusion, threats to self and identity) is not the working class but a diverse set of social movements (e.g., ecological, feminist) based primarily on identity.

At the heart of Castells's analysis is what he calls the information technology paradigm with five basic characteristics. First, these are technologies that act on information. Second, since information is part of all human activity, these technologies have a pervasive effect. Third, all systems using information technologies are defined by a "networking logic" that allows them to affect a wide variety of processes and organizations. Fourth, the new technologies are highly flexible, allowing them to adapt and change constantly. Finally, the specific technologies associated with information are merging into a highly integrated system.

In the 1980s there emerged a new, increasingly profitable global informational economy. "It is *informational* because the productivity and competitiveness of units or agents in this economy (be it firms, regions, or nations) fundamentally depend upon their capacity to generate, process, and apply efficiently knowledge-based information" (Castells, 1996:66). It is global because it has the "*capacity to work as a unit in real time on a planetary scale*" (Castells, 1996:92). This was made possible, for the first time, by the new information and communication technologies. And it is "informational, not just information-based, because the cultural-institutional attributes of the whole social system must be included in the diffusion and implementation of the new technological paradigm" (Castells, 1996:91). Although it is global, there are differences, and Castells distinguishes among regions that lie at the heart of the new global economy (North America, the European Union, and the Asian Pacific). Thus, we are talking about a regionalized, global economy. In addition, there is considerable diversity within each region, and of crucial importance is the fact that while some areas of the globe are included, others are excluded and suffer grave negative consequences. Whole areas of the world (e.g., sub-Saharan Africa) are excluded, as are parts of the privileged regions, such as the inner cities in the United States.

Accompanying the rise of the new global informational economy is the emergence of a new organizational form, the network enterprise. Among other things, the network enterprise is characterized by flexible (rather than mass) production, new management systems (frequently adapted from Japanese models), organizations based on a horizontal rather than a vertical model, and the intertwining of large corporations in strategic alliances. However, most important, the fundamental component of organizations is a series of networks. It is this that leads Castells (1996:171) to argue that "a new organizational form has emerged as characteristic of the informational/global economy: the *network enterprise*" defined as *"that specific form of enterprise whose system of means is constituted by the intersection of segments of autonomous systems of goals."* The network enterprise is the materialization of the culture of the global informational economy, and it makes possible the transformation of signals into commodities through the processing of knowledge. As a result, the nature of work is being transformed (e.g., the individualization of work through such things as flex-time), although the precise nature of this transformation varies from one nation to another.

Castells (1996:373) also discusses the emergence (accompanying the development of multimedia out of the fusion of the mass media and computers) of the culture of *real virtuality, "a system in which reality itself (that is, people's material/symbolic existence) is entirely captured, fully immersed in a virtual image setting, in the world of make-believe, in which appearances are not just on the screen through which experience is communicated, but they become the experience."* In contrast to the past dominated by "the space of places" (e.g., cities like New York or London), a new spatial logic, the "space of flows," has emerged. We have become a world dominated by processes rather than physical locations (although the latter obviously continue to exist). Similarly, we have entered an era of "timeless time" in which, for example, information is instantly available anywhere on the globe.

Going beyond the network enterprise, Castells (1996:469, 470; italics added) argues that the "dominant functions and processes in the information age are increasingly organized around *networks*" defined as sets of "interconnected nodes." Networks are open, capable of unlimited expansion, dynamic, and able to innovate without disrupting the system. However, the fact that our age is defined by networks (the "network society") does not mean the end of capitalism. In fact, at least at the moment, networks allow capitalism to become, for the first time, truly global and organized on the basis of global financial flows, exemplified by the much-discussed global "financial casino" that is a wonderful example of not only a network but also an informational system. Money won and lost here is now far more important than that earned through the production process. Money has come to be separated from production; we are in a capitalist age defined by the endless search for money.

However, as we saw above, Castells does not see the development of networks, the culture of real virtuality, informationalism, and especially their use in informational capitalism as going unchallenged. These are opposed by individuals and collectivities with identities of their own that they seek to defend. Thus, "God, nation, family, and community will provide unbreakable, eternal codes around which a counter-offensive will be mounted" (Castells, 1997:66). However, it is important to recognize that these countermovements must rely on information and networks in order to succeed. Thus, they are deeply implicated in the new order. In this context, Castells describes a wide range of social movements including the Zapatistas in Chiapas, Mexico, the American militia, the Japanese cult Aum Shinrikyo, environmentalism, feminism, and the gay movement.

What of the state? In Castells's view, it is increasingly powerless in this new world of the globalization of the economy and its dependence on global capital markets. Thus, for example, states have become unable to protect their welfare programs because imbalances around the globe will lead capital to gravitate toward those states with low welfare costs. Also eroding the power of the state are global communications that flow freely in and out of any country. Then there is the globalization of crime and the creation of global networks that are beyond the control of any single state. Also weakening the state is the growth of multilateralism, the emergence of super nation-states such as the European Union, and internal divisions. While they will continue to exist, Castells (1997:304) sees states becoming *"nodes of a broader network of power."* The dilemma facing the state is that if it represents its national constituencies, it will be less effective in the global system, but if it focuses on the latter, it will fail to represent its constituencies adequately.

An example of the failure of the state is the Soviet Union. It simply was incapable of adapting to the new informationalism and world of networks. For example, the Soviet state monopolized information, but this was incompatible with a world in which success is associated with the free flow of information. As it fell apart, the old Soviet Union proved easy prey for global criminal elements. Ironically, although in its early years Russia was excluded from the global information society, it was (and is) deeply implicated in global criminality.

Given his critical orientation, especially to informational capitalism and its threats to self, identity, welfare, as well as its exclusion of vast portions of the world, Castells (1998:359) concludes that as they are currently constituted, our "economy, society and culture . . . limit collective creativity, confiscate the harvest of information technology, and deviate our energy into self-destructive confrontation." However, it need not be this way because there "is nothing that cannot be changed by conscious, purposive social action" (Castells, 1998:360).

Castells offers the first sustained sociological analysis of our new computerized world, and there are many insights to be derived from his work. Two major weaknesses stand out. First, this is primarily an empirical study (relying on secondary data), and Castells takes pains to avoid using a series of theoretical resources that might have enhanced his work. Second, he remains locked in a productivist perspective and fails to deal with the implications of his analysis for consumption. Nonetheless, Castells has clearly offered us an important beginning in our effort to gain a better understanding of the emerging world he describes.

The discussion of Castells's work represents a perfect transition to the next chapter, on globalization theory, because, as we have seen, much of his theory relates to global issues and is often discussed as a theory of globalization. Much of globalization theory can be seen as modern (we will encounter other ideas of some of the modern theorists encountered in this chapter—Giddens, Beck, Bauman—in the next chapter), and it has its roots in modern perspectives such as modernization theory and dependency theory. However, globalization theory also critiques and reacts against these earlier perspectives as well as, in at least some cases, the basic tenets of many theories of modernity. Although many of the ideas to be encountered in Chapter 15 are quite modern, many others go beyond the modern to implicit (e.g., "glocalization," "hybridization," and "creolization") and explicit ("empire" and "multitude") association with the postmodern ideas that are dealt with in Chapter 16.

Summary

In this chapter we survey a number of theoretical perspectives that continue to see the contemporary world in modern terms. Anthony Giddens sees modernity as a juggernaut that offers a number of advantages but also poses a series of dangers. Among the dangers underscored by Giddens are the risks associated with the modern juggernaut. These dangers are the key issue in Beck's work on the risk society. The modern world is seen as being characterized by risk and the need on the part of people to prevent risk and protect themselves from it. Bauman sees the Holocaust as the paradigm of rationality and modernity. An emphasis on the Holocaust indicates the irrationalities, and more generally the dangers, associated with modernity and increasing rationalization. Late Modernity, to Bauman, is defined by its liquidity in comparison to the solidity of earlier epochs. Next, we discuss Habermas's work on modernity as an unfinished project. Habermas, too, focuses on rationality, but his concern is with the dominance of system rationality and the impoverishment of the rationality of the life-world. Habermas sees the completion of modernity in the mutually enriching rationalization of system and life-world.

The next section covers the work of Charles Taylor, who focuses on the cultural frames and moral ideals that ground modern societies. In particular he talks about the way that selves are constructed through modern narratives. He also uses the concept of the modern social imaginary to talk about the organization of modern social life. Most recently, he has described the various belief systems at work in the process of secularization.

The final section is devoted to a discussion of the work of Manuel Castells. Castells is concerned with the growth of informationalism and the development of the network society. It is mainly the computer and the information flows it permits that have transformed the world and in the process created a series of problems such as the exclusion of great parts of the world, and even some pockets in the United States, from this system and its rewards.

Globalization Theory

Chapter Outline

It is likely that no single topic has received as much popular and academic attention in recent years as globalization. (For an extensive overview of the state of our knowledge of globalization, see George Ritzer's [2012] five-volume *The Wiley-Blackwell Encyclopedia of Globalization*.) The academic concern is motivated, in large part, by the extraordinary public importance of, interest in, and worry over globalization. However, reasons internal to the academic world (e.g., reactions against early and narrow approaches to what is now called globalization) also have led to a near-obsession with this topic. Social theorists, including many of those discussed in this chapter and elsewhere in this book, have been no exception to this trend toward a focal concern with globalization. It is beyond the scope of this chapter to offer anything like a complete overview of the voluminous work of social theorists on this topic, to say nothing of a review of the entire literature on globalization. What follows is a brief survey of some of the most important theoretical work on globalization.

Globalization is the spread of worldwide practices, relations, consciousness, and organization of social life. Nearly every nation and the lives of billions of people throughout the world are being transformed, often quite dramatically, by globalization. The degree and significance of its impact can be seen almost everywhere one looks, most visibly in the now common protests that accompany high-level meetings of global organizations such as the World Trade Organization (WTO) and the International Monetary Fund (IMF) (G. Thomas, 2007). As both the magnitude of the issues before these organizations and the level of protest against these organizations make clear, people throughout the world feel strongly that they are confronting matters of great moment.

Globalization theory (Robinson, 2007) also emerged as a result of a series of developments internal to social theory, notably the reaction against earlier perspectives such as modernization theory. Among the defining characteristics of this theory were its Western bias, the preeminence accorded to developments in the West, and the idea that the rest of the world had little choice but to become increasingly like the West. Although there are many different versions of globalization theory, there is a tendency in nearly all of them to shift away dramatically from a focus on the West (including and especially the United States) and to examine not only transnational processes that flow in many different directions but also those that are, at least to some degree, autonomous and independent of any single nation or area of the world (see the discussion of Appadurai's work below).

Globalization can be analyzed culturally, economically, politically, and institutionally. For each type of analysis, a key difference is whether one sees increasing homogeneity or heterogeneity. At the extremes, the globalization of culture can be seen either as the transnational expansion of common codes and practices (homogeneity) or as a process in which many global and local cultural inputs interact to create a kind of pastiche, or a blend, leading to a variety of cultural hybrids (heterogeneity). The trend toward homogeneity is often associated with *cultural imperialism,* the influence of a particular culture on a wide range of other cultures. There are many varieties of cultural imperialism, including those that emphasize the role played by American culture, the West, or core countries (Crothers, 2010; de Grazia, 2005). Roland Robertson (1992, 2001), however, among many others, opposes the idea, although he doesn't use the term *cultural imperialism.* His famous concept of glocalization (see below) sees the global as interacting with the local to produce that which is distinctive: the glocal.

Theorists who focus on economic factors tend to emphasize their growing importance and homogenizing effect on the world. They generally see globalization as the spread of neoliberalism, capitalism, and the market economy (Antonio, 2007a) throughout many different regions of the world. For example, some have focused on globalization and the expansion of trade. Joseph E. Stiglitz (2002), a Nobel Prize–winning economist and former chairman of the Council of Economic Advisors, issued a stinging attack on the World Bank, the WTO, and especially the IMF for their roles in worsening, rather than resolving, global economic crises. Among other things, Stiglitz criticizes the IMF for its homogenizing, "one-size-fits-all" approach that fails to take into account national differences. The IMF in particular, and globalization in general, have worked to the advantage of the wealthy nations, especially the United States (which effectively has veto power over IMF decisions), and to the detriment of poor nations. The gap between rich and poor has actually *increased* as a result of globalization.

Although those who focus on economic issues tend to emphasize homogeneity, some differentiation (heterogeneity) is acknowledged to continue to exist at least at the margins of the global economy. Indeed, Stiglitz argues for the need for more differentiated policies by the IMF and other global economic organizations. Other forms of heterogeneity in the economic realm involve, for example, the commodification of local cultures and the existence of flexible specialization that permits the tailoring of many products to the needs of various local specifications. More generally, those who emphasize heterogenization (Tomlinson, 1999) argue that the interaction of the global market with local markets leads to the creation of unique "glocal" markets that integrate the demands of the global market with the realities of the local market.

Political/institutional orientations, too, tend to emphasize either homogeneity or heterogeneity. For example, some of those who operate with a homogenization perspective in this domain focus on the worldwide spread of models of the nation-state and the emergence of similar forms of governance throughout the globe—in other words, the growth of a more-or-less single model of governance around the world (Meyer, Boli, and Ramirez, 1997). More broadly, there is a concern with increasing homogenization in a multiplicity of institutions (Boli and Lechner, 2005). As we will see, some see the growth of transnational institutions and organizations as greatly diminishing the power of both the nation-state and other, more local, social structures to make a difference in people's lives. One of the most extreme views of homogenization in the political realm is Benjamin Barber's (1995) thinking on "McWorld," or the growth of a single political[1] orientation that is increasingly pervasive throughout the world.

Interestingly, Barber also articulates, as an alternative perspective, the idea of "Jihad"—localized, ethnic, and reactionary political forces (including "rogue states") that involve an intensification of nationalism and that lead to greater political heterogeneity throughout the world. The interaction of McWorld and Jihad at the local level may produce unique, glocal political formations that integrate elements of both the former (e.g., use of the Internet to attract supporters) and the latter (e.g., use of traditional ideas and rhetoric).

The issue of homogenization/heterogenization cuts across a broad swath of globalization theory, but it is clearly not exhaustive. That will become clear in the following discussion of major theories of globalization, which certainly touches in various ways on homogenization/heterogenization but also highlights a number of other facets of globalization theory. This discussion is divided into four sections. First we look at the perspectives on globalization of some of the major contemporary theorists (Giddens, Beck, and Bauman) encountered earlier in this book. Then we turn to the aforementioned three broad categories of theorizing globalization: cultural, economic, and political/institutional.

Major Contemporary Theorists on Globalization

Anthony Giddens on the "Runaway World" of Globalization

Giddens's (2000) views on globalization are closely related to, and overlap with, his thinking on the juggernaut of modernity (see Chapter 14). Giddens also sees a close link between globalization and risk, especially the rise of what he calls manufactured risk. Much of the runaway world of globalization is beyond our control, but Giddens is not totally pessimistic. We can limit the problems created by the runaway world, but we can never control it completely. He holds out some hope for democracy, especially international and transnational forms of democracy such as the European Union.

---

[1] Barber's view of McWorld is not restricted to politics. Barber sees many other domains following the model of McWorld.

Giddens is one of those who emphasizes the role of the West in general, and the United States in particular, in globalization. However, he also recognizes that globalization is a two-way process with America and the West being strongly influenced by it. Furthermore, he argues that globalization is becoming increasingly decentered as nations outside the West (e.g., China, India) play an increasingly large role in it. He also recognizes that globalization has both undermined local cultures *and* served to revive them. And he makes the innovative point that globalization "squeezes sideways," producing new areas that may cut across nations. He offers as an example an area around Barcelona in northern Spain that extends into France.

A key clash taking place at the global level today is that between fundamentalism and cosmopolitanism. In the end, Giddens sees the emergence of a "global cosmopolitan society." Yet even the main force in opposition to it—fundamentalism—is itself a product of globalization. Furthermore, fundamentalism uses global forces (e.g., the mass media) in order to further its ends. Fundamentalism can take various forms—religious, ethnic, nationalist, political—but whatever form it takes, Giddens thinks that fundamentalism is problematic, both because it is at odds with cosmopolitanism and because it is linked to violence (see the discussion of Huntington's work below).

Ulrich Beck, the Politics of Globalization, and Cosmopolitanism

We can get at the essence of Beck's (2000) thinking on this issue by discussing his distinction between globalism and globality. *Globalism* is the view that the world is dominated by economics and that we are witnessing the emergence of the hegemony of the capitalist world market and the neoliberal ideology that underpins it. To Beck, this view involves both monocausal and linear thinking. The multidimensionality of global developments—ecology, politics, culture, and civil society—is wrongly reduced to a single economic dimension. And that economic dimension is seen, again erroneously, as evolving in a linear direction of ever-increasing dependence on the world market. Clearly, Beck sees the world in much more multidimensional and multidirectional terms. In addition, he is very sensitive to the problems associated with the capitalist world market, including the fact that there are all sorts of barriers to free trade and that there are not only winners in this world market but also (many) losers.

Even though Beck is a critic of the viewpoint of globalism, he sees much merit in the idea of *globality,* in which closed spaces, especially those associated with nations, are seen as growing increasingly illusory. They are growing illusory because of globalization, which involves transnational actors, with varying degrees of power, identities, and the like, crisscrossing and undermining nation-states. These transnational processes are not simply economic but also involve ecology, culture, politics, and civil society. Such transnational processes traverse national borders, rendering them porous if not increasingly irrelevant. Nothing is any longer limited to the local. That which takes place locally, including both advances and catastrophes, including the risks discussed in Chapter 14 (Beck, 2007), affects the entire world.

Transnational processes have long existed; nevertheless, globality is new for at least three reasons. First, its influence over geographic space is far more extensive than ever before. Second, its influence over time is far more stable; it is of continuing influence from one time to another. Third, there is far greater density to its various elements including transnational relationships and networks. Beck also lists a number of other things that are distinctive about globality in comparison to earlier manifestations of transnationality:

1. Everyday life and interactions across national borders are being profoundly affected.
2. There is a self-perception of this transnationality in such realms as the mass media, consumption, and tourism.
3. Community, labor, and capital are increasingly placeless.
4. There is a growing awareness of global ecological dangers and of actions to be taken to deal with them.
5. There is an increasing perception of transcultural others in our lives.
6. Global culture industries circulate at unprecedented levels.
7. There is an increase in the number and strength of transnational agreements, actors, and institutions.

This leads Beck to refine his previously discussed (see Chapter 14) thinking on modernity and to argue that globality, and the inability to reverse it, are associated with what he now calls "second modernity." Above all, however, what defines the latter is the decline of the power of the nations and the national borders that went to the heart of "first modernity." The central premise of first modernity is (was) that we live in self-enclosed nation-states. (Beck dismisses this notion as a "container theory" of society.) Thus globality, and second modernity, mean denationalization and, Beck hopes, the rise of transnational organizations and perhaps a transnational state.

Much of Beck's recent work, including his thinking on globalization, is linked to the idea of *cosmopolitanism,* which among other things seeks to overcome the traditional sociological focus on the spatially fixed nation and to replace it with a more fluid transnational focus (Beck and Grande, 2010; Beck and Sznaider, 2005, 2006). More generally, it involves a transcendence of the local restraints on thought and action. Thus, in the era of globalization people are no longer rooted in a given cosmos (e.g., the United States) but instead are rooted in "different cities, territories, ethnicities, hierarchies, nations, religions, and so on at the same time" (Beck and Sznaider, 2005:159). This involves a moving-away from a traditional kind of either/or thinking associated, for example, with nation-based perspectives, and a moving-toward a more hybrid, "this-as-well-as-that" sense of the world. Clearly, such a cosmopolitan approach is derived from, and has a close linkage to, globalization.

In *Power in the Global Age,* Beck (2005b:xi–xii) argues that a cosmopolitan orientation must go beyond national and international relations to global politics that involve a "meta-game whose outcome is completely open-ended. It is a game in which boundaries, basic rules and basic distinctions are being renegotiated—not only those between the 'national' and 'international' spheres, but also those between global business and the state, transnational civil society movements, supranational organizations and national governments and societies." It is this reality that requires a change in vision from a national to a cosmopolitan perspective that is better able to comprehend and deal with this meta-game.

Zygmunt Bauman on the Human Consequences of Globalization

Bauman (1998) sees globalization in terms of a "space war." In his view, it is mobility that has become the most important and differentiating factor in social stratification in the world today. Thus, the winners of the space war are those who are mobile, able to move freely throughout the globe and in the process to create meaning for themselves. They can float relatively free of space, and when they must "land" somewhere, they isolate themselves in walled and policed spaces in which they are safe from those who are the losers in the space war. The losers not only lack mobility but are relegated and confined to territories denuded of meaning and even of the ability to offer meaning. Thus, while the elite are likely intoxicated by their mobility opportunities, the rest are more likely to feel imprisoned in their home territories, from which they have little prospect of moving. Furthermore, the latter are likely to feel humiliated by the lack of their own mobility and the sight of elites free to move about at will. As a result, territories become battlefields where the losers and winners of the space war face off in a very uneven conflict.

The winners can be said to live in time rather than space; they are able to virtually span every space quickly, if not instantaneously. In contrast, the losers can be seen as living in space. That space is beyond their control, heavy, resilient, resistant, untouchable, able to tie time down. However, it is important to distinguish among those who have at least some mobility. The *tourists* are those who are on the move because they want to be. They are attracted by something, find it irresistible, and move toward it. The *vagabonds* are those who are on the move because they find their environs unbearable, inhospitable for any number of reasons. The positive aspects of what we applaud as globalization are those that are associated with tourists, while an unavoidable side effect is that many others are transformed into vagabonds. Most people, however, exist between these two extremes. They are unsure exactly where they now stand, but wherever it is, they are not sure they will be in the same place tomorrow. Thus, globalization translates into uneasiness for most of us.

However, even the seeming winners in globalization—the tourists—have their problems. First, there is the burden associated with the impossibility of slowing down; it is hard to always be on the move and at high speed. Second, mobility means an unending string of choices, and each choice has a measure of uncertainty associated with it. Third, each choice also carries with it a series of risks and dangers. Endless mobility and continual choice eventually become troublesome if not burdensome.

It is worth noting that Bauman employs the idea of "liquidity" in a variety of books written in the early twenty-first century (for example, Bauman, 2005). Clearly, a global world is increasingly a liquid world characterized by innumerable "flows" of all types. As a result, the global world is constantly changing its form, and it is becoming increasingly difficult either to control or to gain a solid understanding of it. The idea of liquidity has wide applicability to the process of globalization.

Given the globalization theories of some of today's major social theorists, we turn now to the major types of globalization theory, often with examples from other major social thinkers.

Cultural Theory

Jan Nederveen Pieterse (2004) has identified three major paradigms in theorizing the cultural aspects of globalization, specifically on the centrally important issue of whether cultures around the globe are eternally different, converging, or creating new "hybrid" forms out of the unique combination of global and local cultures. Let us look at each of these paradigms and a representative example (or examples) of each.

Cultural Differentialism

Those who adopt this paradigm argue that among and between cultures there are lasting differences that are largely unaffected by globalization or by any other bi-, inter-, multi-, or transcultural processes. This is not to say that culture is unaffected by any of these processes, especially globalization. But it is to say that at their core cultures are largely unaffected by them; they remain much as they always have been. In this perspective globalization occurs only on the surface, and the deep structure of cultures is largely, if not totally, unaffected by it. Cultures are seen as largely closed not only to globalization but also to the influences of other cultures. In one image, the world is envisioned as a mosaic of largely separate cultures. More menacing is a billiard-ball image, with billiard balls (representing cultures) seen as bouncing off other billiard balls (representing other cultures). This image is more menacing because it indicates the possibility of dangerous and potentially catastrophic collisions among and between world cultures.

The cultural differential paradigm has a long history, but it has attracted increasing attention and adherents (as well as critics) in recent years because of two sets of current events. One is the terrorist attacks of September 11, 2001, and the subsequent wars in Afghanistan and Iraq. Many people saw these events as the product of a clash between Western and Islamic cultures and the eternal cultural differences between them. The other set of current events is the increasing multiculturalism of both the United States (largely the growth of the Hispanic population) and of western European countries (largely the growing Muslim populations) and the vast differences, and enmity, between majority and minority populations.

The most famous and controversial example of this paradigm is Samuel Huntington's *Clash of Civilizations and the Remaking of World Order* (1996). Huntington traces the beginnings of the current world situation to the end of the Cold War and the reconfiguring of the world from one differentiated on a political-economic basis (democratic/capitalist versus totalitarian/communist) to one based on cultural differences. Such cultural differences are nothing new, but they were largely submerged (as in the old Yugoslavia and the differences between, among others, Serbs and Croats) by the overwhelming political-economic differences of the Cold War era. What we have seen resurfacing in the last two decades are ancient identities, adversaries, and enemies. Huntington uses the term *civilization* to describe the broadest level of these cultures and cultural identities (indeed, to him civilization is culture "writ large"). What he sees is the emergence of fault lines among and between these civilizations, and he considers this a highly dangerous situation given the historic enmities among at least some of these civilizations.

Huntington differentiates between a number of world civilizations: Sinic (Chinese); Japan (sometimes combined with "Sinic" as "Far Eastern"); Hindu; Islamic; Orthodox (centered in Russia); Western Europe; North America (along with the closely aligned Australia, New Zealand); Latin America; and (possibly) Africa. He sees these civilizations as differing greatly on basic philosophical assumptions, underlying values, social relations, customs, and overall outlooks on life. To Huntington, human history is in effect the history of civilizations, especially these civilizations. Civilizations share a number of characteristics including the fact that there is great agreement on what they are (although they lack clear beginnings and there are no clear-cut boundaries between civilizations, which, nonetheless, are quite real). Civilizations

1. are among the most enduring of human associations (although they do change over time).
2. are the broadest level of cultural identity (short of humanity in its entirety).
3. are the broadest source of subjective self-identification.
4. usually span more than one state (although they do not perform state functions).
5. are a totality.
6. are closely aligned with both religion and race.

Huntington offers a modern grand narrative of the relationships among civilizations. For more than three thousand years (approximately 1500 BC to AD 1500) civilizations tended to be widely separated in terms of both time and space. As a result, contacts among them were likely to be nonexistent. When they occurred, they tended to be on a limited or intermittent basis, and they were likely quite intense.

The next phase, roughly from 1500 to the close of World War II, was characterized by the sustained, overpowering, and unidirectional impact of Western civilization on all other civilizations. Huntington attributes this impact to various structural characteristics of the West, including the rise there of cities, commerce, and state bureaucracy and an emerging sense of national consciousness. However, the most immediate cause was technological, especially in ocean navigation and the military, including superior military organization, discipline and training, and, of course, weaponry. In the end, the West excelled in organized violence, and although those in the West sometimes forget this, those in other parts of the world have not. Thus, by 1910, just before the First World War, the world came closer, in Huntington's view, than at any time in history to being one world, one civilization—Western civilization.

The third phase—the multicivilizational system—is traceable to the end of the expansion of the West and the beginning of the revolt against it. The period after World War I and until about 1990 was characterized by a clash of ideas, especially capitalist and communist ideologies; but since the fall of communism the major clashes in the world now revolve around religion, culture, and ultimately civilizations. The West continues to be dominant, but Huntington foresees its decline. The decline will be slow, it will not occur in a straight line, and it will involve a waning (at least relatively) of the West's resources—population, economic product, and military capability. The decline in military capability will be traceable to such things as the decline of U.S. forces and to the globalization of the defense industries, which will make generally available many weapons formerly available only or largely in the West. Increasingly, other civilizations will reject the West, but they will embrace and utilize the advances of modernization, which can and should be distinguished from Westernization.

While the West declines, the resurgence of two other civilizations is of greatest importance. The first is the economic growth of Asian societies, especially Sinic civilization. Huntington foresees the continuing growth of Asian economies, which will soon surpass the economics of the West. Important in itself, this will translate into increasing power for the East and a corresponding decline in the ability of the West to impose its standards on the East. Huntington sees the economic ascendancy of the East as largely traceable to the superior aspects of its culture(s), especially its collectivism in contrast to the individuality that dominates the West. Also helpful to the economic rise of the East are various other commonalities among the nations of the region (e.g., religion, especially Confucianism). The successes of Asian economies will be important not only in themselves but also for the role they will play as models for other non-Western societies.

This first of Huntington's arguments is not that surprising or original. After all, we witnessed the dramatic growth of the post–World War II Japanese economy, and we are now witnessing the amazing economic transformation of China and India. Projecting present economic trends, few would disagree with the view that the economy of China will become the largest in the world in the not-too-distant future.

More controversial is Huntington's second major contention, which involves the resurgence of Islam. The Sinic emergence is rooted in the economy, but Islamic growth is rooted in dramatic population growth and the mobilization of the population. This growth of Islam has touched nearly every Muslim society, usually first culturally and then sociopolitically. It can be seen as part of the global revival of religion. It also can be seen both as a product of, and as an effort to come to grips with, modernization.

Huntington goes beyond pointing to this development to paint a dire portrait of the future of the relations between the West and these other two civilizations, especially Islam. The Cold War conflict between capitalism and communism has been replaced by conflict that is to be found at the "fault lines" among and between civilizations, especially the Western, Sinic, and Islamic civilizations. Thus, he foresees dangerous clashes between the West (and what he calls its "arrogance"), Islam (and its "intolerance"), and Sinic "assertiveness." Much of the conflict revolves around the West's view of itself as possessing "universal culture," its desire to export that culture to the rest of the world, and its declining ability to do so. Furthermore, what the West sees as universalism, the rest of the world, especially Islamic civilization, sees as imperialism. More specifically, the West wants to limit weapons proliferation, whereas other civilizations want weapons, especially "weapons of mass destruction." The West also seeks to export democracy to, and even impose it on, other societies and civilizations, which often resist democracy as part of the West's idea of universal culture. And the West seeks to control and to limit immigration (especially from Islamic civilization), although many from those civilizations have found their way into the West or want to be there. As these processes increase, Huntington sees cleft societies developing *within* both Europe and the United States. In the latter, fault lines will develop not only between Westerners and Muslims but also between Anglos and Hispanics (Huntington, 2004).

What has earned Huntington numerous criticisms and the greatest enmity are his controversial statements about Islamic civilization and Muslims (Huntington, 1996). For example, he argues that wherever Muslims and non-Muslims live in close proximity to one another, violent conflict and intense antagonism are pervasive, and he puts much of the blame for this on Muslims and their propensity toward violent conflict. He argues that from the beginning, Islam has been a religion of the sword, it has glorified military values, and there is a history of Islamic conquest. The relationship between Islam and other civilizations has historically been one of mutual indigestibility. Of course, Western imperialism—often with Islam as a target—has played a key role in this. Islam also lacks a strong core state to exert control over the civilization. But of greatest importance to Huntington are the pressures created by the demographic explosion within Islam.

Huntington is concerned about the decline of the West, especially of the United States. He sees the United States, indeed all societies, as threatened by their increasing multicivilizational or multicultural character. For him, the demise of the United States effectively means the demise of Western civilization. Without a powerful, unicivilizational United States, the West is minuscule. For the West to survive and prosper, the United States must do two things. First, it must reaffirm its identity as a Western (rather than a multicivilizational) nation. Second, it must reaffirm and reassert its role as the leader of Western civilization around the globe. The reassertion and acceptance of Western civilization (which would also involve a renunciation of universalism), indeed all civilizations, is the surest way to prevent warfare between civilizations. The real danger, for Huntington, is multiculturalism within the West and all other civilizations. Thus, Huntington ultimately comes down on the side of cultural continuity and something approaching cultural purity within civilizations. For him, at least in some ideal sense, globalization becomes a process by which civilizations continue to exist and move in roughly parallel fashion in the coming years. This constitutes a reaffirmation of the importance of civilization—that is, culture—in the epoch of globalization.

Cultural Convergence

The preceding paradigm is rooted in the idea of lasting differences among and between cultures and civilizations as a result of, or in spite of, globalization. In contrast, the cultural convergence paradigm is based on the idea of globalization leading to increasing sameness throughout the world. While thinkers like Huntington emphasize the persistence of cultures and civilizations in the face of globalization, those who support the convergence perspective see those cultures changing, sometimes radically, as a result of globalization. The cultures of the world are seen as growing increasingly similar, at least to some degree and in some ways. There is a tendency to see global assimilation in the direction of dominant groups and societies in the world. Those who operate from this perspective focus on such things as "cultural imperialism," global capitalism, Westernization, Americanization, "McDonaldization," and "world culture" (Boli and Lechner, 2005; Lechner, 2012). At its extreme, globalization becomes Westernization, Americanization (de Grazia, 2005; Marling, 2006), and McDonaldization writ large.

In what follows we discuss two versions of this basic argument that are closely associated with Ritzer's work on this topic. However, a note of warning and clarification is needed. Although Ritzer's work focuses on cultural convergence, it certainly does *not* argue that this is all that is happening in globalization, or that local cultures are disappearing completely or even necessarily being altered in some fundamental way. Rather, the argument is that global processes are bringing the same or similar phenomena (e.g., McDonald's restaurants in 120-plus countries in the world) to many parts of the world and, in that sense, there is cultural convergence. However, side-by-side with such global phenomena exist local phenomena (e.g., local open-air food markets or craft fairs) that continue to be vibrant and important. Furthermore, it may well be that the arrival of these global forms spurs the revival or development of new local forms. Although the last two points are certainly meritorious, in accepting them we must not lose sight of the fact that some, perhaps a great deal of, cultural convergence is also occurring (the spread of Wal-Mart into Mexico and other nations is another example).

"McDonaldization"

Although it is based on Max Weber's ideas about the rationalization of the West (see Chapter 4), the McDonaldization thesis (Ritzer, 2006, 2013) adopts a different model: Weber focused on the bureaucracy; Ritzer concentrates on the fast-food restaurant. Also, the McDonaldization thesis brings the theory into the twenty-first century and views rationalization as extending its reach into more sectors of society and into more areas of the world than Weber ever imagined. Of greatest concern in the context of this section is the fact that McDonaldization is, as we will see, a force in globalization, especially increasing cultural homogenization.

McDonaldization is the process by which the principles of the fast-food restaurant are coming to dominate more and more sectors of American society, as well as the rest of the world. The nature of the McDonaldization process may be delineated by outlining its five basic dimensions: efficiency, calculability, predictability, control through the substitution of technology for people, and, paradoxically, the irrationality of rationality.

Efficiency   A McDonaldizing society emphasizes *efficiency,* the effort to discover the best possible means to achieve whatever end is desired. Workers in fast-food restaurants clearly must work efficiently. For example, burgers are assembled, and sometimes even cooked, in an assembly-line fashion. Customers want, and are expected, to acquire and consume their meals efficiently. The drive-through window is a highly efficient means for customers to obtain, and for employees to dole out, meals. Overall, various norms, rules, regulations, procedures, and structures have been put in place in the fast-food restaurant to ensure that *both* employees and customers act in an efficient manner. Furthermore, the efficiency of one party helps to ensure that the other will behave in a similar manner.

Calculability   Great importance is given to *calculability,* to an emphasis on quantity, often to the detriment of quality. Various aspects of the work of employees at fast-food restaurants are timed. This emphasis on speed often serves to adversely affect the quality of the work, from the point of view of the employee, resulting in dissatisfaction, alienation, and high turnover rates. Similarly, customers are expected to spend as little time as possible in the fast-food restaurant. The drive-through window reduces this time to zero, but if customers desire to eat in the restaurant, the chairs may be designed to impel them to leave after about 20 minutes. This emphasis on speed clearly has a negative effect on the quality of the dining experience at a fast-food restaurant. Furthermore, the emphasis on how fast the work is to be done means that customers cannot be served high-quality food that, almost by definition, would require a good deal of time to prepare.

Predictability   Because McDonaldization involves an emphasis on predictability, things (products, settings, employee and customer behavior, and so on) are pretty much the same from one geographic setting to another and from one time to another. Employees are expected to perform their work in a predictable manner, and customers are expected to respond with similarly predictable behavior. Thus, when customers enter, employees ask, following scripts, what they wish to order. Customers are expected to know what they want, or where to look to find what they want, and they are expected to order, pay, and leave quickly. Employees (following another script) are expected to thank them when they do leave. A highly predictable ritual is played out in the fast-food restaurant—one that involves highly predictable foods that vary little from one time or place to another.

Control by Means of Technology   Great control exists in McDonaldized systems, and a good deal of that control comes from technologies. These technologies currently dominate employees, but increasingly they will be replacing them. Employees are clearly controlled by such technologies as french-fry machines that ring when the fries are done and even automatically lift the fries out of the hot oil. For their part, customers are controlled by the employees who are constrained by such technologies as well as more directly by the technologies themselves. Thus, the automatic fry machine makes it impossible for a customer to request well-done, well-browned fries.

Irrationality of Rationality   Both employees and customers suffer from the irrationality of rationality that seems inevitably to accompany McDonaldization. Paradoxically, rationality seems often to lead to its exact opposite—irrationality. For example, the efficiency of the fast-food restaurant is often replaced by the inefficiencies associated with long lines of people at the counters or long lines of cars at the drive-through window. Although there are many other irrationalities, the ultimate irrationality is dehumanization. Employees are forced to work in dehumanizing jobs, and customers are forced to eat in dehumanizing settings and circumstances. The fast-food restaurant is a source of degradation for employees and customers alike.

McDonaldization, Expansionism, and Globalization

McDonald's has been a resounding success in the international arena. Over half of McDonald's restaurants are outside the United States (in the mid-1980s only 25 percent of McDonald's were outside the United States). The vast majority of new restaurants opened each year are overseas. Well over half of McDonald's profits come from its overseas operations. The highly McDonaldized Starbucks has become an increasingly global force and is now a presence in Latin America, Europe (it is particularly visible in London), the Middle East, and the Pacific Rim.

Many highly McDonaldized firms outside of the fast-food industry have also had success globally. For example, Wal-Mart opened its first international store (in Mexico) in 1991 and now operates over 1,500 stores overseas (compared to over 3,800 in the United States, including supercenters and Sam's Club).

Another indicator of globalization is the fact that other nations have developed their own variants of this American institution. Canada has a chain of coffee shops, Tim Hortons (merged with Wendy's a few years ago), that has 3,800 outlets (622 in the United States). Paris, a city whose love for fine cuisine might lead you to think it would prove immune to fast food, has a large number of fast-food croissanteries; the revered French bread has also been McDonaldized. India has a chain of fast-food restaurants, Nirula's, that sells mutton burgers (about 80 percent of Indians are Hindus, who eat no beef) as well as local Indian cuisine. Mos Burger is a Japanese chain with over 1,600 restaurants that, in addition to the usual fare, sell teriyaki chicken burgers, rice burgers, and oshiruko with brown rice cake. Russkoye Bistro, a Russian chain, sells traditional Russian fare like pirogi (meat and vegetable dumplings), blini (thin pancakes), Cossack apricot curd tart, and, of course, vodka. Perhaps the most unlikely spot for an indigenous fast-food restaurant, war-ravaged Beirut of 1984, witnessed the opening of Juicy Burger, with a rainbow instead of golden arches and J.B. the Clown standing in for Ronald McDonald. Its owners hoped that it would become the McDonald's of the Arab world. After the 2003 invasion of Iraq, a number of clones of McDonald's ("Madonal," "Matbax") quickly opened.

Now McDonaldization is coming full circle. Other countries with their own McDonaldized institutions have begun to export them to the United States. The Body Shop, an ecologically sensitive British cosmetics chain, had over 2,500 shops in 60 nations in 2011, of which 300 were in the United States. Furthermore, American firms are now opening copies of this British chain, such as Bath and Body Works. Pollo Campero, a Guatemalan chain specializing in chicken, is currently in six countries and is spreading rapidly throughout the United States.

McDonald's, as the model of the process of McDonaldization, has come to occupy a central position throughout the world. At the opening of McDonald's in Moscow, it was described as the ultimate American icon. When Pizza Hut opened in Moscow in 1990, customers saw it as a small piece of America. Reflecting on the growth of fast-food restaurants in Brazil, an executive associated with Pizza Hut of Brazil said that his nation is passionate about things American.

The "Globalization of Nothing"

The "globalization of nothing" (Ritzer, 2007c), like McDonaldization, implies increasing homogenization as more and more nations have an increasing number of the various forms of nothing. Ritzer is *not* arguing that globalization is nothing; indeed it is clear that the process is of enormous significance. Rather, the argument is that there is an *elective affinity* (a term borrowed from Weber) between globalization and nothing: one does not cause the other, but they do tend to vary together.

What is central here is the idea of *grobalization* (a companion to the notion of glocalization), or the imperialistic ambitions of nations, corporations, organizations, and the like and their desire, indeed need, to impose themselves on various geographic areas (see J. M. Ryan, 2007). Their main interest is in seeing their power, influence, and in some cases profits *grow* (hence the term *gro*balization) throughout the world. Grobalization involves a variety of subprocesses. Three of them—capitalism, Americanization, and McDonaldization—are central driving forces in grobalization and are of great significance in the worldwide spread of nothingness.

By *nothing,* Ritzer means (largely) empty forms, forms devoid of distinctive content. (Conversely, *something* would be defined as [largely] full forms, forms rich in distinctive content.) It is easier to export empty forms (nothing) throughout the globe than it is to export forms that are loaded with content (something). The latter are more likely to be rejected by at least some cultures and societies because the content conflicts, is at variance with, local content. In contrast, empty forms, largely devoid of distinctive content, are less likely to come into conflict with the local. In addition, empty forms have other advantages from the point of view of globalization. For example, they are easy to replicate over and over because they are so minimalist, and they have a cost advantage because they are relatively inexpensive to reproduce. A good example of nothing in these terms is the shopping mall (e.g., any of the malls owned by the Mills Corporation—Potomac Mills, Sawgrass Mills, etc.), which is an empty (largely) structure that is easily replicated around the world. These malls *could* be filled with an endless array of specific content (e.g., local shops, local foods, etc.—something!) that *could* vary enormously from one locale to another. However, increasingly, they are filled with chain stores carrying a wide range of various types of . . . nothing! Since more and more countries have these malls, this is an example of the grobalization of nothing and of increasing global homogenization.

There are four subtypes of nothing, and all of them are largely empty of distinctive content and are being globalized: (1) "nonplaces," or settings that are largely empty of content (e.g., the malls discussed above); (2) "nonthings," items such as credit cards in which there is little to distinguish one from the billions of others and all of them work in exactly the same way for all who use them anywhere in the world; (3) "nonpeople," or the kind of employees associated with nonplaces, for example, telemarketers, who may be nearly anywhere in the world and who interact with all customers in much the same way, relying heavily on scripts; and (4) "nonservices," services such as those provided by ATMs (the services provided are identical; the customer does all the work needed to obtain the services) as opposed to human bank tellers. The grobal proliferation of nonplaces, nonthings, nonpeople, and nonservices is another indication of increasing homogenization.

Cultural Hybridization

The third paradigm emphasizes the mixing of cultures as a result of globalization and the production, out of the integration of the global and the local, of new and unique hybrid cultures that are not reducible to either the local or the global culture. From this perspective, McDonaldization and the grobalization of nothing may be taking place, but they are largely superficial changes. Much more important is the integration of these and other global processes with various local realities to produce new and distinctive hybrid forms that indicate continued heterogenization rather than homogenization. Hybridization is a very positive, even romantic, view of globalization as a profoundly creative process out of which emerge new cultural realities and continuing if not increasing heterogeneity in many different locales.

The concept that gets to the heart of cultural hybridization, as well as to what many contemporary theorists interested in globalization think about the nature of transnational processes, is glocalization. *Glocalization* can be defined as the interpenetration of the global and the local resulting in unique outcomes in different geographic areas. While grobalization, as discussed above, tends to be associated with the proliferation of nothing, glocalization tends to be tied more to something and therefore stands opposed, at least partially (and along with the local itself), to the spread of nothing. Following Roland Robertson (2001; see also M. Smith, 2007), the following are the essential elements of the perspective on globalization adopted by those who emphasize glocalization:

1. The world is growing more pluralistic. Glocalization theory is exceptionally alert to differences within and between areas of the world.
2. Individuals and local groups have great power to adapt, innovate, and maneuver within a glocalized world. Glocalization theory sees local individuals and groups as important and creative agents.
3. Social processes are relational and contingent. Grobalization provokes a variety of reactions—ranging from nationalist entrenchment to cosmopolitan embrace—that feed back on and transform it, that produce glocalization.
4. Commodities and the media are seen *not* as (totally) coercive but rather as providing material to be used in individual and group creation throughout the glocalized areas of the world.

Those who emphasize glocalization tend to see it as militating against the grobalization of nothing and, in fact, view it as leading to the creation of a wide array of new, "glocal" forms of something. In contrast, those who emphasize grobalization see it as a powerful contributor to the spread of nothingness throughout the world.

A discussion of some closely related terms (and related examples) will be of considerable help in getting a better sense of glocalization, as well as the broader issue of cultural hybridization (Garcia Canclini, 1995; Pieterse, 2004). Of course, *hybridization* itself is one such term emphasizing increasing diversity associated with the unique mixtures of the global and the local as opposed to the *uniformity* associated with grobalization. A cultural hybrid would involve the combination of two or more elements from different cultures or parts of the world. Among the examples of hybridization (and heterogenization, glocalization) are Ugandan tourists visiting Amsterdam to watch two Moroccan women engage in Thai boxing, Argentinians watching Asian rap performed by a South American band at a London club owned by a Saudi Arabian, and the more mundane experiences of Americans eating such concoctions as Irish bagels, Chinese tacos, and kosher pizza. Obviously, the list of such hybrids is long and growing rapidly with increasing hybridization. The contrast of course would be such uniform experiences as eating hamburgers in the United States, quiche in France, or sushi in Japan.

Yet another concept that is closely related to glocalization is *creolization* (Hannerz, 1987). The term *creole* generally refers to people of mixed race, but it has been extended to the idea of the creolization of language and culture, involving a combination of languages and cultures that were previously unintelligible to one another.

All of the above—glocalization, hybridization, creolization—should give the reader a good feel for what is being discussed here under the heading "cultural hybridization."

Appadurai's "Landscapes"

In *Modernity at Large: Cultural Dimensions of Globalization* (1996), Arjun Appadurai emphasizes global flows and the disjunctures among them. These serve to produce unique cultural realities around the world; they tend to produce culture hybrids.

Appadurai discusses five global flows: ethnoscapes, mediascapes, technoscapes, financescapes, and ideoscapes. The use of the suffix *-scape* allows Appadurai to communicate the idea that these processes have fluid, irregular, and variable shapes and are therefore consistent with the idea of heterogenization and not homogenization. The fact that there are a number of these scapes and that they operate independently of one another to some degree, and perhaps are even in conflict with one another, makes this perspective also in tune with perspectives that emphasize cultural diversity and heterogeneity. Furthermore, these scapes are interpreted differently by different agents ranging all the way from individuals to face-to-face groups, subnational groups, multinational corporations, and even nation-states. And these scapes are ultimately navigated by individuals and groups on the basis of their own subjective interpretations of them. In other words, these are imagined worlds, and those doing the imagining can range from those who control them to those who live in and traverse them.

Although power obviously lies with those in control and their imaginings, this perspective gives to those who merely live in or pass through them the power to redefine and ultimately subvert them.

At the center of Appadurai's thinking are the five landscapes mentioned above:

1. *Ethnoscapes* involve the mobile groups and individuals (tourists, refugees, guest workers) who play such an important role in the ever-changing world in which we increasingly live. This involves actual movement as well as fantasies about moving. In an ever-changing world, people cannot afford to allow their imaginations to rest too long and thus must keep such fantasies alive.

2. *Technoscapes* are the ever-fluid, global configurations of high and low, mechanical and informational technology and the wide range of material (downloading files, e-mail) that now moves so freely and quickly around the globe and across borders that at one time were impervious to such movement (or at least thought to be).

3. *Financescapes* involve the processes by which huge sums of money move through nations and around the world at great speed through commodity speculations, currency markets, national stock exchanges, and the like.

4. *Mediascapes* involve both the electronic capability to produce and transmit information around the world and the images of the world that these media create and disseminate. Involved here are those who write "blogs" for the Internet, global filmmakers and film distributors, television stations (CNN and al-Jazeera are notable examples), and newspapers and magazines.

5. *Ideoscapes,* like mediascapes, are sets of images. However, they are largely restricted to political images produced by states and in line with their ideology, or to images and counterideologies produced by movements that seek to supplant those in power or at least to gain a piece of that power.

Three things are especially worth noting about Appadurai's landscapes. First, they can be seen as global process that are partly or wholly independent of any given nation-state. Second, global flows occur not only through the landscapes but also increasingly in and through the *disjunctures* among them. Thus, to give one example of such a disjuncture, the Japanese are open to ideas (ideoscapes, mediascapes) but notoriously closed to immigration (at least one of the ethnoscapes). More generally, the free movement of some landscapes may be at variance with blockages of others. Studies in this area must be attuned to such disjunctures and to their implications for globalization. Third, territories are going to be affected differently by the five landscapes and their disjunctures. This will lead to important differences among and between cultures. The focus on landscapes and their disjunctures points globalization studies in a set of unique directions. However, the focus on landscapes is in line with the idea that globalization is much more associated with heterogenization than homogenization, and globalization is much more associated with glocalization than grobalization.

Economic Theory

There are many theories about the economic aspects of globalization. The most important perspectives, at least in sociology, tend to be those associated with Marxian theory; they are neo-Marxian in nature. Two major examples are discussed in this section.

Transnational Capitalism

Leslie Sklair (2002) distinguishes between two systems of globalization. The first—the capitalist system of globalization—is the one that is now predominant. The other—the socialist system—is not yet in existence but is foreshadowed by current anti-globalization movements, especially those oriented toward greater human rights throughout the world. The antiglobalization movements, and the possibility of a socialist form, are made possible by the problems in the current system of globalization, especially class polarization and the increasing ecological unsustainability of capitalist globalization.

Although the nation-state remains important, Sklair focuses on transnational practices that are able to cut across boundaries—including those created by states—with the implication that territorial boundaries are of declining importance in capitalist globalization. As a Marxist, Sklair accords priority to economic transnational practices, and it is in this context that *transnational corporations*—one of the central aspects of his analysis—predominate. Underlying this emphasis on transnational corporations is the idea that capitalism has moved away from being an international system (because the nation[-state] is of declining significance) and toward becoming a globalizing system that is decoupled from any specific geographic territory or state.

The second transnational practice of great importance is political, and here the *transnational capitalist class* predominates. However, it is not made up of capitalists in the traditional Marxian sense of the term—that is, the transnational capitalist class does not necessarily own the means of production. Sklair differentiates among four "fractions" of the transnational capitalist class: (1) the *corporate fraction* made up of executives of transnational corporations and their local affiliates; (2) a *state fraction* composed of globalizing state and interstate bureaucrats and politicians; (3) a *technical fraction* made up of globalizing professionals; and (4) the *consumerist fraction* encompassing merchants and media executives. This is obviously a very different group than Marx thought of when conceptualizing the capitalist.

The transnational capitalist class may not be capitalist in a traditional sense of the term, but it is transnational in various ways. First, its "members" tend to share global (as well as local) interests. Second, they seek to exert various types of control across nations. That is, they exert economic control in the workplace, political control in both domestic and international politics, and culture-ideological control in everyday life across international borders. Third, they tend to share a global rather than a local perspective on a wide range of issues. Fourth, they come from many different countries, but increasingly they see themselves as citizens of the world and not just of their place of birth. Finally, wherever they may be at any given time, they share similar lifestyles, especially in terms of the goods and services they consume.

The third transnational practice is culture-ideology, and here Sklair accords great importance to the *culture-ideology of consumerism* in capitalist globalization. Although the focus is on culture and ideology, the emphasis on consumerism ultimately involves the economy by adding an interest in consumption to the traditional concern with production (and transnational corporations) in economic approaches in general and in Marxian theories in particular. In this realm the ability to exert ideological control over people scattered widely throughout the globe has increased dramatically, primarily through the greater reach and sophistication of advertising and the media and the bewildering array of consumer goods that are marketed by and through them. Ultimately, they all serve to create a global mood to consume that benefits transnational corporations, as well as advertising and media corporations, which are examples of such corporations and profit from them.

Ultimately, Sklair is interested in the relationship among the transnational practices and the institutions that dominate such practice, and he argues that transnational corporations utilize the transnational capitalist class to develop and solidify the consumerist culture and ideology that is increasingly necessary to feed the demands of the capitalist system of production. Indeed, it is this relationship that defines global capitalism today, and it is the most important force in ongoing changes in the world.

As a Marxist, Sklair is interested not only in critically analyzing capitalist globalization but in articulating an alternative to it and its abuses. He sees some promising signs in the protectionism of some countries that see themselves as exploited by transnational corporations. Also hopeful are new social movements such as the green movement seeking a more sustainable environment and the various antiglobalization groups that have sprung up in recent years. He is particularly interested in various human rights movements in which, he believes, can be found the seeds of the alternative to capitalist globalization—that is, socialist globalization. He predicts that these and other movements will gain momentum in the twenty-first century as they increasingly resist the ways in which globalization has been appropriated by transnational corporations. In fact, in good Marxian dialectical terms, he sees the success of capitalist globalization sowing the seeds of its own destruction as its expansion tends to provide its opponents with resources (derived from the economic success of transnational capitalism), organizational forms (copied from the successful organizations in global capitalism), and most obviously a clarity of purpose. As the transnational corporations grow more successful, their abuses will become more blatant, and the need to supplant them as the central players in the global system will intensify.

Empire

The most important and widely discussed and debated Marxian approach to globalization is Michael Hardt and Antonio Negri's *Empire* (2000; Passavant, 2012a) and *Multitude* (2004; Passavant, 2012b). Although Hardt and Negri have reservations about postmodern social theory, they analyze the postmodernization of the global economy. They associate modernity with *imperialism,* the defining characteristic of which is one or more nations at the center that control and exploit, especially economically, a number of areas throughout the world. In a postmodern move, Hardt and

Negri "decenter" this imperialism, thereby defining empire as a postmodern reality in which such dominance exists but no single nation (or any other entity) is at its center. To put this another way, *modern* sovereignty can be traced to a *place,* but in its *postmodern* form as empire, sovereignty exists in a nonplace. The empire has no center; it is deterritorialized; it exists only in the realm of ideas communicated through the media. And as a result, the spectacle of the empire is everywhere; it is omnipresent.

Empire does not yet exist fully. It is in formation at the moment, but we can get a sense of its parameters. Empire governs the world with a single logic of rule, but there is no single power at the heart of empire. Instead of a single source of command, in empire power is dispersed throughout society and the globe. Even the United States, in spite of its seeming hegemony in the world today, is not an empire in these terms, nor does it lie at the heart of Hardt and Negri's sense of an empire. However, the sovereignty of the United States does constitute an important precursor to empire, and the United States continues to occupy a privileged position in the world. However, it is being supplanted by empire.

Empire is (or will be) lacking in geographic or territorial boundaries. It also can be seen as lacking temporal boundaries in the sense that it seeks (albeit unsuccessfully) to suspend history and to exist for all eternity. It also can be seen as lacking a lower boundary in that it seeks to expand down into the depths of the social world. This means that it seeks not only to control the basics of the social world (thought, action, interaction, groups), but to go even further in an effort to use biopower to control human nature and population—*both* people's brains and their bodies. In a way, empire is far more ambitious than imperialism in that it seeks to control the entirety of life down to its most basic levels.

The key to the global power of empire lies in the fact that it is (or seeks to be) a new juridical power. It is based on such things as the constitution of order, norms, ethical truths, and a common notion of what is right. This juridical formation is the source of power of empire. Thus, in the name of what is "right," it can intervene anywhere in the world in order to deal with what it considers humanitarian problems, to guarantee accords, and to impose peace on those who may not want peace or even see the empire's goal as peace. More specifically, it can engage in "just wars" in the name of this juridical formation; the latter legitimates the former. Such wars become a kind of sacred undertaking. The enemy is anyone or anything that the juridical formation sees as a threat to ethical order in the world. Thus the right to engage in just war is seen as boundless, encompassing the entire space of civilization. The right to engage in just war also is seen as boundless in time; it is permanent, eternal. In a just war, ethically grounded military action is legitimate, and its goal is to achieve the desired order and peace. Thus empire is based not on force per se but on the ability to project force in the service of that which is right (precursors of this notion can be seen in the two U.S. invasions of Iraq, as well as the incursion into Afghanistan).

Empire is based on a triple imperative. First, it seeks to incorporate all that it can. It appears to be magnanimous, and it operates with a liberal facade. However, in the process of inclusion, it creates a smooth world in which differences, resistance, and conflict are eliminated. Second, empire differentiates and affirms differences. Although those who are different are celebrated culturally, they are set aside juridically.

Third, once the differences are in place, empire seeks to hierarchize and to manage the hierarchy and the differences embedded in it. It is hierarchization and management that is the real power of empire.

Empire is, then, a postmodern Marxian perspective on globalization and on the exertion of power around the world. However, instead of capitalists or capitalist nations exerting that power, it is the much more nebulous empire that is in control. If there are no more capitalists in empire, what about the proletariat? To Hardt and Negri, the time of the proletariat is over. But if the proletariat no longer exists to oppose empire, where is the opposition to come from? Operating from a Marxian perspective, Hardt and Negri must come up with an oppositional force, and they do not disappoint on this score and label the oppositional group the "multitude." This is an interesting choice of terms. For one thing it is much more general and abstract than "proletariat" and also moves us away from a limited focus on the economy. Second, it makes clear that there are lots of at least potential opponents of the empire; indeed, those in control in the empire constitute only a small minority vis-à-vis the multitude.

Hardt and Negri's *multitude* is that collection of people throughout the world that sustains empire in various ways, including but *not* restricted to its labor (it is the real productive force in empire). Among other ways, it also sustains it by buying into the culture-ideology of consumption and, more important, in actually consuming a variety of its offerings. Like capitalism and its relationship to the proletariat, empire is a parasite on the multitude and on its creativity and productivity. Like Marx's proletariat (which all but disappears in this theory), the multitude is a force for creativity in empire. Also like the proletariat, the multitude is capable of overthrowing empire through the autonomous creation of a counter-empire. The counter-empire, like empire, is, or would be, a global phenomenon created out of, and becoming, global flows and exchanges. Globalization leads to deterritorialization (the multitude itself is a force in deterritorialization and is deterritorialized), and deterritorialization is a prerequisite to the global liberation of the multitude. With deterritorialization, social revolution can, as Marx predicted, occur, perhaps for the first time, on a global level.

Hardt and Negri are certainly critics of globalization, whether it be modern capitalist imperialism or postmodern empire, but they also see a utopian potential in globalization. Thus, globalization per se is *not* the problem; instead, the problem is the form that has taken, or takes, in imperialism and empire. That utopian potential has always been present, but in the past it was smothered by modern sovereign powers through ideological control or military force. Empire now occupies, or soon will, that controlling position, but its need to suppress that potential is counterbalanced by the multitude's need to manifest and express it. Ultimately, there exists in globalization the potential for universal freedom and equality. Further, globalization prevents us from falling back into the particularism and isolationism that have characterized much of human history. Those processes, of course, would serve to impede the global change sought by the multitude. More positively, as globalization progresses, it serves to push us more and more in the direction of the creation of counter-empire. This focus on the global serves to distinguish Hardt and Negri from other postmodernists and post-Marxists, who tend to focus on the local and the problems and potential that exist there. In contrast, in their view, a focus on the local serves to obscure the fact that the sources of both our major problems and our liberation exist at the global level, in empire.

While Hardt and Negri foresee counter-empire, they, like Marx in the case of communism, offer no blueprint for how to get there or what counter-empire might look like. Like communism to Marx, counter-empire will arise out of actual practice (*praxis*), especially that of the multitude. Counter-empire must be global, it must be everywhere, and it must be opposed to empire. Counter-empire is made increasingly likely because empire is losing its ability to control the multitude. Thus, empire must redouble its efforts (e.g., through police power), and this serves to mobilize the multitude and make counter-empire more likely. As postmodernists, Hardt and Negri reject a focus on the agent of the type found in Marxian theory, specifically the centrality accorded to the proletarian revolutionary agent who is increasingly conscious of exploitation by capitalism. Instead, they focus on such nonagential, collective actions by the multitude as desertion, migration, and nomadism. In accord with their postmodern orientation and its focus on the body, Hardt and Negri urge a new "barbarism" involving new bodily forms of the kind that are now appearing in the realm of gender, sexuality, and aesthetic mutations (such as tattooing and body piercing). Such bodies are less likely to submit to external control and more likely to create a new life—the basis of counter-empire. Thus, the revolutionary force is not a conscious agent but new bodily, corporeal forms.

Although Hardt and Negri retain a Marxian interest in production, they do recognize a new world of production and work in which immaterial, intellectual, and communicative types of labor are increasingly central. Thus, control over individuals engaged in such work—a key element and increasing proportion of the multitude—is of increasing importance. However, although they are controlled through global communication and ideology (especially via the media), it is also through communication and ideology that the revolutionary potential of the multitude will be expressed. The key thing about communication is that it flows easily and effectively across the globe. This makes it easier for empire to exert control, to organize production globally, and to make its justification of itself and its actions immanent within that communication. Conversely, of course, it is also the mechanism by which the multitude can ultimately create counter-empire.

Political Theory

Several theories, more deeply rooted in political science than in sociology, deal with globalization. *International relations* (IR) focuses on the relations among and between nation-states (Clark, 2007; Elliott, 2012), which are viewed as distinct actors in the world, occupying well-defined territories, and as sovereign within their own borders. There is also an emphasis on a distinct and well-defined interstate system.

Within IR, *political realism* begins with the premise that international politics is based on power, organized violence, and ultimately war (Keohane and Nye, 2000). It assumes that nation-states are the predominant actors on the global stage; that they act as coherent units in the global arena; that force is not only a usable but an effective method by which nation-states wield power on the global stage; and that military issues are of utmost importance in world politics.

Complex interdependence sees nation-states as relating to one another through multiple channels, both formally and informally, and through normal channels and so-called back channels. Complex interdependence differs from realism in the importance accorded to these informal channels where, for example, entities other than the state, such as multinational corporations (MNCs), connect societies to one another. There is no clear hierarchy of interstate relationships, and it is certainly not the case that military issues always, or even often, predominate. Coalitions arise within and between nation-states on these issues. Conflict may or may not arise, and, if conflict arises, it varies greatly in degree of intensity. Complex interdependence tends to lead to the decline in, or even the disappearance of, the use of military force by one nation-state against other(s) within a given region or alliance, although military action may continue to occur outside that region or bloc. International organizations have only a minor role to play in the realist view of the world, but they play an expanded role from the perspective of complex interdependence. Such organizations bring together representatives from various countries, set agendas, serve as catalysts for the formation of coalitions, serve as arenas from which political initiatives arise, and are helpful to weak states in playing a larger role in the international arena. Thus the complex interdependence perspective continues to focus on relationships among nation-states, but it takes a much wider and broader view of the nature of those relationships.

A variety of positions at variance with IR and its derivatives offer fundamental challenges to it. Among these are a wide range of other scholars (e.g., Cerny, 1995, 2003, 2010) associated with IPE (international political economy). Among other things, they focus more on power and critique the state-centrism of IR, which ignores other entities with political and economic power, especially the corporation.

An overriding interest in the literature on globalization and politics is the fate of the nation-state in the age of globalization (Hershkovitz, 2012). Many see the nation-state as threatened by various global processes, especially global economic flows (Ohmae, 1996; Strange, 1996). Some argue that the state is now a minor player globally when compared to a huge and growing borderless global economy that nation-states are unable to control. Whereas nation-states once controlled markets, now markets often control nation-states.

A variety of other factors threaten the autonomy of the nation-state, including flows of information, illegal immigrants, new social movements, terrorists, criminals, drugs, money (including laundered money and other financial instruments), sex-trafficking, and much else. Many of these flows have been made possible by the development and continual refinement of technologies of all sorts. The nation-state also has been weakened by the growing power of global and transnational organizations (for example, the EU) that operate largely free of the control of nation-states. Another factor is the growth of global problems (AIDS, TB) that cannot be handled, or handled very well, by a nation-state operating on its own. A more specific historical factor is the end of the Cold War, which had been a powerful force in unifying, or at least holding together, some nation-states. One example is Yugoslavia and its dissolution with the end of the Cold War, but the main one, of course, is the dissolution of the Soviet Union into a number of independent nation-states (Russia, Ukraine, Georgia, etc.). Then there are "failed states" (e.g., Somalia) in which there is, in effect, no functioning national government as well as states in the process of breaking down (Boas and Jennings, 2007). Clearly, failed states and disintegrating states are in no position to adequately maintain their borders.

One way of summarizing much of this is to say that the nation-state has become increasingly *porous*. Although this seems to be supported by a great deal of evidence, the fact is that no nation-state has *ever* been able to control its borders completely (Bauman, 1992). Thus, it is not the porosity of the nation-state that is new but rather the dramatic *increase* in that porosity and of the kinds of flows able to pass through national borders.

Some critics contest these conclusions, stating that rumors of the demise of the nation-state are greatly exaggerated (Wolf, 2005), that the nation-state continues to be *the* major player on the global stage (Gilpin, 2001), that it retains at least some power in the face of globalization (Conley and Weiner, 2002), and that nation-states vary greatly in their efficacy in the face of globalization (Mann, 2007).

Some scholars see the role of the state not only enduring but increasing in the world today (Beland, 2008) because of four major sources of collective insecurity: terrorism, economic globalization leading to problems such as outsourcing and pressures toward downsizing, threats to national identity due to immigration, and the spread of global diseases such as AIDS. Further, the state may actually find it in its interest to exaggerate or even create dangers and thereby make its citizens more insecure. Prior to the 2003 war with Iraq, the U.S. and British governments both argued that Saddam Hussein had weapons of mass destruction (WMDs) that posed a direct threat to them. The United States even claimed that Iraq could kill millions by using offshore ships to lob canisters containing lethal chemical or biological material into American cities. The collective insecurity created by such outrageous claims helped foster public opinion in favor of invading Iraq and overthrowing Saddam Hussein.

The other side of this argument in support of the nation-state is that global processes of various kinds just are not as powerful as many believe. For example, global business pales in comparison to business *within* many countries, including the United States. For another, some question the porosity of the nation-state by pointing, for example, to the fact that migration to the United States and other countries has *declined* substantially since its heights in the late nineteenth and early twentieth centuries (Gilpin, 2001).

A related point is that it would be a mistake to see globalization simply as a threat to or a constraint on the nation-state; it can also be an *opportunity* for the nation-state (Conley and Weiner, 2002). For example, the demands of globalization were used as a basis to make needed changes (at least from a neoliberal point of view) in Australian society, specifically enabling it to move away from protectionism and in the direction of (neo-)liberalization, to transform state enterprises into private enterprises, and to streamline social welfare. The rhetoric of globalization, especially an exaggeration of it and its effects, was useful to those politicians who desired such changes. In other words, Australian politicians used globalization as an ideology in order to reform Australian society.

Neoliberalism

Neoliberalism is a theory particularly applicable to economics (especially to the market and to trade) and politics (especially to the need to limit the government's involvement in, and control over, the market and trade). It is an important theory in itself, but it also has strongly influenced other thinking and theorizing about both of those domains. This is especially the case with various neo-Marxian economic theories (see above) that are highly critical of neoliberalism.

A number of well-known scholars, especially economists (e.g., Milton Friedman), are associated with neoliberalism. We briefly examine some of the ideas of one neoliberal economist, William Easterly (2006a, 2006b), to provide a sense of this perspective from the point of view of one of its supporters.

Easterly is opposed to any form of collectivism and state planning, either as they were espoused and practiced in, for example, the Soviet Union or are today by the UN, other economists, and so on. Collectivism failed in the Soviet Union and, in Easterly's view, it will fail today. It will fail because it inhibits, if not destroys, freedom, and freedom, especially economic freedom, is highly correlated with economic success. This is the case because economic freedom allows for searches for success that are decentralized; such searches go the heart of the idea of a free market. Economic freedom and the free market are great favorites of neoliberal economists.

Easterly offers several advantages economic freedom provides that encourage economic success. First, it is extremely difficult to know in advance which economic actions will succeed and which will fail. Economic freedom permits a multitude of actions, and those that fail are weeded out. Over time, what remains, in the main, are the successful actions, and they serve to facilitate a higher standard of living. Central planners can never have nearly as much knowledge as myriad individuals seeking success and learning from their failures and from those of others. Second, markets offer continuous feedback on which actions are succeeding and failing; central planners lack such feedback. Third, economic freedom leads to the ruthless reallocation of resources to those actions that are succeeding; central planners often have vested interests that prevent such a reallocation. Fourth, economic freedom permits large and rapid increases in scale by financial markets and corporate organizations; central planners lack the flexibility to make large-scale changes rapidly. Finally, because of sophisticated contractual protections, individuals and corporations are willing to take great risks; central planners are risk averse because of their personal vulnerability if things go wrong.

Created by John Locke (1632–1704), Adam Smith (1723–1790), and others, classical *liberal theory* came to be termed neoliberalism, at least by some, as a result of developments in the 1930s (Fourcade-Gourinchas and Babb, 2002). The term *neoliberalism* involves a combination of the political commitment to individual liberty and *neo*classical economics, which is devoted to the free market and opposed to state intervention in that market (Harvey, 2005). Entrepreneurs are to be liberated, markets and trade are to be free, states are to be supportive of this and to keep interventions to a minimum, and there are to be strong property rights.

Neoliberalism emerged during the Depression era, at least in part in reaction to Keynesian economics and its impact on the larger society. Inspired by the then-predominant theories of John Maynard Keynes (1883–1946), market, entrepreneurs, and corporations came to be limited by a number of constraints (social and political) and a strong regulative environment. Calls for a revitalization of liberal ideas also were spurred by the need to counter the collectivism (Marxian theory) that dominated much thinking and many political systems in the early twentieth century.

The intellectual leaders of this revitalization were economists, especially members of the Austrian school, including Friedrich van Hayek (1899–1992) and Ludwig von Mises (1881–1973). An organization devoted to liberal ideas—the Mont Pelerin Society (MPS)—was created in 1947. Its members were alarmed by the expansion of collectivist socialism (especially in, and sponsored by, the Soviet Union) and the aggressive intervention by liberal governments in the market (e.g., Franklin Roosevelt's "New Deal"). Those associated with MPS, especially the famous and highly influential Chicago economist Milton Friedman (1912–2006), played a key role in efforts to protect traditional liberal ideas, to develop neoliberal theory, and to sponsor their utilization by countries throughout the world.

Neoliberalism comes in various forms, but all are undergirded by some or all of the following ideas (Antonio, 2007a; for a critique of the kind of generalizations about neoliberalism to follow, see Collier, 2011):

- Great faith is placed in the *free market* and its rationality. The market needs to be allowed to operate free of any impediments, especially those imposed by the nation-state and other political entities. The free operation of the market will, in the "long run," advantage just about everyone and bring about both improved economic welfare and greater individual freedom (and a democratic political system). To achieve that end, it is important to champion, support, and expand a wide range of technological, legal, and institutional arrangements that support the market and its freedom. The free market is so important that neoliberals equate it with capitalism. Further, the principles of the free market are not restricted to the economy (and the polity); transactions in every sphere of life (family, education, culture) *should* also be free.
- The key, if not only, actor in the market is the *individual;* neoliberalism is radically individualistic.
- Related to the belief in the free market is a parallel belief in *free trade.*
- Where there are restraints on the free market and free trade, *deregulation* should be pursued to limit or eliminate such restraints. Free markets and free trade are linked to a *democratic political system.* Thus the political system, especially the freedom of democracy, is associated with economic well-being and with the freedom of individuals to amass great individual wealth.
- There is a commitment to *low taxes* and to *tax cuts* (especially for the wealthy whose taxes are deemed too high and too burdensome). Low taxes and tax cuts are believed to stimulate the economy by encouraging people to earn more and ultimately to invest and to spend more.
- *Tax cuts for business and industry* are encouraged with the idea that they would use the tax savings to invest more in their operations and

infrastructure, thereby generating more business, income, and profits. This is seen as benefiting not only business and industry but society as whole. Higher profits would "trickle down" and benefit most people in society.

- Spending on *welfare should be minimized* and the *safety net* for the poor should be *greatly reduced* because these policies hurt economic growth and even harm the poor. Cuts in welfare are designed to reduce government expenditures and allow government to cut taxes or to invest in more "productive" undertakings. Without the safety net, more poor people will be forced to find work, often at minimum wage or with low pay, which will enable companies to increase productivity and profits. Reduction of the safety net also creates a larger "reserve army" that business can draw on in good economic times to expand its workforce.

- There is a strong and generalized belief in *limited government* because no government or government agency can do things as well as the market (the failure of the Soviet Union is seen as proof of that). Among other things, this leaves government at least theoretically less able, or unable, to intervene in the market. It also presumably means a less expensive government, one that would need to collect less in taxes. This, in turn, puts more money in the hands of the public, especially the wealthier members of society who, in recent years, have benefited most from tax cuts. The state must be limited, and its job is to cooperate with open global markets.

- There is great belief in the need for the *global capitalist system to continue to expand.* It is presumed that such expansion would bring with it increased prosperity (but for which members of society?) and decreased poverty.

Most of these ideas focus on the neoliberal economy, but a few ideas apply to the closely linked neoliberal state (Harvey, 2006). More concretely and directly, the neoliberal state should:

- Provide a climate supportive of business and its ability to accumulate capital. This should be done even if certain actions (e.g., raising interest rates by the Federal Reserve) lead to higher unemployment for the larger population.

- Focus on furthering, facilitating, and stimulating (where necessary) the interests of business. This is done in the belief that business success will benefit everyone, but many believe that neoliberalism has benefited comparatively few people and areas of the world.

- Privatize sectors formerly run by the state (e.g., education, telecommunications, transportation) to open these areas for business and profit-making and ensure that those sectors that cannot be privatized are "cost effective" and "accountable."

- Work to allow the free movement of capital among and between economic sectors and geographic regions.

- Extol the virtues of free competition, although it is widely believed that the state actually works in support of the monopolization of markets by business interests.

- Work against groups (e.g., unions, social movements) that operate to restrain business interests and their efforts to accumulate capital.

- Reduce barriers to the free movement of capital across national borders and to the creation of new markets.
- Bail out financial institutions when they are in danger of collapse (for example, as was done in 2008–2009 for Bear Stearns, AIG, Citibank, and others).

Overall, critics argue that the neoliberal state favors elites but seeks to conceal that fact by seeming to be democratic; in fact, it is in the eyes of many deeply antidemocratic as the emphasis on freedom and liberty is largely restricted to the market.

Contrary to the established view, neoliberalism has not made the state irrelevant. Rather, the institutions and practices of the state have been transformed to better attune them to the needs and interests of the neoliberal market and economy.

However, the neoliberal state is riddled with internal contradictions. For one thing, its authoritarianism coexists uncomfortably with its supposed interest in individual freedom and democracy. For another, although committed to stability, its operations, especially in support of financial (and other) speculation, lead to increased instability. Although overtly committed to competition, it operates on behalf of monopolization. Most generally, there is the contradiction that its public support for the well-being of everyone is given the lie by its actions in support of economic elites.

Critiquing Neoliberalism

The Early Thinking of Karl Polanyi

Much of the contemporary critique of neoliberalism, especially as it relates to economics, can be traced to the work of Karl Polanyi (1886–1964), especially his 1944 book, *The Great Transformation: The Political and Economic Origins of Our Time.* He is the great critic of a limited focus on the economy, especially the focus of economic liberalism on the self-regulating or unregulated market, as well as on basing all on self-interest. In his view, these are not universal principles but rather were unprecedented developments associated with the advent of capitalism. Polanyi (1944) shows that the laissez-faire system came into existence with the help of the state, and it was able to continue to function as a result of state actions. Furthermore, if the laissez-faire system was left to itself, it threatened to destroy society. Indeed, it was such threats, as well as real dangers, that led to counterreactions by society and the state (e.g., socialism, communism, the New Deal) to protect themselves from the problems of a free market, especially protection of the products of, and those who labored in, it (Munck, 2002). Expansion of the laissez-faire market and the self-protective reaction against it by the state and society is called the *double movement* (D. Hall, 2007). Economic liberalism saw such counterreactions (including any form of protectionism) as "mistakes" that disrupted the operation of the markets, but Polanyi saw them as necessary and desirable reactions to the evils of the free market. Polanyi believed that the self-regulating market was an absurd idea. He derided the liberal idea that socialists, communists, New Dealers, and so on were involved in a conspiracy against liberalism and the free market. Rather than being a conspiracy, what took place was a natural, "spontaneous," collective reaction by society and its various elements that were threatened by the free market. In his time, Polanyi saw a reversal of the tendency for the economic system to dominate society. This promised to end the evils produced by the dominance of the free market system, and also to produce *more*, rather than less, freedom. That is, Polanyi believed that collective planning and control would produce more freedom for all than was then available in the liberal economic system.

It is interesting to look back on Polanyi's ideas with the passage of more than sixty years and especially with the rise of a global economy dominated by the kind of free market system he so feared and despised. Polanyi's hope lay with society and the nation-state, but they have been rendered far less powerful with the rise of globalization, especially the global economy. Very telling here is Margaret Thatcher's (in)famous statement: "there is no such thing as society."[2] Without powerful social and political influences, the excesses of the market cannot be contained. Clearly, such planning and control are more inadequate than ever in the global age. Beyond that, one wonders whether truly global planning and control is either possible or desirable. Nevertheless, were he alive today, it is likely that the logic of Polanyi's position would lead him to favor global planning and control because of his great fears of a free market economy, now far more powerful and dangerous because it exists on a global scale.

The great global economic crisis of 2007–2008 underscores the importance of Polanyi's ideas. The market had experienced unprecedented freedom; restraints on it turned out to be limited or nonexistent. The result was a series of excesses (mortgage loans to those who should not have qualified for them; excessively risky undertakings by financial institutions; financial instruments that were opaque [e.g., "derivatives"] and that diffused responsibility for bad loans [mortgage-backed securities], etc.) that led to the collapse of the American housing market, the credit crunch, and eventually a global economic meltdown. Polanyi would have said that the cause of all of this was a lack of state control over the market. In fact, in the wake of the crisis, we are witnessing a resurfacing of interest in regulating the market and the economy.

(More) Contemporary Criticisms of Neoliberalism

Among the problems with neoliberalism is the fact that it assumes that everyone in the world wants very narrow and specific types of economic well-being (to be well-off economically, if not rich) and political freedom (democracy). In fact, there are great cultural differences in the ways well-being (e.g., to not have to work very hard) and freedom (e.g., to be unfettered by the state even if it is not democratically chosen) are defined. Neoliberalism very often comes down to the United States and a few global organizations (e.g., International Monetary Fund) seeking to impose *their* definitions of well-being and freedom on peoples in other parts of the world.

In addition, neoliberalism conceals or obscures the social and material interests of those who push such an economic system with its associated technological, legal, and institutional systems. These ends are *not* being pursued because everyone in the world wants them or will benefit from them, but because *some*, usually in the north, are greatly advantaged by them and therefore push them.

---

[2] For the full text of the speech, go to www.margaretthatcher.org/speeches.

Among the other criticisms of neoliberalism are the fact that it has produced financial crises in various countries throughout the world (e.g., Mexico, Argentina), its economic record has been dismal in that it has redistributed wealth (from poor to rich) rather than generating new wealth, it has sought to commodify *everything*, and it has helped to degrade the environment (Harvey, 2005). Furthermore, there are signs that it is failing (deficit financing in the United States and China), signs of more immediate crisis (burgeoning budget deficits, the bailout of financial institutions), and evidence that U.S. global hegemony is crumbling.

The Death of Neoliberalism?

It is arguable that the recent and ongoing economic crisis will spell the beginning of the end of neoliberalism. In a speech in late 2008, French President Sarkozy said: "The idea of the absolute power of the markets that should not be constrained by any rule, by any political intervention, was a mad idea. The idea that markets are always right was a mad idea." Referring implicitly to the global economic system dominated to that point by neoliberalism, Sarkozy argued that "we need to rebuild the whole world financial and monetary system from scratch." In other words, we need to scuttle the remnants of the global neoliberal economic system, just as the Keynesian system was scuttled as neoliberalism gained ascendancy, and replace it with some as yet undefined alternative. Where and how far this goes remains to be seen, but believers in neoliberalism have not disappeared, and their ideas, perhaps in some new form, are likely to resurface when the dust of the recent economic crisis settles.

Other Theories

This chapter gives only a sense of a few of the types of theorizing about globalization. There are many other well-known theories of globalization—for example, ones that draw on network theory (Castells, 1996, 1997, 1998; see Chapter 14) and complexity theory (Urry, 2003), or that focus on religion, sport, or the city. However, the preceding conveys at least a sense of the most important broad types of theorizing on, and specific theories of, globalization. Of course, the process of globalization continues, is expanding, and is constantly changing. As a result, we can expect the continuing development of theorizing about globalization, including new and innovative approaches to the topic.

Summary

Globalization theory emerged as a result of developments and changes both in the world as a whole and in academia. Globalization can be analyzed culturally, economically, politically, and institutionally. A concern for homogenization/heterogenization cuts across work in all of these areas. Central to the work of Giddens on globalization is losing control over the juggernaut of modernity and creating a runaway world. Beck sees hope in globality with the decline of the nation-state and the emergence of transnational organizations and possibly a transnational state. To Bauman, what defines the global world is a "space war" between those who have and those who do not have mobility. However, even those with mobility face grave problems.

Cultural theories of globalization may be divided into three paradigms: cultural differentialism, cultural convergence, and cultural hybridization. Cultural differentialism adopts the view that there are lasting differences among and between cultures and that those differences are largely unaffected by globalization. Huntington offers the best-known example of cultural differentialism with his focus on civilizations, the major civilizations of the world, and the likelihood of economic conflict between Sinic and Western civilization and warfare between Islamic and Western civilization. Cultural convergence takes the view that globalization is leading to increasing sameness around the world. Two examples of cultural convergence are the McDonaldization thesis and the idea that the world is increasingly dominated by the "grobalization" of nothing. Cultural hybridization adopts the perspective that globalization is bringing with it the mixing of cultures, producing new and unique cultures that are not reducible to either global or local. A number of theoretical ideas are associated with cultural hybridization, including glocalization, hybridization, and creolization. A major theory included under the "cultural hybridization" heading is Appadurai's thinking on landscapes and the disjunctures among and between them.

Economic theories of globalization are illustrated with two examples. Leslie Sklair develops a neo-Marxian economic theory of globalization that focuses on transnational capitalism, especially transnational corporations, the transnational capitalist class, and the culture-ideology of consumption. Sklair argues that transnational capitalism is providing the basis for the emergence of socialist globalization. According to Hardt and Negri, we are in the midst of a transition from capitalist imperialism to the dominance of empire. Empire lacks a center and is based on juridical power. The multitude sustains empire, but it also has, at least potentially, the power to overthrow empire and create counter-empire.

International relations theory encompasses various political approaches to globalization, including political realism, complex interdependence, and international political economy. Much of this discussion centers on the fate of the nation-state in the global age. The chapter closes with a detailed discussion of neoliberalism, which is important in both economic and political thinking on globalization. The fundamental tenets of neoliberalism are discussed, as are the major criticisms (including those of Karl Polanyi).

Structuralism, Poststructuralism, and Postmodern Social Theory

Chapter Outline

Structuralism

Poststructuralism

Postmodern Social Theory

Criticisms and Post-Postmodern Social Theory

This book is largely about *modern* social theory. However, in the latter half of the twentieth century there arose a significant challenge to the modern approach to social theory. This *postmodern* approach to theory developed in fields as diverse as art, architecture, literature, sociology, and others. The implication is not only that these things come after the modern, but that there were problems with the modern that the postmodernists were pointing out and endeavoring to deal with. While in North America, the interest in and development of postmodern theory reached its height in the 1980s and 1990s, postmodernism has had a clear impact on the development of social theory in general. In this chapter we discuss the main postmodern theories and consider the continuing significance of these perspectives.

In discussing postmodern social theory it is necessary to shift our focus from *sociological* theories to *social* theories. *Sociological* theories tend to reflect developments that have occurred largely within sociology and that are of interest mainly to sociologists. *Social* theories tend to be multidisciplinary. The distinction between the two, however, is not clear-cut. In fact, at least some of the theories discussed earlier in this book, especially the neo-Marxian and agency-structure theories, might be better described as social theories. In any case, it is clear that postmodern theories are best viewed as social theories.

In this chapter, we deal with the emergence of what, in fact, does come after modern social theory by tracing the line of development from structuralism to poststructuralism and ultimately to what has come to be known as postmodern social theory. Following Lash (1991:ix), we take "the structuralism which swept through French social thought in the 1960s" as the starting point for the emergence of poststructuralism and postmodernism.

Structuralism was a reaction against French humanism, especially the existentialism of Jean-Paul Sartre (Craib and Wernick, 2005; Margolis, 2007). In his early work Sartre focused on the individual, especially individual freedom At that point he adhered to the view that what people do is determined by them and not by social laws or larger social structures. However, later in his career Sartre was more drawn to Marxian theory, and while he continued to focus on the "free individual," that individual was now "situated in a massive and oppressive social structure which limits and alienates his activities" (Craib, 1976:9).

In her analysis of Sartre's work, Gila Hayim (1980) sees continuity between his early and his late work. In *Being and Nothingness,* published in 1943, Sartre focuses more on the free individual and takes the view that "existence is defined by and through one's acts. . . . *One is what one does*" (Hayim, 1980:3). At the same time, Sartre attacks the structuralist view of "objective structures as completely deterministic of behavior" (Hayim, 1980:5). For Sartre and existentialists in general, actors have the capacity to go beyond the present, to move toward the future. For Sartre, then, people are free; they are responsible for everything they do; they have no excuses. In some senses, these "staggering responsibilities of freedom" (Hayim, 1980:17) are a tremendous source of anguish to people. In other senses, this responsibility is a source of optimism to people—their fates are in their hands. In the *Critique of Dialectical Reason,* published in 1963, Sartre devotes more attention to social structures, but even here he emphasizes the "human prerogative for transcendence—the surpassing of the given" (Hayim, 1980:16). Sartre is critical of various Marxists (structural Marxists) who overemphasize the role and place of social structure. "Dogmatic Marxists have, by Sartre's view, eliminated the humanistic component of Marx's original idea" (Hayim, 1980:72). As an existentialist, Sartre *always* retained this humanism. It is against the backdrop of the humanism of existentialism that one must see the rise of structuralism, poststructuralism, and postmodernism.

Structuralism

Structuralism obviously involves a focus on structures, but they are not in the main the same structures that concern the structural functionalists (see Chapter 7). While the latter and indeed most sociologists are concerned with *social* structures, of primary concern to structuralists are *linguistic* structures. This shift from social to linguistic structures is what has come to be known as the *linguistic turn,* which dramatically altered the nature of the social sciences (Lash, 1991:ix). The focus of a good many social scientists shifted from social structure to language (see, for example, the earlier discussions of Habermas's work on communication [in Chapter 8] and the conversation analyses of some ethnomethodologists [in Chapter 10]) or more generally to signs of various sorts.

Roots in Linguistics

Structuralism emerged from diverse developments in various fields (Dosse, 1998). The source of modern structuralism and its strongest bastion to this day is linguistics. The work of the Swiss linguist Ferdinand de Saussure (1857–1913) stands out in the development of structural linguistics and, ultimately, structuralism in various other fields (Culler, 1976; Thibault, 2005a). Of particular interest to us is Saussure's differentiation between *langue* and *parole,* which was to have enormous significance. *Langue* is the formal, grammatical system of language. It is a system of phonic elements whose relationships are governed, Saussure and his followers believed, by determinate laws. Much of linguistics since Saussure's time has been oriented to the discovery of those laws. The existence of *langue* makes *parole* possible (Bakker, 2007b). *Parole* is actual speech, the way speakers use language to express themselves. Although Saussure recognized the significance of people's use of language in subjective and often idiosyncratic ways, he believed that the individual's use of language cannot be the concern of the scientifically oriented linguist. Such a linguist must look at *langue,* the formal system of language, not at the subjective ways in which it is used by actors.

Langue, then, can be viewed as a system of signs—a structure—and the meaning of each sign is produced by the relationship among signs within the system. Especially important here are relations of difference, including binary oppositions. Thus, for example, the meaning of the word *hot* comes not from some intrinsic properties of the word but from the word's relationship with, its binary opposition to, the word *cold.* Meanings, the mind, and ultimately the social world are shaped by the structure of language. Thus, instead of an existential world of people shaping their surroundings, we have here a world in which people, as well as other aspects of the social world, are shaped by the structure of language.

The concern for structure has been extended beyond language to the study of all sign systems. This focus on the structure of sign systems has been labeled "semiotics" and has attracted many followers (Gottdiener, 1994; Hawkes, 1977; Thibault, 2005b). *Semiotics* is broader than structural linguistics because it encompasses not only language but also other sign and symbol systems, such as facial expressions, body language, literary texts, indeed all forms of communication.

Roland Barthes (Perry, 2007) often is seen as the true founder of semiotics. Barthes extended Saussure's ideas to all areas of social life. Not only language but also social behaviors are representations, or signs: "Not just language, but wrestling matches are also signifying practices, as are TV shows, fashions, cooking and just about everything else in everyday life" (Lash, 1991:xi). The "linguistic turn" came to encompass all social phenomena, which, in turn, came to be reinterpreted as signs.

Anthropological Structuralism: Claude Lévi-Strauss

A central figure in French structuralism—Kurzweil (1980:13) calls him "the father of structuralism"—is the French anthropologist Claude Lévi-Strauss (I. Rossi, 2005). Although structure takes various forms in Lévi-Strauss's work, what is important for our purposes is that he can be seen as extending Saussure's work on language to anthropological issues—for example, to myths in primitive societies. However, Lévi-Strauss also applied structuralism more broadly to all forms of communication. His major innovation was to reconceptualize a wide array of social phenomena (for instance, kinship systems) as systems of communication, thereby making them amenable to structural analyses. The exchange of spouses, for example, can be analyzed in the same way as the exchange of words; both are social exchanges that can be studied through the use of structural anthropology.

We can illustrate Lévi-Strauss's (1967) thinking with the example of the similarities between linguistic systems and kinship systems. First, terms used to describe kinship, like phonemes in language, are basic units of analysis to the structural anthropologist. Second, neither the kinship terms nor the phonemes have meaning in themselves. Instead, both acquire meaning only when they are integral parts of a larger system. Lévi-Strauss even used a system of binary oppositions in his anthropology (for example, the raw and the cooked) much like those employed by Saussure in linguistics. Third, Lévi-Strauss admitted that there is empirical variation from setting to setting in both phonemic and kinship systems, but even these variations can be traced to the operation of general, although implicit, laws.

All of this is very much in line with the linguistic turn, but Lévi-Strauss ultimately went off in a number of directions that are at odds with that turn. Most important, he argued that both phonemic systems and kinship systems are the products of the structures of the mind. However, they are not the products of a conscious process. Instead, they are the products of the unconscious, logical structure of the mind. These systems, as well as the logical structure of the mind from which they are derived, operate on the basis of general laws. Most of those who have followed the linguistic turn have not followed Lévi-Strauss in the direction of defining the underlying structure of the mind as the most fundamental structure.

Structural Marxism

Another variant of structuralism that enjoyed considerable success in France (and many other parts of the world) was structuralist Marxism (Lechte, 2005), especially the work of Louis Althusser (K. Tucker, 2007), Nicos Poulantzas, and Maurice Godelier.

Although we have presented the case that modern structuralism began with Saussure's work in linguistics, there are those who argue that it started with the work of Karl Marx: "When Marx assumes that structure is not to be confused with visible relations and explains their hidden logic, he inaugurates the modern structuralist tradition" (Godelier, 1972b:336). Although structural Marxism and structuralism in general are both interested in "structures," each field conceptualizes structure differently.

At least some structural Marxists share with structuralists an interest in the study of structure as a prerequisite to the study of history. As Maurice Godelier said, "The study of the internal functioning of a structure must precede and illuminate the study of its genesis and evolution" (1972b:343). In another work, Godelier said, "The inner *logic* of these systems must be analyzed *before* their *origin* is analyzed" (1972a:xxi). Another view shared by structuralists and structural Marxists is that structuralism should be concerned with the structures, or systems, that are formed out of the interplay of social relations. Both schools see structures as real (albeit invisible), although they differ markedly on the nature of the structure that they consider real. For Lévi-Strauss the focus is on the structure of the mind, whereas for structural Marxists it is on the underlying structure of society.

Perhaps most important, both structuralism and structural Marxism reject empiricism and accept a concern for underlying invisible structures. Godelier argued: "What both structuralists and Marxists reject are the empiricist definitions of what constitutes a social structure" (1972a:xviii). Godelier also made this statement:

> For Marx as for Lévi-Strauss a structure is *not* a reality that is *directly* visible, and so directly observable, but a *level of reality* that exists *beyond* the visible relations between men, and the functioning of which constitutes the underlying logic of the system, the subjacent order by which the apparent order is to be explained.
>
> (Godelier, 1972a:xix)

Godelier went even further and argued that such a pursuit defines all science: "What is visible is a *reality* concealing *another,* deeper reality, which is hidden and the discovery of which is the very purpose of scientific cognition" (1972a:xxiv).

In spite of these similarities, structural Marxism did not in the main participate in the linguistic turn then taking place in the social sciences. For example, the focal concern continued to be social and economic, not linguistic, structures. Moreover, structural Marxism continued to be associated with Marxian theory, and many French social thinkers were becoming at least as impatient with Marxian theory as they were with existentialism.

Poststructuralism

Although it is impossible to pinpoint such a transition with any precision, Charles Lemert (1990) traces the beginning of poststructuralism to a 1966 speech by Jacques Derrida, one of the acknowledged leaders of this approach (Lipscomb, 2007; J. Phillips, 2005), in which he proclaimed the dawning of a new poststructuralist age. In contrast to the structuralists, especially those who followed the linguistic turn and who saw people as being constrained by the structure of language, Derrida reduced language to "writing" that does not constrain its subjects. Furthermore, Derrida also saw social institutions as nothing but writing and therefore as unable to constrain people. In contemporary terms, Derrida deconstructed language and social institutions (Trifonas, 1996), and when he had finished, all he found there was writing. While there is still a focus here on language, writing is *not* a structure that constrains people. Furthermore, while the structuralists saw order and stability in the language system, Derrida sees language as disorderly and unstable. Different contexts give words different meanings. As a result, the language system cannot have the constraining power over people that the structuralists think it does. Furthermore, it is impossible for scientists to search for the underlying laws of language. Thus, Derrida offers what is ultimately a subversive, deconstructive perspective. As we will see, subversion and deconstruction become even more important with the emergence of postmodernism, and it is poststructuralism that laid the groundwork for postmodernism.

The object of Derrida's hostility is the *logocentrism* (the search for a universal system of thought that reveals what is true, right, beautiful, and so on) that has dominated Western social thought. This approach has contributed to what Derrida describes as the "historical repression and suppression of writing since Plato"

(1978:196). Logocentrism has led to the closure not only of philosophy, but also to that of the human sciences. Derrida is interested in deconstructing, or "dismantling," the sources of this closure—this repression—thereby freeing writing from the things that enslave it. An apt phrase to describe Derrida's focus is "the deconstruction of logocentrism" (1978:230). More generally, *deconstruction* involves the decomposition of unities in order to uncover hidden differences (D. N. Smith, 1996:208).

A good concrete example of Derrida's thinking is his discussion of what he calls the "theatre of cruelty." He contrasts this concept with the traditional theater, which he sees as dominated by a system of thought that he calls representational logic (a similar logic has dominated social theory). That is, what takes place on the stage "represents" what takes place in "real life," as well as the expectations of writers, directors, and so on. This "representationalism" is the theater's god, and it renders the traditional theater theological. A theological theater is a controlled, enslaved theater:

> The stage is theological for as long as its structure, following the entirety of tradition, comports the following elements: an author-creator who, absent and from afar, is armed with a text and keeps watch over, assembles, regulates the time or the meaning of representation. . . . He lets representation represent him through representatives, directors or actors, *enslaved* interpreters . . . who . . . more or less directly represent the thought of the "creator." *Interpretive slaves* who faithfully execute the providential designs of the "master." . . . Finally, the theological stage comports a *passive*, seated public, a public of spectators, of consumers, of enjoyers.
> (Derrida, 1978:235; italics added)

Derrida envisions an alternative stage (an alternative society?) in which "speech will cease to govern the stage" (1978:239). That is, the stage no longer will be governed by, for example, authors and texts. The actors will no longer take dictation; the writers will no longer be the dictators of what transpires on the stage. However, this does not mean that the stage will become anarchic. While Derrida is not crystal clear on his alternative stage, we get a hint when he discusses the "construction of a stage whose clamor has not yet been pacified into words" (1978:240). Or, "the theatre of cruelty would be the art of difference and of expenditure without economy, without reserve, without return, without history" (Derrida, 1978:247).

It is clear that Derrida is calling for a radical deconstruction of the traditional theater. More generally, he is implying a critique of society in general, which is in the thrall of logocentrism. Just as he wants to free the theater from the dictatorship of the writer, he wants to see society free of the ideas of all the intellectual authorities who have created the dominant discourse. In other words, Derrida wants to see us all be free to be writers.

Implied here is another well-known concern of the poststructuralists (and postmodernists): *decentering.* In a sense, Derrida wants the theater to move away from its traditional "center," its focus on writers (the authorities) and their expectations, and to give the actors more free play. This point, too, can be generalized to society as a whole. Derrida associates the center with *the* answer and therefore ultimately with death. The center is linked with the absence of that which is essential to Derrida:

"play and difference"[1] (1978:297). Theater or society without play and difference—that is, static theater or society—can be seen as being dead. In contrast, a theater or a world without a center would be infinitely open, ongoing, and self-reflexive. Derrida concludes that the future "is neither to be awaited nor to be refound" (1978:300). His point is that we are not going to find the future in the past, nor should we passively await our fate. Rather, the future is to be found, is being made, is being written, in what we are doing.

Having debunked Western logocentrism and intellectual authority, in the end Derrida leaves us without an answer; in fact, there is *no* single answer (Cadieux, 1995). The search for the answer, the search for Logos, has been destructive and enslaving. All we are left with is the process of writing, of acting, with play and with difference.

The Ideas of Michel Foucault

Although Derrida is an extremely important poststructuralist, the most important thinker associated with this approach is Michel Foucault (Smart, 2000; Venn. 2011). Foucault's work illustrates yet another difference between poststructuralism and structuralism. While structuralism was overwhelmingly influenced by linguistics, Foucault's approach, and poststructuralism more generally, shows a variety of theoretical inputs (Smart, 1985). This variety makes Foucault's work provocative and difficult to handle. Furthermore, the ideas are not simply adopted from other thinkers but are transformed as they are integrated into Foucault's unusual theoretical orientation. Thus, Weber's theory of rationalization has an impact, but to Foucault it is found only in certain "key sites," and it is not an "iron cage"; there is always resistance. Marxian ideas (Smart, 1983) are found in Foucault's work, but Foucault does not restrict himself to the economy; he focuses on a range of institutions. He is more interested in the "micro-politics of power" than in the traditional Marxian concern with power at the societal level. He practices hermeneutics in order to better understand the social phenomena of concern to him. Moreover, Foucault has no sense of some deep, ultimate truth; there are simply ever more layers to be peeled away. There is a phenomenological influence, but Foucault rejects the idea of an autonomous, meaning-giving subject. There is a strong element of structuralism but no formal rule-governed model of behavior. Finally, and perhaps most important, Foucault adopts Nietzsche's interest in the relationship between power and knowledge, but that link is analyzed much more sociologically by Foucault. This multitude of theoretical inputs is one of the reasons Foucault is thought of as a poststructuralist.

There is yet another sense in which Foucault's work is clearly poststructuralist. That is, in his early work Foucault was heavily influenced by structuralism, but as his work progressed, that influence declined and other inputs moved his theory in a variety of other directions. Let us look at the evolution of Foucault's work.

Two ideas are at the core of Foucault's methodology—"archaeology of knowledge" (Foucault, 1966) and "genealogy of power" (Foucault, 1969; Valverde, 2007).

---

[1] Difference, or *différence,* another key concept to Derrida, involves the idea that to understand something we must grasp the way it relates to other things (Ramji, 2007).

Although there is a sense in his work that the latter succeeds the former, Mitchell Dean (1994) has made a convincing case that the two coexist and mutually support one another in his substantive work.

Alan Sheridan (1980:48) contends that Foucault's archaeology of knowledge (Scheurich and McKenzie, 2007) involves a search for "a set of rules that determine the conditions of possibility for all that can be said within the particular discourse at any given time." To put it another way, archaeology is the search for the "general system of the formation and transformation of statements [into discursive formations]" (Dean, 1994:16). The search for such a "general system," or such "rules," as well as the focus on *discourse* (Lemert, 2005b)—spoken and written "documents"—reflects the early influence of structuralism on Foucault's work. In analyzing these documents, Foucault does not seek to "understand" them as would a hermeneuticist. Rather, Foucault's archaeology "organises the document, divides it up, distributes it, orders, arranges it in levels, establishes series, distinguishes between what is relevant and what is not, discovers elements, defines unities, describes relations" (Dean, 1994:15). Discourse and the documents it produces are to be analyzed, described, and organized; they are irreducible and not subject to interpretation seeking some "deeper" level of understanding. Also ruled out by Foucault is the search for origins; it is the documents themselves that are important, not their point of origination.

Foucault is particularly interested in those discourses "that seek to rationalise or systematise themselves in relation to particular ways of 'saying the true'" (Dean, 1994:32). As we will see, this concern leads him in the direction of the study of discourses that relate to the formation of human sciences such as psychology. Archaeology is able to distance and detach itself from "the norms and criteria of validity of established sciences and disciplines in favour of the internal intelligibility of the ensembles so located, their conditions of emergence, existence, and transformation" (Dean, 1994:36).

The concern for "saying the truth" relates directly to Foucault's genealogy of power because, as Foucault comes to see it, knowledge and power are inextricably intertwined (Foucault is here heavily indebted to the philosophy of Nietzsche [Fuller, 2007b; Lemert, 2005a]). Genealogy is a very distinctive type of intellectual history, "a way of linking historical contents into organised and ordered *trajectories* that are neither the simple unfolding of their origins nor the necessary realisation of their ends. It is a way of analysing multiple, open-ended, heterogeneous trajectories of discourses, practices, and events, and of establishing their patterned relationships, without recourse to regimes of truth that claim pseudo-naturalistic laws or global necessities" (Dean, 1994:35–36; italics added). Thus, genealogy is at odds with other types of historical studies that accord centrality to such laws or necessities. Everything is contingent from a genealogical perspective. Genealogy is inherently critical, involving a "tireless interrogation of what is held to be given, necessary, natural or neutral" (Dean, 1994:20).

More specifically, genealogy is concerned with the relationship between knowledge and power within the human sciences and their "practices concerned with the regulation of bodies, the government of conduct, and the formation of self" (Dean, 1994:154). Foucault is interested in the "conditions which hold at any one moment for the 'saying the true'" within the human sciences (Dean, 1994:24). Thus, "where

MICHEL FOUCAULT

A Biographical Sketch

When he died of AIDS in 1984 at 57 years of age (Lemert, 2005a), "Michel Foucault was perhaps the single most famous intellectual in the world" (J. Miller, 1993:13). That fame was derived from a fascinating body of work that has influenced thinkers in a number of different fields, including sociology. Foucault also led an extremely interesting life, and the themes that characterized his life tended to define his work as well. In fact, it could be argued that through his work Foucault was seeking to better understand himself and the forces that led him to lead the life that he led.

Among Foucault's last works was a trilogy devoted to sex—*The History of Sexuality* (1980a), *The Care of the Self* (1984), and *The Use of Pleasure* (1985). These works reflected Foucault's lifelong obsession with sex. A good deal of Foucault's life seems to have been defined by this obsession, in particular his homosexuality and his sadomasochism. During a trip to San Francisco in 1975, Foucault visited and was deeply attracted to the city's flourishing gay community. Foucault appears to have been drawn to the impersonal sex that flourished in the infamous bathhouses of that time and place. His interest and participation in these settings and activities were part of a lifelong interest in "'the overwhelming, the unspeakable, the creepy, the stupefying, the ecstatic'" (cited in J. Miller, 1993:27). In other words, in his life (and his work) Foucault was deeply interested in "limit experiences" (where people [including himself] purposely push their minds and bodies to the breaking point) such as the impersonal sadomasochistic activities that took place in and around those bathhouses. It was Foucault's belief that it was during such limit experiences that great personal and intellectual breakthroughs and revelations became possible.

Thus, sex was related to limit experiences, and both, in turn, were related in his view to death: "'I think the kind of pleasure I would consider as the real pleasure would be so deep, so intense, so overwhelming that I couldn't survive

archaeology had earlier addressed the rules of formation of discourse, the new critical and genealogical description addresses both the rarity of statements and the power of the affirmative" (Dean, 1994:33). In terms of the relationship between Foucault's two methods, archaeology performs tasks that are necessary in order to do genealogy. Specifically, archaeology involves empirical analyses of historical discourses, whereas genealogy undertakes a serial and critical analysis of these historical discourses and their relationship to issues of concern in the contemporary world.

Thus, genealogy is to be a "history of the present." However, this is not to be confused with "presentism," which involves the "unwitting projection of a structure of

the mad, who are progressively unable to protect themselves from this "help." He sees the mad as being sentenced by so-called scientific advancement to a "gigantic moral imprisonment."

Needless to say, Foucault here rejects the idea that over the years we have seen scientific, medical, and humanitarian advances in the treatment of the mad. What he sees, instead, are increases in the ability of the sane and their agents (physicians, psychologists, psychiatrists) to oppress and repress the mad, who, we should not forget, had been on equal footing with the sane in the seventeenth century. The most recent development is that now the mad are less judged by these external agents; "madness is ceaselessly called upon to judge itself" (Foucault, 1965:265). In many senses such internalized control is the most repressive form of control. Clearly, Foucault's archaeology of knowledge leads him to conclusions very different from those of traditional historians about the history and current status of the mad and their relationship to the sane (and their agents). In addition, he is looking at the roots of the human sciences (especially psychology and psychiatry) in the distinction between the mad and the sane and the exertion of moral control over the mad. This is part of his more general thesis about the role of the human sciences in the moral control of people.

As for Foucault's structuralism in this early work, he argues that madness occurs at two "levels," and at "a deeper level madness is a form of discourse" (1965:96). Specifically, madness, at least in the classical age, is not mental or physical changes; instead, "delirious language is the ultimate truth of madness" (Foucault, 1965:97). But there is an even broader structuralism operating in this early work: "Let classical culture formulate, *in its general structure,* the experience it had of madness, an experience which crops up with the same meanings, in the identical order of its inner logic, in both the order of speculation and in the order of institutions, in *both discourse and decree,* in both word and watchword—wherever, in fact, a signifying element can assume for us the value of a language" (Foucault, 1965:116; italics added).

Foucault continues to use a structuralist method in *The Birth of the Clinic,* in which he focuses on medical discourse and its underlying structure: "What counts in the things said by men is not so much what they may have thought or the extent to which these things represent their thoughts, as *that which systematizes them from the outset,* thus making them thereafter endlessly accessible to new discourses and open to the task of transforming them" (1975:xiv; italics added).

In *Madness and Civilization,* medicine was an important precursor of the human sciences, and that is an even more central theme in *The Birth of the Clinic.* (As Foucault said, "The science of man . . . was medically . . . based" [1975:36].) Prior to the nineteenth century, medicine was a classificatory science, and the focus was on a clearly ordered system of diseases. But in the nineteenth century, medicine came to focus on diseases as they existed in individuals and the larger society (epidemics). Medicine came to be extended to healthy people (preventive care), and it adopted a normative posture distinguishing between healthy and unhealthy and, later, normal and pathological states. Medicine had become, again, a forerunner of the human sciences that were to adopt this normal-pathological stance toward people.

As yet, however, there was no clinical structure in medicine. The key was the development of the clinic, where patients were observed in bed. Here Foucault uses a key term, the *gaze,* in this case a "gaze that was at the same time knowledge" (1975:81). In other words, knowledge was derived from what physicians could see in contrast to what they read in books. As a structuralist, Foucault saw the gaze as a kind of language, "a language without words" (1975:68), and he was interested in the deep structure of that "language." The ability to see and touch (especially in autopsies) sick (or dead) people was a crucial change and an important source of knowledge. Foucault says of the autopsy, "The living night is dissipated in the brightness of death" (1975:146). Foucault sees the anatomo-clinical gaze as the "great break" in Western medicine. Thus, there was not an evolution of knowledge but an epistemic change. Doctors were no longer playing the same game; it was a different game with different rules. The game was that people (patients) had become the object of scientific knowledge and practice (instead of the disease as an entity). In terms of his structuralist orientation, what had changed was the nature of discourse—names of diseases, groupings, field of objects, and so forth (Foucault, 1975:54).

Once again, medicine takes on for Foucault the role of forerunner to the human sciences. "It is understandable, then, that medicine should have had such importance in the constitution of the sciences of man—an importance that is not only methodological, but ontological, in that it concerns man's becoming an object of positive knowledge" (Foucault, 1975:197). Specifically on the medical autopsy, Foucault says, "Death left its old tragic heaven and became the lyrical core of man: his invisible truth, his visible secret" (1975:172). In fact, for Foucault the broader change is the individual as subject and object of his own knowledge, and the change in medicine is but one "of the more visible witnesses to these changes in the fundamental structures of experience" (1975:199).

Many of the same themes appear in *Discipline and Punish* (Foucault, 1979), but now we see more of the genealogy of power and much less on structuralism, discourse, and the like. Here "power and knowledge directly imply one another" (Foucault, 1979:27). In this work Foucault is concerned with the period between 1757 and the 1830s, a period during which the torture of prisoners was replaced by control over them by prison rules. (Characteristically, Foucault sees this change developing in an irregular way; it does not evolve rationally.) The general view is that this shift from torture to rules represented a humanization of the treatment of criminals; it had grown more kind, less painful, and less cruel. The reality, from Foucault's point of view, was that punishment had grown more rationalized ("the executioner [in the guillotine] need be no more than a meticulous watchman" [1979:13]) and in many ways impinged more on prisoners. The early torture of prisoners may have made for good public displays, but it was "a bad economy of power" because it tended to incite unrest among the viewers of the spectacle (Foucault, 1979:79). The link between knowledge and power was clear in the case of torture; with the development of rules, that link became far less clear. The new system of rules was "more regular, more effective, more constant, and more detailed in its effects; in short, which increase its effects while diminishing its economic cost" (Foucault, 1979:80–81). The new system was not designed to be more humane, but "to punish better . . . to insert the power to punish more deeply into the social body" (Foucault, 1979:82). In contrast to torture, this new technology of the power to punish occurred earlier in the deviance process; was more numerous, more bureaucratized, more efficient, more impersonal, more invariable, and more sober; and involved the surveillance not just of criminals but of the entire society. It is this theory of society that is of paramount interest, and it could be argued that it would continue to be of interest even if everything that Foucault said about prisons was wrong (Alford, 2000).

This new technology, a technology of disciplinary power, was based on the military model. It involved not a single overarching power system, but rather a system of micro powers. Foucault describes a "micro-physics of power" with "innumerable points of confrontation" (1979:26–27) and resistance (Brenner, 1994). He identifies three instruments of disciplinary power. First is *hierarchical observation*, or the ability of officials to oversee all they control with a single *gaze*. Second is the ability to make *normalizing judgments* and to punish those who violate the norms. Thus, one might be negatively judged and punished on the dimensions of time (for being late), activity (for being inattentive), and behavior (for being impolite). Third is the use of *examination* to observe subjects and to make normalizing judgments about people. The third instrument of disciplinary power involves the other two.

Foucault does not simply take a negative view toward the growth of the disciplinary society; he sees that it has positive consequences as well. For example, he sees discipline as functioning well within the military and in industrial factories. However, Foucault communicates a genuine fear of the spread of discipline, especially as it moves into the state-police network for which the entire society becomes a field of perception and an object of discipline.

Foucault does not see discipline sweeping uniformly through society. Instead, he sees it "swarming" through society and affecting bits and pieces of society as it goes. Eventually, however, most major institutions are affected. Foucault asks rhetorically, "Is it surprising that prisons resemble factories, schools, barracks, hospitals, which all resemble prisons?" (1979:228). In the end, Foucault sees the development of a carceral system in which discipline is transported "from the penal institution to the entire social body" (1979:298). Although there is an iron-cage image here, as usual Foucault sees the operation of forces in opposition to the carceral system; there is an ongoing structural dialectic in Foucault's work.

Although Foucault's greater emphasis on power in *Discipline and Punish* is evident in the discussion to this point, he also is concerned in this work with his usual theme of the emergence of the human sciences. The transition from torture to prison rules constituted a switch from punishment of the body to punishment of the soul or the will. This change, in turn, brought with it considerations of normality and morality. Prison officials and the police came to judge the normality and morality of the prisoner. Eventually, this ability to judge was extended to other "small-scale judges," such as psychiatrists and educators. From all this adjudication emerged new bodies of scientific penal knowledge, which served as the base of the modern "scientifico-legal complex." The new mode of subjugation was that people were defined as the object of knowledge, of scientific discourse. The key point is that the modern human sciences have their roots here. Foucault bitterly depicts the roots of the human sciences in the disciplines: "These sciences, which have so delighted our 'humanity' for over a century, have their technical matrix in the petty, malicious minutiae of the disciplines and their investigations" (1979:226).

One other point about *Discipline and Punish* is worth mentioning. Foucault is interested in the way that knowledge gives birth to technologies that exert power. In this context, he deals with the Panopticon. A *Panopticon* is a structure that gives officials the possibility of complete surveillance (Lyon, 2007; G. Marx, 2005) of criminals. In fact, officials need not always be present; the mere existence of the structure (and the possibility that officials might be there) constrains criminals. The Panopticon might take the form of a tower in the center of a circular prison from which guards could see into all cells. The Panopticon is a tremendous source of power for prison officials because it gives them the possibility of total surveillance. More important, its power is enhanced because the prisoners come to control themselves; they stop themselves from doing various things because they fear that they *might* be seen by the guards. There is a clear link here among knowledge, technology, and power. Furthermore, Foucault returns to his concern for the human sciences, for he sees the Panopticon as a kind of laboratory for the gathering of information about people. It was the forerunner of the social-scientific laboratory and other social-science techniques for gathering information about people. At still another level, Foucault sees the Panopticon as the base of "a whole type of society" (1979:216), the disciplinary society.[2]

Finally, we can look at the first volume of *The History of Sexuality* (Foucault, 1980a). Again, the emphasis is on the genealogy of power. To Foucault, sexuality is "an especially dense transfer point for relations of power" (1980a:103). He sees his goal as being to "define the regime of power-knowledge-pleasure that *sustains* the discourse on human sexuality in our part of the world" (Foucault, 1980a:11). He examines the way sex is put into discourse and the way power permeates that discourse.

Foucault takes issue with the conventional view that Victorianism led to the repression of sexuality in general and of sexual discourse in particular. In fact, he argues the exact opposite position—that Victorianism led to an explosion in discourses on sexuality. As a result of Victorianism, there was more analysis, stocktaking, classification, specification, and quantitative/causal study of sexuality. Said Foucault, "People will ask themselves why we were so bent on ending the rule of silence regarding what was the noisiest of our preoccupations" (1980a:158). This was especially the case in schools, where instead of repression of sexuality, "the question of sex was a constant preoccupation" (1980a:27). Here is the way Foucault sums up the Victorian hypothesis and his alternative view:

> We must therefore abandon the hypothesis that modern industrial societies ushered in an age of increased sexual repression. We have not only witnessed a visible explosion of unorthodox sexualities . . . never have there existed more centers of power; never more attention manifested and verbalized . . . never more sites where the intensity of pleasures and the persistency of power catch hold, only to spread elsewhere.
>
> (Foucault, 1980a:49)

Once again, Foucault accords a special place to medicine and its discourses on sexuality. Whereas to most, medicine is oriented to the scientific analysis of sexuality, Foucault sees more morality than science in the concerns of medicine. (In fact,

---

[2] For an interesting use of this idea, see Zuboff (1988), who views the computer as a modern Panopticon that gives superiors nearly unlimited surveillance over subordinates.

Foucault is characteristically hard on medicine, seeing the aim of its discourse "not to state the truth, but to prevent its very emergence" [1980a:55].) Also involved in the morality of sexuality is religion, especially Western Christianity, the confession, and the need for the subject to tell the truth about sexuality. All this is related to the human sciences and their interest in gaining knowledge of the subject. Just as people confessed to their priests, they also confessed to their doctors, their psychiatrists, and their sociologists. The confession, especially the sexual confession, came to be cloaked in scientific terms.

In the West, "the project of the science of the subject has gravitated, in ever-narrowing circles, around the question of sex" (Foucault, 1980a:70). Questions aimed at ascertaining who we are increasingly have come to be directed to sex. Foucault sums this all up: "Sex, the explanation of everything" (1980a:78).

Instead of focusing on the repression of sexuality, Foucault argues that the scientific study of sex should focus on the relationship between sex and power. Again, that power does not reside in one central source; it exists in a variety of micro settings. Furthermore, as is always the case with Foucault, there is resistance to the imposition of power over sex. Power and the resistance to power are everywhere.

Prior to the eighteenth century, society sought control over death, but beginning in that century, the focus shifted to control over life, especially sex. Power over life (and sex) took two forms. First, there was the "anatomo-politics of the human body," in which the goal was to discipline the human body (and its sexuality). Second, there was the "bio-politics of population," in which the object was to control and regulate population growth, health, life expectancy, and so forth. In both cases, society came to see "life as a political object" (Foucault, 1980a:145). Sex was central in both cases: "Sex was a means of access both to the life of the body and the life of the species" (Foucault, 1980a:146). In the modern West, sex has become more important than the soul (and we know how important that is in Foucault's work) and almost as important as life itself. Through knowledge of sexuality, society is coming to exercise more power over life itself. Yet despite this increase in control, Foucault holds out the hope of emancipation:

> It is the agency of sex that we must break away from, if we aim—through a tactical reversal of the various mechanisms of sexuality—to counter the grips of power with the claims of bodies, pleasures, and knowledges, in their multiplicity and their possibility of resistance. The rallying point for the counterattack against the deployment of sexuality ought not to be sex-desire, but bodies and pleasures.
> (Foucault, 1980a:157)

Dean (1994) argues that from the late 1970s until his death in 1984, Foucault's work shifted from the micro politics of power in the direction of a concern for *governmentalities,* or the "heterogeneous, non-subjective processes in which practices and techniques of governance have come to depend on discursive representations of their fields of intervention and operation" (Dean, 1994:78; Fejes, 2008; Walter, 2008). In contrast to other theorists, Foucault's focus is not specifically on the state, but "the practices and rationalities that compose the means of rule and government" (Dean, 1994:153). Thus, in terms of the will to knowledge in the human sciences, Foucault is concerned with the way bodies are regulated, the way conduct is governed, and the ways in which the self is formed. More generally, he was concerned with self-government, the government of others, and the government of the state. In most general terms, government to Foucault is concerned with "the conduct of conduct" (Dean, 1994:176; Lemert, 2005d).

The Ideas of Giorgio Agamben

Giorgio Agamben (b. 1942) is an Italian philosopher who in recent years has become increasingly oriented to developing a social theory. Although his primary intellectual debts are to philosophers (e.g., Aristotle, Martin Heidegger) and political thinkers (especially Carl Schmitt,[3] Hannah Arendt[4]), his work also shows the influence of social theorists such as Max Weber,[5] Emile Durkheim,[6] Walter Benjamin,[7] and especially Michel Foucault (see below). His set of ideas resembles many of the major social theories and includes a grand narrative of recent social history as well as an effort to identify a phenomenon that lies at the heart of modern society (much as Weber did with the bureaucracy). It is difficult to classify Agamben's work, but given the strong influence of Foucault's ideas, it is best to think of him as a poststructuralist. In addition, he uses a number of poststructuralist (and structuralist) ideas in his thinking.

To get a preliminary sense of Agamben's thinking before discussing his highly esoteric theoretical ideas, let us look at his thinking on Adolph Hitler and the Nazis. Soon after gaining power, the Nazis suspended the articles of the Weimar Constitution that dealt with civil liberties; a suspension that lasted for the duration of their twelve-year rule. This allowed them to engage in a "legal civil war" against their citizens, especially the Jews. The Nazis had created a "zone of exception" that allowed them to murder Jews and others whom they disliked. However, Agamben is not interested in such zones and the harm that is created in and by them as merely historical phenomena. He sees the creation of such zones, and the dangers associated with them, as contemporary phenomena (one of his favorite examples is the prison camp at Guantanamo Bay). Furthermore, he sees the zones of exception increasing over time, and, controversially and highly questionably, he argues that they pose a greater threat today than they did in Nazi Germany. Further, this greater threat is not restricted to totalitarian regimes but also is found in democratic societies.

Basic Concepts

We need to understand a number of basic concepts before we can get to a substantive discussion of Agamben's theory. He begins with the Greek concepts of *zoe* and *bios*.

---

[3] He was crucial in his work on sovereignty (see below).
[4] Agamben argues that she saw the link between totalitarianism and the camp (see below), but lacked a biopolitical perspective.
[5] Agamben discusses Weber's concept of charisma, especially as it is associated with Hitler, although he fails to see that charisma is not just a characteristic of the leader but is also created by the disciples.
[6] For example, Agamben uses Durkheim's concept of anomie, but he criticizes the way the concept is used in *Suicide*.
[7] He was important to Agamben for adding the idea of "pure" or "divine" violence—violence that is unrelated to, or outside, the law (e.g., revolutionary violence)—to violence that serves to make law or preserve law. Agamben (2002/2005:54) appreciates Benjamin's pure violence because it is outside the law and involves "wholly anomic human action" (note the use of Durkheim's concept here).

Zoe is our biological bodies (or "the simple fact of living common to all living beings" [Agamben, 1995/1998:1]), and *bios* is our political bodies (Agamben, 1995/1998:184). These are, for classical philosophy and for Agamben, inherently separate and separable phenomena. However, over time, zoe has come to be politicized; that is, the line between zoe and bios has grown less clear or been obliterated completely. As Agamben (1995/1998:188) puts it, there is no longer anything left of the classical distinction between them; that distinction has been "taken from us forever." As we will soon see, this is no mere philosophical or terminological issue but an issue of great importance to the modern world.

Very close to the idea of zoe is an idea of *bare life,* "the pure fact of birth" (Agamben, 1995/1998:127), which plays a prominent role in his thinking. In an argument similar to the one above, Agamben contends that bare life, like zoe, has been increasingly politicized and that that "constitutes *the decisive event of modernity* and signals a radical transformation" of classical thought (Agamben, 1995/1998:4; italics added). Bare life has always been political, although it long existed at the margins of the polity. Over time, it has been drawn increasingly into the polity, and this "constitutes the original—if concealed—nucleus of sovereign power" (Agamben, 1995/1998:6).

The Jews of Nazi Germany were an example of bare life. That is, they were Jews simply by the pure fact that they were born Jews. Furthermore, being Jewish was highly politicized by the Nazis. The Nazis created the Jews, or at least a particular symbol of the Jews, and then defined them as a people "whose presence [they] can no longer tolerate in any way" (Agamben, 1995/1998:179).

Bare life is closely related to yet another central concept to Agamben (1995/1998:8), *homo sacer* (or sacred man); bare life is "the life of *homo sacer.*" Zoe refers to bare life in general, whereas homo sacer is "bare life insofar as it is included in the political order" (DeCaroli, 2007:52). Thus zoe, at least theoretically and historically, can be and was separated from the polity (it was separated in Aristotle's perfect community), whereas homo sacer is by definition implicated in the political.

Central to the concept of homo sacer is the idea that it involves a person "who *may be killed and yet not sacrificed*" (Agamben, 1995/1998:8). This is the case because homo sacer has been separated politically from the rest of humankind by being defined as lying outside political boundaries. Because homo sacer is outside those limits, many things can be done to this person that cannot be done to other humans, including being killed at will by anyone. Further, whoever does this is not committing homicide and cannot be convicted of such a crime because homo sacer is outside the law and, more generally, the polity. This brings us back to our example (and Agamben's) of the Jews in Nazi Germany whom Agamben sees as a "flagrant case of *homo sacer.*" So, we can see the first part of the definition of homo sacer—one who can be killed—but what about the idea that homo sacer cannot be sacrificed? Here, Agamben has a traditional sense of sacrifice, especially the idea that to be sacrificed one must be part of the community. Because homo sacer is by definition not part of the (political) community, he or she cannot be sacrificed in this traditional sense of the term. Why is such a person "sacred"? As Antonio Negri (2007:121) puts it, he is "sacred in the sense of the assumption of a punishment that separated him from the common." It is being set apart and being punished that makes homo sacer sacred.

The *state of exception* is a topological zone; a "space without law" (Agamben, 2002/2005:51). As such, it is space in which homo sacer resides; it was the abstract space in which the Jews of Nazi Germany were placed. Because of the existence of such a space, the sovereign power (e.g., Hitler as the Fuhrer) is able to decide on his own who can and will be killed. Further, because those killed are outside the confines of the law, their murder is *not* a homicide. Thus, in the context of Nazi Germany and its zone of exclusion, the six million Jews could be murdered without it being considered murder, at least by the Nazis. Furthermore, the state of exception is unique not only in terms of death but, more important today, in terms of life. Thus, today the "overly comatose" person on life-support machines is in a zone of exception wherein it is possible to decide whether the person should live (keep the machines running) or die (turn the machines off and in doing so *not* commit homicide). The latter is crucial for Agamben because it represents the fact that not just death, but life, is now within the state of exception; this gives those in authority power not only over death but increasingly of life. As we will see, this thinking owes a major debt to the theories of Michel Foucault, especially on biopolitics.

Although the state of exception is outside the law, it is important, even essential, to the law. The law is able to define itself, and make its validity possible, with reference to that which lies outside it. It is also characteristic of the zone of exception that it is possible to do something in it that is not possible elsewhere in the political realm—that is the "abolition of the distinction among legislative, executive, and judicial powers" (Agamben, 2002/2005:7). This abolition, in turn, permits the executive (e.g., Hitler, as the German Fuhrer) to gain control over the other branches of government; to institute totalitarian rule (see below). Further, the zone of exception has a characteristic of many other aspects of Agamben's thinking in that it is *both* inside and outside the law; it is included in the law merely by the fact that the law excludes it. As Agamben (1995/1998:17–18) puts it: "The exception is a kind of exclusion. . . . But . . . what is excluded in it is not, on account of being excluded, absolutely without relation to the rule. . . . *The rule applies to the exception in no longer applying, in withdrawing from it.*" Thus, there is a dialectical relationship (there are many dialectical aspects of Agamben's thinking; see, for example, Negri, 2007) between the zone in which law resides and the state of exception, which is devoid of law.

Agamben draws his conceptualization of sovereignty from the work of Carl Schmitt (cited in Agamben, 1995/1998:11) who contends: "Sovereign is he who decides on the state of exception." Thus the sovereign and Agamben's core idea of the state of exception are inextricably intertwined; "exception is the structure of sovereignty" (Agamben, 1995/1998:28). The sovereign has (or takes) a variety of legal powers, including the power to create a state of exception; to "suspend the validity of law" (Agamben, 1995/1998:15). More alarmingly, Agamben (1995/1998:32) argues that "the sovereign is the point of indistinction between violence and law, the threshold on which violence passes over into law and law passes over into violence." It was this threshold that the Nazis, with Hitler as sovereign, passed over with great impunity. Although sovereignty is generally discussed in political terms, Agamben extends it to others in the modern world such as physicians and scientists.

Totalitarianism, at least in its modern form, is defined "as the establishment, by means of the state of exception, of a legal civil war that allows for the physical elimination not only of political adversaries but of entire categories of citizens" (Agamben, 2002/2005:2). The Nazis, of course, created a paradigmatic example of a totalitarian regime, and they used their power not only to murder anyone who opposed them politically but to attempt to eliminate the Jews as an entire category of citizens, not just in Germany but in all of Europe. In doing so, the Nazis waged a "legal civil war" against Jews and other selected categories (gypsies, homosexuals) of the German people, and ultimately people throughout Europe.

Auschwitz and the Camp

All of the above are illustrated in the case of the Nazi concentration camp, especially Auschwitz, to which Agamben (2002) devoted an entire book, *Remnants of Auschwitz: The Witness and the Archive.* The concentration camp (or more generally the camp; see below) is a zone of irresponsibility within that state of exception. Within it, the guards and others are free to behave irresponsibly and even to kill indiscriminately. It is a "gray zone" where distinctions between good and evil and ethical and legal become unclear, confused. It is also a "limit" situation (Foucault was very much interested in this as well) existing at the limits of the good and the ethical; edging, if not diving headlong, into the evil, the illegal, the unethical. The prisoners exist in a zone of exception and hence can be killed with their murder *not* considered a homicide. They were reduced to their bare life, and then their bare lives were taken from them.

Auschwitz, as a concentration camp, was at the core of Nazism and at the "core of the camp" was the *Musselmann*[8] (Agamben, 2002:81). If the camp was a limit situation, then Musselmann in general were limit people who existed in limit situations. They were the limit of a progression that saw them go from non-Aryans, to Jews, to deportees, to prisoners, and then to Musselmann; the only step remaining for them was death. They existed in a moving threshold between life and death ("walking corpse" [Agamben, 2002:70]); between human and nonhuman (they were dehumanized).

Auschwitz in itself was important to Agamben, but it was also the major example of the more general idea of the *camp.* The camp is where the state of exception "acquires a permanent spatial arrangement" (Agamben, in DeCaroli, 2007:52); it is a "materialization of the state of exception" (Agamben, 1995/1998:174); "the pure space of exception" (Agamben, 1995/1998:134). However, the camp did not end with the destruction of Nazism and its concentration camps. It is not merely a historical fact, or even a past anomaly, "but in some ways . . . the hidden matrix and *nomos*[9] of political space in which we are still living" (Agamben, 1995/1998:166). Thus, it is not just that there are still camps; we are increasingly living in camps and in a society that is increasingly camplike. This leads to the conclusion that we are living in a permanent state of exception that is "now given a permanent spatial arrangement" in

---

[8] Literally, 'the Muslim." The Muslim is one who submits unconditionally to God; the Musselmann submitted unconditionally to the concentration camp and its dictates.

[9] A form that people take for granted as normal.

the camp. Thus the camp can be seen as "the hidden paradigm of the political space of modernity" (Agamben, 1995/1998:123). It is paradigmatic in that it is "the space of this absolute impossibility of deciding between fact and law, rule and application, exception and rule, which nevertheless incessantly decides between them" (Agamben, 1995/1998:173). However, those decisions are arbitrary and no longer guided by law. Rather, they are decided on by the sovereign (e.g., Hitler in the case of Nazi Germany), and the camp, then, is a place where "sovereignty exists but the law does not" (DeCaroli, 2007:53). No act committed by the sovereign, or those who act on his behalf, could be considered a crime. As Adolph Eichmann said, "the words of the Fuhrer have the force of law" (cited in Agamben, 2002/2005:38).

Biopolitics and the Influence of the Work of Michel Foucault

Agamben (1995/1998:122) is interested in the biopolitics (which he defines in his own terms [Foucault had no sense of "bare life"] as the "care, control, and use of bare life") of the Nazi concentration camp, the camp more generally, as well as the larger society that has become a camp. It is in his thinking on biopolitics that Agamben was most influenced by Michel Foucault and his seminal work on that topic. As Agamben saw it (1995/1998:3), biopolitics as the concept was developed by Foucault involved "the species and the individual as a simple living body becom[ing] what is at stake in a society's political strategies." However, while to Foucault this development was relatively recent, to Agamben it is an ancient phenomenon (DeCaroli, 2007:53; for other differences[10] between the two thinkers, see Mills, 2007). To Agamben (1995/1998):

> The decisive fact is that, together with the process by which the exception everywhere becomes the rule, the realm of bare life—which is originally situated at the margins of the political order—gradually begins to coincide with the political realm, and exclusion and inclusion, outside and inside, *bios* and *zoe*, right and fact, enter into a zone of irreducible indistinction. At once excluding bare life from and capturing it within the political order, the state of exception actually constituted, in its very separateness, the hidden foundations on which the entire political system rested . . . the bare life . . . becomes . . . the one place for the organization of State power and emancipation from it.
>
> (Agamben, 1995/1998:9)

In the above, bare life becomes the objective of biopolitics and the linkage between the work of Foucault and Agamben.

Foucault focused on the prison as the key site for the practice of biopolitics, but Agamben (1995/1998:20) argued that that site was the camp, "not the prison." Thus, Agamben (1995/1998:119) critiques Foucault because he "never brought his insights to bear on what could well have appeared to be the exemplary place of modern biopolitics: the politics of the great totalitarian states of the twentieth century." Foucault should have seen, for example, that Nazism and the concentration camps were the "point at which the integration of medicine and politics, which is one of the essential

---

[10] For example, Foucault did a genealogical analysis, whereas Agamben was more ontological in his approach (although Agamben [2002/2005:50] did do genealogical analyses of his own, but not on the core issue of biopolitics).

characteristics of modern biopolitics, began to assume its final form . . . the physician and the sovereign seem to exchange roles" (Agamben, 1995/1998:143).

Agamben also differs from Foucault in terms of their outlook for the future. Foucault has a reasonably optimistic outlook involving the future emergence of a "different economy of bodies and liberation" (Agamben, 1995/1998:187). Agamben is more cautious, even pessimistic, but he does have a vision of a possible future in which the distinction between bios and zoe can be undone. For this, however, Agamben proposes a radical break with the history of Western civilization and the emergence of a "happy life . . . in which it is no longer possible to isolate bare life as a political project" (C. Mills, 2011:474). Though, as Mills points out, it is unclear what exactly Agamben means by the happy life, the idea is informed by the work of Walter Benjamin and Judeo-Christian conceptions of messianic time. Mills adds that any use of Agamben's theory must come to terms with the messianic politics that accompany his theory about homo sacer and the state of exception. To date social theorists have kept the two aspects of Agamben's theory separate.

Foucault, of course, was a poststructuralist, and even beyond the impact of Foucault's thinking, there is abundant evidence of the influence of poststructuralism (and structuralism) on his thinking.[11] This is clearest in his concept of "force-of-law," with the word law "under erasure" or crossed out. This procedure is traceable to, and is common in, the work of one of the leading postructuralists, Jacques Derrida. The idea here is that "law" was connected to law at one time, and that connection may still be faintly visible, but the law has been eliminated ("erased"), leaving only force, or the force of law without the law.

Building, at least implicitly, on another key idea in structuralism and poststructuralism—the floating signifier—Agamben (2002/2005:39) argues that "in extreme situations 'force of law' floats as an indeterminate element that can be claimed both by state authorities . . . and by a revolutionary organization. The state of exception is an anomic space in which what is at stake is a force of law without law (which should therefore be written as force-of-law . . . law seeks to annex anomie itself." Because the force of law floats free, there is no internal connection between the law (and norms) and its application. It can be applied freely and differentially by not only various agents of the law (who, like the Nazis, may well have nefarious goals in doing so) but also by revolutionary agents.

Agamben's Grand Narrative and Ultimate Goals

Although Agamben's work shows the influence of poststructuralism, there is no sense that he has been similarly influenced by postmodernism. The result is that he has no compunctions about offering "grand narratives," which may take various forms.

First, he sees the progressive expansion of the state of exception over time: "in our age, the state of exception comes more and more to the foreground as the fundamental political structure and ultimately begins to become the rule" (1995/1998:20; see also Agamben, 2002/2005:2; this view is associated with Benjamin, 1942). Similarly, but in

---

[11] Among other things, Agamben refers to language, *langue* and *parole*, signification, Derrida, and Lévi-Strauss.

greater detail, he argues: "When life and politics—originally divided, and linked together by means of the no-man's-land of the state of exception that is inhabited by bare life—begin to become one, all life becomes sacred and all politics becomes the exception" (Agamben, 1995/1998:148). Most extremely, Agamben (2002/2005:87) argues that the "state of exception has today reached its maximum worldwide deployment."

Second, he sees the progressive expansion of control over biology by politics; the expansion of biopolitics. Over time, for example, the "state decides to assume directly the care of the nation's biological life as one of its proper tasks" (Agamben, 1995/1998:175). Furthermore, this opens the doors for others to control biological life. In modernity, "the physician and the scientist move in the no-man's-land into which at one point the sovereign alone could penetrate" (Agamben, 1995/1998:159).

Third, the camp has expanded and become more central. "The camp, which is now securely lodged within the city's interior, is the new biopolitical *nomos* of the planet" (Agamben, 1995/1998:176). The camp, linked as it is to the Nazi concentration camp, is also tied to the "system's inability to function without being transformed into a lethal machine" (Agamben, 1995/1998:175). This is related to the "unstoppable progression" of global civil war (Agamben, 2002/2005:2). Even democratic states are involved in this civil war, with the result that there is increasingly little difference between democratic and totalitarian states.

Given these trends, what would Agamben like to see instead? He rejects looking backward to some lost original state or looking forward within "the modern political project, with its patriotic narratives and exhausted antagonisms" (DeCaroli, 2007:44). Rather, he articulates only very abstract or general ideas about the future. For example, he favors "a politics in which bare life is no longer separated and excerpted, either in the state order or in the figure of human rights" (Agamben, 1995/1998:134). Or he seeks to open a space for human action (action that is pure means without ends) and that would allow it to once again claim for itself the name of politics. In other words, he wants to see a reintegration of human action and politics. DeCaroli (2007:45) puts this slightly differently, contending that Agamben's goal is the creation of the "'coming community'" involving "the inseparability of politics and subjectivity."

Critiques

The most important critiques of Agamben's work relate to his grand narratives, especially some of his outrageous views, his "wild statements" (Laclau, 2007:21) and "rhetoric of histrionic hyperbole" (LaCapra, 2007:136), about the contemporary world. As LaCapra (2007:133) puts it, "He seems constrained to raise the stakes or 'up the ante' (which is clearly astronomically high) in theoretically daring, jarringly disconcerting claims if he is to make a significant mark as a major theorist." Among the claims that fall into this category are that the modern world is worse than the world created by the Nazis, there is little or nothing to choose today between totalitarian and democratic regimes, the camp is the political space, or the *nomos*, of modernity itself, and "the extreme and absurd paradigm of the concentration camp" (Laclau, 2007:22). Such views are major distortions, if not absurdities, that block "any possible exploration of the emancipatory possibilities opened by our modern heritage" (Laclau, 2007:22).

It certainly does seem as if Agamben is overreaching, especially when he suggests a grand narrative or engages in a critique of the contemporary world. It is hard to accept the idea that the current world, whatever its degree of problems (and there are many), is worse than the world of the Nazis and their concentration camps. The American prison at Guantanamo Bay in Cuba is an abomination, and well reflects ideas such as the state of exception and the camp, but it does not come anywhere close to being the human calamity that was Auschwitz, to say nothing of the many other concentration camps as well as myriad other offenses committed by the Nazis.

Postmodern Social Theory

When postmodern theory emerged in the 1980s it was considered "the hottest game in town" (Kellner, 1989b). It challenged conventional sociological thought and offered the possibility for previously unheard-of (or at least underappreciated) forms of theory and writing. At the time, many considered postmodernism a fad, and while few now call themselves postmodernists, its impact on social theory is unmistakable. For example, a number of the theories that we discuss in Chapter 17 (queer theory, actor-network theory, affect theory) can be seen as extensions of both poststructuralist and postmodern theory. In short, while many have backed down from some of the stronger claims made by postmodernists, they have also incorporated its key insights.

Given the importance of postmodern social theory and the heat it has generated, the objective here is to offer at least a brief introduction to postmodern thinking (Antonio, 1998; Ritzer, 1997; Ritzer and Goodman, 2001). However, this is no easy matter. For one thing, there is great diversity among the generally highly idiosyncratic postmodern thinkers, and so it is difficult to offer generalizations on which the majority would agree. Smart (1993), for example, has differentiated among three postmodernist positions.[12] The first, or extreme, postmodernist position is that there has been a radical rupture and modern society has been replaced by a postmodern society. Exponents of this point of view include Jean Baudrillard (Armitage, 2005), Gilles Deleuze, and Felix Guattari (Deleuze and Guattari, 1972/1983, 1980/1987; Binkley, 2007c; Bogard, 1998; Genosko, 2007; *Theory, Culture and Society,* 1997). The second position is that although a change has taken place, postmodernism grows out of, and is continuous with, modernism. This orientation is adhered to by Marxian thinkers such as Fredric Jameson, Ernesto Laclau, and Chantal Mouffe and by postmodern feminists such as Nancy Fraser and Linda Nicholson. Finally, there is the position, adopted by Smart himself, that rather than viewing modernism and postmodernism as epochs, we can see them as engaged in a long-running and ongoing set of relationships, with postmodernism continually pointing out the limitations of modernism.

Despite the fact that the term *postmodern* is widely used in social theory, there is enormous ambiguity and controversy over exactly what it means. For clarity it is useful to distinguish among the terms *postmodernity, postmodernism,* and *postmodern social theory.*[13] *Postmodernity* refers to a historical epoch that generally is seen as

---

[12] Pauline Rosenau (1992) distinguishes between skeptical and affirmative postmodern thinkers.
[13] Here we follow the distinction made by Best and Kellner (1991:5).

following the modern era, *postmodernism* to cultural products (in art, movies, architecture, and so on) that differ from modern cultural products (Taylor, 2007), and *postmodern social theory* to a way of thinking that is distinct from modern social theory. Thus, the postmodern encompasses *a new historical epoch, new cultural products,* and *a new type of theorizing about the social world.* All these, of course, share the perspective that something new and different has happened in recent years that no longer can be described by the term *modern,* and that those new developments are replacing modern realities.

    To address the first of these concepts, there is a widespread belief that the modern era is ending, or has ended, and we have entered a new historical epoch of *postmodernity.* Lemert argues that the birth of postmodernism can be traced, at least symbolically, to

> the death of modernist architecture at 3:32 P.M., July 15, 1972—the moment at which the Pruitt-Igoe housing project in St. Louis was destroyed. . . . This massive housing project in St. Louis represented modernist architecture's arrogant belief that by building the biggest and best public housing planners and architects could eradicate poverty and human misery. To have recognized, and destroyed the symbol of that idea was to admit the failure of modernist architecture, and by implication modernity itself.
>
> (Lemert, 1990:233; following Jencks, 1977)

The destruction of Pruitt-Igoe is a reflection of differences between modernists and postmodernists over whether it is possible to find rational solutions to society's problems. For modernists it is possible to find rational solutions. For postmodernists it is not. To take another example, Lyndon Johnson's war on poverty in the 1960s was typical of the way modern society believed it could discover and implement rational solutions to its problems. It could be argued that in the 1980s the Reagan administration with its general unwillingness to develop massive programs to deal with such problems was representative of a postmodern society and the belief that there is no single rational answer to various problems. Thus, we might conclude that somewhere between the presidential administrations of Kennedy and Johnson and that of Reagan, the United States moved from being a modern to being a postmodern society. In fact, the destruction of Pruitt-Igoe occurred within that time frame.

    The second concept, *postmodernism,* relates to the cultural realm in which it is argued that postmodern products have tended to supplant modern products. In art, as we will see shortly, Jameson (1984) contrasts Andy Warhol's postmodern, almost photographic and unemotional painting of Marilyn Monroe to Edvard Munch's modern and highly painful *The Scream.* In the realm of television, the show *Twin Peaks* generally is taken to be a good example of postmodernism, and *Father Knows Best* is a good example of a modern television program. In the movies, *Blade Runner* may be seen as a postmodern work, whereas *The Ten Commandments* would certainly qualify as a modern movie.

    Third, and of much more direct relevance to us here, is the emergence of *postmodern social theory* and its differences from modern theory. Modern social theory sought a universal, ahistorical, rational foundation for its analysis and critique of society. For Marx that foundation was species-being, while for Habermas it was communicative reason. Postmodern thinking rejects this "foundationalism" and tends to be relativistic, irrational, and nihilistic. Following Nietzsche and Foucault, among others, postmodernists have come to question such foundations, believing that they tend to privilege some groups and downgrade the significance of others, give some groups power and render other groups powerless.

Similarly, postmodernists reject the ideas of a grand narrative or a metanarrative. It is in the rejection of these ideas that we encounter one of the most important postmodernists, Jean-François Lyotard. Lyotard (1984:xxiii) begins by identifying modern (scientific) knowledge with the kind of single grand synthesis (or "metadiscourse") we have associated with the work of theorists such as Marx and Parsons. The kinds of grand narratives he associates with modern science include "the dialectics of Spirit, the hermeneutics of meaning, the emancipation of the rational or working subject, or the creation of wealth" (Lyotard, 1984:xxiii).

If modern knowledge is identified in Lyotard's view with metanarratives, then postmodern knowledge involves a rejection of such grand narratives. As Lyotard puts it: "Simplifying to the extreme, I define *postmodern* as incredulity to metanarratives" (1984:xxiv). More strongly, he argues: "Let us wage war on totality . . . let us activate the differences" (Lyotard, 1984:82). In fact, postmodern social theory becomes a celebration of a range of different theoretical perspectives: "Postmodern knowledge is not simply a tool of authorities; it refines our sensitivity to differences and reinforces our ability to tolerate the incommensurable" (Lyotard, 1984:xxv). In these terms, sociology has moved beyond the modern period, into the postmodern period, in its search for a range of more specific syntheses. In the view of Fraser and Nicholson, Lyotard prefers "smallish, localized narrative[s]" to the metanarratives, or grand narratives, of modernity (1988:89).

While Lyotard rejects the grand narrative in general, Baudrillard rejects the idea of a grand narrative in sociology. For one thing, Baudrillard rejects the whole idea of the social. For another, rejecting the social leads to a rejection of the metanarrative of sociology that is associated with modernity:

> . . . the great organizing principle, the grand narrative of the Social which found its
> support and justification in ideas on the rational contract, civil society, progress,
> power, production—that all this may have pointed to something that once existed,
> but exists no longer. The age of the perspective of the social (coinciding rightly
> with that ill-defined period known as modernity) . . . is over.
>
> (Bogard, 1990:10)

Thus, postmodern social theory stands for the rejection of metanarratives in general and of grand narratives within sociology in particular.

Postmodern social theory has, to a large degree, been the product of nonsociologists (Lyotard, Derrida, Jameson, and others). In recent years, a number of sociologists have begun to operate within a postmodern perspective, and postmodern social theory can be seen, at least to some degree, as *part* of the classical sociological tradition. Take, for example, the reinterpretation of the work of Georg Simmel entitled *Postmodern(ized) Simmel* (Weinstein and Weinstein, 1993, 1998). Weinstein and Weinstein recognize that there is a strong case to be made for Simmel as a liberal modernist who offers a grand narrative of the historical trend toward the dominance of objective culture—the "tragedy of culture." However, they also argue that an equally strong case can be made for Simmel as a postmodern theorist. Thus, they acknowledge that both alternatives have validity and, in fact, that one is no more true than the other. Weinstein and Weinstein argue: "To our minds 'modernism' and 'postmodernism' are not exclusive alternatives but discursive domains bordering each other" (1993:21). They note that they could be doing a modernist interpretation of Simmel but feel that a postmodernist explication is more useful. Thus, they express a very postmodern view: "There is no essential Simmel, only different Simmels read through the various positions in contemporary discourse formations" (Weinstein and Weinstein, 1993:55).

What sorts of arguments do Weinstein and Weinstein make in defense of a postmodernized Simmel? For one thing, Simmel is seen as being generally opposed to totalizations; indeed, he is inclined to detotalize modernity. In spite of, and aside from, the theory of the "tragedy of culture," Simmel was primarily an essayist and a storyteller, and he dealt mainly with a range of specific issues rather than with the totality of the social world.

Simmel also is described by Weinstein and Weinstein, as he is by others, as a *flaneur,* or someone who is something of an idler. More specifically, Simmel is described as a sociologist who idled away his time analyzing a wide range of social phenomena. He was interested in all of them for their aesthetic qualities; they all existed "to titillate, astonish, please or delight him" (Weinstein and Weinstein, 1993:60). Simmel is described as spending his intellectual life wandering through a wide range of social phenomena, describing one or another as the mood moved him. This approach led Simmel away from a totalized view of the world and toward a concern for a number of discrete, but important, elements of that world.

Bricoleur is another term used to describe Simmel. A *bricoleur* is a kind of intellectual handyman who makes do with whatever happens to be available to him. Available to Simmel are a wide range of fragments of the social world, or "shards of objective culture," as Weinstein and Weinstein (1993:70) describe them in Simmelian terms. As a *bricoleur* Simmel cobbles together whatever ideas he can find in order to shed light on the social world.

There is no need to go too deeply into the details of Weinstein and Weinstein's interpretation of a postmodernized Simmel. The illustrative points already discussed make it clear that such an interpretation is as reasonable as the modernized vision is. It would be far harder to come up with similar postmodern views of the other major classical theorists, although one certainly could find aspects of their work that are consistent with postmodern social theory. Thus, as Seidman (1991) makes clear, most of sociological theory *is* modernist, but as the case of Simmel illustrates, there are postmodern intimations in even that most modernist of traditions (see also the discussion of Weber and postmodernism in Gane, 2002).

Another place to look for intimations of postmodern social theory is among the critics of modern theory *within* sociological theory. As several observers (Antonio, 1991; Best and Kellner, 1991; Smart, 1993) have pointed out, a key position is occupied by C. Wright Mills (1959). First, Mills actually used the term *postmodern* to describe the post-Enlightenment era that we were entering: "We are at the ending of what is called The Modern Age. . . . The Modern Age is being succeeded by a post-modern period" (Mills, 1959:165–166). Second, he was a severe critic of modern grand theory in sociology, especially as it was practiced by Talcott Parsons. Third, Mills favored a socially and morally engaged sociology. In his terms, he wanted a sociology that linked broad public issues to specific private troubles.

While there are intimations of postmodern social theory in the work of Simmel and Mills (and many others), it is not there that we find postmodern theory itself. For example, Best and Kellner contend that Mills "is very much a modernist, given to sweeping sociological generalization, totalizing surveys of sociology and history, and a belief in the power of the sociological imagination to illuminate social reality and to change society" (1991:8).

Given this general background, let us turn to a more concrete discussion of post-modern social theory. We will focus on a few of the ideas associated with two of the most important postmodern social theorists: Fredric Jameson and Jean Baudrillard.

Moderate Postmodern Social Theory: Fredric Jameson

The dominant position on the issue of postmodernity is clearly that there is a radical disjuncture between modernity and postmodernity. However, there are some postmodern theorists who argue that while postmodernity has important differences from modernity, there are also continuities between them. The best known of these arguments is made by Fredric Jameson (1984; Kellner, 2005b) in an essay entitled "Postmodernism, or The Cultural Logic of Late Capitalism," as well as later in a book of essays with the same title (Jameson, 1991). That title is clearly indicative of Jameson's Marxian position that capitalism, now in its "late" phase, continues to be the dominant feature in today's world but has spawned a new cultural logic—postmodernism. In other words, although the cultural logic may have changed, the underlying economic structure is continuous with earlier forms of capitalism. Furthermore, capitalism continues to be up to its same old tricks of spawning a cultural logic to help it maintain itself.

In writing in this vein, Jameson is clearly rejecting the claim made by many postmodernists (for example, Lyotard, Baudrillard) that Marxian theory is perhaps the grand narrative par excellence and therefore has no place in, or relevance to, postmodernity. Jameson is not only rescuing Marxian theory, but endeavoring to show that it offers the best theoretical explanation of postmodernity. Interestingly, although Jameson generally is praised for his insights into the culture of postmodernism, he often is criticized, especially by Marxists, for offering an inadequate analysis of the economic base of this new cultural world.

Also consistent with the work of Marx, and unlike most theorists of postmodernism, Jameson (1984:86) sees both positive and negative characteristics, "catastrophe and progress all together," associated with postmodern society. Marx, of course, saw capitalism in this way: productive of liberation and very valuable advancements and *at the same time* the height of exploitation and alienation.

Jameson begins by recognizing that postmodernism usually is associated with a radical break, but then, after discussing a number of things usually associated with postmodernism, he asks, "Does it imply any more fundamental change or break than the periodic style—and fashion—changes determined by an older high modernist imperative of stylistic innovation?" (1984:54). He responds that there certainly have been aesthetic changes, but those changes continue to be a function of underlying economic dynamics:

> What has happened is that aesthetic production today has become integrated into commodity production generally: the frantic economic urgency of producing fresh waves of ever more novel-seeming goods (from clothing to airplanes), at ever greater rates of turnover, now assigns an increasingly essential structural function and position to aesthetic innovation and experimentation. Such economic necessities then find recognition in the institutional support of all kinds available for the newer art, from foundations and grants to museums and other forms of patronage.
>
> (Jameson, 1984:56)

The continuity with the past is even clearer and more dramatic in the following:

> This whole global, yet American, postmodern culture is the internal and superstructural expression of a whole new wave of American military and economic domination throughout the world: in this sense, as throughout class history, the underside of culture is blood, torture, death and horror.
>
> (Jameson, 1984:57)

Jameson (following Ernest Mandel) sees three stages in the history of capitalism. The first stage, analyzed by Marx, is market capitalism, or the emergence of unified national markets. The second stage, analyzed by Lenin, is the imperialist stage with the emergence of a global capitalist network. The third stage, labeled by Mandel (1975) and Jameson as "late capitalism," involves "a prodigious expansion of capital into hitherto uncommodified areas" (Jameson, 1984:78). This expansion, "far from being inconsistent with Marx's great nineteenth-century analysis, constitutes on the contrary the purest form of capital yet to have emerged" (Jameson, 1984:78). Said Jameson, "The Marxist framework is still indispensable for understanding the new historical content, which demands not modification of the Marxist framework, but an expansion of it" (cited in Stephanson, 1989:54). For Jameson, the key to modern capitalism is its multinational character and the fact that it has greatly increased the range of commodification.

These changes in the economic structure have been reflected in cultural changes. Thus, Jameson associates realist culture with market capitalism, modernist culture with monopoly capitalism, and postmodern culture with multinational capitalism. This view seems to be an updated version of Marx's base-superstructure argument, and many have criticized Jameson for adopting such a simplistic perspective. However, Jameson has tried hard to avoid such a "vulgar" position and has described a more complex relationship between the economy and culture. Nonetheless, even a sympathetic critic such as Featherstone concludes, "It is clear that his view of culture largely works within the confines of a base-superstructure model" (1989:119).

Capitalism has gone from a stage in monopoly capitalism in which culture was at least to some degree autonomous to an explosion of culture in multinational capitalism:

> A prodigious expansion of culture throughout the social realm, to the point at which everything in our social life—from economic value and state power to practices and to the very structure of the psyche itself—can be said to have become

"cultural" in some original and as yet untheorized sense. This perhaps startling proposition is, however, substantively quite consistent with the previous diagnosis of a society of the image or the simulacrum [this term will be defined shortly], and a transformation of the "real" into so many pseudo-events.

(Jameson, 1984:87)

Jameson describes this new form as a "cultural dominant." As a cultural dominant, postmodernism is described as a "force field in which very different kinds of cultural impulses . . . must make their way" (Jameson, 1984:57). Thus, while postmodernism is "a new systematic cultural norm," it is made up of a range of quite heterogeneous elements (Jameson, 1984:57). By using the term *cultural dominant,* Jameson also clearly means that while postmodern culture is controlling, there are various other forces that exist within today's culture.

Fredric Jameson offers a comparatively clear image of a postmodern society composed of four basic elements (a fifth, its late capitalistic character, has already been discussed). First, postmodern society is characterized by superficiality and lack of depth. Its cultural products are satisfied with surface images and do not delve deeply into the underlying meanings. A good example is Andy Warhol's famous painting of Campbell soup cans that appear to be nothing more than perfect representations of those cans. To use a key term associated with postmodern theory, a picture is a *simulacrum* in which one cannot distinguish between the original and the copy. A simulacrum is also a copy of a copy; Warhol was reputed to have painted his soup cans not from the cans themselves but from a photograph of the cans. Jameson describes a simulacrum as "the identical copy for which no original ever existed" (1984:66). A simulacrum is, by definition, superficial, lacking in depth.

Second, postmodernism is characterized by a waning of emotion or affect. As his example, Jameson contrasts another of Warhol's paintings—another near-photographic representation, this time of Marilyn Monroe—to a classic modernist piece of art—Edvard Munch's *The Scream. The Scream* is a surreal painting of a person expressing the depth of despair, or in sociological terms, anomie or alienation. Warhol's painting of Marilyn Monroe is superficial and expresses no genuine emotion. This reflects the fact that to the postmodernists, the alienation and anomie that caused the kind of reaction depicted by Munch is part of the now-past modern world. In the postmodern world alienation has been replaced by fragmentation. Since the world and the people in it have become fragmented, the affect that remains is "free-floating and impersonal" (Jameson, 1984:64). There is a peculiar kind of euphoria associated with these postmodern feelings, or what Jameson prefers to call "intensities." He gives as an example a photorealist cityscape "where even automobile wrecks gleam with some new hallucinatory splendour" (Jameson, 1984:76). Euphoria based on automobile disasters in the midst of urban squalor is, indeed, a peculiar kind of emotion. Postmodern intensity also occurs when "the body is plugged into the new electronic media" (Donougho, 1989:85).

Third, there is a loss of historicity. We cannot know the past. All we have access to are texts about the past, and all we can do is produce yet other texts about that topic. This loss of historicity has led to the "random cannibalization of all styles of the past" (Jameson, 1984:65–66). The result leads us to another key term in postmodern thinking—*pastiche*. Because it is impossible for historians to find the truth about the past, or even to put together a coherent story about it, they are satisfied with creating pastiches, or hodgepodges of ideas, sometimes contradictory and confused, about the past. Further, there is no clear sense of historical development, of time passing. Past and present are inextricably intertwined. For example, in historical novels such as E. L. Doctorow's *Ragtime,* we see the "disappearance of the historical referent. This historical novel can no longer set out to represent historical past; it can only 'represent' our ideas and stereotypes about that past" (Jameson, 1984:71). Another example is the movie *Body Heat,* which, while clearly about the present, creates an atmosphere reminiscent of the 1930s. In order to do this,

> the object world of the present-day—artifacts and appliances, even automobiles, whose styling would serve to date the image—is elaborately edited out. Everything in the film, therefore, conspires to blur its official contemporaneity and to make it possible for you to receive the narrative as though it were set in some eternal Thirties, beyond historical time.
>
> (Jameson, 1984:68)

A movie like *Body Heat* or a novel like *Ragtime* is "an elaborated symptom of the waning of our historicity" (Jameson, 1984:68). This loss of temporality, this inability to distinguish between past, present, and future, is manifested at the individual level in a kind of schizophrenia. For the postmodern individual, events are fragmented and discontinuous.

Fourth, there is a new technology associated with postmodern society. Instead of productive technologies such as the automobile assembly line, we have the dominance of *re*productive technologies, especially electronic media such as the television set and the computer. Rather than the "exciting" technology of the Industrial Revolution, we have technologies such as television, "which articulates nothing but rather implodes, carrying its flattened image surface within itself" (Jameson, 1984:79). The implosive, flattening technologies of the postmodern era give birth to very different cultural products than the explosive, expanding technologies of the modern era did.

In sum, Jameson presents us with an image of postmodernity in which people are adrift and unable to comprehend the multinational capitalist system or the explosively growing culture in which they live. As a paradigm of this world, and of one's place in it, Jameson offers the example of Los Angeles's Hotel Bonaventure, designed by a famous postmodern architect, John Portman. One of the points Jameson makes about the hotel is that one is unable to get one's bearings in the lobby. The lobby is an example of what Jameson means by *hyperspace,* an area where modern conceptions of space are useless in helping us orient ourselves. In this case, the lobby is surrounded by four absolutely symmetrical towers that contain the rooms. In fact, the hotel had to add color coding and directional signals to help people find their way. But the key point is that, as it was designed, people had great difficulty getting their bearings in the hotel lobby.

This situation in the lobby of the Hotel Bonaventure is a metaphor for our inability to get our bearings in the multinational economy and cultural explosion of late capitalism. Unlike many postmodernists, Jameson as a Marxist is unwilling to leave it at that and comes up with at least a partial solution to the problem of living in a postmodern society. What we need, he says, are cognitive maps in order to find our way around (Jagtenberg and McKie, 1997). Yet these are not, cannot be, the maps of old. Thus, Jameson awaits a

> breakthrough to some as yet unimaginable new mode of representing . . . [late capitalism], in which we may again begin to grasp our positioning as individual and collective subjects and regain a capacity to act and struggle which is at present neutralized by our spatial as well as our social confusion. The political form of postmodernism, if there ever is any, will have as its vocation the invention and projection of a global cognitive mapping, on a social as well as a spatial scale.
>
> (Jameson, 1984:92)

These cognitive maps can come from various sources—social theorists (including Jameson himself, who can be seen as providing such a map in his work), novelists, and people on an everyday basis who can map their own spaces. Of course, the maps are not ends in themselves to a Marxist like Jameson but are to be used as the basis for radical political action in postmodern society.

The need for maps is linked to Jameson's view that we have moved from a world that is defined temporally to one that is defined spatially. Indeed, the idea of hyperspace and the example of the lobby of the Hotel Bonaventure reflect the dominance of space in the postmodern world. Thus, for Jameson, the central problem today is "the loss of our ability to *position ourselves within this space and to cognitively map it*" (Jameson, in Stephanson, 1989:48).

Interestingly, Jameson links the idea of cognitive maps to Marxian theory, specifically the idea of class consciousness: "'Cognitive mapping' was in reality nothing but a code word for 'class consciousness' . . . only it proposed the need for class consciousness of a new and hitherto undreamed of kind, while it also inflected the account in the direction of that new spatiality implicit in the postmodern" (1989:387).

The great strength of Jameson's work is his effort to synthesize Marxian theory and postmodernism. While he should be praised for this effort, the fact is that his work often displeases *both* Marxists and postmodernists. According to Best and Kellner, "His work is an example of the potential hazards of an eclectic, multiperspectival theory which attempts to incorporate a myriad of positions, some of them in tension or contradiction with each other, as when he produces the uneasy alliance between classical Marxism and extreme postmodernism" (1991:192). More specifically, for example, some Marxists object to the degree to which Jameson has accepted postmodernism as a cultural dominant, and some postmodernists criticize his acceptance of a totalizing theory of the world.

Extreme Postmodern Social Theory: Jean Baudrillard

If Jameson is among the more moderate postmodern social theorists, Jean Baudrillard is one of the most radical and outrageous of this genre. Unlike Jameson, Baudrillard was trained as a sociologist (Genosko, 2005; Wernick, 2000), but his work has long since left the confines of that discipline. Indeed, it cannot be contained by any discipline, and Baudrillard would in any case reject the whole idea of disciplinary boundaries.

Following Kellner (1989d, 2011), we offer a brief overview of the twists and turns in Baudrillard's work. His earliest work, going back to the 1960s, was both modernist (Baudrillard did not use the term *postmodernism* until the 1980s) and Marxian in its orientation. His early works involved a Marxian critique of the consumer society. However, this work was already heavily influenced by linguistics and semiotics, with the result that Kellner contends that it is best to see this early work as "a semiological supplement to Marx's theory of political economy." However, it was not long before Baudrillard began to criticize the Marxian approach (as well as structuralism) and ultimately to leave it behind.

In *The Mirror of Production,* Baudrillard (1973/1975) came to view the Marxian perspective as the mirror image of conservative political economy. In other words, Marx (and the Marxists) bought into the same worldview as the conservative supporters of capitalism. In Baudrillard's view, Marx was infected by the "virus of bourgeois thought" (1973/1975:39). Specifically, Marx's approach was infused with conservative ideas such as "work" and "value." What was needed was a new, more radical orientation.

Baudrillard articulated the idea of symbolic exchange as an alternative to—the radical negation of—economic exchange (D. Cook, 1994). Symbolic exchange involved an uninterrupted *cycle* of "taking and returning, giving and receiving," a "*cycle* of gifts and countergifts" (Baudrillard, 1973/1975:83). Here was an idea that did not fall into the trap that ensnared Marx; symbolic exchange was clearly outside of, and opposed to, the logic of capitalism. The idea of symbolic exchange implied a political program aimed at creating a society characterized by such exchange. For example, Baudrillard is critical of the working class and seems more positive toward the new left or hippies. However, Baudrillard soon gave up on *all* political objectives.

Instead, Baudrillard turned his attention to the analysis of contemporary society, which, as he sees it, is dominated no longer by production, but rather by the "media, cybernetic models and steering systems, computers, information processing, entertainment and knowledge industries, and so forth" (Kellner, 1989d:61). Emanating from these systems is a veritable explosion of signs (D. Harris, 1996). It could be said that we have moved from a society dominated by the mode of production to one controlled by the code of production. The objective has shifted from exploitation and profit to domination by the signs and the systems that produce them. Furthermore, while there was a time when the signs stood for something real, now they refer to little more than themselves and other signs; signs have become self-referential. We can no longer tell what is real; the distinction between signs and reality has *imploded.* More generally, the postmodern world (for now Baudrillard is operating squarely within that world) is a world characterized by such implosion as distinguished from the explosions (of productive systems, of commodities, of technologies, and so on) that characterized modern society. Thus, just as the modern world underwent a process of differentiation, the postmodern world can be seen as undergoing *de-differentiation.*

Another way that Baudrillard, like Jameson, describes the postmodern world is that it is characterized by *simulations;* we live in "the age of simulation" (Baudrillard, 1983:4; Der Derian, 1994). The process of simulation leads to the creation of *simulacra,* or "reproductions of objects or events" (Kellner, 1989d:78). With the distinction between signs and reality imploding, it is increasingly difficult to tell the real from those things that simulate the real. For example, Baudrillard talks of "the dissolution of TV into life, the dissolution of life into TV" (1983:55). Eventually, it is the representations of the real, the simulations, that come to be predominant. We are in the thrall of these simulations, which "form a spiralling, circular system with no beginning or end" (Kellner, 1989d:83).

Baudrillard (1983) describes this world as *hyperreality*. For example, the media cease to be a mirror of reality but become that reality, or even more real than that reality. The tabloid news shows that are so popular on TV these days (for example, *Inside Edition*) are good examples (another is "infomercials" and so-called "reality TV" programs) because the falsehoods and distortions they peddle to viewers are more than reality—they are hyperreality. The result is that what is real comes to be subordinated and ultimately dissolved altogether. It becomes impossible to distinguish the real from the spectacle. In fact, "real" events increasingly take on the character of the hyperreal. For example, the trial of former football great O. J. Simpson for the murders of Nicole Simpson and Ronald Goldman seemed hyperreal and perfect fodder for hyperreal TV shows like *Inside Edition*. In the end, there is no more reality, only hyperreality.

In all this, Baudrillard is focusing on culture, which he sees as undergoing a massive and "catastrophic" revolution. That revolution involves the masses becoming increasingly passive, rather than increasingly rebellious, as they were to the Marxists. Thus, the mass is seen as a " 'black hole' [that] absorbs all meaning, information, communication, messages and so on, thereby rendering them meaningless . . . masses go sullenly on their ways, ignoring attempts to manipulate them" (Kellner, 1989d:85). Indifference, apathy, and inertia are all good terms to describe the masses saturated with media signs, simulacra, and hyperreality. The masses are not seen as manipulated by the media, but the media are being forced to supply their escalating demands for objects and spectacles. In a sense, society itself is imploding into the black hole that is the masses. Summing up much of this theory, Kellner concludes,

> Acceleration of inertia, the implosion of meaning in the media, the implosion of the social in the mass, the implosion of the mass in a dark hole of nihilism and meaninglessness; such is the Baudrillardian postmodern vision.
>
> (Kellner, 1989d:118)

As extraordinary as this analysis may seem, Baudrillard was even more bizarre, scandalous, irreverent, promiscuous, and playful, or as Kellner says, "carnivalesque," in *Symbolic Exchange and Death* (1976/1993). Baudrillard sees contemporary society as a death culture, with death being the "paradigm of all social exclusion and discrimination" (Kellner, 1989d:104). The emphasis on death also reflects the binary opposition of life and death. In contrast, societies characterized by symbolic exchange end binary oppositions in general and more specifically the opposition between life and death (and, in the process, the exclusion and discrimination that accompany a death culture). It is anxiety about death and exclusion that leads people to plunge themselves even more deeply into the consumer culture.

Holding up symbolic exchange as the preferred alternative to contemporary society began to seem too primitive to Baudrillard (1979/1990), and he came to regard *seduction* as the preferred alternative, perhaps because it fit better with his emerging sense of postmodernism. Seduction "involves the charms of pure and mere games, superficial rituals" (Kellner, 1989d:149). Baudrillard is extolling the power and virtues of seduction, with its meaninglessness, playfulness, depthlessness, "non-sense," and irrationality, over a world characterized by production.

In the end, Baudrillard is offering a fatal theory. Thus, in one of his later works, *America,* Baudrillard says that in his visit to that country, he "sought the finished form of the future catastrophe" (1986/1989:5). There is no revolutionary hope as there is in Marx's work. Nor is there even the possibility of reforming society as Durkheim hoped. Rather, we seem doomed to a life of simulations, hyperreality, and implosion of everything into an incomprehensible black hole.

Interestingly, as a result of the events of 9-11, Baudrillard seemed to back down from some of his stronger, more radical, postmodern claims about hyperreality. As part of his description of the hyperreal, Baudrillard had claimed that the contemporary world is characterized by "weak events" (Kellner, 2011). Weak events are historical events that don't change the basic function of the code and the hyperreal. In this spirit, for example, Baudrillard claimed that the 1991 "Gulf war never happened" (Baudrillard, 1995). In contrast, the events of 9-11 were a "strong event . . . the ultimate event, the mother of all events, the pure event uniting within itself all the events that have never taken place" (Baudrillard quoted in Kellner, 2011:331). Though Baudrillard remained controversial until his death in 2007, Kellner suggests that 9-11 reignited his social theory, giving rise to analyses of difference, conflict, terrorism, and global capitalism. Contrary to his earlier idea that the code absorbs and assimilates all that is in its path, Baudrillard now argued that global capitalism has lost its capacity to absorb all conflicts within the system. This opens the world up to massive possibilities for social change, for good or for bad.

Criticisms and Post-Postmodern Social Theory

Debates about poststructural and postmodern social theory generated an enormous amount of heat. Supporters were often gushing in their praise, while detractors frequently were driven into what can only be described as a blind rage. For example, John O'Neill (1995) writes of "the insanity of postmodernism" (p. 16); he describes it as offering "a great black sky of nonsense" (p. 191) and as "an already dead moment of the mind" (p. 199). Leaving aside the extreme rhetoric, what are some of the major criticisms of postmodern social theory (bearing in mind that given the diversity of postmodern social theories, general criticisms of those theories are of questionable validity and utility)?

1. Postmodern theory is criticized for its failure to live up to modern scientific standards, standards that postmodernists eschew. To the scientifically oriented modernist, it is impossible to know whether the contentions of postmodernists are true. To put it in more formal terms, almost everything that the postmodernists have to say is viewed by modernists as not being falsifiable—that is, their ideas cannot be disproved, especially by empirical research

(Frow, 1991; Kumar, 1995). Of course, this criticism assumes the existence of a scientific model, of reality, and of a search for and existence of truth. All these assumptions would, naturally, be rejected by postmodernists.

2. Since the knowledge produced by postmodernists cannot be seen as constituting a body of scientific ideas, it might be better to look at postmodern social theory as ideology (Kumar, 1995). Once we do that, it is no longer a matter of whether the ideas are true, but simply whether we believe in them. Those who believe in one set of ideas have no grounds to argue that their ideas are any better or worse than any other set of ideas.

3. Because they are unconstrained by the norms of science, postmodernists are free to do as they please, to "play" with a wide range of ideas. Broad generalizations are offered, often without qualification. Furthermore, in expressing their positions, postmodern social theorists are not restricted to the dispassionate rhetoric of the modern scientist. The excessive nature of much of postmodern discourse makes it difficult for most of those outside the perspective to accept its basic tenets.

4. Postmodern ideas are often so vague and abstract that it is difficult, if not impossible, to connect them to the social world (Calhoun, 1993b). Relatedly, meanings of concepts tend to change over the course of a postmodernist's work, but the reader, unaware of the original meanings, is unclear about any changes.

5. Despite their propensity to criticize the grand narratives of modern theorists, postmodern social theorists often offer their own varieties of such narratives. For example, Jameson often is accused of employing Marxian grand narratives and totalizations.

6. In their analyses, postmodern social theorists often offer critiques of modern society, but those critiques are of questionable validity because they generally lack a normative basis from which to make such judgments.

7. Given their rejection of an interest in the subject and subjectivity, postmodernists often lack a theory of agency.

8. Postmodern social theorists are best at critiquing society, but they lack any vision of what society ought to be.

9. Postmodern social theory leads to profound pessimism.

10. While postmodern social theorists grapple with what they consider major social issues, they often end up ignoring what many consider the key problems of our time.

11. Although one can find adherents among them, as we saw in Chapter 12, the feminists have been particularly strong critics of postmodern social theory. Feminists have tended to be critical of postmodern social theory's rejection of the subject, of its opposition to universal, cross-cultural categories (such as gender and gender oppression), of its excessive concern with difference, of its rejection of truth, and of its inability to develop a critical political agenda.

By the beginning of the twenty-first century, the debates surrounding postmodern social theory had exhausted themselves and few would identify themselves as postmodernists (though it's not clear that many would have in the first place). This is not to say that postmodernism has not had an impact. Many of the core ideas of post-modernism have been incorporated into social theory in general and remain important: decentering of the subject, the role of media and consumer codes in constructing con-temporary persons, the importance of language and semiotic systems for the construction of social reality, and even the persistent questioning of scientific authority.

In addition, many of the theorists we have discussed here continue to influence the field. Foucault, in particular, is widely discussed and cited. Baudrillard's work, though less influential, continues to inspire research programs, especially under the aegis of the *International Journal of Baudrillard Studies*. The work of Gilles Deleuze is currently quite influential. Foucault identified Deleuze as one of the most important philosophers of the twentieth century (Buchanan, 2011). Recently, his writings have inspired the development of a new social ontology based around the concepts of assemblage and social complexity (De Landa, 2006). His work is also cited by actor-network theorists (see Chapter 17) and his ideas about life energy and affect are central building blocks for the emerging perspective of affect theory (see Chapter 17).

The influence of postmodern theory is also reflected in the way that theorists have responded to it. Much poststructural and postmodern theory originated in France and therefore was taken up in France earlier than in North America. As a result French social theorists have had a head start in developing "post-postmodern theories." Given their rejection of the human subject, the postmodernists are accused of antihumanism (Ferry and Renaut, 1985/1990:30). Thus, the post-postmodernists are seeking to rescue humanism (and subjectivity) from the postmodern critique that presumably left such an idea for dead. For example, Lilla (1994:20) argues that what is being sought is "a new defense of universal, rational norms in morals and politics, and especially a defense of human rights."

Another strand of "post-postmodern social theory" involves an effort to rein-state the importance of liberalism in the face of the postmodern assault on the liberal grand narrative (Lilla, 1994). The works of the poststructuralists/postmodernists (e.g., Foucault's *Discipline and Punish*), even when they were couched in highly abstract theoretical terms, were read by some French scholars as attacks on structures in general, especially the structure of liberal bourgeois society and its "governmentalities." Not only did postmodern theorists question such a society, this also led to the view that there was no way of escaping the reach of that society's power structure. Issues thought dead during the heyday of postmodern theory—"human rights, constitutional government, representation, class, individualism" (Lilla, 1994:16)—have attracted renewed attention. The nihilism of postmodernism has been replaced by a variety of orientations sympathetic to liberal society. One could say that this revival of interest in liberalism (as well as humanism) indicates a restoration of interest in, and sympathy for, modern society.

Other aspects of post-postmodern social theory are made clear in Gilles Lipovetsky's (1987/1994) *The Empire of Fashion: Dressing Modern Democracy*. Lipovetsky takes on, quite explicitly, the poststructuralists and postmodernists. Here is the way he articulates the position taken by them and to which he is opposed, at least to some degree:

> In our societies, fashion is in the driver's seat. In less than half a century,
> attractiveness and evanescence have become the organizing principles of modern
> collective life. We live in societies where the trivial predominates. . . . Should we
> be dismayed by this? Does it announce the slow but inexorable decline of the
> West? Must we take it as a sign of the decadence of the democratic ideal? Nothing
> is more commonplace or widespread than the tendency to stigmatize—not without
> cause, moreover—the consumerist bent of democracies; they are represented as
> devoid of any great mobilizing collective projects, lulled into a stupor by the
> private orgies of consumerism, infantilized by "instant" culture, by advertising, by
> politics-as-theater.
>
> (Lipovetsky, 1987/1994:6)

In contrast, while he recognizes the problems associated with it, Lipovetsky (1987/1994:6) argues that fashion is "the primary agent of the spiraling movement toward individualism and the consolidation of liberal societies." Thus, Lipovetsky does not share the gloomy view of the postmodernists; he sees not only the negative, but also the positive, side of fashion and has a generally optimistic view of the future of society.

While Lipovetsky has much that is positive to say about fashion, consumerism, individualism, democracy, and modern society, he also recognizes the problems associated with each one. He concludes that we live in "neither the best of worlds nor the worst. . . . Fashion is neither angel nor devil. . . . Such is the greatness of fashion, which always refers us, as individuals, back to ourselves; such is the misery of fashion, which renders us increasingly problematic to ourselves and others" (Lipovetsky, 1987/1994:240–241). Intellectuals are warned not to dismiss fashion (and the rest) just because it offends their intellectual sympathies. It is for being dismissive of such important phenomena as fashion (and liberalism, democracy, and so on) that Lipovetsky attacks the poststructuralists/postmodernists and others (e.g., critical theorists). In any case, the assault on fashion (and other aspects of modern society) has led us to lose sight of the fact that "the age of fashion remains the major factor in the process that has drawn men and women collectively away from obscurantism and fanaticism, has instituted an open public space and shaped a more lawful, more mature, more skeptical humanity" (Lipovetsky, 1987/1994:12).

While his paradigm is clothing, Lipovetsky argues that fashion is a form of social change that is a distinctive product of the Occident. In contrast to the postmodernists, who were resistant to the idea of origins, Lipovetsky traces the origins of fashion to the upper classes in the West in the late Middle Ages. Fashion is a form of change characterized by a brief time span, largely fanciful shifts, and the ability to affect a wide variety of sectors of the social world. A number of factors came together in the West to give birth to the fashion form, especially its consecration of both individuality and novelty.

Fashion has been a force in the rise of individuality by allowing people to express themselves and their individuality in their clothing even while they might also be attending to collective changes in fashion. Similarly, it has been a factor in greater equality by allowing those lower in the stratification system to at least dress like those who ranked above them. Fashion also has permitted frivolous self-expression. Most generally, it is linked to increasing individualism and the democratization of society as a whole.

While all kinds of theories have directly or indirectly opposed themselves to postmodernism in the UK and North America, two particular perspectives are worth noting because of the growing attention they are receiving in contemporary sociology. First, *critical realism* directly challenges the antifoundationalist theory of knowledge promoted by postmodern theory. Though the origins of critical realism go back to philosopher Roy Bhaskar's (2008) work in the 1970s, it has recently become quite influential in the UK and Canada. Critical realism holds the line between positivist sociology and postmodern, relativist sociology. Where many varieties of postmodernism argue that reality is a social construction, critical realists contend that the social world is organized by deep structures. However, unlike most positivist philosophies it does not treat these deep structures as entities that determine social life. Rather, because humans have the capacity for thought and interpretation, the effect of deep structures can be manifold. Clearly there is overlap between critical realism and numerous other theoretical perspectives. For example, Morgan (2007) notes that it addresses many of the issues handled by Giddens in his structuration theory. This said, the perspective is one around which a large number of contemporary theorists are gathering.

Finally, in the United States, Jeffrey Alexander (2003) is developing a perspective that he calls *cultural sociology*. Like poststructuralists and postmodernists Alexander places culture at the center of analysis. However, in contrast to poststructural and postmodern analysis Alexander believes that cultural analysis can generate accurate and more or less true accounts of the world. In particular, it can reveal the ways in which culture determines action. From his perspective all action "is embedded to some extent in a horizon of affect and meaning" (2003:12). In developing his form of cultural analysis Alexander (in an essay written with Philip Smith, 2001) distinguishes *cultural sociology* from the more commonplace *sociology of culture*. Where the sociology of culture treats culture as a derivative of other, presumably more important, social forces (such as the economy), cultural sociology treats culture as an entity unto itself.

Here Alexander argues for a *strong program* in the study of culture. The strong program is comprised of three elements. First, it insists upon the autonomy of culture, meaning that culture must be treated as a social force independent of social structure. For example, Alexander is critical of Marxist analyses of culture (see, for example, the discussion of Jameson earlier in this chapter) that treat culture seriously but nevertheless see it as connected to political economic structures. More relevant to the focus of this chapter, Alexander criticizes poststructuralists like Foucault for not taking culture seriously enough. Foucault placed discourse analysis front and center. However, by emphasizing the relationship between power and knowledge he grounded discourse/culture in material, political economic regimes. For Alexander, culture must be understood as an entity that can shape action independent of these other forces.

The second element of the strong program is the use of a hermeneutic, or interpretive, technique. Here Alexander (2003) relies upon Clifford Geertz's notion of "thick description," a method by which one describes the "webs of meaning" out of which people live (2003:13; see also Alexander, Smith, and Norton, 2011). However he wants to go further than Geertz and argues in favor of a *structural hermeneutics*, which Alexander describes as "an effort to understand culture not just as a text (ala Geertz) but rather as a text that is underpinned by signs and symbols that are in patterned relationships to each other" (2003:24). In fact, here Alexander returns to the insights of structuralism, arguing that it is necessary to study the binary oppositions that are coded within culture. The classical example is the distinction between sacred and profane that Durkheim identified as one of the central dichotomies of religious practice. The third element of Alexander's strong program is to show how culture directs action. Here again we see a difference between the postmodern analysis of culture and Alexander's cultural sociology. For Alexander culture causes certain forms of action. The problem for a cultural sociology, then, is to treat culture as a force unto itself, with its own organizing logic, that has a direct influence on human action. To this end Alexander has applied his cultural sociology to phenomena such as civil society, the Watergate scandal, and the Holocaust, among others. In all of this, like postmodernists, Alexander questions the relevance of traditional sociological approaches to culture. However, he proposes an alternative, more realist version of cultural analysis than imagined by the postmodernists.

Summary

This chapter covers a wide range of important and interrelated developments in the recent history of sociological theory. The source of many of these developments is the revolution that took place in linguistics and led to a search for the underlying structures of language. Structuralism, as this revolution came to be called, affected a number of fields, including anthropology (especially the work of Lévi-Strauss) and Marxian theory (structural Marxism in particular).

While structuralism continues to affect the thinking of social theorists, it gave birth to a movement known as poststructuralism. As the name suggests, poststructuralism built on the ideas of structuralism but went well beyond them to create a distinctive mode of thought. The most important of the poststructuralists is Michel Foucault. In a series of important books, Foucault created a number of theoretical ideas that are likely to be influential for many decades to come. Also of importance is the work of Giorgio Agamben, especially his thinking on bare life, state of exception, and the camp.

Emerging, in part, out of poststructuralism is an enormously influential development known as postmodern theory. Many fields have been influenced by postmodern thinking—art, architecture, philosophy, and sociology. There are a wide variety of postmodern social theories, and this chapter examines a moderate version offered by Fredric Jameson and a radical alternative offered by Jean Baudrillard. At the minimum, postmodern social theory represents a challenge to sociological theory. At the maximum, it stands as a rejection of much, if not all, sociological theory. The chapter closes with some of the major criticisms of postmodern social theory, a discussion of the significance of post-postmodern social theory, and a review of some particularly important emerging alternatives to postmodern theory.

Social Theory in the Twenty-First Century

Chapter Outline

Critical Theories of Race and Racism

Queer Theory

Actor-Network Theory, Posthumanism, and Postsociality

Affect Theory

Our goal in this final chapter is to bring theory as up-to-date as possible by describing a number of theories that have become important to social theory in the last twenty years. We have noted some of these theories in the Chapter 6 historical review and a number of these theories have already been addressed in this book. For example, globalization theory, described in Chapter 15, is of central importance in the contemporary moment. As a group, the four theories presented in this chapter were not chosen to reflect any common theoretical agenda. However, it is worth noting that there are a number of overlapping themes among the theories discussed here. This indicates some prevailing concerns that occupy the present moment.

Alongside globalization, theories concerned with *identity* have become particularly important in recent years. The theoretical focus on identity is a product of the civil rights and postcolonial movements of the mid-twentieth century, but more recently the cultural intermingling brought about by globalization. In these instances identity relates to questions of citizenship and the formation of multicultural societies. As Bryan Turner (2009) has argued, the issue of citizenship, who belongs and is entitled to social and political rights, is of central importance to the contemporary historical moment. In particular, recent theories of identity have focused on the construction of marginalized identities—those whose right to belong is questioned. In this chapter, we consider two theoretical perspectives that describe the social processes surrounding marginalized identity. *Critical theories of race and racism* theorize the creation of racialized identities. *Queer theory* concerns itself with the study of sexuality, in particular the creation of sexual identifications.

Another major area of inquiry in contemporary theory is the impact of science and technology on contemporary societies. Where previous social theories treated science as one of many social institutions, contemporary theories of science and

technology treat science as a force central to the constitution of contemporary societies. As a representative of this area of development we describe *actor-network theory*
and related theories of *posthumanism* and *postsociality*. As we will see, these theoretical perspectives have also addressed questions of identity. In the contemporary
moment, the construction of identity is shaped by scientific ideas and practices. This
is particularly the case with the next area of theoretical inquiry introduced here: affect
theory. *Affect theory* is one of the most recent developments in social theory. It draws
on many postmodernist and poststructuralist ideas and is heavily influenced by work
in the area of cultural studies. Briefly, affect theory studies the way in which social
orders and identities are produced through affective, or emotive, processes. Part of the
argument made by affect theorists is that we have entered an era in which social life
is primarily governed through affect.

Critical Theories of Race and Racism[1]

As discussed in detail in Chapter 12, there has long been a body of feminist theory
dealing with sex (and gender) and sexism. Feminist theories are the first to have
theories on the construction of marginalized identities, in particular the inequalities
that accompany the distinction between male and female. Theories of race and racism,
though part of multicultural social theory, have tended to lag behind feminist theory.
(Of course, there is no clear dividing line between these theories. Mohanty [2002:2],
for example, describes herself as an "antiracist feminist." Some of the most important
developments in feminist theory and multiculturalism [e.g., P. H. Collins, 1990, 1998]
relate to giving black women their due in such theorizing.) This is not to say that
scholars have ignored theorizing about race and racism. Certainly, W.E.B. Du Bois,
for one, has long been recognized as an important theorist of race and racism, and
evidence of his importance has increased significantly in recent years (see Chapter 11
in *Classical Sociological Theory* [Ritzer, 2008]; Goldberg and Essed, 2002; P. Taylor,
2011). However, in the last decade or two, theories of race and racism have begun to
expand dramatically.

Although sociologists and other social scientists have been making significant
contributions to theories of racism since Du Bois's work around the turn of the twentieth century and before, the recent boom in this mode of theorizing received an
important impetus from the development of "critical race theory" largely in the field
of law (Delgado and Stefancic, 2001:3; Valdes, Culp, and Harris, 2002). That theory
came about as a result of the growing realization that the civil rights movement of
the 1960s had lost its momentum, if not been reversed, and there was a need not only
for a revivified social activism but also for new theorizing about race. The ideas
associated with critical race theory developed from a wide range of sources, but some
of them are quite familiar to social theorists, such as those derived from Marxian
theory (e.g., Gramsci), poststructuralism (e.g., Derrida), feminist theory, and, of
course, Du Bois's contributions.

---

1. We here employing a title used by Patricia Hill Collins rather than the more common label "race theory."

Delgado and Stefancic, as well as Matsuda et al. (2003), outline at least a provisional list of the basic tenets of critical race theory:

- Racism is not an aberration; it is "normal" and endemic to American life. This makes it difficult to deal with.
- Much of the population has little incentive to eradicate racism. White elites gain from it materially (through exploitation of blacks and other minorities). Working-class whites also gain materially as well as psychically by having a group of people to whom they can favorably compare themselves in spite of their own difficulties.
- Race is not an objective or fixed reality. It is a social construction that changes over time (this idea aligns critical race theory broadly with the social-constructionist approach in sociology; see Berger and Luckmann, 1967). To emphasize that it is a social construction, critical race theorists generally do not talk about race, because this term suggests that race is a fixed and inherent characteristic of persons (i.e., we are all born with a race). Rather, critical race theorists, and theorists of race and racism in general, refer to *racialization*—the ever-active processes that construct the social category of race. Such social constructions are created, manipulated, and sometimes even retired, though usually to be replaced by new social constructions. This social-constructionist orientation is related to skepticism about the supposed ahistoricism of American law and skepticism about legal claims of neutrality, objectivity, color blindness, and meritocracy. That is, they all may be seen as social constructions that can be manipulated, revised, or even jettisoned when such actions are deemed necessary.
- Differential racialization "involves the ways the dominant society racializes different minority groups at different times, in response to shifting needs such as the labor market" (Delgado and Stefancic, 2001:8). Thus, although blacks have been racialized since practically the inception of the United States, other minorities have come to be racialized over time. Examples include the Japanese during World War II, Muslims after September 11, 2001, and Mexican Americans in recent years as a result of growing concern over legal and illegal immigration.
- As in feminist theory, intersectionality (P. Collins, 1990, 1998) and anti-essentialism are key ideas in critical race theory. Thus, blacks (and other minorities) have no "single, easily stated, unitary identity" (Delgado and Stefancic, 2001:9). Rather, they, as is true of all others, exist, at least potentially, at the intersection of "conflicting, overlapping identities, loyalties, and allegiances" (Delgado and Stefancic, 2001:9). These may include religion, social class, gender, sexual orientation, and political preference.
- Great importance is accorded to the experiential knowledge of people of color and to communities of origin.
- The emphasis on the experiential knowledge of people of color is related to, but also somewhat in contrast with, the anti-essentialism of critical race theory. It suggests the highly controversial idea (given the postmodern critique

of essentialism) that blacks and other racial minorities are uniquely able to speak and write about race and racism because of their specific histories and experiences with oppression. Beyond its essentialism, another of the reasons this emphasis is controversial is that it could be argued that the unique history and experiences of whites in and with systems of oppression give whites a similarly specific, albeit different, perspective on race and racism. The history and experience of whites would seemingly make it as legitimate for them to speak on racial matters as it is for blacks.

• As part of a broader goal of eliminating all forms of oppression, critical race theory is oriented to the elimination of racial oppression.

Critical theories of race and racism (CTRR) have much in common with critical race theory, including the goal of dealing with social injustices, the reduction or elimination of social inequalities, and a strong focus on intersectionality. However, there are also important differences stemming from the fact that CTRR are rooted much more in the social sciences, including sociology, than is critical race theory with its base in legal scholarship and activism. This difference serves to sensitize CTRR to and involve them in cutting-edge issues in theory such as the relationship between race and racism and agency-structure, political economy, and globalization. Included in or related to globalization is a concern for race and racism as it relates to nation-states, nationalism, and ethnonationalism (Connor, 2007), transnationalism (Remennick, 2007), colonialism, neocolonialism (Go, 2007a), decolonization (Go, 2007b), imperialism, empire, and so on. Thus, while critical race theory focuses on the United States and U.S. law, CTRR have a much broader, even global focus (Goldberg and Essed, 2002:4). In addition, CTRR are open to a much wider array of classical and contemporary theories as they apply to race. For example, Darder and Torres (2004:23) adopt a political economy approach to race, one that is heavily indebted to Marx and that adopts a "historical materialist approach." In articulating their approach, Darder and Torres criticize critical race theory for ignoring issues of political economy.

A far broader theoretical approach is adopted by Michael Brown et al. (2003) in *Whitewashing Race*. They operate from a macrostructural and macrocultural approach to race. They explicitly contrast their orientation to what they call "realist analysis," which adopts a micro-focus on individuals and their intentions and choices, thereby ignoring larger structures and institutions.

The realist focus leads to a concern with individual prejudice and discrimination (Law, 2007) and allows for the conclusion that white racism has ended, or is at least in decline. In contrast, Michael Brown and colleagues focus on a wide range of social structures and institutions that, in their view, have led to white accumulation and black disaccumulation, to cumulative structural inequality in society. They look not only at the structure of law but also at racial stratification, labor markets, housing markets, government policies, and so on. Racial disparities have existed in these structures historically, and they continue to exist. Thus, blacks continue to face racial discrimination, and they must deal with the legacy of racial discrimination in these domains. It is therefore not enough to deal with the operation of contemporary structures and institutions; the legacy of discrimination at these levels needs to be confronted and rectified.

A more general conclusion to be derived from critical theories of race and racism is that, as Cornell West (1994) pointed out, "race matters" and that it continues to matter not only in the legal system but throughout the structures and institutions of society.

Many other scholars show that race continues to matter in the United States. For example, Guinier and Torres (2002) draw an analogy between race and the miner's canary used to indicate problems, indeed impending human death, in mines. Race in the United States is like the miner's canary in the sense that problems associated with it point to broader, perhaps fatal problems in the larger society. Guinier and Torres (2002:12), however, do not limit their analysis to blacks but develop a broader concept of "political race" that, among other things, includes various minorities and even some whites (see also Bonilla-Silva, 2003). Nevertheless, it is still people of color who will take the lead in social change movements reflective of the political dimension of political race.

Guinier and Torres explicitly seek to embed their work within critical race theory. However, they also go beyond it in various ways (e.g., shifting the focus from law to politics), and in doing so they move toward CTRR.

A more clearly CTRR effort with an American focus is Bonilla-Silva's (2003) study and critique of color-blind racism (Guinier and Torres also attack this idea) in the United States. Bonilla-Silva is also critical of the view that racism today is of little more than historical interest. Rather, he sees color-blindness as a smoke screen that allows white Americans to continue to perpetuate racial discrimination. He concludes that color-blind racism provides a "sanitized . . . way of calling minorities niggers [Kennedy, 2002], spics, or chinks" (Bonilla-Silva, 2003:181). Based on this conclusion, Bonilla-Silva (2003:185) proposes a variety of practical steps (such an orientation toward praxis is common in the CTRR literature) to combat the problem of "'new racism' practices and color-blind idiocy."

Increasingly, race theorists have focused on the relationship between science and the construction of race. Scientific categories and tools have been used in the construction of race for the last two centuries. Eighteenth- and nineteenth-century scholars, coming from both the natural and social sciences, developed categories and hierarchies that legitimated racial oppression. For example, the science of craniometry claimed that differences in intelligence between races could be measured by skull size (Gould, 1981/1996). Not only, as Gould has demonstrated, were the scientific claims based on faulty measures, but this kind of science actually helped to create the idea of racial difference rather than reflect a presumed preexisting set of racial differences. This kind of *scientific racism*, of course, is best reflected in the atrocities of the Holocaust.

Even though scientific theories are now rarely used to create explicit hierarchies of racial difference,[2] critical theorists have argued that recent work in the *new genomics* and the *genetics of disease* threatens to construct, albeit in a more subtle way,

---

2. An exception is the work of Herrnstein and Murray (1994), whose book, *The Bell Curve,* attracted widespread attention and debate in the 1990s. The book revived the idea that intelligence (IQ) is innately tied to race. Gould (1981/1996) demonstrates the falsity of their thesis.

a relationship between race and biology (Fujimura et al., 2008). Contemporary biomedical researchers, for example, study genetics in order to determine disease variation among populations. While these researchers claim that the research is about differences among populations, critics point out that this is in fact research about differences among so-called races. At the same time, this genetic research has led to the development of pharmaceuticals that are then marketed to particular racialized groups, further consolidating the view that specific "races" have particular biological characteristics and capacities. Rather than seeking remedies for disease within genetic differences, critics argue that it would be more valuable to concentrate on the proximate, social causes of disease—for example, social inequalities that lead to increased rates of diabetes among particular social groups.

Although there is much focus in CTRR on race in the United States, others associated with this orientation seek to demonstrate that race also matters globally. Thus, for example, Winant (2001) deals with race historically and in the United States, as well as in South Africa, Brazil, and Europe.

CTRR are still in the early stages of development and that makes it difficult to delineate clearly their fundamental characteristics, but Patricia Hill Collins delineates the following distinguishing features of critical theories of race and racism:[3]

1. CTRR do not simply study race and racism; they seek to deal with social inequalities and to advance social justice.
2. CTRR eschew all binary oppositions and look at everything from the perspective of intersecting entities. Such a view requires the use of multifaceted research methods.
3. CTRR are inherently multidisciplinary.
4. CTRR draw upon and advance intersectionality, looking at the relationship between race and racism and gender, ethnicity, class, sexuality, and nation.
5. CTRR are increasingly drawn to materialist (political economic) analyses of race and racism, as well as to how race and racism relate to globalization.
6. Structures of power are increasingly central to CTRR. Earlier concerns with the power of the American social welfare and criminal justice systems have been extended to topics such as nation-states and nationalism, democracy, empire, transnationalism, and imperialism.

This enumeration, especially the last three items, clearly aligns CTRR with other very contemporary, if not cutting-edge issues in social theory.

In conclusion, however, it is safe to say that there is as yet no "theory," critical or otherwise, of race and racism. But there is a historical body of theory to draw on (e.g., Du Bois, Said), a plethora of theoretical ideas and perspectives of great relevance (e.g., critical theory, Gramsci on hegemony, Hardt and Negri on empire), as well as a series of ideas developed from within CTRR (e.g., intersectionality). Out of this array of ideas, and undoubtedly many others, critical theories of race and racism will crystallize and expand their theoretical perspective in coming years.

---

3. The following enumeration is derived from the syllabus of Collins's graduate course Critical Theories of Race and Racism, University of Maryland (Fall, 2005).

Queer Theory[4]

Another area of theoretical inquiry concerned with questions of identity formation is queer theory. As we saw in the previous section, there is a tension in critical theories of race and racism between essentialist and anti-essentialist claims. On the one hand, critical theorists of race and racism demonstrate that the category of race is socially constructed: an anti-essentialist position. On the other hand, critical theorists of race and racism argue that it is important to take the experiences and narratives of marginalized racial groups seriously. That is, even though they do not explicitly adopt any essentialist notions of race, they nevertheless argue that the identities and experiences of racialized people are an important resource for theoretical understanding and political activism. In other words, in some cases identity is treated as a worthwhile and important theoretical concept. This is not the case in queer theory, which generally challenges any appeals to real identities and the truth of personal narratives.

Here we should distinguish between queer theory and the area of sociological inquiry called gay and lesbian studies (for more on this, see Giffney, 2004). Gay and lesbian studies takes seriously the concept of identity. It studies and theorizes the lives and experiences of gay and lesbian persons. This is an important task because historically these experiences have been marginalized and silenced. Even though, as we will see, queer theory is also concerned with the political problem of marginalization, it is nevertheless wary of identity thinking. In this respect where gay and lesbian studies are aligned with standpoint theories (see Chapter 12), queer theory is aligned with poststructuralist and postmodern thought (see Chapter 16).

Consistent with the assumptions of postmodernism, queer theorists argue that the concept of identity mistakenly assumes that all persons have essential, in-built character traits and, in the case of sexuality, essential sexual desires. As a postmodern perspective, queer theory rejects essentialist thinking and tries to open conceptual and practical spaces in which we can articulate forms of desire that are not captured within existing categories. The purpose is not merely to speak up for marginalized sexualities, but to establish the basis for descriptions of uncategorized and unmarked desires and forms of social relationship. For this reason, queer theory does not promote the truth or reality of homosexual desire alongside heterosexual desire. Instead it develops theoretical tools that demonstrate the contingency of all identities and then describes the processes through which sexual identifications are achieved. Queer theory "queers" social life by drawing attention to the in-betweens, the hidden spaces, and the invisible zones that both exist alongside but also help to constitute the meaning of identities and desires.

What Is Queer Theory?

The term *queer* has a number of different meanings. To some people it is a derogatory term for individuals with a same-sex desire. To others, *queer* has become an all-inclusive umbrella term for, among others, gay, lesbian, bisexual, transgendered,

---

4. This is a modified version of a piece originally written by Michael J. Ryan.

transsexual, curious, intersexed, questioning, and allied identities. To still others, including many queer theorists, it refers to such a broad multiplicity of identities that it implies a sort of anti-identity or even a nonidentity. Piontek (2006:2) has suggested using the term *queer* "to refer not to an identity but to a questioning stance, a cluster of methodologies that lets us explore the taken for granted and the familiar from new vantage points." *Queer* also can be used as a noun to describe such an identity or a nonidentity; as an adjective to modify a particular noun such as *theory;* or as a verb, turning something into that which is not normal. In the context of queer theory, the word has come to be used in all three ways as part of a broad intellectual and political project.

It is impossible to develop a comprehensive list of the identifying characteristics of queer theory, but Arlene Stein and Ken Plummer (1994) have noted four prominent "hallmarks":

1. "A conceptualization of sexuality which sees sexual power embodied in different levels of social life, expressed discursively and enforced through boundaries and binary divides" (Stein and Plummer, 1994:181–182). Any understanding of sexuality relies on relations of sexual power that are found in multiple forms of social life, even those forms not traditionally thought of as immediately sexual, such as popular culture, politics, education, and economics. This power is maintained by a constant reenactment, reproduction, and policing of the boundaries between sexual categories.
2. "Problematization of sexual and gender categories, and of identities in general. Identities are always on uncertain ground, entailing displacement of identification and knowing" (Stein and Plummer, 1994:182). The very boundaries that are used to construct and maintain sexual power as a basis of conceptualized sexuality are put into question. Sexual categories such as "homosexual" and "heterosexual" have been shifted from starting points as units of analysis and have become discursively produced subjects for research. They are viewed as ways of "doing" rather than as ways of "being." Behaviors, knowledge, and confessions are all examples of phenomena that are used to challenge dominant categorizations of sex, gender, and sexuality. Identity is viewed not as a stable, knowable category but rather as one that rests on ever-shifting and unknowable grounds.
3. "Rejection of civil rights strategies in favor of a politics of carnival, transgression, and parody which leads to deconstruction, decentering, revisionist readings, and an anti-assimilationist politics" (Stein and Plummer, 1994:182). Political claims based on identity, such as the claims made by the gay and lesbian rights movement, are shunned in favor of a more ironic, transgressive, and playful approach. Here queer theory, quite controversially, challenges the *identity politics* that drove political activism from the 1960s through to the 1990s. Identity politics refers to a particular kind of political activism in which marginalized groups seek recognition for their distinct identities. In their challenge to identity politics queer theorists argue that advocating for rights based on a minority identity only legitimates the very

power structure against which one is fighting. To resist is to legitimate the position of one's oppressor. The alternative approach, advocated by queer theorists, is to demonstrate the contingency and constructed nature of identity and thereby open up spaces for new kinds of political formations and alliances.

4. "A willingness to interrogate areas which normally would not be seen as the terrain of sexuality, and to conduct queer 'readings' of ostensibly heterosexual or nonsexualized texts" (Stein and Plummer, 1994:182). Areas of social life such as the media (Walters, 2001), music festivals (B. Morris, 2003), popular culture (Sullivan, 2003), education (Kosciw, 2004), American literature (Lindemann, 2000), social movements (Gamson, 1995), and even archaeology (Dowson, 2002) are all investigated as sites where sexuality is an active player. No area of social life is seen as immune from the influence of sexuality, and even the most seemingly innocuous of texts are open to an interpretation through the lens of sexuality. This speaks to a larger point. Queer theory is not primarily a theory of gay and lesbian identity or even of sexuality more generally. *Like all major social theories, queer theory is a theory of social life.* The main claim of argument of queer theory, then, is that social life is organized around desire (and in particular sexual desire) and that to understand the social world we must understand the processes that activate and govern desire.

With these general points in mind, we turn to a few of the key theoretical concepts developed by queer theorists.

The Heterosexual/Homosexual Binary

As noted, queer theory draws heavily on poststructuralist philosophy. Important here is that according to poststructuralists, language is a system of power that constructs and orders social reality. In the modern West, reality has been constructed through linguistic binaries: male versus female, white versus black, inside versus outside, and in the case of modern sexuality, heterosexual versus homosexual. These categories define what people can be and do in a given time and place. Through the technique of deconstruction poststructuralists show that even though these binaries appear to be natural realities, they are in fact linguistic creations.

For example, Michel Foucault, whom we have already discussed at length in Chapter 16, is often viewed as a major influence on queer theory. In the first volume of his *History of Sexuality* (1978) Foucault traces the construction of sexuality, homosexuality, and heterosexuality in the nineteenth century. Prior to this historical period there was no such thing as a sexual identity, at least in the sense understood today. People engaged in sexual acts such as same-sex sodomy, but it was not believed that these acts expressed something fundamental about the person who engaged in them. The development of the sciences of sex, such as psychoanalysis and sexology, alongside transformations in industrial and domestic life, led to the identification of particular sex acts with character types. The twentieth-century conceptualization of homosexuality emerges, then, when the act of sodomy is associated with the identity of homosexuality. Furthermore, the identity of homosexuality is defined in contrast to the identity of heterosexuality, itself a newly invented concept. Following poststructuralist logic, a central claim of queer theory is that, as binaries, heterosexuality and homosexuality define each other and hence depend for their meaning on each other. This binary has structured modern forms of sexual desire and social life more generally.

Beyond the idea that identities are constructed through binaries, another central poststructuralist idea is that one element in the binary structure is always viewed as inferior to the other. For example, as constructed in patriarchal societies, masculinity is superior to femininity, or as constructed in early-twentieth-century racialized America (and even into the present, as was discussed above), white is superior to black. So too, queer theorists demonstrate that homosexual identity has been constructed as inferior to heterosexuality. In fact, modern Western social life has been organized around the presumed naturalness and primacy of heterosexuality. In other words, modern social life is governed by what Judith Butler (1990) calls a *heterosexual matrix*. The heterosexual matrix is the cultural framework that makes it appear as if heterosexuality is the natural form of sexuality. Further, the heterosexual matrix imposes *compulsory heterosexuality* (Rich, 1980). This refers to a social system in which the only viable, intelligible, and respectable form of sexuality is heterosexuality accompanied by the related accoutrements of middle-class suburban life. Any alternative expression of desire is treated as unnatural and unintelligible. It is frequently disparaged and sometimes met with violence.

Queer theorist Eve Kosofsky Sedgwick (1985, 1990) further describes the logic of contemporary sexual culture through her concept of the *epistemology of the closet*. Epistemology is the field of philosophy that studies the various ways in which humans know and can know the world. The closet refers to the now-popular idea that an identity can be closeted; that is kept secret, hidden from view, maintained in a private and safe place. Sedgwick analyzes the concept of the closet as a means of understanding how the relationship between heterosexuality and homosexuality has shaped modern ways of knowing and relating to sexuality. It is not only that homosexuality is treated as inferior to heterosexuality, but that this relationship of dependency is hidden from view, unspoken, or closeted. This has given rise to central components of identity formation in our times. For one, in contrast to the open public image of heterosexuality, homosexuality and other queer sexualities have largely been developed in hidden spaces. This has resulted in feelings of shame being associated with queer identities. And, as we will see in the section on affect theory, when it goes unspoken and unaddressed shame can make people vulnerable to social control (see also Scheff's work as described in Chapter 9). Further, as a result of its identification with the closet, the act of "coming out" of the closet has, for good or bad, been a defining feature of queer experience in the last thirty years.

Finally, because homosexuality has been closeted, people who identify themselves as heterosexual are unable to understand the relationship between their sexuality and queer sexuality. As already described, queer theorists argue that there is a mutually constitutive relationship between homosexuality and heterosexuality. Moreover, drawing on psychoanalytic theory, queer theorists argue that sexuality, in general, is never classifiable or set in stone. Instead, sexual desire is fluid and open to transformation. Desire is locked into strict categories only through historical and social processes. Following this, queer theorists make a very subversive point: Heterosexual persons contain within themselves the potentials of queer sexuality. When social institutions repress or deny queer sexuality they do not eliminate it but only hide it from view. This can be dangerous. For example, Sedgwick (1990) argues that *homosexual panic*—the fearful and violent reactions that homosexuality arouses in heterosexual society (often described as homophobia)—is a product of the closeting of queer desire. Because it has so insistently denied the homosexuality within itself, the heterosexual culture strikes back against public manifestations of queer sexuality. Making a related point, Judith Butler (1990) argues that modern Western persons suffer *homosexual melancholy*. Homosexual melancholy is the persistent sadness that emerges when heterosexual culture denies its own homosexuality. In both of these examples, even though it is denied, homosexual desire, the queer side of the modern subject, continues to haunt heterosexuality, and vice versa. The task of queer theory, then, is to show the ways that queer desire is and always has been a central component of sociocultural life.

Performing Sex

Judith Butler (1990, 1993, 2004a) is one of the most important queer theorists. Butler is famous for her claim that gender and sex are created through social performances. In feminist theories gender refers to the social roles played by men and women. These roles are generally regarded as social constructions. Sex refers to the biological makeup of males and females. Butler agrees with other feminists that gender roles are social constructions but she takes the argument a step further and says that sex is also a social construction. Even though Western society believes that there are only two sexes—male and female—Butler insists that our perception of this difference is a cultural and historical achievement. The distinction overlooks the many intersex bodies that do not clearly fit into the category of male or female (see also Fausto-Sterling, 2000). It also overlooks the many identities constituted through the combination and recombination of conventional sex and gender categories as well as the desires they enact. For example, Judith Halberstam (1998) analyzes performances of *female masculinity,* and Riki Ann Wilchins (1997) analyzes the challenge posed by transgender people to gender and identity norms.

   With these ideas in hand we can turn to the concept of performance. From Butler's perspective, sex, gender, and desire are not automatic possessions of a body but rather they are brought into existence in performance. The successful achievement of sex identity (to see oneself as a "real man") and accompanying ideas about sex attraction depend upon the successful performance of a gender role. This is similar to Goffman's idea that the self is not an inborn entity but rather an effect of social performances (see Chapter 9). In the same way, then, that a person builds a self over time in social performances, so too sex, gender, and sexual desire are produced through performance. For example, male heteronormative gender performances link together male bodies with male gender performances and male expressions of desire for females. These connections between bodies, desires, and social roles are not automatically given but rather are cultural and personal achievements.

To demonstrate the performed and constructed nature of sexuality and gender Butler (1990) famously uses the example of the drag performer. The drag queen is a man who performs as a woman. A successful performance reveals that gender is a performance and so too is the desire generated by the drag performer in the audience. Butler also provides an analysis of "butch" identity. In queer culture the butch is a lesbian who adopts the posture of masculinity. The Hollywood star James Dean is an iconic figure whom some butch lesbians try to imitate in their everyday identifications (Halberstam, 1998). Butler says that the butch is not simply a woman who adopts a male role. Rather, in juxtaposing sex and gender in new ways the butch generates new forms of sexuality and desire. These examples don't make sex and sexual desire any less concrete or real. Instead, they show that very real feelings and identities originate in sociocultural play.

In connection with this, Butler (1993) also argues that certain culturally sanctioned performances produce "bodies that matter." Butler plays on the double meaning of the word *matter*. On the one hand, "matter" describes the way that identities become embodied. Distinctions made in language are built into the body through its performances so that they are felt and lived as real and uncontestable. At the same time, "matter" describes a political process. Sexuality is constructed and then materialized within social structures that privilege some forms of sexuality and desire over others. There are bodies that matter and there are bodies that don't matter. The bodies that don't matter are marginalized and submitted to social and political violence. Indeed, this focus on the construction of bodies that matter has led Butler into more general theoretical questions about hate speech (1997a), interpersonal ethics (2005), war, violence, and mourning (2004b). Here, echoing themes examined by Giorgio Agamben (see Chapter 16), Butler has consistently been concerned with the question of the "livable life." Whose life is deemed worthwhile, whose life is considered expendable, and what kinds of social worlds do these distinctions allow (Lloyd, 2011)?

The concept of performance, then, is crucial for queer theory. If sex and gender are performed, then the viability of dominant sexualities depends upon their continued performance. Through the concept of performance Butler denaturalizes heterosexuality in a very concrete way. She doesn't merely reveal it to be a social construction, but also shows that it is a performance that has to be chosen to be sustained. To be a woman you need to walk and talk and act like a woman. This does not automatically happen but must be practiced. In addition, the concept of performance grounds Butler's challenge to the heterosexual matrix. Contrary to gay rights activists, Butler does not call for the creation of a space for gays and lesbians within heterosexual culture. Nor does she call for the replacement of heterosexual social organization with a presumably more open and liberating homosexual social organization. Each of those moves would merely reinstantiate a normative social order and in particular reaffirm heterosexuality as the binary opposite of homosexuality. Queer theory tries to move beyond utopias, essentialisms, and binaries and instead sees sexuality as a constant and ongoing set of activities through which sexuality and desire are created.

Critiques

Queer theory has faced criticism. Many argue that its amorphous politics of inclusion and rejection of single characteristics of identity such as race, class, or sex undermine the potential for real political action (e.g., T. Edwards, 1998; Kirsch, 2000). This rejection, in turn, ignores the everyday lived materiality of experience (Stein and Plummer, 1994) and the role of the social in constructing the sexual (A. Green, 2002). If identity is not a motivation for action, then how do groups dealing with the manifest means of oppression organize and fight for justice? There is also an argument that the more queer theory is accepted into academic discourse, the farther removed it is from its revolutionary potential. Halperin (1995:113) has noted that "the more it verges on becoming a normative academic discipline, the less queer 'queer theory' can plausibly claim to be." By being enshrined in academia, it is losing its power to transform; by being normalized, it loses its ability to queer.

In light of these critiques, some have tried to find ways to modify queer theory in such a way as to make it more socially sensitive to the position and lived experiences of actors and the more politically astute. Max Kirsch (2000) has offered a potential solution by arguing that we need to differentiate between identifying *with* and identifying *as,* with a preference for the latter, in order to maintain a basis of identification while still distancing ourselves from the problems of identity. Thus, identity is used as "a mode of affiliation rather than strictly as a category of personal definition" (Kirsch, 2000:7). This approach is thereby able to maintain the critical stance of queer theory toward the dangers of essentializing or concretizing identity, while at the same time still allowing for identity by association to remain a powerful tool for collective social action.

Adam Isaiah Green (2002) has identified at least two strains of queer theory. The first, *radical deconstructionism,* "superimposes a postmodern self-concept onto the homosexual subject, thereby glossing over the enduring institutional organization of sexuality" (Green, 2002:523). The second, *radical subversion,* "superimposes a politically marginal self-concept onto the homosexual subject, thereby grossly oversimplifying complex developmental processes attendant to sexual identification" (Green, 2002:523). At base, each strand is seen as not giving sufficient priority to the materially lived and institutionally dependent situation of actors. Green (2002:537), therefore, calls for a postqueer study of sexuality, one that "brings to bear the categorical scrutiny of queer theory on concrete, empirical case studies."

These critiques, however, do not detract from the important impact that queer theory has had on contemporary social theory. Queer theory illuminates the sphere of sexuality, especially queer sexuality, but it speaks to social theory more generally. For one, it demonstrates that sexuality and desire are central features of social life and have been for some time. This means that any serious social theory must incorporate the study of sex, gender, and sexuality into its analysis. In addition, queer theory provides tools to help understand how various sexualities have been and continue to be constructed and performed. Finally, queer theory shows that as a society we are not locked into preset social and bodily roles. Rather, in the spirit of all social theories that have sought social change, queer theory argues that by playing with new combinations of bodies and roles we can create more equitable and satisfying social relationships and social institutions.

Actor-Network Theory, Posthumanism, and Postsociality

Actor-network theory (ANT) is an influential perspective that grows out of the more general area of science and technology studies. The study of science and technology has a long history in sociology and even social theory. For example, in the 1970s Robert Merton (see Chapter 7) used his functionalist approach to study science. He treated science as a middle-range social institution that was governed by norms. Other theorists have drawn on ethnographic and ethnomethodological techniques (see Chapter 10) to study laboratory practices. For example, Bruno Latour and Steve Woolgar (1986) developed some of the basic terms of ANT analysis in their study of a laboratory at the Salk Institute in California. Others have studied science from the perspectives of cultural studies, feminism, and race theory, among others (see Hess, 1997). In contrast to Merton, these later positions do not see science as simply one of many independent social institutions available for sociological analysis. Rather, science is seen as a form of knowledge and practice that, increasingly, organizes society and constitutes identities. In fact, in grappling with the interrelationship of science, technology, and society, science and technology scholars have had to develop new theoretical languages. Society is thus rethought through the lens of science.

ANT is one of the best examples of the way that the social study of science has led to a rethinking of social theory. While in this section we review a number of ANT concepts, the most significant idea is that society is not made up of human actors alone (Latour [1993] says it never has been). Rather, society is an accomplishment that draws together both human and nonhuman actors (e.g., animals, electrons, computers, and so on) into a "collective" (2007:14; for more on nonhumans see Donna Haraway, 1991, 2008). Latour replaces the term *society* with the term *collective* because "society," at least as it is conventionally understood, implies the existence of some transcendent entity that directs human action from outside. Here he is particularly critical of Durkheim's concept of the *social fact* upon which, he argues, much contemporary sociology and social theory is grounded.[5] The practice of science and technology, or *technoscience*, is crucial to the formation of these networked collectives as it allows practitioners to hook together actors in previously unconceivable assemblages. For example, using a high-powered microscope the biologist can "discover" and thereby "recruit" a new biological agent into the collective. This focus on the networking of human and nonhuman agents is also reflected in posthumanist and postsocial theories, which we address toward the end of this section.

"Actor-network theory," in the words of John Law, "is a ruthless application of *semiotics*. It tells us that entities take their form and acquire their attributes as a result

---

5. See Restivo (2011) for more detail on Latour's refusal of Durkheimian sociology as well as the problems and misconceptions that have accompanied that refusal.

of their relations with other entities. In this scheme of things entities have no inherent qualities" (Law, 1999:3). The idea of the relativity of *subjects* is shared by a number of theoretical perspectives. What is new here is that *material objects* as well are seen as being created and acquiring meaning in a *network* of relationship to other objects. Thus, "action-network theory may be understood as a *semiotics of materiality.* It takes the semiotic insight, that of the relativity of entities, the notion that they are produced in relations, and applies this ruthlessly to all materials—and not simply those that are linguistic" (Law, 1999:4).

That perspective is drawn more from structuralism, but other basic ANT perspectives are drawn from poststructuralism. Implied above is the idea of *anti-essentialism.* That is, entities are lacking in inherent qualities; what they are is a result of their relationship to other entities. In other words, there is *no* essence to any entity or material object, including people. In addition, ANT is *opposed* to the very modern idea of the *search for origins,* either in history or contemporaneously in the idea that human agents are at the root of everything. Like poststructuralism (and postmodernism), ANT is also *antifoundational*—that is, it is opposed to the idea that underlying everything is a basic structure and it is the task of the analyst to uncover that structure.

However, the poststructural concept that goes to the essence of ANT is *decentering.* Generally, this means shifting focus from the center (or essence, or origin, and so on) to the periphery. More specifically, it means in ANT the shift from a focus on the agent taking some action to that which exists, especially networks and nonhuman objects. The actor becomes part of the network; we can think in terms of the " 'networkization' of the 'actor' " (Gomart and Hennion, 1999:223). Actors are subordinated to networks and, in a way, are creatures of networks: "actors are network effects, they take the attributes of the entities which they include" (Law, 1999:5). The focus shifts from the modern concern with the agent to the network and to objects, nonmaterial entities. This, as we will see, is one of the most distinctive contributions of ANT: it "opened the social sciences to nonhumans" (Callon, 1999:182). (By the way, nonhumans and the relationship of humans to them is a significant aspect of what Knorr-Cetina [2001] calls *postsocial relations.*) We will have more to say about this below, but although it is important to focus on the nonhuman, we must remember that "objects are *inferior* partners" to the human (Gomart and Hennion, 1999:223).

ANT leads to a rejection of both micro-macro and agency-structure theory (see Chapter 13). For one thing, those two continua are seen as examples of the kind of modern dualities that are rejected by poststructuralists and postmodernists. (According to Law [1999:3], "all of these divides have been rubbished.") In addition, the problem with both continua is that a shift to one pole of the continuum inevitably leads to dissatisfaction with what is learned about the other pole. More important, the continua are focusing on the wrong things. The central topic is *not* agency/micro or structure/ macro but rather social processes as circulating entities. In other words, the real focus should be on the network, another key topic discussed below. As Latour (1999:22) puts it, ANT is a theory not of the social but rather "of the space of fluids circulating in a nonmodern situation."

That observation leads us to a very useful definition of ANT:[6]

We may conceive of only basic formal units of substance (actants) which enter into relationships (networks) by way of encounters (trials of force) wherein questions regarding the powers and identities of these selfsame units come to be temporarily settled by reference to the overall compound nexus of relationships within which they are now embedded.

(Brown and Capdevila, 1999:34)

The term *actant* (borrowed from semiotics [Fuller, 2007c]) is worth clarifying. It is meant to imply that it is not just humans that act. Nonhuman entities can act—can be actants! As a result, the same explanatory frame should be used for actants of both types.

As Crawford (2005:2) puts it: "Investigators should never shift registers to examine individuals and organizations, bugs and collectors, or computers and their programmers." Furthermore, in discussing the actant, the focus once again shifts from the actor to the network. As Latour (1999:18) puts it, "actantability is not what an actor does . . . but what *provides* actants with their actions, with their subjectivity, with their intentionality, with their morality. When you hook up with this circulating entity, then you are partially provided with consciousness, subjectivity, actoriality, etc. . . . To become an actor is . . . a local achievement." Even something as seemingly human and individual as intentionality is defined in network terms as a "circulating capacity . . . partially gained or lost by hooking up to certain bodies of practice" (Latour, 1999:23).

Basically, actors (or actants) cannot be understood apart from the networks in which they exist and of which they are part. In fact, actor and network are "two faces of the same phenomenon" (Latour, 1999:19). Thus, actor-network theorists seek to bypass the micro-macro and agency-structure dichotomies that have characterized much of social theory (see Chapter 13).

The idea of networks is hard to get at, but Crawford (2005:1) does a good job of defining them and relating them to actants: "Networks are processual, built activities, performed by actants out of which they are composed." Most generally it implies a series of transformations and translations. A more specific sense arises in Latour's (1999:17) argument that a network is not society or an anonymous field of forces but is "the *summing up* of interactions through various kinds of devices, inscriptions, forms and formulae, into a very local, very practical, very tiny locus." Thus, a focus on networks leads one closer to, rather than farther away from, the local. This idea is closely linked to the roots of ANT in science studies, especially the detailed and local study of, for example, the operations of scientific laboratories. However, ANT rejects the micro-macro distinction. Thus, in discussing the local, or the network, and even the actant, there is a sense that the micro-macro, as well as the local-general, cannot be distinguished from one another. More specifically, the macro should be viewed not as "big," "but [as] connected . . . local, mediated, related" (Latour, 1999:18).

---

6. Actually, this is offered as a definition of the "sociology of translation" seen as the generic form of ANT (Brown and Capdevila, 1999).

Related to the idea of network is *performativity*. This means that entities do not exist in any essentialist sense but rather are performed in, by, and through relations, or networks (Law, 1999:4). It is easy to think of human actors as engaging in such performativity, but ANT goes beyond this to see material entities as being characterized by performativity. If people and objects are performed, then "everything is uncertain and reversible" (Law, 1999:4). There are times when durability and fixity result, but the focus is on how those things are performed so that such durability is achieved. In other words, durable networks, to take one example, are performed, and this means that no matter how seemingly durable they are, they can fall apart. Just as networks can be performed into durability, they can be performed into disintegration and even disappearance. However, even ANT theorists recognize some measure of durability, as best exemplified in Latour's concept of "immutable mobiles," which can be defined as "a network of elements that holds its shape as it moves" through space and time (Law and Hetherington, 2002:395–396). Thus, there is a durable network here, but it is one that is in constant movement (and there is the ever-present possibility that it can fall apart).

What is perhaps most distinctive about ANT is its concern with material entities or artifacts: "Material artifacts may exercise something which resembles agency. But this proves to be a peculiar form of *agency,* one entirely *devoid of intentionality*" (Brown and Capdevila, 1999:40). This is one of the reasons, as mentioned above, that material artifacts are "inferior" objects. The key to these artifacts is their lack of meaning; it is this that gives them a "will to connect" with other elements of a network. It is this very blankness that leads the network and its elements to seek to connect with the artifact. To put it another way, by inciting connections, an artifact "drives networks to incorporate and fold around actants" (Brown and Capdevila, 1999:41). Humans can be seen in much the same way: "they perform their own functional blankness . . . incite and form relations on the basis of what they do not present, do not say . . . [they provoke] the will-to-connect to ever greater excesses" (Brown and Capdevila, 1999:40).

Relatedly, there is a concern in ANT with "practical materiality" (Dugdale, 1999). Material artifacts play a key role in constituting networks and subjects. Thus, artifacts are not simply acted upon (e.g., connected with by the network), they also act. Material artifacts, like human agents, are actants. For example, Law and Hetherington (2002:394) discuss how things like carpeting and decor are performative: they act; they "participate in the generation of information, of power relations, of subjectivities and objectivities." Thus, nonhumans are active participants in networks, in social relationships. Of course, material artifacts lack what defines human actors— intentionality! Verran offers a good summary of all of this:

> this interpretive frame avoids any separation of the material and the symbolic in proposing worlds as outcomes of mutually resisting/accommodating participants, where participation goes far beyond the human to encompass the non-living as active in routine (and novel) actions, which constitute the world.
>
> (Verran, 1999:143)

The focus on relations, circulations, and networks obviously has a spatial implication, but ANT has a unique view on spatiality: "different and nonconformable spatialities (e.g., regions and networks) are formed" (Law, 1999:11). Thus, ANT seeks to distance itself from a simple Euclidean view of space. In one of its most distinctive views on space, ANT makes much of the issue of a "fold" in space formed "like a blunt scissors edge across paper, such that what were distant points suddenly become neighbors. Things . . . get crumpled together" (Brown and Capdevila, 1999:29). Also of interest is the fact that Latour (1999:19) argues that the "empty spaces 'in between' the networks, those *terra incognita,* are the most exciting aspects of ANT because they show the extent of our ignorance and the immense reserve that is open to change."

Given its roots in science studies, ANT is oriented to micro-methods (although the term *micro* is anathema to this perspective): "actor-network studies attempt to become part of the networks of which they speak. To be able to trace a network means becoming interior to its activities" (Brown and Capdevila, 1999:43). Or as Latour (1999:20) humbly puts it: "for us, ANT was simply another way of being faithful to the insights of ethnomethodology: actors[7] know what they do and we have to learn from them not only what they do, but how and why they do it. . . . [It is] a very crude method to learn from the actors without imposing on them an *a priori* definition of their world-building capacities" (Latour, 1999:19–20). In fact, as is the case with ethnomethodology, some supporters describe ANT as a method and *not* a theory (Callon, 1999:194).

In terms of the discussion of modernity in Chapter 14 and the treatment of postmodernity in Chapter 16, it is interesting to reflect, in closing, on Bruno Latour's (1993:39) contention that "the modern world never happened." This notion is based, in part, on the fact that we continue to have much in common with premoderns. In addition, it is premised on the idea that it is impossible to identify points of origin or to clearly identify a point at which one epoch ends and another begins. Because we have never been modern (or premodern, for that matter), it follows that we cannot now be postmodern. Thus, ANT rejects the entire distinction between premodernity, modernity, and postmodernity.

Finally, it should be noted that some adherents of ANT are not happy with the directions taken recently by other thinkers associated with the approach, as well as with efforts (like this one) to clearly define and delimit it. For example, Law (1999:9) is concerned about naming, simplifying, and losing complexity— "the theory has been reduced to a few aphorisms that can be quickly passed on." Even more strongly, the leading figure associated with ANT says: "There are four things that do not work with actor-network theory: The word *actor,* the word *network,* the word *theory* and the hyphen. Four nails in the coffin!" (Latour, 1999:15). Key contributors to ANT are thus intent on maintaining the complexity of a theory that seeks to reflect, at least to some degree, the complexity of the social (and material) world. ANT has generated a great deal of research into such diverse issues as pest management (Moore, 2008), sleeping persons (Lee, 2008), methadone maintenance (Valentine, 2007), and tourism (van Der Duim and Caalders, 2008).

---

7. This word seems to be at odds with the earlier point about the broad concern with actants and to imply a focus on human actors. This also tends to support Callon's (1999:182) critique of ANT for offering "an anonymous, ill-defined and indiscernable" perspective on the actor.

Related to the development of actor-network theory are the ideas of posthumanism and the postsocial. *Posthumanism* is defined "by its opposition to humanism, as well as moving beyond it. It rejects the notion of the separability of humanity from the non-human world . . . and the division of knowledge into separate domains" (Franklin, 2007:3548). Because humanism lies at the base of much of sociology, especially microsociologies, posthumanism constitutes a profound challenge to the field. However, it can be seen as an opportunity to extend sociology beyond human actors to a wide range of other phenomena and to encompass them all within a single framework.

The idea of the *postsocial* constitutes a parallel challenge to traditional ideas of sociality. Sociality may continue, but it is declining in importance (social forms are being emptied of social relationships) and taking on new forms. Among the new forms are the relationships emerging with the enormous expansion of objects in the contemporary world such as technologies, consumer goods, and objects of knowledge. As Knorr-Cetina puts it:

> Postsocial relations are human ties triangulated with object relations, and forming only with respect to these relations. . . . Postsocial is what one might call a level of intersubjectivity that is no longer based on face-to-face interaction and may in fact not involve interaction at all. . . . Postsocial systems may arise around the sort of relatedness enabled by the Internet. . . . Postsocial forms are not rich in sociality in the old sense . . . but they may be rich in other ways, and the challenge is to analyze and theorize these constellations.
>
> (Knorr-Cetina, 2007:3580)

The emergence of an increasing number of postsocial relationships is related to the development of new types of work and consumption settings. One example of the former is "virtual organizations" that lack a central headquarters where workers can congregate and interact both to handle work-related tasks and to engage in social relationships. In virtual organizations workers are largely, if not totally, on their own, interacting on a much more limited basis with other workers and with superiors by phone, e-mail, or occasional face-to-face visits.

There are numerous examples of such postsocial relationships in the realm of consumption. For example, instead of interacting with tellers in a bank, we are increasingly likely to interact with ATMs. Other bank-related interactions are now increasingly likely to involve automated telephone contact or online banking. Also, rather than interacting with a salesperson in a bookshop, we are increasingly likely to buy books (and other products) through Amazon.com without ever interacting with a human being. In such instances technologies and other objects replace humans as relationship partners or serve to mediate the relationships among people. We often cannot get to talk to a real person until we have exhausted all the options offered on the automated telephone message.

Increasingly, in many of the best-known consumption sites (what Ritzer [2010a] has called the "cathedrals of consumption"), we find much the same process. For example, in Las Vegas casinos, as well as casinos in many other places in the United States and elsewhere, an increasingly large proportion of floor space is devoted to slot machines, and gamblers interact almost exclusively with these objects. Other forms of gambling—keno, for example—also involve little or no human interaction and are replacing the historic focus of casinos on games (blackjack, poker, roulette, craps, etc.) that require direct interaction with other humans as either employees or fellow players. Similarly, the modern department store has far fewer employees than in the past, and customers are supposed to interact with the store and its products, make selections, and only then bring goods to a human employee in order to pay for those choices.

Of course, the Internet is the postsocial setting *par excellence*. We interact with keyboards, computer screens, Web sites, e-mail, chat rooms, massive multiplayer games, and so on. In some cases Internet relationships may come to involve face-to-face interactions (sometimes with dangerous consequences), but most often whatever human relationships exist on the Internet are mediated by the wide range of technologies associated with it.

Affect Theory

Affect theory is the most recent extension of poststructural and postmodern theory. In addition it draws on elements of queer theory and science and technology studies. As we will see, it shares with those perspectives an interest in deconstruction and decentering the subject. However, it significantly departs from those theoretical perspectives because it emphasizes the independent role that biology or "matter" plays in the construction of reality. In particular, affect theorists are interested in the way that bodies can "affect and be affected" by one another (Blackman and Venn, 2010:9).

While the concept of affect has clear affinities with the concept of emotion (see Chapter 9), affect theorists clearly distinguish between them. To put it simply, affect refers to a more primal or rawer version of emotion. Affect is an indeterminate biological force that energizes and brings vitality to life. Emotion is what happens to affect once it has it has been submitted to social processes that make it conscious and narratable. In other words, *affect* is the word for nonconscious life energies that make life itself possible. Affect theory not only tries to theorize this unique dimension of the social and natural world but also describes the processes by which affect is put to use and managed in societies.

Before getting into more specific concepts it is important to draw attention to two major claims of affect theory. First, affect theorists take seriously the findings of the natural sciences and in particular work in the life sciences (e.g., biology, genetics, neuroscience).[8] This is a major difference from earlier postmodern perspectives that, for the most part, rejected research conducted in the natural sciences on the grounds that most science was a social construction that reproduces normative social categories. For example, as we saw in the earlier section on critical theories of race and racism, some scientific theory has constructed categories of racial difference that have been used to justify colonialism and racial domination.

---

8. Though not all affect theories directly engage scientific ideas. Gregg and Seigworth (2010) identify at least eight different intellectual influences on affect theory, not all of which are connected to the life sciences.

For affect theorists there is a fine line between legitimating what they consider to be problematic versions of normative science and taking the findings of the natural sciences seriously. In what Gregg and Seigworth (2010) consider a founding essay of affect theory, Sedgwick (whom we also discussed under queer theory) and Frank say:

> We have no interest whatever in minimizing the continuing history of racist, sexist, homophobic, or otherwise abusive biologisms, or the urgency of their exposure, that has made the gravamen of so many contemporary projects of critique. At the same time, we fear—with the installation of an automatic antibiologism as the unshifting central tenet of 'theory'—the loss of conceptual access to an entire thought-realm.
>
> (Sedgwick and Frank, 1995:15)

In another founding text, *Parables for the Virtual*, Brian Massumi warns that cultural and social theory has been too quick to distance itself from the natural sciences:

> A common thread running through the varieties of social constructivism currently dominant in cultural theory holds that everything, including nature, is constructed in discourse. . . . In the worst-case solipsist scenario, nature appears as immanent to culture (as its construct). . . . The concepts of nature and culture need serious reworking, in a way that expresses the irreducible *alterity* of the nonhuman in and through its active *connection* to the human and vice versa. (2002:38–9)

Like the actor-network theory discussed above, affect theory takes seriously the agency of nonhumans and criticizes the idea that these other agents are simply cultural constructions. Rather, nature is an "autonomous" force that enters into relations with culture, language, and so on. The problem is to understand how nature and culture interact without reducing one to the other.

Of course, social theorists have relied upon the findings of the natural sciences for many years. *Sociobiology* is a very influential social-theoretical perspective that incorporates the findings of evolutionary theory into social theory (Nielsen, 1994). It's important, though, to distinguish affect theory from perspectives such as sociobiology. For one, sociobiology has been associated with the promotion of the normative social ideals criticized by affect theorists. Most notably, sociobiologists have argued that differences in sex and gender behavior have a genetic foundation. This, as we have seen, is a view that is challenged by queer theorists. So too, it is challenged by affect theorists.

Moreover, sociobiology is a reductivist science. It attempts to explain social life through, what are considered to be foundational genetic and evolutionary processes. In contrast, affect theory tries to use the findings of the natural sciences in ways that are nonreductivist. It treats the findings seriously—gives biology an autonomous power—but also treats social processes seriously. One level of life is not reducible to the other, but rather they intermingle and mutually influence each other. In this spirit, affect theorists have primarily relied on developments in the life sciences that view biology as processual—biology is an ever-changing and dynamic process rather than a concrete set of established structures and mechanisms (Blackman et al., 2010; Fraser et al., 2005). This focus on process opens up the findings of science to sociological concepts central to poststructuralist and postmodern thought.[9]

The second important claim forwarded by affect theorists is that we now live in a society that is governed through affective processes. This again can be read against the earlier postmodern claim that social life is governed through linguistic and symbolic processes. Patricia Clough (2003, 2004) argues that even though Foucauldian poststructuralism theorized the body, it treated the body as a product of discursive forces rather than a biological entity that could act and be acted upon independent of language. This is not to say that the concept of affect was not relevant to previous eras. Two of the major philosophical influences on affect theory wrote in different times and places: Baruch Spinoza was a sixteenth-century Dutch philosopher and Henri Bergson was a nineteenth-century French philosopher. However, the last thirty years have seen significant social, scientific, and technological changes that make the concept of affect more relevant than ever.

For example, the widespread use of psychotropic medications, such as antidepressants, allows people to directly, as a part of their everyday lives, modify bodily affect. This is in contrast to the talk therapies employed by previous generations to modify mood and feeling. Where antidepressants work directly on the neurochemical systems of the body, talk therapy uses roundabout linguistic techniques to modify mood. Affect theorists also have talked about the relation between affect and contemporary consumer culture (Featherstone, 2010), and the way that new media and digital technologies act upon affective systems in unprecedented ways (Hansen, 2004). Affect theory is particularly relevant to a world that operates through the global flows identified by Zygmunt Bauman and Arjun Appadurai (see Chapters 14 and 16). Affect is transmitted faster and with more force than cognition or words. We feel before we see or hear. Indeed, where language tends to fix or hold still, affect tends to flow (though as we will see it can also be held still and controlled). The problem in understanding the management of contemporary populations, then, is understanding the ways that affect is both "captured" and liberated through various social processes and practices (Clough, 2008:3; Massumi, 2002:35).

Basic Concepts

Affect theory is not a micro-social theory *per se,* but in order to get a handle on its basic concepts it is helpful to start at the level of selves/subjects and the relations that they have to their bodies and surrounding environment. Brian Massumi (2002) describes a threefold process out of which mind and consciousness emerge.

1.   Referring to ideas developed by philosophers Spinoza and Bergson, Massumi says that the "subject" exists in an open, decentered field. The word "subject"

---

9. This said, scholars in the humanities and social sciences have been criticized for what some view as their misunderstanding and misuse of scientific concepts. In the 1990s physicist Alan Sokol accused scholars in the humanities of using scientific concepts for ideological purposes. His critique was part of an academic debate referred to as the "science wars." More recently, Papoulias and Callard have directly addressed affect theory to consider the "strange and partial (mis)translation of complex scientific models into the epistemologically distinct space of the humanities and social sciences" (2010:31).

is in quotation marks because there is no subject to speak of at this moment. The field (or more simply, environment) is composed of all the forces and energies bombarding, or impinging upon, the subject. This is the environment as it is experienced before it is perceived and categorized by the subject. This body does not have a point of view. Rather, in the tradition of poststructuralist thought, it is decentered: "being in a state of passional suspension in which it exists more outside of itself, more in the abstracted action of the impinging thing and the abstracted context of the action, than within itself" (2002:31). The term *passional* suggests that this state of being, though inaccessible to consciousness, is an affective or emotional limit point—that point at which one is fully immersed in the surrounding environment.

Even though Massumi does not spend a great deal of time discussing this aspect of experience, it is important because it provides the basic idea that humans are not self-enclosed atoms, fundamentally separate from their world. Rather, at some primal level, humans are deeply interconnected with other bodies and other people. It is a fact of human existence to be caught up in the forces and energies that populate their environments.

2. Even though the body is decentered, at the same time, it positions itself in this environment. That is, it finds ways to distinguish itself, as an autonomous being, from all of these impinging energies and forces. What is particularly important is that this positioning is spontaneously undertaken by the body outside of consciousness. Massumi says: "This is a first order idea produced spontaneously by the body" (2002:32). The biological body has its own self-organizing, or autopoietic principles (see discussion of autopoiesis under systems theory in Chapter 7). The body, in other words, has its own way of "thinking" or processing its relationship to its world. Relying on the ideas of philosopher Gilles Deleuze, Massumi refers to this as an *infolding* of the environment, or the creation of an *intensity*. When affect theorists talk about affect they are generally talking about the bodily experience of this infolding. That is, there is a particular feel to the way that a body moves through its environment nonconsciously experiencing and folding into itself this multitude of forces and energies.

It's important to note that infolding does not result in the separation of the self from the environment and other people. It is rather a state between the full immersion of body in environment under point one, and the achievement of self-actualized consciousness described in the next section. In this state, the body recognizes all of the potentials offered to it by its environment without yet acting on any of them. It is a body in tension—ready to act in many ways, to feel many different things, but not yet acting and feeling.

3. Finally, Massumi defines the mind as conscious reflection upon this infolded sensation: "the autonomic tendency received secondhand from the body is raised to a higher power to become an activity of the mind" (32). Another way of saying this is that even though the body possesses vast potentials for

action and feeling, it actualizes only a few of these potentials. These actualized potentialities of the affected body are what the mind recognizes as conscious experience. As we will see, precisely what gets actualized is heavily influenced by social and cultural processes.

It's also important to point out that even though we've been talking about these states as if they were separate from one another, Massumi is clear that they exist alongside one another, informing one another. Humans, then, exist in a state of tension between the vast possibilities experienced as nonconscious affect and the small set of actions, feelings, and emotions consciously actualized. Historically, sociology has focused only on the latter. For example, symbolic interactionists such as George Herbert Mead tend to focus on the conscious linguistic practices that lead to self-formation. In contrast, Massumi, and other affect theorists argue that nonconscious affect is an equally, if not more important phenomenon for analysis.

These three points aside, for social theory the important focus is the relationship between consciousness and affect. Social theory has a long history of discussing unconscious and nonconscious processes. Critical theory (see Chapter 8) draws on Freudian ideas to discuss the ways that unconscious desires and needs impact human action. Through the concept of practice, Giddens and others introduce the possibility of nonconscious embodied action. This is also captured with the concept of habit and in particular Bourdieu's *habitus*.

But affect theory offers a unique theorization of the nonconscious. For one, it is steeped in scientific ideas not just about the acting body, but about molecular biological processes. Importantly, these biological processes generate their own kind of feeling—affect. Affect is always present, a kind of backdrop energy—buzzing and humming—out of which action emerges, but it is inaccessible to direct experience or even conscious control and management. This is why affect is said to be autonomous. This concept of affect allows social theorists to explain a variety of generally perplexing social and psychological phenomena. These are phenomena that exceed the conceptual grasp of contemporary social science.

For example, Massumi (2002) reviews a number of psychological experiments that show that decisions are made by the body 0.5 seconds before they become conscious. In social theory and the social sciences we usually think of the body as something that is governed by the mind: First we think, and then our bodies carry out our actions. But here, Massumi uses this psychological evidence to argue that the body "thinks" through a problem in advance and the mind registers this decision after the fact. This points to another key characteristic of affect: Affect is faster than thought. On this view, a great deal of human action and interaction occurs in this spontaneous, fast, self-organizing affective realm, and cognitive rationality is better viewed as an afterthought than the driver of action.

The Affective Field

Affect theory is a *relational* theory of human subjectivity and society. This is one of the things that makes affect theory different from theories that assume methodological individualism, such as rational choice and exchange theories (see Chapter 11).

Even though the biological body is taken as a reference point, this body, at least in its first instance, is not thought of as a self-enclosed entity that begins and ends with its skin. We've already seen this idea anticipated under point one above—the subject is immersed across a field of sensations and impingements. It is only through the act of infolding that a body, distinct from its environment, begins to emerge. And even in the moment of infolding, bodies are still affectively connected to other bodies. In this respect, affect is described as prepersonal and presocial, or as Gregg and Seigworth (2010:3) put it, "subpersonal" and "subsocial." Anderson says: "affects are understood as impersonal intensities that do not belong to a subject or an object, nor do they reside in the mediating space between a subject and an object" (2010:161).

Even though analysis of the affective field is central to contemporary affect theory, the concept also can be found at the origins of sociology. For example, Emile Durkheim's (1912/1965) concept of *collective effervescence* describes a presocial collective energy. The social, and in particular, the idea of the social—the collective representation—emerges out of frenzied group dances in which participants give up their individuality and participate in shared energy.

Even though affect theorists have not, as yet, incorporated Durkheim's ideas, they have made use of the ideas of his contemporary Gustav Le Bon, whose theories of crowd behavior were very influential in the late nineteenth century (Borch, 2012). According to Teresa Brennan's (2004) interpretation of Le Bon: "groups have heightened affectivity and a lower level of intellectual functioning" (53). They have an "unconscious irrational component," which can be studied as a social form in itself (53). Specifically, crowds operate via *social contagion* in which affect can directly travel from body to body. The crowd is not simply a collection of individuals but "was capable, ethically, of far more than an individual. An individual would put his own interest first. A crowd need not" (54).

Affect is relational in the sense that it connects and influences people in ways that exceed our usual theories of the self-enclosed body. Brennan puts it like this:

> The transmission of energy and affects is the norm rather than an aberration at the beginning of psychical life. The Western psyche is structured in such a way as to give a person the sense that their affects and feeling are their own, and that they are energetically and emotionally contained in the most literal sense. In other words, people experience themselves as containing their own emotions. (2004:24–25)

The early sociology of crowds offers one example of this transpersonal affective field. Brennan also finds examples in the more intimate spheres described by psychoanalysts. She presents the psychoanalytic relationship as a space in which both analyst (the doctor) and analysand (the client) transfer feelings into each other. More specifically, Brennan extends the psychoanalytic concepts of *projection* and *projective identification* to social interaction more generally. In brief, these terms refer to processes when, in a self-protective move, one individual "dumps" her feelings into another.

> A projection is what I disown in myself and see in you; a projective identification is what I succeed in having you experience in yourself, although it comes from me in the first place. For example, with my projection, I may see you as unimaginative, to

avoid feeling that way myself, although somewhere I probably do. With my projective identification, you actually feel unimaginative, while I do not. (2004:29–30)

In the regular course of social life people not only impose their own desires and feelings on others, but can actually make others feel particular feelings.

Brennan imagines, then, a space in which affect is not self-contained but rather moves back and forth between people. This happens unconsciously and automatically. It constitutes the basis of relationship and forms an affective field. The space of shared affectivity is not simply incidental to relationships—an unusual and troubling occurrence—but rather forms the grounds out of which social life proceeds. First we find ourselves in relational, affective fields and then we carve ourselves out of those fields.

This focus on the prepersonal and presocial affective field has also led affect theorists to theorize phenomena that historically have been considered unusual, odd, and unworthy of scientific study. Some, for example, have written about voice-hearing (Blackman, 2001), telepathy (Blackman, 2010), and mesmerism (Sloterdijk, 1998/2011). All of these are phenomena in which the taken-for-granted distinction between self and other is blurred.

In another line of inquiry, numerous affect theorists invoke the phenomenon of "felt atmosphere." Brennan asks: "Is there anyone who has not, at least once, walked into a room and 'felt the atmosphere'?" (2004:1; see also Berlant, 2010:102; Massumi, 2010:62). Different groups of people, different settings, possess unique atmospheres. Each has its own feel, tone, and smell. The atmosphere is objective and real but can't be described by focusing on individuals and their interactions alone: "the affect in the room is a profoundly social thing. How exactly does it get there?" (Brennan, 2004:68).

To explain how atmosphere "gets there" Brennan turns to research in the field of psychoneuroendocrinology. Atmosphere involves *chemical communication* and *chemical entrainment*. In fact, Brennan argues that chemical entrainment is the mechanism by which affect is transmitted between persons and affective fields are created. As defined by neurologists, entrainment "is a process whereby one person's or one group's nervous and hormonal systems are brought into alignment with another's" (Brennan, 2004:9). Entrainment draws people into one another's spheres, producing an interpersonal connection.

Chemical communication can produce a presocial bond, but it can also produce conflict and domination. It is possible, for example, for one person to be overwhelmed by the pheromones produced by another. This is one form of nonconscious, affective domination—the grounds out of which psychic and social domination can grow. Returning to the idea of atmosphere, Brennan argues that chemical communication can create unique group atmospheres characterized by a particular feel and smell. It is precisely because these atmospheres are a constant, conditioning companion of group life that their importance remains unnoticed.

What is important to emphasize in these numerous examples is that the affective field cannot be reduced to the individual participants in the field. The affective field, in other words, is not simply a product of interpersonal exchanges, but rather is a sphere of its own kind (see also Sloterdijk, 1998/2011). It operates, as we have

noted earlier, according to its own affective logic and is characterized by an indeterminate excess of feeling. Indeed, in order to challenge social and political domination, affect theorists draw attention to and even try to activate the potentials of
what they call "indeterminate zones" (Massumi, 2010:66). The indeterminate zone
is an affective, shared space that is full of unrealized potential. It is present in every
relationship and social formation, but more often than not the potential is restricted
though political control and domination. That is, while affect promises multiple lines
of action and relationship, in the contemporary moment affect has been captured in
political economic formations that allow the continued reproduction of capitalist
society.

The Ethics and Politics of Affect

So far we have described some of the basic conceptual innovations introduced through
affect theory. But the ideas discussed above are really only a starting point in affect
analysis. Most affect theorists have produced politically charged analyses in the spirit
of Marxist theory, critical theory, and queer theory. Here, affect is treated as a site of
potential liberation and freedom. Because it is a site of unrealized potential, the acti-
vation of affect can break old, constraining, harmful attachments and allow for the
creation of new forms of action, feeling, and interaction.

Like poststructuralist, postmodern, and queer theories the affect theorist celebrates the free flow of desire (affective energies) and wants to clear spaces in which
the unpredictable potentials of affect can emerge in various combinations and forms.[10]
In this context, many affect theorists promote a *relational ethic* that welcomes the
unpredictable forms of affect produced when people from different cultures and backgrounds interact with one another. For these reasons, affect theory is frequently
accompanied by expressions of hope for political and economic change (Grossberg,
2010). Indeed, precisely because affect is always unpredictable, slippery, and indeterminate the world can always potentially be other than it is.

At the same time, affect theorists have offered numerous analyses of how contemporary social powers have tried to seize the potential of affect for the purpose of
political economic gain and social control. In affect theory, social control and social
domination are usually described with terms borrowed from the postmodern thinkers
Gilles Deleuze and Felix Guattari (1972/1983, 1980/1987). So, for example, affects
are created and controlled through the construction of "machinic assemblages."
Machinic assemblage is a term that describes the ways that bodies, ideas, and technologies are hooked up in relationship to one another (like the construction of networks in actor-network theory). Particular assemblages produce affects unique to time
and place. When effective these machinic assemblages create populations and citizens
that support the contemporary political and economic status quo (which for most
affect theorists is a problem). In the current moment, affects are produced through
assemblages that hook together capitalist markets, mass media imagery, and biotech-
nologies, among others. When machinic assemblages take over geographical, cultural,

---

10. Though not all affect theorists are committed to this view of political change (see Grossberg, 2010).

and psychical regions this is referred to as *territorialization*. Territorialization is never full or complete and is often met with *deterritorialization* efforts.

Patricia Clough (2008) analyzes the relationship between affect and capitalism through the concept of *biomedia*. Bodies are organized differently in different historical periods. She distinguishes between the *body-as-organism* of the nineteenth century and the *biomediated* body of the present moment. The body-as-organism was a self-enclosed body that was created and reproduced through labor and consumption practices like those described by Marx. The biomediated body, on the other hand, is opened up to the flows and movements that characterize contemporary capitalism. Biomedia are the new technologies that allow historically unique engagements with the biological body. Here affect is "captured" in at least two ways.

First, new media technologies generate and circulate affect in unprecedented ways. This is an era in which populations are not exclusively governed through ideology (i.e., narratives constructed by politicians to secure their power) but also through aesthetic and affective techniques. Media, mass entertainment, and political display work by stimulating and circulating affective energies:

> capital extracts value from affect—around consumer confidence, political fears and so forth, such that the difference between commodification and labor, production and reproduction are collapsed in the modulation of the capacity to circulate affect. (2008: 16)

On a similar note, Anderson (2010) describes how politicians generate "morale" among populations so as to support their "world-making" and "world-destroying" activities (see also Orr, 2006). Morale holds the public body together in times of fear and panic, especially in the midst of war.

The second way that affect is captured is through biomedicine. Biomedicine is the growing sector concerned with the treatment and management of biological health and wellness. It is a high-tech industry connected to the machinations of capitalism. Biomedicine generates *biocapital*. Biocapital is the value—economic wealth—produced through knowledge about bodies and their affective capacities. On the one hand, the biomedical industry profits from the sale of biomedical technologies, for example, drugs. Referring to the writings of Eugene Thacker (2005:85), Clough describes another way that biomedicine produces value:

> On the other hand, what is more lucrative than the sale of drugs is the 'booming industry of diagnostic tests' and the production of databases. There is the economic gain sought in maintaining 'the recirculation of products (pills, testing technologies) back into information (databases, test results, marketing and media campaign.' (Clough, 2008:10)

Like affect theorists, the biomedical industry recognizes that the biological body possesses vast potentials. Biomedicine tries to find ways to manage, control, and capture these otherwise indeterminate and never fully knowable affective forces. These are captured in knowledge databases that describe that various capacities of different kinds of bodies. The question for contemporary biomedicine is: What can particular bodies do and even, what can particular bodies "be made to do" (5)? The biomedical industry assumes that different bodies possess different kinds of genetic makeup and consequently possess unique potentials. For example, some bodies are seen as possessing genetic secrets that could help in the cure of disease (and in gaining the profits that would come from the cure of disease). The challenge for biomedicine is to map and then find ways to capture these potentials.

Here affect theory overlaps with the concerns of critical theories of race and racism outlined in the first part of this chapter. Clough describes, for example, how the biomedical industry revives the scientific racism perpetuated in the nineteenth century. It assumes, for example, that the bodies of different "races" can do different things, each of which can be of unique value:

> What makes the biopolitics of the biomediated body a political economy, then, is the break into biology or 'life itself' by carving out various populations in order to estimate the value of their capacities for life, or more precisely, their capacities to provide life for capital, a deployment of what Foucault described as racism. (18)

Even though affect is never fully captured, biomedicine nevertheless creates a political and economic structure that organizes bodies through assessments of affective worth and value.

Finally, affect theorists have considered the ways that affect is managed in everyday life. Insofar as consumer and popular culture operate in the service of politics and capital, affective capture and control can be found here as well. This is a world in which regulation of populations is achieved not only through the direct manipulation of the biological body (à la Clough) but also through the creation of widespread cultural moods. Common here is the idea that contemporary populations are caught up in shame, humiliation, and other self-degrading (and therefore politically defeating) emotions. Lawrence Grossberg, a cultural theorist recognized for his work on popular culture, writes:

> I want to suggest, for example, that the media today are producing what for the moment I would call a structure of feeling or a mood (I am not sure which, but I do not think it is an emotion) of humiliation and this is a key to understanding much about the articulation of the popular and the political. (2010:330)

Lauren Berlant describes a similar sentiment when she says that contemporary American culture is characterized by "cruel optimism." Optimism is a kind of affect, a feeling, in which one places trust in the promises/potentials "contained in the present moment" (2010:93). In an ideal world, the promises of the moment—in other words, the multiple potentials of affect—would find opportunities for actualization.

Cruel optimism, on the other hand, is the attachment to a set of ideas or objects whose potential cannot be realized. It is "an enabling object that is also disabling" (Berlant, 2010:95). It is a promise that can never be realized. Contemporary America is a place where one lives, paradoxically, in a state of optimism that can never be actualized. The classic example is the myth of the American dream. Although many Americans believe that through hard work and determination they can become wealthy and happy, in fact the capitalist economy requires continuing inequality. Through cruel optimism, then, people are caught up in dreams that can never be realized. The point is that the popular culture and media, in support of the capitalist economy, sets up an appealing, though self-destructive, affective condition. Like most affect theorists Berlant expects that by naming cruel optimism for what it is, we can better free otherwise trapped affective potentials.

Summary

In this chapter we examine four theories that have proven to be of particular significance in the late twentieth and early twenty-first centuries. While each offers a unique set of conceptual tools, they also address overlapping themes such as identity formation, social marginalization, and the impact of science and technology in the formation of society.

Critical theories of race and racism have been part of the discipline since its origins in, for example, the work of W.E.B. Du Bois. The continuing importance of the social category of race is enunciated in the civil rights movements of the 1960s, which in turn gave rise to critical race theories and critical theories of race and racism. These have grown in importance in recent years because of the way that globalization leads to the intermingling of people from various backgrounds. For critical theories of race and racism, race is a social construction, a product of processes of racialization. Critical race theory is a theory that studies the way the law creates and organizes racial identities. From this perspective racism is not merely personal prejudice but a form of inequality and marginalization built into the structure of society. Critical theories of race and racism also view race as built into social structures and expand its analysis of racism into areas like science and technology and globalization.

Queer theory is a perspective that addresses the construction of sex and sexuality. Unlike gay and lesbian studies, it is not an identity theory, that is, it does not believe that people possess a real or true sexual identity. Rather, sexuality is social and discursively produced, a product of a performance, rather than an inherent feature of persons. The nineteenth and twentieth centuries have seen the development of the categories of hetero- and homosexuality. This dichotomy has organized social life into the present moment. Queer theorists seek to deconstruct these taken-for-granted categories so as to allow for the playful reorganization of sexuality, identity, and social life more generally.

Actor-network theory is a perspective that grows out of the larger field of science and technology studies. ANT is most notable for according nonhuman actors their deserved significance in social theory. Affect theory also draws on work in science and technology studies but combines these with work in queer theory and poststructuralism. Affect theory claims to take the findings of the life sciences seriously, but it does this in different ways than perspectives such as sociobiology. In particular, it treats nature and biology as a field of forces and energies. Affect theorists study the ways that these affective energies impact subject formation and the way that they have been submitted to processes of social control and manipulation. Like queer theorists, affect theorists seek a form of social and political organization in which affect (life energy, desire) can flow freely.

The newer theories like those discussed in this chapter continually refresh and challenge sociological theory by adding new themes of study and new ways of thinking not only about them but about many other subjects in the field. It is safe to predict that more new theories will emerge in the coming years, and that they, too, will enrich the field in similar ways.

Appendix

Sociological Metatheorizing and a Metatheoretical Schema for Analyzing Sociological Theory

Appendix Outline
Metatheorizing in Sociology
The Ideas of Thomas Kuhn
Sociology: A Multiple-Paradigm Science
Toward a More Integrated Sociological Paradigm

One important aspect of sociological theory is sociological metatheorizing. While theorists take the social world as their subject matter, metatheorists engage in *the systematic study of the underlying structure of sociological theory* (Ritzer, 1991b; Ritzer, Zhao, and Murphy, 2001; Zhao, 2001, 2005). One goal of this Appendix is to look at the increase in interest in metatheorizing in sociology and at the basic parameters of this approach. The structure of this book rests on a specific set of metatheoretical perspectives developed by the lead author of this text, George Ritzer (1975a, 1981a). Thus, another objective of this Appendix is to present the metatheoretical ideas that inform the text. But first an overview of metatheorizing in sociology will be helpful.

Metatheorizing in Sociology

Sociologists are not the only ones to do meta-analysis (Bakker, 2007c), that is, to reflexively study their own discipline. Others who do such work include philosophers (Radnitzky, 1973), psychologists (Gergen, 1973, 1986, 1994a, 1994b; Schmidt et al., 1984), political scientists (Connolly, 1973), a number of other social scientists (various essays in Fiske and Shweder, 1986), and historians (Hayden White, 1973).

Beyond the fact that meta-analysis occurs in other fields, various kinds of sociologists, not just metatheorists, do this type of analysis (Zhao, 1991). We can group the types of meta-analysis in sociology under the heading "metasociology," which can be defined as *the reflexive study of the underlying structure of sociology in general, as well as of its various components*—substantive areas (for example, Richard Hall's [1983] overview of occupational sociology), concepts (Rubenstein's [1986] analysis of the concept of "structure"), methods (*metamethods,* for example, Brewer and

Hunter's [1989] and Noblit and Hare's [1988] efforts to synthesize sociological methods), data (*meta-data-analysis,*[1] for example, Fendrich, 1984; Hunter, Schmidt, and Jackson, 1982; Polit and Falbo, 1987; F. Wolf, 1986), and theories. It is the last item, *metatheorizing,* that concerns us in this Appendix.

What distinguishes work in this area is not so much the process of metatheorizing (or systematically studying theories, which all metatheorists do) but rather the nature of the end products. There are three varieties of metatheorizing, largely defined by differences in end products (Ritzer, 1991a, 1991b, 1991c, 1992b, 2007b). The first type, *metatheorizing as a means of attaining a deeper understanding of theory* (M_U), involves the study of theory in order to produce a better, more profound understanding of extant theory (Ritzer, 1988). M_U is concerned with the study of theories, theorists, and communities of theorists, as well as the larger intellectual and social contexts of theories and theorists. The second type, *metatheorizing as a prelude to theory development* (M_P), entails the study of extant theory in order to produce new sociological theory. In the third type, *metatheorizing as a source of perspectives that overarch sociological theory* (M_O), the study of theory is oriented toward the goal of producing a perspective—one could say *a* metatheory—that overarches some part or all of sociological theory. (It is this type of metatheorizing that provided the framework used in constructing this book.) Given these definitions, let us examine each type of metatheorizing in detail.

1. The first type of metatheorizing, M_U, is composed of four basic subtypes. All of them involve the formal or informal study of sociological theory to attain a deeper understanding of it.

The first subtype, *internal-intellectual,* focuses on intellectual or cognitive issues that are internal to sociology. Included here are attempts to identify major cognitive paradigms (Ritzer, 1975a, 1975b; see also the discussion below) and "schools of thought" (Sorokin, 1928), more dynamic views of the underlying structure of sociological theory (L. Harvey, 1982, 1987; Holmwood and Stewart, 1994; Nash and Wardell, 1993; Wiley, 1979), and the development of general metatheoretical tools with which to analyze existing sociological theories and to develop new theories (Alexander et al., 1987; Edel, 1959; Gouldner, 1970; Ritzer, 1989, 1990a; Wiley, 1988).

The second subtype, *internal-social,* also looks within sociology, but it focuses on social rather than cognitive factors. The main approach here emphasizes the communal aspects of various sociological theories and includes efforts to identify the major "schools" in the history of sociology (Bulmer, 1984, 1985; Cortese, 1995; Tiryakian, 1979, 1986), the more formal, network approach to the study of the ties among groups of sociologists (Mullins, 1973, 1983), and studies of theorists themselves that examine their institutional affiliations, career patterns, positions within the field of sociology, and so on (Camic, 1992; Gouldner, 1970).

---

[1] The (somewhat awkward) label "meta-data-analysis" is used to differentiate this from the more generic meta-analysis. In meta-data-analysis the goal is to seek ways of cumulating research results across research studies. In his introduction to Wolf's *Meta-Analysis,* Niemi defines *meta-analysis* as "the application of statistical procedures to collections of empirical findings from individual studies for the purpose of integrating, synthesizing, and making sense of them" (F. Wolf, 1986:5).

The third subtype, *external-intellectual,* turns to other academic disciplines for ideas, tools, concepts, and theories that can be used in the analysis of sociological theory (for example, R. Brown, 1987, 1990). Baker (1993) has looked at the implications of chaos theory, with its roots in physics, for sociological theory. Bailey has argued that while explicit attention to metatheorizing may be relatively new in sociology, "general systems theory has long been marked by widespread metatheorizing" (1994:27). Such metatheorizing was made necessary by the multidisciplinary character of systems theory and the need to study and bring together ideas from different fields. He later argues that social-systems theory "embraces metatheorizing" (Bailey, 1994:82). In fact, Bailey uses a metatheoretical approach to analyze developments in systems theory and their relationship to developments in sociological theory.

The fourth subtype, the *external-social approach,* shifts to a more macro level to look at the larger society (national setting, sociocultural setting, etc.) and the nature of its impact on sociological theorizing (for example, Vidich and Lyman, 1985).

Of course, specific metatheoretical efforts can combine two or more types of M_U. For example, Jaworski has shown how Lewis Coser's 1956 book *The Functions of Social Conflict* (see Chapter 7) "was a deeply personal book and a historically situated statement" (1991:116). Thus, Jaworski touches on the impact of his family (internal-social) and of the rise of Hitler in Germany (external-social) on Coser's life and work. Jaworski also deals with the effect of external-intellectual (American radical political thought) and internal-intellectual (industrial sociology) factors on Coser's thinking. Thus, Jaworski combines all four subtypes of M_U in his analysis of Coser's work on social conflict.

2. Most metatheorizing in sociology is not M_U; rather, it is the second type, metatheorizing as a prelude to the development of sociological theory (M_P). Most important classical and contemporary theorists developed their theories, at least in part, on the basis of a careful study of, and reaction to, the work of other theorists. Among the most important examples are Marx's theory of capitalism (see Chapter 2), developed out of a systematic engagement with Hegelian philosophy as well as other ideas, such as political economy and utopian socialism; Parsons's action theory (see Chapter 7) developed out of a systematic study of the work of Durkheim, Weber, Pareto, and Marshall; Alexander's (1982–1983) multidimensional, neofunctional theory, based on a detailed study of the work of Marx, Weber, Durkheim, and Parsons; and Habermas's (1987a) communication theory, based on his examination of the work of various critical theorists, as well as that of Marx, Weber, Parsons, Mead, and Durkheim. Let us look in more detail at M_P as it was practiced by Karl Marx.

In *Economic and Philosophic Manuscripts of 1844,* Marx (1932/1964) develops his theoretical perspective on the basis of a detailed and careful analysis and critique of the works of political economists such as Adam Smith, Jean-Baptiste Say, David Ricardo, and James Mill; philosophers such as G.W.F. Hegel, the Young Hegelians (for example, Bruno Bauer), and Ludwig Feuerbach; utopian socialists such as Etienne Cabet, Robert Owen, Charles Fourier, and Pierre Proudhon; and a variety of other major and minor intellectual schools and figures. It seems safe to say that in almost its entirety the *Manuscripts of 1844* is a metatheoretical treatise in which Marx develops his own ideas out of an engagement with a variety of idea systems.

What of Marx's other works? Are they more empirical? Less metatheoretical? In his preface to *The German Ideology* (Marx and Engels, 1845–1846/1970), C. J. Arthur describes that work as composed mainly of "detailed line by line polemics against the writings of some of their [Marx and Engels's] contemporaries" (1970:1). In fact, Marx himself describes *The German Ideology* as an effort "to set forth together our conception as opposed to the ideological one of German philosophy, in fact to settle accounts with our former philosophical conscience. The intention was carried out in the form of a critique of post-Hegelian philosophy" (1859/1970:22). *The Holy Family* (Marx and Engels, 1845/1956) is, above all, an extended critique of Bruno Bauer, the Young Hegelians, and their propensity toward speculative "critical criticism."[2] In their foreword, Marx and Engels make it clear that this kind of metatheoretical work is a prelude to their coming theorizing: "We therefore give this polemic as a preliminary to the independent works in which we . . . shall present our positive view" (1845/1956:16). In the *Grundrisse* Marx (1857–1858/1974) chooses as his metatheoretical antagonists the political economist David Ricardo and the French socialist Pierre Proudhon (Nicolaus, 1974). Throughout the *Grundrisse* Marx is struggling to solve an array of theoretical problems, in part through a critique of the theories and theorists mentioned here and in part through an application of ideas derived from Hegel. In describing the introduction to the *Grundrisse,* Nicolaus says that it "reflects in its every line the struggle of Marx against Hegel, Ricardo and Proudhon. From it, Marx carried off the most important objective of all, namely the basic principles of writing history dialectically" (1974:42). *A Contribution to the Critique of Political Economy* (Marx, 1859/1970) is, as the title suggests, an effort to build a distinctive economic approach on the basis of a critique of the works of the political economists.

Even *Capital* (1867/1967)—which is admittedly one of Marx's most empirical works, since in it he deals more directly with the reality of the capitalist work world through the use of government statistics and reports—is informed by Marx's earlier metatheoretical work and contains some metatheorizing of its own. In fact, the subtitle, *A Critique of Political Economy,* makes the metatheoretical roots absolutely clear. However, Marx is freer in *Capital* to be much more "positive," that is, to construct his own distinctive theoretical orientation. This freedom is traceable, in part, to his having done much of the metatheoretical groundwork in earlier works. Furthermore, most of the new metatheoretical work is relegated to the so-called fourth volume of *Capital,* published under the title *Theories of Surplus Value* (Marx, 1862–1863/1963, 1862–1863/1968). *Theories* is composed of many extracts from the work of the major political economists (for example, Smith and Ricardo) as well as critical analysis of them by Marx. In sum, it is safe to say that Marx was, largely, a metatheorist, perhaps the *most* metatheoretical of all classical sociological theorists.

3. There are a number of examples of the third type of metatheorizing, M_O—metatheorizing to produce overarching perspectives. They include Walter Wallace's (1988) "disciplinary matrix," Ritzer's (1979, 1981a) "integrated sociological paradigm" (discussed later in this Appendix), Furfey's (1953/1965) positivistic metasociology,

---

[2] In fact, the book is subtitled *Against Bruno Bauer and Co.*

Gross's (1961) "neodialectical" metasociology, Alexander's (1982) "general theoretical logic for sociology," and Alexander's (1995) later effort to develop a postpositivist approach to universalism and rationality. A number of theorists (Bourdieu and Wacquant, 1992; Emirbayer, 1997; Ritzer and Gindoff, 1992, 1994) have been engaged in an effort to create what Ritzer and Gindoff have called "methodological relationism"[3] to complement the extant overarching perspectives of "methodological individualism" (Udehn, 2002) and "methodological holism." Methodological relationism is derived from a study of works on micro-macro and agency-structure integration, as well as a variety of works in social psychology.

The three varieties of metatheory are ideal types. In actual cases there is often considerable overlap in the objectives of metatheoretical works. Nevertheless, those who do one type of metatheorizing tend to be less interested in achieving the objectives of the other two types. Of course, there are sociologists who at one time or another have done all three types of metatheorizing. For example, Alexander (1982–1983) creates overarching perspectives (M_O) in the first volume of *Theoretical Logic in Sociology,* uses them in the next three volumes to achieve a better understanding (M_U) of the classic theorists, and later seeks to help create neofunctionalism (M_P) as a theoretical successor to structural functionalism (Alexander and Colomy, 1990a).

Pierre Bourdieu's Reflexive Sociology

An important contemporary metatheorist (although he resisted that label, indeed any label) is Pierre Bourdieu. Bourdieu calls for a reflexive sociology: "For me, sociology ought to be meta but *always vis-à-vis itself.* It must use its own instruments to find out what it is and what it is doing, to try to know better where it stands" (Bourdieu and Wacquant, 1992:191; see also Meisenhelder, 1997). Or, using an older and less well-defined label ("sociology of sociology") for metasociology, Bourdieu says, "The sociology of sociology is a fundamental dimension of sociological epistemology" (Bourdieu and Wacquant, 1992:68). Sociologists, who spend their careers "objectivizing" the social world, ought to spend some time objectivizing their own practices. Thus, sociology "continually turns back onto itself the scientific weapons it produces" (Bourdieu and Wacquant, 1992:214). Bourdieu even rejects certain kinds of metatheorizing (for example, the internal-social and internal-intellectual forms of M_U) as "a complacent and intimist return upon the private *person* of the sociologist or with a search for the intellectual *Zeitgeist* that animates his or her work" (Bourdieu and Wacquant, 1992:72; for a discussion of Bourdieu's more positive view of even these kinds of metatheorizing, see Wacquant, 1992:38). However, a rejection of certain kinds of metatheorizing does not represent a rejection of the undertaking in its entirety. Clearly, following the logic of *Homo Academicus* (1984b), Bourdieu would favor examining the habitus and practices of sociologists within the fields of sociology as a discipline and the academic world, as well as the relationship between those fields and the fields of stratification and politics. His work *Distinction* (1984a) would

---

[3] Swartz (1997) does a particularly good job of delineating this metatheory as well as the other metatheories that inform Bourdieu's theorizing.

lead Bourdieu to concern himself with the strategies of individual sociologists, as well as of the discipline itself, to achieve distinction. For example, individual sociologists might use jargon to achieve high status in the field, and sociology might wrap itself in a cloak of science so that it could achieve distinction vis-à-vis the world of practice. In fact, Bourdieu has claimed that the scientific claims of sociology and other social sciences "are really euphemized assertions of power" (Robbins, 1991:139). Of course, this position has uncomfortable implications for Bourdieu's own work:

> Bourdieu's main problem during the 1980s has been to sustain his symbolic power whilst simultaneously undermining the scientificity on which it was originally founded. Some would say that he has tied the noose around his own neck and kicked away the stool from beneath his feet.
>
> (Robbins, 1991:150)

Given his commitment to theoretically informed empirical research, Bourdieu also would have little patience with most, if not all, forms of M_O, which he has described as "universal metadiscourse on knowledge of the world" (Bourdieu and Wacquant, 1992:159). More generally, Bourdieu would reject metatheorizing as an autonomous practice, setting metatheorizing apart from theorizing about and empirically studying the social world (see Wacquant, 1992:31).

Bourdieu makes an interesting case for metatheorizing when he argues that sociologists need to *"avoid being the toy of social forces in [their] practice of sociology"* (Bourdieu and Wacquant, 1992:183). The only way to avoid such a fate is to understand the nature of the forces acting on the sociologist at a given point in history. Such forces can be understood only via metatheoretical analysis, or what Bourdieu calls "socioanalysis" (Bourdieu and Wacquant, 1992:210). Once sociologists understand the nature of the forces (especially external-social and external-intellectual) operating on them, they will be in a better position to control the impact of those forces on their work. As Bourdieu puts it, in personal terms, "I continually use sociology to try to cleanse my work of . . . social determinants" (Bourdieu and Wacquant, 1992:211). Thus, the goal of metatheorizing from Bourdieu's point of view is not to undermine sociology, but to free it from those forces which determine it. Of course, what Bourdieu says of his own efforts is equally true of metatheoretical endeavors in general. While he strives to limit the effect of external factors on his work, Bourdieu is aware of the limitations of such efforts: "I do not for one minute believe or claim that I am fully liberated from them [social determinants]" (Bourdieu and Wacquant, 1992:211).

Similarly, Bourdieu wishes to free sociologists from the symbolic violence committed against them by other, more powerful sociologists. This objective invites internal-intellectual and internal-social analyses of sociology in order to uncover the sources and nature of that symbolic violence. Once the latter are understood, sociologists are in a better position to free themselves of, or at least limit, their effects. More generally, sociologists are well positioned to practice "epistemological vigilance" in order to protect themselves from these distorting pressures (Bourdieu, 1984b:15).

What is most distinctive about Bourdieu's metatheoretical approach is his refusal to separate metatheorizing from the other facets of sociology.[4] That is, he believes that sociologists should be continuously reflexive as they are doing their sociological analyses. They should reflect on what they are doing, and especially on how it might be distorting what they are examining, during their analyses. This reflection would limit the amount of "symbolic violence" against the subjects of study.

Although Bourdieu is doing a distinctive kind of metatheoretical work, it is clear that his work is, at least in part, metatheoretical. Given his growing significance in social theory, the association of Bourdieu's work with metatheorizing is likely to contribute further to the growth of interest in metatheorizing in sociology.

With this overview, we now turn to the specific metatheoretical approach that undergirds this book. As will become clear, it involves a combination of M_U and M_O. We begin with a brief review of the work of Thomas Kuhn, and then we examine Ritzer's (M_U) analysis of sociology's multiple paradigms. Finally, we review the metatheoretical tool—the integrated sociological paradigm (M_O)—that is the source of the levels of analysis used to analyze sociological theories throughout this book.

The Ideas of Thomas Kuhn

In 1962 the philosopher of science Thomas Kuhn published a rather slim volume entitled *The Structure of Scientific Revolutions* (Hoyningen-Huene, 1993). Because this work grew out of philosophy, it appeared to be fated to a marginal status within sociology, especially because it focused on the hard sciences (physics, for example) and had little directly to say about the social sciences. However, the theses of the book proved extremely interesting to people in a wide range of fields (for example, Hollinger, 1980, in history; Searle, 1972, in linguistics; Stanfield, 1974, in economics), and to none was it more important than to sociologists. In 1970 Robert Friedrichs published the first important work from a Kuhnian perspective, *A Sociology of Sociology*. After that there was a steady stream of work from this perspective (Eckberg and Hill, 1979; Effrat, 1972; Eisenstadt and Curelaru, 1976; Falk and Zhao, 1990a, 1990b; Friedrichs, 1972; Greisman, 1986; Guba and Lincoln, 1994; Lodahl and Gordon, 1972; D. Phillips, 1973, 1975; Quadagno, 1979; Ritzer, 1975a, 1975b, 1981b; M. Rosenberg, 1989; Snizek, 1976; Snizek, Fuhrman, and Miller, 1979). There is little doubt that Kuhnian theory is an important variety of M_U, but what exactly is Kuhn's approach?

One of Kuhn's goals in *The Structure of Scientific Revolutions* (1962) was to challenge commonly held assumptions about the way in which science changes. In the view of most laypeople and many scientists, science advances in a cumulative manner, with each advance building inexorably on all that preceded it. Science has achieved its present state through slow and steady increments of knowledge. It will advance to even greater heights in the future. This conception of science was enunciated

---

[4] This leads Swartz (1997:11) to argue that "Bourdieu does not share Ritzer's (1988) vision of establishing sociological metatheory as a legitimate subfield within the discipline of sociology."

GEORGE RITZER

Autobiography as a Metatheoretical Tool

Biographical and autobiographical work is useful in helping us understand the work of sociological theorists, and of sociologists generally. The historian of science, Thomas Hankin, explains it this way:

> [A] fully integrated biography of a scientist which includes not only his personality, but also his scientific work and the intellectual and social context of his times, [is] . . . still the best way to get at many of the problems that beset the writing of history of science . . . science is created by individuals, and however much it may be driven by forces outside, these forces work through the scientist himself. Biography is the literary lens through which we can best view this process.
>
> (Hankin, 1979:14)

What Hankin asserts about scientists generally informs my orientation to the biographies of sociological theorists, including myself. This autobiographical snippet is designed to suggest at least a few ways in which biography can be a useful tool for metatheoretical analysis.

Although I have taught in sociology departments for more than thirty years, have written extensively about sociology, and have lectured all over the world on the topic, none of my degrees are in sociology. This lack of a formal background in the field has led to a lifelong study of sociology in general and sociological theory in particular. It has also, at least in one sense, aided my attempt to understand sociological theory. Because I had not been trained in a particular "school," I came to sociological theory with few prior conceptions and biases. Rather, I was a student of all "schools of thought"; they were all equally grist for my theoretical mill.

My first metatheoretical work, *Sociology: A Multiple Paradigm Science* (1975a), sought not only to lay out sociology's separable, and often conflicting, paradigms but also to make the case for paradigm linking, leaping, bridging, and integrating. Uncomfortable with paradigmatic conflict, I wanted to see more harmony and integration in sociology. That desire led to the publication of *Toward an Integrated Sociological Paradigm* (1981a), in which I more fully developed my sense of an integrated paradigm. The interest in resolving theoretical conflict led to a focus on micro-macro (1990a) and agency-structure (Ritzer and Gindoff, 1994) integration as well as the larger issue of theoretical syntheses (1990b).

by the physicist Sir Isaac Newton, who said, "If I have seen further, it is because I stood on the shoulders of giants." But Kuhn regarded this conception of cumulative scientific development as a myth and sought to debunk it.

My interest in metatheoretical work is explained by my desire to understand theory better and to resolve unnecessary conflict within sociological theory. In *Metatheorizing in Sociology* (1991b) and in an edited volume, *Metatheorizing* (1992a), I made a case for the need for the systematic study of sociological theory. I believe that we need to do more of this in order to understand theory better, produce new theory, and produce new overarching theoretical perspectives (or metatheories). Metatheoretical study is also oriented to clarifying contentious issues, resolving disputes, and allowing for greater integration and synthesis.

Having spent many years seeking to clarify the nature of sociological theory, in the early 1990s I grew weary of the abstractions of metatheoretical work. I sought to apply the various theories that I had learned to very concrete aspects of the social world. I had done a little with this in the 1980s, applying Weber's theory of rationalization to fast-food restaurants (1983) and the medical profession (Ritzer and Walczak, 1988). I revisited the 1983 essay, and the result was a book, *The McDonaldization of Society* (1993, 1996, 2013), which argued that while in Weber's day the model of the rationalization process was the bureaucracy, today the fast-food restaurant has become a better model of that process (additional essays on this topic are to be found in *The McDonaldization Thesis* [1998]). In *Expressing America: A Critique of the Global Credit Card Society* (1995), I turned my attention to another everyday economic phenomenon, which I analyzed not only from the perspective of rationalization theory, but from other perspectives, including Georg Simmel's theoretical ideas on money.

This work on fast-food restaurants and credit cards led to the realization that what I was really interested in was the sociology of consumption, a field little developed in the United States, at least in comparison to Great Britain and other European nations. That led to *Enchanting a Disenchanted World: Revolutionizing the Means of Consumption* (1999, 2005a), in which I used Weberian, Marxian, and postmodern theory to analyze the revolutionary impact of a range of new means of consumption (superstores, megamalls, cybermalls, home shopping television, casinos, theme parks, and cruise ships, as well as fast-food restaurants and other franchises) on the way Americans and the rest of the world consume goods and services.

The global reach of McDonald's and McDonaldization, credit cards, and the new means of consumption has led me more directly to an interest in globalization and my latest book, *The Globalization of Nothing* (2004). While I cannot rule out a return to metatheoretical issues, and in fact have recently dealt with them (Ritzer, 2001), my current plans are to continue to use theory to think about the contemporary world, especially consumption (and prosumption) and globalization (Ritzer, 2010b, 2012).

Source: Adapted (and updated) from George Ritzer, "I Never Metatheory I Didn't Like," *Mid-American Review of Sociology,* 15:21–32, 1991. See also Goodman (2005).

Kuhn acknowledged that accumulation plays some role in the advance of science, but the truly major changes come about as a result of revolutions. Kuhn offered a theory of how major changes in science occur. He saw a science at any given time as being dominated by a specific *paradigm* (defined for the moment as a fundamental image of the science's subject matter) (Ritzer, 2005b). *Normal science* is a period of accumulation of knowledge in which scientists work to expand the reigning paradigm. Such scientific work inevitably spawns *anomalies,* or findings that cannot be explained by the reigning paradigm. A *crisis* stage occurs if these anomalies mount, and this crisis ultimately may end in a scientific revolution. The reigning paradigm is overthrown as a new one takes its place at the center of the science. A new dominant paradigm is born, and the stage is set for the cycle to repeat itself. Kuhn's theory can be depicted diagrammatically:

Paradigm I → Normal Science → Anomalies →
Crisis → Revolution → Paradigm II

It is during periods of revolution that the truly great changes in science take place. This view places Kuhn clearly at odds with most conceptions of scientific development.

The key concept in Kuhn's approach, as well as in this section, is the paradigm. Unfortunately, Kuhn is vague on what he means by a paradigm (Alcala-Campos, 1997). According to Margaret Masterman (1970), he used the term in at least twenty-one different ways. We will employ a definition of *paradigm* that Ritzer (1975a) argues is true to the sense and spirit of Kuhn's early work.

A paradigm serves to differentiate one scientific community from another. It can be used to differentiate physics from chemistry or sociology from psychology. These fields have different paradigms. It also can be used to differentiate between different historical stages in the development of a science (Mann, Grimes, and Kemp, 1997). The paradigm that dominated physics in the nineteenth century is different from the one that dominated it in the early twentieth century. There is a third usage of the paradigm concept, and it is the one that is most useful here. Paradigms can differentiate among cognitive groupings *within* the same science. Contemporary psychoanalysis, for example, is differentiated into Freudian, object-relations, and Lacanian paradigms (among others)—that is, there are *multiple paradigms* in psychoanalysis—and the same is true of sociology and most other fields.

We can now offer a definition of *paradigm* that Ritzer feels is true to the sense of Kuhn's original work:

> A paradigm is a fundamental image of the subject matter within a science. It serves to define what should be studied, what questions should be asked, how they should be asked, and what rules should be followed in interpreting the answers obtained. The paradigm is the broadest unit of consensus within a science and serves to differentiate one scientific community (*or subcommunity*) from another. It subsumes, defines, and interrelates the exemplars, *theories* [italics added], and methods and instruments that exist within it.
>
> (Ritzer, 1975a:7)

With this definition we can begin to see the relationship between paradigms and theories. *Theories are only part of larger paradigms.* To put it another way, a paradigm may encompass two or more *theories,* as well as different *images* of the subject matter, *methods* (and instruments), and *exemplars* (specific pieces of scientific work that stand as a model for all those who follow).

Sociology: A Multiple-Paradigm Science

Ritzer's (1975a, 1975b, 1980) work on the paradigmatic status of sociology, beginning in the mid-1970s, provides the basis for the metatheoretical perspective that has guided the analysis of sociological theory throughout much of this book. There are *three* paradigms that dominated sociology, with several others having had the potential to achieve paradigmatic status. The three paradigms are labeled the *social-facts, social-definition,* and *social-behavior* paradigms. Each paradigm is analyzed in terms of the four components of a paradigm.

The Social-Facts Paradigm

1. *Exemplar:* The model for social factists is the work of Emile Durkheim, particularly *The Rules of Sociological Method* and *Suicide.*

2. *Image of the subject matter:* Social factists focus on what Durkheim termed social facts, or large-scale social structures and institutions. Those who subscribe to the social-facts paradigm focus not only on these phenomena but on their effect on individual thought and action.

3. *Methods:* Social factists are more likely than are those who subscribe to the other paradigms to use the interview-questionnaire[5] and historical-comparative methods.

4. *Theories:* The social-facts paradigm encompasses a number of theoretical perspectives. *Structural-functional* theorists tend to see social facts as neatly interrelated and order as maintained by general consensus. *Conflict* theorists tend to emphasize disorder among social facts as well as the notion that order is maintained by coercive forces in society. Although structural functionalism and conflict theory are the dominant theories in this paradigm, there are others, including *systems* theory.

The Social-Definition Paradigm

1. *Exemplar:* To social definitionists, the unifying model is Max Weber's work on social action.

2. *Image of the subject matter:* Weber's work helped lead to an interest among social definitionists in the way actors define their social situations and the effect of these definitions on ensuing action and interaction.

3. *Methods:* Social definitionists, although they are most likely to use the interview-questionnaire method, are more likely to use the observation method than are those in any other paradigm (Prus, 1996). In other words, observation is the distinctive methodology of social definitionists.

4. *Theories:* There are a wide number of theories that can be included within social definitionism: *action theory, symbolic interactionism, phenomenology, ethnomethodology,* and *existentialism.*

---

[5] William Snizek (1976) has shown that the interview-questionnaire is dominant in *all* paradigms.

The Social-Behavior Paradigm

1. *Exemplar:* The model for social behaviorists is the work of the psychologist B. F. Skinner.

2. *Image of the subject matter:* The subject matter of sociology to social behaviorists is the unthinking *behavior* of individuals. Of particular interest are the rewards that elicit desirable behaviors and the punishments that inhibit undesirable behaviors.

3. *Methods:* The distinctive method of social behaviorism is the experiment.

4. *Theories:* Two theoretical approaches in sociology can be included under the heading "social behaviorism." The first is *behavioral sociology,* which is very close to pure psychological behaviorism. The second, which is much more important, is *exchange theory.*[6]

Toward a More Integrated Sociological Paradigm

In addition to detailing the nature of sociology's multiple paradigms, Ritzer sought to make the case for more paradigmatic integration in sociology. Although there is reason for extant paradigms to continue to exist, there is also a need for a more integrated paradigm.[7] Contrary to a claim by Nash and Wardell (1993), Ritzer is *not* arguing for a new hegemonic position in sociology; Ritzer is *not* arguing that "the current diversity represents an undesirable condition needing elimination" (Nash and Wardell, 1993:278). On the contrary, Ritzer argues for *more* diversity through the development of an integrated paradigm to supplement extant paradigms. Like Nash and Wardell, Ritzer *favors* theoretical diversity.

Extant paradigms tend to be one-sided, focusing on specific levels of social analysis while paying little or no attention to the others. This characteristic is reflected in the social factists' concern with macro structures; the social definitionists' concern with action, interaction, and the social construction of reality; and the social behaviorists' concern with behavior. It is this kind of one-sidedness that has led to a growing interest in a more integrated approach among a wide range of sociologists (Ritzer, 1991d). (This is only part of a growing interest in integration within and even among many social sciences; see especially Mitroff and Kilmann, 1978.) For example, Robert Merton, representing social factism, saw it and social definitionism as mutually enriching, as "opposed to one another in about the same sense as ham is opposed to eggs: they are perceptively different but mutually enriching" (1975:30).

The key to an integrated paradigm is the notion of *levels* of social analysis (Ritzer, 1979, 1981a). As the reader is well aware, *the social world is not really divided into levels.* In fact, social reality is best viewed as an enormous variety of

---

[6] Analyses of this paradigm schema include Eckberg and Hill (1979); Friedheim (1979); Harper, Sylvester, and Walczak (1980); Snizek (1976); and Staats (1976).

[7] There are other possibilities, including a postmodern paradigm (Milovanovic, 1995) and more interparadigmatic dialogue (Chriss, 1996).

social phenomena that are involved in continuing interaction and change. Individuals, groups, families, bureaucracies, the polity, and numerous other highly diverse social phenomena represent the bewildering array of phenomena that make up the social world. It is extremely difficult to get a handle on such a large number of wide-ranging and mutually interpenetrating social phenomena. Some sort of conceptual schema is clearly needed, and sociologists have developed a number of such schemas in an effort to deal with the social world. The idea of levels of social analysis employed here should be seen as but one of a large number of such schemas that can be, and have been, used for dealing with the complexities of the social world.

Levels of Social Analysis: An Overview

Although the idea of levels is implicit in much of sociology, it has received relatively little explicit attention. (However, there does seem to be some explicit interest in this issue, as reflected, for example, in the work of Hage [1994], Whitmeyer [1994], and especially Jaffee [1998], Prendergast [2005c], and Smelser [1997].) In concentrating on levels here, we are making explicit what has been implicit in sociology.

Two continua of social reality are useful in developing the major levels of the social world. The first is the *microscopic-macroscopic* continuum. Thinking of the social world as being made up of a series of entities ranging from those large in scale to those small in scale is relatively easy, because it is so familiar. Most people in their day-to-day lives conceive of the social world in these terms. As we saw in Chapter 13, a number of thinkers have worked with a micro-macro continuum. For laypeople and academics alike, the continuum is based on the simple idea that social phenomena vary greatly in size. At the macro end of the continuum are such large-scale social phenomena as groups of societies (for example, the capitalist world-system), societies, and cultures. At the micro end are individual actors and their thoughts and actions. In between are a wide range of meso-level phenomena—groups, collectivities, social classes, and organizations. We have little difficulty recognizing these distinctions and thinking of the world in micro-macro terms. There are no clear dividing lines between the micro social units and the macro units. Instead, there is a continuum ranging from the micro to the macro ends.

The second continuum is the *objective-subjective* dimension of social analysis. At each end of the micro-macro continuum (and everywhere in between) we can differentiate between objective and subjective components. At the micro, or individual, level, there are the subjective mental processes of an actor and the objective patterns of action and interaction in which he or she engages. *Subjective* here refers to something that occurs solely in the realm of ideas; *objective* relates to real, material events. This same differentiation is found at the macro end of the continuum. A society is made up of objective structures, such as governments, bureaucracies, and laws, and subjective phenomena, such as norms and values.

The social world is very complicated, and to get a handle on it, we need relatively simple models. The simple model we are seeking is formed out of the intersection of the two continua of levels of social reality. The first, the microscopic-macroscopic continuum, can be depicted as in Figure A.1.

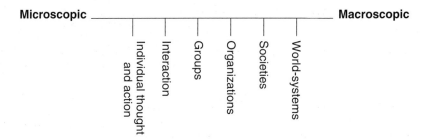

FIGURE A.1   The Microscopic-Macroscopic Continuum, with Identification of Some Key Points on the Continuum

The objective-subjective continuum presents greater problems, yet it is no less important than the micro-macro continuum. In general, an objective social phenomenon has a real, material existence. We can think of the following, among others, as objective social phenomena: actors, action, interaction, bureaucratic structures, law, and the state apparatus. It is possible to see, touch, or chart all these objective phenomena. However, there are social phenomena that exist *solely* in the realm of ideas; they have no material existence. These are sociological phenomena such as mental processes, the social construction of reality (Berger and Luckmann, 1967), norms, values, and many elements of culture. The problem with the objective-subjective continuum is that there are many phenomena in the middle that have *both* objective and subjective elements. The family, for example, has a real material existence as well as a series of subjective mutual understandings, norms, and values. Similarly, the polity is composed of objective laws and bureaucratic structures as well as subjective political norms and values. In fact, it is probably true that the vast majority of social phenomena are mixed types that represent some combination of objective and subjective elements. Thus, it is best to think of the objective-subjective continuum as two polar types with a series of variously mixed types in the middle. Figure A.2 shows the objective-subjective continuum.

Although these continua are interesting in themselves, the interrelationship of the two continua is what concerns us here. Figure 13.1 (see Chapter 13) is a schematic

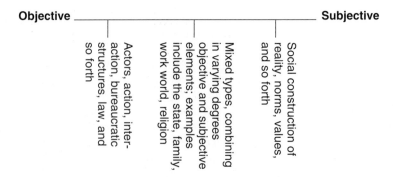

FIGURE A.2   The Objective-Subjective Continuum, with Identification of Some Mixed Types

LEVELS OF SOCIAL REALITY   SOCIOLOGICAL PARADIGMS

Macro-subjective
Macro-objective

Micro-subjective
Micro-objective

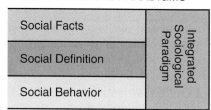

FIGURE A.3 Levels of Social Analysis and the Major Sociological Paradigms

representation of the intersection of these two continua and the four major levels of social analysis derived from it.

The contention here is that an integrated sociological paradigm must deal with the four basic levels of social analysis identified in Figure A.3 and their interrelationships (for similar models, see Alexander, 1985a; Wiley, 1988). It must deal with macro-objective entities such as bureaucracy, macro-subjective realities such as values, micro-objective phenomena such as patterns of interaction, and micro-subjective facts such as the process of reality construction. We must remember that in the real world, all these gradually blend into the others as part of the larger social continuum, but we have made some artificial and rather arbitrary differentiations in order to be able to deal with social reality. These four levels of social analysis are posited for heuristic purposes and are not meant to be accurate depictions of the social world.

Although there is much to be gained from the development of an integrated sociological paradigm, one can expect resistance from many quarters. Reba Lewis has argued that opposition to an integrated paradigm comes from those theorists, "paradigm warriors" (Aldrich, 1988), who are intent on defending their theoretical turf come what may:

> Much of the objection to an integrated paradigm is not on theoretical, but on political grounds; an integrated paradigm threatens the purity and independence— and perhaps even the existence—of theoretical approaches which derive their inspiration from *opposition* to existing theory. . . . An integrated paradigm, such as Ritzer proposes, allows and even encourages a broader perspective than some find comfortable. Adopting an integrated paradigm means relinquishing belief in the ultimate truth of one's favorite theory. . . . Acceptance of an integrated paradigm requires an understanding, and indeed an appreciation, of a broad range of theoretical perspectives—an intellectually challenging task. . . . Although Ritzer does not discuss the issue, this author maintains that overcoming massive *intellectual agoraphobia* presents the greatest challenge to acceptance of an integrated paradigm.
>
> (R. Lewis, 1991:228–229)

An obvious question is how the four levels of the integrated paradigm relate to the three paradigms discussed earlier, as well as to the integrated paradigm. Figure A.3 relates the four levels to the three paradigms.

The social-facts paradigm focuses primarily on the macro-objective and macro-subjective levels. The social-definition paradigm is concerned largely with the micro-subjective world and that part of the micro-objective world that depends on mental processes (action). The social-behavior paradigm deals with that part of the micro-objective world that does not involve the minding process (behavior). Whereas the three extant paradigms cut across the levels of social reality horizontally, an integrated paradigm cuts across vertically. This depiction makes it clear why the integrated paradigm does not supersede the others. Although each of the three existing paradigms deals with a given level or levels in great detail, the integrated paradigm deals with all levels but does not examine any given level in anything like the degree of intensity of the other paradigms. Thus the choice of a paradigm depends on the kind of question being asked. Not all sociological issues require an integrated approach, but at least some do.

What has been outlined in the preceding pages is a model for the image of the subject matter of an integrated sociological paradigm. This sketch needs to be detailed more sharply, but that is a task for another time (see Ritzer, 1981a). The goal of this discussion is not the development of a new sociological paradigm but the delineation of an overarching metatheoretical schema (M_O) that allows us to analyze sociological theory in a coherent fashion. The model developed in Figure 13.1 forms the basis for this book.

Sociological theory is analyzed by using the four levels of social analysis depicted in Figure 13.1. This figure provides us with a metatheoretical tool that can be used in the comparative analysis of sociological theories. It enables us to analyze the concerns of a theory and how they relate to the concerns of all other socio-logical theories.

To be avoided at all costs is the simple identification of a theory or a theorist with specific levels of social analysis. Although it is true, given the preceding description of the current paradigmatic status of sociology, that sociological theorists who adhere to a given paradigm tend to focus on a given level or levels of social analysis, it often does them an injustice simply to equate the breadth of their work with one or more levels. For example, Karl Marx often is thought of as focusing on macro-objective structures—in particular, on the economic structures of capitalism. But the use of the schema in which there are multiple levels of social analysis allows us to see that Marx had rich insights regarding *all* levels of social reality and their inter-relationships. Similarly, symbolic interactionism generally is considered a perspective that deals with micro subjectivity and micro objectivity, but it is not devoid of insights into the macroscopic levels of social analysis (Maines, 1977).

It is also important to remember that the use of levels of social analysis to analyze a theory tends to break up the wholeness, the integrity, and the internal con-sistency of that theory. Although the levels are useful for understanding a theory and comparing it to others, one must take pains to deal with the interrelationship among levels and with the totality of a theory.

In sum, the metatheoretical schema outlined in Figure 13.1, the development of which was traced in this Appendix, provides the basis for the analysis of the socio-logical theories discussed in this book.

References

Abel, Theodore
1948   "The Operation Called Verstehen." *American Journal of Sociology* 54:211–218.

Aboulafia, Mitchell
1986   *The Mediating Self: Mead, Sartre, and Self-Determination.* New Haven: Yale University Press.

Abraham, Gary A.
1992   *Max Weber and the Jewish Question: A Study of the Social Outlook of His Sociology.* Urbana:
                University of Illinois Press.

Abrahamsen, Rita
1997   "The Victory of Popular Forces or Passive Revolution? A Neo-Gramscian Perspective on
                Democratisation." *Journal of Modern African Studies* 35:129–152.

Abrahamson, Mark
1978   *Functionalism.* Englewood Cliffs, N.J.: Prentice-Hall.
2001   "Functional, Conflict and Neofunctional Theories." In George Ritzer and Barry Smart (eds.),
                Handbook of Social Theory. London: Sage: 141–151.

Abrahamsson, Bengt
1970   "Homans on Exchange." *American Journal of Sociology* 76:273–285.

Abrams, Philip
1968   *The Origins of British Sociology: 1834–1914.* Chicago: University of Chicago Press.
1982   *Historical Sociology.* Ithaca, N.Y.: Cornell University Press.

Abrams, Philip, Deem, Rosemary, Finch, Janet, and Rock, Paul
1981   *Practice and Progress: British Sociology 1950–1980.* London: Allen and Unwin.

Acevedo, Gabriel A.
2005   "Turning Anomie on Its Head: Fatalism as Durkheim's Concealed and Multidimensional Alienation
                Theory." *Sociological Theory* 23(1):75–85.

Acker, Joan
1989   *Doing Comparable Worth.* Philadelphia: Temple University Press.
1990   Hierarchies, jobs, and bodies: A theory of gendered organizations. *Gender & Society* 4:139–58.
2008   "Feminist Theory's Unfinished Business: Comment on Andersen." *Gender & Society* 22:104–108.

Adair-Toteff, Christopher
2005   "Max Weber's Charisma." *Journal of Classical Sociology* 5(2):189–204.

Adams, Bert N.
2005   "Pareto, Vilfredo." In George Ritzer (ed.), *Encyclopedia of Social Theory.* Thousand Oaks, Calif.:
                Sage: 544–547.

Adkins, Lisa
1995   *Gendered Work: Sexuality, Family, and the Labour Market.* Bristol, Pa.: Open University Press.
2004a   "Introduction: Feminism, Bourdieu and After." In Lisa Adkins and Beverley Skeggs (eds.),
                Feminism after Bourdieu. Oxford: Blackwell: 3–18
2004b   "Reflexivity: Freedom or Habit of Gender." In Lisa Adkins and Beverley Skeggs (eds.), *Feminism
                after Bourdieu.* Oxford: Blackwell: 191–210.

Adler, Freda, and Laufer, William S. (eds.)
1995   *The Legacy of Anomie Theory.* New Brunswick, N.J.: Transaction Publishers.

R-1

Adorno, Theodor
1966/1973   *Negative Dialectics.* Trans. E. B. Ashton. New York: Continuum.

Agamben, Giorgio
1995/1998   *Homo Sacer: Sovereign Power and Bare Life.* Stanford, Calif.: Stanford University Press.
2002/2005   *State of Exception.* Chicago: University of Chicago Press.
2002   *Remnants of Auschwitz: The Witness and the Archive.* New York: Zone Books.

Agger, Ben
1998   *Critical Social Theories: An Introduction.* Boulder, Colo.: Westview.

Agger, Ben (ed.)
1978   *Western Marxism: An Introduction.* Santa Monica, Calif.: Goodyear.

Ahmed, Sara
2008   "Open Forum Imaginary Prohibitions: Some Preliminary Remarks on the Founding Gestures of the 'New Materialism.'" *The European Journal of Women's Studies* 15(1):23–39.

Alatas, Syed Farid
2011   "Ibn Khaldun." In George Ritzer and Jeffrey Stepnisky, (eds.), *The Wiley-Blackwell Companion to Major Social Theorists: Volume 1—Classical Social Theorists.* Malden, Mass., and Oxford, Eng.: Wiley-Blackwell: 12–29.

Albrow, Martin
1996   *The Global Age.* Cambridge, Eng.: Polity Press.

Albrow, Martin, and King, Elizabeth
1990   *Globalization, Knowledge and Society.* London: Sage.

Alcala-Campos, Raul
1997   "Thomas S. Kuhn: Between Modernity and Postmodernity." *Acta Sociologica* 19:59–77.

Alcoff, Linda Martin
1988   "Cultural Feminism v. Post-Structuralist: The Identity Crisis in Feminist Theory." *Signs,* Spring:405–436.
1998   "What Should White People Do?" *Hypatia* 13:6–26.

Aldrich, Howard
1988   "Paradigm Warriors: Donaldson versus the Critics of Organization Theory." *Organization Studies* 9:19–25.

Aldridge, Alan
1998   "Habitus and Cultural Capital in the Field of Personal Finance." *Sociological Review* 46:1–23.

Alexander, Jeffrey C.
1981   "Revolution, Reaction, and Reform: The Change Theory of Parsons's Middle Period." *Sociological Inquiry* 51:267–280.
1982   *Theoretical Logic in Sociology.* Vol. 1, *Positivism, Presuppositions, and Current Controversies.* Berkeley: University of California Press.
1982–1983   *Theoretical Logic in Sociology.* 4 vols. Berkeley: University of California Press.
1983   *Theoretical Logic in Sociology.* Vol. 4, *The Modern Reconstruction of Classical Thought: Talcott Parsons.* Berkeley: University of California Press.
1985   "The 'Individualist Dilemma' in Phenomenology and Interactionism." In S. N. Eisenstadt and H. J. Helle (eds.), *Macro-Sociological Theory,* Vol. 1. London: Sage: 25–51.
1987a   "Action and Its Environments." In J. C. Alexander et al. (eds.), *The Micro-Macro Link.* Berkeley: University of California Press: 289–318.
1987b   *Twenty Lectures: Sociological Theory since World War II.* New York: Columbia University Press.
1988   "Introduction: Durkheimian Sociology and Cultural Studies Today." In J. C. Alexander (ed.), *Durkheimian Sociology: Cultural Studies.* Cambridge, Eng.: Cambridge University Press: 1–21.
1992   "Shaky Foundations: The Presuppositions and Internal Contradictions of James Coleman's Foundations of Social Theory." *Theory and Society* 21:203–217.
1995   *Fin de Siècle Social Theory: Relativism, Reduction, and the Problem of Reason.* London: Verso.
1998   *Neofunctionalism and After.* London: Blackwell.
2003   *The Meanings of Social Life: A Cultural Sociology.* Oxford, UK: Oxford University Press.

Alexander, Jeffrey C. (ed.)
1985a   *Neofunctionalism.* Beverly Hills, Calif.: Sage.

Alexander, Jeffrey C., and Colomy, Paul
1985   "Toward Neo-Functionalism." *Sociological Theory* 3:11–23.
1990a   "Neofunctionalism: Reconstructing a Theoretical Tradition." In George Ritzer (ed.), *Frontiers of Social Theory: The New Syntheses.* New York: Columbia University Press: 33–67.

Alexander, Jeffrey C., and Colomy, Paul (eds.)
1990b   *Differentiation Theory and Social Change: Comparative and Historical Perspectives.* New York: New York University Press.

Alexander, Jeffrey C., Giesen, Bernhard, Münch, Richard, and Smelser, Neil J. (eds.)
1987   *The Micro-Macro Link.* Berkeley: University of California Press.

Alexander, Jeffrey C., and Smith, Philip
2001   "The Strong Program in Cultural Theory: Elements of a Structural Hermeneutics." In Jonathan H. Turner (ed.), *Handbook of Sociological Theory.* New York: Kluwer Academic/Plenum Publishers: 135–150.

Alexander, Jeffrey C., Smith, Philip, and Norton, Matthew
2011   *Interpreting Clifford Geertz: Cultural Investigation in the Social Sciences.* New York: Palgrave Macmillan.

Alford, C. Fred
2000   "What Would It Matter If Everything Foucault Said about Prison Were Wrong? *Discipline and Punishment* after Twenty Years." *Theory and Society* 29:125–137.

Alford, Robert R., and Friedland, Roger
1985   *Powers of Theory: Capitalism, the State, and Democracy.* Cambridge, Eng.: Cambridge University Press.

Alger, Janet M., and Alger, Steven F.
1997   "Beyond Mead: Symbolic Interaction between Humans and Felines." *Society and Animals* 5:65–81.

Alieva, Dilbar
2008   " 'Catcher in the Rye' of Everyday Life." *Czech Sociological Review* 44:889–922.

Allan, Stuart
2007   "Network Society." In George Ritzer (ed.), *The Blackwell Encyclopedia of Sociology.* Oxford: Blackwell: 3180–3182.

Allen, Judith, A.
2011   "Charlotte Perkins Gilman." In George Ritzer and Jeffrey Stepnisky, (eds.), *The Wiley-Blackwell Companion to Major Social Theorists: Volume 1—Classical Social Theorists.* Malden, Mass., and Oxford, Eng.: Wiley-Blackwell: 283–304.

Allen, Robert Loring
1991a   *Opening Doors: The Life and Work of Joseph Schumpeter: Europe. Vol. 1.* New Brunswick, N.J.: Transaction Publishers.

Alolo, Namawu
2006   "Ethic of Care versus Ethic of Justice? The Gender Corruption Nexus: Testing the New Conventional Wisdom." *Ethics and Economics* 4:2.

Alpert, Harry
1939   *Emile Durkheim and His Sociology.* New York: Columbia University Press.

Alsop, Rachel, Fitzsimons, Annette, and Lennon, Kathleen
2002   *Theorizing Gender,* Cambridge, UK: Polity Press.

Alt, John
1985–1986   "Reclaiming C. Wright Mills." *Telos* 66:6–43.

Althusser, Louis
1969   *For Marx.* Harmondsworth, Eng.: Penguin.

Alway, Joan
1995a   *Critical Theory and Political Possibilities.* Westport, Conn.: Greenwood Press.
1995b   "The Trouble with Gender: Tales of the Still Missing Feminist Revolution in Sociological Theory." *Sociological Theory* 13:209–226.

Amin, Ash (ed.)
1994   *Post-Fordism: A Reader.* Oxford: Blackwell.

Amin, Samirz
1977   *Unequal Development: An Essay on the Social Formations of Peripheral Capitalism.* New York:
              Monthly Review Press.

Andersen, Margaret, and Collins, Patricia Hill
1992   *Race, Class and Gender.* Belmont, Calif.: Wadsworth.

Andersen, Margaret L.
2005   "Thinking about Women: A Quarter Century's View." *Gender & Society* 19(4):437–455.

Anderson, Ben
2010   "Modulating the Excess of Affect: Morale in a State of Total War." In Melissa Gregg and Gregory
              J. Seigworth (eds.), *The Affect Theory Reader.* Durham, N.C.: Duke University Press: 161–185.

Anderson, Benedict
1983   *Imagined Communities: Reflections on the Origin and Spread of Nationalism.* New York: Verso.

Anderson, Kristin
2009   "Gendering Coercive Control." *Violence Against Women* 15(12):1444–1457.

Anderson, Leon, Snow, David A., and Cress, Daniel
1994   "Negotiating the Public Realm: Stigma Management and Collective Action among the Homeless."
              Research in Community Sociology 4, supplement: 121–143.

Anderson, Perry
1984   *In the Tracks of Historical Materialism.* Chicago: University of Chicago Press.
1990a   "A Culture in Contraflow—I." *New Left Review* 180:41–78.
1990b   "A Culture in Contraflow—II." *New Left Review* 182:85–137.

Anderson, R. J., Hughes, J. A., and Sharrock, W. W.
1987   "Executive Problem Finding: Some Material and Initial Observations." *Social Psychology
              Quarterly* 50:143–159.

Andrews, Howard F.
1993   "Durkheim and Social Morphology." In S. P. Turner (ed.), *Emile Durkheim: Sociologist and
              Moralist.* London: Routledge: 111–135.

Anheier, Helmut K., Gerhards, Jurgen, and Romo, Frank P.
1995   "Forms of Capital and Social Structure in Cultural Fields: Examining Bourdieu's Social
              Topography." *American Journal of Sociology* 100:859–903.

Antonio, Robert J.
1981   "Immanent Critique as the Core of Critical Theory: Its Origins and Development in Hegel, Marx and
              Contemporary Thought." *British Journal of Sociology* 32:330–345.
1985   "Values, History and Science: The Metatheoretic Foundations of the Weber-Marx Dialogues." In
              R. J. Antonio and R. M. Glassman (eds.), *A Weber-Marx Dialogue.* Lawrence: University Press of
              Kansas: 20–43.
1991   "Postmodern Storytelling versus Pragmatic Truth-Seeking: The Discursive Bases of Social Theory."
              Sociological Theory 9:154–163.
1998   "Mapping Postmodern Social Theory." In Alan Sica (ed.), *What Is Social Theory? The
              Philosophical Debates.* Oxford: Blackwell: 22–75.
2001   "Nietzsche: Social Theory in the Twilight of the Millennium." In George Ritzer and Barry Smart
              (eds.), *Handbook of Social Theory.* London: Sage: 163–178.
2007a   "The Cultural Construction of Neoliberal Globalization: 'Honey . . . I Think I Shrunk the Kids.' "
              In George Ritzer (ed.), *The Blackwell Companion to Globalization.* Oxford: Blackwell: 67–83.
2007b   "Marx, Karl." In George Ritzer (ed.), *The Blackwell Encyclopedia of Sociology.* Oxford:
              Blackwell: 2805–2828.
2011   "Karl Marx." In George Ritzer and Jeffrey Stepnisky, (eds.), *The Wiley-Blackwell Companion to
              Major Social Theorists: Volume 1—Classical Social Theorists.* Malden, Mass., and Oxford, Eng.:
              Wiley-Blackwell: 115–164.

Antonio, Robert J., and Glassman, Ronald M. (eds.)
1985   *A Weber-Marx Dialogue.* Lawrence: University Press of Kansas.

Antonio, Robert J., and Kellner, Douglas
1994   "The Future of Social Theory and the Limits of Postmodern Critique." In D. R. Dickens and
              A. Fontana (eds.), *Postmodernism and Social Inquiry.* New York: Guilford Press: 127–152.

Anzaldúa, Gloria (ed.)
1990   *Making Face, Making Soul/Hacienda Caras: Creative and Critical Perspectives by Women of Color.* San Francisco: Aunt Lute Foundation Books.

Anzaldúa, Gloria, and Keating, Analouise
2002   *This Bridge We Call Home: Radical Visions for Transformation.* London: Routledge.

Appadurai, Arjun
1996   *Modernity at Large: Cultural Dimensions of Globalization.* Minneapolis: University of Minnesota Press.

Aptheker, Bettina
1989   *Tapestries of Life: Women's Work, Women's Consciousness and the Meaning of Daily Experience.* Amherst: University of Massachusetts Press.

Archer, Margaret S.
1982   "Morphogenesis versus Structuration: On Combining Structure and Action." *British Journal of Sociology* 33:455–483.
1988   *Culture and Agency: The Place of Culture in Social Theory.* Cambridge, Eng.: Cambridge University Press.
1995   *Realist Social Theory: The Morphogenetic Approach.* Cambridge, Eng.: Cambridge University Press.

Arditi, Jorge
1996   "Simmel's Theory of Alienation and the Decline of the Nonrational." *Sociological Theory* 14:93–108.

Arendt, Hannah
2002   "Karl Marx and the Tradition of Western Political Thought." *Social Research* 69:273–361,

Armitage, John
2005   "Deleuze, Gilles." In George Ritzer (ed.), *Encyclopedia of Social Theory.* Thousand Oaks, Calif.: Sage: 190–191.

Aron, Raymond
1965   *Main Currents in Sociological Thought,* Vol. 1. New York: Basic Books.

Aronowitz, Stanley
1994   "The Simmel Revival: A Challenge to American Social Science." *Sociological Quarterly* 35:397–414.
2007   "Lukács, George." In George Ritzer (ed.), *The Blackwell Encyclopedia of Sociology.* Oxford: Blackwell: 2678–2681.

Aronson, Ronald
1995   *After Marxism.* New York: Guilford Press.

Arthur, C. J.
1970   "Editor's Introduction." In K. Marx and F. Engels, *The German Ideology,* Part 1. New York: International Publishers: 4–34.

Asante, Molefi Kete
1996   "The Afrocentric Metatheory and Disciplinary Implications." In Mary F. Rogers (ed.), *Multicultural Experiences, Multicultural Theories.* New York: McGraw-Hill: 61–73.

Athens, Lonnie
1995   "Mead's Vision of the Self: A Pair of 'Flawed Diamonds.' " *Studies in Symbolic Interaction* 18:245–261.
2002   " 'Domination': The Blind Spot in Mead's Analysis of the Social Act." *Journal of Classical Sociology* 2:25–42.

Atkinson, J. Maxwell
1984a   *Our Masters' Voices: The Language and Body Language of Politics.* New York: Methuen.
1984b   "Public Speaking and Audience Responses: Some Techniques for Inviting Applause." In J. M. Atkinson and J. Heritage (eds.), *Structures of Social Action.* Cambridge, Eng.: Cambridge University Press: 370–409.

Atkinson, Paul
1988   "Ethnomethodology: A Critical Review." *Annual Review of Sociology* 14:441–465.

Atkinson, Will
2008   "Not All That Was Solid Has Melted into Air (or Liquid): A Critique of Bauman on Individualization and Class in Liquid Modernity." *Sociological Review* 56:1–17.

Avino, Elvira del Pozo (ed.)
2006   *Integralism, Altruism and Reconstruction: Essays in Honor of Pitirim A. Sorokin.* Valencia, Spain: PUV.

Baber, Zaheer
1991   "Beyond the Structure/Agency Dualism: An Evaluation of Giddens' Theory of Structuration."
            Sociological Inquiry 61:219–230.

Bailey, Cathryn
1997   "Making Waves and Drawing Lines: The Politics of Defining the Vicissitudes of Feminism."
            Hypatia 12:16–28.

Bailey, Kenneth D.
1990   *Social Entropy Theory.* Albany: State University of New York Press.
1994   *Sociology and the New Systems Theory: Toward a Theoretical Synthesis.* Albany: State University
            of New York Press.
1997   "System and Conflict: Toward a Symbiotic Reconciliation." *Quality and Quantity* 31:425–442.
1998   "Structure, Structuration, and Autopoesis: The Emerging Significance of Recursive Theory." In
            Jennifer M. Lehmann (ed.), *Current Perspectives in Social Theory,* Vol. 18. Greenwich, Conn.: JAI
            Press: 131–154.
2001   "Systems Theory." In Jonathan H. Turner (ed.), *Handbook of Sociological Theory.* New York:
            Kluwer Academic/Plenum Publishers: 379–401.
2005   "General Systems Theory." In George Ritzer (ed.), *Encyclopedia of Social Theory.* Thousand Oaks,
            Calif.: Sage: 309–315.

Baker, Peter
2002   "Moscow's Mall-ization." *Washington Post,* October 18:E1, E6.

Baker, Wayne E.
1990   "Market Networks and Corporate Behavior." *American Journal of Sociology* 96:589–625.

Bakker, Hans
2007a   "Economic Determinism." In George Ritzer (ed.), *The Blackwell Encyclopedia of Sociology.*
            Oxford: Blackwell: 1293–1294.
2007b   "Langue and Parole." In George Ritzer (ed.), *The Blackwell Encyclopedia of Sociology.* Oxford:
            Blackwell: 2538–2539.
2007c   "Meta-analysis." In George Ritzer (ed.), *The Blackwell Encyclopedia of Sociology.* Oxford:
            Blackwell: 2963–2964.

Baldwin, Alfred
1961   "The Parsonian Theory of Personality." In M. Black (ed.), *The Social Theories of Talcott Parsons.*
            Englewood Cliffs, N.J.: Prentice-Hall: 153–190.

Baldwin, John C.
1986   *George Herbert Mead: A Unifying Theory for Sociology.* Newbury Park, Calif.: Sage.
1988a   "Mead and Skinner: Agency and Determinism." *Behaviorism* 16:109–127.
1988b   "Mead's Solution to the Problem of Agency." *Sociological Inquiry* 58:139–162.

Baldwin, John D., and Baldwin, Janice I.
1986   *Behavior Principles in Everyday Life.* 2nd ed. Englewood Cliffs, N.J.: Prentice-Hall.

Ball, Richard A.
1978   "Sociology and General Systems Theory." *American Sociologist* 13:65–72.

Ball, Terence
1991   "History: Critique and Irony." In T. Carver (ed.), *The Cambridge Companion to Marx.* Cambridge,
            Eng.: Cambridge University Press: 124–142.

Banks, Alan, Billings, Dwight, and Tice, Karen
1996   "Appalachian Studies and Postmodernism." In Mary F. Rogers (ed.), *Multicultural Experiences,*
            Multicultural Theories. New York: McGraw-Hill: 81–90.

Barad, Karen
2003   "Posthumanist Performativity: Toward an Understanding of How Matter Comes to Matter." *Signs*
            28(3):801–831.

Baran, Paul, and Sweezy, Paul M.
1966   *Monopoly Capital: An Essay on the American Economic and Social Order.* New York: Monthly
            Review Press.

Barbalet, J. M.
1983   *Marx's Construction of Social Theory*. London: Routledge and Kegan Paul.

Barber, Benjamin
1995   *Jihad vs. McWorld*. New York: Times Books.

Barber, Bernard
1993   *Constructing the Social System*. New Brunswick, N.J.: Transaction Publishers.
1994   "Talcott Parsons on the Social System: An Essay in Clarification and Elaboration." *Sociological Theory* 12:101–105.

Bar-Haim, Gabriel
1997   "The Dispersed Sacred: Anomie and the Crisis of Ritual." In Stewart M. Hoover and Knut Lundby (eds.), *Rethinking Media, Religion, and Culture*. Thousand Oaks, Calif.: Sage: 133–145.

Barker, Chris
2007   "Birmingham School." In George Ritzer (ed.), *The Blackwell Encyclopedia of Sociology*. Oxford: Blackwell: 297–301.

Barnes, Barry
2001   "The Macro/Micro Problem and the Problem of Structure and Agency." In George Ritzer and Barry Smart (eds.), *Handbook of Social Theory*. London: Sage: 339–352.

Barry, Kathleen
1979   *Female Sexual Slavery*. Englewood Cliffs, N.J.: Prentice-Hall.
1993   *The Prostitution of Sexuality: The Global Exploitation of Women*. New York: New York University Press.

Bart, Pauline, and Moran, Eileen Geil (eds.)
1993   *Violence against Women: The Bloody Footprints*. Newbury Park, Calif.: Sage.

Bartky, Sandra
1990   *Femininity and Domination: Studies in the Phenomenology of Oppression*. New York, New York: Routledge.

Bartos, Ottomar J.
1996   "Postmodernism, Postindustrialism, and the Future." *Sociological Quarterly* 37:307–325.

Baudrillard, Jean
1970/1998   *The Consumer Society*. London: Sage.
1972/1981   *For a Critique of the Political Economy of the Sign*. St. Louis: Telos Press.
1973/1975   *The Mirror of Production*. St. Louis: Telos Press.
1976/1993   *Symbolic Exchange and Death*. London: Sage.
1979/1990   *Seduction*. New York: St. Martin's.
1983   *Simulations*. New York: Semiotext(e).
1983/1990   *Fatal Strategies*. New York: Semiotext(e).
1986/1989   *America*. London: Verso.
1990/1993   *The Transparency of Evil: Essays on Extreme Phenomena*. London: Verso.
1995   *The Gulf War Never Happened*. Cambridge, Eng.: Polity Press.

Baum, Rainer C., and Lechner, Frank J.
1981   "National Socialism: Toward an Action-Theoretical Perspective." *Sociological Inquiry* 51:281–308.

Bauman, Zygmunt
1976   *Towards a Critical Sociology: An Essay on Commonsense and Emancipation*. London: Routledge and Kegan Paul.
1989   *Modernity and the Holocaust*. Ithaca, N.Y.: Cornell University Press.
1990   "From Pillars to Post." *Marxism Today*, February:20–25.
1991   *Modernity and Ambivalence*. Ithaca, N.Y.: Cornell University Press.
1992   *Intimations of Postmodernity*. London: Routledge.
1998   *Globalization: The Human Consequences*. New York: Columbia University Press.
2000   *Liquid Modernity*. Cambridge, Eng.: Polity Press.
2003   *Liquid Love: On the Frailty of Human Bonds*. Cambridge, Eng.: Polity Press.
2005   *Liquid Life*. Cambridge, Eng.: Polity Press.
2006   *Liquid Fear*. Cambridge, Eng.: Polity Press.
2007a   *Consuming Life*. Cambridge, Eng.: Polity Press.

2007b	*Liquid Times: Living in an Age of Uncertainty.* Cambridge, Eng.: Polity Press.
2010	*44 Letters from the Modern Liquid World.* Cambridge, Eng.: Polity Press.
2011	*Culture in a Liquid Modern World.* Cambridge, Eng.: Polity Press.

Bauman, Zygmunt, and Lyon, David
2012	*Liquid Surveillance: A Conversation.* Cambridge, Eng.: Polity Press.

Beamish, Rob
2007a	"Dialectical Materialism." In George Ritzer (ed.), *The Blackwell Encyclopedia of Sociology.* Oxford: Blackwell: 1150–1151.
2007b	"Species-Being." In George Ritzer (ed.), *The Blackwell Encyclopedia of Sociology.* Oxford: Blackwell: 4637–4638.
2007c	"Use-Value." In George Ritzer (ed.), *The Blackwell Encyclopedia of Sociology.* Oxford: Blackwell: 5155.
2007d	"Exchange-Value." In George Ritzer (ed.), *The Blackwell Encyclopedia of Sociology.* Oxford: Blackwell: 1515–1516.
2007e	"Base and Superstructure." In George Ritzer (ed.), *The Blackwell Encyclopedia of Sociology.* Oxford: Blackwell: 244–246.

Beck, Ulrich
1992	*Risk Society: Towards a New Modernity.* London: Sage.
1996	"World Risk Society as Cosmopolitan Society?" *Theory, Culture and Society* 13:1–32.
2000	*What Is Globalization?* Cambridge, Eng.: Polity Press.
2005a	"Risk Society." In George Ritzer (ed.), *Encyclopedia of Social Theory.* Thousand Oaks, Calif.: Sage: 648–650.
2005b	*Power in the Global Age: A New Global Political Economy.* Cambridge, Eng.: Polity Press.
2007	*World at Risk.* Cambridge, Eng.: Polity Press.

Beck, Ulrich, and Grande, Edgar
2010	"Varieties of Second Modernity: The Cosmopolitan Turn in Social and Political Theory and Research." *British Journal of Sociology,* 61(3):409–443.

Beck, Ulrich, and Sznaider, Natan
2005	"Cosmopolitan Sociology." In George Ritzer (ed.), *Encyclopedia of Social Theory.* Thousand Oaks, Calif.: Sage: 157–161.
2006	"Unpacking Cosmopolitanism for the Social Sciences: A Research Agenda." *British Journal of Sociology,* 57(1):1–23.

Beilharz, Peter
1996	"Negation and Ambivalence: Marx, Simmel and Bolshevism on Money." *Thesis Eleven* 47:21–32.
2005a	"Alienation." In George Ritzer (ed.), *Encyclopedia of Social Theory.* Thousand Oaks, Calif.: Sage: 9–10.
2005b	"Gramsci, Antonio." In George Ritzer (ed.), *Encyclopedia of Social Theory.* Thousand Oaks, Calif.: Sage: 343–344.
2005c	"Bauman, Zygmunt" In George Ritzer (ed.), *Encyclopedia of Social Theory.* Thousand Oaks, Calif.: Sage: 35–40.
2005d	"Post-Marxism." In George Ritzer (ed.), *Encyclopedia of Social Theory.* Thousand Oaks, Calif.: Sage: 578–581.
2005e	"Marx, Karl." In George Ritzer (ed.), *Encyclopedia of Social Theory.* Thousand Oaks, Calif.: Sage: 475–478.
2005f	"Marxism." In George Ritzer (ed.), *Encyclopedia of Social Theory.* Thousand Oaks, Calif.: Sage: 479–483.
2005g	"Socialism" In George Ritzer (ed.), *Encyclopedia of Social Theory.* Thousand Oaks, Calif.: Sage: 769–772.
2011	"Zygmunt Bauman." In George Ritzer and Jeffrey Stepnisky, (eds.), *The Wiley-Blackwell Companion to Major Social Theorists: Volume II—Contemporary Social Theorists.* Malden, Mass., and Oxford, Eng.: Wiley-Blackwell: 155–174.

Beland, Daniel
2008	*States of Global Insecurity: Policy, Politics and Society.* New York: Worth.

Bell, Daniel
1992	"George C. Homans (11 August 1910–29 May 1989)." *Proceedings of the American Philosophical Society* 136:587–593.

Bellah, Robert
1973   "Introduction." In R. Bellah (ed.), *Emile Durkheim: On Morality and Society.* Chicago: University of Chicago Press: ix–lv.

Bellah, Robert N., et al.
1985   *Habits of the Heart: Individualism and Commitment in American Life.* New York: Harper and Row.

Bem, Sandra Lipsitz
1993   *The Lenses of Gender: Transforming Debates on Sexual Inequality.* New Haven: Yale University Press.

Bender, Frederick (ed.)
1970   *Karl Marx: The Essential Writings.* New York: Harper.

Benhabib, Seyla
1995   "The Debate over Women and Moral Authority Revisited." In Johanna Meehan (eds.), *Feminists Read Habermas.* New York: Routledge: 181–204.
1998   "Feminism and Postmodernism: An Uneasy Alliance." *Filosoficky Casopis* 46:803–181.

Benjamin, Jessica
1985   "The Bonds of Love: Rational Violence and Erotic Domination." In H. Eisenstein and A. Jardine (eds.), *The Future of Difference.* New Brunswick, N.J.: Rutgers University Press: 41–70.
1988   *The Bonds of Love: Psychoanalysis, Feminism, and the Problem of Domination.* New York: Pantheon.
1996   "In Defense of Gender Ambiguity." *Gender & Psychoanalysis* 1:27–43.
1998   *Like Subjects, Love Objects: Essays on Recognition and Sexual Difference.* New Haven: Yale University Press.

Benokraitis, Nijole
1997   *Subtle Sexism: Current Practice and Prospects for Change.* Thousand Oaks, Calif.: Sage.

Bergen, Raquel Kennedy
1996   *Wife Rape: Understanding the Response of Survivors and Service Providers.* Thousand Oaks, Calif.: Sage.

Berger, Peter
1963   *Invitation to Sociology.* New York: Doubleday.

Berger, Peter, and Luckmann, Thomas
1967   *The Social Construction of Reality.* Garden City, N.Y.: Anchor.

Bergeson, Albert
1984   "The Critique of World-System Theory: Class Relations or Division of Labor?" In R. Collins (ed.), *Sociological Theory—1984.* San Francisco: Jossey-Bass: 365–372.

Berk, Bernard
2006   "Macro-Micro Relationships in Durkheim's Analysis of Egoistic Suicide." *Sociological Theory* 24(1):58–80.

Berlant, Lauren
2010   "Cruel Optimism." In Melissa Gregg and Gregory J. Seigworth (eds.), *The Affect Theory Reader.* Durham, N.C.: Duke University Press: 93–117.

Bernard, Jessie
1981   *The Female World.* New York: Free Press.
1972/1982   *The Future of Marriage.* 2nd ed. New Haven: Yale University Press.

Bernard, Thomas
1983   *The Consensus-Conflict Debate: Form and Content in Sociological Theories.* New York: Columbia University Press.

Bernstein, J. M.
1995   *Recovering Ethical Life: Jurgen Habermas and the Future of Critical Theory.* London: Routledge.

Bernstein, Richard J.
1989   "Social Theory as Critique." In D. Held and J. B. Thompson (eds.), *Social Theory of Modern Societies: Anthony Giddens and His Critics.* Cambridge, Eng,: Cambridge University Press: 19–33.

Besnard, Philippe
1983   "The 'Année Sociologique' Team." In P. Besnard (ed.), *The Sociological Domain.* Cambridge, Eng.: Cambridge University Press: 11–39.

1993   "Anomie and Fatalism in Durkheim's Theory of Regulation." In S. P. Turner (ed.), *Emile Durkheim: Sociologist and Moralist.* London: Routledge: 169–190.

Best, Steven, and Kellner, Douglas
1991   *Postmodern Theory: Critical Interrogations.* New York: Guilford Press.

Beutel, Ann M., and Marini, Margaret Mooney
1995   "Gender and Values." *American Sociological Review* 60:436–448.

Bhaskar, Roy
2008   *A Realist Theory of Science.* New York: Routledge.

Bian, Yanjie
1997   "Bringing Strong Ties Back In: Indirect Ties, Network Bridges, and Job Searches in China." *American Sociological Review* 62:366–385.

Bienenstock, Elisa Jayne
2005   "Blau, Peter." In George Ritzer (ed.), *Encyclopedia of Social Theory.* Thousand Oaks, Calif.: Sage: 54–57.

Biernacki, Richard
2007   "Practice." In George Ritzer (ed.), *The Blackwell Encyclopedia of Sociology.* Oxford: Blackwell: 3607–3609.

Binkley, Sam
2007a   "Tocqueville, Alexis de." In George Ritzer (ed.), *The Blackwell Encyclopedia of Sociology.* Oxford: Blackwell: 5010–5011.
2007b   "Consumption, Spectacles of." In George Ritzer (ed.), *The Blackwell Encyclopedia of Sociology.* Oxford: Blackwell: 755–760.
2007c   "Deleuze, Gilles." In George Ritzer (ed.), *The Blackwell Encyclopedia of Sociology.* Oxford: Blackwell: 999–1000.
2008   "Liquid Consumption—Anti-Consumerism and the Fetishized De-Fetishization of Commodities." *Cultural Studies* 22:599–623.

Birnbaum, Pierre
2008   *Geography of Hope: Exile, the Enlightenment, Disassimilation.* Stanford, Calif.: Stanford University Press.

Birnbaum, Pierre, and Todd, Jane Marie
1995   "French Jewish Sociologists between Reason and Faith: The Impact of the Dreyfus Affair." *Jewish Social Studies* 2:1–35.

Bittner, Egon
1973   "Objectivity and Realism in Sociology." In G. Psathas (ed.), *Phenomenological Sociology: Issues and Applications.* New York: Wiley: 109–125.

Blackman, Lisa
2001   *Hearing Voices: Contesting the Voice of Reason.* London: Free Association Books.
2010   "Embodying Affect: Voice-Hearing, Telepathy, Suggestion and Modelling the Nonconscious." *Body & Society,* 16(1):163–192.

Blackman, Lisa and Venn, Couze
2010   "Affect." *Body & Society,* 16(1):7–28.

Blackstone, Amy, Uggen, Christopher, and McLaughlin, Heather
2009   "Legal Consciousness and Responses to Sexual Harassment." *Law & Society Review,* 43(3):631–668.

Blakely, Kristin
2008   "Busy Brides and the Business of Family Life: The Wedding-Planning Industry and the Commodity Frontier." *Journal of Family Issues* 29(5):639–682.

Blankenship, Ralph L. (ed.)
1977   *Colleagues in Organization: The Social Construction of Professional Work.* New York: Wiley.

Blau, Peter
1964   *Exchange and Power in Social Life.* New York: Wiley.
1977   *Inequality and Heterogeneity: A Primitive Theory of Social Structure.* New York: Free Press.
1987   "Microprocess and Macrostructure." In K. Cook (ed.), *Social Exchange Theory.* Beverly Hills, Calif.: Sage: 83–100.
1994   *Structural Contexts of Opportunities.* Chicago: University of Chicago Press.

1997   "On Limitations of Rational Choice Theory for Sociology." *American Sociologist* 28:16–21.

Blau, Peter, and Duncan, Otis Dudley
1967   *The American Occupational Structure.* New York: Wiley.

Blau, Peter, and Schwartz, Joseph E.
1997   *Crosscutting Social Circles: Testing a Macrostructural Theory of Intergroup Relations.* New
                Brunswick, N.J.: Transaction Publishers.

Bleich, Harold
1977   *The Philosophy of Herbert Marcuse.* Washington, D.C.: University Press of America.

Bleicher, Josef
1980   *Contemporary Hermeneutics: Hermeneutics as Method, Philosophy and Critique.* London:
                Routledge and Kegan Paul.

Blumer, Herbert
1955/1969   "Attitudes and the Social Act." In H. Blumer, *Symbolic Interaction.* Englewood Cliffs, N.J.:
                Prentice-Hall: 90–100.
1962/1969   "Society as Symbolic Interaction." In H. Blumer, *Symbolic Interaction.* Englewood Cliffs, N.J.:
                Prentice-Hall: 78–89.
1969a   *Symbolic Interaction: Perspective and Method.* Englewood Cliffs, N.J.: Prentice-Hall.
1969b   "The Methodological Position of Symbolic Interactionism." In H. Blumer, *Symbolic Interaction.*
                Englewood Cliffs, N.J.: Prentice-Hall: 1–60.
1990   *Industrialization as an Agent of Social Change: A Critical Analysis.* New York: Aldine de Gruyter.

Boas, Morten, and Jennings, Kathleen M.
2007   "'Failed States' and 'State Failure': Threats or Opportunities?" *Globalizations* 4(4):475–485.

Boden, Deirdre
1990   "The World as It Happens: Ethnomethodology and Conversation Analysis." In George Ritzer (ed.),
                Frontiers of Social Theory: The New Syntheses. New York: Columbia University Press: 185–213.

Bogard, William
1990   "Closing Down the Social: Baudrillard's Challenge to Contemporary Sociology." *Sociological
                Theory* 8:1–15.
1998   "Sense and Segmentarity: Some Markers of a Deleuzian-Guattarian Sociology." *Sociological
                Theory* 16:52–74.

Bogner, Arthur, Baker, Adelheid, and Kilminster, Richard
1992   "The Theory of the Civilizing Process—An Idiographic Theory of Modernization." *Theory, Culture
                and Society* 9:23–52.

Boli, John, and Lechner, Frank
2005   *World Culture: Origins and Consequences.* Oxford: Blackwell.

Boltanski, Luc, and Thevenot, Laurent
1991/2006   *On Justification: Economies of Worth.* Trans. by Catherine Porter. Princeton, N.J.: Princeton
                University Press.

Bonilla-Silva, Eduardo
2003   *Racism without Racists: Color-Blind Racism and the Persistence of Racial Inequality in the United
                States.* Lanham, Md.: Rowman and Littlefield.

Bookman, Ann, and Morgen, Sandra (eds.)
1988   *Women and the Politics of Empowerment.* Philadelphia: Temple University Press.

Bora, Alfons
2007   "Risk, Risk Society, Risk Behavior, and Social Problems." In George Ritzer (ed.), *The Blackwell
                Encyclopedia of Sociology.* Oxford: Blackwell: 3926–3932.

Borch, Christian
2012   *The Politics of Crowds: An Alternate History of Sociology.* New York: Cambridge University Press.

Bordo, Susan
1990   "Feminism, Postmodernism, and Gender-Scepticism." In L. Nicholson (ed.), *Feminism/
                Postmodernism.* New York: Routledge: 133–156.
1993   *Unbearable Weight: Feminism, Western Culture and the Body.* Berkeley: University of California Press.

Bosserman, Phillip
1968   *Dialectical Sociology: An Analysis of the Sociology of Georges Gurvitch.* Boston: Porter Sargent.

Boswell, Terry, and Dixon, William J.
1993   "Marx's Theory of Rebellion: A Cross-National Analysis of Class Exploitation, Economic Development, and Violent Revolt." *American Sociological Review* 58:681–702.

Bottero, Wendy
2007   "Class Consciousness," In George Ritzer (ed.), *The Blackwell Encyclopedia of Sociology.* Oxford: Blackwell: 539–542.

Bottomore, Tom
1984   *The Frankfurt School.* Chichester, Eng.: Ellis Horwood.

Bottomore, Tom, and Frisby, David
1978   Introduction to the translation of Georg Simmel, *The Philosophy of Money* (orig. 1907). London: Routledge and Kegan Paul: 1–49.

Boudon, Raymond
1995   "Should One Still Read Durkheim's Rules after One Hundred Years?" (Interview with Massimo Borlandi), *Schweizerische Zeitschrift fur Soziologie* 21:559–573.

Bourdieu, Pierre
1977   *Outline of a Theory of Practice.* London: Cambridge University Press.
1980/1990   *The Logic of Practice.* Stanford, Calif.: Stanford University Press.
1984a   *Distinction: A Social Critique of the Judgment of Taste.* Cambridge, Mass.: Harvard University Press.
1984b   *Homo Academicus.* Stanford, Calif.: Stanford University Press.
1989   "Social Space and Symbolic Power." *Sociological Theory* 7:14–25.
1990   *In Other Words: Essays toward a Reflexive Sociology.* Cambridge, Eng.: Polity Press.
1993   *The Field of Cultural Production: Essays on Art and Leisure.* New York: Columbia University Press.
1996   *The State Nobility.* Stanford, Calif.: Stanford University Press.
1998   *Practical Reason.* Stanford, Calif.: Stanford University Press.

Bourdieu, Pierre, and Darbel, Alain
1969/1990   *The Love of Art: European Art Museums and Their Public.* Stanford, Calif.: Stanford University Press.

Bourdieu, Pierre, and Passeron, Jean-Claude
1970/1990   *Reproduction in Education, Society and Culture.* London: Sage.

Bourdieu, Pierre, and Wacquant, Loïc J. D.
1992   "The Purpose of Reflexive Sociology (The Chicago Workshop)." In P. Bourdieu and L.J.D. Wacquant (eds.), *An Invitation to Reflexive Sociology.* Chicago: University of Chicago Press: 61–215.

Bourricaud, François
1981   *The Sociology of Talcott Parsons.* Chicago: University of Chicago Press.

Bowring, Finn
1996   "A Lifeworld without a Subject: Habermas and Pathologies of Modernity." *Telos* 106:77–104.

Bradley, Owen
2005a   "Bonald, Louis de." In George Ritzer (ed.), *Encyclopedia of Social Theory.* Thousand Oaks, Calif.: Sage: 65–66.
2005b   "Maistre, Joseph de." In George Ritzer (ed.), *Encyclopedia of Social Theory.* Thousand Oaks, Calif.: Sage: 454–466.

Bramson, Leon
1961   *The Political Context of Sociology.* Princeton, N.J.: Princeton University Press.

Braverman, Harry
1974   *Labor and Monopoly Capital: The Degradation of Work in the Twentieth Century.* New York: Monthly Review Press.

Breen, Margaret Sönser, and Blumenfeld, Warren J.
2005   *Butler Matters: Judith Butler's Impact on Feminist and Queer Studies.* Burlington, Vt.: Ashgate.

Breiner, Peter
2005   "Weber's *The Protestant Ethic* as Hypothetical Narrative of Original Accumulation." *Journal of Classical Sociology* 5(1):11–30.

Brennan, Teresa
2004   *The Transmission of Affect.* Ithaca, N.Y.: Cornell University Press.

Brenner, Neil
1994   "Foucault's New Functionalism." *Theory and Society* 23:679–709.

Brewer, John, and Hunter, Albert
1989   *Multimethod Research: A Synthesis of Styles.* Newbury Park, Calif.: Sage.

Brickell, Chris
2005   "Masculinities, Performativity, and Subversion: A Sociological Reappraisal." *Men and Masculinities* 8(1):24–43

Bronner, Stephen Eric
1995   "Ecology, Politics, and Risk: The Social Theory of Ulrich Beck." *Capital, Nature and Socialism* 6:67–86.

Brown, Michael, et al.
2003   *Whitewashing Race: The Myth of the Color-Blind Society.* Berkeley: University of California Press.

Brown, Richard
1987   *Society as Text: Essays on Rhetoric, Reason and Reality.* Chicago: University of Chicago Press.
1990   "Social Science and the Poetics of Public Truth." *Sociological Forum* 5:55–74.
2005   "Hermeneutics." In George Ritzer (ed.), *Encyclopedia of Social Theory.* Thousand Oaks, Calif.: Sage: 362–364.

Brown, Richard Harvey, and Goodman, Douglas
2001   "Jurgen Habermas' Theory of Communicative Action: An Incomplete Project." In George Ritzer and Barry Smart (eds.), *Handbook of Social Theory.* London: Sage: 201–216.

Brown, Stephen, and Capdevila, Rose
1999   "*Perpetuum Mobile:* Substance, Force and the Sociology of Translation." In John Law and John Hassard (eds.), *Actor Network Theory and After.* Oxford: Blackwell: 26–50.

Brubaker, Rogers
1984   *The Limits of Rationality: An Essay on the Social and Moral Thought of Max Weber.* London: Allen and Unwin.

Bruder, Kurt A.
1998   "Monastic Blessings: Deconstructing and Reconstructing the Self." *Symbolic Interaction* 21:87–116.

Brugger, Bill
1995   "Marxism, Asia, and the 1990s." *Positions* 3:630–641.

Bruun, Hans Henrik
2007   *Science, Values and Politics in Max Weber's Methodology.* Burlington, Vt.: Ashgate.

Bryant, Antony
2007   "Liquid Modernity, Complexity and Turbulence." *Theory Culture & Society* 24:127–135.

Bryant, Christopher G. A.
1985   *Positivism in Social Theory and Research.* New York: St. Martin's.

Bryant, Christopher G. A., and Jary, David
2001a   "The Uses of Structuration Theory: A Typology." In Christopher G. A. Bryant and David Jary (eds.), *The Contemporary Giddens: Social Theory in a Globalizing Age.* New York: Palgrave: 43–62.
2001b   "Anthony Giddens: A Global Social Theorist." In Christopher G. A. Bryant and David Jary (ed.), *The Contemporary Giddens: Social Theory in a Globalizing Age.* New York: Palgrave: 1–26.
2011   "Anthony Giddens." In George Ritzer and Jeffrey Stepnisky, (eds.), *The Wiley-Blackwell Companion to Major Social Theorists: Volume II—Contemporary Social Theorists.* Malden, Mass., and Oxford, Eng.: Wiley-Blackwell: 432–463.

Buchanan, Ian
2011   "Gilles Deleuze." In George Ritzer and Jeffrey Stepnisky, (eds.), *The Wiley-Blackwell Companion to Major Social Theorists: Volume II—Contemporary Social Theorists.* Malden, Mass., and Oxford, Eng.: Wiley-Blackwell: 175–192.

Buchwald, Emilie, Fletcher, Pamela R., and Roth, Martha (eds.)
1993   *Transforming a Rape Culture.* Minneapolis: Milkweed.

Buckley, Kerry W.
1989   *Mechanical Man: John Broadus Watson and the Beginnings of Behaviorism.* New York: Guilford Press.

Buckley, Walter
1967   *Sociology and Modern Systems Theory.* Englewood Cliffs, N.J.: Prentice-Hall.

Buffalohead, W. Roger
1996   "Reflections on Native American Cultural Rights and Resources." In Mary F. Rogers (ed.),
              Multicultural Experiences, Multicultural Theories. New York: McGraw-Hill: 154–156.

Bulmer, Martin
1984   *The Chicago School of Sociology: Institutionalization, Diversity, and the Rise of Sociological
              Research.* Chicago: University of Chicago Press.
1985   "The Chicago School of Sociology: What Made It a 'School'?" *History of Sociology: An
              International Review* 5:62–77.
1996   "The Sociological Contributions to Social Policy Research." In Jon Clark (ed.), *James Coleman.*
              London: Falmer Press: 103–118.

Bunch, Charlotte
1987   *Passionate Politics: Feminist Theory in Action.* New York: St. Martin's.

Bunzel, Dirk
2007   "Rational Legal Authority." In George Ritzer (ed.), *The Blackwell Encyclopedia of Sociology.*
              Oxford: Blackwell: 3805–3808.

Burawoy, Michael
1979   *Manufacturing Consent: Changes in the Labor Process under Monopoly Capitalism.* Chicago:
              University of Chicago Press.
1990   "Marxism as Science: Historical Challenges and Theoretical Growth." *American Sociological
              Review* 55:775–793.

Burawoy, Michael, and Wright, Erik Olin
2001   "Sociological Marxism." In Jonathan H. Turner (ed.), *Handbook of Sociological Theory.* New
              York: Kluwer Academic/Plenum Publishers: 459–486.

Burger, Thomas
1976   *Max Weber's Theory of Concept Formation: History, Laws and Ideal Types.* Durham, N.C.: Duke
              University Press.
1993   "Weber's Sociology and Weber's Personality." *Theory and Society* 22:813–836.

Burns, Tom R.
1986   "Actors, Transactions, and Social Structure: An Introduction to Social Rule System Theory." In
              U. Himmelstrand (ed.), *Sociology: The Aftermath of Crisis.* London: Sage: 8–37.

Burt, Ronald
1982   *Toward a Structural Theory of Action: Network Models of Social Structure, Perception, and Action.*
              New York: Academic Press.
1992   *Structural Holes: The Social Structure of Competition.* Cambridge, Mass.: Harvard University Press.

Bushell, Don, and Burgess, Robert
1969   "Some Basic Principles of Behavior." In R. Burgess and D. Bushell (eds.), *Behavioral Sociology.*
              New York: Columbia University Press: 27–48.

Butera, Karina J.
2008   " 'Neo-mateship' in the 21st Century." *Journal of Sociology* 44:265–281.

Butler, Judith
1990   *Gender Trouble: Feminism and the Subversion of Identity.* New York: Routledge.
1993   *Bodies That Matter: On the Discursive Limits of "Sex."* New York: Routledge.
1995   "Contingent Foundations." In Seyla Benhabib et al. (eds.), *Feminist Contentions.* New York:
              Routledge: 125–147.
1997a   *Excitable Speech: The Politics of the Performative.* London: Routledge.
1997b   "Imitation and Gender Insubordination." In Linda Nicholson (ed.), *The Second Wave: A Reader in
              Feminist Theory.* New York: Routledge: 300–315.
2004a   *Undoing Gender.* London: Routledge.
2004b   *Precarious Life: The Powers of Mourning and Violence.* London: Verso.
2005   *Giving an Account of Oneself.* New York: Fordham University Press.

Buttel, Frederick H. (ed.)
1990   "Symposium: Evolution and Social Change." *Sociological Forum* 5:153–212.

Button, Graham
1987   "Answers as Interactional Products: Two Sequential Practices Used in Interviews." *Social Psychology Quarterly* 50:160–171.

Buxton, William
1985   *Talcott Parsons and the Capitalist Nation-State: Political Sociology as a Strategic Vocation.* Toronto: University of Toronto Press.

Cadieux, R. D.
1995   "Dialectics and the Economy of Difference." *Dialectical Anthropology* 20:319–340.

Calhoun, Craig
1993a   "Habitus, Field, and Capital: The Question of Historical Specificity." In C. Calhoun, E. LiPuma, and M. Postone (eds.), *Bourdieu: Critical Perspectives.* Chicago: University of Chicago Press: 61–88.
1993b   "Postmodernism as Pseudohistory." *Theory, Culture and Society* 10:75–96.
2011   "Pierre Bourdieu." In George Ritzer and Jeffrey Stepnisky, (eds.), *The Wiley-Blackwell Companion to Major Social Theorists: Volume II—Contemporary Social Theorists.* Malden, Mass., and Oxford, Eng.: Wiley-Blackwell: 361–394.

Calhoun, Craig and Derluguian, Georgi (eds.)
2011a   *Business as Usual: The Roots of the Global Financial Meltdown.* New York: New York University Press.
2011b   *The Deepening Crisis: Governance Challenges after Neoliberalism.* New York: New York University Press.
2011c   *Aftermath: A New Global Economic Order?* New York: New York University Press.

Calhoun, Craig, and Karaganis, Joseph
2001   "Critical Theory." In George Ritzer and Barry Smart (eds.), *Handbook of Social Theory.* London: Sage: 179–200.

Callinicos, Alex
1989   "Introduction: Analytical Marxism." In Alex Callinicos (ed.), *Marxist Theory.* Oxford: Oxford University Press, 1989: 1–16.

Callon, Michel
1999   "Actor-Network Theory." In John Law and John Hassard (eds.), *Actor Network Theory and After.* Oxford: Blackwell: 181–195.

Camic, Charles
1990   "An Historical Prologue." *American Sociological Review* 55:313–319.
1992   "Reputation and Predecessor Selection: Parsons and the Institutionalists." *American Sociological Review* 57:421–445.

Camic, Charles (ed.)
1997   *Reclaiming the Sociological Classics: The State of Scholarship.* Oxford: Blackwell.

Campbell, Colin
1982   "A Dubious Distinction? An Inquiry into the Value and Use of Merton's Concepts of Manifest and Latent Function." *American Sociological Review* 47:29–44.

Campbell, J., and Pederson, O. K. (eds.)
2001   *The Rise of Neoliberalism and Institutional Analysis.* Princeton, N.J.: Princeton University Press.

Campbell, Marie and Devault, Marjorie
2011   "Dorothy Smith." In George Ritzer and Jeffrey Stepnisky (eds.), *The Wiley-Blackwell Companion to Major Social Theorists: Volume II—Contemporary Social Theorists.* Malden, Mass., and Oxford, Eng.: Wiley-Blackwell: 268–286.

Campbell, Marie, and Manicom, Ann
1995   *Knowledge, Experience, and Ruling Relations: Studies in the Social Organization of Knowledge.* Toronto: University of Toronto Press.

Caplow, Theodore
1968   *Two against One: Coalition in Triads.* Englewood Cliffs, N.J.: Prentice-Hall.

Capra, Fritjof
2005   "Complexity and Life." *Theory, Culture & Society* 22(5):33–44.

R-16   References

Caputi, Jane
1989   "The Sexual Politics of Murder." *Gender & Society,* 3(4):437–456.

Carter, Michael J.
2007   "Identity Theory." In George Ritzer (ed.), *The Blackwell Encyclopedia of Sociology.* Oxford: Blackwell: 2223–2226.

Carver, Terrell
1983   *Marx and Engels: The Intellectual Relationship.* Bloomington: Indiana University Press.

Castells, Manuel
1996   *The Rise of the Network Society.* Malden, Mass.: Blackwell.
1997   *The Power of Identity.* Malden, Mass.: Blackwell.
1998   *End of Millennium.* Malden, Mass.: Blackwell.

Cerny, Philip G.
1995   "Globalization and the Changing Logic of Collective Action." *International Organization* 49(4):595–625.
2003   "Globalization at the Micro Level: The Uneven Pluralization of World Politics." In Axel Hülsemeyer (ed.), *Globalization in the 21st Century: Convergence and Divergence.* London: Palgrave.
2010   *Rethinking World Politics: A Theory of Transnational Pluralism.* New York: Oxford University Press.

Cerullo, John J.
1994   "The Epistemic Turn: Critical Sociology and the 'Generation of 68.' " *International Journal of Politics, Culture and Society* 8:169–181.

Chafetz, Janet Saltzman
1984   *Sex and Advantage.* Totowa, N.J.: Rowman and Allanhold.
1988   *Feminist Sociology: An Overview of Contemporary Theories.* Itasca, Ill.: Peacock.
1990   *Gender Equity: An Integrated Theory of Stability and Change.* Newbury Park, Calif.: Sage.
1997   "Feminist Theory and Sociology: Underutilized Contributions for Mainstream Theory." *Annual Review of Sociology* 23:97–190.
1999   "Structure, Consciousness, Agency and Social Change in Feminist Sociological Theories: A Conundrum." *Current Perspectives in Social Theory* 19:145–164.
2004   "Bridging Feminist Theory and Research Methodology." *Journal of Family Issues* 25(7):963–977.

Chambliss, Daniel F.
2005   "Frame Analysis." In George Ritzer (ed.), *Encyclopedia of Social Theory.* Thousand Oaks, Calif.: Sage: 289–290.

Chancer, Lynn S.
1992   *Sadomasochism in Everyday Life: The Dynamics of Power and Powerlessness.* New Brunswick, N.J.: Rutgers University Press.

Chancer, Lynn, and Palmer, Craig T.
2001   "A Debate on Sociobiology and Rape." *New Politics (New Series),* 2000: 8:1 (29) Summer: 96–102.

Chapin, Mark
1994   "Functional Conflict Theory: The Alcohol Beverage Industry, and the Alcoholism Treatment Industry." *Journal of Applied Social Sciences* 18:169–182.

Chapoulie, Jean-Michel
1996   "Everett Hughes and the Chicago Tradition." *Sociological Theory* 14:3–29.

Charon, Joel M.
1998   *Symbolic Interactionism: An Introduction, an Interpretation, an Integration.* 6th ed. Englewood Cliffs, N.J.: Prentice-Hall.
2000   *Symbolic Interactionism: An Introduction, an Interpretation, an Integration.* 7th ed. Englewood Cliffs, N.J.: Prentice-Hall.

Chase-Dunn, Christopher
2001   "World-Systems Theory." In Jonathan H. Turner (ed.), *Handbook of Sociological Theory.* New York: Kluwer Academic/Plenum Publishers: 589–612.
2005a   "Wallerstein, Immanuel." In George Ritzer (ed.), *Encyclopedia of Social Theory.* Thousand Oaks, Calif.: Sage: 875–876.
2005b   "World-Systems Theory." In George Ritzer (ed.), *Encyclopedia of Social Theory.* Thousand Oaks, Calif.: Sage: 887–891.

Chase-Dunn, Christopher, and Hall, Thomas D.
1994   "The Historical Evolution of World-Systems." *Sociological Inquiry* 64:257–280.

Chase-Dunn, Christopher, and Inoue, Hiroko
2011   "Immanuel Wallerstein." In George Ritzer and Jeffrey Stepnisky, (eds.), *The Wiley-Blackwell Companion to Major Social Theorists: Volume II—Contemporary Social Theorists*. Malden, Mass., and Oxford, Eng.: Wiley-Blackwell: 395–411.

Chasteen, Amy L.
2001   "Constructing Rape: Feminism, Change, and Women's Everyday Understandings of Sexual Assault." *Sociological Spectrum* 21:101–139.

Cherkaoui, Mohamed
2007   *Good Intentions: Max Weber and the Paradox of Unintended Consequences*. Oxford: Bardwell Press.

Chesler, Phyllis
1994   *Patriarchy: Notes of an Expert Witness*. Monroe, Me.: Common Courage Press.

Chilisa, Bagele, and Ntseane, Gabo
2010   "Resisting Dominant Discourses: Implications of Indigenous, African Feminist Theory and Methods for Gender and Education Research." *Gender and Education* 22(6):617–632.

Chitnis, Anand C.
1976   *The Scottish Enlightenment: A Social History*. Totowa, N.J.: Rowman and Littlefield.

Chodorow, Nancy
1978   *The Reproduction of Mothering: Psychoanalysis and the Sociology of Gender*. Berkeley: University of California Press.
1990   *Feminism and Psychoanalytic Theory*. New Haven: Yale University Press.
1994   *Femininities, Masculinity, Sexualities: Freud and Beyond*. Lexington: University of Kentucky Press.
1999   *The Power of Feelings: Personal Meaning in Psychoanalysis, Gender and Culture*. London: Yale University Press.

Choo, Hae Yeon, and Ferree, Myra Marx
2010   "Practicing Intersectionality in Sociological Research: A Critical Analysis of Inclusions, Interactions and Institutions in Studies of Inequality." *Sociological Theory* 28(2):129–149.

Chopra, Sherry
2004   "In Spite of Challenges by 'Black' and 'Third World' Women, Do Mainstream Feminist Theories Still Reflect the Concerns of White Women?" *Journal of International Women's Studies* 5(2):21–28.

Chriss, James J.
1995   "Testing Gouldner's Coming Crisis Thesis: On the Waxing and Waning of Intellectual Influence." *Current Perspectives in Social Theory* 15:33–61.
1996   "Toward an Interparadigmatic Dialogue on Goffman." *Sociological Perspectives* 39:333–339.
2005a   "Gouldner, Alvin." In George Ritzer (ed.), *Encyclopedia of Social Theory*. Thousand Oaks, Calif.: Sage: 340–342.
2005b   "Mead, George Herbert." In George Ritzer (ed.), *Encyclopedia of Social Theory*. Thousand Oaks, Calif.: Sage: 486–491.
2006   "Giddings and the Social Mind." *Journal of Classical Sociology* 6:123–144.

Christopher, F. S.
2001   *To Dance the Dance: A Symbolic Interactional Exploration of Premarital Sexuality*. Mahwah, N.J.:, Lawrence Erlbaum.

Cicourel, Aaron
1974   *Cognitive Sociology: Language and Meaning in Social Interaction*. New York: Free Press.
1981   "Notes on the Integration of Micro- and Macro-Levels of Analysis." In K. Knorr-Cetina and A. Cicourel (eds.), *Advances in Social Theory and Methodology*. New York: Methuen: 51–79.

Clark, Candace
1987   "Sympathy Biography and Sympathy Margin." *American Journal of Sociology* 93(2):290–321.

Clark, Ian
2007   "International Relations." In Jan Aart Scholte and Roland Robertson (eds.), *Encyclopedia of Globalization*. New York: MTM: 664–669.

Clark, Jon (ed.)
1996   *James S. Coleman*. London: Falmer Press.

Clark, Jon, Modgil, Celia, and Modgil, Sohan (eds.)
1990   *Anthony Giddens: Consensus and Controversy*. London: Falmer Press.

R-18 References

Clark, Nigel
1997   "Panic Ecology: Nature in the Age of Superconductivity." *Theory, Culture and Society* 14:77–96.

Clarke, Simon
1990   "The Crisis of Fordism or the Crisis of Social Democracy?" *Telos* 83:71–98.

Clark-Lewis, Elizabeth
1994   *Living In, Living Out: African American Domestics in Washington, D.C. 1910–1940.* Washington, D.C.: Smithsonian Institution Press.

Clawson, Dan, Neustadtl, Alan, and Bearden, James
1986   "The Logic of Business Unity: Corporate Contributions to the 1980 Congressional Elections." *American Sociological Review* 51:797–811.

Clayman, Steven E.
1993   "Booing: The Anatomy of a Disaffiliative Response." *American Sociological Review* 58:110–130.

Clough, Patricia
2003   "Affect and Control: Rethinking the Body 'Beyond Sex and Gender.'" *Feminist Theory*, 4(3):359–364.
2004   "Technoscience, Global Politics, and Cultural Criticism." *Social Text* 80, 3:1–23.
2008   "The Affective Turn: Political Economy, Biomedia and Bodies." *Theory, Culture & Society*, 25(1):1–22.

Cockerham, William C., Abel, Thomas, and Luschen, Gunther
1993   "Max Weber, Formal Rationality, and Health Lifestyles." *Sociological Quarterly* 34:413–425.

Cohen, G. A.
1978   *Karl Marx's Theory of History: A Defence.* Princeton, N.J.: Princeton University Press.
1978/1986   "Marxism and Functional Explanation." In J. Roemer (ed.), *Analytical Marxism.* Cambridge, Eng.: Cambridge University Press: 221–234.

Cohen, Ira J.
1981   "Introduction to the Transaction Edition." In M. Weber, *General Economic History.* New Brunswick, N.J.: Transaction Books: xv–lxxxiii.
1989   *Structuration Theory.* London: Macmillan.
2005   "Structuration." In George Ritzer (ed.), *Encyclopedia of Social Theory.* Thousand Oaks, Calif.: Sage: 811–814.

Cohen, Percy
1968   *Modern Social Theory.* New York: Basic Books.

Cohen, Philip N.
1998   "Replacing Housework in the Service Economy: Gender, Class, and Race-Ethnicity in Service Spending." *Gender & Society* 12:219–231.

Coleman, James S.
1964   *Introduction to Mathematical Sociology.* New York: Free Press.
1973   *The Mathematics of Collective Action.* London, UK: Heinemann.
1986   "Social Theory, Social Research, and a Theory of Action." *American Journal of Sociology* 91:1309–1335.
1987   "Microfoundations and Macrosocial Behavior." In J. C. Alexander et al. (eds.), *The Micro-Macro Link.* Berkeley: University of California Press: 153–173.
1989   "Rationality and Society." *Rationality and Society* 1:5–9.
1990   *Foundations of Social Theory.* Cambridge, Mass.: Belknap Press of Harvard University Press.
1993a   "The Design of Organizations and the Right to Act." *Sociological Forum* 8:527–546.
1993b   "The Rational Reconstruction of Society." *American Sociological Review* 58:1–15.
1994   "A Vision for Sociology." *Society* 32:29–34.

Collier, Stephen J.
2011   *Post-Soviet Social: Neoliberalism, Social Modernity, Biopolitics.* Princeton, N.J.: Princeton University Press.

Collins, J. L.
2002   "Mapping a Global Labor Market—Gender and Skill in the Globalizing Garment Industry." *Gender & Society* 16:921–940.

Collins, Patricia Hill
1990   *Black Feminist Thought: Knowledge, Consciousness and Empowerment.* Boston: Unwin Hyman.
1998   *Fighting Words: Black Women and the Search for Justice.* Minneapolis: University of Minnesota Press.
1999   "Moving beyond Gender." In Myra Marx Feree, Judith Lorber, and Beth Hess (eds.), *Revisioning Gender.* Thousand Oaks, Calif.: Sage: 261–284.

2000	"Gender, Black Feminism and Black Political Economy." *Annals of the American Academy of Political and Social Science* 568:41–53.
2001	"Like One of the Family: Race, Ethnicity, and the Paradox of US National Identity." *Ethnic and Racial Studies* 24:3–28.
2004	*Black Sexual Politics: African Americans, Gender, and the New Racism.* New York: Routledge.
2012	"Looking Back, Moving Ahead: Scholarship in Service to Social Justice." *Gender & Society* 26:14–22.

Collins, Randall

1975	*Conflict Sociology: Toward an Explanatory Science.* New York: Academic Press.
1979	*The Credential Society.* New York: Academic Press.
1980	"Weber's Last Theory of Capitalism: A Systematization." *American Sociological Review* 45:925–942.
1981a	"On the Microfoundations of Macrosociology." *American Journal of Sociology* 86:984–1014.
1981b	"Micro-Translation as Theory-Building Strategy." In K. Knorr-Cetina and A. Cicourel (eds.), *Advances in Social Theory and Methodology.* New York: Methuen: 81–108.
1985	*Weberian Sociological Theory.* Cambridge, Eng.: Cambridge University Press.
1986a	"Is 1980s Sociology in the Doldrums?" *American Journal of Sociology* 91:1336–1355.
1986b	"The Passing of Intellectual Generations: Reflections on the Death of Erving Goffman." *Sociological Theory* 4:106–113.
1987	"A Micro-Macro Theory of Intellectual Creativity: The Case of German Idealistic Philosophy." *Sociological Theory* 5:47–69.
1988a	"The Micro Contribution to Macro Sociology." *Sociological Theory* 6:242–253.
1988b	"The Durkheimian Tradition in Conflict Sociology." In J. C. Alexander (ed.), *Durkheimian Sociology: Cultural Studies.* Cambridge, Eng.: Cambridge University Press: 107–128.
1990	"Conflict Theory and the Advance of Macro-Historical Sociology." In George Ritzer (ed.), *Frontiers of Social Theory: The New Syntheses.* New York: Columbia University Press: 68–87.
1997a	"An Asian Route to Capitalism: Religious Economy and the Origins of Self-Transforming Growth in Japan." *American Sociological Review* 62:843–865.
1997b	"A Sociological Guilt Trip: Comment on Connell." *American Journal of Sociology* 102:1558–1564.

Collins, Randall, and Makowsky, Michael

| 1998 | *The Discovery of Society.* 6th ed. New York: McGraw-Hill. |

Colomy, Paul

1986	"Recent Developments in the Functionalist Approach to Change." *Sociological Focus* 19:139–158.
1990a	"Introduction: The Functionalist Tradition." In P. Colomy (ed.), *Functionalist Sociology.* Brookfield, Vt.: Elgar Publishing: xiii–lxii.
1990b	"Introduction: The Neofunctionalist Movement." In P. Colomy (ed.), *Neofunctionalist Sociology.* Brookfield, Vt.: Elgar Publishing: xi–xii.
2005	"Alexander, Jeffrey" In George Ritzer (ed.), *Encyclopedia of Social Theory.* Thousand Oaks, Calif.: Sage: 8–9.

Colomy, Paul, and Rhoades, Gary

| 1994 | "Toward a Micro Corrective of Structural Differentiation Theory." *Sociological Perspectives* 37:547–583. |

Conley, Tom, and Wiener, Jarrod

| 2002 | "Globalisation as Constraint and Opportunity: Reconceptualising Policy Capacity in Australia." *Global Society* 16(4):377–399. |

Connell, Catherine

| 2010 | "Doing, Undoing, or Redoing Gender?: Learning from the Workplace Experiences of Transpeople." *Gender & Society* 24(1):31–55. |

Connell, R. W.

1995	*Masculinities.* Berkeley: University of California Press.
1996	"Men and the Women's Movement." In Mary F. Rogers (ed.), *Multicultural Experiences, Multicultural Theories.* New York: McGraw-Hill: 409–415.
1997	"How Is Classical Theory Classical?" *American Journal of Sociology* 102:1511–1557.

Connell, Raewyn

| 2009 | "Accountable Conduct: 'Doing Gender' in Transsexual and Political Retrospect." *Gender & Society* 23(1):104–111. |

Connerton, Paul (ed.)

| 1976 | *Critical Sociology.* Harmondsworth, Eng.: Penguin. |

Connolly, William E.
1973   "Theoretical Self-Consciousness." *Polity* 6:5–35.

Connor, Walker
2007   "Ethnonationalism." In George Ritzer (ed.), *The Blackwell Encyclopedia of Sociology*. Oxford: Blackwell: 1486–1488.

Cook, Deborah
1994   "Symbolic Exchange in Hyperreality." In D. Kellner (ed.), *Baudrillard: A Critical Reader*. Oxford: Blackwell: 150–167.
1996   *The Culture Industry Revisited: Theodor W. Adorno on Mass Culture*. Lanham, Md.: Rowman and Littlefield.

Cook, Gary
1993   *George Herbert Mead: The Making of a Social Pragmatist*. Urbana: University of Illinois Press.

Cook, Karen S.
1987   "Emerson's Contributions to Social Exchange Theory." In K. S. Cook (ed.), *Social Exchange Theory*. Beverly Hills, Calif.: Sage: 209–222.
2005   "Emerson, Richard." In George Ritzer (ed.), *Encyclopedia of Social Theory*. Thousand Oaks, Calif.: Sage: 246–248.

Cook, Karen S., Emerson, Richard M., Gillmore, Mary B., and Yamagishi, Toshio
1983   "The Distribution of Power in Exchange Networks: Theory and Experimental Results." *American Journal of Sociology* 89:275–305.

Cook, Karen S., O'Brien, Jodi, and Kollock, Peter
1990   "Exchange Theory: A Blueprint for Structure and Process." In George Ritzer (ed.), *Frontiers of Social Theory: The New Syntheses*. New York: Columbia University Press: 158–181.

Cook, Karen S., and Rice, Eric R. W.
2001   "Exchange and Power: Issues of Structure and Agency." In Jonathan H. Turner (ed.), *Handbook of Sociological Theory*. New York: Kluwer Academic/Plenum Publishers: 699–719.
2005   "Social Exchange Theory." In George Ritzer (ed.), *Encyclopedia of Social Theory*. Thousand Oaks, Calif.: Sage: 735–740.

Cook, Karen S., and Whitmeyer, J. M.
1992   "Two Approaches to Social Structure: Exchange Theory and Network Analysis." *Annual Review of Sociology* 18:109–127.
2011   "Richard M. Emerson." In George Ritzer and Jeffrey Stepnisky, (eds.), *The Wiley-Blackwell Companion to Major Social Theorists: Volume II—Contemporary Social Theorists*. Malden, Mass., and Oxford, Eng.: Wiley-Blackwell: 193–218.

Cooke, Maeve
1994   *Language and Reason: A Study of Habermas's Pragmatics*. Cambridge, Mass: MIT Press.

Cooley, Charles H.
1902/1964   *Human Nature and the Social Order*. New York: Scribner.

Cooper, Dereck
1991   "On the Concept of Alienation." *International Journal of Contemporary Sociology* 28:7–26.

Cordova, Teresa, Cantu, Norma, Cardena, Gilbert, Garcia, Juan, and Sierra, Christine M. (eds.)
1990   *Chicana Voices: Intersections of Class, Race, and Gender*. Austin, Tex.: National Association for Chicano Studies.

Cortese, Anthony
1995   "The Rise, Hegemony, and Decline of the Chicago School of Sociology, 1892–1945." *Social Science Journal* 32:235–254.

Coser, Lewis
1956   *The Functions of Social Conflict*. New York: Free Press.
1967   *Continuities in the Study of Social Conflict*. New York: Free Press.

Coser, Lewis (ed.)
1965   *Georg Simmel*. Englewood Cliffs, N.J.: Prentice-Hall.

Cott, Nancy F.
1977   *The Bonds of Womanhood: Women's Sphere in New England, 1780–1835*. New Haven: Yale University Press.

Cotterrell, Roger
1999   *Emile Durkheim: Law in a Moral Domain.* Stanford, Calif.: Stanford University Press.

Cottrell, Leonard S., Jr.
1980   "George Herbert Mead: The Legacy of Social Behaviorism." In R. K. Merton and M. W. Riley
                (eds.), *Sociological Traditions from Generation to Generation: Glimpses of the American
                Experience.* Norwood, N.J.: Ablex.

Coulter, Jeff
1983   *Rethinking Cognitive Theory.* New York: St. Martin's.

Craib, Ian
1976   *Existentialism and Sociology: A Study of Jean-Paul Sartre.* Cambridge, Eng.: Cambridge University Press.
1992   *Anthony Giddens.* London: Routledge.
1994   *The Importance of Disappointment.* New York: Routledge.

Craib, Ian, and Wernick, Andrew
2005   "Sartre, Jean-Paul." In George Ritzer (ed.), *Encyclopedia of Social Theory.* Thousand Oaks, Calif.:
                Sage: 663–665.

Crawford, Cassandra
2005   "Actor Network Theory." In George Ritzer (ed.), *Encyclopedia of Social Theory.* Thousand Oaks,
                Calif.: Sage: 1–3.

Crawford, Mary
1995   *Talking Difference: On Gender and Language.* Newbury Park, Calif.: Sage.

Crawley, Sara, L.
2011   "Visible Bodies, Vicarious Masculinity, and 'The Gender Revolution': Comment on Paula
                England." *Gender & Society* 25:108–112.

Crenshaw, Kimberle
1989   "Demarginalizing the Intersection of Race and Sex: A Black Feminist Critique of
                Antidiscrimination Doctrine, Feminist Theory, and Antiracist Politics." *University of Chicago Legal
                Forum:* 139–167.
1991   "Mapping the Margins: Intersectionality, Identity Politics, and Violence against Women of Color."
                Stanford Law Review 43(6):1241–1299.
1997   "Intersectionality and Identity Politics: Learning from Violence against Women of Color." In
                M. Shanley and U. Narayan (eds.), *Reconstructing Political Theory: Feminist Perspectives.*
                University Park: Pennsylvania State University Press.

Crippen, Timothy
1994   "Toward a Neo-Darwinian Sociology: Its Nomological Principles and Some Illustrative
                Applications." *Sociological Perspectives* 37:309–335.

Crook, Stephen
1995   *Adorno: The Stars down to Earth and Other Essays on the Irrational in Culture.* London: Routledge.
2001   "Social Theory and the Postmodern." In George Ritzer and Barry Smart (eds.), *Handbook of
                Social Theory.* London: Sage: 308–338.

Crothers, Charles
2011   "Merton, Robert." In George Ritzer and Jeffrey Stepnisky (eds.), *The Wiley-Blackwell Companion
                to Major Social Theorists: Volume II—Contemporary Social Theorists.* Malden, Mass., and Oxford,
                Eng.: Wiley-Blackwell: 65–88.

Crothers, Lane
2010   *Globalization and American Popular Culture,* 2nd ed. Lanham, Md.: Rowman and Littlefield.

Crozier, Michel, and Friedberg, Erhard
1980   *Actors and Systems: The Politics of Collective Action.* Chicago: University of Chicago Press.

Cubitt, Sean
2005a   "Simulation." In George Ritzer (ed.), *Encyclopedia of Social Theory.* Thousand Oaks, Calif.: Sage:
                704–705.
2005b   "DeBord, Guy." In George Ritzer (ed.), *Encyclopedia of Social Theory.* Thousand Oaks, Calif.:
                Sage: 186–189.
2005c   "Situationists." In George Ritzer (ed.), *Encyclopedia of Social Theory.* Thousand Oaks, Calif.:
                Sage: 706–708.
2007   "Simulation and Virtuality." In George Ritzer (ed.), *The Blackwell Encyclopedia of Sociology.*
                Oxford: Blackwell: 4331–4334.

Culler, Jonathan
1976   *Ferdinand de Saussure.* Harmondsworth, Eng.: Penguin.

Cultural Sociology
2011   Special issue: "On the Shoulders of Pierre Bourdieu: A Contemporary Master in Chiaroscuro." March.

Currie, Dawn H.
1997   "Decoding Femininity: Advertisements and Their Teenage Readers." *Gender & Society*
                 11:453–477.
1999   "Gender Analysis from the Standpoint of Women: The Radical Potential of Women's Studies in
                 Development." *Asian Journal of Women's Studies* 5:9–44.

Curtis, Bruce
1981   *William Graham Sumner.* Boston: Twayne.

Dahme, Heinz-Jurgen
1990   "On the Current Rediscovery of Georg Simmel's Sociology—A European Point of View." In
                 M. Kaern, B. S. Phillips, and R. S. Cohen (eds.), *Georg Simmel and Contemporary Sociology.*
                 Dordrecht, Netherlands: Kluwer: 13–37.

Dahms, Harry
1997   "Theory in Weberian Marxism: Patterns of Critical Social Theory in Lukács and Habermas."
                 Sociological Theory 15:181–214.
1998   "Beyond the Carousel of Reification: Critical Social Theory after Lukács, Adorno, and Habermas."
                 Current Perspectives in Social Theory 18:3–62.
2011a   "Joseph A. Schumpeter." In George Ritzer and Jeffrey Stepnisky, (eds.), *The Wiley-Blackwell
                 Companion to Major Social Theorists: Volume I—Classical Social Theorists.* Malden, Mass., and
                 Oxford, Eng.: Wiley-Blackwell: 448–468.
2011b   "Theodor W. Adorno." In George Ritzer and Jeffrey Stepnisky, (eds.), *The Wiley-Blackwell
                 Companion to Major Social Theorists: Volume 1—Classical Social Theorists.* Malden, Mass., and
                 Oxford, Eng.: Wiley-Blackwell: 559–581.

Dahrendorf, Ralf
1958   "Out of Utopia: Toward a Reorientation of Sociological Analysis." *American Journal of Sociology*
                 64:115–127.
1959   *Class and Class Conflict in Industrial Society.* Stanford, Calif.: Stanford University Press.
1968   *Essays in the Theory of Society.* Stanford, Calif.: Stanford University Press.

Daly, Mary
1973   *Beyond God the Father: Toward a Philosophy of Women's Liberation.* Boston: Beacon Press.
1978   *Gyn/Ecology: The MetaEthics of Radical Feminism.* Boston: Beacon.
1993   *Outercourse: The Be-dazzling Voyage.* San Francisco: Harper.

Dandaneau, Steven P.
1992   "Immanent Critique of Post-Marxism." *Current Perspectives in Social Theory* 12:155–177.
2001   *Taking It Big: Developing Sociological Consciousness in Postmodern Times.* Thousand Oaks,
                 Calif.: Pine Forge Press.
2007a   "Marcuse, Herbert." In George Ritzer (ed.), *The Blackwell Encyclopedia of Sociology.* Oxford:
                 Blackwell: 2759–2761.
2007b   "Mills, C. Wright." In George Ritzer (ed.), *The Blackwell Encyclopedia of Sociology.* Oxford:
                 Blackwell: 3050–3055.

Dant, Tim
1996   "Fetishism and the Social Value of Objects." *Sociological Review* 44:495–516.

Darder, Antonia, and Torres, Rodolfo D.
2004   *After Race: Racism after Multiculturalism.* New York: New York University Press.

Davidson, Alastair
2007   "Gramsci, Antonio." In George Ritzer (ed.), *The Blackwell Encyclopedia of Sociology.* Oxford:
                 Blackwell: 2014–2016.

Davis, Kingsley
1959   "The Myth of Functional Analysis as a Special Method in Sociology and Anthropology." *American
                 Sociological Review* 24:757–772.

Davis, Kingsley, and Moore, Wilbert
1945   "Some Principles of Stratification." *American Sociological Review* 10:242–249.

Davis, Noela
2009   "New Materialism and Feminism's Anti-Biologism: A Response to Sara Ahmed." *The European Journal of Women's Studies* 16(1):67–80.

Dawe, Alan
1978   "Theories of Social Action." In T. Bottomore and R. Nisbet (eds.), *A History of Sociological Analysis*. New York: Basic Books: 362–417.

Day, Kristen
2000   "The Ethic of Care and Women's Experiences of Public Space." *Journal of Environmental Psychology* 20:103–124.

Dean, Mitchell
1994   *Critical and Effective Histories: Foucault's Methods and Historical Sociology*. London: Routledge.
2001   "Michel Foucault: 'A Man in Danger.'" In George Ritzer and Barry Smart (eds.), *Handbook of Social Theory*. London: Sage: 324–338.

de Beauvoir, Simone
1949/1957   *The Second Sex*. New York: Vintage.

DeCaroli, Steven
2007   "Giorgio Agamben and the Field of Sovereignty." In Matthew Calarco and Steven DeCaroli (eds.), *Sovereignty and Life*. Stanford, Calif.: Stanford University Press: 43–69.

Deegan, Mary Jo
1988   *Jane Addams and the Men of the Chicago School, 1892–1918*. New Brunswick, N.J.: Transaction Books.
1991   *Women in Sociology: A Bio-Bibliographical Sourcebook*. Westport, Conn.: Greenwood Press.

Deegan, Mary Jo, and Hill, Michael R. (eds.)
1987   *Women and Symbolic Interaction*. Boston: Allen and Unwin.
1998   *With Her in Ourland: Sequel to "Herland" by Charlotte Perkins Gilman*. Westport, Conn.: Praeger.

Deflem, Matthieu
2003   "The Sociology of the Sociology of Money: Simmel and the Contemporary Battle of the Classics." *Journal of Classical Sociology* 3(1):67–96.
2007   "Anomie." In George Ritzer (ed.), *The Blackwell Encyclopedia of Sociology*. Oxford: Blackwell: 144–146.

de Grazia, Victoria
2005   *Irresistible Empire: America's Advance through Twentieth-Century Europe*. Cambridge, Mass.: Harvard University Press, Belknap Press.

Delamont, Sara
2003   *Feminist Sociology*. London: Sage.

DeLanda, Manuel
2006   *A New Philosophy of Society: Assemblage Theory and Social Complexity*. New York: Continuum.

Delaney, Tim
2005a   "Coser, Lewis." In George Ritzer (ed.), *Encyclopedia of Social Theory*. Thousand Oaks, Calif.: Sage: 155–157.
2005b   "Sumner, William Graham." In George Ritzer (ed.), *Encyclopedia of Social Theory*. Thousand Oaks, Calif.: Sage: 814–815.

Delanty, Gerard
1997   "Habermas and Occidental Rationalism: The Politics of Identity, Social Learning, and the Cultural Limits of Moral Universalism." *Sociological Theory* 15:30–59.
1998   "Editor's Introduction." *European Journal of Social Theory*, 1(1):1–2.
2005   "Citizenship." In George Ritzer (ed.), *Encyclopedia of Social Theory*. Thousand Oaks, Calif.: Sage: 93–98.

de Lauretis, Teresa
1991   "Queer Theory: Lesbian and Gay Sexualities: An Introduction." *differences: A Journal of Feminist Cultural Studies* 3(2):29–313.

Deleuze, Gilles, and Guattari, Felix
1972/1983   *Anti-Oedipus: Capitalism and Schizophrenia*. Minneapolis: University of Minnesota Press.

1980/1987   *A Thousand Plateaus: Capitalism and Schizophrenia.* Trans. B. Massumi. Minneapolis: University of Minnesota Press.

Delgado, Richard, and Stefancic, Jean
2001   *Critical Race Theory: An Introduction.* New York: New York University Press.

Demerath, Nicholas, and Peterson, Richard (eds.)
1967   *System, Change and Conflict.* New York: Free Press.

Dempsey, Ken
2002   "Who Gets the Best Deal from Marriage: Women or Men?" *Journal of Sociology* 38:91–110.

Densimore, Dana
1973   "Independence from the Sexual Revolution." In A. Koedt et al. (eds.), *Radical Feminism.* New York: Quadrangle: 107–118.

Denzin, Norman
1990a   "Harold and Agnes: A Feminist Narrative Undoing." *Sociological Theory* 9:198–216.
1990b   "Reading Rational Choice Theory." *Rationality and Society* 2:172–189.
1991   "Back to Harold and Agnes." *Sociological Theory* 9:280–285.
1993   "Sexuality and Gender: An Interactionist/Poststructuralist Reading." In P. England (ed.), *Theory on Gender/Feminism on Theory.* New York: Aldine de Gruyter: 199–223.

Der Derian, James
1994   "Simulation: The Highest Stage of Capitalism?" In D. Kellner (ed.), *Baudrillard: A Critical Reader.* Oxford: Blackwell: 189–208.

Derrida, Jacques
1978   *Writing and Difference.* Chicago: University of Chicago Press.

Desai, Manisha
2007   "The Messy Relationship between Feminisms and Globalization." *Gender & Society* 21(6): 797–803.

Deutsch, Francine M.
2007   "Undoing Gender." *Gender & Society* 21(1):2007:106–127.

Deutschmann, Christoph
1996   "Money as a Social Construction: On the Actuality of Marx and Simmel." *Thesis Eleven* 47:1–19.

DeVille, Phillippe
1989   "Human Agency and Social Structure in Economic Theory: The General Equilibrium Theory and Beyond." Paper presented at the conference on "Social Theory and Human Agency," Swedish Collegium for Advanced Study in the Social Sciences, Uppsala, Sweden, Sept. 29–Oct. 1.

Diamond, Timothy
1992   *Making Gray Gold.* Chicago: University of Chicago Press.

Dickens, Peter
2005   "Social Darwinism." In George Ritzer (ed.), *Encyclopedia of Social Theory.* Thousand Oaks, Calif.: Sage: 729–731.

Dickerson, Bette J. (ed.)
1995   *African American Single Mothers: Understanding Their Lives and Families.* Newbury Park, Calif.: Sage.

Dietz, Thomas, and Burns, Tom R.
1992   "Human Agency and the Evolutionary Dynamics of Culture." *Acta Sociologica* 35:187–200.

Dill, Bonnie Thornton
1994   *Across the Boundaries of Race and Class: An Exploration of Work and Family among Black Female Domestic Servants.* New York: Garland.

Dill, Jeffrey S.
2007   "Durkheim and Dewey and the Challenge of Contemporary Moral Education." *Journal of Moral Education* 36:221–237.

DiMaggio, Paul J.
2005   "Cultural Capital." In George Ritzer (ed.), *Encyclopedia of Social Theory.* Thousand Oaks, Calif.: Sage: 167–170.

DiMaggio, Paul J., and Powell, Walter W.
1983   "The Iron Cage Revisited: Institutional Isomorphism and Collective Rationality in Organizational Fields." *American Sociological Review* 48:147–160.

Dobb, Maurice
1964   *Studies in the Development of Capitalism.* Rev. ed. New York: International Publishers.

Domhoff, G. William
2005   "Mills, C. Wright." In George Ritzer (ed.), *Encyclopedia of Social Theory.* Thousand Oaks, Calif.: Sage: 503–505.

Donougho, Martin
1989   "Postmodern Jameson." In D. Kellner (ed.), *Postmodernism, Jameson, Critique.* Washington, D.C.: Maisonneuve Press: 75–95.

Donovan, Josephine
1985   *Feminist Theory: The Intellectual Traditions of American Feminism.* New York: Ungar.

Dordoy, Alan, and Mellor, Mary
2000   "Ecosocialism and Feminism: Deep Materialism and the Contradictions of Capitalism." *Capitalism, Nature, Socialism* 11:41–61.

Dorfman, Joseph
1966   *Thorstein Veblen and His America: With New Appendices.* New York: Augustus M. Kelley.

Dosse, Francois
1998   *The History of Structuralism: The Rising Sign, 1945–1966,* Vol. 1. Minneapolis: University of Minnesota Press.

Douglas, Carol Ann
1990   *Love and Politics: Radical Feminist and Lesbian Theories.* San Francisco: Ism Press.

Douglas, Jack
1967   *The Social Meanings of Suicide.* Princeton, N.J.: Princeton University Press.
1980   "Introduction to the Sociologies of Everyday Life." In J. Douglas et al. (eds.), *Introduction to the Sociologies of Everyday Life.* Boston: Allyn and Bacon: 1–19.

Dowd, James J.
1996   "An Act Made Perfect in Habit: The Self in the Postmodern Age." *Current Perspectives in Social Theory* 16:237–263.

Dowson, Thomas A.
2002   "Why Queer Archaeology? An Introduction." *World Archaeology* 12(2):161–165.

Dreher, Jochen
2011   "Alfred Schutz." In George Ritzer and Jeffrey Stepnisky, (eds.), *The Wiley-Blackwell Companion to Major Social Theorists: Volume I—Classical Social Theorists.* Malden, Mass., and Oxford, Eng.: Wiley-Blackwell: 489–510.

Drysdale, John
1996   "How Are Social-Scientific Concepts Formed? A Reconstruction of Max Weber's Theory of Concept Formation." *Sociological Theory* 14:71–88.

DuBois, Ellen Carol
1973/1995   "The Radicalism of the Women's Suffrage Movement." In Claire Goldberg Moses and Heidi Hartmann (eds.), *U.S. Women in Struggle.* Chicago: University of Illinois Press: 42–51.

Du Bois, W.E.B.
1897/1995   "The Conservation of Races." In David Lewis Levering (ed.), *W.E.B. Du Bois: A Reader.* New York: Henry Holt: 20–27.
1899/1996   *The Philadelphia Negro: A Social Study.* Philadelphia: University of Pennsylvania Press.
1903/1996   *The Souls of Black Folk.* New York: Modern Library.
1920/1999   *Darkwater: Voices from within the Veil.* Mineola, N.Y.: Dover.
1935/1998   *Black Reconstruction in America: 1860–1880.* New York: Free Press.
1940/1968   *Dusk of Dawn: An Essay toward an Autobiography of a Race Concept.* New York: Schocken Books.
1968   *The Autobiography of W.E.B. Du Bois: A Soliloquy on Viewing My Life from the Last Decade of Its First Century.* New York: International Publishers.

Dugdale, Annie
1999   "Materiality: Juggling Sameness and Difference." In J. Law and J. Hassard (eds.), *Actor Network and After.* Oxford., Blackwell and the Sociological Review: 113–135.

Duncan, O. D., and Schnore, L. F.
1959   "Cultural, Behavioral and Ecological Perspectives in the Study of Social Organization." *American Journal of Sociology* 65:132–146.

Dunn, Robert G.
1997   "Self, Identity, and Difference: Mead and the Poststructuralists." *Sociological Quarterly* 38:687–705.

Dunning, Eric
1986   "Preface." In N. Elias and E. Dunning, *Quest for Excitement: Sport and Leisure in the Civilizing Process.* Oxford: Blackwell: 1–18.

Durkheim, Emile
1885/1978   "Review of Albert Schaeffle, *Bau und Leben des Sozialen Korpers: Erster Band.*" In Mark Traugott (ed.), *Emile Durkheim on Institutional Analysis.* Chicago: University of Chicago Press: 93–114.
1887/1993   *Ethics and the Sociology of Morals.* Buffalo: Prometheus Books.
1892/1997   *Montesquieu: Quid Secundatus Politicae Scientiae Instituendae Contulerit.* Oxford: Durkheim Press.
1893/1964   *The Division of Labor in Society.* New York: Free Press.
1895/1982   *The Rules of Sociological Method.* New York: Free Press.
1897/1951   *Suicide.* New York: Free Press.
1898/1974   "Individual and Collective Representations." In E. Durkheim, *Sociology and Philosophy.* New York: Free Press: 1–34.
1900/1973   "Sociology in France in the Nineteenth Century." In R. Bellah (ed.), *Emile Durkheim: On Morality and Society.* Chicago: University of Chicago Press: 3–32.
1906/1974   "Determination of Moral Facts." In Emile Durkheim, *Sociology and Philosophy.* New York: Free Press: 35–62.
1912/1965   *The Elementary Forms of Religious Life.* New York: Free Press.
1922/1956   *Education and Sociology.* New York: Free Press.
1925/1961   *Moral Education: A Study in the Theory and Application of the Sociology of Education.* New York: Free Press.
1928/1962   *Socialism.* New York: Collier Books.
1938/1977   *The Evolution of Educational Thought.* London: Routledge and Kegan Paul.
1979   "Durkheim's Review of Georg Simmel's *Philosophie des Geldes.*" *Social Research* 46:321–328.

Durkheim, Emile, and Mauss, Marcel
1903/1963   *Primitive Classification.* Chicago: University of Chicago Press.

Dworkin, Andrea
1989   *Letters from the War Zone: Writings 1976–1987.* New York: Dutton.

Easterly, William
2006a   "Chapter 2: Freedom versus Collectivism in Foreign Aid." *Economic Freedom of the World: 2006 Annual Report.*
2006b   *The White Man's Burden: Why the West's Efforts to Aid the Rest Have Done So Much Ill and So Little Good.* New York: Penguin.

Echols, Alice
1989   *Daring to Be Bad: Radical Feminism in America, 1967–1975.* Minneapolis: University of Minnesota Press.

Eckberg, Douglas Lee, and Hill, Lester
1979   "The Paradigm Concept and Sociology: A Critical Review." *American Sociological Review* 44:925–937.

Edel, Abraham
1959   "The Concept of Levels in Social Theory." In L. Gross (ed.), *Symposium on Sociological Theory.* Evanston, Ill.: Row Peterson: 167–195.

Eder, Klaus
1990   "The rise of counter-cultural movements against modernity: Nature as a new field of class struggle." *Theory, Culture & Society,* 7(4):21–47.

Edin, Kathryn, and Kefalas, Maria
2005   *Promises I Can Keep: Why Poor Women Put Motherhood before Marriage.* Berkeley: University of California Press.

Edin, Kathryn, and Lein, Laura
1997   *Making Ends Meet: How Single Mothers Survive Welfare and Low-Wage Work.* New York: Russell Sage Foundation.

Edwards, Jane
2007   " 'Marriage Is Sacred': The Religious Right's Arguments against 'Gay Marriage' in Australia." *Culture Health and Sexuality* 9:247–261.

Edwards, Richard
1979   *Contested Terrain: The Transformation of the Workplace in the Twentieth Century.* New York: Basic Books.

Edwards, Tim
1998   "Queer Fears: Against the Cultural Turn." *Sexualities* 1(4):471–484.

Effrat, Andrew
1972   "Power to the Paradigms: An Editorial Introduction." *Sociological Inquiry* 42:3–33.

Egeland, Catherine
2006   "Differences That Matter. Or: What Is Feminist Critique?" In E. Morensen (ed.), *Sex, Breath and Force: Sexual Difference in a Post-Feminist Era.* Oxford, Eng.: Lexington Books: 129–144.

Eglitis, Daina Stukuls
2005a   "Means of Production." In George Ritzer (ed.), *Encyclopedia of Social Theory.* Thousand Oaks, Calif.: Sage: 493–494.
2005b   "Means of Consumption." In George Ritzer (ed.), *Encyclopedia of Social Theory.* Thousand Oaks, Calif.: Sage: 491–493.
2005c   "Enchantment/Disenchantment." In George Ritzer (ed.), *Encyclopedia of Social Theory.* Thousand Oaks, Calif.: Sage: 250–251.

Ehrenreich, Barbara
2001   *Nickeled and Dimed: On Not Getting By in America.* New York: Henry Holt.

Eisen, Arnold
1978   "The Meanings and Confusions of Weberian 'Rationality.' " *British Journal of Sociology* 29:57–70.

Eisenberg, Andrew
1998   "Weberian Patrimonialism and Imperial Chinese History." *Theory and Society* 27:83–102.

Eisenberg, Anne F.
2007   "Habitus/Field." In George Ritzer (ed.), *The Blackwell Encyclopedia of Sociology.* Oxford: Blackwell: 2045–2046.

Eisenstadt, S. N., and Curelaru, M.
1976   *The Form of Sociology: Paradigms and Crises.* New York: Wiley.

Eisenstadt, S. N., and Helle, H. J. (eds.)
1985a   *Macro-Sociological Theory: Perspectives on Sociological Theory,* Vol. 1. London: Sage.
1985b   "General Introduction to Perspectives on Sociological Theory." In S. N. Eisenstadt and H. J. Helle (eds.), *Macro-Sociological Theory.* London: Sage: 1–3.

Eisenstein, Zillah
1979   *Capitalist Patriarchy and the Case for Socialist Feminism.* New York: Monthly Review Press.
1994   *The Color of Gender: Reimaging Democracy.* Berkeley: University of California Press.

Ekberg, Merryn
2007   "The Parameters of the Risk Society—A Review and Exploration." *Current Sociology* 55:343–366.

Ekeh, Peter P.
1974   *Social Exchange Theory: The Two Traditions.* Cambridge, Mass.: Harvard University Press.

Eliaeson, Sven
2000   "Constitutional Caesarism: Weber's Politics in Their German Context." In S. Turner (ed.), *The Cambridge Companion to Weber.* Cambridge, Eng.: Cambridge University Press: 131–150.

Elias, Norbert
1939/1978   *The Civilizing Process.* Part 1, *The History of Manners.* New York: Pantheon.

1939/1982	*The Civilizing Process*. Part 2, *Power and Civility*. New York: Pantheon.
1939/1994	*The Civilizing Process*. Oxford: Blackwell.
1968/1994	"Introduction to the 1968 Edition." In N. Elias, *The Civilizing Process*. Oxford: Blackwell: 181–215.
1969/1983	*The Court Society*. New York: Pantheon.
1978	*What Is Sociology?* New York: Columbia University Press.
1986	"Introduction." In N. Elias and E. Dunning, *Quest for Excitement: Sport and Leisure in the Civilizing Process*. Oxford: Blackwell: 19–62.
1993	*Mozart: Portrait of a Genius*. Berkeley: University of California Press.
1994	*Reflections on a Life*. Cambridge, Eng.: Polity Press.
1995	"Technicization and Civilization." *Theory, Culture and Society* 12:7–42.
1997	"Towards a Theory of Social Processes." *British Journal of Sociology* 48:355–383.

Elliott, Anthony
1992	*Social Theory and Psychoanalysis in Transition: Self and Society from Freud to Kristeva*. Oxford: Blackwell.
2004	*Social Theory Since Freud: Traversing Social Imaginaries*. New York: Routledge.

Elliott, Anthony, and Frosh, Stephen
1995	*Psychoanalysis in Contexts: Paths between Theory and Modern Culture*. New York: Routledge.

Elliott, David L.
2007	"Pragmatism." In George Ritzer (ed.), *The Blackwell Encyclopedia of Sociology*. Oxford: Blackwell: 3609–3612.
2012	"International Relations". In George Ritzer (ed.), *The Wiley-Blackwell Encyclopedia of Globalization*, 5 vols. Malden, Mass.: Wiley Blackwell: 1176–1184.

Elster, Jon
1982	"Marxism, Functionalism and Game Theory: The Case for Methodological Individualism." *Theory and Society* 11:453–482.
1985	*Making Sense of Marx*. Cambridge, Eng.: Cambridge University Press.
1986	"Further Thoughts on Marxism, Functionalism, and Game Theory." In J. Roemer (ed.), *Analytical Marxism*. Cambridge, Eng.: Cambridge University Press: 202–220.

Emerson, Richard M.
1962	"Power-Dependence Relations." *American Sociological Review* 27:31–40.
1972a	"Exchange Theory, Part I: A Psychological Basis for Social Exchange." In J. Berger, M. Zelditch Jr., and B. Anderson (eds.), *Sociological Theories in Progress,* Vol. 2. Boston: Houghton Mifflin: 38–57.
1972b	"Exchange Theory, Part II: Exchange Relations and Networks." In J. Berger, M. Zelditch Jr., and B. Anderson (eds.), *Sociological Theories in Progress,* Vol. 2. Boston: Houghton Mifflin: 58–87.
1981	"Social Exchange Theory." In M. Rosenberg and R. H. Turner (eds.), *Social Psychology: Sociological Perspectives*. New York: Basic Books: 30–65.

Emirbayer, Mustafa
1996	"Useful Durkheim." *Sociological Theory* 14:109–130.
1997	"Manifesto for a Relational Sociology." *American Journal of Sociology* 103:281–317.

Engels, Friedrich
1884/1970	*The Origins of the Family, Private Property and the State*. New York: International Publishers.

Engerman, Stanley
2000	"Max Weber as Economist and Economic Historian." In Stephen Turner (ed.), *The Cambridge Companion to Weber*. Cambridge, Eng.: Cambridge University Press: 256–271.

England, Paula
1992	*Comparable Worth: Theories and Evidence*. New York: Aldine de Gruyter.
2010	"The Gender Revolution: Uneven and Stalled." *Gender & Society* 24:149–166.

England, Paula, and Kilbourne, Barbara Stanek
1990	"Feminist Critiques of the Separative Model of the Self." *Rationality and Society* 2:156–171.

Erickson, Bonnie H.
1996	"Culture, Class, and Connections." *American Journal of Sociology* 102:217–251.

Eriksson, Bjorn
1993	"The First Formulation of Sociology: A Discursive Innovation of the 18th Century." *Archives of European Sociology* 34:251–276.

Esposito, Elena
1996   "From Self-Reference to Autology: How to Operationalize a Circular Approach." *Social Science Information* 35:269–281.

Etzkorn, K. Peter (ed.)
1968   *Georg Simmel: The Conflict in Modern Culture and Other Essays.* New York: Teachers College, Columbia University.

Evans, Sara
1980   *Personal Politics: The Roots of the Women's Liberation Movement in the Civil Rights Movement and the New Left.* New York: Vintage.

Faghirzadeh, Saleh
1982   *Sociology of Sociology: In Search of . . . Ibn-Khaldun's Sociology Then and Now.* Teheran: Soroush Press.

Faia, Michael A.
1986   *Dynamic Functionalism: Strategy and Tactics.* Cambridge, Eng.: Cambridge University Press.

Faist, Thomas
2005   "Social Space." In George Ritzer (ed.), *Encyclopedia of Social Theory.* Thousand Oaks, Calif.: Sage: 760–763.

Falk, William, and Zhao, Shanyang
1990a   "Paradigms, Theories and Methods in Contemporary Rural Sociology: A Partial Replication." *Rural Sociology* 54:587–600.
1990b   "Paradigms, Theories and Methods Revisited: We Respond to Our Critics." *Rural Sociology* 55:112–122.

Faludi, Susan
1991   *Backlash: The Undeclared War against American Women.* New York: Crown.

Fararo, Thomas J.
1996   "Foundational Problems in Theoretical Sociology." In Jon Clark (ed.), *James S. Coleman.* London: Falmer Press: 263–284.
2007   "Homans, George." In George Ritzer (ed.), *The Blackwell Encyclopedia of Sociology.* Oxford: Blackwell: 2144–2146.

Farganis, James
1975   "A Preface to Critical Theory." *Theory and Society* 2:483–508.

Faris, R.E.L.
1970   *Chicago Sociology: 1920–1932.* Chicago: University of Chicago Press.

Farrar, Margaret E.
2007   "Foucault, Michel." In George Ritzer (ed.), *The Blackwell Encyclopedia of Sociology.* Oxford: Blackwell: 1774–1778.

Farrell, Chad R.
1997   "Durkheim, Moral Individualism and the Dreyfus Affair." *Current Perspectives in Social Theory* 17:313–330.

Fausto-Sterling, Anne
2000   *Sexing the Body: Gender Politics and the Construction of Sexuality.* New York: Basic Books.

Feather, Howard
2000   *Intersubjectivity and Contemporary Social Theory: The Everyday as Critique.* Aldershot, Eng.: Ashgate.

Featherstone, Mike
1989   "Postmodernism, Cultural Change, and Social Practice." In D. Kellner (ed.), *Postmodernism, Jameson, Critique.* Washington, D.C.: Maisonneuve Press: 117–138.
1991   "Georg Simmel: An Introduction." *Theory, Culture and Society* 8:1–16.
2010   "Body, Image and Affect in Consumer Culture." *Body & Society*, 16, 1:193–221.

Featherstone, Mike (ed.)
1990   *Global Culture: Nationalism, Globalization and Modernity.* London: Sage.

Fechter, Anne-Meike
2010   "Gender, Empire, Global Capitalism: Colonial and Corporate Expatriate Wives." *Journal of Ethnic and Migration Studies* 36(8):1279–1297.

Feenberg, Andrew
1996   "Marcuse or Habermas: Two Critiques of Technology." *Inquiry* 39:45–70.

Fejes, Andreas
2008   "To Be One's Own Confessor: Educational Guidance and Governmentality." *British Journal of Sociology of Education* 29:635–664.

Femia, Joseph
1995   "Pareto's Concept of Demagogic Plutocracy." *Government and Opposition* 30:370–392.

Fendrich, Michael
1984   "Wives' Employment and Husbands' Distress: A Meta-Analysis and a Replication." *Journal of Marriage and the Family* 46:871–879.

Fenstermaker, Sarah, and West, Candace
2002   *Doing Gender, Doing Difference: Inequality, Power, and Institutional Change.* New York: Routledge.

Fenton, Steve
1984   *Durkheim and Modern Sociology.* Cambridge, Eng.: Cambridge University Press.

Ferguson, Harvie
2001   "Phenomenology and Social Theory." In George Ritzer and Barry Smart (eds.), *Handbook of Social Theory.* London: Sage: 232–248.

Ferree, Myra Marx
2009   "Feminist Practice Meets Feminist Theory." *Sociological Theory* 27(1):75–80.

Ferree, M. M., Khan, S. R., and Morimoto, S. A.
2007   "Assessing the Feminist Revolution: The Presence and Absence of Gender." In C. Calhoun (ed.), *Theory and Practice. Sociology in America: A History.* Chicago: University of Chicago Press: 438–479.

Ferree, Myra Marx, Lorber, Judith, and Hess, Beth (eds.)
1999   *Revisioning Gender.* Thousand Oaks, Calif.: Sage.

Ferry, Luc, and Renaut, Alain
1985/1990   *French Philosophy of the Sixties: An Essay on Antihumanism.* Amherst: University of Massachusetts Press.

Fincher, Warren
2007   "Logocentrism." In George Ritzer (ed.), *The Blackwell Encyclopedia of Sociology.* Oxford: Blackwell: 2660–2662.

Fine, Gary Alan
1990   "Symbolic Interactionism in the Post-Blumerian Age." In G. Ritzer (ed.), *Frontiers of Social Theory: The New Syntheses.* New York: Columbia University Press: 117–157.
1992   "Agency, Structure, and Comparative Contexts: Toward a Synthetic Interactionism." *Symbolic Interaction* 15:87–107.
1993   "The Sad Demise, Mysterious Disappearance, and Glorious Triumph of Symbolic Interactionism." *Annual Review of Sociology* 19:61–87.

Fine, Gary Alan, and Manning, Philip
2000   "Erving Goffman." In George Ritzer (ed.), *The Blackwell Companion to Major Social Theorists.* Malden, Mass.: Blackwell.

Fine, William F.
1979   *Progressive Evolutionism and American Sociology, 1890–1920.* Ann Arbor, Mich.: UMI Research Press.

Finlay, Barbara
2007   *Before the Second Wave: Gender in the Sociological Tradition.* Upper Saddle River, N.J.: Prentice-Hall.

Fischer, Norman
1984   "Hegelian Marxism and Ethics." *Canadian Journal of Political and Social Theory* 8:112–138.

Fisher, Sue
1995   *Nursing Wounds: Nurse Practitioners, Doctors, Women Patients and the Negotiation of Meaning.* New Brunswick, N.J.: Rutgers University Press.

Fiske, Donald W., and Shweder, Richard A. (eds.)
1986   *Metatheory in Social Science: Pluralisms and Subjectivities.* Chicago: University of Chicago Press.

Fitzpatrick, Ellen
1990   *Endless Crusade: Women Social Scientists and Progressive Reform.* New York: Oxford University Press.

Foner, Nancy
1994   *The Caregiving Dilemma: Work in an American Nursing Home.* Berkeley: University of California Press.

Fontana, Andrea
2005   "Sociologies of Everyday Life." In George Ritzer (ed.), *Encyclopedia of Social Theory.* Thousand Oaks, Calif.: Sage: 773–775.

Forcey, Linda Rennie
2001   "Feminist Perspectives on Mothering and Peace." *Journal of the Association for Research on Mothering* 3(2):155–174.

Ford, Jackie, and Harding, Nancy
2008   "Fear and Loathing in Harrogate, or a Study of a Conference." *Organization* 15(2):233–250.

Forester, Michael A., and Reason, David
2006   "Competency and Participation in Acquiring a Mastery of Language: A Reconsideration of the Idea of Membership." *Sociological Review* 54:446–466.

Foster, John Bellamy
1994   "Labor and Monopoly Capital Twenty Years After: An Introduction." *Monthly Review* 46:1–13.
2000   *Marx's Ecology: Materialism and Nature.* New York: Monthly Review Press.

Foucault, Michel
1965   *Madness and Civilization: A History of Insanity in the Age of Reason.* New York: Vintage.
1966   *The Order of Things: An Archaeology of the Human Sciences.* New York: Vintage.
1969   *The Archaeology of Knowledge and the Discourse on Language.* New York: Harper Colophon.
1975   *The Birth of the Clinic: An Archaeology of Medical Perception.* New York: Vintage.
1978   *The History of Sexuality.* Vol. 1, *An Introduction.* New York: Pantheon.
1979   *Discipline and Punish: The Birth of the Prison.* New York: Vintage.
1980a   *The History of Sexuality.* Vol. 1, *An Introduction.* New York: Vintage.
1980b   "Questions on Geography." In C. Gordon (ed.), *Power/Knowledge: Selected Interviews and Other Writings, 1972–1977.* New York: Pantheon: 63–77.
1984   *The History of Sexuality.* Vol. 3, *The Care of the Self.* New York: Pantheon.
1985   *The History of Sexuality.* Vol. 2, *The Use of Pleasure.* New York: Pantheon.
1986   "Of Other Spaces." *Diacritics* 16:22–27.
1995   "Madness, the Absence of Work." *Critical Inquiry* 21:290–298.

Fourcade-Gourinchas, Marion, and Babb, Sarah
2002   "The Rebirth of the Liberal Creed: Paths to Neoliberalism in Four Countries." *American Journal of Sociology* 108:3.

Fowler, Bridget
1997   *Pierre Bourdieu and Cultural Theory: Critical Investigations.* London: Sage.

Fox, Renee C.
1997   "Talcott Parsons, My Teacher." *American Scholar* 66:395–410.

Francis, Mark
2007   *Herbert Spencer and the Invention of Modern Life.* Ithaca, N.Y.: Cornell University Press.
2011   "Herbert Spencer." In George Ritzer and Jeffrey Stepnisky, (eds.), *The Wiley-Blackwell Companion to Major Social Theorists: Volume 1—Classical Social Theorists.* Malden, Mass., and Oxford, Eng.: Wiley-Blackwell: 165–184.

Frank, André Gunder
1966/1974   "Functionalism and Dialectics." In R. S. Denisoff, O. Callahan, and M. H. Levine (eds.), *Theories and Paradigms in Contemporary Sociology.* Itasca, Ill.: Peacock: 342–352.

Frank, R. I.
1976   Translator's introduction to Max Weber, *The Agrarian Sociology of Ancient Civilizations.* London: NLB: 7–33.

Frankenberg, Ruth
1993   *White Women, Race Matters: The Social Construction of Whiteness.* Minneapolis: University of Minnesota Press.

Frankfurt Institute for Social Research
1973   *Aspects of Sociology.* London: Heinemann.

Franklin, Adrian
2007   "Posthumanism." In George Ritzer (ed.), *The Blackwell Encyclopedia of Sociology.* Oxford: Blackwell: 3548–3550.

Franks, David D.
2007   "Mind." In George Ritzer (ed.), *The Blackwell Encyclopedia of Sociology.* Oxford: Blackwell: 3055–3057.

Franks, David D., and Gecas, Viktor
1992   "Autonomy and Conformity in Cooley's Self-Theory: The Looking-Glass Self and Beyond." *Symbolic Interaction* 15:49–68.

Fraser, Mariam, Kember, Sarah, and Lury, Celia
2005   "Inventive life." *Theory, Culture & Society* 22(1):1–14.
2006   *Inventive Life: Approaches to the New Vitalism.* London: Sage.

Fraser, Nancy
1989   *Unruly Practices: Power, Discourse and Gender in Contemporary Social Theory.* Minneapolis: University of Minnesota Press.
1992   "Rethinking the Public Sphere: A Contribution to the Critique of Actually Existing Democracy." In Craig Calhoun (ed.), *Habermas and the Public Sphere.* Cambridge, Mass.: MIT Press: 109–142.
1995   "What's Critical about Critical Theory?" In Johanna Meehan (eds.), *Feminists Read Habermas.* New York: Routledge: 21–56.
1997   *Justice Interruptus: Critical Reflections on the "Postsocialist" Condition.* New York: Routledge.

Fraser, Nancy, and Bedford, Katie
2008   "Social Rights and Gender Justice in the Neoliberal Moment: A Conversation about Welfare and Transnational Politics." *Feminist Theory* 9:225–242.

Fraser, Nancy, and Honneth, Axel
2003   *Redistribution or Recognition? A Political-Philosophical Exchange.* London: Verso.

Fraser, Nancy, and Nicholson, Linda
1988   "Social Criticism without Philosophy: An Encounter between Feminism and Postmodernism." In A. Ross (ed.), *Universal Abandon: The Politics of Postmodernism.* Minneapolis: University of Minnesota Press: 83–104.

French, Marilyn
1992   *The War against Women.* New York: Summit.

Freund, Julian
1968   *The Sociology of Max Weber.* New York: Vintage.

Friedan, Betty
1963   *The Feminine Mystique.* New York: Dell.

Friedheim, Elizabeth
1979   "An Empirical Comparison of Ritzer's Paradigms and Similar Metatheories: A Research Note." *Social Forces* 58:59–66.

Friedkin, Noah F.
2005   "Exchange Networks." In George Ritzer (ed.), *Encyclopedia of Social Theory.* Thousand Oaks, Calif.: Sage: 264–265.

Friedman, Debra, and Hechter, Michael
1988   "The Contribution of Rational Choice Theory to Macrosociological Research." *Sociological Theory* 6:201–218.

Friedman, George
1981   *The Political Philosophy of the Frankfurt School.* Ithaca, N.Y.: Cornell University Press.

Friedman, Thomas L.
2000   *The Lexus and the Olive Tree: Understanding Globalization.* New York: Anchor Books.
2005   *The World Is Flat: A Brief History of the Twenty-first Century.* New York: Farrar, Straus, Reese, and Giroux.

Friedrichs, Robert
1970   *A Sociology of Sociology.* New York: Free Press.
1972   "Dialectical Sociology: Toward a Resolution of Current 'Crises' in Western Sociology." *British Journal of Sociology* 13:263–274.

Frisby, David
1981   *Sociological Impressionism: A Reassessment of Georg Simmel's Social Theory.* London: Heinemann.
1984   *Georg Simmel.* Chichester, Eng.: Ellis Horwood.
1992   *Simmel and Since: Essays on Georg Simmel's Social Theory.* London: Routledge.

Frisby, David (ed.)
1994   *Georg Simmel: Critical Assessments.* 3 vols. London: Routledge.

Frow, John
1991   *What Was Postmodernism?* Sydney: Local Consumption Publications.

Frye, Marilyn
1983   *The Politics of Reality: Essays in Feminist Theory.* Trumansburg, N.Y.: Crossings Press.

Fuery, Patrick, and Mansfield, Nick
2000   *Cultural Studies and Critical Theory.* New York: Oxford University Press.

Fuhrman, Ellsworth R.
1980   *The Sociology of Knowledge in America: 1883–1915.* Charlottesville: University of Virginia Press.

Fujimura, Joan H., Duster, Troy, and Rajagopalan, Ramya
2008   "Introduction: Race, Genetics, and Disease: Questions of Evidence, Matters of Consequence." *Social Studies of Science* 38(5):643–656.

Fulbrook, Mary
1978   "Max Weber's 'Interpretive Sociology.'" *British Journal of Sociology* 29:71–82.

Fuller, Steve
1998   "From Content to Context: A Social Epistemology of the Structure-Agency Craze." In Alan Sica (ed.), *What Is Social Theory? The Philosophical Debates.* Oxford: Blackwell: 92–117.
2007a   "Positivism." In George Ritzer (ed.), *The Blackwell Encyclopedia of Sociology.* Oxford: Blackwell: 3544–3547.
2007b   "Nietzsche." In George Ritzer (ed.), *The Blackwell Encyclopedia of Sociology.* Oxford: Blackwell: 3213–3217.
2007c   "Actor-Network Theory, Actants." In George Ritzer (ed.), *The Blackwell Encyclopedia of Sociology.* Oxford: Blackwell: 21–23.

Furfey, Paul
1953/1965   *The Scope and Method of Sociology: A Metasociological Treatise.* New York: Cooper Square Publishers.

Gadamer, Hans Georg
1989   *Truth and Method.* 2nd rev. ed. New York: Crossroad.

Galic, Branka
2011   "Women and Work in Modern Society—the Importance of 'Gendered' Work." *Sociologija i prostor* 49(1):25–48.

Gamson, Joshua
1995   "Must Identity Movements Self-Destruct? A Queer Dilemma." *Social Problems* 42(3):390–407.

Gandy, D. Ross
1979   *Marx and History: From Primitive Society to the Communist Future.* Austin: University of Texas Press.

Gane, Mike
1988   *On Durkheim's Rules of Sociological Method.* London: Routledge.
2001   "Durkheim's Project for a Sociological Science." In George Ritzer and Barry Smart (eds.), *Handbook of Social Theory.* London: Sage: 79–88.
2003   *French Social Theory.* London: Sage.

Gane, Nicholas
1997   "Max Weber on the Ethical Irrationality of Political Leadership." *Sociology* 31:549–564.
2002   *Max Weber and Postmodern Theory: Rationalization versus Re-Enchantment.* New York: Palgrave.

Gans, Herbert J.
1972   "The Positive Functions of Poverty." *American Journal of Sociology* 78:275–289.
1994   "Positive Functions of the Undeserving Poor: Uses of the Underclass in America." *Politics and Society* 22:269–283.

Garcia, Alma M.
1989   "The Development of Chicana Feminist Discourse, 1970–1980." *Gender & Society* 3:217–238.

Garcia, Angela
1991   "Dispute Resolution without Disputing: How the Interactional Organization of Mediation Hearings Minimizes Argument." *American Sociological Review* 56:818–835.

Garcia Canclini, Nestor
1995   *Hybrid Cultures: Strategies for Entering and Leaving Modernity.* Minneapolis: University of Minneapolis Press.

Gardner, Carol Brooks
1995   *Passing By: Gender and Public Harassment.* Los Angeles: University of California Press.

Garfinkel, Harold
1963   "A Conception of, and Experiments with, 'Trust' as a Condition of Stable and Concerted Actions." In O. J. Harvey (ed.), *Motivation in Social Interaction.* New York: Ronald: 187–238.
1967   *Studies in Ethnomethodology.* Englewood Cliffs, N.J.: Prentice-Hall.
1988   "Evidence for Locally Produced, Naturally Accountable Phenomena of Order, Logic, Reason, Meaning, Method, etc., in and as of the Essential Quiddity of Immortal Ordinary Society (I of IV): An Announcement of Studies." *Sociological Theory* 6:103–109.
1991   "Respecification: Evidence for Locally Produced, Naturally Accountable Phenomena of Order, Logic, Reason, Meaning, Method, etc., in and as of the Essential Haecceity of Immortal Ordinary Society (I): An Announcement of Studies." In G. Button (ed.), *Ethnomethodology and the Human Sciences.* Cambridge, Eng.: Cambridge University Press: 10–19.
2002   *Ethnomethodology's Program: Working Out Durkheim's Aphorism.* Edited by A. Rawls. Lanham, Md.: Rowman and Littlefield.

Garland, Anne Witte
1988   *Women Activists: Challenging the Abuse of Power.* New York: Feminist Press.

Garnham, Nicholas
2007   "Culture Industries." In George Ritzer (ed.), *The Blackwell Encyclopedia of Sociology.* Oxford: Blackwell: 942–945.

Gartman, David
1998   "Postmodernism; or, the Cultural Logic of Post-Fordism?" *Sociological Quarterly* 39:119–137.

Gaziano, Emanuel
1996   "Ecological Metaphors as Scientific Boundary Work: Innovation and Authority in Interwar Sociology and Biology." *American Journal of Sociology* 101:874–907.

Gellner, David
1982   "Max Weber, Capitalism and the Religion of India." *Sociology* 16:526–543.

Genosko, Gary
2005   "Baudrillard, Jean." In George Ritzer (ed.), *Encyclopedia of Social Theory.* Thousand Oaks, Calif.: Sage: 29–35.
2007   "Guattari, Felix." In George Ritzer (ed.), *The Blackwell Encyclopedia of Sociology.* Oxford: Blackwell: 2037–2038.

Geras, Norman
1983   *Marx and Human Nature: Refutation of a Legend.* London: NLB.
1987   "Post-Marxism?" *New Left Review* 163:40–82.

Gergen, Kenneth J.
1973   "Social Psychology as History." *Journal of Personality and Social Psychology* 26:309–320.
1986   "Correspondence versus Autonomy in the Language of Understanding Human Action." In D. W. Fiske and R. A. Shweder (eds.), *Metatheory in Social Science: Pluralisms and Subjectivities.* Chicago: University of Chicago Press: 136–162.
1994a   *Toward Transformation in Social Knowledge*, 2nd ed. Thousand Oaks, CA: Sage.
1994b   *Realities and Relationships: Soundings in Social Construction.* Cambridge, Mass.: Harvard University Press.

Gerhardt, Uta
2011   *The Social Thought of Talcott Parsons: Methodology and American Ethos.* Burlington, Vt.: Ashgate.

Gerstein, Dean R.
1983   "Durkeim's Paradigm: Reconstructing a Social Theory." *Sociological Theory* 1:234–258.

Gerth, Hans, and Mills, C. Wright (eds.)
1953   *Character and Social Structure.* New York: Harcourt, Brace and World.
1958   *From Max Weber.* New York: Oxford University Press.

Gerth, Nobuko
1993   "Hans H. Gerth and C. Wright Mills: Partnership and Partisanship." *International Journal of Politics, Culture and Society* 7:133–154.

Gibbs, Jack P.
2003   "A Formal Restatement of Durkheim's 'Division of Labor' Theory." *Sociological Theory* 21(2):103–127.

Gibson, David
2000   "Seizing the Moment: The Problem of Conversational Agency." *Sociological Theory* 18:368–382.

Gibson, Diane
1996   "Broken Down by Age and Gender: 'The Problem of Old Women' Redefined." *Gender & Society* 10:433–448.

Giddens, Anthony
1972   "Introduction: Durkheim's Writings in Sociology and Social Philosophy." In A. Giddens (ed.), *Emile Durkheim: Selected Writings.* Cambridge, Eng.: Cambridge University Press: 1–50.
1975   *The Class Structure of Advanced Societies.* New York: Harper and Row.
1976   *New Rules of Sociological Method: A Positive Critique of Interpretive Sociologies.* New York: Basic Books.
1979   *Central Problems in Social Theory: Action, Structure and Contradiction in Social Analysis.* Berkeley: University of California Press.
1984   *The Constitution of Society: Outline of the Theory of Structuration.* Berkeley: University of California Press.
1989   "A Reply to My Critics." In D. Held and J. B. Thompson (eds.), *Social Theory of Modern Societies: Anthony Giddens and His Critics.* Cambridge, Eng.: Cambridge University Press: 249–301.
1990   *The Consequences of Modernity.* Stanford, Calif.: Stanford University Press.
1991   *Modernity and Self-Identity: Self and Society in the Late Modern Age.* Stanford, Calif.: Stanford University Press.
1992   *The Transformation of Intimacy: Sexuality, Love and Eroticism in Modern Societies.* Stanford, Calif.: Stanford University Press.
1994   *Beyond Left and Right: The Future of Radical Politics.* Stanford, Calif.: Stanford University Press.
1995   *Politics, Sociology and Social Theory: Encounters with Classical and Contemporary Social Thought.* Stanford, Calif.: Stanford University Press.
1998   *The Third Way: The Renewal of Social Democracy.* Cambridge, Eng.: Polity Press.
2000   *Runaway World: How Globalization Is Reshaping Our Lives.* New York: Routledge.
2009   *The Politics of Climate Change.* Cambridge, Eng.: Polity Press.

Giddings, Paula
1984   *When and Where I Enter: The Impact of Black Women on Race and Sex in America.* New York: Morrow.

Gieryn, Thomas F.
2000   "A Space for Place in Sociology." *Annual Review of Sociology* 26:463–496.

Giffney, Noreen
2004   "Denormatizing Queer Theory: More Than (Simply) Gay and Lesbian Studies." *Feminist Theory* 5(1):73–8.

Gilbert, Margaret
1994   "Durkheim and Social Facts." In W.S.F. Pickering and H. Martins (eds.), *Debating Durkheim.* London: Routledge: 86–109.

Gilligan, Carol
1982   *In a Different Voice: Psychological Theory and Women's Development.* Cambridge, Mass.: Harvard University Press.

Gilligan, Carol, and Attanuci, Jane
1988   "Two Moral Orientations: Gender Differences and Similarities." *Merrill Palmer Quarterly* 34:223–237.

R-36   References

Gilman, Charlotte Perkins
1898   *Women and Economics.* Boston: Small and Maynard.

Gilpin, Robert
2001   *Global Political Economy.* Princeton, N.J.: Princeton University Press.

Gimenez, Martha E.
2005   "Capitalism and the Oppression of Women: Marx Revisited." *Science & Society* 69(1):11–32.

Gimenez-Nadal, Jose Ignacio, and Sevilla-Sanz, Almudena
2011   "The Time-Crunch Paradox." *Social Indicators Research* 102(2):181–196.

Glatzer, Wolfgang
1998   "The German Sociological Association: Origins and Developments." Paper presented at the meetings of the International Sociological Association, Montreal, Canada.

Glenn, Evelyn Nakano
1999   "The Social Construction and Institutionalization of Gender and Race: An Integrative Framework." In Myra Marx Feree, Judith Lorber, and Beth Hess (eds.), *Revisioning Gender.* Thousand Oaks, Calif: Sage: 3–43.

Glenn, Evelyn Nakano, Chang, Grace, and Forcey, Linda Rennie (eds.)
1993   *Mothering.* New York: Routledge.

Glenn, Phillip J.
1989   "Initiating Shared Laughter in Multi-Party Conversations." *Western Journal of Speech Communications* 53:127–149.

Glennon, Lynda M.
1979   *Women and Dualism.* New York: Longman.

Go, Julian
2007a   "Colonialism (neo-colonialism)." In George Ritzer (ed.), *The Blackwell Encyclopedia of Sociology.* Oxford: Blackwell: 602–604.
2007b   "Decolonization." In George Ritzer (ed.), *The Blackwell Encyclopedia of Sociology.* Oxford: Blackwell: 984–986.

Godelier, Maurice
1972a   *Rationality and Irrationality in Economics.* London: NLB.
1972b   "Structure and Contradiction in Capital." In R. Blackburn (ed.), *Readings in Critical Social Theory.* London: Fontana: 334–368.

Goffman, Erving
1959   *Presentation of Self in Everyday Life.* Garden City, N.Y.: Anchor.
1961   *Encounters: Two Studies in the Sociology of Interaction.* Indianapolis: Bobbs-Merrill.
1963   *Stigma: Notes on the Management of Spoiled Identity.* Englewood Cliffs, N.J.: Prentice-Hall.
1967   *Interaction Ritual: Essays on Face-to-Face Behavior.* New York: Anchor Books.
1974   *Frame Analysis: An Essay on the Organization of Experience.* New York: Harper Colophon.
1979   *Gender Advertisements.* New York: Harper and Row.

Goldberg, Chad A.
2008   "Introduction to Emile Durkheim's 'Anti Semitism and Social Crisis.' " *Australian and New Zealand Journal of Criminology* 41:333–344.

Goldberg, David Theo, and Essed, Philomena
2002   "Introduction: From Racial Demarcations to Multiple Identifications." In Philomena Essed and David Theo Goldberg (eds.), *Race Critical Theories.* Malden, Mass.: Blackwell: 1–11.

Goldfield, Michael, and Gilbert, Alan
1997   "The Limits of Rational Choice Theory." *National Political Science Review* 6:205–228.

Goldman, Michael, and Schurman, Rachel A.
2000   "Closing the 'Great Divide': New Social Theory on Society and Nature." *Annual Review of Sociology* 26:563–584.

Gomart, Emilie, and Hennion, Antoine
1999   "The Sociology of Attachment: Music Amateurs, Drug Users." In John Law and John Hassard (eds.), *Actor Network Theory and After.* Oxford: Blackwell: 220–247.

Gonos, George
1977   " 'Situation' versus 'Frame': The 'Interactionist' and the 'Structuralist' Analyses of Everyday Life."
        American Sociological Review 42:854–867.
1980   "The Class Position of Goffman's Sociology: Social Origins of an American Structuralism." In
        J. Ditton (ed.), *The View from Goffman.* New York: St. Martin's: 134–169.

Goode, William J.
1960   "A Theory of Role Strain." *American Sociological Review* 25:483–496.

Goodman, Douglas J.
2005   "Ritzer, George." In George Ritzer (ed.), *Encyclopedia of Social Theory.* Thousand Oaks, Calif.:
        Sage: 650–651.

Goodwin, Charles
1979   "The Interactive Construction of a Sentence in Natural Conversation." In G. Psathas (ed.),
        Everyday Language: Studies in Ethnomethodology. New York: Irvington: 97–121.
1984   "Notes on Story Structure and the Organization of Participation." In J. M. Atkinson and J. Heritage
        (eds.), *Structures of Social Action.* Cambridge, Eng.: Cambridge University Press: 225–246.

Goodwin, Jan
1994   *Price of Honor: Muslim Women Lift the Veil of Silence on the Islamic World.* New York: Little,
        Brown.

Goonewardena, Kanishka
2011   "Henri Lefebvre." In George Ritzer and Jeffrey Stepnisky, (eds.), *The Wiley-Blackwell Companion
        to Major Social Theorists: Volume II—Contemporary Social Theorists.* Malden, Mass., and Oxford,
        Eng.: Wiley-Blackwell: 44–54.

Gordon, Linda
1994   *Pitied but Not Entitled: Single Mothers and the History of Welfare.* New York: Free Press.

Gottdiener, Mark
1994   "Semiotics and Postmodernism." In D. R. Dickens and A. Fontana (eds.), *Postmodernism and
        Social Inquiry.* New York: Guilford Press: 155–181.

Gould, Stephen Jay
1981/1996   *The Mismeasure of Man,* revised and expanded. New York: W.W. Norton.

Gouldner, Alvin
1958   "Introduction." In E. Durkheim, *Socialism and Saint-Simon.* Yellow Springs, Ohio: Antioch Press.
1959/1967   "Reciprocity and Autonomy in Functional Theory." In N. Demerath and R. Peterson (eds.), *System,
        Change and Conflict.* New York: Free Press: 141–169.
1962   "Introduction." In E. Durkheim, *Socialism.* New York: Collier Books: 7–31.
1970   *The Coming Crisis of Western Sociology.* New York: Basic Books.

Graf, Nikki L., and Schwartz, Christine R.
2011   "The Uneven Pace of Change in Heterosexual Romantic Relationships." *Gender & Society*
        25(1):101–107.

Gramsci, Antonio
1917/1977   "The Revolution against *Capital.*" In Q. Hoare (ed.), *Antonio Gramsci: Selections from Political
        Writings (1910–1920).* New York: International Publishers: 34–37.
1932/1975   *Letters from Prison: Antonio Gramsci.* Ed. Lynne Lawner. New York: Harper Colophon.
1971   *Selections from the Prison Notebooks.* New York: International Publishers.

Granovetter, Mark
1973   "The Strength of Weak Ties." *American Journal of Sociology* 78:1360–1380.
1983   "The Strength of Weak Ties: A Network Theory Revisited." In R. Collins (ed.), *Sociological
        Theory—1983.* San Francisco: Jossey-Bass: 201–233.
1985   "Economic Action and Social Structure: The Problem of Embeddedness." *American Journal of
        Sociology* 91:481–510.
2005   "Strength of Weak Ties." In George Ritzer (ed.), *Encyclopedia of Social Theory.* Thousand Oaks,
        Calif.: Sage: 801–802.

Greatbatch, David, and Dingwall, Robert
1997   "Argumentative Talk in Divorce Mediation Sessions." *American Sociological Review* 62:151–170.

Green, Adam Isaiah
2002   "Gay but Not Queer: Toward a Post-Queer Study of Sexuality." *Theory and Society* 31(4):
            521–545.

Green, Donald, and Shapiro, Ian
1994   *Pathologies of Rational Choice Theory: A Critique of Applications in Political Science.*
            New Haven: Yale University Press.

Green, Karen
1995   *The Woman of Reason: Feminism, Humanism, and Political Thought.* New York: Continuum.

Gregg, Melissa, and Seigworth, Gregory J.
2010   "An Inventory of Shimmers." In Melissa Gregg and Gregory J. Seigworth (eds.), *The Affect Theory
            Reader.* Durham, N.C.: Duke University Press: 1–28.

Gregory, Derek
1989   "Presences and Absences: Time-Space Relations and Structuration Theory." In D. Held and J. B.
            Thompson (eds.), *Social Theory of Modern Societies: Anthony Giddens and His Critics.*
            Cambridge, Eng.: Cambridge University Press: 185–214.

Gregson, Nicki, and Lowe, Michelle
1994   *Servicing the Middle Class: Class, Gender and Waged Domestic Labor.* New York: Routledge.

Greisman, Harvey C.
1986   "The Paradigm That Failed." In R. C. Monk (ed.), *Structures of Knowing.* Lanham, Md.:
            University Press of America: 273–291.

Gronow, Jukka
1997   *The Sociology of Taste.* London: Routledge.

Gross, Llewellyn
1961   "Preface to a Metatheoretical Framework for Sociology." *American Journal of Sociology* 67:
            125–136.

Grossberg, Lawrence
2010   "Affect's Future: Rediscovering the Virtual and the Actual." In Melissa Gregg and Gregory J.
            Seigworth (eds.), *The Affect Theory Reader.* Durham, N.C.: Duke University Press: 309–338.

Grossberg, Lawrence, and Nelson, Cary
1988   "Introduction: The Territory of Marxism." In C. Nelson and L. Grossberg (eds.), *Marxism and the
            Interpretation of Culture.* Urbana: University of Illinois Press: 1–13.

Guba, Egon G., and Lincoln, Yvonna S.
1994   "Competing Paradigms in Qualitative Research." In Norman K. Denzin and Yvonna S. Lincoln
            (eds.), *Handbook of Qualitative Research.* Thousand Oaks, Calif.: Sage: 105–117.

Gubbay, Jon
1997   "A Marxist Critique of Weberian Class Analyses." *Sociology* 31:73–89.

Guignon, Charles
2004   *On Being Authentic.* New York: Routledge.

Guilhot, Nicolas
2002   " 'The Transition to the Human World of Democracy': Notes for a History of the Concept of
            Transition, from Early Marxism to 1989." *European Journal of Social Theory* 5:219–243.

Guillory, John
2000   "Bourdieu's Refusal." In Nicholas Brown and Imre Szeman (eds.), *Pierre Bourdieu: Fieldwork in
            Culture.* Lanham, Md.: Rowman and Littlefield: 87–99.

Guinier, Lani, and Torres, Gerald
2002   *The Miner's Canary: Enlisting Race, Resisting Power, Transforming Democracy.* Cambridge, Mass.:
            Harvard University Press.

Gurney, Patrick J.
1981   "Historical Origins of Ideological Denial: The Case of Marx in American Sociology." *American
            Sociologist* 16:196–201.

Gurvitch, Georges
1964   *The Spectrum of Social Time.* Dordrecht, Netherlands: D. Reidel.

Haaken, Jan
2008   "When White Buffalo Calf Woman Meets Oedipus on the Road: Lakota Psychology, Feminist
                Psychoanalysis, and Male Violence." *Theory and Psychology* 18(2):195–208.

Habermas, Jurgen
1970   *Toward a Rational Society.* Boston: Beacon Press.
1971   *Knowledge and Human Interests.* Boston: Beacon Press.
1973   *Theory and Practice.* Boston: Beacon Press.
1975   *Legitimation Crisis.* Boston: Beacon Press.
1979   *Communication and the Evolution of Society.* Boston: Beacon Press.
1981   "Modernity versus Postmodernity." *New German Critique* 22:3–14.
1984   *The Theory of Communicative Action.* Vol. 1, *Reason and the Rationalization of Society.* Boston:
                Beacon Press.
1986   *Autonomy and Solidarity: Interviews.* Ed. Peter Dews. London: Verso.
1987a   *The Theory of Communicative Action.* Vol. 2, *Lifeworld and System: A Critique of Functionalist
                Reason.* Boston: Beacon Press.
1987b   *The Philosophical Discourse of Modernity: Twelve Lectures.* Cambridge, Mass.: MIT Press.
1991   "A Reply." In A. Honneth and H. Joas (eds.), *Communicative Action: Essays on Jurgen
                Habermas's* The Theory of Communicative Action. Cambridge, Eng.: Cambridge University Press:
                215–264.
1994   *The Past as Future.* Interviewed by Michael Haller. Lincoln: University of Nebraska Press.

Hacker, Helen Mayer
1951   "Women as a Minority Group." *Social Forces* 30:60–69.

Hagan, John, and Kay, Fiona
1995   *Gender in Practice: A Study of Lawyers' Lives.* New York: Oxford University Press.

Hage, Jerald
1994   "Constructing Bridges between Sociological Paradigms and Levels: Trying to Make Sociological
                Theory More Complex, Less Fragmented, and Politicized." In J. Hage (ed.), *Formal Theory in
                Sociology: Opportunity or Pitfall?* Albany: State University Press of New York: 152–168.

Haines, Valerie
1988   "Is Spencer's Theory an Evolutionary Theory? *American Journal of Sociology* 93:1200–1223.
1992   "Spencer's Philosophy of Science." *British Journal of Sociology* 43:155–172.
2005   "Spencer, Herbert." In George Ritzer (ed.), *Encyclopedia of Social Theory.* Thousand Oaks, Calif.:
                Sage: 781–787.

Hakim, Catherine
2010   "Erotic Capital." *European Sociological Review* 26(5):499–518.
2011   "Erotic Capital: The Power of Attraction in the Boardroom and the Bedroom." New York: Basic Books.

Halas, Elzbieta
2005   "Znaniecki, Florian Witold." In George Ritzer (ed.), *Encyclopedia of Social Theory.* Thousand
                Oaks, Calif.: Sage: 896–898.

Halberstam, Judith
1998   *Female Masculinity.* Durham, N.C.: Duke University Press.

Halfpenny, Peter
1982   *Positivism and Sociology: Explaining Social Life.* London: Allen and Unwin.
2001   "Positivism in the Twentieth Century." In George Ritzer and Barry Smart (eds.), *Handbook of
                Social Theory.* London: Sage: 371–385.
2005   "Positivism." In George Ritzer (ed.), *Encyclopedia of Social Theory.* Thousand Oaks, Calif.: Sage:
                571–575.

Hall, Derek
2007   "Double Movement." In Jan Aart Scholte and Roland Robertson (eds.), *Encyclopedia of
                Globalization.* New York: MTM: 338–340.

Hall, John R.
2007   "Annales School." In George Ritzer (ed.), *The Blackwell Encyclopedia of Sociology.* Oxford:
                Blackwell: 142–144.

Hall, Richard
1983   "Theoretical Trends in the Sociology of Occupations." *Sociological Quarterly* 24:5–23.

Hall, Robert T.
1987   *Emile Durkheim: Ethics and the Sociology of Morals.* New York: Greenwood Press.

Hall, Stuart
1988   "Brave New World." *Marxism Today* October:24–29.

Halliday, Fred
1990   "The Ends of the Cold War." *New Left Review* 180:5–23.

Halls, W. D.
1996   "The Cultural and Educational Influences of Durkheim, 1900–1945." *Durkheimian Studies* 2:122–132.

Halperin, David
1995   *Saint Foucault: Towards a Gay Hagiography.* New York: Oxford University Press.

Hamlin, Cynthia Lins, and Brym, Robert J.
2006   "The Return of the Native: A Cultural and Social-Psychological Critique of Durkheim's *Suicide* Based on the Guarani-Kaiowa of Southwestern Brazil." *Sociological Theory* 24(1):42–57.

Hammer, Rhonda
2002   *Antifeminism and Family Terrorism: A Critical Feminist Perspective.* Lanham, Md.: Rowman and Littlefield.

Handel, Warren
1982   *Ethnomethodology: How People Make Sense.* Englewood Cliffs, N.J.: Prentice-Hall.

Haney, Lynne
1996   "Homeboys, Babies, Men in Suits: The State and the Reproduction of Male Dominance." *American Sociological Review* 61:759–778.

Hankin, Thomas L.
1979   "In Defense of Biography: The Use of Biography in the History of Science." *History of Science* 17:1–16.

Hannerz, Ulf
1987   "The World in Creolisation." *Africa* 57:546–559.
1990   "Cosmopolitans and Locals in World Culture." In Mike Featherstone (ed.), *Global Culture: Nationalism, Globalization and Modernity.* London: Sage.

Hansen, Mark
2004   "The Time of Affect, or Bearing Witness to Life." *Critical Inquiry*, 30:584–626.

Haraway, Donna
1988   "Situated Knowledge: The Science Question in Feminism and the Privilege of Partial Perspective." *Feminist Studies* 14:575–600.
1991   *Simians, Cyborgs, and Women: The Reinvention of Nature.* New York and London: Routledge.
2008   *When Species Meet.* Minneapolis: University of Minnesota Press.

Harding, Sandra
1986   *The Science Question in Sociology.* Ithaca, N.Y.: Cornell University Press.

Hardt, Michael, and Negri, Antonio
2000   *Empire.* Cambridge, Mass.: Harvard University Press.
2004   *Multitude: War and Democracy in the Age of Empire.* New York: Penguin.

Harnois, Catherine
2012   "Race, Gender and the Black Woman's Standpoint." *Sociological Forum* 25(1):68–85.

Harper, Diane Blake, Sylvester, Joan, and Walczak, David
1980   "An Empirical Comparison of Ritzer's Paradigms and Similar Metatheories: Comment on Friedheim." *Social Forces* 59:513–517.

Harré, Rom
2002   "Social Reality and the Myth of Social Structure." *European Journal of Social Theory* 5:111–123.

Harris, David
1996   *A Society of Signs?* London: Routledge.

Harris, Kathleen Mullan
1996   "Life after Welfare: Women, Work, and Repeat Dependency." *American Sociological Review* 61:407–426.

Harris, Scott
2001   "What Can Interactionism Contribute to the Study of Inequality? The Case of Marriage and
            Beyond." *Symbolic Interaction* 25:455–480.

Hart, Randle, and MacKinnon, Andrew
2010   Sociological Epistemology: Durkheim's Paradox and Dorothy E. Smith's Actuality. *Sociology,*
            44(6):1038–1054.

Hartmann, Heidi
1979   "Capitalism, Patriarchy and Job Segregation by Sex." In Z. Eisenstein (ed.), *Capitalist Patriarchy
            and the Case for Socialist Feminism.* New York: Monthly Review Press: 206–247.
1981   "The Unhappy Marriage of Marxism and Feminism: Towards a More Progressive Union." In Lydia
            Sargent (ed.), *Women and Revolution.* Boston: South End Press.

Hartsock, Nancy
1983   *Money, Sex and Power: Towards a Feminist Historical Materialism.* New York: Longman.
1990   "Foucault on Power: A Theory for Women?" In L. Nicholson (ed.), *Feminism/Postmodernism.*
            New York: Routledge: 157–175.

Harvey, David
1969   *Explanation in Human Geography.* New York: St. Martin's.
1973   *Social Justice and the City.* Baltimore: Johns Hopkins University Press.
1989   *The Condition of Postmodernity: An Enquiry into the Origins of Cultural Change.* Oxford: Blackwell.
2000   *Spaces of Hope.* Berkeley: University of California Press.
2005   *A Brief History of NeoLiberalism.* Oxford: Oxford University Press.
2006   *Spaces of Global Capitalism: Towards a Theory of Uneven Geographical Development.* London: Verso.

Harvey, Lee
1982   "The Use and Abuse of Kuhnian Paradigms in the Sociology of Knowledge." *British Journal of
            Sociology* 16:85–101.
1987   "The Nature of 'Schools' in the Sociology of Knowledge: The Case of the 'Chicago School.'"
            Sociological Review 35:245–278.

Hawkes, Terence
1977   *Structuralism and Semiotics.* London: Methuen.

Hawthorn, Geoffrey
1976   *Enlightenment and Despair.* Cambridge, Eng.: Cambridge University Press.

Hayden, Tom
2006   *Radical Nomad: C. Wright Mills and his Times.* Boulder, CO: Paradigm Publishers.

Hayim, Gila
1980   *The Existential Sociology of Jean-Paul Sartre.* Amherst: University of Massachusetts Press.

Hays, Sharon
2003   *Flat Broke with Children.* Oxford: Oxford University Press.

Hazelrigg, Lawrence
1972   "Class, Property and Authority: Dahrendorf's Critique of Marx's Theory of Class." *Social Forces*
            50:473–487.

Hearn, Jeff
2004   "From Hegemonic Masculinity to the Hegemony of Men." *Feminist Theory* 5(1):49–72.

Heberle, Rudolph
1965   "Simmel's Methods." In L. Coser (ed.), *Georg Simmel.* Englewood Cliffs, N.J.: Prentice-Hall: 116–121.

Hechter, Michael, and Kanazawa, Satoshi
1997   "Sociological Rational Choice Theory." In John Hagan and Karen S. Cook (eds.), *Annual Review
            of Sociology,* Vol. 23. Palo Alto, Calif.: Annual Reviews: 191–214.

Heckathorn, Douglas D.
1997   "Overview: The Paradoxical Relationship between Sociology and Rational Choice." *The American
            Sociologist* 28:6–15.
2005   "Rational Choice." In George Ritzer (ed.), *Encyclopedia of Social Theory.* Thousand Oaks, Calif.:
            Sage: 620–624.

Heckathorn, Douglas D., and Broadhead, Robert S.
1996   "Rational Choice, Public Policy and AIDS." *Rationality and Society* 8:235–260.

Hedstrom, Peter, and Swedberg, Richard
1996   "Rational Choice, Empirical Research, and the Sociological Tradition." *European Sociological Review* 12:127–146.

Hegel, G.W.F.
1807/1967   *The Phenomenology of Mind.* New York: Harper Colophon.
1821/1967   *The Philosophy of Right.* Oxford: Clarendon Press.

Hegtvedt, Karen A., Thompson, Elaine A., and Cook, Karen S.
1993   "Power and Equity: What Counts in Attributions for Exchange Outcomes?" *Social Psychology Quarterly* 56:100–119.

Heilbron, Johan
1995   *The Rise of Social Theory.* London: Polity Press.

Heilbrun, Carolyn
1988   *Writing a Woman's Life.* New York: Norton.

Heins, Volker
1993   "Weber's Ethic and the Spirit of Anti-Capitalism." *Political Studies* 41:269–283.

Hekman, Susan
1983   *Weber, the Ideal Type, and Contemporary Social Theory.* Notre Dame, Ind.: University of Notre Dame Press.

Held, David, and Thompson, John B.
1989   "Editors' Introduction." In D. Held and J. B. Thompson (eds.), *Social Theory of Modern Societies: Anthony Giddens and His Critics.* Cambridge, Eng.: Cambridge University Press: 1–18.

Held, Virginia
1993   *Feminist Morality: Transforming Culture, Society and Politics.* Chicago: University of Chicago Press.

Helle, Horst Jurgen
2005   "Simmel, George." In George Ritzer (ed.), *Encyclopedia of Social Theory.* Thousand Oaks, Calif.: Sage: 698–703.

Helle, H. J., and Eisenstadt, S. N. (eds.)
1985   *Micro-Sociological Theory: Perspectives on Sociological Theory,* Vol. 2. London: Sage.

Hennessey, Rosemary, and Ingraham, Chrys
1997   "Introduction: Reclaiming Anticapitalist Feminism." In R. Hennessey and C. Ingraham (eds.), *Materialist Feminism.* New York: Routledge: 1–14.

Hennis, Wilhelm
1994   "The Meaning of 'Wertfreiheit': On the Background and Motives of Max Weber's 'Postulate.'" *Sociological Theory* 12:113–125.

Heritage, John
1984   *Garfinkel and Ethnomethodology.* Cambridge, Eng.: Polity Press.

Heritage, John, and Atkinson, J. Maxwell
1984   "Introduction." In J. M. Atkinson and J. Heritage (eds.), *Structures of Social Action.* Cambridge, Eng.: Cambridge University Press: 1–15.

Heritage, John, and Greatbatch, David
1986   "Generating Applause: A Study of Rhetoric and Response in Party Political Conferences." *American Journal of Sociology* 92:110–157.

Herrnstein, Richard, and Murray, Charles.
1994   *The Bell Curve: The Reshaping of American Life by Difference in Intelligence.* New York: Free Press.

Hershkovitz, Shay
2012   "Nation-state." In George Ritzer (ed.), *The Wiley-Blackwell Encyclopedia of Globalization*, 5 vols. Malden, Mass.: Wiley Blackwell: 1492–1496.

Herva, Soma
1988   "The Genesis of Max Weber's *Verstehende Sociologie.*" *Acta Sociologica* 31:143–156.

Hess, David J.
1997   *Science Studies: An Advanced Introduction.* New York: New York University Press.

Hesse, Mary
1995   "Habermas and the Force of Dialectical Argument." *History of European Ideas* 21:367–378.

Hewitt, John P. and Shulman, David
2011   *Self and Society: A Symbolic Interactionist Social Psychology.* 11th ed. Boston: Allyn and Bacon.

Heyl, John D., and Heyl, Barbara S.
1976   "The Sumner-Porter Controversy at Yale: Pre-Paradigmatic Sociology and Institutional Crisis." *Sociological Inquiry* 46:41–49.

Hiatt, L. R.
1996   *Arguments about Aborigines: Australia and the Evolution of Social Anthropology.* Cambridge, Eng.: Cambridge University Press.

Hilbert, Richard A.
1986   "Anomie and Moral Regulation of Reality: The Durkheimian Tradition in Modern Relief." *Sociological Theory* 4:1–19.
1990   "Ethnomethodology and the Micro-Macro Order." *American Sociological Review* 55:794–808.
1991   "Norman and Sigmund: Comment on Denzin's 'Harold and Agnes'" *Sociological Theory* 9:264–268.
1992   *The Classical Roots of Ethnomethodology: Durkheim, Weber and Garfinkel.* Chapel Hill: University of North Carolina Press.
2005   "Ethnomethodology." In George Ritzer (ed.), *Encyclopedia of Social Theory.* Thousand Oaks, Calif.: Sage: 252–257.

Hill, Greg
1997   "History, Necessity, and Rational Choice Theory." *Rationality and Society* 9:189–213.

Hill, Lisa
1996   "Anticipations of Nineteenth and Twentieth Century Social Thought in the Work of Adam Ferguson." *Archives Européenes de Sociologie* 37:203–228.

Hill, Michael R.
1989   "Empiricism and Reason in Harriet Martineau's Sociology." Introduction to M. Hill (ed.), *"How to Observe Morals and Manners"* by Harriet Martineau. Sequicentennial edition. New Brunswick, NJ: Transaction, pp. xv–lx.
2007   "Ward, Lester Frank." In George Ritzer (ed.), *The Blackwell Encyclopedia of Sociology.* Oxford: Blackwell: 5216.

Hill, Shirley A., and Sprague, Joey
1999   "Parenting in Black and White Families: The Interaction of Gender with Race and Class." *Gender & Society* 13:480–502.

Himes, Joseph
1966   "The Functions of Racial Conflict." *Social Forces* 45:1–10.

Hinkle, Roscoe
1980   *Founding Theory of American Sociology: 1881–1915.* London: Routledge and Kegan Paul.
1994   *Developments in American Sociological Theory: 1915–1950.* Albany: State University of New York Press.

Hinkle, Roscoe, and Hinkle, Gisela
1954   *The Development of American Sociology.* New York: Random House.

Hird, Myra J.
2004   "Feminist Matters: New Materialist Considerations of Sexual Difference." *Feminist Theory* 5:223–232.

Hirschmann, Nancy J., and Di Stefano, Christine (eds.)
1996   *Revisioning the Political: Feminist Reconstructions of Traditional Concepts in Western Political Theory.* Boulder, Colo.: Westview.

Hobsbawm, Eric J.
1965   *Primitive Rebels.* New York: Norton.

Hochschild, Arlie
1997   *The Time Bind: When Work Becomes Home and Home Becomes Work.* New York: Metropolitan Books.
2000   "The Nanny Chain." *The American Prospect* 11:1–4.
1983/2003   *The Managed Heart: Commercialization of Human Feeling*, 20th Anniversary Edition. Berkeley: University of California Press.
2003   *The Commercialization of Intimate Life: Notes from Home and Work.* Berkeley: University of California Press.

Hochschild, Arlie, with Machung, Anne
1989   *The Second Shift.* New York: Avon Books.

Hoecker-Drysdale, Susan
1994   *Harriet Martineau: First Woman Sociologist.* New York: Berg.
2011   "Harriet Martineau." In George Ritzer and Jeffrey Stepnisky (eds.), *The Wiley-Blackwell Companion to Major Social Theorists: Volume 1—Classical Social Theorists.* Malden, Mass., and Oxford, Eng.: Wiley-Blackwell: 61–95.

Hofstadter, Richard
1959   *Social Darwinism in American Thought.* New York: Braziller.

Hollinger, David
1980   "T. S. Kuhn's Theory of Science and Its Implications for History." In G. Gutting (ed.), *Paradigms and Revolutions.* Notre Dame, Ind.: Notre Dame University Press: 195–222.

Holmwood, John
1996   *Founding Sociology: Talcott Parsons and the Idea of General Theory.* Essex: Longman.

Holmwood, John, and Stewart, Alexander
1994   "Synthesis and Fragmentation in Social Theory: A Progressive Solution." *Sociological Theory* 12:83–100.

Holton, Robert J.
2000   "Bourdieu and Common Sense." In Nicholas Brown and Imre Szeman (eds.), *Pierre Bourdieu: Fieldwork in Culture.* Lanham, Md.: Rowman and Littlefield: 87–99.
2001   "Talcott Parsons: Conservative Apologist or Irreplaceable Icon?" In George Ritzer and Barry Smart (eds.), *Handbook of Social Theory.* London: Sage: 152–162.

Holton, Robert J., and Turner, Bryan S.
1986   *Talcott Parsons on Economy and Society.* London: Routledge and Kegan Paul.

Holub, Robert C.
1991   *Jurgen Habermas: Critic in the Public Sphere.* London: Routledge.

Homans, George C.
1950   *The Human Group.* New York: Harcourt Brace.
1961   *Social Behavior: Its Elementary Forms.* New York: Harcourt, Brace and World.
1962   *Sentiments and Activities.* New York: Free Press.
1967   *The Nature of Social Science.* New York: Harcourt, Brace and World.
1969   "The Sociological Relevance of Behaviorism." In R. Burgess and D. Bushell (eds.), *Behavioral Sociology.* New York: Columbia University Press: 1–24.
1974   *Social Behavior: Its Elementary Forms.* Rev. ed. New York: Harcourt Brace Jovanovich.
1984   *Coming to My Senses: The Autobiography of a Sociologist.* New Brunswick, N.J.: Transaction Books.

Homans, George C., and Curtis, Charles
1934   *An Introduction to Pareto, His Sociology.* New York: Knopf.

Honneth, Axel
1985/1991   *The Critique of Power: Reflective Stages in a Critical Social Theory.* Cambridge, Mass.: MIT Press.
1990/1995   *The Fragmented World of the Social.* Albany, N.Y.: State University of New York Press.
1992/1994   *The Struggle for Recognition: The Moral Grammar of Social Conflicts.* Cambridge, Eng.: Polity Press.
2000/2007   *Disrespect: The Normative Foundations of Critical Theory.* Cambridge, Eng.: Polity Press.
2008   *Reification: A New Look at an Old Idea.* Oxford, Eng.: Oxford University Press.

Hook, Sidney
1965   "Pareto's Sociological System." In J. H. Meisel (ed.), *Pareto and Mosca.* Englewood Cliffs, N.J.: Prentice-Hall: 57–61.

hooks, bell
1984   *Feminist Theory: From Margin to Center.* Boston: South End Press.
1990   *Yearning: Race, Gender, and Cultural Politics.* Boston: South End Press.

Horowitz, Irving L.
1962/1967   "Consensus, Conflict, and Cooperation." In N. Demerath and R. Peterson (eds.), *System, Change and Conflict.* New York: Free Press: 265–279.
1983   *C. Wright Mills: An American Utopian.* New York: Free Press.

Howard, Michael, and King, John E.
2005   "Political Economy." In George Ritzer (ed.), *Encyclopedia of Social Theory.* Thousand Oaks,
              Calif.: Sage: 563–568.

Hoyningen-Huene, Paul
1993   *Reconstructing Scientific Revolutions: Thomas S. Kuhn's Philosophy of Science.* Chicago:
              University of Chicago Press.

Huaco, George
1966   "The Functionalist Theory of Stratification: Two Decades of Controversy." *Inquiry* 9:215–240.
1986   "Ideology and General Theory: The Case of Sociological Functionalism." *Comparative Studies in
              Society and History* 28:34–54.

Hudelson, Richard
1993   "Has History Refuted Marxism?" *Philosophy of the Social Sciences* 23:180–198.

Hughes, John A., Martin, Peter J., and Sharrock, W. W.
1995   *Understanding Classical Sociology: Marx, Weber and Durkheim.* London: Sage.

Humphery, Kim
1998   *Shelf Life: Supermarkets and the Changing Cultures of Consumption.* Cambridge, Eng.: Cambridge
              University Press.

Hunnicutt, Gwen
2009   "Varieties of Patriarchy and Violence against Women: Resurrecting 'Patriarchy' as a Theoretical
              Tool." *Violence Against Women* 15(5):553–573.

Hunter, Allen
1988   "Post-Marxism and the New Social Movements." *Theory and Society* 17:885–900.

Hunter, J. E., Schmidt, F. L., and Jackson, G. B.
1982   *Meta-Analysis: Cumulating Research Findings across Studies.* Beverly Hills, Calif.: Sage.

Huntington, Samuel P.
1996   *The Clash of Civilizations and the Remaking of World Order.* New York: Simon and Schuster.
2004   "The Hispanic Challenge." *Foreign Policy,* March/April:30–45.

Imber, Jonathan B. (ed.)
1997   "The Place of Rational Choice in Sociology." *American Sociologist* 28:3–87.

Inbar, Michael
1996   "The Violation of Normative Rules and the Issue of Rationality in Individual Judgments." In Jon
              Clark (ed.), *James S. Coleman.* London: Falmer Press: 227–262.

Ingraham, Chrys
1999   *White Weddings: Romancing Heterosexuality in Popular Culture.* New York: Routledge.
2008   *White Weddings: Romancing Heterosexuality in Popular Culture.* New York: Routledge.

Israel, Joachim
1971   *Alienation: From Marx to Modern Sociology.* Boston: Allyn and Bacon.

Jackman, Mary R.
1994   *The Velvet Glove: Paternalism and Conflict in Gender, Class, and Race Relations.* Berkeley:
              University of California Press.

Jackson, S.
2001   "Why a Materialist Feminism Is (Still) Possible—And Necessary." *Women's Studies International
              Forum* 24:283–293.

Jacobs, Glenn
2006   *Charles Horton Cooley: Imagining Social Reality.* Amherst: University of Massachusetts Press.

Jacobs, Mark D.
2007a   "Interaction Order." In George Ritzer (ed.), *The Blackwell Encyclopedia of Sociology.* Oxford:
              Blackwell: 2365–2366.
2007b   "Dewey, John." In George Ritzer (ed.), *The Blackwell Encyclopedia of Sociology.* Oxford:
              Blackwell: 1145–1146.

Jacobsen, Martin M.
2007   "Sacks, Harvey." In George Ritzer (ed.), *The Blackwell Encyclopedia of Sociology.* Oxford:
              Blackwell: 3971.

Jaffee, David
1998   *Levels of Socio-Economic Development Theory.* Westport, Conn.: Praeger.

Jaggar, Alison M.
1983   *Feminist Politics and Human Nature.* Totowa, N.J.: Rowman and Allanheld.

Jaggar, Alison M., and Bordo, Susan (eds.)
1989   *Gender/Body/Knowledge: Feminist Reconstructions of Being and Knowing.* New Brunswick, N.J.:
                Rutgers University Press.

Jaggar, Alison M., and Rothenberg, Paula (eds.)
1984   *Feminist Frameworks.* 2nd ed. New York: McGraw-Hill.

Jagtenberg, Tom, and McKie, David
1997   *Eco-Impacts and the Greening of Postmodernity: New Maps for Communication Studies, Cultural
                Studies and Sociology.* Thousand Oaks, Calif.: Sage.

James, Stanlie M., and Busia, Abema P. A. (eds.)
1993   *Theorizing Black Feminisms.* New York: Routledge.

Jameson, Fredric
1984   "Postmodernism, or the Cultural Logic of Late Capitalism." *New Left Review* 146:53–92.
1989   "Afterword—Marxism and Postmodernism." In D. Kellner (ed.), *Postmodernism, Jameson,
                Critique.* Washington, D.C.: Maisonneuve Press: 369–387.
1991   *Postmodernism, or, The Cultural Logic of Late Capitalism.* Durham, N.C.: Duke University Press.

Janara, Laura
2011   "Alexis de Tocqueville." In George Ritzer and Jeffrey Stepnisky (eds.), *The Wiley-Blackwell
                Companion to Major Social Theorists: Volume I—Classical Social Theorists.* Malden, Mass., and
                Oxford, Eng.: Wiley-Blackwell: 96–114.

Jansen, Robert S.
2008   "Jurassic Technology? Sustaining Presumptions of Intersubjectivity in a Disruptive Environment."
                Theory and Society 37:127–159.

Jasso, Guillermina
2000   "Some of Robert K. Merton's Contributions to Justice Theory." *Sociological Theory* 18:331–339.
2001   "Formal Theory." In Jonathan H. Turner (ed.), *Handbook of Sociological Theory.* New York:
                Kluwer Academic/Plenum Publishers: 37–68.
2011   "James S. Coleman." In George Ritzer and Jeffrey Stepnisky (eds.), *The Wiley-Blackwell
                Companion to Major Social Theorists: Volume II—Contemporary Social Theorists.* Malden, Mass.,
                and Oxford, Eng.: Wiley-Blackwell: 219–239.

Jaworski, Gary Dean
1991   "The Historical and Contemporary Importance of Coser's Functions." *Sociological Theory*
                9:116–123.
1995   "Simmel in Early American Sociology: Translation as Social Action." *International Journal of
                Politics, Culture and Society* 8:389–417.
1997   *Georg Simmel and the American Prospect.* Albany: State University of New York Press.

Jay, Martin
1973   *The Dialectical Imagination.* Boston: Little, Brown.
1984   *Marxism and Totality: The Adventures of a Concept from Lukács to Habermas.* Berkeley:
                University of California Press.
1988   *Fin-de-Siècle Socialism and Other Essays.* New York: Routledge.
2010   "Liquidity Crisis: Zygmunt Bauman and the Incredible Lightness of Modernity." *Theory, Culture
                & Society,* 27(6):95–106.

Jedlowski, Paolo
1990   "Simmel on Memory." In M. Kaern, B. S. Phillips, and R. S. Cohen (eds.), *Georg Simmel and
                Contemporary Sociology.* Dordrecht, Netherlands: Kluwer: 131–154.

Jefferson, Gail
1979   "A Technique for Inviting Laughter and Its Subsequent Acceptance Declination." In G. Psathas
                (ed.), *Everyday Language: Studies in Ethnomethodology.* New York: Irvington: 79–96.
1984   "On the Organization of Laughter in Talk about Troubles." In J. M. Atkinson and J. Heritage
                (eds.), *Structures of Social Action.* Cambridge, Eng.: Cambridge University Press: 346–369.

Jeffries, Vincent
2005   "Sorokin, Pitirim." In George Ritzer (ed.), *Encyclopedia of Social Theory.* Thousand Oaks, Calif.:
              Sage: 777–778.

Jencks, Charles
1977   *The Language of Post-Modern Architecture.* New York: Rizzoli.

Jenkins, Richard
1992   *Pierre Bourdieu.* London: Routledge.
2005a   "Bourdieu, Pierre." In George Ritzer (ed.), *Encyclopedia of Social Theory.* Thousand Oaks, Calif.:
              Sage: 66–71.
2005b   "Habitus." In George Ritzer (ed.), *Encyclopedia of Social Theory.* Thousand Oaks, Calif.: Sage:
              352–353.

Jensen, Mette, and Blok, Anders
2008   "Pesticides in the Risk Society: The View from Everyday Life." *Current Sociology* 56:757–778.

Joas, Hans
1981   "George Herbert Mead and the 'Division of Labor': Macrosociological Implications of Mead's
              Social Psychology." *Symbolic Interaction* 4:177–190.
1985   *G. H. Mead: A Contemporary Re-examination of His Thought.* Cambridge, Mass.: MIT Press.
1993   *Pragmatism and Social Theory.* Chicago: University of Chicago Press.
1996   *The Creativity of Action.* Chicago: University of Chicago Press.
1998   "Bauman in Germany: Modern Violence and the Problems of German Self-Understanding."
              Theory, Culture and Society 15:47–55.
2001   "The Emergence of the New: Mead's Theory and Its Contemporary Potential." In George Ritzer
              and Barry Smart (eds.), *Handbook of Social Theory.* London: Sage: 89–99.

Johnson, Alan
1997   *The Gender Knot.* Philadelphia: Temple Press.

Johnson, Chalmers
1966   *Revolutionary Change.* Boston: Little, Brown.

Johnson, Miriam
1989   "Feminism and the Theories of Talcott Parsons." In R. A. Wallace (ed.), *Feminism and
              Sociological Theory.* Newbury Park, Calif.: Sage: 101–118.

Johnston, Barry V.
1995   *Pitirim Sorokin: An Intellectual Biography.* Lawrence: University of Kansas Press.
2007   "Merton, Robert K." In George Ritzer (ed.), *The Blackwell Encyclopedia of Sociology.* Oxford:
              Blackwell: 2958–2961.

Jones, Greta
1980   *Social Darwinism and English Thought: The Interaction between Biological and Social Theory.*
              Atlantic Highlands, N.J.: Humanities Press.

Jones, Harold B.
1997   "The Protestant Ethic: Weber's Model and the Empirical Literature." *Human Relations* 50:757–778.

Jones, Mark Peter
1996   "Posthuman Agency: Between Theoretical Traditions." *Sociological Theory* 14:290–309.

Jones, Robert Alun
1994   "The Positive Science of Ethics in France: German Influences in *De la Division du Travail
              Social.*" *Sociological Forum* 9:37–57.
2000   "Emile Durkheim." In George Ritzer (ed.), *The Blackwell Companion to Major Social Theorists.*
              Malden, Mass.: Blackwell: 205–250.

Jones, Susan Stedman
1996   "What Does Durkheim Mean by 'Thing'?" *Durkheimian Studies* 2:43–59.

Jordan, June
1992   *Technical Difficulties: African-American Notes on the State of the Union.* New York: Pantheon.

Kaern, Michael, Phillips, Bernard S., and Cohen, Robert S. (eds.)
1990   *Georg Simmel and Contemporary Sociology.* Dordrecht, Netherlands: Kluwer.

Kalberg, Stephen
1980   "Max Weber's Types of Rationality: Cornerstones for the Analysis of Rationalization Processes in History." *American Journal of Sociology* 85:1145–1179.
1985   "The Role of Ideal Interests in Max Weber's Comparative Historical Sociology." In R. J. Antonio and R. M. Glassman (eds.), *A Weber-Marx Dialogue.* Lawrence: University Press of Kansas: 46–67.
1990   "The Rationalization of Action in Max Weber's Sociology of Religion." *Sociological Theory* 8:58–84.
1994   *Max Weber's Comparative-Historical Sociology.* Chicago: University of Chicago Press.
1996   "On the Neglect of Weber's Protestant Ethic as a Theoretical Treatise: Demarcating the Parameters of Postwar American Sociological Theory." *Sociological Theory* 14:49–70.
1997   "Max Weber's Sociology: Research Strategies and Modes of Analysis." In Charles Camic (ed.), *Reclaiming the Sociological Classics: The State of Scholarship.* Oxford: Blackwell: 208–241.
2001   "Should the 'Dynamic Autonomy' of Ideas Matter to Sociologists? Max Weber on the Origin of Other-Worldly Salvation Religions and the Constitution of Groups in American Society Today." *Journal of Classical Sociology* 1:291–327.
2011   "Max Weber." In George Ritzer and Jeffrey Stepnisky (eds.), *The Wiley-Blackwell Companion to Major Social Theorists: Volume 1—Classical Social Theorists.* Malden, Mass., and Oxford, Eng.: Wiley-Blackwell: 305–372.

Kaldor, Mary
1990   "After the Cold War." *New Left Review* 180:25–40.

Kalekin-Fishman, Devorah
2008   " 'False Consciousness': How 'Ideology' Emerges from the Encounter of Body Practices and Hegemonic Ideas." *Current Sociology* 56:535–553.

Kall, Lisa Folkmarson
2006   "Sexual Difference as Nomadic Strategy." *NORA* 14:3:195–206.
2008   "Sexual Difference as Nomadic Strategy." *NORA—Nordic Journal of Feminist and Gender Research* 14(3):195–206.

Kaminsky, Amy
1994   "Gender, Race, Raza." *Feminist Studies* 20:7–31.

Kamolnick, Paul
2001   "Simmel's Legacy for Contemporary Value Theory: A Critical Assessment." *Sociological Theory* 19:65–85.

Kan, Man Yee, Sullivan, Oriel, and Gershuny, Jonathan
2011   "Gender Convergence in Domestic Work: Discerning the Effects of Interactional and Institutional Barriers from Large-scale Data." *Sociology* 45(2):234–251.

Kanigel, Robert
1997   *The One Best Way: Frederick Winslow Taylor and the Enigma of Efficiency.* New York: Viking.

Karady, Victor
1983   "The Durkheimians in Academe: A Reconsideration." In P. Besnard (ed.), *The Sociological Domain.* Cambridge, Eng.: Cambridge University Press.

Kasler, Dirk
1985   "Jewishness as a Central Formation-Milieu of Early German Sociology." *History of Sociology: An International Review* 6:69–86.

Kasperson, Lars Bo, and Gabriel, Norman
2008   "The Importance of Survival Units for Norbert Elias's Figurational Perspective." *Sociological Review* 56:370–387.

Kaye, Howard L.
1991   "A False Convergence: Freud and the Hobbesian Problem of Order." *Sociological Theory* 9:87–105.
2003   "Was Freud a Medical Scientist or a Social Theorist? The Mysterious 'Development of the Hero.'" *Sociological Theory* 21:375–397.

Keller, Evelyn Fox
1985   *Reflections on Gender and Science.* New Haven: Yale University Press.

Kellner, Douglas
1989b   "Introduction: Jameson, Marxism, and Postmodernism." In D. Kellner (ed.), *Postmodernism,*
             Jameson, Critique. Washington, D.C.: Maisonneuve Press: 1–42.
1990   *Television and the Crisis of Democracy.* Boulder, Colo.: Westview.
1993   "Critical Theory Today: Revisiting the Classics." *Theory, Culture and Society* 10:43–60.
1995   "Marxism, the Information Superhighway, and the Struggle for the Future." *Humanity and Society*
             19:41–56.
2002   "Theorizing Globalization." *Sociological Theory* 20:285–305.
2005a   "Cultural Marxism and British Cultural Studies." In George Ritzer (ed.), *Encyclopedia of Social*
             Theory. Thousand Oaks, Calif.: Sage: 171–177.
2005b   "Jameson, Frederic." In George Ritzer (ed.), *Encyclopedia of Social Theory.* Thousand Oaks,
             Calif.: Sage: 421–422.
2005c   "Frankfurt School." In George Ritzer (ed.), *Encyclopedia of Social Theory.* Thousand Oaks, Calif.:
             Sage: 290–293.
2011   "Jean Baudrillard." In George Ritzer and Jeffrey Stepnisky (eds.), *The Wiley-Blackwell Companion*
             to Major Social Theorists: Volume II—Contemporary Social Theorists. Malden, Mass., and Oxford,
             Eng.: Wiley-Blackwell: 310–338.

Kellner, Douglas (ed.)
1989a   *Postmodernism, Jameson, Critique.* Washington, D.C.: Maisonneuve Press.
1989b   *Jean Baudrillard: From Marxism to Postmodernism and Beyond.* Cambridge, Eng.: Polity Press.

Kellner, Douglas, and Lewis, Tyson
2007   "Cultural Critique." In George Ritzer (ed.), *The Blackwell Encyclopedia of Sociology.* Oxford:
             Blackwell: 896–898.

Kelly, Erin L., Ammons, Samantha K., Chermack, Kelly, and Moen, Phyllis
2010   "Gendered Challenge, Gendered Response: Confronting the Ideal Worker Norm in a White-Collar
             Organization." *Gender & Society* 24(3):281–303.

Kemeny, Jim
1976   "Perspectives on the Micro-Macro Distinction." *Sociological Review* 24:731–752.

Kemper, Theodore D. (ed.)
1990   *Research Agendas in the Sociology of Emotions.* Albany: State University of New York Press.

Ken, Ivy
2008   "Beyond the Intersection: A New Culinary Metaphor for Race-Class-Gender Studies." *Sociological*
             Theory 26:152–172.

Kennedy, Randall
2002   *Nigger: The Strange Career of a Troublesome Word.* New York: Vintage Books.

Keohane, Robert O., and Nye, Joseph S.
1989   *Power and Interdependence.* Boston: Little, Brown.
2000   *Power and Independence.* 3rd ed. New York: Addison-Wesley.

Kettler, David, and Meja, Volker
1995   *Karl Mannheim and the Crisis of Liberalism.* New Brunswick, N.J.: Transaction Publishers.

Khanna, Ranjana
2010   "Unbelonging: In Motion." *Differences* 21(1):109–123.

Kiely, Ray
1998   "Globalization, Post-Fordism and the Contemporary Context of Development." *International*
             Sociology 13:95–115.

Kilminster, Richard
1993   "Norbert Elias and Karl Mannheim: Closeness and Distance." *Theory, Culture and Society* 10:81–114.

Kilminster, Richard, and Mennell, Stephen
2011   "Norbert Elias." In George Ritzer and Jeffrey Stepnisky (eds.), *The Wiley-Blackwell Companion to*
             Major Social Theorists: Volume II—Contemporary Social Theorists. Malden, Mass., and Oxford,
             Eng.: Wiley-Blackwell: 13–43.

Kimmel, Michael
1996   *Manhood in America: A Cultural History.* New York: Free Press.

2002   "'Gender Symmetry' in Domestic Violence: A Substantive and Methodological Research Review." *Violence against Women* 8:1332–1363.

Kimmel, Michael S., and Messner, Michael A. (eds.)
1992   *Men's Lives.* New York: Macmillan.

Kirk, Gwyn
1997   "Standing on Solid Ground: A Materialist Ecological Feminism." In Rosemary Hennessy and Chrys Ingraham (eds.), *Materialist Feminism.* London: Routledge: 345–363.

Kirk, Gwyn, and Okazawa-Rey, Margo (eds.)
1998   *Women's Lives: Multicultural Perspectives.* Mountain View, Calif.: Mayfield.

Kirkpatrick, Graeme
1994   "Philosophical Foundations of Analytical Marxism." *Science and Society* 58:34–52.

Kirsch, Max H.
2000   *Queer Theory and Social Change.* London: Routledge.

Klagge, Jay
1997   "Approaches to the Iron Cage: Reconstructing the Bars of Weber's Metaphor." *Administration and Society* 29:63–77.

Klasnic, Ksenija
2011   "Economic Violence Against Women in Intimate Relationships In Croatian Society—A Conceptual." *Socijalna Ekologija* 20(3):335–355.

Kleiner, Marcus S.
2005   "German Idealism." In George Ritzer (ed.), *Encyclopedia of Social Theory.* Thousand Oaks, Calif.: Sage: 316–321.

Knorr-Cetina, Karin D.
1981   "Introduction: The Micro-Sociological Challenge of Macro-Sociology: Towards a Reconstruction of Social Theory and Methodology." In K. Knorr-Cetina and A. Cicourel (eds.), *Advances in Social Theory and Methodology.* New York: Methuen: 1–47.
2001   "Postsocial Relations: Theorizing Sociality in a Postsocial Environment." In George Ritzer and Barry Smart (eds.), *Handbook of Social Theory.* London: Sage: 520–537.
2005   "Postsocial." In George Ritzer (ed.), *Encyclopedia of Social Theory.* Thousand Oaks, Calif.: Sage: 585–590.
2007   "Postsocial." In George Ritzer (ed.), *The Blackwell Encyclopedia of Sociology.* Oxford: Blackwell: 3578–3580.
2009   "The Synthetic Situation: Interactionism for a Global World." *Symbolic Interaction* 32(1):61–87.

Kohn, Melvin L.
1976   "Occupational Structure and Alienation." *American Journal of Sociology* 82:111–127.

Kolb, William L.
1944   "A Critical Evaluation of Mead's 'I' and 'Me' Concepts." *Social Forces* 22:291–296.

Kollock, Peter
1994   "The Emergence of Exchange Structures: An Experimental Study of Uncertainty, Commitment, and Trust." *American Journal of Sociology* 100:313–345.

Komarovsky, Mirra
1946   "Cultural Contradictions in Sex Roles." *American Journal of Sociology* 52:184–189.

Korllos, Thomas S.
1994   "Uncovering Simmel's Forms and Social Types." *International Social Science Review* 69:17–22.

Koscianska, Agnieszka
2009   "The 'Power of Silence': Spirituality and Women's Agency beyond the Catholic Church in Poland." *European Journal of Anthropology* 53:56–71.

Kosciw, Joseph G.
2004   *The 2003 National School Climate Survey: The School-Related Experiences of Our Nation's Lesbian, Gay, Bisexual, and Transgender Youth.* New York: GLSEN.

Krais, Beate
1993   "Gender and Symbolic Violence: Female Oppression in the Light of Pierre Bourdieu's Theory of Social Practice." In C. Calhoun, E. LiPuma, and M. Postone (eds.), *Bourdieu: Critical Perspectives.* Chicago: University of Chicago Press: 156–177.

Kripke, Saul A.
1982   *Wittgenstein on Rules and Private Language: An Elementary Exposition.* Cambridge, Mass.:
              Harvard University Press.

Kuhn, Annette, and Wolpe, Ann Marie (eds.)
1978   *Feminism and Materialism: Women and Modes of Production.* London: Routledge.

Kuhn, Manford
1964   "Major Trends in Symbolic Interaction Theory in the Past Twenty-five Years." *Sociological
              Quarterly* 5:61–84.

Kuhn, Thomas
1962   *The Structure of Scientific Revolutions.* Chicago: University of Chicago Press.
1970   *The Structure of Scientific Revolutions.* 2nd ed. Chicago: University of Chicago Press.

Kumar, Krishan
1995   *From Post-Industrial to Post-Modern Society: New Theories of the Contemporary World.* Oxford,
              Eng.: Blackwell.

Kurasawa, Fuyuki
2005   "Lefebvre, Henri." In George Ritzer (ed.), *Encyclopedia of Social Theory.* Thousand Oaks, Calif.:
              Sage: 438–440.

Kurzweil, Edith
1980   *The Age of Structuralism: Lévi-Strauss to Foucault.* New York: Columbia University Press.
1995   *Freudians and Feminists.* Boulder, Colo.: Westview.

LaCapra, Dominick
2007   "Approaching Limit Events: Siting Agamben." In Matthew Calarco and Steven DeCaroli (eds.),
              Sovereignty and Life. Stanford, Calif.: Stanford University Press: 126–162.

Lachman, L. M.
1971   *The Legacy of Max Weber.* Berkeley, Calif.: Glendessary Press.

Laclau, Ernesto
1990   "Coming Up for Air." *Marxism Today,* March:25, 27.
2007   "Bare Life or Social Indeterminacy?" In Matthew Calarco and Steven DeCaroli (eds.), *Sovereignty
              and Life.* Stanford, Calif.: Stanford University Press: 11–22.

Laclau, Ernesto, and Mouffe, Chantal
1985   *Hegemony and Socialist Strategy: Towards a Radical Democratic Politics.* London: Verso.
1987   "Post-Marxism without Apologies." *New Left Review* 166:79–106.

Lamont, Michelle
2000   *The Dignity of Working Men: Morality and the Boundaries of Race, Class and Immigration.* New
              York: Russell Sage.

Landreau, John C.
2011   "Queer Intersubjectivity: Doing and Undoing Masculinity in Women's Studies." *Men and
              Masculinities* 14(2):155–172.

Landry, Lorraine Y.
2000   *Marx and the Postmodernism Debates: An Agenda for Critical Theory.* Westport, Conn.: Praeger.

Langford, Wendy
1999   *Revolutions of the Heart: Gender, Power, and the Delusions of Love.* London: Routledge.

Langman, Lauren
2007   "Critical Theory/Frankfurt School." In George Ritzer (ed.), *The Blackwell Encyclopedia of
              Sociology.* Oxford: Blackwell: 873–877.

Langsdorf, Lenore
1995   "Treating Method and Form as Phenomena: An Appreciation of Garfinkel's Phenomenology of
              Social Action." *Human Studies* 18:177–188.

Lareau, Annette
2003   *Unequal Childhoods: Race, Class and Family Life.* Berkeley: University of California Press.

Larrain, Jorge
1979   *The Concept of Ideology.* London: Hutchinson.

Lash, Scott
1991   "Introduction." In *Post-Structuralist and Post-Modernist Sociology.* Aldershot, Eng.: Edward Elgar: ix–xv.

Lash, Scott, and Lury, Celia
2007   *Global Culture Industry.* Cambridge, Eng.: Polity Press.

Lash, Scott, and Urry, John
1987   *The End of Organized Capitalism.* Cambridge, Eng.: Polity Press.

Latour, Bruno
1993   *We Have Never Been Modern.* New York: Harvester Wheatsheaf.
1999   "On Recalling ANT." In John Law and John Hassard (eds.), *Actor Network Theory and After.*
                Oxford: Blackwell: 15–25.
2007   *Reassembling the Social: An Introduction to Actor Network Theory.* Oxford: Oxford University
                Press.

Latour, Bruno, and Woolgar, Steve
1986   *Laboratory Life: The Construction of Social Facts.* Princeton, N.J.: Princeton University Press.

Latshaw, Beth A.
2011   "The More Things Change, the More They Remain the Same? Paradoxes of Men's Unpaid Labor
                Since 'The Second Shift.'" *Sociology Compass* 5, 7(Jul 2011):653–665.

Law, Ian
2007   "Discrimination." In George Ritzer (ed.), *The Blackwell Encyclopedia of Sociology.* Oxford:
                Blackwell: 1182–1184.

Law, John
1999   "After ANT: Complexity, Naming and Topology." In John Law and John Hassard (eds.), *Actor
                Network Theory and After.* Oxford: Blackwell: 1–14.

Law, John, and Hetherington, Kevin
2002   "Materialities, Spatialities, Globalities." In Michael J. Dear and Steven Flusty (eds.), *The Spaces of
                Postmodernity: Readings in Human Geography.* Oxford: Blackwell: 390–401.

Layder, Derek
1985   "Power, Structure and Agency." *Journal for the Theory of Social Behaviour* 15:131–149.

Layder, Derek, Ashton, David, and Sung, Johnny
1991   "The Empirical Correlates of Action and Structure: The Transition from School to Work."
                Sociology 25:447–464.

Lechte, John
2005   "Structuralist Marxism." In George Ritzer (ed.), *Encyclopedia of Social Theory.* Thousand Oaks,
                Calif.: Sage: 805–811.

Lechner, Frank
2012   "World Culture." In George Ritzer (ed.), *The Wiley-Blackwell Encyclopedia of Globalization,*
                5 vols. Malden, Mass.: Wiley-Blackwell: 2279–2285.

Leck, Ralph Matthew
2000   *Georg Simmel and Avant-Garde Sociology: The Birth of Modernity, 1880–1920.* Amherst, N.Y.:
                Humanity Books.

Lee, Nick
2008   "Awake, Asleep, Adult, Child: An A-humanist Account of Persons." *Body & Society* 14:57–74.

Lefebvre, Henri
1962/1995   *Introduction to Modernity.* London: Verso.
1968   *The Sociology of Marx.* New York: Vintage.
1974/1991   *The Production of Space.* Oxford: Blackwell.

Leggewie, Claus
2005   "Herrschaft (Rule)." In George Ritzer (ed.), *Encyclopedia of Social Theory.* Thousand Oaks, Calif.:
                Sage: 364–369.

Lehmann, Jennifer M.
1993a   *Deconstructing Durkheim: A Post-Post-Structuralist Critique.* London: Routledge.
1993b   *Durkheim and Women: The Problematic Relationship.* Lincoln: University of Nebraska Press.

Leik, Robert K.
1992   "New Directions for Network Exchange Theory: Strategic Manipulation of Network Linkages."
                Social Networks 14:309–323.

Lemert, Charles
1990   "The Uses of French Structuralisms in Sociology." In George Ritzer (ed.), *Frontiers of Social
                Theory: The New Syntheses.* New York: Columbia University Press: 230–254.
1994a   "The Canonical Limits of Durkheim's First Classic." *Sociological Forum* 9:87–92.
1994b   "Social Theory at the Early End of a Short Century." *Sociological Theory* 12:140–152.
2000   "W.E.B. Du Bois." In George Ritzer (ed.), *The Blackwell Companion to Major Social Theorists.*
                Malden, Mass.: 345–366.
2001   "Multiculturalism." In George Ritzer and Barry Smart (eds.), *Handbook of Social Theory.* London:
                Sage: 297–307.
2005a   "Foucault, Michel." In George Ritzer (ed.), *Encyclopedia of Social Theory.* Thousand Oaks, Calif.:
                Sage: 284–289.
2005b   "Discourse." In George Ritzer (ed.), *Encyclopedia of Social Theory.* Thousand Oaks, Calif.: Sage:
                203–205.
2005c   "Genealogy." In George Ritzer (ed.), *Encyclopedia of Social Theory.* Thousand Oaks, Calif.: Sage:
                307–309.
2005d   "Governmentality." In George Ritzer (ed.), *Encyclopedia of Social Theory.* Thousand Oaks, Calif.:
                Sage: 342–343.
2005e   "Du Bois, William Edward Burghardt (W.E.B.)" In George Ritzer (ed.), *Encyclopedia of Social
                Theory.* Thousand Oaks, Calif.: Sage: 213–218.

Lengermann, Patricia Madoo
1979   "The Founding of the American Sociological Review." *American Sociological Review* 44:185–198.

Lengermann, Patricia Madoo, and Niebrugge-Brantley, Jill
1995   "Intersubjectivity and Domination: A Feminist Analysis of the Sociology of Alfred Schutz."
                Sociological Theory 13:25–36.
1998   *The Women Founders: Sociology and Social Theory, 1830–1930.* New York: McGraw-Hill.

Lengermann, Patricia Madoo, and Niebrugge, Gillian
2013   *Charlotte Perkins Gilman: Essays in Classical Sociology.* London: Ashgate Publishers.

Lenin, Vladimir Ilich
1972   *Collected Works.* Moscow: Progress Publishers.

Lenzer, Gertrud (ed.)
1975   *Auguste Comte and Positivism: The Essential Writings.* Magnolia, Mass.: Peter Smith.

Leonard, Thomas
2009   "Origins of the Myth of Social Darwinism: The Ambiguous Legacy of Richard Hofstader's 'Social
                Darwinism in American Thought.'" *Journal of Economic Behavior and Organization* 71:37–51.

Lepenies, Wolf
1988   *Between Literature and Science: The Rise of Sociology.* Cambridge, Eng.: Cambridge University Press.

Lerner, Gerda
1986   *The Creation of Patriarchy.* New York: Oxford University Press.
1993   *The Creation of Feminist Consciousness.* New York: Oxford University Press.

Lester, David (ed.)
1994   *Emile Durkheim: Le Suicide One Hundred Years Later.* Philadelphia: Charles Press.

Levi, Margaret, Cook, Karen S., O'Brien, Jodi A., and Faye, Howard
1990   "The Limits of Rationality." In K. S. Cook and M. Levi (eds.), *The Limits of Rationality.* Chicago:
                University of Chicago Press.

Levidow, Les
1990   "Foreclosing the Future." *Science as Culture* 8:59–90.

Levine, Andrew, Sober, Elliot, and Wright, Erik Olin
1987   "Marxism and Methodological Individualism." *New Left Review* 162:67–84.

Levine, Donald
1971   "Introduction." In D. Levine (ed.), *Georg Simmel: Individuality and Social Forms.* Chicago:
                University of Chicago Press: ix–xiv.

1981a	"Rationality and Freedom: Weber and Beyond." *Sociological Inquiry* 51:5–25.
1981b	"Sociology's Quest for the Classics: The Case of Simmel." In B. Rhea (ed.), *The Future of the Sociological Classics*. London: George Allen and Unwin: 60–80.
1985	"Ambivalent Encounters: Disavowals of Simmel by Durkheim, Weber, Lukács, Park and Parsons." In D. Levine (ed.), *The Flight from Ambiguity: Essays in Social and Cultural Theory*. Chicago: University of Chicago Press: 89–141.
1989	"Simmel as a Resource for Sociological Metatheory." *Sociological Theory* 7:161–174.
1991a	"Simmel and Parsons Reconsidered." *American Journal of Sociology* 96:1097–1116.
1991b	"Simmel as Educator: On Individuality and Modern Culture." *Theory, Culture and Society* 8:99–118.
1995	*Visions of the Sociological Tradition*. Chicago: University of Chicago Press.
1997	"Simmel Reappraised: Old Images, New Scholarship." In Charles Camic (ed.), *Reclaiming the Sociological Classics: The State of Scholarship*. Oxford: Blackwell: 173–207.
2000	"On the Critique of 'Utilitarian' Theories of Action: Newly Identified Convergences among Simmel, Weber and Parsons." *Theory, Culture and Society* 17:63–78.

Levine, Donald, Carter, Ellwood B., and Gorman, Eleanor Miller
1976a	"Simmel's Influence on American Sociology—I." *American Journal of Sociology* 81:813–845.
1976b	"Simmel's Influence on American Sociology—II." *American Journal of Sociology* 81:1112–1132.

Lévi-Strauss, Claude
1967	*Structural Anthropology*. Garden City, N.Y.: Anchor.

Lewis, David Levering
1993	*W.E.B. Du Bois: Biography of a Race, 1869–1919*. New York: Holt.
2000	*W.E.B. Du Bois: The Fight for Equality and the American Century, 1919–1963*. New York: Holt.

Lewis, Helen
1971	*Shame and Guilt in Neurosis*. New York: International University Press.

Lewis, J. David, and Smith, Richard L.
1980	*American Sociology and Pragmatism: Mead, Chicago Sociology, and Symbolic Interaction*. Chicago: University of Chicago Press.

Lewis, Reba Rowe
1991	"Forging New Syntheses: Theories and Theorists." *American Sociologist* Fall/Winter:221–230.

Li, Rebecca S. K.
2005	"Collins, Randall." In George Ritzer (ed.), *Encyclopedia of Social Theory*. Thousand Oaks, Calif.: Sage: 123–123.

Lichtblau, Klaus, and Ritter, Mark
1991	"Causality or Interaction? Simmel, Weber and Interpretive Sociology." *Theory, Culture and Society* 8:33–62.

Lidz, Victor
2007	"Parsons, Talcott." In George Ritzer (ed.), *The Blackwell Encyclopedia of Sociology*. Oxford: Blackwell: 3365–3368.

Lidz, Victor (ed.)
2011a	*Talcott Parsons*. Surrey, UK: Ashgate.
2011b	"Talcott Parsons." In George Ritzer and Jeffrey Stepnisky (eds.), *The Wiley-Blackwell Companion to Major Social Theorists: Volume 1—Classical Social Theorists*. Malden, Mass., and Oxford, Eng.: Wiley-Blackwell: 511–558.

Lilla, Mark
1994	"The Legitimacy of the Liberal Age." In M. Lilla (ed.), *New French Thought: Political Philosophy*. Princeton, N.J.: Princeton University Press: 3–34.

Lindbekk, Tore
1992	"The Weberian Ideal-Type: Development and Continuities." *Acta Sociologica* 35:285–297.

Lindemann, Marilee
2000	"Who's Afraid of the Big Bad Witch? Queer Studies in American Literature." *American Literary History* 12(4):757–770.

Lindenberg, Siegwart
2000	"James Coleman." In George Ritzer (ed.), *The Blackwell Companion to Major Social Theorists*. Malden, Mass.: Blackwell: 513–544.

2001   "Social Rationality versus Rational Egoism." In Jonathan H. Turner (ed.), *Handbook of Sociological Theory.* New York: Kluwer Academic/Plenum Publishers: 635–668.
2005   "Coleman, James." In George Ritzer (ed.), *Encyclopedia of Social Theory.* Thousand Oaks, Calif.: Sage: 111–115.

Lindner, Rolf
1996   *The Reportage of Urban Culture: Robert Park and the Chicago School.* Cambridge, Eng.: Cambridge University Press.

Linstead, Stephen
2006   "Ethnomethodology and Sociology: An Introduction." *Sociological Review* 54:399–404.
2007   "Postmodern Organizations." In George Ritzer (ed.), *The Blackwell Encyclopedia of Sociology.* Oxford: Blackwell: 3563–3568.

Lipovetsky, Gilles
1987/1994   *The Empire of Fashion: Dressing Modern Democracy.* Princeton, N.J.: Princeton University Press.

Lipscomb, Michael
2007   "Derrida, Jacques." In George Ritzer (ed.), *The Blackwell Encyclopedia of Sociology.* Oxford: Blackwell: 1062–1064.

Lipset, Seymour Martin, Trow, Martin, and Coleman, James S.
1956   *Union Democracy: The Internal Politics of the International Typographical Union.* New York: Free Press.

Liska, Allen E.
1990   "The Significance of Aggregate Dependent Variables and Contextual Independent Variables for Linking Macro and Micro Theories." *Social Psychology Quarterly* 53:292–301.

Lloyd, Moya
2011   "Judith Butler." In George Ritzer and Jeffrey Stepnisky, (eds.), *The Wiley-Blackwell Companion to Major Social Theorists: Volume II - Contemporary Social Theorists.* Malden, Mass., and Oxford, Eng.: Wiley-Blackwell: 541–560.

Loader, Colin
2011   "Karl Mannheim." In George Ritzer and Jeffrey Stepnisky (eds.), *The Wiley-Blackwell Companion to Major Social Theorists: Volume I—Classical Social Theorists.* Malden, Mass., and Oxford, Eng.: Wiley-Blackwell: 469–488.

Loader, Colin, and Alexander, Jeffrey C.
1985   "Max Weber on Churches and Sects in North America: An Alternative Path toward Rationalization." *Sociological Theory* 3:1–6.

Lockwood, David
1956   "Some Remarks on the Social System." *British Journal of Sociology* 7:134–146.

Lodahl, Janice B., and Gordon, Gerald
1972   "The Structure of Scientific Fields and the Functioning of University Graduate Departments." *American Sociological Review* 37:57–72.

Lodge, Peter
1986   "Connections: W. I. Thomas, European Social Thought and American Sociology." In R. C. Monk (ed.), *Structures of Knowing.* Lanham, Md.: University Press of America: 135–160.

Lofland, Lyn H.
1985   "The Social Shaping of Emotion: The Case of Grief." *Symbolic Interaction* 8(2):171–190.

Lohmann, Georg, and Wilkes, Geoff
1996   "The Adaptation of Inner Life to the Inner Infinity of the Metropolis: Forms of Individualization in Simmel." *Thesis Eleven* 44:1–11.

Lopata, Helena Znaniecka
1996   *Current Widowhood: Myths and Realities.* Thousand Oaks, Calif.: Sage.

Lorber, Judith
1994   *Paradoxes of Gender.* New Haven: Yale University Press.
2000   "Using Gender to Undo Gender: A Feminist Degendering Movement." *Feminist Theory* 1:79–95.
2001   "It's the 21st Century—Do You Know What Gender You Are?" *Advances in Gender Research* 5:119–137.

Lorde, Audre
1984   *Sister Outsider: Essays and Speeches.* Trumansburg, N.Y.: Crossings Press.

Lovaglia, Michael J.
2007   "Social Exchange Theory." In George Ritzer (ed.), *The Blackwell Encyclopedia of Sociology*.
              Oxford: Blackwell: 4408–4410.

Love, John
2000   "Max Weber's Orient." In Stephen Turner (ed.), *The Cambridge Companion to Weber*. Cambridge,
              Eng.: Cambridge University Press: 172–199.

Lovell, David W.
1992   "Socialism, Utopianism and the 'Utopian Socialists.'" *History of European Ideas* 14:185–201.

Low, Jacqueline
2008   "Structure, Agency, and Social Reality in Blumerian Symbolic Interactionism: The Influence of
              Georg Simmel." *Symbolic Interaction* 31:325–343.

Lowy, Michael
1996   "Figures of Weberian Marxism." *Theory and Society* 25:431–446.

Luhmann, Niklas
1977   "Differentiation of Society." *Canadian Journal of Sociology*, 2(1):29–53.
1982   *The Differentiation of Society*. New York: Columbia University Press.
1984/1995   *Soziale Systeme. Grundreiner allgemeinen Theorie/Social Systems: Outline of a General Theory*.
              Frankfurt am Main: Suhrkamp/Stanford, Calif.: Stanford University Press.
1986/1989   *Okologische Kommunikation. Kann die moderne Gesellschaft sich auf okologische Gefahrdungen
              einstellen?/Ecological Communication*. Opladen: Westdeutscher Verlag/Cambridge, Eng.: Polity Press.
1987   "Modern Systems Theory and the Theory of Society." In V. Meja, D. Misgeld, and N. Stehr (eds.),
              Modern German Sociology. New York: Columbia University Press: 173–186.
1988   *Die Wirtschaft der Gesellschaft*. Frankfurt am Main: Suhrkamp.
1990   *Die Wissenschaft der Gesellschaft*. Frankfurt am Main: Suhrkamp.
1991   *Soziologie des Risikos*. Berlin: de Gruyter.
1993   *Das Recht der Gesellschaft*. Frankfurt am Main: Suhrkamp.
1997/2012   *Theory of Society*, Vol. 1. Trans. Rhodes Barrett. Palo Alto, Calif.: Stanford University Press.

Lukács, Georg
1922/1968   *History and Class Consciousness*. Cambridge, Mass.: MIT Press.
1991   "Georg Simmel." *Theory, Culture and Society* 8:145–150.

Lukes, Steven
1972   *Emile Durkheim: His Life and Work*. New York: Harper and Row.
1977   "Power and Structure." In S. Lukes, *Essays in Social Theory*. London: Macmillan: 3–29.

Lynch, Michael
1985   *Art and Artifact in Laboratory Science: A Study of Shop Work and Shop Talk in a Research
              Laboratory*. London: Routledge and Kegan Paul.
1991   "Pictures of Nothing? Visual Construals in Social Theory." *Sociological Theory* 9:1–21.
1993   *Scientific Practice and Ordinary Action: Ethnomethodology and Social Studies of Science*.
              Cambridge, Eng.: Cambridge University Press.
1999   "Silence in Context: Ethnomethodology and Social Theory." *Human Studies* 22:211–233.
2005   "Social Studies of Science." In George Ritzer (ed.), *Encyclopedia of Social Theory*. Thousand
              Oaks, Calif.: Sage: 764–768.

Lynch, Michael, and Bogen, David
1991   "In Defense of Dada-Driven Analysis." *Sociological Theory* 9:269–276.

Lynch, Michael, and Sharrock, Wes (eds.)
2003   *Harold Garfinkel: 4 volumes*. Thousand Oaks, Calif.: Sage.

Lyon, David
2007   "Surveillance." In George Ritzer (ed.), *The Blackwell Encyclopedia of Sociology*. Oxford:
              Blackwell: 4895–4898.

Lyotard, Jean-François
1984   *The Postmodern Condition*. Minneapolis: University of Minnesota Press.

Mackay, Robert W.
1974   "Words, Utterances and Activities." In R. Turner (ed.), *Ethnomethodology: Selected Readings*.
              Harmondsworth, Eng.: Penguin: 197–215.

MacKinnon, Catherine
1979   *Sexual Harassment of Working Women.* New Haven: Yale University Press.
1989   *Towards a Feminist Theory of the State.* Cambridge, Mass.: Harvard University Press.
1993   *Only Words.* Cambridge, Mass.: Harvard University Press.

MacKinnon, Malcolm H.
2001   "Max Weber's Disenchantment: Lineages of Kant and Channing." *Journal of Classical Sociology*
              1:329–351.

MacPherson, C. B.
1962   *The Political Theory of Possessive Individualism.* Oxford: Clarendon Press.

MacRae, Donald G.
1974   *Max Weber.* Harmondsworth, Eng.: Penguin.

Macy, Michael W., and Van de Rijt, Arnout
2007   "Game Theory." In George Ritzer (ed.), *The Blackwell Encyclopedia of Sociology.* Oxford:
              Blackwell: 1822–1825.

Mahoney, Maureen A., and Yngvesson, Barbara
1992   "The Construction of Subjectivity and the Paradox of Resistance: Reintegrating Feminist
              Anthropology and Psychology." *Signs* 18:44–73.

Maines, David R.
1977   "Social Organization and Social Structure in Symbolic Interactionist Thought." In A. Inkeles,
              J. Coleman, and N. Smelser (eds.), *Annual Review of Sociology,* Vol. 3. Palo Alto, Calif.: Annual
              Reviews: 259–285.
1988   "Myth, Text, and Interactionist Complicity in the Neglect of Blumer's Macrosociology." *Symbolic
              Interaction* 11:43–57.
1989a   "Repackaging Blumer: The Myth of Herbert Blumer's Astructural Bias." *Symbolic Interaction*
              10:383–413.
1989b   "Herbert Blumer on the Possibility of Science in the Practice of Sociology: Further Thoughts."
              Journal of Contemporary Ethnography 18:160–177.
2001   *The Faultline of Consciousness: A View of Interactionism in Sociology.* New York: Aldine de Gruyter.
2005   "Blumer, Herbert." In George Ritzer (ed.), *Encyclopedia of Social Theory.* Thousand Oaks, Calif.:
              Sage: 58–62.

Maines, David, Bridger, Jeffrey C., and Ulmer, Jeffery T.
1996   "Mythic Facts and Park's Pragmatism: On Predecessor-Selection and Theorizing in Human
              Ecology." *Sociological Quarterly* 37:521–549.

Maines, David R., and Morrione, Thomas J.
1990   "On the Breadth and Relevance of Blumer's Perspective: Introduction to His Analysis of
              Industrialization." In H. Blumer, *Industrialization as an Agent of Social Change: A Critical
              Analysis.* New York: Aldine de Gruyter.

Maldonado, L. A.
1995   "Symposium: On West and Fenstermaker's 'Doing Difference.'" *Gender & Society* 9:494–496.

Mancini, Mathew
1994   *Alexis de Tocqueville.* New York: Twayne.

Mandel, Ernest
1975   *Late Capitalism.* London: New Left Books.

Mandelbaum, Jenny
1989   "Interpersonal Activities in Conversational Storytelling." *Western Journal of Speech
              Communications* 53:114–126.

Mandes, Evans
2007   "Behaviorism." In George Ritzer (ed.), *The Blackwell Encyclopedia of Sociology.* Oxford:
              Blackwell: 256–258.

Manent, Pierre
1994/1998   *The City of Man.* Princeton, N.J.: Princeton University Press.

Manis, Jerome, and Meltzer, Bernard (eds.)
1978   *Symbolic Interaction: A Reader in Social Psychology.* 3rd ed. Boston: Allyn and Bacon.

R-58   References

Mann, Michael
2007   "Has Globalization Ended the Rise and Rise of the Nation-State?" *Review of International Political Economy* 4(3):472–496.

Mann, Susan A., Grimes, Michael D., and Kemp, Alice Abel
1997   "Paradigm Shifts in Family Sociology? Evidence from Three Decades of Family Textbooks." *Journal of Family Issues* 18:315–349.

Mannheim, Karl
1931/1936   "The Sociology of Knowledge." In K. Mannheim, *Ideology and Utopia*. New York: Harcourt, Brace and World: 264–311.

Manning, Philip
1991   "Drama as Life: The Significance of Goffman's Changing Use of the Theatrical Metaphor." *Sociological Theory* 9:70–86.
1992   *Erving Goffman and Modern Sociology*. Stanford, Calif.: Stanford University Press.
2005a   "Dramaturgy." In George Ritzer (ed.), *Encyclopedia of Social Theory*. Thousand Oaks, Calif.: Sage: 210–213.
2005b   "Goffman, Erving." In George Ritzer (ed.), *Encyclopedia of Social Theory*. Thousand Oaks, Calif.: Sage: 333–339.
2005c   "Impression Management." In George Ritzer (ed.), *Encyclopedia of Social Theory*. Thousand Oaks, Calif.: Sage: 397–399.
2007   "Dramaturgy." In George Ritzer (ed.), *The Blackwell Encyclopedia of Sociology*. Oxford: Blackwell: 1226–1229.

Manning, Philip, and Ray, George
1993   "Shyness, Self-Confidence, and Social Interaction." *Social Psychology Quarterly* 56:178–192.

Manning, Robert
2000   *Credit Card Nation*. New York: Basic Books.

Manuel, Frank
1962   *The Prophets of Paris*. Cambridge, Mass.: Harvard University Press.
1992   "A Requiem for Karl Marx." *Daedalus* 121:1–19.

Marcus, Judith (ed.)
1999   *Surviving the Twentieth Century: Social Philosophy from the Frankfurt School to the Columbia Faculty Seminars*. New Brunswick, N.J.: Transaction Publishers.

Marcuse, Herbert
1958   *Soviet Marxism: A Critical Analysis*. New York: Columbia University Press.
1964   *One-Dimensional Man*. Boston: Beacon Press.
1969   *An Essay on Liberation*. Boston: Beacon Press.
1971   "Industrialization and Capitalism." In O. Stammer (ed.), *Max Weber and Sociology Today*. New York: Harper and Row.

Mardorossian, C. M.
2002   "Toward a New Feminist Theory of Rape." *Signs* 27(3):743–775.

Margolis, Eric
2007   "Sartre, Jean-Paul." In George Ritzer (ed.), *The Blackwell Encyclopedia of Sociology*. Oxford: Blackwell: 4009–4010.

Markovsky, Barry
2005   "Network Exchange Theory." In George Ritzer (ed.), *Encyclopedia of Social Theory*. Thousand Oaks, Calif.: Sage: 530–534.
2007   "Theory and Methods." In George Ritzer (ed.), *The Blackwell Encyclopedia of Sociology*. Oxford: Blackwell: 4993–4995.

Markovsky, Barry, Willer, David, and Patton, Travis
1988   "Power Relations in Exchange Networks." *American Sociological Review* 53:220–236.

Markus, Gyorgy
2005   "Lukács, Gyorgy." In George Ritzer (ed.), *Encyclopedia of Social Theory*. Thousand Oaks, Calif.: Sage: 458–460.

Marling, William H.
2006   *How American Is Globalization?* Baltimore: Johns Hopkins University Press.

Marsden, Peter V.
2007   "Coleman, James." In George Ritzer (ed.), *The Blackwell Encyclopedia of Sociology.* Oxford: Blackwell: 569–575.

Martin, Donald D., and Wilson, Janelle L.
2005   "Role Theory." In George Ritzer (ed.), *Encyclopedia of Social Theory.* Thousand Oaks, Calif.: Sage: 651–655.

Martin, K., Vieraitis, L. M., and Britto, S.
2006   "Gender Equality and Women's Absolute Status: A Test of the Feminist Models of Rape." *Violence against Women* 12(4):321–339.

Martin, Michael
2000   *Verstehen: The Uses of Understanding in Social Science.* New Brunswick, N.J.: Transaction Publishers.

Martin, Patricia Yancy
2004   "Gender as a Social Institution." *Social Forces* 82 (June):1249–1273.

Marx, Gary T.
2005   "Surveillance and Society." In George Ritzer (ed.), *Encyclopedia of Social Theory.* Thousand Oaks, Calif.: Sage: 816–821.

Marx, Karl
1842/1977   "Communism and the *Augsburger Allegemeine Zeitung.*" In D. McLellan (ed.), *Karl Marx: Selected Writings.* New York: Oxford University Press: 20.
1843/1970   "A Contribution to the Critique of Hegel's Philosophy of Right." In *Marx/Engels Collected Works,* Vol. 3. New York: International Publishers: 3–129.
1847/1963   *The Poverty of Philosophy.* New York: International Publishers.
1850/1964   *The Class Struggles in France, 1848–1850.* New York: International Publishers.
1852/1970   "The Eighteenth Brumaire of Louis Bonaparte." In R. C. Tucker (ed.), *The Marx-Engels Reader.* New York: Norton: 436–525.
1857–1858/ *Pre-Capitalist Economic Formations.* Ed. Eric J. Hobsbawm. New York:
1964   International Publishers.
1857–1858/ *The Grundrisse: Foundations of the Critique of Political Economy.* New York:
1974   Random House.
1859/1970   *A Contribution to the Critique of Political Economy.* New York: International Publishers.
1862–1863/ *Theories of Surplus Value,* Part I. Moscow: Progress Publishers.
1963
1862–1863/ *Theories of Surplus Value,* Part II. Moscow: Progress Publishers.
1968
1867/1967   *Capital: A Critique of Political Economy,* Vol. 1. New York: International Publishers.
1869/1963   *The 18th Brumaire of Louis Bonaparte.* New York: International Publishers.
1884/1891   *Capital,* Vol. 2. New York: Vintage Books.
1932/1964   *The Economic and Philosophic Manuscripts of 1844.* Ed. Dirk J. Struik. New York: International Publishers.

Marx, Karl, and Engels, Friedrich
1845/1956   *The Holy Family.* Moscow: Foreign Language Publishing House.
1845–1846/ *The German Ideology,* Part 1. Ed. C. J. Arthur. New York: International
1970   Publishers.
1848/1948   *Manifesto of the Communist Party.* New York: International Publishers.

Maryanski, Alexandra
2005   "Evolutionary Theory." In George Ritzer (ed.), *Encyclopedia of Social Theory.* Thousand Oaks, Calif.: Sage: 257–263.

Maryanski, Alexandra, and Turner, Jonathan H.
1992   *The Social Cage: Human Nature and the Evolution of Society.* Stanford, Calif.: Stanford University Press.

Massumi, Brian
2002   *Parables for the Virtual: Movement, Affect, Sensation.* Durham, N.C.: Duke University Press.
2010   "The Future Birth of the Affective Fact: The Political Ontology of Threat." In Melissa Gregg and Gregory J. Seigworth (eds.), *The Affect Theory Reader.* Durham, N.C.: Duke University Press: 52–70.

Masterman, Margaret
1970   "The Nature of a Paradigm." In I. Lakatos and A. Musgrove (eds.), *Criticism and the Growth of Knowledge*. Cambridge, Eng.: Cambridge University Press: 59–89.

Matsuda, Marie, et al.
2003   *Words That Wound: Critical Race Theory, Assaultive Speech, and the First Amendment*. Boulder, Colo.: Westview.

Matthews, Fred H.
1977   *Quest for an American Sociology: Robert E. Park and the Chicago School*. Montreal: McGill University Press.

Maturana, Humberto, and Varela, Francisco
1980   *Autopoeisis and Cognition*. Dordrecht: Reidel.

Mayall, Margery
2007   "Attached to Their Style: Traders, Technical Analysis and Postsocial Relationships." *Journal of Sociology* 43:421–437.

Mayer, Tom
1994   *Analytical Marxism*. Thousand Oaks, Calif.: Sage.

Mayhew, Bruce
1980   "Structuralism versus Individualism: Part I, Shadowboxing in the Dark." *Social Forces* 59:335–375.

Maynard, Douglas W.
1991   "Goffman, Garfinkel and Games." *Sociological Theory* 9:277–279.
2011   "Harold Garfinkel (1917–2011): A Sociologist for the Ages." *Symbolic Interaction* 35(1):88–96.

Maynard, Douglas W., and Clayman, Steven E.
1991   "The Diversity of Ethnomethodology." *Annual Review of Sociology* 17:385–418.

Maynard, Douglas W., and Kardash, Teddy
2007   "Ethnomethodology." In George Ritzer (ed.), *The Blackwell Encyclopedia of Sociology*. Oxford: Blackwell: 1483–1486.

Mazlish, Bruce
1984   The Meaning of Karl Marx. Oxford, UK: Oxford University Press.

McBride, William
2000   "Habermas and the Marxian Tradition." In Lewis Hahn (ed.), *Perspectives on Habermas*. Chicago: Open Court.

McCann, Stewart J. H.
1997   "Threatening Times and the Election of Charismatic U.S. Presidents: With and without FDR." *Journal of Psychology* 131:393–400.

McCarthy, E. Doyle
1996   *Knowledge as Culture: The New Sociology of Knowledge*. New York: Routledge.
2007   "Knowledge, Sociology of." In George Ritzer (ed.), *The Blackwell Encyclopedia of Sociology*. Oxford: Blackwell: 2482–2485.

McCarthy, Thomas
1982   *The Critical Theory of Jurgen Habermas*. Cambridge, Mass.: MIT Press.
2005   "Thomas, William Isaac." In George Ritzer (ed.), *Encyclopedia of Social Theory*. Thousand Oaks, Calif.: Sage: 834–835.

McCaughey, Martha
1997   *Real Knockouts: The Physical Feminism of Women's Self-Defense*. New York: New York University Press.
2008   *The Caveman Mystique: Pop-Darwinism and the Debates over Sex, Violence, and Science*. New York: Routledge.

McCormick, Charles
2007   "Poststructuralism." In George Ritzer (ed.), *The Blackwell Encyclopedia of Sociology*. Oxford: Blackwell: 3580–3584.

McCormick, Ken
2011   "Thorstein Veblen." In George Ritzer and Jeffrey Stepnisky (eds.), *The Wiley-Blackwell Companion to Major Social Theorists: Volume I—Classical Social Theorists*. Malden, Mass., and Oxford, Eng.: Wiley-Blackwell: 185–204.

McCraw, Thomas K.
2007   *Prophet of Innovation: Joseph Schumpeter and Creative Destruction.* Cambridge, Mass.: Belknap
              Press of Harvard University Press.

McDowell, Linda
2008   "The New Economy: Class Condescension and Caring Labour: Changing Formations of Class and
              Gender." *NORA—Nordic Journal of Feminist and Gender Research* 16(3):150–165.

McFalls, Laurence H.
2007   *Max Weber's 'Objectivity' Reconsidered.* Toronto: University of Toronto Press.

McGregor, Gaile
1995   "Gender Advertisements Then and Now: Symbolic Interactionism and the Problem of History."
              Studies in Symbolic Interactionism 27:17–42.

McGuigan, Jim
2002   *Cultural Populism.* London: Routledge.
2005   "Cultural Studies and the New Populism." In George Ritzer (ed.), *Encyclopedia of Social Theory.*
              Thousand Oaks, Calif.: Sage: 177–181.

McKinney, John C.
1966   *Constructive Typology and Social Theory.* New York: Appleton-Century-Crofts.

McLaughlin, Neil
2007   "Fromm, Erich." In George Ritzer (ed.), *The Blackwell Encyclopedia of Sociology.* Oxford:
              Blackwell: 1804–1808.

McLaughlin, Peter
2001   *What Functions Explain: Functional Explanation and Self-Reproducing Systems.* Cambridge, Eng.:
              Cambridge University Press.

McLean, Paul D.
1998   "A Frame Analysis of Favor Seeking in the Renaissance: Agency, Networks, and Political Culture."
              American Journal of Sociology 104:51–91.

McLellan, David
1973   *Karl Marx: His Life and Thought.* New York: Harper Colophon.

McLennan, Gregor
2001   "Maintaining Marx." In George Ritzer and Barry Smart (eds.), *Handbook of Social Theory.*
              London: Sage: 43–53.

McMurty, John
1978   *The Structure of Marx's World-View.* Princeton, N.J.: Princeton University Press.

McVeigh, Rory, and Sikkink, David
2005   "Organized Racism and the Stranger." *Sociological Forum* 20:497–522.

Mead, George Herbert
1934/1962   *Mind, Self and Society: From the Standpoint of a Social Behaviorist.* Chicago: University of
              Chicago Press.
1936   *Movements of Thought in the Nineteenth Century.* Chicago: University of Chicago Press.
1938/1972   *The Philosophy of the Act.* Chicago: University of Chicago Press.
1959   *The Philosophy of the Present.* LaSalle, Ill.: Open Court.
1982   *The Individual and the Social Self: Unpublished Work of George Herbert Mead.* Chicago:
              University of Chicago Press.

Meeker, Barbara
1971   "Decisions and Exchange." *American Sociological Review* 36:485–495.

Meeks, Chet
2007   "Queer Theory." In George Ritzer (ed.), *The Blackwell Encyclopedia of Sociology.* Oxford:
              Blackwell: 3728–3780.

Mehan, Hugh, and Wood, Houston
1975   *The Reality of Ethnomethodology.* New York: Wiley.

Meiksins, Peter
1994   "Labor and Monopoly Capital for the 1990s: A Review and Critique of the Labor Process Debate."
              Monthly Review 46:45–59.

Meisenhelder, Tom
1991   "Toward a Marxist Analysis of Subjectivity." *Nature, Society, and Thought* 4:103–125.
1997   "Pierre Bourdieu and the Call for a Reflexive Sociology." *Current Perspectives in Social Theory* 17:159–183.

Meltzer, Bernard
1964/1978   "Mead's Social Psychology." In J. Manis and B. Meltzer (eds.), *Symbolic Interaction: A Reader in Social Psychology*. 3rd ed. Boston: Allyn and Bacon: 15–27.

Meltzer, Bernard, Petras, James, and Reynolds, Larry
1975   *Symbolic Interactionism: Genesis, Varieties and Criticisms*. London: Routledge and Kegan Paul.

Menard, Scott
1995   "A Developmental Test of Mertonian Anomie Theory." *Journal of Research in Crime and Delinquency* 32:136–174.

Mennell, Stephen
1992   *Norbert Elias: An Introduction*. Oxford: Blackwell.
2005a   "Figurational Sociology." In George Ritzer (ed.), *Encyclopedia of Social Theory*. Thousand Oaks, Calif.: Sage: 279–280.
2005b   "Civilizing Processes." In George Ritzer (ed.), *Encyclopedia of Social Theory*. Thousand Oaks, Calif.: Sage: 105–107.

Mennell, Stephen, and Goudsblom, Johan (eds.)
1998   *Norbert Elias: On Civilization, Power, and Knowledge*. Chicago: University of Chicago Press.

Merton, Robert K.
1949/1968   "Manifest and Latent Functions." In R. K. Merton, *Social Theory and Social Structure*. New York: Free Press: 73–138.
1968   *Social Theory and Social Structure*. New York: Free Press.
1975   "Structural Analysis in Sociology." In P. Blau (ed.), *Approaches to the Study of Social Structure*. New York: Free Press: 21–52.
1980   "Remembering the Young Talcott Parsons." *American Sociologist* 15:68–71.
1995   "Opportunity Structure: The Emergence, Diffusion, and Differentiation of a Sociological Concept, 1930s–1950s." In F. Adler and W. S. Laufer (eds.), *The Legacy of Anomie Theory*. New Brunswick, N.J.: Transaction Publishers.

Messerchmidt, James
2009   "'Doing Gender': The Impact and Future of a Salient Sociological Concept." *Gender & Society* 23(1):85–88.

Messner, Michael A.
1997   *Politics of Masculinities: Men in Movements*. Thousand Oaks, Calif.: Sage.

Mestrovic, Stjepan G.
1988   *Emile Durkheim and the Reformation of Sociology*. Totowa, N.J.: Rowman and Littlefield.
1998   *Anthony Giddens: The Last Modernist*. London: Routledge.

Mészáros, István
1970   *Marx's Theory of Alienation*. New York: Harper Torchbooks.
1995   *Beyond Capital*. New York: Monthly Review Press.

Meyer, John, Boli, J., Thomas, G., and Ramirez, F.
1997   "World Society and the Nation State." *American Journal of Sociology* 103:144–181.

Milbrandt, Tara, and Pearce, Frank
2011   "Emile Durkheim." In George Ritzer and Jeffrey Stepnisky (eds.), *The Wiley-Blackwell Companion to Major Social Theorists: Volume I—Classical Social Theorists*. Malden, Mass., and Oxford, Eng.: Wiley-Blackwell: 236–282.

Milkie, Melissa A., Raley, Sara B., and Bianchi, Suzanne M.
2009   "Taking on the Second Shift: Time Allocations and Time Pressures of U.S. Parents with Preschoolers." *Social Forces* 88(2):487–518.

Miller, Dan E.
2011   "Toward Theory of Interaction: The Iowa School." *Symbolic Interaction* 34(3):340–348.

Miller, David
1973   *George Herbert Mead: Self, Language and the World.* Austin: University of Texas Press.
1981   "The Meaning of Role-Taking." *Symbolic Interaction* 4:167–175.
1982a   "Introduction." In G. H. Mead, *The Individual and the Social Self: Unpublished Work of George Herbert Mead.* Chicago: University of Chicago Press: 1–26.
1982b   Review of J. David Lewis and Richard L. Smith, *American Sociology and Pragmatism. Journal of the History of Sociology* 4:108–114.
1985   "Concerning J. David Lewis' Response to My Review of American Sociology and Pragmatism." *Journal of the History of Sociology* 5:131–133.

Miller, James
1993   *The Passion of Michel Foucault.* New York: Anchor Books.

Miller, Richard
1991   "Social and Political Theory: Class, State, Revolution." In Terrell Carver (ed.), *The Cambridge Companion to Marx.* Cambridge, Eng.: Cambridge University Press: 55–105.

Miller, W. Watts
1993   "Durkheim's Montesquieu." *British Journal of Sociology* 44:693–712.

Mills, C. Wright
1951   *White Collar.* New York: Oxford University Press.
1956   *The Power Elite.* New York: Oxford University Press.
1959   *The Sociological Imagination.* New York: Oxford University Press.

Mills, Catherine
2007   "Biopolitics, Liberal Eugenics, and Nihilism." In Matthew Calarco and Steven DeCaroli (eds.), *Sovereignty and Life.* Stanford, Calif.: Stanford University Press: 180–202.
2011   "Giorgio Agamben." In George Ritzer and Jeffrey Stepnisky (eds.), *The Wiley-Blackwell Companion to Major Social Theorists: Volume II—Contemporary Social Theorists.* Malden, Mass., and Oxford, Eng.: Wiley-Blackwell: 464–479.

Milovantovic, Dragan
1995   "Dueling Paradigms: Modernist versus Postmodernist Thought." *Humanity and Society* 19:19–44.

Miriam, Kathy
2007   "Towards a Phenomenology of Ex-Right: Reviving Radical Feminist Theory of Compulsory Heterosexuality." *Hypatia* 22(1):210–228.

Mirowsky, John, and Ross, Catherine E.
1995   "Sex Differences in Distress: Real or Artifact?" *American Sociological Review* 60:449–468.

Misra, Joya (ed.)
2012   "Symposia on the Contributions of Patricia Hill Collins." *Gender & Society* 26:6.

Misztal, B.
2001   "Normality and Trust in Goffman's Theory of Interaction Order." *Sociological Theory* 19:312–324.

Mitchell, Jack N.
1978   *Social Exchange, Dramaturgy and Ethnomethodology: Toward a Paradigmatic Synthesis.* New York: Elsevier.

Mitroff, Ian
1974   "Norms and Counter-Norms in a Select Group of the Apollo Moon Scientists: A Case Study of the Ambivalence of Scientists." *American Sociological Review* 39:579–595.

Mitroff, Ian, and Kilmann, Ralph
1978   *Methodological Approaches to Social Science.* San Francisco: Jossey-Bass.

Mitzman, Arthur
1969/1971   *The Iron Cage: An Historical Interpretation of Max Weber.* New York: Grosset and Dunlap.
1970   *The Iron Cage: An Historical Interpretation of Max Weber.* New York: Alfred A. Knopf.

Miyahara, Kojiro
1983   "Charisma: From Weber to Contemporary Sociology." *Sociological Inquiry* 55:368–388.

Mizruchi, Mark S.
1990   "Cohesion, Structural Equivalence, and Similarity of Behavior: An Approach to the Study of Corporate Political Power." *Sociological Theory* 8:16–32.

1994   "Social Network Analysis: Recent Achievements and Current Controversies." *Acta Sociologica* 37:329–343.
2005   "Network Exchange Theory." In George Ritzer (ed.), *Encyclopedia of Social Theory.* Thousand Oaks, Calif.: Sage: 530–540.

Mizruchi, Mark S., and Koenig, Thomas
1986   "Economic Sources of Corporate Political Consensus: An Examination of Interindustry Relations." *American Sociological Review* 51:482–491.

Mohanty, Chandra Talpade
1991   "Under Western Eyes: Feminist Scholarship and Colonial Discourses." In C. Mohanty, A. Russo, and L. Torres (eds.), *Third World Women and the Politics of Feminism.* Bloomington: Indiana University Press.
2002   *Feminism without Borders: Decolonizing Theory, Practicing Solidarity.* Durham, N.C.: Duke University Press.

Moi, Toril
1991   "Appropriating Bourdieu: Feminist Theory in Pierre Bordieu's Sociology of Culture." *New Literary History* 22:1017–1049.
1999   *What Is a Woman?* Oxford: Oxford University Press.

Molm, Linda D.
1988   "The Structure and Use of Power: A Comparison of Reward and Punishment Power." *Social Psychology Quarterly* 51:108–122.
1989   "Punishment Power: A Balancing Process in Power-Dependence Relations." *American Journal of Sociology* 94:1392–1418.
1994   "Is Punishment Effective? Coercive Strategies in Social Exchange." *Social Psychology Quarterly* 57:75–94.
1997   *Coercive Power in Exchange.* Cambridge, Eng.: Cambridge University Press.
2001   "Theories of Social Exchange and Exchange Networks." In George Ritzer and Barry Smart (eds.), *Handbook of Social Theory.* London: Sage: 260–272.
2005a   "Behaviorism." In George Ritzer (ed.), *Encyclopedia of Social Theory.* Thousand Oaks, Calif.: Sage: 44–47.
2005b   "Homans, George." In George Ritzer (ed.), *Encyclopedia of Social Theory.* Thousand Oaks, Calif.: Sage: 381–385.
2007   "Power-Dependence Theory." In George Ritzer (ed.), *The Blackwell Encyclopedia of Sociology.* Oxford: Blackwell: 3598–3602.

Molm, Linda D., and Cook, Karen S.
1995   "Social Exchange and Exchange Networks." In K. S. Cook, G. A. Fine, and J. S. House (eds.), *Sociological Perspectives on Social Psychology.* Boston: Allyn and Bacon: 209–235.

Molm, Linda D., Quist, Theron M., and Wisely, Phillip A.
1994   "Imbalanced Structures, Unfair Strategies: Power and Justice in Social Exchange." *American Sociological Review* 59:98–121.

Mommsen, Wolfgang J.
1974   *The Age of Bureaucracy.* New York: Harper and Row.

Monnier, Christine A.
2007   "Bourdieu, Pierre." In George Ritzer (ed.), *The Blackwell Encyclopedia of Sociology.* Oxford: Blackwell: 347–350.

Monrow, Paul T,
2007   "Intersubjectivity." In George Ritzer (ed.), *The Blackwell Encyclopedia of Sociology.* Oxford: Blackwell: 2400–2402.

Moore, Keith M.
2008   "Network Framing of Pest Management Knowledge and Practice." *Rural Sociology* 73:414–439.

Moore, Wilbert E.
1966   "Global Sociology: The World as a Singular System." *American Journal of Sociology* 71:475–482.
1978   "Functionalism." In T. Bottomore and R. Nisbet (eds.), *A History of Sociological Analysis.* New York: Basic Books: 321–361.

Morgan, Jamie
2007   "Critical Realism." In George Ritzer (ed.), *Blackwell Encyclopedia of Sociology.* Oxford: Blackwell.

Morgan, Robin
1970   *Sisterhood Is Powerful: An Anthology of Writings from the Women's Liberation Movement.*
                New York: Vintage.

Morrione, Thomas J.
1988   "Herbert G. Blumer (1900–1987): A Legacy of Concepts, Criticisms, and Contributions." *Symbolic
                Interaction* 11:1–12.
2007   "Blumer, Herbert George." In George Ritzer (ed.), *The Blackwell Encyclopedia of Sociology.*
                Oxford: Blackwell: 318–322.

Morris, Bonnie
2003   "At the Michigan Womyn's Music Festival." *The Gay and Lesbian Review Worldwide* 10(5):16–18.

Morris, Martin
2001   *Rethinking the Communicative Turn: Adorno, Habermas, and the Problem of Communicative
                Freedom.* Albany: State University of New York Press.

Morrow, Raymond A.
1994   "Critical Theory, Poststructuralism, and Critical Theory." *Current Perspectives in Social Theory*
                14:27–51.

Morrow, Raymond A., and Brown, David D.
1994   *Critical Theory and Methodology.* Thousand Oaks, Calif.: Sage.

Morse, Chandler
1961   "The Functional Imperatives." In M. Black (ed.), *The Social Theories of Talcott Parsons.*
                Englewood Cliffs, N.J.: Prentice-Hall: 100–152.

Mortensen, Ellen (ed.)
2006   *Sex, Breath, and Force: Sexual Difference in a Post-Feminist Era.* Lanham, Md.: Lexington Books.

Moscovici, Serge
1993   *The Invention of Society.* Cambridge, Eng.: Polity Press.

Mouffe, Chantal
1988   "Radical Democracy: Modern or Postmodern?" In A. Ross (ed.), *Universal Abandon? The Politics of
                Postmodernism.* Minneapolis: University of Minnesota Press: 31–45.

Mouzelis, Nicos
1997   "In Defence of the Sociological Canon: A Reply to David Parker." *Sociological Review*
                97:244–253.

Movahedi, Siamak
2007   "Psychoanalysis." In George Ritzer (ed.), *The Blackwell Encyclopedia of Sociology.* Oxford:
                Blackwell: 3694–3696.

Mozetič, Gerald
2007   "Pareto, Vilfredo." In George Ritzer (ed.), *The Blackwell Encyclopedia of Sociology.* Oxford:
                Blackwell: 3360–3362.

Muller, Hans-Peter
1994   "Social Differentiation and Organic Solidarity: The Division of Labor Revisited." *Sociological
                Forum* 9:73–86.

Mullins, Beverly
2005   "Women Rule? Globalization and the Feminization of Managerial Professional Workspaces in the
                Caribbean." *Gender, Place and Culture* 12(1):1–27.

Mullins, Nicholas
1973   *Theories and Theory Groups in Contemporary American Sociology.* New York: Harper and Row.
1983   "Theories and Theory Groups Revisited." In R. Collins (ed.), *Sociological Theory—1983.* San
                Francisco: Jossey-Bass: 319–337.

Münch, Richard
1987   "The Interpenetration of Microinteraction and Macrostructures in a Complex and Contingent
                Institutional Order." In J. C. Alexander et al. (eds.), *The Micro-Macro Link.* Berkeley: University
                of California Press: 319–336.
2005   "Parsons, Talcott." In George Ritzer (ed.), *Encyclopedia of Social Theory.* Thousand Oaks, Calif.:
                Sage: 550–555.

Münch, Richard, and Smelser, Neil J.
1987   "Relating the Micro and Macro." In J. C. Alexander et al. (eds.), *The Micro-Macro Link.* Berkeley: University of California Press: 356–387.

Munck, Ronaldo
2002   "Globalization and Democracy: A New Great Transformation." *Annals* 581, May:10–21.

Musolf, Gil Richard
1994   "William James and Symbolic Interactionism." *Sociological Focus* 27:303–314.

Myles, John
1999   "From Habitus to Mouth: Language and Class in Bourdieu's Sociology of Language." *Theory and Society* 28:879–901.

Nafassi, Mohammed R.
1998   "Reframing Orientalism: Weber and Islam." *Economy and Society* 27:97–118.

Nagel, Joane
2003   *Race, Ethnicity, and Sexuality: Intimate Intersections, Forbidden Frontiers.* New York: Oxford University Press.

Nagel, Mechthild
1997   "Critical Theory Meets the Ethic of Care." *Social Theory and Practice* 23:307–326.

Nash, Bradley, Jr., and Wardell, Mark
1993   "The Control of Sociological Theory: In Praise of the Interregnum." *Sociological Inquiry* 63:276–292.

Nass, Clifford I.
1986   "Bureaucracy, Technical Expertise, and Professionals: A Weberian Approach." *Sociological Theory* 4:61–70.

Nedelmann, Birgitta
1990   "Georg Simmel as an Analyst of Autonomous Dynamics: The Merry-Go-Round of Fashion." In M. Kaern, B. S. Phillips, and R. S. Cohen (eds.), *Georg Simmel and Contemporary Sociology.* Dordrecht, Netherlands: Kluwer: 225–241.
2001   "The Continuing Relevance of Georg Simmel: Staking Out Anew the Field of Sociology." In George Ritzer and Barry Smart (eds.), *Handbook of Social Theory.* London: Sage: 66–78.

Nedelmann, Birgitta, and Sztompka, Piotr
1993   "Introduction." In B. Nedelmann and P. Sztompka (eds.), *Sociology in Europe: In Search of Identity.* Berlin: Walter de Gruyter: 1–23.

Negri, Antonio
2007   "The Discreet Taste of the Dialectic." Matthew Calarco and Steven DeCaroli (eds.), *Sovereignty and Life.* Stanford, Calif.: Stanford University Press: 109–125.

Nemedi, Denes
1995   "Collective Consciousness, Morphology, and Collective Representations: Durkheim's Sociology of Knowledge, 1894–1900." *Sociological Perspectives* 38:41–56.

Nettl, J. P., and Robertson, Roland
1968   *International Systems and the Modernization of Societies.* New York: Basic Books.

Nicolaus, Martin
1974   "Foreword." In K. Marx, *The Grundrisse.* New York: Random House: 7–63.

Niebrugge, G., Lengermann, P., and Dickerson, B.
2010   "Women's leadership in Sociology." In Karen O'Connor (ed.), *Gender and Women's Leadership: A Reference Handbook.* Thousand Oaks, Calif: Sage.

Nielsen, Donald A.
1999   *Three Faces of God: Society, Religion, and the Categories of Totality in the Philosophy of Emile Durkheim.* Albany: State University of New York Press.
2005a   "Social Facts." In George Ritzer (ed.), *Encyclopedia of Social Theory.* Thousand Oaks, Calif.: Sage: 740–744.
2005b   "Annales School." In George Ritzer (ed.), *Encyclopedia of Social Theory.* Thousand Oaks, Calif.: Sage: 12–16.
2007a   "Social Fact." In George Ritzer (ed.), *Encyclopedia of Sociology.* Oxford: Blackwell: 4414–4416.
2007b   "Functionalism/Neo-Functionalism." In George Ritzer (ed.), *The Blackwell Encyclopedia of Sociology.* Oxford: Blackwell: 1810–1813.

Nielsen, Francois
1994   "Sociobiology and Sociology." *Annual Review of Sociology*, 20:267–303.

Nisbet, Robert
1953   *Community and Power.* New York: Galaxy Books.
1959   "Comment." *American Sociological Review* 24:479–481.
1967   *The Sociological Tradition.* New York: Basic Books.
1976–1977   "Many Tocquevilles." *The American Scholar* 46:59–75.

Noblit, George W., and Hare, R. Dwight
1988   *Meta-Ethnography: Synthesizing Qualitative Studies.* Newbury Park, Calif.: Sage.

Nollman, Gerd
2005a   "Luhmann, Niklas." In George Ritzer (ed.), *Encyclopedia of Social Theory.* Thousand Oaks, Calif.:
            Sage: 454–458.
2005b   "Habermas, Jurgen." In George Ritzer (ed.), *Encyclopedia of Social Theory.* Thousand Oaks,
            Calif.: Sage: 351–352.

Norkus, Zenonus
2000   "Max Weber's interpretive sociology and rational choice approach." *Rationality and Society,*
            12(3):259–282.

Oakes, Guy (ed.)
1984   *Georg Simmel on Women, Sexuality and Love.* New Haven: Yale University Press.

Oakes, Len
1997   *Prophetic Charisma: The Psychology of Revolutionary Religious Personalities.* Syracuse, N.Y.:
            Syracuse University Press.

Oberhauser, Ann M., and Pratt, Amy
2004   "Women's Collective Economic Strategies and Political Transformation in South Africa." *Gender,
            Place and Culture* 11(2):209–228.

Ohmae, E.
1996   *The End of the Nation-State: The Rise of Regional Economies.* New York: Free Press.

Oksala, Johanna
2011   "Sexual Experience: Foucault, Phenomenology and Feminist Theory." *Hypatia* 26(1):207–223.

Oliver, Ivan
1983   "The 'Old' and the 'New' Hermeneutic in Sociological Theory." *British Journal of Sociology* 34:519–553.

Oliver, Kelly
2006   "The Depressed Sex: Sublimation and Sexual Difference." In E. Morensen (ed.) *Sex, Breath and
            Force: Sexual Difference in a Post-Feminist Era.* Oxford, Eng.: Lexington Books: 97–110.

Ollman, Bertell
1976   *Alienation.* 2nd ed. Cambridge, Eng.: Cambridge University Press.

Olson, Richard
1993   *The Emergence of the Social Sciences, 1642–1792.* New York: Twayne.

O'Neill, John
1995   *The Poverty of Postmodernism.* London: Routledge.

Ono, Michikuni
1996   "Collective Effervescence and Symbolism." *Durkheimian Studies* 2:79–98.

Orbuch, Terri L.
1997   "People's Accounts Count: The Sociology of Accounts." In John Hagan and Karen S. Cook (eds.),
            Annual Review of Sociology, Vol. 23. Palo Alto, Calif.: Annual Reviews: 455–478.

Orenstein, David Michael
2007   "Comte, Auguste." In George Ritzer (ed.), *The Blackwell Encyclopedia of Sociology.* Oxford:
            Blackwell: 650–656.

Orme, J.
2002   "Social Work: Gender, Care and Justice." *British Journal of Social Work* 32:799–814.

Orr, Catherine M.
1997   "Charting the Currents of the Third Wave." *Hypatia* 12:29–43.

Orr, Jackie
2006   *Panic Diaries: A Genealogy of Panic Disorder.* Durham, N.C.: Duke University Press.

Outhwaite, William
1994   *Habermas: A Critical Introduction.* Stanford, Calif.: Stanford University Press.
2011   "Jurgen Habermas." In George Ritzer and Jeffrey Stepnisky (eds.), *The Wiley-Blackwell Companion to Major Social Theorists: Volume II—Contemporary Social Theorists.* Malden, Mass., and Oxford, Eng.: Wiley-Blackwell: 339–360.

Owen, Margaret
1996   *A World of Widows.* Atlantic Heights, N.J.: Zed Books.

Paap, Kris
2008   "Power and Embodiment: Comment on Andersen." *Gender & Society* 22:99–103.

Papoulias, Constantian, and Callard, Felicity
2010   "Biology's Gift: Interrogating the Turn to Affect." *Body & Society*, 16(1):29–56.

Pareto, Vilfredo
1935   *A Treatise on General Sociology.* 4 vols. New York: Dover.

Park, Robert E.
1927/1973   "Life History." *American Journal of Sociology* 79:251–260.

Park, Robert, and Burgess, Ernest
1921   *Introduction to the Science of Sociology.* Chicago: University of Chicago Press.

Parker, David
1997   "Why Bother with Durkheim?" *Sociological Review* 45:122–146.

Parker, Mike, and Slaughter, Jane
1990   "Management-by-Stress: The Team Concept in the US Auto Industry." *Science as Culture* 8:27–58.

Parsons, Talcott
1937   *The Structure of Social Action.* New York: McGraw-Hill.
1942   "Some Sociological Aspects of the Fascist Movements." *Social Forces* 21:138–147.
1947   "Certain Primary Sources and Patterns of Aggression in the Social Structure of the Western World." *Psychiatry* 10:167–181.
1949   *The Structure of Social Action.* 2nd ed. New York: McGraw-Hill.
1951   *The Social System.* Glencoe, Ill.: Free Press.
1966   *Societies.* Englewood Cliffs, N.J.: Prentice-Hall.
1970   *Social Structure and Personality.* New York: Free Press.
1971   *The System of Modern Societies.* Englewood Cliffs, N.J.: Prentice-Hall.
1975   "Social Structure and the Symbolic Media of Interchange." In P. Blau (ed.), *Approaches to the Study of Social Structure.* New York: Free Press: 94–100.
1977   "On Building Social System Theory: A Personal History." In T. Parsons (ed.), *Social Systems and the Evolution of Action Theory.* New York: Free Press: 22–76.
1990   "Prolegomena to a Theory of Social Institutions." *American Sociological Review* 55:319–333.

Parsons, Talcott, and Platt, Gerald
1973   *The American University.* Cambridge, Mass.: Harvard University Press.

Parsons, Talcott, and Shils, Edward A. (eds.)
1951   *Toward a General Theory of Action.* Cambridge, Mass.: Harvard University Press.

Passavant, Paul
2012a   "Empire." In George Ritzer (ed.), *The Wiley-Blackwell Encyclopedia of Globalization*, 5 vols. Malden, Mass.: Wiley-Blackwell: 500–505.
2012b   "Multitude." In George Ritzer (ed.), *The Wiley-Blackwell Encyclopedia of Globalization*, 5 vols. Malden, Mass.: Wiley-Blackwell: 1473–1481.

Pateman, Carole.
1999   "Beyond the Sexual Contract?" In Geoff Dench (ed.), *Rewriting the Sexual Contract.* New Brunswick, N.J.: Transaction Publishers: 1–9.

Paul, Axel
2001   "Organizing Husserl: On the Phenomenological Foundations of Luhmann's Systems Theory." *Journal of Classical Sociology* 1:371–394.

Paulsen, Michael B., and Feldman, Kenneth A.
1995   "Toward a Reconceptualization of Scholarship: A Human Action System with Functional Imperatives." *Journal of Higher Education* 66:615–640.

Pearce, Frank
1989   *The Radical Durkheim.* London: Unwin Hyman.
2005   "Durkheim, Emile." In George Ritzer (ed.), *Encyclopedia of Social Theory.* Thousand Oaks, Calif.:
            Sage: 218–223.

Peel, J.D.Y.
1971   *Herbert Spencer: The Evolution of a Sociologist.* New York: Basic Books.

Pelaez, Eloina, and Holloway, John
1990   "Learning to Bow: Post-Fordism and Technological Determinism." *Science as Culture* 8:15–26.

Perakyla, Anssi
2007   "Conversation Analysis." In George Ritzer (ed.), *The Blackwell Encyclopedia of Sociology.*
            Oxford: Blackwell: 791–794.

Perinbanayagam, Robert S.
1985   *Signifying Acts: Structure and Meaning in Everyday Life.* Carbondale: Southern Illinois University
            Press.

Perrin, Robert
1976   "Herbert Spencer's Four Theories of Social Evolution." *American Journal of Sociology* 81:1339–1359.
1995   "Emile Durkheim's Division of Labor and the Shadow of Herbert Spencer." *Sociological Quarterly*
            36:791–808.

Perry, Nick
2007   "Barthes, Roland." In George Ritzer (ed.), *The Blackwell Encyclopedia of Sociology.* Oxford:
            Blackwell: 242–244.

Perry, Wilhelmia E., Abbott, James R., and Hutter, Mark
1997   "The Symbolic Interactionist Paradigm and Urban Sociology." *Research in Urban Sociology*
            4:59–92.

Peters, Michael
1994   "Habermas, Post-Structuralism and the Question of Postmodernity: The Defiant Periphery." *Social
            Analysis* 36:3–20.

Peterson, Gretchen
2005   "Molm, Linda." In George Ritzer (ed.), *Encyclopedia of Social Theory.* Thousand Oaks, Calif.:
            Sage: 511–512.

Phelan, Shane
1994   *Getting Specific: Postmodern Lesbian Politics.* Minneapolis: University of Minnesota Press.

Phillips, Anne
1993   *Democracy and Difference.* University Park: Pennsylvania State University Press.

Phillips, Derek
1973   "Paradigms, Falsifications and Sociology." *Acta Sociologica* 16:13–31.
1975   "Paradigms and Incommensurability." *Theory and Society* 2:37–62.

Phillips, John William
2005   "Derrida, Jacques." In George Ritzer (ed.), *Encyclopedia of Social Theory.* Thousand Oaks, Calif.:
            Sage: 196–197.

Piccone, Paul
1990   "Paradoxes of Perestroika." *Telos* 84:3–32.

Pickering, Mary
1993   *Auguste Comte: An Intellectual Biography,* Vol. 1. Cambridge, Eng.: Cambridge University Press.
1997   "A New Look at Auguste Comte." In Charles Camic (ed.), *Reclaiming the Sociological Classics:
            The State of Scholarship.* Oxford: Blackwell: 11–44.
2011   "Auguste Comte." In George Ritzer and Jeffrey Stepnisky (eds.), *The Wiley-Blackwell Companion
            to Major Social Theorists: Volume I—Classical Social Theorists.* Malden, Mass., and Oxford,
            Eng.: Wiley-Blackwell: 30–60.

Pierce, Jennifer
1995   *Gender Trials: Emotional Lives in Contemporary Law Firms.* Berkeley: University of California
            Press.

Pieterse, Jan N.
2004   *Globalization and Culture: Global Melange.* Lanham, Md.: Rowman and Littlefield.

Piontek, Thomas
2006   *Queering Gay and Lesbian Studies.* Urbana: University of Illinois Press.

Poggi, Gianfranco
1993   *Money and the Modern Mind: Georg Simmel's Philosophy of Money.* Berkeley: University of
                California Press.
1996   "Three Aspects of Modernity in Simmel's *Philosophie des Geldes:* Its Epiphanic Significance, the
                Centrality of Money and the Prevalence of Alienation." In Richard Kilminster and Ian Varcoe
                (eds.), *Culture, Modernity and Revolution: Essays in Honour of Zygmunt Bauman.* London:
                Routledge: 42–65.

Polit, Denise F., and Falbo, Toni
1987   "Only Children and Personality Development: A Quantitative Review." *Journal of Marriage and
                the Family* 49:309–325.

Polanyi, Karl
1944   *The Great Transformation: The Political and Economic Origins of Our Time.* Boston: Beacon Press.

Pollner, Melvin
1987   *Mundane Reason: Reality in Everyday and Sociological Discourse.* Cambridge, Eng.: Cambridge
                University Press.
1991   "Left of Ethnomethodology: The Rise and Decline of Radical Reflexivity." *American Sociological
                Review* 56:370–380.

Pollock, Griselda
2010   "Moments and Temporalities of the Avant-Garde in, of, and from the Feminine." *New Literary
                History: A Journal of Theory and Interpretation* 41(4):795–820.

Pope, Whitney
1976   *Durkheim's Suicide: A Classic Analyzed.* Chicago: University of Chicago Press.

Portes, Alejandro, and Landolt, Patricia
1996   "The Downside of Social Capital." *American Prospect* 26:18–21.

Postone, Moishe, LiPuma, Edward, and Calhoun, Craig
1993   "Introduction: Bourdieu and Social Theory." In C. Calhoun, E. LiPuma, and M. Postone (eds.),
                Bourdieu: Critical Perspectives. Chicago: University of Chicago Press: 1–13.

Powell, Jason, and Owen, Tim (eds.)
2008   *Reconstructing Postmodernism.* New York: Nova Science.

Powers, Charles H.
1986   *Vilfredo Pareto.* Newbury Park, Calif.: Sage.
2005a   "Turner, Jonathan." In George Ritzer (ed.), *Encyclopedia of Social Theory.* Thousand Oaks, Calif.:
                Sage: 850–851.
2005b   "Veblen, Thorstein." In George Ritzer (ed.), *Encyclopedia of Social Theory.* Thousand Oaks, Calif.:
                Sage: 863–864.

Prendergast, Christopher
2005a   "Schutz, Alfred." In George Ritzer (ed.), *Encyclopedia of Social Theory.* Thousand Oaks, Calif.:
                Sage: 674–675.
2005b   "Social Capital." In George Ritzer (ed.), *Encyclopedia of Social Theory.* Thousand Oaks, Calif.:
                Sage: 715–716.
2005c   "Levels of Social Structure." In George Ritzer (ed.), *Encyclopedia of Social Theory.* Thousand
                Oaks, Calif.: Sage: 441–443.

Press, Andrea
2009   "The End of Television? Its Impact on the World (So Far): Gender and Family in Television's
                Golden Age and Beyond." *The Annals of the American Academy of Political and Social Science*
                625:139–150.

Pressler, Charles A., and Dasilva, Fabio
1996   *Sociology and Interpretation: From Weber to Habermas.* Albany: State University of New York
                Press.

Prus, Robert
1996   *Symbolic Interaction and Ethnographic Research: Intersubjectivity and the Study of Human Lived Experience.* Albany: State University of New York Press.

Przeworski, Adam
1985   *Capitalism and Social Democracy.* Cambridge, Eng.: Cambridge University Press.

Purcell, Elizabeth
2011   "Fetishizing Ontology: Julia Kristeva and Slavoj Zizek on the structure of desire." *Radical Philosophy Review* 14(1):67–104.

Purkayastha, Bandana
2012   "Intersectionality in a Transnational World." *Gender & Society* 26:55–62.

Putnam, Robert
2001   *Bowling Alone: The Collapse and Revival of American Community.* New York: Simon and Schuster.

Quadagno, Jill
1979   "Paradigms in Evolutionary Theory: The Sociobiological Model of Natural Selection." *American Sociological Review* 44:100–109.

Quine, W. V.
1972   "Methodological Reflections on Current Linguistic Theory." In Donald Davidson and Gilbert Harman (eds.), *Semantics of Natural Language.* Dordrecht, Netherlands: Reidel: 442–454.

Rachlin, Allan
1991   "Rehumanizing Dialectic: Toward an Understanding of the Interpenetration of Structure and Subjectivity." *Current Perspectives in Social Theory* 11:255–269.

Radkau, Joshua
2009   *Max Weber.* Cambridge, Eng.: Polity Press.

Radnitzky, Gerard
1973   *Contemporary Schools of Metascience.* Chicago: Regnery.

Rambo, Eric
1995   "Conceiving Best Outcomes within a Theory of Utility Maximization: A Culture-Level Critique." *Sociological Theory* 13:145–162.

Ramet, Sabrina P.
1991   *Social Currents in Eastern Europe: The Sources and Meaning of the Great Transformation.* Durham, N.C.: Duke University Press.

Ramji, Hasmita
2007   "Difference." In George Ritzer (ed.), *The Blackwell Encyclopedia of Sociology.* Oxford: Blackwell: 1153–1155.

Rammstedt, Otthein
1991   "On Simmel's Aesthetics: Argumentation in the Journal *Jugend,* 1897–1906." *Theory, Culture and Society* 8:125–144.

Rasch, William
2000   *Niklas Luhmann's Modernity: The Paradoxes of Differentiation.* Stanford, Calif.: Stanford University Press.

Rattansi, Ali
1982   *Marx and the Division of Labour.* London: Macmillan.

Rawls, Anne Warfield
1996   "Durkheim's Epistemology: The Neglected Argument." *American Journal of Sociology* 102: 430–482.
2001   "Durkheim's Treatment of Practice: Concrete Practice vs Representations as the Foundation of Reason." *Journal of Classical Sociology* 1:33–68.
2005a   "Conversation Analysis." In George Ritzer (ed.), *Encyclopedia of Social Theory.* Thousand Oaks, Calif.: Sage: 145–149.
2005b   "Garfinkel, Harold." In George Ritzer (ed.), *Encyclopedia of Social Theory.* Thousand Oaks, Calif.: Sage: 301–304.
2007   "Durkheim, Emile." In George Ritzer (ed.), *The Blackwell Encyclopedia of Sociology.* Oxford: Blackwell: 1250–1261.

2011   "Harold Garfinkel." In George Ritzer and Jeffrey Stepnisky (eds.), *The Wiley-Blackwell Companion to Major Social Theorists: Volume II—Contemporary Social Theorists*. Malden, Mass., and Oxford, Eng.: Wiley-Blackwell: 89–124.

Reagon, Bernice Johnson
1982/1995   "My Black Mothers and Sisters; or, On Beginning a Cultural Autobiography." In C. Goldberg and H. Hartmann (eds.), *U.S. Women in Struggle*. Urbana: University of Illinois Press: 296–310.

Reckwitz, Andreas
2002   "Toward a Theory of Social Practices: A Development in Culturalist Theorizing." *European Journal of Social Theory* 5(2):243–263.
2007   "Practice Theory." In George Ritzer (ed.), *The Blackwell Encyclopedia of Sociology*. Oxford: Blackwell.

Reddock, Rhoda
2000   "Feminist Theory and Critical Reconceptualization in Sociology: The Challenge of the 1990s." In Stella Quah and Arnaud Sales (eds.), *The International Handbook of Sociology*. London: Sage: 84–100.

Reedy, W. Jay
1994   "The Historical Imaginary of Social Science in Post-Revolutionary France: Bonald, Saint-Simon, Comte." *History of the Human Sciences* 7:1–26.

Reich, Robert
2000   *The Future of Success*. New York: Knopf.

Reiger, K.
1999   "'Sort of Part of the Women's Movement. But Different': Mothers' Organisations and Australian Feminism." *Women's Studies International Forum* 22(6):585–595.

Reitz-Pustejovsky, M.
2002   "Is the Care We Provide Homeless People Just? The Ethic of Justice Informing the Ethic of Care." *Journal of Social Distress and the Homeless* 11:233–248.

Remennick, Larissa
2007   "Transnationalism." In George Ritzer (ed.), *The Blackwell Encyclopedia of Sociology*. Oxford: Blackwell: 5064–5066.

Reskin, Barbara, and Maroto, Michelle L.
2011   "What Trends? Whose Choices?: Comment on England." *Gender & Society* 25:81–87.

Reskin, Barbara, and Padavic, Irene
1994   *Women and Men at Work*. Thousand Oaks, Calif.: Pine Forge Press.

Restivo, Sal
2011   "Bruno Latour." In George Ritzer and Jeffrey Stepnisky (eds.), *The Wiley-Blackwell Companion to Major Social Theorists: Volume II—Contemporary Social Theorists*. Malden, Mass., and Oxford, Eng.: Wiley-Blackwell: 520–540.

Rhoades, Lawrence J.
1981   *A History of the American Sociological Association*. Washington, D.C.: American Sociological Association.

Rhodes, Jacqueline
2005   *Radical Feminism, Writing, and Critical Agency*. Albany: State University of New York Press.

Rich, Adrienne
1976   *Of Woman Born: Motherhood as Experience and Institution*. New York: Norton.
1980   "Compulsory Heterosexual and Lesbian Experience." In C. R. Stimson and E. S. Person (eds.), *Women, Sex, and Sexuality*. Chicago: University of Chicago Press: 62–91.

Ridgeway, Cecelia
1997   "Interaction and the Conservation of Gender Inequality: Considering Employment." *American Sociological Review* 62:218–235.
2011   *Framed by Gender: How Gender Inequality Persists in the Modern World*. Oxford: Oxford University Press.

Riesman, David
1950   *The Lonely Crowd*. New Haven: Yale University Press.

Ringer, Fritz
1997   *Max Weber's Methodology: The Unification of the Cultural and Social Sciences*. Cambridge, Mass.: Harvard University Press.

Risman, Barbara J.
2001   "Calling the Bluff of Value-Free Science." *American Sociological Review* 66:605–611.
2004   "Gender as a Social Structure: Theory Wrestling with Activism." *Gender & Society* 18(4):429–450.
2009   "From Doing to Undoing: Gender as We Know It." *Gender & Society* 23:81–84.

Risman, Barbara J., and Ferree, Myra Marx
1995   "Making Gender Visible: Comment on Coleman's Rational Reconstruction of Society." *American Sociological Review* 60:5.

Ritzer, George
1975a   *Sociology: A Multiple Paradigm Science.* Boston: Allyn and Bacon.
1975b   "Sociology: A Multiple Paradigm Science." *American Sociologist* 10:156–167.
1975c   "Professionalization, Bureaucratization and Rationalization: The Views of
            Max Weber." *Social Forces* 53:627–634.
1979   "Toward an Integrated Sociological Paradigm." In W. Snizek et al. (eds.), *Contemporary Issues in
            Theory and Research.* Westport, Conn.: Greenwood Press: 25–46.
1980   *Sociology: A Multiple Paradigm Science.* Rev. ed. Boston: Allyn and Bacon.
1981a   *Toward an Integrated Sociological Paradigm: The Search for an Exemplar and an Image of the
            Subject Matter.* Boston: Allyn and Bacon.
1981b   "Paradigm Analysis in Sociology: Clarifying the Issues." *American Sociological Review* 46:245–248.
1983   "The McDonaldization of Society." *Journal of American Culture* 6:100–107.
1985   "The Rise of Micro-Sociological Theory." *Sociological Theory* 3:88–98.
1988   "Sociological Metatheory: Defending a Subfield by Delineating Its Parameters." *Sociological
            Theory* 6:187–200.
1989   "Of Levels and 'Intellectual Amnesia.'" *Sociological Theory* 7:226–229.
1990a   "Micro-Macro Linkage in Sociological Theory: Applying a Metatheoretical Tool." In George Ritzer
            (ed.), *Frontiers of Social Theory: The New Syntheses.* New York: Columbia University Press: 347–370.
1990b   "The Current Status of Sociological Theory: The New Syntheses." In George Ritzer (ed.),
            Frontiers of Social Theory: The New Syntheses. New York: Columbia University Press: 1–30.
1991a   "Metatheorizing in Sociology." *Sociological Forum* 5:3–15.
1991b   *Metatheorizing in Sociology.* Lexington, Mass.: Lexington Books.
1991d   "The Recent History and the Emerging Reality of American Sociological Theory: A
            Metatheoretical Interpretation." *Sociological Forum* 6:269–287.
1992b   "Metatheorizing in Sociology: Explaining the Coming of Age." In George Ritzer (ed.),
            Metatheorizing. Newbury Park, Calif.: Sage: 7–26.
1993   *The McDonaldization of Society.* Thousand Oaks, Calif.: Pine Forge Press.
1995   *Expressing America: A Critique of the Global Credit Card Society.* Thousand Oaks, Calif.: Pine
            Forge Press.
1996   *The McDonaldization of Society.* Rev. ed. Thousand Oaks, Calif.: Pine Forge Press.
1997   *Postmodern Social Theory.* New York: McGraw-Hill.
1998   *The McDonaldization Thesis.* London: Sage.
2001   "From Exclusion to Inclusion to Chaos (?) in Sociological Theory." In George Ritzer (ed.),
            Explorations in Social Theory: From Metatheorizing to Rationalization. London: Sage: 145–153.
2003   *The Blackwell Companion to Major Contemporary Social Theorists.* Oxford: Blackwell.
2004   *The Globalization of Nothing.* Thousand Oaks, Calif.: Pine Forge Press.
2005b   "Paradigm." In George Ritzer (ed.), *Encyclopedia of Social Theory.* Thousand Oaks, Calif.: Sage:
            543–544.
2007a   "Elias, Norbert." In George Ritzer (ed.), *The Blackwell Encyclopedia of Sociology.* Oxford:
            Blackwell: 1357–1359.
2007b   "Metatheory." In George Ritzer (ed.), *The Blackwell Encyclopedia of Sociology.* Oxford:
            Blackwell: 2964–2967.
2007c   *The Globalization of Nothing 2.* Thousand Oaks, Calif.: Pine Forge Press.
2008   *Classical Sociological Theory.* New York: McGraw-Hill.
2009   "Focusing on the Prosumer: On Correcting an Error in the History of Social Theory." Paper
            presented at Conference on the Prosumer, Frankfurt, Germany, April.
2010a   *Enchanting a Disenchanted World: Continuity and Change in the Cathedrals of Consumption.*
            3rd ed. Thousand Oaks, Calif.: Pine Forge Press.
2010b   *Globalization: A Basic Text.* Oxford: Wiley-Blackwell.
2013   The *McDonaldization of Society*, 7th ed. Thousand Oaks, Calif.: Pine Forge Press.

Ritzer, George (ed.)
1991c   "Recent Explorations in Sociological Metatheorizing." *Sociological Perspectives* 34:237–390.

1992a	*Metatheorizing.* Newbury Park, Calif.: Sage.
2000	*The Blackwell Companion to Major Social Theorists.* Malden, Mass.: Blackwell.
2002	*McDonaldization: The Reader.* Thousand Oaks, Calif.: Pine Forge Press.
2006	*McDonaldization: The Reader.* 2nd ed. Thousand Oaks, Calif.: Sage.
2012	*The Wiley-Blackwell Encyclopedia of Globalization*, 5 vols. Malden, Mass.: Wiley-Blackwell.

Ritzer, George, Dean, Paul, and Jurgensen, Nathan
2012   "The Coming Age of the Prosumer." *American Behavioral Scientist* 56(4):379–398.

Ritzer, George, and Gindoff, Pamela
1992   "Methodological Relationism: Lessons for and from Social Psychology." *Social Psychology Quarterly* 55:128–140.
1994   "Agency-Structure, Micro-Macro, Individualism-Holism-Relationism: A Metatheoretical Explanation of Theoretical Convergence between the United States and Europe." In P. Sztompka (ed.), *Agency and Structure: Reorienting Social Theory.* Amsterdam: Gordon and Breach: 3–23.

Ritzer, George, and Goodman, Douglas
2001   "Postmodern Social Theory." In Jonathan H. Turner (ed.), *Handbook of Sociological Theory.* New York: Kluwer Academic/Plenum Publishers: 151–169.

Ritzer, George, Goodman, Douglas, and Wiedenhoft, Wendy
2001   "Theories of Consumption." In George Ritzer and Barry Smart (eds.), *Handbook of Social Theory.* London: Sage: 410–427.

Ritzer, George, and Jeffrey, Stepnisky, eds.
2011   *The Wiley-Blackwell Companion to Major Social Theorists: Volume I—Classical Social Theorists.* Malden, Mass., and Oxford, England: Wiley-Blackwell.
2011   *The Wiley-Blackwell Companion to Major Social Theorists: Volume II—Contemporary Social Theorists.* Malden, Mass., and Oxford, England: Wiley-Blackwell.

Ritzer, George, and Walczak, David
1988   "Rationalization and the Deprofessionalization of Physicians." *Social Forces* 67:1–22.

Ritzer, George, Zhao, Shanyang, and Murphy, Jim
2001   "Metatheorizing in Sociology: The Basic Parameters and the Potential Contributions of Postmodernism." In Jonathan H. Turner (ed.), *Handbook of Sociological Theory.* New York: Kluwer Academic/Plenum Publishers: 113–131.

Robbins, Derek
1991   *The Work of Pierre Bourdieu.* Boulder, Colo.: Westview.

Robertson, Roland
1992   *Globalization: Social Theory and Global Culture.* London: Sage.
2001   "Globalization Theory 2000+: Major Problematics." In George Ritzer and Berry Smart (eds.), *Handbook of Social Theory.* London: Sage: 458–471.

Robinson, F.
2001   *Globalizing Care: Ethics, Feminist Theory, and International Relations.* Binghampton, N.Y.: Haworth Press.

Robinson, W. I.
2004   *A Theory of Global Capitalism.* Baltimore.: Johns Hopkins University Press.
2007   "Theories of Globalization." In George Ritzer (ed.), *The Blackwell Companion to Globalization.* Oxford: Blackwell: 125–143.

Rocher, Guy
1975   *Talcott Parsons and American Sociology.* New York: Barnes and Noble.

Rock, Paul
1979   *The Making of Symbolic Interactionism.* Totowa, N.J.: Rowman and Littlefield.

Rockmore, Tom
2002   *Marx after Marxism: The Philosophy of Karl Marx.* Malden, Mass.: Blackwell.

Roemer, John
1982   *A General Theory of Exploitation and Class.* Cambridge, Mass.: Harvard University Press.
1986a   "Introduction." In J. Roemer (ed.), *Analytical Marxism.* Cambridge, Eng.: Cambridge University Press: 1–7.

| 1986b | "'Rational Choice' Marxism: Some Issues of Method and Substance." In J. Roemer (ed.), *Analytical Marxism.* Cambridge, Eng.: Cambridge University Press: 191–201. |

Rogers, Mary F.

1996b	"Theory—What? Why? How?" In Mary F. Rogers (ed.), *Multicultural Experiences, Multicultural Theories.* New York: McGraw-Hill: 11–16.
2000	"Alfred Schutz." In George Ritzer (ed.), *The Blackwell Companion to Major Social Theorists.* Malden, Mass.: Blackwell: 367–387.
2001	"Contemporary Feminist Theory." In George Ritzer and Barry Smart (eds.), *Handbook of Social Theory.* London: Sage: 285–296.

Rogers, Mary F. (ed.)

| 1996a | *Multicultural Experiences, Multicultural Theories.* New York: McGraw-Hill. |

Rogowski, Ralf

| 2007 | "Luhmann, Niklas." In George Ritzer (ed.), *The Blackwell Encyclopedia of Sociology.* Oxford: Blackwell: 2675–2678. |

Rojek, Chris

| 2003 | *Stuart Hall.* Cambridge, Eng.: Polity Press. |
| 2005 | "Hall, Stuart." In George Ritzer (ed.), *Encyclopedia of Social Theory.* Thousand Oaks, Calif.: Sage: 353–356. |

Rose, Arnold

| 1962 | "A Systematic Summary of Symbolic Interaction Theory." In A. Rose (ed.), *Human Behavior and Social Processes.* Boston: Houghton Mifflin. |

Rose, Nancy E.

| 1995 | *Workfare or Fair Work: Women, Welfare, and Government Work Programs.* New Brunswick, N.J.: Rutgers University Press. |

Rosenau, James N.

| 2003 | *Distant Proximities: Dynamics beyond Globalization.* Princeton, N.J.: Princeton University Press. |

Rosenau, Pauline Marie

| 1992 | *Post-Modernism and the Social Sciences: Insights, Inroads, and Intrusions.* Princeton, N.J.: Princeton University Press. |

Rosenberg, Julius

| 2005 | "Globalization Theory: A Post Mortem." *International Politics* 42:2–74. |

Rosenberg, Morris

| 1989 | "Self-Concept Research: A Historical Review." *Social Forces* 68:34–44. |

Rosenberg, Rosalind

| 1982 | *Beyond Separate Spheres: Intellectual Roots of Modern Feminism.* New Haven: Yale University Press. |
| 1992 | *Divided Lives: American Women in the Twentieth Century.* New York: Hill and Wang. |

Rosenfeld, Rachel A., Cunningham, David, and Schmidt, Kathryn

| 1997 | "American Sociological Association Elections, 1975 to 1996: Exploring Explanations for 'Feminization.'" *American Sociological Review* 62:746–759. |

Rosenthal, Naomi, Fingrutd, Meryl, Ethier, Michele, Karant, Roberta, and McDonald, David

| 1985 | "Social Movements and Network Analysis: A Case Study of Nineteenth-Century Women's Reform in New York State." *American Journal of Sociology* 90:1022–1054. |

Ross, Dorothy

| 1991 | *The Origins of American Social Science.* Cambridge, Eng.: Cambridge University Press. |

Rossel, Jorg, and Collins, Randall

| 2001 | "Conflict Theory and Interaction Rituals." In Jonathan H. Turner (ed.), *Handbook of Sociological Theory.* New York: Kluwer Academic/Plenum Publishers: 509–531. |

Rossi, Alice

1964	"Equality of the Sexes: An Immodest Proposal." *Daedalus* 93:607–652.
1974	*The Feminist Papers: From Adams to de Beauvoir.* New York: Bantam.
1977	"A Biosocial Perspective on Parenting." *Daedalus* 106:9–31.
1983	"Gender and Parenthood." *American Sociological Review* 49:1–19.

Rossi, Ino
2005   "Lévi-Strauss, Claude." In George Ritzer (ed.), *Encyclopedia of Social Theory*. Thousand Oaks,
             Calif.: Sage: 443–446.

Rossler, Beate
2007   "Work, Recognition, Emancipation." In Bert Van Den Brink and David Owen (eds.), *Recognition
             and Power: Axel Honneth and the Tradition of Critical Theory*. Cambridge, Eng.: Cambridge
             University Press: 135–165.

Roth, Guenther
1968   "Introduction." In G. Roth and C. Wittich (eds.), *Max Weber, Economy and Society*, Vol. 1.
             Totowa, N.J.: Bedminster Press: xxvii–civ.
1971   "Sociological Typology and Historical Explanations." In G. Roth and R. Bendix (eds.), *Scholarship
             and Partisanship: Essays on Max Weber*. Berkeley: University of California Press: 109–128.
1976   "History and Sociology in the Work of Max Weber." *British Journal of Sociology* 27:306–318.
2000   "Global Capitalism and Multi-Ethnicity: Max Weber Then and Now." In S. Turner (ed.), *The
             Cambridge Companion to Weber*. Cambridge, Eng.: Cambridge University Press: 117–130.

Roth, Louise Marie
1999   "The Right to Privacy Is Political: Power, the Boundary between Public and Private, and Sexual
             Harassment." *Law and Social Inquiry* 24(1):45–71.

Rowe, A.M.C.
2000   "Locating Feminism's Subject: The Paradox of White Femininity and the Struggle to Forge
             Feminist Alliances." *Communication Theory* 10:64–80.

Rubenstein, David
1986   "The Concept of Structure in Sociology." In M. L. Wardell and S. P. Turner (eds.), *Sociological
             Theory in Transition*. Boston: Allen and Unwin: 80–94.

Ruddick, Sara
1980   "Maternal Thinking." *Feminist Studies* 6:342–367.
1994   "Notes towards a Feminist Maternal Peace Politics." In A. Jaggar (ed.), *Living with Contradictions:
             Controversies in Feminist Social Ethics*. Boulder, Colo.: Westview.

Rudy, Kathy
2001   "Radical Feminism, Lesbian Separatism, and Queer Theory." *Feminist Studies* 27:191–222.

Ruef, Martin
2007   "Mannheim, Karl." In George Ritzer (ed.), *The Blackwell Encyclopedia of Sociology*. Oxford:
             Blackwell: 2756–2759.

Rueschemeyer, Dietrich
1994   "Variations on Two Themes in Durkheim's *Division du Travail:* Power, Solidarity, and Meaning in
             Division of Labor." *Sociological Forum* 9:59–71.

Rundell, John
2001   "Modernity, Enlightenment, Revolution and Romanticism: Creating Social Theory." In George
             Ritzer and Barry Smart (eds.), *Handbook of Social Theory*. London: Sage: 13–29.
2005   "Elias, Norbert." In George Ritzer (ed.), *Encyclopedia of Social Theory*. Thousand Oaks, Calif.:
             Sage: 239–245.

Russell, Diana E.
1998   *Dangerous Relationships: Pornography, Misogyny, and Rape*. Thousand Oaks, Calif.: Sage.

Ryan, J. Michael
2005a   "Micro-Macro Integration." In George Ritzer (ed.), *Encyclopedia of Social Theory*. Thousand Oaks,
             Calif.: Sage: 501–503.
2005b   "Agency-Structure Integration." In George Ritzer (ed.), *Encyclopedia of Social Theory*. Thousand
             Oaks, Calif.: Sage: 5–6.
2007   "Grobalization." In George Ritzer (ed.), *The Blackwell Encyclopedia of Sociology*. Oxford:
             Blackwell: 2022–2023.

Ryan, William
1971   *Blaming the Victim*. New York: Pantheon.

Sadri, Ahmad
1992   *Max Weber's Sociology of Intellectuals*. New York: Oxford University Press.

Salamini, Leonardo
1981   *The Sociology of Political Praxis: An Introduction to Gramsci's Theory.* London: Routledge and
                Kegan Paul.

Sallee, Margaret W.
2008   "A Feminist Perspective on Parental Leave Policies." *Innovations in Higher Education* 32:
                181–194.

Salomon, A.
1945   "German Sociology." In G. Gurvitch and W. F. Moore (eds.), *Twentieth Century Sociology.* New
                York: Philosophical Library: 586–614.
1963/1997   "Georg Simmel Reconsidered." In Gary D. Jaworski, *Georg Simmel and the American Prospect.*
                Albany: State University of New York Press: 91–108.

Sanday, Peggy Reeves
1996   *A Woman Scorned: Acquaintance Rape on Trial.* New York: Doubleday.

Sanderson, Stephen K.
2001   "Evolutionary Theorizing." In Jonathan H. Turner (ed.), *Handbook of Sociological Theory.* New
                York: Kluwer Academic/Plenum Publishers: 439–455.
2007   "Conflict Theory." In George Ritzer (ed.), *The Blackwell Encyclopedia of Sociology.* Oxford:
                Blackwell: 662–665.

Sandstrom, Kent L., and Kleinman, Sherry
2005   "Symbolic Interaction." In George Ritzer (ed.), *Encyclopedia of Social Theory.* Thousand Oaks,
                Calif.: Sage: 821–826.

Sandstrom, Kent L., Martin, Daniel D., and Fine, Gary Alan
2001   "Symbolic Interactionism at the End of the Century." In George Ritzer and Barry Smart (eds.),
                Handbook of Social Theory. London: Sage: 217–231.

Sassen, Saskia
1998   *Globalizatoin and Its Discontents.* New York: New Press.
2004   "Local Actors in Global Politics." *Current Sociology* 52:649–670.

Satoshi, Kamata
1982   *Japan in the Passing Lane.* New York: Pantheon.

Saunders, Peter
1989   "Space, Urbanism and the Created Environment." In D. Held and J. B. Thompson (eds.), *Social
                Theory of Modern Societies: Anthony Giddens and His Critics.* Cambridge, Eng.: Cambridge
                University Press: 215–234.

Sawyer, R. Keith
2002   "Durkheim's Dilemma: Toward a Sociology of Emergence." *Sociological Theory* 20:227–247.
2005   "Emergence." In George Ritzer (ed.), *Encyclopedia of Social Theory.* Thousand Oaks, Calif.: Sage:
                245–246.
2007   "Complexity and Emergence." In George Ritzer (ed.), *The Blackwell Encyclopedia of Sociology.*
                Oxford: Blackwell: 633–636.

Sayce, Susan
2012   "Being a Female Pension Trustee." *Equality, Diversity and Inclusion: An International Journal*
                31(3):298–314.

Sayer, Derek
1991   *Capitalism and Modernity: An Excursus on Marx and Weber.* New York: Routledge.

Sayers, Sean
2007   "The Concept of Labor: Marx and His Critics." *Science and Society* 71:431–454.

Scaff, Lawrence A.
1989   *Fleeing the Iron Cage: Culture, Politics, and Modernity in the Thought of Max Weber.* Berkeley:
                University of California Press.
2005   "Rationalization." In George Ritzer (ed.), *Encyclopedia of Social Theory.* Thousand Oaks, Calif.:
                Sage: 624–628.
2011   "Georg Simmel." In George Ritzer and Jeffrey Stepnisky (eds.), *The Wiley-Blackwell Companion
                to Major Social Theorists: Volume 1—Classical Social Theorists.* Malden, Mass., and Oxford,
                Eng.: Wiley-Blackwell: 205–235.

Scambler, Graham
1996   "The 'Project of Modernity' and the Parameters for a Critical Sociology: An Argument with Illustrations from Medical Sociology." *Sociology* 30:567–581.

Schaeffer, D.
2001   "Feminism and Liberalism Reconsidered: The Case of Catharine MacKinnon." *American Political Science Review* 95:699–708.

Schatzki, Theodore R.
1996   *Social Practices: A Wittgensteinian Approach to Human Activity and the Social.* Cambridge, Eng.: Cambridge University Press.

Schatzki, Theodore R., Knorr-Cetina, Karin, and von Savigny, E. (eds.)
2001   *The Practice Turn in Contemporary Theory.* London: Routledge.

Scheff, Thomas
1997   *Microsociology: Discourse, Emotion, and Social Structure.* Chicago: University of Chicago Press.
2000   "Shame and the Social Bond: A Sociological Theory." *Sociological Theory* 18(1):84-99.
2003   "Shame in Self and Society." *Symbolic Interaction* 26(2):239-262.
2006   *Goffman Unbound! A New Paradigm for Social Science.* Boulder, Colo.: Paradigm.
2007   "Microsociology." In George Ritzer (ed.), *The Blackwell Encyclopedia of Sociology.* Oxford: Blackwell: 3005–3008.

Schegloff, Emanuel
1979   "Identification and Recognition in Telephone Conversation Openings." In G. Psathas (ed.), *Everyday Language: Studies in Ethnomethodology.* New York: Irvington: 23–78.
2001   "Accounts of Conduct in Interaction: Interruption, Overlap, and Turn-Taking." In Jonathan H. Turner (ed.), *Handbook of Sociological Theory.* New York: Kluwer Academic/Plenum Publishers: 287–321.
2007   *Sequence Organization in Interaction: A Primer in Conversation Analysis.* Cambridge: Cambridge University Press.

Scheurich, James Joseph, and McKenzie, Kathryn Bell
2007   "Foucaldian Archeological Analysis." In George Ritzer (ed.), *The Blackwell Encyclopedia of Sociology.* Oxford: Blackwell: 1771–1774.

Schilt, Kristen
2008   "The Unfinished Business of Sexuality: Comment on Andersen." *Gender & Society* 22:109–114.

Schluchter, Wolfgang
1981   *The Rise of Western Rationalism: Max Weber's Developmental History.* Berkeley: University of California Press.
1996   *Paradoxes of Modernity: Culture and Conduct in the Theory of Max Weber.* Stanford, Calif.: Stanford University Press.

Schmaus, Warren
1994   *Durkheim's Philosophy of Science and the Sociology of Knowledge: Creating an Intellectual Niche.* Chicago: University of Chicago Press.

Schmidt, Neal, Gooding, Richard Z., Noe, Raymond A., and Kirsch, Michael
1984   "Meta-Analyses of Validity Studies Published between 1964 and 1982 and the Investigation of Study Characteristics." *Personnel Psychology* 37:407–422.

Schmitt, Raymond L., and Schmitt, Tiffani Mari
1996   "Community Fear of AIDS as Enacted Emotion: A Comparative Investigation of Mead's Concept of the Social Act." *Studies in Symbolic Interaction* 20:91–119.

Schmutz, Corinne
1996   "The Service Industry and Marx's Fetishism of Commodities." *Humanity and Society* 20:102–105.

Schneider, Louis
1967   *The Scottish Moralists: On Human Nature and Society.* Chicago: University of Chicago Press.
1971   "Dialectic in Sociology." *American Sociological Review* 36:667–678.

Schneider, Mark A.
1993   *Culture and Disenchantment.* Chicago: University of Chicago Press.

Schneidhofer, Thomas M., Schiffinger, Michael, and Mayrhofer, Wolfgang
2012   "Still a Man's World? The Influence of Gender and Gender Role Type on Income in Two Business School Graduate Cohorts over Time." *Equality, Diversity and Inclusion: An International Journal* 31(1):65–82.

Schroeter, Gerd
1985 "Dialogue, Debate, or Dissent? The Difficulties of Assessing Max Weber's Relation to Marx." In R. J. Antonio and R. M. Glassman (eds.), *A Weber-Marx Dialogue.* Lawrence: University of Kansas Press: 2–13.

Schroyer, Trent
1970 "Toward a Critical Theory of Advanced Industrial Society." In H. P. Dreitzel (ed.), *Recent Sociology: No. 2.* New York: Macmillan: 210–234.
1973 *The Critique of Domination.* Boston: Beacon Press.

Schubert, Hans-Joachim
2005 "Cooley, Charles Horton." In George Ritzer (ed.), *Encyclopedia of Social Theory.* Thousand Oaks, Calif.: Sage: 150–155.
2007 "Cooley, Charles Horton." In George Ritzer (ed.), *The Blackwell Encyclopedia of Sociology.* Oxford: Blackwell: 798–801.

Schultz, Ruth W.
1995 "The Improbable Adventures of an American Scholar: Robert K. Merton." *American Sociologist* 26:68–77.

Schulz, Markus S.
2007a "Horkheimer, Max." In George Ritzer (ed.), *The Blackwell Encyclopedia of Sociology.* Oxford: Blackwell: 2163–2165.
2007b "Adorno, Theodor W." In George Ritzer (ed.), *The Blackwell Encyclopedia of Sociology.* Oxford: Blackwell: 27–30.

Schumpeter, Joseph Alois
1976 *Capitalism, Socialism and Democracy.* 5th ed. London: Allen and Unwin.

Schutte, Gerhard
2007 "Phenomenology." In George Ritzer (ed.), *The Blackwell Encyclopedia of Sociology.* Oxford: Blackwell: 3401–3404.

Schutz, Alfred
1932/1967 *The Phenomenology of the Social World.* Evanston, Ill.: Northwestern University Press.

Schwalbe, Michael L.
1993 "Goffman against Postmodernism: Emotion and the Reality of the Self." *Symbolic Interaction* 16:333–350.
1996 *Unlocking the Iron Cage: The Men's Movement, Gender Politics and American Culture.* New York: Oxford University Press.
2005 "Self and Self-Concept." In George Ritzer (ed.), *Encyclopedia of Social Theory.* Thousand Oaks, Calif.: Sage: 684–687.

Schwanenberg, Enno
1971 "The Two Problems of Order in Parsons' Theory: An Analysis from Within." *Social Forces* 49:569–581.

Schwartz, Barry
1998 "Postmodernity and Historical Reputation: Abraham Lincoln in Late Twentieth-Century American Memory." *Social Forces* 77:63–103.

Schwartz, Justin
1995 "In Defence of Exploitation." *Economics and Philosophy* 11:275–307.

Schwartz, Pepper
1994 *Peer Marriage: How Love between Equals Really Works.* New York: Free Press.

Schweber, Silvan S.
1991 "Auguste Comte and the Nebular Hypothesis." In R. T. Bienvenu and M. Feingold (eds.), *In the Presence of the Past: Essays in Honor of Frank Manuel.* Dordrecht, Netherlands: Kluwer: 131–191.

Schwendinger, Julia, and Schwendinger, Herman
1974 *Sociologists of the Chair.* New York: Basic Books.

Schwinn, Thomas
1998 "False Connections: Systems and Action Theories in Neofunctionalism and in Jurgen Habermas." *Sociological Theory* 16:75–95.

Scimecca, Joseph
1977 *The Sociological Theory of C. Wright Mills.* Port Washington, N.Y.: Kennikat Press.

Sciulli, David, and Gerstein, Dean
1985   "Social Theory and Talcott Parsons in the 1980s." *Annual Review of Sociology* 11:369–387.

Scully, Diana
1990   *Understanding Sexual Violence: A Study of Convicted Rapists.* Boston: Unwin Hyman.

Searle, John
1972   "Chomsky's Revolution in Linguistics." *New York Review of Books* 18:16–24.

Sedgwick, Eve Kosofsky
1985   *Between Men: English Literature and Male Homosexual Desire.* New York: Columbia University
            Press.
1990   *Epistemology of the Closet.* Berkeley: University of California Press.

Sedgwick, Eve Kosofsky, and Frank, Adam
1995   "Shame in the Cybernetic Fold: Reading Silvan Tomkins." In Eve Kosfsky Sedgwick and Adam
            Frank (eds.), *Shame and Its Sisters: A Silvan Tomkins Reader.* Durham, N.C.: Duke University
            Press: 1–28.

Segura, Denise A., and Pierce, Jennifer
1993   "Chicana/o Family Structure and Gender Personality: Chodorow, Familism, and Psychoanalytic
            Sociology Revisited." *Signs* 19:62–91.

Seidman, Steven
1983   *Liberalism and the Origins of European Social Theory.* Berkeley: University of California Press.
1989   "Introduction." In S. Seidman (ed.), *Jurgen Habermas on Society and Politics: A Reader.* Boston:
            Beacon Press: 1–25.
1991   "The End of Sociological Theory: The Postmodern Hope." *Sociological Theory* 9:131–146.

Seidman, Steven, and Alexander, Jeffrey (eds.)
2001   *The New Social Theory Reader.* New York: Routledge.

Seigel, Jerrold E.
1978   *Marx's Fate: The Shape of a Life.* Princeton, N.J.: Princeton University Press.

Seligman, Adam B.
1993   "The Representation of Society and the Privatization of Charisma." *Praxis International* 13:68–84.

Sellerberg, Ann-Mari
1994   *A Blend of Contradictions: Georg Simmel in Theory and Practice.* New Brunswick, N.J.:
            Transaction Publishers.

Sewart, John J.
1978   "Critical Theory and the Critique of Conservative Method." *American Sociologist* 13:15–22.

Shalin, Dmitri
1986   "Pragmatism and Social Interactionism." *American Sociological Review* 51:9–29.
2011   "George Herbert Mead." In George Ritzer and Jeffrey Stepnisky (eds.), *The Wiley-Blackwell
            Companion to Major Social Theorists: Volume 1—Classical Social Theorists.* Malden, Mass., and
            Oxford, Eng.: Wiley-Blackwell: 373–425.

Shamir, Ronen
1993   "Formal and Substantive Rationality in American Law: A Weberian Perspective." *Social and Legal
            Studies* 2:45–72.

Sharrock, Wes
2001   "Fundamentals of Ethnomethodology." In George Ritzer and Barry Smart (eds.), *Handbook of
            Social Theory.* London: Sage: 249–259.

Sharrock, Wes, and Anderson, Bob
1986   *The Ethnomethodologists.* Chichester, Eng.: Ellis Horwood.

Shelton, Beth Anne
2000   "Understanding the Distribution of Housework between Husbands and Wives." In Linda J. Waite,
            Christine Bachrach, Michelle Hindin, Elizabeth Thomson, and Arland Thornton (eds.), *The Ties
            That Bind: Perspectives on Marriage and Cohabitation.* New York: Aldine de Gruyter: 343–355.

Shelton, Beth Anne, and Agger, Ben
1993   "Shotgun Wedding, Unhappy Marriage, No-Fault Divorce? Rethinking the Feminism-Marxism
            Relationship." In P. England (ed.), *Theory on Gender/Gender on Theory.* New York: Aldine de Gruyter.

Sheridan, Alan
1980   *Michel Foucault: The Will to Truth.* London: Tavistock.

Sherlock, Steve
1997   "The Future of Commodity Fetishism." *Sociological Focus* 30:61–78.

Shields, Rob
1996   "Meeting or Mis-Meeting? The Dialogical Challenge to Verstehen." *British Journal of Sociology* 47:275–294.

Shilling, Chris
1997   "The Undersocialised Conception of the Embodied Agent in Modern Sociology." *Sociology* 31:737–754.

Shilling, Chris, and Mellor, Philip A.
1996   "Embodiment, Structuration Theory and Modernity: Mind/Body Dualism and the Repression of Sensuality." *Body and Society* 2:1–15.

Shils, Edward
1996   "The Sociology of Robert E. Park." *American Sociologist* 27:88–106.

Shows, Carla, and Gerstel, Naomi
2009   "Fathering, Class, and Gender: A Comparison of Physicians and Emergency Medical Technicians." *Gender & Society* 23:161–187.

Shreve, Anita
1989   *Women Together, Women Alone: The Legacy of the Consciousness Raising Movement.* New York: Viking.

Sica, Alan
1986   "Hermeneutics and Axiology: The Ethical Content of Interpretation." In M. L. Wardell and S. P. Turner (eds.), *Sociological Theory in Transition.* Boston: Allen and Unwin: 142–157.
1988   *Weber, Irrationality and Social Order.* Berkeley: University of California Press.
2001   "Weberian Theory Today: The Public Face." In Jonathan H. Turner (ed.), *Handbook of Sociological Theory.* New York: Kluwer Academic/Plenum Publishers: 487–507.
2005   "Modernity." In George Ritzer (ed.), *Encyclopedia of Social Theory.* Thousand Oaks, Calif.: Sage: 505–511.

Silber, Ilanna Friedrich
2003   "Pragmatic Sociology as Cultural Sociology: Beyond Repertoire Theory?" *European Journal of Social Theory* 6(4):427–449.

Silver, Beverly J. and Arrighi, Giovanni
2011   "The End of the Long Twentieth Century." In C. Calhoun and G. Derluguian (eds.), *Business as Usual: The Roots of the Global Financial Meltdown.* New York: New York University Press: 53–68.

Simmel, Georg
1903/1971   "The Metropolis and Mental Life." In D. Levine (ed.), *Georg Simmel.* Chicago: University of Chicago Press: 324–339.
1904/1971   "Fashion." In D. Levine (ed.), *Georg Simmel.* Chicago: University of Chicago Press: 294–323.
1906/1950   "The Secret and the Secret Society." In K. H. Wolff (ed.), *The Sociology of Georg Simmel.* New York: Free Press: 307–376.
1907/1978   *The Philosophy of Money.* Ed. and trans. Tom Bottomore and David Frisby. London: Routledge and Kegan Paul.
1908/1950a   "Subordination under a Principle." In K. Wolff (ed. and trans.), *The Sociology of Georg Simmel.* New York: Free Press: 250–267.
1908/1950b   "Types of Social Relationships by Degrees of Reciprocal Knowledge of the Participants." In K. Wolff (ed. and trans.), *The Sociology of Georg Simmel.* New York: Free Press: 317–329.
1908/1955   *Conflict and the Web of Group Affiliations.* New York: Free Press.
1908/1959a   "How Is Society Possible?" In K. Wolff (ed.), *Essays in Sociology, Philosophy and Aesthetics.* New York: Harper Torchbooks: 337–356.
1908/1959b   "The Problem of Sociology." In K. Wolff (ed.), *Essays in Sociology, Philosophy and Aesthetics.* New York: Harper Torchbooks: 310–336.
1908/1971a   "Group Expansions and the Development of Individuality." In D. Levine (ed.), *Georg Simmel.* Chicago: University of Chicago Press: 251–293.

1908/1971b	"The Stranger." In D. Levine (ed.), *Georg Simmel.* Chicago: University of Chicago Press: 143–149.
1908/1971c	"The Poor." In D. Levine (ed.), *Georg Simmel.* Chicago: University of Chicago Press: 150–178.
1908/1971d	"Domination." In D. Levine (ed.), *Georg Simmel.* Chicago: University of Chicago Press: 96–120.
1917/1950	"The Problem Areas of Sociology." In K. H. Wolff (ed.), *The Sociology of Georg Simmel.* New York: Free Press: 16–25.
1918/1971	"The Transcendent Character of Life." In D. Levine (ed.), *Georg Simmel.* Chicago: University of Chicago Press: 353–374.
1921/1968	"The Conflict in Modern Culture." In K. P. Etzkorn (ed.), *Georg Simmel.* New York: Teachers College, Columbia University: 11–25.
1950	*The Sociology of Georg Simmel,* Ed. and trans. Kurt Wolff. New York: Free Press.
1984	*On Women, Sexuality and Love.* Trans. Guy Oakes. New Haven: Yale University Press.
1991	"Money in Modern Culture." *Theory, Culture and Society* 8:17–31.

Simon, Herbert
1957   *Administrative Behavior.* New York: Free Press.

Simpson, Brent
2007   "Rational Choice Theories." In George Ritzer (ed.), *The Blackwell Encyclopedia of Sociology.* Oxford: Blackwell: 3794–3799.

Singer, Brian C. J.
2005a   "Rousseau, Jean-Jacques." In George Ritzer (ed.), *Encyclopedia of Social Theory.* Thousand Oaks, Calif.: Sage: 656–658.
2005b   "Montesquieu, Charles Louis de Secondat." In George Ritzer (ed.), *Encyclopedia of Social Theory.* Thousand Oaks, Calif.: Sage: 512–515.

Singer, Peter
1980   *Marx.* Oxford: Oxford University Press.

Sitton, John F.
1996   "Disembodied Capitalism: Habermas's Conception of the Economy." *Sociological Forum* 13:61–83.

Sjoberg, Gideon, Gill, Elizabeth, Littrell, Boyd, and Williams, Norma
1997   "The Reemergence of John Dewey and American Pragmatism." In Norman K. Denzin (ed.), *Studies in Symbolic Interaction,* Vol. 21. Greenwich, Conn.: AI Press: 73–92.

Skeggs, Beverley
2008   "The Dirty History of Feminism and Sociology: Or the War of Conceptual Attrition." *The Sociological Review* 56(5):670–690.

Sklair, Leslie
2002   *Globalization: Capitalism and Its Alternatives.* Oxford: Oxford University Press.

Skocpol, Theda
1979   *States and Social Revolutions.* Cambridge, Eng.: Cambridge University Press.

Skog, Ole-Jorgen
1991   "Alcohol and Suicide—Durkheim Revisited." *Acta Sociologica* 34:193–206.

Slater, Don
1997   *Consumer Culture and Modernity.* Cambridge, Eng.: Polity Press.
2005   "Consumer Culture." In George Ritzer (ed.), *Encyclopedia of Social Theory.* Thousand Oaks, Calif.: Sage: 139–145.

Sloterdijk, Peter
1998/2011   *Bubbles: Spheres Volume 1: Microspherology.* Los Angeles: Semiotext(e).

Smart, Barry
1983   *Foucault, Marxism and Critique.* London: Routledge and Kegan Paul.
1985   *Michel Foucault.* Chichester, Eng.: Ellis Horwood.
1993   *Postmodernity.* London: Routledge.
2000   "Michel Foucault." In George Ritzer (ed.), *The Blackwell Companion to Major Social Theorists.* Malden, Mass.: Blackwell: 630–650.

Smelser, Neil
1959   *Social Change in the Industrial Revolution.* Chicago: University of Chicago Press.
1962   *Theory of Collective Behavior.* New York: Free Press.

1992   "The Rational Choice Perspective: A Theoretical Assessment." *Rationality and Society* 4:381–410.

1997   *Problematics of Sociology: The Georg Simmel Lectures, 1995.* Berkeley: University of California Press.

Smith, Cyril
1997   "Friedrich Engels and Marx's Critique of Political Economy." *Capital and Class* 62:123–142.

Smith, David Norman
1996   "The Social Construction of Enemies: Jews and the Representation of Evil." *Sociological Theory* 14:203–240.
1998   "Faith, Reason, and Charisma: Rodolf Sohm, Max Weber, and the Theology of Grace." *Sociological Inquiry* 68:32–60.

Smith, Dennis
1999   "The Civilizing Process and the History of Sexuality: Comparing Norbert Elias and Michel Foucault." *Theory and Society* 28:79–100.
2001   *Norbert Elias and Modern Social Theory.* Thousand Oaks, Calif.: Sage.

Smith, Dorothy E.
1979   "A Sociology for Women." In J. A. Sherman and E. T. Beck (eds.), *The Prism of Sex: Essays in the Sociology of Knowledge.* Madison: University of Wisconsin Press.
1987   *The Everyday World as Problematic: A Feminist Sociology.* Boston: Northeastern University Press.
1989   "Sociological Theory: Methods of Writing Patriarchy." In R. A. Wallace (ed.), *Feminism and Sociological Theory.* Newbury Park, Calif.: Sage: 34–64.
1990a   *The Conceptual Practices of Power: A Feminist Sociology of Knowledge.* Boston: Northeastern University Press.
1990b   *Texts, Facts and Femininity: Exploring the Relations of Ruling.* London: Routledge and Kegan Paul.
1999a   "From Women's Standpoint to a Sociology for People." In Janet L. Abu-Lughod (ed.), *Sociology for the Twenty-first Century.* Chicago: University of Chicago Press: 65–82.
1999b   *Writing the Social: Critique, Theory, and Investigations.* Toronto: University of Toronto Press.
2000   "Schooling for Inequality." *Signs* 25:1147–1151.
2004a   "Ideology, Science and Social Relations: A Reinterpretation of Marx's Epistemology." *European Journal of Social Theory* 7(4):445–462.
2004b   *Institutional Ethnography: A Sociology for People.* Palo Alto, Calif.: Altamira Press.
2004c   "Institutional Ethnography—Towards a Productive Sociology: An Interview with Dorothy E. Smith." *Sosiologisk tidsskrift* 12(2):179–184.
2006   *Institutional Ethnography as Practice.* Lanham, Md.: Rowman and Littlefield.
2009   "Categories Are Not Enough." *Gender & Society* 23(1):76–80.

Smith, Gregory W. H.
2006   *Erving Goffman.* New York: Routledge.
2007   "Goffman, Erving." In George Ritzer (ed.), *The Blackwell Encyclopedia of Sociology.* Oxford: Blackwell: 1995–1999.
2011   "Erving Goffman." In George Ritzer and Jeffrey Stepnisky (eds.), *The Wiley-Blackwell Companion to Major Social Theorists: Volume II—Contemporary Social Theorists.* Malden, Mass., and Oxford, Eng.: Wiley-Blackwell: 125–154.

Smith, Ken
2007   "Operationalizing Max Weber's Probability Concept of Class Situation: The Concept of Social Class." *British Journal of Sociology* 58:87–104.

Smith, Melanie
2007   "Glocalization." In George Ritzer (ed.), *The Blackwell Encyclopedia of Sociology.* Oxford: Blackwell: 1994–1995.

Smith, Norman Erik
1979   "William Graham Sumner as an Anti-Social Darwinist." *Pacific Sociological Review* 22:332–347.

Smith, Philip
2008   "Durkheim and Criminology: Reconstructing the Legacy." *Australian and New Zealand Journal of Criminology* 26:299–323.

Smith, T. V.
1931   "The Social Philosophy of George Herbert Mead." *American Journal of Sociology* 37:368–385.

Smythe, Deborah
2009   "A Few Laced Genes: Women's Standpoint in the Feminist Ancestry of Dorothy E. Smith."
            History of the Human Sciences 22(2):22–57.

Snitow, Ann Barr, Stansell, Christine, and Thompson, Sharon
1983   *Powers of Desire: The Politics of Sexuality.* New York: Monthly Review Press.

Snizek, William E.
1976   "An Empirical Assessment of 'Sociology: A Multiple Paradigm Science.'" *American Sociologist*
            11:217–219.

Snizek, William E., Fuhrman, Ellsworth, R., and Miller, Michael K. (eds.)
1979   *Contemporary Issues in Theory and Research.* Westport, Conn.: Greenwood Press.

Snow, David A.
1986   "Frame Alignment Processes, Micromobilization, and Movement Participation." *American
            Sociological Review* 51:464–481.
2001   "Extending and Broadening Blumer's Conceptualization of Symbolic Interactionism." *Symbolic
            Interaction* 24:367–377.
2007   "Frame." In George Ritzer (ed.), *The Blackwell Encyclopedia of Sociology.* Oxford: Blackwell.
            1778–1780.

So, Alvin Y., and Suwarsono
1990   "Class Theory or Class Analysis? A Reexamination of Marx's Unfinished Chapter on Class."
            Critical Sociology 17:35–55.

Sociological Perspectives
1995   Vol. 38. (Special edition)

Soeffner, Hans-Georg
2005   "Verstehen." In George Ritzer (ed.), *Encyclopedia of Social Theory.* Thousand Oaks, Calif.: Sage:
            864–868.

Soja, Edward W.
1989   *Postmodern Geographies: The Reassertion of Space in Critical Theory.* London: Verso.
1996   *Thirdspace: Journeys to Los Angeles and the Real-and-Imagined Places.* Malden, Mass.: Blackwell.
2000   *Postmetropolis: Critical Studies of Cities and Regions.* Malden, Mass.: Blackwell.

Sokoloff, Natalie
1980   *Between Money and Love: The Dialectics of Women's Home and Market Work.* New York: Praeger.

Solinger, Rickie (ed.)
1998   *Abortion Wars: A Half Century of Struggle, 1950–2000.* Berkeley: University of California Press.

Song, Jesook
2010   "'A Room of One's Own': The Meaning of Spatial Autonomy for Unmarried Women in Neoliberal
            South Korea." *Gender, Place and Culture* 17(2):131–149.

Sorokin, Pitirim
1928   *Contemporary Sociological Theories.* New York: Harper.

Speier, Matthew
1970   "The Everyday World of the Child." In J. Douglas (ed.), *Understanding Everyday Life.* Chicago:
            Aldine: 188–217.

Spender, Dale
1982   *Women of Ideas (And What Men Have Done to Them).* London: Routledge and Kegan Paul.

Spender, Dale (ed.)
1983   *Feminist Theorists: Three Centuries of Key Women Thinkers.* New York: Random House.

Spykman, Nicholas
1925/1966   *Social Theory of Georg Simmel.* Chicago: Aldine.

Srubar, Ilja
2005   "Phenomenology." In George Ritzer (ed.), *Encyclopedia of Social Theory.* Thousand Oaks, Calif.:
            Sage: 557–562.

Staats, Arthur W.
1976   "Skinnerian Behaviorism: Social Behaviorism or Radical Behaviorism?" *American Sociologist* 11:59–60.

Stacey, Judith, and Thorne, Barrie
1985   "The Missing Feminist Revolution in Sociology." *Social Problems* 32:301–316.
1996   "Is Sociology Still Missing Its Feminist Revolution?" *Perspectives: The ASA Theory Section Newsletter* 18:1–3.

Stanfield, Ron
1974   "Kuhnian Scientific Revolutions and the Keynesian Revolution." *Journal of Economic Issues* 8:97–109.

Staples, Clifford
2007   "Feuerbach, Ludwig." In George Ritzer (ed.), *The Blackwell Encyclopedia of Sociology.* Oxford: Blackwell: 1747–1749.

Starks, Brian, and Junisbai, Azamat
2007   "False Consciousness." In George Ritzer (ed.), *The Blackwell Encyclopedia of Sociology.* Oxford: Blackwell: 1568–1570.

Starosta, Guido
2008   "The Commodity-Form and the Dialectical Method: On the Structure of Marx's Exposition in Chapter 1 of *Capital.*" *Science and Society* 72:295–318.

Stauth, Georg
1997   "'Elias in Singapore': Civilizing Processes in a Tropical City." *Thesis Eleven* 50:51–70.

Stebbins, Robert
2007a   "Thomas, W. I." In George Ritzer (ed.), *The Blackwell Encyclopedia of Sociology.* Oxford: Blackwell: 5000.
2007b   "Znaniecki, Florian." In George Ritzer (ed.), *The Blackwell Encyclopedia of Sociology.* Oxford: Blackwell: 5316–5317.

Stehr, Nico
2001   "Modern Societies as Knowledge Societies." In George Ritzer and Barry Smart (eds.), *Handbook of Social Theory.* London: Sage: 494–508.

Steil, Janice M.
1997   *Marital Equality: Its Relationship to the Well-Being of Husbands and Wives.* Thousand Oaks, Calif.: Sage.

Stein, Arlene, and Plummer, Ken
1994   "'I Can't Even Think Straight': 'Queer' Theory and the Missing Revolution in Sociology." *Sociological Theory* 12(2):178–187.

Steinmetz, George
2007   "Marxism and Sociology." In George Ritzer (ed.), *The Blackwell Encyclopedia of Sociology.* Oxford: Blackwell: 2815–2818.

Stephanson, Anders
1989   "Regarding Postmodernism: A Conversation with Fredric Jameson." In D. Kellner (ed.), *Postmodernism, Jameson, Critique.* Washington, D.C.: Maisonneuve Press: 43–74.

Stichweh, Rudolph
2011   "Niklas Luhman." In George Ritzer and Jeffrey Stepnisky (eds.), *The Wiley-Blackwell Companion to Major Social Theorists: Volume II—Contemporary Social Theorists.* Malden, Mass., and Oxford, Eng.: Wiley-Blackwell: 287–309.

Stiglitz, Joseph E.
2002   *Globalization and Its Discontents.* New York: Norton.

Stiglmayer, Alexandra (ed.)
1994   *Mass Rape: The War against Women in Bosnia-Herzegovina.* Translations by Marion Faber. Lincoln: University of Nebraska Press.

Stokoe, Elizabeth
2006   "On Ethnomethodology, Feminism, and the Analysis of Categorical Reference to Gender in Talk-in-Interaction." *Sociological Review* 54:467–494.

Stones, Rob
2005a   "Giddens, Anthony." In George Ritzer (ed.), *Encyclopedia of Social Theory.* Thousand Oaks, Calif.: Sage: 321–327.

2005b   *Structuration Theory.* Cambridge: Palgrave McMillan.
2007a   "Structuration Theory." In George Ritzer (ed.), *The Blackwell Encyclopedia of Sociology.* Oxford:
               Blackwell: 4859–4861.
2007b   "Structure and Agency." In George Ritzer (ed.), *The Blackwell Encyclopedia of Sociology.* Oxford:
               Blackwell: 4861–4864.

Storey, John
2007   "Cultural Studies, British." In George Ritzer (ed.), *The Blackwell Encyclopedia of Sociology.*
               Oxford: Blackwell: 918–919.

Strange, Susan
1996   *The Retreat of the State: The Diffusion of Power in the World Economy.* Cambridge, Eng.:
               Cambridge University Press.

Strasser, Hermann, and Nollman, Gerd
2005   "Dahrendorf, Ralf." In George Ritzer (ed.), *Encyclopedia of Social Theory.* Thousand Oaks, Calif.:
               Sage: 183–185.

Strauss, Anselm
1996   "Everett Hughes: Sociology's Mission." *Symbolic Interaction* 19:271–283.

Strenski, Ivan
1997   *Durkheim and the Jews of France.* Chicago: University of Chicago Press.

Strydom, Piet
2005   "The Scottish Enlightenment." In George Ritzer (ed.), *Encyclopedia of Social Theory.* Thousand
               Oaks, Calif.: Sage: 675–680.

Stryker, Robin
2007   "Function." In George Ritzer (ed.), *The Blackwell Encyclopedia of Sociology.* Oxford: Blackwell:
               1808–1810.

Stryker, Sean
1998   "Communicative Action in New Social Movements: The Experience of the Students for a
               Democratic Society." *Current Perspectives in Social Theory* 18:79–98.

Stryker, Sheldon
1980   *Symbolic Interactionism: A Social Structural Version.* Menlo Park, Calif.: Benjamin/Cummings.
2001   "Traditional Symbolic Interactionism, Role Theory, and Structural Symbolic Interactionism: The
               Road to Identity Theory." In Jonathan H. Turner (ed.), *Handbook of Sociological Theory.* New
               York: Kluwer Academic/Plenum Publishers: 211–231.

Sullivan, Nikki
2003   *A Critical Introduction to Queer Theory.* New York: New York University Press.

Summers-Effler, Erika
2002   "The Micro Potential for Social Change: Emotion, Consciousness, and Social Movement
               Formation." *Sociological Theory* 20:41–60.

Swartz, David
1997   *Culture and Power: The Sociology of Pierre Bourdieu.* Chicago: University of Chicago Press.

Swatos, William H., Jr.
2007   "Constructionism." In George Ritzer (ed.), *The Blackwell Encyclopedia of Sociology.* Oxford:
               Blackwell: 686–687.

Swedberg, Richard
1991   "Introduction: The Man and His Work." In R. Swedberg (ed.), *The Economics and Sociology of
               Capitalism.* Princeton, N.J.: Princeton University Press: 3–98.
1996   "Analyzing the Economy: On the Contribution of James S. Coleman." In Jon Clark (ed.), *James S.
               Coleman.* London: Falmer Press: 313–328.
1998   *Max Weber and the Idea of Economic Sociology.* Princeton, N.J.: Princeton University Press.

Symbolic Interaction
2010   Special issue on the Internet, 33(4).

Szmatka, Jacek, and Mazur, Joanna
1996   "Theoretical Research Programs in Social Exchange Theory." *Polish Sociological Review* 3:265–288.

Sznaider, Natan
2005   "Ulrich Beck." In George Ritzer (ed.), *Encyclopedia of Social Theory.* Thousand Oaks, Calif.: Sage: 41–42.

Sztompka, Piotr
1974   *System and Function: Toward a Theory of Society.* New York: Academic Press.
1991   *Society in Action: The Theory of Social Becoming.* Chicago: University of Chicago Press.
1994   *Agency and Structure: Reorienting Social Theory.* Amsterdam: Gordon and Breach.
2000   "Robert Merton." In George Ritzer (ed.), *The Blackwell Companion to Major Social Theorists.* Malden, Mass.: Blackwell: 435–456.
2005   "Merton, Robert." In George Ritzer (ed.), *Encyclopedia of Social Theory.* Thousand Oaks, Calif.: Sage: 499–500.

Tabboni, Simonetta
1995   "The Stranger and Modernity: From Equality of Rights to Recognition of Difference." *Thesis Eleven* 43:17–27.

Takayama, K. Peter
1998   "Rationalization of State and Society: A Weberian View of Early Japan." *Sociology of Religion* 59:65–88.

Takla, Tendzin, and Pope, Whitney
1985   "The Force Imagery in Durkheim: The Integration of Theory, Metatheory and Method." *Sociological Theory* 3:74–88.

Tannen, Deborah
1990   *You Just Don't Understand: Women and Men in Conversation.* New York: Morrow.
1994   *Gender and Discourse.* New York: Oxford University Press.

Tannen, Deborah (ed.)
1993   *Gender and Conversational Interaction.* New York: Oxford University Press.

Tar, Zoltan
1977   *The Frankfurt School: The Critical Theories of Max Horkheimer and Theodor W. Adorno.* London: Routledge and Kegan Paul.

Tarrant, Shira
2006   *When Sex Became Gender.* New York: Routledge.

Taylor, Charles
1989   *Sources of the Self: The Making of the Modern Identity.* New York: Cambridge University Press.
2004   *Modern Social Imaginaries.* Durham, N.C.: Duke University Press.
2007   *A Secular Age.* Cambridge, Mass.: Harvard University Press.

Taylor, Paul C.
2011   "William Edward Burghardt Du Bois." In George Ritzer and Jeffrey Stepnisky (eds.), *The Wiley-Blackwell Companion to Major Social Theorists: Volume 1—Classical Social Theorists.* Malden, Mass., and Oxford, Eng.: Wiley-Blackwell: 448–468.

Taylor, Verta, and Rupp, Leila
1993   "Women's Culture and Lesbian Feminist Activism: A Reconsideration of Cultural Feminism." *Signs* 19:1–61.

Taylor, Victor E.
2007   "Postmodern Culture." In George Ritzer (ed.), *The Blackwell Encyclopedia of Sociology.* Oxford: Blackwell: 3556–3558.

Telos
1989–1990   "Does Critical Theory Have a Future? The Elizabethtown Telos Conference (February 23–25, 1990)." *Telos* 82:111–130.

Tenbruck, F. H.
1959   "Formal Sociology." In K. Wolff (ed.), *Essays on Sociology, Philosophy and Aesthetics.* New York: Harper Torchbooks: 61–99.

Ten Have, Paul
1995   "Medical Ethnomethodology: An Overview." *Human Studies* 18:245–261.

Terkel, Studs
1974   *Working.* New York: Pantheon.

Tester, Griff
2008   "An Intersectional Analysis of Sexual Harassment in Housing." *Gender & Society* 22:349–366.

Thacker, Eugene
2005   *The Global Genome, Biotechnology, Politics and Culture.* Cambridge, Mass.: MIT Press.

Then, Gabe
2007   "Reappraising the Risk Society Thesis: Telescopic Sight or Myopic Vision?" *Current Sociology* 55:793–813.

Theory, Culture and Society
1997   "Gilles Deleuze: A Symposium." 14:1–88.

Thibault, Paul J.
2005a   "Saussure, Ferdinand de." In George Ritzer (ed.), *Encyclopedia of Social Theory.* Thousand Oaks, Calif.: Sage: 665–672.
2005b   "Semiology." In George Ritzer (ed.), *Encyclopedia of Social Theory,* Thousand Oaks, Calif.: Sage: 687–693.

Thibaut, John W., and Kelley, Harold H.
1959   *The Social Psychology of Groups.* New York: Wiley.

Thistle, Susan
2000   "The Trouble with Modernity: Gender and the Remaking of Social Theory." *Sociological Theory* 18:275–288.
2002   "Gender, Class and Welfare State Formation in the 21st Century." *Current Perspectives in Social Theory* 21:115–142.

Thomas, George M.
2007   "Globalization: The Major Players." In George Ritzer (ed.), *The Blackwell Companion to Globalization.* Oxford: Blackwell: 84–102.

Thomas, William I., and Thomas, Dorothy S.
1928   *The Child in America: Behavior Problems and Programs.* New York: Knopf.

Thomas, William I., and Znaniecki, Florian
1918/1958   *The Polish Peasant in Europe and America.* New York: Dover Publications.

Thompson, Becky W.
1994   *A Hunger So Wide and So Deep: American Women Speak Out on Eating Problems.* Minneapolis: University of Minnesota Press.

Thompson, John B.
1989   "The Theory of Structuration." In D. Held and J. B. Thompson (eds.), *Social Theory of Modern Societies: Anthony Giddens and His Critics.* Cambridge, Eng.: Cambridge University Press: 56–76.

Thompson, Kenneth
1975   *Auguste Comte: The Foundation of Sociology.* New York: Halstead Press.

Thomson, Ernie
1994   "The Sparks That Dazzle Rather Than Illuminate: A New Look at Marx's 'Theses on Feuerbach.'" *Nature, Society and Thought* 7:299–323.

Thorne, Barrie
1995   "Symposium: On West and Fenstermaker's 'Doing Difference.'" *Gender & Society* 9:497–499.

Tilly, Charles
1997   "James S. Coleman as a Guide to Social Research." *American Sociologist* 28:82–87.

Tilman, Rick
1984   *C. Wright Mills: A Native Radical and His American Intellectual Roots.* University Park: Pennsylvania State University Press.
1992   *Thorstein Veblen and His Critics, 1891–1963: Conservative, Liberal, and Radical Perspectives.* Princeton, N.J.: Princeton University Press, 1992.

Tindall, D. B., and Malinick, Todd E.
2007   "Weak Ties (Strength of)." In George Ritzer (ed.), *The Blackwell Encyclopedia of Sociology.*
            Oxford: Blackwell: 5222–5225.

Tiryakian, Edward A.
1974   "Review of *Emile Durkheim on Morality and Society.*" *American Journal of Sociology* 80:769–771.
1979   "The Significance of Schools in the Development of Sociology." In W. Snizek, E. Fuhrman, and
            M. Miller (eds.), *Contemporary Issues in Theory and Research.* Westport, Conn.: Greenwood
            Press: 211–233.
1981   "The Sociological Import of Metaphor." *Sociological Inquiry* 51:27–33.
1986   "Hegemonic Schools and the Development of Sociology: Rethinking the History of the Discipline."
            In R. C. Monk (ed.), *Structures of Knowing.* Lanham, Md.: University Press of America: 417–441.
1994   "Revisiting Sociology's First Classic: *The Division of Labor in Society* and Its Actuality."
            Sociological Forum 9:3–16.
1995   "Collective Effervescence, Social Change and Charisma: Durkheim, Weber and 1989."
            International Sociology 10:269–281.
2007a   "Durkheim, Emile, and Social Change." In George Ritzer (ed.), *The Blackwell Encyclopedia of
            Sociology.* Oxford: Blackwell: 1261–1264.
2007b   "Sorokin, Pitirim A." In George Ritzer (ed.), *The Blackwell Encyclopedia of Sociology.* Oxford:
            Blackwell: 4619–4624.

Tiryakian, Edward A. (ed.)
1991   "Symposium: Robert K. Merton in Review." *Contemporary Sociology* 20:506–530.

Titunik, Regina F.
1997   "A Continuation of History: Max Weber and the Advent of a New Aristocracy." *Journal of Politics*
            59:680–700.

Toby, Jackson
1977   "Parsons' Theory of Societal Evolution." In T. Parsons, *The Evolution of Societies.* Englewood
            Cliffs, N.J.: Prentice-Hall: 1–23.

Tocqueville, Alexis de
1835–1840/ *Democracy in America.* Garden City, N.Y.: Doubleday.
1969
1856/1983   *The Old Regime and the French Revolution.* New York: Doubleday.
1893/1959   *The Recollections of Alexis de Tocqueville.* New York: Meridian Books.

Tomlinson, John
1999   *Globalization and Culture.* Chicago: University of Chicago Press.

Tong, Rosemarie
1998   *Feminist Thought: A More Comprehensive Introduction.* Boulder, Colo.: Westview.
2009   *Feminist Thought: A More Comprehensive Introduction,* 3rd ed. Boulder, CO: Westview Press.

Toscano, Alberto
2007a   "Situationists." In George Ritzer (ed.), *The Blackwell Encyclopedia of Sociology.* Oxford:
            Blackwell: 4335–4336.
2007b   "Neo-Marxism." In George Ritzer (ed.), *The Blackwell Encyclopedia of Sociology.* Oxford:
            Blackwell: 3178–3180.

Touraine, Alain
1977   *The Self-Production of Society.* Chicago: University of Chicago Press.
1995   *Critique of Modernity.* Oxford: Blackwell.

Travers, Andrew
1992   "The Conversion of Self in Everyday Life." *Human Studies* 15:169–238.

Treviño, A. Javier
2005   "Parsons's Action-System Requisite Model and Weber's Elective Affinity." *Journal of Classical
            Sociology* 5:319–348.

Trexler, Richard C.
1995   *Sex and Conquest: Gendered Violence, Political Order, and the European Conquest of the
            Americas.* Ithaca, N.Y.: Cornell University Press.

Tribe, Keith
1989   "Introduction." In K. Tribe (ed.), *Reading Weber.* London: Routledge: 1–14.

Trifonas, Peter
1996   "The Ends of Pedagogy: From the Dialectic of Memory to the Deconstruction of the Institution."
            Educational Theory 46:303–333.

Troyer, William
1946   "Mead's Social and Functional Theory of Mind." *American Sociological Review* 11:198–202.

Tseelon, Efrat
1992   "Is the Presented Self Sincere? Goffman, Impression Management and the Postmodern Self."
            Theory, Culture and Society 9:115–128.

Tucker, Kenneth H., Jr.
2007   "Althusser, Louis." In George Ritzer (ed.), *The Blackwell Encyclopedia of Sociology.* Oxford:
            Blackwell: 125–127.

Tucker, Robert C. (ed.)
1970   *The Marx-Engels Reader.* New York: Norton.

Tumin, Melvin
1953   "Some Principles of Stratification: A Critical Analysis." *American Sociological Review* 18:387–394.

Turner, Bryan S.
1974   *Weber and Islam: A Critical Study.* London: Routledge and Kegan Paul.
1981   *For Weber: Essays in the Sociology of Fate.* Boston: Routledge and Kegan Paul.
1985   *The Body and Society: Explorations in Social Theory.* Oxford: Blackwell.
1986   "Simmel, Rationalization and the Sociology of Money." *Sociological Review* 34:93–114.
1991   *Religion and Social Theory.* Thousand Oaks, Calif.: Sage.
1995   "Karl Mannheim's Ideology and Utopia." *Political Studies* 43:718–727.
2007   "Body and Cultural Sociology." In George Ritzer (ed.), *The Blackwell Encyclopedia of Sociology.*
            Oxford: Blackwell: 324–328.
2009   "Introduction: A New Agenda for Social Theory?" In Bryan S. Turner (ed.), *The New Blackwell
            Companion to Social Theory.* Malden, Mass.: Blackwell.

Turner, Jonathan H.
1973   "From Utopia to Where? A Strategy for Reformulating the Dahrendorf Conflict Model." *Social
            Forces* 52:236–244.
1975   "A Strategy for Reformulating the Dialectical and Functional Theories of Conflict." *Social Forces*
            53:433–444.
1982   *The Structure of Sociological Theory.* 3rd ed. Homewood, Ill.: Dorsey Press.
1985   "In Defense of Positivism." *Sociological Theory* 3:24–30.
1986   *The Structure of Sociological Theory.* 4th ed. Chicago: Dorsey Press.
1987   "Social Exchange Theory: Future Directions." In K. S. Cook (ed.), *Social Exchange Theory.*
            Beverly Hills, Calif.: Sage: 223–238.
1995   "Can Symbolic Interactionism Really Contribute to Macro Sociology?" *Current Perspectives in
            Social Theory* 15:181–197.
2000   "Herbert Spencer." In George Ritzer (ed.), *The Blackwell Companion to Major Social Theorists.*
            Malden, Mass.: Blackwell: 81–104.
2001   "The Origins of Positivism: The Contributions of Auguste Comte and Herbert Spencer." In George
            Ritzer and Barry Smart (eds.), *Handbook of Social Theory.* London: Sage: 30–42.
2005   "Conflict Theory." In George Ritzer (ed.), *Encyclopedia of Social Theory.* Thousand Oaks, Calif.:
            Sage: 134–139.
2007a   "Spencer, Herbert." In George Ritzer (ed.), *The Blackwell Encyclopedia of Sociology.* Oxford:
            Blackwell: 4638–4641.
2007b   "Micro-Macro Links." In George Ritzer (ed.), *The Blackwell Encyclopedia of Sociology.* Oxford:
            Blackwell: 2997–3005.

Turner, Jonathan H., and Boyns, David E.
2001   "The Return of Grand Theory." In Jonathan H. Turner (ed.), *Handbook of Sociological Theory.*
            New York: Kluwer Academic/Plenum Publishers: 353–378.

Turner, Jonathan H., and Maryanski, A. Z.
1979   *Functionalism.* Menlo Park, Calif.: Benjamin/Cummings.
1988   "Is 'Neofunctionalism' Really Functional?" *Sociological Theory* 6:110–121.

Turner, Jonathan H., and Stets, Jan E.
2005   *The Sociology of Emotions.* New York: Cambridge University Press.

Turner, Roy
1970   "Words, Utterances and Activities." In J. Douglas (ed.), *Understanding Everyday Life.* Chicago:
              Aldine: 161–187.

Turner, Stephen P.
1983   "Weber on Action." *American Sociological Review* 48:506–519.
1991   "Social Constructionism and Social Theory." *Sociological Theory* 9:22–33.
1993   "Introduction: Reconnecting the Sociologist to the Moralist." In S. P. Turner (ed.), *Emile
              Durkheim: Sociologist and Moralist.* London: Routledge: 1–22.
1994   *The Social Theory of Practices: Tradition, Tacit Knowledge, and Presuppositions.* Chicago:
              University of Chicago Press.
1998   "Who's Afraid of the History of Sociology?" *Schwezerische Zeistschrift fur Soziologie* 24:3–10.
2003   "Charisma Reconsidered." *Journal of Classical Sociology* 3(1):5–26.
2004   "The Maturity of Social Theory." In Charles Camic and Hans Joas (eds.), *The Dialogical Turn:
              New Roles for Sociology in the Post-Disciplinary Age.* Lanham, Md.: Rowman and Littlefield:
              141–170.

Turner, Stephen P., and Factor, Regis A.
1994   *Max Weber: The Lawyer as Social Thinker.* London: Routledge.

Udehn, Lars
1981   "The Conflict between Methodology and Rationalization in the Work of Max Weber." *Acta
              Sociologica* 24:131–147.
2002   "The Changing Face of Methodological Individualism." In John Hagan et al. (eds.), *Annual Review
              of Sociology.* Palo Alto, Calif.: Annual Reviews, pp. 479–507.

Uehara, Edwina
1990   "Dual Exchange Theory, Social Networks, and Informal Social Support." *American Journal of
              Sociology* 96:521–557.

Ullmann-Margalit, Edna
1997   "The Invisible Hand and the Cunning of Reason." *Social Research* 64:181–198.

Ulmer, Jeffery T.
2007   "Mesostructure." In George Ritzer (ed.), *The Blackwell Encyclopedia of Sociology.* Oxford:
              Blackwell: 2961–2963.

Ungar, Sheldon
1984   "Self-Mockery: An Alternative Form of Self-Presentation." *Symbolic Interaction* 7:121–133.

Urry, John
1995   *Consuming Places.* London: Routledge.
2003   *Global Complexity.* Cambridge, Eng.: Polity Press.

Vail, D. Angus
2007a   "Preparatory Stage." In George Ritzer (ed.), *The Blackwell Encyclopedia of Sociology.* Oxford:
              Blackwell: 3617.
2007b   "Play Stage." In George Ritzer (ed.), *The Blackwell Encyclopedia of Sociology.* Oxford: Blackwell:
              3417–3418.
2007c   "Game Stage." In George Ritzer (ed.), *The Blackwell Encyclopedia of Sociology.* Oxford:
              Blackwell: 1821–1822.
2007d   "Generalized Other." In George Ritzer (ed.), *The Blackwell Encyclopedia of Sociology.* Oxford:
              Blackwell: 1899–1900.

Valdes, Francisco, Culp, Jerome McCristal, and Harris, Angela P. (eds.)
2002   *Crossroads, Directions and a New Critical Race Theory.* Philadelphia: Temple University Press.

Valentine, Kylie
2007   "Methadone Maintenance Treatment and Making Up People." *Sociology—The Journal of the
              British Sociological Association* 41:497–514.

Valverde, Mariana
2007   "Genealogies of European States: Foucauldian Reflections." *Economy and Society* 36:159–178.

van den Berg, Axel
1980   "Critical Theory: Is There Still Hope?" *American Journal of Sociology* 86:449–478.

Vandenberghe, Frederic
2005   "Historical Materialism." In George Ritzer (ed.), *Encyclopedia of Social Theory.* Thousand Oaks,
             Calif.: Sage: 373–375.

van den Berghe, Pierre
1963   "Dialectic and Functionalism: Toward Reconciliation." *American Sociological Review* 28:695–705.

Van Den Brink, Bert, and Owen, David (eds.)
2007a   *Recognition and Power: Axel Honneth and the Tradition of Critical Theory.* Cambridge, Eng.:
             Cambridge University Press.
2007b   "Introduction." In Bert Van Den Brink and David Owen (eds.), *Recognition and Power: Axel
             Honneth and the Tradition of Critical Theory.* Cambridge, Eng.: Cambridge University Press: 1–30.

Van Der Duim, V. R., and Caalders, J.
2008   "Tourism Chains and Pro-Poor Tourism Development: An Actor-Network Analysis of a Pilot
             Project in Costa Rica." *Current Issues in Tourism* 11:109–125.

Vanderstraeten, Raf
2005   "System and Environment: Notes on the Autopoiesis of Modern Society." *Systems Research and
             Behavioral Science* 22:471–481.

Van Krieken, Robert
1998   *Norbert Elias.* London: Routledge.
2001   "Norbert Elias and Process Sociology." In George Ritzer and Barry Smart (eds.), *Handbook of
             Social Theory.* London: Sage: 353–367.

Varcoe, Ian
1998   "Identity and the Limits of Comparison: Bauman's Reception in Germany." *Theory, Culture and
             Society* 15:57–72.

Varga, Ivan
2006   "Social Morals, the Sacred and State Regulation in Durkheim's Sociology." *Social Compass*
             53:457–466.

Varley, Ann
2008   "A Place Like This? Stories of Dementia, Home and the Self." *Environment and Planning*
             26(1):47–67.

Varul, Matthias Zick
2007   "Veblen, Thorstein" In George Ritzer (ed.), *The Blackwell Encyclopedia of Sociology.* Oxford:
             Blackwell: 5186.

Veblen, Thorstein
1899/1994   *The Theory of the Leisure Class.* New York: Penguin Books.
1914/1964   *The Instinct of Workmanship and the State of the Industrial Arts.* New York: Augustus M. Kelly.

Veneziani, Roberto
2008   "A Future for (Analytical) Marxism?" *Philosophy of the Social Sciences* 38:388–399.

Venkatesh, Alladi
2007   "Postmodern Consumption." In George Ritzer (ed.), *The Blackwell Encyclopedia of Sociology.*
             Oxford: Blackwell: 3552–3556.

Venn, Couze
2011   In George Ritzer and Jeffrey Stepnisky (eds.), *The Wiley-Blackwell Companion to Major Social
             Theorists: Volume II—Contemporary Social Theorists.* Malden, Mass., and Oxford, England:
             Wiley-Blackwell:240–267.

Verran, Helen
1999   "Staying True to the Laughter in Nigerian Classrooms." In John Law and John Hassard (eds.),
             Actor Network Theory and After. Oxford: Blackwell: 136–155.

Vespa, Jonathan
2009   "Gender Ideology Construction: A Life Course and Intersectional Approach." *Gender & Society*
             23(3):363–387.

Vetter, Lisa P.
2008   "Harriet Martineau on the Theory and Practice of Democracy in America." *Political Theory*
             36:424–455.

Vidich, Arthur J., and Lyman, Stanford M.
1985   *American Sociology: Worldly Rejections of Religion and Their Directions.* New Haven: Yale
            University Press.

Vidler, Anthony
1991   "Agoraphobia: Spatial Estrangement in Georg Simmel and Siegfried Kracauer." *New German
            Critique* 54:31–45.

Villalon, Roberta
2010   "Passage to Citizenship and the Nuances of Agency: Latina Battered Immigrants." *Women's Studies
            International Forum* 33(6):552–560.

Vogel, Lise
1995   *Woman Questions: Essays for a Materialist Feminism.* New York: Routledge.

Wacquant, Loïc J. D.
1989   "Towards a Reflexive Sociology: A Workshop with Pierre Bourdieu." *Sociological Theory* 7:26–63.
1992   "Toward a Social Praxeology: The Structure and Logic of Bourdieu's Sociology." In P. Bourdieu
            and L.J.D. Wacquant (eds.), *An Invitation to Reflexive Sociology.* Chicago: University of Chicago
            Press: 2–59.

Wagner, Gerhard
1998   "Differentiation as Absolute Concept? Toward the Revision of a Sociological Category."
            International Journal of Politics, Culture and Society 11:451–474.

Wagner, Helmut
1964   "Displacement of Scope: A Problem of the Relationship between Small Scale and Large Scale
            Sociological Theories." *American Journal of Sociology* 69:571–584.

Wagner, Peter
1994   *A Sociology of Modernity: Liberty and Discipline.* London: Routledge.

Walby, Sylvia
2009   *Globalization and Inequalities: Complexities and Contested Modernities.* London: Sage.

Waldfogel, Jane
1997   "The Effect of Children on Women's Wages." *American Sociological Review* 62:209–217.

Wallace, Walter
1969   "Overview of Contemporary Sociological Theory." In W. Wallace (ed.), *Sociological Theory.*
            Chicago: University of Chicago Press: 1–59.
1988   "Toward a Disciplinary Matrix in Sociology." In N. Smelser (ed.), *Handbook of Sociology.*
            Newbury Park, Calif.: Sage: 23–76.

Wallerstein, Immanuel
1974/2011   *The Modern World-System I: Capitalist Agriculture and the Origins of the European World-
            Economy in the 16th Century.* Berkeley: University of California Press.
1980/2011   *The Modern World-System II: Mercantilism and the Consolidation of the European World-
            Economy, 1600–1750.* Berkeley: University of California Press.
1986   "Marxisms as Utopias: Evolving Ideologies." *American Journal of Sociology* 91:1295–1308.
1989/2011   *The Modern World-System III: The Second Era of Great Expansion of the Capitalist World-
            Economy, 1730–1840.* New York: Academic Press.
1992   "America and the World: Today, Yesterday, and Tomorrow." *Theory and Society* 21:1–28.
1995   "The End of What Modernity?" *Theory and Society* 24:471–488.
1999   *The End of the World as We Know It: Social Science for the Twenty-first Century.* Minneapolis:
            University of Minnesota Press.
2000   *The Essential Wallerstein.* New York: New Press.
2007   "Braudel, Fernand." In George Ritzer (ed.), *The Blackwell Encyclopedia of Sociology.* Oxford:
            Blackwell: 360–363.
2011a   The Modern World-System IV: Centrist Liberalism Triumphant, 1789–1914. Berkeley: University
            of California Press.
2011b   "Dynamics of Unresolved Global Crisis." In C. Calhoun and G. Derluguian (eds.), *Business as
            Usual: The Roots of the Global Financial Meltdown.* New York: New York University Press: 69–88.

Wallimann, Isidor
1981   *Estrangement: Marx's Conception of Human Nature and the Division of Labor.* Westport, Conn.:
            Greenwood Press.

Walter, Ryan
2008   "Governmentality Accounts of the Economy: A Liberal Bias?" *Economy and Society* 37:94–114.

Walters, Suzanna Danuta
2001   *All the Rage: The Story of Gay Visibility in America.* Chicago: University of Chicago Press.

Ward, Kathryn B.
1988   "Women in the Global Economy." In B. Glick et al. (eds.), *Women and Work.* Beverly Hills, Calif.:
                     Sage: 17–48.
1994   "Lifting as We Climb: How Scholarship about Women of Color Has Shaped My Life as a White
                     Feminist." In G. Young and B. Dickerson (eds.), *Color, Class, and Country: Experiences of
                     Gender.* Atlantic Highlands, N.J.: Zed Books.

Wardell, Mark L., and Turner, Stephen P. (eds.)
1986   *Sociological Theory in Transition.* Boston: Allen and Unwin.

Wartenberg, Thomas E.
1982   "'Species-Being' and 'Human Nature' in Marx." *Human Studies* 5:77–95.

Wasserman, Stanley, and Faust, Katherine
1994   *Social Network Analysis: Methods and Application.* Cambridge, Eng.: Cambridge University Press.

Weakliem, David, and Heath, Anthony
1994   "Rational Choice and Class Voting." *Rationality and Society* 6:243–270.

Weber, Lynn
1995   "Symposium: On West and Fenstermaker's 'Doing Difference.'" *Gender & Society* 9:499–503.
1999   *Understanding Race, Class, Gender: A Conceptual Framework.* New York: McGraw-Hill.
2009   *Understanding Race, Class, Gender: A Conceptual Framework.* Second Edition. Oxford: Oxford
                     University Press.

Weber, Marianne
1975   *Max Weber: A Biography.* Ed. and trans. Harry Zohn. New York: Wiley.

Weber, Max
1896–1906/   *The Agrarian Sociology of Ancient Civilizations.* London: NLB.
1976
1903–1906/   *Roscher and Knies: The Logical Problems of Historical Economics.* New York:
1975   Free Press.
1903–1917/   *The Methodology of the Social Sciences.* Ed. Edward Shils and Henry Finch.
1949   New York: Free Press.
1904–1905/   *The Protestant Ethic and the Spirit of Capitalism.* New York: Scribner.
1958
1906/1985   "'Churches' and 'Sects' in North America: An Ecclesiastical Socio-Political Sketch." *Sociological
                     Theory* 3:7–13.
1915/1958   "Religious Rejections of the World and Their Directions." In H. H. Gerth and C. W. Mills (eds.),
                     From Max Weber: Essays in Sociology. New York: Oxford University Press: 323–359.
1916/1964   *The Religion of China: Confucianism and Taoism.* New York: Macmillan.
1916–1917/   *The Religion of India: The Sociology of Hinduism and Buddhism.* Glencoe,
1958   Ill.: Free Press.
1921/1958   *The Rational and Social Foundations of Music.* Carbondale: Southern Illinois University Press.
1921/1963   *The Sociology of Religion.* Boston: Beacon Press.
1921/1968   *Economy and Society.* 3 vols. Totowa, N.J.: Bedminster Press.
1922–1923/   "The Social Psychology of the World Religions." In H. H. Gerth and C. W. Mills
1958   (eds.), *From Max Weber: Essays in Sociology.* New York: Oxford University Press: 267–301.
1927/1981   *General Economic History.* New Brunswick, N.J.: Transaction Books.

Wedgwood, Nikki
2009   "Connell's Theory of Masculinity—Its Origins and Influences on the Study of Gender." *Journal of
                     Gender Studies* 18(4):329–339.

Weigert, Andrew
1981   *Sociology of Everyday Life.* New York: Longman.

Weiler, Bernd
2007a   "Social Darwinism." In George Ritzer (ed.), *The Blackwell Encyclopedia of Sociology.* Oxford:
                     Blackwell: 4390–4392.

2007b   "Sumner, William Graham." In George Ritzer (ed.), *The Blackwell Encyclopedia of Sociology.* Oxford: Blackwell: 4884–4886.

Weingart, Peter
1969   "Beyond Parsons? A Critique of Ralf Dahrendorf's Conflict Theory." *Social Forces* 48:151–165.

Weingartner, Rudolph H.
1959   "Form and Content in Simmel's Philosophy of Life." In K. Wolff (ed.), *Essays on Sociology, Philosophy and Aesthetics.* New York: Harper Torchbooks: 33–60.

Weinstein, Deena, and Weinstein, Michael A.
1993   *Postmodern(ized) Simmel.* London: Routledge.
1998   "Simmel-Eco vs. Simmel-Marx: Ironized Alienation." *Current Perspectives in Social Theory* 18:63–77.

Weinstein, Eugene A., and Tanur, Judith M.
1976   "Meanings, Purposes and Structural Resources in Social Interaction." *Cornell Journal of Social Relations* 11:105–110.

Weiss, Johannes
1987   "On the Irreversibility of Western Rationalization and Max Weber's Alleged Fatalism." In S. Whimster and S. Lash (eds.), *Max Weber, Rationality and Modernity.* London: Allen and Unwin.

Weldes, Jutta
1989   "Marxism and Methodological Individualism." *Theory and Society* 18:353–386.

Weldon, Laurel, S.
2006   "The Structure of Intersectionality: A Comparative Politics of Gender." *Politics & Gender* 2(2):235–248.

Wellman, Barry
1983   "Network Analysis: Some Basic Principles." In R. Collins (ed.), *Sociological Theory—1983.* San Francisco: Jossey-Bass: 155–200.

Wellman, Barry, and Berkowitz, S. D. (eds.)
1988/1997   *Social Structures: A Network Approach.* Greenwich, Conn.: JAI Press.

Wellman, Barry, and Wortley, Scot
1990   "Different Strokes for Different Folks: Community Ties and Social Support." *American Journal of Sociology* 96:558–588.

Wells, Gordon C., and Baehr, Peter
1995   "Editors' Introduction." In *Max Weber, The Russian Revolutions.* Ithaca, N.Y.: Cornell University Press.

Werbner, Pnina, and Basu, Helene
1998   *Embodying Charisma: Modernity, Locality and the Performance of Emotion in Sufi Cults.* London: Routledge.

Wernick, Andrew
2000   "From Comte to Baudrillard: Socio-Theology after the End of the Social." *Theory, Culture and Society* 17:55–75.
2005a   "Comte, Auguste." In George Ritzer (ed.), *Encyclopedia of Social Theory.* Thousand Oaks, Calif.: Sage: 128–134.
2005b   *Auguste Comte and the Religion of Humanity: The Post-theistic Program in French Social Theory.* New York: Cambridge University Press.

West, Candace, and Fenstermaker, Sarah
1993   "Power, Inequality and the Accomplishment of Gender: An Ethnomethodological View." In P. England (ed.), *Theory on Gender/Feminism on Theory.* New York: Aldine de Gruyter: 223–254.
1995   "Doing Difference." *Gender & Society* 9:8–20.
2002   "Central Problematics: An Agenda for Feminist Sociology." In Sarah Fenstermaker and Candace West (eds.), *Doing Gender, Doing Difference: Inequality, Power, and Institutional Change.* New York: Routledge: 217–220.

West, Candace, and Zimmerman, Don
1987   "Doing Gender." *Gender & Society* 2:125–151.

West, Cornell
1994   *Race Matters.* New York: Vintage.

Wexler, Philip (ed.)
1991   *Critical Theory Now.* London: Falmer Press.

Whalen, Jack, Zimmerman, Don H., and Whalen, Marilyn R.
1988   "When Words Fail: A Single Case Analysis." *Social Problems* 35:335–361.

Whalen, Marilyn R., and Zimmerman, Don H.
1987   "Sequential and Institutional Contexts in Calls for Help." *Social Psychology Quarterly* 50:172–185.

Wharton, Amy (ed.)
2006   " 'This Missing Feminist Revolution in Sociology' Twenty Years Later: Looking Back, Looking Ahead." *Social Problems* 53(4):443–562.

Wheatland, Thomas
2009   *The Frankfurt School in Exile.* Minneapolis: University of Minnesota Press.

Whimster, Sam
2001   "Max Weber: Work and Interpretation." In George Ritzer and Barry Smart (eds.), *Handbook of Social Theory.* London: Sage: 54–65.
2005   "Weber, Max." In George Ritzer (ed.), *Encyclopedia of Social Theory.* Thousand Oaks, Calif.: Sage: 877–882.

White, Everett
1961   "Introduction." In E. Durkheim, *Moral Education.* New York: Free Press: ix–xxviii.

White, Harrison
1992   *Identity and Control: A Structural Theory of Social Action.* Princeton, N.J.: Princeton University Press.

White, Harrison C., Boorman, Scott A., and Breiger, Ronald L.
1976   "Social Structure from Multiple Networks: Parts 1 and 2." *American Journal of Sociology* 91:730–780, 1384–1446.

White, Hayden
1973   *The Historical Imagination in Nineteenth-Century Europe.* Baltimore: Johns Hopkins University Press.

Whitehead, Jaye Cee
2007   "Feminist Prison Activism: An Assessment of Empowerment." *Feminist Theory* 8(3):299–312.

Whitmeyer, Joseph M.
1994   "Why Actor Models Are Integral to Structural Analysis." *Sociological Theory* 12:153–165.
2005a   "Cook, Karen." In George Ritzer (ed.), *Encyclopedia of Social Theory.* Thousand Oaks, Calif.: Sage: 149–150.
2005b   "Power-Dependence Relations." In George Ritzer (ed.), *Encyclopedia of Social Theory.* Thousand Oaks, Calif.: Sage: 594–595.

Widerberg, Karin
2008   "In the Home of Others—Exploring New Sites and Methods When Investigating the Doings of Gender, Class, and Ethnicity." *Sociologisk Forskning* 4:7–23.

Wiedenhoft, Wendy
2005   "Fordism and Post-Fordism." In George Ritzer (ed.), *Encyclopedia of Social Theory.* Thousand Oaks, Calif.: Sage: 282–283.

Wiggershaus, Rolf
1994   *The Frankfurt School: Its History, Theories, and Political Significance.* Cambridge, Mass.: MIT Press.

Wilchins, Riki Anne
1997   *Read My Lips: Sexual Subversion and the End of Gender.* Ann Arbor, Mich.: Firebrand Books.

Wilde, Lawrence
1991   "Logic: Dialectic and Contradiction." In T. Carver (ed.), *The Cambridge Companion to Marx.* Cambridge, Eng.: Cambridge University Press: 275–295.

Wiley, Norbert
1979   "The Rise and Fall of Dominating Theories in American Sociology." In W. Snizek, E. Fuhrman, and M. Miller (eds.), *Contemporary Issues in Theory and Research.* Westport, Conn.: Greenwood Press: 47–79.
1985   "The Current Interregnum in American Sociology." *Social Research* 52:179–207.
1986   "Early American Sociology and *The Polish Peasant*." *Sociological Theory* 4:20–40.
1988   "The Micro-Macro Problem in Social Theory." *Sociological Theory* 6:254–261.
2007   "Znaniecki's Key Insight: The Merger of Pragmatism and Neo-Kantianism." *Polish Sociological Review* 158:133–143.

Wilkinson, Iain
2011   "Ulrich Beck." In George Ritzer and Jeffrey Stepnisky (eds.), *The Wiley-Blackwell Companion to Major Social Theorists: Volume II—Contemporary Social Theorists.* Malden, Mass., and Oxford, Eng.: Wiley-Blackwell: 480–499.

Willer, David
1999   "Developing Network Exchange Theory." In David Willer (ed.), *Network Exchange Theory.* Westport, Conn.: Praeger: 285–308.

Willer, David, and Emanuelson, Pamela
2008   "Testing Ten Theories." *Journal of Mathematical Sociology* 32:165–203.

Willer, David, Markovsky, Barry, and Patton, Travis
1989   "Power Structures: Derivations and Applications of Elementary Theory." In J. Berger, M. Zelditch Jr., and B. Anderson (eds.), *Sociological Theories in Progress: New Formulations.* Newbury Park, Calif.: Sage: 313–353.

Willer, David, and Patton, Travis
1987   "The Development of Network Exchange Theory." In E. J. Lawler and B. Markovsky (eds.), *Advances in Group Processes,* Vol. 4. Greenwich, Conn.: JAI Press: 199–242

Williams, Christine
2006   Still missing? Comments on the twentieth anniversary of "The missing feminist revolution in sociology." *Social Problems,* 53(4):454–458.

Williams, Joan
2000   *Unbending Gender.* Oxford: Oxford University Press.

Williams, Joyce
2007   "Small, Albion W." In George Ritzer (ed.), *The Blackwell Encyclopedia of Sociology.* Oxford: Blackwell: 4341–4342.

Williams, Patricia
1991   *The Alchemy of Race and Rights: Diary of a Law Professor.* Cambridge, Mass.: Harvard University Press.

Williams, Simon Johnson
1986   "Appraising Goffman." *British Journal of Sociology* 37:348–369.

Williamson, John
1990   "What Washington Means by Policy Reform." In John Williamson (ed.), *Latin American Adjustment: How Much Has Happened?* Washington, D.C.: Institute for International Economics: 7–20.
1997   "The Washington Consensus Reassessed." In Louis Emmerij (ed.), *Economic and Social Development into the XXI Century.* Washington, D.C.: Inter-American Development Bank: 48–61.

Wilson, John, and Musick, Mark
1997   "Who Cares? Toward an Integrated Theory of Volunteer Work." *American Sociological Review* 60:694–713.

Wiltshire, David
1978   *The Social and Political Thought of Herbert Spencer.* London: Oxford University Press.

Winant, Howard
2001   *The World Is a Ghetto: Race and Democracy since World War II.* New York: Basic Books.

Winterer, Caroline
1994   "A Happy Medium: The Sociology of Charles Horton Cooley." *Journal of the History of the Behavioral Sciences* 30:19–27.

Wirth-Cauchon, Janet
2011   "Donna Haraway." In George Ritzer and Jeffrey Stepnisky (eds.), *The Wiley-Blackwell Companion to Major Social Theorists: Volume II—Contemporary Social Theorists.* Malden, Mass., and Oxford, Eng.: Wiley-Blackwell: 500–519.

Wittgenstein, Ludwig
1953   *Philosophical Investigations.* Oxford: Blackwell.

Wolf, Frederick M.
1986   *Meta-Analysis: Quantitative Methods for Research Synthesis.* Beverly Hills, Calif.: Sage.

Wolf, Harald
2005a   "Capital." In George Ritzer (ed.), *Encyclopedia of Social Theory.* Thousand Oaks, Calif.: Sage: 75–76.
2005b   "Capitalism." In George Ritzer (ed.), *Encyclopedia of Social Theory.* Thousand Oaks, Calif.: Sage: 76–80.

Wolf, Martin
2005   *Why Globalization Works.* New Haven: Yale University Press.

Wolf, Naomi
1991   *The Beauty Myth: How Images Are Used against Women.* New York: Morrow.

Wolfe, Cary (ed.)
2000   *Observing Complexity: Systems Theory and Postmodernity.* Minneapolis: University of Minnesota Press.

Womack, James P., Jones, Daniel T., and Roos, Daniel
1990   *The Machine That Changed the World.* New York: Rawson.

Wood, Ellen Meiksins
1986   *The Retreat from Class: The New "True" Socialism.* London: Verso.
1989   "Rational Choice Marxism: Is the Game Worth the Candle?" *New Left Review* 177:41–88.
1995   *Democracy against Capitalism.* Cambridge, Eng.: Cambridge University Press.
1997   "Modernity, Postmodernity or Capitalism?" *Review of International Political Economy* 4:539–560.

Wood, Ellen Meiksins, and Foster, John Bellamy (eds.)
1997   *In Defense of History: Marxism and the Postmodern Agenda.* New York: Monthly Review Press.

Wood, Michael, and Wardell, Mark L.
1983   "G. H. Mead's Social Behaviorism vs. the Astructural Bias of Symbolic Interactionism." *Symbolic Interaction* 6:85–96.

Worsley, Peter
1982   *Marx and Marxism.* Chichester, Eng.: Ellis Horwood.

Wortmann, Susan
2007   "Praxis." In George Ritzer (ed.), *The Blackwell Encyclopedia of Sociology.* Oxford: Blackwell: 3612–3613.

Wright, Erik Olin
1985   *Classes.* London: Verso.
1987   "Towards a Post-Marxist Radical Social Theory." *Contemporary Sociology* 16:748–753.

Wrigley, Julia
1995   *Other People's Children: An Intimate Account of the Dilemma Facing Middle-Class Parents and the Women They Hire to Raise Their Children.* New York: Basic Books.

Wrong, Dennis
1994   *The Problem of Order: What Unites and Divides Society.* New York: Free Press.
1997   "Is Rational Choice Humanity's Most Distinctive Trait?" *American Sociologist* 28:73–81.

Yamagishi, Toshio
1995   "Social Dilemmas." In K. S. Cook, G. A. Fine, and J. S. House (eds.), *Sociological Perspectives on Social Psychology.* Boston: Allyn and Bacon: 311–335.
2005   "Social Dilemma." In George Ritzer (ed.), *Encyclopedia of Social Theory.* Thousand Oaks, Calif.: Sage: 731–735.

Yamagishi, Toshio, and Cook, Karen S.
1993   "Generalized Exchange and Social Dilemmas." *Social Psychology Quarterly* 56:235–248.

Yamagishi, Toshio, Gillmore, Mary R., and Cook, Karen S.
1988   "Network Connections and the Distribution of Power in Exchange Networks." *American Journal of Sociology* 93:833–851.

Yancy, George
2000   "Feminism and the Subtext of Whiteness: Black Women's Experiences as a Site of Identity Formation and Contestation of Whiteness." *Western Journal of Black Studies* 24:156–166.

Young, Robert L.
1997   "Account Sequences." *Symbolic Interaction* 20:291–305.

Yuval-Davis, Nira
2012   "Dialogical Epistemology—An Intersectional Resistance to the Oppression Olympics." *Gender & Society* 26:46.

Zablocki, Benjamin
1996   "Methodological Individualism and Collective Behavior." In Jon Clark (ed.), *James S. Coleman*.
            London: Falmer Press: 147–160.

Zafirovski, Milan
2001   "Parsons and Sorokin: A Comparison of the Founding of American Sociological Theory Schools."
            Journal of Classical Sociology 1:227–256.

Zannettino, Lana
2008   "Imagining Womanhood: Psychodynamic Processes in the 'Textual' and Discursive Formation of
            Girls' Subjectivities and Desires for the Future." *Gender and Education* 20(5):465–479.

Zaslavsky, Victor
1988   "Three Years of Perestroika." *Telos* 74:31–41.

Zeitlin, Irving M.
1996   *Ideology and the Development of Sociological Theory.* 6th ed. Englewood Cliffs, N.J.: Prentice-Hall.

Zerai, Assata
2000   "Agents of Knowledge and Action: Selected Africana Scholars and Their Contributions to the
            Understanding of Race, Class and Gender Intersectionality." *Cultural Dynamics* 12:182–222.

Zerilli, Linda M. G.
2005   *Feminism and the Abyss of Freedom*. Chicago: University of Chicago Press.

Zhao, Shanyang
1991   "Metatheory, Metamethod, Meta-Data-Analysis." *Sociological Perspectives* 34:377–390.
2001   "Metatheorizing in Sociology." In George Ritzer and Barry Smart (eds.), *Handbook of Social
            Theory.* London: Sage: 386–394.
2005   "Metatheory." In George Ritzer (ed.), *Encyclopedia of Social Theory.* Thousand Oaks, Calif.: Sage:
            500–501.

Zijderveld, Anton C.
2005   "Ideal Type." In George Ritzer (ed.), *Encyclopedia of Social Theory.* Thousand Oaks, Calif.: Sage:
            389–390.

Zimmerman, Don
1978   "Ethnomethodology." *American Sociologist* 13:5–15.
1988   "The Conversation: The Conversation Analytic Perspective." *Communication Yearbook* 11:406–432.

Zimmerman, Don, and Pollner, Melvin
1970   "The Everyday World as a Phenomenon." In J. Douglas (ed.), *Understanding Everyday Life.*
            Chicago: Aldine: 80–103.

Zimmerman, Don, and Wieder, D. Lawrence
1970   "Ethnomethodology and the Problem of Order: Comment on Denzin." In J. Douglas (ed.),
            Understanding Everyday Life. Chicago: Aldine: 285–298.

Zinn, Jens
2007a   "Reflexive Modernization." In George Ritzer (ed.), *The Blackwell Encyclopedia of Sociology.*
            Oxford: Blackwell: 3829–3830.
2007b   "Autopoesis." In George Ritzer (ed.), *The Blackwell Encyclopedia of Sociology.* Oxford: Blackwell:
            232–233.

Zipes, Jack
1994   "Adorno May Still Be Right." *Telos* 101:157–167.

Zosky, D. L.
1999   "The Application of Object Relations Theory to Domestic Violence." *Clinical Social Work Journal*
            27:55–69.

Zuboff, Shoshana
1988   *In the Age of the Smart Machine.* New York: Basic Books.

Zunz, Olivier, and Kahan, Alan S. (eds.)
2002   *The Tocqueville Reader: A Life in Letters and Politics.* Oxford: Blackwell.

Zweigenhaft, Richard L., and Domhoff, G. William
2006   *Diversity in the Power Elite: How It Happened, Why It Matters.* Lanham, Md.: Rowman and Littlefield.

Photo Credits

Page 12: © Time Life Pictures/Getty Images; p. 16: © Apic/Getty Images; p. 33: Courtesy of the Library of Congress; p. 38: © Edward Gooch/Getty Images; p. 50: Courtesy of the Library of Congress; p. 86: © Bettmann/CORBIS; p. 114: © Hulton Archive/Getty Images; p. 160: © INTERFOTO/Alamy; p. 196: © Bettmann/CORBIS; p. 198: © Imagno/Getty Images; p. 202: Courtesy of the American Sociological Association; p. 208: Courtesy of the Library of Congress; p. 216: © Fritz Goro/Time Life Pictures/Getty Images; p. 240: Courtesy of the American Sociological Association; p. 254: Courtesy of the American Sociological Association; p. 307: © Alexei Kouprianov/Wikimedia Commons; p. 338: Courtesy of the University of Chicago; p. 356: Courtesy of the American Sociological Association; p. 378: © Arlene Garfinkel/Wikimedia Commons; p. 404: Courtesy of the American Sociological Association; p. 412: Courtesy of the American Sociological Association; p. 418: Courtesy of the University of Washington; p. 432: Courtesy of the American Sociological Association; p. 462: Courtesy of Dorothy E. Smith; p. 468: Courtesy of Patricia Hill Collins; p. 492: Courtesy of Jeffrey C. Alexander; p. 498: Courtesy of Randall Collins, Ph.D.; p. 502: HyperElias©WorldCatalogue/Wikimedia Commons; p. 518: © Pierre Verdy/AFP/Getty Images; p. 542: © Szusi/Wikimedia Commons; p. 558: © Wolfram Huke/Wikimedia commons; p. 610: © Bettmann/CORBIS; p. A-8: Courtesy of George Ritzer.

Name Index

Subject Index